# Churchill

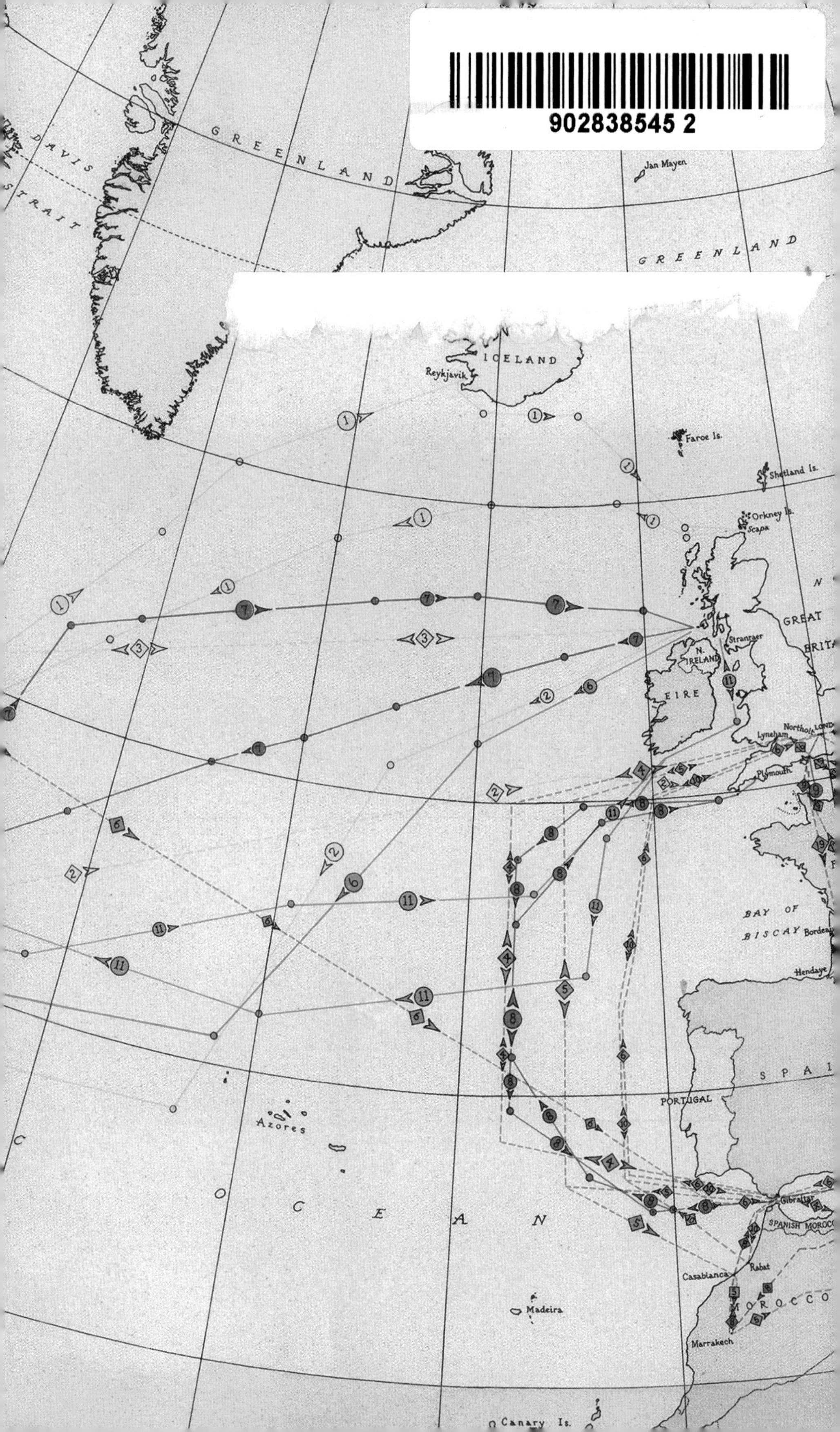

DAVIS STRAIT
GREENLAND
Jan Mayen
GREENLAND
ICELAND
Reykjavik
Faroe Is.
Shetland Is.
Orkney Is.
Scapa
GREAT
N. IRELAND
Stranraer
EIRE
Lyneham
Plymouth
BAY OF BISCAY
Hendaye
PORTUGAL
Gibraltar
Rabat
Casablanca
Marrakech
Azores
Madeira
O C E A N
Canary Is.

ANDREW ROBERTS

# Churchill

## *Walking with Destiny*

ALLEN LANE
*an imprint of*
PENGUIN BOOKS

ALLEN LANE

UK | USA | Canada | Ireland | Australia
India | New Zealand | South Africa

Allen Lane is part of the Penguin Random House group of companies whose addresses can be found at global.penguinrandomhouse.com

First published 2018
006



Set in 10.2/13.5 pt Sabon LT Std
Typeset by Jouve (UK), Milton Keynes
Printed and bound in Great Britain by Clays Ltd, Elcograf S.p.A.

A CIP catalogue record for this book is available from the British Library

ISBN: 978–0–241–20563–1

www.greenpenguin.co.uk

Penguin Random House is committed to a sustainable future for our business, our readers and our planet. This book is made from Forest Stewardship Council® certified paper.

*For Henry and Cassia*
*From their proud father*

*If you can meet with Triumph and Disaster,*
*And treat those two impostors just the same . . .*

Rudyard Kipling, 'If'

*Study history, study history. In history lie all the secrets of statecraft.*

Churchill to an American student before
a Coronation luncheon in Westminster Hall, 27 May 1953

# *Contents*

## PART TWO
## The Trial

# *List of Illustrations*

All material from the Churchill Archives Centre is reproduced by kind permission of The Master, Fellows and Scholars of Churchill College, Cambridge. Every effort has been made to contact all copyright holders. The publishers will be happy to amend in future editions any errors or omissions brought to their attention.

The endpapers are adapted from Lieutenant-Commander Frank A. de Vine Hunt's map of the journeys undertaken by Churchill during the Second World War, originally printed and published in 1947 by George Philip & Son, Ltd., London, in association with *Time and Tide*.

# *Acknowledgements*

I should like to acknowledge the gracious permission of Her Majesty Queen Elizabeth II to make use of material from the Royal Archives, Windsor, and especially for allowing me to be the first Churchill biographer to be given unfettered access to the whole of her late father King George VI's wartime diaries.

I have used many papers not in the public domain, and would in particular like to thank David Cameron for allowing me to work on the Chequers visitors' books for 1940–45 and 1951–5; George and Frances Osborne for allowing me to see the visitors' books and the Golden Book of Corinthian Bagatelle at Dorneywood; Sir Nicholas Soames for allowing me to be the first Churchill biographer since Sir Martin Gilbert to research the Other Club records; Petronella Wyatt for permission to consult the Woodrow Wyatt diaries; the Walker family for Marian Holmes's wartime diaries; John Townsend for permission to consult the papers of the 2nd Earl of Birkenhead; the Marquess of Salisbury for his memories of Churchill and for permission to quote from the Gascoyne-Cecil papers at Hatfield House, where Robin Harcourt Williams could not have been more helpful. Hugo Vickers kindly allowed me to investigate Churchill's share dealings using the huge ledgers kept by his grandfather Cecil Vickers, founder of the stockbroking firm Vickers da Costa; Judge Richard Parkes has allowed me to quote from his grandfather's unpublished memoirs of Antwerp and Gallipoli, Ben Strickland from Captain Smyth's account of the Battle of Omdurman, and Nick Thorne for the diaries of Lieutenant-Commander Vivian Cox. Michael F. Bishop of the National Churchill Library and Center (NCLC) in Washington, DC – and also the fine Director of the International Churchill Society – and Elisabeth Kaplan at the Gelman Library of George Washington University allowed me to research Churchill's wartime monthly engagement cards before the NCLC was officially opened, for which many thanks.

I would also like to thank Lady Williams of Elvel for her memories of working for Churchill; Jerry del Missier for our 500-mile round trip in central Cuba to see where Churchill heard his first shot fired in anger; Joy Hunter for her memories of working in the War Cabinet's Joint Planning Secretariat; Mervyn King for checking my passage about Churchill's decision to rejoin the Gold Standard; Laurence Geller and David Freeman of the International Churchill Society; Rodney Francis of the Public Schools Fencing Competition; Bill and Alex Roedy for showing me Churchill's flat at 11 Morpeth Mansions; Simon Ekins of Churchill's solicitors, Fladgate's; Carrie Starren at the Hurlingham Club; John Forster, Lady Henrietta Spencer-Churchill, Karen Wiseman and Michael Dey at Blenheim Palace; Jeremy McIlwaine at the Weston Library in the Bodleian Library, Oxford; Bill Stockting and Allison Derrett at the Royal Archives; Jean Cannon at the Hoover Institution at Stanford University; Jane Fish at the Imperial War Museum; Hal Kleepak and Ricardo Guardaramo Roman for their help in Cuba; Susan Scott, Corinne Conrath and Lady Williams of Elvel for help with the Other Club records; Larry Arnn, Soren Geiger and all the Churchill documents team at Hillsdale College, Michigan, for the truly magnificent work they are doing in documenting all of Churchill's written legacy; Clare Kavanagh and the staff at Nuffield College Archives, Oxford; Claire Batley at the House of Lords Records Office for her help over Freedom of Information; Mark Foster-Brown for his grandfather Rear Admiral Roy Foster-Brown's memories of Churchill's visit to Athens in December 1944; Tace Fox at the Harrow School Archives; Imam Ahmed Abdel-Rahman al Mahdi for his thoughts on his grandfather, the Mahdi; P. W. H. Brown at the British Academy; Dr Kate Harris at the Longleat Archives; Dr Rob Havers of the George C. Marshall Foundation; Diana Manipud at the Liddell Hart Archives in the Department of War Studies at King's College London; Rodney Melville and Francesca McCoy for my day with the Chequers visitors' books; Janina Gruhner of Zurich University for showing me the podium Churchill spoke from in 1946; John Lee for taking me to where Churchill crossed the Rhine in March 1945 and our battlefield tour of Churchill's trench positions at Ploegsteert; Rafael Serrano for showing me around the Old Admiralty Building; Lady Avon for permission to research Anthony Eden's papers; Timothy Shuttleworth of Gray's Inn, where Churchill and Franklin Roosevelt first met; Heather Johnson of the National Naval Museum; Zoë Colbeck and Katherine Barnett at Chartwell; the captain and crew of the USS *Winston Churchill*; Dr John Mather for our discussions on Churchill's health; Christopher Clement-Davies for his insight into his grandfather's relations with Churchill; Barnaby Lennon for inviting me to speak at the Churchill Songs at Harrow School; Gregory Fremont-Barnes and Dr Anthony Morton at Sandhurst, and Geoffrey Partington for his reminiscences. Donatella Flick very kindly showed me 28 Hyde Park Gate, where Churchill died.

I have benefited enormously from discussions about Churchill with fellow historians. In particular I would like to thank Jonathan Aitken, Larry Arnn, Wilfred Attenborough, Christopher M. Bell, John Bew, Paul Bew, Conrad Black, Jeremy Black, Jonathan Black, Robin Brodhurst, Stefan Buczacki, Michael Burleigh, Dr Peter Caddick-Adams, David Cannadine, Ronald I. Cohen, Paul Courtenay, Rodney Croft, Barry De Morgan, David Dilks, Warren Dockter, Lady Antonia Fraser, Marcus Frost, Soren Geiger, Richard Griffiths, Rafe Heydel-Mankoo, James Holland, Sir Michael Howard, John Hughes-Wilson, Sir Ian Kershaw, Warren Kimball, Albert Knapp, Jim Lancaster, Celia Lee, John Lee, Lewis E. Lehrman, Michael McMenamin, Allan Mallinson, John H. Maurer, William Morrissey, James Muller, Philip Reed, Kenneth Rendell, Larry Robinson, Kevin Ruane, Douglas Russell, Celia Sandys, Peter Saville, Richard W. Smith, Gillian Somerscales, Nicholas Stargardt, Cita Stelzer, Ben Strickland, Bradley P. Tolppanen and Curt Zoller. The distinguished Churchill historian Paul Addison read the proofs of the book, and I would like to thank him very much for his comments.

I should also like to thank the staff at the Museo de Arroyo Blanco in Cuba; the National Archives at Kew; the Cadbury Research Library, Birmingham University; Cambridge University Library; the New York Public Library Berg Collection; the Imperial War Museum, Duxford; the Churchill War Rooms; the Inglaterra and Nacional Hotels in Havana for showing me where Churchill stayed on his 1895 and 1946 visits; the Mamounia Hotel, Marrakesh; the Plug Street Experience Centre, Ploegsteert, Belgium, and the staff of the Liddell Hart Centre, King's College London.

For reading the manuscript before publication and suggesting alterations, I should like to thank Paul Addison, Gregg Berman, Michael F. Bishop, Robin Brodhurst, Rudy Carmenaty, Richard Cohen, Paul Courtenay, my brother-in-law Paul Daly, Marc Feigen, Alan Hobson, Richard Langworth, John Lee, Jerry del Missier, Richard Munro, Stephen Parker, Lee Pollock, Professor Elihu Rose, Peter Saville, Max Schapiro, Gilles Vauclair, Moshe Wander and Peter Wyllie. I should also like to acknowledge other very useful help from Merlin Armstrong, Richard Cohen, my son Henry Roberts, Matthew Sadler and Gabriel Whitwam.

I would especially like to thank Allen Packwood and all the staff at the Churchill Archives Centre, Churchill College, Cambridge, including Katharine Thomson, Heidi Egginton, Sarah Lewery, Natasha Swainston and Andrew Riley. These wonderful archivists have put up with TV crews, translated Churchillian hieroglyphics, provided photographs and lunched with me over the years, and have always been exceptionally kind, friendly, helpful and efficient.

The Churchill family could not have been more supportive and encouraging, especially Randolph Churchill, Edwina Sandys, Celia Sandys, Minnie Churchill, Emma Soames and Sir Nicholas Soames, and the late Mary, Lady Soames. Likewise, Michael F. Bishop has been a rock.

I can hardly overstate my debt to Richard Langworth, of the magnificent Hillsdale Churchill Project, without whom this book could not have been written. The numbers of emails between us, and also Paul Courtenay, on every conceivable aspect of Churchilliana over the years long ago entered four figures, and their knowledge and wisdom permeate every page, though there are doubtless still plenty of things with which they will disagree. My interaction with them was one of the greatest pleasures of writing this book.

'Writing a long and substantial book is like having a friend and companion at your side,' wrote Churchill of his *A History of the English-Speaking Peoples*, 'to whom you can always turn for comfort and amusement, and whose society becomes more attractive as a new and widening field of interest is lighted in the mind.' My thanks to my editors, Stuart Proffitt and Joy de Menil, my agent Georgina Capel, and my copy-editor, the eagle-eyed Peter James, as well as my picture editor Cecilia Mackay, and Richard Duguid and Ben Sinyor at Penguin, for their friendship, good humour, Stakhanovite work and superb professionalism. Stephen Ryan was once again a superlative proofreader.

I cannot thank my wife Susan enough for visiting Gallipoli, Cuba and Hiroshima with me, and for living with this book for more than four years, giving me unfailing help, support and encouragement all along the way. As Churchill put it in the final words of *My Early Life*, 'I married and lived happily ever afterwards.'

Andrew Roberts
July 2018

# Note on Money Conversion

£1 in today's money was roughly worth £80 when Churchill was born in 1874, £101 in 1900, £91 in 1914, £41 in 1920, £50 in 1930, £52 in 1940, £35 in 1945, £28 in 1950, and £16 when he died in 1965. The pound sterling was worth \$4.86 until 1914, \$3.66 in 1920, \$4.80 in 1930, \$4.03 in 1940, \$4.00 in 1945, and \$2.80 from 1950 to 1965.

## Churchill's extended family during his lifetime

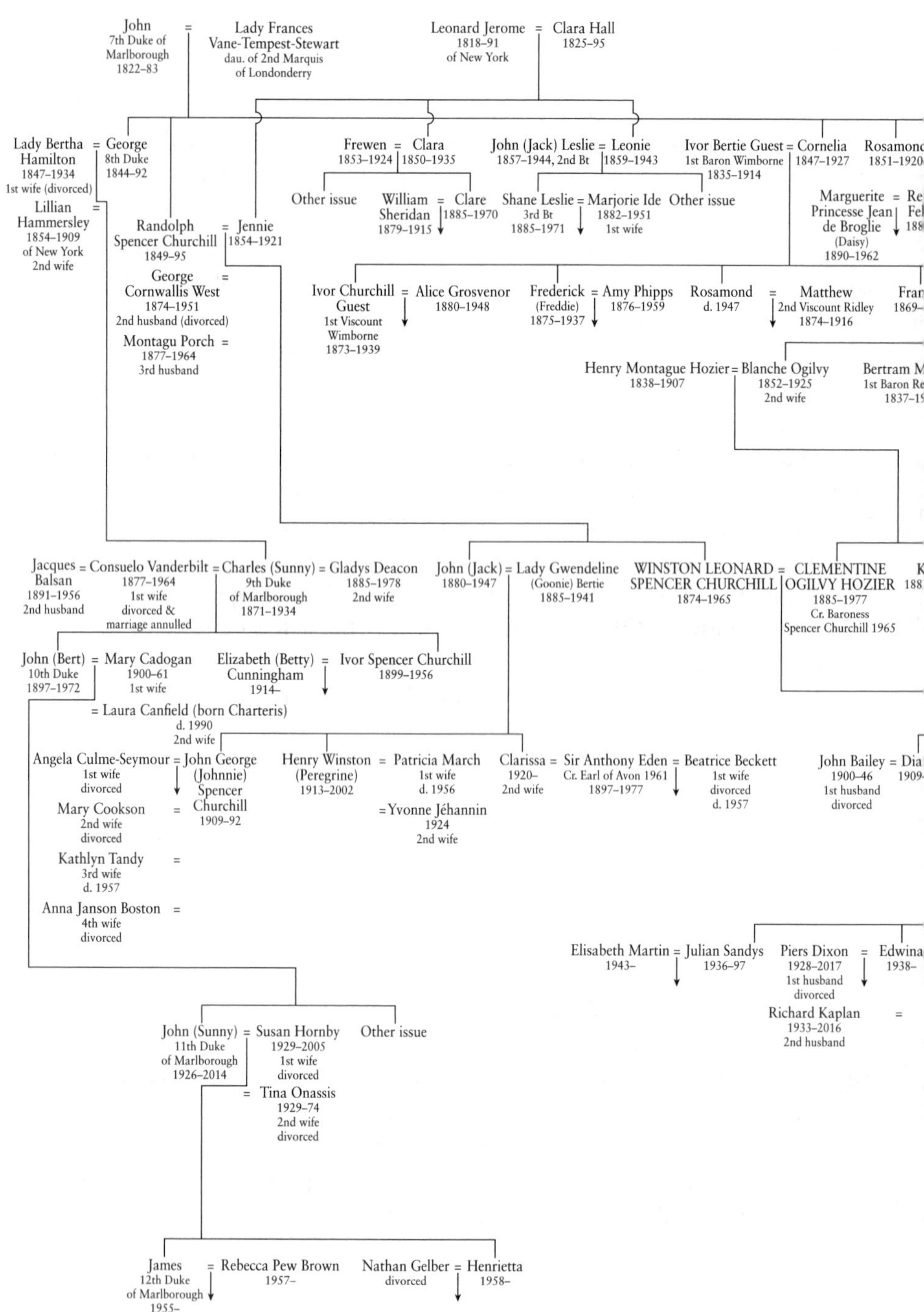

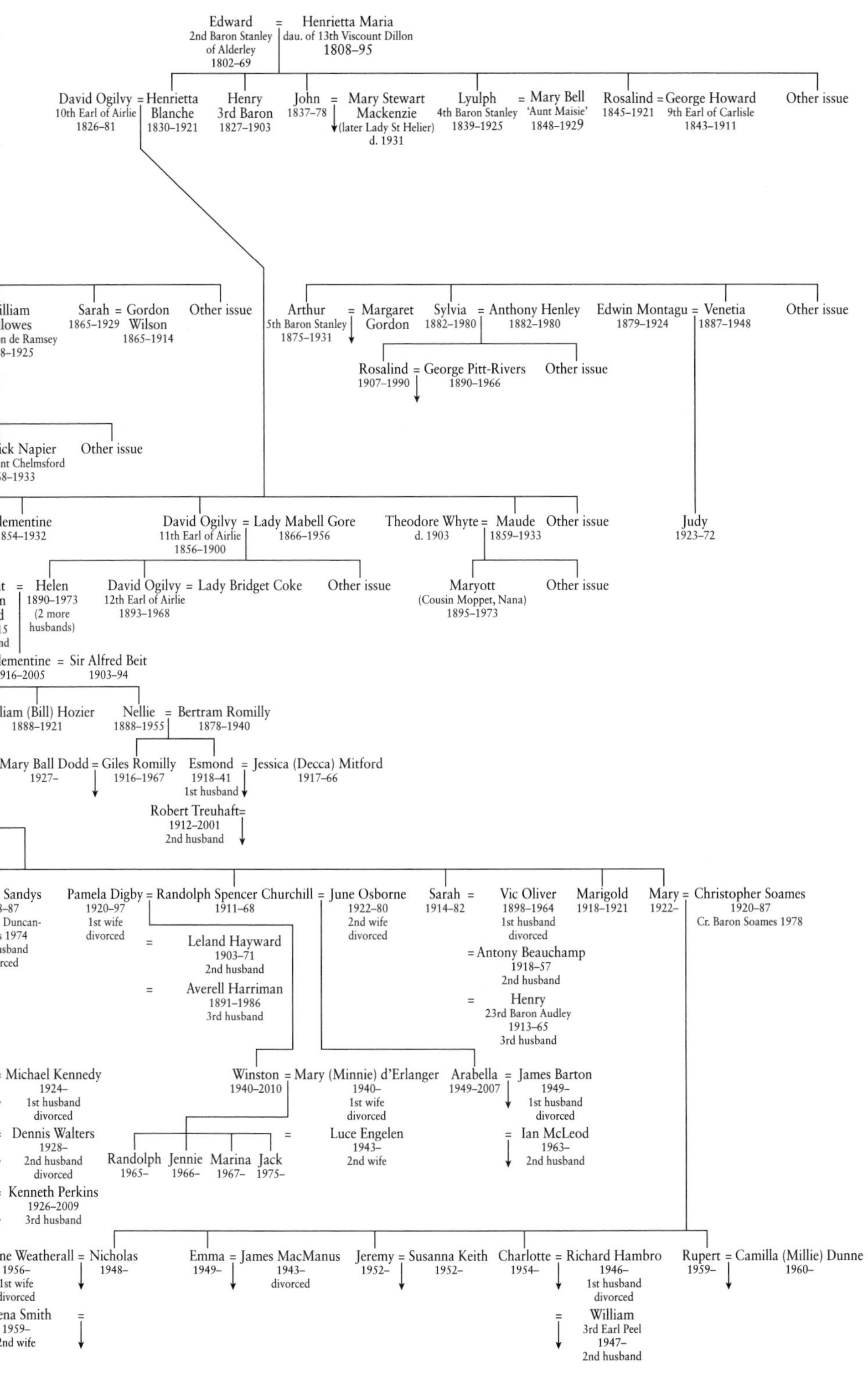

Edward 2nd Baron Stanley of Alderley 1802–69 = Henrietta Maria dau. of 13th Viscount Dillon 1808–95
David Ogilvy 10th Earl of Airlie 1826–81 = Henrietta Blanche 1830–1921
Henry 3rd Baron 1827–1903
John 1837–78 = Mary Stewart Mackenzie (later Lady St Helier) d. 1931
Lyulph 4th Baron Stanley 1839–1925 = Mary Bell 'Aunt Maisie' 1848–1929
Rosalind 1845–1921 = George Howard 9th Earl of Carlisle 1843–1911
Other issue
illiam llowes n de Ramsey 8–1925
Sarah 1865–1929 = Gordon Wilson 1865–1914
Other issue
Arthur 5th Baron Stanley 1875–1931 = Margaret Gordon
Sylvia 1882–1980 = Anthony Henley 1882–1980
Edwin Montagu 1879–1924 = Venetia 1887–1948
Other issue
Rosalind 1907–1990 = George Pitt-Rivers 1890–1966
Other issue
ck Napier nt Chelmsford 8–1933
Other issue
lementine 854–1932
David Ogilvy 11th Earl of Airlie 1856–1900 = Lady Mabell Gore 1866–1956
Theodore Whyte d. 1903 = Maude 1859–1933
Other issue
Judy 1923–72
t n d 5 nd = Helen 1890–1973 (2 more husbands)
David Ogilvy 12th Earl of Airlie 1893–1968 = Lady Bridget Coke
Other issue
Maryott (Cousin Moppet, Nana) 1895–1973
Other issue
lementine 916–2005 = Sir Alfred Beit 1903–94
liam (Bill) Hozier 1888–1921
Nellie 1888–1955 = Bertram Romilly 1878–1940
Mary Ball Dodd 1927– = Giles Romilly 1916–1967
Esmond 1918–41 1st husband = Jessica (Decca) Mitford 1917–66
Robert Treuhaft= 1912–2001 2nd husband
Sandys 3–87 Duncan- s 1974 usband rced
Pamela Digby 1920–97 1st wife divorced = Randolph Spencer Churchill 1911–68 = June Osborne 1922–80 2nd wife divorced
= Leland Hayward 1903–71 2nd husband
= Averell Harriman 1891–1986 3rd husband
Sarah 1914–82 = Vic Oliver 1898–1964 1st husband divorced
= Antony Beauchamp 1918–57 2nd husband
= Henry 23rd Baron Audley 1913–65 3rd husband
Marigold 1918–1921
Mary 1922– = Christopher Soames 1920–87 Cr. Baron Soames 1978
Michael Kennedy 1924– 1st husband divorced
Dennis Walters 1928– 2nd husband divorced
Kenneth Perkins 1926–2009 3rd husband
Winston 1940–2010 = Mary (Minnie) d'Erlanger 1940– 1st wife divorced
= Luce Engelen 1943– 2nd wife
Randolph 1965–
Jennie 1966–
Marina 1967–
Jack 1975–
Arabella 1949–2007 = James Barton 1949– 1st husband divorced
= Ian McLeod 1963– 2nd husband
ne Weatherall 1956– 1st wife divorced = Nicholas 1948–
na Smith 1959– 2nd wife =
Emma 1949– = James MacManus 1943– divorced
Jeremy 1952– = Susanna Keith 1952–
Charlotte 1954– = Richard Hambro 1946– 1st husband divorced
= William 3rd Earl Peel 1947– 2nd husband
Rupert 1959– = Camilla (Millie) Dunne 1960–

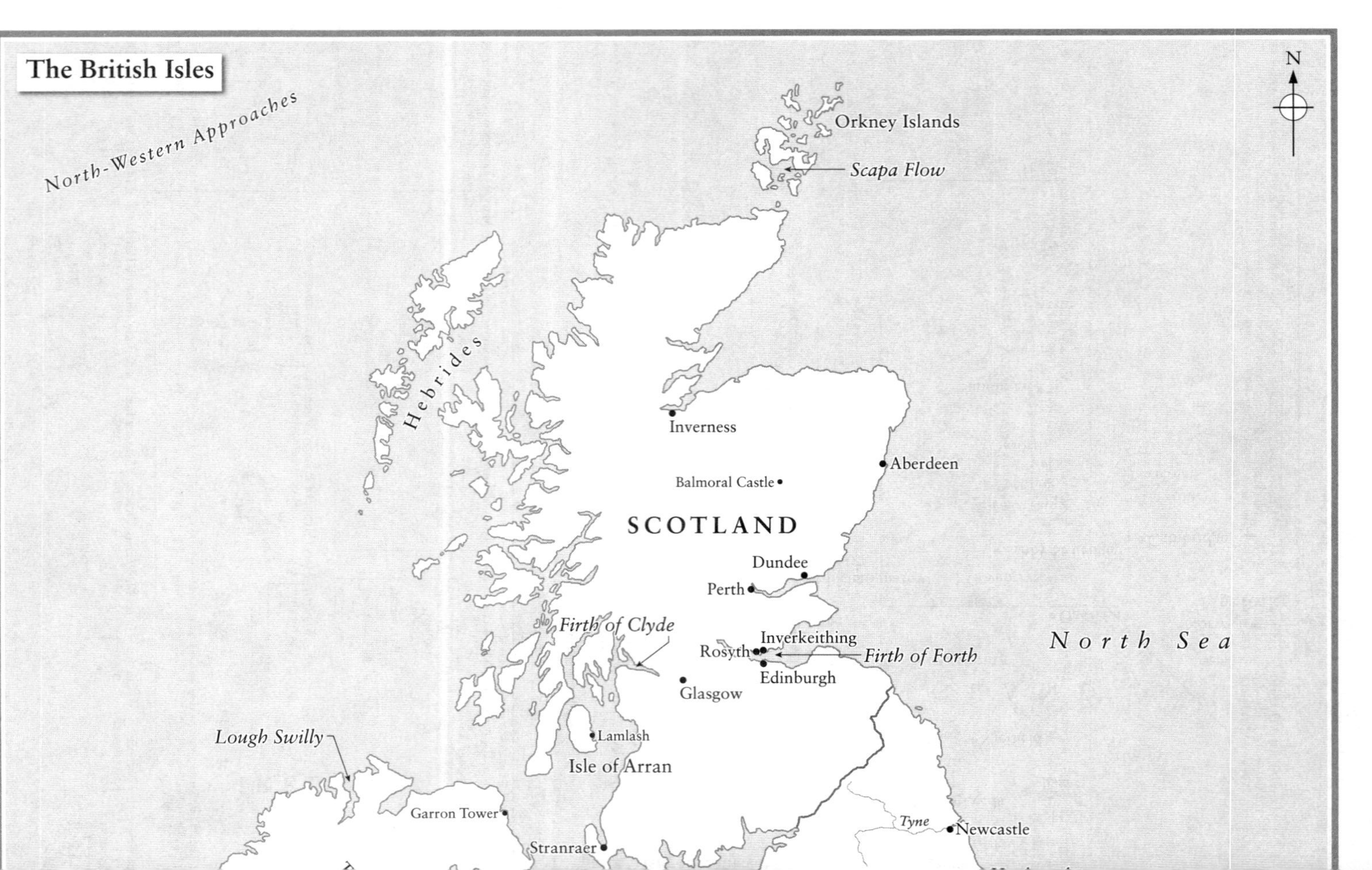
The British Isles
N
North-Western Approaches
Orkney Islands
Scapa Flow
Hebrides
Inverness
Aberdeen
Balmoral Castle
SCOTLAND
Dundee
Perth
Firth of Clyde
Inverkeithing
Rosyth
Firth of Forth
Edinburgh
Glasgow
North Sea
Lough Swilly
Lamlash
Isle of Arran
Garron Tower
Tyne
Newcastle
Stranraer

Isle of Man
Dundalk
IRELAND
Irish Sea
Dublin
Kingstown
The Curragh
Cork
Berehaven
York
Blackpool
Burnley
Leeds
Hull
Humber
Grimsby
Bolton
Oldham
Manchester
Sheffield
Liverpool
Llandudno
ENGLAND
Nottingham
Overstrand
Norwich
Norfolk
Oakham
Leicester
Birmingham
Coventry
Ashby St Ledgers
Cambridge
Severn
WALES
Bletchley Park
Ditchley Park
Woodstock
Blenheim Palace
Bladon
Chequers
Oxford
Waltham Abbey
Nazeing
Theydon Bois
Shoeburyness
Thanet
Margate
Rhondda Valley
Llanelli
Swansea
Tonypandy
Cardiff
Thames
Bristol
Bath
Lyneham
Sandhurst
London
Chartwell
Canterbury
Kent
Walmer Castle
Dover
Godalming
East Grinstead
Ashdown Forest
Southampton
Portsmouth
Brighton
Pevensey
Dungeness
Wimborne
Bournemouth
Cowes
Spithead
Solent
Isle of Wight
Plymouth
Portland Bill
English Channel
100 miles
100 kms
0

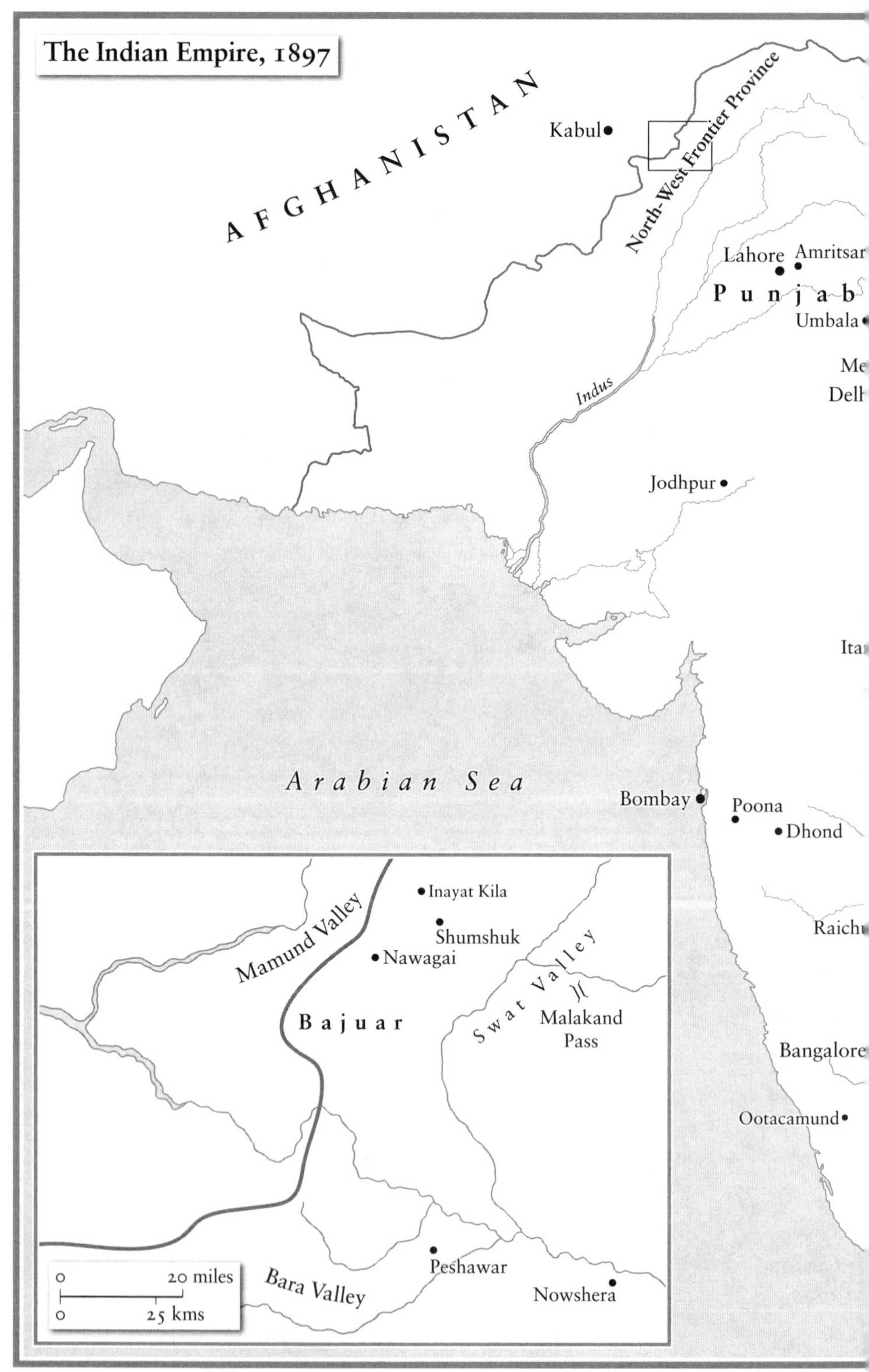

The Indian Empire, 1897
AFGHANISTAN
Kabul
North-West Frontier Province
Lahore
Amritsar
Punjab
Umbala
Indus
Jodhpur
Arabian Sea
Bombay
Poona
Dhond
Bangalore
Ootacamund
Inayat Kila
Shumshuk
Nawagai
Mamund Valley
Bajuar
Swat Valley
Malakand Pass
Peshawar
Nowshera
Bara Valley
0 20 miles
0 25 kms

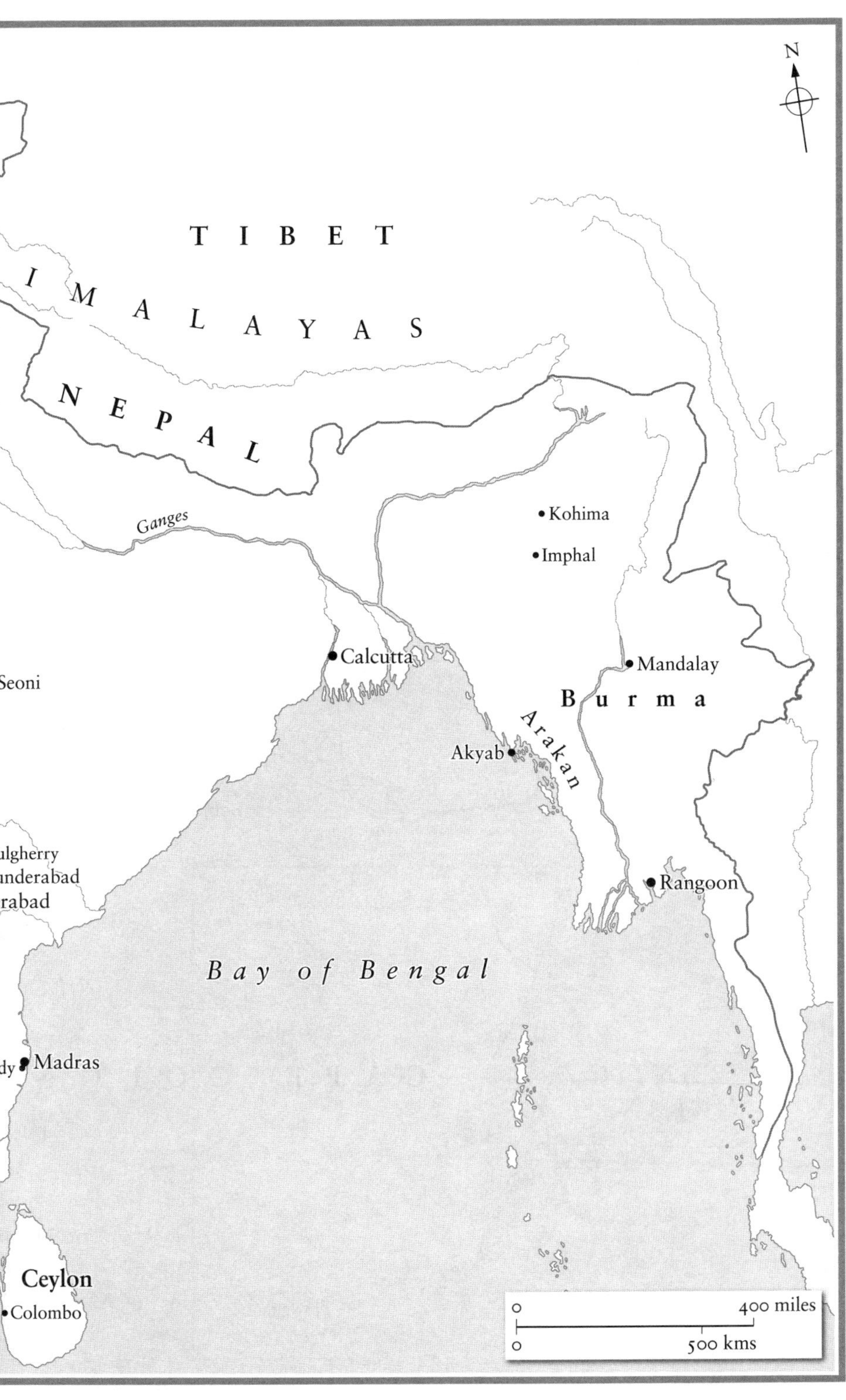
N
TIBET
IMALAYAS
NEPAL
Ganges
Kohima
Imphal
Calcutta
Mandalay
Seoni
Burma
Arakan
Akyab
Rangoon
Bay of Bengal
Madras
Ceylon
Colombo
0
400 miles
0
500 kms

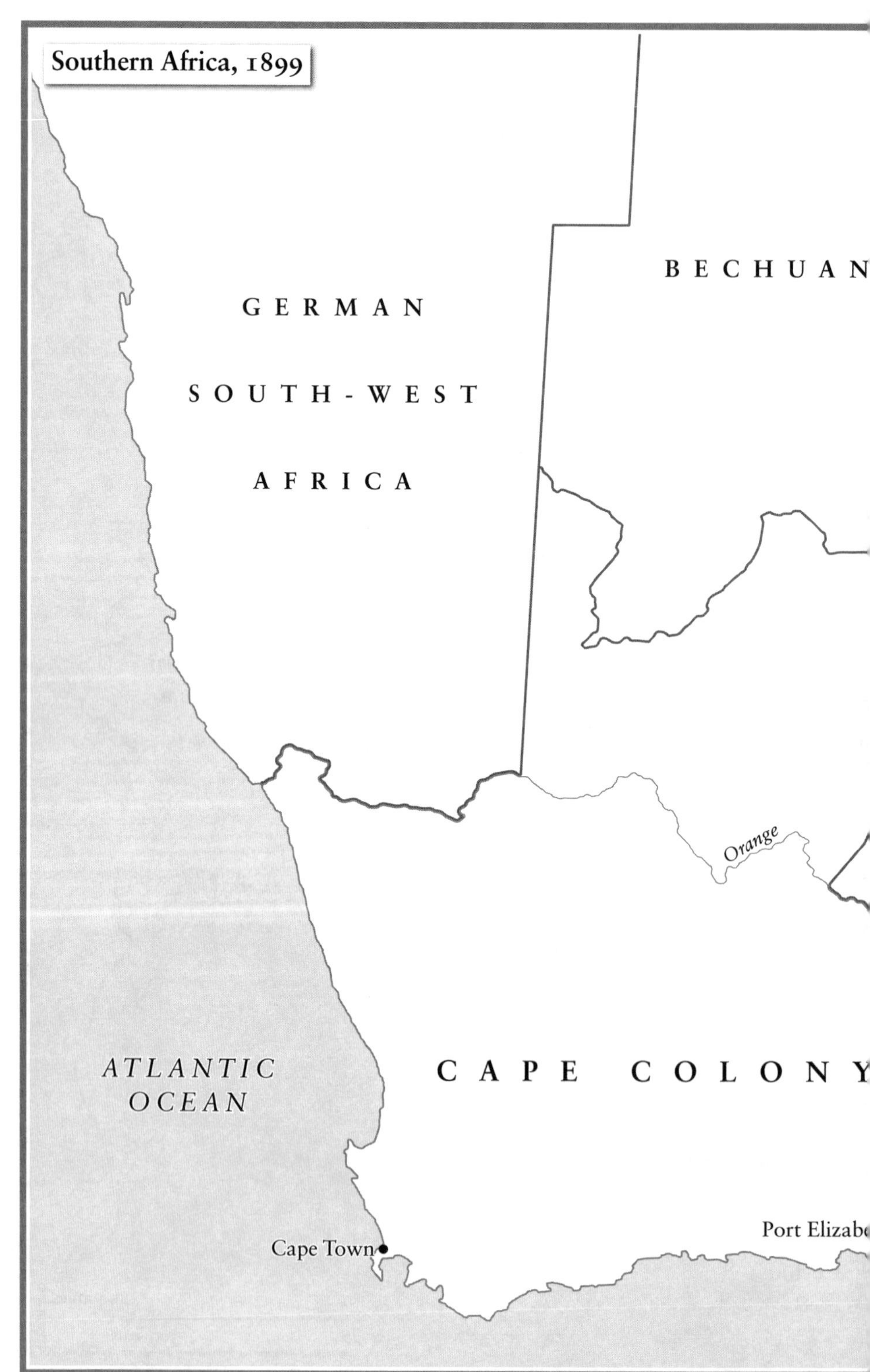
Southern Africa, 1899
GERMAN
SOUTH-WEST
AFRICA
Orange
ATLANTIC
OCEAN
CAPE COLONY
Cape Town

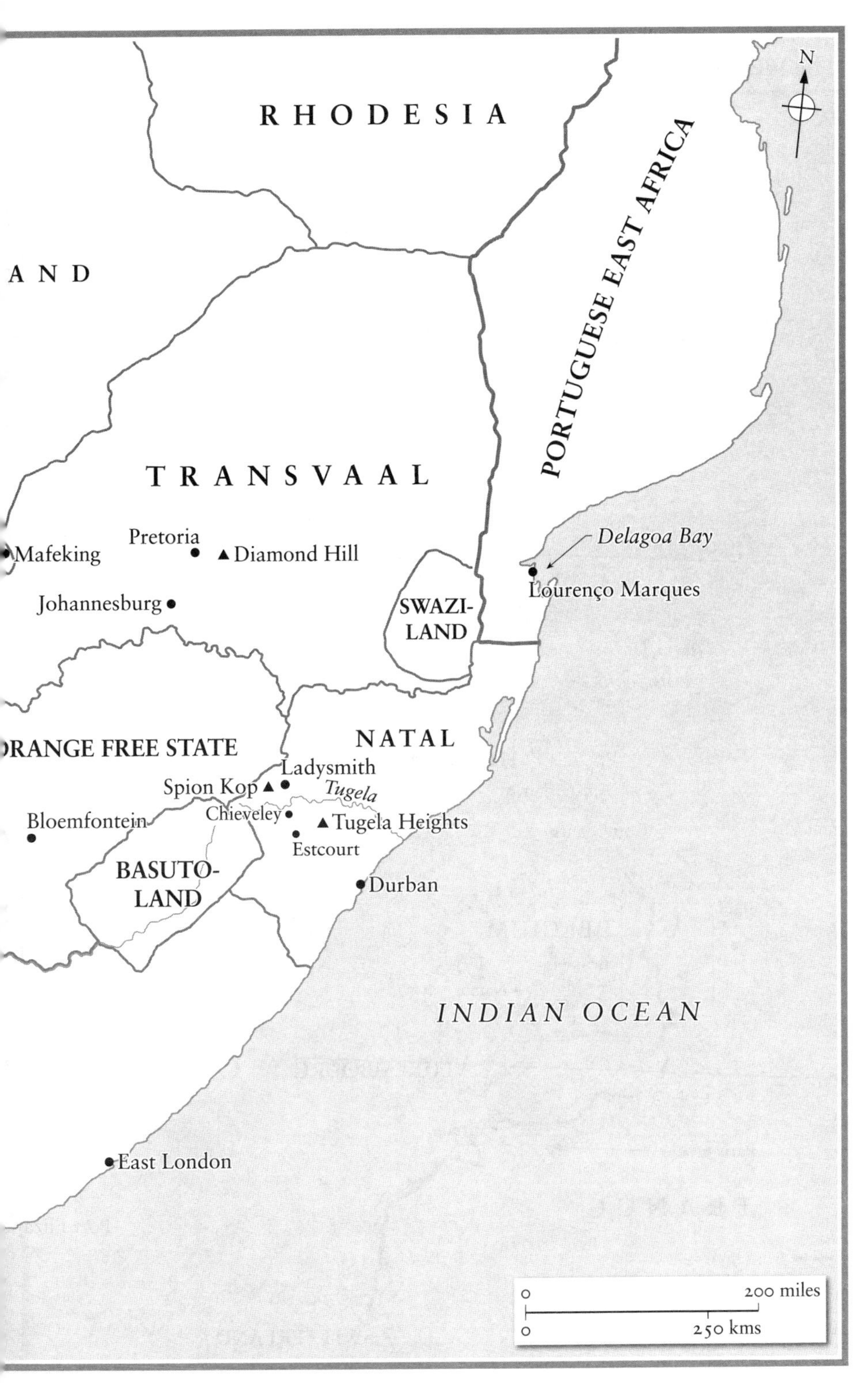
RHODESIA
AND
PORTUGUESE EAST AFRICA
N
TRANSVAAL
Pretoria
Mafeking
Diamond Hill
Johannesburg
Delagoa Bay
Lourenço Marques
SWAZI-
LAND
ORANGE FREE STATE
NATAL
Ladysmith
Spion Kop
Tugela
Chieveley
Tugela Heights
Bloemfontein
Estcourt
BASUTO-
LAND
Durban
INDIAN OCEAN
East London
0
200 miles
0
250 kms

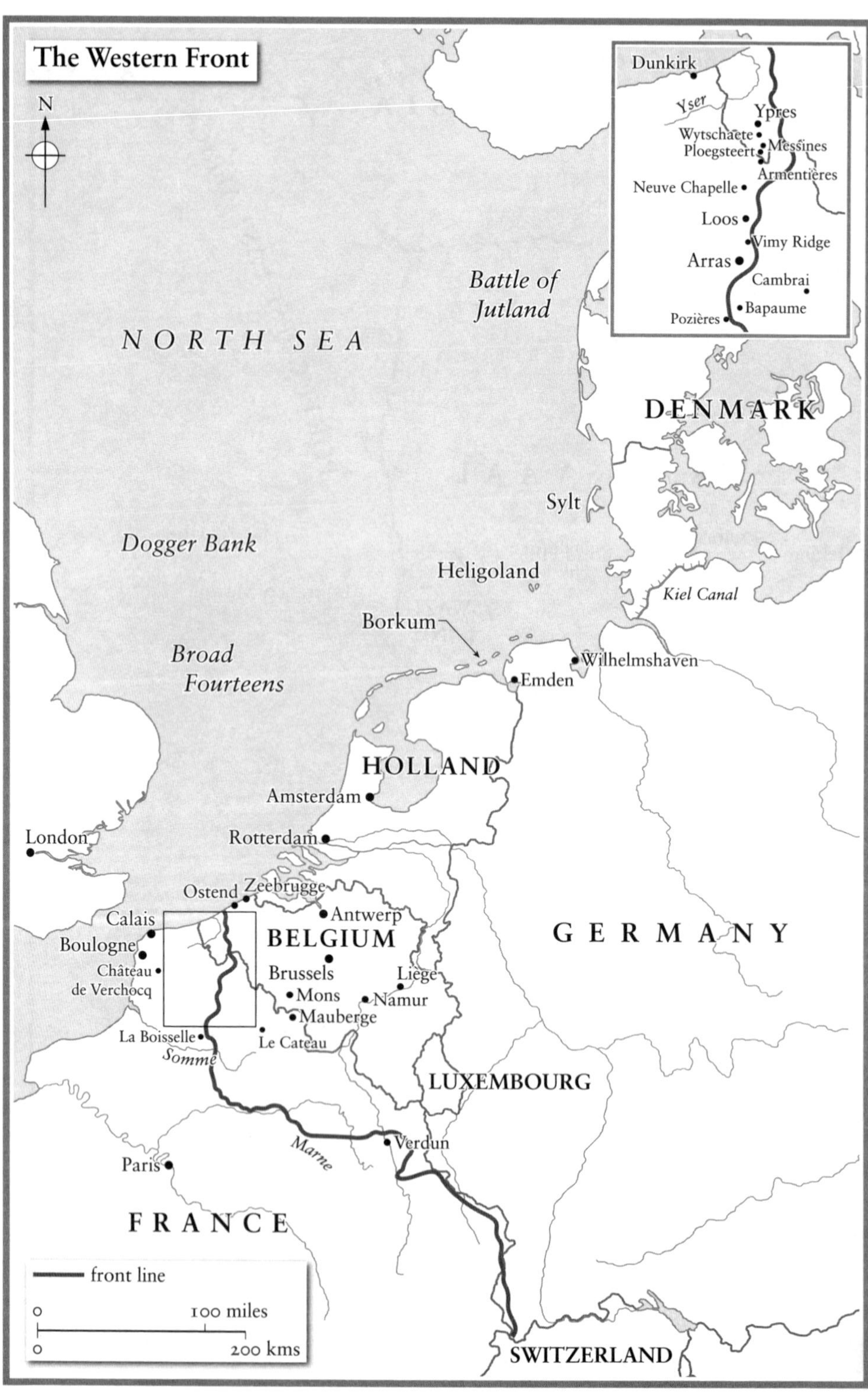
The Western Front
N
Dunkirk
Yser
Ypres
Wytschaete
Messines
Ploegsteert
Armentières
Neuve Chapelle
Loos
Vimy Ridge
Arras
Cambrai
Bapaume
Pozières
Battle of Jutland
NORTH SEA
DENMARK
Sylt
Dogger Bank
Heligoland
Kiel Canal
Borkum
Broad Fourteens
Wilhelmshaven
Emden
HOLLAND
Amsterdam
London
Rotterdam
Ostend
Zeebrugge
Calais
Antwerp
Boulogne
BELGIUM
GERMANY
Château de Verchocq
Brussels
Liège
Mons
Namur
Mauberge
La Boisselle
Le Cateau
Somme
LUXEMBOURG
Verdun
Marne
Paris
FRANCE
front line
0 100 miles
0 200 kms
SWITZERLAND

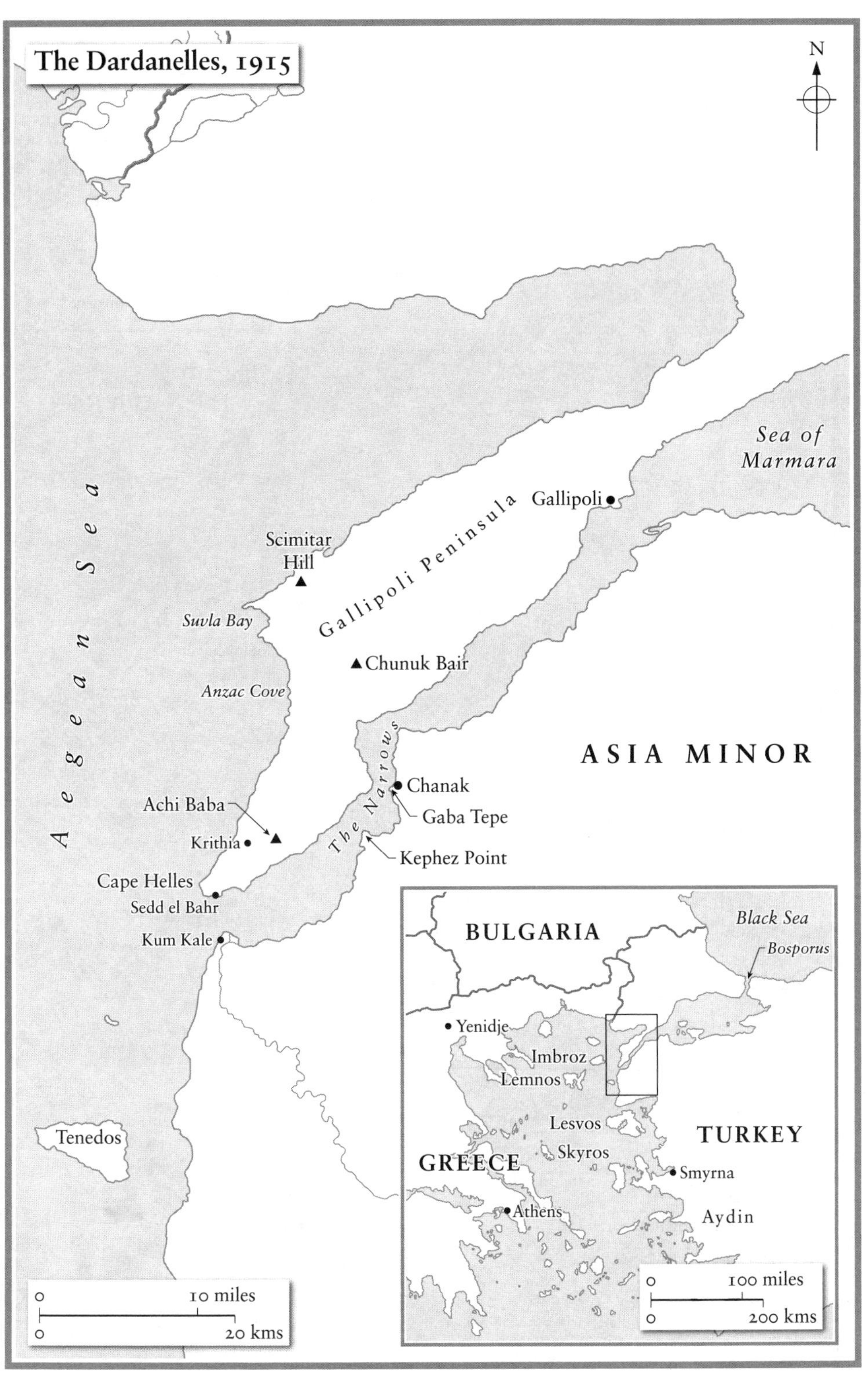
The Dardanelles, 1915
N
Sea of Marmara
Gallipoli
Gallipoli Peninsula
Scimitar Hill
Suvla Bay
Chunuk Bair
Anzac Cove
Aegean Sea
The Narrows
ASIA MINOR
Chanak
Gaba Tepe
Achi Baba
Krithia
Kephez Point
Cape Helles
Sedd el Bahr
Kum Kale
Tenedos
0 10 miles
0 20 kms
BULGARIA
Black Sea
Bosporus
Yenidje
Imbroz
Lemnos
Lesvos
Skyros
TURKEY
GREECE
Smyrna
Athens
Aydin
0 100 miles
0 200 kms

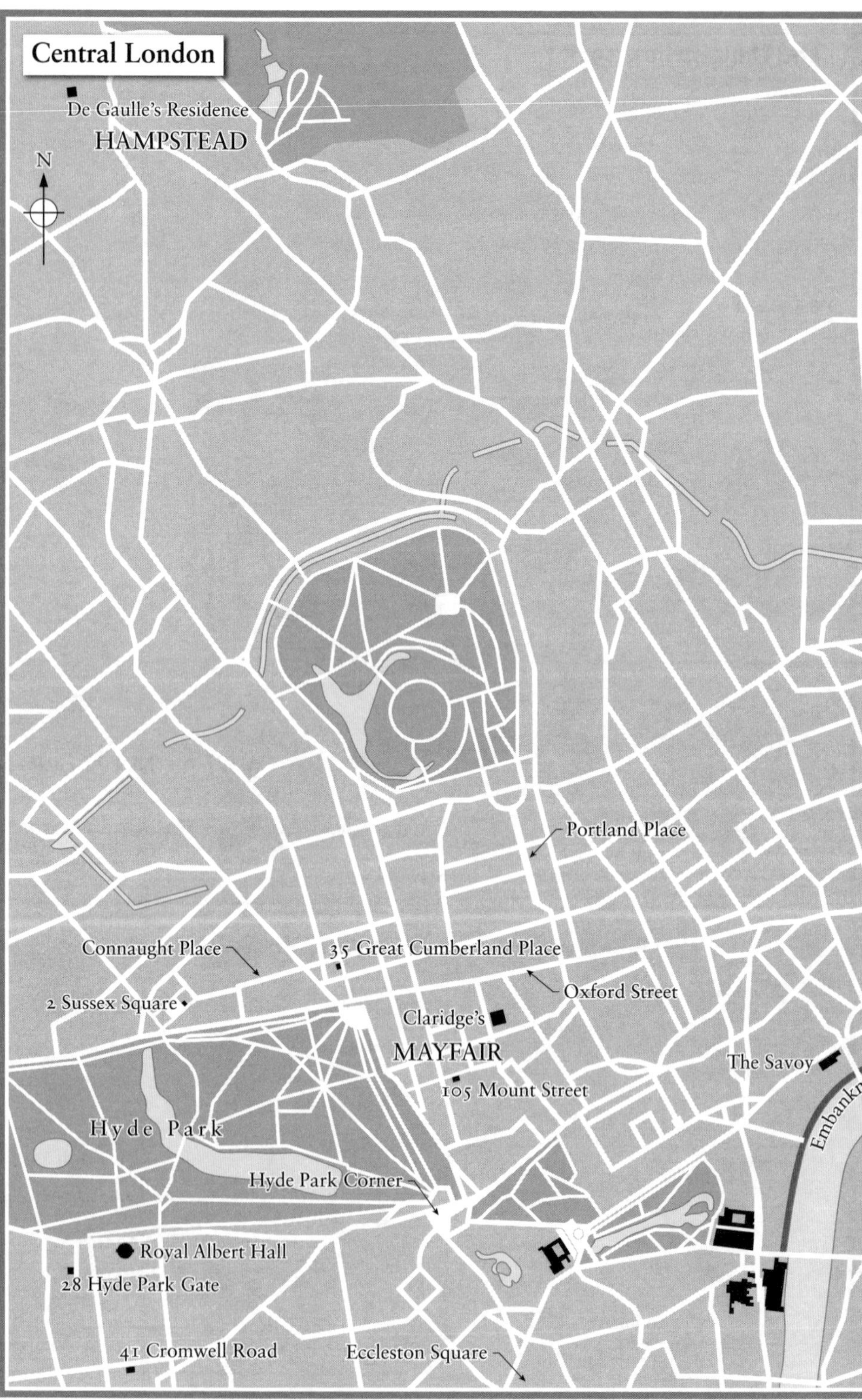

Central London
De Gaulle's Residence
HAMPSTEAD
N
Portland Place
Connaught Place
35 Great Cumberland Place
Oxford Street
2 Sussex Square
Claridge's
MAYFAIR
The Savoy
105 Mount Street
Hyde Park
Hyde Park Corner
Royal Albert Hall
28 Hyde Park Gate
41 Cromwell Road
Eccleston Square

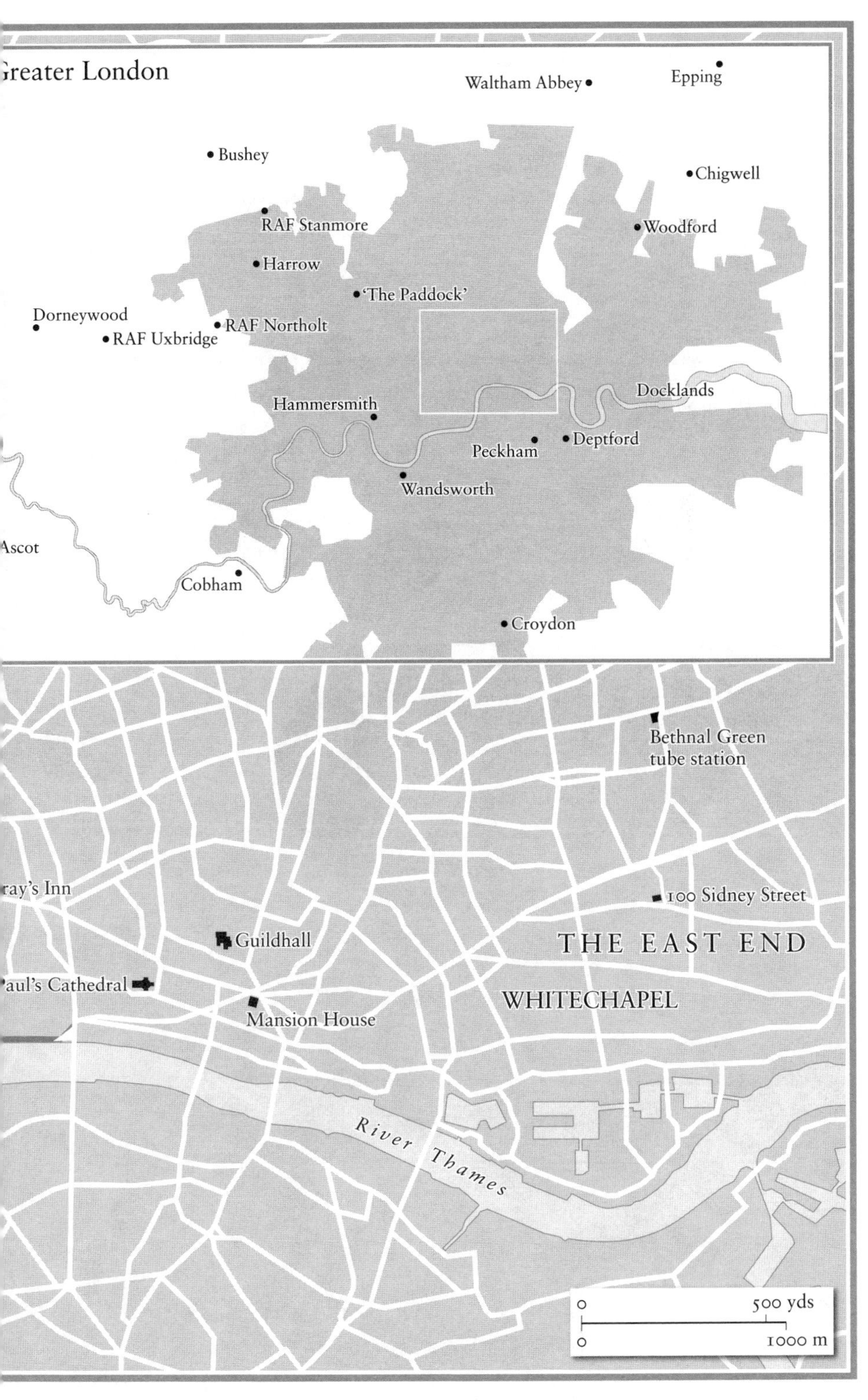

Greater London
Waltham Abbey
Epping
Bushey
Chigwell
RAF Stanmore
Woodford
Harrow
'The Paddock'
Dorneywood
RAF Northolt
RAF Uxbridge
Docklands
Hammersmith
Deptford
Peckham
Wandsworth
Ascot
Cobham
Croydon
Bethnal Green
tube station
ray's Inn
100 Sidney Street
Guildhall
THE EAST END
aul's Cathedral
WHITECHAPEL
Mansion House
River Thames
0
500 yds
0
1000 m

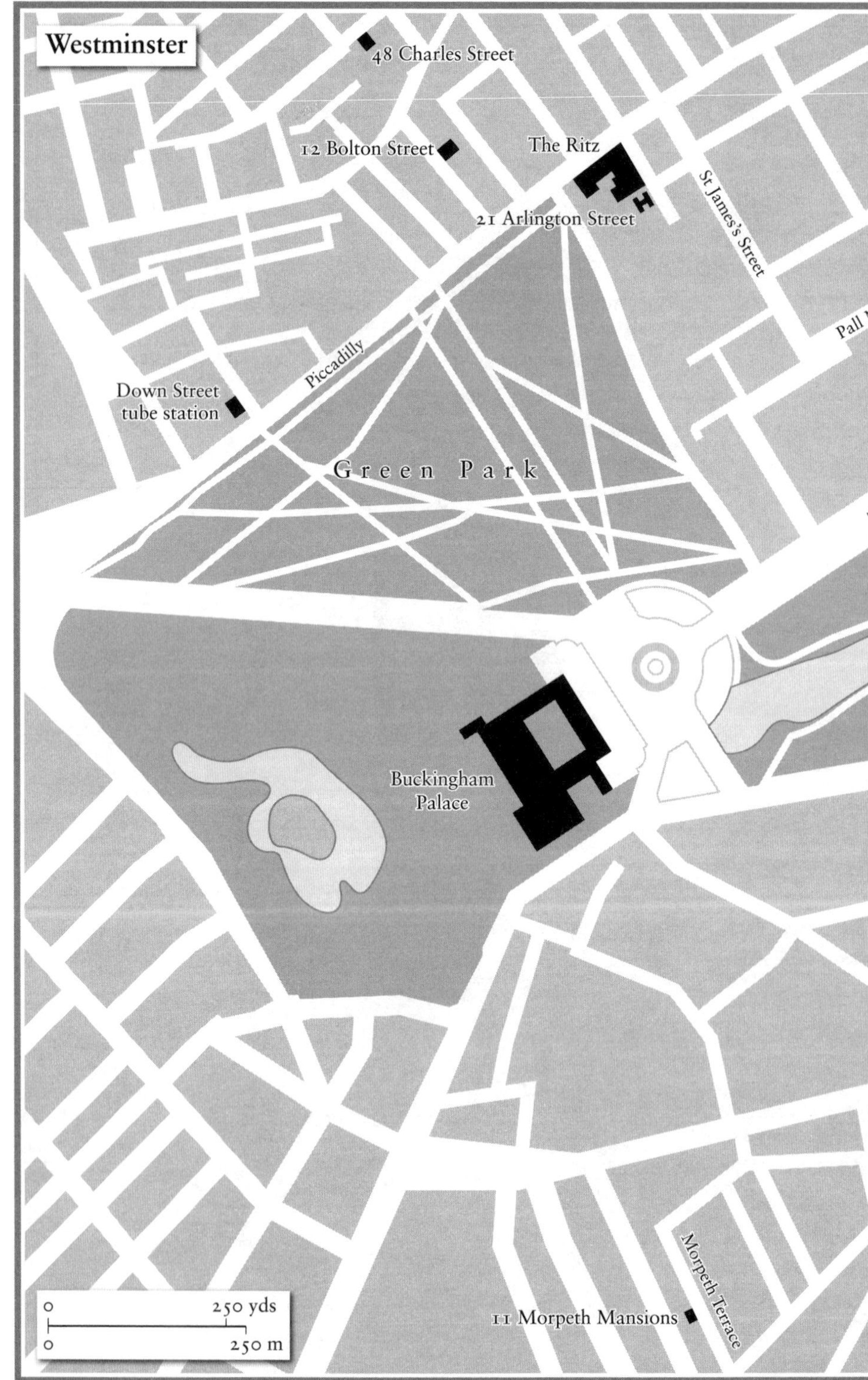
Westminster
48 Charles Street
12 Bolton Street
The Ritz
21 Arlington Street
St James's Street
Pall M
Piccadilly
Down Street
tube station
Green Park
T
Buckingham
Palace
Morpeth Terrace
11 Morpeth Mansions
0
250 yds
0
250 m

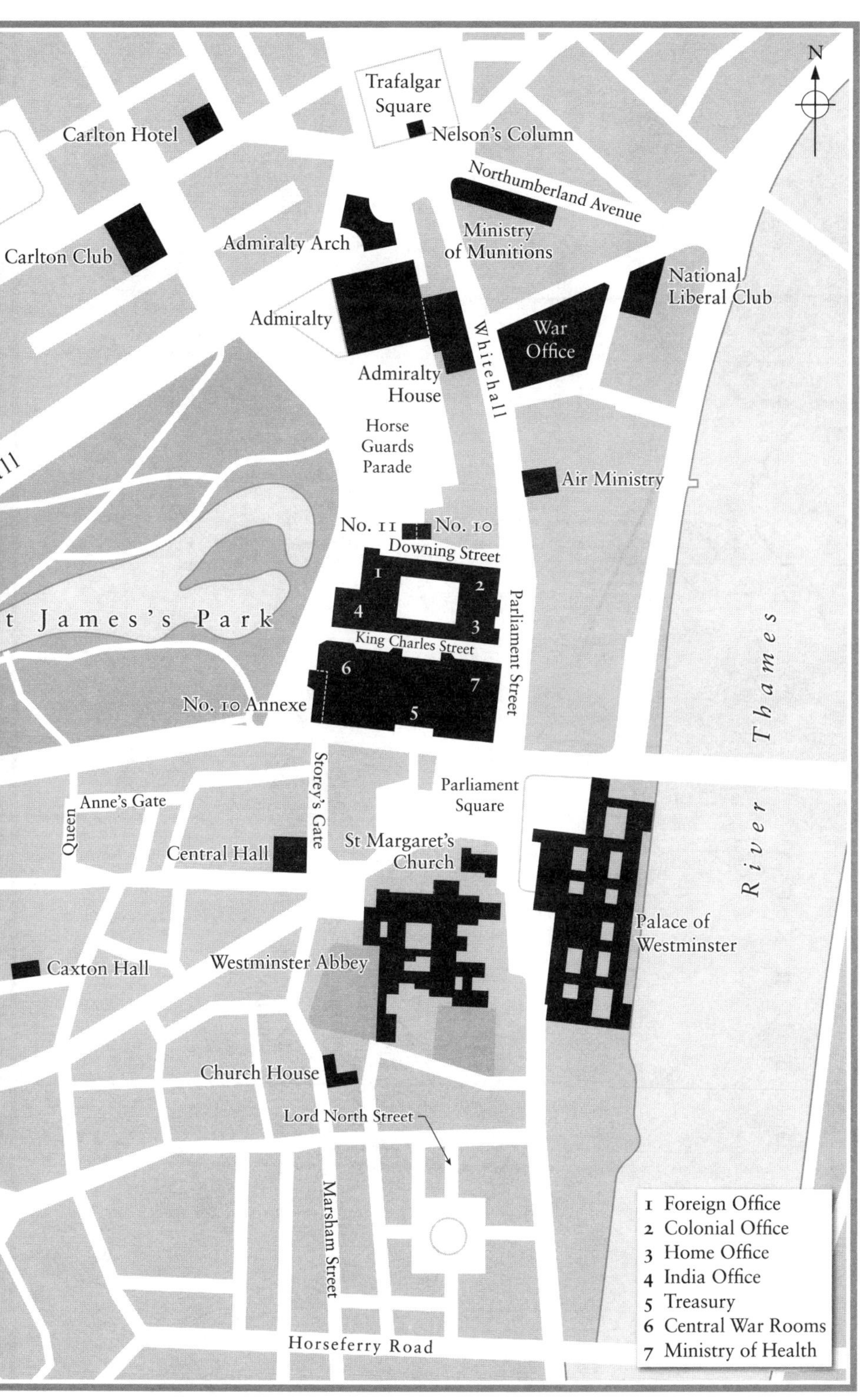
N
Trafalgar Square
Nelson's Column
Carlton Hotel
Northumberland Avenue
Carlton Club
Admiralty Arch
Ministry of Munitions
National Liberal Club
Admiralty
War Office
Whitehall
Admiralty House
Horse Guards Parade
Air Ministry
No. 11
No. 10
Downing Street
1
2
4
3
t James's Park
King Charles Street
Parliament Street
6
7
5
No. 10 Annexe
Thames
Storey's Gate
Parliament Square
Queen Anne's Gate
Central Hall
St Margaret's Church
River
Palace of Westminster
Caxton Hall
Westminster Abbey
Church House
Lord North Street
Marsham Street
Horseferry Road
1 Foreign Office
2 Colonial Office
3 Home Office
4 India Office
5 Treasury
6 Central War Rooms
7 Ministry of Health

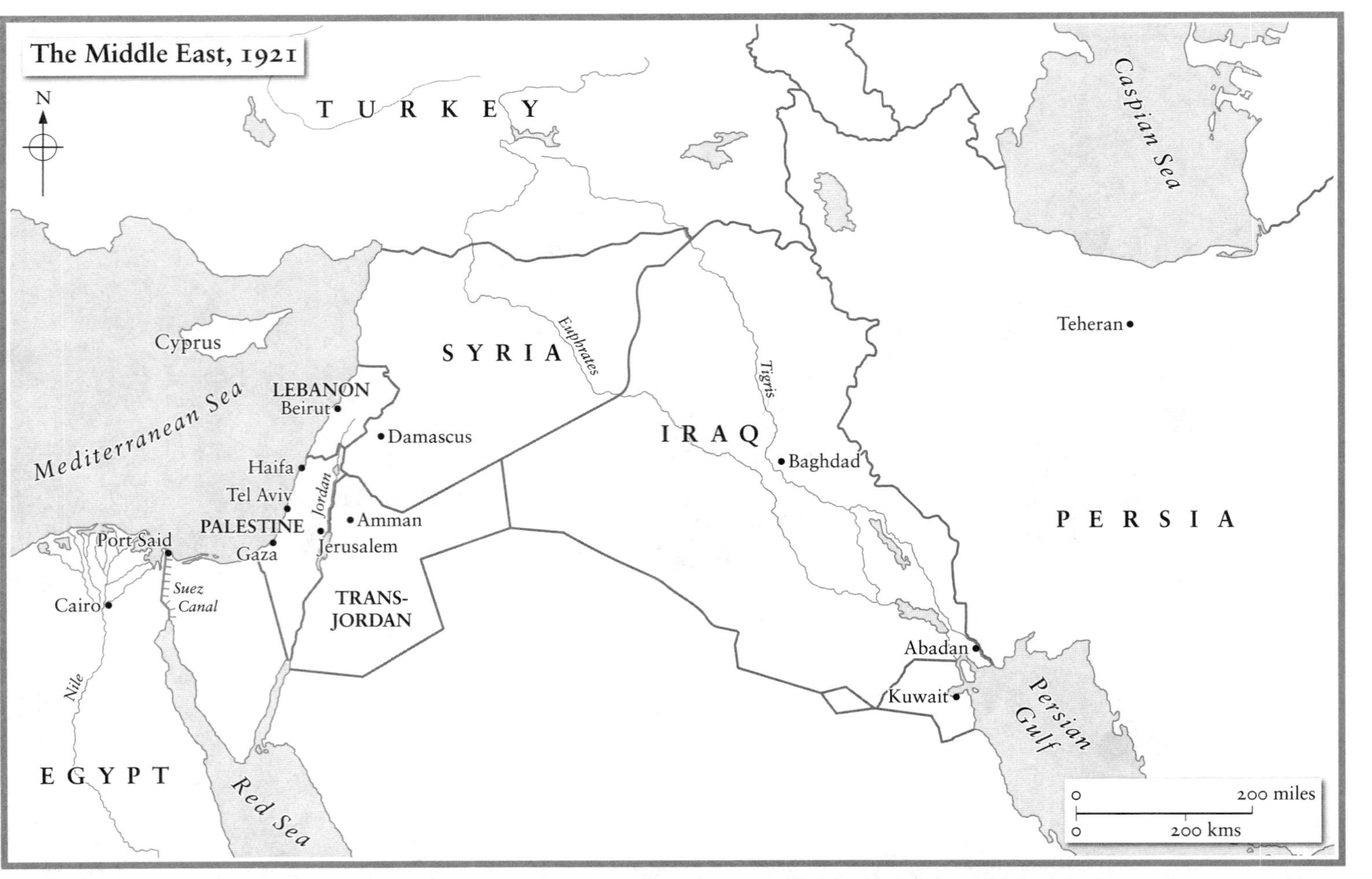
The Middle East, 1921
N
TURKEY
Caspian Sea
Teheran
PERSIA
SYRIA
Euphrates
Tigris
IRAQ
Baghdad
Cyprus
Mediterranean Sea
LEBANON
Beirut
Damascus
Haifa
Tel Aviv
Jordan
Amman
PALESTINE
Jerusalem
Gaza
Port Said
Suez Canal
Cairo
TRANS-JORDAN
Abadan
Kuwait
Persian Gulf
Nile
EGYPT
Red Sea
0
200 miles
0
200 kms

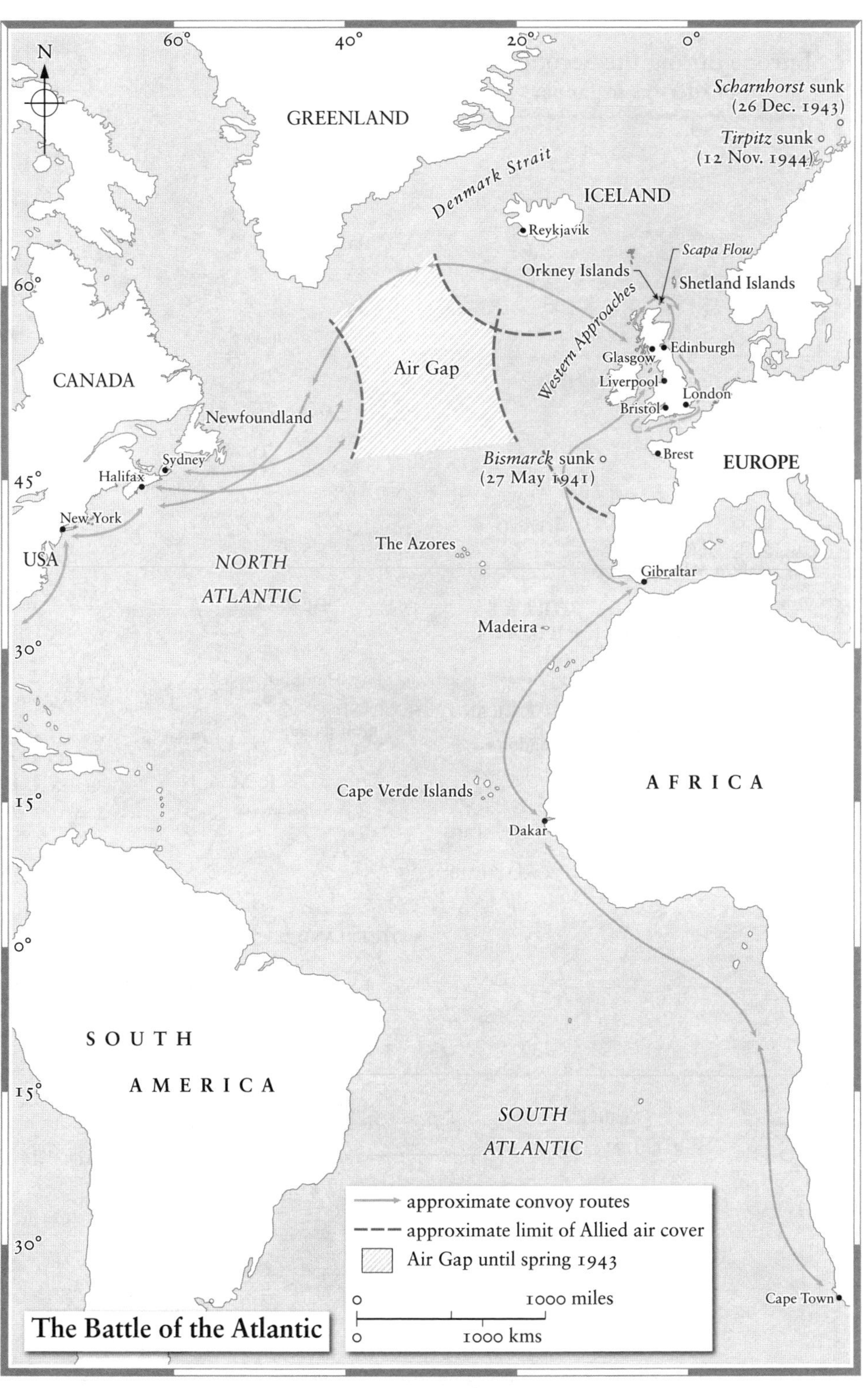

N
60°
40°
20°
0°
GREENLAND
Scharnhorst sunk
(26 Dec. 1943)
Tirpitz sunk
(12 Nov. 1944)
Denmark Strait
ICELAND
Reykjavik
Scapa Flow
Orkney Islands
Shetland Islands
Western Approaches
Air Gap
CANADA
Glasgow
Edinburgh
Liverpool
London
Bristol
Newfoundland
Sydney
Halifax
Brest
Bismarck sunk
(27 May 1941)
EUROPE
45°
New York
USA
The Azores
NORTH
ATLANTIC
Gibraltar
Madeira
30°
Cape Verde Islands
AFRICA
15°
Dakar
0°
SOUTH
AMERICA
15°
SOUTH
ATLANTIC
approximate convoy routes
approximate limit of Allied air cover
Air Gap until spring 1943
30°
0
1000 miles
0
1000 kms
Cape Town

The Battle of the Atlantic

Europe during the Second World War
borders as in January 1938
N
ATLANTIC OCEAN
Narvik
NORWAY
SWEDEN
Trondheim
Åndalsnes
Bergen
Oslo
Rjukan
Stavanger
Stockholm
Jösing Fjord
Skagerrak
SCOTLAND
NORTHERN IRELAND
North Sea
DENMARK
Copenhagen
Baltic Sea
GREAT BRITAIN
IRELAND
Dublin
Sylt
Danzig
EAST PRUSSIA
WALES
Hamburg
Lübeck
Stettin
ENGLAND
HOLLAND
Lek
Amsterdam
Bergen-Belsen
Berlin
Potsdam
London
Nijmegen
Torgau
GERMANY
Breslau
Lublin
BELGIUM
Rhine
Buchenwald
Elbe
Kraków
Paris
CZECHOSLOVAK
LUXEMBOURG
Danube
Vienna
FRANCE
AUSTRIA
SWITZERLAND
Carinthia
HUNGARY
Ljubljana Gap
Ljubljana
Po
Trieste
YUGOSLAVIA
Florence
Metauro
Adriatic Sea
ITALY
Corsica
Ajaccio
Lazio
Rome
Anzio
Isernia
Monte Cassino
Bari
ALBANIA
Naples
Salerno
Sardinia
Corfu
PORTUGAL
Madrid
SPAIN
Mediterranean Sea
Gibraltar
Pantelleria
Malta

Curzon Line
Baku–Batumi railway
Gothic Line
0
500 miles
0
500 kms
White Sea
Archangel
UNION OF SOVIET SOCIALIST REPUBLICS
Leningrad
Moscow
Volga
Katyń
Orel
Minsk
BELORUSSIA
Stalingrad
Dnieper
Kiev
UKRAINE
Caspian Sea
Odessa
CRIMEA
Balaklava
Baku
Sevastopol
Yalta
GEORGIA
Batumi
AZERBAIJAN
Bucharest
Black Sea
Istanbul
TURKEY
Leros
Dodecanese
Sounion
Rhodes
Nicosia
Cyprus
Crete
Maleme

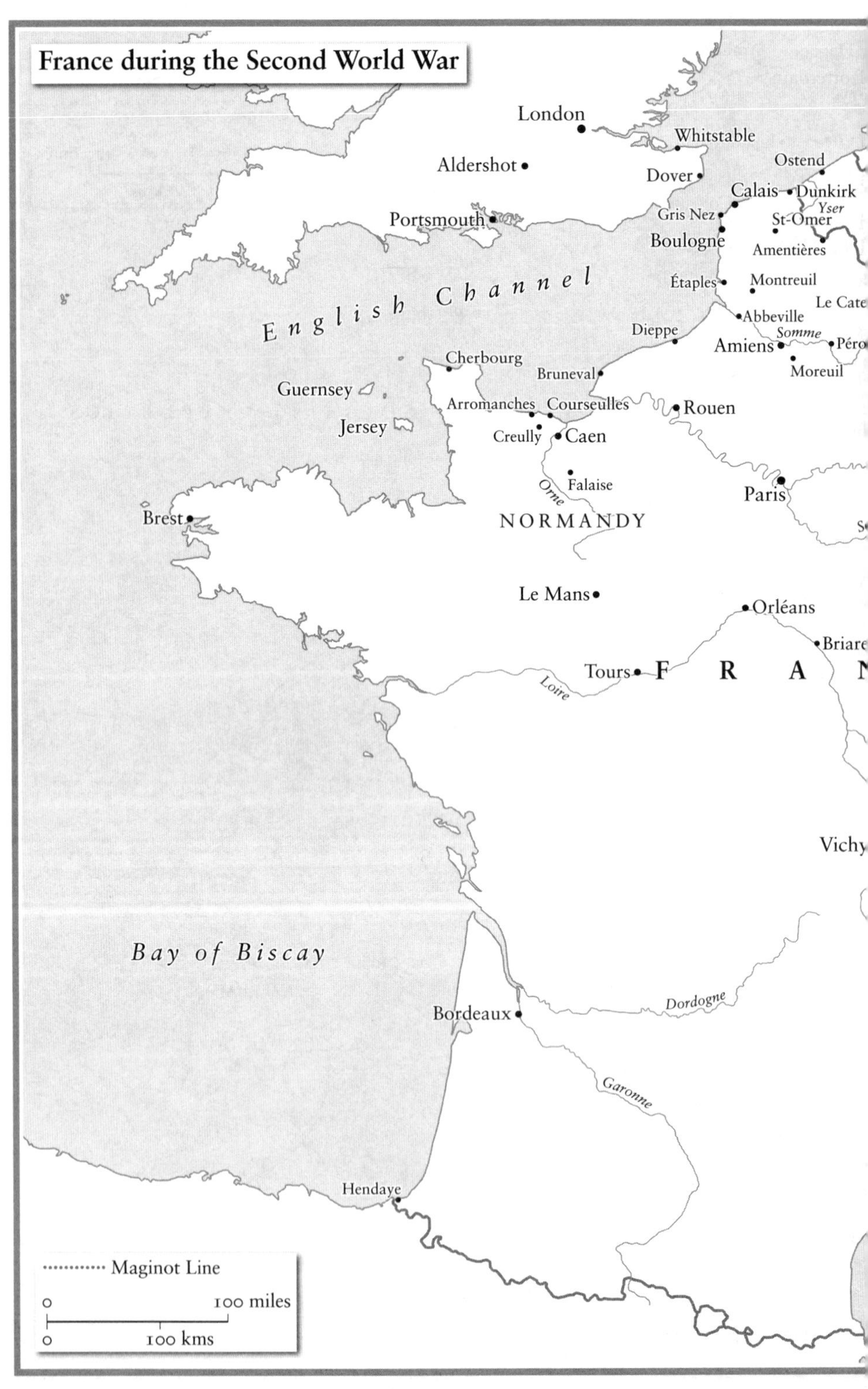
France during the Second World War
London
Whitstable
Aldershot
Dover
Ostend
Calais
Dunkirk
Yser
Portsmouth
Gris Nez
St-Omer
Boulogne
Amentières
English Channel
Étaples
Montreuil
Le Cate
Abbeville
Dieppe
Somme
Amiens
Péro
Cherbourg
Bruneval
Moreuil
Guernsey
Arromanches
Courseulles
Rouen
Jersey
Creully
Caen
Falaise
Orne
Paris
Brest
NORMANDY
Le Mans
Orléans
Briare
Tours
F R A N
Loire
Vichy
Bay of Biscay
Dordogne
Bordeaux
Garonne
Hendaye
Maginot Line
0 100 miles
0 100 kms

N
Hague
Arnhem
Rotterdam
Wesel
RUHR
Waal
Leipzig
Dresden
Eindhoven
Antwerp
Büderich
Wuppertal
RHINELAND
GERMANY
Lidice
Prague
Cologne
Rhine
Brussels
Remagen
LGIUM
Liège
Meuse
amur
Malmédy
Würzburg
Moselle
Bastogne
Nuremberg
Trier
tcornet
Sedan
LUXEMBOURG
RDENNES
ufchâtel
heims
Meuse
Blenheim
Linz
Marne
Strasbourg
Munich
Rhine
Sochaux
AUSTRIA
Maîche
Zurich
E
Bern
SWITZERLAND
Lake Geneva
Lake Como
Zermatt
Baveno
Lake Maggiore
Venice
Lyon
Aix-les-Bains
Milan
Turin
Genoa
ITALY
Rhône
Cap d'Ail
Roquebrune
n-de-Provence
Golfe-Juan
Monte Carlo
x-en-Provence
Cannes
Marseilles
Toulon
Mediterranean Sea
Corsica

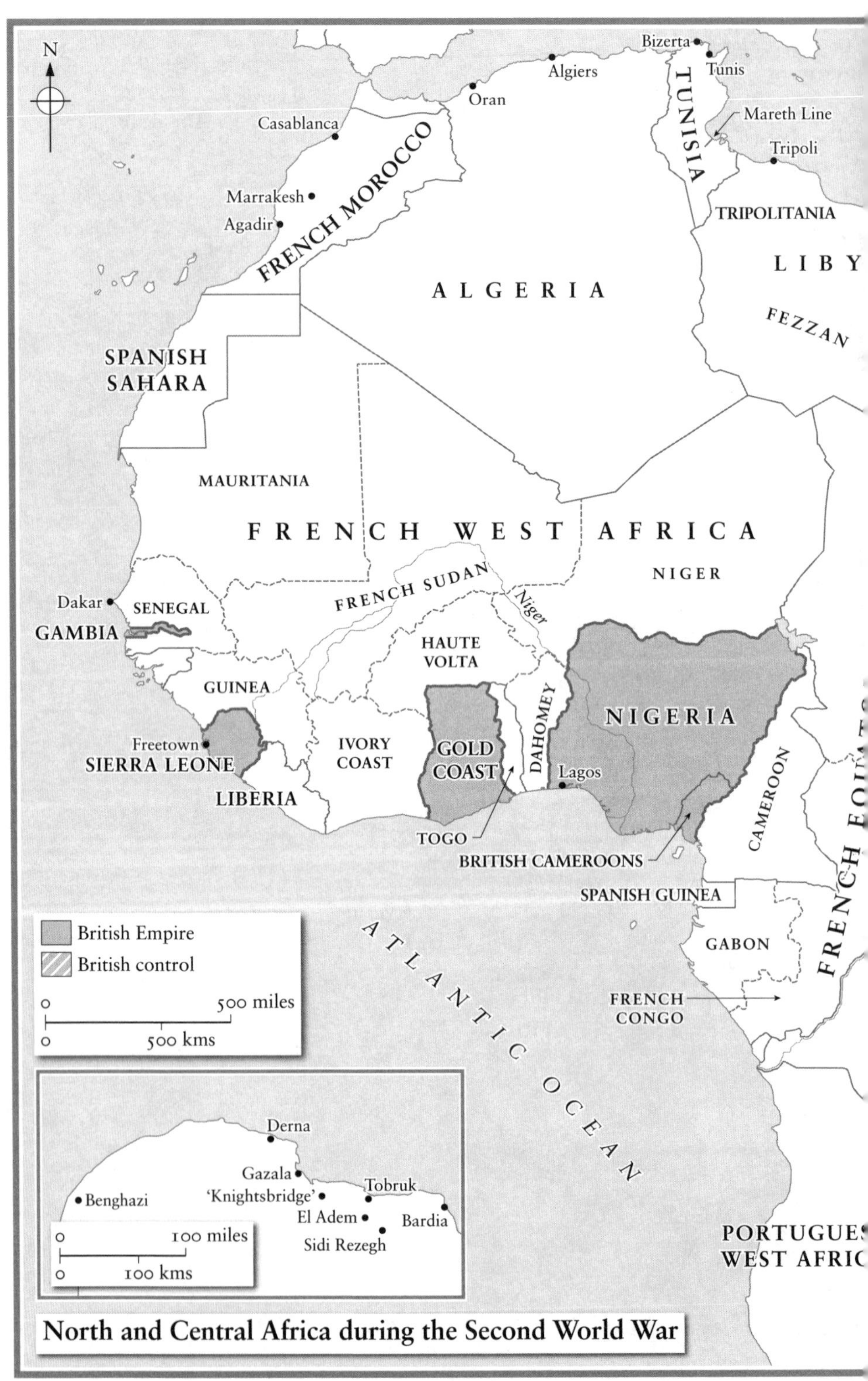

North and Central Africa during the Second World War

CYPRUS
editerranean Sea
LEBANON
SYRIA
IRAQ
Teheran
PERSIA
PALESTINE
Jerusalem
Alexandria
Mersa Matruh
El Alamein
TRANSJORDAN
attara Depression
Cairo
Suez
Fayoum Oasis
Suez Canal
RENAICA
EGYPT
KUWAIT
Persian Gulf
QATAR
Luxor
Aswan
ARABIA
OMAN
Red Sea
Mecca
Wadi Halfa
MUSCAT
Nile
Omdurman
Khartoum
Atbara
IAD
Massowah
YEMEN
ADEN PROTECTORATE
ERITREA
SUDAN
Aden
Djibouti
BRITISH SOMALILAND
ITALIAN EAST AFRICA
ONGO
ETHIOPIA
Murchison Falls
UGANDA
Lake Albert
KENYA
Congo
Kampala
Ripon Falls
Mount Kenya
Entebbe
Lake Naivasha
Nairobi
BELGIAN CONGO
Lake Victoria
BRITISH EAST AFRICA
Mombasa
ZANZIBAR
TANGANYIKA
INDIAN OCEAN
NYASALAND
NORTHERN RHODESIA
PORTUGUESE EAST AFRICA
S.RHODESIA
MADAGASCAR

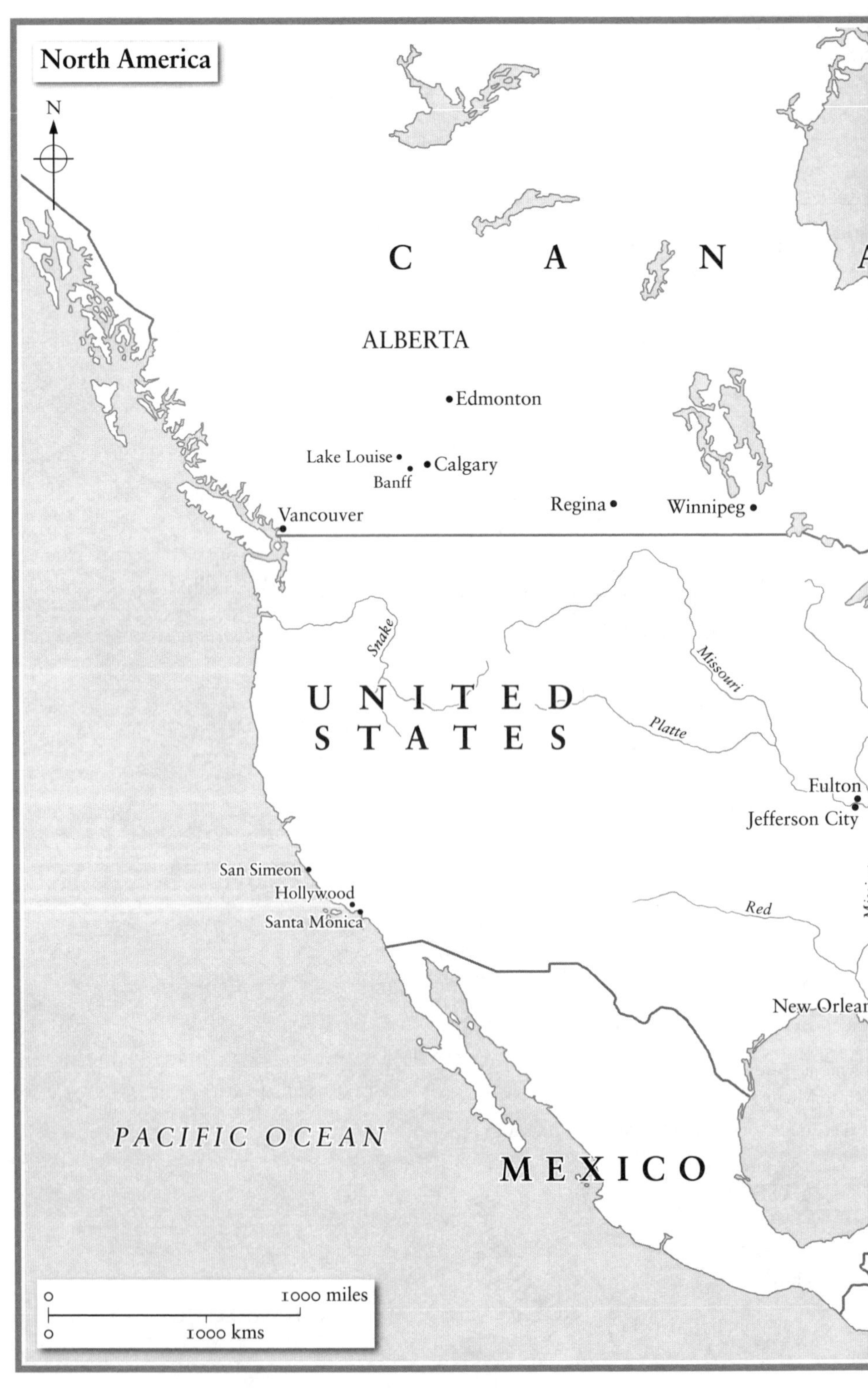
North America
N
CANADA
ALBERTA
Edmonton
Lake Louise
Banff
Calgary
Regina
Winnipeg
Vancouver
Snake
Missouri
Platte
UNITED STATES
Fulton
Jefferson City
San Simeon
Hollywood
Santa Monica
Red
New Orleans
PACIFIC OCEAN
MEXICO
0
1000 miles
0
1000 kms

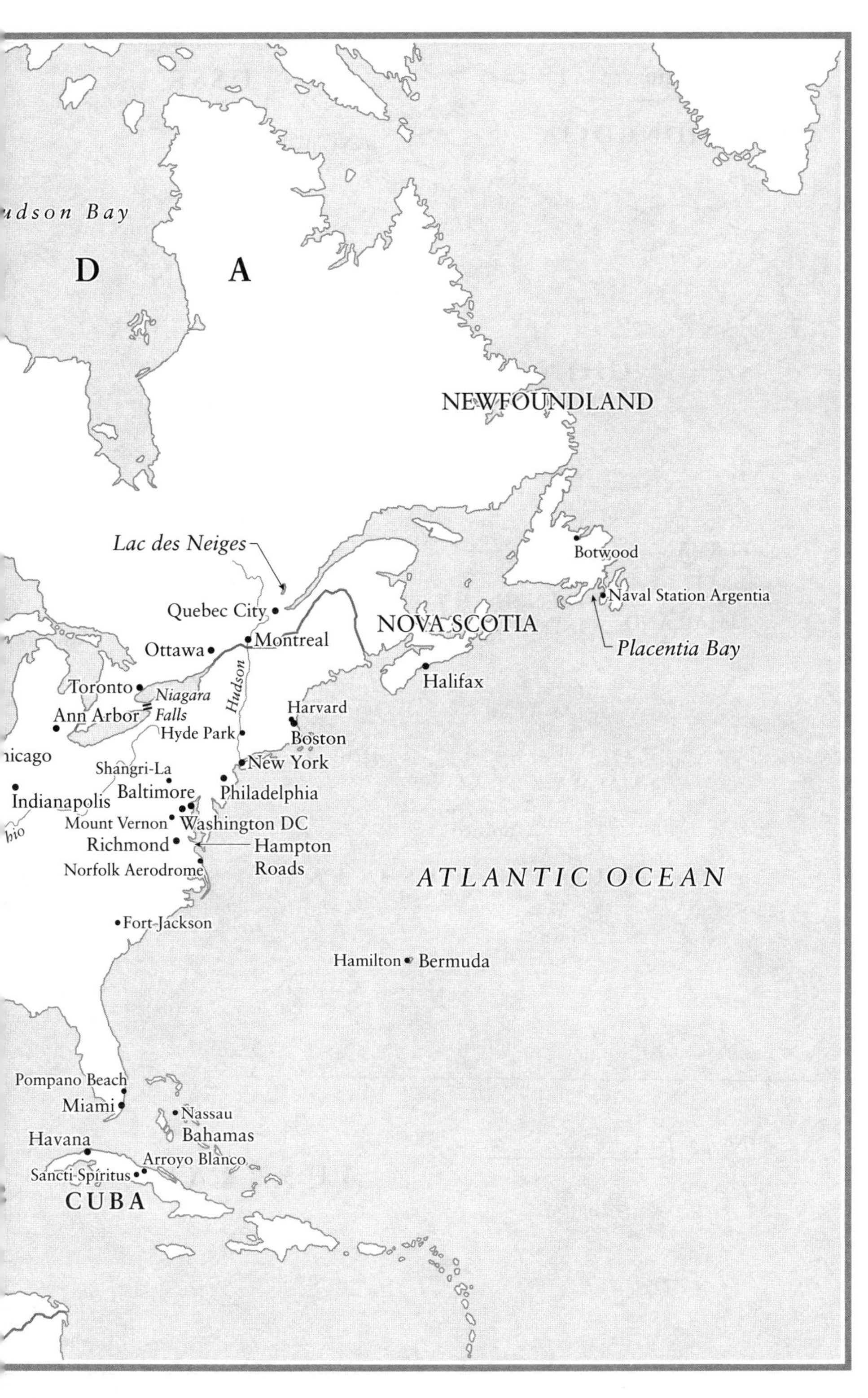

udson Bay
D
A
NEWFOUNDLAND
Lac des Neiges
Botwood
Naval Station Argentia
Quebec City
NOVA SCOTIA
Placentia Bay
Montreal
Ottawa
Hudson
Halifax
Toronto
Niagara
Falls
Ann Arbor
Harvard
Hyde Park
Boston
icago
New York
Shangri-La
Baltimore
Philadelphia
Indianapolis
Mount Vernon
Washington DC
hio
Richmond
Hampton
Roads
Norfolk Aerodrome
ATLANTIC OCEAN
Fort Jackson
Hamilton
Bermuda
Pompano Beach
Miami
Nassau
Bahamas
Havana
Arroyo Blanco
Sancti Spíritus
CUBA

The Pacific Theatre
MONGOLIA
MANCHURIA
USSR
Vladivostok
Peking
Wei-hei-wei
KOREA
Tokyo
Hiroshima
Kyoto
Nagasaki
JAPAN
CHINA
Shanghai
Yangtze
Burma Road
Kohima
Imphal
Irrawaddy
Mandalay
Hanoi
Hong Kong
Akyab
BURMA
Rangoon
THAILAND
Bangkok
FRENCH INDO-CHINA
Luzon
PHILIPPINES
Bataan
Guam
Straits of Malacca
Prince of Wales and Repulse sunk (10 Dec. 1941)
MALAYA
Singapore
Sumatra
Borneo
DUTCH EAST INDIES
Java
Port Darwin
INDIAN OCEAN
AUSTRALIA
Perth
Sydney
Canberra
40°
20°
0°
20°
100°
120°
140°

0 1000 miles
0 1000 kms

N

Midway

Pearl Harbor

Hawaii

P A C I F I C O C E A N

[Sol]omon Islands

NEW ZEALAND

160°

180°

200°

# Introduction

On Thursday, 20 December 1945, the editor of the *Sunday Dispatch*, Charles Eade, lunched with Winston Churchill and his wife Clementine at their new home in Knightsbridge in London. Eade was editing the former Prime Minister's wartime speeches for publication, and they were due to discuss the latest volume.

Before lunch, Eade had waited in what he later described as 'a beautiful room with bookshelves let into the wall and carrying superbly bound volumes of French and English books', which Churchill called his 'snob library'. The walls were adorned with pictures of Churchill's great ancestor, the 1st Duke of Marlborough, and a portrait of Churchill painted by Sir John Lavery during the First World War.

The lunch reflected post-war British rationing: an egg dish, cold turkey and salad, plum pudding and coffee. They drank a bottle of claret that the Mayor of Bordeaux had just sent over. Churchill told the trusted journalist, who had lunched with him several times during the war, that he 'had got very drunk' at a dinner at the French Embassy the previous night, adding with a chuckle, 'drunker than usual'.

Over several glasses of brandy and a cigar – whose band Eade took away as a souvenir – Churchill got down to discussing the best way to publish the wartime speeches he had delivered when the House of Commons had been in secret session during the war. In the course of their hour-long talk, he showed Eade the sixty-eight volumes of minutes, messages and memoranda that he had sent to various Cabinet ministers and the Chiefs of Staff between 1940 and 1945, allowing him to open them at random.

When Eade naturally expressed surprise at the sheer volume of work that Churchill had managed to get through as prime minister, 'He explained to me that he was able to handle all these affairs at the centre, because his whole life had been a training for the high office he had filled during the war.' It was a sentiment that Churchill had expressed two years earlier to the Canadian Prime Minister, William Mackenzie King, during the Quebec Conference in August 1943. When King told Churchill that no one else could have saved the British Empire in 1940, he replied that 'he had had very exceptional training, having been through a previous war, and having had large experience in government.' King rejoined, 'Yes, it almost confirmed the old Presbyterian idea of pre-destination or pre-ordination; of his having been the man selected for this task.' This idea was reiterated by the Conservative politician Lord Hailsham, who had been a junior minister in Churchill's wartime government, when he said, 'The one case in which I think I can see the finger of God in contemporary history is Churchill's arrival at the premiership at that precise moment in 1940.'

Churchill put his remarks to King and Eade far more poetically three years later in the final lines of his book *The Gathering Storm*, the first volume of his war memoirs. Recalling the evening of Friday, 10 May 1940, when he had become prime minister only hours after Adolf Hitler had unleashed his Blitzkrieg on the West, Churchill wrote, 'I felt as if I were walking with destiny, and that all my past life had been but a preparation for this hour and for this trial . . . I could not be reproached either for making the war or with want of preparation for it. I thought I knew a good deal about it all, and I was sure I should not fail.'

He had believed in his own destiny since at least the age of sixteen, when he told a friend that he would save Britain from a foreign invasion. His lifelong admiration of Napoleon and his own ancestor, John Churchill, 1st Duke of Marlborough, coloured his belief that he too was a man of destiny. His aristocratic birth, as the holder of the two famous names of Spencer and Churchill, gave him a tremendous self-confidence that meant that he was not personally hurt by criticism. In the courageous and often lonely stands he was to take against the twin totalitarian threats of Fascism and Communism, he cared far more for what he imagined would have been the good opinion of his fallen comrades of the Great War than for what was said by his living colleagues on the benches of the House of Commons.

The memory of his friends killed in war or by accidents (such as Lawrence of Arabia) or alcoholism (such as F. E. Smith) very often moved Churchill to tears, but so did many other things, as this book will relate. Churchill's passions and emotions often mastered him, and he never minded crying in public, even as prime minister, in an age that admired the stiff upper lip. This was just one phenomenon of many that made him a profoundly unusual person.

This book explores the extraordinary degree to which in 1940

Churchill's past life had indeed been but a preparation for his leadership in the Second World War. It investigates the myriad lessons that he learned in the sixty-five years before he became prime minister – years of error and tragedy as well as of hard work and inspiring leadership – then it looks at the ways that he put those lessons to use during civilization's most testing hour and trial. For although he was indeed walking with destiny in May 1940, it was a destiny that he had consciously spent a lifetime shaping.

# PART ONE

# The Preparation

# I

# A Famous Name, November 1874–January 1895

*It is said that famous men are usually the product of unhappy childhood. The stern compression of circumstances, the twinges of adversity, the spur of slights and taunts in early years, are needed to evoke that ruthless fixity of purpose and tenacious mother-wit without which great actions are seldom accomplished.*

Churchill, *Marlborough*[1]

*Half English aristocrat and half American gambler.*

Harold Macmillan on Churchill[2]

Winston Leonard Spencer-Churchill was born in a small ground-floor room, the nearest bedroom to the main entrance of Blenheim Palace in Oxfordshire, at 1.30 a.m. on Monday, 30 November 1874. It was a worrying birth as the baby was at least six weeks premature, and his mother, the beautiful American socialite Jennie Jerome, had suffered a fall a few days earlier. She had also been shaken by a pony-cart the day before the birth, following which her labour-pains started. In the event there were no abnormalities, and the baby's father, Lord Randolph Churchill, the younger son of the 7th Duke of Marlborough, was soon describing him as 'wonderfully pretty' with 'dark eyes and hair and very healthy'.[3] (The hair soon went strawberry blond, and great tresses of it from when he was five can be seen in the birth room at the Palace today; thereafter Churchill was red-headed.)

The name 'Winston' recalled both Sir Winston Churchill, the child's ancestor who had fought for King Charles I in the English Civil War, and Lord Randolph's elder brother, who had died aged four. 'Leonard' honoured the baby's maternal grandfather, a risk-taking American financier and railway-owner who had already made and lost two great fortunes on Wall Street. 'Spencer' had been hyphenated with 'Churchill' since 1817, the result of a marital alliance with the rich Spencer family of Althorp, Northamptonshire, who at that time held the earldom of Sunderland and were later to become the Earls Spencer. Proud of his Spencer forebears, he signed himself Winston S. Churchill, and in 1942 told an American trade unionist that 'of course his real name was Spencer-Churchill and it is in this way that he is described, for example, in Court Circulars when he goes to see the King.'[4]

The child's paternal grandfather was John Winston Spencer-Churchill, owner of Blenheim Palace, which has been described both as the English Versailles and as 'the greatest war memorial ever built'.[5] Named after the most glorious of the battles won by John Churchill, 1st Duke of Marlborough, in the War of Spanish Succession in 1704, its magnificent structure, tapestries, busts, paintings and furnishings commemorated a victory in a conflict that had saved Britain from domination by a European superpower – in this case, the France of Louis XIV – a message that the young Winston did not fail to imbibe. 'We have nothing to equal this,' King George III admitted when he visited Blenheim Palace in 1786.

'We shape our buildings,' Winston Churchill was later to say, 'and afterwards our buildings shape us.'[6] Although he never lived at Blenheim, he was profoundly influenced by the splendour of the Palace's 500-foot frontage, its 7 acres of rooms and its 2,700-acre estate. He absorbed its magnificence during the many holidays and weekends he stayed there with his cousins. The Palace was – still is – pervaded with the spirit of the 1st Duke, the greatest soldier-statesman in British history, who, as Churchill was to describe him in his biography of his ancestor, was a duke 'in days when dukes were dukes'.[7]

For his late Victorian contemporaries, the young Winston Churchill's name conjured up two images: the splendour of the 1st Duke's military reputation and Palace of course, but also the adventurous career of Lord Randolph Churchill, the child's father. Lord Randolph had been elected a Member of Parliament nine months before Churchill was born, and was one of the leaders of the Conservative Party from the child's sixth birthday onwards. He was controversial, mercurial, opportunistic, politically ruthless, a brilliant speaker both on public platforms and in the House of Commons, and was marked out as a future prime minister – as long as his inherent tendency to recklessness did not get the better of him. In politics, he followed the precepts of the Conservative leader Benjamin Disraeli, which combined imperialism abroad with a progressive programme of social reform at home. Lord Randolph was to call his version Tory Democracy, and it was to be imbibed in full by Winston. His slogan, 'Trust the People', was to be used many times in his son's career.

Although Lord Randolph was the son of a duke, he was not rich, at least relative to most of the rest of his class. As an aristocratic younger son in the era of primogeniture, he could not expect to inherit much from his father; and although the father of his American wife Jennie Jerome had been enormously rich in the recent past – he was once nicknamed 'the King of New York' – he had seen massive reverses in the American stock-market crash of 1873. Nevertheless, Leonard Jerome still lived in a house that covered an entire block on Madison Avenue and 26th Street, and which boasted extensive stabling and a full-size theatre. He had owned the land where the Jerome Park Reservoir is today, founded the American Jockey Club and co-owned the *New York Times*.

By the time of Jennie's wedding the year after the crash, however, Jerome could settle only £2,000 per annum on his beautiful daughter, the Duke of Marlborough contributing £1,200 per annum for his son. Along with the leasehold on a house at 48 Charles Street in Mayfair, courtesy of Jerome, that ought to have been enough for the couple to live upon comfortably, had they not both been notorious spendthrifts. 'We were not rich,' their son recalled during the Second World War. 'I suppose we had about three thousand pounds a year and spent six thousand.'[8]

Lord Randolph had met Jennie at Cowes Regatta on the Isle of Wight in August 1873. After only three days he had proposed and been accepted. They married in the British Embassy in Paris after a seven-month engagement, on 15 April 1874. Although the Marlboroughs gave their formal blessing to the union, they were absent from the wedding, because the Duke – who had sent agents to New York and Washington to try to ascertain Jerome's genuine net worth – thought it a *mésalliance* and Jerome 'a vulgar kind of man', 'a *bad* character' from 'the class of speculators'.[9]

Churchill was proud that his parents had married for love. Writing in 1937 about a libel action he was launching against a book which had described him as 'the first-fruit of the first famous snob-dollar marriage', he told a friend:

> The reference to my mother and father's marriage is not only very painful to me, but as you know is utterly devoid of foundation. This was a love-match if ever there was one, with very little money on either side. In fact they could only live in the very smallest way possible to people in London Society. If the marriage became famous afterwards it was because my father, an unknown sprig of the aristocracy, became famous, and also because my mother, as all her photographs attest, was by general consent one of the beauties of her time.[10]

(He eventually won £500 in damages from the publisher for the libel, plus £250 in costs, but not the apology for which he had been hoping.)

Winston Churchill was born into a caste that held immense political and economic power in the largest empire in world history, and that had not yet become plagued by insecurity and self-doubt. Churchill's sublime self-confidence and self-reliance stemmed directly from the assurance he instinctively felt in who he was and where he came from. In his obituary of his cousin 'Sunny',* the 9th Duke of Marlborough, he wrote that he had been born into one of 'the three or four hundred families which had for three or four hundred years guided the fortunes of the nation'.[11] He knew he came from the apex of the social pyramid, and one of the key attributes of that class at that time was not to care overmuch what people further down it thought of them. As his greatest friend, the Tory MP and barrister F. E. Smith, later Lord Birkenhead, was to write of him, 'He was shielded in his own mind from self-distrust.'[12] This was to prove invaluable to Churchill at the periods – of which there were many – when no one else seemed to trust him.

The social life of the Victorian and Edwardian upper classes was partly based upon staying in the country houses of friends and acquaintances for the 'Friday-to-Monday' extended weekend. Over the coming years, Churchill was to stay with the Lyttons at Knebworth, his cousins the Londonderrys at Mount Stewart, the Rothschilds at Tring, the Grenfells at Taplow and Panshanger, the Roseberys at Dalmeny, the Cecils at Hatfield, the Duke of Westminster at Eaton Hall and on his yacht *Flying Cloud*, his cousins Lord and Lady Wimborne at Canford Manor, the John Astors at Hever and the Waldorf Astors at Cliveden, as well as paying frequent visits to Blenheim and very many other such houses. Although he occasionally experienced social ostracism as a result of his politics in later life, he always had an extensive and immensely grand social network upon which he could fall back. This largely aristocratic cocoon of friendship and kinship was to sustain him in the bad times to come.

The Victorian English aristocracy was a distinct tribe, with its own hierarchies, accents, clubs, schools, colleges, career-paths, vocabulary, honour-codes, love-rituals, loyalties, traditions, sports and sense of humour. Some of these were quite intricate and almost impenetrable to outsiders. When as a young subaltern Churchill was introduced to the caste system in India, he understood it instantly. His political opinions essentially stemmed from Disraeli's Young England movement of the 1840s, whose sense of *noblesse oblige* assumed eternal superiority but also instinctively appreciated the duties of the privileged towards the less well off. The interpretation Churchill gave to the obligations of aristocracy was that he and his class had a profound responsibility towards his country, which had the right to expect his lifelong service to it.

* So nicknamed because of his earliest courtesy title, the Earl of Sunderland, rather than because of his disposition.

The British upper classes of the last quarter of the nineteenth century could on occasion seem quite separate from the rest of society. Lord Hartington, heir to the dukedom of Devonshire, had never heard of napkin-rings, for example (because he assumed that table linen was washed after every meal); the statesman Lord Curzon was reputed to have taken a bus only once in his life, when he was outraged that the driver refused to take him where he was ordered. Similarly, the first time that Churchill dialled a telephone number himself was when he was seventy-three.[13] (It was to the speaking clock, which he thanked politely.) He did not believe he depended on household servants quite as much as he did. 'I shall cook for myself,' he once proudly told his wife in the 1950s. 'I can boil an egg. I've seen it done.'[14] (In the end, he did not.) Aged fifteen, one of the postscripts to his letters reads: 'Milbanke is writing this for me as I am having a bath.'[15]* Two years later he complained bitterly about having to travel in a second-class compartment, writing, 'I won't travel Second again by Jove.'[16] When older, he rarely went anywhere without a valet, even to the battlefields of the Boer War and Second World War, and while in prison in South Africa he had a barber come in to shave him. He ordered food at the Savoy that wasn't on the menu, and as prime minister, if he wanted a fly swatted, he asked his secretary to call for his valet to 'Wring its bloody neck.'[17] Churchill was emphatically not representative of the coming Age of the Common Man.

Like a true aristocrat, he was no snob. 'What is the sense of being against a man simply because of his birth?' he wanted to ask Adolf Hitler of the Jews.[18] His closest friends were taken from a wide social circle; indeed, if anything, he had something of a weakness for parvenus, such as his friends Brendan Bracken and Maxine Elliott. 'Imbued with a historic sense of tradition,' a close friend wrote, 'he was quite untrammelled by convention.'[19] This was seen in his eccentric dress-sense such as siren suits and zip-shoes, as well as the highly irregular hours he kept. He enjoyed disregarding the rules of hierarchy, often to others' fury. 'I am arrogant,' he once said of himself in a perceptive piece of self-analysis, 'but not conceited.'[20] In the modern world, a sense of aristocratic entitlement is considered reprehensible, but Churchill was replete with it and it affected his attitude towards everything – it explains, for example, his readiness blithely to spend money that he did not have. He lived his life in an aristocratic way even if he could not afford it, but that was in itself aristocratic. He demanded extended credit, gambled heavily in casinos and as soon as he was properly solvent – which was not until he was in his seventies – he bought racehorses.

* Sir John 'Jack' Milbanke later won the Victoria Cross in the Boer War.

Many are the memoirs that condemn Churchill for his insensitivity to other people and their views, but they fail to appreciate that just such a rhinocerine hide was essential for someone who was to become as addicted to controversy as he was. 'You are one of the few who have it in their power to bestow judgments which I respect,' he wrote to Lord Craigavon who had fought in the Boer War and was prime minister of Northern Ireland, in December 1938, at one of the lowest points in his life.[21] Like the Marquess of Lansdowne, who promoted peace with Germany during the First World War, or the Marquess of Tavistock, who much more reprehensibly did so during the Second, the aristocrat in Churchill encouraged him to say fully and exactly what he thought, regardless of the consequences.

Churchill spent his early years in Dublin, where his parents lived at Little Lodge, close to the Viceregal Lodge* in Phoenix Park, where Lord Randolph worked as private secretary to his father. The 7th Duke had been appointed viceroy and lord lieutenant of Ireland by Disraeli in January 1877; Lord Randolph had to leave London because he was being socially ostracized by the Prince of Wales after trying unsuccessfully to blackmail him over a scandal involving Randolph's elder brother, the Marquess of Blandford, some compromising love-letters and a married former mistress of the Prince. It was one of the very many unedifying scrapes in which Lord Randolph found himself during his short, unstable but undeniably exciting life. The elephantine Prince had a long memory, and Lord Randolph was not permitted to return to London for over three years.

Churchill's earliest memory was suitably martial, of his grandfather unveiling a statue to Lord Gough, the Anglo-Irish imperial hero, in Phoenix Park in 1878. The Duke made a speech which included the phrase 'And with a withering volley he shattered the enemy's line,' which Churchill claimed he understood even at the age of three.[22] With his grandfather representing Queen Victoria and discharging her ceremonial duties in Ireland, Churchill acquired a profound reverence for monarchy that was to stay with him for the rest of his life. His next memory came the following March, in 1879, when he was riding a donkey in the Park and came across what his governess feared was an Irish republican demonstration, but which was probably in fact only a march by the Rifle Brigade. 'I was thrown off and had concussion of the brain,' he later recalled. 'This was my first introduction to Irish politics!'[23] His next came in 1882 when Thomas Burke, the Under-Secretary of Ireland, who had given Churchill

* Áras an Uachtaráin, where the president of Ireland lives today.

a toy drum, was stabbed to death in Phoenix Park by Irish republican terrorists along with the newly appointed Chief Secretary, Lord Frederick Cavendish, profoundly shocking the household.

Churchill's younger brother Jack was born – also prematurely – in February 1880, while the family was still in Ireland, but that April Lord Randolph's social exile came to an end and he returned to set up house at 29 St James's Place in London. Churchill's next political memory was the death of Disraeli in April 1881, when he was six. 'I followed his illness from day to day with great anxiety,' he recalled, 'because everyone said what a loss he would be to his country and how no one else could stop Mr Gladstone from working his wicked will upon us all.'[24] The Liberal William Gladstone had won a general election in the month the Churchills returned to London, becoming prime minister for the second time. In 1883, Lord Randolph founded the Primrose League, a grass-roots Tory political organization, named after Disraeli's supposed favourite flower. It existed principally to promote his father's career and the Tory Democracy political programme, and Winston joined its Brighton branch when he was twelve.

'My dear Mamma, I hope you are quite well,' he wrote from Blenheim Palace in his first surviving letter, in January 1882, after his parents had celebrated Christmas elsewhere. 'I thank you very very much for the beautiful presents those Soldiers and Flags and Castle they are so nice it was so kind of you and dear Papa I send you my love and a great many kisses, Your loving Winston.'[25] Many boys had toy soldiers, but one of Churchill's cousins later recalled that 'His playroom contained from one end to the other a plank table on trestles, upon which were thousands of lead soldiers arranged for battle. He organized wars. The lead battalions were manoeuvred into action, peas and pebbles committed great casualties, forts were stormed, cavalry charged, bridges were destroyed.'[26] These battles were 'played with an interest that was no ordinary child game'. The enormous lead army implies generosity from his parents for the boy whom his grandmother was by then describing as 'a naughty, sandy-haired little bulldog'.[27] Yet the fact that his parents had spent Christmas away from him was indicative of a persistent physical as well as emotional distance that would today be regarded as verging on the abusive. His brother Jack's son Peregrine was possibly correct in his belief that his uncle had not been neglected by his parents more than most upper-class Victorian children of the period, but that his sensitive nature rebelled against it more than most.

Lord Randolph Churchill's political career and Jennie's active social life meant that they had relatively little time for their son. On one occasion Lord Randolph gave a speech in Brighton without bothering to visit Winston at school less than 2 miles away in Hove. After a dinner in the late

1930s, Winston was to say to his own son, 'We have this evening had a longer period of continuous conversation together than the total which I ever had with my father in the whole course of his life.'[28] Jennie noted in her diary each of the thirteen occasions that she saw her sons during the first seven months of 1882, such as 'Found the children pretty well' or 'Saw the children'.[29] She also went shopping eleven times, painted twenty-five times, had lunch or tea with her friend Lady Blanche Hozier twenty-six times and had tea with the Conservative MP Arthur Balfour ten times. She went out in the evenings so often that she mentioned instead the very rare occasions when she 'did not go out to any parties, too sleepy'. Otherwise she hunted, spent weekends in house parties in the country, had 'tremendous chaff' with the famous beau Captain Bay Middleton at tea and 'mostly frivolous larking' with friends at lunch, played the piano, dined at the Café Royal, played billiards, lunched at St James's Palace, watched Sarah Bernhardt and Lilly Langtry on stage, 'stayed in bed till 2 p.m.', played tennis and generally lived the crowded life of a much sought-after Society beauty.[30]

'Went to the Salisburys' party', reads a typical entry in Jennie's diary, 'afterwards to Cornelia's ball. The Prince and Princess there. Not wildly amusing.'[31] Since she could hardly have found 'Little Win' wildly amusing at seven, he had to take his place in the long queue for her attention and affection, as she lived the socially accomplished if somewhat vacuous life of the wife of a Victorian aristocrat and politician. On a single occasion she went out with Consuelo, Duchess of Marlborough, 'to give away blankets, etc' to the poor, two days after she had 'Shopped all morning'.[32] Winston was later famously to write of his mother, 'She shone for me like the evening star. I loved her dearly – but at a distance.'[33]

Much of Churchill's well-documented naughtiness at the various schools to which he was sent seems to have stemmed from the desire to draw attention to himself, for unlike the archetypal child of the Victorian era he was determined to be both seen and heard. It is rare for anyone to depict themselves as less intelligent than they genuinely are, but Churchill did so in his autobiography *My Early Life* in 1930, which needs to be read in the context of his colourful self-mythologizing rather than as strictly accurate history. His school reports utterly belie his claims to have been an academic dunce. Those from St George's Preparatory School in Ascot, which he entered just before his eighth birthday in 1882, record him in six successive terms as having come in the top half or usually top third of the class.[34]

Churchill was regularly beaten at St George's, but this was not because of his work – his History results were always 'good', 'very good' or 'exceedingly good' – but because his headmaster, H. W. Sneyd-Kinnersley, was a sadist described by one alumnus as 'an unconscious sodomite', who enjoyed beating young boys on their bare bottoms until they bled.[35] Ostensibly the reason for these fortnightly beatings derived from Churchill's bad conduct, which was described as '*very* naughty', 'still troublesome', 'exceedingly bad', 'very disgraceful' and so on.[36] 'He cannot be trusted to behave himself anywhere,' wrote Sneyd-Kinnersley in April 1884, but in the very next sentence: 'He has very good abilities.'[37]

'Dreadful legends were told about Winston Churchill,' recalled the writer Maurice Baring, a near-contemporary at St George's. 'His naughtiness appeared to have surpassed anything. He had been flogged for taking sugar from the pantry, and so far from being penitent, he had taken the headmaster's sacred straw hat from where it hung over the door and kicked it to pieces. His sojourn at this school [was] one long feud with authority. The boys did not seem to sympathize with him. Their point of view was conventional and priggish.'[38] (This lack of friendly support from conventional and priggish contemporaries was to dog Churchill for almost the rest of his life.)

At this distance of time it is impossible to tell whether Churchill's bad behaviour had genuinely warranted punishment, or whether Sneyd-Kinnersley's craving to hurt children was more to blame, but before Churchill was ten years old the beatings had so damaged his health that his parents took him away from St George's and sent him to a far kinder school in Hove, run by two sisters both called Miss Thomson.

In *My Early Life* Churchill calls St George's 'St James's', perhaps out of tact, but more likely because he had sensibly put the place out of his mind for nearly half a century.[39] The person who had first spotted the lashes wrought on the young boy by Sneyd-Kinnersley was Churchill's fifty-two-year-old spinster nanny, Elizabeth Everest. 'My nurse was my confidante,' Churchill later recalled. 'It was to her I poured out my many troubles.'[40] One doesn't have to embrace Freudianism to find his nicknames for her – 'Woom' and 'Woomany' – poignant in a child looking for a mother-surrogate while his real mother was dazzling the Prince of Wales's Marlborough House Set* with her beauty, high spirits and sexual allure. Other maternal figures sometimes stepped in: his grandmother often had him to stay at Blenheim, and his aunt Lady Wimborne, Lord Randolph's sister, hosted him at Bournemouth during school holidays, but the woman who was by far the closest to him was Mrs Everest. 'Lots of love and kisses from your loving WOOM,' she would write to 'My darling Winny' when they were apart.[41] The Churchills unceremoniously sacked

* So called because they met at the Prince's London residence, Marlborough House.

her when he was nineteen and Jack thirteen, leaving the elder boy distraught. When she fell ill from peritonitis a short while later, he paid for her nursing and rushed to her bedside when she was dying, aged sixty-two. 'She had lived such an innocent and loving life of service to others and held such a simple faith', he later wrote of her death, 'that she had no fears at all, and did not seem to mind very much. She had been my dearest and most intimate friend during the whole of the twenty years I had lived.'[42] Subsequently he paid for the upkeep of her grave for the rest of his life.* Close friends were to predecease him throughout his life, but few were closer to him than Elizabeth Everest.

Aside from a lacerated bottom, Churchill took away from St George's a photographic and phonographic memory, perhaps as a means to avoid floggings by memorizing things by heart that he did not properly understand. He claimed in his autobiography that, because he could not master the first declension of Latin, 'there was one thing I could do: I could learn by heart.'[43] His capacity for memorizing huge amounts of prose and verse stayed with him for life, and would continue to astonish contemporaries well into old age. Many were the occasions that he would quote reams of poetry or songs or speeches half a century after having learned them. He was omnivorous in what his mind's ear chose to retain, which included long Shakespeare soliloquies, but also much of the repertoires of music-hall performers such as Marie Lloyd, George Robey, 'Little Tich' and George Chirgwin ('the White-Eyed Kaffir').[44]

At Hove, Churchill read voraciously, especially epic tales of heroic, often imperial, adventure, such as *Treasure Island*, *King Solomon's Mines* and the works of G. A. Henty.[45] He came first in Classics, third in French and fourth in English in 1885, further belying his later claims to have been an academic failure, while he continued to be either near or at the bottom of the entire school for conduct.[46] His unpunctuality was to be a lifelong trait; even as prime minister he would arrive late or with only minutes to spare for meetings with Cabinets and monarchs and for debates in Parliament. As his exasperated wife was to say, 'Winston always likes to give the train a sporting chance to get away.'[47]

Churchill knew from an early age that his father was famous, and he asked him for autographs to sell to his classmates.[48] When he was taken to a pantomime at Brighton where an actor playing Lord Randolph was hissed by the audience, he burst into tears and turned furiously on a man behind him, shouting, 'Stop that row, you snub-nosed Radical!'[49] In the summer of 1883, when Churchill was eight, his father took him to Paris.

* The Churchill Family Graves Trust undertakes the task today.

As they drove together through the Place de la Concorde, Churchill noticed that one of the monuments was covered with black crêpe and he asked his father why. 'These are monuments of the provinces of France,' replied Lord Randolph, but 'Alsace and Lorraine have been taken from France by the Germans in the last war [that is, the Franco-Prussian War of 1870–71]. The French are very unhappy about it and hope some day to get them back.' Churchill remembered 'quite distinctly thinking to myself, "I hope they will get them back."'[50] It was his first introduction to what he was to call 'the long feud between Teuton and Gaul'. His Francophilia was to remain long after Alsace and Lorraine had been restored to France by the Versailles Treaty in 1919.

Hove was kinder than St George's, but there were two dangerous incidents there. The first came in December 1884 when the ten-year-old Winston was stabbed in the chest with a penknife by a boy whose ear he was yanking. It turned out to be merely a flesh wound. The second came in March 1886 when he contracted pneumonia, his temperature reached 104.3 degrees Fahrenheit (40.2 Celsius), and he became delirious, an illness so serious that it even persuaded his parents to visit him.[51] Part of the cure was the regular administration of relatively large doses of brandy, both orally and rectally.[52] 'My boy at school at Brighton nearly died of inflammation of the lungs* last week,' his father informed the 3rd Marquess of Salisbury, the Conservative Party leader.[53] Overall, however, Churchill was happy at Hove, where he could pursue the activities that interested him, primarily French, History, riding, swimming and learning reams of poetry by heart.[54]

In June 1885, Lord Salisbury appointed Randolph Churchill secretary of state for India. It was in recognition of his talents and his ability to cause trouble rather than for any loyalty he had shown. As the leader of the tiny so-called Fourth Party of Tory MPs, Lord Randolph had often rebelled against the Conservative Party leadership in the Commons, making jokes at its expense. Salisbury hoped that an important Cabinet office might discipline him.

In February 1886 Lord Randolph annexed Upper Burma, a country five times the size of England, to the British Empire (which was already thrice the size of the Roman Empire at its height).[55] He had earlier opposed Gladstone's bombardment of Alexandria in 1882 as too much of a 'Forward' imperialist policy, yet only four years later he went further. Similarly, he had given assurances to Charles Stewart Parnell, the Irish nationalist leader, in 1885 that he would endorse Irish Home Rule, assurances which

* In fact, it was only his right lung.

in 1886 he completely reneged upon, declaring that the northern Protestants would start a civil war sooner than join a united Ireland. 'Ulster will fight,' he said provocatively in a public letter of 7 May 1886, 'and Ulster will be right.' Lord Randolph also made private remarks in favour of 'Fair Trade' – then a code for Imperial Protectionism – before publicly advocating Free Trade. His principles may have been flexible, but audiences that turned out to hear him speak were enormous, sometimes numbering in their tens of thousands, because he was an electrifying orator. His obvious ambition and opportunism, however, made him distrusted by Lord Salisbury and the Tory Establishment.

In the summer of 1886, when Winston was eleven, Lord Randolph and Jennie became estranged, and rumours spread of a formal separation.[56] She was spending even more of her time with the Marlborough House Set, pursuing an affair with the dashing Austrian Ambassador to London, Prince Karl Kinsky, which lasted at least until 1892, when she began another with the handsome Freddy, Lord Wolverton.[57] Lord Randolph meanwhile, when he was not in the Commons or the Carlton Club, spent a good deal of time in Paris, where people presumed he was womanizing. 'Tell Mary she is a fool not to forgive Billy,' he once wrote to Jennie about two of their friends. 'What does one occasional cook or housemaid matter?'[58] It was indicative of his attitude, but nonetheless surprising to express it in a letter to his wife.

The general election of July 1886 saw the Conservatives and their anti-Irish Home Rule allies the Liberal Unionists (henceforth together the Unionists) win an outright victory. In recognition of Lord Randolph's key role in enthusing massive audiences around the country and attacking Gladstone with wit and eloquence, Lord Salisbury, the Prime Minister, appointed him both chancellor of the Exchequer and leader of the House of Commons. As Salisbury was almost twenty years older, and sat in the Lords rather than the Commons, Lord Randolph seemed to be the heir apparent for the premiership. He was also in a key position to promote the Disraelian concept of Tory Democracy which he had adopted as his political philosophy. When asked by a friend to explain what it meant in 1885, he only half joked, 'I believe it to be principally opportunism.'[59] Forced to define it publicly three years later, he waffled, 'It invokes the idea of a Government who . . . are animated by lofty and liberal ideas.'

After only five months in office, Lord Randolph threatened to resign from the Cabinet over the military budget (the Estimates), which he considered too high, despite having supported higher defence expenditure in opposition. Behind this was an attempt to wrest power inside the Cabinet from the Prime Minister. Instead of backing down, as he had done several times in the past, Lord Salisbury simply accepted the resignation. Lord Randolph was never to hold public office again. He had behaved like a prima donna for years and ridden roughshod over his colleagues, and not a single Cabinet minister supported him.

In the biography of his father that Churchill was later to write, he connected the resignation with the onset of the mysterious disease that was to kill Lord Randolph within a decade: 'That frail body, driven forward by its nervous energies, had all these last five years been at the utmost strain. Good fortune had sustained it; but disaster, obloquy, and inaction now suddenly descended with crushing force, and the hurt was mortal.'[60] The boy was profoundly affected by his father's entirely self-inflicted disaster, from which he learned several important lessons. The most important was not to threaten to resign unless one is prepared to go into the wilderness. If one is not so prepared, then only threaten to resign along with several other people capable of bringing down the Government.

The attempted power-grab having spectacularly failed, Lord Randolph did indeed start to decline politically, mentally and personally. There were still some social occasions where the Churchills performed together in public – despite their informal separation, they still lived in the same house – although these grew fewer and fewer. On 8 August 1887, the diary of Prince George of Wales (the future King George V) records that at the time of Queen Victoria's Golden Jubilee 'the Randolph Churchills & Winny & Jack' went aboard the Royal Yacht *Osborne* at Spithead.[61] The twelve-year-old Churchill had the thrill of sailing on the Royal Yacht through the battle-fleet of twelve warships commanded by Vice Admiral Sir William Hewett VC, many of them names redolent of British history: HMS *Agincourt*, *Black Prince* and *Iron Duke* among them. That evening they went aboard the newly launched ironclad flagship HMS *Collingwood*.

'Did you go to Harrow or Eton?' Churchill asked his father in October 1887.[62] It seems extraordinary that he did not know his father had gone to Eton, but he himself was destined for Harrow, largely because of the supposed health benefits of Harrow Hill's sunlit uplands over Eton's misty lowlands. Founded in 1572, Harrow was one of the great public schools of England, which among ancient buildings provided an elite, largely classical education informed by equally ancient traditions for the future gentlemen who were expected to go on to run the country and Empire. He passed the entrance exam in March 1888, after working through the second book of Virgil's *Aeneid*.[63] In September 1941 he reminisced about Harrow to his private secretary John 'Jock' Colville, himself an Old

Harrovian, saying that this was 'where he had spent the unhappiest days of his life'.[64] He wrote to his parents in November of this second year, 'Don't imagine I am happy here.' He nonetheless returned to Harrow frequently between 1938 and 1962.

In *My Early Life*, Churchill boasted of how badly he had done in the entrance exam, and one of his school contemporaries, Sir Gerald Woods Wollaston (later Garter King of Arms), recalled that 'The inconvenience likely to be caused by the rejection of Lord Randolph Churchill's son' probably played a part in his acceptance.[65] Churchill claimed that 'In all the twelve years I was at school no one ever succeeded in making me write a Latin verse or learn any Greek except the alphabet.'[66] This was untrue, as his school reports show. He nonetheless recalled his schooldays as 'a sombre patch upon the chart of my journey' and 'a time of discomfort, restriction and purposeless monotony'.[67] On the day he entered Harrow, 17 April 1888, the boy three above him in the school list was Archibald Campbell-Colquhoun, who lived at Chartwell Manor at Westerham in Kent.[68]

For all his later denials, Churchill was in fact something of a success at Harrow. At fourteen he won a prize for reciting no fewer than 1,200 lines of Macaulay's *Lays of Ancient Rome* without error, and a contemporary recalled that 'he could quote whole scenes of Shakespeare's plays and had no hesitation in correcting his masters if they misquoted.'[69] He enjoyed Macaulay's tales of heroism set in the ancient world. 'If I had to make my literary will and my literary acknowledgements,' he told an acquaintance in 1946, 'I should have to own that I owe more to Macaulay than to any other English writer.'[70] The talented schoolmaster Robert Somervell taught Churchill English grammar at Harrow. 'Thus I got into my bones the essential structure of the ordinary British sentence,' Churchill wrote, 'which is a noble thing.'[71] Less noble was his sole attempt at poetry, an ode entitled 'Influenza'. The fourth of twelve stanzas goes:

On Moscow's fair and famous town,
Where fell the first Napoleon's crown,
It made a direful swoop;
The rich, the poor, the high, the low,
Alike the various symptoms know,
Alike before it droop.[72]

Churchill kept himself busy with all manner of eclectic pastimes. He was a member of his victorious House swimming team; wrote for the school magazine the *Harrovian*; collected stamps, birds' eggs and autographs; built a model theatre; played chess; bred silkworms; drew landscapes, and played the cello. In April 1892 he won the Public Schools

Fencing Championship Cup at Aldershot, using a foil. Despite being smaller and lighter than the other competitors, he won, according to the *Harrovian*, 'chiefly due to his quick and dashing attack which quite took his opponents by surprise'.[73]

Importantly for later life, Churchill also polished a talent for cheeky repartee. When Mr Mayo, a Harrow teacher, expostulated to a class rhetorically, 'I don't know what to do with you boys!' the fourteen-year-old Churchill retorted, 'Teach us, sir!'[74] Later, when the Headmaster, the formidable Dr Welldon, said, 'Churchill, I have very grave reason to be displeased with you,' he received the less witty but equally brave reply, 'And I, sir, have very grave reason to be displeased with you!'[75] Churchill displayed similar courage when he showed his nanny Mrs Everest all over Harrow, 'to her immense delight', as Wollaston recalled, 'and not content with this, he marched arm-in-arm with her up the high street for all who cared to see.'[76] The story of Churchill and his nanny 'went like wildfire through the school, and did not then, I regret to say, add favourably to his schoolboy reputation', his cousin Shane Leslie remembered. 'When he walked about with her, a few jeering friends followed him down to the station where he had the courage to kiss her.'[77] Churchill was not about to allow the sneers of his snobbish contemporaries to mar the happiness of the woman who had showed him unquestioning love all his life. As Leslie noted, 'He owed much health and probably his life to her devotion.'

Churchill enjoyed lectures on the battles of Waterloo and Sedan (where Germany had sealed France's fate in 1870 and would again in 1940), on Alpine climbing by the famous mountaineer Edward Whymper of Zermatt, and on natural selection in butterflies, from which possibly stemmed his lifelong love of them. Asked what he intended to do as a profession, he replied, 'The Army, of course, so long as there's any fighting to be had. When that's over, I shall have a shot at politics.'[78] The Harrow Archives contain an extraordinary document written when Churchill was fourteen, a 1,500-word essay set in the future about a British invasion of Russia, complete with six pages of battle plans. Written in the first person by 'Colonel Seymour' and dated 7 July 1914, it is full of military manoeuvres, 'glittering bayonets', 'dark clouds of Cossacks', heroic derring-do and aides-de-camp charging across limb-strewn battlefields carrying vital orders between commanders. 'The fields which this morning were green', Churchill wrote, 'are now tinged with the blood of seventeen thousand.'[79] A quarter of a century before the Great War, he understood that as a result of advances in military technology 'The front line was no place for cavalry now.' Like Churchill's hero Napoleon, 'Colonel Seymour' was nonetheless kept busy on horseback. 'As I galloped off to obey the order,' he writes, 'I looked over my shoulder at the spot on which General C— was standing, even while I was looking a nine-pound shell burst within three paces of him, exactly where I had been standing for half an hour. "Chance," you say, but that was more than chance.'[80]

A brave cavalry charge in which the 17th Lancers and the 10th and 11th Hussars attack the Odessa and Dnieper regiments sees the British lose one-third of their men, especially once 'A crackle of musketry mixes with the cannonade.'[81] There are lots of military commands such as 'With case shot at a hundred yards, fire', 'Action right', 'Independent firing' and other orders he had learned from the Harrow School Rifle Volunteer Corps. Seymour is captured, but, in the chaos of battle, 'Seeing my opportunity I jumped on a stray horse and rode for my life.'[82] In the rest of the campaign, 'The enemy retreated slowly and deliberately at first, but at the River Volga they became broken and our cavalry, light and heavy, executed a most brilliant charge which completed the confusion' and showed 'the superiority of John Bull over the Russian Bear'.[83] The hero of the story was thus able 'to sleep tonight under the influence of victory which is the best narcotic in the world'. Churchill finally notes that 'Colonel Seymour' died gallantly on 21 September 1914, 'endeavouring to hold a fortification on the heights of Woronzoff'.[84]

Churchill's teenage juvenilia might not seem worth recording except that later in life he took part in a cavalry charge of the 21st Lancers (which later amalgamated with the 17th Lancers of the story), was captured by an enemy but later escaped, oversaw the fate of a British Expeditionary Force to Russia and nearly died after a shell landed where he had been standing moments earlier, during a war that broke out within a month of Churchill's speculative dating of such an event twenty-five years earlier. Stalingrad, where the German invasion of Russia was broken in 1943, lies on the River Volga. 'Chance, you say . . .'

This was not his only moment of extraordinary prescience. On a Sunday evening in July 1891, in a basement room of Dr Welldon's house after evensong in chapel, he was discussing his life plans with his friend Murland Evans. 'I can see vast changes coming over a now peaceful world,' Churchill told Evans,

> great upheavals, terrible struggles; wars such as one cannot imagine; and I tell you London will be in danger – London will be attacked and I shall be very prominent in the defence of London. I see further ahead than you do. I see into the future. This country will be subjected somehow, to a tremendous invasion, by what means I do not know, but I tell you I shall be in command of the defences of London and I shall save London and England from disaster . . . dreams of the future are blurred but the main objective is clear. I

> repeat – London will be in danger and in the high position I shall occupy, it will fall to me to save the capital and save the Empire.[85]

Evans went on to work in the War Office and was a man whose powers of recollection can be depended on.

'I am always ready to learn,' Churchill was to say in 1952, 'although I do not always like being taught.'[86] He continued to be beaten at Harrow, because, as a contemporary recalled, 'He consistently broke almost every rule made by masters or boys, was quite incorrigible, and had an unlimited vocabulary of backchat.'[87] On 25 May 1891, for example, he was 'swished' (caned) seven times on the backside for 'breaking into premises and doing damage' in a disused factory in Harrow. This did not make him unusual; according to the Harrow punishment book, fourteen boys received seven swishes that month. Churchill kept a bulldog, against school rules, and used to walk him with one of the townspeople. He did odd jobs for Nugent Hicks, the head boy, who gave him a 'whopping' for failing to perform his duties. 'I shall be a greater man than you,' Churchill told him during one of these swishings, with spectacularly poor timing. Hicks, who later became bishop of Lincoln, replied: 'You can take two more for that.'[88]

Little would induce his parents to visit him at school. 'Please do do do do do do come down to see me,' he begged in February 1891. 'Please do come I have been so disappointed so many times about your coming.'[89] They did not. 'Dearest boy, don't be so lazy and neglectful about writing,' Jennie wrote to him in a typical letter. 'You only seem to do so when you want something – and then you are very prolific with your pen!'[90] Her hypocrisy can be measured precisely: in the seven years from 1885 to 1892, Churchill wrote to his parents seventy-six times; they to him six times. The huge majority of Churchill's letters were not asking for anything, except, between the lines, for love and attention. Their letters to him on the other hand contained constant remonstrations. 'I would go down to you – but I have so many things to arrange for the Ascot party next week that I can't manage it,' Jennie wrote in June 1890. 'I have much to say to you, I'm afraid not of a pleasant nature . . . your Father is very angry with you' (for using a typewriter).[91] Of his schoolwork, 'Your father and I are both more disappointed than we can say . . . I daresay you have a thousand excuses . . . You make me very unhappy . . . your work is an insult to your intelligence . . . It is that thoughtlessness of yours which is your greatest enemy . . . I must say that you repay his kindness to you badly.'[92]

When the seventeen-year-old Churchill tried to get out of being sent to a French family to learn French over Christmas 1891, Jennie wrote, 'I have only read one page of your letter and I send it back to you as its style does not please me.'[93] 'My darling Mummy,' he replied, 'never would I have believed you would have been so unkind. I am utterly miserable . . . I can't tell you how wretched you have made me feel . . . Oh my Mummy! . . . I expect you were too busy with your parties and arrangements for Christmas. I comfort myself by this.'[94] As a postscript he added, 'I am more unhappy than I can possibly say . . . your loving son, Winny.'[95]

There were many more such letters. On 18 December he wrote, 'I am so wretched. Even now I weep. Please my darling Mummy be kind to your loving son. Don't let my silly letter make you angry. Let me at least think that you love me – Darling Mummy I despair. I am so wretched. I don't know what to do. Don't be angry I am so miserable.'[96] 'I can't tell you what trouble I have had with Winston,' Jennie wrote to her husband, neglecting to bother with a reply to her son. 'Of course it is a great disappointment to him not being home for Xmas but he makes as much fuss as tho' he were going to Australia for two years . . . I think I have arranged everything satisfactorily.'[97] Jennie did not want her son in London as it would have inconvenienced her in her affair with Count Kinsky. The only person who comforted Winston and supported his bid to spend Christmas with his family was Mrs Everest, who of course had no say in the matter.

The Harrow School Songs, sung by the houses each term and by the whole school annually, were written by masters to encourage pupils to identify with the school, its famous alumni and Britain's glorious past. One of these, 'Stet Fortuna Domus', first performed in 1891 when Churchill was at the school, includes the stanza:

> Tonight we praise the former days
> In patriotic chorus,
> And celebrate the good and great
> Who trod the Hill before us;
> Where Sheridan and Peel began,
> In days of Whig and Tory,
> Where Ashley vow'd to serve the Crowd
> And Byron rose to Glory.

Another song, 'When Raleigh Rose', connected the school, which had been founded during Queen Elizabeth I's reign, to the heroes who defeated the Spanish Armada. In 'Giants', Harrovians were enjoined to remember that 'the hero-race may come and go, / But it doesn't exactly die! . . . For all of we, / Whoever we be, / Come up to the giants of old, you see.' The most famous of the Songs, 'Forty Years On', written in 1872, had a stanza that ran:

Routs and discomfitures, rushes and rallies,
Bases attempted and rescued and won,
Strife without anger, and art without malice –
How will it seem to you, forty years on?
Then, you will say, not a feverish minute
Strained the weak heart and the wavering knee,
Never the battle raged hottest, but in it,
Neither the last nor the faintest were we![98]

'Listening to those boys singing all those well-remembered songs,' Churchill told his son after he had visited the school during the London Blitz in 1940, 'I could see myself fifty years before singing with them those tales of great deeds and of great men and wondering with intensity how I could ever do something glorious for my country.'[99] His son believed that 'The stirring patriotism these verses evoked abided with him for ever and were the mainspring of his political conduct.'[100] The message of the school and of these songs was strong and clear: it was incumbent on Harrovians to try to become great men. After Churchill had pushed his diminutive fellow pupil Leopold Amery into Ducker, the school swimming pool, not realizing that Amery was in fact in the senior year, Churchill apologized by saying, 'My father, who is a great man, is also small.'[101]

Churchill had a long run of illnesses and accidents throughout his time at Harrow, with a toothache, biliousness (cured by Eno's Salts), a concussion from falling off a bicycle, 'severe fever', measles and an incipient hernia in the groin.[102] In January 1893, playing a game of chase with his cousins at their estate in Wimborne aged eighteen, he jumped off a footbridge, hoping the branches of the trees below him would snap off and break his descent, which they did not. He fell nearly thirty feet on to hard ground, was concussed for three days and confined to bed for nearly three months with a ruptured kidney and a broken bone in his mid-back that was only discovered in an X-ray in 1962. 'For a year I looked at life round a corner,' he wrote.[103]

While convalescing, Churchill visited Parliament. He listened to and occasionally had a chance to meet the leading figures of late Victorian politics, including Arthur Balfour, Joseph Chamberlain, Lord Rosebery, Herbert Asquith and John Morley, introduced by his father. 'Politics seemed very important and vivid to my eyes in those days,' he reminisced.[104] On 21 April 1893, he was in the gallery to witness perhaps the most climactic parliamentary debate of the era, when William Gladstone presented the Second Irish Home Rule Bill to the House of Commons. As a great parliamentary occasion, the drama was only to be exceeded half a century later, and then by Churchill himself. Churchill's plan was to distinguish himself as a soldier, before entering the House of Commons to further his father's Tory Democrat legacy.

When Lord Randolph agreed to let his son join the British Army after Harrow, Winston believed that 'my father with his experience and flair had discerned in me the qualities of military genius.'[105] He continued in this delusion for several years, until he was told that his father had in fact merely thought he was not clever enough to become a barrister, let alone a help in his political career. 'If ever I began to show the slightest idea of comradeship,' Churchill recalled, 'he was immediately offended, and when once I suggested that I might help his private secretary to write some of his letters, he froze me into stone.' He recorded that in the autumn of 1892 'I had one of the three or four long intimate conversations with him that are all that I can boast.' He found his father captivating, though Lord Randolph ended the conversation in a characteristically self-absorbed way, 'Do remember things do not always go right with me. My every action is misjudged and every word distorted ... So make some allowances.'[106] His son later regretted that he had not been able to leave Harrow early. 'I should have got to know my father,' he wrote, 'which would have been a joy to me.'[107] But it was not to be.

Churchill took the exam for the Royal Military College at Sandhurst in June 1893, helped by a crammer because his higher mathematics was so bad. He passed on his third attempt, but came ninety-fifth out of 389, meaning he would have to join the cavalry rather than the infantry. 'My dear Winston,' his father wrote to his eighteen-year-old son on 9 August,

> There are two ways of winning an examination, one creditable and the other the reverse. You have unfortunately chosen the latter method, and appear to be much pleased with your success. The first extremely discreditable failure of your performance was missing the infantry, for in that failure is demonstrated beyond refutation your slovenly happy-go-lucky harum scarum style of work for which you have been distinguished at your different schools. Never have I received a really good report of your conduct in your work from any master or tutor ... Always behind-hand, never advancing in your class, incessant complaints of total want of application ... With all the advantages you had, with all the abilities which you foolishly think yourself to possess ... this is the grand result that you come up among the second rate and third rate who are only good for commissions in a cavalry regiment ... You imposed on me an extra charge of some £200 a year. Do not think that I am going to take the trouble of writing you long letters after every failure and folly you commit and undergo ... because I no longer attach the slightest weight to anything you may say about your own

> accomplishments and exploits. Make this position indelibly impressed on your mind, that if your conduct and action is similar to what it has been in the other establishments ... then ... my responsibility for you is over. I shall leave you to depend on yourself giving you merely such assistance as may be necessary to permit of a respectable life. Because I am certain that if you cannot prevent yourself from leading the idle useless unprofitable life that you have had during your schooldays and later months, you will become a mere social wastrel, one of hundreds of the public school failures, and you will degenerate into a shabby, unhappy and futile existence. If that is so you will have to bear all the blame for such misfortunes yourself.
>
> Your affectionate father, Randolph SC[108]

By then, Lord Randolph's judgement was badly clouded by mental degeneration.[109] He was experiencing problems with his speech, hearing, balance and concentration, resulting in depression and violent outbursts, from an as yet undiagnosed illness.[110] Yet his son was able to quote from that letter from memory thirty-seven years later, showing how much its message of distrust and contempt from the man he worshipped had seared him. Nor was it tossed off in a rage, for Lord Randolph had also written to his mother the Duchess four days earlier in similar terms: 'I have told you often and you would never believe me that he has little [claim] to cleverness, to knowledge or any capacity for settled work. He has great talent for show off exaggeration and make-believe ... I will not conceal from you it is a great disappointment to me.'[111] Jennie also wrote to say, 'Papa is not very pleased at your getting in by the skin of your teeth and missing the Infantry by eighteen marks. He is not as pleased with your exploits as you seem to be!'[112] Years later, Churchill's closest friend was to observe that Lord Randolph 'discerned nothing remarkable, nothing of singular promise in a very remarkable and original boy'.[113]

That summer, before Winston entered Sandhurst, he and his brother Jack went on a walking tour of Switzerland with a tutor. Staying in Zermatt, they climbed the 15,000-foot Monte Rosa in sixteen hours, as well as the Wetterhorn. They travelled widely before Winston again cheated death in Lake Geneva, when he and someone he described as a 'companion' went swimming alone off a boat in the middle of the lake, and a light breeze started to blow the boat away from them. 'I saw Death as near as I believe I have ever seen him,' he wrote in *My Early Life*. 'He was swimming in the water at our side, whispering from time to time in the rising wind which continued to carry the boat away from us at about the same speed we could swim. No help was near. Unaided we could never reach the shore ... I now swam for life ... I scrambled in, and rowed back for my companion who, though tired, had not apparently realised the dull yellow glare of mortal peril that had so suddenly played around us.'[114] The younger companion was in fact Jack, but Churchill presumably did not want his readers to know that he had put his younger brother in such mortal peril.

Churchill entered Sandhurst on 1 September 1893. He was 5 foot 6½ inches tall and had a chest measurement of only 31 inches. He had delicate skin, slightly protruding very light blue eyes and a handsome face. He enjoyed his time at Britain's premier military academy, especially the study of tactics and fortifications, and the constant riding, at which he became highly proficient, taking up steeplechasing, polo and occasionally amateur horse-racing.[115] The pathos of his correspondence with his parents continued. 'I am awfully sorry that Papa does not approve of my letters,' he told his mother on 17 September. 'I take a great deal of pain over them and often rewrite entire pages. If I write a descriptive account of my life here, I receive a hint from you that my style is too sententious and stilted. If on the other hand I write a plain and excessively simple letter it is put down as slovenly. I never can do anything right.'[116] When he accidentally dropped into a stream a pocket watch that his father had given him, he was so terrified of confessing the loss that he launched a desperate salvage operation. This involved mobilizing twenty-three men from an infantry company to search for it, then hiring a fire engine to dredge the stream, before he diverted the headwaters and was finally able to retrieve it. When Lord Randolph discovered what had happened from the watch-repairer, he was predictably furious and scornful.[117]

By 1894, Lord Randolph was starting to die of what much medical opinion today believes to have been a rare and incurable brain disease, but which, because it shared some symptoms with syphilis, was diagnosed as that by his doctors. Lord Randolph left with Jennie on a round-the-world tour in June. Churchill later recalled, 'I never saw him again, except as a swiftly fading shadow.'[118] After he had spoken to his father's doctors, Robson Roose and Thomas Buzzard, and was given the probable diagnosis, he wrote in early November 1894 an alarmed letter to his mother, who was by then in Singapore: 'I asked Dr Roose and he told me everything and showed me the medical reports. I have told no one . . . I need not tell you how anxious I am. I had never realised how ill Papa had been and had never until now believed there was anything serious the matter . . . Do, my darling mamma when you write let me know *exactly* what you think.'[119]

Churchill understandably did not speak or write about the possible cause of his father's illness, and only on a single occasion did he ever mention it.

In 1951 or 1952, he told his private secretary, Anthony Montague Browne, 'You know my father died of Locomotorataxia, the child of syphilis.'[120] In fact Locomotorataxia is a general descriptive term for a neurological disturbance and is certainly not unique to syphilis. It is likely that Churchill laboured for a lifetime under the shame of his father's death of a disease from which he did not in fact suffer. Yet it never lessened his hero-worship of this proud, aloof, disdainful man. 'He embodied that force, caprice and charm which so often springs from genius,' Churchill wrote of him.[121] As Churchill's great friend Violet Bonham Carter (née Asquith) was to put it: 'He worshipped at the altar of his unknown father.'[122]

While his parents were on the other side of the world, Churchill gave his first public speech, on the most unlikely of platforms. That summer Mrs Ormiston Chant, a member of the London County Council, led a social purity campaign directed against the promenade of the Empire Theatre in Leicester Square, a bar area behind the dress circle where young men drank and met unchaperoned young women, some of whom were ladies of easy virtue. The outraged Mrs Chant had managed to get wood and canvas partitions put up to keep the sexes apart, which on 3 November 1894 a crowd that included Churchill rowdily destroyed. A witness recalled that Churchill and his friends 'broke down the palisades separating them from the ladies of the town and addressed the rioters. He and a future general drove off in a hansom [taxicab] waving trophies.'[123] The speech he made on top of the debris was sadly not recorded, but began with the pun, 'Ladies of the Empire, I stand for liberty!'[124] Someone else present recalled him 'dodging about in the foyer', slapping women on their bottoms, with a bouncer in hot pursuit.[125] It was an unlikely inauguration to the public-speaking career of the greatest orator of the coming century.

Churchill graduated from Sandhurst in December 1894 ranked twentieth out of 130 cadets,* and second in the arduous riding competition. By then Lord Randolph was too ill to notice, let alone congratulate his son. 'My father died on January 24 in the early morning,' Churchill recalled thirty-five years later. 'Summoned from a neighbouring house where I was sleeping, I ran in the darkness across Grosvenor Square, then lapped in snow. His end was quite painless. Indeed he had long been in stupor. All my dreams of comradeship with him, of entering Parliament at his side and in his support, were ended. There remained for me only to pursue his aims and vindicate his memory.'[126] Half a century later, he told his daughter that his father's death had left him utterly prostrate with grief for a whole day and night.[127]

* Not eighth out of 150 'with honours', as he claimed in *My Early Life*.

Despite being largely separated, Jennie had nursed Lord Randolph faithfully in his final illness, resolutely if absurdly blaming his death on the Tory leader, Lord Salisbury. 'There is not the slightest doubt that worry and overwork started the disease,' she told a friend, 'and I know you will agree with me that Lord S. has a lot to answer for. There was a time a few years ago when a generous hand stretched out would have saved everything and R would now be with us as he was. But Lord S. and the others were too jealous of him – I feel all this deeply – and hope one of these days it will be known.'[128] Churchill was fortunate that his father died while still an MP. Had he lived long enough to retire from the House of Commons after the election that came six months later, he would almost certainly have been awarded a peerage, which would soon have devolved upon his eldest son – meaning that Churchill could not have had the career he did in the Commons, with a correspondingly small chance of his becoming prime minister in 1940.

The funeral was held at Blenheim Palace's parish church in the neighbouring village of Bladon. The congregation sang 'Rock of Ages' and 'Now the Labourer's Task is O'er', and heard the words 'Man that is born of a woman hath but a short time to live, and is full of misery.'[129] The 5th Earl of Rosebery, who had become prime minister in March 1894, delivered the eulogy. Afterwards, Churchill, Jennie and Jack stood at the snow-covered grave and scattered lilies-of-the-valley on the coffin. 'Over the landscape, brilliant with sunshine, snow had spread a glittering pall,' he later recalled.[130]

The neglect and emotional cruelty at the hands of his parents that could have crushed a lesser person instead gave Churchill an unquenchable desire to succeed in life, not only in general but in his father's chosen profession of politics. His father-worship extended to learning several of Lord Randolph's more famous speeches by heart; visiting his father's friends such as Lord Rosebery and Lord Justice Gerald FitzGibbon principally to listen to stories about him; adopting his characteristic speaking pose of putting his hand facing down on his hip. As we shall see, he also wrote a filial two-volume biography; mentioned him regularly in speeches; wore his father's chancellor of the Exchequer robes when he assumed the same office; named his only son Randolph and wrote about a daydream in which he met his father over half a century after his death.

Churchill told the parliamentary lobby correspondent A. G. Gardiner that he had copied his father's practice of using pauses while speaking, even of deliberately fumbling in his pockets for a note he did not want or need, in order to concentrate his listeners' attention.[131] It might have been understandable if he had rebelled against his harsh, distant father, but part of his greatness of character is that instead he regarded his life's work as promoting his father's Disraelian and Tory Democrat ideas, based on *Imperium et Libertas*. 'I took my politics almost unquestioningly from him,' he wrote in 1931, saying that although his father lived and died a loyal Tory 'He saw no reason why the old glories of Church and State, of King and Country, should not be reconciled with modern democracy; or why the masses of working people should not become the chief defenders of those ancient institutions by which their liberties and progress had been achieved.'[132] Winston wanted, if possible, to wreak a terrible revenge on what he regarded as the Tory Establishment cabal whom he blamed for bringing his father down.

It was said of Emperor Napoleon III that he bore a name that was simultaneously his making and his undoing. Winston Leonard Spencer-Churchill similarly carried a name that marked him out among his contemporaries and created expectations that only a very remarkable person could fulfil. 'A medal glitters,' he once wrote, 'but it also casts a shadow.' That was also true of his name. It is notoriously hard to be the child of a famous parent, yet among his many achievements Churchill succeeded at that too.

Churchill believed he had only a short time to live, and regularly referred to his father's death at forty-five as the explanation for his own thrusting nature. His contemporaries thought him pushy, and so he was, but there was a cold actuarial reason behind it. Three of his father's siblings had died at ten months, two years and four years old, and his father's sisters were to die aged forty-five and fifty-one, and their brother the 8th Duke of Marlborough at forty-eight. His ever-present fear of an early death suggests that Churchill believed that it might have been a non-sexual form of Locomotorataxia that had killed his father. Whatever it was, he felt he did not have long to make his mark.

If there were ideal conditions for the creation of a future hero of the Empire, by the end of January 1895 Churchill had fulfilled all of them. A famous name, selfish and unimpressed parents, a patchy but patriotic schooling that taught him how great men can change history by great feats, a first-class military education, a schoolboy ambition to save the Empire, not enough money to become indolent, appreciation of English prose and a reverence for the British history that he felt ran through his aristocratic veins. Above all, an aloof, famous father who had annexed Burma aged thirty-six and was dead at forty-five. Now twenty and freed from his father's stultifying influence, Churchill was about to make his own name. Few have set out with more cold-blooded deliberation to become first a hero and then a Great Man.

# 2

# Ambition under Fire
# January 1895–July 1898

*Solitary trees, if they grow at all, grow strong: and a boy deprived of a father's care often developes, if he escape the perils of youth, an independence and vigour of thought which may restore in after life the heavy loss of early days.*

Churchill, *The River War*[1]

*His school was the barrack-room; his university the battlefield.*

A. G. Gardiner on Churchill in *Prophets, Priests and Kings*[2]

'To understand a man,' Napoleon once said, 'look at the world when he was twenty.' When Churchill was twenty, the British Empire covered more than one-fifth of the earth's land surface, and its Navy – easily the largest in the world – dominated its oceans. London was a great seaport and financial capital, the British constitution was unchallenged domestically, and although there were international disputes in the offing – principally with America over commerce and France and Russia over faraway colonial borders – these were not considered life-threatening. To Churchill the late Victorian imperial world seemed secure, permanent and benevolent, so long as people like himself dedicated themselves to its service. He was shaped by a frame of mind that saw a lifetime of duty as the price to be paid for historically unprecedented greatness.

'I was now in the main the master of my fortunes,' Churchill wrote of the period immediately after his father's death. In *My Early Life* he claimed that his father's estate 'almost exactly equalled his debts', but that was untrue. Once all outstanding debts had been paid off, the family was left with £54,237 (around £5.5 million in today's money) in trust, with the income going to Jennie for her lifetime and the capital belonging to Winston and Jack. If Jennie remarried, the trustees had discretion to divert half the income to her sons.[3] In the short term, therefore, Winston was dependent on his mother. Now that he was no longer a boring child, the distance between them shrank and their relationship became, as he put it, 'more like brother and sister than mother and son'.[4] Cash was a problem: his Army salary was a mere £120 per annum, scarcely enough to cover his mess bills; at least another £500 per annum was needed for other essential military accoutrements such as his magnificent uniform, a second charger, saddlery and polo ponies.

'I have had a very sad time of it these last six weeks or so,' he wrote to a Sandhurst friend in early February 1895, 'but now that is all over one can turn to the business of living again and try and leave one's sorrows behind.'[5] On 1 April, Second Lieutenant Churchill was gazetted to the 4th Queen's Own Hussars, then under the command of the charismatic Colonel John Brabazon, a friend of his mother's. Founded in 1685, the regiment had fought in the Peninsular War and taken part in the Charge of the Light Brigade in 1854. In the various favours for access and advancement he was to ask of people over the next couple of years, it did Churchill no harm that since his father's death he had become the direct heir to the dukedom of Marlborough, and would remain so until the future 10th Duke was born in September 1897.

Soon after joining up, Churchill strained his sartorius muscle running down the length of the thigh and on which a rider's grip on a horse depends. 'In consequence I suffered tortures,' he recalled later. 'One simply had to go on tearing at a lacerated muscle with the awful penalty of being thought a booby if one begged off even for a day.'[6] In another accident, Churchill was thrown while steeplechasing, nearly breaking his leg and obliging him to rest in bed for three days. He promised his mother he wouldn't race again, but five days later 'Mr Spencer' finished third in the Sandhurst Challenge Cup, on a fellow subaltern's horse.[7] Churchill loved the life of a cavalry officer, even the ostensibly tedious parts. 'The stir of the horses, the clank of their equipment, the thrill of motion, the sense of incorporation in a living machine, the suave dignity of the uniform,' he wrote, 'all combine to make cavalry drill a fine thing in itself.' He took part in parades of the 25,000-strong Aldershot garrison, marching past Queen Victoria in her carriage at the saluting point. On one occasion he was drilled by a Captain Douglas Haig.

Although Churchill enjoyed the Army, it was only ever a means to an end: he wanted to make his name as a soldier prior to becoming a great statesman, as he thought his father had been. After Lord Salisbury had won the general election of 1895, he told his mother, 'It is a fine game to play – the game of politics – and it is well worth waiting for a good hand before really plunging.' He thus prescribed himself 'four years of healthy and pleasant existence . . . The more I see of soldiering the more I like it, but the more I feel convinced that it is not my *métier*.'[8] Sure enough, four years after sending that letter he was standing for Parliament. But in the meantime what could he do to win medals and distinction when his regiment was stationed in Aldershot, rather than on active service?

In the summer of 1895, with ten weeks' leave looming, and insufficient funds to buy the quality of horse necessary to spend the fox-hunting season in England, Churchill looked to see where he could take part in a war. He systematically scoured the world map for a place where he could have as high profile an adventure as possible. The Cubans were then fighting a guerrilla war against their Spanish imperial masters, so he persuaded Lieutenant Reginald 'Reggie' Barnes, a brother-officer in the regiment, to go there with him, securing the accreditation necessary to accompany the Spanish forces from his father's friend Sir Henry Drummond-Wolff, then Ambassador in Madrid. Before they left, Colonel Edward Chapman, the Director of Military Intelligence, asked Churchill and Barnes to discover anything they could about the penetration and striking power of the Spanish Army's new type of bullet. This was Churchill's inauguration into the world of secret intelligence.

Jennie paid for the transatlantic ticket, but to help finance the rest of the expedition Churchill persuaded the *Daily Graphic*, for which his father had written five years earlier, to hire him as a war correspondent at five guineas an article. As long as the individual's commanding officer agreed and his military duties were not impaired, officers were permitted to write about campaigns for the newspapers, although it was not actively encouraged.

Relatively penniless, Churchill was already learning how to dun creditors or make them wait inordinately long for payment, in the long-established aristocratic manner. Despite being only a ducal heartbeat away from the ownership of Blenheim, he needed an alternative form of income to maternal generosity. Journalism provided it – which was just as well as Jennie had started extensively redecorating a new apartment on the Champs-Élysées and a seven-storey leasehold house at 35 Great Cumberland Place, near Marble Arch in London, where she had a discreet lift installed to take her lover, the obese Prince of Wales, from the street level to her boudoir.

Churchill was under no illusions about his mother's extravagance, and the absolute necessity of providing for himself independently as soon as possible. 'Except for my name, all the rest I had to work for, to fight for,' he reminisced years later. 'When I was twenty-two, with my small Army pay not covering expenses, I realized that I was . . . unable to live my life as I wanted to. I wanted learning and I wanted funds. I wanted freedom. I realized there was no freedom without funds. I had to make money to get essential independence; for only with independence can you let your own life express itself naturally. To be tied down to someone else's routine, doing things you dislike – that is not life – not for me . . . So I set to work. I studied, I wrote. I lectured . . . I can hardly remember a day when I had nothing to do.'[9]

The key was the 'noble' English sentence. Once Churchill had discovered that he was capable of writing vividly to the right length under tight deadlines in war zones, he demanded ever higher rates and within five years he was the world's best-paid war correspondent. From that, together with his books and related lectures, he had by 1901 amassed a fortune equivalent to £1 million today, enough to allow him to enter politics. Journalism taught him to be pithy and to hold his readers' attention. Such clarity and liveliness were to be as evident in his political speeches as in his highly readable articles. But for most of his life money continued to be an issue and he wrote regularly for the press until 1939.

In early November 1895 Churchill sailed for New York, the city of his mother's birth, on his way to Cuba in the first of fourteen visits he made to the United States over the next sixty-seven years. He was met off the boat by Bourke Cockran, a forty-one-year-old congressman and admirer of Jennie's, who put him and Reggie up in his luxurious home on Fifth Avenue. Cockran played an important role in Churchill's life over the next ten years, as father-figure and as political role-model, but more importantly as the man who profoundly affected both his conversational and his oratorical styles. 'I have never seen his like,' Churchill wrote in the early 1930s, 'or in some respects his equal . . . He was pacifist, individualist, democrat, capitalist and a "Gold-Bug"' (advocate of the Gold Standard). Above all he was a Free Trader, and, as Churchill added, 'Thus he was equally opposed to socialists, inflationists and Protectionists, and he resisted them on all occasions. In consequence there was in his life no lack of fighting.'[10] Churchill was never a pacifist, but he would adopt all the rest of Cockran's stances during his own political career. Cockran changed parties four times, even more inconsistent in his affiliations than Churchill himself would be.

Cockran represented New York as a congressman for five non-consecutive terms between 1887 and his death in 1923, and was famed for his witty retorts against hecklers. His biographer described his speeches (he sometimes spoke to audiences of over 20,000 in Madison Square Garden) as those of 'a finished literary craftsman'.[11] Although Churchill never heard Cockran speak in public, he read all his speeches and learned his oratorical techniques. 'He taught me to use every note of the human voice as if playing an organ,' Churchill wrote. 'He could play on every emotion and hold thousands of people riveted in great political rallies when he spoke.'[12] And Cockran's private conversation, 'in point, in pith, in rotundity, in antithesis and in comprehension, exceeded anything I have ever heard'.[13] His use of classical and historical allusions, his extravagant vocabulary, facial expressions and occasional dramatic gestures, were imbibed by the young Churchill, who quoted his phrases for decades afterwards. 'Never before in the history of the English-speaking people', Cockran had said of the Irish Home Rule Bill two years earlier, 'has there been a victory which was so great a triumph as that attained by Mr Gladstone.'[14] Cadences and phrases such as these were filed away in Churchill's already astoundingly capacious memory. In 1955, the American politician Adlai Stevenson was amazed when Churchill started to quote long excerpts from Cockran's speeches of sixty years before, and told him, 'He was my model.'[15]

'What an extraordinary people the Americans are!' Churchill wrote to his mother on 10 November. 'Their hospitality is a revelation to me and they make you feel at home and at ease in a way that I have never before experienced.'[16] He and Barnes dined at the Waldorf Astoria, visited West Point, watched a murder trial, saw a staged fire being put out by the New York Fire Department especially for them and attended the opening of the New York Horse Show. 'This is a very great country my dear Jack,' Churchill told his brother. 'Not pretty or romantic but great and utilitarian. There seems to be no such thing as reverence or tradition. Everything is eminently practical and thus is judged from a matter of fact standpoint.'[17]

'Picture to yourself the American people as a great, lusty youth,' Churchill continued, 'who treads on all your sensibilities, perpetrates every possible horror of ill-manners – whom neither age nor just tradition inspire with reverence – but who moves about his affairs with a good-hearted freshness which may well be the envy of older nations of the earth.'[18] It could have been a description of Churchill himself at this stage of his life.

On 17 November, Churchill and Barnes left New York by train for Tampa, Florida, and took a boat to Havana the next day. 'Here was a place where something would certainly happen,' Churchill later wrote of Cuba. 'Here I might leave my bones.'[19] They met the Spanish Commander-in-Chief, General Martínez Campos, who permitted them to visit the front, first by train to Sancti Spíritus and then with a military column, arriving at the fortified outpost of Arroyo Blanco on the 28th. Churchill was later critical of the way the Spanish Army 'moved like Napoleon's convoys in the Peninsula', which is to say, very ponderously. Both Napoleon and Campos were fighting guerrillas, and outside Arroyo Blanco were the same near-jungle conditions that still exist there today.

'You might call it tomfoolery,' Churchill later wrote of the expedition. 'To travel thousands of miles with money we could ill afford, and get up at four o'clock in the morning in the hope of getting into a scrape in the company of perfect strangers, is certainly hardly a rational proceeding.'[20] Yet they were seeing action while their brother-officers back home were fox-hunting. Churchill won in Cuba the first of his thirty-seven decorations, the Red Cross of Spain for Military Merit First Class, a courtesy decoration which he later wore in blithe contravention of War Office regulations.[21]

Churchill sympathized with the Cuban rebels, although he could not do so openly considering the Spanish were his hosts. He used the evocative simile that Cuba was for Spain 'like a dumb-bell held at arm's length'.[22] Although his claim to have heard his first shots fired in anger on his twenty-first birthday was untrue, he did hear them the very next day, 1 December, en route from Arroyo Blanco to La Reforma.[23] 'A ragged volley rang out from the edge of the forest,' he later wrote. 'The horse immediately next to me – not my horse – gave a bound.'[24] It had been shot in the ribs, and 'I could not help reflecting that the bullet which had struck the chestnut had certainly passed within a foot of my head. So at any rate I had been "under fire". That was something. Nevertheless, I began to take a more thoughtful view of our enterprise than I had hitherto done.'[25] He was under heavy fire for more than ten minutes and more sporadic fire for a day and a half. 'There were sounds about us sometimes like a sigh, sometimes like a whistle and at others like the buzz of an offended hornet,' but effective counter-measures were impossible because of the impenetrability of the jungle.[26]

It was during this campaign (if eighteen days of military tourism can be dignified with such a term) that Churchill demonstrated an adeptness for sketching, which much later developed into a love of painting. It was not true, as Lord Mountbatten was later to claim, that 'He left Cuba with three great predilections for the whole of his life – active service, siestas, and cigars.'[27] Churchill already smoked cigars* and did not start taking regular afternoon naps until 1914. Yet the trip did encompass his first time outside Europe, his first experience of espionage, his first nationally published articles (signed 'W.S.C.') and his baptism of fire. In an interview

* He considered cigarettes 'atrocious things', although he did occasionally make an exception for Turkish cigarettes (Murray, *Bodyguard* p. 87).

on the dockside in New York before recrossing the Atlantic on 14 December, he amused pressmen with his banter, saying of the rebels, 'They are not good soldiers but as runners would be hard to beat.'[28]

Before the 4th Hussars were posted to India in September 1896, Churchill spent what he later called 'the only idle spell I have ever had' – playing polo, living with his mother, meeting senior politicians socially and extracting a promise from General Sir Bindon Blood, the commander of a recent expedition to the Malakand Pass on India's North-West Frontier, that if he ever led another one he would allow him to join it.[29] Otherwise, he did the social rounds expected of a young, upper-class Englishman with a famous name. 'I realized that I must be on my best behaviour,' as he later put it, 'punctual, subdued, reserved; in short, display all the qualities with which I am least endowed.'[30]

Churchill's sense of sheer thrust was evident in a letter to his mother of 4 August 1896, written from his Army base at Hounslow in west London, while he was preparing to go out to what he called 'useless and unprofitable exile' in 'the tedious land of India'.[31] He did not want to waste his life on garrison duty in Bangalore, and having discovered that the 9th Lancers might be sent to quell an uprising in Matabeleland in southern Africa, he applied to join them as a supernumerary (that is, unpaid) subaltern. Otherwise, 'I am guilty of an indolent folly that I shall regret all my life. A few months in South Africa would earn me the SA medal and in all probability the [British South African] Company's Star.* Thence hot foot to Egypt – to return with two more decorations in a year or two – and beat my sword into an iron dispatch box . . . It is useless to preach the gospel of patience to me. Others as young are making the running now and what chance have I of ever catching up.'[32]

The Matabele inconveniently surrendered too soon for Churchill's plan to materialize, so he set sail instead with his regiment from Southampton on 11 September on the twenty-three-day journey to Bombay (modern-day Mumbai). As his launch came alongside the Sassoon Dock there, he reached out for an iron ring set in a stone wall, just as a 5-foot wave swung the boat down, severely dislocating his right shoulder. 'I scrambled up all right,' he recalled, 'made a few remarks of a general nature, mostly beginning with the early letters of the alphabet, hugged my shoulder and soon thought no more about it.'[33] It turned out that he had sustained a lifelong injury, which meant that he had to play polo with the upper part of his arm strapped to his body. He was still able to hit the ball, but without

* He got his Medal, but not the Star.

reaching the highest point forwards or backwards. 'When you make some great mistake,' he philosophized, 'it may very easily serve you better than the best-advised decision. Life is a whole, and luck is a whole, and no part of them can be separated from the rest.'[34] That would turn out to be true of his accident in Bombay.

Arriving at Bangalore, the military headquarters of the Madras (today's Chennai) Presidency, on 3 October 1896, Churchill, Barnes and their fellow officer Hugo Baring pooled their resources and took a comfortable bungalow with valets, grooms and butlers. It was Churchill's first time in the Empire, and he quickly fell hopelessly in love, imbuing it with a veneration that stayed with him for the rest of his life and was profoundly to influence his career again and again. It was in Bangalore that he learned to admire what he later called the 'great work that England was doing in India and of her high mission to rule these primitive but agreeable races for their welfare and our own'.[35] He told a friend that, although imperialism was sometimes a burden to Britain, 'It is justified if it is undertaken in an altruistic spirit for the good of the subject races,' which he had no doubt it was.[36] The 150,000 or so Britons in India could not maintain their Raj (literally, 'rule') without the active cooperation of vast numbers of the more than 300 million Indians, and Churchill understood that this could be done only through maintaining the prestige and power of the rulers. 'Nothing is so remarkable as the ascendancy which the British officer maintains over the native soldier,' he was to write a year later. 'The dark *sowars* [cavalrymen] follow the young English soldier who commands them with a strange devotion . . . To save his life they will sacrifice their own.'[37]

Today, of course, we know imperialism and colonialism to be evil and exploitative concepts, but Churchill's first-hand experience of the British Raj did not strike him that way. He admired the way the British had brought internal peace for the first time in Indian history, as well as railways, vast irrigation projects, mass education, newspapers, the possibilities for extensive international trade, standardized units of exchange, bridges, roads, aqueducts, docks, universities, an uncorrupt legal system, medical advances, anti-famine coordination, the English language as the first national lingua franca, telegraphic communications and military protection from the Russian, French, Afghan, Afridi and other outside threats, while also abolishing *suttee* (the practice of burning widows on funeral pyres), *thugee* (the ritualized murder of travellers) and other abuses. For Churchill this was not the sinister and paternalist oppression that we now know it to have been. Instead, he took the firm and irrevocable decision to dedicate his life to the defence of the British Empire against all its enemies, at home and abroad. Time and again throughout his political career, he would put his allegiance to his ideal of the Empire before his own best interests.

'As a young subaltern in India,' one of Churchill's secretaries recalled him saying in 1944, 'he found himself often at a loss to understand references in conversation. He decided to be better informed. He began to spend after-siesta time lying on his *charpoy* [bed] reading.'[38] Harrow had left him with large gaps in his education, so in the winter of 1896 he embarked upon a supremely ambitious reading programme which within two years was to leave him easily as well read as those of his contemporaries who had gone to Oxford or Cambridge. 'I pity undergraduates,' he was later to write, 'when I see what frivolous lives many of them lead in the midst of precious fleeting opportunity. After all, a man's life must be nailed to a cross of either Thought or Action.'[39] His own life was to prove that someone could comprehensively cover both.

Churchill's reading programme began with Edward Gibbon's 4,000-page *The Decline and Fall of the Roman Empire* – which he was to re-read twice more over the course of his life, and parts of which he could quote from memory. He followed it with Gibbon's autobiography and then read Macaulay's six-volume *History of England*, which he loved (except for the attacks on the 1st Duke of Marlborough) and the *Lays of Ancient Rome*.[40] After that he read Jowett's translation of Plato's *Republic*, and the key texts of Schopenhauer, Malthus, Darwin, Adam Smith, Henry Hallam, Samuel Laing, William Lecky, the Marquis de Rochefort and very many others – though no novels. The sheer breadth of his reading matter was astonishing, and it gave him enormous intellectual self-confidence, to add to the other kinds he already had. A friend recalled lending Dr Welldon's translation of Aristotle's *Ethics* to Churchill. It was very good, he rejoined, 'But it is extraordinary how much of it I had already thought out for myself.'[41] Churchill told his mother that he wanted his reading to give him 'a scaffolding of logical and consistent views'.[42] She replied to say that his bank had bounced a cheque for £11, which she would nonetheless honour. Churchill's autodidacticism meant that there were inevitably gaps in his knowledge. As late as 1906 he had not heard of Keats's 'Ode to a Nightingale', and he confused the poet William Blake with the admiral Robert Blake. But once this was pointed out, a friend recorded, 'the next time I met him, he had learned not merely this, but all the odes of Keats by heart – and he recited them to me mercilessly from start to finish, not sparing me a syllable!'[43]

Churchill also spent a good deal of his time in Bangalore learning about politics. He asked his mother to send him as many copies as possible of the political almanac *The Annual Register*, which today are at the Churchill Archives at Cambridge University, complete with his very extensive annotations which show us something of how he schooled himself in the subject. He chose the volumes that covered Benjamin Disraeli's 1874–80 premiership and read them extremely carefully, covering them with marginalia and occasional underlinings, which highlighted aspects of imperialism, foreign policy and the Conservatives' social-reform agenda. In the three volumes for 1874, 1875 and 1876, which covered all the legislation debated in Parliament at the time of his birth and infancy, he even wrote out the speeches that he would have delivered had he been in politics at the time, which he then pasted into the books.[44] The Scotch Church Patronage Bill, the Endowed Schools Act Amendment Bill, the Judicature Amendment Act: nothing was too obscure for Churchill's considered reactions. Of the Indian famine of 1873–4, for example, he imagined his support for the then Viceroy of India, Lord Northbrook, in not halting the export of grain: 'I am astounded that such a prohibition should have ever been advised. I should have thought that famine prices would immediately attract the grain without any law being necessary. I am opposed to any interference by Government with private trade.'[45] Churchill even critiqued the *Register*'s language. Where it likened a statement of Gladstone's to 'a thunderbolt falling from a calm empyrean', he wrote in the margin: 'Why not say a bolt from the blue?'[46] In the 1874 volume are marks of emphasis in pencil, sometimes as many as five strokes for important passages, such as Disraeli's attack on Lord Salisbury as 'a great master of gibes and flouts and jeers' – and references to his grandfather the Duke of Marlborough.[47]

In the 1875 volume, the speeches of R. A. Cross, the social-reforming Home Secretary, were annotated, as well as Samuel Plimsoll MP – the reformer who campaigned for a line to be painted on ships' hulls indicating the maximum safety draught – telling the Speaker, 'I will unmask the villains who sent brave men to death,' and 'Never will I withdraw; I will expose them all.'[48] Churchill's comment was: 'I can imagine no finer or more glorious memorial of a noble life devoted [to] the benefit of the human race than "the Plimsoll Mark".'[49] The attraction of politics through dramatic parliamentary engagements was being drummed into him by his own diligent reading.

In foreign policy, Churchill annotated an essay outlining 'the Buffer State idea', which argued for the wisdom of having several states separating the British and Russian Empires.[50] Disraeli's phrase about Britain's 'determination to maintain our empire' was noted approvingly, while the

Liberal Robert Lowe's questioning of Britain's right to rule over India was crossed out with the words 'A most nefarious speech, W.S.C.' written right across the page.

The notes he pasted into these volumes provide an acute insight into his views as a neophyte political thinker. 'Progress is the principle of the human race,' he wrote in the 1877 volume of the proposal to extend the franchise to the working classes.[51] Of the Artisans' Dwelling Act, by which slums had been compulsorily purchased for redevelopment, he asked, 'Who would not lend assistance to put out a neighbour's conflagration? Neither charity nor pity can inspire the acts of a Government. The interests of the community as a whole must direct them.'[52] He supported capital punishment because 'In this imperfect world it is necessary to do many hard and unchristian things.' He believed in its deterrent effect. 'Because the door of hope is definitely shut,' he nonetheless admitted, 'the idea of killing a man in cold blood by machinery appeals with horror to the human race.'[53]

In the 1880 volume he noted that his father had been described as an 'extreme freelance' in the Irish land question, who 'spoke sarcastically', was involved in 'angry discussion' and made an 'incisive speech' to give a bill 'grudging support'.[54] In the 1882 volume he extensively annotated the pages covering Boer complaints against the British before the First Anglo-Boer War of 1881 and marked up the speeches of Joseph Chamberlain heavily in the margins, and in the 1885 volume he noted the way that the Conservatives' Housing of the Working Classes Bill and Medical Relief Bill had 'indicate[d] the bias of the new Toryism towards State Socialism'.[55]

Churchill was working out for himself, very soon after his father's death, that social reform was not the exclusive preserve of the Liberals but could be appropriated by what he called 'the Tory democracy'.[56] To that end, he was in favour of a progressive income tax, with total exemptions for the poor and a higher rate for unearned than for earned income. His beliefs were not entirely inherited from his father, growing also out of a close reading of recent political history.

Flashes of what was to become a characteristically Churchillian sense of humour were occasionally evident here too. The Royal Titles Bill, by which Queen Victoria had become Empress of India, had been attacked in 1875 for appealing to 'the lovers of novelty and high-sounding titles', prompting Churchill to note, 'I must array myself with those who "love high sounding titles", since no title that is not high sounding is worth having . . . There would not be much satisfaction in being styled "Your Insignificance" or "Your Squalidity".'[57] On the issue of women voting, the young Churchill was profoundly chauvinist, arguing that 'only the most undesirable class of women are eager for the right,' and that 'Those women who discharge their duty to the state viz. marrying and giving birth to children, are adequately represented by their husbands,' therefore 'I shall unswervingly oppose this ridiculous movement.' This was partly because 'If you give women votes you must ultimately allow women to sit as members of Parliament,' after which inevitably 'all power passes to their hands.'[58] These were not his views later on, and he notably married a woman who supported female suffrage, but it would have been surprising if an aristocratic Victorian Army officer had had different ones a decade before female suffrage came to the forefront of the political agenda.

The *Annual Register* volumes show us that already his heroes were Gibbon as writer and moralist, Disraeli as statesman and orator, and Lord Randolph Churchill, whose speeches were marked up diligently. Another author whose work had a powerful effect on Churchill, for both good and ill, was Charles Darwin. Like so many of his contemporaries, he extended the implications of Darwin's ideas into the human sphere, and came to believe that different races evolved at different speeds, just as animals and plants had over the millennia. Where he fundamentally differed from other Social Darwinists is that he believed that the stronger and more 'advanced' races – in which he included the Anglo-Saxons and the Jews – had a proportionately more profound moral responsibility towards what he saw as the weaker and less advanced ones. This fitted well with his strong sense of *noblesse oblige* and his Tory Democrat principles.

Unlike many other imperialists of the day, Churchill's sense of the moral responsibility of the rulers towards the ruled had little to do with Christianity. Although he did occasionally hint in later life that he believed in the existence of an Almighty – whose primary duty seems to have been to protect Winston Churchill – he did not acknowledge the divinity of Jesus Christ. Of all the five million words he uttered in his speeches, he never said the word 'Jesus' and only said the word 'Christ' once, and then not in a context acknowledging him as Saviour. His views on religion were influenced by his reading of Gibbon and by Winwood Reade's *Martyrdom of Man*, published in 1872, which argued that all religions were essentially the same.

Churchill did have a belief-system, which was acquired in – of all unlikely places – the officers' mess of the 4th Hussars at Bangalore. 'In the regiment we sometimes used to argue questions like "Whether we should live again in another world after this was over?" [and] "Whether we have ever lived before?" . . .' he recalled in *My Early Life*. 'There was general agreement that if you tried your best to live an honourable life and did your duty and were faithful to friends and not unkind to the weak and poor, it did not matter much what you believed or disbelieved. This would nowadays I suppose be called "The Religion of Healthy-Mindedness".'[59] This has been described as a form of Gibbonian deism, and it was certainly not in any sense Christian.[60]

Although Churchill had no belief in any revealed religion, he was a lifelong nominal Anglican, as almost all Conservative politicians of the day were, and he made regular references to the Almighty in his Second World War speeches.[61] But as he told his private secretary in the 1950s, 'I am not a pillar of the church but a buttress. I support it, from the outside.'[62] He was certainly not opposed to others having Christian (or any other kind of) faith, and he fully acknowledged Jesus Christ as having been the finest moralist of history, but his own core beliefs were of a different kind. 'For orthodox religion,' wrote one astute biographer, 'Churchill substituted a secular belief in historical progress, with a strong emphasis on the civilizing mission of Britain and the British Empire.'[63] Central to many key decisions of his life was this belief that Britain and her Empire were not just political entities but also spiritual ones; imperialism was in effect a substitute for religion. He imbibed, largely from his extensive reading of Macaulay and the Whig historians, a theory of historical progress that put the English-speaking peoples' adoption of Magna Carta, the Bill of Rights, the American Constitution and parliamentary institutions at the apex of civilizational development. These advantages were slowly and carefully being imparted to those parts of the world over which they ruled. In the absence of Christian faith, therefore, the British Empire became in a sense Churchill's creed.

There was more to Churchill's life at Bangalore than self-education, political reading and spiritual pondering: he played a great deal of polo. The 4th Hussars won the prestigious Golconda Cup in Hyderabad within two months of their arrival and they set their heart on winning the Inter-Regimental Cup, even though it had never been won by a cavalry regiment from southern India. He also collected butterflies. 'My garden is full of Purple Emperors, White Admirals and Swallow Tails and many other beautiful and rare insects,' he told Jack – before his collection was eaten by a rat.

It was at Secunderabad on 3 November 1896 that Churchill met Pamela Plowden, the twenty-two-year-old daughter of Sir Trevor Chichele Plowden, a senior member of the Indian Civil Service and former MP. 'I must say that she is the most beautiful girl I have ever seen,' Churchill wrote to his mother the next day. 'We are going to try and do the City of Hyderabad together on an elephant.'[64] The courtship continued to a point in August 1899 when he felt able to tell his mother that, despite her other active titled suitors, 'Now she loves me.'[65] He had no money to marry, however, and although he got unofficially engaged to her, Jack learned that no fewer than three other men considered themselves to be in the same position.[66]

It was regularly claimed during the Indian self-government debates of the 1930s that Churchill did not properly know India. While it was true that by then he had not visited for thirty years, he certainly travelled around it extensively when he was there, writing letters from Bangalore, the Upper Swat Valley, Poona, Trimulgherry in the Deccan, the Mamund Valley, Seoni, Guindy, Dhond, Itarsi, Nawagai, Umbala, Inayat Kila, Bajaur, Hyderabad, Raichur, Meerut, Peshawar, the Bara Valley, Bombay, Ootacamund, Madras, Jodhpur and Calcutta. 'You could lift the heat with your hands,' he wrote of its hot season, 'it sat on your shoulders like a knapsack, it rested on your head like a nightmare.'[67]

It was also in India that Churchill learned how to drink (mostly whisky, diluted with very large amounts of soda) and in particular how not to get drunk. Throughout his life he enjoyed depicting himself as a heavy drinker, but it is remarkable on how few occasions anybody else thought him to have been drunk. (There is only one occasion during the whole of the Second World War, with all its strains and stresses.) 'I have been brought up and trained to have the utmost contempt for people who got drunk,' he wrote, 'except on very exceptional occasions and a few anniversaries.'[68] For all the later Nazi propaganda, and his own jokes about his drinking, Churchill had an extraordinary capacity for alcohol and it rarely affected his judgement. 'A single glass of champagne imparts a feeling of exhilaration,' he was to write. 'The nerves are braced; the imagination is agreeably stirred; the wits become more nimble. A bottle produces a contrary effect. Excess causes a comatose insensibility. So it is with war, and the quality of both is best discovered by sipping.'[69] The overwhelming evidence is that Churchill loved alcohol, drank steadily by sipping, had a hardy constitution and was only very rarely affected by it.

Accidents continued to befall him. In March he fell from a pony and injured his left shoulder on rock-hard ground – but continued to play polo with his reins fastened to his wrist – and the following month a bullet misfired leaving shards in his hand. By May, when he sailed to England on three months' accumulated leave, he was keen to get away, describing India as 'this godless land of snobs and bores'.[70] In between bouts of 'fearful' seasickness on the boat home, he befriended Colonel Ian Hamilton, who was in charge of musketry training in India, and visited Pompeii and Rome (luckily for the latter, as he refused to countenance its bombing in 1944).[71]

On 26 July 1897, Churchill made his first official public speech, to an audience of about a hundred members of the Primrose League at Claverton Down, near Bath. After a brief reference to Queen Victoria's Diamond

Jubilee the previous month, he spoke of the Workmen's Compensation Bill. 'The British workman has more to hope for from the rising tide of Tory Democracy than from the dried-up drain-pipe of Radicalism,' he said with flair.[72] He got both laughter and cheers, and then made a few jokes at the expense of the Radicals and Liberals, ending with a peroration about the Empire:

> There are . . . those who say that in this Jubilee year our Empire has reached the height of its glory and power, and that now we shall begin to decline, as Babylon, Carthage, Rome declined. Do not believe these croakers, but give the lie to their dismal croaking by showing by our actions that the vigour and vitality of our race is unimpaired and that our determination is to uphold the Empire that we have inherited from our fathers as Englishmen, that our flag shall fly high upon the sea, our voice be heard in the councils of Europe, our Sovereign supported by the love of her subjects, then shall we continue to pursue that course marked out for us by an all-wise hand and carry out our mission of bearing peace, Civilization and good government to the uttermost ends of the earth.[73]

It was a classic statement of pugnacious late Victorian imperialism. Churchill recalled in *My Early Life* that the audience 'cheered a lot in all the right places when I paused on purpose to give them a chance, and even at others which I had not foreseen. At the end they clapped loudly and for quite a long time. So I could do it after all!'[74] The Tory-supporting *Morning Post* had sent along a reporter, and published a short leader announcing a new arrival on the political scene, although the *Eastern Morning News* sniffed that 'political talent is the least hereditary of our tendencies'. In fact, Churchill turned out to be far more politically talented than his father had ever been, and the Claverton speech made him confident that, with practice, he could become adept at public speaking.

Lord Salisbury, who had been re-elected in August 1895, adopted a 'Forward' policy designed to protect the Empire by proactively defending its borders wherever threatened. Churchill was soon in a position to carry out a mission for the Empire at 'the uttermost ends of the earth'. In August 1897 he heard that a Pathan revolt on the North-West Frontier had led to Sir Bindon Blood being given the command of a three-brigade Malakand Field Force (MFF). He immediately asked Blood for a place on it, despite the fact that the 4th Hussars were not to be included, only to receive the reply, 'Very difficult; no vacancies; come up as a correspondent; will try to fit you in.'[75] So Churchill asked for six weeks' further leave of absence from his regiment, took a train over 2,000 miles in five days of sweltering heat from Bangalore to Nowshera, the MFF railhead, and reported for duty. He also bought a grey – that is, white – horse, a conscious act of self-advertisement, and a potentially suicidal one. 'I am more ambitious for a reputation for physical courage than for anything else in the world,' he told his mother, who helped negotiate a contract for him with the *Daily Telegraph* that paid £5 a column.[76] He was nonetheless a soldier first, wearing his 4th Hussars uniform, and a journalist second.

On 16 September 1897, the 12,000-strong Malakand Field Force marched into the Mamund Valley. It was a punitive expedition to burn the enemy's crops, chop down trees, fill up wells, destroy reservoirs and raze villages in retaliation for repeated raids on British-controlled areas. 'Of course it is cruel and barbarous,' wrote Churchill, 'as is everything else in war, but it is only an unphilosophic mind that will hold it legitimate to take a man's life and illegitimate to destroy his property.'[77] The tribesmen made occasional sudden and lethal counter-attacks, and to be captured meant being tortured to death. Churchill personally disapproved of the expedition, though not on humanitarian grounds. Although he liked and admired Blood, he blamed the enterprise on Lord Salisbury's imperial 'Forward' policy. 'Financially it is ruinous,' he told his mother. 'Morally it is wicked. Militarily it is an open question, and politically it is a blunder. But we can't pull up now.'[78]

Churchill fought bravely, and was mentioned in dispatches for 'courage and resolution' and for having 'made himself useful at a critical moment', but he did not win the gallantry medal for which he longed.[79] 'I rode on my grey pony all along the skirmish line where everyone else was lying down in cover,' he boasted to his mother. 'Foolish perhaps, but I play for high stakes and given an audience there is nothing too daring or too noble. Without the gallery, things are different.'[80] Years later he took a more fatalistic view of the expedition. 'They wanted to shoot at us and we wanted to shoot at them. So a lot of people were killed, and on our side their widows have had to be pensioned by the Imperial Government, and others were badly wounded and hopped around for the rest of their lives, and it was all very exciting and, for those who did not get killed or hurt, very jolly.'[81] Less jolly for him at the time was the death of his friend Lieutenant William Browne-Clayton, of the Royal West Kent Regiment, who was 'literally cut to pieces on a stretcher', he told his mother. 'I must rank as a rare instance the fact that I cried,' he wrote.[82] In fact, in later life, Churchill was to cry extraordinarily easily.

Back in Bangalore in October, he started to write his first book, *The Story of the Malakand Field Force: An Episode of Frontier War*, furious to discover that his articles had been published in the *Telegraph* under the byline 'A Young Officer' rather than his own name. He complained bitterly to his mother that they had been written with the intention 'of bringing my personality before the electorate. I had hoped that some political advantage might have accrued.'[83] She replied that an Army officer writing press articles was 'very unusual and might get you into trouble'.[84] 'If I am to avoid doing "unusual" things it is difficult to see what chance I have of being more than an average person,' he wrote back. 'I was proud of the letters and anxious to stake my reputation on them.' Fear of becoming an average person amounted almost to a terror for the young Churchill, who desperately needed to be seen as remarkable if he was going to woo parliamentary constituencies: at that time political associations had autonomy over who stood for them and well-heeled Tory candidates who could promise to contribute to the association's coffers would otherwise have an advantage over him.

In November 1897 the twenty-three-year-old Churchill wrote an article entitled 'The Scaffolding of Rhetoric'. Although he had so far given only two speeches, one of which had been to an audience of rakes and prostitutes during a semi-riot at the back of a music hall, it showed that he had completely mastered the theory of public speaking if not yet the practice. Much of what he wrote at this early age was to prove true time and again in his life:

> Of all the talents bestowed upon men, none is so precious as the gift of oratory. He who enjoys it wields a power more durable than that of a great king. He is an independent force in the world. Abandoned by his party, betrayed by his friends, stripped of his offices, whoever can command this power is still formidable . . . A meeting of grave citizens, protected by all the cynicism of these prosaic days, is unable to resist its influence. From unresponsive silence they advance to grudging approval and thence to complete agreement with the speaker. The cheers become louder and more frequent; the enthusiasm momentarily increases; until they are convulsed by emotions they are unable to control and shaken by passions of which they have resigned the direction . . . It appears there are certain features common to all the finest speeches in the English language . . . Rhetorical power is neither wholly bestowed nor wholly acquired, but cultivated. The peculiar temperament and talents of the orator must be his by nature, their development is encouraged by practice. The orator is real. The rhetoric is partly artificial . . . The orator is the embodiment of the passions of the multitude . . . Before he can move their tears his own must flow. To convince them he must himself believe. He may be often inconsistent. He is never consciously insincere.[85]

Of no one was that to be truer than Churchill himself.

'Sometimes a slight and not unpleasant stammer or impediment has been of some assistance in securing the attention of the audience,' Churchill wrote in his essay, 'but usually a clear and resonant voice gives expression of the thoughts.' From early youth he had pronounced the letter 's' as 'sh'. He had received treatment from the royal physician, Sir Felix Semon, who told him that only practice and perseverance could cure it, as there was no organic defect to his mouth or tongue. He therefore repeated the phrase, 'The Spanish ships I cannot see for they are not in sight,' over and over again.[86] In 1905 he asked Semon to cut out what he thought was an extraneous ligament on his tongue, which thankfully the doctor refused to do.[87] For many years thereafter his sibilant 's' was clearly noticeable; even as late as 1913 a lobby journalist wrote, 'That defect of speech alone would have destroyed most men. Mr Churchill makes you forget it by the sheer energy of his mind and manner.'[88] As his essay shows, Churchill recognized the impediment but did not consider it a hindrance to a political career.

Churchill believed there were five 'elements' to great oratory. First was the 'exact appreciation of words', that is, 'the continual employment of the best possible word'. He instanced 'dour' to describe the Scots. He believed in using 'short, homely words of common usage'. Although the words should be short, sentences did not need to be, provided they had an internal rhythm. The second element of oratory was sound: 'The influence of sound on the human brain is well known,' he wrote. 'The sentences of the orator when he appeals to his art become long, rolling and sonorous. The peculiar balance of the phrases produces a cadence which resembles blank verse rather than prose.'[89] His reference to blank verse reflects his lifelong love of Shakespeare, whose works had a profound effect on his oratory, written style and sense of British exceptionalism, and influenced his later practice of writing out his speech notes in blank-verse form. (He also playfully developed a line in cod-Shakespeare, which often fooled those less familiar with the plays than he was.)

The third element in oratory was the steady accumulation of argument. 'A series of facts is brought forward all pointing in a common direction,' he wrote. 'The crowd anticipate the conclusion and the last words fall amid a thunder of assent.'[90] Fourth was the use of analogy, which can 'translate an established truth into simple language', and of which he gave examples from the speeches of Lord Salisbury and Macaulay, as well as his own father's remark that 'Our rule in India is, as it were, a sheet of oil spread over and keeping free from storms a vast and profound ocean of humanity.'[91] Churchill used analogy constantly in his speeches, seemingly naturally, but, as this essay shows, it was all part of a highly considered artistry.

'A tendency to wild extravagance of language – to extravagance so wild that reason recoils – is evident in most perorations,' Churchill wrote of his fifth and last element. 'The emotions of the speaker and the listeners are alike aroused and some expression must be found that will represent all they are feeling. This usually embodies in an extreme form the principles they are supporting . . . The effect of such extravagances on a political struggle is tremendous. They become the watchwords of parties and the creeds of nationalities.'[92] He cited speeches by William Pitt the Elder and the great American orator William Jennings Bryan, arguing that the orator cannot 'resist the desire to express his opinions in an extreme form or to carry his argument to the culmination'.[93]

Throughout his political career, Churchill was criticized for using exaggerated, extreme language in his speeches. Few people appreciated that this was entirely intentional, indeed an integral part of his oratorical technique. These 'extravagances', as he termed them, were designed to win him fame and attention, and to keep him at the centre of debate, but they were also to lead him into controversies and to inspire bitter distrust. By the time the Second World War loomed, the rise of Hitler at last fully justified the hyperbole that he had been employing on different, lesser issues for decades.

He also liked using deliberately old-fashioned words. He ended a letter to his mother in 1898, 'I end ere I weary you . . . Adieu' – which was archaic language even for the late Victorian period. Anachronistic vocabulary was often used to great effect in his wartime speeches, employing words like 'foe' instead of 'enemy' and phrases like 'as in the olden time'.

It was fortunate for Churchill that 'The Scaffolding of Rhetoric' was never published, as it would have undermined his future deliveries. Yet it is extraordinary how many of his greatest Second World War speeches conform to each of the five elements of this seminal essay, written more than forty years earlier. Well-chosen words; carefully crafted sentences; accumulation of argument; use of analogy; deployment of extravagances: those were the five scaffolds of the rhetoric of the greatest orator of his age. Churchill ended his article with a Gibbonian sentence: 'The student of rhetoric may indulge in the hope that nature will finally yield to observation and perseverance, the key to the hearts of men.'[94]

There is a constant sense in Churchill's letters to his mother and others at this time that he was already writing for posterity. 'Bullets – to a philosopher my dear Mamma – are not worth considering,' he told her from Bangalore just before Christmas 1897. 'Besides I am so conceited I do not believe the Gods would create so potent a being as myself for so prosaic an ending. Anyway it does not matter . . . Fame, sneered at, melodramatised, degraded, is still the finest thing on earth.'[95] As so often in Churchill's correspondence it is important to remember that he was at least half joking; detractors have frequently ignored the fact that much of what he said and wrote was intended to charm and amuse rather than be taken at precisely face value. But there was a self-mocking quality to his vanity that kept it from being unattractive. As he put it in another letter to his mother, 'Of course – as you have known for some time – I believe in myself.'[96]

'I shall devote my life to the preservation of this great Empire and to trying to maintain the progress of the English people,' he wrote in the same December 1897 letter. 'Nor shall anyone be able to say that vulgar consideration of personal safety ever influenced me. I know myself pretty well and am not blind to the tawdry and dismal side of my character but if there is one situation in which I do not feel ashamed of myself it is in the field.'[97] Cowardice in battle was 'vulgar'.

In January 1898 Churchill took ten days' Christmas leave in Calcutta, where he stayed with the Earl of Elgin, the Viceroy of India, and used the time to lobby for a posting on a new expedition on the North-West Frontier in the Tirah Valley, pulling every string he could, up to and including the Commander-in-Chief. He was helped most by Ian Hamilton and the expedition commander's aide-de-camp, Captain Aylmer Haldane, but to Churchill's great chagrin the expedition ended in negotiation with the tribesmen. There was to be no *Story of the Tirah Field Force*. 'It is a pushing age and we must shove with the best,' he told his mother.[98] Perhaps not surprisingly, contemporaries were beginning to regard him as a thrusting self-advertiser and medal hunter. 'I often saw a fresh-faced, fair-haired subaltern of the 4th Hussars who talked a great deal,' recalled Captain Hubert Gough.

> It was Winston Churchill. He had just returned from the fighting north of Peshawar . . . He used to take his stand in front of the fire . . . and he would lecture all and sundry on the conduct of operations with complete confidence . . . Brought up in the 16th Lancers, I did not at all approve of this somewhat bumptious attitude. Such style would never have been tolerated in our mess, but in the Gunners' mess at Peshawar neither the many generals who gathered there nor anyone else attempted to check him. I used to wonder how the generals stood it, but even then I was dimly aware that they were rather afraid of him and his pen.[99]

Gough and his other military detractors gave Churchill little credit for the fact that he was always thrusting his way towards places of mortal danger rather than away from them.

Churchill returned to Bangalore in late January to troubling financial news. In order to restructure her finances, Jennie wanted to take out a loan of £17,000 (approximately £1.7 million today), which required his consent – Jack was still under-age – as it would be guaranteed against Lord Randolph's trust. 'Speaking quite frankly on the subject,' Churchill told her, 'there is no doubt we are both you and I equally thoughtless – spendthrift and extravagant. We both know what is good – and we both like to have it. Arrangements for paying are left to the future . . . The pinch of the matter is we are damned poor.'[100] He nonetheless signed the documents, writing Jack a despondent letter saying, 'The only thing that worries me in life is – money.'[101]

On 15 March, *The Story of the Malakand Field Force* was published to excellent reviews, earning the author the equivalent of two years' pay. It had been shockingly badly proofread by Moreton Frewen, Churchill's uncle, whom he subsequently nicknamed 'Mortal Ruin', but nonetheless its Augustan style contained plenty of Churchillian epigrams and generalizations, such as 'Courage is not only common, but cosmopolitan,' and 'Every influence, every motive, that provokes the spirit of murder among men, impels these mountaineers to deeds of treachery and violence,' and 'It is better to be making the news than taking it; to be an actor rather than a critic,' and 'Nothing in life is so exhilarating as to be shot at without result.'[102]

The book covered more than just the tactics of the Malakand campaign, and contained Churchill's thoughts on wider strategy and the nature of the enemy the British Empire faced on what is today the Afghan–Pakistan border. It was critical of British generalship, though not of Bindon Blood himself. 'The general who avoids all "dash",' he wrote, 'who never starts in the morning looking for a fight and without any definite intention, who does not attempt heroic achievements, and who keeps his eye on his watch, will have few casualties and little glory.'[103] He was also highly critical of the Talibs, the tribe from whom the modern Taliban derive their name; they were, he wrote, 'as degraded a race as any on the fringe of humanity: fierce as a tiger but less cleanly; as dangerous, not so graceful'.[104] He believed their insistence on a rigid form of Islam kept the Afghan people in 'the grip of miserable superstition'.[105] His view was that their 'religion, which above all others was founded and propagated by the sword . . . stimulates a wild and merciless fanaticism'.[106] Islam, he further stated,

> increases, instead of lessening, the fury of intolerance. It was originally propagated by the sword, and ever since its votaries have been subject, above the people of all other creeds, to this form of madness. In a moment the fruits of patient toil, the prospects of material prosperity, the fear of death itself, are flung aside. The more emotional Pathans are powerless to resist. All rational considerations are forgotten. Seizing their weapons, they become Ghazis [anti-infidel fanatics] – as dangerous and as sensible as mad dogs: fit only to be treated as such.

'Civilization is confronted with militant Mahommedanism,' he concluded. 'The forces of progress clash with those of reaction. The religion of blood and war is face to face with that of peace. Luckily the religion of peace is usually the better armed.'[107] On the North-West Frontier and soon again in the Sudan, Churchill saw Islamic fundamentalism up close. It was a form of fanaticism that in many key features – its sheer implacability, contempt for Christianity, opposition to liberal Western values, addiction to violence, demand for total allegiance and so on – was not unlike the political fanaticism that he was to encounter forty years later. None of the three British prime ministers of the 1930s – Ramsay MacDonald, Stanley Baldwin and Neville Chamberlain – had ever personally encountered such extremism in their personal lives, and they were tragically slow to discern the nature of Nazi ideology. Churchill had fought against fanaticism in his youth, and recognized its salient features earlier than anyone else.

Far from India, a conflict was brewing between the British Empire and an Islamic power that would not be settled by negotiation. At its height in 1898, the Mahdist Empire under Abdullah al-Taashi, known as the Khalifa, covered the Sudan and South Sudan and some parts of Ethiopia and Eritrea. A full thirteen years after the Khalifa's predecessor, Muhammad Ahmad (the 'Mahdi'), had captured Khartoum and killed the British general Charles Gordon, Lord Salisbury's government was finally ready to send an Anglo-Egyptian expedition under Major-General Sir Herbert Kitchener to exact revenge and protect the southern part of British-controlled Egypt.

Churchill was desperate to fight in the coming Sudan campaign. 'Redouble your efforts in this direction,' he instructed his mother. 'My plans for the future will be much influenced by this.'[108] He could be caustic to his mother, who put considerable effort into promoting his career and negotiating his contracts, but after her death he admitted that 'In my interest she left no wire unpulled, no stone unturned, no cutlet uncooked.'[109] Her appreciation of his talents and ambition had finally ignited her maternal instincts. Their problem was that both Kitchener and Douglas Haig, his staff officer, were totally opposed to having journalists on the expedition, especially one as thrusting and high-profile as Churchill, with a reputation for criticizing generals in print.[110] 'It was a case of dislike before first sight,' Churchill later wrote.[111] Yet the decision was not really personal. Kitchener told a *Times* correspondent that the fact that Churchill had no intention of staying in the Army and 'was only making a convenience of it' meant he should not go 'in place of others whose professions were at stake'.[112]

Back in Britain on leave, Churchill received a letter from Lord Salisbury's private secretary asking him to visit the Prime Minister in his rooms at the Foreign Office. 'He met me at the door', Churchill later recalled, 'and with a charming gesture of welcome and salute conducted me to a seat on a small sofa in the middle of his vast room.'[113] Salisbury had destroyed Lord Randolph's political career overnight, but he said he would like to help his son. This might have been a mere pleasantry, but it was one upon which Churchill immediately took him up.[114] Salisbury wrote to Lord Cromer, the High Commissioner in Egypt, asking him to write to Kitchener on Churchill's behalf – yet still Kitchener proved unwilling. It was eventually through Lady Jeune, the wife of a family friend who was in turn a friend of Sir Evelyn Wood, the Adjutant-General, that Churchill got a post as a supernumerary lieutenant attached to the 21st Lancers, and then only because a Lieutenant P. Chapman had died, creating a vacancy. It was the only British cavalry regiment in Kitchener's Anglo-Egyptian Army.

Churchill was ordered to the regimental headquarters at Cairo post-haste. 'It is understood that you will proceed at your own expense,' the War Office letter stated, 'and that in the event of your being killed or wounded in the impending operations, or for any other reason, no charge of any kind will fall on British Army funds.'[115] Churchill arranged through his friend Oliver Borthwick, whose father owned the *Morning Post*, to be hired at £15 per column, three times his Malakand rate. He got to Cairo in six days, taking a tramp steamer from Marseilles for part of the journey in order to be incommunicado from the Indian Army, from which he had asked for yet more leave. Once he reached Egypt, he reasoned, he could not easily be recalled.

# 3
# From Omdurman to Oldham via Pretoria August 1898–October 1900

*You would rise in the world? . . . You must work while others amuse themselves. Are you desirous of a reputation for courage? You must risk your life.*

Churchill, *Savrola*[1]

*A great sight. It made me weep and my heart throbbed wildly. The rugged, dirty, begrimed troops looked tanned and hard as steel, and the defenders with trim uniforms and wan pale faces.*

Churchill to Sir George Riddell on the entry of the British troops into Ladysmith[2]

By 2 August 1898, Churchill was on parade in his khaki uniform, gaiters and Sam Brown belt, with his revolver and field glasses, at the Abbassia Barracks in Cairo. From there he made his way to Kitchener's headquarters outside Khartoum by way of Luxor, Aswan, the Temple of Philae and Wadi Halfa, crossing 400 miles of desert on the railway built expressly for the campaign. A fortnight later he was at Khartoum, 175 miles from where 'the waters of the Atbara flow into the mighty Nile.'[3] The journey was not without its dangers: the officer who had taken a troop of lancers from Cairo just before him was ambushed and killed along with all his men.[4] Churchill spent a miserable night without food or water lost in the desert in mid-August when he got separated from the convoy. He wandered for 70 miles before finding it again through the use of 'the glorious constellation of Orion. Never did the giant look more splendid,' he later wrote. It had directed him towards the Nile, and probably saved his life.[5]

On 28 August, the Anglo-Egyptian Army set off on its advance. 'One felt the sun leaning down upon one and piercing our bodies with his burning rays,' Churchill recalled.[6] After only four days, he was sent by Colonel Rowland Martin, the regimental commanding officer, to report to Kitchener that the Khalifa's army of slightly more than 50,000 Dervish warriors was advancing quickly towards them in a column 4 or 5 miles long.

Churchill cantered over 6 miles of desert in forty minutes and found Kitchener's army advancing in battle array. Kitchener asked him how long he thought he had before the two forces met. 'You have got at least an hour,' Churchill estimated, 'probably an hour and a half, sir, even if they come on at their present rate.'[7] Instead the Dervishes halted and waited for morning at Omdurman on the outskirts of Khartoum, as Kitchener's 25,800-strong force took up position with their backs to the Nile.

Churchill returned to his regiment, and was hailed by Lieutenant David Beatty, an officer commanding a gunboat on the river, who threw a bottle of champagne to him. 'It fell in the waters of the Nile,' Churchill recalled, 'but happily where a gracious Providence decreed them to be shallow and the bottom soft. I nipped into the water up to my knees, and reaching down seized the precious gift which we bore in triumph back to our Mess.'[8] The following year he told an American acquaintance how that night the young officers had amused themselves reciting nursery rhymes, of which Churchill himself had 'a large assortment, which he would quote in a very witty manner when the occasion called for them'.[9]

'The sun no longer seemed hot or the hours long,' Churchill wrote the following year. 'After all, they [the Dervishes] were there. We had not toiled up on a fruitless errand. The fatigues of the march, the heat, the insects, the discomforts – all were forgotten. We were "in touch"; and that is a glorious thing to be, since it makes all the features of life wear a bright and vivid flush of excitement, which the pleasures of the chase, of art, of intellect, or love can never excel and rarely equal.'[10] Thirty years later, he would write, 'Talk of Fun! Where will you beat this! On horseback, at daybreak, within shot of an advancing army, seeing everything, and corresponding with Headquarters.'[11] It was small wonder, writing sentences like these, that Churchill was to acquire a reputation for loving war, even though he was always at pains to point out that the fighting he had been describing was a world away from the industrialized horrors of the First World War. In the only other known first-hand account of the period immediately before the action, that of Captain Robert Smyth, Churchill was called 'The Correspondent' and blamed for exposing himself by remaining mounted while others got off their horses during a reconnaissance mission. 'Riflemen in the centre see this and fire two volleys,' recorded Smyth. 'Bullets whistling and splashing on rocks very close.'[12] Luckily they were ordered to retire at once, and when the regimental adjutant upbraided Smyth for unnecessarily exposing himself he correctly said, 'It was The Correspondent's fault.'

The charge of the 21st Lancers at the Battle of Omdurman on Friday, 2 September 1898, was the largest British cavalry charge since the Crimean War forty-four years earlier. Although there were a few afterwards in the Boer War and Great War, it was the last significant cavalry charge in British history. Churchill, riding 'a handy, sure-footed, grey Arab polo pony', commanded a troop of twenty-five lancers. Many of the Dervishes they attacked were hidden in a dried-out watercourse when the regiment set off, and it was only after the charge had begun that the regiment realized they were outnumbered by approximately ten to one.[13] 'We were going at a fast but steady gallop,' Churchill wrote later. 'There was too much trampling and rifle fire to hear any bullets. After this glance to the right and left and at my troop, I looked again towards the enemy. The scene seemed entirely transformed. The blue-black men were still firing, but behind them there now came into view a depression like a shallow sunken road. This was crowded and crammed with men rising up from the ground where they had hidden. Bright flags appeared as if by magic.'

As Churchill got closer, he quickly saw what needed to be done.

> The Dervishes appeared to be ten or twelve deep at the thickest, a great grey mass gleaming with steel, filling the dry watercourse. In the same twinkling of an eye I saw that our right overlapped their left, that my troop would just strike the edge of their array, and that the troop on my right would charge into air. My subaltern comrade on the right, Wormald of the 7th Hussars, could see the situation too; and we both increased our speed to the very fastest gallop and curved inwards like the horns of the moon. One really had not time to be frightened or to think of anything else but these particularly necessary actions . . . They completely occupied mind and senses.[14]

As he rode down into the watercourse, having lost the momentum of the charge by his necessary change of course, Churchill reached his moment of maximum personal danger. 'I found myself surrounded by what seemed to be dozens of men,' he recalled.

> Straight before me a man threw himself on the ground . . . I saw the gleam of his curved sword as he drew it back for a ham-stringing cut [to Churchill's horse's legs]. I had room and time enough to turn my pony out of his reach, and leaning over the offside I fired two shots into him at about three yards. As I straightened myself in the saddle, I saw before me another figure with uplifted sword. I raised my pistol and fired. So close were we that the pistol itself actually struck him. Man and sword disappeared below and behind me.

> On my left, ten yards away, was an Arab horseman in a bright-coloured tunic and steel helmet, with chain-mail hangings. I fired at him. He turned aside.[15]

Churchill saw that the other three troops of the squadron were re-forming close by. 'Suddenly in the middle of the troop up sprung a Dervish . . . I shot him at less than a yard.'[16] In the close and confused fighting he killed four men with the ten-shot Mauser automatic pistol that he was fortunately using instead of his sword, as a result of his shoulder injury in Bombay.[17] Soon afterwards the Khalifa's men disengaged. 'Now,' Churchill recalled, 'from the direction of the enemy there came a succession of grisly apparitions; horses spouting blood, struggling on three legs, men staggering on foot, men bleeding from terrible wounds, fish-hook spears stuck right through them, arms and faces cut to pieces, bowels protruding, men gasping, crying, collapsing, expiring.'[18] It was a scene he was later to invoke when he wanted to remind people of the horrors of war.

'I never felt the slightest nervousness and felt as cool as I do now,' he wrote to his mother of the charge two days later.[19] The importance of staying calm and retaining high morale in the face of heavy odds was brought home vividly at Omdurman. After the charge he found over twenty lancers 'so hacked and mutilated as to be almost unrecognizable'.[20] In the two or three minutes of the action, the regiment had lost five officers and sixty-five men either killed or wounded – almost a quarter of those who had charged – as well as 120 horses. 'There was nothing *dulce et decorum** about the Dervish dead,' Churchill later wrote; 'nothing of the dignity of unconquerable manhood; all was filthy corruption. Yet these were as brave men as ever walked the earth . . . destroyed, not conquered, by machinery.'[21]

The Battle of Omdurman saw the Khalifa's army routed by the highly disciplined Anglo-Egyptian Army's modern weaponry, including no fewer than fifty-two Maxim machine guns, against the Dervishes' spears and swords. In the first edition of his book about the campaign, *The River War*, Churchill denounced Kitchener for having ordered the desecration of the Mahdi's tomb after the battle, which was blown up after the body (except for the skull) had been thrown into the Nile. Churchill confided his suspicions to the poet Wilfrid Scawen Blunt in 1909, saying, 'Kitchener behaved like a blackguard in that business. He pretended to have sent the [Mahdi's] head back to the Sudan in a kerosene tin, but the tin may have contained anything, perhaps ham sandwiches. He kept the head, and has it still . . . I always hated Kitchener, though I did not know him personally . . . he blew up the body and kept the head.'[22] When he discovered

* In Horace's *Odes*, 'Dulce et decorum est pro patria mori' translates as 'It is sweet and noble to die for one's country.'

that Kitchener had banned his staff from providing him with any information to help him write the book, Churchill described the general to his mother, with unusual snobbishness, as 'a vulgar common man'.[23]

The memory of the brutal treatment of the enemy wounded after Omdurman, when several thousand were killed in cold blood, was to stay with Churchill for a long time, although he himself took no part in it. Three years later, he told a friend that he had seen the 21st Lancers 'spearing the wounded and leaning with their whole weight on their lances after the charge to get the points through the thick clothes the wounded Dervishes wore as they lay on the ground. As the points went in, the Dervishes would kick up their feet and hands. One trooper had boasted of his kindness at putting only four inches of steel into his man. "He ought to be thankful", he had said, "to find himself in the hands of a good-natured chap like me."'[24]*

On 5 September, the 21st Lancers started their march home. In Cairo, Churchill found that Major Richard Molyneux, the son of the Earl of Sefton, had been seriously wounded by a sword cut to his wrist and urgently needed a skin graft. Churchill volunteered to give his skin to save his brother-officer. 'Ye've heeard of a man being flayed aloive?' Churchill recalled the Irish doctor saying to him in his strong brogue. 'Well, this is what it feels loike.'[25] He took flesh about the size of a modern ten-pence piece from Churchill's left forearm without any anaesthetic and grafted it straight on to Molyneux's wound, which healed up. 'My sensations as he sawed the razor to and fro fully justified his description,' he later recalled. When Molyneux died in 1954, Churchill remarked, 'He will take my skin with him, a kind of advance guard, into the next world.'[26]

On his return to London he continued his wooing of Pamela Plowden, asking to see her before he left to rejoin his regiment in India. 'Why do you say I am incapable of affection,' he asked her in a letter from his mother's house in Great Cumberland Place on 28 November. 'Perish the thought. I love one above all others. And I shall be constant. I am no fickle gallant capriciously following the fancy of the hour. My love is deep and strong. Nothing will ever change it.'[27] As he had earlier in the same letter written, 'I met a young lady the other day who is – I think – I judge only from the standpoint of reason – nearly as clever and wise as you,' he was clearly trying to make her jealous. It did not work.[28] 'I have lived all my life seeing the most beautiful women London produces,' Churchill wrote in March 1899. 'Then I met you . . . Were I dreamer of dreams, I would

* To set against that, Churchill also saw the twenty-seven-year-old Lord Tullibardine, heir to the dukedom of Atholl, extract a bullet from the leg of a Dervish 'through the agency of a buttonhook', as he told a dinner that Tullibardine was chairing in 1941(*CS* II p. 2221).

say . . . "Marry me – and I would conquer the world and lay it at your feet." Marriage, however, requires two conditions to be met. Money and the consent of both parties. One certainly, both probably are absent.'[29] Although the date of his formal proposal to her is contested, it is agreed that it took place in a punt while they were staying at Warwick Castle, and that she refused.[30] She married the 2nd Earl of Lytton instead in April 1902, and she and Churchill remained good friends for the rest of his life.

No sooner was the Sudan campaign over than Churchill started work on *The River War*, writing in Egypt, in London and on the boat to rejoin his regiment in India, where he went largely to play in the Inter-Regimental Polo Tournament before he left the Army in April. Writing to Captain Haldane on the train between Bombay and Bangalore in mid-December, he worried that his India General Service Medal with its 'Punjab Frontier 1897–98' clasp had still not arrived. 'I naturally want to wear my medals while I still have a uniform to wear them on,' he complained. 'They have already sent me the Egyptian one. I cannot think why the Frontier one has not arrived . . . Do try and get mine for me as soon as possible. Otherwise it will never be worn . . . Will you try to get the medal sent me – there is only the general clasp – so that there should be no great difficulty.' He signed off: 'Write to me at Bangalore and do what you can about the medal.'[31]

Churchill arrived in India on 8 February. Not long afterwards, on the night before leaving Jodhpur for the championships at Meerut, he fell down a flight of stone stairs, dislocating his right shoulder again and spraining both his ankles. 'I trust the misfortune will propitiate the gods,' he told his mother, 'offended perhaps at my success and luck elsewhere.'[32] He was to dislocate his right shoulder for the third time in a hunting accident, and nearly again while making an expansive gesture in the House of Commons.[33] He played in the game on 24 February with his upper right arm strapped, and the 4th Hussars won the Inter-Regimental Polo Tournament for the first time in the match's sixty-two-year history. Despite his injury, Churchill scored three of the four goals that secured the 4–3 victory.

Churchill resigned his Army commission at the end of April and returned to London to pursue a political career. On board the steamer SS *Carthage*, he met a pretty young American woman, Christine Conover, who recalled:

> The gangplank was about to be raised when down the wharf ran a freckled, red-haired young man in a rumpled suit carrying an immense tin cake box. Although he had nearly missed the boat, he seemed utterly unruffled . . . At lunch, or tiffin as it was called then, we found ourselves sitting directly opposite Mr Churchill. Hardly had he been seated when he bent across the

table and said, 'You are American, aren't you?' When we said he was right he exclaimed, 'I love Americans. My mother is an American.'

Remembering the occasion much later, she wrote, 'Though far from handsome, he had a charming smile and a slight hesitation in his speech.'[34] The cake box contained the manuscript of *The River War*, on which he continued to work during the journey. 'Perhaps his one fault at this time was being a little too sure about everything,' thought Miss Conover, 'which the other young people did not always appreciate.'[35]

*The River War: An Historical Account of the Reconquest of the Soudan* would be published in two volumes by Longmans seven months later, on 6 November. All told it was over 950 pages long. The book was dedicated to Lord Salisbury, who had not required him to delete any of the negative references to Kitchener.[36] Churchill had chosen as the epigraph of his Malakand book a line from one of Salisbury's speeches about frontier wars – 'They are but the surf that marks the edge and the advance of the wave of Civilization' – an analogy he had chosen to illustrate his fourth element of the art of oratory in 'The Scaffolding of Rhetoric'.

The influence of Gibbon on Churchill's writing is clear in the aphorisms and generalizations that pepper *The River War*. 'At once slovenly and uxorious,' he wrote of the Sudanese soldier, 'he detested his drills and loved his wives with equal earnestness.'[37] Or this on the joy of the Khalifa's wives at his downfall: 'Since they were henceforth to be doomed to an enforced and inviolable chastity, the cause of their satisfaction is as obscure as its manifestation was unnatural.'[38] There were also some poetic moments such as his description of the African night: 'We are left sad and sorrowful in the dark, until the stars light up and remind us that there is always something beyond.'[39] Churchill wrote of how in a Sudanese school 'The simplicity of the instruction was aided by the zeal of the students, and learning grew beneath the palm trees more quickly perhaps than in the more magnificent schools of Civilization.'[40] Sometimes the application of eighteenth-century idiom to events on the eve of the twentieth century became slightly ridiculous, as when in the smoke of a steam engine 'The malodorous incense of Civilization was offered to the startled gods of Egypt.'[41] Churchill's frequent references to Civilization in his writings underlined his belief that in these imperial frontier wars the Muslim tribesmen represented barbarism, whereas the British Empire stood in direct succession to the great civilizations of Greece, Rome and Christendom.

In the first edition of the book, Churchill damned Kitchener with faint praise, saying that he deserved 'certainly the third, and possibly even the second place' in the list of Britons responsible for destroying the Dervish

Empire, after Salisbury and Lord Cromer. In the second edition, published in one volume in 1902, Kitchener was promoted to the second place and one-third of the book was excised, including the line, 'By Sir Herbert Kitchener's order, the [Mahdi's] Tomb had been profaned and razed to the ground.' The first edition garnered generally excellent reviews – although the *Saturday Review* commented that 'the annoying feature of the book is the irrepressible egoism of its author.' In the Army the book was referred to as 'A Subaltern's Hint to Generals'.[42]

Churchill praised the courage of the Dervish enemy in fighting for their way of life. 'I hope that if evil days should come upon our own country,' he wrote, 'and the last army which a collapsing Empire could interpose between London and the invader were dissolving in rout and ruin . . . there would be some – even in these modern days – who would not care to accustom themselves to a new order of things and tamely survive the disaster.'[43] Churchill would express precisely the same sentiments to his ministers when discussing a possible Nazi invasion of Britain on 28 May 1940. Another passage that he removed from the condensed 1902 edition, as he was by then hoping to hold office in an empire comprising tens of millions of Muslims, was one which read,

> How dreadful are the curses which Mohammedanism lays on its votaries! Besides the fanatical frenzy, which is as dangerous in a man as hydrophobia in a dog, there is this fearful fatalistic apathy. The effects are apparent in many countries. Improvident habits, slovenly systems of agriculture, sluggish methods of commerce, and insecurity of property exist wherever the followers of the Prophet rule or live. A degraded sensualism deprives this life of its grace and refinement; the next of its dignity and sanctity. The fact that in Mohammedan law every woman must *belong* to some man as his absolute property – either as a child, a wife, or a concubine – must delay the final extinction of slavery until the faith of Islam has ceased to be a Great power among men. Individual Moslems may show splendid qualities . . . but the influence of the religion paralyses the social development of those who follow it. No stronger retrograde force exists in the world. Far from being moribund, Mohammedanism is a militant and proselytising faith. It has already spread throughout Central Africa, raising fearless warriors at every step; and were it not that Christianity is sheltered in the strong arms of science – the science against which it had vainly struggled – the civilisation of modern Europe might fall, as fell the civilisation of ancient Rome.[44]

Back in London, Churchill was preoccupied about his future. On 3 May he wrote to the Society palm-reader Mrs Robinson of Wimpole Street, sending her a cheque for two guineas and complimenting her on her 'strange skill in palmistry'. She had told him that 'He would pass great difficulties but reach the top of his profession,' which prompted him three days later to tell her, 'I would rather not have my hand published to the world: although I trust you may be right in your forecast.'[45] Two days later the Scottish Tory MP Ian Malcolm, Chief of the Clan Malcolm and 17th Laird of Poltalloch, organized a lunch for some other MPs of the 1895 intake to meet Churchill. One of their number, David Lindsay, later the 27th Earl of Crawford, wrote in his diary, 'Here is a coming man: pugnacious, obstinate and nervous – he cannot sit still. A curious halting shuffle in his voice which must make it difficult for an audience to hear him ... There is a bumptiousness about him which will soon wear off ... If he will consent to be humble and obscure for a few years there is no reason why he should not become a power in the land. In some ways he resembles his father closely.'[46] He was certainly not content to be either humble or obscure for a moment, let alone for a few years, but the MP's prediction otherwise turned out to be no less accurate than the palm-reader's.

The political situation that Churchill found on returning to Britain was complicated. The Conservative Party led by Lord Salisbury was in a permanent alliance with the Liberal Unionists led by Joseph Chamberlain and the Duke of Devonshire. The Liberal Unionists had left the Liberal Party in 1886 to oppose Gladstone's Irish Home Rule Bill. Gladstone had died in 1898 and the Liberal Party itself was informally split between the Liberal Imperialists, led by the former Prime Minister Lord Rosebery, and the Radicals.

By 20 June, Churchill had agreed to an approach from the Oldham Conservative Association in Lancashire to fight the seat in a by-election for the Unionists. The constituency had been represented by two Conservatives in the previous Parliament, one of whom had died and the other had retired. Churchill fought hard in the constituency, giving three or four speeches a night, despite having to spray an inflamed left tonsil with a special mixture sent from Dr Roose. He was keenly aware of walking in his father's footsteps and spoke of him in several speeches. 'The present Government owe more than they always remember,' he said of his father's legacy on one occasion, 'or at any rate more than they confess.'[47] 'No doubt the Radicals will say I am trading on my father's name,' he conceded at the Cooperative Hall in Oldham. 'Well, and why should I not? Did not you think it is a good name to trade with?'[48]

The pressing issue at Oldham was the Clerical Tithes Bill, which benefited Anglican clergy at the expense of the Nonconformists and Methodists who made up a good proportion of the constituency. Three days before the poll, Churchill stated that had he been in the Commons he would have voted against it. This was an act of pure opportunism, but not one that persuaded the Nonconformists to vote for him. It did lead Lord Salisbury's nephew and Jennie's old friend Arthur Balfour to quip, 'I thought he was a young man of promise, but it appears he is a young man of promises.'[49] Churchill recognized that he had made a mistake. 'It is not the slightest use defending governments or parties', he was later to say, 'unless you defend the very worst thing about which they are attacked.'[50]

On 6 July, Churchill won 11,477 votes, losing by a narrow margin to two Radical Liberals, Alfred Emmott and Walter Runciman, who won 12,976 and 12,770 respectively. 'Everyone threw the blame on me,' he later wrote wryly. 'I have noticed that they nearly always do. I suppose it is because they think I shall be able to bear it best.'[51] He returned to London, as he was to put it in his memoirs, 'with those feelings of deflation which a bottle of champagne or even soda-water represents when it is half emptied and left uncorked for a night'.[52] Christine Conover, with whom he stayed in touch for some months, confided to her diary that 'Although he was greatly disappointed, he told me he intended to try again and hoped someday even to be Prime Minister of England.'[53]

'He might have been defeated,' reported the *Manchester Courier*, 'but he was conscious that in this fight he had not been disgraced.' Churchill fully agreed, thanking the newspaper proprietor Lord Northcliffe for his support in the *Daily Mail* and saying that he thought his career would not be 'seriously damaged' by the defeat.[54] He made his excuses to Balfour who responded encouragingly, 'This small reverse will have no permanent ill effect upon your political fortunes.'[55] He was still only twenty-four.

As was so often the case in Churchill's life, what looked like a reverse at the time turned out in retrospect to have been good fortune. Had he squeaked into the House of Commons in 1899, he would not have gone to South Africa and would not have had the opportunity to make not just a local or national reputation for himself, but a truly international one.

There was a strong air of unfinished business to Lord Salisbury's 'Forward' policy in Africa. Britain had been defeated in the First Boer War of 1880–81 in South Africa at the hands of the Dutch-descended Afrikaners, who controlled the independent Transvaal and Orange Free State republics to the north of the British-controlled Cape Colony and Natal. Joseph Chamberlain, the British Colonial Secretary, and Lord Milner, the High Commissioner of Cape Colony, had so encroached on the Afrikaner republics by October 1899 that Paul Kruger, their leader, suddenly invaded Cape Colony and Natal, hoping to capture them before the British Empire could respond.

'He has the reputation of being bumptious,' Chamberlain warned Milner, after an interview with Churchill at the Colonial Office. 'Put him on the right lines.'[56] If Churchill was going to cover this, his fourth war in four years, he would need money. He secured from the *Morning Post* the huge salary of £1,000 for the first four months of the war, followed by £200 a month plus expenses, and booked himself on to the Royal Mail Ship *Dunottar Castle* which was also taking General Sir Redvers Buller, the British Commander-in-Chief, to Cape Town. Like most other commentators, Churchill did not believe that the quarter-million Boers could last long against the 350-million-strong British Empire, and he expected to be back in time for the Derby horse-race at the end of May.

On 14 October, three days after war had been declared, Churchill set sail, taking six cases of claret, champagne and spirits with him. (This was not all for personal consumption: alcohol was a useful currency in war zones.) Also on board was John Atkins, a *Manchester Guardian* journalist, who described him as 'slim, slightly reddish-haired, pale, lively, frequently plunging along the deck "with neck out-thrust", as Browning fancied Napoleon . . . when the prospects of a career like that of his father, Lord Randolph, excited him, then such a gleam shot from him that he was almost transfigured. I had not before encountered this sort of ambition, unabashed, frankly egotistical, communicating its excitement, and extorting sympathy.'[57] 'It was not that he was without the faculty of self-criticism,' added Atkins. 'He could laugh at his dreams of glory, and he had an impish fun.'[58] This kind of unabashed ambition might have extorted sympathy from Atkins, but in a culture that promoted the cult of the inspired amateur it would often arouse resentment.

On 29 October the *Dunottar Castle* passed a small tramp steamer that had left Cape Town three days earlier. The news chalked on a long blackboard as they sailed past read, 'Boers Defeated – Three Battles – Penn Symons killed'.[59] Despite the mortal wounding of General Sir William Penn Symons at the Battle of Talana Hill, and the retreat of his forces to the town of Ladysmith in Natal, the main anxiety of Churchill and his fellow passengers was that the war might be over before they disembarked at Cape Town two days later. Churchill wasted no time on landing and immediately tried to get to Ladysmith, 140 miles north-west of Durban. By then the Boers had cut the rail link on the Tugela River, and on 2 November they laid siege to the town. Once again Churchill had been fortunate in his misfortune: had he succeeded in getting into Ladysmith he would have been incarcerated there and unable to file dispatches until its relief nearly four months later. Churchill decided to travel to Estcourt in Natal to wait for an opening to get into Ladysmith, where General Sir

George White and Churchill's friend Colonel Ian Hamilton were besieged. He shared a tent in the Estcourt railway yard with Atkins. He showed him his *Morning Post* articles, and asked, 'Is the interest due to any merit in me or is it only because I am Randolph's son?' Atkins replied that he did not think they would have excited so much interest if he himself had written them. 'A fair verdict,' Churchill replied. 'But how long will my father's memory help me?'[60] Atkins thought another two to three years, whereupon Churchill said, 'My father died too young. I must try to accomplish whatever I can by the time I am forty.'[61]

In the same discussion, Churchill argued that military strategy and tactics were 'just a matter of common sense'. 'Put all the elements of a problem before a civilian of first-rate ability and enough imagination, and he would reach the right solution, and any soldier could afterwards put his solution into military terms.'[62] This belief, combined with the gross errors he witnessed at first hand by British generals in the Boer War, was profoundly to affect his thinking about civil–military relations in the far greater twentieth-century wars to come.

On Wednesday, 15 November 1899 one such idiotic military decision was to change Churchill's life. Shortly after dawn, Colonel Charles Long, the British commander of the Estcourt garrison, sent Captain Aylmer Haldane out on an armoured train on patrol, manned by a company of Dublin Fusiliers and Durham Light Infantry in three trucks, along with a 7-pound naval gun. They were not accompanied by mounted troops, a decision Buller later ascribed to 'inconceivable stupidity'.[63] Churchill need not have gone on the expedition, but, as he admitted later, he was 'eager for trouble', telling Atkins, 'I have a feeling, a sort of intuition, that if I go something will come of it. It's illogical, I know.'[64] Atkins passed up the opportunity for himself, as did the *Times*'s chief war correspondent in South Africa, Churchill's Harrow contemporary Leo Amery.

The train was an absurdly easy target for Louis Botha, the Boer commando leader, who allowed it to steam north to Chieveley before putting rocks across the track as it was approaching a bend close to the Blauuw Krantz River on the return journey.[65] Although they had spotted Botha's men on the way to Chieveley, Churchill persuaded Haldane not to turn back, so he was in part responsible for giving the Boers enough time to lay their ambush.[66] He later told Major-General H. J. T. Hildyard a story that emphasized his and Haldane's hubris that day, admitting that 'They ran confidently on to within range of the Boers, being unaware that they had [artillery] guns with them, and hoping to give them a lesson.'[67] When it hit the rocks the train's engine somehow remained on the rails, but the three trucks were derailed and the front one knocked entirely off the line.

Boer artillery and snipers fired shells and bullets into the overturned trucks, and soon silenced the naval gun.

Churchill displayed great bravery and initiative in leading some survivors out on to the track and then spending half an hour heaving the two overturned trucks off the line so that the badly damaged engine with fifty survivors could escape back to Estcourt, most of them wounded, while he stayed to rally the rest of the trapped and outnumbered troops.[68] In all he spent about ninety minutes under almost continuous fire. The Boers were famously accurate snipers, and he was lucky to have survived. Back in Estcourt, Atkins met a dozen of the escaped fugitives and pieced together what had happened. 'We heard how Churchill had walked round and round the wreckage while the bullets were hitting against the iron walls, and had called for volunteers to free the engine; how he had said "Keep cool, men," and again, "This will be interesting for my paper!"; and again how, when the train driver was grazed on the head and was about to run off, he had jumped in to help him and had said, "No man is hit twice on the same day."'[69] (Eleven years later, Churchill recommended the driver and his stoker for the Albert Medal.) Those who made it out alive on the engine gave Churchill, who stayed behind with the majority of the troops, much of the credit for their escape.

With the engine gone, six men dead and thirty-five wounded out of the complement of 120 (a casualty rate of over one-third, even higher than at the charge at Omdurman), there was nothing for the remaining men to do but surrender. Churchill later told Atkins that the Boers had rounded up the prisoners 'like cattle! The greatest indignity of my life!'[70]* Churchill subsequently claimed that he had been captured by Louis Botha, who was elsewhere at the time, but it was a tiny embellishment on an otherwise extraordinarily commendable performance. He was fortunately unarmed when he was captured, as he had left his Mauser in the engine during the effort to dislodge the trucks. Even so, there was some debate among the Boers about whether he should be shot as a spy, whereas he told Louis de Souza, the Boer War Minister, that as a journalist he should be freed.

The Afrikaner State-Attorney who interrogated him, the Cambridge-educated lawyer Jan Christian Smuts, initially opposed his release. 'I

* In December 1902 he wrote a short story, 'On the Flank of the Army', for the Boston publication *Youth's Companion*. It was an exciting fictional tale about an upper-class Old Harrovian Lancer, Lieutenant Henry Morelande, who was captured by a Boer Commando but escaped with the help of a Boer whose son's life he had nobly spared. Morelande/Churchill was appalled at being captured. 'Shame, disgust, and anger plunged the subaltern in the deepest gloom . . . And then to lose all the opportunities of the campaign – to be a miserable prisoner! He groaned aloud' (*Windsor Magazine*, March 1903).

remember when we met,' Churchill said over half a century later. 'I was wet and draggle-tailed. He was examining me on the part I had played . . . a difficult moment.'[71] Since Churchill had instinctively behaved like a combatant army officer rather than a non-combatant war correspondent, he was imprisoned.

The first of Churchill's sixty-six telegrams and thirty-five letters from the war was published in the *Morning Post* on 16 November, but there were to be no more in the immediate future as Churchill was on his way to the State Model School Prison in Pretoria, housed in a hastily converted school. On 18 November, in a postscript to a letter written to his mother when he arrived there, he wrote: 'Cox's [Bank] should be instructed to cash any cheques I draw.'[72] He saw no reason why imprisonment should interfere with his creature comforts.

It was during this period of his captivity that Churchill came to understand why the Boers had such an aversion to British rule, which he put down to 'the abiding fear and hatred of the movement that seeks to place the native on a level with the white man'.[73] Churchill had no sympathy for the aggressive white supremacism of the Afrikaner, from which his own paternalistic instincts were entirely different. He wrote of a future South African society in which 'Black is to be proclaimed the same as white . . . to be constituted his legal equal, to be armed with political rights,' a prospect that infuriated Afrikaners no less than would be 'a tigress robbed of her cubs'.

As might be expected from someone so desperate to achieve as much as possible in life as quickly as possible, the prospect of spending time behind bars drove Churchill to despair. 'I am twenty-five today,' he wrote to Cockran on 30 November. 'It is terrible to think how little time remains.'[74] He later wrote, 'Hours crawl like paralytic centipedes. Nothing amuses you. Reading is difficult, writing, impossible. I certainly hated every minute of my captivity more than I have ever hated any period of my life.'[75] He exercised in the compound, and indulged his burgeoning interest in butterflies.* He was also permitted to write letters, and started at the top.

'I venture to think that Your Royal Highness will be interested to receive a letter from me and from this address,' Churchill wrote to the Prince of Wales, on very thin, prison-issue paper, 'although of course the censorship excludes me from writing freely . . . I consider myself unfortunate in having been captured so early in the operations, and I would have liked to have written some general account of the war. However it is something to be alive and well and when I saw so many soldiers and volunteers torn with such

* The butterfly expert Hugh Newman later described Churchill as 'If not a fully-fledged lepidopterist, at least a disciple in the field' (*FH* no. 89 p. 35).

horrible injuries, I could not help feeling thankful that I had been preserved – even though as a prisoner.'[76] He said that clearing the railway line had been 'very dangerous and exciting', and added, 'what an astonishing din the great projectiles exploding and crashing among the iron trucks made'.

On the night of Tuesday, 12 December 1899, Churchill climbed over the iron lattice-work palings of the prison behind the lavatory, when the guard's back was turned. 'I had come to the conclusion that we should waste the whole night in hesitations unless the matter were clinched once and for all,' he was later to write about his fellow escapees, Haldane and a Sergeant Brockie, who were having doubts about the timing of the escape. 'And as the sentry turned to light his pipe, I jumped on to the ledge of the wall and in a few seconds had dropped into the garden safely on the other side. Here I crouched down and waited for the others to come. I expected them to come every minute. My position in the garden was a very anxious one because I had only a few small and leafless bushes to hide behind, and people kept passing to and fro, and the lights of the house were burning. Altogether I waited more than an hour and a half in the garden for the others to join me. Twice a man from the house walked along a path within seven or eight yards of me.'[77] As he told Leo Amery thirty years later, 'He had given the others every chance but they wouldn't take it, urged him to come back which he wouldn't do (they talked through the lattice), so they gave him . . . their blessing.'[78]

Having waited as long as he could, Churchill walked through the Boer capital at night, intending to make his way to neutral Portuguese East Africa (modern-day Mozambique). He had to cross 300 miles of enemy territory with no map, compass, food, money, firearm or knowledge of Afrikaans. The lack of a compass did not seem to concern him, as he would orient himself by the stars, one star in particular. 'Orion shone brightly,' he later recalled. 'Scarcely a year before he had guided me when lost in the desert to the banks of the Nile. He had given me water. Now he should lead me to freedom.'[79] People often believe in their stars in a general way; Churchill actually specified which one it was.

With superb effrontery, he left in his cell a letter to de Souza to tell him that because he did not consider the Pretoria Government had any right to detain him, 'I have decided to escape from your custody.' He readily accepted that the Boer treatment of prisoners was 'correct and humane', however, and promised that 'When I return to the British lines I will make a public statement to this effect.' He also thanked him for his personal civility, and expressed the hope 'that we may meet again at Pretoria before very long, and under different circumstances'.[80]

A year later he summed up his escape route in a speech at the Waldorf

Astoria Hotel in New York: 'I passed through the streets of Pretoria unobserved and managed to board a coal train on which I hid among the sacks of coal. When I found the train was not going in the direction I wanted, I jumped off.'[81] Having jumped both on to and off a moving train, Churchill was now hungry. He entered a small grove of trees which grew on the side of a deep ravine, hoping to wait till dusk. 'I had one consolation,' he wrote later, 'no one in the world knew where I was – I did not know myself . . . My sole companion was a gigantic vulture, who manifested an extravagant interest in my condition, and made hideous and ominous gurglings from time to time.'[82] Six years later he told an audience in the Central Hall, Manchester, to loud applause and laughter, 'I travelled for some distance in a coal-truck, from which I jumped in the night, head over heels, and took refuge in a thicket. It was in this thicket that I met the vulture. Nobody will believe in my vulture. I don't care whether anybody believes it or not. There was a vulture.'[83] The escape was the one occasion in his life, he later told his nephew, when he 'prayed very earnestly'.[84] 'I wandered about aimlessly for a long time, suffering from hunger,' he recalled, 'and at last I decided that I must seek aid at all risks. I knocked at the door of a kraal, expecting to find a Boer, and to my joy, found it occupied by an Englishman named Herbert Howard, who ultimately helped me to reach the British lines.'[85]

John Howard – Churchill had slightly changed his name to protect him – was a British mining engineer who hid him down his mine for three days, amid rats that scuttled over his face when the candles guttered out, and who, along with some other brave Britons there, including a Mr Dewsnap, helped stow him at the bottom of a railway coal-wagon to Lourenço Marques (modern-day Maputo), the capital of Portuguese East Africa. Churchill's absence from the prison might not have been spotted so early if he had only cancelled his appointment with the barber, who arrived to give him a haircut and shave the following morning and raised the alarm when he could not find him.[86] That he might have attended to his toilette himself while in prison seems not to have occurred to him. The Boers launched a manhunt for him covering hundreds of miles and including door-to-door searches, but to no avail.*

When he reached the British Consulate at Lourenço Marques on 22 December, armed Britons arrived to prevent his being recaptured by the local Boers. The British Consul let him take a hot bath and had his filthy clothes

* Sadly, the famous '£25 dead or alive poster' for Churchill's capture was a forgery: no such reward was offered; it was not put out by the Boer police; the man who ostensibly signed the document did not hold the job attributed to him at the time, and some versions used a typeface that did not exist until 1928. Churchill was not to know that, though, and took great pleasure from it in later life.

burned. 'What a pity,' Churchill said when he found out; 'I wanted them for Madame Tussaud.'[87] He took a boat to Durban, where he arrived on 23 December a popular hero. Unbeknown to him, his sensational escape had been the sole bright moment in an otherwise disastrous time for the Empire. The British Army had been defeated in no fewer than three battles, at Stromberg, Magersfontein and Colenso – the notorious 'Black Week' of 10 to 17 December, when 2,700 men had been killed, wounded or captured.

A large and excited crowd welcomed Churchill ashore at the docks, where he climbed up on a rickshaw and delivered an impromptu speech. 'We are in the midst of a fierce struggle with a vast military power, he said, 'which is resolved at all costs to gratify its reckless ambition by beating the British out of South Africa.' There were cries of 'Never!' and a voice called out, 'Never, while we have such fine fellows as you!' Churchill continued:

> It is for the people of South Africa, for those of the Cape Colony, and those in Natal to say whether or not the British flag is going to be hauled down in this country. When I see around me such a crowd as this, such determination and such enthusiasm, I am satisfied that, no matter what the difficulties, no matter what the dangers and what the force they may bring against us, we shall be successful in the end.

There were more cheers and an old man shouted, 'God bless you, my boy.'[88]

Over the coming years, attempts were made to question the heroism of Churchill's prison escape. A libel suit in 1912 alleged that he had deliberately left Haldane and Brockie behind. It was true that Brockie had abused Churchill for his ungentlemanly behaviour after he had gone, but Haldane pointed out in April 1931, after Churchill's account of the escape had been published in *My Early Life*, that there was a provision in the Army Act stating (in Haldane's paraphrase) that 'If any officer, a prisoner, sees the opportunity of escaping and does not take it, he can be punished.'[89] Churchill had seen his chance and taken it, while the others had not. As he was to acknowledge in *My Early Life*, the escape and the immense fame it brought him both in Britain and around the world 'was to lay down the foundations of my later life'.[90]

On the morning of 6 January 1941, when Churchill had many more pressing matters on his mind, he told his private secretary that he always remembered the anniversary of the day in 1900 when General Buller had given him his lieutenancy in the 700-strong South African Light Horse,*

* Nicknamed the 'Cockyolibirds' because of the plume cockades on their hats.

without requiring him to give up his war correspondent's job.[91] Buller had told him he would not get paid for serving, but that did not matter as he was receiving a stipend from the *Morning Post*.

Many war correspondents would have taken no further risks during that war, and some would have returned home after the prison escape. Churchill went straight back to the front, now formally a soldier again. Four days later, he volunteered to take a message 18 miles from his commanding officer, Colonel Julian 'Bungo' Byng, to General Sir Francis Clery. Byng 'thought his offer was a gallant one, as neither he nor I knew what parties of Boers might be lurking in the neighbourhood'.[92] He told Byng that he wanted to win the Distinguished Service Order, 'as it would look so nice on the robes of the Chancellor of the Exchequer'.[93] Byng told him that 'he must first get into Parliament, if he could get any constituency to have him!' By then, Churchill could fairly surmise that he would have his choice of constituencies once he returned home.

'Ah, horrible war,' Churchill wrote in his dispatch for the *Morning Post* of 22 January 1900, 'amazing medley of the glorious and the squalid, the pitiful and the sublime, if modern men of light and leading saw your face closer, simple folk would see it hardly ever.'[94] Over the next two days, Churchill saw a good deal of the pitiful and squalid side of war, acting as liaison officer between General Sir Charles Warren, one of the worst generals of the Boer War, and Colonel Alexander Thorneycroft, who led the initial assault – on the wrong hill – during the appallingly mismanaged Battle of Spion Kop, another British military disaster.* Churchill was too junior an officer for any blame to attach to him, but it gave him a close view of the military incompetence that plagued the Army. In the fighting he experienced several near-misses from bullets, including one which parted the long sakabula-bird tail-feathers adorning his hat.[95] As he put it on an earlier occasion, 'The bullet is brutally indiscriminating, and before it the brain of a hero or the quarters of a horse stand exactly the same chance to the vertical square inch.'[96] On 12 February, he and his brother Jack, who had volunteered for military service, carried out a reconnaissance on Hussar Hill, where Jack was shot in the leg.† 'It was his baptism of fire,' Churchill wrote later, 'and I have since wondered at the strange caprice which strikes down one man in his first skirmish and protects another time after time. But I suppose all pitchers will get broken in the end. Outwardly I sympathised with my brother in his misfortune . . .

* Elsewhere on the same battlefield Mohandas Gandhi was serving as a stretcher-bearer.

† Jack had to be invalided for a month on the hospital ship on which their mother had sailed to Cape Town and for which she had enterprisingly and patriotically found donors, before having it fully kitted out.

but secretly I confess myself well content that this young gentleman should be honourably out of harm's way for a month.'[97] For Atkins, 'It seemed as though [Jack] had paid his brother's debts.'[98]

Ladysmith was finally relieved on 28 February 1900, after a gruelling 118-day siege, with the defenders having only half a week's rations left. Churchill was present, and for him it was the greatest scoop of the war. In *My Early Life*, he described how he 'galloped across the scrub-dotted plain' with two squadrons of the South African Light Horse and entered Ladysmith. 'On we pressed, and at the head of a battered street of tin-roofed houses met Sir George White on horseback, faultlessly attired. Then we all rode together into the long beleaguered, almost starved-out, Ladysmith. It was a thrilling moment. I dined with the Headquarters staff that night.'[99]*

Churchill's Boer War adventures continued unabated after Ladysmith: he had a horse shot from under him in late April; he cycled in civilian clothes through Boer-held Johannesburg at the end of May; he met Milner in Cape Town and hunted jackals with his aide-de-camp the Duke of Westminster on Table Mountain.[100] On 16 May he published a book about these adventures, *London to Ladysmith via Pretoria*, which quickly sold out its initial print run of 10,000 copies. On 5 June 1900 he entered Pretoria with the South African Light Horse and liberated the prison in which he had been held, tearing down the Boer flag as his former cell-mate Major Cecil Grimshaw replaced it with a Union Jack that he carried up the flagpole in his teeth.

Six days later Churchill fought at the Battle of Diamond Hill with what the British commander, Ian Hamilton, described as 'conspicuous gallantry'.[101] He kept a large piece of shrapnel that had landed between himself and his cousin Sunny, the Duke of Marlborough, during the battle, which he was to give to the Duke, inscribed in silver with the words 'This fragment of a 30lb shrapnel shell fell between us and might have separated us forever, but is now a token of union.' (It is on display today in Blenheim Palace.) Hamilton tried to get Churchill a gallantry award for his valour

* This account, which implies that Churchill was present when White was relieved at 6 p.m., and had dinner with him on the night of the relief, was comprehensively contradicted in 1954 by General Sir Hubert Gough, who wrote in his autobiography *Soldiering On* that Churchill and his commanding officer, the Earl of Dundonald, were not seen in Ladysmith until 8 p.m., after darkness had fallen and once the Imperial Light Horse and Natal Carabineers had already relieved the town. Gough added that his remarks 'may not show him as a very pleasant and popular young man, but one can recognise in them his energy, his capacity for emotional excitement, which could stir him so deeply and which were the foundations of his power for leadership' (Gough, *Soldiering On* p. 81). Churchill would hardly have been the first war correspondent to have embroidered the truth, but the autobiographies of Dundonald and Field Marshal Lord Birdwood, also both eyewitnesses, whose memoirs were published in 1934 and 1941, much earlier than Gough's, fully support Churchill's account.

at the battle, but this was blocked, possibly by Kitchener, on the grounds that he was a press correspondent first and a soldier second.[102] A photo of Churchill in uniform taken at this time shows him with a wispy moustache, which he soon shaved off because it was too light coloured, and his Spanish medal.[103] In all, Churchill was awarded no fewer than six clasps to his Queen's South Africa Medal: Diamond Hill, Johannesburg, Relief of Ladysmith, Orange Free State, Tugela Heights and Cape Colony. Churchill's experiences in the Boer War had won him great fame, given him several chances to display tremendous physical courage, earned him good money as a journalist and made him several friends for life, such as Hamilton and Westminster, whose best man he was to be in 1930.

In February 1900, *Savrola*, a 70,000-word novel, was published in Boston and London. Churchill had written a quarter of it in India three years earlier, but had to stop to publish his other two books first. His only book of fiction, it was dedicated to his fellow officers of the 4th Hussars. Although he was later to joke, 'I have consistently urged my friends to abstain from reading it,' *Savrola* deserves examination for the opportunity it offers, in the words many years later of the novelist Sir Compton Mackenzie, 'to pry into the dreams of a young man of destiny, not merely about his own future but also about the political future of dictators and Communists'.[104] It is said that most first novels are at least partly autobiographical, and *Savrola* is no exception, although the eponymous hero seems to have a good deal of Churchill's father in him as well. (Mrs Everest also appears as the hero's devotedly loyal housekeeper, Bettine.)

The novel is set in a fictional Balkan country called Laurania, ruled by the dictator President Antonio Molara five years after a brutal civil war. The pro-democracy National Party is led by the handsome, well-bred thirty-two-year-old Savrola, a thinker as well as a man of action. The story opens just as Molara is about to disenfranchise half the electorate to ensure victory in the coming elections. Savrola, who is very well read – 'a volume of Macaulay's *Essays* lay on the writing-table' – was the de facto leader of the opposition. 'Ambition was the motive force,' we are told, 'and he was powerless to resist it.'[105] Molara's beautiful wife Lucile leaves the presidential palace just as Savrola is arriving to protest against the killing of forty demonstrators the previous day, and there is a powerful mutual attraction. Molara's odious, Iago-like secretary Miguel suggests to Molara that Savrola should meet with 'an accident' before being elected to the Senate, but Molara fears this would provoke revolution. Instead he asks Lucile to uncover Savrola's plans.

Lucile secretly witnesses Savrola giving a rousing speech to 7,000 people. He spots her just in time and rescues her from being crushed by the crowd. There is then an insurgency, invasion, intervention by a British warship and a kiss between Savrola and Lucile that is interrupted by Molara and Miguel. Revolvers are pointed and much melodrama ensues, including Molara striking his 'strumpet!' wife with the back of his hand.[106] In the closing scenes, Molara dies, Miguel changes sides twice and Savrola is forced into exile with Lucile, but 'after the tumults had subsided, the hearts of the people turned again to the illustrious exile who had won them freedom and whom they had deserted in the hour of victory.'[107]

*Savrola* was a financial success, earning Churchill £700 – around six years of Army pay. It boasted several memorable lines such as 'Chivalrous gallantry is not among the peculiar characteristics of excited democracy,' and 'It is hard, if not impossible, to snub a beautiful woman; they remain beautiful and the rebuke recoils.' He never, however, wrote another novel.

Magnanimity after victory was a policy Churchill was to adopt regularly throughout his career. In a letter to the *Natal Witness* in March 1900, he now urged lenient treatment of the Boers, arguing that the spirit of revenge was wrong, 'first of all because it is morally wicked, and secondly because it is practically foolish. Revenge may be sweet, but it is also most expensive ... We must also make it easy for the enemy to accept defeat. We must tempt as well as compel.'[108] He could not know that it would ultimately fall to him to integrate the Transvaal and Orange Free State into the British Empire.

On 20 July 1900, Churchill returned to Britain as a national hero. He received offers from no fewer than eleven Conservative constituency associations to stand in the general election in late September, in which Lord Salisbury hoped to capitalize upon support for the Boer War. Churchill chose to refight the two-member constituency of Oldham, telling Arthur Balfour that he believed his fame could win a seat in Parliament not only for himself but also for his Tory running mate: 'I might have chosen other safer seats but I am particularly anxious to win these two seats back for the party, and indeed I think there is a pretty good chance of success.'[109]

In his stump speeches, Churchill certainly employed just the extravagances and similes he had recommended in 'The Scaffolding of Rhetoric', calling Liberals 'prigs, prudes and faddists' and accusing them of hiding their ideology 'from the public view like a toad in a hole, but when it stands forth in all its hideousness the Tories will have to hew the filthy object limb from limb'.[110] The election saw him face down slander for the first time. 'It was said that I was habitually drunk,' he told a meeting in Oldham; 'that I had been drummed out of the Army; that I had had a quarrel with my [Conservative] colleague [in Oldham], Mr. Crisp, and that I had so far forgotten myself that I had struck him in the face. In order to give the lie some colour a disreputable scoundrel threw a brick at and cut Mr. Crisp's face.'[111]

In one of the election meetings, at Oldham's Theatre Royal, Churchill praised Dan Dewsnap, an Oldham resident and one of his saviours during his prison escape. 'His wife's in the gallery!' shouted a member of the audience, a fact which led to 'general jubilation'.[112] It was the kind of political advertising that money could not buy. Most of his actual election expenses were fortunately picked up by the Duke of Marlborough.[113] Churchill was wrong when he boasted to Balfour that his fame could win the Conservatives both seats. On 1 October he was elected with 12,931 votes, just trailing Alfred Emmott with 12,947 and thus taking the seat from Walter Runciman who got 12,709, ahead of Charles Crisp with 12,555. Extraordinarily, there were only 392 votes separating the top candidate from the bottom out of over 50,000 cast.

'It is clear to me from the figures that nothing but personal popularity arising out of the late South African War carried me in,' he reported to Lord Salisbury. 'Without the personal – probably non-political vote – I should have been behind Mr Runciman.'[114] The caption of a 'Spy' cartoon in *Vanity Fair* magazine soon afterwards analysed the situation perfectly: 'He is ambitious; he means to get on, and he loves his country. But he can hardly be regarded as a slave of any party.' Churchill's extremely narrow victory was part of a massive landslide for Lord Salisbury's Unionist coalition, with 402 Conservatives and Liberal Unionist MPs elected to support the Government, against 184 Liberals, two MPs from the new Labour Party (formed that February) and eighty-two Irish Nationalists.

Before the new MP had even taken his seat, he had fought in four wars, published five books (the most recent, *Ian Hamilton's March*, the sequel to *From London to Ladysmith*, appeared twelve days after his election), written 215 newspaper and magazine articles, participated in the greatest cavalry charge in half a century and made a spectacular escape from prison. 'At twenty-five he had fought in more continents than any soldier in history save Napoleon,' a contemporary profile of him was to proclaim, 'and seen as many campaigns as any living general.'[115]

Churchill was undeniably pushy. He cut corners and deliberately employed 'extravagances' and exaggeration for political effect, and he had been criticized as a thruster. He had also learned how to write and speak extraordinarily well, had boundless self-confidence, had developed an elephantine hide against criticism, could speak well in public and had shown a great deal of moral as well as physical courage. His prison escape showed that he could grasp an opportunity when it came his way. He was, in short, ready for a life in politics.

# 4

# Crossing the Floor October 1900–December 1905

*The House of Commons ... is a kind of college or theatre in which men of rising talent have a chance of revealing, not only their aptitude for parliamentary and public affairs, but their character and personality.*

Churchill speech to a lobby lunch, February 1940[1]

*Reasonable care for a man's own interest is neither a public nor a private vice. It is affectation to pretend that statesmen and soldiers who have gained fame in history have been indifferent to their own advancement, incapable of resenting injuries, or guided in their public action only by altruism.*

Churchill, *Marlborough*[2]

On 28 July 1900, Jennie Churchill married George Cornwallis-West, a handsome Army officer, born two weeks before her eldest son, who had little means of financial support. Churchill had warned her the previous year that 'Fine sentiments and empty stomachs do not accord,' and sure enough the couple were very soon to run out of money.[3] It was a stormy marriage which ended with Cornwallis-West's public desertion of Jennie and a divorce in 1913. But clearly Churchill could not now expect much from his trust fund. Since MPs were unpaid until 1911, he needed to make money.

Parliament was in recess until mid-February 1901 and Churchill spent the time after his election giving lucrative public speeches in Britain and North America, mainly about his adventures in South Africa, illustrated by slides from a 'magic lantern' projector. He was careful not to be too vainglorious. At one dinner he joked, 'I have been reading a book called *Twice Captured*, an extraordinary title for it is perfectly easy to be captured. A man might just as easily call his book "Twice Bankrupt".'[4] The

British tour earned Churchill £3,782 for twenty-nine performances. Ian Hamilton, who used to visit him in his flat at 105 Mount Street in Mayfair (lent to Churchill rent free by Sunny Marlborough), remembered 'his joy in telling me that he found he could hop like a bird off the bough of a tree away from his prepared speech into impromptu and then hop back again before anyone could catch him'.[5] In November 1900, Churchill was elected to the Carlton Club, almost a prerequisite for Conservative politicians, coincidentally on the same day as another new MP, the Canadian-born businessman Andrew Bonar Law.

Churchill arrived in New York on 8 December 1900 on board the Cunard steamer *Lucania*. 'I pursue profit not pleasure in the States this time,' he told Bourke Cockran, admitting to feeling 'no small trepidation at embarking upon the stormy sea of American thought and discussion'.[6] 'I am not here to marry anybody,' he told reporters waiting for him at the dock. 'I am not going to get married and I would like to have that stated positively.'[7] When asked whether an Afrikaner maiden or Providence had helped him escape from prison, he replied enigmatically, 'It is sometimes the same thing.'[8] That night at the Press Club, enjoying the post-prandial brandy and cigars, he said, 'After seeing many nations, after travelling through Europe, and after having been a prisoner of the Boers, I have come to see that, after all, the chief characteristic of the English-speaking people as compared with other white people is that they wash, and wash at regular periods. England and America are divided by a great ocean of salt water, but united by an eternal bathtub of soap and water.'[9] It was hardly a noble inauguration of the concept of the English-speaking peoples' 'fraternal association' that he was one day to make his own.

On 10 December, Churchill met Vice President-elect Theodore Roosevelt in Albany, the capital of New York State, but they did not get along. 'I saw the Englishman* Winston Churchill here,' Roosevelt wrote to a friend, 'and although he is not an attractive fellow, I was interested in some of the things he said.'[10] Roosevelt's daughter later perceptively concluded that they had not bonded because they were so much alike. No less a figure than Mark Twain introduced Churchill at his first New York lecture six days later, saying, 'Mr. Churchill by his father is an Englishman, by his mother he is an American, no doubt a blend that makes the perfect man.'[11]

Like many Americans, Twain had opposed the Boer War, and on a tour of the University of Michigan at Ann Arbor Churchill was loudly booed and hissed. He worked out a clever way of deflecting pro-Boer hostility

* To differentiate him from the popular American novelist of the same name.

in the Irish-American audience in Chicago, however, an audience that had arrived with animosity 'and with whisky' to barrack him loudly. Altering the strict historical narrative of a battle, Churchill presented the British as being on the verge of crushing defeat when, 'In this desperate situation, the Dublin Fusiliers arrived! Trumpeters sounded the charge and the enemy were swept from the field.'[12] The audience, torn for a moment between Anglophobia and consanguinity, went with their hearts and cheered the supposedly Irish victory.

'I am very proud of the fact that there is not one person in a million who at my age could have earned £10,000 [roughly £1 million today] without any capital in less than two years,' Churchill boasted to his mother on the first day of the new century. 'But sometimes it is very unpleasant work. For instance, last week I arrived to lecture in an American town and found [the organizer Major James B.] Pond had not arranged any public lecture, but that I was hired out for £40 to perform at an evening party in a private house – like a conjurer.'[13] The money Churchill raked in was profitably invested for him by his father's friend, the financier Sir Ernest Cassel.

Queen Victoria died on 22 January 1901, when Churchill was lecturing in Winnipeg. 'I am curious to know about the King.' Churchill asked his mother satirically about the newly acceded Edward VII, one of her former lovers: 'Will it entirely revolutionise his way of life? Will he sell his horses and scatter his Jews [as Prince of Wales he had borrowed heavily from Jewish financiers] or will Reuben Sassoon be enshrined among the crown jewels and other regalia? Will he become desperately serious? Will he continue to be friendly to you? Will the Keppel* be appointed the 1st Lady of the Bedchamber?'[14] The next day he placed a £100 wager with James C. Young, an American industrialist in Minneapolis, opposing Young's contention that the British Empire would be 'substantially reduced' over the next decade.[15] He certainly won, but it is not known whether he ever collected.

He embarked for England on 2 February, and on his return bought a motor car, a French Mors (the only non-British car he ever owned), even though he could not yet drive. Years later he told a friend that 'He had never thought of being taught but had simply taken delivery and set off.' He admitted to having 'a little trouble with a bus' at Hyde Park Corner, 'resulting in some damage', but 'we got that patched up' and the next year he drove from London to York in a day.[16] Churchill habitually drove fast, routinely jumped traffic lights and occasionally went up on to the

* Alice Keppel was the new King's favourite mistress, in a crowded field.

pavement when faced with traffic congestion.[17] His impatience behind the wheel and ignoring of the rules of the road seem completely at one with his general attitude to life.

Churchill took his seat in the House of Commons on 14 February 1901. 'It was an honour to take part in the deliberations of this famous assembly,' he was later to write, 'which for centuries had guided England through numberless perils forward on the path of Empire.'[18] Surprisingly for him, the first words he uttered there were not his own initiative. The speaker who preceded him, the Liberal firebrand David Lloyd George, had proposed a moderately phrased amendment to the Bill being debated, but he did so in a bitter and animated speech against the Tories.[19] So, prompted by the Tory MP Thomas Bowles, Churchill started his maiden speech on 18 February by saying, 'It might perhaps have been better, upon the whole, if the honourable Member, instead of making his speech without moving his Amendment, had moved his Amendment without making his speech.'[20] The Tories laughed at this sally, and the House noted that Churchill might be someone to whom it was enjoyable and profitable to listen. They were less amused by the rest of Churchill's maiden speech, which proposed leniency towards the Boers once they were defeated, and included the line, 'If I were a Boer fighting in the field – and if I were a Boer I hope I should be fighting in the field . . . '[21] At that Joseph Chamberlain was heard to remark from the Government front bench, 'That's the way to throw away seats.'[22] Churchill continued: 'From what I saw of the war – and I sometimes saw something of it – I believe that as compared with other wars, especially those in which a civil population took part, this war in South Africa has been on the whole carried on with unusual humanity and generosity.' (The internment of Boer civilians in concentration camps was initially for their protection in the absence of their husbands and brothers; it was only later that the diseases broke out that killed 16,000 of them.)

Churchill said he hoped that after the British victory the Boers, 'those brave and unhappy men who are fighting in the field', would be given 'a full guarantee for the security of their property and religion, an assurance of equal rights, a promise of representative institutions, and last of all, but not least of all, what the British Army would most readily accord to a brave and enduring foe – all the honours of war'.[23] His peroration celebrated the way in which the war had solidified the unity of the Empire. 'Whatever we may have lost in doubtful friends in Cape Colony,' he said, 'we have gained ten times, or perhaps twenty times, over in Canada and Australia, where the people – down to the humblest farmer in the most distant provinces – have by their effective participation in the conflict been able to realise, as they never could realise before, that they belong to the Empire, and that the Empire belongs to them.'[24] He ended with a moving reference to his father: 'I cannot sit down without saying how very grateful I am for the kindness and patience with which the House has heard me, and which have been extended to me, I well know, not on my own account, but because of a certain splendid memory which many honourable Members still preserve.'[25] The speech was widely reported because Churchill had released the text to the press beforehand, a practice which in those days was considered disrespectful, indeed almost sharp practice.

When Lord Randolph Churchill had entered the Commons in 1874, he had joined a group of rebels who became known as the Fourth Party because they rebelled so often against the Conservative leadership. His son did much the same thing in his first years in Parliament, joining a small group of aristocratic rebels gathered around Lord Hugh 'Linky' Cecil, the Marquess of Salisbury's son, who were nicknamed the 'Hughligans'. Although Cecil was a reactionary and Churchill a Tory Democrat, the Hughligans often dined and voted together, and were generally seen as bright young men who were being rebellious in order to draw attention to themselves in the hopes of gaining office. They were unsurprisingly viewed with some resentment by the less well-born but more loyal bulk of Tory backbenchers.

Churchill did not have to wait long for his chance to rebel. When St John Brodrick, the Secretary for War, in March 1901 announced an increase in the size of the Army of 50 per cent, Churchill saw an opportunity to vindicate his father's memory. He took a crash course in orthodox economics from Sir Francis Mowatt, a friend at the Treasury, and advocated a reduction in income tax from its current level of 5.8 per cent, which was considered dangerously high. This was to be paid for by a cut rather than an increase in military spending. Churchill took six weeks to prepare his attack on Brodrick's Army Estimates. His second Commons speech, on 13 May, came almost three months after his maiden. 'I learnt it so thoroughly off by heart', he told a journalist, 'that it hardly mattered where I began it or how I turned it.'[26] He did not refer to his notes once in the entire hour he spoke.*

Brodrick had ambitious plans for a British Army of six corps, of which three would be ready for dispatch to the continent in the event of war. 'They are enough to irritate,' Churchill said of the six corps, 'they are not

* In Churchill's first eleven months in the House of Commons he made only nine speeches there, but thirty others in the countryside and twenty in towns, clearly indicating that he wanted to remain nationally known. In that time he also spent twelve days playing polo, fourteen hunting, two shooting and eighteen on holiday abroad. (OB II p. 29.)

enough to overawe.'[27] He believed that the Navy protected Britain, whereas the Army only ever needed to be an imperial police force, rather than something that might involve Britain in continental military commitments. He quoted his father writing to Lord Salisbury days before his resignation: 'I decline to be a party to encouraging the military and militant circle of the War Office and Admiralty to join in the high and desperate stakes which other nations seem to be forced to risk.' He ended his speech with the words 'I am very glad the House has allowed me, after an interval of fifteen years, to lift again the tattered flag of retrenchment and economy.'[28] He described himself as 'a Conservative by tradition, whose fortunes are linked indissolubly to the Tory party', but who nonetheless wanted to argue the unpopular cause of defence cuts, 'for this is a cause I have inherited, and a cause for which the late Lord Randolph Churchill made the greatest sacrifice of any minister of modern times'.[29]

'A European war cannot be anything but a cruel, heart-rending struggle,' Churchill predicted, 'which, if we are ever to enjoy the bitter fruits of victory, must demand, perhaps for several years, the whole manhood of the nation, the entire suspension of peaceful industries, and the concentrating to one end of every vital energy in the community.' He argued that the whole nature of war had fundamentally changed from the days of small regular armies of professional soldiers fighting limited actions. Instead, fifteen years before conscription and the Total War of 1916, he perceptively stated, 'A European war can only end in the ruin of the vanquished and the scarcely less fatal commercial dislocation and exhaustion of the conquerors. Democracy is more vindictive than Cabinets. The wars of peoples will be more terrible than those of kings.'[30]

Churchill wrote out this extraordinarily prescient speech no fewer than six times before memorizing it. In the words of one political correspondent it 'electrified the House by its grasp of the problems of national defence'. Only seventeen Conservatives voted against what he had described as an 'ill-considered conglomeration of absurdities', but Brodrick nonetheless withdrew his scheme. Churchill had made his name in Parliament very swiftly – albeit by fighting against his own side.

When in early 1903 Brodrick brought forward new expansion plans for the British Army, Churchill launched further attacks, turning to ridicule and humour whenever possible. 'When I was walking by Whitehall the other day,' he told an Oldham audience in January, 'I noticed that the new War Office building is to be put up on the site previously occupied by the Asylums Board and the offices of the Lunacy Commissioners.'[31] Instead of a large standing army, Churchill believed in a strong navy. He said that he 'did not defend unpreparedness, but, with a supreme Navy, unpreparedness could be redeemed; without it, all preparation, however careful, painstaking or ingenious, could not be to any avail.'[32] In April he published a book of his speeches on the issue, entitled *Mr Brodrick's Army*, something he was to do regularly on other subjects throughout his career.

Churchill meanwhile wrote to Joseph Chamberlain, the Colonial Secretary, asking whether he 'might get some sort of military mention or decoration' for his bravery in the train ambush. 'I suspect the authorities think the whole thing a piece of journalistic humbug,' he wrote, 'which it was not. Of course in common with all other Members of Parliament I care nothing for the glittering baubles of honour for *my own sake*: but I have like others, as you know, to "think of my constituents" – and perhaps I ought also to consider the feelings of any possible wife.'[33] He got nothing beyond an enhanced reputation for pushiness. The story also went around that when the editor of the *Morning Post* had sent Churchill a proof copy of one of his speeches, which included the bracketed word 'cheers' after one of his remarks, he had returned it with the edited addition, 'loud and prolonged applause'.[34]

Churchill gave speeches around the country to ever-growing audiences and grew more confident with every successful outing.[35] He also managed, for the moment at least, to keep in check the resentment he felt towards those senior Tory politicians who had destroyed his father's political career. He had, after all, dedicated *The River War* to Lord Salisbury and joined the Hughligans, led by Salisbury's son. The Conservative Party leader in the Commons, Arthur Balfour, was Salisbury's nephew and anointed successor (hence, it is sometimes said, the phrase 'Bob's your uncle'). Balfour had been Lord Randolph Churchill's friend and occasional ally in the late 1870s and early 1880s, but had resolutely stuck with Salisbury in the crisis moment of Lord Randolph's resignation.

By December 1901, Churchill was acquiring a powerful social conscience, largely precipitated by his reading of Benjamin Seebohm Rowntree's book *Poverty: A Study of Town Life*. 'I see little glory in an Empire which can rule the waves and is unable to flush its sewers,' he wrote to J. Moore Bayley, a friend of his father's. 'What is wanted is a well-balanced policy . . . that will coordinate development and expansion with the progress of social comfort and health.'[36] Rowntree's 400-page book, which went through five editions in two years, was an extremely detailed investigation into the appalling poverty and squalor of the slums of York. 'In this land of abounding wealth,' it concluded, 'during a time of perhaps unexampled prosperity, probably more than one-fourth of the population are living in poverty.'[37] Its message fitted in perfectly with the social-reform aspect of Tory Democracy that Churchill had inherited from his father, and his father from Disraeli.

Churchill wrote a long but unpublished review of Rowntree's book. After sections on the definitions of poverty, the lack of nutrition in the diets of the poor, the wretched life of the casual labourer and issues of housing and rent, he addressed what was to his mind the central issue: that poverty was 'a serious hindrance to recruiting' for the Army and Navy, and bemoaned the future for the British Empire 'supposing the common people shall be so stunted and deformed in body as to be unfit to fill the ranks the army corps may lack. And thus – strange as it may seem, eccentric, almost incredible to write – our imperial reputation is actually involved in their condition.'[38] Churchill concluded that statesmen 'must in some degree be held responsible if the manhood of the British nation deteriorates so much that she can no longer provide a status of recruits fit to fall in line with our colonial brothers'.[39] Far from an aberration separate from his belief in the Empire, his interest in social reform was in fact intimately bound up with it.

Churchill's interest in social reform and combating poverty introduced him to left-wing intellectuals whom he might not otherwise have met. 'Went in to dinner with Winston Churchill,' wrote Beatrice Webb, the leading socialist thinker, in her diary on 8 July 1903. 'First impression: restless, almost intolerably so, without capacity for sustained and unexcited labour, egotistical, bumptious, shallow-minded and reactionary, but with a certain personal magnetism, great pluck and some originality, not of intellect but of character. More of the American speculator than the English aristocrat. Talked exclusively about himself and his electioneering plans . . . "I never do any brainwork that anyone else can do for me."'[40] (That was obviously a joke, but the humourless sociologist took it seriously.) 'But I dare say he has a better side, which the ordinary cheap cynicism of his position and career covers up to a casual dinner acquaintance,' she continued. 'No notion of scientific research, philosophy, literature or art, still less of religion. But his pluck, courage, resourcefulness and great traditions may carry him far, unless he knocks himself to pieces like his father.'[41]

Webb's estimation was flawed in several respects – Churchill certainly did have a notion of religion, he simply didn't subscribe to it – but offered some useful insights about his charisma and originality. Where she was completely wrong was over Churchill's capacity for hard work; if he thought something was important, he could focus his mind upon it completely, and direct his gargantuan memory for facts, quotations and statistics to master the subject so that no journalist, heckler or parliamentary antagonist could get the better of him.

Along with the development of Churchill's social thinking came an interest in the idea of a centre party in politics that would combine the best and most moderate elements of the Conservative and Liberal parties, both shorn of their extreme wings. This dream of a grand coalition of reasonable, liberal-minded centrist politicians ruling in virtual perpetuity was to stay with him until the early 1950s. When the former Prime Minister Lord Rosebery made a speech roughly along those lines at Chesterfield in December 1901, Hugh Cecil had to remind Churchill that 'As to joining a Middle Party, that may be a very proper course when there is a Middle Party to join. Now there is none . . . If for instance you were offered office in a Rosebery administration, now it would be madness not to remain unequivocally Unionist.'[42] Yet Churchill continued to hanker after a coalition that would keep out the socialists and occupy the centre ground in British politics. The difficulty was that any intriguing for such a realignment in British politics was sure to become known, whereupon he would understandably be seen as a plotter and party traitor.

Churchill began the research for a two-volume biography of his father in 1902, which had the effect on him of reopening the old antagonisms over Lord Randolph's supposed ill-treatment at the hands of the Tory hierarchy. When Salisbury resigned in July 1902, Balfour succeeded to the premiership that Churchill might have thought would under different circumstances have gone to his father. In his book *Great Contemporaries*, published after Balfour's death, he was to write, after much favourable comment about Balfour's intelligence and charm, that 'underneath all this was a cool ruthlessness where public affairs were concerned. He rarely allowed political antagonism to be a barrier in private life; neither did he . . . let personal friendship, however sealed and cemented, hamper his solutions to the problems of State.'[43]

In researching the book, Churchill borrowed the correspondence of his father's friends with Lord Randolph, but it was his mother who had the most bitter letters. 'Tory Democracy, the genuine article, is at an end,' he had told her in 1891. 'No power on earth will make me lift a hand or foot or voice for the Tories.' 'I expect I have made great mistakes; but there has been no consideration, no indulgence, no memory or gratitude – nothing but spite, malice and abuse. I am quite tired and dead-sick of it all, and will not continue political life any longer.'[44] Self-pitying letters like this one – why should he have expected indulgence or gratitude when he had tried to bring down his party leader? – left his son raw in his relationship with Balfour and the Tory leadership, even though he sat on the same benches. Lord Winterton, a fellow Tory MP, recalled that in those early days Churchill 'seemed to enjoy causing resentment. He appeared to have, in modern parlance, "a chip on his shoulder".'[45]

'Distinguished people frequently ask why I go about quoting my father,' Churchill told the Blackpool Conservative Association in January 1902, 'and I reply that I am quite willing to quote anybody else when I find that their published opinions express the views to which I feel myself morally and mentally bound. But there is a great need nowadays for men to lead this country. There are of course old men who cannot be expected to pay much attention to anything, and young men to whom nobody can be expected to pay much attention.'[46] There was laughter at this, just as there was at many of his jokes.

Asked in an interview in 1902 about the qualities desirable in a politician, Churchill said, 'The ability to foretell what is going to happen tomorrow, next week, next month, and next year – and . . . to explain why it didn't happen.'[47] He could quip of the job of an MP, 'He is asked to stand, he wants to sit and is expected to lie.'[48] Wit mattered a great deal to Churchill, and he turned it into an effective weapon in his political armoury – to deflect criticism, ridicule opponents and calm situations that were getting fraught. He understood how in the Victorian era of long political speeches he needed to entertain if he was to instruct, persuade and inspire. He has been compared with his contemporaries Hilaire Belloc, Noël Coward and P. G. Wodehouse as a humorist, with a comic timing akin to Groucho Marx's. A. P. Herbert, the great parliamentary wit, pointed out that words on the printed page could not do Churchill justice 'without some knowledge of the scene, the circumstances, the unique and vibrant voice, the pause, the chuckle, the mischievous and boyish twinkle on the face'.[49] Even in the worst days of the Second World War, Churchill constantly managed to inject humour into his speeches. By contrast, premiers such as Stanley Baldwin, Ramsay MacDonald and Neville Chamberlain rarely brought witty repartee into the Chamber, some because they were incapable of it, others because they thought it unbecoming. By contrast, Churchill constantly employed humour, both of the self-deprecating kind and as a way of pricking an antagonist's pomposity. Expectation of a quotable witticism from him often filled up the Chamber as he rose to speak.

Churchill's highly ambivalent feelings about the Tories meant that his political activities in the Commons revolved around the Hughligans, who were only semi-attached to the official Unionist Party. The dining book of the Hughligans in the House of Lords Archive is a virtual Who's Who of the Edwardian Unionist Party. The club gave Thursday-night dinners in honour of ministers and influential MPs, and Churchill was present at almost all of them. There would be toasts to 'Purity, Parsimony and the Persian Gulf' or 'Profligacy, Personality and the Press'. The leading lights after Cecil and Churchill were the Scottish aristocrat Ian Malcolm, Arthur Stanley, son of the 16th Earl of Derby, and Earl Percy, the eldest son of the 7th Duke of Northumberland. Among those whom the Hughligans fêted in their brief but influential existence as a parliamentary pressure group were St John Brodrick (despite Churchill's barbs against him), Joseph Chamberlain's son Austen, Arthur Balfour, the Liberal MP Sir Edward Grey, Lord Rosebery and the Liberal orator John Morley.

Sometimes they met at Blenheim but the most important meeting the Hughligans ever threw took place in the House of Commons on 25 April 1902. It was in honour of Joseph Chamberlain, who was about to split the Unionist Party over Tariff Reform just as completely as in 1886 he had split the Liberal Party over Irish Home Rule. This giant of late nineteenth-century politics paused at the door as he was leaving, turned and said with much deliberation, 'You young gentlemen have entertained me royally, and in return I will give you a priceless secret. Tariffs! They are the politics of the future, and of the near future.'[50] The meeting crystallized Churchill's opposition to Tariff Reform (also known as Imperial Preference), which was ultimately to propel him out of the Unionist Party. The revolution that Chamberlain was about to propose involved levying high Protectionist duties on imports from countries outside the Empire, which would encourage trade within the Empire, but would also inevitably result in higher food prices. Making the working classes pay more for food was anathema to liberal Tories such as Churchill. He wrote to Rosebery about 'the chance of a central coalition' if Chamberlain was serious, saying that he felt that ' "Tory-Liberal" was a much better name than "Tory-Democrat" or "Liberal Imperialist" . . . The one real difficulty I have to encounter is the suspicion that I am moved by mere restless ambition: and if some issue such as the Tariff were to arise, that difficulty would disappear.'[51] His father had been completely unprincipled over the issue, proposing both Free Trade and Imperial Preference in his time and almost simultaneously, and he did not quote from letters in his filial biography which made that obvious.

True to his word, Chamberlain began advocating a comprehensive package of Tariff Reforms, and Churchill saw this as his moment. On 25 May, he wrote to Balfour warning him that Chamberlain's recent speeches advocating preferential tariffs with the colonies 'revealed plain Protectionist intention'. 'I am utterly opposed to anything that will alter the Free Trade character of this country,' he warned, 'and I consider such an issue superior in importance to any other now before us. Preferential tariffs . . .

are dangerous and objectionable . . . Once this policy is begun it must lead to the establishment of a complete Protective system, involving commercial disaster and the Americanisation of English politics.'[52] This is a particularly histrionic example of the thin-end-of-the-wedge argument that Churchill was often to employ, because of course there were plenty of stopping points between full-scale Free Trade and Protectionism. The pejorative reference to American politics was probably a nod to what one historian has described as 'the log-rolling, the intrigue, the corruption generated by the American tariff system of that time.[53] Churchill said it despite his general admiration for America and recognition of its growing importance on the world stage. A month later, on 22 June, he said in a debate on the Budget that 'He had always thought that it ought to be the main end of English statecraft over a long period of years to cultivate good relations with the United States.'[54] This had become easier after the Boers' surrender and the signing of the Peace of Vereeniging in May.

'My dear Winston,' Balfour replied frostily, 'I have never understood that Chamberlain advocated Protection, though, no doubt, he is ready, and indeed anxious – for a duty on foodstuffs which may incidentally be protective in its character . . . But undoubtedly the matter is of extreme difficulty, and requires the most wary walking.'[55] Balfour's attempt to walk that middle course was to wreck his premiership and draw Churchill's searing ire, but it is hard in retrospect to see what else he could have done considering how riven his party was from top to bottom. Years later, Churchill admitted that such was his antipathy to the Party's harsh treatment of the defeated Boers, Army reform and exploitation of its recent electoral victory that by the time 'the Protection issue was raised I was already disposed to view all their actions in the most critical light'.[56] In other words, he was spoiling for a fight.

The clash became public on 28 May 1903. Churchill spoke immediately after Chamberlain in the Commons after the Colonial Secretary had formally advocated Tariff Reform. Briefed by Mowatt, he had studied trade policy intensely and put himself forward as one of the leaders of sixty or so Conservative rebels known as the Free Fooders, who opposed Tariff Reform. 'These are matters which must be dealt with in the prolonged course of what will be the greatest controversy in the history of our country,' he began, with deliberate exaggeration. He predicted that under Protection 'The old Conservative Party, with its religious convictions and constitutional principles, will disappear, and a new Party will arise like perhaps the Republican Party of the United States of America – rich, materialist, and secular – whose opinions will turn on tariffs, and who will cause the lobbies to be crowded with the touts of protected industries.'[57]

The battle within the Unionist Party over Tariff Reform wore on over the next thirty months, with Cabinet resignations from both sides. Churchill told Charles Eade that one of the reasons for his father's rise to prominence had been that 'he attacked Gladstone more rudely than anyone else.'[58] It was true, and Churchill's own attacks on Arthur Balfour for his fence-sitting over Tariff Reform were intended to achieve the same result. In the debate on the Sugar Conventions Bill on 29 July 1903, Churchill described his own front bench as 'All good men, all honest men, who are ready to make great sacrifices for their opinions, but they have no opinions. They are ready to die for the truth, if they only knew what the truth was. Their opinions are only in the "advance proof stage" and will be carefully corrected and revised by the Prime Minister before they are actually made public.'[59] Such sallies soon started to provoke a response from the Tories sitting around him. Colonel Claude Lowther said that he feared that Churchill might have caught beriberi in South Africa, 'because I have heard that the most marked characteristic of the disease is a terrific swelling of the head'.[60]

By August 1903, Churchill was convinced that the next election would see a Liberal landslide. 'The smug contentment and self-satisfaction of the Government will be astonished by what is coming to meet them,' he wrote to Lord Northcliffe, the owner of *The Times*. 'With a little care we might set up a great Central Government neither Protectionist nor pro-Boer, that is, Radical Liberal, which will deal with the shocking administrative inefficiency which prevails.'[61] He put this idea in print that autumn in the *Monthly Review*, arguing that 'The position which many moderate reasonable people occupy today is one of great difficulty. They lie between the party organizations.' Referring to the harsh terms Salisbury and Chamberlain had imposed on the Boers in the peace treaty, Churchill said that moderate people 'take a sincere pride and pleasure in the development and consolidation of the Empire, but they are not prepared to see Imperialism exploited as a mere electioneering dodge . . . The great question is – are political organizations made for men or men for political organizations?'[62]

On 24 October, Churchill wrote a letter to Hugh Cecil, his closest friend in politics, a fellow Tory who was committed to reforming the Conservative-dominated Unionist Party from the inside. 'I am an English Liberal,' he wrote. 'I hate the Tory party, their men, their words and their methods. I feel no sort of sympathy with them – except to my own people at Oldham. I want to take up a clear practical position which masses of people can understand.'[63] Churchill never sent the letter, and as with many of his unsent letters over the years it should probably be seen more as a way of letting off steam than as a reasoned analysis of his beliefs, yet it was indicative of the way he was moving politically.

'He is a little, square-headed fellow of no very striking appearance, but of wit, intelligence, and originality,' Wilfrid Scawen Blunt noted on 31 October. 'In mind and manner he is a strange replica of his father, with all his father's suddenness and assurance and I should say more than his father's ability. There is just the same *gaminerie* and contempt of the conventional and the same engaging plain spokenness and readiness to understand.'[64]

Churchill's physical courage was on full display when he went to speak at the Birmingham Town Hall, in the very heart of Chamberlain country, on 11 November. The local Chief Constable had to erect special barriers outside the building and use a fire engine to scatter the 'howling crowd' outside. 'Suddenly a carriage and pair drove into the midst of the hostile crowd,' recorded a journalist. 'It contained only Mr Churchill; open, palpable, flagrant; a challenge that might mean lynching. For a moment there was a pause: then the crowd, captured by the spirit of the thing, burst into cheers.'[65]

Once inside the hall, where he was subjected to loud interruptions and cries of 'Chuck him out!', Churchill said, 'I ask this great assemblage of Englishmen, in a great city in the van of progress and enlightenment, to give me and Lord Hugh Cecil a fair hearing.'[66] They did, and in the course of his speech Churchill won over at least part of the room. 'You may, by the arbitrary and sterile act of Government,' he said, 'for, remember, Governments create nothing and have nothing to give but what they have first taken away – you may put money in the pocket of one set of Englishmen, but it will be money taken from the pockets of another set of Englishmen, and the greater part will be spilled on the way.'[67] He ended by saying that 'High protective tariffs, although they might increase the profits of capital, are to the poor and the poorest of the poor a cursed engine of robbery and oppression.'

When, in December, Balfour suggested a commission to investigate Tariff Reform – a classic governmental delaying tactic – Churchill asked a public meeting in Halifax, 'Is it appointed by the Prime Minister? Is there any Prime Minister?'[68] When the laughter died down, Churchill, who had by then mastered the art of comic timing, asked, 'Where is Mr. Balfour? Where does he come in? What is his part in all this strange performance?'[69] Such an attack on the leader of his own party was bound to have consequences, and two days later the Oldham Conservative Association wrote to say they had no confidence in him. He offered to resign and force a by-election, but fearing they would lose they agreed he should continue to represent them until the next election. By late January 1904, Churchill was no longer receiving the Tory whip.

'They say that the Protectionist manufacturers are in favour of

Mr. Chamberlain's proposals because they love the working man,' Churchill said in Manchester in February. 'They love the working man, and they love to see him work.'[70] Later in that speech he said, 'To think you can make a man richer by putting on a tax is like a man thinking that he can stand in a bucket and lift himself up by the handle.'[71] On 29 March, just as Churchill rose to speak in the Commons, Balfour walked out of the Chamber. When Churchill protested at this 'lack of deference and respect', the entire ministerial bench trooped out, and then the backbenchers present too, over 200 in all, some of whom jeered at Churchill from the Bar of the House, in what Sir John Gorst, Lord Randolph's Fourth Party colleague, described as 'the most marked discourtesy which I think I have ever seen'.[72] Only a small group of Unionist Free Traders stayed on the benches beside Churchill.[73] 'It was the highest tribute ever paid to a parliamentary orator,' one political correspondent was to write. 'It was as though the enemy fled at his appearance.'[74]

Churchill said that people wanted to know what 'the Prime Minister really thought about the subject that was vexing the country, and he did not think it was unreasonable that they should ask this because, after all, there was a difference in a policy when it was put forward on the faith and honour of a public man and when it was put forward avowedly as a matter of convenient political tactics'.[75] A little over a fortnight later, at the inaugural meeting of the Free Trade League in Oldham on 15 April 1904, he announced that 'until this great Protectionist agitation is laid to rest again, I trust forever, I have no politics but Free Trade. I will work with or for any Free Trader, whatever his politics, whatever his party, and I will work against any Protectionist, whatever his politics, whatever his party.'[76]

Churchill had been memorizing his speeches, even those lasting an hour. During a debate on the Trade Disputes Bill on 22 April, after speaking for forty-five minutes he completely forgot what he intended to say, and abruptly sat down. The official parliamentary record, Hansard, recorded that 'The honourable Member here faltered in the conclusion of his speech, and, amid sympathetic cheers, resumed his seat, after thanking the House for having listened to him.'[77] The next day's headlines were 'Mr Churchill Breaks Down' and 'Moving Incident in the House'.[78] The reason it was moving was that something similar had happened to his father when his illness descended. Churchill told Cockran that 'The slip was purely mechanical,' but ever afterwards he ensured that he had the key words in each sentence written out in notes, in what he called psalm form. Churchill was not unnerved by the humiliation, a friend recalled of the incident, but he learned from it.[79]

Churchill did not want to fight against his old comrades in Oldham, so a week later it was announced that he had been adopted as the Free Trade candidate for Manchester North West for the next election, with Liberal support. Leslie Hore-Belisha, a ten-year-old schoolboy there, remembered his calling on his uncle, a prominent local Liberal. Churchill was 'a masterful, slightly stooping figure. The pink face was topped by reddish fair hair . . . He was dressed in a frock coat with silk facings and below his chin was a large winged collar with a black bow-tie. He strode into the room with an unmistakable lisp.' Yet it wasn't Hore-Belisha's uncle who got Churchill adopted but Churchill's own uncle, the Liberal former Cabinet minister Lord Tweedmouth, who was married to Lord Randolph's sister Fanny. Churchill's fame would almost certainly have secured him a seat somewhere, but Tweedmouth secured him one in the home of Free Trade.

Churchill gave a powerful performance at Manchester's Free Trade Hall on 13 May, describing the Unionists as 'a party of great vested interests, banded together in a formidable confederation; corruption at home, aggression to cover it up abroad; the trickery of tariff juggles, the tyranny of a party machine; sentiment by the bucketful; patriotism by the imperial pint; the open hand at the public exchequer, the open door at the public-house; dear food for the million, cheap labour for the millionaire'. To loud cheers he declared: 'That is the policy of Birmingham, and we are going to erect against that policy of Birmingham the policy of Manchester.'[80] He went on to repeat his message in front of thousands in halls and theatres across the country. There was a good deal of knockabout in these speeches, but there was much reasoned argument too. Part of Churchill's belief in Free Trade was based on the widespread conviction that it promoted world peace. 'The dangers which threaten the tranquillity of the modern world come not from those Powers that have become interdependent upon others, interwoven by commerce with other States,' he would say in March 1905, 'they come from those Powers which are more or less detached, which stand more or less aloof from the general intercourse of mankind, and are comparatively independent and self-supporting.'[81] It was a specious argument, sadly, for in 1914 Britain's largest trading partner was Imperial Germany.

In Churchill's last speech from the Government benches, on 16 May, he attacked Chamberlain and what he called the 'New Imperialism', sharply distinguishing the noble imperialism of the British Army from that of the political 'caucus'.* Although his father had lived and died a

* It was a word he was often to use pejoratively, later calling Hitler 'a squalid caucus boss and butcher'.

Tory, the twenty-nine-year-old Churchill's other two greatest heroes had both changed sides spectacularly (and very successfully) early on in their careers. The 1st Duke of Marlborough was thirty-eight when he betrayed King James II for William of Orange, and Napoleon was thirty when he overthrew the Directory and made himself first consul. The precedents for what Churchill was about to do were good.

On Tuesday, 31 May 1904, on what the *Manchester Guardian* called 'the twilight of a rainy afternoon', Churchill entered the Chamber of the House of Commons and walked forward a few paces and bowed to the Speaker's chair. But then, instead of turning left to sit on the Tory benches, he 'swerved suddenly to the right' and took his place among the Liberals, sitting down next to David Lloyd George, the Welsh MP for Caernarvon Boroughs, whom he had so disparaged in his maiden speech a little over three years earlier.[82]

Lloyd George was a leading figure on the Radical wing of the Liberal Party, and one of its greatest orators. Churchill did not like him on early acquaintance, describing him as 'a vulgar, chattering little cad'.[83] By July 1903, however, he had warmed to him enough to invite him to Blenheim, and by October of the following year their friendship was firm, at least on Churchill's side. 'Very ambitious, very clever' was how Lloyd George described him to his brother at the time.[84] Speaking of Lloyd George's 'energy and courage' in his constituency of Carnarvon Boroughs, Churchill called him 'the best fighting general in the Liberal ranks'.[85] They enjoyed each other's company, but could not fail to recognize that one day they might become rivals.

Churchill took the much coveted corner-seat below the Opposition gangway from which his father had for years poured scorn on both Gladstone and the Tory benches.[86] He was soon afterwards followed by his cousins Ivor and Freddie Guest, and his friend Jack Seeley. Although the Liberal Unionists had 'crossed the floor' en masse during the Irish Home Rule crisis nearly twenty years earlier, individuals did it only very rarely, and it was a far more serious step in Edwardian politics than in Regency or Victorian times, when parties were more fluid. He was soon even more hated on the Tory benches than Lloyd George, who, as a radical Welsh Nonconformist, was not expected to be anything but hostile to them. From being regarded as loud, bumptious and pushy – a 'thruster' in the vocabulary of the day – Churchill was now seen as a traitor to his party, and very soon a traitor to his class too.

'Absorbed in his own affairs,' an aide was later to say of him, 'he seemed to many people brusque, vain, intolerant and overbearing.'[87] A regular criticism was that he lacked 'some intuitive tactile sense to tell him what others were thinking and (especially) feeling'.[88] Yet he hardly needed such a sense in the summer of 1904, when Unionists showed little restraint in letting the new MP know precisely what they were thinking and feeling about him. Many assumed he had 'ratted', as they put it, for personal advantage. Joseph Chamberlain's son Austen, the Chancellor of the Exchequer, said that Churchill's 'conversion to Radicalism coincided with his personal interests'. Alfred Lyttelton, another Cabinet minister, thought that 'He trims his sails with every passing wind.' Leo Maxse, editor of the *National Review*, wrote that he was 'half alien and wholly undesirable', and the future Prime Minister Andrew Bonar Law – whose maiden speech had been completely overshadowed by Churchill's on the same evening – called him a 'turncoat'.[89] Such views were not expressed just behind his back: a year later he said that crossing the floor had led to 'every odious circumstance of abuse'.[90]

It might have also led to his political demise. Churchill had attacked the Liberals extravagantly, after all, and there was no guarantee they would take to him. It seemed to everyone – himself included – that he had lost any possible chance of ever returning to the Party in which, as he later put it, he had been brought up from childhood and where nearly all his friends and family were.[91] Furthermore, his close friend the MP F. E. Smith was later to argue, if he had not crossed the floor, by 1914 'he would, in my judgment, unquestionably have been the leader of the Unionist party'.[92] Churchill had paid a high price for his Free Trade principles.

When the 4th Marquess of Salisbury, the son of the former Prime Minister, cut Churchill socially, he wrote to explain that 'In my heart I think it was not your act but your demeanour in so acting that led me to be rude.'[93] Churchill replied:

> I readily admit that my conduct is open to criticism, not – thank heaven – on the score of its sincerity, but from the point of view of taste. I had to choose between fighting and standing aside. No doubt the latter was the more decorous. But I wanted to fight – I felt I could fight with my whole heart and soul – so there it is . . . Of course politics is a form of tournament in which mud-slinging and invective are recognized weapons. But taking part in such an ugly brawl does not in my mind prejudice personal relations.[94]

The last sentence here was an attitude Churchill sustained all through his life. His extraordinary ability to separate politics from personal friendship, remaining privately affable with people he publicly denounced and who denounced him in similar terms, was often misunderstood by people who assumed he was being insincere either in the friendship or in the politics. In fact he was being neither.

On the same day he crossed the floor, Churchill published a letter in *The Times*, *Manchester Guardian* and *Jewish Chronicle* denouncing the Unionist Government's Aliens Bill, which was intended to restrict the immigration into Britain of Jews escaping from pogroms in Tsarist Russia. 'It is expected to appeal to insular prejudices against foreigners,' he wrote of the Bill, 'to racial prejudice against Jews, and to labour prejudice against competition.'[95] The British population then stood at 32.5 million. He pointed out that only one in 140 were not born in Britain. Jewish immigration amounted to only about 7,000 a year.[96] The letter was itself intended as an electoral gambit – one-third of his new constituency's voters were Jewish, against 0.7 per cent of the general population – but it also reflected a curious anomaly in this upper-class Victorian: he was a lifelong philo-Semite.

As with so many of his early opinions, Churchill's liking of the Jewish race stemmed from his father, who had been friendly with Nathaniel Meyer, 1st Baron Rothschild, Sir Felix Semon and Sir Ernest Cassel. 'What, Lord Randolph, you've not brought your Jewish friends?' his father was asked teasingly at a country-house weekend. 'No,' he retorted, 'I didn't think they would be very amused by the company.'[97] Both father and son were admirers of Disraeli. As a young man, Winston Churchill stayed in Paris with Baron Maurice de Hirsch, and on his summer holidays in Europe in 1906 with Cassel, Lionel Rothschild and Baron de Forest, Baron de Hirsch's adopted son.[98] 'Bravo Zola!' Churchill had written to his mother during the Dreyfus Affair six days after the Battle of Omdurman. 'I am delighted to witness the complete debacle of this monstrous conspiracy.'[99]

So he was not acting solely out of political opportunism when he opposed the Aliens Bill. He started to make contributions to his constituency's Jewish Soup Kitchen, Jewish Lads' Club and the Jewish Tennis and Cricket Club, as well as visiting the Jewish Hospital, Talmud Torah religious school and Jewish Working Men's Club, where he commended the emphasis on communal self-help.[100] 'While never an uncritical supporter of Zionism,' Sir Martin Gilbert, Churchill's official biographer, has written, 'he was one of its most persistent friends and advocates. In a world where Jews were often the objects of scorn, dislike, distrust and hostility, Churchill held them in high esteem, and wanted them to have their rightful place in the world.'[101] This helped Churchill in the 1930s, giving him the ability – denied to many anti-Semites across the political spectrum – to spot very clearly and early what kind of a man Adolf Hitler was. As one of the rare philo-Semites of his class and background, and sitting for a heavily Jewish constituency over a quarter of a century before Hitler became chancellor of Germany, his antennae were more highly attuned than those of his parliamentary colleagues.*

Churchill made his first speech from the Opposition benches on 8 June 1904, opposing the Aliens Bill. (*The Sun* claimed he did so on the orders of Lord Rothschild, the first of many baseless accusations that he was in the pay of the Jews.)[102] Churchill and three other Liberals were so tenacious in the committee stage of the Bill (when its provisions are scrutinized in detail) that the Government initially abandoned it, only to reintroduce and pass it the following year. In December 1905, Churchill shared a platform opposing the Tsarist pogroms with the Russian-born chemistry lecturer Dr Chaim Weizmann, who was later to play a formative part in his thinking on Zionism.

When, in July 1904, a Tory MP by the name of Colonel William Kenyon-Slaney accused Churchill and Ivor Guest of being 'renegades and traitors' for their lenient stance over the Boers, Churchill had an opportunity for one of his acidic ripostes. 'I have often noticed that when political controversy becomes excited,' he said, 'persons of choleric dispositions and limited intelligences are apt to become rude. I had the honour of serving in the field for our country while this gallant, fire-eating colonel was content to kill Kruger with his mouth in the comfortable security of England.'[103] Churchill was alluding to the second line of Rudyard Kipling's poem 'The Absent-Minded Beggar' – 'When you've finished killing Kruger with your mouth' – which would have been instantly recognizable to his audience. This was harsh on Kenyon-Slaney, who had been decorated at the Battle of Tel-el-Kebir in 1882 and had retired from the Army ten years later, but it reminded people that if they attacked Churchill they must be prepared for a withering riposte.

The following month, Churchill dismissively pointed out that Balfour's 'leadership of the House has been much praised in the newspapers whose editors he had ennobled or promoted'.[104] Before long, abusing the Prime Minister seemed to be his favourite pastime. 'My piece of advice is,' he said of Tariff Reform in Manchester in January 1905, 'in politics when you are in doubt what to do, do nothing. In politics when you are in doubt what to say, say what you really think. If the Prime Minister from the beginning of this controversy had acted on these principles it would have

* When Gilbert, who was Jewish, interviewed Churchill's colleague General Sir Louis Spears, he was intrigued by his statement 'Even Winston had a fault.' He leaned forward, eager to discover his hero's Achilles heel, only to hear: 'He was too fond of Jews.' (Gilbert, *Churchill and the Jews* p. xv.) Spears was himself Jewish, though he changed his name from Speirs to hide the fact.

been much better for our country, much better for his own reputation, and much better for the party organization to which he attaches such extraordinary and undue importance.'[105] Later that month Churchill was widely thought to have overstepped the mark when he said, 'Abdications have taken place in the history of the world, but if you look at the course of history you will see that they have usually been made by masculine rather than by feminine monarchs. Kings have abdicated but never queens, and it is one of the attractive qualities of Mr. Balfour that his nature displays a certain femininity.'[106] Attacks such as these continued to get him noticed, and disliked.

The first biography of Churchill was published by the journalist Alexander MacCallum Scott in 1905. 'The youth of thirty is confidently spoken of by his admirers as a future Prime Minister,' Scott wrote, likening Churchill's attack on Chamberlain to a David and Goliath struggle, and noting of Balfour that 'the Prime Minister fled from his presence.'[107] The estimation that Churchill 'is of the race of giants' seemed hyperbolic in 1905 and not everyone was so impressed. In May 1905 he was blackballed from the Hurlingham Club in London, something that he told the Liberal Chief Whip, the Master of Elibank,* was 'almost without precedent in the history of the Club – as polo players are always welcomed. I do not think you and your Liberal friends realize the intense political bitterness which is felt against me on the other side.'[108] He had resigned from the Carlton Club the previous month, telling his cousin Lord Londonderry, 'Old friendships have been snapped and on the other hand new obligations have been contracted.'[109]

When in late July Balfour lost a vote in the Commons by 200–196 but refused to resign, as was the time-honoured custom, Churchill, outraged, thundered, 'The power given to Lord Salisbury had been assumed by another with whom the nation had not yet had any direct dealings, and whose character the House had only gradually and lately discovered.'[110] Churchill took aim at Balfour's 'gross, unpardonable ignorance' and his 'slipshod, slapdash, haphazard manner of doing business'. He joked that 'the dignity of a Prime Minister, like a lady's virtue, is not susceptible of partial diminution'.[111] 'To keep in office for a few more weeks and months there is no principle which the Government are not prepared to betray,' he added, 'and no quantity of dust and filth they are not prepared to eat.'[112] Churchill did not really believe the philosopher Balfour, a Fellow of the British Academy, to be ignorant, or any of the rest of it; for him these extravagances were all part of the general cut and thrust of the great game

* The courtesy title given to the heirs to the Scottish barony of Elibank.

of politics. He was quite prepared to take any 'dust and filth' the Unionists cared to throw back at him. For many staid Edwardian gentlemen, however, including King Edward VII himself, it was deemed unacceptable.

'Winston, I am told, made one of the most insolent speeches ever heard in Parliament,' the courtier Lord Esher wrote to his son.[113] Lord Crawford noted in his diary, 'The King is excessively angry at Winston Churchill's attack on A.J.B., and makes no secret of his opinion that Churchill is a born cad.'[114] This biting political invective appeared to augur a new viciousness in parliamentary discourse, although those with a better historical knowledge understood that such sallies had in fact been the norm for centuries.

Conspicuous speeches continued to flow from him. A clash in India between Lord Curzon, the Viceroy, and Lord Kitchener, the Commander-in-Chief, over army reorganization, had led to Curzon's resignation in August 1905. This gave Churchill an opportunity to exact revenge on Kitchener. In a debate in October, he said of Curzon, 'The contemptuous manner in which he has been driven from the country has practically created the Commander-in-Chief the military dictator, and the power of the Viceroy and the prestige of the civil power have been gravely if not permanently affected.'[115] Once again, he was employing deliberate exaggeration for effect – as well as using the word 'dictator' in a pejorative way for the first time.

Balfour finally resigned on 4 December 1905, whereupon the King sent for Sir Henry Campbell-Bannerman, the Liberal Leader of the Opposition, who formed a minority caretaker government with the sole aim of calling an election, which he did for 12 January 1906. Sir Edward Grey was appointed foreign secretary, Asquith chancellor of the Exchequer and Lloyd George president of the Board of Trade. Campbell-Bannerman offered Churchill the post of financial secretary to the Treasury, the most senior post below Cabinet rank, but he politely refused it in favour of the nominally lowlier position of under-secretary of state for the colonies. It was a canny move that allowed Churchill to represent that important department in the Commons, because the Secretary of State, the Earl of Elgin, the former Viceroy of India (and the grandson of the man who had bought the Parthenon Marbles), was in the House of Lords.

Churchill asked Eddie Marsh, a clerk in the West African Department of the Colonial Office and friend of Churchill's former girlfriend Pamela Plowden (now the Countess of Lytton), to become his private secretary.*

* Marsh was homosexual, and there was no trace of prejudice in Churchill's makeup. His friends were to include homosexuals, bisexuals and asexuals such as Rupert Brooke, Noël Coward, Harold Nicolson, Philip Sassoon, Ivor Novello, Bob Boothby and T. E. Lawrence.

He remained in this post for over thirty years in eight governmental departments. 'I was two years older than my prospective master,' Marsh recalled, 'and furthermore I was a little afraid of him . . . Though I had thought him the most brilliant person I had ever come across he struck me as rather truculent and overbearing.'[116] Before taking on the job, Marsh asked Lady Lytton for her advice. 'The first time you meet Winston you see all his faults,' she told him, 'and the rest of your life you spend in discovering his virtues.'[117]

# 5
# Liberal Imperialist
# January 1906–April 1908

*He had the showman's knack of drawing public attention to everything he said or did.*

Churchill on his father, 1906[1]

*Let us have only one measure for treating people subject to our rule, and that a measure of justice.*

Churchill on the Transvaal, July 1906[2]

On New Year's Day 1906, Churchill published his election manifesto to the electors of Manchester North West, alliteratively denouncing the idea of 'Seven more years of dodge and dole and dawdle! Seven years of tinker and tax and trifle! Seven years of shuffle, shout and sham! Do not be taken in again.'[3] The very next day he published his biography of his father, for which he had been paid the huge advance of £8,000. As with all his works, even the histories, it contained strong elements of either conscious or subconscious autobiography. 'No smooth path of patronage was opened to him,' he wrote. 'No glittering wheels of royal favour aided and accelerated his journey. Whatever power he acquired was grudgingly conceded and hastily snatched away. Like Disraeli, he had to fight every mile in all his marches.'[4]

This might have been what Churchill felt about himself but it was hardly true of Lord Randolph, who had been born in Belgravia the son of a duke, had been educated at Eton and Oxford and had virtually inherited his parliamentary seat at Woodstock near Blenheim at the age of twenty-five. He could easily have enjoyed the glittering wheels of royal favour if he had not tried to blackmail the Prince of Wales. Nowhere in the book did Churchill try to account for the dislike and distrust his father aroused, or his lack of self-awareness over it, though these were not the least of the characteristics the son shared with him.

Lord Randolph's modern biographer Roy Foster has perceptively pointed out that *Lord Randolph Churchill* 'was at least partially intended as an explanation of the political somersaults being executed by the author at the time of writing it'.[5] The book reads well, but it has not survived the test of time as history because of its lack of objectivity, as well as its author's willingness, indeed eagerness, to ignore any evidence that undermined his case. 'I very often yield to the temptation of adapting my facts to my phrases,' he had told his mother of his journalism in December 1897, and it was true of this book too.[6] Lord Randolph Churchill's rudeness about dead former colleagues was excised; evidence of his opportunism was ignored; selective quotation was employed on a massive scale and all contemporary and later criticism of his annexation of Burma was passed over. His father's secret sympathies with Irish Home Rule in 1885 went unmentioned. Understandably he chose to skip over his parents' marital difficulties, and the rumour of syphilis, but neither did important figures such as Nathaniel Rothschild appear, despite his having been Lord Randolph's closest confidant at the Treasury.[7] The Government business that Lord Randolph had given Rothschild's bank and the £12,758 he owed it on his death were also ignored.[8]

Churchill failed to use ellipses in his book to indicate where he had excised sentences, and even changed direct quotations, so 'I shall get everything out of [Joseph Chamberlain]' becomes 'I shall learn more', and 'I should give anything to form a government' is rendered as 'I should like to form a government.' Lord Randolph's grosser acts of political self-interest were somehow presented as magnificent acts of altruism and he was made to sound far more centrist than he actually was. His constant attempts at interference in Lord Salisbury's foreign policy were presented as collegial, which they had not been.[9] Nor did it end there: Lord Randolph's intriguing and leaking to journalists were ignored, and the supposedly off-the-cuff circumstances of his resignation contradicted facts that Churchill knew.

In the years that followed, Churchill did not allow others the necessary archival wherewithal to contradict him. Foster believes there was 'a good deal of judicious weeding before the papers were made publicly available', so ultimately the portrait that emerges was one in which 'Churchill not only discovered his father, but also refashioned him in his own image.'[10] Uncomfortable facts were not allowed to get in the way of Churchill's elegant recruitment of his dead father as a posthumous mentor for himself. The distance between myth and reality did not go unnoticed. Ivor Guest opined that 'Few fathers had done less for their sons. Few sons have done more for their fathers.'[11] With this book, which became an overnight bestseller, Churchill had finally dragooned his father into doing something useful for him.

'He possessed the strange quality, unconsciously exerted and not by any means to be simulated, of compelling attention, and of getting himself talked about,' Churchill wrote.[12] He must have known that there was nothing unconscious about his father's implausibly high wing collars, massive moustache, hand upside down on his hip while speaking, deliberate attacks on his own party and creation of the Fourth Party faction within the Conservatives. These exertions to compel attention were to Churchill perfectly acceptable manoeuvres with a mass electorate, and this lesson too he had taken to heart. 'There is an England of wise men who gaze without self-deception at the failings and follies of both political parties,' the book offers in conclusion, 'of brave and earnest men who find in neither faction fair scope for the effort that is within them . . . It was to that England that Lord Randolph appealed; it was that England he so nearly won; it is by that England that he will be justly judged.'[13] The critical reception of the book was overwhelmingly positive, although the anonymous reviewer in the *Telegraph* was not wholly persuaded of its idealized portrait: 'His treatment of his friends was often atrocious, sometimes not even honourable; he was very careless of the truth.'[14]

That Churchill had published his manifesto on one day and his biography on the next was no coincidence. He was in the midst of a challenging campaign and had to justify his desertion of his party, and convince the voters of Manchester that he would be more loyal to them. On 11 January 1906, in his eve-of-poll speech, he told a crowd in Manchester:

> I admit I have changed my party. I don't deny it. I am proud of it. When I think of all the labours which Lord Randolph Churchill gave to the fortunes of the Conservative party and the ungrateful way in which he was treated by them when they obtained the power they would never have had but for him, I am delighted that circumstances have enabled me to break with them while I am still young and still have the first energies of my life to give to the popular cause.[15]

The ghost of his father was ever on his mind, yet his budding social conscience was also prompting him to carve out his own path. Walking with Eddie Marsh through the slums of Manchester the previous week, he had said, 'Fancy living in one of those streets, never seeing anything beautiful, never eating anything savoury, *never saying anything clever*!'[16*]

* Marsh wrote that the italics were Churchill's rather than his, since 'it would be impossible to give a better rendition of italics in the spoken word' (Marsh, *Number* p. 150).

That has been taken as snobbish and condescending, and so in some degree it was, but it also shows something of his thinking about the need for social legislation to improve the educational and living conditions, and not to adopt food taxes that would leave the slum-dwellers yet poorer.

Although Churchill had voted for an early measure of female suffrage in March 1904 in the House of Commons, in the 1906 election his high profile made him a particular target for the suffragettes' disruptive tactics that had been adopted by their radical wing for several months. During an election rally in Manchester, a young woman in the gallery interrupted his speech, whereupon he offered to give her five minutes to speak at the end, and promised to answer any questions she had about women's suffrage. She refused and after half an hour's disruption Churchill pointed out that the right of public meeting was one of the most valuable democratic privileges the people possessed, and that it would 'be absurd to admit the right of a single individual to bring it to naught'.[17] At the end of the meeting, another campaigner, Flora Drummond, spokeswoman for the Women's Suffrage Association, was invited on to the platform by Churchill to make her case, which she did forcefully.

Churchill was then asked for his views. He chose his words carefully. 'I voted in favour of the enfranchisement of women in the session before last,' he said. 'Although I think this a question of great difficulty, I was steadily moving forward to the position of a whole-hearted supporter of their case. But I have been much put off by what has happened in the last few months.' He did not want to be seen to be 'giving way to the violent interruptions which have happened at my meetings'.[18] He always wanted to show magnanimity in victory, but was instinctively defiant when he felt himself under attack. On 5 January 1906 his meeting in Cheetham Hill was disrupted by Adela Pankhurst, the daughter of the suffragette leader Emmeline Pankhurst. Churchill also offered to allow her on to the platform, telling the crowd,

> The young lady bears a name which is greatly and deservedly respected in Manchester. I recognize the conscientious zeal which makes her do these things, but they are wholly undemocratic and for anyone who desires to show how fit women are to receive the franchise I cannot imagine a more foolish course to pursue. I am not so hostile to the proposal as I thought it right to say just now, but I am not going to be hen-pecked on a question of such grave public importance.[19]

Four days later, when yet another meeting was disrupted, he insisted that the woman involved should be treated with 'courtesy and chivalry'. But he was clearly irritated by the suffragettes' practices. Now all he would say on the subject of women's suffrage was 'Having regard to the perpetual disturbance of public meetings at this election, I utterly decline to pledge myself.'[20]

Churchill was elected for Manchester North West on 13 January 1906, with 5,639 votes against his Conservative opponent William Joynson-Hicks's 4,398. Some 89 per cent of voters had turned out. In the 1900 election the nine Manchester seats had been represented by eight Unionists (including Arthur Balfour) and one Liberal, but in 1906 the Liberals won seven seats and the Labour Party the other two. Balfour experienced the biggest general election landslide of the era against him, and lost his own seat too, providing more than enough *Schadenfreude* for Churchill. As the voting was spread over several weeks, Churchill set off to be a celebrity speaker in several other constituencies. The final results did not come through until 7 February. Four hundred Liberal MPs, 157 Unionists, eighty-three Irish Nationalists and thirty Labour MPs would be forming the next Parliament. 'This election is the vindication of my father's life,' Churchill told a family friend, 'and points to the moral of my book. The one crowning irretrievable catastrophe which he always dreaded has now overtaken the old gang, and with them, the great party they misruled.'[21] Churchill was not always successful in his timing, but choosing to leave the Conservative Party just as it was about to go into opposition for over a decade was inspired, even though for a time, as Lord Winterton later recalled, it gave him 'the distinction of being the most unpopular figure in the House'.[22] The Tories were to exact a terrible revenge on him when they finally returned to government, but that lay a long way in the future.

Churchill's first action on entering the Colonial Office the previous December had been to place a small bronze bust of Napoleon on his desk, but his imperial policy was far more pacific than this might have indicated. When the Munshi tribe of Nigeria burned down the Niger Company's station at Abinsi on the last day of 1905, Sir Frederick Lugard, the High Commissioner, proposed a punitive expedition against them. Churchill had been on such expeditions in India and thought them expensive and often ineffective. 'The chronic bloodshed which stains the West African seasons is odious and disquieting,' he wrote to Lord Elgin. 'Moreover the whole enterprise is liable to be represented by persons unacquainted with Imperial terminology as the murdering of natives and the stealing of their lands.'[23] Elgin agreed, but by then the expedition had advanced too far to be stopped. Churchill took a similar stance in April, when he condemned the Government of Natal in South Africa for putting twelve Zulu rebels on trial under martial law. (In doing so he employed one of the similes that he recommended as an element in public speaking: 'Of course all martial law is illegal, and an attempt to introduce illegalities into martial law, which is not military law, is like attempting to add salt water to the sea.')[24] His colonial policy often sympathized with the natives of the Empire, although as a junior minister he did not always get his way.

With Campbell-Bannerman returned to Downing Street after the election, Churchill resumed his place at the Colonial Office. He was given the thorny matter of how to deal with the defeated Boer republics, which had surrendered in 1902, and by 1906 seemed ready for the introduction of responsible self-government. It was a complex problem, and he was to answer 500 parliamentary questions on South African issues over the next two years. On 19 January 1906, he met Jan Smuts, who had interrogated him after his capture by the Boers in 1899. Smuts had left the law to become a successful Commando general, but had been in favour of the Peace of Vereeniging that had ended the conflict in 1902. 'The officials were alarmed at the prospect of a young and untried minister encountering this formidable and sinister man,' Churchill teasingly recalled half a century later of the meeting at the Colonial Office. 'Accordingly a large screen was erected in the corner of the room, behind which Eddie Marsh was installed – the idea being that if I said anything dangerous to the State, Eddie could deny that I had said it.'[25]

Churchill and Smuts agreed there should be a fresh start based on a policy of impartiality between Briton and Boer, a proposal which was accepted by the Cabinet and led to internal self-government for the two republics within a year. This in turn led to the formation in 1910 of a self-governing Union of South Africa, a Dominion of the Empire with equal status to Canada, Australia and New Zealand. In respect of the treatment of the native African population, Churchill's hands were completely tied by the terms of the Treaty of Vereeniging. 'It is undoubted that the Boers would regard it as a breach of that treaty if the franchise were in the first instance extended to any persons who are not white men as opposed to coloured people,' he told the Commons. 'We may regret that decision. We may regret that there is no willingness in the Transvaal and Orange River Colony to make arrangements which have been found not altogether harmful in Cape Colony. But we are bound by this treaty.'[26] Churchill nonetheless ensured that Britain retained control of large tribal areas such as Basutoland (modern-day Lesotho), Bechuanaland (Botswana) and Swaziland (eSwatini), where the native populations were treated in a more benevolent fashion than they had been by the Boers.[27]

For all the Tories' accusations that Churchill had shown weakness towards Britain's old enemy, the settlement was hailed as an extraordinary departure from the bitterness of 1902. The fact that South Africa subsequently fought beside Britain in both world wars was a tribute to Churchill, Smuts and the friendship that developed between them.[28] In October 1942, Smuts reminisced to King George VI how 'Winston could not understand a late enemy coming to ask for his country back only four years after he had been defeated, and asked Smuts if it had ever been done before, to which Smuts said "I don't think so."'[29]

Churchill was handed several contentious problems as under-secretary, the worst being that of the more than 50,000 Chinese workers who were being exploited by mine-owners in South Africa to such an extent that several Liberal newspapers and politicians freely used the term 'Chinese slavery'. Churchill told Parliament in February that 'It cannot in the opinion of His Majesty's Government be classified as slavery in the extreme acceptance of the word without some risk of terminological inexactitude.'[30]* Despite his insistence that it not be called slavery, Churchill unequivocally denounced the treatment of the Chinese workforce in South Africa, calling it 'as degrading, hideous, and pathetic as any this civilized and Christian nation has made itself responsible for in modern years'.[31] Lord Milner when high commissioner had authorized the corporal punishment of Chinese manual labourers whom their employers believed were slacking or engaging in 'unnatural vice' (that is, sodomy).[32] Milner argued that this had been done in legal accordance with the local labour code, but Radical Liberal MPs disagreed and wanted him prosecuted. On 21 March 1906 Churchill moved a Government amendment that 'This House, while recording its condemnation of the flogging of Chinese coolies in breach of the law, desires, in the interests of peace and conciliation in South Africa, to refrain from passing censure upon individuals.'

Churchill's speech moving the amendment was to prove one of his most controversial in a career that was already no stranger to it. Alfred Milner, who had retired in April 1905, was a hero to many Unionist MPs for his single-minded promotion of British interests in South Africa before, during and after the Boer War, and they expected a forthright defence of him from the Government against the Radicals' attack. Churchill tried to defend Milner, while criticizing his policy. 'Having exercised great authority he now exerts no authority,' he said. 'Having held high employment

* With that phrase 'terminological inexactitude', Churchill showed he knew how far he could go under parliamentary etiquette in using the word 'lie'. It was unparliamentary language, for example, to call one's opponent a fool, but when interrupted by jeering laughter on one occasion he said, 'The crackling of thorns under a pot does not disturb me,' a reference to Ecclesiastes 7: 6, which began 'For as the crackling of thorns under a pot, so is the laughter of fools.'

he now has no employment. Having disposed of events which have shaped the course of history, he is now unable to deflect in the smallest degree the policy of the day . . . Is it worthwhile to pursue him any further? . . . [He] sees the ideals, the principles, the policies for which he has toiled utterly discredited . . . Lord Milner has ceased to be a factor in public events.'[33] The amendment was carried by 355 to 135; Milner was safe.

Eddie Marsh claimed that, when Churchill had practised the speech beforehand in his office, he (Marsh) 'had been positively moved by the generosity of its spirit! . . . But the effect in the House was quite different – something went wrong in the delivery . . . and he appeared to be taunting a discredited statesman with the evil days on which he had fallen.'[34] It is hard to reconcile Marsh's excuses with the actual words Churchill used. The Unionists' fury was unbounded. 'His many enemies in the Conservative party exultantly claimed he was finished,' recalled Lord Winterton.[35] Margot Asquith, the acerbic wife of the Home Secretary, thought the speech 'ungenerous, patronizing and tactless'.[36] The *National Review* wrote of Churchill, 'He always plays up to the loudest gallery. He is a transatlantic type of demagogue.'[37] The King described his behaviour as 'simply scandalous'.[38] Joseph Chamberlain's daughter Hilda, who was in the gallery, reported to her brother Neville that 'Churchill's manner made it if possible more insolent and insulting even than the words,' and noted that 'there was only a most perfunctory cheer when he sat down.'[39] Against this background, it was unsurprising that Churchill failed miserably when he tried to get cross-party support for the granting of self-government to the South African republics in July. 'With all our majority we can only make it the gift of a party,' he said. 'They [the Unionists] can make it the gift of England.'[40] They refused.

By 1906 Churchill had already spotted a problem that was to become much more serious in the years ahead: the Unionist-dominated House of Lords was increasingly using its power of veto over Liberal legislation. 'I am a man of peace,' he told an audience at his aunt's estate, Canford Park, in August, to much laughter. 'Nothing would cause me greater pain than that we should have to get into an angry dispute with those lordly people.'[41] That his phrase 'I am a man of peace' was greeted with laughter shows that Churchill had already won a reputation for aggression, or at least truculence. 'For my own part I have always felt that a politician is to be judged by the animosities that he excites among his opponents,' he told the Institute of Journalists dinner in November. 'I have always set myself not merely to relish but to deserve thoroughly their censure.'[42] He was beginning to enjoy performing at the dispatch box, despite his poor start over Milner. 'I hope you admire my ministerial manner in making colonial pronouncements,' he told J. A. Spender, editor of the *Westminster Gazette*. 'Vacuity, obscurity, ambiguity and pomposity are not much less difficult to practise than their opposites.'[43]

Churchill was a reservist officer, having held a commission in the Queen's Own Oxfordshire Hussars in the Territorial Army since 1902. He wore its uniform when he visited the German Army manoeuvres in Breslau in September 1906, at the invitation of Kaiser Wilhelm II, who spoke English and with whom he spent twenty minutes in conversation. 'He was very friendly and is certainly a most fascinating personality,' he told Lord Elgin.[44] Churchill was impressed by the German Army's 'numbers, quality, discipline and organization'. He told his aunt Leonie Leslie that he was 'thankful that there is a sea between that army and England'.[45] Having met the Kaiser in 1906, and again in 1909, helped guard him against the mistake made by a number of British politicians, of thinking that Adolf Hitler was simply another version of the petulant Emperor.

At a speech in Glasgow in October 1906, Churchill discussed his political philosophy. He said that he had opposed socialism all his life, but had come around to the idea that 'The State should increasingly assume the position of the reserve employer of labour.'[46] He also supported 'the universal establishment of minimum standards of life and labour, and their progressive elevation as the increasing energies of production may permit'.[47] This 'minimum standard' concept, which was also being adopted at that time by other influential Liberals such as David Lloyd George and Charles Masterman, was later to evolve into the modern welfare state. Churchill sought to calm those Liberal MPs who were worried by the Labour Party, likening it to a balloon that 'goes up quite easily for a certain distance, but after a certain distance it refuses to go up any farther, because the air is too rarefied to float it and sustain it'.[48] Churchill was to make many spectacularly bad predictions in his career, and this was one of them.

The support that Tory Democracy gave to the free market and competition still mattered to him. 'We do not want to pull down the structures of science and civilization,' he told his Glaswegian audience:

> but to spread a net over the abyss; and I am sure that if the vision of a fair Utopia which cheers the hearts and lights the imagination of the toiling multitudes, should ever break into reality, it will be by developments through, and modifications in, and by improvements out of, the existing competitive organization of society . . . Where you find that State enterprise is likely to be ineffective, then utilize private enterprises, and do not grudge them their profits.[49]

Churchill's political stance was constantly evolving, under the influence of Bourke Cockran, Lloyd George, Beatrice Webb and even to an extent Clementine, who was a lifelong Liberal. Yet central to his essentially Tory Democrat ideas was the concept of free enterprise, from which he never resiled.

Two of Churchill's most important friendships were formed in 1906, with the Tory MP and one of the most brilliant barristers of his generation F. E. Smith (later Lord Birkenhead) and Violet Asquith (later Lady Violet Bonham Carter), the daughter of Herbert Asquith. They were both powerful, heartfelt and lifelong friendships, but they had a practical aspect too. 'F.E.', as he was universally known, was a useful conduit into the Tory Party and Violet's father was the Chancellor of the Exchequer and heir to the Liberal leadership. Some months into 1906, Churchill was introduced to Smith, who was two years his senior, as he was about to enter the Commons Chamber before an important vote.[50] Smith drank heavily, but as Churchill's future wife was later to say, 'Winston is always ready to be accompanied by those with considerable imperfections.'[51] They holidayed together in the summer of 1907 and when F.E.'s first son, Freddie, was born that December, Churchill stood godfather. The two great wits sparked off each other constantly, and Churchill was later to say that Smith was the dearest friend he had in life.[52]

Churchill met Violet Asquith at a dinner in the early summer of 1906, at which other luminaries such as Balfour, George Wyndham and Hilaire Belloc were also present. She had eyes only for Churchill, however, and for what she later described as 'his unabashed confidence, unsquashable resilience, his push and dash and flair for taking shortcuts through life, his contempt for humdrum conformity'.[53] She was placed next to him, and he 'seemed to me quite different from any other young man I had ever met'. He asked her how old she was and when she told him she was nineteen, he said he was thirty-two,* 'Younger than anyone else who *counts*, though.' He then added, 'Curse ruthless time! Curse our mortality! How cruelly short is the allotted span for all we must cram into it!'[54] The death of both of Churchill's paternal aunts – Fanny Tweedmouth in 1904 at fifty-one and Georgiana Howe in 1906 at forty-five – had made it clearer than ever to him that he did not have long to live. 'We are all worms,' he told Violet in forthright conclusion. 'But I do believe that I am a glow-worm.'[55]

Violet developed an intellectual and emotional crush on Churchill that

* In fact he was thirty-one; her memory was fallible.

was to remain for life. 'When I proclaimed to others my discovery,' she later recalled,

> I found ... my estimate of Winston Churchill was not sympathetically received. In fact I was mocked by many. The attitude of the general public towards him at the time was, at best, one of expectant interest, curiosity and tolerant amusement, at worst one of mistrust and acid reprobation. In Tory and social circles he had for some years past been a red rag which turned the mildest cows into infuriated bulls. He was an outsider, a pusher, thruster and self-advertiser. After he crossed the Floor he became, in addition, a rat, a turncoat, an *arriviste* and, worst crime of all, one who had certainly arrived.[56]

As a young minister, Churchill honed his ability to cut to the heart of the matter, a quality which proved invaluable in later life. One of his Colonial Office memoranda of January 1907 regarding the difficult question of whether Australian state premiers ought to be invited to the Colonial Conference in London opened with the sentence: 'The main reason for inviting the state premiers of Australia to the Colonial Conference is that they want to come.'[57] He happily admitted that 'the Conference is not likely to lead to large practical results', because the new Government opposed Imperial Preference and the colonial governments had shown no interest in contributing meaningfully to the imperial fleets and armies.

Yet for all that his portfolio encouraged him to look overseas, Churchill understood that the Liberals' domestic agenda would ultimately determine its electoral fate. As the Unionist-dominated House of Lords started to disrupt the elected Government's legislative programme, Churchill showed how far he was prepared to go to put his new party's agenda above the ancient legislative rights of his own class. 'I have no time to deal to-night with the plain absurdities in the composition of our hereditary Chamber,' he told a Manchester audience in February 1907:

> where a man acquires legislative functions simply through his virtue in being born, where the great majority of the members never come near the place from year's end to year's end, where if they go mad or are convicted of a crime or become mentally incompetent to manage their estates, or acquire an unwholesome acquaintance with intoxicating beverages, nevertheless they are still considered perfectly fit to exercise the highest legislative functions. I pass that over, and say nothing about it. I might be betrayed into using disrespectful language if I did, and I am sure you would all be very sorry for that.[58]

Churchill went on to point out that, despite having lost the election, Balfour, who had by then returned to Parliament representing a different constituency, had 'his hand on the throttle-valve of obstruction', because he 'has the power to write a note on a half sheet of notepaper, and to give it to a messenger and send it two hundred yards down the corridor to the House of Lords. And by writing that note he can mutilate or reject or pass into law any clause or any bill which the House of Commons may have spent weeks in discussing.'[59]

In June, Churchill attacked the House of Lords as 'one-sided, hereditary, unpurged, unrepresentative, irresponsible, absentee'.[60] He asked whether it had ever got anything right in the past, citing its uniformly reactionary stances over Catholic Emancipation, the right of Jews to sit as MPs, the extension of the franchise, secret balloting in elections, the purchasing of Army commissions and so on. 'I defy the Party opposite to produce a single instance of a settled controversy in which the House of Lords was right,' he said.[61] Although such sallies infuriated the Conservatives, they endeared him to a Liberal Party still distrustful of the way he had joined them just as they were winning. 'The applause of the House is the breath of his nostrils,' Lloyd George told his brother William in July. 'He is just like an actor. He likes the limelight and the approbation of the pit.'[62] It was true – though somewhat hypocritical of Lloyd George to criticize another politician for traits he possessed in abundance himself.

That summer, Churchill attended the French military manoeuvres, and fell in love with the French Army. 'When I saw the great masses of the French infantry storming the position, while the bands played the "Marseillaise", I felt that by those valiant bayonets the Rights of Man had been gained and that by them the rights and liberties of Europe would be faithfully guarded.'[63] He was right, but he did not compute fully the effect that guarding those rights and liberties would soon have on the French Army and nation.

During the Autumn Recess from late October 1907 to early January 1908, Churchill went on a tour of Britain's East African possessions, travelling extensively in Egypt, Sudan, British East Africa (modern-day Kenya and Tanzania) and Uganda. He started in Mombasa, where he was taken in a British warship, and ended in Alexandria. The journey took in Nairobi, Mount Kenya, Lake Naivasha, Entebbe, Kampala, the Murchison Falls (where he crawled on his stomach 'to look actually down upon the foaming hell beneath'), Lake Victoria and the Ripon Falls, as well as Khartoum and Cairo, which left him with an even greater love, and a much better understanding, of the Empire and its opportunities and problems.[64] He ensured that it was a financially as well as an educationally and ideologically profitable trip, signing a contract to write five articles for the *Strand Magazine* at £150 each and a book, *My African Journey*, for £500. Churchill took along his uncle Colonel Gordon Wilson, the husband of Lord Randolph's sister Sarah, his manservant George Scrivings and Eddie Marsh. He also packed a large number of books on socialism, telling a friend, 'I'm going to see what the Socialist case really is.'[65] (These volumes hardened him in his opposition.)

Arriving in Mombasa in October 1907, Churchill's party took what he called 'one of the most romantic and most wonderful railways in the world', from which they watched herds of antelopes and gazelles, a dazzle of 500 zebras, long files of black wildebeest, herds of red kongoni antelope and wild ostriches, a dozen giraffes lolloping, and six lions which walked 'in a leisurely mood across the rails in broad daylight'.[66] Elsewhere he saw troops of baboons 'who seemed as large as men'.

Sport was an important aspect of the trip as well as fact-finding, and, although none of the animals Churchill shot were endangered species in those days, there were an awful lot of them. He shot crocodiles (for which he seems to have conceived a lifelong dislike), a hippopotamus 'who sunk with a harsh sort of scream', waterbuck, two reedbucks, 'a few' gazelle and two roan antelope, 'who walked slowly down to water past our ambuscade'.[67] He also shot a white rhinoceros with a double-barrelled .450 rifle.[68] 'The manner of killing a rhinoceros in the open is crudely simple . . .' Churchill wrote; 'you walk up as near as possible to him from any side except the windward, and then shoot him in the head or heart . . . I fired. The thud of a bullet which strikes with the impact of a ton and a quarter, tearing through hide and muscle and bone with the hideous energy of cordite, came back distinctly.'[69] He did not kill it with his first shot, and it 'bore straight down upon us in a peculiar trot, nearly as fast as a horse's gallop, with an activity surprising in so huge a beast, and instinct with unmistakable purpose. Great is the moral effect of a foe who advances. Everybody fired.'[70]

Churchill's respect for the lion was even greater than for the rhino. 'Broken limbs, broken jaws, a body raked from end to end, lungs pierced through and through, entrails torn and protruding – none of these count,' he wrote. 'It must be death – instant and utter – for the lion, or down goes the man, mauled by septic claws and fetid teeth, crushed and crunched, and poisoned afterwards to make doubly sure.'[71] A different sport – pig-sticking warthogs – was much more hazardous than polo, because 'The pig cannot be overtaken and speared except by a horse absolutely at full gallop,' and if one fell 'The warthog would certainly attack the unhorsed cavalier.'[72] At one point a column of marching soldier-ants that he 'could not resist interfering with' chased him off to 'a respectful distance'.[73] By contrast, Churchill loved the many butterflies he saw, and he found that he 'could pick them up quite gently in my fingers without the need of any net at all'.[74]

The party travelled by every conceivable means: train, horseback, rickshaw, canoe and steel sailing boat. They were sometimes carried in litters on the shoulders of porters, which Churchill described as 'quite as uncomfortable as it sounds', though it was presumably worse for the porters.[75] Reconnoitring a railway extension between Lakes Albert and Victoria involved no fewer than 400 porters, who carried an average of 65 pounds 10 or 12 miles a day.[76] He had an armchair attached to the cowcatcher on the front of the train to Lake Victoria so that he could absorb the passing landscape to the full, with no apparent worry about what would happen if it came into contact with a cow.

'Churchill arrived here yesterday,' noted Henry Hesketh Bell, the Governor of the Uganda Protectorate, on 19 November. 'He landed in a white uniform and a galaxy of medals.'[77] Three days later, during a three-hour rickshaw ride, pushed and pulled by three Ugandan men, Churchill asked Bell how old he was. On being told that he was forty-three, the thirty-two-year-old Churchill said, 'I wonder where I shall be when I am your age.' 'Where do you think you'll be?' asked Bell. 'P.M.,' Churchill said, in what Bell called 'a tone characteristic of acute determination'.[78] When they reached the Ugandan chiefs wearing their splendid gala robes, Churchill was 'a perfect nuisance, dodging about with his camera all the time, taking snapshots'. In trying to explain to the chiefs that Churchill was the King-Emperor's Colonial Under-Secretary, the translator told them that he was a *toto*, 'a small black urchin' who assisted at table and was paid in scraps and left-overs.[79] 'He is a difficult fellow to handle, but I can't help liking him,' Bell recorded in his diary. 'He sees things *en grand* and appreciates the great possibilities that are latent in this remarkable country.'[80]

Whether the Colonial Office would act on Churchill's recommendations when he returned was another matter. The senior civil servant there, Sir Francis Hopwood, wrote to Elgin in December: 'He is most tiresome to deal with and will, I fear, give trouble – as his father did – in any position to which he may be called. The restless energy, uncontrollable desire for notoriety and the lack of moral perception makes him an anxiety indeed!'[81] Yet even Hopwood came round to admiring him in time.

Eddie Marsh enjoyed Churchill's puns and jokes along the way. When an administrator spoke of the regrettable spread of venereal disease among the natives, Churchill dubbed it the 'Pox Britannica'. An attractive feature was his readiness to make fun of his own loquacity. On the struggle between Civilization and the jungle, he said, 'On this we talked – or at least I talked – while we scrambled across the stumps of fallen trees or waded in an emerald twilight from one sunbeam to another across the creeper flood.'[82] On another occasion, 'I was as tired of making "brief and appropriate" speeches as my companions must have been of hearing them.'[83]

As one would expect at that period in history and stage of scientific development, Churchill's assumption of white racial superiority was palpable throughout his articles and subsequent book, *My African Journey*. 'It is unquestionably an advantage that the East African negro should develop a taste for civilized attire,' he wrote in the latter. 'His life will gradually be made more complicated, more varied, less crudely animal, and himself raised to a higher level of economic utility.' At another point he wrote, 'A Government runs risks when it intrudes upon the domain of fashion; but when a veritable abyss of knowledge and science separates the rulers from the ruled, when authority is dealing with a native race still plunged in its primary squalor, without religion, without clothes, without morals, but willing to emerge and capable of emerging, such risks may fairly be accepted.'[84] That the local people had their own religions, tribal dress and systems of morality and justice did not seem to occur to him. In Kenya he noted, 'Now that their inter-tribal fighting has been stopped, white officers ride freely about among their villages without even carrying a pistol.' He was impressed by the ability of only a handful of Britons to pacify vast stretches of land. 'Two young white officers', he wrote, 'preside from this centre of authority, far from the telegraph, over the peace and order of an area as large as an English county, and regulate the conduct and fortunes of some seventy-five thousand natives, who have never previously known or acknowledged any law but violence or terror.'[85]

Churchill felt a genuine and profound sense of paternalist duty towards the natives of the British Empire. It was the duty of the Government, to his mind, to protect the natives against what he called 'a petty white community, with the harsh and selfish ideas which mark the jealous contact of races and the exploitation of the weaker'.[86] For that reason he was pleased that the local British administrators 'regard themselves as guardians of native interests and native rights against those who only care about exploiting the country and its people'.[87] 'No one can travel even for a little while among the Kikuyu tribes without acquiring a liking for these light-hearted, tractable, if brutish children, or without feeling that they are capable of being instructed and raised from their present degradation,' he wrote. 'It will be an ill day for these native races when their fortunes are removed from the impartial and august administration of the Crown and abandoned to the fierce self-interest of a small white population.'[88]

Although he used language that today would shock even the least politically correct, Churchill believed in the notion of civilizational progress and potential. 'I ask myself if there is any other spot in the whole earth where the dreams and hopes of the negrophile, so often mocked by results and stubborn facts, have ever attained such a happy realization,' he wrote.[89] He described the Kingdom of Uganda as 'a fairy-tale' where 'An elegance of manners springing from a naïve simplicity of character pervades all classes.'[90]

The King had asked Churchill to write to him about his East African possessions, and much of the long letter Churchill sent was about the spirillum tick and 'the dreaded tsetse fly'.[91] 'Uganda is defended by its insects,' he later wrote.[92] Whole areas were being depopulated by the then-incurable sleeping sickness carried by the tsetse fly, one of which was flicked off Churchill's bare shoulder moments after it had landed, possibly adding to his already long list of close shaves.

At Khartoum, Churchill witnessed a huge change in the near-decade since the Omdurman campaign: slavery had been abolished, the railway reached the southern bank of the Blue Nile, broad thoroughfares had electric lights, education, craftsmanship and agriculture had been transformed, there were European shops, steam tramways, ferries and the Gordon Memorial College for training primary school teachers – in sum, the benefits of British imperial rule.[93] Yet it was also at Khartoum that tragedy struck. Scrivings died suddenly of Asiatic cholera, a violent internal inflammation. Churchill arranged a military burial for him, a ceremony Marsh found 'moving in the extreme', and recorded how, nine years after burying his Omdurman comrades, 'I again found myself standing at an open grave, while the yellow glare of the departed sun still lingered over the desert, and the sound of funeral volleys broke its silence.'[94]

He returned to England on 17 January 1908, and soon afterwards spoke at the National Liberal Club to promote the idea of a 135-mile Ugandan railway (never to be built). He argued that the native populations should never be 'handed over from the careful, the disinterested control of British officials to the mere self-interest of some small local community'.[95] He also argued passionately that social reform was necessary if the Empire was going to be maintained. 'If the British people will have a great Empire,' he told the audience, 'if any ray of true glory is to fall upon it, they will need an imperial race to support the burden. They will never erect that great fabric upon the shoulders of stinted millions crowded together in the slums of cities, trampled in the slush of dismal streets. Not that way lies the future of the British race.'[96]

Churchill continued his public speaking all over the country, sometimes criticizing 'that mighty press-gang gathered together under the august headship of the *Daily Mail* and the *Daily Express*'. He took aim at socialism with snappy lines like 'The Socialism of the Christian era was based on the idea that "All mine is yours," but the Socialism of [the Independent Labour Party MP] Mr. [Victor] Grayson is based on the idea that "All yours is mine."'[97]

His articles on his African journey appeared in nine parts in the *Strand* in March. *My African Journey* followed in December. In February, he published another book of speeches, this time on Free Trade, and that month he also spoke to the Authors' Club. 'To be able to make your work your pleasure', he said, 'is the one class distinction in the world worth striving for.'[98] Of the joy he found in writing, he said, 'To sit at one's table on a sunny morning, with four clear hours of uninterruptible security, plenty of nice white paper, and a Squeezer pen* – that is true happiness.' He spoke passionately about his admiration for the power and expressive range of the English language:

> If an English writer cannot say what he has to say in English, and in simple English, depend upon it, it is probably not worth saying . . . Someone† – I forget who – has said: 'Words are the only things which last forever.' That is, to my mind, always a wonderful thought. The most durable structures raised in stone by the strength of man, the mightiest monuments of his power, crumble into dust, while the words spoken with fleeting breath, the passing expression of the unstable fancies of his mind, endure not as echoes of the past, not as mere archaeological curiosities or venerable relics, but with a force and life as new and strong, and sometimes far stronger than when they were first spoken, and leaping across the gulf of three thousand years, they light the world for us to-day.[99]

With speeches such as this one, full of Shakespearian echoes, Churchill marked himself out as different from those politicians who concentrated solely on politics. They made him more interesting to the public, and allowed him to reach across the political divide. But most importantly they were evidence of a hinterland that gave him solace when politics went badly for him, which given his willingness – indeed, eagerness – to break with party orthodoxy, it so often did.

On 7 March, Churchill wrote a long letter to the editor of the centre-left magazine the *Nation*, published under the title 'The Untrodden Field in Politics'. In what amounted to a personal manifesto, he made the case for 'the minimum standard', setting out the areas where he would like to see state intervention. These included labour exchanges, licensing bills to counter 'the excessive consumption of strong drink', wages boards in

* A pen that used rubber to suck up the ink.

† William Hazlitt.

certain 'notoriously sweated industries', technical colleges, railway nationalization, public works to fight unemployment ('to urge forward the social march'), all to be paid for by a tax on dividends.[100] Most of these ideas (except railway nationalization) were Tory Democrat ones. His embrace of German-style social reform was no more socialist or egalitarian in origin than Otto von Bismarck's had been, and he consciously used Germany as his model. It was partly intended to take the most popular policies of the socialists' platform and to co-opt them as his own, and partly to promote the Tory Democrat ideas he had held all his life. 'I am in favour of government of the people, for the people, but not by the people,' he joked to the Liberal MP Charles Masterman.[101] Therein lay the difference between paternalistic Tory Democracy and Liberalism or socialism.

'Winston is full of the poor, whom he has just discovered,' Masterman wrote to his wife Lucy at this time. 'He thinks he is called by Providence to do something for them.' He quoted his dramatic plea for social reform, 'Why have I been kept safe within a hair's breadth of death, except to do something like this? I'm not going to live long.'[102] Masterman's summation was 'He is just an extraordinarily gifted boy, with genius and astonishing energy.'[103] When he teased Churchill about his enjoyment of speaking to huge crowds, Churchill replied, 'Of course I do. Thou shalt not muzzle the ox when he treadeth out the corn.* That shall be my plea at the Day of Judgment ... Sometimes I feel as if I could lift the whole world on my shoulders.'[104]

In March 1908, the thirty-three-year-old Churchill attended a dinner party given by Lady St Helier, a friend of his mother's, where he met the beautiful, intelligent and strong-willed twenty-three-year-old Clementine Hozier. They had met once before, at a ball held by the future Marquess of Crewe in the summer of 1904. Although he had asked his mother to effect an introduction on that occasion – Clementine's mother, Lady Blanche Hozier, had been Jennie's best friend years before – he was for once completely lost for words and unable to speak. Another man took Clementine off to dance, remarking, out of earshot, that he was surprised that she had been talking to 'that frightful fellow Winston Churchill'.[105]

In the intervening years, Clementine had been engaged twice to Sidney Peel, the third son of Viscount Peel, and later to Lionel Earle, a civil servant nearly twice her age. She had broken off the engagements – one of them after the wedding presents had started to arrive – when she realized they were not the right men for her.[106] (Her mother had also intended her to marry Lord Bessborough, and she 'had been left in a maze with him

* Deuteronomy 25: 4.

all one afternoon'.)[107] Churchill meanwhile had himself been unofficially engaged to Pamela Plowden, and after a courtship that he described to his mother as 'tranquil *banalité*', proposed to Muriel Wilson, the daughter of a rich Hull shipowner, in 1906, who rejected him as too poor. He also proposed to the American actress Ethel Barrymore, who felt she could not 'cope with the great world of politics'.[108] None of these were much more than dalliances conducted in the formal Edwardian manner, and nothing like the great lifelong love affair that beckoned.

Churchill and Clementine were thus both unattached when they met again at Lady St Helier's. Clementine had only been invited at the last moment to prevent there being thirteen around the table, and she had wanted to refuse because she was tired and had no clean white gloves. Churchill had spent the day working at the Colonial Office, and was similarly disinclined to go, but was told by Eddie Marsh that it was rude to drop out at the last minute. He arrived late, but was immediately smitten with Clementine, completely ignoring the lady on his other side.[109] According to Clementine's recollection years later, his opening remark, somewhat abrupt, was 'Have you read my book?' She admitted she had not, whereupon he said he would send it round the next day in a hansom cab.[110]

When the men joined the ladies after dinner, Clementine was cornered by Lord Tweedmouth, the husband of Lord Randolph's sister Fanny, who was then first lord of the Admiralty. Churchill sent him off to look at a portrait of Nelson in the corridor and then 'promptly appropriated' the chair next to Clementine. They talked for the rest of the evening. They were the last people to leave, and he took her home. He never sent round a copy of *Lord Randolph Churchill*, but he had fallen in love with her. He invited Clementine and her mother to Jennie's country house, Salisbury Hall near St Albans, for the weekend of 11–12 April 1908.

Not for the last time, politics intervened.

# 6

# Love and Liberalism
# April 1908–February 1910

*I could not conceive myself forming any other attachment than that to which I have fastened the happiness of my life.*

Churchill to Clementine, November 1909[1]

*I avow my faith that we are marching towards better days.*

Churchill, October 1908[2]

On 8 April 1908, Sir Henry Campbell-Bannerman resigned the premiership after suffering a heart attack. He died fourteen days later at No. 10. He was succeeded by Herbert Asquith, who offered Churchill the post of president of the Board of Trade, responsible for industrial relations, where he would be in a position to enact several of the ideas contained in his article 'The Untrodden Field in Politics'. (He said that he was pleased not to have been sent to the Local Government Board, as 'I refuse to be shut up in a soup kitchen with Mrs [Beatrice] Webb.')[3] At thirty-three, Churchill became the youngest Cabinet minister in over forty years. Because an economic downturn had led to sharp wage reductions, he had to deal with major strikes: of shipwrights in January; of engineers in February; of Tyne, Clyde and Merseyside shipbuilders in May, and of the clothing industry over the summer. The Edwardian age is often depicted as a halcyon period of domestic peace, but it was a profoundly disturbed one in the factories and shipyards, and Churchill was closely involved in trying to settle disputes fairly.

Yet before he could do anything he needed to get re-elected because an ancient constitutional rule required that a new Cabinet minister had to be re-elected to the Commons. The Opposition regularly waived this provision in order to avoid the expense of a contest, but in Churchill's case the Conservatives announced that William Joynson-Hicks would refight Manchester North West. The hoped-for long weekend with Clementine was therefore truncated by a series of election meetings.

His speeches in Manchester were nothing if not exhaustive; one he gave at the Grand Theatre in April was 7,600 words long. So many people attended another that he stood on the roof of a car in the street immediately outside and repeated it verbatim. There were light moments in response to hecklers. 'What would be the consequence if this seat were lost to Liberalism and to Free Trade?' he asked his audience rhetorically. When someone shouted out 'Beer!', Churchill immediately replied, 'That might be the cause. I am talking of the consequence.'[4] After another heckler yelled 'Rot!' at one of his points, Churchill retorted, 'When my friend in the gallery says "Rot" he is no doubt expressing very fully what he has in his mind.'[5] Such sallies were part of what people had come for, and the word 'laughter' appeared more than forty times in the newspaper report of one meeting.

'I seize this fleeting hour of leisure to write and tell you how much I liked our long talk on Sunday,' Churchill wrote to Clementine on 16 April, 'and what a comfort and pleasure it was to meet a girl with so much intellectual quality and such strong reserves of noble sentiment . . . We may lay the foundations of a frank and clear-eyed friendship which I should certainly value and cherish with many serious feelings of respect.'[6] It was more romantic in the Edwardian idiom than it reads today, and was the first of no fewer than 1,700 letters, billets-doux and telegrams Winston and Clementine were to send to each other over the course of their lives. 'If it were not for the excitement of reading about Manchester every day in the belated newspapers,' Clementine replied, 'I should feel as if I were living in another world than the delightful one we inhabited together for a day at Salisbury Hall.'[7] She said she was reading his biography of his father (she had procured a copy anyway), and signed herself, as he had, 'Yours very sincerely'.

On 23 April, to Churchill's intense disappointment, Joynson-Hicks won Manchester North West by 5,417 to 4,988 votes, a majority of 429 votes in a 6.4 per cent swing. Churchill publicly put his defeat down to 'the low and blatant influence' of the Tory press, but in private to 'those sulky Irish Catholics changing sides at the last moment under priestly pressure'.[8] (The Liberals' Education Bill seemed to threaten Catholic voluntary schools.) Churchill's political opponents took savage satisfaction from his defeat: Sir Edward Carson, the Irish-born Unionist MP, told Lady Londonderry, who was married to Churchill's cousin, 'I think W. Churchill really degrades public life more than anyone of any position in politics, and I doubt if he will ever mature into the kind of serious and reliable politician the majority of people have confidence in.'[9] The Prince of Wales (later King George V) noted in his diary, 'We were all very excited when we heard that Winston Churchill has been beaten.'[10] The King had recently told his son that Churchill 'is almost more of a cad in office than in opposition'.[11]

'I was under the dull clouds of reaction on Saturday after all the effort and excitement of that tiresome election,' Churchill wrote to Clementine on 27 April. Such was his popularity in the Liberal Party, however, that eight or nine safe seats propositioned him to represent them. 'The election may well prove a blessing in disguise,' he told Clementine. 'If I had won Manchester now, I should probably have lost it at the general election. Losing it now I shall I hope get a seat which will make me secure for many years.' 'How I should have liked you to have been there,' he wrote in closing. 'Write to me again – I am a solitary creature in the midst of crowds. Be kind to me.'[12] It was hardly the signing-off of someone who only wanted a frank and clear-eyed friendship.

Churchill accepted the offer of the Liberal Association of the solidly working-class Scottish constituency of Dundee, where the long-term danger seemed more likely to come from Labour than from the Tories. The sitting MP, Edmund Robertson, a junior minister whose health was failing, was awarded a peerage as Lord Lochee in order to create a vacancy, further indication of Churchill's importance to the Party. On the second day of his campaign in Dundee in early May, Churchill was asked about Home Rule for Scotland. 'I would not deny Scotland any liberty that you give to Ireland,' he replied, 'but I am not at all sure that Scotland is in a hurry to give up the great influence that she exerts upon the Government of England.'[13] The implication that Ireland did not have 'liberty' was the first step he took away from his father's legacy. '*The Times* is speechless, and takes three columns to express its speechlessness,' he proclaimed of the Liberal Party's support for Irish Home Rule, 'and thousands of people who never under any circumstances voted Liberal before are saying that under no circumstances will they ever vote Liberal again.'[14]

Throughout the campaign in Dundee Churchill was followed by Mary Maloney, an Irish suffragette, who rang a large bell whenever he got up to speak, drowning him out. All he did was to doff his cap to her and drive off, hoping to finish his next event before she arrived.[15] When he finally could be heard, he said of the House of Lords, 'The old doddering peers are there, the cute financial magnates are there, the clever wirepullers are there, the big brewers with bulbous noses are there. All the enemies of progress are there: the weaklings, the sleek, smug, comfortable, selfish individuals.'[16] His attacks on 'sleek' and 'comfortable' members of the upper classes were somewhat hypocritical: Churchill spent no less than £80 a year (approximately £8,000 today) on silk underwear from the Army

& Navy Stores.[17] (When Violet Asquith teased him about this, he told her that it 'is essential to my being. I have a very delicate and sensitive cuticle [outer skin] which demands the finest covering.')[18] He only ever patronized the best St James's and Oxford Street shoemakers (Lobb's), slipper cobblers (Hook, Knowles & Co.; he liked grey antelope), booksellers (Hatchard's), tobacconists (Robert Lewis), hatters (Scott's and Chapman & Moore), uniform tailors (E. Tautz & Sons), wine merchants (Berry Bros. and Randolph Payne & Sons) and stationers (Smythson's).[19] 'Mr Churchill is easily satisfied with the best,' said F. E. Smith.[20] Churchill was elected for Dundee with 7,079 votes on 9 May 1908, a handsome margin of 2,709 over the Unionist candidate. Coming last, with only 655 votes, was the Prohibitionist candidate, Edwin Scrymgeour, who, as we shall see, was not discouraged. Churchill told his mother he thought Dundee was a 'life seat', but he was not without detractors.[21] The next time he visited, in June, no fewer than six suffragettes had to be ejected from the meeting in Kinnaird Hall for what he called their 'pantomime antics', although he insisted, as always, on the absolute minimum use of force.[22]

Churchill and Clementine saw each other several times in June and July at social occasions with chaperones present. They arranged to meet at Salisbury Hall with their mothers again in mid-August.[23] Otherwise, he involved himself in the question of Army Estimates in the Cabinet, which was well outside his portfolio, gave speeches in favour of temperance legislation – though nothing so unChurchillian as full-scale Prohibition – and was installed as a member of the Albion Lodge of the Ancient Order of Druids.

On 4 August, his brother Jack married Lady Gwendeline Bertie,* the daughter of the 7th Earl of Abingdon. After the wedding, Churchill and some friends went on to stay at Burley Hall near Oakham in Rutland – 'one of the stateliest homes of England' – which was rented by his cousin Freddie Guest. At one o'clock on the morning of 6 August, when everyone had gone to bed, a maid discovered that a fire had broken out as a result of a faulty new heating system. It spread to the beams and an entire wing of the house was razed to the ground. House-guests scrambled from their bedrooms in 'scanty clothing'; Churchill saved his ministerial papers, but F. E. Smith lost his entire wardrobe. 'Winston commandeered a fireman's helmet and assumed the direction of operations,' Eddie Marsh recalled, but they didn't manage to save the priceless Elizabethan manuscripts.[24] 'As Churchill was carrying two marble busts to safety,' *The Times*

* Pronounced Barty; she was nicknamed 'Goonie'.

reported, 'the blazing roof fell in behind him.'[25] Fortunately, the only life lost was that of a canary.

With unconscionable cruelty, a member of the Dudley Ward family told Clementine that Churchill had died in the fire, and then followed her to the post office where she hoped to get more news. Instead, there was a telegram from the Duke of Marlborough saying that Churchill was safe.[26] She telegraphed her relief, writing, 'My dear my heart stood still with terror.' She signed off, 'Yours, Clementine H.'[27] He wrote back, his eyes still smarting from the heat, 'The Fire was great fun and we all enjoyed it thoroughly. It is a pity such jolly entertainments are so costly.'[28] He suggested they stay at Blenheim that weekend before going on to Salisbury Hall: 'We shall find lots of places to talk in and lots of things to talk about . . . Write and tell me . . . whether you have thought of me at all. If the newspapers have not jogged your memory! You know the answer that I want to this.'[29] He ended, 'Always yours.'

On Tuesday, 11 August 1908, Winston Churchill proposed to Clementine Hozier in the impossibly romantic setting of the Temple of Diana in the park of Blenheim Palace. On the morning that he was going to take her on a walk in the gardens after breakfast to propose, he had overslept. Chagrined, Clementine seriously considered returning to London, but Sunny Marlborough took her on a buggy tour around the estate and told a servant to warn Churchill of his faux pas. He was there when they returned and took her off to the Temple of Diana.[30] He promised her he would keep the engagement secret until she had told her mother, but crossing the lawn only minutes later he could not stop himself from blurting out the news to Sunny and his guests.[31] 'I am not rich nor powerfully established,' he wrote to Lady Blanche Hozier, 'but your daughter loves me, and with that love I feel strong enough to assume this great and sacred responsibility; and I think I can make her happy and give her a station and a career worthy of her beauty and her virtues.'[32]

For all that Clementine's first cousin was the Earl of Airlie, the Hoziers were quite poor, indeed Clementine had had to give French lessons at two shillings and sixpence an hour to supplement her small allowance.[33] (She was fluent in French as her mother had moved to Dieppe for financial reasons after her parents separated when she was six.) As Mary Soames later recalled, when her father proposed, Clementine 'was down to her last laundered and starched dress and, having no personal maid, she would have to make this one last the unexpected visit' to Blenheim.[34] The couple knew they would not have much money when they married, and for the first six months they had to live in Churchill's bachelor flat at 12 Bolton

Street, before moving to a much larger flat at 33 Eccleston Square in downmarket Pimlico.

'Je t'aime passionnément,' Clementine wrote two days after the engagement. 'I feel less shy in French.'[35] Churchill replied, 'There are no words to convey to you the feelings of love and joy by which my being is possessed.'[36] Later that month she wrote: 'I do long for you so much. I wonder how I have lived twenty-three years without you.'[37] Churchill asked Hugh Cecil to be his best man, and after Lord Salisbury had written to congratulate him on his engagement, he replied from the Board of Trade, 'This auspicious event in a remote manner connects me with your family: and the union between Churchills and Cecils which was unsuccessfully attempted in two generations in the political sphere, may now perhaps be more prosperously approached from the private side.'[38] Even at that happy moment, Churchill could not forbear to mention his father's political destruction at the hands of Salisbury's father.

The wedding took place at St Margaret's Westminster on Saturday, 12 September 1908. Churchill talked shop with Lloyd George in the vestry during the signing of the register, leading the latter to tell a mutual friend that 'he had never met anyone with such a passion for politics.'[39] The church was packed and there was a large and enthusiastic crowd outside. Dr Welldon, Churchill's former headmaster at Harrow who had since briefly been bishop of Calcutta, delivered the address and 1,300 guests attended the reception afterward at Lady St Helier's house. The *Tailor & Cutter* magazine described Churchill's outfit as 'one of the greatest failures as a wedding garment we have ever seen, giving the wearer a sort of glorified coachman appearance'.[40] The King gave Churchill a gold-capped Malacca cane and the Cabinet presented a silver tray autographed by his colleagues.* That same day, Madame Tussaud's put its waxwork of Churchill on to permanent exhibition, thereby fulfilling the prediction he had made to the British Consul in Lourenço Marques almost a decade earlier.

The honeymoon was spent at Blenheim, then in Baveno on Lake Maggiore, then in Venice and finally back at Blenheim again. But politics was ever on his mind. Even while at Baveno, Churchill wrote to Masterman, who was parliamentary secretary at the Local Government Board (LGB), asking him to:

> let me know privately what the LGB is really doing and not doing. I have circularized the Cabinet once already about the state of industry and warned them of the distress which the winter would bring to the poor, but all that

* Both are on display at the Churchill War Rooms.

> Asquith said was that Burns* thought differently . . . Do let me know how things really are behind the grinning mask of official assurance . . . But you had better write to me 'Secret' at the B[oard] of T[rade].[41]

This is quintessential Churchill: asking a friend in a different department to help him clandestinely discover the truth about what was going on in Whitehall, and worrying about it even while on honeymoon. 'We have only loitered and loved,' Churchill wrote to his mother from Venice, 'a good and serious occupation for which the histories furnish respectable precedents.'[42]

Although it was a genuine love-match, after their honeymoon Churchill and Clementine tended to holiday separately throughout their lives. One of the reasons that there are so very many letters and billets-doux and telegrams between them is that they were often apart, which was probably good for their marriage as Churchill was exhausting company. He recognized it, and did not mind when Clementine felt she had to take time away from him. They quickly devised pet names for each other. 'The poor pug pules [cries] disconsolately,' he wrote to her. 'Sweet cat – I will come back tomorrow by the 6.15.' He was 'Amber Dog', 'Puggy Wow', 'little pug', then 'Pug' and later on 'Pig'; she was 'Cat' or 'Kat', sometimes 'Bird', 'Clemmie Cat', 'woo-Kat' and even 'Clem Pussy Bird'. He would draw pictures of pigs, pugs and cats on his letters to her, and when she became pregnant, the cats followed suit.[43]

On one occasion in the early days of the marriage, when Churchill said he wanted roast duck for dinner, Clementine tried to put him off by telling him that duck was expensive because it was out of season. But he had read in the papers that alligators at the Zoo were being fed ducks, and he said that if they could eat them he could not see why he should not.[44] Clementine admitted to Freddie Birkenhead in her old age that their financial situation 'could not have been *really* bad, as they had five servants, but said that it [having many servants] was a matter of course in those days.'[45] When Beatrice Webb lunched with them a month after the engagement, she recorded, 'his bride – a charming lady, well-bred and pretty, and earnest withal – but not rich, by no means a good match, which is to Winston's credit'.[46]

Clementine would give birth to their first child, Diana, on 11 July 1909. Churchill nicknamed her 'the cream-gold kitten', 'puppy kitten' and 'P.K.'.

* John Burns, the President of the Local Government Board, at that time was 'frankly hostile to the aggressive pretensions of Lloyd George and Winston whom he calls the "Bounding Brothers"' (eds. Thorpe and Toye, *Parliament* p. 35).

Lloyd George supposedly told the Mastermans that he had asked Churchill whether Diana was a pretty child. '"The prettiest child ever seen," said Winston beaming. "Like her mother, I suppose?" "No," said Winston still more gravely, "she is exactly like me."'[47]*

'Soon, very soon our brief lives will be lived away,' he told his Dundee audience in October.

> Uncounted generations will trample heedlessly upon our tombs. What is the use of living if it be not to strive for noble causes and to make this muddled world a better place for those who will live in it after we are gone? How else can we put ourselves in harmonious relation with the great verities and consolations of the infinite and the eternal? . . . Humanity will not be cast down. We are going on – swinging bravely forward along the grand high road – and already behind the distant mountains is the promise of the sun.[48]

His high, uplifting oratory during the Second World War was clearly prefigured more than thirty years earlier.

In the calendar year 1908, Churchill made no fewer than ninety-six speeches, travelling nearly 5,400 miles, mainly by train, to venues all over the country. In 1899 he had made fourteen speeches (travelling over 700 miles) and in 1900 ten (1,500 miles), in 1901 twenty-one (1,600 miles) and in 1902 thirteen (over 800 miles). These earlier numbers and distances were normal for an MP, who had to visit his constituency at least occasionally. Yet after 1903 the mileages shot up dramatically, a sign not only of his growing ambition and confidence in his speaking ability, but also of the ever-increasing flow of invitations he received from all over the country as the word spread of what an entertaining, indeed electrifying, public speaker he could be. These speeches were a good way of building up goodwill among local MPs whose support he might one day need in a leadership bid. Thus in 1903 he made twenty-nine speeches (travelling over 2,200 miles), in 1904 thirty-eight (5,500 miles), in 1905 forty-four (over 3,700 miles), in 1906 fifty-nine (3,800 miles) and in 1907 (despite his East African trip) forty-two. These speeches of often more than 5,000 words each required a great deal of concentration in writing – he very rarely repeated himself – and continual practice. He kept up this extraordinarily high level of activity even after the peak year of 1908, with sixty-nine speeches in 1909, seventy-seven in 1910 and sixty-five in 1911, travelling a total of almost 10,000 miles to deliver them. By the outbreak of the Second World

* Almost every time he was mentioned by Lloyd George in Lucy Masterman's extensive diaries, it was to belittle him, so this story might well be apocryphal.

War, Churchill had made about 1,700 speeches and travelled about 82,000 miles – over three times the circumference of the earth – to deliver them. It was an extraordinary display of energy, far more than normal politicians even of the front rank. He had become a vastly experienced and assured public speaker, capable of gauging any audience in an instant.

His attack on the Unionists, and in particular on their leader, did not dissipate with his by-election victory in Dundee. 'Mr Balfour used very strong language on this subject,' he said of the Licensing Bill, which Churchill hoped would curb alcoholism by restricting the number of public houses. 'Now, strong language is often used by weak men and it is never used more strongly than on a weak case.'[49] Churchill had become a prominent, if unlikely, temperance advocate since joining the Liberal Party, just as he had embraced Irish Home Rule and other Liberal measures he had shown little or no interest in as a Tory. The drinks industry had for decades been closely connected to the Conservative Party, which largely explains the irony of Churchill, who greatly enjoyed alcohol (though almost never excessively), attacking it. Now, with the Lords threatening to veto the Bill, he accused the Tories of becoming 'the champions of property gone mad, the champions of private right at any cost'.[50]

Churchill's continuing attacks on the House of Lords were, in Liberal eyes at least, all the more admirable because of the large number of his family members there. As well as his first cousins the Duke of Marlborough and the Duke of Roxburghe (the son of Lord Randolph's sister Anne), other kinsmen included his uncles Lords Tweedmouth and Wimborne, his second cousin the Marquess of Londonderry, his uncle by marriage Earl Howe, Clementine's first cousin the Earl of Airlie and Jack's father-in-law the Earl of Abingdon. Unsurprisingly, several did not appreciate his anti-Lords stance, which even led to a certain froideur from Sunny Marlborough, his friend, cousin and Boer War comrade. After the Lords had rejected the Licensing Bill in November, Masterman recorded that Churchill 'stabbed at his bread, would hardly speak' and then pronounced, 'We shall send them a Budget in June as shall terrify them; they have started the class war, they had better be careful.'[51] He seemed impervious to the fact that it was his own class he was threatening to assault.

At a meeting in Nottingham on 30 January 1909, Churchill made a remark that was to be hung around his neck for years afterwards. He described the Tories as 'the party of the rich against the poor, of the classes and their dependents against the masses, of the lucky, the wealthy, the happy, and the strong against the left-out and the shut-out millions of the weak and poor'.[52] Even as late as 1944, left-wing journalists would quote these words against him.[53]

In 1904 Britain had entered into an Entente Cordiale (effectively an alliance) with France, concerned at the increasingly aggressive tendencies of the German Empire, especially with regard to its naval building programme which could have no other motive than to threaten the Royal Navy. Churchill nonetheless kept up his unpopular belief that defence spending should be kept as low as possible. On 9 February he, Lloyd George, Sir Edward Grey and John Morley, the pacifist Secretary of State for India, threatened Asquith with resignation if Reginald McKenna, the First Lord of the Admiralty, got his way over building the six new dreadnoughts which John 'Jacky' Fisher, the First Sea Lord, insisted were necessary to keep abreast of Germany's new naval building programme. The combination of the heavy-calibre guns and steam-turbine propulsion of these ironclad battleships made all other warships obsolete. Churchill had learned from his father's experience that a threat to resign over the Defence Estimates needed to be done en masse, not singly. 'I am not one of those who admire politicians who think it worthwhile to win cheap cheers by advocating a braggart and sensational policy of expenditure upon armaments,' he told a Manchester audience. 'I have always been against that, as my father was before me.'[54] Yet the rest of the Cabinet opposed the four ministers and, as Whitehall wags put it, McKenna wanted six dreadnoughts, Lloyd George and Churchill wanted four, so the Government compromised on eight.

Partly in order to save money, but also because of his naturally restless mind, Churchill was constantly looking out for technological breakthroughs in the military sphere. As early as February 1909, very early in the history of aeronautics, he began to think about the military application of air power, when he told the Committee of Imperial Defence's subcommittee on aerial navigation, 'The problem of the use of aeroplanes was a most important one, and we should place ourselves in communication with Mr Wright himself, and avail ourselves of his knowledge.'[55] Churchill was to remain a powerful advocate of air power, establishing the Royal Naval Air Service as soon as he was in a position to do so, and arguing for the proper funding of the Royal Flying Corps and its successor the Royal Air Force.[56]

On 24 March, Churchill proposed the Trade Boards Bill, his first major piece of legislation, intended to establish minimum rates of pay and conditions in the 'sweated labour' industries, mainly clothing. It was a very Tory Democrat measure, giving Government the power to fine employers who treated their workers badly, and introducing a minimum wage for the first time. Churchill learned how to pilot a bill into law, with all the hard work and mastery of mind-numbing detail that was required.

Committees and select committees; the first, second and third readings of the Bill; amendments; debate procedure; parliamentary guillotines (closure motions) and all the other procedures by which laws were made in Parliament all became second nature to him over the coming years of hard legislative slog.

Working closely together between 1908 and 1911, Churchill and Lloyd George, now chancellor of the Exchequer, established their reputations as the foremost social reformers of the era. The increase in unemployment since the 1907–8 economic downturn persuaded Churchill to introduce labour exchanges, where unemployed workers were put in touch with potential employers. He recruited William Beveridge to establish them, and by March 1910 there were 214. He won shopworkers a half-holiday. The Old Age Pensions Act 1908 introduced a pension of five shillings a week (approximately £23 in today's money) for 600,000 old people for the first time, costing £4 million per annum. 'It is not much,' Churchill was to say of the very modest pension provision, 'unless you have not got it.'[57] Lloyd George and Churchill introduced the first nationwide compulsory unemployment insurance scheme in 1911, which by October 1913 had insured 14.7 million people through 236 local insurance committees and 23,500 societies and branches. Together they established the Port of London Authority, and passed the Coal Mines (Eight Hours) Act of 1908, which cut the number of hours that miners could be compelled to work, and the Coal Mines Act of 1911, which improved mining safety (and incidentally lessened the harshness of pit-ponies' lives). They also planned to introduce an income tax allowance for parents, which was soon nicknamed the 'Brat'.

Churchill found a military metaphor for the process of helping the poor, equating it with 'going back to bring the rear-guard in'. He viewed all these as evolutionary, Tory Democrat measures, which would make Britain stronger in future crises, and especially in the event of war. The paternalist in Churchill wanted, in Masterman's critical but essentially accurate phrase, 'a state of things where a benign upper class dispensed benefits to an industrious, *bien pensant*, and grateful working class'.[58]

These reforms and others in the pipeline were extremely expensive. When the cost of eight new dreadnoughts was added, a significant new income stream for the Treasury would be necessary to fund them. In April 1909 Lloyd George unleashed the naked class war that Churchill had predicted five months earlier, with his Finance Bill, soon nicknamed by Liberals the 'People's Budget'. In order to raise the extra £16 million, income tax would rise from 1s to 1s 2d in the pound (that is, from 5 to 5.83 per cent), a super-tax would be introduced on high incomes, as well as taxes on tobacco, alcohol, motor cars and petrol, and a halfpenny tax per pound on the value of undeveloped land, with death duties of 25 per cent on property valued over £1 million, and a 20 per cent capital gains tax on land. This represented wealth redistribution on a scale unprecedented in recent British history, and could be guaranteed to provoke the Unionists' opposition in the Lords.* If that opposition could not be mollified or overcome and the Lords refused to pass the Budget there would be a profound constitutional crisis.

'Tomorrow is the day of wrath!' Churchill told Clementine on 28 April, before a key vote on the Finance Bill. 'I feel this Budget will be kill or cure: either we shall secure ample pounds for great reforms next year, or the Lords will force a Dissolution in September.'[59] Churchill believed, as he told the City Liberal Club in June, that 'All taxes are bad,' but he considered these ones necessary.[60] The King's response to the crisis was to make a rather juvenile joke, saying that Churchill's 'initials – W.C. – are well named!'[61]

'This Budget will go through,' Churchill assured an audience in Manchester in May, to loud cheers. 'It will vindicate the power of the House of Commons.'[62] He described it as insurance against dangers at home and abroad, and added,

> If I had my way I would write the word 'insure' over the door of every cottage and upon the blotting-book of every public man, because I am convinced that by sacrifices which are inconceivably small, which are all within the reach of the very poorest man in regular work, families can be secured against catastrophes which otherwise would split them up forever . . . when through the death, the illness, or the invalidity of the bread-winner, the frail boat in which the fortunes of the family are embarked founders, and the women and children are left to struggle helplessly in the dark waters of a friendless world.[63]

A week later, after taking part in Territorial Army field manoeuvres with the Queen's Own Oxfordshire Hussars and seven other regiments, Churchill told Clementine something she had probably already guessed, that he would have loved to have been a general. 'I have much confidence in my judgment on things,' he told her, 'which I see clearly, but on nothing

* Churchill made a three-minute vinyl record in defence of the People's Budget, which was distributed widely. It was the earliest recording of his voice, and although there are some cadences that are recognizable from the famous Second World War speeches, it was higher-pitched, more sing-song, and had a much more noticeable sibilant lisp. He pronounced words differently from later on in his career, such as 'pro-tective' and 'systeem'. His pronunciation as well as his timbre of voice would mature over the next thirty years and gain a gravelly growl that was not evident in his mid-thirties.

do I seem to *feel* the truth more than in tactical formations. It is a vain and foolish thing to say – but *you* will not laugh at it. I am sure I have the root of the matter in me but never I fear in this state of existence will it have a chance of flowering – in bright red blossom.'[64]

Years later, Clementine told Freddie Birkenhead that during this period 'Winston was "completely under Lloyd George's thumb". He was completely fascinated by him.'[65] The Chancellor himself, by contrast, was jealous that Churchill's frequent, well-attended speeches stole some of the publicity from his Budget. Driving to Brighton with Charles and Lucy Masterman, Lloyd George 'commented with some contempt on the idea that Winston Churchill was the author of the Budget. "Winston", he said, "is opposed to pretty nearly every item in the Budget except the 'Brat' and that was because he was expecting soon to be a father himself."'[66] That was untrue – indeed Lloyd George had just written to his brother about Churchill's support for the Budget – but it was a sign of Lloyd George's concern at the advance of a rival, albeit one still very much his junior in legislative achievement.[67]

On 4 September, Churchill made a further incendiary denunciation of the House of Lords at the Palace Theatre in Leicester. 'The wealthy', he said in the course of a nearly 7,000-word speech, 'so far from being self-reliant, are dependent on the constant attention and waiting of scores and sometimes even hundreds of persons who are employed in ministering to their wants.'[68] (He had clearly forgotten the 400 porters carrying his baggage in East Africa.) By then the Budget had spent 600 hours in Commons committees, where the Government had made some concessions, though tempers had frayed. He continued in his Leicester speech:

> The issue will be whether the British people in the year of grace 1909 are going to . . . allow themselves to be dictated to and domineered over by a miserable minority of titled persons, who represent nobody, who are responsible to nobody, and who only scurry up to London to vote in their party interests, in their class interests, and in their own interests.[69]

He now wanted the House of Lords to be stripped of its equality with the Commons, and therefore no longer capable of vetoing legislation sent to it by the democratically elected lower Chamber. Churchill's criticism of the Lords did not extend to his wanting a unicameral legislature or an elected second chamber. His stance would have been instantly recognizable to eighteenth-century Whigs such as Charles James Fox and Lord Melbourne.

Churchill's speech shocked many Tories, and led to protests from both the King and Prime Minister. Lord Knollys, the King's private secretary, wrote a letter of protest to *The Times*.[70] 'He and the King must really have gone mad,' Churchill told Clementine. 'This looks to me like a rather remarkable royal intervention and shows the bitterness which is felt in those circles. I shall take no notice of it.'[71] Even Asquith thought Churchill had gone too far, however, and Churchill did need to take notice of him.

Later in September, Churchill and Marsh visited the battlefields of the Franco-Prussian War, especially the decisive Sedan, and watched the German Army manoeuvres as a guest of the Kaiser again, this time near Würzburg. Marsh found Churchill's explanations 'so lucid that for a fleeting instant I saw the campaign with the clear eye of History, or at least of topography'.[72] The Conservative MP Lord Crawford noted a rumour about 'the caddish tactlessness of Churchill', in which it was claimed that he had asked for a French officer to take him around Sedan.[73] This was completely untrue. 'Much as war attracts me and fascinates my mind with its tremendous situations,' Churchill wrote to Clementine from the Kronprinz Hotel in Würzburg, 'I feel more deeply every year . . . what vile and wicked folly and barbarism it all is.'[74]* Churchill was concerned, even at that early date, by the growing might of the German Navy. 'It was no good shutting one's eyes to facts,' he told Count Paul von Metternich, the German Ambassador, in early September, 'and however hard Governments and individuals worked to make a spirit of real trust and confidence between two countries they would make very little headway while there was a continually booming naval policy in Germany.'[75]

Because of the coming German threat, the following month, despite being president of the Board of Trade with no formal *locus standi* in intelligence matters, Churchill was closely involved in the creation of the Secret Service Bureau which was later to become MI5 and MI6. This was done without informing Parliament, and as home secretary in August 1911 he also helped rush the Official Secrets Act through the legislature deftly and almost without debate. It remained on the statute book for seventy-eight years. These initiatives, built on a lifetime's fascination with espionage, signals intelligence and human intelligence, meant that by the 1920s he had studied more espionage-related documents over a longer period and more attentively than any other politician alive.

In October, the King summoned Balfour and Lord Lansdowne, the Unionist leader in the Lords, to Buckingham Palace. He urged them to pass the

* Churchill was unimpressed by the Tiepolos on the ceiling above the staircase of the Residenz, thinking they belonged 'to the whipped cream and sponge cake style of painting' (*CV* II Part 2 p. 911).

Budget and thus preserve their legislative veto, but they told him that their 'Diehard' followers could not be controlled. 'I look on him as my enemy,' Churchill said of Balfour, but he was also 'the most courageous man alive. I believe that if you held a pistol to his face it would not frighten him.'[76] The Liberals certainly seemed to be holding a pistol to the head of the Upper House, but Balfour was not about to back down. In October, Churchill stoked the fire further and told a Dundee audience that it was 'an extraordinary thing' that 10,000 'should own practically the whole land of Great Britain and that the rest should be trespassers on the soil on which they were born'.[77]

The day before, staying at the Queen's Hotel in Dundee, he had half eaten a kipper 'when a huge maggot crept out and flashed his teeth at me!' he told Clementine. 'Such are the trials which great and good men endure in the service of their country!'[78] Their finances were another trial. Having sent Clementine £60 for housekeeping in October, he told her, 'The pug is *décassé* [out of money] for the moment.'[79] (Like her, he was obviously less shy in French.) They would have to holiday in England, but he would be paid £50 when *Liberalism and the Social Problem*, another collection of speeches, was published in November. It was an indication of how hand-to-mouth the newlyweds' financial situation could sometimes be. She replied that they could easily stay in Eccleston Square and miss out on a holiday altogether, for 'My crowning joy will be when I can really be a help to you in your life and a comfort to you in disappointments and deceptions.'[80] Yet Clementine had begun to worry that Churchill was somehow being unfaithful, despite there being no evidence. In his next letter he said in a postscript, 'I have not spoken to a single cat of any sort except my mother!!!!!' Then, a week later, 'Dearest it worries me very much that you should seem to nurse such absolutely wild suspicions which are so dishonouring to all the love and loyalty I bear you, and will please God bear you while I breathe – they are unworthy of you and me. We do not live in a world of small intrigues, but of serious and important affairs [not the aptest of words]. You ought to trust me for I do not love and will never love any woman in the world but you . . . Your sweetness & beauty have cast a glory upon my life.'[81] It was true, and beneath the pug-dog picture on the letter were the words 'wistful but unashamed'. When Clementine re-read this letter half a century later, she could not even remember what it could have been about.

On 4 November 1909, the People's Budget passed the House of Commons by 397 votes to 156. Even after concessions, it retained the higher land taxes and the introduction of a super-tax on incomes over £3,000 (approximately £300,000 today). The consequences of the Lords' rejection of it, Churchill was authorized by Asquith to make clear during the debate, would be a general election.[82] Ten days later, a suffragette named Theresa Garnett assaulted him with a riding-whip at Bristol Temple Meads railway station, even though he was surrounded by detectives.[83] 'He saw the blow coming and grappled with the woman,' recorded *The Times*. 'For a moment there was a struggle . . . The woman was shouting frantically and the words "Take that, you brute, you brute!" could be heard. Mr Churchill wrenched the whip from his assailant's hands.'[84] He went ahead with his meeting at the Colston Hall, though it was badly disrupted by suffragettes, who attempted to break up the meetings of all prominent Liberal politicians, not just Churchill. Garnett was sentenced to one month's imprisonment for disturbing the peace.

*Liberalism and the Social Problem* was published on 26 November. On that same day Lord Milner, one of the leaders of the Tory Diehards, said of the Budget, 'It is our duty to prevent it and to damn the consequences.'[85] Clementine threw a thirty-fifth birthday party for Churchill at Eccleston Square four days later. One of the guests, Lord Esher, reported to his son,

> He has a charming double room on the first floor, all books . . . He had a birthday cake with thirty-five candles. And *crackers*. He sat all the evening with a paper cap, from a cracker, on his head. A queer sight, if all the thousands who go to his meetings could have seen him . . . He and she sit on the same sofa, and he holds her hand. I never saw two people more in love. If he goes out of office, he has not a penny. He would have to earn a living, but he says it is well worth it if you live with someone you love. He would loathe it, but he is ready to live in a lodging – just two rooms – with her and the baby![86]

The dinner ended early so that the party could go to the Lords to watch the vote. The Budget was rejected by 350 to 75. Parliament was dissolved two days later and an election called, voting to get under way on 14 January 1910, which the Liberals would fight on the slogan 'The Peers versus the People'.

During the campaign, Churchill quickly published *The People's Rights*, a distillation of his speeches on Lords reform, the Budget, Free Trade and taxation. He threw himself into the campaign with a flurry of further jibes against his favourite foe. 'Mr. Balfour, of course, is a leader who does whatever his followers tell him,' he told one audience, 'only, when he knows his followers are wrong, he does it half-heartedly.'[87] Lord Curzon, the former Viceroy of India, offered a defence of aristocracy at Oldham, in which he asked, rhetorically, whether Churchill owed anything to his father. 'Why, of course. I owe everything to my father,' Churchill replied in Burnley a few days later.

> But what defence is all this of a House of hereditary legislators? Because my father was member for Woodstock, I do not suggest that I should be permanently member for Woodstock, irrespective of what the people of Woodstock may think of me. It is quite true that some instances can be cited of men who have succeeded distinguished fathers and have attained equal and even greater distinction themselves. But how many cases can be shown of the contrary? You can almost count the hereditary instances on your fingers. In fact Lord Curzon did not cite as many instances as there are fingers on his hands. But only consider the enormous number of contrary instances which have been veiled in a decent and merciful obscurity.[88]

He well understood how rare it was for someone with a distinguished father to succeed in life.

Curzon had quoted the nineteenth-century French philosopher Ernest Renan, who had said, 'All civilization has been the work of aristocracies.' 'They liked that in Oldham,' Churchill said of his predominantly working-class former constituency. 'There was not a duke, not an earl, not a marquis, not a viscount in Oldham who did not feel that a compliment had been paid to him . . . Why, it would be much more true to say the upkeep of the aristocracy has been the hard work of all civilizations.'[89] Curzon complained that Churchill had the 'manners of the mudlark', Lord Newton spoke of the 'nauseous cant of Winston Churchill' and the Duke of Beaufort said he would like to see Churchill and Lloyd George 'in the middle of twenty couples of drag-hounds'. Churchill delightedly reported all this to an audience in Warrington soon afterwards.[90] The clash was covered so widely that the next day the *Washington Post* reported that Churchill was being cut in the Turf Club and that the club servants served him there only 'with evident disinclination'.[91]

Churchill was sent many postcards during the election entitled 'The Rat's Reward' with a picture of a little red rat eating a pot of honey alongside the words 'Salary of the President of the Board of Trade: £2,000 a year'.[92] All sorts of vicious rumours were circulated about the Churchills.* Freddie Birkenhead later recorded Clementine telling him of this period, 'The atmosphere in which they moved was hostile in the extreme. People like Lady Londonderry cut them stone dead. Peggy [Marchioness of]

* When Earl Percy, one of the Hughligans, was found dead in mysterious circumstances in Paris on 30 December – he was in a cheap hotel bedroom near the Gare du Nord, which he had booked under the name Mr Percy – the rumour went around that he had been Clementine's lover and had been killed by Jack Churchill, sent to Paris because his brother was too cowardly to murder him himself (Birkenhead Papers 65/A3). The post-mortem stated he had died of pleurisy, but there were also rumours that he had been killed in a duel.

Crewe, although a Liberal, also behaved oddly, and told her that Winston's association with Lloyd George was embarrassing her and should be stopped. Margot Asquith . . . was hostile and unfriendly.'[93] Clementine, however, 'regarded the hatred as a compliment'. When she was involved in an accident in a cab that caused some blood to flow on the pavement and in the hall of the house in Eccleston Square, 'This immediately caused rumours that Winston was in the habit of beating his wife.'[94] Churchill stopped reading press cuttings about himself. When he visited Harrow he was booed.[95]

Voting in the general election began on 14 January 1910, and continued until 10 February. On 22 January, Churchill was re-elected for Dundee with a slim margin of 10,747 votes against 10,365 for Labour, 4,552 for the Conservative, 4,339 for the Liberal Unionist and 1,512 for the persistent Prohibitionist Edwin Scrymgeour. Across the nation, the result was just as tight, with 275 Liberals elected, 273 Unionists, 82 Irish Nationalists and 40 Labour. Whereas the Liberals had polled 2.88 million votes and Labour 505,000, the Unionists had polled 3.13 million. The Liberals had lost 104 seats and their great majority of 1906, only four years into what could have been a seven-year term. Yet they were still the largest party and Asquith remained in office; with the support of the Irish Nationalists and Labour they had enough votes to pass the People's Budget.

Two days after the last results came in, Asquith offered Churchill the post of chief secretary of Ireland. 'For myself I would like to go either to the Admiralty,' he boldly replied, 'or to the Home Office. It is fitting, if you will allow me to say so – that ministers should occupy a position in the Government which corresponded to some extent with their influence in the country.'[96] Asquith acquiesced, and Churchill became at thirty-five the youngest home secretary since Sir Robert Peel in 1822. He was also the only home secretary (so far) to have been to prison, let alone to have escaped from one.

# 7
# Home Secretary February 1910–September 1911

*If you have an important point to make, don't try to be subtle or clever. Use a pile driver. Hit the point once. Then come back and hit it again. Then hit it a third time.*

Churchill's advice to the Prince of Wales on public speaking, 1919[1]

*My conscience is a good girl. I can always come to terms with her.*

Churchill to General de Gaulle, August 1942[2]

On Monday, 21 February 1910, one week into his job as home secretary, Churchill signed his first death warrant. Since everyone under sentence of death had the right of final appeal for clemency before they were hanged, he had to review every case. Talking to Ian Hamilton's wife Jean at dinner that night, it was clear that the decision had 'weighed on him'. The man in question had taken a child up an alley and brutally cut her throat. ' "Think", he said rather savagely, "of a society that forces a man to do that." ' She thought he was in a 'sensitive and in an excitable mood – alive'.[3] Churchill found the decision-making in these cases 'most painful'. As his son put it years later, 'Conscious of his direct responsibility, he would brood long and hard over each case.'[4] Of the forty-three capital cases presented to him for review, Churchill reprieved twenty-one, a higher rate than the 40 per cent reprieved by his predecessors over the previous decade.[5] He told Wilfrid Blunt 'how it had become a nightmare to him having to exercise his power of life and death in the case of condemned criminals, on an average of one a fortnight. Nearly all the cases of murder are a combination of love and drink.'[6] He nonetheless supported the death penalty, telling Sir Edward Grey, 'To most men – including all the best – a life sentence is worse than a death sentence.'[7] This reflected his personal belief, and was very much the stoical attitude common to soldiers. He also held that in certain circumstances such as 'an incurable disease or disgrace' suicide was acceptable.[8] 'After all,' he told Jean Hamilton, 'we make too much of death.'[9]

On 17 August 1909, Churchill had been able to look beyond his love of the Raj to acknowledge the bravery of the Indian revolutionary Madan Lal Dhingra, who was executed at Pentonville Prison for the assassination of a former viceregal aide-de-camp, Lieutenant-Colonel Sir Curzon Wyllie, in furtherance of a terrorist campaign to get the British to quit India. 'The only lesson required in India at present is to learn how to die,' Dhingra had said just before he was hanged, 'and the only way to teach it is by dying ourselves. Therefore I die, and glory in my martyrdom.'[10] Churchill told Wilfrid Blunt that Dhingra would be remembered in 2,000 years 'as we remember Regulus and Caractacus and Plutarch's heroes', and quoted his last words as 'the finest ever made in the name of patriotism'.[11] He believed it would have been 'an additional torture to have commuted the sentence'. Churchill's open respect for the bravery of his enemies, be they Pathan, Dervish, Boer, Indian revolutionary or, later, the Irish republican Michael Collins and the German General Erwin Rommel, was an attractive feature of his makeup.

Churchill years later told an aide that when he had been home secretary 'His nerves were in a very bad state and he was assailed by worries.'[12] He discovered that the best remedy was 'to write down on a piece of paper all the various matters which are troubling one, from which it will appear that some are merely trivial, some are irremediable, and there are thus only one or two on which one need concentrate one's energies'. Over the centuries, the Home Office had become a portmanteau department for whatever did not fit in elsewhere, so as well as clemency and commutation the list of things Churchill now had to worry about included policing, prisons, probation, the regulation of working conditions, public-house licensing and workmen's compensation for injury.

On 31 March, Lloyd George introduced a Parliament Bill to end the Lords' power to veto legislation connected in any way to money, which came simultaneously with a semi-public threat by Asquith to create 500 new peers overnight, to swamp the Unionist opposition if it failed to pass. Faced with this, and the Unionists having lost two elections in a row, the People's Budget was passed by the Lords in April without a vote. Yet this was not enough to appease the Liberal Government, which wanted fundamentally to alter the constitution and neuter the aristocracy as a political force in Britain. Diehards in the Lords were not about to surrender their veto rights without another fight, one that Asquith, Lloyd George and Churchill were more than willing to give them. Despite the passing of the Budget, the Parliament Bill was not withdrawn.

As home secretary, Churchill had to perform various ceremonial duties, and the sudden death of King Edward VII on 6 May 1910 ought to have provided him with the opportunity of establishing better relations with King George V. It did not happen. The new King was, according to Lord Crawford, personally affronted by the way senior Liberals such as Churchill had supposedly almost bullied his father during the Budget and Parliament Bill crises, although there is no evidence, even if they had, that it had affected his health. 'He did feel the affront deeply,' recorded Crawford: 'so much so that the new King can hardly conceal his sentiments on the matter. Cecil Manners* tells me that when Churchill, as home secretary, was summoned to the Palace when a demise seemed imminent, he was left *downstairs*: not even admitted to an antechamber of the royal apartments.'[13] Crawford could not resist adding 'That Churchill is without conscience or scruple, without a glimmer of the comities of public reserve and deference, we all know, and all, even his closest friends, admit.' His closest friends actually made no such admission.

In the short period of political truce during the public obsequies, Churchill suggested to F. E. Smith that a Liberal–Conservative coalition might find a consensus for Lords reform, federal Home Rule for Ireland, compulsory state-assisted National Insurance, land reform and compulsory military service.[14] Lloyd George supported this idea for a short period, and Smith pressed Balfour and Andrew Bonar Law to follow it up, not least because the King's private secretary Lord Knollys supported it, but nothing came of it. Charles Masterman, who helped Lloyd George design the Budget and opposed a coalition, believed that Churchill's 'passionate' and constant yearning for centrist government revealed 'the aboriginal and unchanging Tory in him', though in fact it was more specifically revealing the unchanging Tory Democrat.[15] In June Churchill had dinner with Lloyd George in the Café Royal, where, he reported to Clementine, 'We renewed treaties of alliance for another seven years.'[16]

An important part of Churchill's new job was to keep public order during the many long and hard-fought strikes that punctuated this period as the result of a generally weak economy and increasing trade union power. In May there was unrest at Newport docks. Churchill agreed to the local authorities' requests to provide 250 foot and 50 mounted policemen to keep order.[17] Sir Edward Troup, the Permanent Under-Secretary at the Home Office, noted that Churchill was 'most anxious' that the military should not be called in.[18] 'Once a week or oftener,' he recalled, 'Mr Churchill came into the office bringing with him some adventurous

* Lord Cecil Manners was a former Tory MP with connections at Court.

or impossible projects; but after half an hour's discussion something was evolved which was still adventurous but not impossible.'[19]

In July, a moderate Parliamentary Franchise (Women) Bill came before the House. In the spring Churchill had supported the establishment of an all-party Conciliation Committee under the chairmanship of his friend Lord Lytton, with Noel Brailsford its secretary, to try to take the issue out of partisan politics. The vote at the time was limited to between six and seven million males on the criterion of homeownership, and if the same criterion were extended to women around one million would have qualified, which seemed to many as if it should be the basis for a compromise.[20] Before the Commons debate on the Bill, Churchill wrote a memorandum detailing all his conversations and meetings on the issue of female suffrage and concluding that he did not intend to vote against it. He changed his mind, however, two days before the debate. He said he thought it 'deeply injurious to the Liberal cause', and decided that as Asquith and Lloyd George were opposing it he would look cowardly in abstaining.[21] Brailsford now described Churchill's stance as 'treacherous' and Lytton accused him of hypocrisy, but Churchill answered that any private views he might have held earlier in favour had to be subject to the view of the Home Office civil servants, a somewhat unconvincing excuse since he had never hidden behind officials' expert advice before.[22]

There were undoubtedly party political considerations at work. What if the propertied women voted Tory?* 'I do not believe that the great mass of women want a vote,' Churchill said in the debate. 'I think they have made singularly little use of the immense opportunities of local and municipal government which have been thrown open to them. Although there are numerous brilliant exceptions, these exceptions do not alter the actual fact.'[23] Neither side was impressed with his position, and although the Bill was passed by a majority of over a hundred on a free vote, it got no further because votes would be whipped against it by the Liberal Government.

'Winston is in a rather tepid manner a suffragist (his wife is very keen) and he came down to the Home Office intending to vote for the Bill,' Lucy Masterman recorded. When her husband Charles, who opposed it, gave Churchill some rhetorical lines about how divorcees and some 'fallen women' (prostitutes) would get the vote under the terms of the Bill because they were property-owners, whereas a blameless mother of a family might not, 'Winston began to see the opportunity for a speech on these lines,

* As they did in the 1955, 1959 and 1970 elections, which would have been won by Labour under solely male suffrage.

and as he paced up and down the room, began to roll them off in long phrases. By the end of the morning he was convinced that he had always been hostile to the Bill and that he had already thought of all these points himself. The result was a speech of such violence and harshness that Lady Maclean [wife of Liberal MP Sir Donald] wept in the gallery and Lord Lytton cut him in public.'[24] Even though he must have known that it would apply in only a small number of cases, Churchill told the Commons, 'There is no end to the grotesque absurdities that would follow the passing of this measure. It would be possible for women to have a vote while living in a state of prostitution; if she married and became an honest woman she would lose that vote, but she could regain it through divorce.'[25] A regular criticism of Churchill was that, as Asquith put it to his close friend Venetia Stanley,* 'Winston thinks with his mouth,' meaning that he adopted policies because they sounded good in speeches.[26] (This was a charge also sometimes levelled by the Chiefs of Staff during the Second World War.) It was usually unfair, but not in the case of female suffrage. Churchill could hardly have been surprised when the suffragettes redoubled their efforts after this to disrupt his public meetings.

By total contrast, Churchill's speech on prison reform on 10 July reflected a profound liberalism. His own very short experience of incarceration had filled him with a horror of captivity. He told the Commons,

> The mood and temper of the public in regard to the treatment of crime and criminals is one of the most unfailing tests of the civilization of any country. A calm and dispassionate recognition of the rights of the accused against the State, and even of convicted criminals against the State, a constant heart-searching by all charged with the duty of punishment, a desire and eagerness to rehabilitate in the world of industry all those who have paid their dues in the hard coinage of punishment, tireless efforts towards the discovery of curative and regenerating processes, and an unfaltering faith that there is a treasure, if you can only find it, in the heart of every man – these are the symbols which in the treatment of crime and criminals mark and measure the stored-up strength of a nation, and are the sign and proof of the living virtue in it.[27]

In 1908 and 1909 over 180,000 people were in prison in Britain, around half for failure to pay a fine on time.[28] Churchill argued that more time should be allowed for payment, since the best principle for a prison system

* Asquith wrote her numerous love-letters, but their relationship was probably not consummated.

should be to 'prevent as many people as possible from getting there'.[29] He set in motion processes by which the number of people imprisoned for failing to pay a fine for drunkenness was reduced from 62,000 to 1,600 over the next decade.[30]

Churchill also searched for alternative punishments for petty offences, especially by children, as he saw prison as a place of last resort for serious offenders.[31] When he visited Pentonville Prison in October, he released youths imprisoned for minor offences and although he was not at the Home Office long enough to reform the penal system as a whole, he reduced the sentences of nearly 400 individuals.[32] He also introduced music and libraries into prisons, tried to improve the conditions of suffragettes imprisoned for disturbing the peace and reduced the maximum amount of time that prisoners could be kept in solitary confinement to thirty days.

Churchill was lambasted in the press and Parliament when a Dartmoor shepherd called David Davies, a burglar whose sentence he had commuted, was caught housebreaking again soon after his release.[33] Years later Clementine recalled that Davies 'was quite alright when he was tending sheep, but whenever he fell on hard times, he rifled poor boxes in churches. When he was asked why he did this, he used to reply that the boxes were labelled "For the Poor", and as he was certainly poor, the money was obviously for him.'[34]

In the summer of 1910, Churchill embarked on a two-month cruise in the Mediterranean on board *Honor*, the yacht of the Baron de Forest, a fellow Liberal MP who shared an early interest in aviation and often hosted him. 'You will be glad to hear that I visited the Monte Carlo Gambling Hell on four occasions,' he reported to Marsh from Naples, 'and took away from them altogether upwards of £160.'[35] Official pouches of Home Office work reached him at Athens and Smyrna, and he sat on the cowcatcher of a special train the whole 260 miles of the British-built railway to Aydin in Turkey's Aegean region. There was 'no better way', he told Sir Edward Grey, 'of seeing a country in a flash'. They sailed through the Dardanelles to Constantinople, where he learned about the successes of German, and the difficulties of British, diplomacy with Turkey.[36]

'The only view I have formed about this part of the world of ruined civilizations and harshly jumbled races is this,' he told the Foreign Secretary: 'why can't England and Germany come together in strong action and for general advantage?'[37] He doubted this would be possible, however, telling Wilfrid Blunt on a shooting weekend in mid-October, 'We should hold on to Egypt as we hold on to India. It was not that it brought us any advantage but it was impossible to go back on what we had undertaken, a necessity of Empire. The fate of Egypt would be decided by the issue of the coming war with Germany.'[38]

Probably under the influence of his reading of Darwin, Churchill was briefly a convinced eugenicist. In October 1910 he noted that there were at least 120,000 'feeble-minded people at large in our midst' in Britain whom he thought should be 'segregated under proper conditions so that their curse died with them and was not transmitted to future generations'.[39] He was interested in the possibility of sterilization, telling Asquith in December that the 'multiplication of the [mentally] unfit' constituted 'a very terrible danger to the race'.[40] He saw sterilization as a liberating measure that would protect the feeble-minded from incarceration, but it was never introduced in Britain.

As well as being an (absent) member of the first international Eugenics Conference in July 1912, Churchill was one of the early drafters of the Mental Deficiency Act 1913, which defined four grades of what it called 'mental defectives' who could be incarcerated, namely 'idiots', 'imbeciles', 'the feeble-minded' and 'moral defectives', although it rejected sterilization. This thinking was so uncontroversial across all the parties in those days that the Bill passed with only three votes cast against. As with his views on race, Churchill's support for eugenics needs to be seen in the context of the scientific beliefs of the day, which were shared by thinkers on the left such as H. G. Wells, Sydney Webb, John Maynard Keynes and William Beveridge and distinguished jurists such as Oliver Wendell Holmes.

In early November, 25,000 miners went on strike in the Rhondda Valley in South Wales over pay. The Chief Constable of Glamorgan had 1,400 policemen there, but asked for more, and also for troops. Churchill sent 300 Metropolitan Police officers, and although troops were dispatched to the area under the command of General Sir Nevil Macready they were not deployed after serious rioting broke out on 7 and 8 November in Tonypandy in the Rhondda Valley, where sixty-three shops were damaged and looted. One striker was killed, even though the police used rolled-up raincoats to control the violence.[41] Churchill's decision not to use troops was criticized by *The Times* for showing weakness but praised by the *Manchester Guardian* as having 'saved many lives'.[42] Yet in Labour mythology Churchill was for decades held personally responsible for brutally suppressing the innocent workers of Tonypandy through military action.

'Looking back at it now it is difficult to see what else a resolute Home Secretary could have done,' admitted George Isaacs, a senior trade unionist at the time and later chairman of the Trades Union Congress. 'On later occasions it could be said that Churchill was too ready to use troops, but on this occasion his influence seems to have been a moderating one.'[43] Churchill was in fact far from the ideological opponent of organized labour that he has been made to seem. At that point he had good relations with the trade unions, telling the TUC Parliamentary Committee in March 1911 that he was 'powerfully impressed with the enormous value of the work which the Trade Union body are doing . . . It is of the greatest use to a public department like the Home Office that the study of these [industrial relations] questions . . . should be supplemented by the constant experience that you gentlemen . . . are alone able to bring to bear upon the problems.'[44]

At a strike in Llanelli in South Wales in August 1911, events grew so out of hand that Churchill did send in troops. They shot dead two rioters who had attacked a train under military protection, had refused to disperse and had beaten its engineer unconscious. The rioting in Monmouthshire and eastern parts of Glamorgan took on a darker and more disturbing aspect when a mob of 250 people attacked Jewish-owned businesses in what has been termed the 'Tredegar pogrom'. Churchill and Lord Haldane, the Secretary for War, were quick to send troops there too, to protect the Jews. Troops were also used to quell riots in Liverpool, including cavalry who had orders to fire over the heads of the crowd (there were no injuries).

To deal with Britain's first national rail strike, in mid-August, Churchill sent thousands of troops to rail centres throughout the country, with twenty rounds of ammunition each, and gave the local commanders wide powers.[45] The Labour Party leader, Ramsay MacDonald, called this move 'diabolical'. 'This is not a medieval state and it is not Russia,' he said, 'it is not even Germany.' Even Masterman referred to Churchill's 'whiff-of-grapeshot' attitude, referring to Napoleon putting down the Paris mob in 1795.[46]

Churchill defended his strike-breaking action, on the grounds that much of the country's food moved by rail. 'If [the strike] had not been interrupted it would have hurled the whole of that great community into an abyss of horror which no man can dare to contemplate,' he said with his customary extravagance.[47] He nonetheless cleared the trade union officials of responsibility for the disorders, and shepherded through the Commons the Trade Union Bill of 1913, which allowed trade unions to use funds for political purposes. 'Representation in Parliament is absolutely necessary to trade unions,' he said. 'I consider that every workman is well advised to join a trade union . . . to protect the rights and interests of labour.'[48]

The London dock strike of late July was resolved peacefully in early

August. Ben Tillett, the dockers' leader, wrote that Churchill had been a moderating influence:

> Slightly bent, hesitant of speech, almost an apologetic manner, youth left in mobile features, ready for boyish fun, the cares of office sitting lightly on a good-sized brow, eyes that sparkle with a wistfulness almost sweet – this was the modern Nero, whose terrible power had been threatened against us. The responsible person for the South Wales riots and shootings, who had ultimately to be responsible for the shooting in Llanelly.

Tillett accepted that Churchill had 'turned a deaf ear to [the] clamours of the cowardly crew who would . . . have gloated over the killing of their fellow-creatures'.[49]

On 18 November, 117 women and one man were arrested at a full-scale riot in and around Parliament Square in London, on what the suffragettes termed 'Black Friday'. Churchill ordered their release, but the suffragette leaders blamed him for the police brutality that had taken place, including instances of, in Brailsford's words to Masterman, 'kicking them with the knee between the legs from behind which is dangerous and painful as well as disgusting, and twisting or handling the breasts. Also of course arm twisting and forcing back the thumb.'[50] Masterman noted 'Seen by S[ecretary of]/S[tate]' on the letter. This does not mean, as has been alleged, that Churchill had turned a blind eye, let alone approved of what had happened; indeed he is likely to have been just as disgusted as Brailsford. He considered suing Christabel Pankhurst for libel when she accused him of having ordered the police brutality, but he was persuaded not to by Sir John Simon, the Solicitor-General, on grounds of setting a dangerous precedent. Churchill did upbraid Sir Edward Henry, the head of the Metropolitan Police, saying that 'very regrettable scenes occurred. It was my desire to avoid this even at some risk . . . In future I must ask for a strict adherence to the policy' of treating women with respect and with minimum violence.[51] He did not, however, order an inquiry.

Four days later, Augustine Birrell, the Chief Secretary of Ireland, was beaten up by a group of suffragettes, leaving him temporarily lame and in danger of losing his kneecap. That same day, in what was later termed the Battle of Downing Street, a group of suffragettes including Anne Cobden-Sanderson, whom Churchill knew socially, attacked Asquith outside No. 10. Churchill happened to be on the scene. 'Take that woman away,' he told the police, 'she is obviously one of the ringleaders.'[52] This was overheard by Hugh Franklin, an undergraduate at Caius College, Cambridge, and a militant suffragist who had also been at the Black Friday demonstration. On 26 November, having addressed a meeting in Bradford, Churchill was on his way to the dining car in the train home when Franklin attacked him with a horsewhip, shouting, 'Take that, you dirty cur!'[53] He was overpowered and sentenced to six weeks in prison for assault. Churchill considered suing Franklin for libel for stating in print that on Black Friday he had ordered 'his thousands of trained servants to become a real set of hooligans', but as with the Pankhurst libel Simon persuaded him against it, this time because it would give his opponents free publicity.

Parliament was dissolved in November 1910 for a second general election that year, to be held between 2 and 19 December, in order to decide the momentous issue of the Lords' veto powers. The King had promised Asquith that if the Liberals won he would create enough new peers to pass the Parliament Bill (two of whom, Churchill recommended, should be Ian Hamilton and Wilfrid Blunt). During the campaign, both male and female suffragists had to be ejected from Churchill's meetings on 22, 26, 28 and 30 November and 9 December. The election provided Churchill with an opportunity to make it clear that he did not consider women's sex to be the reason that he opposed female suffrage, but that he was, as he said in Dundee on 2 December 1910, 'in favour of the principle of women being enfranchised'. But he said he 'would not vote for any Bill which he considered would have the effect of unfairly altering the balance between the parties by giving an undoubted preponderance to the property [that is, Tory] vote; and he would not vote for any Bill unless he was convinced that it had behind it the genuine majority of electors'.[54]

Churchill remained unfailingly polite to the female disruptors but he was predictably rumbustious towards the male ones, saying in a speech in Lambeth, 'I am told that individuals are to be singled out for villainous assaults. If that is so there is only one word for it, and that is "come on". If a public man were to allow his course to be altered by mere threats of personal violence, he would be unworthy of the slightest respect or confidence.'[55] In the same speech he attacked Smith, his closest friend but a Tory supporter of the Lords' veto, saying that 'whereas Mr. Lloyd George is invariably witty, Mr. F. E. Smith is invariably vulgar.'[56] As always, politics was never allowed to get in the way of friendship, but also vice versa.

The same was true of others. On 8 December, when someone mentioned Churchill to Lloyd George, Charles Masterman recorded that the Chancellor 'got a little indignant. It is difficult to say whether a tiny element of jealousy does not enter in.' Lloyd George said of Churchill, who had baulked at confiscatory taxation of the rich, that he had had to 'remind him that no man can rat twice. Oh, he'll come to heel alright. He always

1. Churchill thought this portrait by Sir William Orpen to be the best likeness of the many made of him. It was painted in 1916, when he was out of office after the Dardanelles defeat.

2. The front façade of Blenheim Palace in Oxfordshire, home of the dukes of Marlborough, where Churchill was born in 1874. 'We have nothing to equal this,' said King George III when he visited.

3. Lord Randolph Churchill, Winston's aloof, distant, reproachful father, whom he spent a lifetime trying to impress.

4. Jennie Jerome, Winston's beautiful, headstrong and usually absent American socialite mother.

5. Elizabeth Everest, Churchill's beloved nanny.

6. Aristocratic entitlement in a seven-year-old's pose.

THE CHARTWELL TRUST

My dear Mamma

I hope you will come and see me soon. Did Everest give you my flour I sent you. Give my love to my ants and tell not to forget to come down. I am comeinge home In a month.

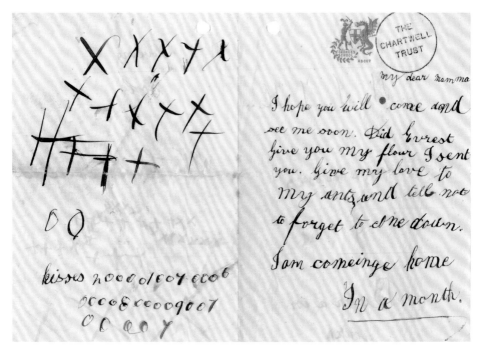

7. The eight-year-old Winston's letters begging his mother to visit him at school went largely unheeded.

8. 'General Conduct: Very bad – is a constant trouble to everybody, and is always in some scrape or other. Headmaster's Remarks: He cannot be trusted to behave himself anywhere. He has very good abilities.' Churchill's school reports reveal him not to be the dunce he depicted himself to be in his autobiography, though he was consistently among the naughtiest pupils of every school he attended.

9. Dr Welldon's house photo at Harrow in 1892; Churchill is leaning over the railings. Behind him is George Hoare, who died of wounds sustained in 1915. Eleven of the boys in this photograph were dead by the end of the First World War.

10. Churchill's brother Jack was the first officer casualty on board the hospital ship *Maine*, which their mother Jennie fitted out and took to the Boer War.

11. Churchill in South Africa in 1899. He wore his Spanish Cross of the Order of Military Merit medal ribbon against Army regulations. He soon shaved off his moustache because it was too light coloured.

12. He returned to Durban a hero, after having escaped from a prisoner-of-war camp in Pretoria in November 1899.

13. With Kaiser Wilhelm II watching German Imperial Army manoeuvres in 1906.

14. Sitting on the cowcatcher of his train in East Africa are (*left to right*) Eddie Marsh, Churchill's uncle Colonel Gordon Wilson, Sir James Hayes Sadler (Commissioner of Uganda), Churchill.

15. Clementine Hozier, just before her marriage to Churchill.

16. The couple emerging from St Margaret's, Westminster, after their wedding on 12 September 1908.

17. The Irish suffragette Mary Maloney rang a large bell to drown out Churchill's stump speeches during the May 1908 by-election in Dundee.

18. On board the Admiralty yacht HMS *Enchantress* in the Mediterranean in 1912 are (*left to right*) Herbert Asquith, his daughter Violet (later Lady Violet Bonham Carter), Churchill and Churchill's private secretaries James Masterton-Smith and Eddie Marsh.

19. Admiral Lord 'Jacky' Fisher: Churchill's mercurial colleague, friend and nemesis.

20. David Lloyd George sowed the seeds of the welfare state with Churchill, but thereafter their relations alternated between friendly and fractious until Lloyd George's death in 1945.

does when he sees which way the wind is turning. The question is how long he takes about it and how much harm he does in the meantime.'[57] Although Churchill did not realize it, Lloyd George's political alliance with him was only ever that: political. 'If we put in a special clause in the Budget exempting Sunny from taxation,' Lloyd George remarked, 'Winston would let us do what we liked.'[58] That was totally untrue and unfair, but a typical jibe behind his back. Churchill was entirely unaware of Lloyd George's private antipathy, and accepted his hospitality. When out walking with Lloyd George at his house in Criccieth, Wales, that year, Churchill fell into a stream. 'He was not in the least angry,' recalled a fellow guest, 'and when he got up said cheerfully, "As I am wet through, I may as well have some fun out of it," and stayed for half an hour wallowing in the stream and damming up the flow with stones, during which his wife sat on the edge with a very short skirt which she had pulled well above her knees. [Lloyd] George stood watching him.'[59]

The final election results revealed that the Liberals and Unionists had each won 272 seats, alongside eighty-four Irish Nationalists and forty-two Labour. The Unionists had won 2.42 million votes, the Liberals 2.30 million and Labour 372,000. Asquith continued in power, but was dependent on Irish Nationalist support, whose price was nothing short of Home Rule.

On the morning of 3 January 1911, Churchill wrote to Asquith from Eccleston Square. He thought the Liberals should compromise with the Unionists over large areas of their legislative programme, but only if they would agree to thoroughgoing constitutional change, including the Parliament Bill, which would end the House of Lords' power of veto over legislation. 'After the veto has been restricted,' he wrote, 'I hope we may be able to pursue *une politique d'apaisement*.'* This would include an Order of Merit for Joseph Chamberlain, privy councillorships for Bonar Law and Smith, 'a liberal grant of honours' for leading Unionist MPs and newspaper proprietors, an offer to 'confer' on Ireland, the Poor Law, child labour and National Insurance, and an undertaking that Balfour should be given 'full access to all Admiralty information'. Meanwhile, death duties ought not to fall on landed estates more than once in a quarter of a century.[60] He was even willing to countenance small tariffs on French and Portuguese wine, a significant retreat from his earlier stance of not giving, as he had said in one speech, 'a farthing's preference on a single peppercorn'.[61]

While Churchill was writing this letter, a Home Office messenger

* His first recorded use of the word 'appeasement' was therefore positive, and in French.

arrived with news that earlier that morning three Russian anarchist-terrorist would-be jewel thieves, armed with Mausers and led by the mysterious Riga-born Peter Straume (alias 'Peter the Painter'), had been trapped by police at a house in Sidney Street in London's East End. On 16 December they had killed three policemen and wounded two more, after which a pistol, 750 cartridges, nitroglycerine and bottles of nitric acid had been found at their safe house in nearby Gold Street. On the morning of 3 January, more shots had been exchanged and a sergeant wounded.[62] Churchill went to Sidney Street to observe the situation, which the local police were dealing with.[63] 'Now and again a pistol shot, fired, one would say, more in general defiance than with deliberate aim, would come from an attic window of No. 100,' a journalist recorded.[64]

Churchill did not issue any orders, but he did make the sensible suggestion that steel plates be brought from the Woolwich Armoury to provide portable cover for snipers.[65] (Churchill was one of the few people present with personal knowledge of the effectiveness of the Mauser automatic pistols the terrorists were using.) Otherwise, his sole contributions were to call up a platoon of Scots Guards from where they were protecting the Crown Jewels at the Tower of London, and approve the decision to do nothing when the building unexpectedly caught fire shortly after 1 p.m.[66] 'I thought it better to let the house burn down, than spend good British lives in rescuing these ferocious rascals,' he later explained to Asquith.[67]

Churchill was photographed in a top hat and fur-lined overcoat with astrakhan collar, taking cover in the doorway of a warehouse with the heads of the Criminal Investigation Department, Metropolitan Police and Scotland Yard's Political Section, occasionally peering around a corner towards No. 100, in what was soon dubbed the Sidney Street Siege or the Battle of Stepney. Two bodies were found in the charred remains of the house; one with a bullet wound, the other asphyxiated. Peter the Painter was never apprehended.

When, back at the Home Office, Masterman criticized Churchill for having gone to Sidney Street, Churchill lisped: 'Now Charlie. Don't be croth. It was such fun.'[68] On returning to Eccleston Square he continued his interrupted letter to the Prime Minister, giving him an animated account – 'firing from every window, bullets chipping the brickwork, police and Scots Guards armed with loaded weapons, artillery jingling up, etc.'.[69] Yet because the physical presence of the Home Secretary was not necessary for this operation his judgement was soon called into question. It seemed to fit into a narrative of Churchillian self-advertisement, what in a different context Lucy Masterman described as 'his appetite for applause, which is very nearly insatiable . . . He cannot resist the limelight in any form.'[70] Even the normally supportive journalist A. G. Gardiner was to write the next year, 'He is always unconsciously playing a part – an heroic part. And he is himself his most astonished spectator.'[71]

When Churchill's image came on to the Pathé newsreels reporting the Siege in cinemas after the incident, it was booed.[72] The Siege also gave Balfour a long-awaited chance for a jibe; in the Commons on 6 February he said, 'He was, I understand, in military phrase, in what is known as the zone of fire – he and a photographer were both risking valuable lives. I understand what the photographer was doing, but what was the right honourable Gentleman doing?'[73] Years later Churchill admitted that he had been wrong to go, and that his 'convictions of duty were supported by a strong sense of curiosity which perhaps it would have been well to keep in check'.[74] Yet in the long run his willingness to go to the scene of action would serve his country well.

Besides attending royal births and deaths, one of the Home Secretary's vestigial duties was to write regular letters to the King summarizing what had happened in Parliament each day. Edward VII had enjoyed the tone that Churchill employed – which was more jocular than was customary in home secretaries – but George V did not. 'As for tramps and wastrels, there ought to be proper labour colonies where they could be sent,' Churchill wrote on 10 February. 'It must not, however, be forgotten that there are idlers and wastrels at both ends of the social scale.'[75] The King found these views 'very socialistic' and they prompted an exchange of letters between Churchill and Knollys in which Churchill suggested that someone other than the busy Home Secretary could undertake the task of daily parliamentary reporter, before the King relented and admitted that Churchill's letters were 'always very interesting'.[76] Knollys, perfectly representing Establishment thinking, and expressing it with predictable cliché, simply thought Churchill was 'rather like a bull in a china shop'.[77]

Churchill certainly appeared that way in a debate on the Revenue Bill on 9 March, after Hugh Cecil had accused the Government of breaking its word in a way that, if an individual had behaved similarly in pecuniary matters, would have led to prison. 'I am so much accustomed to the controversial methods of the noble lord who deals always in taunts and in insults,' Churchill said of his own best man.[78] Crawford noted the next day that 'Churchill succeeded in disgusting his friends and foes indiscriminately. What a cad he is.'[79] But barbs that might have crushed a lesser figure never so much as dented Churchill's carapace. 'I never complain of hard words across the floor of the House,' he said in a debate on the Parliament Bill on 4 April 1911, 'but I claim to be allowed to match them with arguments equal to the attack which has been made' – and he always did.[80]

One problem facing the Cabinet during this period was the amount that Asquith was drinking (one of his nicknames was 'Squiffy'). 'On Thursday night the PM was very bad,' Churchill told Clementine,

> and I squirmed with embarrassment. He could hardly speak and many people noticed. He continues most friendly and benevolent and entrusts me with everything after dinner. Up till that time he is at his best – but thereafter! It is an awful pity, and only the persistent freemasonry of the H[ouse] of C[ommons] prevents a scandal. I like the old boy and admire both his intellect and his character. But what risks to run. We only got him away the other night just before Balfour began the negotiations [on the Parliament Bill] which I conducted, but which otherwise would have fallen to him – with disastrous consequences. The next day he was serene, efficient, undisturbed.[81]

The House of Lords finally passed the Parliament Bill on 10 August 1911. It had taken two years and two general elections, but now the elected House of Commons was supreme over the hereditary and appointed House of Lords. Churchill had negotiated much of the eventual deal. It made him deeply distrusted and disliked among the Tory Diehards, and by many of his own class, but it brought Britain closer to becoming a fully functioning modern democracy.

On Thursday, 18 May 1911, the Other Club met for the first time. It was in time to become an important part of Churchill's social life, and of his political career, in a way not often fully recognized. It is untrue that it owed its existence to Churchill and F. E. Smith's having been blackballed from The Club, a leading Establishment dining club of the day. The Other Club had a very definite political purpose, that of promoting cross-party cooperation, and even perhaps one day of bringing about the Liberal–Conservative coalition after which Churchill always hankered, one that would allow sensible centrists to rule without the need to pander to Irish Nationalists, socialists or the extremes of the Unionist and Liberal parties.

The Other Club was originally intended to meet fortnightly in the Pinafore Room at the Savoy Hotel whenever Parliament was in session. The table there was only 2½ feet wide, encouraging the congenial atmosphere its founders sought, and although the room was renovated in 1925 it has stayed exactly the same ever since.* It was intended to have twelve MPs from each of the two major parties as members, as well as a few

* The urinals down the corridor are the same as in 1911 too.

distinguished outsiders. To emphasize the non-partisan ideal behind the club, Lord Knollys chaired the first dinner, and the King's deputy private secretary, Sir Arthur Bigge (later Lord Stamfordham), was also present.

Since both the joint secretaries, liable in the Club rules for 'all unforeseen obligations', Bolton Eyres-Monsell and Freddie Guest, were party whips, parliamentary pairing for votes was easily arranged so that dinner wasn't interrupted by divisions in the Commons. The early Liberal members included Charles Masterman, William Dudley Ward (whose wife Freda was to be the Prince of Wales's mistress before Wallis Simpson) and Rufus Isaacs. The Conservatives included Admiral Lord Charles Beresford, who was a bitter critic of Churchill's, Waldorf Astor and several Tory Democrat social-reforming MPs with whom Churchill had worked before he crossed the floor. Lord Winterton was a member too, despite occasionally being a strong critic of Churchill, and so was Churchill's friend the Liberal MP Jack Seely, a Boer War hero who had crossed the floor with him and taken over from him as under-secretary at the Colonial Office. The Radical Liberal MP Arthur Ponsonby was pressed to join, but distrusted Churchill too much to do so.

Membership required a fairly sturdy constitution: a bill of fare (the term Churchill preferred to 'menu') from one of the early dinners announced six courses, of Oeuf Pluvier, Consommé, Tay Salmon, Medallions of Veal, Aylesbury Farci Anglais and Canapé Diane. The Club rules included 'The names of the Executive Committee shall be wrapped in impenetrable mystery,' and 'Nothing in the rules or intercourse of the Club shall interfere with the rancour or asperity of party politics.'[82] Yet it was set up precisely to assuage rancour, and to provide a forum where senior Liberal and Conservative politicians could meet socially, only three months before the deeply divisive Parliament Act. Lloyd George and Bonar Law initially went there quite often – both of them dined three times in May and June 1911. Lloyd George also came three times in 1912–13 and Law another three times up to November 1911. After that, party asperity was such that Bonar Law did not return until the outbreak of the Great War, when the Club met only once – on 5 August 1914, the day after war had been declared – before March 1916. Bonar Law was the key figure (along with Balfour) for any hope of coalition, and when he ceased attending, Churchill's major ambition for the Club was effectively dead.

Only after its immediate raison d'être had disappeared did the Club start to reflect Churchill's and Smith's personal friendships, although there was always much more to it than that. In the words of one of its members, 'The Club had never been just an assembly of Churchill's cronies. It had been a tonic, not merely a featherbed.'[83] Later members included his brother

Jack, cousins Viscount Castlereagh and Sunny Marlborough, as well as powerful newspapermen such as J. L. Garvin, Sir George Riddell and Lords Northcliffe, Beaverbrook and Rothermere. Non-political members included a wide galère of Smith's and Churchill's friends and acquaintances over the years, including the actor-manager Sir Herbert Beerbohm Tree, architect Sir Edwin Lutyens, industrialist Sir Harry McGowan and a large number of writers including H. G. Wells, P. G. Wodehouse, John Buchan and Anthony Hope, the author of *The Prisoner of Zenda*. There were several soldiers such as Sir John French, Jan Smuts and, perhaps surprisingly in light of his and Churchill's past relations, Lord Kitchener. Several members had insights on the Middle East: Sir Mark Sykes co-authored the Sykes–Picot Agreement that split the region into zones of influence after the Great War, and Air Marshal Sir John Salmond policed Iraq from the air in 1919. There was also one Irish Nationalist MP, T. P. O'Connor, although he was probably elected for the books he wrote, including one on Napoleon. The Club inevitably had its black sheep – Lord Kylsant was imprisoned for fraud, and Sir Oswald Mosley for Fascism.

The Club's Betting Book gives an indication of the eclectic nature of the subjects discussed. These include dates of dissolutions of Parliament, outcomes of court cases and tennis matches, the fate of Lloyd George's would-be assassins after suffragettes bombed his country house, the extent of military advances on battlefields, who was better at translating certain Greek verses, whether 'the marriage between A and B on 1st December 1920 proves fruitful',* who would be the next prime minister,† the contents of books, the level of stock prices during the Great Depression, Grand National winners, the Boat Race, the age of Sir Kenneth Clark, the next American president, and several in which the writing is sadly illegible, possibly as a result of drink. When there were thirteen around the table, Churchill had a 2-foot-high wooden black cat called Kaspar placed on an empty chair.‡ A napkin was tied around Kaspar's neck, and he would be served the whole meal, dish after dish.

Churchill was to attend more than 300 dinners of the Other Club, by far the largest number of meals he ever had in one place other than with his own family.[84] Clementine did not begrudge him his Club evenings, despite his 'coming home very late. I don't mind. He ought to see his friends.'[85] Yet with Churchill there was very often a political angle to friendship, as became powerfully evident in his great crisis of 1940, when

* The Duke of Marlborough's forty-five-year-old daughter Lady Norah Spencer-Churchill married the forty-six-year-old Francis Bradley-Birt; they did have issue.

† Birkenhead bet John Seely £300 to £10 it wouldn't be himself.

‡ He can be seen today in the foyer of the Savoy.

an extraordinarily large number of Other Club members came together in several different ways to help make him prime minister, and then to serve in his wartime Government. The Other Club might have failed to contribute towards national coalition-building before the First World War, but in keeping it alive for another three decades Churchill created something that was to make a real contribution to just that in the Second, long after many of its original founders were dead.

On 28 May 1911, Randolph Churchill, nicknamed 'the Chumbolly' (Farsi for a healthy, chubby newborn baby), was born at Eccleston Square. The baby's name was chosen out of filial piety, and his middle names, Frederick and Edward, after his godfathers F. E. Smith and Sir Edward Grey.[86] In his autobiography, written in January 1959, Randolph recalled being a 'very naughty' child, throwing his nursery-maid's wristwatch out of a top-storey window and singing, 'Nanny's going, nanny's going, hurrah! Hurrah!' at the departure of each successive incumbent, few of whom stayed very long. 'Diana was more docile than I was,' he admitted. 'I could never brook authority or discipline.'[87] Randolph's great misfortune was that he inherited a full measure of his father's ambition, unconventionality and self-confidence, but not a fraction of his charm, self-discipline or sensitivity. He developed a particularly bad relationship with his mother, Clementine, who invariably took her husband's side in rows between them.[88]

Clementine feared she would not be able to attend the Coronation of King George V on 22 June, so soon after Randolph's birth, but the King offered her a place in his private box and sent one of the royal broughams to take her from Eccleston Square to Westminster Abbey and back again. (As soon as she heard this, Jennie made sure to take Clementine's place next to Winston in the Abbey.)[89] As home secretary, Churchill rode in a state coach with the Duchess of Devonshire and the Countess of Minto. He was both cheered and booed along the route. 'It was rather embarrassing for these two Tory dames,' he told Clementine. 'They got awfully depressed when the cheering was very loud, but bucked up a little around the Mansion House when there were more hostile demonstrations . . . I did not acknowledge any cheering and paid no attention at all to the crowds.'[90] As home secretary, Churchill also played a major part in the Investiture of Edward as the Prince of Wales (later King Edward VIII and then Duke of Windsor) at Carnarvon Castle on 14 July. 'He is a very nice boy,' he wrote from the Royal Yacht *Victoria & Albert*, 'quite simple and terribly kept in order.'[91] Churchill's friendship with the Prince, who turned out not to be a very nice boy at all when his father was no longer there to keep him in order, was to cause him much trouble in the years ahead.

That same month, Germany caused a war scare when she sent the gunboat *Panther* to the Moroccan port of Agadir. This was a clear provocation of France, in whose zone of influence Agadir lay. The incident had a profound effect on Churchill, convincing him of Britain's need to be allied with France and, he hoped, Russia too, if Germany was to be prevented from dominating the European continent.[92] He supported Lloyd George's warning to Germany against adventurism, and the dispatching of a British fleet to Morocco to monitor developments. 'I hope we are going to be firm with those treacherous Germans,' he told Clementine.[93]

The Agadir Crisis prompted Churchill to write a Cabinet paper entitled 'Military Aspects of the Continental Problem'. This remarkable document set out what he thought would happen in the opening stages of a war with Germany. 'The German armies advancing through Belgium and onwards into France will be relatively weakened,' he wrote.

> By the fortieth day, Germany should be extended at full strain both internally and on her war fronts, and this strain will become daily more severe and ultimately overwhelming, unless it is relieved by decisive victories in France. If the French army has not been squandered by precipitate or desperate action, the balance of forces should be favourable after the fortieth day, and will improve steadily as time passes.[94]

Brigadier Henry Wilson, the Director of Military Operations at the War Office, dismissed the idea of Germany violating Belgian neutrality, and described the paper as 'ridiculous and fantastic'. In the event, the fortieth day after German mobilization three years later fell on 9 September 1914, the very day that the British Expeditionary Force counter-attacked across the Marne, so helping to prevent the Germans from taking Paris. By that time the French had suffered 210,000 casualties, including 10 per cent of their officer corps.[95]

On 23 August 1911 the Committee of Imperial Defence held a full day's discussion, chaired by Asquith, on what the War Office and Admiralty planned to do in the event of a German invasion of France. Churchill had been invited as home secretary, as the author of the Agadir paper and because he was the only Cabinet minister besides Lord Pentland, the Secretary of State for Scotland, who had served in the armed forces. The meeting provoked so severe a crisis that Churchill had to be moved from the Home Office after only twenty months in the job in order to sort out the chaos in British strategy.

Brigadier Wilson, standing by an enormous map, examined the probable German plan for unleashing 110 divisions against the 85 French in north-west France, and explained how a British Expeditionary Force (BEF) of six divisions would need to be sent immediately to the French extreme left to help repulse the German first wave. Admiral Sir Arthur Wilson, the First Sea Lord, the most senior officer in the Royal Navy, then expounded the principle of a close blockade of the enemy's ports in which the Army's role was reduced to carrying out raids in the Baltic once the German High Seas Fleet had been defeated. 'It was very soon apparent that a profound difference existed between the War Office and Admiralty view,' recalled Churchill.[96]

The Admiralty thought that if the BEF were not sent to France but instead used in counter-strikes on the German coast it would draw off more than its weight in numbers from the German fighting line. Admiral Wilson's view was 'violently combated' by Brigadier Wilson, and the meeting descended into 'complete discord'.[97] (It predictably became known as the Battle of the Wilsons.)[98] When Admiral Wilson refused to give assurances that the Navy would transport six divisions to France in the event of war, Churchill recognized that he and the political head of the Navy, Reginald McKenna, the First Lord of the Admiralty, needed to be replaced as soon as possible. Asquith told Haldane, the War Secretary, on 31 August that the Army plan would be adopted, as he thought the Navy one 'puerile and wholly impracticable'.[99] Churchill agreed. 'I cannot help feeling uncomfortable about the Admiralty,' he told Lloyd George. 'They are so cocksure, insouciant and apathetic ... I cannot feel much confidence in [Admiral] Wilson's sagacity after his performance the other day.'[100]

The CID meeting had exposed the complete chaos in British strategy. After they had played a game of golf together at his Scottish home at Archerfield on 30 September, the Prime Minister asked Churchill whether he would like to become first lord of the Admiralty, swapping jobs with McKenna. 'Indeed I would,' he replied.

'Your father has just offered me the Admiralty,' he told Violet immediately, as 'the fading light of evening disclosed in the far distance the silhouettes of two battleships steaming slowly out of the Firth of Forth. They seemed invested with a new significance to me ... Look at the people I have had to deal with so far – judges and convicts! This is the big thing – the biggest thing that has ever come my way – the chance I should have chosen before all the others. I shall pour into it everything I've got.' She later wrote, 'Never, before or since, have I seen him more completely and profoundly happy.'[101]

# 8

# First Lord of the Admiralty October 1911–August 1914

*The world on the verge of its catastrophe was very brilliant. Nations and empires crowned with princes and potentates rose majestically on every side, lapped in the accumulated treasures of the long peace.*

Churchill, *The World Crisis*[1]

*Germany clanked obstinately, recklessly, awkwardly, towards the crater, and dragged us all in with her.*

Churchill, *The World Crisis*[2]

Winston Churchill's time at the Admiralty from October 1911 to May 1915 was one of the most productive and turbulent periods in its long history. He would soon become its most controversial first lord. He entered office with a brief to change the war strategy of the most powerful navy in the world, but he changed many other things there besides. Much of the strength of his reputation in the period up to 1940 rested on the fact that he had 'got the Navy ready' for the outbreak of the Great War. Yet in the process he also made powerful enemies in an institution with intimate ties to the Conservative Party and much influence throughout the Establishment.

Admirals were a powerful caste in post-Edwardian Britain, and some were among the most famous celebrities of the day. Yet at one point at the end of 1913 all four sea lords were contemplating resignation.[3] Churchill could be peremptory. He showed no more respect to admirals than to generals, telling one who had been in the Navy since Churchill was aged two that his reports were 'mere jottings of passing impressions hurriedly put together without sequence', and lecturing another, who was twenty-two years his senior, on the importance of fleet exercises.[4] Having hitherto been a deeply dovish advocate of defence cuts, Churchill now aligned himself with the hawkish, imperialist wing of the Liberal Party, once led by Lord Rosebery and now by Sir Edward Grey. He was naturally accused of opportunism, although after the Agadir Crisis the international situation now fully justified his volte-face. Germany – which had supported Austria-Hungary in fomenting anti-Russian unrest in the Balkans, formed a strategic entente with Turkey, built a powerful navy to complement her already formidable Army, sabre-rattled in Jerusalem and Agadir and secretly formulated the Schlieffen Plan to capture Paris with armies sweeping through neutral Belgium – was hoping to dominate the European continent in a way that had not been seen since Napoleon or Louis XIV or Philip II. Britain had opposed those three monarchs in the name of preserving the balance of continental power and of denying a powerful enemy with continent-wide ambitions the use of the Channel ports for an invasion of the British Isles. Now she was doing the same thing with a fourth.

Traditionally, the duty of the first lord of the Admiralty was to defend the Royal Navy's interest in the Cabinet and to present the annual Naval Estimates to Parliament. He was expected to take the Board of the Admiralty's advice on strategy, appointments, naval building, gunnery, technical matters, training and so on. Churchill was to be a completely different type of first lord, one whose extensive constitutional powers, dormant for decades, were about to be revived, extended and continuously exercised.

One of Churchill's key allies was the charismatic former First Sea Lord Admiral Lord 'Jacky' Fisher, who during his tenure from 1906 to 1910 had been the chief advocate of the dreadnought, that class of steam turbine-powered, fast, heavily armed battleship that had already revolutionized naval construction. Churchill had first met Fisher on holiday in Biarritz in 1907. Fisher 'fell desperately in love' (his phrase) with Churchill, whom he found to be 'quite the nicest fellow I ever met and such a quick brain that it's a delight to talk to him'.[5] It was to prove the most fruitful and subsequently the most toxic working relationship of Churchill's life. 'He told me wonderful stories of the Navy and of his plans,' Churchill recalled sixteen years later, which covered dreadnoughts, submarines, a new education system for the Navy, Horatio Nelson, the Bible and the island of Borkum off the north-west German coast, which Fisher longed to capture and use as a British naval base.[6]

In June 1912, Churchill asked Fisher to return to the Admiralty as his most senior adviser. 'You need a plough to draw,' he told him, mixing his metaphors magnificently. 'Your propellers are racing in air.'[7] Fisher did not return to the Admiralty officially, but chaired a Royal Commission for Churchill and advised him regularly on changes needed there.[8] The hurricane that swept through the Admiralty between 1912 and 1915, throwing up outraged opposition at almost everything that was done, was a joint Churchill–Fisher phenomenon. Like others who had helped Churchill in his career, such as John Brabazon, Bindon Blood and Bourke Cockran, Fisher was much older than him, in his case by thirty-three years.

Churchill's first reform was to create a Naval War Staff, divided between Operations, Intelligence and Mobilization. Admiral Wilson's opposition, on the grounds that it would sideline the Board in operational matters, gave Churchill an opportunity to force him into retirement in December 1911, albeit with the award of the Order of Merit. He was replaced as first sea lord by Sir Francis Bridgeman, who accepted the need for a War Staff. After a meeting on 8 January 1912, the day it came into being, Brigadier Wilson, the Director of Military Operations at the War Office, wrote of Churchill that 'He, at all events, is alive to the German danger.'[9]

Once set up and properly staffed, the Mobilization Department drew up a plan comprising tonnages, timetables, embarkation and disembarkation, for transporting the British Expeditionary Force across the Channel in the event of a German assault on France, which had been feared since even before the Agadir Crisis of 1911. It undertook this in tandem with the waspish but highly efficient secretary of the Committee of Imperial Defence, Maurice Hankey, Fisher's protégé.[10] Hankey's first impression of Churchill, in March 1912, was 'A bit impetuous, but extraordinarily hard working.'[11]

Churchill set about building new, Queen Elizabeth-class battleships with 15-inch guns, the largest calibre that had ever existed afloat.* These had a muzzle velocity of 2,458 feet per second and a range of 19,000 yards (10.8 miles), well beyond the maximum range of any German naval gun. He managed to get naval spending increased from £39 million to £50 million per annum, making him unpopular with other ministers whose own departmental spending had to be cut back.[12] He urged a policy of building 60 per cent more warships than Germany. 'Nothing', he wrote to Fisher in February 1912, 'would more surely dishearten Germany than the certain proof that as a result of all her present and prospective efforts she will only be more hopelessly behindhand.'[13]

To power these new 'super-dreadnoughts', Churchill insisted that the Navy's fuel should be changed from coal to oil. This made the vessels lighter and consequently faster, and put the Royal Navy ahead of the rest of the world, with the Germans coming very late to the change.[14] Ships no longer had to sail from coaling-station to coaling-station and could now

* Two of these guns can be seen outside the Imperial War Museum in Lambeth today.

stay at sea for much longer. Yet the change had other profound strategic implications for Britain in the Middle East. In order to ensure the necessary smooth supply of high-quality oil, Churchill negotiated massive long-term contracts with both Shell Oil and the Anglo-Persian Oil Company, and oversaw the British Government's purchase of a controlling 51 per cent stake in Anglo-Persian weeks before war broke out.[15] Lloyd George was unimpressed, complaining to the Mastermans that Churchill 'was getting more and more absorbed in boilers'.[16] He told the newspaper proprietor Sir George Riddell, somewhat scornfully, that all Churchill could ever think about was how to sink the German Fleet as soon as war broke out.

Churchill's great strategic change was to strengthen the North Sea Fleet at the expense of the Mediterranean by at least six battleships. For this to work he needed the French to agree to take up more responsibility for the Mediterranean, in return for a promise to protect the Channel ports, deliver an expeditionary force in the event of an invasion and blockade Germany. As there was no formal Anglo-French defensive treaty, this required a good deal of trust on both sides. 'Your new scheme of Fleet organization is admirable,' Fisher wrote to Churchill on 5 March 1912. 'Let the French take care of the Mediterranean.'[17] In May he added, 'It is futile to be strong in the subsidiary theatre of war and not overwhelmingly supreme in the decisive theatre.'[18]

Churchill tried to persuade the influential Lord Chancellor, Lord Haldane, the former Secretary for War, of this strategy, telling him in May that Britain could not possibly hold the Mediterranean or guarantee British interests there until the Germans had been defeated in the North Sea. 'It would be very foolish to lose England in safeguarding Egypt. Of course if the Cabinet and the House of Commons like to build another fleet of Dreadnoughts for the Mediterranean, the attitude of the Admiralty will be like that of a cat to a nice fresh dish of cream. But I do not look upon this as practical politics.' He quoted Clausewitz's 'first of all the laws of war – overpowering strength at the decisive point'.[19]

The new strategy was opposed by the Foreign Office, the War Office, important elements in the Admiralty and Lord Kitchener, the Commander-in-Chief in Egypt, but it was nonetheless adopted, and proved to be the correct one. Churchill kept Balfour closely informed of Committee of Imperial Defence decisions, sending him top-secret documents (with Asquith's permission) in the hope that what he was doing would not be reversed should the Government lose office.[20] Bonar Law suspiciously interpreted Churchill's rapprochement with Balfour as yet another attempt to promote a cross-party coalition, which on this occasion it was not.[21]

Yet naval strategy was only part of the changes Churchill pushed through at the Admiralty. He also introduced better pay for the Navy's 136,000 seamen, although Lloyd George cut back the money available for the increase from £750,000 to £350,000. There were also improved prospects of promotion for able seamen who showed promise. Further up the service, the senior officers he promoted, such as Prince Louis of Battenberg, David Beatty, Roger Keyes and Sir John Jellicoe, were much better than the many whom he retired early or sacked.[22] To the diehards who complained about his violating naval traditions, he is said to have rejoined, 'Naval tradition? Naval tradition? Monstrous. Nothing but rum, sodomy, prayers, and the lash.'[23] (When this famous list is cited, prayers are sometimes omitted.)

Churchill created the Royal Naval Air Service, which had fifty planes by 1914, and pioneered the concept of aerial bombing of Zeppelin airship aerodromes and German lines of communication. The first successful launch of a plane off the deck of a battleship took place in January 1912, and some military historians see Churchill as the father of the modern aircraft carrier.[24] He launched the *Naval Review* magazine and appointed a new commodore of destroyers and director of naval ordnance. 'He has a great belief in the submarine as the weapon of the future,' recorded Wilfrid Blunt in October 1912, 'and is pushing that branch of the service all he can.'[25] He thought the submarine would be used only against warships, telling Fisher in January 1914 that he did not believe that 'the use of submarines to sink merchant vessels . . . would ever be done by a civilized power'.[26]

Churchill also presided over the creation of the first British signals intelligence agency, named Room 40, after the room in the Admiralty where it started. He drew up Room 40's charter in his own hand, specifying that the circulation of decrypts must be limited to half a dozen of the most senior members of the Naval Staff. He liked to receive the raw intelligence data himself, before it was processed by committee.

Continuing his practice of wanting to see everything for himself, in the three years before 1914 Churchill spent no fewer than eight months aboard the 3,800-ton, eighty-crew Admiralty yacht *Enchantress*, visiting naval dockyards, shipyards, training establishments, warships and submarines, in home waters and the Mediterranean.[27] After a night-firing exercise at Portland Bill on the south coast with the Home Fleet, which then consisted of seventeen dreadnoughts, Churchill asked the officers' wardroom of the fleet flagship questions about every aspect of control systems and gun and searchlight performance.[28] When in March 1912 he was told that the electric turrets of HMS *Invincible* needed to be replaced by hydraulics at the vast cost of £150,000, he went to sit in one and ordered the guns to be fired eight times in quick succession. He described the experience as 'a stern and terrible picture of the wrath of Man', while obviously enjoying every moment.[29]

Herbert, Margot and Violet Asquith joined the Churchills in the *Enchantress* in May 1912, sailing to Malta and watching naval exercises in the Mediterranean. Margot and Violet did not get on, but otherwise there was a friendly, family atmosphere on board. 'As we leaned side by side against the taffrail, gliding past the lovely, smiling coast-line of the Adriatic, bathed in sun, and I remarked, "How perfect!",' Violet recalled years afterwards, 'he startled me by his reply: "Yes – range perfect, visibility perfect – if we had got some six-inch guns on board how easily we could bombard . . ." etc, etc.'[30] One difference between the young man Violet had once wanted to marry and her father was well illustrated by Churchill's hunger for newspapers and work pouches at each port of call, while her father, despite being prime minister, was relieved by their absence.

The Churchills did not move into Admiralty House in Whitehall until April 1913, because the First Lord was expected to pay for the twelve servants there, far more than the four or five they had at Eccleston Square. As well as holidaying with the Prime Minister, Churchill had kept him closely informed with long, detailed memoranda posing as letters, something he was also to do for President Roosevelt during the Second World War. He needed Asquith's support, as there were rows within the Admiralty over most of his reforms.

The sacking of Admiral Bridgeman, the First Sea Lord, in December 1912 was badly handled. Churchill did it on grounds of ill-health, despite Bridgeman's indignant protests that he was perfectly well.[31] Bonar Law supported Bridgeman and the King commiserated with him. One of Churchill's most aggressive critics over the Bridgeman sacking was the Tory MP Admiral Lord Charles Beresford. 'I am not one of those who take the Noble Lord too seriously,' Churchill said of him in a debate. 'He is one of those orators of whom it was well said, "Before they get up, they do not know what they are going to say; when they are speaking, they do not know what they are saying; and when they have sat down, they do not know what they have said."'[32] The sacking of Bridgeman was an unpleasant episode. In the course of it, Churchill behaved badly by quoting from private letters he should not have, and at one point he threatened to reveal that Bridgeman had been able to attend only three out of six meetings of the CID, one of which he had been forced to leave from sudden faintness.[33] 'Winston Churchill seems to have made a great mess of it,' the King wrote in his diary, which in this case was an accurate assessment.

At another point, Churchill faced the threat of resignation from the whole Admiralty Board when he announced his intention of sacking Admiral Sir Richard Poore, Commander-in-Chief at The Nore, who resented the way he took junior officers' advice over his. This, too, became political.[34] Ultimately Churchill got his way in these and many other controversies, though at a greater cost than he realized at the time.

When Andrew Bonar Law was elected leader of the Conservative Party on the resignation of the exhausted and thrice-defeated Balfour in November 1911, Churchill wrote him a friendly letter of congratulation. Bonar Law told him in reply that he looked forward to seeing Churchill at the Other Club, while simultaneously writing to Riddell that the Club would have to be disbanded.[35] For his part, Churchill had drafted a crushing line about Bonar Law for use in the Commons – 'The raw and rowdy Under-Secretary, whom the nakedness of the land, and the jealousies of his betters, have promoted to the leadership of the Tory party' – which in the event he did not use.[36] He also wrote to Balfour, regretting that he had had to be 'in an antagonistic and disagreeable political relation to you: and no doubt my own faults of character and manner have unnecessarily aggravated this evil state of things', but adding that 'some of the talks we have had have been among the most pleasant and memorable experiences of my life.'[37] By this he meant their discussions about his father. If Balfour felt pretty cynical about such a half-apology, given the number and severity of Churchill's assaults on him over the past seven years, it would have been understandable.

On 27 November, Churchill proposed the names of the four new battleships – *Africa*, *Liberty*, *Assiduous* and *Oliver Cromwell* – and sent them to the King for approval.[38] The King agreed to *Africa* but not the others, instead suggesting *Delhi*, *Wellington* and *Marlborough*. Instead of taking the last as a compliment and letting the matter drop, Churchill dug in his heels. So did the King. A year went by and Churchill tried to have the name *Cromwell* approved again, this time for one of the four Queen Elizabeth-class super-dreadnoughts for 1912, on the grounds that 'Oliver Cromwell was one of the founders of the Navy and scarcely any man did so much for it.'[39] Despite Cromwell's repressive legacy, Churchill also admired him for readmitting the Jews into Britain, and ending monarchical dictatorship. Instead of taking the hint that the King was not about to honour a regicide, Churchill persisted, trying to persuade Lord Stamfordham that 'His Majesty is the heir of all the glories of the nation, and there is no chapter of English history from which he should feel himself divided.'[40]

There was something almost comic about the obstinacy he showed and the ingenious arguments he put, none of them to any avail. The King and Stamfordham had several arguments of their own, not least that the gesture would infuriate the Irish Nationalists because of Cromwell's notorious massacres at Drogheda and Wexford in 1649. In 1913, Churchill proposed the names *Ark Royal* and *Pitt*. The King had various arguments against *Ark Royal*, thinking it would be nicknamed 'Noah's Ark', but he rejected *Pitt* on an intuition derived from his own many years at sea that there was 'always the danger of the men giving the ship nicknames of ill-conditioned words rhyming with it'.[41] Churchill grumbled that this suggestion was 'unworthy of the royal mind'.[42] The four ships eventually went to sea with the names *Iron Duke* (which Churchill liked better than *Wellington*), *Marlborough*, *Emperor of India* and *Benbow* (after the great late seventeenth-century Admiral John Benbow). Churchill would in all likelihood have continued the unequal struggle indefinitely had Admiral Prince Louis of Battenberg, his new first sea lord, whom he admired and trusted, not persuaded him to drop it.[43] He had to wait for thirty-two years before he was able to christen a medium-weight tank the Cromwell.

The 1913 dreadnoughts, the last of the pre-war building programme, were in the end given the names *Royal Sovereign*, *Royal Oak*, *Resolution*, *Revenge* and *Ramillies*, the last another tribute to Marlborough, as it was the name of his great victory of 1706.[44] In May 1912 Churchill wrote privately to Clementine, 'The King talked more stupidly about the Navy than I have ever heard him before. Really it is disheartening to hear the cheap and silly drivel with which he lets himself be filled up.'[45]

If he tussled over the naming of battleships, Churchill sailed into much more treacherous waters with his vocal advocacy of Irish Home Rule. 'It must always be a guiding star of British statesmanship', he wrote in December 1911, 'not only to federate the Empire, but to draw nearer in bonds of friendship and association to the United States. The road to the unity of the English-speaking races is no doubt a long one, and we cannot see the end of it. But it is an open road, and an Irish parliament, loyal to the Crown, and free to make the best of the Emerald Isle, is assuredly the first milestone upon it.'[46] Although there was in fact no chance whatever that an independent Ireland would remain loyal to the Crown in the long run, Churchill's mind was starting to move along the lines that were to climax with his suggestion of joint Anglo-American citizenship at Harvard in 1943. This was one of his earliest statements about the confederation of the English-speaking peoples, a concept he would pioneer and see as central to Britain's continuing relevance in the world.

Yet his support for even a limited form of Home Rule was profoundly unpopular in the Protestant North. He showed great personal courage in going to speak in Belfast on the issue in February 1912. Clementine bravely went with him, though this looked foolhardy when Orangemen protesters took over the Ulster Hall just as he was about to speak – the same place where his father had declared in 1886 that Ulster would be right to fight – and the situation looked like it might get violent. The War Office wanted to put three brigades on standby to keep the peace, but Churchill held up that order, while telling the authorities that he would go ahead with his speech.[47] It was eventually moved to the Celtic Football Ground in the nationalist Falls Road part of Belfast, as the police drew a cordon between the two parts of the city.[48]

Churchill and Clementine were threatened by a hostile Loyalist mob at their hotel, and their car was nearly overturned on the way to the Falls Road, but once they reached the Celtic Football Ground they were fêted in the pouring rain by 5,000 Nationalists. 'Would not the arrival of an Irish Parliament upon the brilliantly lighted stage of the modern world be an enrichment and an added glory to the treasures of the British Empire?' he asked the crowd. 'And what of all this vain and foolish chatter about separation? The separation of Ireland from Great Britain is absolutely impossible.'[49] Clementine told Riddell when they returned that 'Winston was not nervous and that the opposition and threats seemed to "ginger him up"'.[50] In fact, male suffragists gave more trouble than Irish Loyalists, and 'Winston threatened to smash the face of one of the male tormentors who forced his way into their compartment on the train.'[51]

The Irish Home Rule Bill was given its first reading on 16 April. In the past, Churchill had described an Irish Parliament in Dublin as 'dangerous and impracticable', but with the Irish Nationalists now holding the balance of power he had completely come around to supporting it, as his speech at the football ground showed, although he did believe that the Ulstermen needed 'a moratorium of several years before they had to join'.[52] It was an unheroic stance, but a commonsensical compromise. The Unionists never gave him credit for insisting on concessions to the Ulster Protestants that many of the Radicals and Irish Nationalists on his own side did not want to make.[53] 'Never before has so little been asked,' he said of the Bill, 'never before have so many people asked for it.'

On the second reading of the Bill on 30 April, Churchill made a harsh attack on Bonar Law and Sir Edward Carson, the Ulster Unionist leader. He pilloried them for their 'incitements to the Orangemen', describing Bonar Law's statements that Ulster would oppose Home Rule by force as an 'almost treasonable activity'. The Home Rule struggle became progressively more bitter over the course of the year. On 11 November, the

Conservatives won a surprise vote on a minor amendment and chanted 'Resign! Resign!' as Liberal ministers left the chamber, calling out 'Good-bye, good-bye; take your pensions: good-bye!' The vote was overturned on the 13th, and as Churchill left the Chamber with Jack Seely – to opposition cries of 'Rats!' – they mockingly waved their handkerchiefs at the Opposition benches, whereupon Ronald McNeill, an Old Harrovian Ulster-born Conservative MP sitting for a Kent constituency, threw a small leather-bound copy of the Speaker's Standing Orders* at Churchill, hitting him in the face and drawing blood.[54] (He apologized the next day.)

While all the time preparing for war, Churchill also made several comprehensive peace offers to Germany. On 18 March 1912, when he presented his first Naval Estimates to a packed House of Commons, he had offered what was later termed a 'naval holiday', the temporary halting of all new naval construction by both countries. He first made the assertion that, for every new capital ship built by Germany, Britain would build 60 per cent more, 'because when we consider our naval strength we are not thinking of our commerce, but of our freedom'.[55] Then came his promise that 'Any retardation or reduction in German construction will . . . be promptly followed here . . . by large and fully proportioned reductions.'[56] If Germany did not build the three capital ships that she was planning for 1913, Churchill promised to 'blot out' the five super-dreadnoughts Britain planned to build. 'This keen and costly naval rivalry can be at any time abated,' he announced.[57]

Germany rejected the offer. The Kaiser wrote a 'courteous' message, saying that this 'would only be possible between allies', but privately he described Churchill's speech as 'arrogant'.[58] Theobald von Bethmann-Hollweg, the German Chancellor, dismissed Churchill as 'a firebrand past praying for' and made no public response. Churchill, undeterred, made the same offer twice more in 1913, telling Grey that it ought not 'to be stifled just because it is unwelcome to the ruling classes in Germany'.[59] Churchill thought for ever afterwards, as he put it in an *Evening Standard* article in September 1937, that 'If this had been accepted, it would have enormously eased the European tension, and possibly have averted the catastrophe.'[60] It certainly absolves him of any blame for the events of the next thirty months: naval holidays are not generally the policy of warmongers.

The sinking of the *Titanic* on 15 April 1912 filled Churchill with pride that the women and children had been taken off the stricken ship first. He felt, as he told Clementine, who was convalescing in Paris, that this 'reflects

* Ironically, the parliamentary rulebook.

nothing but honour upon our civilization'. Characteristically he saw this event in historical terms and drew racial and political conclusions:

> I cannot help feeling proud of our race and its traditions as proved by this event. Boatloads of women and children tossing on the sea safe and sound – and the rest – silence. Honour to their memory. In spite of all the inequalities and artificialities of our modern life, at the bottom – tested to its foundations, our civilization is humane, Christian, and absolutely democratic. How differently Imperial Rome or Ancient Greece would have settled the problem. The swells and potentates would have gone off with their concubines and pet slaves and soldier guards, and . . . whoever could bribe the crew would have had the preference and the rest could go to hell. But such ethics could neither build *Titanics* with science nor lose them with honour.[61]

In late March 1912, Clementine had suffered a miscarriage, which was followed by months of ill-health. She had continued to hunt regularly during her pregnancy, and the Ulster trip may have contributed to the strain. 'My darling I do hope that you are not fretting and that all is going on well,' Churchill wrote from the *Enchantress*. 'It is probably for the best. I felt so awfully guilty to have imposed such a heavy task upon you so soon after your recovery.* No wonder you have not felt well for the last month. Poor lamb. Anyhow you will be able to have a jolly year and hunt again in the winter. And there is plenty of time.'[62]

'It is so strange to have all the same sensations that one has after a real Baby, but with no result,' Clementine wrote back with restrained honesty. 'I hope I shall not have such another accident again.'[63] Despite the pain and disappointment, she drew on inner reserves of strength and was soon back on fighting form. Within a week, she was writing a humorous letter to *The Times*, ridiculing the pompous anti-suffragist letters there, and saying, 'The question seems no longer to be "Should women have votes?" but "Ought women not to be abolished altogether?"' Her letter was signed, 'C.S.C. ("One of the Doomed")'.[64] Asquith, though adamantly against female suffrage, found it 'much the best thing' he had read on the subject. Unfortunately, the very next day her husband sounded exactly like the kind of person she had been satirizing, telling Sir George Riddell, 'The truth is that we have enough ignorant voters and we don't need any more.'[65]

On 13 November, Churchill and Clementine were attacked at the theatre by suffragettes, although Jennie, who was also present, 'went for the

* This sentence about Churchill's guilt at making his wife pregnant so soon after Diana's birth was replaced by an ellipsis in Mary Soames's edition of her parents' letters (ed. Soames, *Speaking* p. 61).

suffragettes and told them that they should be forcibly fed with common sense!'[66] Parcels could not be opened at home for fear of suffragettes' bombs, which exploded at Lloyd George's house in Surrey, under the Coronation Chair at Westminster Abbey and elsewhere. Hundreds of shop windows were smashed with hammers, paintings were slashed at art galleries and acid was poured into hundreds of postboxes. 'These harpies are quite capable of trying to burn us out,' Churchill warned Clementine. Kidnap threats against the Churchill children meant that they had to have police protection for their walks in the park.[67]

The campaign for votes for women was suspended on the outbreak of the Great War, and such was the contribution made by women that in February 1918 women aged thirty or over finally got the right to vote in parliamentary elections, with Churchill voting in favour. In December 1919, Nancy, Lady Astor, became the first woman to take her seat in the House of Commons. She sensed that Churchill, whom she knew socially, was acting coldly towards her, and when she asked why, he replied, 'I feel as if you have come into my bathroom and I have only a sponge with which to defend myself.'[68] (He could on very rare occasions be ungallant: when in the 1950s a friend told him that the practice of men giving women seats on buses was dying out, he replied, 'Serves them right! They want to be equal. Let them stand!')[69]

Even in the toxic atmosphere of pre-Great War politics, with profound ructions over Ireland, female suffrage, rearmament, social reform, the Lords' veto and industrial relations, Churchill did not give up his dream of a centrist national party. During a wet golf match at Walton Heath in March 1913, he told George Riddell, 'The time will soon be ripe for a fusion of the two parties.' The Conservatives would agree to a minimum wage for agricultural workers, and in return Liberals would accept compulsory military conscription. 'In both parties there are fools at one end and crackpots at the other,' he said, 'but the great body in the middle is sound and wise.'[70] Lloyd George was uninterested in the project, and refused to give Churchill any credit for promoting it. 'It is no earthly good talking principles or anything like that with Winston,' he complained to the Mastermans in late November 1912. 'I told him straight, "I regard you as one might regard a leading barrister that you don't want your opponent in a case to get, so you retain him yourself. I think your fees rather excessive but I am willing to go with you as far as I can in reason."'[71] This explains Lloyd George's retention of Churchill in future ministries far more than affection, regard or political accord. 'I don't know anyone who, with a good and healthy standard in his private relationships, is so totally without any apparent principle where public matters come in,' he continued.[72] For a long time Churchill regarded Lloyd George as one of his closest friends in politics; this was not how Lloyd George saw the relationship.

The rift between the parties was deepened in the summer of 1912 by the revelation that Lloyd George, still chancellor of the Exchequer, and Sir Rufus Isaacs, the Attorney-General, had bought shares in the American Marconi Company without declaring them for a full four months after telling the Commons that they did not have shares in its sister-company, the British Marconi Company, where Isaacs's brother was managing director. A big British Government contract had trebled the share price in the British company, and it was suggested that the ministers had been insider dealing. No actual corruption was involved, as the two companies were officially different entities, but the circumstances seemed damning.[73]

Churchill supported his friends publicly and unequivocally. He told Riddell he had 'great concern for LG and Rufus Isaacs in regard to the Marconi incident, and said that his heart bled for them. He described LG as "that brave, honest little man, on whom so much depended".'[74] Riddell concluded that Churchill was 'a loyal, affectionate creature' and Lloyd George's brother agreed. 'Chief amongst the friends who rallied around him in the days of this determined attack on his reputation', he recalled in his memoirs, 'were Mr Winston Churchill and Mr C. P. Scott of the *Manchester Guardian*. It is said of the former that he seemed to worry over the matter quite as much as Lloyd George himself did,' and he paid tribute to 'the help he gave to keep the fire under control and to prevent it spreading'.[75] Churchill persuaded Lord Northcliffe not to allow *The Times* to go on the attack and F. E. Smith to represent Lloyd George and Sir Rufus Isaacs in their successful libel action against the French newspaper *Le Matin*. He also negotiated the exact wording of Asquith's speech in the debate on the report of the Commons Select Committee investigating the matter.

When a witness suggested that Churchill himself had been involved in the share-buying, he was given a one-hour summons to appear before the Select Committee. 'Mr. Churchill came into the Committee Room like a whirlwind,' one observer wrote, 'sat down for a moment, deathly pale with anger, and was immediately summoned to the witness-chair,' whereupon the chairman asked if he had had any dealings in Marconi shares.[76] Churchill's reply was a masterpiece of outraged and eloquent denial that had the Committee Room laughing and applauding:

> I have never at any time, in any circumstances, directly or indirectly, had any investments or any interests of any kind, however vaguely it may be described,

> in Marconi telegraphic shares or any other shares of that description, in this or any other country in the inhabited globe, and if anybody at any time has said so, that person is a liar and a slanderer, and if anybody has repeated this statement and said he had no evidence and he believed it to be false, but that there it was, the only difference between that person and a liar and a slanderer is that he is a coward in addition.[77]

When Lord Robert Cecil, Lord Hugh's brother and a Tory MP, suggested that Churchill must have appreciated this opportunity to clear his name, Churchill replied that since no evidence had been produced beyond an overheard rumour that had been passed on by a man who himself disbelieved it, he should not have been called at all.[78] The eight Liberals on the Select Committee outvoted the six Conservatives, and so Rufus Isaacs and Lloyd George escaped official criticism. Churchill also used the opportunity of a speech at the National Liberal Club on 1 July to defend Lloyd George and Isaacs, and to attack their tormentor, Cecil, for having made a speech whose insinuations were 'odious and contemptible . . . uttered by one who has been fraudulently posing as a fair-minded, impartial man, and lending a smooth pretence of gentlemanly culture to the dirty work he has set himself to do'.[79] This was one of the lowest points in Churchill's long love-hate relationship with the Cecil family.

An invitation to go stag-hunting at Balmoral Castle in late September – where the King found Churchill 'sensible and fairly reasonable' – gave him an opportunity to connect with the nineteen-year-old Prince of Wales. Churchill went through the Prince's red dispatch boxes with him, advising him on the government papers within.[80] 'He is so nice, and we have made rather friends,' Churchill reported to Clementine. 'He requires to fall in love with a pretty cat, who will prevent him from getting too strenuous.'[81] It did not turn out that way.

Most of the time at Balmoral was spent on country pursuits rather than in discussing politics. Churchill was pleased when he managed to kill a stag with 'a really difficult shot – downhill, half-covered and running fast'. His attempt to persuade his fellow guest Bonar Law to agree to Irish Home Rule, even with Ulster having special rights outside the overall framework, was less successful.[82] 'History teaches us that in such cases British common sense generally triumphs,' Churchill told him. He made the case that Catholic Ireland would not 'stand by and see the cup, almost at her lips, dashed to the ground', but Bonar Law would not budge.[83]

When for the third time Churchill proposed a naval de-escalation or 'holiday' with Germany in a speech in the Free Trade Hall in Manchester in October 1913, four months went by before the Anglophobic Admiral

Alfred von Tirpitz, the powerful and long-serving German Naval Minister, formally replied in the Reichstag explicitly rejecting the offer. The Kaiser described British arms-limitation offers as 'a bad insult to the German people and their Emperor', adding, 'They bite on granite.'[84] Churchill made these offers in public because they had been rejected in private and hoped to mobilize German public opinion behind them. Part of the Kaiser's fury probably stemmed from a realization that they cast him undeniably as the warmonger in the naval arms race. One conservative paper, the *Deutsche Tageszeitung*, remarked that Churchill should take a holiday from making speeches.[85] But the British opposition press was not much more receptive to the proposal. The *National Review* denounced 'the mountebank at the Admiralty' for promoting 'the disarmament craze', which, it said, played 'into the hands of the vast army of Anglophobes who preach *jihad* against this country'.[86] They could not know that Churchill, convinced that war was coming, was privately demanding four more super-dreadnoughts and large increases in naval spending, especially for submarines.[87] There was no hypocrisy in his offering peace publicly while preparing for war in Cabinet. In the face of aggressive German militarism, it made sense.

Churchill had started taking dancing lessons in 1912, and now began taking flying lessons too. He told a friend that they 'had done him much good and given a new zest to life'.[88] On 22 October 1913, a monoplane in which he was due to have flown 'side-slipped' and was totally wrecked, but he was not deterred.[89] The very next day he flew an Astra-Torres airship, invented five years earlier, for an hour. After inspecting seaplanes at the Sheerness dockyard, he told Clementine, 'It has been as good as one of those old days in the South African War, and I have lived entirely in the moment, with no care for all those tiresome party politics and searching newspapers, and awkward by-elections, and sulky Orangemen, and obnoxious Cecils and little smugs like Runciman.'[90] Clementine wrote back, 'Please be kind and don't fly any more just now.'[91] Churchill selfishly refused her request, despite the fact that aeronautics was still very much in its infancy, as were his two children under the age of five. 'Do not be vexed with me,' he told her on 29 November, claiming that flying was not 'a serious risk'.[92] Three days later his instructor, Captain Gilbert Wildman-Lushington, was killed in a flying accident. Lieutenant-Colonel Hugh Trenchard, the commandant of the Central Flying School in Portsmouth, did not believe Churchill to be a natural pilot. 'He seemed altogether too impatient for a good pupil,' he recalled. 'He would arrive unexpectedly . . . see what he wanted to see, and stay the night – or what was left of it when he'd finished talking. Everything, including flying, was subordinated in his mind to a single purpose – getting the Fleet ready for a war in which Germany would be the enemy.'[93]

On 29 May 1914, Churchill told Clementine that he hadn't written because he had been flying at the Central Flying School and had not wanted to worry her. Six days earlier, he had been on the welcoming committee for the German aviator Gustav Hamel, who was crossing the Channel but died en route when his plane crashed into the sea. A lieutenant who had taken Churchill up only the week before had also died in the same plane they had used on that previous flight, as had his co-pilot.[94] Clementine replied that her pleas were 'like beating one's head against a stone wall'.[95] He had to admit that insurance companies 'try to charge excessive premiums on my life – political strain, short-lived parentage and of course flying'.[96] Any insurance agent evaluating his life up to that point – especially if he had guessed what it would involve in the future – would have been insane to have given him coverage. On 6 June, he finally promised that, even though he was on the verge of getting his pilot's licence or 'wings', 'I give it up decidedly for many months and perhaps forever. This is a gift – so stupidly am I made – which costs me more than anything which could be bought with money.'[97] He had flown nearly 140 times in seven months with many pilots in many different types of planes, and felt he now knew enough 'to understand all the questions of policy which will arise in the near future'.[98]

Churchill's negative reference to Walter Runciman, the Minister for Agriculture, stemmed from the Cabinet row over naval spending. His demands for an extra £3 million had been adamantly opposed by Runciman, as well as by Herbert Samuel the Postmaster-General, Sir John Simon the Attorney-General, Reginald McKenna the Home Secretary and Lloyd George. Only Asquith and Jack Seely, the Secretary for War, supported him. The press baron Max Aitken, later Lord Beaverbrook, pithily summed up the Unionists' attitude to 'the leader of the War party in the Cabinet' at this time: 'He was hated, he was mistrusted, and he was feared.'[99] Almost the same thing could be said of the attitude to Churchill in the Cabinet itself.

In the end, Asquith's support swung the Cabinet behind providing the extra £3 million. 'Never can I forget the support he gave me,' Churchill recalled in 1950. 'We had more than twenty Cabinet meetings [about the Estimates] and I should never have survived as a minister but for his commanding authority.'[100] Lloyd George tried to goad Churchill in an interview with the *Daily Chronicle* on New Year's Day 1914, saying that the prospects for world peace had never been better, that large military expenditure was a folly and that one of his predecessors as chancellor, Lord Randolph

Churchill, had resigned rather than accept 'bloated' military budgets. Churchill, who rightly construed this as a deliberate provocation, refused to make a statement 'upon a matter which is being considered by the Cabinet'.[101] He was fortunate that his opponents could not agree on a possible successor if Churchill was ousted: McKenna doubted that Herbert Samuel would be a good fit at the Admiralty, as 'They would not like a Jew.'[102]

On 31 December 1913, Churchill signed a long-term contract for Shell Oil to supply the Royal Navy with 200,000 tons of oil per annum. 'We have always found them courteous, considerate, ready to oblige, anxious to serve the Admiralty and to promote the interests of the British Navy and the British Empire – at a price!' he said in the Commons.[103] He later emphasized the point: 'The only difficulty has been price. On that point, of course, we have been treated with the full rigours of the game.' This won him the support of the Labour benches, but at the Shell Annual General Meeting six days later Sir Marcus Samuel, the chairman, denied Churchill's allegations and invited him either to disclose the price or let him do so. Churchill refused both. It was only in 1966, after Churchill's death, that the figures were finally published. These showed that in fact Shell had at first made a loss supplying the Navy at far below the prevailing market rate, and that the company had even offered the Admiralty a seat on its board.[104]

By late January 1914, several Cabinet ministers, led by McKenna, were intent on forcing Churchill out of the Cabinet because of his insistence on higher defence spending. 'If I resign,' Churchill told Riddell in mid-February, 'I shall take a small house in Carnoustie, near Dundee, and deliver a series of speeches setting out my political views. That will be my platform.'[105] Asked if he would rejoin the Tories, he said, 'No, certainly not! On no account. I am a Free Trader, and quite out of sympathy with their attitude to the working classes.'[106] Commenting on his adamant refusal to reduce the number of British capital ships in home waters below twenty-nine – facing the Germans' twenty-two – he told Riddell, 'LG is accustomed to deal with people who can be bluffed and frightened, but I am not to be bluffed or frightened! He says that some of the Cabinet will resign. Let them resign!'[107]

On 17 March, Churchill introduced the new Naval Estimates in a marathon two-and-a-half-hour speech, in which spoke of the importance of air defences by 'guns which fire upwards, and by searchlights which train throughout the entire arc, but the only real security upon which sound military principles will rely is that you should be master of your own air'.[108] He employed a startling image to explain how the offensive power of modern battleships was now out of all proportion to their defensive power. 'If you want to make a true picture in your mind of a battle between great modern ironclad ships you must not think of it as if it were two men in armour striking at each other with heavy swords,' he said. 'It is more like a battle between two egg-shells striking each other with hammers.'[109] He spoke too of 'the power of the submarine and the decisive part which this weapon, aided perhaps in some respects by the seaplane, may play in the naval warfare of the future'.[110] Churchill's constant interest in the next generation of weaponry was to stay with him throughout his life, up to and including the invention of the atomic bomb.

In the spring of 1914 a crisis developed in Ireland that almost led to full-scale civil war. When an Irish Home Rule Bill was introduced in the Commons – the third since 1886 – the leader of the Ulster Protestants, Sir Edward Carson, set up a paramilitary Ulster Volunteer Force (UVF) in the north. The Irish Volunteers soon sprang up in the Catholic south in reply. The Unionists, whose raison d'être was evident in their official name – 'the Conservative and Unionist Party' – rejected Asquith's compromise federal solution on 9 March, so any hope of bipartisan agreement was lost. Two days later Asquith appointed a Cabinet committee chaired by Lord Crewe, on which both Churchill and Seeley served, to consider the danger posed by the Ulster Volunteer Force.

Brigadier Lord Gleichen, commander of the 15th Infantry Brigade in Belfast, reported that a Loyalist force armed with machine guns and 80,000 rifles was preparing to storm arms depots and sabotage communications in Ulster.[111] Three days later, General Sir Arthur Paget, who commanded the Army in Ireland, was ordered by the War Office to take 'special precautions' against 'evil-disposed persons' raiding ammunition stores. He replied that he had issued instructions to protect the depots but did not propose sending more troops there, whereupon he was summoned to London to discuss the situation.

On 14 March, Churchill gave a speech at the St George's Hall in Bradford that threw fuel on to an already highly combustible situation. He had been authorized by Asquith to make it clear that the Government was prepared to confront rebellion in Ulster, but this was probably not the right moment for him to deploy his deliberate extravagances. 'Mr. Bonar Law is really in some respects a public danger,' Churchill told his large audience.

> He quite sincerely thinks, if I may judge from his speeches, that he has only to continue to terrorize the Government to wreck the Home Rule Bill and force his way into the councils of the Sovereign ... Behind every strident

> sentence which he rasps out you can always hear the whisper of the party manager – 'We must have an election . . . Ulster is our best card. It is our only card' . . . Bloodshed, gentlemen, no doubt is lamentable. I have seen some of it – more perhaps than many of those who talk about it with such levity. But there are worse things than bloodshed, even on an extreme scale. An eclipse of the central Government of the British Empire would be worse. The abandonment by our public men of the righteous aims to which they are pledged in honour would be worse. The cowardly abdication of responsibility by the Executive would be worse. The trampling down of law and order which, under the conditions of a civilized state, assure life, liberty, and the pursuit of happiness, all this would be worse than bloodshed.

If there were no wish for peace and every concession was spurned, Churchill concluded, and especially if the Loyalists really had 'a sinister and revolutionary purpose – then, gentlemen, I can only say to you let us go forward together and put these grave matters to the proof'.[112]* Leo Amery spoke for many Conservatives when he wrote that this was Government policy announced 'in its most uncompromising and menacing form'.[113]

General Paget arrived in London on 18 March. He was told by Jack Seely, Sir John French, the Chief of the Imperial General Staff, and Sir John Ewart, the Army's Adjutant-General, that while there was no question of the British Army attacking Ulstermen, troops would need to be moved there to aid the civil power in an emergency. The next day, Churchill ordered eight battleships of the 3rd Battle Squadron, then on manoeuvres off Spain, to 'proceed at once at ordinary speed' to Lamlash on the Isle of Arran in the Firth of Clyde, 60 miles from Ulster. Simultaneously, HMS *Gibraltar* and *Royal Arthur* were 'to proceed at once to Kingstown, Ireland, to embark tomorrow 550 infantry equally divided and to proceed to Dundalk', halfway between Dublin and Belfast.[114] He also put five destroyers at Irish ports on standby to carry troops, as Loyalist railwaymen were threatening to close the railway lines. His measures received Cabinet approval and were intended to be preventative, in case Carson's UVF attempted to set itself up as a provisional government in Ulster. Many Tories believed, however wrongly, that Churchill was deliberately

* This was the second time Churchill had used the phrase 'Let us go forward together'; the first had been in March 1910 with reference to the Parliament Bill. But when he found a phrase that worked – and this one gained 'loud cheers' in Bradford – he was wont to use it again in different contexts. This was a phrase he used on at least nineteen occasions to audiences (and at least once to his dog Rufus). It was usually issued as a call for unity, but in March 1914 it was considered to be the opposite, a provocative call to arms.

trying to provoke armed resistance in the north that could be smashed, so that Home Rule could be imposed across the whole island by force.[115]

The fleet had only reached as far as the Scilly Isles before Asquith countermanded the order on 21 March. By then the situation had been greatly complicated when Brigadier Hubert Gough and fifty-seven of the seventy officers of the 3rd Cavalry Brigade stationed at the Curragh, the main British Army camp in Ireland, declared they would sooner be dismissed than serve in any coercion of Ulster. Although at no point did any officer refuse to obey any order that had actually been given, this became known as the Curragh Mutiny. 'Winston talked very big about bringing the officers over in a battleship to be tried by court martial,' recalled Ewart. 'I however urged that we should wait to see what the senior officers concerned had to say.'[116] Gough was summoned to the War Office where he and Seely agreed it had all been a misunderstanding, and a three-paragraph memorandum to that effect received Cabinet assent. Seely later added two paragraphs of his own, stating that the Army would not be used to coerce the Ulstermen opposing Home Rule. This, when leaked to the press, made it seem as if the Mutiny had forced the Government into a climbdown. When the Cabinet repudiated the extra two paragraphs, Seely and French were forced to resign.

Churchill had been intimately involved in all of this, visiting his friend Seely's house at Chester Square in London, Asquith at No. 10 and Buckingham Palace during the crisis, as well as sitting in on the Cabinets and giving orders to the fleet. But rumours of his involvement blossomed into a conspiracy theory of massive proportions. The so-called plot was given the name of the Ulster Pogrom, although no actual blood was shed. Even as late as 1954 General Sir Hubert Gough (as he had become) noted, 'My impressions of these few exciting days are that it was Winston Churchill who was the driving force behind these warlike preparations against Ulster, that Seely was a mere tool in his hands, and that Paget was equally so.'[117] Churchill had allegedly told French 'that if Belfast showed fight his fleet would have the town in ruins in twenty-four hours'.[118]

Lord Crawford, who was in 1912 the Conservative Chief Whip, naturally put the worst possible construction on Churchill's involvement. 'There was clear evidence of an elaborate conspiracy,' he wrote, 'hatched I doubt not by Churchill, and probably not communicated to Asquith and the respectable members of the Cabinet.'[119] Crawford put it down to ancestry and 'the Indo-Mexican* strains in Churchill's blood which explains

* The Jeromes were (wrongly) reputed to have Native American blood; where the Mexican idea came from is not known.

the unaccountable fits of madness'.[120] F. E. Smith, who supported Carson, equally unjustifiably accused Churchill of 'finessing the firing of the first shot' (which of course was never fired).[121] Beresford accused Churchill at a Unionist rally in Hyde Park of being 'a Lilliput Napoleon, a man with an unbalanced mind, an egomaniac', adding, 'As long as Mr Winston Churchill remains in office, the State is in danger.'[122]

All through these weeks the situation in the Commons Chamber was febrile. Leo Amery asked Churchill on 1 April 'whether he expected and hoped that purely precautionary movements to look after stores would lead to fighting and bloodshed?'[123] Churchill called that a 'hellish insinuation', which the Speaker forced Amery to withdraw. With the Conservatives yelling 'Resign! Traitor! Withdraw!' at him, Churchill made matters worse by stating that Bonar Law was willing 'to show that it is always right for soldiers to shoot down a Radical or Labour man'. Yet on 27 March, in the middle of this maelstrom over Ulster, the Liberal MP Cecil Harmsworth found 'Winston singing blithely to himself in the lavatory behind the Speaker's Chair. I thank him for his reassuring cheerfulness and he tells me that it is his habit to confront difficulties with an outward serenity of aspect.'[124]

In the Commons on 27 April, two days after the Ulster Volunteers had landed a large shipment of guns and ammunition, Churchill characterized Tory attacks as 'uncannily like a vote of censure by the criminal classes upon the police', which prompted Balfour's retort that only one character was more immoral than the meanest criminal, and that was the agent provocateur.[125] Despite the inherent unlikeliness that Churchill should want to raze Belfast, one of the great cities of the Empire he loved, the myth of the Ulster Pogrom stuck in the Tory memory, and the undoubtedly inflammatory Bradford speech has been used to cast doubt upon Churchill's judgement ever since. 'It is no disparagement of Winston's extraordinary qualities to say that his judgement is not quite equal to his abilities,' wrote Sir Almeric Fitzroy, the Clerk of the Privy Council, in his diary, 'nor his abilities quite equal to his ambitions. His defect is that he sees everything through the magnifying glass of his self-confidence.'[126] This was indeed a defect for most of his life, until the moment when it emerged as a tremendous strength. In fact, his Ulster policy was much more concessionary than many appreciated at the time.[127]

The Government of Ireland Bill (known as the Third Irish Home Rule Bill) received its third and therefore last reading in the Commons on 21 May 1914 and received Royal Assent on 18 September, because the Parliament Act did not permit the House of Lords to reject it a third time. Yet on the outbreak of war the Unionists and Liberals declared a political truce for the duration of the conflict, and the provisions of the Bill were also suspended, so none of the consequences threatened by the chief actors in the two years since it had been introduced in Parliament transpired. Indeed, some 200,000 Irishmen joined the fight against Germany.

'No part of the Great War compares in interest with its opening,' Churchill later wrote. 'The measured, silent drawing together of gigantic forces, the uncertainty of their movements and positions, the number of unknown and unknowable facts made the first collision a drama never surpassed.'[128] On 17 June, he secured the Shell deal for Persian oil for the Royal Navy. Eleven days later Archduke Franz Ferdinand of Austria was assassinated in Sarajevo, triggering a series of events through July that led to the outbreak of war. At the beginning of the month, the Churchills were holidaying in Pear Tree Cottage in Overstrand, near Cromer in Norfolk, where Churchill enjoyed playing with the children on the beach. He nonetheless attended the Spithead Review of 400 vessels on 17 and 18 July, which he described as 'the greatest assemblage of naval power ever witnessed in the history of the world'.[129]

On 25 July, the Cabinet was discussing Irish Home Rule when Sir Edward Grey interrupted to read out a note he had received announcing Austria-Hungary's drastic demands on Serbia, which was accused of harbouring terrorists involved in the Archduke's assassination. Vienna was fully supported by Germany, which saw an opportunity to provoke Serbia's protector, Russia, which was in turn allied to France. As Churchill listened to Grey, he realized that:

> This note was clearly an ultimatum; but it was an ultimatum such as has never been penned in modern times. As the reading of it proceeded it seemed absolutely impossible that any State in the world could accept it, or that any acceptance, however abject, could satisfy the aggressor. The parishes of Fermanagh and Tyrone faded back into the mists and squalls of Ireland, and a strange light began immediately, but by perceptible gradations, to fall and grow upon the map of Europe.[130]

In that meeting, Churchill supported Asquith and Grey in wanting Britain actively to intervene in the European crisis in support of France should Germany declare war against her, not because he was a warmonger but because a firm position might persuade Germany and Austria to back away from war. On the night of 25 July, he dined with the German shipping magnate Albert Ballin, who knew the Kaiser well, and told him that a Franco-German war might well engender an Anglo-German one. With tears in his eyes, Churchill begged Ballin to do all he could to prevent a

German war with France.[131] Yet the majority of the Cabinet, led by John Morley and John Burns, wanted Britain to remain neutral. Morley wrote in his posthumously published *Memorandum on Resignation* that the interventionist case 'was being openly worked with his best daemonic energy by Winston'.[132] At one point between 25 and 27 July, Morley 'tapped Winston on the shoulder, as he took his seat next to me. "Winston, we have beaten you after all."' He claimed that Churchill in response 'smiled cheerfully'.[133]

Lloyd George, who had opposed the Boer War, was, in the words of his brother William, 'extremely reluctant to commit himself to a policy which would involve the country in war . . . Mr Winston Churchill felt no hesitation over the matter, and made strong personal appeals to my brother to come over to his side, reminding him in forcible terms of their past close associations. According to the tenor of those appeals, Churchill and Daffyd [David] had, in effect, come to the parting of the ways: the choice put before my brother by Churchill was to become "Comrades or opponents" for the rest of their lives.'[134] Churchill particularly mentioned the provocative part Lloyd George had played during the Agadir Crisis, 'a shrewd shot which, no doubt, reached its target'. When in late July Lloyd George declared himself in favour of war, Morley put it down to Churchill, 'the splendid *condottiere* at the Admiralty'. In fact Lloyd George was of course more than capable of making up his own mind.

On Sunday, 26 July, when Churchill was back at Overstrand, Prince Louis Battenberg, the First Sea Lord, took the decision to halt the dispersal of the Fleet after the end of the trial mobilization manoeuvres off Portland on the south coast. This was promptly endorsed by Churchill, on his own initiative and without Cabinet sanction. He took the next train back to London. The Fleet was sent to Scapa Flow, the sheltered anchorage in the Orkney Islands which afforded protection from a surprise attack from the North Sea. Its passing through the Straits of Dover without lights gave rise to one of the poetic passages in *The World Crisis*, Churchill's memoir of the First World War:

> We may now picture this great Fleet, with its flotillas and cruisers, steaming slowly out of Portland Harbour, squadron by squadron, scores of gigantic castles of steel wending their way across the misty, shining sea, like giants bowed in anxious thought. We may picture them again as darkness fell, eighteen miles of warships, running at high speed and in absolute blackness through the narrow Straits, bearing with them into the broad waters of the North the safeguard of considerable affairs . . . The King's ships were at sea.[135]

On 28 July, Austria declared war on Serbia, and the next day the Fleet arrived at its battle stations at Orkney.

At midnight on 28 July, Churchill wrote to Clementine. 'My darling One and beautiful,' it reads,

> Everything trends towards catastrophe and collapse. I am interested, geared-up and happy. Is it not horrible to be built like that? The preparations have a hideous fascination for me. I pray to God to forgive me for such fearful moods of levity. Yet I would do my best for peace, and nothing would induce me wrongfully to strike the blow – I cannot feel that we in this island are in any serious degree responsible for the wave of madness which has swept the mind of Christendom . . . I wondered whether those stupid Kings and Emperors could not assemble together and revivify Kingship by saving the nations from hell, but we all drift on in a kind of dull cataleptic trance. As if it was somebody else's operation![136]

Churchill's detractors rarely quote beyond the fifth sentence, but when read in its entirety the letter makes much more sense. Churchill was fascinated not just by the preparations but by war itself, while also having seen four wars at close enough quarters to know how obscene war is, and therefore also to deprecate his own fascination with it. It was not horrible for him to be built like that, but fortunate that the Cabinet had at least one member of a martial bent at such a time. He even proposed the 'kingly conference' idea in Cabinet on 29 July, but nothing came of it.[137]

After a short digression to Clementine on the black 'darling cygnet' in St James's Park (which was given four adjectives – 'grey, fluffy, precious and unique'), Churchill proudly continued, speaking now specifically of the Navy, 'Everything is ready as it has never been before. And we are awake to the tips of our fingers . . . I feel sure however that if war comes we will give them a good drubbing.'[138] He asked Clementine to phone him at fixed times, warning her, 'But talk in parables – for they all listen.'[139] He was referring to the General Post Office switchboard operators rather than foreign agents, but it was as well to be security conscious at such a time, and the Churchills already had a nickname-laden language they could use. He also worried that Overstrand might be dangerous for his family in the event of a German raid on Cromer, as it 'has a good landing place near'.[140]

On Wednesday, 29 July, Churchill was still attempting to bring Lloyd George over on to his side in Cabinet. 'Together we can carry a wide social policy,' he told him. 'The naval war will be cheap.'[141] He did not know at that stage that the British Expeditionary Force would be dispatched to the continent: the force itself was ready and the plans had been in place since

1911, but the Cabinet had not yet decided the nature of British involvement in a European conflict. Even as late as 3 August, as the Germans were starting to invade Belgium, General Sir John French, who would command the BEF, was told by Downing Street that there was no question of an army being sent to France.[142] If Britain had simply fought a naval war it would indeed have been cheap, at least in comparison to the one she did fight. Churchill passed a note to Lloyd George over the table at that same Cabinet saying, 'Keep Friday night [that is, 31 July] clear. F.E. inquiring.'[143] F. E. Smith was approaching Bonar Law, Max Aitken (later Lord Beaverbrook) and others about joining a national government in coalition with the Liberals, but Bonar Law once again rejected the idea.

'Winston Churchill came to see me,' wrote the King in his diary on Friday, 31 July; 'the Navy is all ready for war, but please God it will not come.'[144] Churchill fully agreed with those sentiments, as is clear from his letter to Clementine that day from the Admiralty, which he told her was 'Not to be left about – but locked up or burned.' 'There is still some hope although the clouds are blacker and blacker,' he wrote.

> Germany is realizing I think how great are the forces against her, and is trying tardily to restrain her idiot ally. We are working to soothe Russia. But everybody is preparing swiftly for war and at any moment now the stroke may fall. We are ready . . . Germany has sent a proposal to us to be neutral if she promises not to take French territory nor to invade Holland – She must take French colonies and she cannot promise not to invade Belgium – which she is by treaty bound not merely to respect but to defend. Grey has replied that these proposals are impossible and disgraceful. Everything points therefore to a collision on these issues. Still hope is not dead.[145]

Late on Saturday, 1 August, Germany declared war on Russia. When Grey, Haldane and the Marquess of Crewe, the Lord Privy Seal, went to No. 10 with the news, they had to wait for an hour before Asquith and the ladies had finished their game of bridge. (Crewe likened it to playing on the top of a coffin.) Churchill however immediately mobilized the Navy, again without Cabinet authority. 'He was not depressed, he was not elated; he was not surprised,' recalled Aitken. 'He went straight out like a man going to a well-accustomed job.'[146] He informed Asquith, who said nothing but looked 'quite content', and the Cabinet gave its formal assent the next morning.[147]

'The news tonight opens again hope,' Churchill wrote to Lord Robert Cecil at 10.30 that night from the Admiralty. 'There seems to be a prospect of Austria and Russia resuming negotiations on a formula which Germany has proposed: and every exertion will be made to that end. But a collision between the armies may arise at any moment out of an incident or an accident. And I hold that in all the circumstances if we allowed Belgian neutrality to be trampled down by Germany without exerting ourselves to aid France we should be in a very melancholy position both in regard to our interests and our honour.'[148]

On the afternoon of Monday, 3 August, German troops invaded Belgium in accordance with the Schlieffen Plan to defeat France which had been in existence since 1905 and whose main provisions Churchill had guessed with eerie accuracy in 1911. At the Cabinet that morning, Grey admitted that Britain was not bound by any signed agreement to go to the aid of France, a point he reiterated at 3 p.m. in the House of Commons. He nonetheless believed that the honour, prestige and strategic interests of Britain, which, like Germany, had guaranteed Belgium's independence in 1839, were at stake, and the Commons agreed with him, although extraordinarily, for such an important decision, no vote was taken. A twenty-four-hour ultimatum was sent to Germany, set to expire at 11 p.m. on Tuesday, 4 August.

Churchill asked Asquith and Grey permission to put the Anglo-French naval war plans into operation to protect the Channel before the ultimatum's expiration. This, he told them, 'implies no offensive action and no warlike action unless we are attacked'.[149] The next morning *The Times* described Churchill as the one minister 'whose grasp of the situation and whose efforts to meet it have been above all praise'.[150] On 4 August, before the British ultimatum expired, the German battlecruiser *Goeben* bombarded Philippeville (modern Skikda) and the light cruiser *Breslau* bombarded Bône (modern Annaba) in French Algeria. Then both escaped eastwards, heading for Turkey, despite the Royal Navy shadowing them. 'It would be a great misfortune to lose these vessels as is possible in the dark hours,' Churchill told Asquith and Grey, begging for permission to engage them.[151]

'Winston, who has got on all his war-paint, is longing for a sea-fight in the early hours of tomorrow morning to result in the sinking of the *Goeben*,' Asquith wrote to Venetia Stanley. 'The whole thing fills me with sadness.' The Cabinet refused permission for any offensive action to take place before eleven o'clock that night. After dinner at the Admiralty, Churchill was asked by a French naval delegation if they could have another naval base in the Mediterranean. 'Use Malta as if it were Toulon,' came the reply.[152]

Churchill was in the Admiralty at 11 p.m. on 4 August when the ultimatum expired. 'Along the Mall from the direction of the Palace the sound of an immense concourse singing "God Save the King" floated in,' he later recalled. 'On this deep wave there broke the sounds of Big Ben; and, as the first stroke of the hour boomed out, a rustle of movement swept across the room. The war telegram, which meant "Commence hostilities against Germany", was flashed to the ships and establishments under the White Ensign all over the world.'[153]

Rear Admiral Troubridge, commander of the 1st Cruiser Squadron in the Mediterranean, received the telegram while still in contact with *Goeben* and *Breslau*, but failed to engage them, and they escaped unharmed through the Dardanelles, to become part of the Turkish Navy. This put Turkey, which craved British-owned Cyprus and hated Russia, even more firmly on the side of the Central Powers of Germany and Austria-Hungary. (The *Goeben* became the *Yavuz* and remained the main Turkish flagship until 1950.) At a dinner with his friends the Hamiltons soon afterwards, Churchill said that 'Admiral Troubridge is a ruined man, and will probably be court-martialled and shot – like [the eighteenth-century sailor who failed to capture Minorca] Admiral Byng.'[154] In the event Troubridge was acquitted at his court martial, but his career was effectively over.

In order to prevent a similar incident, Churchill sent a company from the Sherwood Foresters Regiment to the Armstrong shipyard on the Tyne and seized a Turkish dreadnought that was almost completed. The *Reshadieh* was renamed the *Erin* and sent to Scapa Flow. A second Turkish battleship under construction, the *Sultan Osman I*, became the *Agincourt*. The Turks were infuriated, despite a generous financial offer from Britain for the use of the ships for the duration of hostilities.[155] The ships had been bought by public subscription – Turkish women had even sold their hair to raise the money – and the country was in uproar over their confiscation. McKenna, Lloyd George and many others were later to claim that Churchill had forced Turkey on to the Central Powers' side with these seizures, but it was untrue: on 2 August Turkey had secretly undertaken to join Germany and Austria, as soon as the time was ripe.

After the expiration of the 11 p.m. ultimatum on 4 August, Churchill went over to No. 10, although Lloyd George later claimed that he recalled sitting with Asquith in the Cabinet Room waiting for the ultimatum to expire when the double doors were suddenly flung open and Churchill came in to say that he was about to order the Fleet to action stations. 'Winston dashed into the room, radiant, his face bright, his manner keen, one word pouring out on another,' Lloyd George claimed. 'You could see he was a really happy man. I wondered if this was the state of mind to be in at the opening of such a fearful war as this.'[156] Churchill's exuberance that night has long been held against him, but it was the heightened emotion of someone who had not wanted the war to break out and had offered

Germany the naval holiday three times. He had nonetheless planned meticulously what his department would do if war came.

In 1913, A. G. Gardiner had accused Churchill of presenting an 'horrific picture of the German menace. He believes it all because his mind once seized with an idea works with enormous velocity round it, intensifies it, enlarges it, makes it shadow the whole sky. In the theatre of his mind it is always the hour of fate and the crack of doom . . . He will write his name big on our future. Let us take care he does not write it in blood.'[157] Elsewhere in that essay Gardiner wrote, 'He thinks of Napoleon; he thinks of his great ancestor. Thus did they bear themselves; thus in this rugged and awful crisis will he bear himself. It is not make-believe, it is not insincerity: it is that in that fervid and picturesque imagination there are always great deeds afoot with himself cast by destiny in the Agamemnon rôle.'[158] Gardiner was clearly goading the thirty-nine-year-old First Lord in that last full year of peace, but if Churchill had died before 1939 he would principally be known as the man who got the Royal Navy ready for the Great War.

# 9
# 'This Glorious, Delicious War' August 1914–March 1915

*The war will be long and sombre.*

Churchill, September 1914[1]

*Criticism is always advantageous. I have derived continued benefit from criticism at all periods of my life, and I do not remember any time when I was ever short of it.*

Churchill, House of Commons, November 1914[2]

Churchill embarked on the Great War like a dynamo. He set up the Admiralty War Group, which met daily – sometimes several times a day – and which consisted of himself, the First Sea Lord (Prince Louis of Battenberg), the Second Sea Lord (Vice Admiral Sir Frederick Hamilton), the Chief of the Naval War Staff (Vice Admiral Sir Doveton Sturdee) and the Naval Secretary (Rear Admiral Sir Horace Hood), thereby subtly shifting executive power away from the Board of the Admiralty which had traditionally run the Navy. The War Group agreed that the Royal Navy's overriding strategic objectives must be to transport the BEF to France, blockade Germany, confine the German High Seas Fleet to its Baltic and North Sea ports and sink it if it emerged, and keep the Empire's global trade routes open. Churchill and Fisher – but not many others at the Admiralty – also dreamed of taking strategic points such as the island of Borkum in the Ems estuary or Heligoland (a persistent fascination for Fisher), or perhaps even landing an army in northern Germany once the situation in France had stabilized.

Outside the Admiralty, however, the organization of the war was ridiculously haphazard. Decisions were made by a few ministers called together ad hoc in emergencies with no one taking minutes. Only at the end of November 1914 was a War Council of eight members formed, which met around an octagonal table with Hankey as secretary, although it soon grew to thirteen. The Cabinet had twenty-two sub-committees by September, and thirty-eight by March 1916, many of which overlapped in their responsibilities and personnel.[3] Asquith completely failed to grasp, as Churchill and all too few others did, that this struggle was going to be totally different from anything they had seen before.

Although only two days earlier No. 10 had deprecated the idea of the BEF going to France, the invasion of Belgium that day and the British declaration of war the next changed everything. At a War Council meeting on 5 August 1914, Churchill argued that the BEF should be sent to France as soon as possible, and found general support. He did not want it simply to join the French line at the front at Mauberge, and argued that it should concentrate on building up its strength in Tours – equidistant between Saint-Nazaire and Paris – as a strategic reserve able to exploit weak spots in the German line and fight a war of manoeuvre. However the new Secretary for War, Lord Kitchener, who had been appointed that day on Churchill's advice, supported the plan of Major-General Henry Wilson, the Director of Military Operations at the War Office – which had long been in existence but kept secret from the Cabinet – to place the BEF on the left of the French line.

At the Other Club that evening, Kitchener proposed that Admiral Jellicoe be elected. Recently appointed, at Churchill's insistence, as commander-in-chief of the Home Fleet, Jellicoe was responsible for the operation to get the four infantry and one cavalry division of the BEF over to France between 9 and 22 August, which was extraordinarily successful. (Indeed, by the end of 1914, the Navy had transported 809,000 men, 203,000 horses and 250,000 tons of stores across the Channel without loss.)[4] At the end of dinner, Churchill rose and said he intended to disregard the rule against any toasts but the Loyal Toast. He then proposed that the Club drink to 'Success to British Arms'.

The next day General Wilson called in at the Admiralty to say farewell before leaving for France. The Irish-born Wilson had distrusted Churchill over the 'Ulster Pogrom', when the general had actively encouraged the Curragh mutineers. He told Churchill that, while they 'had often differed and never been afraid to cross swords', he had 'behaved like a hero at Downing Street on the 5th' in insisting that Britain support France on the continent. 'I wished to shake hands with him and to bid him goodbye,' Wilson wrote in his diary. 'He began to tell me he was sure I would "Lead to victory" and then he completely broke down and cried. I never liked him so much.'[5] Wilson put the BEF at Mons, on the left of the French line, as planned.

The King, Lloyd George and Kitchener grandly took a pledge not to consume any alcohol during the war. Churchill pointedly did not join them. It did not help the war effort – Britain's ally, France, needed exports, after all – but showed a degree of self-sacrifice. The King and Kitchener kept their pledge, becoming somewhat irritable as a result. Lloyd George soon broke his, though he pretended he had not. 'Churchill put on a grand air,' recounted Frances Stevenson, Lloyd George's secretary and mistress, 'and announced that he was not going to be influenced by the King, and refused to give up his liquor – he thought the whole thing was absurd.'[6] In January 1919, he laughingly instructed Riddell, a teetotaller, on the 'merits of a reasonable quantity of strong drink [which] alters one's outlook on life. At the end of a troublesome, gloomy day it makes things look happier and it is invaluable as an adjunct to oratory and social intercourse.'[7]

When it was recognized by 16 August that there would be between 20,000 and 30,000 Royal Navy reservists for whom there would not be room on ships, Churchill set up the first three brigades of a new Royal Naval Division (RND), a new infantry force under the control of the Admiralty rather than the Army. The division was ultimately to see action in many of the bloodiest engagements of the war, including Gallipoli, the Somme and the Third Battle of Ypres (Passchendaele). Many of Churchill's friends and acquaintances served in it – 'salamanders born in the furnace', as he called them – and several were killed, including Rupert Brooke, Vere Harmsworth, Patrick Shaw-Stewart, Alan Campbell and William Ker. Two who survived, the Prime Minister's son Arthur 'Oc' Asquith and Bernard Freyberg, sustained more than a dozen wounds between them.[8]

The RND kept naval ranks, customs, language and traditions. They wore beards, drank to the King's health seated, had battalions named after admirals such as Nelson, Drake, Hawke and Hood, and so on – differentiating them from the Army divisions in the BEF. Churchill, ever attuned to the warrior psychology, noted that it was 'strange how men . . . confronted with the cruellest trials and under the constant menace amounting almost to certainty of death, find comfort and revivifying strength in little things which to others, freed from these circumstances, living in an easy and exalted sphere, only appear trivial and, perhaps, absurd'.[9] Towards the end of the war an attempt was made to disband the division. It was resisted by Sir Edward Carson, then First Lord of the Admiralty, earning Churchill's respect for what he ruefully called Carson's 'ample controversial powers'. In 1923 Churchill's preface to the history of the division was one of his most moving pieces of writing.

In accordance with a by now well-established practice of seeing for himself what was going on, on 19 August he visited the mayors of Calais and Dunkirk to discuss the redoubts they were building to keep the Germans at bay. After the Allied defeats at Namur and Mons between 22 and 24 August, the key invasion ports of Dunkirk, Calais and Boulogne were, in Churchill's phrase, left 'naked'. 'No one can tell how far this great adventure may carry us all,' he told his brother Jack. 'Unless we win, I do not want to live any more. But win we will.'[10]

On 26 August, Britain's Russian allies captured the code and cipher books from the German light cruiser *Magdeburg* after it ran aground on the Estonian coast. These allowed the Room 40 cryptographers to start decoding German signals in real time. Churchill did not inform the Cabinet, or anyone who might be captured at sea, but kept the secret within the Admiralty War Group.[11]

While II Corps of the BEF were engaged in desperate rearguard fighting at Le Cateau on 26 August, Roger Keyes, whom Churchill had appointed commodore of submarines in 1912, put into operation a plan to surprise and destroy German light forces in the Heligoland Bight. The plan was based on baiting a trap and catching the German destroyers at low tide when their dreadnoughts could not cross the Jade Bar sandbanks, but it had been rejected by the Admiralty as too risky. Keyes took it straight to Churchill, who approved it, and Jellicoe dispatched Beatty to command the operation. On 28 August three German light cruisers were sunk and three more damaged, and Tirpitz's son was captured. Afterwards, Churchill boarded the British flagship at Sheerness to hail what he called 'a brilliant episode'.[12] 'Winston had a little scheme on foot,' Asquith told Venetia. 'It has come off very well . . . and some set-off to our sad losses on land.'[13]

On 1 September, Churchill wrote to Sir Charles Douglas, the new Chief of the Imperial General Staff (CIGS), to ask that the War Office and Admiralty start 'to examine and work out a plan for the seizure, by means of a Greek army of adequate strength, of the Gallipoli Peninsula, with a view to admitting a British fleet to the Sea of Marmara'.[14] The Dardanelles is a narrow strait that separates the eastern Mediterranean from the Sea of Marmara and thus Asia from Europe, which had been last forced by Admiral Sir John Duckworth during the Napoleonic Wars. It is noteworthy that Churchill assumed that, in order to get a British fleet through it, an army would first have to seize the Gallipoli Peninsula on its western side.

Between 7 and 13 September the German advance towards Paris was finally stopped at the Battle of the Marne. In 1911, Churchill had predicted that would happen on the fortieth day of the war, which fell on 13

September. But by then a new threat had emerged. On 7 September, the Belgian Government asked for a force of 25,000 men to defend Antwerp against the German Army which was moving rapidly towards it. 'The Admiralty regard the sustained and effective defence of Antwerp as a matter of high consequence,' Churchill told Asquith, Kitchener and Grey. 'It preserves the life of the Belgian nation: it safeguards a strategic point which, if captured, would be of the utmost menace.'[15] He proposed supplying Antwerp via the Scheldt, but the Cabinet rejected that and no other proposal was submitted nor any other contingency plan considered.

'We entered upon this war reluctantly after we had made every effort compatible with honour to avoid being drawn in,' Churchill told the National Liberal Club in a speech on 11 September, 'and we entered upon it with a full realization of the sufferings, losses, disappointments, vexations, and anxieties, and of the appalling and sustaining exertions which would be entailed upon us by our action.'[16] He did not believe in minimizing the danger or horror of war. His father's motto 'Trust the people' had convinced him that they could hear the worst, so long as it was not put in a demoralizing way. He also likened British sea power to the way 'the nose of the bulldog has been slanted backwards so that he can breathe with comfort without letting go'.[17] The *Manchester Guardian* pointed out how much he himself looked like a bulldog as he said it.

In mid-September, on his way to inspect naval installations in the Scottish Highlands, Churchill was involved in an incident that he would years later write about in an entertaining essay which he entitled 'My Spy Story'. He was accompanied by three senior officers in uniform, including Sir Henry Oliver, the Director of Naval Intelligence, one of whom spotted that a house on the coast had a searchlight on its roof, which they feared might be intended to send messages to U-boats. 'Suspicion and curiosity went hand in hand,' Churchill recalled, 'and the excitement of adventure spurred them both.'[18] They approached the front door, armed with revolvers. The house belonged to Sir Arthur Bignold, a highly respectable former MP, whose butler 'seemed startled at such a visit'. The searchlight turned out to be for locating hillside game so as to give stalkers a head start, but Churchill had it dismantled all the same.[19] Although he has been criticized for having 'fully shared in the spy paranoia' of the time, in fact no fewer than twenty-two German spies were arrested on the outbreak of war, half of whom were shot by firing squad in the Tower of London.[20] British intelligence caught most of them through the interception of their correspondence under Home Office warrants, a system he had pioneered.[21]

On 21 September, speaking to an all-party recruiting rally of 15,000 people at the Tournament Hall in Liverpool, Churchill made an error, though not one of policy. 'Although we hope that a decision at sea will be a feature of this war,' he said, and 'we hope that our men will have a chance of settling the question with the German Fleet, yet if they do not come out and fight in time of war they will be dug out like rats in a hole.'[22] The phrase drew loud cheers at the time, but the Establishment did not like its rumbustious tone. The King found it 'undignified and ungentlemanly', and the Earl of Selborne, a senior Tory politician, considered that 'The fundamental fault of his system is his restlessness.' When reminded of his statement in a debate eighteen months later, Churchill said, 'It was a very foolish phrase, and I regret that it slipped out.' Of course Churchill's rhetorical phrases did not 'slip out' – they were carefully written out in psalm form like all his other speeches. It would probably have been forgotten, or at least forgiven, if the very next day three cruisers, HMS *Aboukir*, *Hogue* and *Cressy*, had not been sunk by a single U-boat in broad daylight, with the loss of 1,459 men. Nicknamed the 'Live-Bait Squadron', they were patrolling the Broad Fourteens, a southern part of the North Sea. 'These cruisers ought not to continue on this beat,' Churchill had written to Battenberg four days earlier. 'The risk to such ships is not justified by any services they can render.'[23] The King was heard to remark sardonically that 'The rats came out of their own accord and to our cost.' The Tory press, always ready to pounce, was receiving leaks from Churchill's enemies at the Admiralty and sharpened its knives. McKenna, who had been roundly criticizing Churchill in private, now had yet more ammunition in Cabinet.[24] (Still bitter at having had to swap jobs with Churchill in 1911, McKenna told Riddell only ten days after the outbreak of war that Churchill had let the *Goeben* 'slip through our fingers', should not have seized the Turkish ships under construction and should have mined the German coast.)[25]

By 28 September, the Austrian-made Skoda howitzers that had smashed Namur and also Liège were being turned on Antwerp, as Churchill had predicted. Three days later, General Joseph Joffre, Commander-in-Chief of French forces on the Western Front, offered two divisions to relieve the city, but in the end he only sent their Fusiliers Marins, thus reducing any potential Allied relief force from 53,000 men to 22,000. Sir John French, who was racing up from Armentières to Ypres, also resiled from his original statement to Kitchener that the relief of Antwerp was 'of first importance'.[26] So Churchill suggested flinging the Royal Naval Division into Antwerp, until it could be relieved by a new regular corps under Sir Henry Rawlinson that was not yet quite ready to deploy. Asquith privately mused that 'it would be idle butchery to send a force like Winston's little army there,' but he didn't officially object to the deployment, even though it contained his own son Arthur, whom he told would be envied 'being sent off after three days to the front'.[27]

In the early hours of Saturday, 3 October, with the Prime Minister in Wales, Grey and Kitchener agreed that Churchill himself should go to Antwerp with the RND to assess the situation and reinforce the Belgians' resolve to hold the city. It was of course highly irregular for a minister to take command of troops in a war zone. Churchill told the Belgian authorities that 2,000 Royal Marines would arrive that day, followed by 8,000 troops of the RND within three days, and an entire corps (Rawlinson's) within ten. As the naval brigades numbered only 6,000 men at the time, Churchill clearly intended to send even the rawest recruits.[28] Asquith supported the idea, telling Venetia Stanley, 'I cannot but think he will stiffen them [the Belgians] up to the sticking point.'[29] Churchill did indeed stiffen them up, persuading the Belgian Prime Minister to continue to defend Antwerp if the Allies could protect the Belgian Field Army's retreat through the city.[30]

Doubts in the Admiralty about what Churchill was trying to do with the RND can be gauged from the diary entry of the acerbic Captain Herbert Richmond, the Assistant Director of Military Operations. He wrote on Sunday, 4 October, 'It is a tragedy that the Navy should be in such lunatic hands at this time.' Beatty told his wife: 'The man must have been mad to have thought he could relieve [Antwerp] . . . by putting eight thousand half-trained troops into it.'[31] Yet Antwerp had a treble line of forts and inundations, and seemed highly defensible.

'I am willing to resign my office and undertake command of relieving and defensive forces assigned to Antwerp in conjunction with the Belgian Army,' Churchill wrote formally to the Cabinet on Monday, 5 October, 'provided that I am given necessary military rank and authority and full powers of a commander of a detached force in the field. I feel it is my duty to offer my services because I am sure this arrangement will afford the best prospects of a victorious result.'[32] When this was read to the Cabinet it gave rise to what Asquith told Venetia was 'Homeric' laughter – that is, the loud and unrestrained laughter of the gods.[33] Kitchener, on the other hand, thought it was a perfectly reasonable suggestion, and was willing to make Churchill a lieutenant-general while Sir Henry Rawlinson was readying his force for Antwerp.[34]

Churchill left for Antwerp immediately, but instead of wearing a military uniform he wore that of an Elder Brother of Trinity House, Britain's lighthouse authority, founded in 1514 to protect the wellbeing of seafarers, which featured a naval cap and badge and a pea jacket. The story goes that when asked by a Belgian of ambassadorial rank what his uniform signified, Churchill replied in his inimitable, execrable French, 'Moi, je suis un frère aîné de la Trinité'* 'Mon Dieu!' replied the Belgian. 'La Trinité?!'[35] On Wednesday, 7 October, while Churchill was in Antwerp, Sarah, his third child, was born at Admiralty House. She was named after the great Sarah Churchill, Duchess of Marlborough, who had built Blenheim, but was quickly nicknamed 'Bumblebee'.

On that day and on the 8th, King Albert of the Belgians led his Field Army south and west out of Antwerp to take a line of defence on the Yser River. The RND joined this defence of the line, and with the Belgian 2nd Division and garrison troops covered the retirement of the Field Army over the Scheldt.[36] Although the wisdom of Churchill's going to Antwerp with untrained men can be questioned, his characteristic raw physical courage there cannot be. 'He repeatedly exposed himself upon the firing-line,' reported the American journalist E. Alexander Powell, 'and on one occasion, near Waelhem, had a rather narrow escape, a shell bursting in his immediate vicinity.'[37]

'I thought it was going to be my great opportunity,' Churchill said of the Antwerp expedition years later.[38] Without the diversion of the large French reinforcements that Joffre had initially promised, however, the Belgians were losing heart. There was no real hope that Churchill could prevent Antwerp from falling to the Germans, with only 8,000 brave but untrained RND troops. It was only surprising that it held out as long as it did, finally falling on 10 October. Some 215 British troops were killed or wounded, 936 were taken prisoner and 1,500 were interned for the rest of the war by the neutral Dutch.[39]

Churchill has been much criticized for sending the RND into Antwerp, but it is worth remembering that they were the only troops available in Britain at the time. The Belgians had been expected to surrender Antwerp on 3 October: it held out for an extra week, and much of that delay can be put down to Churchill's prompt action. 'This last week, which has delayed the fall of Antwerp by at least seven days,' Asquith wrote to Venetia Stanley, 'and has prevented the Germans from linking up their forces – has not been thrown away and may . . . have even been of vital value.'[40] Some military historians consider that the week gained allowed Sir John French to stop the Germans at the First Battle of Ypres, and so prevent Dunkirk and Calais from falling into German hands.

Churchill returned to Britain on 9 October, the day before Antwerp surrendered. Lloyd George offered his 'congratulations' on his 'brilliant

* 'I am an elder brother of the Trinity.'

effort'. 'Winston has returned,' Frances Stephenson told her diary, 'admitting failure, and blaming Kitchener and the War Office for lack of foresight.'[41] Kitchener in turn blamed Joffre.[42] Yet Haldane called it 'a great and heroic episode', and Grey said he felt 'a glow imparted by the thought that I am sitting next to a hero'.[43] Churchill asked Asquith for a military command. 'His mouth waters at the sight and thought of Kitchener's new armies,' the Prime Minister wrote to Venetia Stanley:

> Are these 'glittering commands' to be entrusted to 'dug-out trash'* bred on the obsolete tactics of twenty-five years ago, 'mediocrities who have led a sheltered life mouldering in military routine,' etc., etc? For about a quarter of an hour he poured forth a ceaseless cataract of invective and appeal, and I much regretted that there was no shorthand writer within hearing, as some of his unpremeditated phrases were quite priceless. He was, however, three parts serious and declared that a political career was nothing to him in comparison with military glory ... He is a wonderful creature, with a curious dash of schoolboy simplicity ... and what someone said of genius – 'a zigzag streak of lightning in the brain'.[44]

Within days, the tide had turned against Churchill over the Antwerp expedition, especially in the press, once the rawness of the returning RND had become apparent. 'Winston is becoming a great danger,' Lloyd George told Riddell. He likened him to a self-destructing torpedo. Bonar Law wrote that he 'seems to have an entirely unbalanced mind which is a real danger at a time like this'.[45] Asquith now believed it a 'wicked folly' for Churchill to have sent 'a callow crowd of the rawest tyros, most of whom had never fired off a rifle' and told Venetia Stanley, 'It was like sending sheep to the shambles [abattoir].'[46] The *Morning Post* described Antwerp as 'a costly blunder'; for the *Daily Mail* it was 'a gross example of malorganization'. On 19 October the *Morning Post* added, 'This severe lesson ought to teach him that he is not ... a Napoleon, but a Minister of the Crown with no time either to organize or lead armies in the field ... To be photographed and cinematographed under fire at Antwerp is an entirely unnecessary addition to the risks and horrors of war.' Four days later it went further: 'When Mr Churchill became First Lord he set himself more directly to undermine the power of the Board and to establish himself as Dictator ... the Navy is governed no longer by a Board of experts, but by a brilliant and erratic amateur.'[47]

In 1931 Churchill reflected on the whole episode in his essay 'A Second

* 'Dug-out' was a slang expression for ex-officers re-employed for military duties, as well as being the term for shelters in trenches. Churchill was using it in the former sense.

Choice'. 'I ought, for instance, never to have gone to Antwerp,' he wrote. 'I ought to have remained in London . . . Those who are charged with the direction of supreme affairs must sit on the mountain-tops of control; they must never descend into the valleys of direct physical and personal action.'[48] He would say much the same about his appearance at Sidney Street. In going to Antwerp, he showed the same absence of restraint he had shown there and was to show again and again in the future, as he climbed on to rooftops during the London Blitz, tried to watch D-Day from the Channel, attended Operation Dragoon in a warship, visited the front line in Italy, crossed the Rhine in a landing craft, and so on. But he not only enjoyed descending into the valleys: doing so gave him insights into conflicts that he could not get from the mountain-tops.

Churchill gave vent to his strategic frustrations at a dinner with Captain Richmond on 24 October. The Captain recorded him 'in low spirits, oppressed with the impossibility of doing anything. The attitude of waiting, threatened all the time by submarines, unable to strike back at their fleet, which lies behind the dock-gates of the [Kiel] Canal, Emden or Wilhelmshaven, and the inability of the staff to make any suggestions, seem to bother him. I have not seen him so despondent before.'[49] Although blockade was an unromantic strategy, unsuited to Churchill's restless mind, it worked well, causing Germany great privation. Some 221 German merchant ships lay idle in German ports, with a further 245 detained in Allied ports and 1,059 in neutral ports.

Three days later, the battleship HMS *Audacious* hit a mine off Lough Swilly while carrying out firing practice, but with no loss of life. Usually the public was informed of the loss of ships, but Churchill decided to keep this one secret as a declaration of war from Turkey seemed to be in the balance. Belgian coastal operations were in progress, and he did not want to advertise that the Grand Fleet was north of Ireland, and thus in no position to assist them. 'Trust the people' occasionally had to be tempered by common sense.

That same day, Churchill had the unpleasant task of asking Battenberg to resign as first sea lord. The xenophobic whispering campaign against the German-born admiral was not the only reason, although that had spilt out into public speeches, a poison-pen letter campaign and attacks in the press. (Lord Crawford wrote in his diary that Battenberg was 'not only a German, but a German *who employs German servants*'.)[50] The personal attacks, the losses at sea and perhaps also Battenberg's chronic gout – his gargantuan breakfasts, Henry Oliver noted, were 'enough to have fed an officers' mess' – had left him depressed and off form.[51] Churchill had to tread carefully as Battenberg was the King's cousin by marriage. The admiral was mollified by being appointed to the Privy Council on his resignation.

In Battenberg's place, against the protestations of the King and others, Churchill appointed the seventy-three-year-old Lord Fisher, whom he described as 'a veritable volcano of knowledge and of inspiration'.[52] Yet despite Churchill's claim that 'He left me with the impression of a terrific engine of mental and physical power burning and throbbing in that ancient frame,' Fisher's own naval assistant, Commander Dudley Pound, told a friend that in fact Fisher was 'a very old man, and really only put in about two hours work a day at the Admiralty'.[53] Fisher addressed his letters 'Beloved Winston', leaked information to newspapers, conspired with the Tory opposition, wrote long letters full of triple underlinings and multiple exclamation marks, openly opposed several of Churchill's policies and generally behaved like an irascible, impossible martinet.[54] He would have been fine as an adviser, but Churchill made an error in appointing him to the most senior position in the Navy after his own.

On the day that Fisher took up his post, the newly Turkish ships *Goeben* and *Breslau* shelled Odessa and Sevastopol in the Black Sea. The closure of the Dardanelles by Turkey meant that, if ever the Allies had aid or armaments for Russia in future, they could not be sent via the Mediterranean. Allied prestige was also thought to have suffered in the neutral countries of the region, including Italy, Greece, Romania and Bulgaria. Churchill ordered Vice Admiral Sackville Carden, the Commander-in-Chief of the British squadron in the Mediterranean, to bombard the Turkish Outer Forts of Sedd el Bahr and Kum Kale in the Dardanelles, which was duly done on 4 November, the day before Britain and France declared war on Turkey.[55] To commence hostilities without a formal declaration of war was a serious matter, but this was not the last time Churchill would do it.

At about this time, Lloyd George started deliberately briefing against Churchill, and no longer in the sly, half-joking way he had in the past. Their alliance that had been badly frayed before the war over defence spending had effectively fallen apart. If the war was won at sea, Lloyd George's contribution at the Treasury was unlikely to be lauded as much as that of his erstwhile friend and supposed Cabinet ally. 'Churchill went to the Front waving his sword,' Lloyd George told C. P. Scott, the editor of the *Manchester Guardian*, 'but the net result was that the evacuation was delayed a few days, that the Belgians lost twenty thousand men interned and we about two thousand and that Antwerp was half ruined.'[56] Scott asked if there had been any strategic gain from the delay, and Lloyd George untruthfully answered 'None.' 'Through all this narrative there was obvious a strong personal antagonism to Churchill,' Scott noted to himself. The seven-year 'treaties of alliance' agreed at the Café Royal in June 1910 had barely lasted half that time.

Back on 1 October, Churchill had minuted on a telegram from Rear Admiral Sir Christopher Cradock, whose squadron was off the west coast of South America, 'It would be best for the British ships to keep within supporting distance of one another, whether in the [Magellan] Straits or near the Falklands, and to postpone the cruise along the west coast until the present uncertainty about the [whereabouts of] *Scharnhorst* and *Gneisenau* is cleared up.'[57] These battleships, under the command of Admiral Graf Maximilian von Spee, surprised Cradock on 1 November near the Chilean port of Coronel. Two British cruisers were sunk, and Cradock was killed. Fisher sent off two modern battle cruisers, HMS *Invincible* and *Inflexible*, to track down von Spee's force, which they succeeded in doing in the only decisive naval battle of the war, off the Falkland Islands on 8 December. The German overseas squadron was destroyed and von Spee killed. The defeat at Coronel was widely blamed by the Tory press on an overly interventionist Churchill, however, who was not given credit for the Falklands victory.[58]

'The British people have taken for themselves this motto,' Churchill declared at the Lord Mayor's Banquet at the Guildhall on 9 November, '"Business carried on as usual during alterations on the map of Europe."'[59] The phrase 'Business as usual' was to be employed frequently during the Second World War, when it raised morale after being chalked up on seemingly bombed-out enterprises during the Blitz. Later in November 1914, Churchill openly confronted the prospect of having to fight on without France: 'But even if we were single-handed, as we were in the days of the Napoleonic wars, we should have no reason to despair of our capacity – no doubt we should suffer discomfort and privation and loss – but we should have no reason to despair of our capacity to go on indefinitely.'[60]

At the first meeting of the new War Council on 25 November, Churchill floated the notion of the Navy forcing the Dardanelles, sailing through the Sea of Marmara and anchoring off Constantinople (modern-day Istanbul), and then either shelling the city into submission or occupying it, or both. This was, however, no longer presented initially as a land operation, as it had been when he first envisaged opening up the strait. Kitchener, Lloyd George and Hankey all liked the idea, though there was not enough support in the War Council for it to be put into execution. Churchill nonetheless kept a squadron of ships at Suez to convoy troops for a future operation.

On 16 December a squadron of the German Navy under Admiral Franz von Hipper slipped past the Royal Navy blockade of the North Sea and bombarded Hartlepool and Scarborough, which seemed an inexplicable humiliation for the world's greatest naval power of over a thousand vessels. The German warships involved had in fact very nearly come to grief at the hands of Beatty, but Churchill could not reveal that without giving away operational secrets and had to weather a good deal more press criticism of himself and the Admiralty.

The front in France and Flanders was quickly solidifying into static trench warfare. 'I think it quite possible that neither side will have the strength to penetrate the other's line in the Western theatre,' Churchill wrote to Asquith on 29 December. 'The position of both armies is not likely to undergo any decisive change – although no doubt several hundred thousand men will be spent to satisfy the military mind on the point . . . Are there not other alternatives than sending our armies to chew barbed wire in Flanders?'[61] Only four days later, the perfect alternative seemed to present itself.

On 2 January 1915, Grand Duke Nicholas of Russia urged Britain to undertake a diversionary attack, no more than a 'demonstration' as he put it, against Turkey, which was attacking Russia heavily in the Caucasus.[62] When Churchill and Kitchener discussed this proposal, Kitchener said the Army was too small and fully committed to undertake anything significant, but reminded Churchill of their discussions at the War Council and suggested that the Dardanelles would make a good target, 'particularly if . . . reports could be spread at the same time that Constantinople was threatened'.[63]

The problem was that the 41 miles of the Dardanelles were only 4 miles wide at their greatest extent and less than a mile at their narrowest, sown with underwater minefields in the strait and with Turkish forts on both banks, as well as moveable mortars and artillery. There were also strong currents running from the Black Sea to the Mediterranean, which would cause problems for any minesweepers attempting to clear a path. Back in 1904, Fisher had described any putative attack on the Dardanelles as 'mightily hazardous'.[64] That same year, Haldane had said 'there would be a grave risk of a reverse'.[65] Churchill himself had written in 1911 that 'It is no longer possible to force the Dardanelles, and nobody should expose a modern fleet to such peril.'[66] When asked in 1914 whether he could contribute to such a plan, Joffre said he could spare no men from the Western Front.

Yet, for all the operational problems, the scheme seemed to offer huge strategic advantages if it could somehow be brought off. It would use the Royal Navy for something other than blockade work in the North Sea;

the Ottoman First Army would be cut off in the Gallipoli Peninsula; it might even provoke a coup d'état in Constantinople and a new pro-Allied Turkish government; it might conceivably bring over Romania and Bulgaria and therefore help the Serbs against the Austrians, and encourage the Italians and Greeks to join the Allies. Beyond this, it could open a warm-water route to supply the hard-pressed Russians should the Allies one day have any surplus to give them.[67] One of the soldiers who fought at Gallipoli, a thirty-two-year-old Captain Clement Attlee of the South Lancashire Regiment, believed all his life that, as he put it, 'the strategic conception was sound'.[68]

On 3 January 1915, Churchill telegraphed Carden asking for his views. Carden replied that the strait could not be rushed but a large fleet and a methodical campaign might succeed.[69] Carden's plan was to silence the Outer Forts, clear the minefield, destroy the Inner Forts at the Narrows and only then sail through the Sea of Marmara, bombard key Ottoman installations and go on to Constantinople. The main Turkish arsenal was on the Bosporus, and would be well within the range of British guns. Churchill asked the planning staff at the Admiralty, which was highly doubtful about the project, to investigate the possibility of forcing the strait using some mothballed but heavily armoured pre-dreadnought battleships. He telegraphed Carden: 'Importance of results would justify severe loss.' This sounds heartless – but, if the result was indeed to force Turkey out of the war, was no more than the truth.[70]

The 4th of January saw the first of many resignation threats from Fisher, not over the Dardanelles or his plan to attack the German coast in the North Sea or Baltic, but over the rejection of his proposal to execute a German hostage for every Briton killed in Zeppelin raids. Churchill ignored the resignation threat, and Fisher behaved as if nothing had happened.* In retrospect, Churchill should have simply accepted one of Fisher's early resignation threats, but he liked and admired the charismatic, if deeply neurotic, sailor, even as he was making his opposition more and more public.

Instead he wrote to Fisher the same day, 'I think we had better hear what others have to say about the Turkish plans before taking a decided line. I would not grudge a hundred thousand men because of the great political effects in the Balkan Peninsula: but Germany is the foe, and it is bad war to seek cheaper victories and easier antagonists.'[71] The very next

* The Royal Naval Air Service continued to bomb the Zeppelins in their hangars and manufacturing sites as far afield as Friedrichshafen in southern Germany, destroying six in the first year of the war.

day, Carden telegraphed his view that 'The Dardanelles might be forced by extended operations with large number of ships.'[72] Churchill's reservations of twenty-four hours earlier evaporated, and he replied, 'High authorities here concur in your opinion.' This was misleading; Churchill had briefly discussed the issue with two admirals, both of whom had been fairly guarded in their responses, and had not yet mentioned it to the War Staff Group of the Admiralty.

At the time, the Dardanelles was not the most important item on Churchill's agenda. On the day he telegraphed Carden, he pressed Asquith about an invention he hoped might break the stalemate on the Western Front, where a solid line of trenches and barbed wire now stretched all the way from the English Channel to Switzerland, more than 400 miles. 'It would be quite easy in a short time to fit up a number of steam tractors with small armoured shelters, in which men and machine guns could be placed, which would be bullet-proof,' he suggested. 'Used at night they would not be affected by artillery fire to any extent. The caterpillar system would enable trenches to be crossed quite easily, and the weight of the machine would destroy all wire entanglements.'[73] As he later wrote in his war memoirs, 'As we could not go round the trenches, it was evidently necessary to go over them.'[74] He provided the enormous sum of £70,000 for research into the tank concept from the Admiralty budget, despite its clearly being a land weapon. His early, strong and sustained support for its development makes it plausible for him to be described as the father of the tank.

Despite the island's distance from Britain and close proximity to the German naval base of Emden, on 7 January the War Council approved Fisher's proposal to undertake detailed planning for the seizure of Borkum in Lower Saxony, an initiative for which he had been building up naval strength ever since becoming first sea lord. Churchill had supported Fisher over Borkum until the Dardanelles adventure laid out the prospect of a far more alluring prize. Much of the Admiralty was adamantly opposed to the Borkum expedition, and part of Fisher's later opposition to the Gallipoli expedition stemmed from the way it eclipsed this pet project that he had been promoting for years.

On 8 January, Kitchener read to the War Council a report from his department. 'The Dardanelles appeared to be a most suitable objective,' it stated, 'in cooperation with the Fleet.'[75] Kitchener now thought it should not be solely a naval operation, but could be done with 150,000 men – a force certainly not yet available. Lloyd George thought it would require more.[76] Sir John French's view, that there should not be an attack in the East until success in the West had proved impossible, was overruled.[77] But

Churchill's original intention that the Greeks could support the operation with ground troops was impossible in the face of continued Greek neutrality.

On 10 January, Churchill sat next to Margot Asquith at dinner in Kent. He told her that he no longer wanted to be viceroy of India, which had been his previous interim ambition on the way to the premiership. Now it was only the war that mattered to him. 'My God,' he told her. '*This* is living History ... It will be read by a thousand generations – think of *that*!! Why, I would not be out of this glorious, delicious war for anything the world could give me ... I say, don't repeat that I said the word "*delicious*" – you know what I mean.'[78] She only told her diary, but it was foolish to say such a thing to someone who so distrusted him. Her husband and much of the Establishment were so affronted by the moral horrors of the war that any enthusiasm for it – let alone the kind of jubilant obsession with it that Churchill personified – was considered tasteless and unbecoming.

On 11 January, Carden produced a four-point operational plan for the Dardanelles which involved the destruction of the Outer Forts, action against the strait, bombardment of the Inner Forts by shelling at 10,000 yards' range and then sweeping a passage through the minefield.[79] Churchill enthusiastically endorsed this, saying later, 'Both the First Sea Lord and the Chief of Staff [Admiral Sir Henry Oliver] seemed favourable to it ... The four or five great naval authorities ... all rated it as an extremely interesting and hopeful proposal.' Churchill added that Admiral Sir Henry Jackson, the Chief of the Naval War Staff, 'approved its detail. Right or wrong, it was a Service plan ... I did not and I could not make the plan.'[80] In fact Jackson had been highly sceptical. Sir Percy Scott, the Admiralty gunnery expert, thought it 'an impossible task', and Fisher denied having been asked his opinion at that time. The next day Churchill wrote a memorandum for the War Council in favour of forcing the Dardanelles, which ended 'Definite plans should be worked out accordingly.'[81] It is hard to escape the impression that by 11 January he had set his heart on the expedition, believing that it might be the key to breaking the Western deadlock.

At noon on Wednesday, 13 January 1915, the War Council held a key, four-hour meeting. Asquith was flanked by Sir John French and Arthur Balfour (who had been invited to attend meetings of the War Council, despite being a member of the Opposition). Next to French was Kitchener, then Fisher, Churchill and Sir Arthur Wilson (who at seventy-two had been recalled to the Admiralty by Churchill and was prepared in the emergency of war to forget past differences), and beyond them Crewe,

Grey and Lloyd George. 'You won't often see a stranger collection of men around one table,' Asquith told Venetia Stanley.[82] French began by putting forward a plan for an advance along the Channel coast, which was rejected by Lloyd George and Balfour. There were extended discussions about the attritional fighting on the Western Front.

At what seemed like the end of a long, ineffectual meeting, Churchill read out Carden's signal and produced the plan for an attack on the Dardanelles by the Navy alone. 'The idea caught on at once,' Hankey wrote later.

> The whole atmosphere changed. Fatigue was forgotten . . . Churchill unfolded his plans . . . lucidly but quietly and without exaggerated optimism. The War Council turned eagerly from the dreary vista of a 'slogging match' on the Western Front to brighter prospects, as they seemed, in the Mediterranean. The Navy, in whom everyone had implicit confidence, and whose opportunities had so far been few and far between, was to come into the front line.[83]

Hankey later suspected that Churchill pushed the Dardanelles plan in order to recoup his reputational loss at Antwerp, but at the time he himself was as keen as everyone else.[84]

Churchill suggested that the Turkish forts would be destroyed 'within a few weeks' by naval bombardment. The field guns on the banks of the strait would be 'merely an inconvenience'. Once through, the fleet would sink the *Goeben*. Because Churchill seemed to be giving the Admiralty's collective view, none of the politicians asked Fisher or Wilson for their thoughts, and they remained silent throughout the meeting. It was therefore assumed they were in favour, which they were not. 'Neither made any remark and I certainly thought that they agreed,' Churchill wrote later.[85] 'He was my chief,' Fisher would say, 'and it was silence or resignation.' As Churchill was to emphasize in November 1915, 'The War Council was immensely impressed with the political advantages of the plan if it could be carried out, and they pressed the Admiralty to find a way to carry it out. No one spoke against the methods proposed. No expert adviser indicated any dissent.'[86]

Kitchener said that no troops could be spared from the Western Front. Despite the earlier War Office assessment that the operation would require 150,000 men, Carden's opinion that the Dardanelles could be forced by ships alone persuaded the War Council to resolve that the Admiralty 'should also prepare for a naval expedition in February to bombard and take the Gallipoli Peninsula, with Constantinople as its objective'. Yet the wording made no sense: the Navy could 'take' neither the peninsula nor Constantinople without the Army's support.[87] The word 'prepare' was also interpreted differently by the various participants. To Churchill it meant 'prepare to launch' but to Asquith 'prepare to investigate further'. The real reason that Fisher and other Admiralty figures allowed their silence to be taken as endorsement was that it initially seemed to be a low-risk venture. They thought they could cut their losses if the pre-dreadnought vessels did not get through.[88] These were ships that could be lost without the Navy's all-important position in the North Sea being threatened. The prize seemed worth the possible cost.

'Everyone seemed alive to its advantages,' Churchill wrote of the plan in his war memoirs. 'If successful, the operation would open communications with Russia, enabling her to export her wheat and to receive munitions.'[89] In an excited note, Balfour also emphasized this aspect, pointing out that if Russia could resume her wheat exports 'This would restore the Russian exchanges' as well as 'cut the Turkish Army in two', 'put Constantinople under our control' and 'open a passage to the Danube'.[90] Yet the Allies were suffering a severe shell shortage of their own on the Western Front in the spring of 1915. If supplying the Russians with munitions was a motive for the operation, it could only have ever been a very long-term one.

On the day of the crucial meeting, Asquith, who was sixty-two, wrote two long love-letters to Venetia Stanley, who was twenty-seven, in addition to the one he had written after midnight the previous night. 'And you – my most dearly beloved,' he had written, 'to whom every day and night, I give you my best thoughts, my most intimate confidence, my unceasing devotion, my fears and hopes, my strength and weakness, my past my present my future.'[91] One letter was written at 3.30 p.m. during the War Council meeting, of which he said, 'A most interesting discussion, but so confidential and secret that I won't put anything down on paper, but will talk fully to you tomorrow.'[92] He read her last love-letter to him during the meeting. In the second letter he added, 'The Council is now over, having arrived harmoniously at four conclusions suggested by me, which will keep both Navy and Army busy till March. I am keen to tell you all about it, and see if it meets with your approval . . . Winston showed a great deal of rugged fluency.'[93] The 300,000 words Asquith wrote to Venetia between January 1913 and May 1915 allow us a unique insight into the mind of the Prime Minister during the early part of the Great War, but also remind us that he was not concentrating fully on the Gallipoli campaign, where hundreds of thousands of lives would shortly be at stake.

While Asquith was keeping Venetia informed of these secret military operations (in direct contravention of the Official Secrets Act which his own Government had drawn up), Lloyd George was telling Frances Stevenson that 'Churchill favours an attack through the Kattegat, as involving more honour and glory to himself.'[94] In fact, Churchill's support for Fisher's operations in the Baltic and landings in Schleswig-Holstein had dwindled once the War Council showed its preference for the Dardanelles operation.

Yet even as these meetings were taking place the original reason for the Dardanelles operation evaporated with Turkey's smashing defeat at the hands of the Russians at the Battle of Sarykamysh in the Caucasus, where by 17 January they had suffered 78,000 casualties out of 90,000 men engaged.[95] Russia was no longer in danger from Turkey, but by then the Dardanelles had opened up more glittering vistas for the hard-pressed War Council than merely helping the Russians in the Caucasus, including changing the balance of power in the Balkans and knocking Turkey out of the war. On 19 January, Churchill wrote to the Grand Duke Nicholas, 'It has been determined to attempt to force the passage of the Dardanelles,' which was not strictly true, as he had only been authorized to 'prepare' for such an expedition.[96]

Seeing his Borkum operation sidelined, Fisher now rallied opposition to the Dardanelles campaign. 'There is only one way out and that is to resign!' Fisher told Jellicoe on 19 January. 'I don't agree with a single step taken.'[97] Two days later he wrote, 'I just abominate the Dardanelles operation, unless a great change is made and it is settled to be a military operation with two hundred thousand [men] in conjunction with the Fleet.'[98] Yet he did not resign. Churchill told the official Government inquiry into the Gallipoli debacle, known as the Dardanelles Commission, that the first he heard of Fisher's opposition was when he read a memorandum from him on 25 January. This carried the title 'The Position of the British Fleet and its Policy of Steady Pressure', in which he stated that 'The pressure of sea power . . . requires great patience . . . husbanding our resources.'[99] It did not oppose the attack on the Dardanelles per se, but it discouraged any purely naval attack, stating, 'We play into Germany's hands if we risk fighting ships in any subsidiary operations such as coastal bombardments or the attack of fortified places without military cooperation . . . Even the older ships should not be risked, for they cannot be lost without losing men, and they form our only reserve behind the Grand Fleet.'[100]

Fisher was right: a huge combined-operations surprise attack in February would have had a far greater chance of success than the solely naval attack that took place on 18 March, followed by the Army's assault on 25 April. Yet Kitchener did not have that kind of force available at that time. 'People are beginning to get rather dissatisfied with Winston,' Frances Stevenson noted in her diary, parroting the thoughts of her lover. 'Fisher says they try to argue with him at the Admiralty, but he simply overrides them and talks them down. If he continues his domineering course they fear there may be a catastrophe.'[101]

Churchill decided against circulating Fisher's memorandum to the War Council, even though its only actual direct mention of the Dardanelles was in favour of a combined-forces attack in order to bring the Turkish Navy into the open. It might have been the Appendix to which Churchill objected, which quoted an unnamed naval officer in the *New York Times* who argued that time and 'the policy of watchful waiting' were on the Allies' side and 'those amateur strategists who demand that the British Fleet should charge madly over minefields to get to the Germans simply ask England to commit suicide.'[102]

Fisher did however send his memorandum to Asquith, who requested a meeting with him and Churchill before the next War Council meeting at 11.30 a.m. on 28 January. There Fisher told Asquith that he preferred the alternative schemes in the North Sea to the Dardanelles, but, crucially, in the words of the post-mortem Dardanelles Report of 1917, he 'did not criticize the attack on the Gallipoli Peninsula on its own merits'. When Churchill then presented a detailed account of the proposed operation to the War Council, using a large map of the strait, Hankey reported that he elucidated the Navy's proposals at considerable length, including all the potential risks and drawbacks. 'He fully explained the plan,' Hankey recalled. 'He explained it in very great detail. There he was standing up at the end of a long table with a map and the members crowding round him . . . He was reading from a document and explaining the whole thing in detail.'[103]

Fisher and Wilson were both present and a prolonged discussion ensued in which, as Churchill was later to point out, 'again no adverse opinions were expressed, and . . . Lord Fisher contented himself with saying that he had expressed his opinion to the Prime Minister – the operation was definitely sanctioned, and we were directed to execute it.'[104] During the meeting, Fisher rose from the table in irritation and went to the window. Kitchener joined him and persuaded him not to resign.[105] Later that same day, Churchill and Fisher discussed the operation again and Fisher agreed to go along with it. As he later admitted to the Commission, 'I went in the whole hog, *totus porcus*.'[106]

'Another personal matter which rather worries me is the growing friction between Winston and Fisher,' Asquith confided to Venetia Stanley.

> They came to see me this morning before the War Council, and gave tongue to their mutual grievances. I tried to compose their differences by a compromise, under which Winston was to give up for the present his bombardment

> of Zeebrugge, Fisher withdrawing his opposition to the Dardanelles. When at the Council we came to discuss the matter – which is warmly supported by Kitchener and Grey, and enthusiastically by A.J.B[alfour], old 'Jacky' maintained an obstinate and ominous silence. He is always threatening to resign and writes an almost daily letter to Winston.

'Winston, very ignorant, believes he can capture the Dardanelles without troops,' wrote Captain Richmond in his diary on 9 February.[107] In his evidence to the Commission, Admiral Wilson stated that Churchill thought 'he could do it without the Army' not least because 'he generally minimized the risks from mobile guns.'[108] Various individuals in the Admiralty tried to impress on Churchill the vital importance of having a major military element to the naval attack, at the minimum to assist the Marines in occupying any forts which the Navy had destroyed and passed by but which they did not want the enemy to seize when the fleet had inevitably to come back out again. This might have been one of the few times that Churchill's great knowledge of history led him astray. In 1807, Admiral Sir John Duckworth had successfully forced the strait by ships alone, losing only ten men on the way there and twenty-nine on the way back. The accuracy of military weaponry, and above all the use of underwater mines, had changed everything in the intervening 108 years.

Despite Richmond's view and the fact that the War Council had not yet formally authorized the expedition, what remained of the Royal Naval Division was sent to the Aegean, setting up a base at Lemnos. On 16 February it was agreed that the 29th Division of British regulars should be dispatched there from Britain, and the Australian and New Zealand Army Corps (ANZAC) in Egypt were earmarked for future deployment too. Kitchener's words to Churchill at the War Council were 'You get through! I'll find the men.'[109] But only four days later Kitchener changed his mind and the orders to the 29th Division were rescinded.

On 19 February, Carden began his bombardment of the Outer Forts in the south of the Dardanelles, Kum Kale and Sedd el Bahr. This was followed by sporadic shelling of other forts in the strait until 16 March. 'I know a curse should rest on me – because I *love* this war,' Churchill told Violet Asquith at dinner at the Admiralty on 22 February. 'I know it's smashing and shattering the lives of thousands every moment – and yet – I *can't* help it – I enjoy every second of it.'[110] When the Royal Naval Division went 'marching . . . into Constantinople . . . That will make them sit up,' he said of 'the swine who snarled at the Naval Division' during the Antwerp adventure. 'This reflection seems to afford him even more balm than the prospect of the impending downfall of the Ottoman Empire,' Violet concluded.[111]

'With proper military and naval cooperation, and with forces which are available, we can make certain of taking Constantinople by the end of March, and capturing or destroying all Turkish forces in Europe,' he informed the War Council on 25 February. 'The effect on the whole of the Balkans will be decisive. It will eliminate Turkey as a military factor.'[112] Though he believed this implicitly, it was foolish to commit such predictions to paper. The next day he told the War Council that troops would not be needed to force the strait, but only to occupy Constantinople, 'after the fleet had obtained command of the Sea of Marmara'. He even used the phrase 'reap the fruits of the naval success'.[113]

Churchill was undoubtedly on strong ground when he later attempted to share the blame for Gallipoli with Kitchener, who changed his mind no fewer than five times about what to do with the 29th Division between 7 January and mid-March.[114] The poster-image of the resolute Kitchener hid a man capable of painful vacillations. 'It seems clear now that when Lord Kitchener went back upon his undertaking to send the 29th Division to reinforce the army gathering in Egypt for the Dardanelles expedition and delayed it for nearly three weeks,' Churchill wrote years later, 'I should have been prudent then to have broken off the naval attack. It would have been quite easy to do so, and all arrangements were made upon that basis. I did not do it, and from that moment I became accountable for an operation the vital control of which had passed to other hands.'[115]

Kitchener appointed General Sir Ian Hamilton, Churchill's greatest friend in the Army, to command in Gallipoli, who in turn chose Jack Churchill to join his staff. Hamilton was far from the idiotic Blimp he was later made out to be. He was highly experienced and well educated, a Liberal in politics (very unusual for Great War generals), a published poet and a thinking soldier who had won victories in the Boer War. If he had a fault, it was that he tended to be too gentlemanly in dealing with the substandard generals he was given to serve under him.

On 12 March, British minesweepers reached the edge of Kephez Point minefield in the strait, but artillery and howitzer fire forced them back. They were wooden-hulled North Sea trawlers crewed mainly by fishermen which advanced slowly: the outflow from the Black Sea through the Dardanelles was sometimes 6 knots and manoeuvring was difficult. To make matters worse, Carden suffered something akin to a mental breakdown. Two days before the attack, now scheduled for 18 March, he had to be replaced by his second-in-command, Vice Admiral John de Robeck, who was doubtful about the operation, despite having the pugnacious Roger Keyes as his deputy.[116] One positive aspect was that the French Mediterranean Fleet was closely integrated into it; after the successful bombardment of the Outer Forts on 25 February, Admiral Émile Guépratte, the commander of the French squadron, said it had been 'An excellent day, allowing us to augur well for the success on the campaign.'[117]

Militating against that was the fact that the Turks had already laid between 350 and 400 mines in the strait. On the night of 17 March, the minelayer *Nusret* laid an extra twenty-six parallel to the shore at Eren Keui Bay, which had been earmarked by Allied planners as the place for the fleet to swing to starboard in the strait after discharging their fire at the forts.[118] 'The more surprise was absent,' Churchill was to write about the Dardanelles, 'the more intensity was vital.'[119] There could be no surprise as Carden had bombarded the Outer Forts in November, but neither could there be any doubt about the intensity of the firepower of de Robeck's nine-battleship squadron as it prepared to assault the Dardanelles Inner Forts on 18 March. Would it be enough?

# 10
# Gallipoli
# March–November 1915

*The Admiral, signalling for half-speed, picked his way . . . towards the mouth of the channel cautiously. It was so contrived that a vessel in passing must be exposed to a cross-fire from the heavy guns in the batteries. The actual passage was nearly a mile wide, but the navigable channel itself was dangerously narrow and extremely difficult.*

Churchill, *Savrola*[1]

*Politicians rise by toils and struggles. They expect to fall; they hope to rise again.*

Churchill, *Great Contemporaries*[2]

On Thursday, 18 March 1915, Rear Admiral John de Robeck's Anglo-French fleet attempted to force the strait, and failed. Two British pre-dreadnought capital ships, HMS *Ocean* and HMS *Irresistible*, and one French ship, the *Bouvet*, were sunk by mines. Three more ships were badly damaged before de Robeck called off the attack at dusk. The Inner Forts were battered, but of 176 Turkish guns in fixed positions, only four were destroyed. Allied ships were hit 139 times.[3] One line of mines was successfully swept, but there were nine further lines intact.[4]

In *The World Crisis*, Churchill dismissively referred to 'less than thirty British lives and two or three worthless ships' being lost, thus ignoring the capsizing of the *Bouvet*, which killed all but thirty-five of its crew of 674.[5] He also argued that 'If they had tried again they would have found the door was open,' but that cannot be substantiated, partly because of the minefields and also because (as recent research has established) the Turks had plenty of ammunition left over with more on its way.[6]

At the War Council the morning after the attack, Hankey recorded that everyone was 'rather upset by Churchill reading telegrams . . . Lord

F[isher] and I in the rather unenviable position of being able to say "I told you so."' Hankey said he had 'begged Churchill to have troops to cooperate but he wouldn't listen'.[7] The Council then had a long discussion on the partition of Turkey, which Hankey wrote, with some understatement, was 'premature I think'. Churchill wanted Admiral de Robeck – whom, with his inability to resist a pun, he was later to nickname 'Admiral Rowback' – to persevere with the attack.[8] Fisher, Wilson and Jackson adamantly disagreed. 'For the first time since the war began,' recalled Churchill, 'high words were used around the octagonal table.'[9]

The War Council decided that Allied infantry should capture the Gallipoli Peninsula, 50 miles long and between 4 and 12 miles wide, on the European side of the strait, in order to give the Navy another chance to get through. With the peninsula in Allied hands, they could clear away the Turkish mobile field artillery on the European side, which had caused the ships as much damage as the forts themselves. They could then try to neutralize the artillery on the Asiatic side, so the minesweepers – which by then would be converted destroyers rather than civilian-manned trawlers – would have an easier time clearing a path through the minefields.

Once past the strait, it was hoped that Roebuck's powerful fleet could get to Constantinople where, if the Turkish Government had not evacuated and moved inland, they might be forced to renounce their alliance with the Central Powers.[10]* As Churchill had written in *The River War*, 'We live in a world of "ifs".'[11] Because the campaign was ultimately to cost the British Empire over 114,000 battle casualties, for no strategic advantage whatever, we now know that the Council should have abandoned its strategy after this first disastrous day. But in late February Kitchener had declared, 'The effect of a defeat in the Orient would be very serious.'[12] It was felt that to admit defeat at the hands of a Muslim power would weaken the British Empire, which ruled over tens of millions of Muslims – and in India particularly prestige was more important than sheer military power. Since the Empire was Churchill's secular religion, this was an argument that had particular force with him. Instead of cutting their losses, therefore, the War Council planned an even greater commitment. Yet nothing was put to the vote, nor did the War Council once look at the campaign in the overall context of imperial resources and objectives.

As well as overestimating the firepower of naval guns firing at a flat trajectory against land defences, Churchill and others, extrapolating from

* In January 1916 the Turkish leader Enver Pasha stated that, even if a British fleet had broken through and appeared off Constantinople, his contingency plan 'was to repair our army to the surrounding hills and to Asia Minor' (*The Times* 26 January 1916).

Turkish defeats in the recent Balkan Wars and in the Holy Land, fatefully assumed that 'Johnnie Turk' was not much of soldier.[13] The reverse side of Churchill's unquestioning belief in the greatness of the British race – which so fortified him in the Second World War – was his dangerous assumption of the inferiority of other races, which served him very ill with regard to the Turks in 1915 and the Japanese in 1942.

What happened next was well summed up by Hankey: 'Behind each episode there lay a whole history of rumour, contradiction, conjecture, planning, preliminary movement, discussion, decision, indecision, order, counter-order, before the climax was reached, often in a welter of bloodshed and destruction.'[14] A modern historian has pointed out that 'There were four distinct variations of the concept: an attack by the navy alone; then by the navy then the army; by the navy and army together; and by the army then the navy.' As for the ultimate objectives, 'Different views on these goals were held concurrently by different actors, and virtually everyone's views changed over time.'[15]

The 1913 edition of the *Manual for Combined Naval and Military Operations* had not envisaged the possibility of a full-blown assault on defended beaches anywhere, yet Hamilton was only given thirty-three days to plan the first ever amphibious attack on a coast defended by modern weapons of war. His troops were currently stationed in Alexandria, which meant he had to go there and back, while the German commander in the peninsula, Liman von Sanders, had the Turkish Fifth Army feverishly preparing the defence: building roads, digging trenches, rolling out barbed wire, choosing fields of fire for machine-gun emplacements and so on.[16] On 6 April Churchill was still telling Hankey that 'He anticipated no difficulty in effecting a landing.'[17]

An underlying problem was that Britain simply could not afford two major offensive operations in 1915. Every man, gun and shell was needed by the BEF in France and Belgium. Yet Kitchener was now under Cabinet orders to send troops to Gallipoli, even though that would commit Britain to a war on two fronts, the very aspect that was bleeding Germany dry. The War Office tried to carry out the campaign on the cheap, initially sending Hamilton only 75,000 men for an operation that every previous report had said would require between 150,000 and 200,000.

Brigadier Herbert Studd, who had served in the planning department of the War Office before the war, wrote to his friend Neville Chamberlain, the Lord Mayor of Birmingham and younger son of Joseph Chamberlain, 'I fear that the Dardanelles enterprise with its great expenditure of ammunition will prove, even if successful, a severe handicap on our main effort in France and Belgium. If it fails it will be a very serious business. I am afraid it was started without being thought out in consequence of some heated impulse of Winston Churchill, who could not be content with the limited opportunities that the Germans give the Fleet.'[18]

Was Churchill at this point only putting on a brave front? 'Churchill is very worried about the whole affair, and looking very ill,' Lloyd George told his mistress on 8 April. 'He is touchy too.'[19] He had certainly given up boasting that the Dardanelles had all been his idea and was more tempered in his endorsement. When Balfour expressed worries to him about the coming attack, Churchill replied,

> You must not be unduly apprehensive of the military operation. The soldiers think they can do it . . . The military attack is in addition to, and not in substitution for, or derogation from, the naval attack. Both attacks mutually aid each other, and either by succeeding would be decisive . . . I think there is nothing for it but to go through with the business, and I do not at all regret that this should be so. No one can count with certainty on the issue of a battle. But we have the chances in our favour, and play for vital gains with non-vital stakes.[20]

Misgivings about the operation were building, and few doubted where to lay the blame if it went wrong. 'Churchill is a serious danger to the State,' Lord Charles Beresford wrote to the Tory editor of the *National Review* Leo Maxse. 'After Antwerp, and now the Dardanelles, the Government really ought to get rid of him.'[21]

On 23 April, the poet Rupert Brooke died of sepsis from an infected mosquito bite on his way to Gallipoli, a month before another friend, Julian Grenfell, was also killed. Churchill had met Brooke through their mutual friend Eddie Marsh, and admired his poetry. 'Rupert Brooke is dead,' he wrote in a eulogy in *The Times*.

> A telegram from the Admiral at Lemnos tells that this life has closed at the moment when it seemed to have reached its springtime. A voice had become audible, a note had been struck, more true, more thrilling, more able to do justice to the nobility of our youth in arms engaged in this present war, than any other – more able to express their thoughts of self-surrender, and with a power to carry comfort to those who watch them so intently from afar. The voice has been swiftly stilled. Only the echoes and the memory remain; but they will linger.[22]

In the first draft of his original handwritten obituary, written on Admiralty writing paper, Churchill had written the word 'pagan' in a sentence lauding Brooke's 'Pagan sympathy of mind and body'. He changed this to 'classic', probably to avoid antagonizing religious sentiment.[23] In 1923,

Churchill wrote of the officers of the Royal Naval Division that 'On the scented Island of Skyros, the little band of friends, themselves nearly all marked for death, gathered at the grave in which they buried Rupert Brooke and his dawning genius.'[24] For the rest of his life, Churchill would be surrounded by the ghosts of the 'Lost Generation', and it would profoundly affect his outlook during his Wilderness Years.

On Sunday, 25 April 1915, the 29th Division, the Royal Naval Division, two ANZAC divisions and a French division were ranged against six Turkish divisions, who knew they were about to be attacked and were defending their own territory at a time when the military strategists believed that assaulting troops needed to be three times the number of defenders if they were to succeed. Of the 9,000 men of the 29th Division who landed on five beaches, 3,000 were killed or wounded, even after a massive supportive naval bombardment.[25] The ANZACs suffered over 2,000 casualties that day, and evacuation was briefly considered, but Hamilton ordered 'Dig, dig, dig, until you are safe.'[26] So trenches were dug, in a replica of the Western Front, exactly what the campaign had been intended to avoid.

Hamilton did succeed in a brilliant deceptive operation at Kum Kale, where his French division pinned down two Turkish ones. A naval feint at Bulair occupied another two Turkish divisions, and featured the New Zealander Bernard Freyberg swimming ashore and lighting decoy fires. Hamilton got four divisions ashore at Cape Helles and Gaba Tepe. But the Royal Navy failed to suppress the Turkish beach defences with their murderous fields of fire. The first day's objectives – Achi Baba and Chunuk Bair – were not captured that day, or at all.

This lack of success led the Tory *Morning Post* to denounce Churchill as 'a danger to the country'.[27] He seems never to have realized that Fisher was leaking classified information on the campaign to that newspaper. Then, in early May, Fisher did something almost more reprehensible than breaking the Official Secrets Act. He told Clementine, during a lunch to which she had invited him while her husband was in Paris negotiating Italy's entry into the war, that he was actually with a mistress there. Clementine was sufficiently confident of Churchill's affections to dismiss the suggestion out of hand. 'Be quiet you silly old man,' she told him, 'and get out.'[28]

Churchill might have survived the battering from the Tory press had he had the support of Asquith and Lloyd George. But on 8 May Lloyd George told Margot Asquith, 'Winston is a difficult fellow: he has not merely bad judgement, but he has *none*. His Dardanelles expedition gave the Turk a frightful long start. He . . . got us at war with the Turk, which he need never have done . . . Now Fisher gasses about all over the place saying he was against the expedition – and he *was*, but he should have said so . . . Winston said he would do this thing with ships.'[29] When Margot Asquith said in response, 'Winston has no imagination of the heart,' Lloyd George agreed, saying, 'He has none.'[30]

When the unarmed British passenger liner the *Lusitania* was sunk by a U-boat on 7 May 1915, with the loss of over 1,400 lives, including 128 Americans, Churchill was accused by conspiracy theorists at the time and in the 1930s, in the 1970s and even today of being somehow involved, but this is completely false.[31] It was true that after the Germans announced the introduction of unrestricted submarine warfare Churchill had seen a ruthless way of using that against them. 'My dear Walter,' he wrote to Runciman, the President of the Board of Trade, on 12 February, 'It is most important to attract neutral shipping to our shores, in the hope especially of embroiling the United States with Germany . . . We want the traffic – the more the better; and if some of it gets into trouble, better still.'[32] This injudicious letter has provided fodder for conspiracy theorists who claim that Churchill directed the *Lusitania* to sail directly where he knew the *U-20* was lying in wait (even though no such order was given). Churchill certainly regretted that Woodrow Wilson did not declare war against Germany over the outrage, writing in *The World Crisis* that if he had, instead of waiting two more years, 'what abridgement of the slaughter; what sparing of the agony; what ruin, what catastrophes would have been prevented; in how many million homes would an empty chair be occupied to-day; how different would [be] the shattered world in which victors and vanquished alike are condemned to live'.[33]

In the second and third weeks of May 1915, a concatenation of events created a ministerial crisis that forced Churchill out of the Admiralty. On 11 May, Venetia Stanley broke the news to Asquith that she was going to marry Edwin Montagu, one of his Cabinet ministers. The Prime Minister told her that this would break his heart. The next morning he went into his wife Margot's bedroom for solace. 'My heart went out to him,' she reported in her diary. 'I jumped out of bed and put my arms round him,' and consoled him that maybe it wouldn't happen.[34] But it did, and he was distracted for weeks afterwards. The very next day, Fisher again attempted to resign, but was again persuaded not to. There was much talk in the press of a coalition government being formed, with the Conservatives entering only on the condition that Churchill should leave the Admiralty.

'What a satire if the coming coalition Government of which Winston has gassed so much should not contain him!' chortled Margot Asquith to her diary on 13 May. 'There is no doubt if [her husband] Henry wanted to make himself supremely popular with every party, *ours and the others*, he would exclude Winston.'[35] That same day, Churchill sent a telegram moving two submarines from the home squadron to the Mediterranean reinforcements list. Fisher objected, telling Churchill it was a 'casus belli' between them.[36] Churchill was forced to cancel the telegram and send one approved by Fisher instead.

On 14 May, Colonel Charles Repington, the highly respected military correspondent for *The Times*, reported that the BEF was running short of high-explosive shells, thereby suggesting that soldiers were dying as a result of political incompetence, which predictably caused a sensation. General Sir John French was clearly behind the story, something which he later did not even bother to deny.[37] Although Churchill was in no way responsible for this, the ensuing crisis contributed to his fall.

The War Council met that day in an atmosphere that he later described as 'sulphurous'.[38] Kitchener stated that, in his opinion, they would never get through the Dardanelles, and said he had been misled over the number of men required.[39] When the War Council informed Fisher that 'the great projects in northern waters' (such as the capture of Borkum) would not take place because of the Gallipoli and other commitments, he decided he really would resign, claiming to have opposed the operation from the start.[40] This prompted Churchill to write to Asquith to point out that 'The First Sea Lord has agreed in writing to every executive telegram on which the operations have been conducted.'[41]

On Saturday, 15 May, Fisher did at last resign – his eighth and final attempt since rejoining the Admiralty. He disappeared and went to the Charing Cross Hotel to lie low, possibly after a period of meditation in Westminster Abbey.[42] When No. 10 finally tracked him down, Asquith commanded him 'in the King's name' to return to the Admiralty.[43] Instead, Fisher sent the Prime Minister a long list of conditions, including the removal of HMS *Queen Elizabeth* from the Dardanelles and Churchill from the Admiralty, adding that the First Lord was 'a bigger danger than the Germans'.[44] Asquith told the King that the letter 'showed signs of mental aberration'.[45] Asquith was not about to be blackmailed and accepted Fisher's resignation instead.

When Bonar Law heard of this, he visited No. 10, ostensibly to seek confirmation of the rumours but in fact to tell Asquith and Lloyd George that Fisher's resignation meant that unless Churchill were removed from the Admiralty the political truce between the parties was at an end. It had taken a world war to bring the truce about and it was now threatened at a time of maximum turmoil. After consultations lasting several days, made ever more fraught by the shells scandal, Asquith, Lloyd George and Bonar Law agreed to form a new coalition government, on condition that Churchill and Lord Haldane, the Lord Chancellor and Asquith's close friend, who had been at university in Germany and was known to admire German culture, were removed from their posts. In the end, the Admiralty and Colonial Office were the only major posts the Conservatives received. What Asquith could not have known as he made this Faustian compact was that no purely Liberal government would ever hold power in Britain again.

Lloyd George needed no persuasion to throw over his old friend and ally. The price of the Conservatives joining a national government was that Churchill should be sent to a sinecure post with no executive portfolio attached. 'It is the Nemesis of the man who has fought for this war for years,' Lloyd George told Frances Stevenson that day. 'When the war came he saw in it the chance of glory for himself, and has accordingly entered on a risky campaign without caring a straw for the misery and hardship it would bring to thousands, in the hope that he would be the outstanding man in this war.'[46] There was bitterness and jealousy in that remark, but little factual accuracy. At the time, Churchill naively believed that Lloyd George was still his supporter.

The Tories were about to exact revenge for over a decade of perceived treachery. There were the jibes against Lord Milner, the attacks on Balfour's weakness and femininity, his closeness to Lloyd George, the Sidney Street Siege, the People's Budget and Parliament Act, the Wilson and Bridgeman sackings, the mock-waving of his handkerchief during the Irish Home Rule debates, the so-called Ulster Pogrom, the Bradford and 'rats in a hole' speeches, the Antwerp adventure, the Dardanelles and the Battle of Coronel. No senior Liberals were willing to say Churchill ought to remain at the Admiralty; indeed McKenna told Asquith, 'Winston is a real danger.'[47]

'Winston is far the most disliked man in my Cabinet by his colleagues,' Asquith told his wife. 'Oh! he is intolerable! Noisy, long-winded and full of perorations.'[48] At about this time he also said, 'It is a pity Winston hasn't a better sense of proportion . . . He will never get to the top in British politics, with all his wonderful gifts.'[49] Lloyd George's mistress noted that 'It seems strange that Churchill should have been in politics all these years, and yet not won the confidence of a single party in the country, or a single colleague in the Cabinet.'[50] This was to be true right up to the moment he became prime minister. His mercurial enthusiasms, brilliant aperçus, sudden about-turns, willingness to embrace unpopular causes and just as bravely reject popular ones made it hard to follow him. Only his cousin

Freddie Guest and Jack Seely did. Without a following in the Commons, Churchill was expendable.

'A man who can plot the Ulster Pogrom, plan Antwerp and carry out the Dardanelles fiasco is worth watching,' Sir Henry Wilson wrote to Bonar Law. 'He and the Government have got to cover up their tracks and the means employed will not be too nice.'[51] That evening Churchill and Clementine went down to Asquith's country house, The Wharf, in Oxfordshire. 'By dint of talking loud, he managed to silence the table,' recorded the ever-acerbic Margot, 'and with the glee of a schoolboy he harangued in his habitual, highly-coloured, amusing way.'[52] Churchill knew he was fighting for his political life, even though Violet Asquith believed he was 'as impervious to atmosphere as a diver in his bell'.[53]

'I am strongly in favour of a national Government,' Churchill wrote to Asquith on 17 May, 'and no personal claims or interests should stand in its way at the present crisis.' He also wrote to Bonar Law and Fisher, hoping to save the job he loved. Fisher meanwhile told Lord Esher, as the latter recorded, that 'It was impossible for him to stay any longer at the Admiralty with Churchill. He had disapproved of the Dardanelles operations from the beginning; he gave all his reasons to the Prime Minister at the time, but was overruled.'[54] On the same day, Ian Hamilton came up with a plan to break out of the beachheads, one which required extensive reinforcements. He telegraphed London for approval, but because of the ministerial crisis his plan was not considered by the War Council for three whole weeks. 'As a consequence the dispatch of the reinforcements asked for by Sir Ian Hamilton in his appreciation was postponed for six weeks,' an official report concluded – six weeks in which men were dying and the Turks were strengthening their positions.[55]

'I shall form a Coalition Government,' Asquith told his wife on the 17th. 'I've just seen Bonar Law. He was pleased and happy.'[56] Of Fisher and Churchill, Bonar Law simply said, 'They had both better go.'[57] At one point, Bonar Law and Balfour offered Lloyd George the premiership, but he turned it down out of loyalty to Asquith, or so he told his mistress.[58] Lloyd George was supposedly also offered the War Office on the basis that Kitchener 'had misled the Government on the subject of ammunition – chiefly explosives – and was not fit to be in charge'.[59] The Asquith Government's failure fully to mobilize the war economy had really been responsible for the shells shortage, which was made worse by the serious overextension of the military effort across the Western Front and the Dardanelles and the lesser fronts in the Middle East and Africa, but it was useful to have a scapegoat. Kitchener – though secretive, erratic and domineering within the War Office and contemptuously refusing to inform even the War Council of the reasoning behind his decisions – was wildly popular in the country and not about to be removed by anyone. Knowing himself to be virtually unsackable rendered him dangerous. He made a magnificent recruiting poster, but an almost impossible colleague.

It took someone who was neither a politician nor a soldier to assess the situation succinctly. 'The Cabinet has crashed!' Ian Hamilton's wife Jean wrote in her diary on 18 May. 'Brought down I fear by Winston's mistake in bombarding the Dardanelles front by the Fleet before they were supported by the troops, and that old rat, Lord Fisher, has ground a hole in the sinking ship.'[60] 'I feel like a wounded man,' Churchill told Lloyd George that day. 'I know I am hurt, but as yet I cannot tell how badly. Later on I shall know the extent to which I am damaged, but now I only feel the shock.'[61] He had recovered enough by the next day for Frances Stevenson to write in her diary, 'Today, Churchill seems to be going to put up a fight.'[62] He showed Lloyd George and Grey a long letter justifying his conduct that he intended to publish. Lloyd George pointed out that it would publicly question the success of the Dardanelles expedition for the first time. Once Churchill saw that both Grey and Lloyd George assumed he would have to resign, he 'completely lost his temper'.[63] The letter, like so many that Churchill used to vent his feelings over the years, was never sent.

'You don't care what becomes of me,' he told Lloyd George. 'You don't care if I am trampled underfoot by my enemies. You don't care for my personal reputation.' 'No,' Lloyd George claimed to have replied, 'I don't care for my own at the present moment. The only thing I care about now is that we win this war.'[64] It sounded more like a lovers' tiff than a discussion between statesmen, but it taught Churchill how little friendship counted at the top of politics, as Lord Haldane was about to learn too. That evening, in a desperate act designed to save his own position, Churchill offered Fisher a seat in the Cabinet if he would rescind his resignation, despite having no authority to do so. Fisher histrionically told Bonar Law, 'I rejected the thirty pieces of silver to betray my country.'[65] The editor of the *Morning Post* meanwhile proclaimed himself 'very cock-a-whoop' at the prospect of Churchill's fall.[66]

The King was delighted by the creation of a national government. 'Only by that means can we get rid of Churchill from the Admiralty,' he wrote in his diary. 'He is intriguing also with French against Kitchener, he is the real danger.'[67] The Prince of Wales agreed, telling his father, 'It is a great relief to know that Winston is leaving the Admiralty . . . one does feel that he launches the country on mad ventures which are fearfully expensive both as regards men and munitions and which don't attain their object.'

It was for this feckless young man that Churchill would later nearly sacrifice his career.

On 20 May, Clementine wrote a remarkable, heartfelt letter to Asquith in a last-ditch attempt to save her husband. 'My dear Mr Asquith,' she wrote,

> For nearly four years Winston has worked to master every detail of naval science. There is no man in this country who possesses equal knowledge, capacity and vigour. If he goes, the injury to Admiralty business will not be reparable for many months . . . Why would you part with Winston? Unless indeed you have lost confidence in his work and ability? But I know that cannot be the reason. Is not the reason expediency – 'to restore public confidence'. I suggest to you that public confidence will be restored in *Germany* by Winston's downfall . . . If you throw Winston overboard you will be committing an act of weakness and your Coalition Government will not be as formidable a war machine as the present Government. Winston may in your eyes and in those with whom he had to work have faults but he has the supreme quality which I venture to say very few of your present or future Cabinet possess – the power, the imagination, the deadliness to fight Germany. If you send him to another place he will no longer be fighting – if you waste this valuable war material you will be doing an injury to this Country.[68]

Asquith showed the letter to Margot. 'It shows the soul of a servant,' she confided to her diary. 'That touch of blackmail and insolence, and the revelation of black ingratitude and want of affection, justifies everything I have thought of this shallow couple.'[69] When Asquith tried to defend it as 'the letter of a wife', Margot replied, 'A fishwife, you mean!!'

There was some debate among the family about whether Churchill had seen the letter before Clementine sent it. Maurice Bonham Carter, Asquith's private secretary (who later married Violet) called it a 'bêtise' and discovered that, although Churchill had not inspired it, he had let Clementine send it. Asquith never even bothered to reply, though he did read it out aloud 'with amused relish' to his lunch guests, and told Venetia Stanley it was 'the letter of a maniac'.[70] A truer estimation was that of the historian who judged it 'a plea so passionate, albeit so imprudent, that one cannot read it without thinking that any man would rejoice to have a wife believe in him to that extent'.[71]

Churchill himself, still working at the Admiralty, told Riddell that same day, 'I am finished!' When Riddell expressed surprise, saying that he was only forty and still had 'remarkable powers', Churchill replied, 'Yes, finished in respect of all I care for – waging war, the defeat of the Germans.'[72] On 21 May he wrote to Bonar Law, urging him not to allow 'a newspaper campaign, necessarily conducted in ignorance and not untinged with prejudice', to force his resignation, but rather let him be 'judged fairly, deliberately and with knowledge'.[73] Bonar Law replied that his resignation was now 'inevitable'.[74] Churchill then wrote to Asquith:

> My responsibility is terrible. But I know I could sustain it, and without the slightest impairment . . . could bring this vast Dardanelles business safely through . . . Arthur Wilson and I together can do it. We know the whole position. But fancy my feelings if, at this critical moment – on mere uninformed newspaper hostility – the whole intricate affair is taken out of our hands, and put into the hands of a stranger without the knowledge, or worst of all into the hands of a deadly foe to the whole plan. It is no clinging to office or to this particular office or my own interest or advantage which moves me. I am clinging to my *task* and to my *duty*. I am straining to make good the formidable undertaking in which we are engaged; and which I know – with Arthur Wilson – I can alone discharge. I did not believe it was possible to endure such anxiety . . . I can only look to you. Let me stand or fall by the Dardanelles – but do not take it from my hands.[75]

Asquith merely replied, 'You must take it as settled that you are not to remain at the Admiralty . . . I hope to retain your services as a member of the new Cabinet, being, as I am, sincerely grateful for the splendid work you have done both before and since the war.'[76] Asquith could treat Churchill harshly partly because the First Lord had so few supporters. One of them was James Masterton Smith, Churchill's private secretary, who bravely told the Asquiths and Bonham Carter that he 'still hankers after Churchill as First Lord, owing to his great driving power and capacity for work'.[77]

'I hope Balfour will become First Lord of the Admiralty in place of Churchill who has become impossible,' the King wrote in his diary on 22 May.[78] He did. Remarkably, despite having been sacked by him before the war, Admiral Wilson refused to serve as first sea lord under anyone but Churchill, so the job went to Admiral Jackson. The Government was reconstituted as a coalition, with Asquith as prime minister, Lloyd George as minister for munitions (to deal with the shells shortage), Bonar Law as colonial secretary, McKenna as chancellor of the Exchequer and Grey staying at the Foreign Office. 'I wanted us to go to the Tories when we were strong,' Churchill told Violet, 'not in misfortune to be made an honest woman of.'[79]

Churchill never forgot the humiliation of May 1915 as his fingers were prised off the Admiralty, telling his aides much later in life that the month of May was always his least favourite. 'I cannot forget that when I left the

Admiralty in May 1915 the first and, with one exception, the only one of my colleagues who paid me a visit of ceremony was the over-burdened Titan whose disapprobation had been one of the disconcerting experiences of my youth,' Churchill wrote of Kitchener years later.[80] At that meeting, Kitchener, who had not been involved in the machinations to remove him, told Churchill 'in the impressive and almost majestic manner that was natural to him, "Well, there is one thing at any rate they cannot take from you. The Fleet was ready."'[81]

The Admiralty rejoiced at Churchill's departure, at least privately. Jellicoe called Churchill 'a public danger to the Empire'; Beatty wrote, 'The Navy breathes freer now it is rid of the succubus Churchill'; Richmond denounced the 'personal vanity' of this 'shouting amateur'.[82] The press similarly gloated over his fall – all but J. L. Garvin who predicted in the *Observer* that 'His hour of triumph will come.'[83]

Churchill had not been cashiered altogether, however. He retained a post in the Cabinet and the War Council, with no executive power. From commanding the thousand-ship Royal Navy, his new post of chancellor of the Duchy of Lancaster gave him the role of appointing rural justices of the peace. His salary was halved to £2,000. His official duty as chancellor was to oversee the management of the King's private estate (the Duchy of Lancaster), which took less than one day a week; the rest of the time he was a minister without portfolio. Balfour allowed Churchill and Clementine to stay at the Admiralty until mid-June, after which (because Grey had rented their flat at Eccleston Square) they moved in with Ivor Guest at 21 Arlington Street and then into Jack's house at 41 Cromwell Road, almost opposite the Natural History Museum.

After visiting Clementine at Admiralty house on 26 May, Edwin Montagu wrote to his fiancée Venetia Stanley: 'She was so sweet but so miserable and crying all the time.'[84] The extent to which the campaign had permeated every aspect of the Churchills' family life is evident from the four-year-old Randolph's nightly prayers which went: 'God bless Mummy and Papa. God bless the Dardanelles and make me a good boy. Amen.'[85]

For the next six months, Churchill continued to attend meetings and give advice, but from a position of no authority. He persuaded Balfour to continue funding work on the prototype 'land battleship' – that is, the tank – and even secured a surge of extra forces for the Dardanelles. 'Like a sea-beast fished up from the depths, or a diver too suddenly hoisted,' he later recalled, 'my veins threatened to burst from the fall in pressure. At the moment when every fibre of my being was inflamed to action, I was forced to remain a spectator of the tragedy, placed cruelly in a front seat.'[86]

Although Churchill had been demoted, his acknowledged expertise in every aspect of the campaign meant that the Cabinet still needed him, not least because his successor Balfour had very little experience in naval matters. 'The position at the Dardanelles is at once hopeful and dangerous,' he wrote in a Cabinet memorandum on 1 June. After the Third Battle of Krithia in early June, the Dardanelles Committee, which consisted of the thirteen most powerful men in the Government, decided to reinforce Hamilton with six more divisions, partly on Churchill's urging.[87] 'Through the Narrows of the Dardanelles and along the ridges of the Gallipoli Peninsula', he told a Dundee audience on 5 June, 'lie some of the shortest paths to a triumphant peace . . . Beyond those few miles of ridge and scrub on which our soldiers, our French comrades, our gallant Australians, and our New Zealand fellow-subjects are now battling, lie the downfall of a hostile empire, the destruction of an enemy's fleet and army, the fall of a world-famous capital, and probably the accession of powerful allies.'[88]

On 9 June he told his friend Major Archie Sinclair of the 2nd Life Guards,

> One must try to bear misfortune with a smile . . . But the hour is bitter: and idleness torture. Here I am in a fat sinecure, very well received and treated by the new Cabinet who have adopted my policy and taken all the steps I was pressing for and more . . . But now all that is settled and I cannot endure sitting here to wait for a turn of the political wind. I do not want office, but only war direction: that perhaps never again. Everything else – not that. At least so I feel in my evil moments . . . Fisher is a mystery. Was it a mental breakdown or a coup d'etat? Or more likely than either both combined. And synchronizing with this Lloyd George striking out for power in alliance with Northcliffe: and Asquith affectionate but weak and indolent and seeking self-preservation at all costs. I am presently unsettled: and cannot use my gift . . . I do not feel that my judgment has been falsified, or that the determined pursuance of my policy through all the necessary risks was wrong . . . I do not feel at all attracted by a political prospect and am repelled by the political game. Between me and LG *tout est fini*. I want a breath of fresh air.[89]

The crisis had finally allowed him to see through Lloyd George. 'You are a clever fellow!' he told him to his face. 'You have been scheming for this for months, and have left no stone unturned to get what you wanted.'[90]

Before he could bring himself to leave the Government and find redemption in the trenches, Churchill needed to fight for the maximum support to Ian Hamilton, in the hope that he could turn around the Dardanelles campaign and thereby explode the damning narrative that had got him expelled from the Admiralty. If the Gallipoli campaign succeeded, he would be vindicated. His arguments were supported by the terrible facts on the Western Front, where Joffre's May offensive had cost nearly a quarter of a million casualties, after which, as Churchill told his colleagues on 18 June, 'Of approximately 18,500 square miles of France and Belgium in German hands, we have recovered about eight.'[91] Against that dismal record he continued to hold out for what he called the 'prize' of Constantinople, 'the prize, and the only prize, which lies within reach this year. It can certainly be won, without unreasonable expense, and within a comparatively short time.'[92]

The Churchill family spent the weekends at Hoe Farm, a converted Tudor farmhouse they rented jointly with Jack in Surrey during the summer of 1915. 'The garden gleams with summer jewellery,' Churchill told Jack, who was serving with Hamilton. 'We live very simply – but with the essentials of life well understood and well provided for – hot baths, cold champagne, new peas and old brandy.'[93] It was there that Churchill discovered another essential for his life. In early July he watched his sister-in-law Goonie painting, and decided to try it himself.[94] What started as a form of post-Admiralty therapy – 'If it weren't for painting, I could not live; I could not bear the strain of things,' he said – quickly turned into a lifelong passion. He was ultimately to paint more than 540 canvases, and became very good indeed.[95] 'Had he chosen painting instead of statesmanship,' said no less an authority than his teacher, the painter Sir John Lavery, 'I believe he would have been a great master with the brush.'[96]

Churchill's considerable innate artistic talent was nurtured by Walter Sickert, under whose tutelage he developed his technical skills. Sickert had studied at the Slade School of Fine Art, had been apprenticed to J. A. Whistler and was a friend of Degas. As well as Lavery and Sickert, Churchill was also taught by Sir William Nicholson and the Anglo-French painter Paul Maze. Churchill has often been dismissed as a mere 'Sunday painter', but he reached a high level of technical proficiency. In 1925 an artistic panel comprising Sir Oswald Birley, Lord Duveen and Kenneth Clark judged an anonymous painting, *Winter Sunshine*, in a public competition for amateurs. Duveen did not want to award it the prize because it had to his mind clearly been painted by a professional artist. Clark said they had to trust the contenders not to have cheated. It was by Churchill.

'Painting is complete as a distraction,' Churchill wrote. 'I know of nothing which, without exhausting the body, more entirely absorbs the mind.'[97] He gave most of what he modestly called his 'daubs' to family and friends, occasionally to staff and, during the Second World War, to Franklin Roosevelt and Harry Truman as well as Generals Eisenhower, Montgomery and Marshall. He painted all genres – still lifes, flowers, architectural scenes (including the Pyramids), tapestries at Blenheim, landscapes, weeds at Fontaine de Vaucluse and portraits – and sometimes painted from photographs. When an aide saw him projecting a magic-lantern image on to his canvas and said, 'Looks a bit like cheating,' Churchill retorted, 'If the finished product looks like a work of art, then it *is* a work of art!'[98] Asked why he preferred landscapes to portraits, Churchill replied, 'A tree doesn't complain that I haven't done it justice.'[99]

'I cannot pretend to feel impartial about colours,' Churchill wrote in 'Painting as a Pastime', an article of 1921 that was published in book form in 1948. 'I rejoice with the brilliant ones, and genuinely feel sorry for the poor browns. When I go to Heaven I mean to spend a considerable portion of my first million years in painting, and so get to the bottom of the subject.'[100]* Given a large bottle of brandy as a present during the 1930s, he sent his children and nephew Peregrine all around his house to collect more bottles for a painting, saying, 'Fetch me associate and fraternal bottles to form a bodyguard to this majestic container.'[101] They quickly found eleven more bottles and some large cigar boxes, and he called that painting *Bottlescape*. Nor did Churchill confine himself to painting; when Oscar Nemon sculpted him in the 1950s, he spent his sittings sculpting Oscar Nemon.

Kitchener asked Churchill to visit the Dardanelles in mid-July 1915 to discover from Ian Hamilton why the campaign had degenerated into a trench deadlock every bit as bad as the original on the Western Front. Before his departure, he wrote a letter to Clementine to be opened in the event of his death there. He set out the very modest financial support with which she would find herself, of about £450 per annum. He asked her to 'get hold of all my papers, especially those which refer to my Admiralty administration', as she was his literary executor and he wanted a book written:

> Some day I should like the truth to be known. Randolph will carry on the lamp. Do not grieve for me too much. I am a spirit confident of my rights. Death is only an incident, and not the most important which happens to us in this state of being. On the whole, especially since I met you my darling one, I have been happy, and you have taught me how noble a woman's heart can be. If there is anywhere else I shall be on the lookout for you. Meanwhile look forward, feel free [presumably to remarry], cherish the children, guard my memory. God bless you.[102]

* It was in that essay that he also wrote, 'Nothing makes a man more reverent than a library' (WSC, *Painting* p. 10).

Jean Hamilton lunched with the Churchills the day before he was due to leave, and recorded that he 'still maintains the Fleet could have got through the Narrows unassisted by the troops'.[103] He was also 'full of confidence that a great victory is coming at the Dardanelles, and wants to be there to see it – he is off early tomorrow'. The Cabinet cancelled the trip at the last moment, not wanting him to return with more reasons to reinforce a losing campaign. 'I have now much time on my hands and can feel thoroughly every twinge,' he told Archie Sinclair. 'It is a horrible experience remaining here in the midst of things knowing everything, caring passionately, conscious of capacity for service, yet paralysed nearly always. It is like being in a cataleptic trance while all you value is being hazarded.' For as long as the Gallipoli expedition still had a chance of success, Churchill knew he needed to stay in London arguing for it, but he knew where his duty lay thereafter, telling Sinclair, 'It will comfort my soul to come out for a few months and serve with my regiment, and my mind turns more and more in its malaise to that. But till victory is won in the Dardanelles my post is plainly here.'[104]

Many other ministers before and since have been demoted or dismissed on the failure of their signature policy. Yet the pain Churchill felt at the humiliation, and his desperation to be vindicated, gnawed at him whenever he was not at the easel. 'The Dardanelles haunted him for the rest of his life,' Clementine told Martin Gilbert. 'He always believed in it. When he left the Admiralty he thought he was finished . . . I thought he would never get over the Dardanelles. I thought he would die of grief.'[105] To Freddie Birkenhead she specified how that might happen: 'Winston was filled with such a black despair that she felt that he would never recover from it, and even feared at one time that he might commit suicide.'[106] Like the Romans, he believed that there was nothing ignoble about committing suicide to atone for disgrace.

On 11 July 1911, Churchill had had dinner with his cousin Ivor Guest and his wife Alice. 'Alice interested me a great deal in her talk about her doctor in Germany,' he reported from the Home Office to Clementine afterwards, who was on holiday in Seaford in East Sussex, 'who completely cured her depression. I think this man might be useful to me – if my black dog returns. He seems quite a way from me now. It is such a relief. All the colours came back into the picture. Brightest of all your dear face, my Darling.'[107] This is the only reference Churchill ever made to his so-called 'black dog' depression (a term used by Victorian and Edwardian nannies to describe their charges as out of sorts or ill-tempered). Lord Moran, his doctor, mentions it only five times in his 800-page book on Churchill, and then for the most part speculatively. The diary entries published by Moran for 14 August 1944 and 2 August 1945, upon which almost all the evidence for Churchill's 'black dog' has been based, do not correspond to the manuscript versions in his private papers.[108]

Churchill never missed a single day off work because of this supposed depression, although he certainly felt low on occasion, such as during the defeats in the early part of the Second World War. His private secretaries and family never heard him use the term 'black dog', although some did say that they felt apprehensive about his moods at certain times, such as when he was 'fratchetty' before important setpiece speeches.[109] It is unlikely that Churchill was a depressive at all, let alone a manic one, and this sole reference of July 1911 can be explained in terms of an incorrect self-diagnosis, the hypochondria of a man who took his own temperature daily and believed he had a 'sensitive cuticle'. (More recent amateur diagnoses that he was bipolar can be similarly dismissed.) When something as catastrophic as the Dardanelles disaster happened, Churchill got depressed, as anyone else would have in the same circumstances.

'This Government of able men and opposed parties does not develop any of the qualities required for war,' Churchill told Archie Sinclair only two months after the coalition had taken office. 'The personal and party elements neutralize each other: and there are many opinions, much politeness, unlimited decorum – but little action. The predisposition towards the negative is very marked. Meanwhile there are restless movements which I watch attentively without joining.'[110] Of course that might be because he was still considered too toxic for anyone in the Opposition to invite him to join. Lloyd George, he generously wrote, 'is necessary to the State. He has the war-making quality. I do not intend to allow any personal feelings to prevent my working with him. But distrust based on experience is a terrible barrier. It is strange to look back on a year ago . . . My part in events is woefully shrunken. But I still think I shall have work to do, though not for many months. The war must be fought to the bitter end. Any half-measured peace will only be a truce. We must at all costs have a decisive result. We are not doing all we should. Would you believe it – I pass my days painting. It keeps my mind at peace . . . Do not let my letters fall into the hands of the Germans when they storm your trenches. The swine will rejoice . . . It is better to burn letters.'[111] As so often, it was a phrase that ensured their careful safe-keeping.

Hamilton's imaginative plan to turn the Turkish flank at Suvla Bay and break out from the ANZAC area was launched on 6 August, but despite the great bravery of the Australians and New Zealanders who stormed the shores, it failed. The Turks by that stage had sixteen divisions in the peninsula, facing Hamilton's fourteen. Allied units were landed in the wrong place, faced sheer cliffs and deep gullies and got lost because of bad maps. The quality of the senior officers was generally abysmal because the Western Front was always the first priority. (One general had been resident in a lunatic asylum as recently as 1912.) When there were advances, Lieutenant-General Sir Frederick Stopford, commander of IX Corps, threw away opportunities that were never to recur. Stopford was relieved of his command on 16 August, but by then it was too late: all fronts were stalemated.

Although Churchill depicted the chancellorship of the Duchy of Lancaster, a post dating to the fourteenth century, as a sinecure and a backwater, it at least allowed him to sit on a high-powered Cabinet committee in mid-August 'to examine the resources of this country and of our allies for the prosecution of the war to the end of 1916'. In twelve meetings over three weeks, the Committee took evidence from dozens of senior political and military figures – including half the Cabinet. Churchill asked probing questions of all of them. He asked Balfour about the regulation of mercantile shipping; demanded more accurate figures from the Director of Recruitment; questioned Lloyd George about 18-pounder shells and compulsory military service; expressed shock to the Secretary of the War Office that nearly a quarter of a million Britons had been discharged as medically unfit for service, and asked Walter Runciman how to free some of the 200,000 people employed on the railways for service in the armed forces. He asked politicians and civil servants about population statistics and French exports, and had at his fingertips the total number of males between seventeen and forty-five in the furniture and timber trades. He questioned Rear Admiral Morgan Singer on Maxim guns on ships, Hotchkiss anti-aircraft guns, automatic fuses, shells, rifles and carbines from America, asking, 'Are you alright for cordite now?'[112] There was no subject or issue too small, and his relish for statistics was unbounded.

In early September, on hearing that a major French assault on the Western Front was going to be cancelled and the divisions sent to the Dardanelles, Churchill passed Lloyd George a note in Cabinet: 'I feel like a man who was about to be shot, and who instead is left a large fortune.'[113] Unfortunately, Hamilton's valiant attempts to break out of Suvla would still come to naught. By this time, supported by Clementine who sensed his frustration with politics, Churchill was offering to leave the Cabinet and go to the front. He wanted to be a major-general and be given an Army corps, which Kitchener found 'embarrassing', knowing it would 'offend the army' if he complied.[114]

Churchill was under no illusions about Lloyd George's role in his removal from the Admiralty. 'I have done you many a good turn,' he told him in mid-September, probably in reference to the Marconi scandal, 'you might have said the word that would have kept me there.'[115] Lloyd George answered bluntly that the Dardanelles had been a mistake. By late September there was talk of evacuating Gallipoli altogether, and forming a new War Council without Churchill. Despite his graciousness when Churchill was removed, Kitchener in particular now said he could not work with Churchill any longer; Hankey recalled that Kitchener was 'almost in an hysterical condition' and threatening to resign rather than have Churchill continue on the War Council.[116] The feeling by then was entirely mutual: when C. P. Scott, the editor of the *Manchester Guardian*, visited Churchill in his Duchy offices in Downing Street, he found him 'chafing desperately at having virtually no work to do and spoke of perhaps resigning and rejoining his regiment'. When Scott 'put it to him what would he do to bring about a real change for the better he hesitated for a moment and then said, in absolute confidence, first get rid of Kitchener'.[117] Churchill suggested to Scott that the roles of secretary for war and overall grand strategist should then be split. The present combination, he said, 'was now seen to have been a mistake and would never be repeated. In addition, there should be an inner Cabinet responsible for the conduct of the war and meeting daily.' This was precisely what Churchill created when he became prime minister in 1940.

The first half of October 1915 saw the British defeat at the Battle of Loos in France, and Bulgaria's decision to join the Central Powers. Churchill could not come up with any better way to remedy the situation beyond renewing the naval attack on the Dardanelles. 'I believe we have been all these months in the position of the Spanish prisoner', he wrote to Balfour on 6 October, 'who languished for twenty years in a dungeon until one morning the idea struck him to push the door, which had been open all the time.'[118] It was a terrible analogy. Gallipoli was hardly an easy or obvious solution. The land campaign was completely stalemated by then. What would the Turkish artillery have done to ships trying to pass the Narrows? The forts might have been overwhelmed by the sheer audacity of a surprise attack, but the Turks had a large amount of artillery in the peninsula by then and would have reacted swiftly and aggressively against any naval attack. Any ships that survived this assault would then have confronted the minefields.

On 14 October, the War Council decided to recall Sir Ian Hamilton and replace him with General Sir Charles Monro, who soon recommended an evacuation from the peninsula. 'General Monro was an officer of swift decision,' Churchill quipped a few years later. 'He came, he saw, he capitulated.'[119] (He called Lieutenant-General Sir James Wolfe Murray, who agreed with Monro, 'Sheep' Murray.) 'Nothing leads more surely to disaster than that a military plan should be pursued with crippled steps and in a lukewarm spirit in the face of continual nagging within the executive circle,' Churchill wrote in a Cabinet memorandum in response to Bonar Law's demands for such an evacuation. 'Even in politics such methods are unhealthy. In war they are a crime.'[120]

Churchill went on to predict, somewhat hyperbolically even for him, that the proposed evacuation would be the worst military decision since the loss of the American colonies. Bonar Law was unmoved and threatened resignation unless there was an evacuation. By then he was certainly right. On 5 November, a newly constituted War Council met for the first time, consisting of Asquith, Balfour, Grey, Lloyd George, Bonar Law, McKenna, Grey and Kitchener, but not Churchill.[121] Lloyd George told Frances Stevenson that Churchill 'was very sick at not being put on the small War Committee', but by that stage he could hardly have been surprised.[122]

Three days later, Asquith threw his weight behind evacuation, and on Thursday, 11 November 1915 Churchill resigned from the Government. 'I am in cordial agreement with the decision to form a small War Council,' he wrote to Asquith.

> I make no complaint at all that your scheme should be changed. But with that change my work in the Government comes naturally to a close. Knowing what I do about the present situation, and the instrument of executive power, I could not accept a position of general responsibility for war policy without an effective share in its guidance and control . . . Nor do I feel able in times like these to remain in well-paid inactivity. I therefore ask you to submit my resignation to the King. I am an officer, and I place myself unreservedly at the disposal of the military authorities, observing that my regiment is in France. I have a clear conscience which enables me to bear my responsibility for past events with composure. Time will vindicate my administration of the Admiralty, and assign me my due share in the vast series of preparations and operations which have secured us the complete command of the seas. With much respect and unaltered personal friendship, I bid you goodbye.'[123]

The last sentence was untrue, the rest sublime.

There was some discussion about sending Churchill out to command the British forces in East Africa, which surprisingly both Bonar Law and Carson supported but the War Office blocked.[124] Hankey suggested he ought to be sent to north Russia to stimulate the importation of munitions.[125] It is probably no coincidence that both places were a very long way from London. Meanwhile, Violet Asquith sent Churchill Rudyard Kipling's poem 'If', probably chosen for its apposite line about meeting with Triumph and Disaster and treating 'those two impostors just the same'. She added, 'Remember that England trusts and needs you.'[126]

In his resignation speech in the Commons on 15 November, Churchill tackled the question of the Dardanelles:

> I will not have it said that this was a civilian plan, foisted by a political amateur upon reluctant officers and experts. I am not going to embark upon any reproaches this afternoon, but I must say I did not receive from the First Sea Lord [Fisher] either the clear guidance before the event or the firm support after which I was entitled to expect. If he did not approve the operation, he should have spoken out in the War Council. War is a hard and brutal job, and there is no place in it for misgivings or reserves . . . When the moment of action is come, the hour of misgivings is passed. It is often not possible to go backward from a course which has been adopted in war. A man must answer 'Aye' or 'No' to the great questions which are put, and by that decision he must be bound.[127]

He nonetheless took full responsibility for the naval operations:

> Not a line, not a word, not a syllable that was produced by naval and expert brains of high competency, without the slightest non-expert interference, but I approved of the plan; I backed the plan; I was satisfied that in all the circumstances that were known to me – military, economic, and diplomatic – it was a plan that ought to be tried, and tried then.[128]

After this he fatefully said, 'I recommended it to the War Council, and to the French Government, not as a certainty, but as a legitimate war gamble, with stakes that we could afford to lose for a prize of inestimable value – a prize which, in the opinion of the highest experts, there was a fair reasonable chance of our winning, a prize which at that time could be won by no other means.'[129] Referring to the expedition as 'a legitimate war gamble' allowed detractors for ever afterwards to allege that his gambler's instinct had led him to gamble away men's lives, and indeed there is no getting away from the terrible losses. The British Empire killed and wounded numbered 114,743, of whom 21,882 died in action and 8,899 in hospital. The French had 17,235 recorded burials.

Churchill was by no means the sole person responsible for the decision to occupy Gallipoli, but he was the politician most closely associated with the catastrophe and he did allow himself to become scapegoat-in-chief. This was partly because it was indeed his original plan – however many other people had initially supported it – but also because he insisted on seeing it through to the end, long after others had distanced themselves from it. Had Ian Hamilton not been the Army commander, Churchill might possibly have drawn back before the campaign derailed his career, but that too is doubtful. In the Second World War his bulldog obstinacy proved invaluable; during the Gallipoli campaign it left him appallingly vulnerable.

The Dardanelles debacle taught Churchill a great deal that was to stand him in excellent stead during the Second World War. 'A single, prolonged conference, between the allied chiefs, civil and martial, in January 1915, might have saved us from inestimable misfortune,' he wrote in *The World Crisis*, and he held many such conferences later.[130] He learned much about his own limitations, never once overruling his Chiefs of Staff when they unanimously rejected his schemes, and he did not encourage or become complicit in their silence if they disagreed with him, as he had with Fisher. Churchill also learned that it was sometimes better to cut one's losses than massively to increase the stakes. So in Norway, Dakar, Greece and elsewhere – and especially with RAF fighter squadrons over France in mid-May 1940 – he vigilantly guarded against mission-creep, and disengaged without allowing considerations of prestige to suck him into deeper military commitments.

Above all, he would not in future allow overmighty Service chiefs to amass power that properly belonged to elected politicians. Churchill differentiated between the 'brass-hats' of the military and the 'frock-coats' of the politicians, and thought that all too often in the Great War the former – using their immense authority with the press and public – decided which battles and campaigns were fought where, while the politicians all too often had to accept it. In his war memoirs after the Second World War he declared that after the failure of the naval attack of 18 March 1915 he had been wrong in 'trying to carry out a major and cardinal operation of war from a subordinate position'.[131] So on becoming prime minister in 1940 he appointed himself to the new position of minister of defence as well. He would come up against some tough and even domineering Service chiefs in the Second World War, Alan Brooke, Andrew Cunningham and Arthur Harris among them, but they knew themselves always to be in a subordinate position.

'I should have made nothing if I had not made mistakes,' Churchill wrote to Clementine soon after resigning.[132] He had made colossal mistakes during the Dardanelles debacle, but the lessons he learned from them were of immense value a quarter of a century later. General Stopford's performance at Suvla Bay in particular joined those of the Boer War generals in a long catalogue of military incompetence. One of the reasons why Churchill sacked so many generals in the Second World War was that he had formed a low opinion of the caste in his wide personal experience up to that point.

It was to be many long years before 'What about the Dardanelles?!' was no longer shouted at Churchill at public meetings. Even the five-year-old Randolph had contemporaries tell him, 'Your father killed mine at the Dardanelles.'[133] ('I am sorry to say that it made me feel immensely proud,' recalled Randolph, 'and I realized my father was a boss man who could order other fathers about.')[134] The Dowager Countess of Longford, whose husband had died at Scimitar Hill fighting with the 29th Division, would not enter a house in the 1920s if Clementine, let alone Churchill himself, was present.[135]

Churchill's resignation speech marked his last in the Commons before he left for the Western Front two days later. 'When it was over there was hardly a Member of Parliament present who was not cheering,' *The Times* reported. 'Punctuated by cheers from all parts of the House, and accorded an ovation at the close, the speech was an undoubted parliamentary triumph.'[136] Violet wrote the next day, 'I thought your speech quite flawless. I have seldom been more moved. It was a fine and generous speech. How thankful I am you said what you did about that wicked old lunatic [Fisher].' On 18 November, Major Churchill put on the uniform of his yeomanry regiment, the Queen's Own Oxfordshire Hussars, and reported for duty in France.

# 11

# Plug Street to Victory
# November 1915–November 1918

*In war, which is an intense form of life, Chance casts aside all veils and disguises and presents herself nakedly from moment to moment as the direct arbiter over all persons and events.*

Churchill, *Thoughts and Adventures*[1]

*Hatred plays the same part in Government as acids in chemistry.*

Churchill, *The World Crisis*[2]

Churchill was under absolutely no obligation to join the Army and fight in the trenches. Conscription was not extended to married men up to the age of forty-one until May 1916, by which time he was in his forty-second year. It was extraordinary for a minister to resign on a point of principle during a war and go to fight on the front line. Although Churchill did not consider himself disgraced by his stance over the Dardanelles, he knew the honourable path. He was now in the political wilderness, and thought that when his country was at war, if he could not serve it in politics he should do so by fighting.

There was undoubtedly also a powerful sense of personal redemption in his decision to enlist and share the dangers of the troops at the front. (When in the Second World War an MP disgraced himself, Churchill suggested that he join a bomb-disposal unit as the best way of regaining people's regard.) He wrote afterwards that the soldiers at the front 'and their regimental officers, armed with a cause, would by their virtue in the end retrieve the mistakes and ignorance of Staffs and Cabinets, of Admirals, Generals and politicians – including, no doubt, many of my own. But alas, at what a needless cost!'[3]

On landing at Boulogne on 18 November 1915, Churchill visited Sir John French at his headquarters at Saint-Omer, who offered him the choice of a staff appointment or command of a brigade in the field. He gladly chose the latter, requesting only that he serve 'a month or two in the line to measure the novel conditions'.[4] As a brigadier-general he would not have faced direct contact with the enemy, and he did not want a high command without having had that first. So the Earl of Cavan, who commanded the Guards Division of the BEF, attached Churchill to the 2nd Battalion of the Grenadier Guards, commanded by Lieutenant-Colonel George 'Ma' Jeffreys, whose battalion was going into the line at Neuve Chapelle the next day.

Churchill liked the fact that the Grenadiers had been the Duke of Marlborough's first regiment. One of its officers, Harold Macmillan, later recalled that 'There was great opposition to "the damned politician", but in two days he had won them all over.'[5] This was to be the story of his time in the army: initial opposition from mainly Tory officers because he was a politician, a Liberal and Winston Churchill, followed by quick acceptance as a result of his charm, bravery and willingness to learn.

'I expect to go into the line on Saturday for a week or two,' Churchill told Clementine. 'You must not let this fret you in the least. No action is contemplated and only a very general and ordinary risk need be contemplated . . . It is indeed much safer than going into the line with the Queen's Own [Oxfordshire Hussars] . . . Do not suppose I shall run any foolish risks or do anything which is not obviously required.'[6] Clementine had fully supported his decision to go to the front, despite its obvious risk. She herself joined the Munition Workers' Auxiliary Committee, which organized canteens for arms-factory workers in north London.

'Although it's only a few miles you seem to me as far away as the stars,' she wrote back, 'lost among a million khaki figures.'[7] By the time he left the Army in early May 1916 he had written over a hundred letters to his wife, which allow us to peer into his mind better than at any other period of his life. 'I am very happy here,' Churchill wrote in one letter to her on 19 November 1915. 'I did not know what release from care meant. It is a blessed peace.'[8] He added of his time as chancellor of the Duchy of Lancaster, 'How I could have spent so many months in impotent misery, which might have been spent in war, I cannot tell.'[9] Although some fifteen Grenadiers were killed or wounded per day, he told her, 'It will make me very sulky if I think you are allowing yourself to be made anxious by any risk.'[10] That risk was increased by Churchill's enjoyment of alcohol, because his battalion headquarters at Ebenezer Farm was strictly dry. 'As I have always believed in the moderate and regular use of alcohol,' he wrote years later, 'especially under conditions of winter war, I gladly moved my belongings from Ebenezer Farm to a company in the line.'[11]

'We don't want to seem inhospitable,' Jeffreys told Churchill, 'but I think it only right to say that you coming was not a matter in which we were given any choice.'[12] He accompanied the lieutenant-colonel on his twice-daily tours of the trenches through the snow and mud for two to three hours, commenting on German marksmanship when they were shot at, and Churchill was soon treated like any other officer. He quickly learned a good deal about trench warfare. The regimental adjutant had provided only one spare pair of socks and a shaving kit, so he wrote home asking for a warm leather waistcoat, wading boots, waterproof clothing, a periscope, sheepskin sleeping bag, khaki trousers, sardines, chocolates and potted meats to be sent 'with the utmost speed'.[13] Later on he also asked for Shakespeare, big cigars, a typewriter, Stilton, raisins and three bottles of brandy to be sent every ten days, the last of which were shared with his brother officers.[14]

No major offensives were in the offing, but the trenches were under unceasing fire of one kind or another, and no one was ever wholly dry or warm. 'Everything is very quiet,' Churchill told Clementine on 21 November. 'A few men are hit now and again by stray bullets skimming over the trenches, or accurate sniping. But we are able to walk right into the trenches without crawling along a sap [trench], and even in the five trenches in the front line there is great tranquillity.'[15] His company was commanded by Edward Grigg, who, like Harold Macmillan in the same regiment, was one day to become a minister in Churchill's wartime Government.

On 23 November, Kitchener recommended to the War Council that the Gallipoli Peninsula be evacuated. 'My scorn for Kitchener is intense,' Churchill told Clementine. 'If they evacuate in disaster – all the facts shall come out. They will be incredible to the world. The reckoning will be heavy and I shall make sure it is exacted.'[16] He was wrong; unlike so much of that campaign, the evacuation that took place in December and January was a model operation of retiring in the presence of the enemy and is still taught in some staff colleges today. It was achieved without loss; indeed nothing became Gallipoli so well as the leaving it. At 3.30 p.m. on 20 December Captain Clement Attlee of the 6th Battalion, South Lancashire Regiment, became the last man but one to leave Suvla Bay.[17] Attlee was convinced that the Dardanelles strategy had been a bold and correct one, which, in the view of one of his biographers, 'gave him his lifelong admiration for Churchill as a military strategist which contributed enormously to their working relationship in the Second World War'.[18]

'Thank God they got off [Cape] Helles all right,' Churchill wrote to Clementine when it was all over. 'I expect the Turks were as exhausted as our men, and only too glad to let them get away. Also perhaps a little money changed hands: and rendered this scuttle of "imperishable memory" less dangerous than it looked.'[19] He was raw and angry, but it was nonetheless still a thoroughly unwarranted speculation based on the old imperialist assumption that 'Johnny Turk' was corrupt and easily bribed.

On the same day as Kitchener's momentous decision to evacuate, Churchill wrote to Clementine. Despite corpses 'breaking through the soil, water and muck on all sides', he wrote, 'troops of enormous rats . . . and the venomous whining and whirring of the bullets which pass overhead, amid these surroundings, aided by wet and cold, and every minor discomfort, I have found happiness and content such as I have not known for many months.'[20]

On Wednesday, 24 November 1915, Churchill had a transformative experience, which he described to Clementine, presumably so as not to alarm her unduly, merely as 'a curious thing'. He was in his dugout when he received a message that Lieutenant-General Sir Richard Haking, the commander of XI Corps, was sending a car to pick him up at 4.30 p.m., which required him to walk for 3 miles 'across sopping fields on which stray bullets are always falling, along tracks periodically shelled'. He and his soldier-servant (his 'batman') walked for an hour, only to learn from a staff officer that the meeting had been cancelled. 'Oh, it was nothing in particular,' the staff officer said nonchalantly. 'He thought as he was coming up this way, he would like to have a talk with you.'[21] So Churchill walked back for another hour, across 'sopping fields now plunged in darkness', abusing 'the complacency of this General' for dragging him out 'in rain and mud for nothing'.[22] When he finally got back to his dugout, a sergeant told him, 'Better not go in there, Sir, it's in an awful mess . . . About five minutes after you left, a whizzbang [German high-explosive shell] came in through the roof and blew [his mess orderly's] head off.'[23] His anger at General Haking evaporated. 'Now see from this how vain it is to worry about things,' he told Clementine. 'It is all chance or destiny and our wayward footsteps are best planted without too much calculation. One must yield oneself simply and naturally to the mood of the game: and trust in God which is another way of saying the same thing.'[24] Writing of this incident in the *Pall Mall Gazette* in 1927, he said he felt 'the strong sensation that a hand had been stretched out to move me in the nick of time from a fatal spot'.[25]

That same night in the trenches, Churchill found a sentry asleep at his post. 'I frightened him dreadfully but did not charge him with the crime,' he told Clementine. 'He was only a lad . . . the penalty is death or at least two years.'[26] Instead, he kept watch so that others could sleep. In a similar spirit, when a young officer returning from a daring trench-raid accidentally let off his revolver and shot one of his own Grenadiers dead, the nine others in the company kept this secret and pretended it had been done by the enemy. 'Such men you never saw,' Churchill told Clementine, 'these terrific warriors, in jerkins and steel helmets with their bloody clubs in hand – looking pictures of ruthless war – was one to stay in the memory. C'est très bon.'[27] His men knew they could trust him not to be officious over such an unfortunate (though by no means isolated) friendly-fire incident, and to tell the dead Guardsman's family that he had died heroically. Sometimes in war, as he was to say later, the truth has to be defended by a bodyguard of lies.

'A total indifference to death or casualties prevails,' Churchill told Clementine of the thirty-five casualties the battalion had suffered in less than a week.[28] In a conversation at dinner at the Admiralty in February 1915, Churchill had told Violet Asquith 'that when one watches the extraordinarily arbitrary and haphazard way in which death and destruction are meted out by Providence – no guiding principle of justice or expediency apparently at work – one feels more than ever convinced of the unimportance of life. It *cannot* matter as much as one thinks whether one is alive or dead. The *absolute* planlessness here makes one suspect a bigger plan elsewhere.'[29] Now he was among others who were equally fatalistic.

'I do not feel the least revolt at the turn of events,' Churchill wrote on 27 November. Lloyd George, McKenna and 'the old block', by which he meant Asquith, were 'far away and look like the mandarins of some remote province of China'.[30] Yet he also asked her to 'Keep in touch with the Government. Show complete confidence in our fortunes. Hold your head very high . . . Above all, do not worry about me. If my destiny has not already been accomplished I shall be guarded surely.'[31] She replied that if he was killed because he had overexposed himself 'the world might think that you had sought death out of grief for your share in the Dardanelles. It is your duty to the country to try and live (consistent with your honour as a soldier).'[32]

Between 1 and 10 December, back at Saint-Omer, he spent time with three people who would be extremely important to him later: Louis Spears, Max Aitken and Archie Sinclair. These friendships forged in war were different and stronger than those acquired in peace. 'Nothing influenced him more in a man's favour than gallantry on the field of battle,' one of his aides would write years later. So it was unsurprising that he took to Spears, the first British officer to arrive at the front in August 1914, who had been wounded several times and had won the Military Cross.[33]*

* When Churchill visited the French XXXIII Corps with Spears, its commander gave him a distinctive *poilu* helmet, which he thought superior to the round British 'soup bowl' steel helmet and which he wore thereafter. 'It looks so nice and will perhaps protect my valuable cranium,' he told Clementine, saying it was 'the cause of much envy. I look most martial in

When he was wounded yet again in October 1916, Churchill wrote to him: 'My dear Louis, I read your name this morning in the casualty list for the fourth time with keen emotion. You are indeed a Paladin worthy to rank with the truest knights of the great days of romance.'[34] Paladin, meaning a knight errant, became a favourite description for his many close friends who had shown bravery in war.

Sir Max Aitken (from 1917, Lord Beaverbrook) was a Tory MP and friend of Bonar Law who, like Law, was from New Brunswick. He had a somewhat shady reputation deriving from his business practices back in his native Canada, but in Britain he owned the *Globe* newspaper, had a secret stake in the *Daily Express* (which he was soon to buy outright) and had tried to take over the *Evening Standard* (which he also eventually bought). Churchill was always highly solicitous of newspaper proprietors. As well as political ambition and an interest in history, he and Aitken shared a conviction that Asquith was mismanaging the war.

Sir Archie Sinclair was a twenty-five-year-old Scottish baronet and soldier, who had been in the Life Guards since 1910 but was now in the Machine Gun Regiment, a man whom Churchill admired for his bravery and charm.[35] Serving in the trenches brought them together for life, and many of the most visceral letters that Churchill wrote about politics at this time were those to Sinclair, who was a Liberal in politics and was to rise to become the Party's leader.

Churchill studied the quartermaster side of the supply system at Saint-Omer: 'I am to follow the course of a biscuit from the base to the trenches, etc,' he wrote.[36] But he was interested in more than biscuits. A paper he submitted to the Committee for Imperial Defence, entitled 'Variants of the Offensive', foresaw the tank tactics that were to bring some advantages to the BEF from 1916 onwards, but also huge victories to the Germans in 1940. 'They are capable of traversing any ordinary obstacle, ditch, breastwork or trench,' he wrote of what he still called Caterpillars. 'They carry two or three Maxims each, and can be fitted with flame-apparatus. Nothing but a direct hit from a field gun will stop them. On reaching the enemy's wire they turn right or left and run down parallel to the enemy's trench, sweeping his parapet with their fire.'[37] He hoped that Sir John French might put these ideas into operation when the machines became available, but told Clementine, 'That odious Asquith and his pack of

---

it – like a Cromwellian – I always intend to wear it under fire, but chiefly for the appearance' (ed. Soames, *Speaking* pp. 132, 129). His new headgear underlined his Francophilia, and his lifelong love of unusual hats, which he felt was useful for cartoonists.

incompetents and intriguers ruin everything.' He told her that he kissed her photograph each night before going to sleep.[38]

Although Lord Cavan persuaded Churchill that he should command a battalion (approximately 700 men) before taking on a brigade (of 2,800), on 4 December General French, fearing that he was about to be recalled as commander-in-chief of the BEF by Asquith, changed Churchill's mind back to commanding a brigade. Clementine was against this, thinking that many people would consider he had not done enough time in the trenches to warrant it. She was right, and anyway he needed far more practical experience on the Western Front before taking on such an onerous task. Nonetheless, Churchill believed he was going to be given the command of the 56th Brigade in the 19th Division, and wanted to appoint Spears as his major and Sinclair as staff captain. He told Clementine he did not care that there would be 'criticism and carping', because even if he had taken a battalion he would have faced the criticism that he was using it 'merely as a stepping stone, etc'.[39] He therefore asked her to buy the necessary accoutrements for a brigadier-general's uniform.

'My conviction that the greatest of my work is still to be done is strong within me: and I ride reposefully along the gale,' he told his wife. 'The hour of Asquith's punishment and K's exposure draws nearer. The wretched men have nearly wrecked our chances. It may fall to me to strike the blow. I shall do it without compunction.'[40] On 15 December, however, French was replaced by General Sir Douglas Haig, who rescinded Churchill's appointment to brigadier-general on the orders of Asquith, who was about to be asked a hostile question about it in the House of Commons. When Churchill was told, he wrote to Clementine, 'Altogether I am inclined to think that [Asquith's] conduct reached the limit of meanness and ungenerousness . . . Personally I feel that every link is severed . . . all relationship should cease.'[41] On 20 December he wrote that 'Asquith will throw anyone to the wolves to keep himself in office.'[42] Despite such strong feelings, he visited the Prime Minister's son Raymond in the trenches, and saw Asquith himself when he was back in London on a three-day Christmas leave. Clementine had been entertaining people strategically with an eye to his eventual rehabilitation, and her advice was not to 'burn any boats', since the Prime Minister had treated him no worse than Lloyd George had. Of the latter she wrote, 'I assure you he is the direct descendant of Judas Iscariot.'[43]

On New Year's Eve, Churchill visited Haig at his headquarters, as he was to do several times during the war. They always got on perfectly well face to face, whatever they might write or say about each other over the years in private. (On one occasion Haig thanked Churchill for a memorandum which he said he would read 'with great interest', but upon which he had already written 'What rubbish.')[44] Churchill was unimpressed by the way Brigadier-General John Charteris, Haig's intelligence chief, emphasized evidence to support Haig's preconceived theories. 'The temptation to tell a chief in a great position the things he most likes to hear is one of the commonest explanations of mistaken policy,' he later wrote in *The World Crisis*; 'the outlook of the leader on whose decisions fateful events depend is usually far more sanguine than the brutal facts admit.'[45]

On New Year's Day, he wrote a remarkably buoyant letter to Clementine about the coming year 1916: 'I think it will be better for us than the last – which was not too bad. At any rate our fortunes have more room to expand and less to decline than in January last.'[46] Even after easily the worst year of his life, he showed unbounded optimism. 'I can't help longing for the power to give those wide directions which occupied my Admiralty days,' he admitted. 'As for the Navy – it has dozed off under that old tabby [Balfour].' He asked Clementine to keep in touch with Lloyd George, despite her antipathy towards him: 'A situation might develop at any time, which would throw us inevitably together. Our relations are now good – and should be kept so. Of course I could not leave the Army in the field for any position which did not give me an effective share in the direction of the war.'[47] A few days later he added, 'I must rely on you to keep constant touch with the friends and pseudo-friends I have.'[48] He was finally under no illusion about which category Lloyd George fell into.

On 5 January 1916 Churchill took command of the 6th Battalion, The Royal Scots Fusiliers, as its lieutenant-colonel. He asked Clementine for a copy of Robert Burns's poetry. 'I will soothe and cheer their spirits by quotations from it. I shall have to be careful not to drop into mimicry of their accent! You know I am a great admirer of that race. A wife, a constituency, and now a regiment attest to the sincerity of my choice!'[49] The battalion had been badly depleted at the horrific Battle of Loos, losing nearly half the men and three-quarters of their officers. This allowed Churchill to appoint Sinclair as his second-in-command. It had nearly 1,000 yards of the front line to hold, flat and featureless terrain near the village of Ploegsteert, north of Armentières and just below Messines on the southernmost part of the Ypres salient, which the men immediately dubbed 'Plug Street'. It was one of the quieter sectors of the line, from which most of the civilians had been removed during gas attacks the previous spring. Churchill divided his time between his advanced battalion headquarters at Laurence Farm, near the hamlet of Le Gheer, and his battalion headquarters, 500 yards behind the lines, at the Sisters of Zion hospice in Ploegsteert. At the same time, Adolf Hitler was serving with the 16th Bavarian Reserve Infantry Battalion at Fromelles, 10 miles away.

Churchill's first words to the battalion were, 'War is declared, gentlemen – on the lice.'[50] Andrew Dewar Gibb, one of his officers, who wrote a superb memoir of Churchill in the trenches, recalled, 'With these words was inaugurated such a discourse on *pulex Europaeus* [in fact, a genus of fleas], its origin, growth and nature, its habitat and importance as a factor in wars ancient and modern, as left one agape with wonder at the erudition and force of its author.' As well as fighting lice, Churchill emphasized the other practical aspects of soldiering – gas practice, keeping rifles in good order, trench discipline and routine, precise drill and marching, and so on. When out of the line he introduced sports, concerts and much communal singing. He quickly got his section of the line dry with boarded and drained trenches, and provided his men with thick parapets, good wire and clear fields of fire. 'No more popular officer ever commanded,' wrote Gibb. 'He left behind men who will always be his loyal partisans and admirers.' Noting that Churchill encouraged the battalion medical officer to talk on his own subjects, Gibb also spotted that 'Winston had a *flair* for a good man of science.'[51]

Churchill did not go out looking for a Military Cross, but nor was it normal for a lieutenant-colonel to take part in officers' patrols in the 300 yards of no man's land, which he did on more than thirty occasions. On several of these patrols he got so close he could hear the Germans talking to each other. One of his junior officers, Edmund Hakewill Smith, recalled, 'He would often go into no-man's-land. It was a nerve-wracking experience to go with him. He would call out in his low gruff voice – far too loud it seemed to us – "You go that way, I will go this . . . Come here, I have found a gap in the German wire. Come over here at once!" He was like a baby elephant out in no-man's-land at night.'[52] The same officer wrote, 'He never fell when a shell went off; he never ducked when a bullet went past with its loud crack. He used to say after watching me duck, "It's no damn use ducking; the bullet has gone a long way past you by now."'[53] Gibb believed that 'There was no such thing as fear in him.'[54] When a general complained that recent shelling had made a part of the trench dangerous, Churchill replied, to the delight of the fusiliers within earshot, 'Yes sir, but, you know, this is a very dangerous war.'[55]

In his four months commanding the battalion, Churchill lost a total of fifteen men killed and 123 wounded. Eleven of the dead lie in the Lancashire Cottage Cemetery at Ploegsteert. They came from Ayr, Kilmarnock, Glasgow, Edinburgh, Leicester and Oldham. Private W. Russell was nineteen years old when he was killed on 7 February 1916. Though every loss was a tragedy to a family, fifteen fatalities was a very small number over such a long period on the Western Front, and represents a success for Churchill's intensive training programme.

On 17 January, Churchill and Jack Seely attended a lecture for senior officers on the lessons of the Battle of Loos. Afterwards the organizers asked what was the lesson of the lecture. 'I restrained an impulse to reply "Don't do it again,"' Churchill told Clementine. 'But they will – I have no doubt.'[56] His absolute opposition to the kind of attritional fighting that Haig had embraced and was soon to put into such painful operation at the Somme was the most important of the many lessons he learned from the war. 'All the Allied plans are flowing into a vast offensive for which no one has yet found the method,' Churchill wrote on New Year's Day 1916.[57] They were not to find that method by the time of the first day of the Somme Offensive on 1 July.

On 23 January, the day before his return to the front line, Churchill wrote to 'My dearest Randolph', telling the four-year-old:

> I am living here in a little farm. It is not so pretty as Hoe Farm, and there are no nice flowers and no pond or trees to play [the Churchill family game] gorilla but there are three large fat dirty pigs. Like the ones we saw in the wood . . . Soon we are going to go close up to the Germans and then we shall shoot back at them and try to kill them. This is because they have done wrong and caused all this war and sorrow.[58]

'Laugh a little, and teach your men to laugh,' he ordered his officers as they went into the front line; 'war is a game that is played with a smile. If you can't smile grin. If you can't grin keep out of the way till you can.'[59] He was living cheek by jowl with the working classes for the first time in his life, and he admired his men as soldiers. That did not mean he had to rely solely on their tough and tasteless meat ration, however, and he asked Clementine to send him 'large slabs of corned beef', as well as cream, Stilton cheese, hams, sardines, dried fruits and 'a big beefsteak pie, but not tinned grouse or fancy tinned things'.[60] He took the men's military experiences into account when it came to disciplining them. 'It was found that if a man was put in front of Winston for some misdemeanour he would ask them if they had fought at Loos,' Gibb noticed. 'If the answer was in the affirmative the Colonel would dismiss the charge. Inevitably, word got around and before long everyone in the battalion claimed to have fought at Loos.'[61]

While being shelled at Ploegsteert on 1 February, Churchill was accurately forecasting the next major realignment in British politics, after the anticipated fall of Asquith. 'The group I want to work with and form into an effective governing instrument', he told Clementine, were Lloyd George, Bonar Law, Carson, Smith and Curzon. 'Keep that steadily in mind. It is the alternative Government, when "wait and see"* is over.'[62] The last two named came out to visit him in France, but Clementine was still unpersuaded about Lloyd George, describing him as a 'shabby little tike . . . I feel contempt and almost pity for him . . . Ishmael!'[63]† Churchill's distance from influence was beginning to wear on him. 'By God I would make them skip if I had the power,' he wrote, 'even for a month.'[64]

Early February saw another lucky escape when a shell exploded 'at no great distance' from him while lunching at Laurence Farm with Archie Sinclair and others. Then, as Sinclair suggested they go to the dugout in the nearby barn, 'there was a tremendous crash, dust and splinters came flying through the room, plates were smashed, chairs broken. Everyone was covered with debris and the Adjutant (he is only 18) hit on the finger . . . The wonderful good luck is that this shell (a 4.2) [artillery shell] did not – could not have – burst properly.'[65] On another occasion, what Churchill called 'the goddess Nicotine' probably saved his life, for as he told *Strand* magazine readers years later, 'If I had not turned back to get that matchbox which I left behind in my dugout in Flanders, might I not just have walked into the shell that pitched so harmlessly a hundred yards ahead?'[66] At 6 a.m. on 14 February he was 'saluted on my doorstep by a very sulky bullet'.[67] Six days later a 30-pound shell entered the bedroom he shared with Sinclair, passed completely through it and penetrated the cellar. 'This is now the third time in a fortnight that our bedroom has been pierced by shells,' Churchill told Clementine. 'One lives calmly on the brink of the abyss.'[68]

By early March, several of Churchill's friends, including J. L. Garvin, C. P. Scott, Max Aitken and Francis Hopwood, were urging him to leave the Army (which, as an MP, he could do), return to Westminster and oppose the Government. Clementine disagreed, even though she worried about him constantly. Back on leave, he dined at the Other Club on 5 March, with Masterman, Riddell, Aitken, Smith and Rufus Isaacs (now the Marquess of Reading), none of whom dissuaded him from criticizing the Government. Neither did its Chancellor, Lloyd George, who lunched with him the following day and reported to his brother, 'He is anxious to come back. Sick of the trenches.'[69]

On Tuesday, 7 March 1916, Churchill made a speech in the Commons

* The catchphrase associated with Asquith's statesmanship after he repeated it four times during the Parliament Bill furore in April 1910.

† It was foretold of Ishmael that 'his hand will be against everyone and everyone's hand against him' (Genesis 16: 12).

that destroyed any hope he might have had for an early comeback, and further added to his enemies' long catalogue of his misjudgements. He started by making a measured but determined attack on the Admiralty. 'You cannot afford to indulge even for the shortest period of time in resting on your oars,' he said. 'You must continually drive the vast machine forward at its utmost speed. To lose momentum is not merely to stop, but to fall.'[70] He was listened to respectfully, but then at the end of his speech he made what he called a 'practical proposal' of 'recalling Lord Fisher to his post as First Sea Lord'. The House was astounded, as historians have also been, considering that he knew how volatile a figure Fisher was, for all his brilliance in earlier years.

This ludicrous proposal to turn back to the man who had destroyed his career allowed Balfour to launch a blistering counter-attack. The result was politically disastrous for Churchill. The *Spectator* wrote of 'the restless egoism of the political gambler', and Margot Asquith of the speech's 'farcical folly! . . . He is a dangerous maniac.' Lord Charles Beresford referred to Churchill's 'wicked statement', and Geoffrey Dawson of *The Times* wrote, 'the whole intrigue was a miserable fiasco, and Mr Balfour wiped up what was left of Winston the next afternoon in a tremendous dialectical onslaught.'[71]

Churchill knew he had made a bad misstep. He asked Violet to come to his mother's house in Marble Arch that night; there she found him alone. 'I shall never forget the pain of the talk which followed,' she wrote.

> He looked pale, defiant, on the defensive. I knew better than to criticize, reproach or even ask the question that gnawed at me – 'What possessed you? *Why* did you do it?' I saw at once that, whatever his motive, he realized that he had hopelessly failed to accomplish what he had set out to do. His lance was broken. What he had conceived as a great gesture of magnanimity – the forgiveness of the wrongs Fisher had done to him for the sake of a greater aim, our naval supremacy – had not been interpreted as such. It was regarded instead as a clumsy gambler's throw for his own ends.[72]

Violet, who still loved Churchill platonically, kindly but firmly advised him to return to France, which she called 'a difficult and agonizing task because I did not want to enhance his sense of failure by stressing the fact that he had fatally weakened his own position by his speech, and that by leaving the army now he would weaken it still further. But far worse was the dreadful thought that if my words had any effect at all I might be urging him to go back to his death.'[73] The next day Churchill went to No. 10 to see Asquith, who advised him not to follow the example of his father, who 'had committed political suicide through one impulsive action'.[74]

When Churchill spoke of his supporters, Asquith replied frankly, 'At the moment you have none that count at all.' 'Winston had tears in his eyes when they parted,' Violet recalled. Asquith further told his daughter that 'It was strange how little Winston knew of the attitude of others towards himself.'[75] The next day, Churchill returned to the trenches.

'When next I see you I hope there will be a little time for us both alone,' the twenty-nine-year-old Clementine wrote to her husband on 25 March, in one of her only references to the physical side of their marriage. 'We are still young, but Time flies stealing love away and leaving only friendship which is very peaceful but not stimulating or warming.'[76] It was a plea to make time for lovemaking among all the politicking she knew he would be doing during his next period of leave. He replied, 'Oh my darling do not write of "friendship" to me – I love you more each month that passes and feel the need of you and all your beauty.' He told her how much he wanted to go to 'some lovely spot' in Italy or Spain, 'and just paint and wander about together'.[77]

He was less thoughtful three days later when, apropos of a shell that had just missed him, he envisaged his own death, writing of 'No more tangles to unravel, no more anxieties to face, no more hatreds and injustices to encounter: joy of all my foes, relief of that old rogue [Asquith], a good ending to a chequered life, a final gift – unvalued – to an ungrateful country – an impoverishment of the war-making power of Britain which no one would ever know or measure or mourn.'[78] There was some self-pity there, certainly, but also some objective analysis, especially in the last phrase. 'Sometimes also I think I would not mind stopping living very much,' he told her. 'I am so devoured by egoism that I would like to have another soul in another world and meet you in another setting, and pay you all the love and honour of the great romances.'[79]

Clementine believed in her husband implicitly, both personally and politically, but counselled strongly against an overhasty return from the trenches that would surely be misinterpreted. 'I know (barring all tragic accidents) that you will prevail,' she wrote on 6 April, 'and that someday perhaps soon, perhaps not for five years, you will have a great and commanding position in this country. You will be held in the people's hearts and in their respect.'[80] Yet by then Churchill was feeling much as he had in the prisoner-of-war camp in Pretoria, and replied harshly, 'You are deluded if you think that by remaining here and doing nothing, I shall recover my influence on affairs.'[81]

Clementine nevertheless stood her ground and gave Churchill some of the best advice he ever got, saying that he would look like an adventurer if he returned to the Commons too soon, whereas remaining at the front 'you are in an honourable, *comprehensible* position until such time as a portion of the country demand your services for the State. If you come back before the call you may blunt yourself . . . my Darling Love – *For once only* I pray be patient. It will come if you wait . . . I could not bear you to lose your military halo . . . You are always an interesting figure, be a great one my darling.'[82]

Churchill stayed. Then, in early May, several battalions had to be amalgamated following heavy losses in the division. As the 6th Battalion was one of them, and as another colonel had seniority over him, Churchill was free to return to London honourably. 'It is really a most fortunate and natural conclusion,' he told Clementine, 'and well worth having waited for.'[83] His departure from the Army after only six months in the trenches was of course twisted by his enemies. 'The Arch-Mountebank has shown himself a supreme cad in his methods many times before,' wrote Alan 'Tommy' Lascelles, a future courtier, who was serving with the Bedfordshire Yeomanry, to a friend. 'It is only the harlequin-politician who can lay aside the King's uniform the moment it becomes unpleasantly stiff with trench-mud . . . He's not a Cabinet minister; he has not got a following in the country; he has been tried and found wanting at home. He is of military age. Why can't he be content to try and learn to fight the Germans in the flesh and hold his tongue?'[84]

He chose to do quite the opposite. Privately he had told his brother Jack that 'Asquith reigns sodden, supine, supreme.' And in public he launched into a series of speeches over the next fourteen months that convinced people – most especially Lloyd George – that he was far more dangerous outside the Government than inside. In May he called for the establishment of a separate Air Ministry, saying that air defences were effective 'over 95 per cent of the time. This truth is incontrovertible. Panic may resent it, ignorance may deride it, malice may distort it, but there it is.'[85] As he himself had taken charge of Britain's air defences in the early part of the war, he could take credit for it. A week later, in a debate on the Army, Churchill combined his two favourite periods in history to observe, 'If the Germans are to be beaten decisively, they will be beaten like Napoleon was beaten and like the Confederates were beaten – that is to say, by being opposed by superior numbers along fronts so extensive that they cannot maintain them or replace the losses incurred along them.'[86] There were still few serving politicians so familiar with military strategy.

On the afternoon and evening of 31 May and the morning of 1 June 1916, the last high seas fleet battle in British history was fought, off Jutland. It was a pyrrhic victory for Britain, which lost three battlecruisers and two cruisers sunk, the armoured cruiser HMS *Warrior* disabled and abandoned, five destroyers lost and six unaccounted for – heavier losses than those suffered by the Germans in both men and ships. Yet the German fleet was forced to return to port and never came out again for the rest of the war. Churchill later said of Admiral Jellicoe, 'He was the only man on either side who could lose the war in an afternoon.'[87] Although Churchill's time at the Admiralty has been blamed for the problems at Jutland, HMS *Indefatigable*, *Queen Mary* and *Invincible*, the three battlecruisers which blew up during the battle, were all launched or laid down before he became first lord.

The Admiralty released an initial communiqué about the battle on 2 June, and a second one in the early hours of the next morning. Their announcement of the serious losses caused consternation in Britain, so Balfour asked Churchill to write a more upbeat appreciation of the situation, which he immediately did in a third Admiralty communiqué on 3 June, saying that the battle had been 'a definite step towards the attainment of complete victory'.[88]*

Coincidentally, on 1 June the Government announced that a full-scale Commission of Inquiry would be held into the Dardanelles defeat, which Churchill had been demanding for months in the hope that it would clear his name. It was announced that all the relevant official papers would be released, but Asquith then changed his mind, ostensibly on security grounds. Churchill worked hard with Ian Hamilton to show that Kitchener's continual alterations of the plan had hobbled the operation, rather than anything they had done. 'Winston seems unbalanced and excitable just now,' Jean Hamilton noted in her diary on 29 May, 'but he has go, and vision, and is the enemy of caution and "Wait and See" . . . He walked around the room, declaiming, shouting, trying his oratory on me . . . He was terribly excited talking about Lord Kitchener, said he had a spitting toad inside his head, he pressed his hands over his own head and eyes to show the baffled weariness of trying to deal with such a fool.'[89]

Churchill and Hamilton were working on their case at 41 Cromwell Road at lunchtime on 6 June when, as Hamilton recalled, 'We heard someone in the street crying out Kitchener's name.' It was a newsvendor with a bundle of papers under his arm shouting, 'Kitchener drowned! No

* The battle long fascinated Churchill; in January 1928, the diarist James Lees-Milne described how after midnight at Chartwell 'Mr Churchill spent a blissful two hours demonstrating with decanters and wine-glasses how the Battle of Jutland was fought. It was a thrilling experience. He was fascinating. He got worked up like a schoolboy, making barking noises in imitation of gunfire and blowing cigar smoke across the battle scene in imitation of gun-smoke' (Gilbert, *A Life* pp. 483–4).

survivors!' The armoured cruiser HMS *Hampshire*, which had been taking Kitchener to Russia to discuss munition supply and military strategy with the Tsar – much the same job as Hankey had suggested for Churchill – had hit a mine and sunk the day before. 'When we came in the dining room,' Hamilton recalled, 'Winston signed to everyone to be seated and then, before taking his own seat, very solemnly quoted, "Fortunate was he in the hour of his death!"' Churchill and Hamilton were preparing what they believed was an unanswerable case against Kitchener, which they could now not launch against a dead hero. 'It was a nightmare lunch – no small talk,' recalled Hamilton, 'Winston said K might yet turn up but I told the company that he always had a horror of cold water.'[90]

The Battle of the Somme, which began on 1 July, was to exceed in the number of Allied casualties in the first three weeks that of the whole eight-month Gallipoli campaign.[91] Churchill did not believe the high figures the War Office was giving about German losses during the battle, complaining that 'A Government is entitled to know the facts from its servants.'[92] He was right; they were far too large. In November, once the tragedy had become fully apparent to all, he circulated a paper for the Cabinet and CID entitled 'The Greater Application of Mechanical Power to the Prosecution of an Offensive on Land'. He went into great detail about what could be achieved by bombing from aeroplanes, mustard and other gases, trench mortars, artillery attached to railway tracks, but mostly by tanks and other caterpillar-tracked vehicles. It was ignored, so he wrote a shorter version a year later, complete with a recommendation to cease the costly assaults Haig and General Sir William Robertson, the CIGS, apparently favoured just 'because it was better than doing nothing'.[93]*

Churchill also circulated a paper on the tactics of the Somme at this time. 'We could have held the Germans on our front just as well by threatening an offensive as by making one,' he argued. 'So long as an army possesses a strong offensive power it rivets its adversaries' attention. But when the kick is out of it . . . the enemy's anxiety is relieved and he recovers his freedom of movement.'[94] On Asquith's copy, someone, possibly his private secretary Maurice Bonham Carter, scribbled question marks and words such as 'Rubbish'.[95] On 15 September, Raymond Asquith, the Prime Minister's son, was killed. Churchill was later to write of his friend, 'When the Grenadiers strode into the crash and thunder of the Somme, he went

* The private attacks on Churchill during this period were personal and sometimes bizarre. After Churchill had described the losses on the Somme as 'disastrous' and the territorial gains as 'barren', Haig wrote to the King, 'I also expect that Winston's head is gone from his taking drugs' (Sheffield, *The Chief* p. 91).

to his fate cool, poised, resolute, matter-of-fact, debonair.'[96] Writing to Asquith, Churchill said,

> He was so brave and true that nothing less than the most dangerous and intensely personal service would content him ... His was a character of singular charm and distinction – so gifted and yet so devoid of personal ambition, so critically detached from ordinary affairs yet capable of the utmost willing sacrifice. Altogether he seemed to be above the worldly sum of things, yet so full of enjoyment of them and purpose in them ... I mourn with you the cruel cutting off of this rare and precious life so dearly beloved.[97]

The Battle of the Somme destroyed any faith Churchill might have had in Haig, whom he liked well enough personally but wanted Lloyd George to sack, preferably with Robertson too. 'Battles are won by slaughter and manoeuvre,' he wrote in *The World Crisis*. 'The greater the general, the more he contributes in manoeuvre, the less he demands in slaughter.'[98] Reviewing Alfred Duff Cooper's biography of Haig in the *Daily Mail* in October 1935, he wrote that Haig's mind had been thoroughly orthodox and unoriginal: 'No one can discern a spark of that mysterious, visionary, often sinister genius which has enabled the great captains of history to dominate the material factors, save slaughter, and confront their foes with the triumph of novel apparitions.'[99]

The Dardanelles Commission convened in August 1916, and after twenty-two hearings published an interim report in February 1917 that cleared Churchill of acting alone during the decision-making. 'I am hopeful that the truth may be published,' he told Seely before its first meeting. 'But failure and tragedy are all that are left to divide.'[100] The Commission held a further sixty-eight hearings after that, taking evidence from 170 witnesses, and presented its final report on 4 December 1917. The two truths Churchill wanted to see included were Fisher's initial lack of vocal opposition and Kitchener's failure to send troops in support of the naval attack.

Churchill begged Asquith to publish all the telegrams between himself and de Robeck, and all the War Council discussions, but, advised by Hankey that these would compromise national security, Asquith refused. (Only much later, under tremendous political pressure, did he relent.) Churchill meanwhile kept up his attack on the Government in the Commons. 'We cannot go on treating the War as if it were an emergency which can be met by makeshifts,' he said in August. 'It is, until it is ended, the one vast, all-embracing industry of the nation, and it is until it is ended the sole aim and purpose of all our lives. Everything in the State ought now to be devised and regulated with a view to the development and maintenance of our war power at the absolute maximum for an indefinite period. If you want to shorten the War, do this.'[101] Again in November he spoke with complete directness. 'This nation at war is an army,' he told the Commons; 'it must be looked upon as an army; it must be organised like an army; it must be directed like an army; and it ought to be rationed and provided and supplied like an army. That is the brutal fact to which we are being hurried remorselessly by events which we cannot in the least control.'[102] He urged the Government to regulate food prices for reasons of civilian morale, nationalize shipping and prevent 'the accumulation of extortionate profits in the hands of private individuals'.[103] This speech was his first advocacy of 'War Socialism' measures; they were not adopted in the First World War but were in the Second.

'The Admiralty is fast asleep and lethargy and inertia are the order of the day,' he wrote to Clementine's brother Bill Hozier on 30 September. 'However, everybody seems delighted – so there is nothing to be said. No plans, no enterprise, no struggle to aid the general cause. Just sit on the spacious throne and snooze.'[104] His criticisms irritated the Establishment. On 2 September, the *Spectator* claimed that 'his influence on our political life is almost wholly bad because it is wholly disassociated from any motive except that of personal advancement.'[105] Churchill was ferociously ambitious all his life, but the idea that he had no other motive is absurd: evident in his letters of this period is a burning desire to overthrow the dilatory Asquith and put in place a ministry that would pursue the war energetically and more effectively. By the end of the year, and especially after the carnage of the Somme that ended in stalemate in mid-November, Churchill's view of Asquith was shared by an overwhelming majority of Tory MPs.[106] They wanted a change, but they did not want Churchill to benefit from it.

On 5 December 1916, the long-awaited coup was finally launched when five Cabinet ministers led by Lloyd George and Bonar Law resigned from the Government over Asquith's direction of the war, forcing Asquith also to resign that same evening. Although the King offered Bonar Law the premiership, he turned it down in favour of Lloyd George, in accordance with the terms of the plot. So Lloyd George became prime minister and Bonar Law became chancellor, taking with him to the Treasury an unknown MP new to politics named Stanley Baldwin.

'One noticeable feature of the crisis of December 1916 and its aftermath', recalled Bonar Law's private secretary J. C. C. Davidson, 'was the evidence of Bonar's dislike for Winston. It was a combination of dislike and distrust. The feeling was reciprocated.'[107] With the Dardanelles Inquiry still ongoing, Lloyd George and Bonar Law could not have given Churchill a place in the new coalition Government even had they wanted to, and they did not. Lloyd George had by now reversed his earlier judgement, and asked Bonar Law, 'Is he more dangerous for you than when he is against you?', to which Bonar Law replied, 'I would rather have him against us every time.'[108] When the new Government was announced, *The Times* reported that it had learned 'with relief and satisfaction that Mr Churchill will not be offered any post in the new administration'. Churchill himself was distraught about it, and years later was quoted as recalling his exclusion from power by his supposed ally Lloyd George in December 1916 as the 'toughest moment of his life'.[109] The new War Council was composed of Lloyd George, Bonar Law, Curzon, Lord Milner and Arthur Henderson of the Labour Party. Balfour became foreign secretary, prompting Churchill to write years later, 'He passed from one Cabinet to the other . . . like a powerful, graceful cat walking delicately and unsoiled across a rather muddy street.'[110]

The interim report of the Dardanelles Commission, published on 12 February 1917, dealt with the origins and inception of the attack. Of the crucial War Council meetings of 13 and 28 January 1915, which had initiated the concept, it sagely concluded:

> Mr Churchill thought that he was correctly representing the collective views of the Admiralty experts. But, without in any way wishing to impugn his good faith, it seems clear that he was carried away by his sanguine temperament and his firm belief in the success of the undertaking which he advocated . . . Mr Churchill had obtained their support to a less extent than he himself imagined . . . Other members of the Council, and more especially the Chairman [Asquith], should have encouraged the experts to give their opinion, and, indeed, should have insisted upon their doing so.[111]

A collective 'groupthink' permeated the meeting of 13 January, encouraging optimism and discouraging incisive questioning, a problem made all the worse by Fisher's and Jackson's culpable silence. 'The views entertained by Mr Churchill at the time as to the prospect of success of a purely naval operation were somewhat more optimistic than was warranted by the opinion of the experts,' the Commission reported. 'Under these circumstances, Lord Kitchener grasped, perhaps rather too eagerly, at the proposal to act through the agency of the Fleet alone.'

Both the Dardanelles Commission and the official history of the war published in 1932–3 largely exonerated Churchill, although there were criticisms of the way he had been 'carried away' by his hopes for its success, which was fair. Its main criticism was of Asquith, for the absence of War Council meetings between 19 March and 14 May, and for an 'atmosphere of vagueness and want of precision which seems to have characterised the proceedings of the War Council'.[112] Kitchener, the commissioners concluded, 'did not sufficiently avail himself of the services of his General Staff, with the result that more work was undertaken by him than was possible for one man to do, and confusion and want of efficiency resulted'.[113]

One of the major problems was that both Kitchener and his military secretary had drowned on the *Hampshire*, and Kitchener had, as the Inquiry noted, 'seldom communicated his intentions or his reasons for action to anyone'.[114] Churchill was cross-examined on 26, 28 and 29 March, longer than anyone else, but he was well prepared and performed well. 'A fifth of the resources, the effort, the loyalty, the resolution, the perseverance vainly employed in the battle of the Somme to gain a few shattered villages and a few square miles of devastated ground', he told the Inquiry, 'would in the Gallipoli Peninsula, used in time, have united the Balkans on our side, joined hands with Russia, and cut Turkey out of the war.'[115]

The final report, published in December 1917, concluded that the campaign had been fatally compromised by a number of factors. The difficulties of a military attack on the peninsula had been severely underestimated and insufficient resources had been diverted from the Western Front to ensure its success. Both of the Allied landings on the peninsula, on 25 April and 6 August 1915, had been flawed. The report did not find Churchill principally responsible, but was much harder on Hamilton and Kitchener, and especially Stopford.[116] In the Commons debate on the report, Churchill said of the parts that were critical of the planners, 'Your Commission may condemn the men who tried to force the Dardanelles, but your children will keep their condemnation for all who did not rally to their aid.'[117]

Yet, for all his certainty, many of Churchill's closest friends doubted him. After a lunch with the Hamiltons, the diarist Marie Belloc Lowndes, elder sister of Churchill's friend Hilaire Belloc, recorded in her diary that 'There was great discussion concerning Winston Churchill. He is evidently coming back into public life. I said I hoped he would . . . but everyone else expressed fear lest this happened. This from people who declared that they were warmly attached to him.'[118] The heavy losses in the Gallipoli campaign explain much of the personal animosity to Churchill at this time, although they were merely the latest in a long accumulation of factors. The simple fact was that his judgement was no longer trusted, and his explanations no longer believed.

The United States entered the war on 6 April 1917, after Room 40 had intercepted a telegram from Arthur Zimmermann, the German Foreign Minister, encouraging the Mexicans to recapture Texas, Arizona and New

Mexico. Without it, Churchill later wrote, the war 'would have ended in a peace by negotiation, or, in other words, a German victory'.[119] That victory might have come about through the U-boats starving Britain, which could not feed its population from home produce alone. It was not until 26 April 1917 that the Admiralty finally adopted the convoy system to protect merchantmen. Churchill had long argued for a system whereby merchantmen moved only in large groups protected by warships, regardless of the fact that they would inevitably attract far more attention from U-boats. 'No story of the Great War is more remarkable or more full of guidance than this,' wrote Churchill in a review of the official history of the naval war published in 1931. 'It was a long, intense, violent struggle between the amateur politicians, thrown by democratic parliamentary institutions to the head of affairs, on the one hand, and the competent, trained, experienced experts of the Admiralty and their great sea officers on the other. The astonishing fact is that the politicians were right, and the Admiralty authorities were wrong.'[120]

Despite his general optimism that Britain would eventually win the war, he was not confident that it would happen soon. At the Other Club on 21 June, Colonel Charles Sofer Whitburn wagered him £50 at evens that the Germans would be driven over the Rhine by Christmas. Churchill wrote underneath, 'I hope to God they will. *But*.'[121] In fact they were never driven back over the Rhine at all: when the war ended, all German armies were still stationed on Allied soil.

'Is it not obvious that we ought not to squander the remaining armies in France and Britain in precipitate offensives before the American power begins to be felt on battlefields,' he told a secret session of the Commons on 10 May, predicting that, since 'We have not the numerical superiority necessary for such a successful offensive,' new assaults in 1917 would be 'bloody and disastrous adventures' and should be called off 'for a decisive effort in a later year'.[122] He was ignored and the slaughter continued, particularly between July and November at the Third Battle of Ypres, known as Passchendaele. There were some victories, such as General Plumer's at Messines, but most of the year was spent in a bloody stalemate.[123]

Churchill continued to put immense effort into his speeches. 'He never appeared at his hostess's table until tea-time,' a journalist reported. 'All day he might be heard booming away in his bedroom, rehearsing his facts and his flourishes to the accompaniment of resounding knocks on the furniture.'[124] He performed so well at the secret session – a debate where only MPs were allowed into the Chamber, while strategy was discussed – that it put his career back on track. Afterwards, in a conversation behind the Speaker's chair, Lloyd George told him he would bring him back into the Government in a reshuffle. This was not because Churchill had a party, faction or friends to offer, but because he had his voice.

Rumours that Churchill would return to government sent the Unionist Establishment into a tailspin. 'The power of Winston for good and evil is, I should say, very considerable,' Lord Esher told Haig. 'His temperament is of wax and quicksilver.'[125] Lord Charles Beresford wrote to Bonar Law to say he had evidence of Churchill's 'orders to the Fleet at the time of the Ulster Rebellion . . . to fire on Belfast' (which he could not have, since there were none).[126] Balfour wrote to Bonar Law to remind him that 'Some of us only joined the Government on the distinct understanding that W.C. was not to be a member.'[127] Sir George Younger, the chairman of the Conservative Party, told Bonar Law that the Party would not countenance Churchill's return.

So when Lloyd George unilaterally appointed him minister of munitions on 17 July 1917, the reaction was predictably furious, even though the post was not in the Cabinet. One hundred Conservative MPs signed a Commons motion deploring the decision. 'Although we have not yet invented the unsinkable ship, we have discovered the unsinkable politician,' the *Morning Post* fulminated. 'We confidently anticipate that he will continue to make colossal blunders at the cost of the nation.'[128] Lord Curzon was extremely angry; the Earl of Derby threatened to resign as secretary for war, thinking Churchill a 'great danger' and predicting interference from him.[129] Walter Long, the Colonial Secretary, wrote a pained letter to Bonar Law. The *Sunday Times* described Churchill as 'a grave danger to the Administration and the Empire as a whole', and the National Unionist Council, the voluntary body of the Conservative Party, carried a motion, to resounding cheers, that Churchill's appointment was 'an insult to the Navy and the Army'.[130] Lloyd George later wrote, 'For a short while the very existence of the Government was in jeopardy,' but he knew that Bonar Law was not about to put Asquith back in power, so he presented him with a fait accompli, announcing the appointment to the press and then avoiding him for the rest of the day.[131] Churchill meanwhile had to refight Dundee, which he won with a 5,226 majority, although the votes for Edwin Scrymgeour, the dogged Prohibitionist, went up to 30 per cent of the total.

The Ministry of Munitions of War, as it was formally called, headquartered in the former Metropole Hotel on Northumberland Avenue, off Trafalgar Square, employed two and a half million workers and was the biggest purchasing business and industrial employer in the world. When he came in, Churchill completely reorganized its 12,000 civil servants into twelve sections, and appointed an overall Advisory Council largely made up of successful businessmen. He took an all-embracing approach to the supply and strategy of mechanical warfare, especially with regard to trench mortars, tanks and aeroplanes.[132] By the end of the war the number of ministry officials had risen to 25,000. Ten years later he likened his own position as minister to riding 'comfortably on an elephant, whose trunk could pick up a pin or uproot a tree with equal ease, and from whose back a wide scene lay open'.[133] Of course it rankled with him that he was not in the Cabinet – although he attended Cabinet meetings that overlapped with the work of his department, and managed to inveigle himself into plenty of them. Despite Lloyd George's assurances to the Conservatives that he wouldn't interfere in other ministers' business, he took part in general discussions, and of course could not stop himself from coming up with ideas for military operations.

In February, Churchill had bought the Tudor mansion Lullenden Manor in East Grinstead in West Sussex. He invited Hankey and his wife down in July, when they went 'rambling around his wild and beautiful property'. Hankey recalled that 'On the whole he was in a chastened mood. He admitted to me that he had been "a bit above himself" at the Admiralty, and surprised me by saying that he had had no idea of the depth of public opinion against his return to public life, until his appointment was made.' Yet he was not so chastened that he did not use the opportunity of Hankey's visit to put forward an idea of a naval attack on the Turkish Mediterranean port of Alexandretta (modern-day Iskenderun). Hankey noted that Churchill was 'hot' for the operation, before his guest laid out all the objections and difficulties.[134]

A week later, the head of the Admiralty's planning section, Captain Dudley Pound, had to do the same to Churchill's detailed proposals for a 'close and aggressive blockade' of the German coast around the Heligoland Bight, intended to prevent the egress of submarines.[135] The French and Americans found the idea impractical and refused to supply any ships, but the Dardanelles had clearly not deterred Churchill from promoting offensive naval projects. Pound, who had distinguished himself at Jutland, pointed out the dangers presented by submarines and mines and the severe drain on the Fleet's resources.[136] It was now that he learned the importance of not saying no directly to Churchill, but rather of explaining in full all the advantages and implications of a particular course of action. 'Churchill was essentially a fair man and usually prepared to accept a professional opinion provided it was not defeatist,' recorded the seaman's biographer. 'The methodology was to remain with Pound and was to be frequently used in the next war.'[137] (Churchill also suggested to Lloyd George the idea of using artificial floating harbours to attack the Frisian Islands of Borkum and Sylt in 1917, a precursor to the use of the Mulberry harbours off the Normandy coast on D-Day.)

The Third Battle of Ypres began on 31 July. Churchill was furious that British generals continued to take the offensive even after 26 October, when Haig threw four Canadian divisions into the assault. He later wrote in *The World Crisis*, 'It cannot be said that "the Soldiers", that is to say the Staff, did not have their way. They tried their sombre experiment to its conclusion. They took all they required from Britain. They wore down alike the manhood and the guns of the British Army almost to destruction. They did it in the face of the plainest warnings, and of arguments which they could not answer.'[138] He suggested in 1919 that the mountain of rubble that was the centre of Ypres should be left for ever as a memorial to the devastation of war. The idea did not gain favour, although the destroyed medieval Cloth Hall was not restored in his lifetime.[139]

The new Minister of Munitions oversaw enormous increases in the production of tanks and machine guns, aircraft and mustard gas. He faced criticism, of course – one general described the tank as 'Winston's folly' – but this in no way deterred him.[140] It was at this time that he developed the practice of demanding information 'on a single sheet of paper', something he was also to do in the Second World War.[141] In October 1917 he gave munitions workers a 12.5 per cent pay rise, and during his time as minister provided large quantities of arms for the American Expeditionary Force, including 164 heavy guns, 300,000 grenades, 11 million bullets, 4,553 trucks, 8,100 cars and 452 aeroplanes.[142] At the Battle of Cambrai in November, 378 British tanks helped capture 10,000 German prisoners. In his final dispatch in 1919, Haig acknowledged that 'Only in 1918 was it possible to conduct artillery operations independent of any limiting consideration other than that of transport.'[143] Churchill's staff had those words printed on a graph that showed how the production of guns and gun-carriages had increased exponentially during his time at the ministry.

Churchill continued to visit the front, making another journey to Haig's headquarters in mid-September 1917. Eddie Marsh later wrote that when they reached Wytschaete 'no sooner did we walk along the ridge than six-inch shells began to burst around us . . . Columns of smoke rose from the ground sixty to a hundred yards from us, and bits of shell fell quite close – five or six yards off.'[144] The next day they visited the headquarters of I ANZAC Corps, where Jack Churchill was camp commandant, in the company of Major Desmond Morton, Haig's aide-de-camp. Morton, another Paladin, had won the Military Cross at the Battle of Arras earlier that year, and despite being shot in the heart continued to serve for two more years with the bullet still inside him. He was to become one of Churchill's three personal assistants (with special responsibility for intelligence) during the Second World War. Marsh recalled that on that trip they saw a cemetery 'packed tight with I should think two thousand crosses, and a stack of spare crosses just outside, waiting for the next push'.[145]

The next day at Pozières and La Boisselle, Churchill and Marsh saw '*everywhere* the tiny nameless white crosses, single or in clusters, "like snowdrops" as Winston said'.[146] They passed the massive crater of La Boisselle where the German lines began and went on to Bapaume and then 'through a succession of camps and disembowelled villages till we came to Arras [where] hardly a house is untouched'. Churchill discussed gas requirements with the experts of XV Army Corps, before going on to visit his old regiment, the Royal Scots Fusiliers, near by. Later, he spent half an hour walking towards a battle – 'shells whistling over our heads'. 'W's disregard of time, when there's anything he wants to do,' Marsh recorded, 'is sublime – he firmly believes that it waits for him.'[147] When soldiers marching past cheered and waved to him, indicating that hostility to him was by no means universal, 'he was as pleased as Punch.'[148]

There is a fine sketch of Churchill towards the end of September 1917 from the poet Siegfried Sassoon, whom he tried to recruit into the Ministry of Munitions. 'Pacing the room, with a huge cigar in his mouth,' Sassoon recalled,

> he gave me an emphatic vindication of militarism as an instrument of policy and stimulator of glorious individual achievements, not only in the mechanism of warfare but in the spheres of social progress. The present war, he argued, had brought about inventive discoveries which would ameliorate the condition of Mankind. For example, there had been immense improvements of sanitation.[149]

Even if we take the last sentence as satirical, he could also have mentioned air-to-air communication, hydrophones, plastic surgery, the mobile use of X-rays, blood transfusion, daylight-saving, female emancipation, pub closing times and the beginning of the end of colonialism in his list, although he would not necessarily have hailed the last three. 'From time to time he advanced on me,' Sassoon remembered, 'head thrust well forward and hands clasped behind his back, to deliver the culminating phrases of some resounding period.'[150] Sassoon was unpersuaded. 'He had made me feel that he was extremely likeable as a human being,' he wrote. 'Yet there was no doubt that I disagreed with almost every opinion he had uttered.'[151] When Churchill had said that war was 'the normal occupation of Man', Churchill qualified the statement by adding 'and gardening'.[152]

On 7 November, the Bolsheviks seized power in Petrograd, the former St Petersburg, which they later renamed Leningrad. 'Of all the tyrannies in history, the Bolshevik tyranny is the worst,' Churchill said shortly after the war, 'the most destructive, the most degrading . . . far worse than German militarism.'[153] It was true, yet the time would soon come when Lloyd George was to warn him that his 'obsession' with Bolshevism was 'upsetting [his] balance'.[154] Churchill described the Russian Revolution as 'a tide of ruin in which perhaps a score of millions of human beings have been engulfed. The consequences of these events . . . will darken the world for our children's children.'[155] This was both prophetic and numerically precise – at least twenty million people died under Soviet tyranny – yet his anti-Communism was to cost him a great deal politically. Lloyd George would allege in 1939 that Churchill's attitude towards the Bolsheviks was coloured by his class background: 'His ducal blood revolted against the wholesale elimination of Grand Dukes in Russia.'[156] Yet that background had not prevented him from leaving the Tory Party, endorsing the People's Budget, haranguing the House of Lords and supporting death duties, land taxes and Irish Home Rule, hardly stances expected of a man of 'ducal blood'; nor was it necessary to be upper class to be revolted by Lenin's execution of the Tsar, Tsarina and their young children. Churchill loathed Communism because of the attack it made 'on the human spirit and human rights', he said in July 1920. 'My hatred of Bolshevism and Bolsheviks is not founded on their silly system of economics, or their absurd doctrine of an impossible equality. It arises from the bloody and devastating terrorism which they practise in every land into which they have broken, and by which alone their criminal regime can be maintained.'[157]

'The longer Britain and America are fighting side by side,' Churchill said at Bedford's Corn Exchange on 10 December, 'the fiercer the struggle, the greater the effort they make together, the more closely that these two branches of the English-speaking family of the Anglo-Saxon world are drawn together, the truer will be their comradeship and the struggle will be a bond between them . . . It is to this that . . . we may rightfully look on the mainstay of the future of the world when the war is over.'[158] Despite America's entry into the war, he told Hugh Trenchard, now the commander of the Royal Flying Corps, it was a conflict that would last a long time.[159]

Visiting Ploegsteert and Ypres in late February with Reggie Barnes, who by then was a general commanding the 57th Division, Churchill found nothing but 'utter ruin'. He told Clementine that there was:

> absolutely nothing except a few tree stumps in acres of brown soil pock-marked with shell holes touching one another. This continues in every direction for 7 or 8 miles . . . Nearly 800,000 of our British men have shed their blood or lost their lives here during 3½ years of unceasing conflict! Many of our friends and my contemporaries all perished here. Death seems as commonplace and as little alarming as the undertaker. Quite a natural ordinary event, which may happen to anyone at any moment.[160]

His response was to write a Cabinet paper advocating the dropping of 'not five tons but five hundred tons of bombs each night on the cities and manufacturing establishments' of the enemy, in order to end the war as soon as possible.[161] The war ended before that became technically possible, but the seeds of future strategy were clearly already in Churchill's mind.

The Germans launched the massive Ludendorff Offensive along the Western Front on 21 March 1918, in the hope of finally breaking through and winning the war before American troops started to arrive in numbers. They overran 1,200 square miles, captured 75,000 British troops and 1,300 guns and got to within 7 miles of Amiens. By May they had reached the Marne, only 45 miles from Paris. By 19 April, Churchill was able to boast to the King 'that every gun that has been lost in this great battle had been replaced'.[162] The Germans took 17 miles in one day on 27 May, a record for the Western Front in the whole war. Churchill was only 10,000 yards behind the British Fifth Army's front. 'There was a rumble of artillery fire, mostly distant, and the thudding explosions of aeroplane raids,' he later recalled. 'And then, exactly as a pianist runs his hands across a keyboard from treble to bass, there rose in less than one minute the most tremendous cannonade I shall ever hear. It swept around us in a wide curve of red flame.'[163] Churchill would reminiscence about the Spring Offensive for years afterwards. In March 1945, he gave a 'vivid description' of it to ministers.[164] It left him with a profound respect for the German capacity for counter-attacking even while seemingly exhausted, and helps explain why he was less surprised than others when the Germans launched their Ardennes Offensive in December 1944.

Churchill was in Paris coordinating munitions production with his French opposite numbers during the Ludendorff Offensive, and on 30 March he discussed the strategic situation with Georges Clemenceau, the French Prime Minister, the senior French generals Ferdinand Foch, Philippe Pétain and Maxime Weygand, as well as Generals Haig and Rawlinson. Churchill relished getting to know the great Clemenceau, who had taken the double portfolio of prime minister and minister of defence on his accession to power in November. 'The old man is very gracious to me and talks in the most confidential way,' he told Clementine.[165] 'He is an extraordinary character . . . His spirit and energy indomitable.' Watching the fighting north of Moreuil with him, Churchill reported, 'I finally persuaded the old tiger to come away from what he called "un moment délicieux".'[166]

In *Great Contemporaries*, published in 1937, Churchill drew a superb pen portrait. 'Clemenceau embodied and expressed France,' he wrote. 'As much as any single human being, miraculously magnified, can ever be a nation, he was France.' Clemenceau's life-story was one of 'fighting, fighting all the way; never at ease'; he had waited half a century for his moment, having had 'to earn his daily bread as . . . a journalist'. 'Everyone had felt the lash of his tongue and of his pen . . . Rarely was a public man in time of peace more cruelly hounded and hunted.'[167] Yet even at his lowest point Clemenceau was 'Not suppliant: never that. Defiant, unconquerable . . . Such was the man who, armed with the experience and loaded with the hatreds of half a century, was called to the helm of France in the worst period of the war . . . It was at that moment . . . that the fierce old man was summoned to what was in fact the dictatorship of France. He returned to power . . . doubted by many, dreaded by all, but doom-sent, inevitable.'[168]

The anticipations of Churchill himself twenty-five years later are heavy. When he delivered his speech to the French Chamber on becoming prime minister in November 1917, Clemenceau – in Churchill's account – found that 'all around him was an assembly which would have done anything to avoid having him there, but having put him there, felt they must obey . . . The last desperate stake had to be played . . . With snarls and growls, the ferocious, aged, dauntless beast of prey went into action. In this fashion did the death-grapple with Germany begin.'[169] In a discussion about the Parisian munition and aircraft factories that were under threat from the German advance, Clemenceau told Churchill, 'I will fight in front of Paris; I will fight in Paris; I will fight behind Paris.'[170] Churchill wrote in *Great Contemporaries*, 'Paris might have been reduced to the ruins of Ypres or Arras. It would not have affected Clemenceau's resolution. He meant to sit on the safety-valve, till he won or till all his world blew up. He had no hope beyond the grave; he mocked at death; he was in his seventy-seventh year. Happy the nation which when its fate quivers in the balance can find such a tyrant and such a champion.'[171] Churchill is often said to have had Marlborough, Lloyd George and Pitt the Younger as his primary role models, but, insofar as he needed one, it was Georges Clemenceau.

In an extraordinary memorandum in April 1918, Churchill suggested that Britain should try to persuade Lenin to re-enter the war after the Bolsheviks had signed a peace treaty with Germany at Brest-Litovsk the previous month. In exchange the Allies would protect the Bolsheviks from counter-revolution. 'Let us never forget that Lenin and Trotsky are fighting with ropes around their necks,' he argued. 'They will leave office for the grave. Show them any real chance of consolidating their power . . . and they would be non-human not to embrace it.'[172] Now as later, he was willing to put aside his bitter ideological anti-Communism to defeat Germany, but the offer was not made, and would certainly have been rejected.

On 23 April – St George's Day – Vice Admiral Roger Keyes led the spectacular Zeebrugge Raid, which blocked the entrance to the canal linking Zeebrugge Harbour to Bruges at low tide. No fewer than eight Victoria Crosses were awarded, the highest number for single engagement since the Zulu War. Churchill wrote that it would 'rank as the finest feat of arms in the Great War, and certainly as an episode unsurpassed in the history of the Royal Navy'.[173] It cemented Churchill's already high regard for Keyes, who had a love for amphibious operations based on surprise and daring and who had wanted to renew the attack on the Dardanelles the day after de Robeck had called it off.

Haig gave Churchill the pretty Napoleonic-era Château de Verchocq in the Pas-de-Calais as a French headquarters for the Ministry of Munitions in May, which Churchill jokingly described as 'a little maison tolérée', or licensed brothel.[174] He made regular flights across the Channel to visit Verchocq and Paris, which he called 'this menaced but always delightful city'. He sometimes piloted the aircraft to and from Verchocq himself. 'I flew all my journey last time,' he told Sinclair on one occasion, 'and very nearly finished an eventful though disappointing life in the salt water of the Channel. We just fluttered back to shore . . . It just takes one hour from Lullenden to G.H.Q! But one must have careful engine supervision.'[175] On 6 June, as the Spring Offensive rolled on only 45 miles away, he told Clementine, 'The fate of the capital hangs in the balance.'[176]

On 1 June 1918, Jennie, Churchill's sixty-four-year-old mother, married the handsome and rich Montagu Porch, who was, at forty-one, two years younger than Churchill. 'He has a future and I have a past, so we should be alright,' she observed.[177] She had been divorced from George Cornwallis-West for four years and had returned to her earlier name of Lady Randolph Churchill.

By then, Clementine was pregnant again. The Churchills were short of money, but it was nonetheless truly extraordinary for Clementine to have spoken as she did on 21 June with the childless Lady Hamilton, who was about to adopt an infant named Harry. According to Jean Hamilton's diary, Clementine 'urged me on no account to adopt Harry . . . she asked if I'd like to have her baby; of course I said I would, and . . . I offered to have her here for it [the birth], as she had been telling me how expensive the nursing home would be – £25 for a room alone – and she said she could not possibly afford it. She said if she had twins I would have one.'[178] Churchill was now on a minister's salary, but he had been living on his MP's salary of only £400 per annum for fourteen months after leaving the Army. Clementine was tired and distraught during what she later said had been the lowest point in her life, so the offer should probably be seen in emotional rather than literal terms, although Jean Hamilton seems to have taken it seriously. Perhaps luckily for their friendship, Clementine did not have twins.

In a speech celebrating America's Fourth of July in 1918, Churchill propounded a message that was to become central to his thinking. 'The Declaration of Independence is not only an American document,' he told his audience in the Westminster Central Hall.

> It follows on the Magna Carta and the Bill of Rights as the third great title-deed on which the liberties of the English-speaking people are founded. By it we lost an Empire, but by it we also preserved an Empire. By applying its principles and learning its lesson we have maintained our communion with the powerful Commonwealths our children have established beyond the seas . . . Deep in the hearts of the people of these islands, in the hearts of those who, in the language of the Declaration of Independence, are styled 'our British brethren', lay the desire to be truly reconciled before all men and all history with their kindred across the Atlantic Ocean, to blot out the reproaches and redeem the blunders of a bygone age, to dwell once more in spirit with them, to stand once more in battle at their side, to create once more a union of hearts, to write once more a history in common.[179]

Churchill often spoke about freedom, but his ideas were always rooted in history, in the Magna Carta and English common law, and in practical politics rather than in the more abstract thought about freedom of philosophers such as Locke, Hume and John Stuart Mill.

In his speech on America's Independence Day, Churchill went so far as to say of the eruption of a million American soldiers on to the battlefields of France under their commander General John Pershing that 'No event since the beginning of the Christian Era is more likely to strengthen and restore Man's faith in the moral governance of the universe.'[180] He insisted, to loud cheers, that 'Germany must be beaten. Germany must know that she is beaten, must feel that she is beaten. Her defeat must be expressed in terms and facts which will for all time deter others from imitating her crimes, and which will make it impossible for her to renew them.'[181] After that speech he told Archie Sinclair, 'If all goes well England and the United States may act permanently together. We are living fifty years in one at this rate.'[182]

Six days later, he appointed Jack Seely, who was back from the trenches after being gassed, as his parliamentary secretary, his second-in-command in the ministry. Seely had been mentioned in dispatches no fewer than five times, had commanded a brigade and had even on one occasion braved the wrath of his superiors to commandeer infantry from another corps to form an ad hoc combat group that captured an enemy stronghold. Among all Churchill's Paladins, Seely, whose eldest son Reginald was killed in action in 1917, was at the forefront.

The German attack at the Second Battle of the Marne on 15 July was, in Churchill's view, 'the supreme crisis' of the war. He later described how, from the heights of Montmartre, 'the horizons could be seen alive with the flashes of artillery.'[183] By 6 August, however, it was clear that it had failed, leaving the Germans exhausted and demoralized at having to fight the Americans as well as the French and British Empires on the Western Front. Only two days later began the great Allied hundred-day counter-offensive that was to win the war.

A week before, on Monday, 29 July 1918, Winston Churchill met Franklin D. Roosevelt, the Assistant Secretary of the US Navy, at a dinner in the hall of Gray's Inn in London, one of the ancient Inns of Court. It ought to have been one of the great encounters of history, but Roosevelt was to take away no higher opinion of Churchill than his cousin Theodore had previously. For all his admiration of Americans in general, Churchill showed little interest in the Assistant Secretary of the Navy, perhaps in part because also present that evening were F. E. Smith, Curzon, Smuts, Geddes, Long, Robert Borden (the Prime Minister of Canada), the dukes of Marlborough, Rutland and Northumberland, Freddie Guest, Mark Sykes and other friends and grandees. According to Joseph P. Kennedy – not a wholly reliable source – Roosevelt later complained that Churchill had 'acted like a stinker' on that occasion, 'lording it all over us'.[184]

Despite the fact that he had been lucky to be invited to rejoin the Government, Churchill was incapable of not interfering with other ministers' departments. On one day – 17 August 1918 – for example, he managed to prompt resignation threats from both of the most important Service ministers: he precipitated a row with Sir Eric Geddes, the First Lord of the Admiralty, with his suggestion that naval guns might be taken out of elderly ships (which could be laid up now that the United States was in the war) and adapted for military use, and another with Lord Derby, the Secretary for War, by proposing that some 6-inch howitzers should be taken from Haig and sent to British forces in Russia.[185] 'What right has he to express an opinion?' the 17th Earl of Derby asked of the Minister of Munitions. 'He is only an ironmonger.'[186]

'I am trying . . . to arrange to give the Germans a good first dose of the Mustard gas before the end of the month,' Churchill wrote to Clementine from the Ritz Hotel in Paris in September. 'Haig is very keen on it and we shall I think have enough to produce a decided effect. Their whining in defeat is very gratifying to hear.'[187] Mustard gas had been used by the Germans at Ypres in July 1917, and the British responded with their own on 28 September 1918. The same happened with chlorine gas, which was far more lethal than mustard gas (though more easily defended against) and had first been used by the Germans at the Second Battle of Ypres in April 1915, and by the British six months later at Loos. It was the Churchills' tenth wedding anniversary and his next words were deeply loving: 'My dearest sweet I hope and pray that future years may bring you serene and smiling days.' He was perfectly capable of writing about 'this hellish poison' one moment and their 'serene and smiling days' together the next.

Despite the deployment by May of over a million Americans on the Western Front, who decisively tipped the balance in favour of the Allies, Churchill was nonetheless surprised by how suddenly the Great War ended. After Turkey and Austria had collapsed in late October, he wrote to Marsh of 'A drizzle of empires, falling through the air'.[188] The sudden end of effective German resistance in November meant that plans he was germinating for intervention against the Bolsheviks had no time to solidify. He later argued of this possibility that 'Had the Great War been prolonged into 1919, Intervention, which had been gathering momentum every week, must have been militarily successful.'[189] Here was yet another of the 'what ifs' he so enjoyed.

The Armistice meant that the Allies would not be fighting for a Russian government that would support a Second Front against the Central Powers; instead most Allied governments wanted to quit Russia as swiftly as possible, if possible without damaging the anti-Bolshevist White Russian cause too badly. Churchill was one of the few who wanted the anti-Bolshevik struggle widened and deepened, believing as he did that otherwise Communism would pose a threat to Germany and eastern Europe. 'We might have to build up the German army,' the Cabinet minutes report him saying on 10 November, the very day before the Armistice, 'as it was important to get Germany on her legs again for fear of the spread of Bolshevism.'[190] After the Armistice, he urged that shiploads of food be sent to Germany, but that was not Lloyd George's policy at all. He was limbering up for a general election based on making Germany pay 'till the pips squeak' (in Geddes's phrase) and much rhetoric about hanging the Kaiser for war crimes. One in ten British men between the ages of twenty and forty-five had died in the war, some 744,000, as well as 14,600 merchant seamen, and 1,000 civilians. A further 150,000 Britons died of Spanish influenza that winter. Against such a background, any fresh military commitments were not going to be popular. The Government was under enormous financial pressure immediately after the war, which affected everything it was trying to do. Of the fifteen million tons of shipping sunk in the conflict, for example, nine million had been British.

'It was a few minutes before the eleventh hour of the eleventh day of the eleventh month,' Churchill later wrote of the moment the Great War ended.

> I stood at the window of my room looking up Northumberland Avenue towards Trafalgar Square, waiting for Big Ben to tell that the war was over . . . And then suddenly the first stroke of the chime. I looked again at the broad street beneath me. It was deserted. From the portals of one of the hotels absorbed by Government departments darted the slight figure of a girl clerk, distractedly gesticulating while another stroke of Big Ben resounded. Then from all sides men and women came scurrying into the street. Streams of people poured out of all the buildings. The bells of London began to clash . . . Flags appeared as if by magic. Swarms of men and women flowed from the Embankment. They mingled with the torrents pouring down the Strand on their way to acclaim the King.[191]

'At the summit true politics and strategy are one,' Churchill wrote in *The World Crisis*. 'The manoeuvre which brings an ally into the field is as serviceable as that which wins a great battle. The manoeuvre which gains an important strategic point may be less valuable than that which placates or overawes a dangerous neutral.'[192] Churchill considered two of Germany's most egregious errors of the war to have been her invasion of Belgium, which precipitated Britain's involvement, and her unrestricted submarine warfare, which brought in the United States three years later. He thought that the Germans should have stayed on the defensive in north-west Europe and concentrated on knocking out the weaker Allied Powers such as Italy and Romania. All this had powerful implications for his strategy for the Allies in the Second World War.[193]

Another great lesson of the many Churchill learned in the First World War was about the importance of unity of command. 'War, which knows no rigid divisions between French, Russian, and British Allies,' he wrote, 'between land, sea, and air, between gaining victories and alliances, between supplies and fighting men, between propaganda and machinery, which is, in fact, simply the sum of all forces and pressures operative at a given period, was dealt with piecemeal. And years of cruel teaching were necessary before the imperfect unifications of study, thought, command and action were achieved.'[194] He admired Marshal Foch's insistence on total Allied unity.

As soon as the war ended, Churchill immediately set about writing *The World Crisis*. It was to be packed with lessons for the future. 'No war is so sanguinary as the war of exhaustion,' he wrote. 'No plan could be more unpromising than the plan of frontal attack. Yet on these two brutal expedients the military authorities of France and Britain consumed, during three successive years, the flower of their national manhood.'[195]

# 12

# Coalition Politics November 1918–November 1922

*For good or ill, right or wrong, in war you must know what you want and what you mean and hurl your whole life and strength into it and accept all hazards inseparable from it.*

Churchill, *Illustrated Sunday Herald*, April 1920[1]

*If I had been properly supported in 1919, I think we might have strangled Bolshevism in its cradle, but everybody turned up their hands and said 'How shocking!'*

Churchill to the National Press Club, Washington, DC, 1954[2]

'The South African War accounted for a large proportion not only of my friends but of my company,' Churchill was to write of his Sandhurst cadet company in *My Early Life*; 'and the Great War killed almost all the others.'[3] His best friend at Harrow, Jack Milbanke VC, had been killed, in Churchill's words, 'leading a forlorn attack in the awful battle of Suvla Bay'.[4] Major Cecil Grimshaw, Churchill's cell-mate in Pretoria, who had raised the Union Flag when Churchill liberated the prison, was killed at Cape Helles. John Morgan, a housemate at Harrow, was killed at Lala Baba. Indeed of the sixty-seven boys in his 1892 house photograph, a total of forty-one served in either the Boer War or Great War or both, and eleven were dead by 1918.

Captain Norman Leslie of the Rifle Brigade, son of Jennie Churchill's sister, was killed by a German sniper at Armentières in northern France in October 1917. Alastair Buchan, John Buchan's brother, who had been wounded serving under Churchill at Ploegsteert, was killed in action in April 1917, aged twenty-two. Eddie Marsh noted that many of the young officers and administrators who had escorted him and Churchill on their East African tour in 1907 were dead by the time of the Armistice.[5] At the Other Club, the standing rule against toasts had been ignored in

November 1917 as one was drunk in silence to 'The Memory of the Brave'. Lord Rosebery's son, the Liberal MP Captain Neil Primrose MC of the Royal Buckinghamshire Hussars, had died of wounds received leading a dismounted attack against the Turks in the Third Battle of Gaza. Another Liberal MP, Thomas Agar-Robartes, had been killed by a sniper while rescuing a wounded comrade at the Battle of Loos. And of course Kitchener had drowned. Churchill wrote obituaries for Rupert Brooke and Valentine Fleming, and had known scores of others who had been killed, including Auberon Herbert, Raymond Asquith and three members of the Other Club. 'There are few homes in Britain where you will not find the empty chair and the aching heart,' he said in a speech in July 1918, and his own home was as full of the shades of family and friends as any.[6]

On 15 November, four days after the Armistice, Churchill and Clementine's third daughter, the red-headed Marigold Frances (the 'Duckadilly'), was born. The following month, as so often before, politics interrupted family life. At the general election in December, Churchill campaigned in Dundee as a Coalition Liberal, now distinct from the Asquithian Liberals who had not been reconciled to the Lloyd George Government in December 1916. He received an endorsement, nicknamed a 'coupon', from both Lloyd George and Bonar Law that was invaluable electorally, so popular was the Prime Minister at the moment of victory. (Indeed, with those candidates in receipt of the coupon doing very well at the polls, and candidates without it correspondingly badly, it became known as the Coupon Election.) Churchill's domestic platform was much the same as the Liberal one in pre-war days, such as rail nationalization and a forty-hour week, although this time he wanted heavy taxation of war profits, which was both popular with the public and in keeping with his own distaste for profiteering. He suggested to Lloyd George that a 100 per cent tax be levied on war profits of over £10,000 (approximately £910,000 in today's money) to help reduce the War Debt. 'Why *should* anybody make a great fortune out of the war?' he asked the Prime Minister. 'While everybody has been serving the country, profiteers and contractors and shipping speculators have gained fortunes of a gigantic character. Why should we bear the unpopularity of defending old Runciman's ill-gotten gain?'[7]*

Churchill's speech in Dundee on 26 November, much heckled by pro-Bolshevik agitators, presaged a famous Second World War speech, and struck a vigorous note. 'Repair the waste,' he said. 'Rebuild the ruins.

* When Lord Runciman, as he had by then become, died in 1937 he left in his will £2.4 million, approximately £130 million in today's money.

Heal the wounds. Crown the victors. Comfort the broken and broken-hearted. There is the battle we have now to fight. There is the victory we have now to win. Let us go forward together.'[8] He later regretted saying of the starving Germans, 'They were all in it, and they must all suffer for it'[9] He admitted in a book years later, 'I cannot pretend not to have been influenced by the electoral currents so far as verbiage was concerned.'[10] His true policy of advocating large grain shipments to Germany was the one he summed up with admirable brevity to Violet Asquith: 'Kill the Bolshie; Kiss the Hun.'[11]

On 30 November, Churchill celebrated his forty-third birthday. It was the age at which he had predicted to Hesketh Bell in Uganda that he would be prime minister, yet he was not even in the Cabinet. The election took place on 14 December, for the first time on a single day, but the result was not announced till 28 December because the Service vote had to be collected from around the world. The result was an emphatic endorsement of Lloyd George – popularly known as 'the Man Who Won the War' – and of his coalition, but it was Bonar Law who had the parliamentary upper hand in terms of numbers. The Coalition Unionists had 335 MPs in the new Parliament, the Coalition Liberals 133 and Coalition Labour 10 (totalling 478 Coalition supporters out of 707 MPs). Elected to oppose the coalition were seventy-three Sinn Fein MPs, sixty-three Labour, twenty-eight Asquithian Liberals (Asquith himself losing his seat at East Fife), twenty-five Irish Unionists, twenty-three non-Coalition Conservatives and seven Irish Nationalists. The popular vote had come to 3.5 million votes for the Coalition Unionists, 1.46 million for the Coalition Liberals, 2.38 million for Labour, 1.29 million for the Asquithian Liberals and 487,000 for Sinn Fein. The Sinn Feiners refused to take their seats at Westminster, and set up their own alternative assembly in Dublin instead, which they called the Dáil Éireann. They demanded independence, as the Irish Republican Army started a violent campaign against the police and government.

Partly as a result of the coupon, Churchill himself had been returned for Dundee with the immense majority of 15,365. An Air Ministry was about to be created, and, the day after the election, Lloyd George offered him the choice of either the Admiralty or both the War and Air ministries. He asked for a different combination – the Admiralty and Air Ministry – arguing that 'Though aeroplanes will never be a substitute for armies, they will be a substitute for many classes of warships.'[12] Instead, on 10 January 1919, to the press's almost universal displeasure, Churchill became secretary for war and air. 'Character is destiny,' intoned the *Morning Post*; 'there is some tragic flaw in Mr Churchill which determines him on every occasion in the wrong course.'[13]

Churchill faced enormous problems in demobilizing an army of 2.5 million men. His primary task was to get as many men back to their homes and jobs as quickly as possible, but he also needed to find enough troops to police the German occupation zone, Constantinople and the Dardanelles, Palestine and Iraq, and to reinforce a small contingent that in 1918 had been sent to help the White Russians fight the Bolsheviks. He persuaded the Cabinet to drop the prioritization of industrial needs, and instead base release on wounds, age and length of service. This fairer 'first in, first out' scheme extended service for recent recruits to April 1920 but allowed the immediate demobilization of war veterans. 'Let three out of four go,' he said, summarizing his policy in March 1919, 'and pay the fourth double.'[14]

It worked well, although there were some nasty disturbances, including the burning down of Luton Town Hall in July by ex-servicemen protesting against their unemployment. Earlier in the year there had been a general strike in Glasgow, which was put down by imprisoning the ringleaders. When Churchill told the Cabinet in August that 'militarily, we are in a good position to fight the Triple Alliance,' it was not a troika of foreign enemy powers he was talking about, but the mining, railway and dock trade unions. Churchill admitted to Riddell that he was 'often gloomy and abstracted when thinking things out', but in politics 'It does not do to look so. This is the smiling age. In former days, statesmen were depicted as solemn, stately individuals . . . Today, the smile is in fashion.'[15] He told Riddell that he 'had had a happy life on the whole', but it had been 'one constant struggle and fight'.

In 1919, when Prohibition was only months away from being instituted in America, a great military review was held in London. The American Expeditionary Force's commander, General John Pershing, inspected the troops with the King, while Churchill and George C. Marshall, Pershing's aide-de-camp, followed them. There were 3,000 Americans on parade, all over 6 foot tall, with every kind of decoration. Marshall made a number of observations to Churchill as they went along the lines, but elicited no reply. At last, when they had been all around the rear rank and back up the flank, Churchill said to him, 'What a magnificent body of men, and never to look forward to another drink!'[16]

Churchill had been fascinated by the military application of air power since 1909. When he was at the Air Ministry it was nurtured by Sir Hugh Trenchard, another Paladin friend. When Trenchard nearly died during the Spanish flu epidemic in 1919, Churchill repeatedly refused his offers of resignation, saying how much he looked forward to working with him when he was restored to health. Trenchard persuaded Churchill in 1919 that Mesopotamia (modern-day Iraq) could be policed from the air, thus releasing several Army divisions and saving £40 million a year. In the fierce departmental infighting between the Sir Henry Wilson, now CIGS at the War Office, Admiral Beatty, now First Sea Lord at the Admiralty, and Trenchard, Chief of the Air Staff at the nascent Air Ministry, over the cost-cutting proposal to disband the RAF which had only been founded on 1 April 1918 by merging the Royal Flying Corps and the Royal Naval Air Service, Churchill staunchly championed Trenchard.[17] He denounced 'the most mischievous inter-departmental agitation' which attempted to subsume it.[18] 'No compromise is workable . . .' he declared. 'We must create a real air service, not necessarily large but highly efficient.'[19] That the RAF survived as an independent force was very much down to Churchill.[20] In what one historian has described as 'the greatest inter-service squabble of the century', his judgement was true.[21] If Trenchard is rightly known today as 'the Father of the RAF', Churchill was its godfather, protecting the nascent organization from being smothered at birth by its two much older jealous siblings.

When Churchill entered the War Office on 10 January 1919, the decision had already been taken by his predecessor Lord Milner to leave the British contingent in Russia for the time being. There were 30,000 Allied troops – over half of them British – under General Ironside at Murmansk and Archangel, guarding 600,000 tons of munitions. The Royal Navy was blockading the Baltic and Black Sea; British forces occupied the Baku–Batumi railway in the south, with more in Persia (modern-day Iran) and Salonica capable of crossing into Russia if ordered to support British intervention in the Russian Civil War. The White Russian Government under Admiral Kolchak in Omsk had been officially recognized by the British Government, and supplies were being given to General Denikin, the White Russian commander. Although Lloyd George did not want Britain to get into a direct fighting war with the Bolsheviks, recognizing that it would be unpopular, especially on the left, the War Council – which continued in existence – did not want to let the Whites down. 'Winston all against Bolshevism,' Wilson noted in his diary on 15 January, 'and therefore, in this, against Lloyd George.'[22] On 24 January, when Lloyd George suggested inviting the Russians to talks at Prinkipo in Turkey, Churchill wryly remarked, 'One might as well legalize sodomy as recognize the Bolsheviks.'[23]

Churchill's anti-Bolshevist stance was supported – at different times and to different degrees – by Milner, Balfour, Curzon and Wilson in the War Council, and outside the Cabinet by Tory MPs such as Colonel

Claude Lowther, Lieutenant-Colonel Walter Guinness and Brigadier Henry Page Croft.[24] Opposing it were Lloyd George, Austen Chamberlain and other Cabinet ministers who thought that Britain could not make a material difference in the Russian Civil War and did not want to get sucked into another war so soon after the last one.

In mid-February Churchill went to Paris to try to persuade President Woodrow Wilson personally that ending support for the Whites would present the West with 'an interminable vista of violence and misery', but he failed.[25] He had been unimpressed by the way that Wilson had kept the United States out of the war for as long as he had, almost two years after the sinking of the *Lusitania*, and he thought that the President's haughty treatment of the Republicans in 1919 was not the way to build the necessary consensus in Washington for the country to join the new international body set up by Versailles, the League of Nations. His estimation of Wilson in *The World Crisis* was therefore harsh. 'The spacious philanthropy which he exhaled upon Europe stopped quite sharply at the coasts of his own country,' he wrote. 'His gaze was fixed with equal earnestness upon the destiny of mankind and the fortunes of his party candidates. Peace and goodwill among all nations abroad, but no truck with the Republican Party at home. That was his ticket and that was his ruin, and the ruin of much else as well. It is difficult for a man to do great things if he tries to combine a lambent charity embracing the whole world with the sharper forms of populist party strife.'[26]

Yet lack of American support in Russia did not deter Churchill. 'The aid which we can give to those Russian armies which are now engaged in fighting against the foul baboonery of Bolshevism can be given by arms, munitions, equipment, and by the technical services,' he said at the Mansion House in February.[27] Churchill's extravagances in his anti-Communist language served to undermine the very accurate predictions he made about the vast numbers of Russians that the Bolsheviks would kill – those who heard him concentrated on phrases like 'foul baboonery' rather than on the substance of his argument. Churchill was right about the horrors of Communism, which was ultimately responsible for around a hundred million deaths in the twentieth century, including in Chairman Mao's China, but in 1919–22, as fellow-travellers trumpeted its attractions, few wanted to listen to his predictions. Yet simply continuing to speak the uncomfortable truth about this deadly totalitarian ideology prepared Churchill well for the 1930s, when he did the same thing for Bolshevism's sister-creed, Nazism.

In March a 'Hands Off Russia' campaign in the Labour Party and trade unions, combined with American policy and some unrest in the Army against intervention, led Austen Chamberlain, the Chancellor of the Exchequer, to argue for an agreement with the Bolsheviks that would allow British troops to evacuate northern Russia safely. This was anathema to Churchill, who wanted instead to send British NCOs to help train Denikin's armies. The following month, Churchill described Bolshevism as 'That foul combination of criminality and animalism'.[28] Between January 1920 and July 1927 he spoke of the Bolsheviks and Russia as 'the avowed enemies of civilization', 'crocodiles with master-minds', 'an infected Russia, a plague-bearing Russia', 'the blood-dyed tyrants of Moscow', 'a load of shame and degradation', 'filthy butchers of Moscow', 'cosmopolitan conspirators from the underworld', 'the dark conspirators in the Kremlin' and much else besides.[29] All were to be flung in his face when he entered into alliance with Russia in June 1941, but he did not rescind a word.[30] As he made clear, his hatred of Communism had not lessened simply because he needed Russia's help to defeat a closer and even more immediate foe.

Such was the strength of his anti-Communist beliefs that Churchill took a major risk with his career when he sent support to a Czech Legion serving in Siberia in June 1919, even after the Cabinet had turned down the idea.[31] With the White Russian Army only 400 miles from Moscow, he believed that success would justify his actions. 'Bolshevism is not a policy,' he said in a speech on 29 May; 'it is a disease. It is not a creed; it is a pestilence. It presents all the characteristics of a pestilence. It breaks out with great suddenness; it is violently contagious; it throws people into a frenzy of excitement; it spreads with extraordinary rapidity; the mortality is terrible.'[32] Yet from mid-June onwards Admiral Kolchak's Army started to suffer a series of defeats in central Russia. Churchill, undeterred, started to point to some successes of Denikin's in southern Russia instead.

On 27 June, Churchill and Henry Wilson urged that General Ironside be permitted to use 13,000 British and 22,000 White Russian troops to attack 33,700 Bolsheviks at Kotlas in north Russia because, as Churchill argued, 'He did not think we could possibly slink out of the country . . . if we turned round now and cleared off our reputation would suffer irretrievably.'[33] It was the same prestige argument used to justify persisting in the attack on Gallipoli. Similarly, Churchill underestimated the enemy's fighting potential, telling the War Council, 'All experience went to show that the Bolsheviks had never been able to screw up enough courage to offer any prolonged resistance.' In the end, a mutiny in Ironside's force put an end to the Kotlas plan.

Although Churchill was overworked running two ministries – 'You want to be a Statesman,' said Clementine, 'not a juggler' – he was not paid two salaries. He and Clementine became so overextended that they sold Lullenden to Sir Ian and Lady Hamilton.[34] Then their charming Scottish nanny Isabelle died of the Spanish influenza in March 1919. 'She talked fast and loud in an unearthly voice like a chant for several hours,' a distressed Clementine told her husband. She herself was suffering from influenza and had a temperature of 102.[35]

On 13 April 1919, Brigadier-General Reginald Dyer gave orders to fire upon an illegal political demonstration in Amritsar in the Punjab, killing 379 Indians and wounding over a thousand. After Dyer had been disavowed and disciplined by the British authorities and forced to retire, his fate was debated in Parliament on 8 July 1920. Edwin Montagu, the Secretary of State for India, and Churchill, speaking for the Army, justified the treatment of him before an angry and excitable Tory right led by Sir Edward Carson, who were convinced that Dyer had been scapegoated for using ruthless but defensible measures to prevent a revolution in the Punjab. Montagu, who was Jewish, was subjected to anti-Semitic barbs from the Tory backbenches, and also by Carson. Churchill came to his assistance. Measuring his words carefully, he proved that Dyer had not used minimum force in the massacre. 'At Amritsar the crowd was neither armed nor attacking,' he pointed out. 'These are simple tests which it is not too much to expect officers in these difficult circumstances to apply.' He went on to say that Dyer had been indulging in 'terrorism' and 'frightfulness', and said, 'We have to make it absolutely clear, some way or other, that this is not the British way of doing business.'[36] He called the Amritsar Massacre 'an episode which appears to me to be without precedent or parallel in the modern history of the British Empire. It is an event of an entirely different order from any of those tragical occurrences which take place when troops are brought into collision with the civil population. It is an extraordinary event, a monstrous event, an event which stands in singular and sinister isolation.'[37] When Page Croft tried to justify Dyer's actions on the grounds that there had been 'frightfulness on the other side' elsewhere in the Punjab, Churchill said, 'We cannot admit this doctrine in any form. Frightfulness is not a remedy known to the British pharmacopoeia.'[38]

A departmental minute Churchill wrote in the War Office on 12 May 1919 has been used by detractors to suggest that he did indeed think frightfulness was acceptable, once again through selective quotation. 'I do not understand this squeamishness about the use of gas,' he wrote about the British policy in Iraq. 'We have definitely adopted the position at the Peace Conference of arguing in favour of the retention of gas as a permanent method of warfare.'[39] Yet the rest of the minute, which often goes unquoted, makes it clear that Churchill was referring to tear gas, not to chlorine or lethal gases. 'It is sheer affectation to lacerate a man with the poisonous fragment of a bursting shell and to boggle at making his eyes water by means of lachrymatory [tear-causing] gas,' Churchill wrote. 'I am strongly in favour of using poisoned gas against uncivilized tribes. The moral effect should be so good that the loss of life should be reduced to a minimum. It is not necessary to use only the most deadly gasses: gasses can be used which cause great inconvenience and would spread a lively terror and yet would leave no serious permanent effects on most of those affected.'

With Lloyd George away in Paris for the Versailles Peace Conference, Bonar Law chaired many Cabinet meetings in the first half of 1919. He disliked Churchill's loquacity and customary extravagances of language and on 14 May he finally snapped, saying 'very sharply that while he was in the chair he would not allow such speeches as Churchill was making and that if Churchill did not like the present system he could leave it'.[40] The incident was later recalled by Lawrence Burgis, the Cabinet Office stenographer, who apart from Churchill and Smuts was the only person who attended the War Cabinets of both the First and Second World Wars. 'The only time I ever saw Bonar Law lose his temper was when he was in the chair at the Cabinet and Winston made some rather outrageous remark and "BL" fairly flew off the handle,' Burgis recalled. 'But Winston in those days could be very irritating, in fact his stenographer [at the War Office] . . . got so exasperated with him that she threw her shorthand-book at him. Needless to say she got the sack.'[41]

The Versailles Treaty was signed on 28 June 1919. Churchill deplored the harsh economic and financial provisions the Treaty imposed on Germany, which had been insisted upon by Clemenceau, but he was not in a strong enough position to do anything about them. He later described these clauses of the Treaty as 'malignant and silly to an extent that made them obviously futile' and 'a sad story of complicated idiocy'.[42] He instead urged the humane treatment of Germany, warning of the 'grave consequences for the future' should the Russians and Germans ever come together.[43]

Churchill had flown a good deal during the Great War, and he resumed his flying lessons after the Armistice. These finally ended when he had yet another near-death experience on 18 July 1919. He took off with his instructor, Colonel A. J. L. 'Jack' Scott, from Croydon Aerodrome, reached 90 feet, sideslipped and crashed. Scott switched off the ignition seconds before they hit the ground, preventing an explosion and probably saving their lives.[44] Churchill walked away bruised and with a scratched forehead. Scott broke his leg. Churchill nonetheless presided at a dinner in the Commons that evening in General Pershing's honour. 'You know the nation can't spare you,' Spears wrote to him afterwards, 'no one can give you an order but surely you see it is your duty not to run such unnecessary risks.'[45] Trenchard pointed out that a minister who shared his views about the RAF was of much more use to him alive than dead.[46] Churchill finally bowed to these pleas from family and colleagues, and gave up flying for good, although he occasionally relished taking the controls of planes in the Second World War.

According to the Cabinet minutes, in the face of Lloyd George's demands that all British forces in Russia be evacuated, Churchill declared that 'The whole episode was a very painful one, and, to go back into history, reminded him of our operations at Toulon and our desertion of the Catalans.'[47] These references – to the Royal Navy's evacuation of Toulon in 1793 and Britain's botched attempt to open a second front against Napoleon in eastern Spain in 1813 – were typical examples of Churchill's constant use of the past to inform and, he hoped, influence the present. Yet here they signally failed. In September, the row with Lloyd George came to a head. 'I am frankly in despair,' the Prime Minister wrote to him. He rightly accused Churchill of misleading the Cabinet over the Kotlas expedition. It 'was hardly a retiring one to cover the retirement of Ironside's troops', he said. 'It was in the nature to cut through in order to join hands with Kolchak.' The Prime Minister pointed out that Britain could not afford the £100 to £150 million that intervention had already cost, asking, 'I wonder whether it is any use my making one last effort to induce you to throw off this obsession which, if you will forgive me for saying so, is upsetting your balance . . . as you know that you won't find another responsible person in the whole land who will take your view, why waste your energy and your usefulness on this vain fretting which completely paralyses you for other work?'[48]

Churchill replied at great length three days later. He began by saying that he found 'the suggestions of your letter very unkind and I think also unjust'.[49] He explained all the other commitments that were costing huge amounts, on top of demobilization costs which he characterized as necessary 'to restore an army from mutiny to contentment'. He pointed out that when he took over the War Office his predecessor Lord Milner had already sent British troops to Archangel, and the Navy to the Baltic: 'Not I assuredly had sent them there.' He claimed somewhat disingenuously that the only operations he had proposed were the ones recommended by the General Staff 'as essential to the safe withdrawal of the troops', and 'I do not think it is fair to represent operations thus demanded by military men of your own choosing, as if they were so many sugar plums given to please me.'[50] 'I may get rid of my "obsession",' Churchill continued, 'or you may get rid of me: but you will not get rid of Russia: nor of the consequences of a policy which for nearly a year it has been impossible to define . . . I cannot help feeling a most dreadful and ever present sense of responsibility. Am I wrong? How easy for me to shrug my shoulders and say it is on the Cabinet, or on the Paris Conference. I cannot do it.' In a reference to his many long letters to Lloyd George on the issue, he added, 'And surely I am not wrong in writing earnestly and sincerely to my chief and oldest political friend to let him know that things are not all right and are not going to get all right along this road. Surely I was bound to do this.'[51]

The next day, Churchill presented a Cabinet memorandum entitled 'Final Contribution to General Denikin', which argued that since most of the nominally £14 million worth of military supplies he proposed sending was only really worth £2.5 million, as they were 'surplus to British military requirements and are of a non-marketable character', this contribution should be made for military reasons and was also a good investment. If donated over time, it would allow the British Government 'to guide him in a non-reactionary direction'.[52] (The Whites committed anti-Semitic pogroms quite as often as the Reds, and Churchill tried to make the military aid contingent upon Denikin 'preventing by every possible means the ill-treatment of the innocent Jewish population'.)[53]

On the same day, in a discussion with H. A. L. Fisher, the Education Minister and historian, Lloyd George said that Churchill 'is like the Counsel that a solicitor employs not because he is the best man but because he would be dangerous on the other side'.[54] Throughout October, Churchill was absurdly over-optimistic about Russia, putting out press statements describing the Whites as the 'victorious forces who will soon reconstitute the Russian Nation' and writing about the Soviet government in the past tense.[55] Nonetheless, on 29 October 1919, the last British troops left Archangel and Murmansk.

Churchill continued to make inflammatory speeches about Communism, saying in a debate in the Commons on 5 November that 'In Russia a man is called a reactionary if he objects to having his property stolen, and his wife and children murdered.'[56] A fortnight later he recalled that in 1917 the Germans had allowed Lenin to travel through Germany to St Petersburg, 'in the same way that you might send a phial containing a culture of typhoid or of cholera to be poured into the water supply of a great city, and it worked with amazing accuracy'.[57] Ten years later he was to speak of Lenin with undiminished ferocity:

> Implacable vengeance, rising from a frozen pity in a tranquil, sensible, matter-of-fact, good-humoured integument! His weapon logic; his mood opportunist. His sympathies cold and wide as the Arctic Ocean; his hatreds tight as the hangman's noose. His purpose to save the world; his method to blow it up. Absolute principles, but readiness to change them . . . but a good husband; a gentle guest; happy, his biographers assure us, to wash up the dishes or dandle the baby; as mildly amused to stalk a capercailzie as to butcher an Emperor.[58]*

He did not talk down to his readers, expecting them to know (or discover) that integument means husk or rind, and that a capercailzie (also known as capercaillie) is a large wood-grouse.

The Red Army, led by Leon Trotsky, steadily pushed the Whites back. By March 1920, Denikin controlled only the Crimea. 'So ends in practical disaster another of Winston's military attempts,' Henry Wilson noted in his diary, 'Antwerp, Dardanelles, Denikin.'[59] Aiding the White Russians had cost Britain £100 million (approximating £4.1 billion in today's money). Churchill was unrepentant. 'Since the Armistice,' he told Lloyd George on 24 March, 'my policy would have been "Peace with the German people, war on the Bolshevik tyranny." Willingly or unavoidably, you have followed something very near the reverse.'[60] Churchill was never an easy subordinate. In November, three weeks short of his forty-sixth birthday, he reached the age at which his father had died. In *My Early Life* he was to admit that (by 1930) he had come to see his father 'in a somewhat different light from the days when I wrote his biography . . . I understand only too plainly the fatal character of his act of resignation.'[61] He was not about to make the same mistake, but the intemperate language he sometimes employed towards the Prime Minister might have taken the decision out of his hands.

On 19 December, Lord French narrowly evaded assassination at the hands of the IRA, an attempt masterminded by its commander Michael Collins. It was the culmination of eighteen murders in sixty-seven attacks that calendar year. With Sir Henry Wilson in the chair, the Other Club sent French a telegram expressing 'heartfelt rejoicing at your providential escape'.[62] Three days later, the Government of Ireland Bill proposed the partition of the island between twenty-six mainly Catholic southern counties to be ruled from Dublin and the six mainly Protestant northern counties

* When he found out that his wayward Irish cousin Clare Sheridan had gone to Moscow to sculpt a bust of Lenin, she was told that 'Winston would never speak to me again' (Sheridan, *Nuda Veritas* p. 196). In fact he started speaking to her again a year later, and soon afterwards helped her get a job in New York.

of Ulster to be ruled from Belfast. It was the obvious solution to the sectarian divide that had existed on the island of Ireland since the seventeenth century. In the south, an Irish Republican Army had resorted to violence to win independence from the Crown for the whole island, spearheaded by its political wing, Sinn Fein ('Ourselves Alone').

While the Government of Ireland Bill was being discussed, Churchill attempted to crush the rebellion in the south through the use of two paramilitary forces. The first was a Special Emergency Gendarmerie of 1,500 mainly ex-soldiers operating as a unit within the Royal Irish Constabulary (RIC), who were nicknamed the 'Black and Tans' because of their dark tunics, black belts and surplus khaki trousers. The second was the Auxiliary Division of the RIC, or 'Auxis'. Churchill likened them to the anti-gangster units of the New York and Chicago police departments, and wrote of 'their intelligence, their characters and their records in the war'. He defended the way they were sent to strike 'down in the darkness those who struck from the darkness', that is, meet terror with terror.[63] Yet both groups were so violent and ill-disciplined that they achieved the opposite effect of what was intended.

Churchill has been accused of trying to use aeroplanes to bomb peaceful Irish protesters. This stems from the incomplete quotation of what he actually wrote to Trenchard on 1 July 1920, which makes it clear that far from being innocent demonstrations he wished to attack, it was actually republican revolutionaries training for assaults. 'Suppose information is received that Sinn Feiners are accustomed to drill in considerable numbers at any particular place,' he minuted,

> with or without arms, they must be regarded as a rebel gathering. If they can be definitely located and identified from the air, I see no objection from a military point of view, and subject of course to the discretion of the Irish Government and of the authorities on the spot, to aeroplanes being despatched with definite orders in each particular case to disperse them by machine gun fire or bombs, using of course no more force than is necessary to scatter and stampede them.[64]

In December 1920, the Black and Tans burned down a large area of the city of Cork, driving Irish moderates into the arms of Sinn Fein without breaking the IRA's rebellion against the Crown.[65] 'Crush them with iron and unstinted force, or try to give them what they want,' was how Churchill defined the choice before the Government in early 1921. 'These were the only alternatives,' he wrote a few years later, 'and though each had ardent advocates, most people were unprepared for either. Here indeed was the Irish Spectre – horrid and inexorcizable!'[66] Once it was clear that his attempt to crush the IRA had resoundingly failed, Churchill was the first to champion a wide and generous offer to the south, despite opposition from both the Tory right, who thought it went too far, and Sinn Fein, who did not think it went far enough.

On 8 February 1920, Churchill published an article in the *Illustrated Sunday Herald* entitled 'Zionism versus Bolshevism'. 'Some people like Jews and some do not,' he wrote, 'but no thoughtful man can doubt the fact that they are beyond all question the most formidable and the most remarkable race which has ever appeared in the world.' In the article he pointed to the large numbers of Jews in the upper echelons of the Bolshevik movement – 'this sinister confederacy . . . this world-wide conspiracy for the overthrow of civilization' – whom he called 'terrorist Jews'. He went on to argue that the Bolsheviks were 'repudiated vehemently by the great mass of the Jewish race', and added the encomium: 'We owe to the Jews a system of ethics which, even if it were entirely separated from the supernatural, would be incomparably the most precious possession of mankind, worth in fact the fruits of all wisdom and learning put together. On that system and by that faith there has been built out of the wreck of the Roman Empire the whole of our existing civilization.'[67]

Back in November 1917, Churchill had supported Balfour's Declaration in favour of a national homeland for the Jews in Palestine. 'If, as may well happen,' he wrote in the 1920 article, 'there should be created in our own lifetime by the banks of the Jordan a Jewish State under the protection of the British Crown, which might comprise three or four millions of Jews, an event would have occurred in the history of the world which would, from every point of view, be beneficial, and would be especially in harmony with the truest interests of the British Empire.'[68] At the time there were 80,000 Jews in Palestine and 600,000 Arabs, so any possibility of such a Jewish homeland there seemed a long way off.[69]

When it was discovered in November that Sinn Fein intended to kidnap Lloyd George, Churchill and other ministers, Churchill was given a bodyguard. Detective Constable Walter H. Thompson stayed with him off and on from 1921 to 1932 and then again throughout the Second World War. 'When I first became Mr Churchill's personal detective,' Thompson recalled, echoing very many other people who worked for or with him, 'I had found his manner brusque, off-handed, even as I thought then, piggish. But I soon began to see through the rough facade, to wait for the grimness to break up in that boyish smile. It did not take me long to like him. In a little while, I came to love him.'[70]

Irish terrorists were not the only ones from whom Churchill needed Thompson's protection. 'What were a few Churchills or Curzons on lamp-posts compared with the massacre of thousands at Amritsar, or the reprisals on hundreds of Irishmen in Ireland?' the Communist MP Cecil Malone told a mass meeting of the Hands Off Russia movement at the Royal Albert Hall on 7 November 1920. 'What were the punishments of those world criminals compared with the misery that they were causing to thousands of men, women and children in Russia?'[71] When the police raided Malone's flat after his arrest on sedition charges, they found two railway cloakroom tickets, which matched a parcel of military training booklets for an underground British 'Red Army'. As well as lessons for insurgents on bank raids, 'Machine Gun Drill', 'Use of Bombs', 'Use of Revolvers', they also found information on how to seize post offices and telephone exchanges, and propaganda featuring lines such as 'Down with our enemies, the Churchills, the Capitalists, the Imperialists and all their lackeys. Long live the Red Army!'[72]

Churchill lost a key vote in the Cabinet over the reopening of trading relations with Russia on 18 November, which he vehemently opposed. 'He was so upset by the decision that he declared himself unequal to discussing the items on the agenda affecting the Army. He was quite pale, and did not speak again during the meeting,' Hankey recorded, who had to take over one of the items on the agenda originally intended for his colleague.[73] After having it formally minuted that no Cabinet minister would be prevented from making anti-Bolshevist speeches, Churchill went up to the Oxford Union that evening to make just such a speech. 'The policy I will always advocate is the overthrow and destruction of that criminal regime,' he told the undergraduates, adding that he had 'not always been able to give that clear view as full an effect as I would have desired'. After this public act of divergence, Lloyd George began to think of moving Churchill to the Colonial Office. Soon afterwards trading relations with Soviet Russia were established, which amounted to a de facto recognition of the regime.

On 10 August 1920, the Treaty of Sèvres was signed with the Turkish Government, triggering another rift with Lloyd George. Thrace had been awarded to Greece, and Istanbul placed in a 'neutral zone'. General Mustapha Kemal (later known as Kemal Atatürk) had distinguished himself at Gallipoli and now led a nationalist movement in Ankara that rejected the harsh and humiliating terms of the treaty. Churchill, impressed by Kemal's anti-Bolshevism, led the pro-Turkish group in the Cabinet, while Lloyd George was pro-Greek. 'I am very sorry to see how far we are drifting apart on foreign policy,' Churchill wrote to Lloyd George in early December.

> I feel I owe it to you and to your long friendship and many kindnesses to send a solemn warning of the harm which your policy – so largely a personal policy – is doing to the unity and cohesion of several important elements of opinion on which you have hitherto been able to rely. Moreover it seems to me to be a most injurious thing that we, the greatest Mohammedan Empire in the world . . . seem to be becoming the most anti-Turk and the most pro-Bolshevik power in the world: whereas in my judgement we ought to be the exact opposite . . . When one has reached the summit of power and surmounted so many obstacles, there is danger of becoming convinced that one can do anything one likes and that any strong personal view is necessarily acceptable to the nation and can be enforced upon one's subordinates.[74]

He continued with a characteristic military analogy: 'I can never forget the service you did me in bringing me a fresh horse when I was dismounted in the war, and intensely longing to take a real part in the struggle. Office has not now the same attraction for me, and I have other new interests on which I could fall back.* Therefore the counsels I offer are those of a friend and of a sincere friend – but of a friend who cannot part with his independence.'[75] Warning the Prime Minister of hubris carried the distinct risk of alienating his sole benefactor in politics.

On 26 January 1921, Lord Harry Vane-Tempest, brother of the 6th Marquess of Londonderry, died in a railway accident. He was unmarried, and because Churchill's grandmother, Frances, Duchess of Marlborough, had been the daughter of the 3rd Marquess of Londonderry, in his will his Garron Towers estates in County Antrim – worth £4,000 per annum (roughly £164,000 in today's money) – were bequeathed to Churchill. Clementine summed up the effect of the Garron Bequest on their lives succinctly: 'Haunting care had vanished forever from our lives.'[76] She had felt for some time that Churchill's journalism, though fabulously well paid, was being 'discussed trivially' and was dimming his chances of the premiership. 'I have a sort of feeling that the "All Highest" [Lord Curzon] rejoices every time you write an Article and thinks it brings *him* nearer the Premiership.'[77] Churchill had not forsaken that prize, writing to her on 6 February from Chequers in Buckinghamshire, the beautiful Tudor country house which had recently been given to the nation for the use of prime ministers, 'You would like to see this place. Perhaps you will some day! It is just the kind of house you admire – a panelled museum full of history, full of treasures, but insufficiently warmed.'[78]

Churchill's chances of occupying Chequers in his own right moved

* A reference to *The World Crisis*.

significantly forward the next day when he became colonial secretary, and for one week during the reshuffle held the seals of three secretaryships of state – War, Air and Colonies, which he thought was a record.* He accepted the Colonial Office on the condition that he could set up a new department that incorporated responsibility for the Iraq, Transjordan (modern-day Jordan) and Palestine Mandates which had been awarded to Britain after the war under Article 22 of the League of Nations Covenant. The vote in Cabinet went eight to five in favour with two abstentions, which naturally irritated Curzon, the Foreign Secretary, who complained that Churchill was trying to become 'a sort of Asiatic Foreign Secretary'.[79] Churchill was under no illusions. 'Curzon will give me lots of trouble and have to be half flattered and half overborne,' he told Clementine. 'We overlap horribly. I do not think he is much good . . . We are on quite good terms personally. I shall take lots of trouble to bring him along.'[80]

One of Churchill's first actions at the Colonial Office was to recruit T. E. Lawrence ('of Arabia'), the legendary British liaison officer to the leaders of the Arab Revolt against the Turks in the Great War, as his chief adviser on the Middle East. 'I have got Lawrence to put on a bridle and collar' was how he put it.[81] Their plan was to install Arab emirs as client kings of Iraq and Transjordan to ensure the supply of oil to the West (and especially the Royal Navy) and cut the cost of administering the new mandates. As Churchill told Spears, 'it would be possible to install a Sharifian† government that would enable a British Protectorate to be run cheaply.'[82]

The situation in the Middle East was eloquently summed up by Churchill in his chapter on Lawrence in *Great Contemporaries*:

> We had recently suppressed a most dangerous and bloody rebellion in Iraq, and upwards of forty thousand troops at a cost of thirty millions a year were required to preserve order. This could not go on. In Palestine, the strife between the Arabs and the Jews threatened at any moment to take the form of actual violence. The Arab chieftains, driven out of Syria [by the French] with many of their followers – all of them our late allies – lurked furious in the desert beyond the Jordan. Egypt was in ferment. Thus the whole Middle East presented a most melancholy and alarming picture.[83]

In order to calm the situation, establish new emirates as client kingdoms of Britain and draw the new borders necessary, Churchill convened a

* Wrongly, because during his caretaker ministry of November–December 1834 the Duke of Wellington was simultaneously prime minister, foreign secretary, home secretary, war secretary, colonial secretary and leader of the House of Lords.

† Sharif Husayn ibn Ali had been the leader of the Arab Revolt.

conference in Cairo in March 1921 to consult the British administrators in the region.

On 2 March, he, Archie Sinclair, Trenchard, Lawrence and a group of civil servants left London by train bound for Marseilles, where he collected Clementine and boarded a French steamship for Alexandria. There he was met at the docks by a twenty-six-year-old RAF officer, Maxwell Coote, his temporary aide-de-camp for the Cairo Conference.[84] Like so many others, Coote disliked Churchill at first but quickly grew fond of him, enjoying phrases such as his description of a Cabinet as being like a lot of 'reviving vipers'.[85] Before going to bed one night, Churchill asked Coote whether he was 'really happy, bird happy'.[86] On arrival at the main terminus in Cairo on 10 March the party avoided a large student demonstration shouting 'Down with Churchill!' by getting out early and taking backstreets to the Semiramis Hotel, where the Conference was taking place.[87] (The governors of Aden and Somaliland came, the latter bringing two lion cubs, which were kept in the hotel garden.)

Churchill chaired the Conference over the next nine mornings, allowing for painting and working on *The World Crisis* almost every afternoon. (When thrown off a camel on his way to paint the Sphinx, he was offered a horse by a Bedouin. 'I started on a camel and will finish on a camel,' he harrumphed.)[88] Liaison with the Arab delegations was done through Lawrence and the formidable Gertrude Bell, the only female British intelligence officer of the time, who was popular with the Arabs and fluent in Arabic and Persian.

Churchill insisted that he would keep a completely open mind until he had heard the views of the local British administrators, especially those of Sir Percy Cox, the High Commissioner of Iraq. In fact the two sons of Emir Sharif Husayn ibn Ali of Mecca had been favoured before Churchill even left London. Faisal was chosen to rule Iraq, and his brother Abdullah to rule Transjordan. 'The Emir Abdullah is in Transjordania,' Churchill boasted years later, 'where I put him one Sunday afternoon at Jerusalem.'[89] It was essentially true, and today's moderate Arab state of Jordan is one that Churchill brought into being. Between 1921 and 1928, British troops could be entirely withdrawn from Iraq. Giving power to these local rulers allowed Britain to step back from attempting to maintain direct control, which Churchill rightly understood she could not afford.*

* It is quite untrue that the abruptly concave section of Jordan's eastern border with Saudi Arabia was drawn arbitrarily by Churchill following a liquid lunch, as its Arabic nickname, 'Winston's Hiccup', implies. The story has it that as he was drawing the map he hiccupped, causing the large zigzag in the border, but that is a fantasy (Dockter, *Churchill and the Islamic World* pp. 157–8). In fact the borders were drawn after much deliberation by administrators who knew the region well.

Less realistically, Churchill also harboured an idea for a pan-Arab confederation headed by Ibn Saud, Saudi Arabia's first king, a form of wide Middle Eastern federation in which there would be room for a Jewish homeland. Although he also wanted to establish a homeland in northern Iraq for the Kurds – 'to protect the Kurds from some future bully in Iraq', as he put it – that plan was overruled by the Foreign Office. As the price of Jews being allowed to emigrate between the Mediterranean and the River Jordan, they were prevented from going east of that river. 'We covered more work in a fortnight than has ever been got through in a year,' Bell wrote to Cox. Lawrence later declared, 'I must put on record my conviction that England is out of the affair with clean hands.'[90]

When Sinclair was hospitalized with a temperature of 105 degrees, Coote recorded that Churchill 'was most dreadfully upset as he is most awfully fond of Sinclair. Winston is also evidently a bit of a pessimist where illness is concerned and was apt to be very over-anxious.'[91] Coote did not know that the last time Churchill had been to that part of Africa his manservant had died of fever. At dinner that night, 'Conversation did not flow at first even with champagne which Winston insisted on having.'

On 23 March, Churchill left Cairo by train, after dining at the British Residency with a viceroy of India, three high commissioners, a secretary of state and several governors and generals. 'I had, of course, to hustle Winston into his carriage as he was naturally the last in and kept the train waiting,' recalled Coote, who had by then become used to Churchill's unpunctuality.[92] They stopped at Gaza, where a Palestinian mob cheered Churchill and Great Britain. As Coote recorded, 'Their chief cry over which they waxed quite frenzied was "Down with the Jews", "Cut their throats" . . . Winston and [the Jewish High Commissioner of Palestine Sir] Herbert [Samuel] also were quite delighted with their reception, not in the least understanding what was being said.'[93] At a memorial service at the military cemetery in Jerusalem for British Great War dead, Churchill 'was most deeply moved when he spoke', and had tears in his eyes.[94] 'These veteran soldiers lie here where rests the dust of the Khalifs and Crusaders and the Maccabees,' he said. 'Peace to their ashes, honour to their memory and may we not fail to complete the work which they have begun.'[95] There followed three volleys fired by a guard of honour, and the Last Post.

In Jerusalem, the Executive Committee of the Haifa Congress of Palestinian Arabs asked him to abandon the idea of a national homeland for the Jews. 'It is manifestly right that the scattered Jews should have a national centre and a national home in which they might be reunited,' Churchill told them, 'and where else but in Palestine, with which the Jews for three thousand years have been intimately and profoundly associated?

We think it is good for the world, good for the Jews, and good for the British Empire, and it is also good for the Arabs dwelling in Palestine, and we intend it to be so . . . Step by step we shall develop representative institutions, leading to full self-government, but our children's children will have passed away before that is completed.'[96] The following year, when it was suggested that the Jews were not necessary to the development of Palestine, Churchill replied, 'Left to themselves, the Arabs of Palestine would not in a thousand years have taken effective steps towards the irrigation and electrification of Palestine. They would have been quite content to dwell – a handful of philosophic people – in wasted, sun-drenched plains, letting the waters of the Jordan flow unbridled and unharnessed into the Dead Sea.'[97]

He returned from the Middle East in the second week of April, via Alexandria and Genoa. He wanted to get back to London quickly, as he had heard that Austen Chamberlain was about to resign as chancellor of the Exchequer, but on the journey he discovered that Robert Horne, President of the Board of Trade, had been appointed; Horne's place had been taken by Stanley Baldwin, who entered the Cabinet for the first time. Churchill was deeply disappointed and resentful against Lloyd George for being passed over, although one consolation was that Bonar Law had seemingly retired from politics at sixty-two. Chamberlain became the new Tory leader, remarking that Churchill was 'as cross as a bear with a sore head and thinks the world is out of joint'.[98] Churchill did not visit Lloyd George on his return, and started his letters, 'Dear Prime Minister', rather than the previous 'Dear Ll.G.' or even 'My dear David'.[99] Frances Stevenson recorded that the feeling was reciprocated: 'D is so sick with C. I don't think he cares if he does go. Horne says Churchill is criticizing the Government on Finance and Ireland in the clubs and lobbies.'[100]

Churchill stayed on for an extra six weeks as secretary for air at the same time as being colonial secretary until a suitable replacement could be found, who eventually was Freddie Guest. *The Times* was predictably rude about Churchill's stewardship when he handed over the post at the beginning of April: 'Gold braid and metal polish, acres of cantonments, establishments aping the Army, those are the fruits of his well-meaning and laborious, but wholly inadequate rule at the Air Ministry.' In fact the gold braid he introduced for air chief marshals' uniforms, as well as the institutions of non-Army ranks, deliberately avoided aping either of the other two services, while the acres of cantonments were to prove invaluable twenty years later. By the time Churchill left the ministry, the RAF had squadrons in Iraq, Egypt, Palestine, India and Ireland.

As a result of the reshuffle, Edward Wood (later Lord Irwin, then Lord

Halifax) became under-secretary at the Colonial Office, a fact Churchill also resented as he had not appointed him and had wanted to have Guest instead. When Churchill began to snub him, Wood stormed into his office and told him, 'I am prepared to resign and leave this office tomorrow, but, so long as I remain here, I expect to be treated like a gentleman.'[101] Churchill asked him to sit down, apologized, offered him a drink and thereafter behaved better, prompting Wood to remark truthfully: 'He hates doormats.' It was the beginning of what was to prove one of the most important political relationships of Churchill's life.

Five days after the Churchills arrived home from Cairo, Bill Hozier, Clementine's thirty-four-year-old brother, committed suicide in a Paris hotel room. Like his mother and twin sister Nellie, he had had a gambling addiction that led him into financial difficulties.[102] Churchill went to Paris for the funeral and to try – unsuccessfully – to elicit more details about what had happened. Bill had left him a gold-topped malacca cane, which he used for the rest of his life.

Further tragedy befell the family on 29 June, when Churchill's mother Jennie died, at only sixty-seven. At the end of May, she had fallen down some stairs in Dorset and broken her left leg near the ankle. It had become gangrenous and was amputated on 10 June. She seemed to have recovered from the operation, when she suddenly suffered a violent haemorrhage. Churchill ran the short distance down Clifton Place from his house in Sussex Square when he was told about the haemorrhage, but he could not get to Westbourne Street before she slipped into a coma. She died shortly afterwards. 'I wish you could have seen her as she lay at rest,' Churchill wrote to a friend, 'after all the sunshine and storm of life was over. Very beautiful and splendid she looked. Since the morning with its pangs, thirty years had fallen from her brow.'[103] She would have liked that: she had once said, 'I shall never get used to not being the most beautiful woman in the room.'[104] She was buried next to Lord Randolph at Bladon. 'The wine of life was in her veins,' Churchill told Curzon, who had written a moving letter to him. 'On the whole it was a life of sunshine.'[105]

It was around this time, when Randolph was ten years old and a pupil at Sandroyd School in Cobham, Surrey, that a teacher named Wrixon 'undid his trousers and caused me to manipulate his organ'.[106] When Churchill, who was playing polo with his cousin Lord Wimborne at Ashby St Ledgers at the time, discovered what had happened, Randolph recalled, 'I don't think I have ever seen him so angry before or since. He leapt out of bed, ordered his car and drove all across country,' a round trip of 200 miles, to confront the headmaster, who it turned out had already dismissed Wrixon on other grounds. 'Never let anyone do that to you again,' he told Randolph.[107]

In early August, Thomas Walden, Churchill's faithful manservant who had worked for his father before him, and had gone out to the Boer War with him, died. 'Alas my dearest I grieve to have lost this humble friend devoted and true whom I have known since I was a youth,' Churchill wrote to Clementine after the funeral, where he 'wept bitterly' along with the rest of the household of Sussex Square.[108] Few other aristocrats of the day would have described their manservant as a friend and wept for them.

But the year of loss and pain had not even reached its lowest depth. On 23 August, Winston and Clementine's younger daughter Marigold died of septicaemia of the throat, at only two years and nine months. Her parents blamed themselves for trusting the nanny, their cousin Maryott Whyte, who had taken the children on holiday at Broadstairs in Kent and failed to spot the symptoms in time. For many years Clementine could not console herself, because she had been away playing tennis at Eaton Hall in Cheshire with the Westminsters when Marigold fell ill.[109] Marigold had had sore throats and coughs before, so not enough attention was paid when her throat became septic. She became really ill on 14 August, but neither Miss Whyte nor Mademoiselle Rose, their young French governess, called Clementine for two days. Clementine left Eaton Hall as soon as she was told that Marigold was unwell, Churchill came from London, a specialist was called in, but in the age before antibiotics it was too late and nothing could be done.

Churchill and Clementine were with Marigold when she died. Stricken with guilt and grief, they buried her at Kensal Green three days later. In an otherwise chirpy letter from Dunrobin Castle on 18 September, Churchill admitted to Clementine, 'Alas I keep on feeling the hurt of the Duckadilly.'[110] In less than twenty weeks, to add to all the other ghosts in his life, Churchill had lost his mother, daughter, brother-in-law and faithful manservant. 'What changes in a year! What gaps! What a sense of fleeting shadows!' he wrote to Clementine. 'But your sweet love and comradeship is a light that burns the stronger as our brief years pass.'[111]

Although it was in no sense a compensation for the losses of 1921, that August Churchill met the newly appointed Lees Professor of Experimental Philosophy (that is, Physics) and Director of the Clarendon Laboratory at Oxford, Professor Frederick Lindemann, when they were partnered at a charity tennis tournament. They didn't win, despite Lindemann having played at Wimbledon, but they struck up an immediate friendship.[112] Lindemann's father, a successful businessman, had fled his native Alsace when it became German in 1871, and his mother was part American, part Russian. He had a PhD in physics from Berlin University, had studied quantum physics and had been elected a Fellow of the Royal Society in 1920. Einstein called him a friend.

Lindemann was a teetotaller, non-smoker and vegetarian, none of them attitudes which appealed to Churchill. On the other hand, in 1917 he had learned to fly solely in order to test his aerodynamic theory of how pilots could bring planes out of tailspins, which had hitherto almost always proved fatal. This was just the kind of Paladin bravery that Churchill relished.[113] 'It seemed certain death,' he later recalled. 'But his theory worked . . . I did admire him so much.'[114]

'His exterior was conventionally forbidding,' Sarah Churchill wrote of Lindemann, 'the domed cranium, the close-cropped iron-grey hair which had receded as if the brain had shed it away, the iron-grey moustache, the sallow complexion, the little sniff which took the place of what normally would have been a laugh; yet still he could exude a warmth that made scientific thinking unfrightening.'[115] The man the family called 'the Prof' showed Churchill total loyalty, and occasionally picked up bills, especially during the family holidays on which the rich bachelor scientist was regularly invited. He explained to Churchill, who had no scientific education but much scientific interest, the physics behind weaponry and much else. Lindemann's great talent was to be able to boil down complicated scientific subjects on to Churchill's 'one sheet of paper'. He once explained quantum theory in five minutes in words of few syllables to the satisfaction of everyone present, including the children who burst into spontaneous applause. Lindemann was aggressive, sarcastic, arrogant and right wing (but profoundly anti-Fascist), and his biographer said his life was driven by 'absolute loyalty and love for his friends, and sustained rancour towards his enemies'.[116] In April 1924 Churchill asked Lindemann to make enquiries into 'a ray which will kill at a certain distance' and which reportedly could kill mice. 'It may be all a hoax, but my experience has been not to take "No" for an answer.'[117] It was indeed a hoax, but gives an indication of Churchill's questing interest in new scientific weaponry.

On 8 July 1921, an Irish truce was agreed, allowing direct negotiations to begin three days later between the leaders of the IRA and the British Government. As colonial secretary, Churchill could expect to play a leading role in the negotiations, along with F. E. Smith (now Lord Birkenhead), Austen Chamberlain and Lloyd George. 'I do feel that while he is PM it would be better to hunt with him than to lie in the bushes and watch him careering along with a jaundiced eye,' Churchill confided to Clementine.[118]

Three months went by before pre-negotiations with the Irish delegation began at Downing Street on 11 October. Churchill threatened 'a real war – not just bush-ranging' if the Irish refused to sign the Treaty that partitioned the island, which had been on the table since the previous December.[119]*

The Irish delegation was led by the politician Arthur Griffith, but it included the IRA guerrilla leader Michael Collins. Churchill had put a price on Collins's head. When Collins reminded him of it, Churchill retorted, 'At any rate it was a good price – £5,000. Look at me – £25 dead or alive. How would you like that?'[120] The actual negotiations came to a dramatic head on the night of 5 December, when Lloyd George gave the Irish delegation an ultimatum. At 2.20 the next morning the Treaty was signed. It created the Irish Free State of the southern twenty-six counties (which eventually became the Republic of Ireland) and was later approved by the Irish Dáil by sixty-four votes to fifty-seven. Churchill recalled that after the signing 'the British Ministers upon a strong impulse walked round and for the first time shook hands.'[121]

The Irish Free State had won complete domestic independence and practical independence in foreign policy, but agreed to stay in the British Commonwealth under the same Dominion status enjoyed by Canada and Australia. This meant that Irish ministers would be expected to swear at least theoretical allegiance to King George V. Britain also retained three so-called Treaty ports – Berehaven, Lough Swilly and Queenstown – to be used by the Royal Navy. When the wily and opportunistic President of the Dáil, Éamon de Valera, rejected the Treaty on 7 December, it led to a savage ten-month civil war.

In January 1922, Churchill managed to get the Prime Minister of what was now Northern Ireland, Sir James Craig (a member of the Other Club), and Michael Collins together in the same room in the Colonial Office to negotiate the fine-tuning of the Treaty. 'They both glowered magnificently,' he recalled, but they came to an agreement when left alone for several hours.[122] Commending the Irish Free State Bill to the Commons on 16 February, Churchill argued that since the Great War:

> The whole map of Europe has been changed. The position of countries has been violently altered. The modes of thought of men, the whole outlook on affairs, the grouping of parties, all have encountered violent and tremendous

* At the time, Churchill was being equally pugnacious over Chinese demands for the port of Wei-hei-wei (modern-day Weihai) and indemnities for the Boxer Uprising of 1900. 'Why should we melt down the moral capital collected by our forefathers to please a lot of pacifists?' he asked in Cabinet. 'I would send a telegram beginning "Nothing for nothing and precious little for twopence"' (ed. Middlemas, *Whitehall Diary* I p. 181).

> changes in the deluge of the world, but as the deluge subsides and the waters fall short we see the dreary steeples of Fermanagh and Tyrone emerging once again. The integrity of their quarrel is one of the few institutions that has been unaltered in the cataclysm which has swept the world.[123]

That August, Collins was killed in an ambush by anti-Treaty forces. Shortly before his death he had told a friend who was going to London, 'Tell Winston that we could never have done anything without him.'[124]

Churchill was now swiftly caught up in another crisis that was eventually to overwhelm the whole Coalition. In the same month that the Irish Treaty was signed, he urged Lloyd George to end what he called 'this vendetta against the Turks'.[125] He was referring to Lloyd George's bellicose attitude towards Mustapha Kemal's nationalist forces as they started to threaten the British enclaves in Istanbul and the port of Chanak (modern-day Çanakkale). Against Churchill's advice, the Treaty of Sèvres had given the British extensive rights in mainland Turkey, which were now under threat from Kemal's Turkish army, especially at Chanak. The Chanak Crisis is often presented as an example of Churchill's impetuousness, but he had never wanted Britain to have these exposed enclaves, and initially he fought hard against Lloyd George's genuinely impetuous support for Greece, which had large Greek-speaking populations in western Turkey. 'On this world so torn with strife I dread to see you let loose the Greek armies,' he told Lloyd George.[126] But as the Turkish forces became ever more threatening at Chanak, Churchill was forced to abandon his position through a realistic appraisal of the likely outcomes, in much the same way he had in Ireland.

On 22 June 1922, Sir Henry Wilson was assassinated by anti-Treaty IRA gunmen outside his home at 36 Eaton Place in Belgravia. He could have retreated into the house when the first shot missed, but instead he instinctively drew his sword and was shot dead. Bravely hoping to defeat two gunmen with a sword was in essence the same strategy Churchill had accused him of adopting on the Western Front, with much the same result. As it was assumed that the next attempt would be on Churchill, he was accorded two more bodyguards in addition to Walter Thompson.

In July, the Coalition was hit by a financial scandal when it became clear that an agent of the Prime Minister, the extremely shady Maundy Gregory, had effectively been selling honours for contributions to the Lloyd George Fund, set up to fight elections. The South African mining millionaire and war profiteer Sir Joseph Robinson had paid £30,000 for a peerage, but the uproar in Parliament now meant that he never received it. 'The debate on honours was squalid in the extreme and will do nothing but harm to the Government in the country, and to the country in the Empire,' Churchill told Clementine. 'The PM was lamentable and is universally pronounced to have made the worst speech of his career. It is indeed a decline.'[127] On 22 July Churchill wrote to Lloyd George, 'Don't get torpedoed; for if I am left alone your colleagues will eat me.'[128] Yet he himself was not entirely blameless for the state of affairs. Back in 1906, he had recommended Robinson to Campbell-Bannerman for a baronetcy, which he received for helping the Government over Chinese 'slave' labour in the Transvaal. Churchill had written to Campbell-Bannerman saying Robinson wanted an honour, '(baronetcy I presume). I do trust you will give most favourable consideration to this.'[129]

As Parliament adjourned for its summer recess in August, Conservative MPs were angry. Unemployment was at its highest point for decades; the Irish Treaty seemed to have rewarded the IRA; Field Marshal Wilson had been assassinated in Belgravia; de facto recognition of Soviet Russia looked like further appeasement; austerity cuts had damaged education and lowered war pensions, and the honours scandal had thoroughly disgusted MPs, who no longer trusted Lloyd George. With by-election losses in the offing the Coalition looked shaky, and it now also seemed that Kemalist forces were advancing on the Greek population and their British protectors at Chanak. On 15 September Churchill argued that the Empire should send a major force to stop the Kemalists retaking the Gallipoli Peninsula, 'with the graves of so many of its soldiers there'.[130] He drafted both a request for support to Dominion prime ministers and simultaneously a bellicose communiqué for the press, intended to make the Kemalist commander at Chanak draw back. In a disastrous error of timing, the appeal to the premiers went to the press before it reached the premiers themselves, causing further ill-will. Churchill's suggestion that France and Italy supported Britain's stance was then contradicted by both countries. In his defence, Churchill's concentration on the crisis might have been lessened by two domestic events: on the same day an ultimatum to Turkey was being discussed, his fifth and last child, Mary, was born. As he later told his secretary, one should have four children: 'One for Mother, one for Father, one for Accidents, and one for Increase.'[131] On that day, Churchill also bought Chartwell Manor in Kent for £5,500 – without telling Clementine, who had been around it but despaired at where the money for its renovation would come from. Despite the Londonderry inheritance, the Churchills were still living above their means, as Winston seemed constitutionally incapable of curbing his expenses.

Just when complete Cabinet unity was essential for its Near East policy to succeed, Lord Derby, the influential Conservative former Secretary for

War, withdrew his support from the Coalition. On 18 September Lloyd George was contemptuously dismissive to Lord Curzon, his proud foreign secretary, who had severe doubts about the anti-Turkish policy. Churchill chaired a ministerial committee on 22 September at which it was agreed that any Kemalist vessel that attempted to cross the Dardanelles would be sunk.[132] With war looming, Churchill and Austen Chamberlain persuaded Lloyd George not to take the dispute to the League of Nations, which might force Britain to evacuate Chanak. On 27 September Lloyd George was supported by Churchill, Birkenhead, Horne and Freddie Guest in Cabinet in his refusal to evacuate Chanak, but opposed by the Turcophiles Austen Chamberlain, Curzon and several other junior ministers including Stanley Baldwin. By now Churchill was one of the most ardent Turcophobes in the Cabinet, besides Lloyd George. He was not warmongering, however, as he was certain that if the British Empire rallied, Kemal would have to back down.

Two days later, the Cabinet instructed Sir Charles Harington, the British commander of the Army of Occupation in Turkey, to deliver an ultimatum to the Kemalist commander at Chanak warning that if his forces did not withdraw within forty-eight hours all British forces in the region would attack. The Cabinet went into permanent session throughout the 29th and 30th, awaiting the reply. Curzon's requests for an extension were denied. He and Baldwin found the brinkmanship irresponsible, taking Britain into a new war for no discernible reason other than to prevent the Turks reclaiming their own territory. Kemal was ripping up the Sèvres Treaty of 1920 by marching into demilitarized zones in much the same way that Hitler would in the Rhineland in March 1936, when Baldwin also wanted to do nothing whatever about it.

General Harington had not delivered the ultimatum and continued to negotiate with his Turkish opposite number. After the Cabinet meeting on 30 September, Curzon told Lord Crawford, then Minister of Transport, 'Perhaps Churchill wants to recover a strategical prestige already lost at Gallipoli.'[133] The next day, Harington finally wired back to the Cabinet to say that the Turks had withdrawn from the British barbed-wire perimeter at Chanak and that he was going to meet Kemal. There was immense relief. On 7 October, from his retirement, Bonar Law wrote a letter to *The Times* declaring that Britain could no longer be 'the policeman of the world'. This was rightly seen as criticism of Lloyd George's and Churchill's brinkmanship, and an encouragement to Tory MPs to destabilize the Coalition.

On the morning of Monday, 16 October, at this key moment of crisis for the Government, Churchill contracted chronic appendicitis, an extremely serious disease in those days which killed more than 1,600 people a year in Britain.[134] The next day he was operated on in hospital. The operation was a success but his doctors said he would not be able to move for weeks. When he came round, his first thought was to hear the result of the Newport by-election, where the anti-Coalitionist Conservative candidate overturned a 2,000-vote majority, and the Coalition candidate came in third. At a Conservative Party meeting at the Carlton Club on the morning of 19 October, Chamberlain and Balfour spoke in favour of continuing the Coalition and Bonar Law and Baldwin for ending it, the latter making a devastating, highly personal attack on Lloyd George. The vote went 185 to 88 in favour of fighting the next election as an independent party. 'Poor Austen,' F. E. Smith was later to say of Chamberlain. 'He always played the game and always lost it.'[135]

Lloyd George went to the Palace to resign that afternoon, advising the King to send for Bonar Law, who formed what Churchill called 'the Government of the Second Eleven'. Churchill let it be known that he would 'never stifle myself in such a moral and intellectual sepulchre'.[136] This ignored the fact he was the last person they would ask to join. He even made a snobbish remark about Bonar Law, who was ill: 'How is our ambitious invalid? What about our gilded tradesman?'[137] (He had made his fortune in the iron industry.)

Parliament was dissolved and a general election called for 15 November. Despite privately describing the Bonar Law ministry as 'this Government of duds and pipsqueaks', Churchill's own position was not strong in economically depressed Dundee.[138] He was able to go home to Sussex Square on 1 November, but had to write his election address from there while convalescing. 'I stand as a Liberal and a Free Trader,' he wrote, 'but I make it quite clear that I am not going to desert Mr Lloyd George, or the high-minded Conservatives who have stood by him.'[139]

Clementine left for Dundee on 6 November, taking along the seven-week-old Mary. She lodged in the prophetically named Dudhope Terrace and made powerful speeches to large meetings, despite being spat upon in a singularly unpleasant campaign.[140] 'The idea against you seems to be that you are a "War Monger",' she reported to her husband, 'but I am exhibiting you as a Cherub Peace Maker with little fluffy wings around your chubby face.'[141] Birkenhead also went up to speak for Churchill, despite being a Tory.

Churchill's operation prevented him from getting up to Dundee until 11 November, Armistice Day, only four days before the poll. Still weak, but wearing his eleven medals, he had to speak while seated, somewhat groggy from painkillers. 'I was struck by looks of passionate hatred on the faces of some of the younger men and women,' he recalled of the Communist supporters of his opponent William Gallacher. 'Indeed, but for my helpless condition, I am sure they would have attacked me.'[142] Although 5,000 people had come to hear him, the meeting had to be abandoned because of violence. Shaking his fist at the hundred or so Communist demonstrators, he said, 'No voice, no brains; just break up a meeting that they have not the wit to address. The electors will know how to deal with a party whose only weapon is idiotic clamour.'[143]

The extreme unpopularity of the Coalition over the Chanak Crisis and the honours scandal, but primarily over continued high unemployment and economic stagnation, meant that Churchill's large majority from 1918 was overturned by Edwin Scrymgeour, at his fifth attempt, the only MP ever elected on a Prohibitionist ticket, who now had a majority of over 10,000. Churchill polled fewer votes than the Labour candidate. 'If you saw the kind of lives the Dundee folk have to live you would admit they have many excuses,' he wrote to a friend afterwards.[144] Overall, the Conservatives won 345 seats, Labour 142, the National Liberals 62 and the Asquithian Liberals 54. The Conservatives took 5.50 million votes, Labour 4.24 million, Asquithian Liberals 2.52 million and National Liberals 1.67 million. 'In the twinkling of an eye,' Churchill later wrote, 'I found myself without an office, without a seat, without a party, and without an appendix.'[145]

# 13
# Redemption November 1922–May 1926

*In finance, everything that is agreeable is unsound and everything that is sound is disagreeable.*

Churchill speech at the Waldorf Hotel, London, March 1926[1]

*Everybody said that I was the worst Chancellor of the Exchequer that ever was. And now I'm inclined to agree with them. So now the world's unanimous.*

Churchill to Sir Oswald Falk in 1930[2]

Churchill had been an MP for twenty-two years and a minister, with only two short breaks, for seventeen. He now decided to decamp with the family to the Villa Rêve d'Or in Cannes, where he stayed for six months, painting and completing the first and much of the second volume of *The World Crisis*. The Other Club fell into abeyance without him in Parliament, and he only returned to Britain on three short trips: to take his children to and from school, to oversee the building work at Chartwell and to meet his publishers. Detractors accuse him of being a neglectful parent, but as Randolph wrote in his autobiography, 'My father and mother, though they were busy people, always took trouble about us children, particularly in the holidays. From the time I was about twelve we went abroad nearly every summer. Usually we motored through France in a bumbling old Wolseley limousine.'[3]* Churchill, who never smacked his children, visited them at school and wrote them regular letters.[4] It was another example of his learning from mistakes – in this case, those of his own parents.

The first of five volumes of *The World Crisis*, Churchill's 823,000-word

* Churchill owned five Wolseleys between 1923 and 1931, none of them limousines. Randolph was probably thinking of their 1926 car, their only closed Wolseley.

memoir of the Great War, was published in London on 10 April 1923; the last did not come out until 1931. Ten thousand copies sold immediately and it was reprinted within a month. He had considered calling it 'Within the Flag' or 'The Meteor Flag' before finally settling on his title.[5] 'It is not for me with my record and special point of view to pronounce a final conclusion,' he wrote in the preface of the second volume, which covered Gallipoli; it was merely 'a contribution to history'.[6] Its defensiveness over his record makes it clearly the book of a front-rank politician intending to make a comeback before long. As David Reynolds, the biographer of Churchill as historian, has pointed out, it was full of 'truths, half-truths and dubious assertions'.[7] Balfour said it was 'Winston's brilliant autobiography, disguised as a history of the universe.'[8] Yet the autobiographical parts showed a burgeoning self-knowledge. 'Looking back with after-knowledge and increasing years,' he wrote in the opening volume, 'I seem to have been too ready to undertake tasks which are hazardous or even forlorn.'[9]

The first volume told the story of Imperial Germany's war-planning, arms buildup and aggressive attempt to dominate Europe, forcing her neighbours into a defensive alliance. Bonar Law complained that by revealing what ministers said in private the book breached Churchill's oath as a privy councillor; Lloyd George told Frances Stevenson that it was 'Brilliantly written – but too much of an apologia to be of general value,' adding, 'He is not always fair to me.'[10] The *New Statesman*, however, proclaimed it 'honest' and asserted that it would 'certainly survive him'. The reviews were generally, unlike his other press, extremely good.[11] The literary critic Sir Herbert Read criticized it severely on stylistic grounds, however, writing of a passage that covered the fall and death of the Tsar and the entry of America into the war, 'Such eloquence is false because it is artificial: it is one of the pits into which a writer may fall if his conception of "fine writing" is not supported by an inner structure of fine thinking . . . the writer, suspecting the meanness of his theme, attempts to magnify it by grand phrases, thereby hoping to invest his own poor thoughts with the quality of this magnificence.'[12] Churchill clearly did not think that the fall of the Russian Empire or the entry of America into the Great War were mean themes. The book was cited by the Nobel Committee as one of the reasons Churchill won the Literature Prize in 1953, and it certainly bears re-reading a century after publication.

In the second volume Churchill claimed that after the attack of 18 March 1915 the Ottoman forts had almost run out of ammunition, that the minefields were not a continuing threat, that Kitchener's vacillations over the 29th Division were disastrous, that Russia was not collapsing but

Turkey was, that the weeks wasted while the Government was reconstructed in May 1915 gave the Turks time to reinforce the peninsula, and that he could have saved millions of lives by winning the war years earlier if he had not been let down by lily-livered colleagues.[13] Some of these assertions were undoubtedly true, others highly debatable, but it was a powerful narrative to throw back at the hecklers who still yelled 'What about the Dardanelles?' at his public meetings. By the early to mid-1920s, moreover, the public was much more receptive to the argument that any risk had been worth taking that might have avoided the charnel-houses of the Somme and Passchendaele.

Major-General Sir James Edmonds, the editor of the Government's Official War History, helped Churchill on *The World Crisis*, and recorded how he would brief Churchill at Chartwell on each chapter with the relevant documents and maps; Churchill would then dictate the story to his secretary, walking up and down his study. 'I heard what seemed to be a spirit voice whispering to him,' recalled Edmonds, 'but the whispers were his own; he murmured each sentence over to see how it sounded before he dictated it. He took infinite pains to polish up his prose; after two or three typewritten versions, he would have four or five galley-proofs – an expensive business for his publishers . . . He has the soul of an artist.'[14]

Edmonds's papers bulge with files full of Churchill's questions to him from January 1923 onwards, regarding such issues as German violation of Dutch neutrality, Serbia in 1914, the French General Maurice Sarrail's actions in Salonica, the effect on the Germans of 'the wonderful tenacity of our attack' on the Somme, who really invented the 'creeping barrage', German reaction to the Battle of Armentières, Marshal Foch's use of intelligence, the German campaign in Romania, the differences in quantifying British and German casualty numbers, the Battle of Lemberg and very much else. Some of the questions were trivial or technical, such as 'Is it "double-ply" or "double-fly" tents that we lived in in India?' Edmonds stayed for several weekends at Chartwell, noting that his host 'never missed an afternoon sleep on a Napoleon bed with green silk fittings with golden bees on them'.[15]

Churchill sent Edmonds his proofs, counting on his 'vigilant pencil' to strike out inaccuracies.[16] When Edmonds thought Churchill was being too harsh – especially on Haig – he said so, and received replies such as 'Of course the sarcasms and asperities can all be pruned out or softened. I often put things down for the purpose of seeing what they look like in print.'[17] Over the Somme, Churchill stated baldly, 'I am anxious to vindicate my own appreciation of the position at the time, and of course my general argument against these offensives.'[18] He also read every book published on Gallipoli. 'The intervention of Mustapha Kemal on the 25th April [1915, the day of the amphibious landings] is news to me,' he told Ian Hamilton after one of these, 'and profoundly interesting. Destiny was very busy in our affairs.'[19]

Over lunch in May 1923, Robert Horne asked Churchill where he now stood politically, considering that the National Liberals had lost their raison d'être with the demise of the Coalition. 'I am what I have always been,' Churchill replied, 'a Tory Democrat. Force of circumstances has compelled me to serve with another party, but my views have never changed, and I should be glad to give effect to them by rejoining the Conservatives.'[20] This suddenly became possible with the resignation of Bonar Law as prime minister and Conservative Party leader on 20 May, prompted by the cancer from which he died that October. 'Of all the Prime Ministers I ever saw,' Churchill used to say, quoting Hilaire Belloc, 'The least remarkable was Bonar Law.'[21] Curzon was briefly considered, but was stymied by Balfour and the King's private secretary Lord Stamfordham, and Stanley Baldwin acceded to both posts. Churchill had consistently underestimated the new Prime Minister. 'Marshal your baldwins! Marshal your baldwins!' he had said to Asquith as he set out his pawns before a chess game.[22] Yet he hoped that Baldwin would now allow him back into the Conservative Party. For all Churchill's evident ambition, Baldwin had become prime minister only twenty-six months after joining the Cabinet, whereas Churchill was not even in Parliament fifteen years after he first held Cabinet rank.

Churchill won two libel actions in 1923, one over alleged extravagance with taxpayers' money at the Cairo Conference and the other against Lord Alfred Douglas, Oscar Wilde's former lover, who had written a pamphlet accusing Churchill of making money on the New York Stock Exchange through Sir Ernest Cassell, by manipulating the news of the Battle of Jutland.[23] (Douglas equally ludicrously claimed that Lord Kitchener's drowning had been arranged by international Jewry.) Under aggressive cross-examination, Churchill provoked laughter in the High Court when, having been asked, 'Did Lord Fisher refuse to see you and resign?', he replied, 'No, he resigned and refused to see me.'[24] The only witness for the defence, a Captain Spencer, reduced the court to a different kind of laughter with his obvious fabrications.* It took the jury eight minutes to decide on

* Including that he had uncovered Lenin's plan to assassinate the Romanovs but had been arrested and carried off in an Army ambulance in the Balkans, from which he escaped by putting a nurse's Red Cross uniform over his pyjamas and bicycling to the American Consul.

a guilty verdict, after which Douglas was sentenced to six months' imprisonment. (During the Second World War, Douglas wrote a sonnet in Churchill's honour; the latter acknowledged it gracefully with the words, 'Tell him from me that time ends all things.')[25] In 1924, the Irish novelist Frank Harris claimed in his autobiography *My Life and Loves* that Lord Randolph had died of syphilis. The allegation could not be challenged in court, but it spawned further theories about Churchill's supposed instability and lack of judgement. Churchill's eleven-year-old nephew Peregrine was confronted at his prep school by a classmate saying, 'My daddy says all you Churchills have revolting diseases and are quite mad.'[26]

As he was not in Parliament, Churchill was free as a private citizen to act on behalf of Royal Dutch Shell and Burmah Oil in support of their merger with the state-controlled Anglo-Persian Oil Company. This would have positive implications for the security of continued cheap fuel for the Royal Navy, and was certainly in Britain's strategic interests. He lobbied Baldwin personally in August 1923, despite his former private secretary Sir James Masterton-Smith being very much against Churchill's involvement 'on large political grounds'.[27] Churchill entered Downing Street through the Treasury entrance to avoid press comment, which, he told Clementine, 'much amused Baldwin'.[28] He had privately (and wrongly) written Baldwin off as a nonentity, but confided to his wife that the meeting was 'most agreeable. He professed unbounded leisure and received me with the utmost cordiality.'

Their conversation ranged widely. They spoke of the Ruhr, the Admiralty, Air Ministry matters, war reparations, the American debt and general politics. Churchill found the new Prime Minister thoroughly in favour of the merger of the oil companies. 'I am sure it will come off,' Churchill told his wife. 'The only thing I am puzzled about is my own [part in the] affair.'[29] Shell's managing director Sir Robert Waley-Cohen paid Churchill £5,000 (approximately £205,000 in today's money) for the four months of consulting and networking he had done for the deal, a huge sum, but former ministers moving into the private sector after stints in government were not unusual.

Despite his inheritance of the Garron Estate, Churchill needed the money, because he was no longer drawing a ministerial or MP's salary, was running his London house in Sussex Square and also paying for the renovations to Chartwell. Set in 80 acres and only 24 miles from Westminster, the Henry VIII-period house, with several modern extensions, was built on a hillside, giving it dramatic views over the Kentish Weald. Clementine had initially been in favour of buying it, writing in July 1921, 'I can think of nothing but that heavenly tree-crowned hill . . . I do hope we shall get it. If we do I feel that we shall live there a great deal and be very happy.'[30] Once she realized on subsequent visits that it was dilapidated and beset with problems that would cost vast amounts to fix, she changed her mind. By then it was too late, as her husband had fallen in desperate, lifelong love with the house and its grounds.[31] 'A day away from Chartwell is a day wasted,' he would say.[32] On arriving in his car, his secretary Grace Hamblin recalled, 'As we got to the precinct, he'd cast everything aside. All the papers would go flying . . . the dog would be pushed aside, the secretary pushed aside, everything pushed aside, ready to leap out. And he'd say "Ah, Chartwell."'[33] Churchill could work in his study there, with its bust of Napoleon on his desk, better than anywhere else. 'Do not disturb your father,' Clementine would tell Mary, 'he is with speech.'[34]

The costs of renovating and running Chartwell were debilitating. As ever, Churchill decided to resolve the problem by earning more rather than by spending less, however often he told Clementine that they must retrench. The renovations included extensive rewiring, a large extension, new roofs, an orchard, a summerhouse for Mary, an elaborate water-garden of descending pools for his golden orfe carp (which he would sometimes show off to complete strangers who were standing outside his gates, and which were occasionally prey to otters), two large lakes and a swimming pool heated to 75 degrees Fahrenheit. In the 1930s, he had eight indoor servants, two secretaries, a chauffeur and three gardeners. The salaries of fourteen people were thus dependent on his income from books, articles and the scripts of (unfilmed) movies. 'I lived in fact from mouth to hand,' he wrote.[35]

Chartwell was a fine place to entertain guests. The visitors' book, which features the 2,316 signatures of the 780 people who came to stay, records that Lindemann went there eighty-six times, Bernard Montgomery forty-six and Brendan Bracken thirty-one, and also his friends F. E. Smith, Beaverbrook and Eddie Marsh a good deal. It also features the names of Balfour, Lloyd George, T. E. Lawrence – who was one of the few people to whom Churchill would listen intently and without (much) interruption – and Charlie Chaplin.[36] Many more came in the 1930s but for privacy and security reasons did not sign the book, including German anti-Nazi politicians and soldiers, Air Ministry whistle-blowers, Foreign Office anti-appeasement renegades and Desmond Morton's intelligence contacts.

In 1923 Churchill wrote Clementine 'A Dissertation on Dining Room Chairs' which stated that 'The Dining Room chair has certain very marked requisites.' It needed to be comfortable, have arms and be compact, and the back had to be 'almost perpendicularly over the legs'.[37] There also needed to be no fewer than twenty of them. Meals around the circular table in Chartwell's dining room would last two or sometimes three hours as repartee and argument flashed to and fro or long-remembered lines of verse and prose poured forth in torrents. 'Ah, Clemmie,' Churchill would say when she made a move to leave the table. 'It is so nice . . . Do not go. Let us command the moment to remain.'[38]

When Churchill discovered in late May 1928 that the lower pool in his water-garden at Chartwell was 10 feet higher than the water in his new lake, he turned to Lindemann to explain how gravity could be used to regulate the levels in both and to discover how wide the pipes needed to be.[39] As well as a physicist, bomb-sighter, musical theoretician, debate-prepper and ray-gun expert, Churchill expected Lindemann to be a landscape gardener. 'Assuming these 7½ gallons [per minute] were poured into the 1" or 1½" pipe with a ten feet command at two hundred yards distance,' Churchill asked, 'what would be the rate of delivery at the out-flow end? I do hope these problems are not beyond the range of Oxford mathematics!'[40] They were not. Early the next month Churchill telegraphed him at Christ Church: 'Water flowing beautifully according to your calculations, Winston.'[41]

Large numbers of animals lived at Chartwell, too. Over the years, there were two faithful red-orange poodles Rufus and Rufus II (next to which he originally wished to be buried); black swans from Australia; a Canadian goose called 'the Flag Lieutenant' (because he reminded Churchill of a naval officer he once knew) which 'would fall in two or three paces behind his master and march proudly as he made his tour of the estate'; another goose to whom he would bellow 'Ah-wah-wah' across the terrace in order to hear a distant 'honk honk' in reply from lake; a beautiful marmalade cat called Jock* and another, unimaginatively called Cat. (When it ran away Churchill had a sign placed in the window saying, 'If Cat cares to come home, all is forgiven,' and ten days later it did.)[42] After Mary's pug dog had fallen ill, Churchill became 'greatly upset' and composed a poem for her and Sarah to chant:

> Oh, what is the matter with poor Puggy-wug?
> Pet him and kiss him and give him a hug,
> Run and fetch him a suitable drug,
> Wrap him up tenderly all in a rug,
> That is the way to cure Puggy-wug.[43]

It was hardly Keats, but it showed his playful spirit and affection for his daughters. (Puggy-wug recovered.)

Churchill also kept pigs and had a wire brush attached to a long stick

* There is a tradition that there must always be a marmalade cat at Chartwell; the present incumbent is Jock VI.

in order to scratch their backs. 'Dogs look up to you,' he told an aide in 1952, 'cats look down on you. Give me a pig! He looks you in the eye and treats you as an equal.'[44] After the Second World War he also kept tropical fish, and Toby the blue budgerigar, which flew free in his study and left secretaries and visitors, in Mary's words, 'at risk from the bird's indiscretions'.[45] He built a butterfly house but sometimes left the door open, saying, 'I can't bear this captivity.'[46] Sarah recalled, 'My father had very strong views about no animal being slaughtered for food once he had said "Good morning" to it.'[47] Of a particular goose he said, 'You carve, Clemmie. He was a friend of mine.'[48]

In 1934, the Churchills started keeping bees so the family could have their own honey for tea, Clementine having been a member of the Kent Bee-Keepers' Association for several years.[49] Twenty years later, Churchill ordained that the Chartwell strawberries sold to Covent Garden merchants were all to be packed with their noses facing down, to emphasize their freshness.[50]

Churchill was convinced that his ducks knew him. He tried to prove this to Hastings Ismay, his military secretary during the Second World War, by 'uttering seductive cooing sounds until one solitary drake emerged from the reeds and swam slowly over to receive a reward of breadcrumbs from the prime minister's hand'. When he challenged Ismay to exercise the same influence, Ismay imitated Churchill's 'curious call and after a while the same drake paddled across towards him'. Churchill 'eyed it with the more-in-sorrow-than-anger regard of a man whose valued friend had let him down, and then in a voice charged with emotion he said sadly "I *do* wish he hadn't done that."'[51]

In the late 1920s Churchill became a bricklayer and built a wall around the kitchen garden and also a large part of two cottages. (For political reasons, and with singular lack of humour, the national executive of the Amalgamated Union of Building Trade Workers rescinded the membership card he had been given by its local branch.) In the woods on the common land above the Chartwell estate lived Mr and Mrs 'Donkey' Jack, a Romany couple. Churchill paid for 'Donkey' Jack's funeral in 1933, saving him from a pauper's grave, and when his widow was evicted by the local council he offered to get a place in a home for her at his own expense. She nonetheless preferred to camp in a shack in his woodland for the rest of her life, which he allowed.[52] These personal acts of generosity, not known about outside the family at the time, came naturally to him.

'What a swine this Mussolini is,' Churchill wrote to Clementine in September 1923. 'I see Rothermere is supporting him! I am all for the League of Nations.'[53] It would have been better for Churchill's reputation if he had stuck to this opinion about the Italian dictator who had recently seized power in Rome, but as time went on he began to see him as a bulwark against Communism, which he feared would spread westwards in post-war Europe.

In October, Baldwin promised to reintroduce Protection in the hope of fighting unemployment, ending any hopes Churchill might have of readmission to the Tory fold. He swung back towards his old Liberal allegiance and mounted a strong attack on the Government in the general election campaign. Just before it began, on 8 November, he met the twenty-two-year-old Brendan Bracken, who was to become his closest adviser, most faithful follower and, along with Lindemann, his best friend after F. E. Smith's death. Bracken had a past that he kept deliberately mysterious, encouraging the rumour, partly prompted by his red hair, that he was Churchill's illegitimate son, which to Clementine's chagrin Churchill did nothing to scotch. When Clementine probed further, he teasingly replied, 'I looked it up, but the dates don't coincide.'[54] (He had been in South Africa for most of the year before Bracken's birth.) It was a sign of Churchill's love of interesting, intelligent and amusing people, and his lack of concern for their pedigree, that he took to a brazen adventurer like Bracken. The far more conventional Clementine did not come to appreciate him for much longer.

Born in County Tipperary, the son of a well-to-do builder and member of the anti-British, pro-republican Fenian Brotherhood, Bracken was sent to Australia during the Great War from where he returned in 1919. In 1921 at nineteen, posing as an Australian whose parents had perished in a bush fire, he secured a place as a pupil at the public school Sedbergh, in Cumbria.[55]After one term there he spent a year teaching in prep schools, still claiming to have come from Sydney.[56] By the age of twenty-five Bracken was on the board of a newspaper publishing company. He then made his fortune in the mid-1920s revitalizing the publishing business of the financially incompetent and intellectually limited Crosthwaite-Eyre family, culminating in his merging the *Financial News* and the *Financial Times* in 1945. He became Conservative MP for Paddington North in 1929. He was a chancer, undoubtedly, but also a creator, and Churchill appreciated both his unquestioning loyalty and his ability to lift his spirits. As an entirely self-made man, Bracken was also a proselytizer for free enterprise and competitive individualism.[57]

Baldwin described Bracken as Churchill's 'faithful *chela*', a Hindu word meaning devoted disciple. (There were less friendly epithets; the Tory MP John Davidson described him as 'Winston's jackal', and Gladwyn Jebb of the Foreign Office called him 'simply a guttersnipe', though not to his face.)[58] Yet Bracken was much more than a disciple. He was a spin-doctor, as well as trusted adviser and friend, and someone who did not back down before the Churchillian bulldozer. 'He had the most fantastic arguments with Winston,' recalled Harold Macmillan. 'They quarrelled like husband and wife, but Churchill expected that – and it never lasted or affected their true harmony.'[59] Macmillan saw how Bracken 'sometimes helped to keep him on the rails, especially in the war'.

Bracken was also the only person allowed to enter any of Churchill's meetings without knocking and one of the very few people who had free licence to tease Churchill. When Churchill told Bracken that Parisian holders of the Médaille Militaire, which he was awarded in May 1947, could be taken home by taxi at the expense of the French state if they were drunk, Bracken observed, 'You must have made some economies on taxi fares in Paris.' Later, when Churchill appointed an Old Harrovian to a Government post, he told him, 'You only want him because he was at that bloody borstal of yours.'[60] When he cheekily lit his cigarette with the Prime Minister's cigar-end, Churchill told the Chief Whip, 'I have murdered men for less than that.'[61] Yet, for all the jokes and rows, when appeasement of the Nazis was at its height Brendan Bracken was the only non-family MP who spoke up for Churchill, looked out for his interests, took on his enemies and entered every division lobby alongside him, night after night, month after month.

'We are threatened here with another General Election and I have to do a great deal of work for Churchill who is standing for a seat,' Bracken wrote to his (blameless) mother later that month. Just as surprising as Baldwin's elevation to the premiership and embracing of Protectionism had been his calling of a general election four years early when he had a large majority in Parliament, but he felt he needed a new mandate to end Free Trade. Equally surprising was Churchill's choice of Leicester West to fight as a National Liberal Free Trader, when he was offered several winnable seats in Manchester. He later explained it in terms of 'some obscure complex' that led him 'to go off and fight against a Socialist in Leicester, where, being also attacked by the Conservatives, I was of course defeated'.[62] His decision to position himself as more anti-Labour than anti-Tory was to work in his favour in the long run, and so was being out of Parliament in 1923 and thus not beholden to the Liberal whip.

It was a tough election, with 'What about Antwerp?' shouted at him on the hustings, and a brick thrown at his car. 'Mr. Baldwin, our Prime Minister, is a very honest man,' he told his audience, to gales of laughter. 'I for one could have been quite ready to believe that, even if he had not told us so often. It is a fine thing to be honest, but it is also very important for a Prime Minister to be right.'[63] Three days before the election he said, 'Mr. Baldwin does not even know what is a raw material. He does not know whether the tariff he proposes is to be high or low.'[64] Since Baldwin had been successful in the iron and steel industry before entering politics, this was a curious attack on a man who three months earlier he had hoped would take him back into the Conservative Party.

Churchill lost to Frederick Pethick-Lawrence, the Labour candidate, by 4,000 votes, in an election where overall the Conservatives won 258 seats, Labour 191 and the Liberals 159. The Conservatives won 5.54 million votes, Labour 4.44 million, the Liberals 4.31 million. It was the first time Labour had polled more of the popular vote than the Liberals, which it has done ever since. After the election, in Churchill's words, 'The Liberals most unwisely and wrongly put the Socialist minority for the first time into power, thus sealing their own doom.'[65] After the election, the Asquithian Liberals preferred to support a Labour government, whereas the Coalition Liberals preferred a Conservative one, and Churchill became the leading spokesman for the latter group, despite not being in Parliament. 'Free Trade is to be tried by a drumhead court and shot at dawn,' he had told an audience in Manchester during the election, and he could not resile from its support.[66] Nor could he rejoin the Conservatives while they embraced Protectionism.

Churchill set out his position in a letter to *The Times* published on 18 January 1924. 'The enthronement in office of a Socialist Government will be a serious national misfortune such as has usually befallen great states only on the morrow of defeat in war,' he wrote.[67] He professed to see Labour, which wanted to establish full diplomatic relations with Russia, as fellow-travellers with Bolshevism, even though Ramsay MacDonald, the Labour leader, was clearly no Lenin or Trotsky. On 22 January, MacDonald became the first Labour prime minister, with Asquithian Liberal support.

Churchill had a long and friendly talk with Baldwin after the election, and told Clementine on 23 February that the Tory leader 'evidently wants very much to secure my return and cooperation'.[68] He therefore decided to stand in the by-election for the central London constituency of Westminster, Abbey Division, as an Independent Anti-Socialist, the first time since 1906 that the word 'Liberal' did not appear in his electoral nomenclature. The local Conservatives stood a candidate against him, Captain O. W. Nicholson, who was both the nephew of the man whose death had caused the by-election and a large contributor to Party funds. 'I am sure you do not wish to be compelled by technicalities to fire upon the reinforcements

I am bringing to your aid,' Churchill wrote to Baldwin, asking for his support on 7 March, but although Baldwin wanted Churchill in Parliament he would not overrule the local Conservative association.[69]

In his election address on 10 March, Churchill wrote, 'I am a Liberal who wishes to work with the Conservative Party in strong resistance to this menacing attack' – meaning socialism. 'Mr Baldwin has publicly appealed for the co-operation of Liberals. I support him in this policy of putting country before party.'[70] The same day, Clementine sent out a leaflet saying, 'With the single exception of Mr Lloyd George, no public man alive has been responsible for more important acts of social legislation that Mr Churchill.' She further instanced as his successes the Transvaal Constitution, 'the Trades Board Act dealing with sweated industries', labour exchanges, unemployment insurance, the Coal Mines Regulation Act 1910, the abolition of lengthy solitary confinement in prisons, the Shop Hours Act 1911, daylight saving time, 'preparing the Navy against the German menace', saving Dunkirk by holding Antwerp, the way the Dardanelles Commission 'cast no blame of any kind on him', 'ordering the first tanks', setting up an independent Arab kingdom in Mesopotamia ('saving Britain 40 millions') and being a signatory of the Irish treaty.[71]

It was a useful checklist for her husband's life thus far, but the Labour candidate, Fenner Brockway, produced his own version, entitled, 'Winston's Black Record: How He Voted Against the Workers', which instanced the £14 million sent to Denikin (implying it was in cash rather than munitions); Churchill's vote against a Labour motion for an inquiry into coal profiteering; a vote in July 1920 against the repeal of the Protectionist McKenna Duties; 'Mesopotamia adventures which could profit no one but the millionaire oil-profiteers'; sending the Army to railway stations in 1911, and voting against a motion condemning the Black and Tans in November 1920.[72] 'He is a political adventurer,' said Brockway, 'with a genius for acts of mischievous irresponsibility.'[73]

Thirty Conservative MPs supported Churchill, and only one senior Tory, Leo Amery, made a public appeal to vote against him. As a result, Baldwin released a supportive letter from Balfour that he had been holding up. With characteristic élan, Churchill toured the constituency not in a motor car but in a coach-and-four. Nicholson took 8,187 votes, Churchill 8,144, Brockway 6,156 and J. S. Duckers (Liberal) 291. Losing by 43 votes in an electorate of over 22,000 was hard to bear, but Churchill had shown he had a strong personal appeal, and had not denied the Tories their seat. Moreover, as he put it in 1932, he had 'regained for a time at least the goodwill of all those strong Conservative elements, some of whose deepest feelings I share and can at critical moments express, although they have never liked or trusted me'.[74] In 1946 he joked, 'I have fought more contested elections than anyone else, and of all of them the Westminster election was the most exciting and dramatic . . . It was a non-party election because at that Election, all parties were agreed in opposing me.'[75]*

Only two months later, on 7 May 1924, Churchill stood on a Conservative platform for the first time in twenty years, telling the Working Men's Conservative Association in the Sun Hall, Liverpool, that, as he had been 'working in close accord in the Cabinet, or outside' with the Tories for nearly a decade, 'I do not feel, therefore, that my presence at this meeting need be taken as marking any exceptional or extraordinary departure either by my audience or myself.'[76] When, in June, Baldwin renounced his pledge to introduce tariffs, Churchill began searching for a Conservative seat to fight at the next election.

In September, Churchill published an extraordinarily prescient article in the *Pall Mall Gazette* entitled 'Shall We All Commit Suicide?', written with Lindemann's help. Sir Ernest Rutherford had split the atom in 1917, and Churchill attempted to explain the military significance of this fact to his readers. 'Mankind has never been in this position before,' he wrote.

> Without having improved appreciably in virtue or enjoying wiser guidance, it has got into its hands for the first time the tools by which it can unfailingly accomplish its own extermination . . . Death stands at attention, obedient, expectant, ready to serve, ready to sheer away the peoples en masse; ready, if called upon, to pulverize, without hope of repair, what is left of Civilization . . . Might not a bomb no bigger than an orange be found to possess a secret power to destroy a whole block of buildings – nay, to concentrate the force of a thousand tons of cordite and blast a township at a stroke? Could not explosives, even of the existing type, be guided automatically in flying machines by wireless or other rays, without a human pilot, in ceaseless procession upon a hostile city, arsenal, camp or dockyard?[77]

This article anticipated Albert Einstein's letter to President Roosevelt about the possibility of a nuclear bomb by fifteen years, and the Nazis' unmanned V-1 and V-2 missiles by even longer.

'Let it not be thought for a moment that the danger of another explosion in Europe is passed,' Churchill wrote in the same article. 'For the time being the stupor and the collapse which followed the World War

* Churchill's electoral fortunes were relatively undistinguished in his first twelve elections in the quarter-century up to 1924. He had come third in 1899 and second in 1900 in Oldham, first in 1906 and second in 1908 in Manchester North West, then first for the next five elections in Dundee from 1908 to 1918, then fourth in Dundee in 1922 and second in both Leicester West and Westminster Abbey. However, he came top of the poll in all of the following nine.

ensure a sullen passivity, and the horror of war, its carnage and its tyrannies, has sunk into the soul, has dominated the mind, of every class in every race. But the causes of war have in no way been removed; indeed they are in some respects aggravated by the so-called peace treaties.'[78] Writing in such a way about Versailles and its satellite treaties of Trianon, Sèvres, San Remo and so on, was shocking to readers so soon after the end of the war.

Churchill was formally adopted by the Epping Conservative Association on 22 September for the general election now scheduled on 29 October. It was the third election in two years, triggered by the withdrawal of Liberal support for the Labour Government after only ten months in office. He officially stood as a Constitutionalist and Anti-Socialist candidate, but he was finally back in the Tory fold, and in one of the safest seats in the country which, although it later changed its name to Woodford, and still later to Wanstead and Woodford, he was to retain for an unbroken forty years. In his electoral address, Churchill wrote, 'This famous island is the home of Freedom and of representative government. We have led the world along these paths, and we have no need now to seek our inspiration from Moscow or from Munich.'[79] His reference to the attempted Munich Beer-Hall Putsch by Erich Ludendorff and Adolf Hitler of the previous November was an indication that he was closely watching events in Germany.

Churchill won a 9,763-vote majority in that election, and overall the Conservatives won 419 seats, Labour 151 and the Liberals 40, which showed how badly Labour was thought to have failed in its first stint in government. The popular vote went Conservative 8.04 million, Labour 5.49 million and the Liberals 2.93 million. So Churchill's run of three successive defeats in two years was over, and Baldwin was prime minister for the second time. 'It is very unlikely that I shall be invited to join the Government,' Churchill wrote to a supporter, because the size of the parliamentary majority meant it would be composed 'only of impeccable Conservatives'.[80] He could not have been more wrong: two days later Baldwin offered him nothing less than the chancellorship of the Exchequer. Neville Chamberlain, who was Austen's half-brother, had turned it down so that he could pursue major reforms at the Ministry of Health, whereupon Baldwin told him that Churchill 'would be more under control inside than out'.[81]

Churchill later wrote that when Baldwin asked whether he would like the post, increasingly seen as the second most important in government, 'I should have liked to have answered "Will the bloody duck swim?" But as it was a formal and important occasion, I replied "This fulfils my ambition. I still have my father's robes as Chancellor. I shall be proud to serve you in this splendid office."'[82] That his first response to the Prime Minister was not about the state of the economy, taxation, the Gold Standard, the coal industry or any of the problems that were to trouble him over the next five years, but about his father, clearly demonstrates how strong his memory still was, nearly thirty years after Lord Randolph's death. (His mother had 'most carefully preserved' the robes in case he needed them.)[83] When he told Clementine the news, 'I had great difficulty in convincing my wife that I was not merely teasing her.'[84] John Singer Sargent gave Churchill a drawing of him in his Chancellor's robes, one of the last he ever made. 'I wanted to point out the awful concavity of my right cheek,' Churchill said. 'However, one must not look a gift portrait in the mouth.'[85]

Churchill's remark that the chancellorship 'fulfils my ambition' was a coded promise not to intrigue for Baldwin's job, but on the eve of his fiftieth birthday neither man really believed it. 'It would be up to him to be loyal,' Baldwin told Tom Jones, Deputy Secretary to the Cabinet and his trusted adviser, 'if he is capable of loyalty.'[86] Baldwin's real aim was to detach Churchill from Lloyd George, who still led his faction of Liberals, which such a generous offer succeeded in doing – as it turned out, for ever. It would also force him to water down his position on Free Trade, which the astute Baldwin rightly thought Churchill was ready to do in the face of the continuing high unemployment that had bedevilled the post-war economy.[87] The appointment also gave weight to an otherwise uninspiring ministry. Asquith said that Churchill towered like 'a Chimborazo [the highest mountain in Ecuador] or Everest among the sandhills of the Baldwin Cabinet'.[88] Just as in July 1917, Churchill's political career had been saved – advanced – by a prime minister whose primary motivation was the fear of his powerful voice raised in opposition on the backbenches.

Chancellors very often fall out with their prime ministers – perhaps in part because they are neighbours in Downing Street, living next door to the person whom they almost invariably hope to replace – but Churchill and Baldwin got on extremely well personally throughout the five years of the ministry. They were constantly plagued by untrue rumours, invented by ill-wishers, that Churchill was plotting against Baldwin, which the Prime Minister treated with remarkable sangfroid.[89] 'I recognise the truth of Disraeli's remark that the vicissitudes of politics are inexhaustible,' Churchill told his audience at a celebratory dinner in December in Liverpool.[90] As in 1904 when he crossed the floor to become a Liberal, Churchill's timing could hardly have been better, for just as the Liberals were in office for the next sixteen years after 1906, so in 1924 the Conservatives were to be in power for all but two of the next twenty-one years. The Liberals never formed another government. 'Anyone can rat,' Churchill said of his becoming a Tory again, 'but it takes a certain ingenuity to re-rat.'[91]

In 1924 Birkenhead published a book, *Contemporary Personalities*, in which he wrote that Lord Randolph had 'died in complete ignorance of the fact that he had produced a son intellectually greater than himself'.[92] In that short pen-portrait, Birkenhead suggested that Winston Churchill 'walks through the lobbies of the House of Commons with an air appropriate to Napoleon Bonaparte on the morning of the crisis of the 18th Brumaire'.[93]* For all that people saw Churchill as 'insolent, and even domineering', Birkenhead attested that his friends knew he had 'in the intimacy of personal friendship a quality which is almost feminine in its caressing charm. And he has never in all his life failed a friend, however embarrassing the obligations.'[94]

Lord Randolph Churchill had been an undistinguished chancellor of the Exchequer, who referred to decimal points as 'those damned dots'. Economics was not his son's forte either. (As he admitted in October 1943, telling the Commons that losses by strikes and stoppages had been no more than two-thirds of half of 1 per cent, 'We have always to run a great risk in these matters – two-thirds of 0.5 per cent. Neither I nor my father was ever any good at arithmetic.')[95] 'They all talk Persian,' he said of his Treasury advisers – but as his private secretary there Percy Grigg later wrote, 'He would talk himself into a knowledge and understanding of any topic which came before him.'[96]† In 1924, he inherited an economy that was largely dysfunctional as a result of the Great War. Inflation was high, unemployment was over one million – 10 per cent of the workforce – and unevenly distributed geographically. Income tax was at the historically very high figure of five shillings to the pound, or 25 per cent. The coal industry – the largest in the country – employed over a million men, but although Britain had exported 73 million tons of coal in 1913, by 1921 it was down to 25 million.[97] Textiles, one of Britain's other strongest industries, which employed half a million people, were beginning to face stiff Japanese competition. Earlier in 1924 Philip Snowden, the Labour

* The day of Napoleon's coup d'état in 1799.

† One aspect of taxation that Churchill understood perfectly was his own. In order to minimize the income tax on his earnings from writing he officially retired as an author for eighteen months, to allow his royalties to be treated as non-taxable capital gains. He was to do this again after the Second World War started.

Chancellor, had rescinded the McKenna Duties of 1915, the last part of Protectionism.

Ironically for the son of Gladstone's tormentor, Churchill was by the 1920s essentially an orthodox Gladstonian Liberal in finance, believing in retrenchment, balanced budgets, Free Trade and cheese-paring reductions in public expenditure wherever possible. On 28 November, he told Tom Jones that he wanted the Government to concentrate on housing and pensions, especially for war widows. 'I think I see my way to help both of these if I can stop the departments spending in other directions,' he said. 'I was all for the Liberal measures of social reform in the old days, and I want to push the same sort of measures now . . . We cannot have a lot of silly little cruisers, which would be of no use anyway.'[98]

One of the major criticisms of Churchill's chancellorship has been that he so cut defence expenditure, especially in the Navy's cruiser programme and the new naval base at Singapore, that he was much to blame for Britain's weakness against the Axis powers of Germany, Italy and Japan in the 1930s. His own parliamentary private secretary at the Treasury, Bob Boothby, alleged that he was a 'very bad Chancellor of the Exchequer . . . His whole objective was to reduce the income tax by a shilling . . . [which] was the basis for our weakness in the 1930s. Churchill disarmed the country . . . as nobody has ever disarmed this country before.'[99] In the mid-1920s, however, Germany and Japan were not considered future enemies – indeed in 1925 the Locarno Treaty brought Germany back into the international diplomatic mainstream. Although cruisers continued to be built during Churchill's chancellorship, he did indeed resist Admiralty demands for a massive cruiser-building programme. In December he wrote to Baldwin, 'I feel sure that such a policy will not only bring the Government into ruin but might well affect the safety of the State.'[100] He feared 'starting up the whole armament race all over the world and setting the pace towards a new vast war. I cannot conceive any course more certain to result in a Socialist victory.'[101] Baldwin said almost exactly the same thing in 1936, explaining why he had not pressed for rearmament. This was to earn him a stinging rebuke from Churchill in his war memoirs, accusing him of 'putting party before country'.* The key difference in their parallel arguments was that in December 1924 Adolf Hitler was a failed plotter languishing in Landsberg Prison and the Nazi Party had won only 2.3 per cent of the vote in the 1923 German elections, whereas in the mid-1930s he was Führer of Germany and a clear danger to world peace. In September

* This was unfair to Baldwin, who had been referring to a hypothetical election in 1934, not to the actual general election of 1935, but Churchill never corrected his statement.

1939 Britain and her Empire in fact entered the war with fifty-six cruisers, almost as many as Germany, Italy and Japan combined, many of which had been built during Churchill's chancellorship.

Churchill told Baldwin that the Admiralty's expansionist policy in the Far East was 'provocative' to Japan, which had been Britain's ally in the Great War. He asked the generally supportive Foreign Secretary, Austen Chamberlain, to make a Cabinet declaration 'ruling out war with Japan among the reasonable possibilities to be taken into account in the next 10, 15 and 20 years'.[102] The struggle with the Admiralty, led by Lord Bridgeman* as first lord and Lord Beatty as first sea lord, over the 1925–6 Naval Estimates was a long and bruising one, which ended in compromise. In the course of the controversy, Churchill made remarks that were to be proved spectacularly wrong. 'Why should there be a war with Japan?' he wrote in December 1924. 'I do not believe there is the slightest chance of it in my lifetime.'[103] In any case, Churchill pointed out that Britain had forty-three cruisers that were less than ten years old, displacing over 236,000 tons, versus Japan's twenty that displaced 109,000.[104]

In January 1925 Churchill foresaw a 'long peace, such as follows in the wake of great wars'.[105] He could not spend the £90 million that a large rearmament programme would cost while also keeping balanced budgets, cutting unemployment, expanding social welfare, reviving trade and cutting taxes to stimulate growth.[106] Beatty, on the verge of resignation in January 1925, wrote, 'That extraordinary fellow Winston has gone mad, economically mad, and no sacrifice is too great to achieve what in his short-sightedness is the panacea for all evils, to take one shilling off the Income Tax.'[107] Yet the Foreign Office agreed with Churchill, considering a future Japanese attack to be very unlikely and suggesting it would amount to 'national hara-kiri'.[108]

Churchill cut spending on the new naval base at Singapore from the estimated £12 million down to £8 million.[109] If war did break out, he believed that the Royal Navy should stay on the defensive around Singapore, guard trade routes to India and Australasia, and wait until new naval construction could be brought to bear. In the first instance, Britain should 'base a squadron of battle cruisers, or a fast division of battleships, or if possible both, upon Singapore during the period of strained relations, or as soon as may be after the war has begun'.[110] This was what he tried to do with Force Z in December 1941.

There is a canard among his detractors that Churchill always tended to promote the interests of whichever department he was representing at

* No relation to the former first sea lord Sir Francis Bridgeman, fortunately.

the time. His opposition to the much deeper naval cuts pushed for by his Treasury officials, such as Sir George Barstow, belies this.[111] Certainly any alternative chancellor – Neville or Austen Chamberlain and certainly any Labour or Liberal one – would have been much tougher on the Admiralty at this point than Churchill was. Moreover, he was supported by Baldwin and the vast majority of the Cabinet in resisting Admiralty demands. Overall, the naval budget increased during Churchill's chancellorship from £105 million to £113 million.[112]

In January 1925 Churchill went to Paris for a conference to negotiate and restructure international war debts and reparations. Britain's war debt to the United States stood close to £1 billion, but £2 billion was owed to Britain by France, Japan, Belgium and Italy, among others, not including Germany. President Coolidge's attitude towards Britain's war debt was unforgiving: 'They hired the money, didn't they?' It was not an unreasonable stance to take, but it was feared that full and early repayment would damage Britain's economy and thus stifle transatlantic trade, to no one's ultimate advantage.[113] 'Hope flies on wings,' Churchill wrote, 'and international conferences plod afterwards along dusty roads.'[114] After seven days of detailed discussion, it was agreed that Britain would reimburse the USA at a rate directly linked to her own receipts. 'I have had tremendous battles with the Yanks and have beaten them down inch by inch to a reasonable figure,' he reported to Clementine. 'However there was never any ill-will.'[115]

It was his first major international financial negotiation. On his return, the Cabinet officially 'expressed their high appreciation of the success of the Chancellor of the Exchequer's mission'.[116] On 11 March Churchill persuaded ministers to include Germany in the talks that would eventually result in the Locarno Treaty of December 1925, which set in stone Germany's eastern frontier. 'The wars of Frederick the Great as well as those of Peter the Great had arisen from deep causes and ambitions which so far from having passed away', he noted, 'were now associated with great historic memories.'[117] He was thus one of the architects of the inter-war agreement that brought Germany into the international system once again – and set the border tripwires that Hitler was later to trigger.

With the pound sterling floating on the foreign exchange markets within 2.5 per cent of its pre-war figure of $4.86, there was a strong movement in the Government, the Bank of England, the City and the Treasury towards trying to restore the pre-war trade and monetary system, and on Tuesday, 17 March 1925, Churchill held a small dinner party at 11 Downing Street that was to have heavy consequences for the British economy and for his own reputation. 'It is no exaggeration to say that the whole world is watching the efforts of this country to restore the Gold Standard,' *The Times* had proclaimed eleven days earlier. 'Everyone expects us to succeed.'[118] Britain had left the Gold Standard on the outbreak of war in 1914, and in 1918 the Cunliffe Committee, chaired by the Governor of the Bank of England, had recommended an eventual return to the Gold Standard at the pre-war figure of $4.86 to the pound sterling. By 1920 inflation had been arrested, and in July 1922 interest rates were down to the historically low rate of 3 per cent. By early 1923, sterling was trading at $4.63. Montagu Norman, the powerful new Governor of the Bank of England, wanted a return to the Gold Standard, as did Otto Niemeyer, the financial controller at the Treasury and almost all the senior officials there. They hoped it would stabilize prices. The Conservatives, Liberals and even the Labour Party had all promised a return. Both Germany and the United States had returned to the Gold Standard by early 1925.

Churchill knew himself to be no financial expert, and although Bourke Cockran had provided him with several fine phrases in support of the Gold Standard, his instincts were not initially in favour. 'Are we to be at the mercy of a lot of Negro women scrabbling with their toes in the mud of the Zambesi?' he asked officials.[119] Yet in his December letter to Baldwin he had written, 'It will be easy to attain the Gold Standard and indeed almost impossible to avoid taking the decision.'[120]

So on 17 March Churchill invited John Maynard Keynes, the Cambridge economist who had been a dissenting voice on the Cunliffe Committee, Reginald McKenna, the former Chancellor of the Exchequer, Lord Bradbury, the reparations expert, and Niemeyer to dinner at the Treasury to thrash out the issue. Also present was Percy Grigg, who called the meeting 'a sort of Brains Trust', after the popular radio programme. Grigg later recalled that Niemeyer and Bradbury supported the project whereas Keynes and McKenna opposed it. 'The symposium lasted till midnight or after,' he noted.

> I thought at the time that the ayes had it. Keynes' thesis, which was supported in every particular by McKenna, was that the discrepancy between American and British prices was not 2½% as the exchanges indicated, but 10%. If we went back to gold at the old parity we should therefore have to deflate domestic prices by something of that order. This meant unemployment and downward adjustments of wages and prolonged strikes in the heavy industries, at the end of which it would be found that these industries had undergone a permanent contraction. It was much better, therefore, to try to keep domestic prices and nominal wage rates stable and allow the exchanges to fluctuate.[121]

Bradbury pointed out that the Gold Standard was 'knave-proof', in that politicians could not manipulate the value of the pound sterling for political purposes, because the currency was directly linked to gold.[122] The advantage of price stability and therefore no inflation was believed to outweigh the disadvantage of lack of liquidity in the system. To the suggestion that Britain should return at a lower parity, Bradbury thought 'it was silly to create a shock to confidence and to endanger our international reputation for so small and ephemeral an easement.' After much discussion, McKenna had the last word, 'There is no escape; you have got to go back; but it will be hell.'

Keynes, whose *The Economic Consequences of the Peace*, published in 1919, had attacked the financial clauses of the Versailles Treaty, wrote three articles similarly attacking the return to gold, which appeared in the *Evening Standard* in July 1925 and were then republished as a 32-page pamphlet entitled *The Economic Consequences of Mr Churchill*. In it, he argued that because the Gold Standard overvalued sterling, which had been done 'to satisfy the impatience of the City fathers', wages would fall. He explained Churchill's decision as having been taken 'Partly, perhaps, because he has no instinctive judgement to prevent him from making mistakes; partly because, lacking this instinctive judgement, he was deafened by the clamorous voice of conventional finance; and, most of all, because he was gravely misled by experts.'[123] Churchill did not mind this ad hominem attack, which he considered part of the political give-and-take. Nor did he necessarily disagree, telling Niemeyer that overall 'I would rather see Finance less proud and Industry more content,' whereas joining the Gold Standard would have the opposite effect.[124]

Churchill later deeply regretted having nevertheless accepted the advice of Montagu Norman, Lord Bradbury and Philip Snowden to rejoin the Gold Standard, while failing to adjust wage and taxation policy to the new exigencies of gold-backed sterling. One result was that British coal costs became too high in relation to output, at a time when the end of the French occupation of the Ruhr brought enormous quantities of cheaper German coal on to an increasingly competitive international market. 'We are often told that the Gold Standard will shackle us to the United States,' Churchill said in a debate in the Commons. 'I will tell you what it will shackle us to. It will shackle us to reality.'[125] But as early as June the mine-owners warned the Miners' Federation that wages would have to be cut and hours of work increased. Churchill funded a temporary nine-month subsidy to buy industrial peace until the April 1926 Budget. This started off costing £10 million but eventually rose to £23 million. The Cabinet's Supply and Transport Committee was not ready for an all-out coal strike, so this was a piece of strategic appeasement while Churchill argued that 'The Gold Standard is no more responsible for the condition of affairs in the coal industry than is the Gulf Stream.'[126]

Part of Churchill's difficulty was the deflationary environment that was hindering global economic growth. Although Britain had been on the victorious side in the war, she did not find herself well placed to reap the benefits, not least because several of her best pre-war markets had been devastated by the conflict. Few countries prospered between 1913 and 1929, and Britain's post-war failure to enter new markets led to lower growth than that achieved by her European competitors.[127] Coal, shipbuilding and textiles remained her staple export industries, but these now had to face increased competition. France and other industrial countries renovated their factories and machinery along up-to-date technological lines in a way that Britain did not. Restoring the Gold Standard dried up the easy credit that was needed to do this, while not solving any of Britain's underlying economic ills, which were far more serious than her fiscal and monetary ones.

Devaluation would have been a better course of action, and would have made the transition to gold simpler, but the Government thought that that would effectively admit that Britain could not return to her former level of greatness as a superpower.[128] 'Without the development of new industries and a different entrepreneurial spirit,' one study of Churchill's actions concludes, 'no monetary policy could have made the decisive difference.'[129] This did not prevent Churchill from making several political sallies about the Gold Standard at the time. 'We could no doubt keep our export trade continually booming at a loss,' he said at one point, and at another he likened those who wanted to go back at a reduced parity from 1914 to grocers who 'take an ounce off the pound' and tailors who 'snip an inch off the yard'. In another speech he accused Keynes and his followers of wanting to establish a quicksilver standard.[130] These quips were amusing at the time, but Keynes was to be proved right.

In 1945, Churchill admitted privately, 'The biggest blunder of my life was the return to the Gold Standard.'[131] The almost total unanimity of the financial experts in favour of it, when set alongside the views of the admirals about the convoy system, and those of the generals about how to fight both the Boer War and Great War, led Churchill seriously to doubt the wisdom of experts. His willingness to attack the views of the entire Establishment over appeasement might not have been so complete had he not seen its experts proved wrong time and again, and had he not, in the case of the Gold Standard, been forced to take ultimate responsibility.

On 28 April 1925, Churchill introduced the first of his five Budgets, observed from the Commons gallery by Clementine, Randolph and Diana, who was now fifteen. He cut sixpence rather than his hoped-for shilling off income tax (reducing it from 25 to 22.5 per cent), announced the return to the Gold Standard, lowered the pensionable age from seventy to sixty-five and introduced the first state-backed contributory pensions scheme, which covered fifteen million people, while abolishing the hated qualifications for state hand-outs known as the Means Test. 'It is not', he said, 'the sturdy marching troops that need extra reward and indulgence. It's the stragglers, the weak, the wounded, the veterans, the widows and orphans to whom the ambulances of state should be directed.'[132] It was Tory Democracy in action.

Churchill also introduced some very modest measures of Imperial Preference, for West Indian sugar, Kenyan and Rhodesian tobacco, South African and Australian wine and Middle Eastern dried fruits. If that wasn't enough of a volte-face, he added tariffs on luxury imports such as motor cars, silk, watches and movies. He explained this throwing over of his longest-held principle of Free Trade simply in terms of the practical needs of the Treasury, in a world where other countries were also introducing Protectionist duties. 'To some they are a relish,' he told the Commons of tariffs, 'to others a target, and to me a revenue . . . We cannot afford to throw away a revenue like that.'[133] Baldwin reported to the King that 'throughout his speech he showed that he is not only possessed of consummate ability as a parliamentarian, but also all the versatility of an actor.'[134]

Lloyd George predictably attacked the Budget, saying of the Chancellor, 'I admire his dazzling mind, his brilliant mind, so brilliant as to dazzle his judgement. In fact, one of his troubles is that his headlights are rather blinding – and he finds it difficult to drive a straight course on the road, and to avoid smashing into traffic.'[135] Another sceptic, Percy Grigg, disloyally told Tom Jones, 'Within a year Winston will have committed some irretrievable blunder which, if it does not imperil the Government, will bring Winston down.'[136] As old allies fell away, however, new ones appeared on the scene. Anthony Eden, a young, newly elected Tory MP, wrote in his diary that Churchill's Budget had been '2½ hours and a masterly performance'.[137] Ten years earlier, aged seventeen, he had commended Churchill in his diary for being one of the Cabinet ministers who had voted to go to war in 1914, without which, Eden thought, Britain could not have gone on 'without losing all her prestige as a first-class Power'.[138]

'I don't think there can be any dispute but that he has been a source of increased influence and prestige to the government as a whole,' Neville Chamberlain wrote to Baldwin in August. The letter goes further than most others in explaining the relations between Churchill and Chamberlain at that early stage of their long and complicated acquaintanceship. 'What a brilliant creature he is,' he continued. 'But there is somehow a great gulf fixed between him and me which I don't think I shall ever cross. I like him, I like his humour and vitality. I like his courage . . . But not for all the joys of paradise would I be a member of his staff.'[139]

On 20 March 1925, Lord Curzon died unexpectedly of a bladder haemorrhage. 'I do not think the tributes were very generous,' Churchill said immediately after his funeral. '*I* would not have been grateful for such stuff. But he did not inspire affection, nor represent great causes.'[140] Churchill was still raw over Curzon's defection from the Coalition, though he was kinder in his book *Great Contemporaries* in 1937.

The Other Club, which had not met for nearly three years while Churchill was out of Parliament, was revived on 12 April. Twelve members attended, including Sinclair, Seely, Waldorf Astor and the Duke of Marlborough. It resumed meeting regularly thereafter, with Churchill attending whenever he was in London. As Lloyd George had now dropped out completely, it changed from being a political vehicle for rapprochement to an opportunity for the friends of Churchill and Birkenhead to gather. That April evening the two founders signed themselves in mock self-reverence as 'Fundatores pii' (pious founders). New members included James de Rothschild, a Liberal MP who had won the Distinguished Conduct Medal serving in the Jewish Battalion of the Royal Fusiliers in Palestine, Sir Hugh Trenchard, Edward Hilton Young, who had won the Distinguished Service Order and bar, the Distinguished Service Cross and the Croix de Guerre and had lost an arm commanding a rear-gun on the Zeebrugge Raid, and Oliver Locker-Lampson, who had personally funded the Royal Naval Air Service's Armoured Car Division in 1914. Also elected were J. H. Thomas, Labour's former Colonial Secretary, and Sir William Berry (later Lord Camrose), whose family owned the *Daily Telegraph*. A later member, the journalist Colin Coote, recalled that between the wars, when the Loyal Toast was drunk, Churchill 'always added an original touch to this time-honoured ceremony. After "The King" he would add, sotto voce, "And *no war*!"'[141]

Churchill officially rejoined the Conservative Party and also the Carlton Club in late 1925. At the Grand Theatre in strongly working-class Bolton in January 1926 he set about the socialists with relish. 'Let them abandon the utter fallacy,' he said, 'the grotesque, erroneous, fatal blunder of believing that by limiting the enterprise of man, by riveting the shackles of a false equality upon the efforts of all the different forms and different classes of human enterprise, they will increase the well-being of the world.'[142] This sound ideology of liberty was spoilt when six days later he said of Italy, which had settled her war debts with Britain, words he would come to regret, 'It possesses a Government under the commanding leadership of Signor Mussolini which does not shrink from the logical consequences of economic facts and which has the courage to impose the financial remedies required to secure and to stabilize the national recovery.'[143]* However, when in early March Lord Rothermere suggested that a Mussolini-style leader might work for Britain, Churchill told a Chambers of Commerce luncheon in Belfast, 'Our society is very broadly and deeply founded. We are not in the position that we have to choose between various unconstitutional extremes.'[144]

When Clementine and her sister-in-law Goonie visited Rome for a fortnight in March they met the Duce, who gave them a photo of himself signed 'devotamente, Mussolini' that was for a short time displayed in the drawing room at Chartwell. 'He sent you friendly messages and said he would like to meet you,' Clementine reported to her husband. 'I am sure he is a very great person.'[145] 'No doubt he is one of the most wonderful men of our time,' Churchill replied, with a touch of scepticism.[146] Three days later he added, 'I feel sure you are right in regarding him as a prodigy,' but then he quoted the politician Augustine Birrell, who had written, 'It is better to read about a world figure, than to live under his rule!'[147]

Churchill's second Budget was delivered on 27 April 1926. His coal subsidy was coming to an end, with consequent disruption in the mining industry, and all government departments were required to make savings. The Air Ministry's expenditure was reduced from £18 million to £16 million, for example, and the Naval Estimates capped at £57.5 million. Although Churchill and Baldwin tried to stave off the mining crisis, miners arriving for work on 1 May found themselves locked out, with employers stating that they simply could not continue to pay the same wages in the face of shrinking profits. A. J. Cook, the General Secretary of the National Union of Mineworkers (NUM), responded with the slogan, 'Not a penny off the pay, not a minute on the day'. The Trades Union Congress (TUC) then proclaimed a General Strike – nationwide, all-industries – beginning at 11.59 p.m. on 3 May, having informed the Government of its intentions the day before.

Churchill was more sympathetic to the miners than almost anyone else in the Cabinet, but he nonetheless joined the unanimous vote to end the

* On signing the settlement of the debt, Churchill said, 'The best evidence of the fairness of any settlement is the fact that it fully satisfies neither party' (*CS* IV p. 3827).

fruitless negotiations with the TUC on 2 May. As a Tory Democrat, he disliked the mine-owners' version of laissez-faire capitalism. He did not think highly of his own cousin Lord Londonderry, who owned coalmines in Durham and who had rejected the Government's compromise proposals. Churchill sympathized with the men who worked long, dangerous hours underground, yet he also knew that the elected Government could not give in to the threat of a General Strike. 'It is a conflict which, if it is fought out to a conclusion,' he said in the Commons as the Strike began, 'can only end in the overthrow of Parliamentary Government or in its decisive victory. There is no middle course open . . . No door is closed; but, on the other hand, while the situation remains what it is, we have no alternative whatever but to go forward unflinchingly and do our duty.'[148]

On the first day of the strike, Monday, 3 May 1926, Baldwin put Churchill in charge of the Government newspaper the *British Gazette*, which Baldwin's biographers explain was to 'keep him busy and stop him doing worse things'.[149] Using the offices and printing facilities of the *Morning Post* (which were offered by the owners, not commandeered as myth soon had it), Churchill brought out eight daily issues* of the paper and himself wrote much of what appeared in them. His more bellicose editorials were toned down by John Davidson, whom Baldwin had sent to watch him, which naturally led to many clashes.[150] In order to ensure continued publication, 450 tons of paper was ordered from Holland with a company of Royal Engineers deputed to guard it.

Because of his actions when troops clashed with miners at Llanelli in 1911, and his involvement in the events at Tonypandy the previous year, it was easy for the left to portray Churchill as an enemy of the working man and organized labour. The *British Gazette* offered them plenty of ammunition (one modern historian described the paper as 'inflammatory'), but it also gave the former journalist a good opportunity to make the Government's voice heard nationally.[151] Churchill did not want it to be merely a propaganda news-sheet; he wanted to turn it into a proper newspaper (although it was subsidized, it had a cover price of one penny), and its circulation rose from 232,000 on 5 May to over 2.2 million by 13 May.[152] It featured thoughtful articles by statesmen like Asquith and Grey, but also blatant anti-Strike propaganda, despite its purported impartiality. On 11 May it ran a headline entitled 'False News', which read, 'Believe nothing until you see it in an authoritative journal like *The British Gazette*.'

'This great nation,' read the editorial in the first edition, 'on the whole the strongest community which Civilization can show, is for the moment

* There were also two 3 a.m. editions, on 11 and 13 May.

reduced in this respect to the level of African natives dependent only on rumours which are carried from place to place.'[153] The article was unsigned, but its authorship was obvious. Elsewhere in the *Gazette*, strikers were described as 'the enemy', the remarkable early solidity of the stoppage was downplayed and it was presented as 'a direct challenge to ordered Government'. One French newspaper was quoted as claiming that the Bolsheviks were behind the Strike. An editorial in the fourth issue stated that if the armed forces had to take any action that had not been previously authorized they would be supported by the Government, an opinion which even the King thought irresponsible.[154] The Labour politician George Lansbury was described as 'a wild Socialist, passionate and shouting'.

Churchill and Baldwin played contrasting roles during the Strike, with the Prime Minister showing moderation and regard for the other side, while Churchill, through the *Gazette*, demanded nothing less than unconditional victory. Davidson complained to Lord Irwin, who was by then viceroy of India, that Churchill 'regarded the strike as an enemy to be destroyed', and to Baldwin that 'He thinks he is Napoleon.'[155] Irwin's brother-in-law, the Tory MP George Lane-Fox, thought Churchill 'most belligerent and troublesome'.[156] Against that, there were 1,389 prosecutions for violence before the Strike ended, over a hundred a day, which represented genuine belligerence of a non-rhetorical kind.

On 9 May, as the Strike reached its decisive stage, Churchill wanted to commandeer the BBC, which was unnecessary as it subtly supported the Government anyway, but in so doing he made an enemy for life of Sir John Reith, its director-general. Reith subsequently kept him off the airwaves for much of the 1930s and expressed his loathing of him in his diaries, even when he was serving in his wartime Government. 'He was really very stupid,' Reith wrote during the Strike, in a typical entry.[157] Churchill's piratical seizure of large amounts of *The Times*'s paper infuriated its editor, Geoffrey Dawson, who complained bitterly and held it against him for years.

'He simply revels in this affair,' sniffed Neville Chamberlain on 4 May, 'which he *will* continually treat and talk of as if it were 1914.'[158] After Tom Jones had proposed a compromise settlement with the TUC on 7 May, he later recalled, Churchill 'overwhelmed me with a cataract of boiling eloquence', telling him that 'We were at war. Matters had changed from Sunday morning . . . We must go through with it. You must have the nerve.'[159] Churchill recognized that a generous offer on the terms of the miners' pay and employment could be made only once the constitutional threat to the Government had been seen off, and he felt this could not happen after just four or five days. He even went so far as to refuse to publish an appeal for conciliation written by the Archbishop of Canterbury.

'Winston is enjoying himself in editing the *British Gazette*,' Thomas Inskip, the Solicitor-General, reported to Irwin. 'His Budget of £820m no longer interests him very much. I don't say he is wrong in his instinct for the dominant issue of the moment, but he is entertaining in his absorption in "publicity".'[160] Publicity was still something of a dirty word in the 1920s, and considered beneath politicians. Yet, for all the criticism from prominent Conservatives, Churchill's refusal to show any sign of bending, when added to Baldwin's tough response, meant that on 11 May the Strike started to crack. Churchill immediately wrote Baldwin a note that read, 'Surrender today, tomorrow magnanimity'.[161] This was his attitude towards the Boers, the suffragettes and the Germans after both world wars. He had wanted to adopt it towards the Irish republicans too, but – as so often – Ireland turned out to be a case apart.

The TUC called off the General Strike on 13 May, but the NUM fought on alone. In the *New Statesman* later that month, satirically entitled 'Should We Hang Mr Churchill or Not?' its editor wrote, 'Mr Churchill was the villain of the piece. He is reported to have remarked that he thought "a little blood-letting" would be all to the good.'[162] Churchill asked Sir Douglas Hogg, the Attorney-General, whether he could sue, as 'I certainly do not feel inclined to allow such a lie to pass into the general currency of Labour recriminations.'[163] Hogg told him it wasn't worth the trouble, but the General Strike nevertheless left Churchill vilified as a strike-breaker and a diehard, ideological foe of trade unionists, which he was not. He had not been determined to break the Strike until the NUM tried to force the Government into paying further huge subsidies.

During the Second World War, Churchill made sure to appoint senior trade unionists to key positions in his government, and in his peacetime premiership he pursued full-scale appeasement of them. Such were the antagonisms of politics, however, that after the General Strike he seems to have been forgiven more quickly for his victory by his socialist opponents than by his critics in the Tory Establishment, figures such as Davidson, Inskip, Reith, Dawson, Lane-Fox, Crawford and Neville Chamberlain, who were meant to be on his side.

# 14
# Crash
# June 1926–January 1931

*This was a capable, sedate government.*

Churchill on the 1924–9 Conservative Ministry[1]

*I like things to happen and if they don't happen I like to make them happen.*

Churchill to Arthur Ponsonby MP, 1929[2]

On 7 June 1926, Churchill was being driven from Chartwell to London in the mist by Alexander Aley, his chauffeur, when they hit a van driven by a fishmonger, who suffered two broken ribs. Churchill offered him £77 (approximately £3,500) in compensation but he took the case to court. The jury exonerated Churchill, but he nonetheless sent the fishmonger £25.[3] A few years earlier, in February 1920, Churchill had survived a car crash in Whitehall, and, in a different incident, his chauffeur was fined £3 for speeding, despite his statement that he had been urged on by Churchill to get to the War Office faster.[4] Churchill tended to ignore speed limits and traffic lights; he only became less dangerous on the roads when he became prime minister and had a 'clanger' (that is, bell) to warn other drivers of his approach.[5] He was a compulsive risk-taker in peace and war, at the gambling tables and in the stock market, and his all-or-nothing attitude towards driving along roads and staking everything to win the General Strike was no different. On occasion it led to crashes, but in the last case it had helped bring victory.

'I decline utterly to be impartial as between the fire brigade and the fire,' proclaimed Churchill defending the partisanship of the *British Gazette* in a Commons debate on the Strike on 7 July. 'When you are in a great difficulty and in a fight of this kind, however unfortunate it may be, it is absolutely no use people pretending they do not know what side they are on.'[6] He deflected serious criticism, however, as so often in his career, with a well-timed joke, telling the Labour benches, 'Make your minds perfectly clear that if ever you let loose upon us again a General Strike, we will loose upon you another *British Gazette*.'[7] The impact of Churchill's jokes lay in his superb sense of comic timing delivering the punchline, an essential feature of his wit.

Churchill also understood the power of propaganda in all its forms. On 15 August, he was being filmed at the Treasury by Conservative Central Office for an informational movie, in which all Cabinet ministers took part. Several of them intensely disliked doing it, though not Churchill. Neville Chamberlain visited while the filming was taking place and reported to Lord Irwin, 'By Jove! how things hum in that office. The table groaned under mountains of books, Secretaries rushed in and out. Ronald McNeill* sat him down in an attitude of respectful attention and then, lighting a cigar of Brobdingnagian proportions, Winston grimaced, stormed, gesticulated, and orated until the film man got paralysed or his film burst.'[8]

After the humorous part of his letter, Chamberlain got down to the staple criticism of his presumed rival as successor to Baldwin. 'Winston constantly improves his position in the House and in the party,' he told the Viceroy.

> His speeches are extraordinarily brilliant and men flock in to hear him as they would to a first class entertainment at a theatre. The best show in London they say, and there is the weak point. So far as I can judge they think of it as a show and they are not prepared at present to trust his character and still less his judgement. Personally I can't help liking and admiring him more, the more I see of him, but it is always accompanied by a diminution of my intellectual respect for him. I have noticed that in all disputes of a departmental character that I have had with him he has had to give way because his case was not really well founded.[9]

Another explanation for Churchill's giving way would have been that Baldwin liked and trusted Chamberlain, whom he saw as his natural successor as Tory leader, and so tended to support him over his chancellor. In another letter, Chamberlain told Irwin, 'There is too deep a difference between our natures for me to feel at home with him or to regard him with affection. He is a brilliant wayward child who compels admiration but who wears out his guardians with the constant strain he puts upon them.'[10]

When Baldwin, ill with lumbago, went to Aix-les-Bains in eastern France for a three-week holiday on 24 August, he left Churchill in charge of the coal negotiations. Churchill used the opportunity to try to put pressure on the coal-owners to settle. 'Hideous reciprocal injuries are being

* The man who had thrown a book at Churchill in the Commons in 1912 was now his financial secretary at the Treasury.

inflicted by British hands on British throats,' he lamented in the Commons.[11] In the event he failed to find a solution, to his great frustration. The strike was damaging the Treasury's financial calculations, not least because it had to send £250,000 a week in social benefits to the districts affected. On 15 September, the day before Baldwin's return, Churchill's proposal that the Government coerce the coal-owners by instituting a minimum wage for miners was rejected by the Cabinet.

One hundred thousand miners returned to the pits in October, and by the end of November the strike was effectively over. When his coal-owning cousin Lord Londonderry wrote to Churchill to say the mine-owners deserved support because they were 'fighting Socialism', he replied, uncompromisingly, 'Both sides are represented by their worst and most unreasonable elements and by people selected for their obstinacy and combative qualities. It is not the duty of the coal owners, as coal owners, to fight Socialism. If they declare it their duty, how can they blame the Miners' Federation for pursuing political ends?'[12]

In 1927 the Baldwin Government passed the Trade Disputes and Trade Unions Act, which outlawed secondary action – thus making general strikes illegal – and ended the system whereby industrial workers had to pay union dues automatically, which was to lead to a significant drop in the union funding of the Labour Party. The political journalist C. E. Bechhofer Roberts believed that it was due to Churchill's support for this measure that 'the deep breach between Churchill and the Conservative Party has been healed'.[13] The Act was profoundly unpopular with organized labour, but was not repealed until 1947.

In the late summer of 1926, Churchill drew up a list of fourteen ways to save money at Chartwell. It read more like a Treasury minute than a letter to a beloved wife, complete with individually lettered sub-clauses:

> a) No more champagne is to be bought. Unless special directions are given, only the white or red wine, or whisky and soda are to be offered at luncheon, or dinner. The Wine Book is to be shown to me every week. No more port is to be opened without special instructions.
> b) Cigars must be reduced to four a day. None should be put on the table; but only produced out of my case. It is quite usual to offer only cigarettes.
> c) No fruit should be ordered through the household account; but only bought and paid for by you and me on special occasions.
> d) No cream unless specially sanctioned.
> e) When alone we do not need fish. Two courses and a sweet should suffice for dinner and one for luncheon . . .[14]

He also wanted to cut the cost of washing and to ration tins of boot polish. Next to nothing was done about any of it. 'I do not remember shortage of food or drink,' wrote Mary years later; 'or my father wearing dirty, crumpled shirts.'[15] No fewer than eleven guests signed the visitors' book at Chartwell that Christmas, and no diminution is noticeable in the frequency with which the Churchills entertained.

In January 1927, Churchill, his brother Jack and Randolph, who was then at Eton, toured the Mediterranean together. They watched Vesuvius erupt, visited Genoa, Pompeii and Herculaneum (where the fifteen-year-old Randolph was not allowed to see the indecent frescoes) and picnicked at the Parthenon in Athens. Staying at Malta with Admiral Keyes, who was then commander-in-chief of the Mediterranean Fleet, Churchill played his last game of polo, aged fifty-two. In Rome they had an audience with Pope Pius XI at the Vatican. 'The early part of the conversation was a little sticky,' Randolph recalled. 'Then my father and the Pope got on to the subject of the Bolsheviks and had a jolly half hour saying what they thought of them.'[16]

Churchill also met Mussolini in Rome, and released a press statement stating that the Italian Fascisti movement had 'rendered service to the whole world'.[17] Even worse, he added, 'If I had been an Italian, I am sure I should have been whole-heartedly with you from the start to finish in your triumphant struggle against the bestial appetites and passions of Leninism.'[18] This was of course to be intensely embarrassing later on, especially since detractors regularly quote the first twenty-five words but not the last eight. Mussolini had not yet invaded Abyssinia (modern-day Ethiopia), but Churchill's anti-Communism had undoubtedly blinded him, for the moment, to the brutality of Fascism. That anti-Communism was to the fore in February when Churchill supported a Cabinet decision to warn the Soviet Government, which had been secretly sowing Communist sedition in Britain through the Comintern, that if it continued to interfere in British domestic and imperial affairs, a breach of relations would follow. It was a terrible error. Churchill had made inspired use of the Secret Services during the Russian Civil War, actively supporting the work of highly effective agents such as Sidney Reilly and Boris Savinkov. Yet in 1927, in order to prove to Moscow that they knew the Comintern was conducting subversive operations in Britain and India, the Cabinet revealed that the intelligence agencies had broken the Soviet ciphers, which, for a very short-lived political advantage, led Moscow to adopt a new, unbreakable system. Churchill was appalled, and learned that in intelligence matters it was best not to let the enemy know what you know.

January 1927 saw the largest intake of new members in the Other Club's history, including Lindemann, Keynes (further evidence of Churchill's tolerance of well-considered dissent) and the literary critic Desmond MacCarthy. Six months later, the Tory politician Oliver Stanley and the traditionalist painter Alfred Munnings joined too. Churchill was not an admirer of modern art.* Anthony Eden turned down the offer to join as he said he did not like dining clubs. Admiral Keyes was invited to join and when he baulked at the £5 entry fee, Churchill pointed out the other, unspoken aspect of the Club: 'It will keep you in touch with many important people who are active at or near the centre of things.'[19] Keyes joined.

The third volume of *The World Crisis* was serialized in February. Haig was still very popular in Britain, and Churchill's critique of his attritional Western Front strategy was highly controversial. 'In all the British offensives,' Churchill noted, 'the British casualties were never less than three to two and often nearly double the corresponding German losses.'[20] He rightly attributed this to the fact that for most of the conflict Germany was on the defensive. In the book, he asked the central question of the day, indeed of the European twentieth century: 'Will a new generation in their turn be immolated to square the black accounts of Teuton and Gaul? Will our children bleed and gasp again in devastated lands? Or will there spring from the very fires of conflict that reconciliation of the three giant combatants, which would unite their genius and secure to each in safety and freedom a share in rebuilding the glory of Europe?'[21]

Despite Haig's popularity – a million people were to attend his funeral the following year after he had died of a heart attack† – the reviews were generally laudatory. Keynes wrote in the *Nation and Athenaeum* that it was 'a tractate against war – more effective than the work of a pacifist could be'.[22] Keynes had read Churchill's attitude well. Commenting on the proofs of Beaverbrook's new book, *Politicians and the War*, Churchill fulminated, 'Think of all these people – decent educated, the story of the past laid out before them – What to avoid – what to do etc patriotic, loyal, clean – trying their utmost – What a ghastly muddle they made of it! *Unteachable from infancy to tomb* – There is the first and main characteristic of mankind . . . Yours ever, W [P.S.] No more War.'[23]

Such was his reputation as a speaker by this time that the clamour for tickets to the Commons gallery when Churchill presented his third Budget on 11 April 1927 was likened to that for a popular sporting event. The

* 'Alfred,' Churchill once asked Munnings, 'if you met Picasso coming down the street would you join me in kicking his arse?' 'Yes sir, I would,' Munnings replied. (Gilbert, *Other Club* p. 93.)

† This prompted Churchill to tell his son that, although sixty-six was young to die, 'Yet it is the best of exits' (CAC RDCH 1/3/1).

Prince of Wales attended, and Baldwin reported to the King, 'The scene was quite sufficient to show that Mr Churchill as a star turn has a power of attraction which nobody in the House of Commons can excel.'[24] Naval Estimates were again reduced, to £56 million, and taxes on alcohol and tobacco increased, but with the General Strike and the coal dispute leaving a hole in the public finances of £30 million the Chancellor could do little to aid industrial recovery. But he was praised in the press for his austerity Budget. Two days later he declared, 'It only shows the British public, and the great nation which inhabits this somewhat foggy island, are less likely to be grateful for benefits received than they are for evils averted.'[25]

After one of the Budget debates, Lord Monsell congratulated Churchill on a crushing retort and asked him how he did it. 'Bobby, it's patience,' Churchill replied. 'I've waited two years to get that one off.'[26] In a debate on the Finance Bill on 19 May, he made the ideological point that 'If you strike at savings you at once propagate the idea of, "Let us eat, drink and be merry, for to-morrow we die." That is at once the inspiration and the mortal disease by which the Socialist philosophy is affected.'[27] He privately criticized the tendency of bureaucracies to expand unless they were constantly reined back. 'It is really intolerable the way these civil departments browse onwards like a horde of injurious locusts,' he told Clementine.[28]

Although Churchill had supported the idea that the Royal Navy should be at parity in battleships and aircraft carriers with the United States in the Washington Naval Treaty of 1922, five years later, after a huge American naval building programme, the United States also wanted parity in cruisers. 'There can really be no parity between a power whose navy is its life and a power whose navy is only for prestige,' Churchill wrote in a Cabinet memorandum in June 1927. 'It always seems to be assumed that it is our duty to humour the United States and minister to their vanity. They do nothing for us in return but exact their last pound of flesh.'[29] In July he went further, writing that although it was 'quite right in the interests of peace' to keep repeating the mantra that war with the United States was 'unthinkable',

> Everyone knows that this is not true. However foolish and disastrous such a war would be, it is in fact, the only basis upon which the [British–American] Naval discussions . . . are proceeding. We do not wish to put ourselves in the power of the United States. We cannot tell what they might do if at some future date they were in a position to give us orders about our policy, say, in India, or Egypt, or Canada . . . Moreover tonnage parity means that Britain can be starved into obedience to any American decree . . . Evidently on the basis of American naval superiority, speciously disguised as parity, immense dangers overhang the future of the world.[30]

Churchill had been chairman of the English-Speaking Union since 1921, but for him the interests of the Empire trumped even his belief in the fraternal union of the English-speaking peoples. The following year he 'talked very freely about the U.S.A.' to the Conservative politician James Scrymgeour-Wedderburn, after dinner at Chartwell. 'He thinks they are arrogant, fundamentally hostile to us, and that they wish to dominate world politics,' noted the future MP. 'He thinks their "Big Navy" talk is a bluff which we ought to call.'[31] Churchill sensibly confined such blatantly anti-American remarks to the private sphere. In February 1928 he even told the Cabinet that in order to stay in competition with the United States 'We could add £20 or £30 million more to naval estimates if necessary.'[32] It was a far cry from what he had been saying three years earlier about Japan. Though from a later perspective it seems extraordinary, the conversion of Churchill to becoming what was called a 'Big Fleeter' was not down to threats from Germany or Japan, but derived from a sense of competitiveness with the United States.[33]

'Winston remains the figure most interesting to the general public,' Chamberlain wrote to Irwin in August. 'He has materially improved his position in the Party, and it is admitted on all sides that he has no equal in the House of Commons. His manner with the Opposition is so good-humoured that although they often interrupt him, they look forward to his speeches as the finest entertainment the House can offer.'[34] On the third reading of the Trade Unions Bill, for example, Churchill was interrupted by Labour MPs as he built up to his peroration, whereupon he said, 'Of course it is perfectly possible for honourable Members to prevent my speaking, and of course I do not want to cast my pearls before' – long pause – 'those who do not want them.' Chamberlain recorded 'a roar of delight' lasting for several minutes. Later on in the same letter, he could not resist the observation, 'Winston's greatest admirers still distrust his judgement.'[35] Baldwin himself wrote at this time, 'Winston's position is curious. Our people like him. They love listening to him in the House; look on him as a star turn and settle down in the stalls with anticipatory grins. But for the leadership, they would turn him down every time. If anything happened to me, the best men are Neville and Hogg.'[36] Douglas Hogg was attorney-general, and a safe pair of hands, but Chamberlain was always the heir apparent.

Churchill effectively forced Lord Cecil of Chelwood (the former Lord Robert Cecil) to resign as chancellor of the Duchy of Lancaster in October, when he led Cabinet resistance to American proposals at the Geneva Conference on naval disarmament, which had opened in February. Cecil was willing to restrain the size of the British cruiser fleet, which was already the world's largest, but Churchill was not. 'We do completely disagree on the main issue,' Cecil had written to him as early as July. 'You believe that future war is practically certain, that the best way of avoiding it is the old prescription of preparedness, and that in any case the first duty of the Government is to collect such armaments as may be necessary to prevent defeat.'[37] It was indeed an accurate assessment of Churchill's position. By contrast, Cecil argued that collective security through reliance on the League of Nations was the best way to preserve peace. Cecil's elder brother, the 4th Marquess of Salisbury, wrote to Irwin, 'The crisis was reached when Winston avowedly voted for a particular proposition (which was carried in the Cabinet) because he thought it would defeat the Conference. Bob thereupon blew up and said that if the Conference broke down, he would resign. And he did.'[38] Cecil did not hold office again. Four decades after Lord Randolph's resignation, a Cecil had fallen victim to a Churchill. The Conference ended without agreement, to Churchill's relief.

In mid-December, Churchill set out to the Cabinet a radical proposal for completely changing local taxation by cutting industrial rates by 75 per cent and abolishing business and agricultural rates altogether, with central government taking on the rest of the burden. He hoped this would reduce unemployment, relieve small struggling firms of a restrictive tax and stimulate the growth of new industry. Chamberlain wrote that the plan was 'characteristic of Winston in its ingenuity, audacity and vagueness'.[39] The discussions between the two men became fraught. 'I accused Winston of reckless advocacy of schemes the effects of which he himself didn't understand,' Chamberlain reported to Irwin. 'He accused me of pedantry, of inexplicable coolness towards ideas which were not my own, and of personal jealousy of himself. At times feelings became rather acute.'[40] After much deliberation, it was agreed that one-third of the business and agricultural rates would be retained, which Churchill accepted stoically, telling Baldwin that the Cabinet was 'defacing the classical purity of the conception for the sake of an easier passage'.[41]

On 12 February, Clementine underwent two mastoid operations on her middle ear, one conducted at No. 11 at 2.30 p.m. and the next at midnight. 'If you should turn out – which I do not doubt – to be a fearless man, you will know where you get it from,' Churchill wrote to Randolph the next day.[42]* Churchill read passages from the Psalms to her, and Mary

* The previous month, Churchill had written to Randolph at Eton about his handwriting, or what he called the 'calligraphic elucidations' in his son's letters: 'In the early years of manhood, a really venomous and misleading handwriting will be a serious handicap to you. Your handwriting is perverse. One can guess what you mean as a rule, but proper names remain indecipherable.' (The word 'calligraphic' in his own letter was itself virtually indecipherable.) A

later recalled how close the illness had made her parents.[43] By April Clementine had made a complete recovery, and Churchill wrote to her about Randolph's character. He reported an argument on the existence of God that their son had had with Percy Grigg, where 'he more than defended his dismal position. The logical strength of his mind, the courage of his thought, and the brutal and sometimes repulsive character of his rejoinders impressed me very forcibly. He is far more advanced than I was at his age, and quite out of the common – for good or ill.'[44] Sadly it was all too often to be for ill. Randolph started to drink heavily in his mid-twenties and his 'brutal and sometimes repulsive' rejoinders were often directed against a father whose talents he knew he could never approach. It was hard for Randolph to be the son of a brilliant public figure, of course, but his father had himself overcome that difficulty. In her reply, Clementine accurately predicted, 'He is certainly going to be an interest, an anxiety and an excitement in our lives. I do hope he will always care for us.'[45] Tragically, he did not.

In early April, Churchill discovered a new passion to add to that for painting, one on which he would spend considerably more time during the Second World War. 'I am becoming a film fan,' he told Clementine, 'and last week I went to see *The Last Command*, a very fine anti-Bolshevik film, and *Wings* [the first film to win an Oscar for Best Picture] which is all about aeroplane fighting and perfectly marvellous.'[46] It was to be the start of a love affair with the silver screen, from which he was to make a large proportion of his income writing film scripts, though sadly for movies that never got made. His love of film sprang from his romantic and imaginative nature and his eclectic interests, as well as from his fascination with history, politics and propaganda. It was later to become his chief form of relaxation.*

Churchill's fourth Budget speech, on 23 April 1928, was no fewer than 15,000 words long (longer than this chapter). He increased child tax credits, saying that it was 'another application of our general policy of helping the producer'.[47] He was able to announce the de-rating scheme, which listeners did not know had been watered down to incorporate Chamberlain's reservations. ('Neville's letter is tyrannical but let him strut,' he

---

week later he continued, 'Some boobies even have illegible signatures. They can often be punished by having their letters put aside until they choose to write again.' (CAC RDCH 1/3/1.)

* Captain (later Professor Sir) Michael Howard, who guarded him at Chequers, recalls Churchill watching a gangster film. 'From the encouraging noises that came from the depths of the chair it was clear that he was enjoying it hugely. "Go on . . . hit him!" he would growl. "Look out! He's behind the door! Oh you fool!"' (Howard, *Captain Professor* p. 59.)

wrote to Grigg about one set of complaints.)[48] The Budget was considered a major success by the press, and Lord Derby wrote to tell him that it was 'not merely the Budget of an electioneer but of a statesman'.[49] Freddie Guest was even more positive: 'It seems to me that you have taken a sure step towards your future premiership.'[50]

In August 1919 Churchill had supported the introduction of what was called the Ten Year Rule, which decreed that the Defence Estimates would henceforth be based on the assumption that 'the British Empire will not be engaged in any great war during the next ten years and that no Expeditionary Force is required for this purpose'.[51] Intended to realize a peace dividend, it did great damage by encouraging complacency in the Treasury and Service ministries. In July 1928, Churchill made another error of judgement when he persuaded the Committee of Imperial Defence to make the Ten Year Rule a rolling one rather than subject to annual renewal, 'as a standing assumption that at any given date there will be no major war for ten years from that date'.[52] The Cabinet ratified it, against Balfour's objections. It was only finally abolished in March 1932, before Adolf Hitler had come to power but considerably less than ten years before the outbreak of the next war.

Churchill spent the summer at Chartwell finishing the fourth volume of *The World Crisis* and writing an autobiography to be called *My Early Life*.* He put the fact that he had not been chosen to deputize in Cabinet during Baldwin's long summer holiday down to the 'serious . . . handicap I have to carry in the Party by warning them off the Protectionist question . . . Half the Tory party are religiously convinced about tariffs. Really I feel very independent of them all.'[53] Writing to Baldwin, he said, 'I have had a delightful month building a cottage and dictating a book. Two hundred bricks and two thousand words a day.'[54] Yet for all his professed independence and his life outside politics, the Churchills had not given up their ultimate ambition. 'If you are ever made Prime Minister I think you will incur great displeasure here if Charley is not included in the Cabinet,' Clementine wrote of the Marquis of Londonderry from Mount Stewart in Ulster. 'I long for my Pig meanwhile. I am used to him, odious as he sometimes is, and cannot do with these inbred sprogs of the *ancien régime*!'[55]† By the time Churchill did become prime minister, Londonderry had ruled himself out as a candidate for ministerial office by his

* In America, *A Roving Commission*.

† Londonderry explained Churchill's success in life entirely in terms of the Vane-Tempest-Stewart blood inherited from his paternal grandmother, ignoring the several family members who had died insane.

refusal to condemn Hitler, whom he had met several times and greatly admired, until after the outbreak of war.[56]

In September 1928, when shooting stag and grouse with the King at Balmoral, Churchill reported to Clementine on the daughter of the Duke and Duchess of York, Princess Elizabeth, who was then two and a half. He said that she 'is a character. She has an air of authority and reflectiveness astonishing in an infant.'[57] Elizabeth was then third in line to the throne but, as the Prince of Wales had yet to marry, Churchill could hardly have guessed that she would ever be queen, let alone that he would be her first prime minister. His other statement from Balmoral, in reply to Clementine's fretting about 'household matters', came straight from the Victorian aristocrat in him: 'All will be well. Servants exist to save one trouble, and should never be allowed to disturb one's inner peace. There will always be food to eat, and sleep will come even if the beds are not made. Nothing is worse than worrying about trifles.'[58] His anti-Americanism had still not abated either. 'H.M. also shares my views about the Yankees,' he wrote on 27 September, 'and expressed them in picturesque language.'[59]

Herbert Hoover's victory in the presidential election on 7 November seemed to make matters worse, because of his tough stance on the repayment of war debts. 'Poor old England,' Churchill wrote to Clementine, who was ill in a nursing home from blood poisoning caused by infected tonsils, 'she is being slowly but surely forced into the shade.'[60] Here was another indication of his growing sense that Britain – he used the word 'England' interchangeably with 'Britain', to the fury of some Scots – was being eclipsed in power and might by what he called 'the Great Republic'. 'Why can't they let us alone? They have exacted every penny owing from Europe . . .' he wrote to Clementine, 'surely they might leave us to manage our own affairs.'[61] Clementine wrote back that he ought to be foreign secretary, 'But I am afraid your known hostility to America might stand in the way. You would have to try and understand and master America and make her like you.'[62] His hostility to America was not in fact known, as he kept it assiduously and deliberately out of his Commons and public speeches.

Alfred Duff Cooper, a Conservative MP who had won a DSO for gallantry in 1918, was elected to the Other Club in the spring of 1928, as were Lord Rothermere's son Esmond Harmsworth, and Field Marshal Sir Claud Jacob, the Commander-in-Chief of the British Army on the Rhine. In July, Boothby and the comic novelist P. G. Wodehouse also joined. 'I enjoyed the dinners tremendously,' recalled Wodehouse, 'though being overwrought in such company.'[63]* On 31 January 1929, Keynes wagered Churchill £20 to £10 at the Other Club that after the next election the Conservatives would not constitute more than half the House of Commons. Esmond Harmsworth and the owner of the *Daily Telegraph*, Sir William Berry (later Lord Camrose), each bet him £500 to £25 that the Conservatives would not exceed half the House of Commons by fifty seats or more.[64] Continuing high unemployment, the legacy of the General Strike and the Trade Disputes Act, and a long period in power had weakened the Baldwin Government, for which Churchill had some responsibility. Yet once more he was fortunate in his defeat: he would not have wanted to be chancellor of the Exchequer during the Wall Street Crash later that year.

In early March, Churchill published *The Aftermath*, the fourth volume of *The World Crisis*, for which he had been paid a £2,000 advance, more than enough to cover the £60 he would shortly be paying Keynes, Harmsworth and Berry. 'The story of the human race is War,' he wrote towards the end of this work. 'Except for brief and precarious interludes there has never been peace in the world; and before history began murderous strife was universal and unending. But the modern developments surely require severe and active attention.'[65] On 1 March he gave a copy to Chamberlain, who annotated on the back 'June 1929', suggesting that he read it over the next three months.

Churchill then signed a contract for a multi-volume biography of the 1st Duke of Marlborough for the enormous advance of £20,000 (£1 million in today's money). 'How strange it is that the past is so little understood and so quickly forgotten,' he wrote to Raymond Asquith's widow Katharine. 'We live in the most thoughtless of ages. Every day headlines and short views. I have tried to drag history up a little nearer to our own times in case it should be helpful as a guide in present difficulties.'[66]

In Churchill's fifth and last Budget, delivered on 15 April 1929 (only Walpole, Pitt, Peel and Gladstone had delivered as many) taxes on alcohol were raised less than previously, but death duties by more. 'The failure of beer was repaired by the harvest of death,' he said.[67] He attacked waste with the words 'Squandermania . . . is the policy . . . of buying a biscuit early in the morning and walking about all day looking for a dog to give it to.' He abolished the tax on tea and lowered the tax on betting but, despite an election looming on 30 May, that was about all he could responsibly do. Chamberlain had to admit to Irwin that Churchill's Budget

* After Wodehouse, a harmless naïf, had made five (unpolitical) broadcasts for the Germans in 1941, Churchill said, 'Let him go to hell – as soon as there's a vacant passage' (Marian Holmes's Diary p. 17).

speech 'kept the House fascinated and enthralled by its wit, audacity, adroitness and power'.[68] Baldwin wrote, 'I have never heard you speak better, and that's saying a great deal.'[69]

In April 1929 Churchill made his first ever radio broadcast, warning the public to 'avoid chops and changes of policy; avoid thimble-riggers and three-card trick men; avoid all needless borrowings; and above all avoid, as you would the smallpox, class warfare and violent political strife'.[70] He was a natural performer on the radio, and recognized immediately its capacity to project his message into millions of homes free from the distorting prism of newspaper reportage and editorial bias.

Churchill published his election address on 10 May, with a large photograph on the front cover of himself in an astrakhan coat, seated with a cane in his hand. 'Judged by every test that can be applied,' it claimed, 'we are a stronger, richer, more comfortable, more numerous, more fully employed community than we were in 1924 . . . We claim to have conducted the affairs of this country in a clean, honest and disinterested manner, to have promoted peace abroad, to have preserved peace and freedom at home.'[71] He described the General Strike as an 'unconstitutional outrage' which was 'signally defeated', but which 'robbed the Exchequer of £400 millions which would otherwise have provided wages for the unemployed'.[72]

Churchill boasted of his Widows', Orphans' and Old Age Contributory Pensions Act 1925, which introduced a widow's benefit for the first time. 'When I think of the fate of poor old women, so many of whom have no one to look after them and nothing to live on at the end of their lives, I am glad to have had a hand in all that structure of pensions and insurance which no other country can rival and which is especially a help to them.'[73] For the first time in history, all women aged twenty-one and over would be able to vote in this election. Churchill quickly made his peace with the new state of things. In January 1931 he wrote to Lindemann with an idea for an article that would ask, 'To what heights will the ascendancy of women go? Will there be a woman prime minister? . . . A world controlled by women?'[74]

On election night, Churchill sat at a desk at 10 Downing Street keeping the score in red ink as the results came over the ticker-tape machine. Tom Jones recorded him 'sipping whisky and soda, getting redder and redder, rising often and going to glare at the machine himself, hunching his shoulders, bowing his head like a bull about to charge . . . As Labour gain after Labour gain was announced, Winston became more and more flushed with anger, left his seat and confronted the machine in the passage; with his shoulders hunched he glared at the figures, tore the sheets and behaved as though if any more Labour gains came along he would smash the whole apparatus. His ejaculations to the surrounding staff were quite unprintable.'[75] They would have been even worse had he known what a devastating watershed moment it was for him. He had been in office for more than four-fifths of the past twelve years, yet over the next ten he would not hold office at all.

Labour won 288 seats in the 1929 general election, the Conservatives 260 and the Liberals 59. The Conservatives won 8.66 million of the popular vote, Labour 8.39 million and the Liberals trailed with 5.31 million. For the first time over 50,000 Britons voted Communist. Churchill, standing as a Constitutionalist Conservative, won Epping with a 4,967 majority over the Liberal candidate. For a few days after the election he and Baldwin tried to build a coalition with the Liberals to keep MacDonald out, but they were blocked by both Lloyd George and the Tory Protectionists. So on 8 June, when MacDonald became prime minister again, Churchill found himself on the Opposition front bench for the first time in his life.

He decided to use the long parliamentary summer recess to undertake a spectacular three-month tour of Canada and the United States, taking Randolph, Jack and Jack's son Johnny, but not Clementine who had to undergo another operation on her tonsils. They set sail on 3 August on board the *Empress of Australia*. Also aboard was Leo Amery, the former Dominions Secretary whom he had known since Harrow. 'The real thing is to get rid of the blight of Winston at the Treasury,' Amery had written to Chamberlain three months earlier. 'Cannot you convince Stanley that there can be no Imperial policy if the key position in the State is held by one who is definitely hostile to the Empire?'[76] Needless to say, Churchill was anything but hostile to the Empire; he just did not believe that the dearer food that came from Imperial Preference would help endear it to Britons.

Churchill invited Amery for dinner. They discussed 'such themes as if one is really afraid of death when it comes and would one in fact stand up straight to a firing party'.[77] Churchill told Amery that his sole consolation over the Dardanelles disaster 'was that God wished things to be prolonged in order to sicken Mankind of war, and that therefore He had interfered with a project that would have brought the war to a speedier conclusion'.[78] He also declared that the existence of the Almighty could be deduced by 'the existence of Lenin and Trotsky, for whom a Hell [is] needed'.[79] More seriously, he told Amery, a leading Protectionist, that if the Tory Party adopted Imperial Preference he would leave politics and go off to make money. Otherwise, he said, 'I propose to stick to you with all the loyalty of a leech.'[80] He claimed that 'He had been all he ever wanted to be short of the highest post which he saw no prospect of, and anyhow politics were not as they had been. The level was lower.'[81] There were no longer great men of the calibre of Gladstone, Salisbury or Morley. At the end of their discussion, which after they left the restaurant had continued in Churchill's cabin, Amery got up to go and Churchill to dress for bed, putting on 'a long silk nightshirt and a woolly tummy band over it'. Amery concluded, 'The key to Winston is to realize that he is a mid-Victorian, steeped in the politics of his father's period, and unable ever to get the modern point of view.'[82] In fact it was Amery's pan-imperial economic policies that were already out of date and soon to be doomed.

The Churchills arrived in Quebec on 9 August and stayed at the imposing Château Frontenac Hotel, with its magnificent views down the St Lawrence River. From there, Churchill dragooned the local welcoming dignitaries to refight the 1759 Battle of Quebec over the golf course at the top of the Heights of Abraham. He sent Randolph and Johnny to clamber up the cliffs as General James Wolfe's army had done, while he took the position of the Marquis de Montcalm at the top. The party then began their long journey across the continent from Quebec to Vancouver. They travelled in great style thanks to the generosity of both the Canadian Pacific Railways and an American admirer, Charles Schwab of the Bethlehem Steel Corporation, who provided them with a saloon cabin with double beds, an observation room and a dining car. 'Fancy cutting down those beautiful trees we saw this afternoon', Churchill said outside Quebec, 'to make pulp for those bloody newspapers, and calling it Civilization.'[83] After Montreal they went to Ottawa, where they met the 'most kind and cordial' Prime Minister, William Lyon Mackenzie King. (Churchill also recognized the trumpeter of the 4th Hussars from their days in India, who gave him a box of cigars.)[84] Then they passed through Toronto, Niagara Falls, Winnipeg, Regina, Banff, Edmonton, Calgary and the Alberta oilfields. Randolph opined that the oil barons weren't cultured enough to spend their vast wealth properly. 'Cultured people', his father replied, 'are merely the glittering scum which floats upon the deep river of production.'[85] They visited Lake Louise, where Churchill painted the gorgeous scenery. He protected the top of his nose from the sun by taping a piece of gauze over it, which he took off when photographers were present.[86] He made eleven speeches to large and very welcoming audiences across Canada.

'The United States are stretching their tentacles out in all directions,' Churchill reported to Clementine on 15 August, 'but the Canadian national spirit and personality is becoming so powerful and self-contained that I do not think that we need to fear the future.'[87] 'Darling, I am greatly attracted to this country,' he added twelve days later. 'Immense developments are going forward. There are fortunes to be made in many directions.' He was also reflecting on politics and his own career. If Chamberlain became leader of the Conservative Party, 'or anyone else of that kind, I clear out of politics and see if I cannot make you and the kittens a little more comfortable before I die. Only one goal still attracts me . . . However the time to take decisions is not yet.'[88] (Given his attraction to that 'one goal', it was perhaps cavalier of him to leave Britain for three whole months when the future direction of Conservative opposition policy, especially over such important issues as India and Protectionism, would be decided without him.)

After Vancouver, where they saw a bear begging for biscuits, the party entered Prohibition America and were given a bottle of champagne by an admiring customs official who checked their luggage.[89] 'We realize one hundred million pounds sterling a year from our liquor taxes,' Churchill told the *Appleton Post-Crescent* newspaper, 'which I understand you give to your bootleggers.' From Seattle they drove through the Giant Redwood forests in California and stayed with the newspaper magnate William Randolph Hearst, where Churchill was delighted to find that butterflies abounded. They were hosted by Hearst's wife at San Simeon, and later by the actress Marion Davies, his mistress, in Los Angeles. 'Two magnificent establishments, two charming wives,' Churchill reported to Clementine. 'Complete indifference to public opinion, a strong liberal and democratic outlook; a fifteen million daily circulation, oriental hospitalities, extreme personal courtesy (to us at any rate), the appearance of a Quaker elder.'[90] When they went fishing off Hearst's yacht near Santa Catalina Island, Churchill caught a marlin that weighed 188 pounds, which he reeled aboard in under twenty minutes.[91]

On 21 September, Churchill met Charlie Chaplin at a large party given in his honour by Marion Davies at her 110-room Ocean House in Santa Monica. Chaplin was perhaps the most famous actor in the world at the time, and despite his support for Communism Churchill got on very well with him – yet another example of his not allowing politics to prejudice friendship. Chaplin later recalled Churchill standing apart, 'Napoleon-like, with his hand in his waistcoat, watching the dancing'.[92] By 3 a.m. they had decided that, if Chaplin would play Napoleon, Churchill would write the film script. 'Think of the possibilities for humour,' Churchill said. 'Napoleon in his bathtub arguing with his imperious brother who's all dressed up, bedecked in gold braid, and using this opportunity to place Napoleon in a position of inferiority. But Napoleon, in his rage, deliberately splashes water over his brother's fine uniform and he has to exit ignominiously from him. This is not alone clever psychology. It is action and fun.'[93] The two men met several times more, including at the actor's film studio where Chaplin showed Churchill the rushes of his forthcoming movie *City Lights*. Churchill called him 'a marvellous comedian – bolshy [Bolshevik] in politics and delightful in conversation'.[94]*

The Churchill party then crossed the American continent, passing through Yosemite National Park and Chicago before finally arriving in New York on 5 October, where they stayed in the Fifth Avenue house of Bernard Baruch, whom Churchill had befriended when the financier had been chairman of the War Industries Board in 1918. After that, they visited Washington, where they met President Hoover, and went to Richmond, Philadelphia and various Civil War battlefields. Baruch tried to arrange for Churchill to meet Franklin Roosevelt, then governor of New York, at the end of October, but the invitation was declined; nor was one extended to Churchill to visit Roosevelt in Albany.[95] Roosevelt's elusiveness might have been influenced by his recollection of their first meeting, but it is more likely because he was busy dealing with the aftershock of 'Black Thursday', 24 October 1929, when the American stock market crashed.

On 19 September, Churchill had written to Clementine setting out his considerable income since leaving office in June. He listed publishing advances of £7,700, payments for newspaper articles of £1,875, speaking fees of £300, as yet unwritten Canadian and American articles worth £2,750 and profits on shares of £9,200. Added together, it totalled £21,825 (approximately £1.09 million in today's money) in only three and a half months.[96] 'So here we have really recovered in a few weeks a small fortune,' he told her. 'This "mass of manoeuvre"† is of the utmost importance and must not be frittered away.'[97] Despite this stricture, in the same letter he asked her to start building another wing at Chartwell. Six days later, against Baruch's advice, he invested £3,000 in the American stock market. He told his wife this had 'the best possible chances of success'.[98] Churchill was later to blame the Wall Street Crash on what he called 'an orgy of speculation'. If that was so, it was an orgy in which he himself had been an enthusiastic participant.[99] 'I am a member of your profession,' Winston Churchill once wrote to a newspaper editor in 1945. 'I have never had any money except what my pen has brought me.'[100] It was a proud boast, and

* When Chaplin visited Chartwell in 1931, the children managed to persuade him to do his bowler-hat-and-walking-stick routine. Churchill asked him what role he was playing next and Chaplin answered Jesus Christ. Churchill said, 'Have you cleared the rights?' (Churchill, *Tapestry* p. 35.)

† A Napoleonic strategic term meaning a strong central reserve of troops.

largely true, but also an unintended confession that he was a generally unsuccessful stock-market speculator.

The ledger books of his stockbrokers Vickers da Costa reveal that Churchill speculated in a very wide selection of bonds, equities and currencies. In the early 1920s, for example, these included South African and Rhodesian goldmines, the Cunard shipping line, Chinese 4½ per cent bonds, hotel company debentures, the French franc, the British Cellulose Company, British American Tobacco, Eagle Oil, the Burma Corporation, Hungarian 7½ per cent bonds and the Shanghai Electrical Company. He suspended share-dealing during his chancellorship – although Clementine continued to buy small amounts of American equities – but immediately on resigning in June 1929 he bought shares in the Western Union Telegraph, British Oxygen, the Pennroad Corporation, Sherwood Star Goldmining, Canadian Pacific Railways, Western Union Telegraph and the International Nickel Corporation.[101] He was no long-term investor, sometimes buying and selling stock four times in a fortnight; as he told his Canadian commodities trader of an investment in American Rolling Mills in 1929, 'I do not expect to hold these shares for more than a few weeks.'[102]*

His London stockbroker Cecil Vickers urged him to stop dealing in 'gambling stock' that year, but he did not, even though companies such as Strike Oil, in which he had a $2,000 stake, signally failed to live up to its name and went into liquidation. Churchill was a gambler – in 1923 his losses at Biarritz cost him £2,000, more than the cost of the new wing at Chartwell – and he essentially saw stock market speculation as gambling on a much larger scale.[103] When he listened to friends such as Sir Ernest Cassel, Bernard Baruch and Sir Abe Bailey, he tended to make money, as he did when he bet on a certainty, such as in his massive buying of Shell Oil and Shell Transport & Trading Co. stock in early 1924 while advising them on the purchase of Anglo-Persian, which would leave them the largest oil company in the world (a transaction which in those days was neither immoral nor illegal).[104] Otherwise, however, he was no more successful on the Stock Exchange than on the tables at Monte Carlo and Biarritz.

With his preternatural capacity for being at the centre of events when history was being made, Churchill was actually on Wall Street on Black Thursday. The very next day, from directly under his window in the Savoy Plaza Hotel, a man threw himself fifteen storeys down on to the pavement below, causing, as Churchill reported, 'a wild commotion and the arrival

* In March 1931 he traded in the shares of the American mail-order retailer Montgomery Ward sixteen times in four days, on borrowed money.

of the fire brigade'.[105] Churchill himself lost around £10,000 (approximately £500,000) virtually overnight. In the Great Depression that engulfed the industrial world for the next three years, world trade fell by two-thirds, unemployment rose dramatically across the West and the conditions were created in Germany for the rise of Adolf Hitler. Yet even before Churchill left New York on 30 October bound for Southampton – where Clementine met him on the boat-train platform to hear their catastrophic financial news[106] – he was describing the Crash in a newspaper article as 'only a passing episode in the march of a valiant and serviceable people who by fierce endeavour are hewing new paths for men, and showing to all nations much that they should attempt and much that they should avoid'.[107] When someone commiserated with him on his stock market losses, Churchill shot back, 'Yes, how much better if I had spent it. What is money made for except to spend?'[108]

Churchill's journey around America, meeting the President, senators, governors, congressmen and large numbers of ordinary Americans, entirely dissipated his anti-Americanism, and it was never to reappear, despite occasional frustrations with individual Americans during the Second World War. 'You are the friends we would like to see most strongly armed,' he told a dinner of the Iron and Steel Institute in New York on 25 October. 'We welcome every growth and development of every arm of the American Navy.'[109] Needless to say this went down well with his audience, who were providing the materials for building that Navy, but he meant it.

When Churchill returned to England on 5 November, his losses were such that economies had to be made. Chartwell was closed and dust-sheeted. Mary stayed in a cottage on the estate with her nanny, and her parents rented a furnished flat in London, having sold 2 Sussex Square in January 1925. In the past, Jack Churchill, who was a partner at Vickers da Costa, would occasionally cover his brother's losses, but these were too heavy, and by the summer of 1930 the list of his unpaid tradesmen's bills covered two pages.[110] It was also more than his journalism, very well paid though it was, could cover. Churchill's friends stepped forward: Ivor Guest guaranteed a loan, Bailey provided £2,000 and Cassel also helped out. Nonetheless, by the end of 1930, Churchill was £22,000 in debt (approximately £1.1 million in today's money) to various banks and insurance companies such as the Commercial Union, forcing him to put Chartwell on the market at the very high price of £30,000, for which there were no takers. In January 1931, when Jack had found £2,000 to help bail his brother out, Cecil Vickers gave Churchill the excellent advice to take a rest from the stock market until it saw an upturn.[111]

As before, Churchill got out of his financial difficulties by working harder, and by making sure his publishers paid the absolute maximum for his books (which is hardly a cardinal sin). In a sense we can thank his unsuccessful stock market speculation for the fact that so many fine books were written by Churchill in the 1930s. He also wrote screenplays for the Korda brothers, one of which was about Napoleon, and when he had earned £35,000 from his pen he reopened Chartwell. There was nothing hypocritical about Churchill's espousal of hard work and individual enterprise. After the death of Lady Sarah Wilson, Lord Randolph Churchill's sister, at sixty-four in October, only two of the 7th Duke of Marlborough's eleven children were still alive, further strengthening Churchill's belief that he did not have long to live and his conviction that he needed to provide for Clementine and their offspring.

Churchill was on board ship returning to England when Lord Irwin, the Viceroy, announced that the British Government would grant Dominion status to India. A Round Table Conference would be convened in London, attended by Indians, to discuss how it should happen. Dominion status, already enjoyed by Canada, Australia, South Africa, New Zealand, Newfoundland and the Irish Free State, effectively meant self-government, and thus ultimately independence and the removal of the jewel in the crown of the British Empire.

Churchill had no sympathy for or trust in the mainly Hindu professional and intellectual middle class in the big cities who were the driving force behind the independence movement, spearheaded by the Indian National Congress (INC). He resolved to fight both the Labour Government and the Tory Lord Irwin over the granting of Dominion status. 'You have the ideas of a subaltern a generation ago,' Irwin claimed eleven years later to have told Churchill at this time. 'There are a number of interesting Indians coming to the Round Table Conference and I really think it would be very valuable to you to talk to some of them to bring your ideas up to date.' 'I am quite satisfied with my views on India,' Churchill is reported to have replied, 'and I certainly don't want them disturbed by any bloody Indian.'[112] With Baldwin supporting Irwin, Churchill had little support in Parliament for his projected campaign, but much in the Conservative Party grassroots – though not a majority.[113] When Irwin succeeded to the title of Viscount Halifax in 1934, the Churchill family nicknamed him 'the Holy Fox', a hint at his political dexterity as well as a reference to his High Church predilections and love of fox-hunting.

'It is the duty of public men and political parties', Churchill wrote in the *Daily Mail* in November, 'to make it plain without delay that the extension of Dominion Status to India is not practicable at the present time and that any attempt to secure it will encounter the earnest resistance of the British nation.' He further called the idea of Home Rule for India 'criminally mischievous'. His argument was more subtle than the white supremacist one that his detractors made out, both at the time and since, although his own deliberately extravagant language made their job of caricaturing it much easier. At one point he described the Government of India Bill that followed the Round Table Conference as 'a catastrophe which will shake the world'.[114] Churchill believed that what the majority of Indians truly wanted was not representative government but good government, under the rule of law. He further thought that high standards of sanitation and public health, modern communications, the protection of minorities such as the Untouchables and Muslims from majority Hindu domination and balancing the interests of India's numerous and competing religions and regions were more important to Indians than their sovereign independence. He doubted – rightly, as it turned out – that the Indian princes (comprising maharajahs, rajahs, nawabs and others), who ruled over seventy million of India's population of 300 million, could retain their semi-autonomous status in a Congress-ruled sub-continent. Churchill never grasped that, like any other self-respecting peoples, the Indian nationalists wanted self-government first and foremost, from which they believed they would get – or, in this case, keep – good government. 'The odds are very heavy against us,' Churchill wrote of the battle in the Commons against the Bill. 'But I feel a strong sense that I am doing my duty, and expressing my sincere convictions.'[115]

Churchill's stance on India, for which he quite consciously threw away what appeared to be his last chance of winning the premiership, cannot be understood except in the light of the secular religion that he had made of the British Empire, and his Whiggish conviction that it was central to Britain's historical mission of progress. His belief had been strengthened as recently as 1927 by the book *Mother India* by an American sociologist Katherine Mayo, which depicted a sub-continent in the grip of forced marriage before puberty, indigenous medicine, gang-robbery, primitive gynaecology and backward agriculture, problems that the British were battling to overcome in the face of localized religious obscurantism.[116]

Having fought on the North West Frontier, Churchill was fully conscious of what the British Army had been doing militarily since the 1840s to protect northern India from Afghan tribes and the Russians, while keeping the peace between Muslims, Sikhs and Hindus, who he thought might massacre each other in communal riots were the British to leave. (In this, too, he was proved not wholly wrong.) As a Free Trader, he was convinced by Mayo's detailed arguments, supported by a large quantity of evidence, that far from Britain being an economic drain on India, trade had been mutually beneficial.[117] The fact that almost all the richest people in India were Indian merchants or princes, not Britons, struck him as further evidence that the British were not the exploitative colonialists of other European empires in Asia and Africa.

Mayo's paeans to the ways the British were attempting to educate the Untouchables, prevent cruelty to animals and improve medicine – all worthy projects regularly stymied by Hindu religious leaders – increased Churchill's antipathy to Indian independence.[118] 'Once we lose confidence in our mission in the East,' he said in a debate on Egyptian constitutional reform in December – his thoughts of course applied just as much to India – 'once we repudiate our responsibilities to foreigners and to minorities, once we feel ourselves unable calmly and fearlessly to discharge our duties to vast helpless populations, then our presence in those countries will be stripped of every moral sanction, and, resting only upon selfish interests or military requirements, it will be a presence which cannot long endure.'[119]

In June 1930, shortly after Mohandas Gandhi, the INC leader known to his followers as the 'Mahatma' (Great Soul), had been arrested and imprisoned for deliberately breaking salt tax laws in India, the Indian Statutory Commission, appointed by the Labour Government to inquire into constitutional reform and chaired by Sir John Simon, published its report. Much to Churchill's ire, it recommended a major step towards Indian self-government. It was this, not the appeasement of the Nazis, that was to lead to Churchill's break with the Tory leadership, and the start of his long years in the political wilderness.

While India and the stock market crash dominated the news and his public pronouncements, these were by no means his only interests. He also accepted a well-paid non-executive directorship, for the first and only time in his life, of a subsidiary company of Lord Inchcape's Peninsular & Oriental shipping line, and was a regular attendee at its board meetings for eight years. He continued to write articles for newspapers and magazines, read for his Marlborough biography and dictate *My Early Life*. From November 1931 he rented a large fifth-floor maisonette, 11 Morpeth Mansions, in Morpeth Terrace, an eight-minute walk from the House of Commons, whose spacious drawing and dining rooms on the fourth floor looked out on to Westminster Cathedral. It had a large roof terrace with a panoramic view, from which one can see the Houses of Parliament. The master-bedroom floor looks directly out at a mansion block that had the date of its construction – '1886' – prominently emblazoned on it. Every time Churchill looked out of his bedroom window, therefore, he saw the date of his father's resignation, the start of a period in the wilderness – nine years – that was almost exactly to mirror his own.

On 22 April 1930, the London Naval Treaty, which regulated submarine warfare and limited naval shipbuilding, was signed between Britain, Japan, France, Italy and the United States. Britain abandoned her claim for more trade-route protection ships than other maritime powers, and agreed to limit future naval construction in certain areas. Churchill denounced the Treaty: 'What a disastrous instrument it has been, fettering the unique naval knowledge we possess, and forcing us to spend our money on building wrong or undesirable ships.'[120] In May he complained, 'Never since the reign of Charles II has this country been so defenceless as this treaty will make it.'[121] This was unsurprisingly denounced as hypocritical, considering his cuts to the Admiralty's cruiser-building programme as chancellor, but he was fast being seen as the spokesman, on India and defence, of the Tory right.[122] He also kept up his reputation for sharp criticism in the Chamber, congratulating William Graham, the President of the Board of Trade, on his 'excellent speeches, very long, very careful and very lucid speeches, delivered without a note and often without a point'.[123]

In June Churchill delivered the Romanes Lecture at the Sheldonian Theatre at Oxford University, on 'Parliamentary Government and the Economic Problem', in which he proposed a way of taking the issue of Free Trade versus Protection out of the realm of partisan politics. His solution was for an economic sub-parliament made up of one-fifth of MPs plus economists and other technical experts, which could decide fiscal policy instead of the House of Commons. 'Winston is feeling horribly nervous about the Lecture,' Clementine told the Oxford economist Roy Harrod. 'He is overawed at the idea of addressing all the Learned Birds.'[124] (He was never overawed at the idea of addressing anybody, but Harrod would have appreciated the compliment.) 'I do not believe that the true principles can be discovered by our Parliamentary and electoral institutions, not even if they are guided by a faithful and energetic press,' Churchill said in the lecture. 'I doubt, however, whether Democracy, or Parliamentary Government, or even a General Election would make a decisively helpful contribution . . . It must be observed that economic problems, unlike political issues, cannot be solved by any expression, however vehement, of the national will, but only by taking the right action. You cannot cure cancer by a majority.'[125] He had certainly understood the nature of economics but his idea never got anywhere, and in the era of the dictators his critics misinterpreted it as an attempt to step back from parliamentary democracy. He actually hoped it would pave the way for the centrist government he always hankered after, by removing the most contentious matter of the day from the partisan political arena.[126]

When others were losing faith in capitalism during the Depression, Churchill did not. In August a young guest at Chartwell suggested that capitalism was collapsing. 'More mush!' he retorted. 'Capitalism will right itself. What is Capitalism? It is merely the observance of contract, that's all. That's why it will survive.'[127] He quite literally put his money where his mouth was, investing large amounts of the more than £100,000 he earned pre-tax between 1929 and 1937 in shares, buying nearly £3,000 of Marks & Spencer shares in 1930 and £6,760 of General Motors in 1931, and telling Cecil Vickers, his stockbroker, in July 1932, 'I do not think America is going to smash. On the contrary I believe they will quite soon begin to recover.'[128]

In the German elections on 14 September 1930, the Nazi Party received 6.4 million votes, taking 107 seats and becoming, with 18 per cent of the vote, the second largest party in the Reichstag. The Social Democrats won 143 seats, the Communists 77 and the Centre Party 68. A month later, Churchill told Prince Otto von Bismarck, the grandson of the great Chancellor, that he was 'convinced that Hitler or his followers [will] seize the first opportunity to resort to armed force'.[129] That hardly took much prescience – they had already tried in Munich in 1923 – but it showed that Hitler's activities were already of concern to him.

Balfour died on 19 March. 'As I observed him regarding with calm, firm and cheerful gaze the approach of Death,' Churchill wrote, 'I felt how foolish the Stoics were to make such a fuss about an event so natural and so indispensable to Mankind.'[130] (Churchill had organized a subscription of Balfour's friends to buy him a Rolls-Royce for his eightieth birthday in July 1928, and called for three cheers at the celebration.) F. E. Smith, Lord Birkenhead, Churchill's great friend, died of cirrhosis of the liver on 30 September, at only fifty-eight. 'He was a rock,' Churchill told the Other Club, 'a man one could love, a man one could play with, and have jolly times. At this narrow table where he sat so often among us, we feel his loss now . . . I do not think anyone knew him better than I did, and he was, after all, my dearest friend . . . Just at the time when we feel that our public men are lacking in the power to dominate events, he has been taken. This was the occasion, and these were the years, for the full fruition of his service to our country.'[131] Five years later he wrote in the *News of the World*, 'He had all the canine virtues in a remarkable degree – courage, fidelity, vigilance, love of the chase . . . F.E. was the only one of my contemporaries with whom I have derived the same pleasure and profit as I got from Balfour, Morley,

Asquith, Rosebery and Lloyd George . . . He seemed to have a double dose of human nature . . . F.E. banked his treasure in the hearts of his friends, and they will cherish his memory till their time is come.'[132]

It was a political as well as personal blow to Churchill: Birkenhead had supported him from inside the Conservative Party over India, Russia, the American Navy and much else. Had he not self-indulgently drunk himself to death, he could have been a great aid to Churchill in the struggle against the appeasement of Nazi Germany. Several times during the Second World War, Churchill turned to aides to say, 'How I miss F.E.,' believing that his 'presence would have made all the difference to the weight of the burden he had to carry'.[133] Jock Colville told Freddie Birkenhead, his son, that 'None of his later personal relationships were quite comparable, even with Max, Brendan and the Prof, to that with your father.'[134]

On 9 October, Baldwin announced that the Conservatives would seek a 'free hand' for the reintroduction of Protectionism at the next election. 'You will see our programme,' he wrote a week later to Lord Irwin in India. 'I think it probable Winston will resign on it.'[135] Forcing Churchill to resign from the Conservative Business Committee (the precursor to the Shadow Cabinet) might even have been part of the intention, leaving the field clear for Baldwin's preferred candidate, Neville Chamberlain, to succeed him. Yet Churchill did not resign immediately, perhaps recalling his father's fate.[136]

The first print run of 17,000 copies of *My Early Life*, published on 20 October 1930, immediately sold out. Dedicated 'To a New Generation', it is today Churchill's bestselling single-volume book, translated into nineteen languages. The man of letters and future National Labour MP Harold Nicolson said it was 'like a beaker of champagne'. *The Times* praised its 'charm and briskness', as well as its 'humour, headlong excitement, quiet irony, melancholy regret for vanished customs and glories, love of sport, the pleasures of friendship', although it also made the snide point that 'The material is, of course, splendid, as Mr Churchill will agree.'[137] General Sir Hubert Gough, who had fought in two campaigns with Churchill, made annotations in the margins of his copy that questioned its factual accuracy: 'disregard of strict truth', 'pure fabrication', 'Bunk' and so on.[138] The events described had taken place three decades earlier, and time tends to lend embroidery to anecdotes. There were more esoteric complaints, too. Explaining his frustrations with the Tirah expedition of 1897–8, Churchill concluded a chapter, 'Thus the beaver builds his dam, and thus when his fishing is about to begin, comes the flood and sweeps his work and luck and fish away together. So he has to begin again.' He later received a letter from a Canadian informing him that the beaver 'is a strict vegetarian in diet, and neither catches fish nor eats fish'.[139] Yet if there were occasional minor embellishments, there were also superb scenes, beautiful writing and truths that have survived the test of nine decades. 'Never, never, never believe any war will be smooth and easy,' he wrote, 'or that anyone who embarks on that strange voyage can measure the tides and hurricanes he will encounter.'[140] Elsewhere in *My Early Life* he wrote, 'Scarcely anything material or established which I was brought up to believe was permanent or vital, has lasted. Everything I was sure or taught to be sure was impossible, has happened.'[141] Much of the book, which is packed with adventures, is about what constitutes a good death. By the time he wrote it in his mid-fifties, Churchill had seen a great deal of death, and the book, though ostensibly about youth, is full of musings such as how 'Young men have often been ruined through owning horses, or through backing them, but never through riding them: unless of course they break their necks, which, taken at a gallop, is a very good death to die.'[142]

'Come on now, all you young men, all over the world,' Churchill exhorted, in the most famous lines of the book:

> You are needed more than ever now to fill the gap of a generation shorn by the War. You have not an hour to lose. You must take your places in life's fighting line. Twenty to twenty-five! These are the years! Don't be content with things as they are. 'The earth is yours and the fulness thereof.' Enter upon your inheritance, accept your responsibilities . . . Don't take No for an answer. Never submit to failure. Do not be fobbed off with mere personal success or acceptance. You will make all kinds of mistakes; but as long as you are generous and true, and also fierce, you cannot hurt the world or even seriously distress her. She was made to be wooed and won by youth. She has lived and thrived only by repeated subjugations.[143]

Pervading *My Early Life* was the assumption – mistaken as it turned out – that his story would primarily be interesting to future generations because of the glories of the British Empire. 'I was a child of the Victorian era,' Churchill writes, 'when the structure of our country seemed set, when its position in trade and on the seas was unrivalled, and when the realization of the greatness of our Empire and of our duty to preserve it was ever growing stronger.'[144] No one reading *My Early Life* could have doubted how far Churchill would be willing to go to preserve the Empire from Ramsay MacDonald, Lord Simon, 'Mahatma' Gandhi, Lord Irwin and, if necessary, Stanley Baldwin.

On 12 November 1930, the Round Table Conference met in the Royal Gallery of the House of Lords and remained in session for over two months.

It included an Indian delegation, although Gandhi himself was in prison and only released a week after it ended. Although Churchill dismissed the Indian claims as 'absurd and dangerous pretensions', Baldwin was determined to pursue Dominion status for India as a way of giving India effective self-government but keeping it within the Empire.[145] Opposed were a group of about sixty 'Diehard' Conservative MPs. Brigadier J. H. Morgan, their constitutional adviser, recorded of their leaders – Lords Salisbury, Wolmer and Lloyd, and the MPs John Gretton and Sir Henry Page Croft – '*All* of them distrusted Churchill.'[146] This was because they believed that Churchill, as Wolmer put it, 'has no convictions; he has only joined us for what he can get out of it'.[147] This was not true; Churchill could not hope to get anything out of his campaign except to head off the early loss of India to the Empire. It was hardly a route to political advancement. Even if the decision ultimately led to Baldwin's fall, as he was eventually to hope that it would, Churchill knew that he was not the obvious alternative candidate for Tory leader. This campaign was undertaken out of conviction, in defence of the Empire he loved.

'Winston is in the depths of gloom,' Baldwin reported to Davidson on 13 November. 'He wants the Conference to bust up quickly and the Tory Party to go back to pre-war and govern with a strong hand. He has become once more the subaltern of hussars of '96.'[148] That was also unfair, but a potent line of attack. Another was that which Davidson employed, repeating the criticism made so often of him already: 'The diehard Tories who opposed us over India never regarded Churchill as a Conservative at all, but as a renegade Liberal who had crossed the floor. He was regarded as being unstable politically,' he said. 'He was a brilliant man, but it was considered that this very brilliance denoted instability of principles and judgement.'[149]

On Tuesday, 27 January 1931, Churchill resigned from the Conservative Business Committee, and thus from the Tory front bench, over the Party's support of Dominion status for India. The Committee had only been instituted the previous March, so it did not feel like a great renunciation, and his resignation did allow him to speak openly against Party policy. The Tory Establishment was equally pleased to see him go, though he had not been forced out; it had been his choice. In his biography of his father, Churchill had written, 'He resigned at the wrong time, on the wrong issue, and he made no attempt to rally support,' and the same might be said of the son. Hitherto he had been adamantly against resignations, telling Violet Asquith that Curzon had been wrong to resign the viceroyalty of India over his disagreements with Kitchener in 1905. 'I would *never* have resigned,' he said. 'I would have waited my time and fought him on some other issue and beaten him. Never resign.'[150]

Back in 1924, the Labour candidate in the Westminster Abbey by-election, Fenner Brockway, had published a leaflet showing Churchill walking past milestones saying 'Leicester West' and 'Dundee' and then following a signpost pointing 'To the Wilderness'.[151] Now he had arrived there. It is often argued that Churchill should have saved his political capital and not fought against Indian self-government, which was a fait accompli because both front benches supported it, but instead waited among the party leaders to fight against the appeasement of the Nazis. Yet for all the suspicions that Hitler might attempt another putsch, Churchill could not have known that he would come to power in 1933, whereas he could see clearly that what he considered to be the most glorious achievement in Britain's history, her Indian Empire, was about to be given away without a fight.

Churchill's huge political capital in later years rested on the public perception that he told unpopular truths as he saw them, followed his heart, took a lone stand and did not make a personal calculation; rather, he did what he thought right at the time. The battle over the Government of India Bill proved just as much a preparation for later trials as those battles where he had been on the winning side. The public trusted him in 1940 not because they believed he had always, or even generally, been right – all too clearly he had not – but because they knew he had fought bravely for what he believed in, while many other, more self-serving politicians had not.

# 15
# Into the Wilderness
# January 1931–October 1933

*Every prophet has to come from Civilization, but every prophet has to go into the wilderness. He must have a strong impression of a complex society and all that it has to give, and then must serve periods of isolation and meditation. That is the process by which psychic dynamite is made.*

Churchill, *The Sunday Chronicle*, November 1931[1]

*Mighty forces were adrift. The void was open, and into that void after a pause there strode a maniac of ferocious genius, the repository and expression of the most virulent hatreds that have ever corroded the human breast – Corporal Hitler.*

Churchill, *The Gathering Storm*[2]

Despite his now being in the political wilderness, Churchill's parliamentary performances continued to draw the crowds and the laughs. On 28 January 1931, during a debate on the Trade Union Disputes Bill, he gave what Harold Nicolson thought was 'the wittiest speech of his life'.[3] Churchill spoke of Ramsay MacDonald's

> wonderful skill in falling without hurting himself. He falls, but up he comes again, smiling, a little dishevelled, but still smiling . . . I remember, when I was a child, being taken to the celebrated Barnum's Circus which contained an exhibition of freaks and monstrosities, but the exhibit on the programme which I most desired to see was the one described as 'The Boneless Wonder'. My parents judged that that spectacle would be too revolting and demoralizing for my youthful eyes, and I have waited fifty years to see the boneless wonder sitting on the Treasury bench.[4]

Churchill kept up his torrent of speeches all over the country as well as at Westminster, far more than most Opposition politicians, testament both to his energy and to his ambition. In 1930 he gave sixty-one major speeches, then forty-eight in 1931, twenty-eight in 1932, forty-one in 1933, thirty-nine in 1934, fifty-four in 1935, twenty-three in 1936, fifty-five in 1937, thirty-nine in 1938 and thirty-six in 1939, not including hundreds of lesser interventions in Westminster and scores of articles. However much the Party whips were able to sideline him in the Commons, his often well-attended public meetings meant he was a force in British politics that they could never ignore. Mass political meetings were a form of free evening entertainment in the days before television, and there were few celebrity performers of his status or quality.

He certainly spoke with passion on the issue of India. For all that Churchill genuinely wished to protect the princes, Muslims, minorities and Untouchables from the Hindu majority, there was no doubt that part of his intention was also to try to build a coalition against the Congress Party. His Victorian sense of racial superiority was central to his belief that six white-ruled countries were suitable for self-government but, as he put it in a speech in Manchester, 'except as an ultimate visionary goal, Dominion status like that of Canada or Australia is not going to happen in India in any period which we can even remotely foresee.'[5] He trotted out the common prejudice that 'It is never possible to make concessions to Orientals when they think you are weak or are afraid of them.'[6] That was ultimately why he condemned Irwin. 'His attitude towards India has throughout been an apology.' It was a theme he pursued three days later in Liverpool:

> The British lion, so fierce and valiant in bygone days, so unconquerable through all the agony of Armageddon, can now be chased by rabbits from the fields and forests of his former glory. It is not that our strength is yet seriously impaired. We are suffering from a psychological collapse. We have only to stand erect and face our difficulties as in the days of yore, for these same difficulties to be halved.

He instanced the need to stimulate industry and agriculture, develop tighter controls on finance, foster imperial economic unity. 'And as an indisputable preliminary to all those heavy tasks, we have got to throw this wretched, spendthrift, intriguing, grovelling Government into the street.'[7]

Around this time he wrote to Lindemann with the idea for an article on 'Great Fighters in Lost Causes'. He concentrated on Hannibal, Vercingetorix, Harold Godwinson, Charles I and Robert E. Lee, saying, 'Both the lost cause and the greatness of the fighter and fighting should be developed.'[8] Lindemann suggested he read an apocalyptic novel called *Last and*

*First Men* by W. Olaf Stapledon, which moved Churchill to discuss the ordering of the universe for the first time since the 4th Hussars mess endorsed the Religion of Healthy-Mindedness in the late 1890s. Writing to Lindemann of Mankind in the abstract, he said, 'After we have got through the whole of this business, I hope it will be a long time before any of their seed lands upon some innocent and harmless star. Without the explanation of a Supreme spiritual being, all these peregrinations are futile. However, it is a great thing to know that there is lots to do.'[9]

On Monday, 23 February 1931, speaking to the council of his constituency association at Winchester House in Epping, Churchill made perhaps the most notorious speech of his life, explaining his resignation from the Tory front bench. 'I should not be able to serve in any administration about whose Indian policy I was not reassured,' he said.[10]

> It is alarming and also nauseating to see Mr. Gandhi, a seditious Middle Temple lawyer, now posing as a fakir of a type well known in the East, striding half-naked up the steps of the Viceregal palace, while he is still organizing and conducting a defiant campaign of civil disobedience, to parley on equal terms with the representative of the King-Emperor. Such a spectacle can only increase the unrest in India and the danger to which white people there are exposed.[11]

In another passage he described Gandhi as 'this malignant subversive fanatic'.[12]*

A motion of confidence and approval in their Member was carried unanimously, and Churchill described his reception to Clementine as 'loving, ardent and unanimous'.[13] The same has not been true of the verdict of history, especially since Gandhi became a secular saint after his assassination in 1948. It is hard today to appreciate how fraudulent Gandhi seemed to British imperialists in the early 1930s, with his often opaque and ambiguous remarks. They simply did not believe in his sanctity or sincerity and thought him a highly political revolutionary, although most appreciated his doctrine of non-violence. In his attacks on Gandhi, as with his descriptions of Bolshevism, Churchill's oratorical extravagances had started to work against him, to be seen more in the nature of a music-hall turn than as serious public discourse. He was almost becoming too oratorical for the good of his causes.

* In an undelivered letter of 1944, Gandhi replied teasingly to Churchill, 'I have long been trying to be a fakir and that (too) naked – a more difficult task. I, therefore, regard the expression as a compliment, though unintended . . . Your sincere friend, M. K. Gandhi' (*CIHOW* p. 343).

On 4 March, he wrote an article in the *Strand Magazine* entitled 'A Second Choice', about all the twists his life had taken, and how it might have gone otherwise: 'If we look back on our past life we shall see that one of its most usual experiences is that we have been helped by our mistakes and injured by our most sagacious decisions.'[14] Although he wasn't to know it for several years, he was about to be helped enormously by his decision to resign from the Shadow Cabinet over India, which kept him from being responsible for any of the decisions resulting in the appeasement of Germany. Feeling elegiacal about his life, as people often do after completing an autobiography, he concluded the article with the words, 'Let us reconcile ourselves to the mysterious rhythm of our destinies, such as they must be in this world of space and time. Let us treasure our joys but not bewail our sorrows. The glory of light cannot exist without its shadows. Life is a whole, and good and ill must be accepted together. The journey has been enjoyable and well worth making. Once.'[15]

Yet although he was looking back over life, he continued to be focused on the future regarding politics. 'It is astonishing looking back over the last six weeks what a change has been brought in my position,' he told Clementine. 'Anything may happen now if opinion has time to develop.'[16] The support of the Rothermere and Beaverbrook press – especially the *Daily Mail*, *Daily Express* and *Evening Standard* – for the Diehards against Dominion status for India, as well as a revolt among the Tory grassroots over it, severely damaged Baldwin's position as Party leader. Baldwin kept up a perfect composure. (Churchill admitted with rueful respect, 'Fighting Baldwin was like fighting an eiderdown. You gave him what you thought was a knockout blow, and then discovered you had made not the slightest impression.')[17] Yet the Prime Minister had seriously considered resigning on 1 March, and was only dissuaded by two of his closest friends in politics, John Davidson and William Bridgeman.

Baldwin's survival depended on the outcome of a by-election at St George's Westminster, where the Tory candidate, Alfred Duff Cooper, faced Sir Ernest Petter, an Independent Conservative opposed to Dominion status who was vigorously supported by the Rothermere and Beaverbrook newspapers. Prompted by his cousin Rudyard Kipling,* Baldwin rebuked the press barons with the celebrated words, 'What the

* Churchill had always loved the work of Rudyard Kipling, even though Kipling never thought very highly of him. In November 1937 he told the Kipling Memorial Fund dinner at the Grosvenor House Hotel in London that 'Two immortal poems or passages of English command admiration without distinction of party or mood. The "Recessional" hymn upon the Diamond Jubilee and that rule of life contained in the verses entitled "If" should at one time or another

proprietorship of these papers is aiming at is power and power without responsibility – the prerogative of the harlot throughout the ages.' The next day at the Royal Albert Hall, Churchill told the Indian Empire Society:

> To abandon India to the rule of the Brahmins would be an act of cruel and wicked negligence. It would shame for ever those who bore its guilt. These Brahmins who mouth and patter the principles of Western Liberalism, and pose as philosophic and democratic politicians, are the same Brahmins who deny the primary rights of existence to nearly sixty millions of their own fellow countrymen whom they call 'Untouchable', and whom they have by thousands of years of oppression actually taught to accept this sad position . . . And then in a moment they turn round and begin chopping logic with John Stuart Mill, or pleading the rights of man with Jean Jacques Rousseau.[18]

He went on to warn that the departure of the British Army would lead to communal massacres across northern India.[19]

On 19 March 1931, Duff Cooper won St George's by 17,242 to 11,532, a very healthy majority, and Churchill's campaign against the India Bill was dealt a serious setback. He nonetheless decided to fight on. 'I am sure you know that I have no personal feelings of hostility towards you,' he wrote to Irwin, the Viceroy of India. 'I feel the deepest sorrow at the course of events in India, and at the impulsion you have given them. We shall, I fear, be locked in this controversy for several years, and I think it will become the dividing line in England. At any rate you will start with the big battalions on your side.'[20] He was right, and they remained on the side of constitutional reform in India as he became ever more isolated. He did not soften his message to the prevailing political circumstances in any way, however. 'It makes me sick when I hear the Secretary of State saying of India, "She will do this and she will do that,"' he told the Constitutional Club a week later. 'India is no more a political personality than Europe. India is a geographical term. It is no more a united nation than the Equator.'[21]

For all his isolation, Churchill continued to amuse the House. In the Budget debate in April, when some Liberal MPs complimented him on his chancellorship, he replied, 'I suppose a favourable verdict is always to

---

be learned by heart by every good Englishman' (*CS* VI p. 5905). 'Recessional' was a pessimistic warning of the coming end of British imperial grandeur when:

> Far-called our navies melt away;
> On dune and headland sinks the fire:
> Lo, all our pomp of yesterday
> Is one with Nineveh and Tyre!

be valued, even if it comes from an unjust judge or a nobbled umpire.'[22] When he said in another debate, 'We have all heard how Dr Guillotin was executed by the instrument that he invented,' and Sir Herbert Samuel shouted out, 'He was not!', Churchill shot back, 'Well, he ought to have been.'[23] In an article about political cartoons in the *Strand Magazine* in June, Churchill wrote, 'Just as eels are supposed to get used to skinning, so politicians get used to being caricatured.'* Indeed, 'If we must confess it, they are quite offended and downcast when the cartoons stop . . . They murmur: "We are not mauled and maltreated as we used to be. The great days are ended."'[24]

The Wall Street Crash having turned into what was by now unmistakably a Great Depression, Churchill finally embraced the concept of general tariffs for the first time. He agreed with Chamberlain, now Shadow chancellor, that the need for revenue overcame everything, and that it would, as Churchill put it, 'afford occasion for striking those new bargains with foreign countries which are necessary and which, wisely handled, may play an important part in welding together the production and consumption of our Empire, before the present process of dispersal and disintegration has reached its fatal end'.[25] It was the end of the long campaign that had led him to cross the floor in 1904, but with unemployment reaching 2.5 million in June he put reality ahead of economic dogma. It further aligned him with the Tory right, which agreed with him over India.

A severe financial crisis of July 1931 caused by the deepening of the Great Depression ended Ramsay MacDonald's purely Labour Government the next month, and a National Government took office with MacDonald still as prime minister and Philip Snowden as chancellor of the Exchequer, but also featuring the Conservatives Baldwin as lord president of the Council, Neville Chamberlain at Health and Samuel Hoare as secretary for India, with the Liberals Lord Reading as foreign secretary and Sir Herbert Samuel at the Home Office. No call came for Churchill.

'What an extraordinary transformation of the political scene! I am glad I am not responsible for it,' he told Eddie Marsh.[26] 'I can truthfully affirm that I never felt resentment, still less pain, at being so decisively discarded in a moment of national stress,' wrote Churchill in his memoirs seventeen years later.[27] He took solace again in the strange ways of Fortune. 'Sometimes when she scowls most spitefully,' he wrote in the *Sunday Pictorial* on 30 August, 'she is preparing her most dazzling gifts.'[28] It was true. Churchill's opposition to a central plank of the Government's policy,

* Of course, eels don't get used to being skinned; they die.

Dominion status for India, kept him in the political wilderness in the decade in which successive governments allowed, as he was later to put it, 'the locusts to eat'.[29]

A nine-day visit the same month of George Bernard Shaw, whom Churchill liked personally, and Nancy Astor, whom he did not, to Russia, from where they returned full of praise for Stalin and Communism, drove him to predictable outrage. 'The Russians have always been fond of circuses and travelling shows,' he told the readers of the *Pall Mall Gazette*; '. . . here was the World's most famous intellectual clown and pantaloon, and the charming Columbine* of the capitalist pantomime,' for whom 'Arch-Commissar Stalin . . . flung open the closely-guarded sanctuaries of the Kremlin, and pushing aside his morning's budget of death warrants, and *lettres de cachet*, received his guests with smiles of overflowing comradeship.'[30] When at their meeting Stalin asked Lady Astor about Churchill's career, she told him, 'Oh, he's finished!'[31]

On 21 September, the new National Government suspended the Gold Standard and imposed tariffs on all imported manufactured goods, which even the Liberals did not oppose. It also announced a general election for 27 October in order to gain a new mandate. 'In this grave public emergency I come before you as a National and Conservative candidate,' Churchill wrote to the people of Epping in his election leaflet. 'I have always warned you of the evils which Socialist Government would bring upon our country . . . Undue tolerance has been shown to that gospel of envy, hatred and malice borrowed from foreign writings and ceaselessly fanned from abroad. The British nation has realized its peril only on the very brink of the precipice to which it has been lured.'[32] In a stunning volte-face he then wrote, 'As Conservatives we are convinced that an effective measure of protection for British industry and British agriculture must hold a leading place in any scheme of national self-regeneration . . . Only by walking in company together can the races and states of the British Empire preserve their glory and their livelihood.'[33] This was almost precisely what he had for decades on hundreds of public platforms derided the Chamberlain family, Leo Amery and the Imperial Fair Traders for saying, but the Great Depression was reaching its nadir and his concern for people's immediate suffering now trumped his long-term ideal. He also blamed 'the doubting, incoherent policy of the Socialists in India' for bringing 'discord and suffering' on Indians and impairing Britain in the eyes of the world – even though Irwin had been a Conservative all his life.

* 'Mistress of Harlequin' (*Shorter Oxford Dictionary*).

Standing as a Conservative – his fourth party label in seven years, but his final one – Churchill doubled his majority at Epping. He was one of 473 Conservatives elected, alongside 35 National Liberals and 13 National Labour MPs – giving the National Government a total of 554 in a House of Commons of 615. In opposition, Labour had fifty-two seats and the Independent Liberals four. The popular vote went Conservative 11.98 million, Labour 6.65 million, Liberals 1.40 million and National Liberals 0.81 million. Given his opposition to the India Bill, and with the Government enjoying such a huge majority, there was no question of Churchill being offered any office.

He published *The Eastern Front*, the fifth and final volume of *The World Crisis*, in early November. His earlier volumes had by then altered many people's views of the war, and of his part in it. It is said that journalism is the first draft of history, but his memoirs of both the world wars were the true first drafts of the histories of both those conflicts, setting many of the terms of reference of them for decades. Once again he sent a signed copy to Neville Chamberlain, whose annotation 'January 1932' at the end implies that he again read it almost immediately. His opponents never denied his authorial capacities. 'If I had – which God forbid – to deliver an address on you,' Baldwin was to tell him in 1933, 'I should say "Read *Marlborough*."'[34]*

In November 1931 Churchill also published an article entitled 'Fifty Years Hence' in *Maclean's Magazine*, in which he made some absurd predictions – that we would grow only those parts of chickens we wanted to eat, for example – but also some astonishingly accurate ones.[35] 'Wireless telephones and television,' he wrote, long before the commercial production of either, 'following naturally upon their present path of development, would enable their owner to connect up with any room similarly installed, and hear and take part in the conversation as well as if he had put his head in through the window.' Then he added, 'The congregation of men in cities would become superfluous.'[36] He stated that 'Nuclear energy is incomparably greater than the molecular energy which we use today. The coal that a man can get in a day can easily do five hundred times as much work as the man himself. Nuclear energy is at least one million times more powerful still . . . There is no question among scientists that this gigantic source of energy exists. What is lacking is the match to set the bonfire alight.'[37]

The article distilled a number of Churchill's thoughts about the nature

* Churchill dictated his speeches, books, articles and letters while striding around his study at Chartwell, and during the Wilderness Years he used a crude stand-up desk made by a local carpenter on which he laid out documents. For his birthday in 1949, his family bought him an attractive mahogany version. (Singer, *Churchill Style* p. 134; *FH* no. 94 p. 11.)

of Mankind, and reiterated his belief that human nature was not improving at anything like the same rate as technological knowledge was advancing. This could ultimately prove disastrous. 'Certain it is that while men are gathering knowledge and power with ever-increasing and measureless speed,' he wrote,

> their virtues and their wisdom have not shown any notable improvement as the centuries have rolled. The brain of a modern man does not differ in essentials from that of the human beings who fought and lived here millions of years ago. The nature of man has remained hitherto practically unchanged. Under sufficient stress – starvation, terror, warlike passion, or even cold intellectual frenzy – the modern man we know so well will do the most terrible deeds, and his modern woman will back him up.[38]

At least as worrying was the problem that Churchill had already identified in his Romanes Lecture: that the representative institutions democracy relied upon no longer attracted the quality of people necessary for them to function effectively. 'Democracy as a guide or motive to progress has long been known to be incompetent,' he wrote. 'None of the legislative assemblies of the great modern states represents in universal suffrage even a fraction of the strength or wisdom of the community . . . Democratic governments drift along the line of least resistance, taking short views, paying their way with sops and doles, and smoothing their path with pleasant-sounding platitudes.'[39] This has been taken as indicating that Churchill had lost his faith in democracy and was considering embracing dictatorship.[40] In fact the opposite was true; he was calling for a reinvigoration of democracy, and arguing that 'It is therefore above all things important that the moral philosophy and spiritual conceptions of men and nations should hold their own . . . Without an equal growth of Mercy, Pity, Peace and Love, Science herself may destroy all that makes human life majestic and tolerable.'[41]

In J. C. Squire's book of counterfactual history essays, *If It Had Happened Otherwise*, published in 1931, Churchill wrote the chapter entitled 'If Lee Had Not Won the Battle of Gettysburg', which assumes a Confederate victory in the American Civil War; thereafter Robert E. Lee supersedes Jefferson Davis and ends slavery in the Confederacy, an association of the English-speaking peoples prevents the Great War from breaking out and Kaiser Wilhelm becomes the titular head of a peaceful United Europe movement. It is an entertaining tale and shows how far Churchill's thinking on the subject of the English-speaking peoples had developed.

To replenish his coffers after the Wall Street Crash, Churchill sailed to New York with Clementine and Diana on the *Europa* liner for what was intended to be a forty-lecture tour of the United States. He was still accompanied by Walter Thompson, his detective-bodyguard, because of death threats from the Punjabi-Sikh Ghadar terrorist organization, which was believed to have active cells in North America. The themes of his lectures were 'The Pathway of the English-Speaking Peoples' and 'The Economic Crisis'. As he told Archie Sinclair, 'The cruel and criminal deflation of commodities and services which has characterized the last two years, and the artificial enhancement of gold, will receive my outspoken condemnation.'[42]

On Sunday, 13 December 1931, having dined at his hotel, the Waldorf Astoria, on Park Avenue and 49th Street, Churchill took a cab 2 miles uptown to Bernard Baruch's house at 1055 Fifth Avenue, between 86th and 87th Streets. He realized during the journey that he did not know Baruch's address, but he had stayed there in 1929 and was sure he would recognize the building. He paid off his cab on the Central Park side of Fifth Avenue between 76th and 77th Streets, a full ten blocks south of Baruch's home. In those days Fifth Avenue had two-way traffic.* Churchill began crossing the street, wearing a heavy, fur-lined overcoat, but halfway across, momentarily forgetting he was not in England, he looked left instead of right and was knocked down by a northbound car.[43]

The driver, Mario Constasino (or Contasino – accounts differ) of Yonkers, was going at about 35mph. He tried to brake, but it was too late. 'There was one moment – I cannot measure it in time,' Churchill wrote soon afterwards:

> of a world aglare, of a man aghast. I certainly thought quickly enough to achieve the idea 'I am going to be run down and probably killed.' Then came the blow. I felt it on my forehead and across the thighs. But besides the blow there was an impact, a shock, a concussion indescribably violent. It blotted out everything except thought. I do not understand why I was not broken like an eggshell, or squashed like a gooseberry . . . I certainly must be very tough or very lucky, or both.

Thereafter he felt 'wave upon wave of convulsive, painful sensations'.[44]

'A man has been killed!' shouted out a passer-by.[45] A policeman arrived, whom Churchill was able to inform that he himself had been entirely at fault.[46] He was taken to Lenox Hill Hospital, fortunately only two blocks away, lying on the floor of a cab. Churchill found he could not move his hands or feet, but he soon felt 'violent pins and needles'. He was treated

* There is a long-standing mystery here: why, if he was coming from downtown, was he not dropped off on the residential, eastern side of Fifth Avenue, rather than the western, Central Park side?

for concussion, contusions needing sutures on his nose and forehead, and heavy bruising on his right arm, chest and leg, all of which required him to be hospitalized for over a week.[47] When Mr Constasino visited he gave him a signed copy of *The Eastern Front*.

'I had a terrible bump,' he wrote to Sinclair on the 30th, 'and how I was not squashed or shattered I cannot imagine. I was also very lucky in escaping the wheels, which only went over and broke the tips of my toes.'[48] Lindemann explained the physics in a telegram, based on Churchill weighing 200 pounds, which read: 'Delighted good news. Collision equivalent falling thirty feet onto pavement* . . . Equivalent stopping ten-pound brick dropped six hundred feet or two charges buckshot point-blank range . . . Your body transferred during impact at rate 8,000 horsepower. Congratulations on preparing suitable cushion and skill in taking bump.'[49]

Having negotiated no less than £500 for it (approximately £25,000 in today's money), Churchill's article on his accident appeared in the *Daily Mail* on 4 January 1932, under the headline 'My New York Misadventure'. 'With me the nitrous-oxide trance usually takes this form,' he wrote of his concussion, 'the sanctum is occupied by alien powers.'[50] A follow-up article was entitled 'I Was Conscious Through It All'. Churchill went to the Bahamas for three weeks with his family on New Year's Eve, where he had planned to be at Christmas.[51] Sir Bede Clifford, the Governor, 'noticed that he still bore the mark of a villainous wound on his forehead'.[52] (It lasted for many years, and witnesses recalled how it reddened during the Second World War when he got angry.) The family stayed at Government House in Nassau. Churchill 'loved to float face downwards in the water, periodically surfacing for breath', and when his daughter Diana called out that she thought she'd seen a turbot, Churchill rhymed, 'Well don't disturb it.'[53]†

On Churchill's return to Prohibition America, Dr Otto Pickhardt of Lenox Hill Hospital provided him with a universal prescription stating, 'This is to certify that the post-accident convalescence of the Hon. Winston S. Churchill necessitates the use of alcoholic spirits especially at meal times. The quantity is naturally indefinite but the minimum requirements would be 250 cubic centimeters.'[54] Churchill wrote on it in pencil, 'Keep on hand.' On 28 January 1932 he resumed his postponed lecture tour and was able to honour thirty-five of his forty original commitments, a tribute

* Coincidentally the same distance he fell from the tree in Wimborne in 1893.

† He told Clifford that he did not share the common prejudice against puns, and boasted of his best one, which he had produced at Port Said when a group of Arabs had come aboard his ship looking for their Wazir (another word for vizier). 'Yes, he was 'ere a minute ago,' Churchill had told them, 'but I can't see him now.' (Clifford, *Proconsul* p. 189.)

to the recuperative powers of a fifty-seven-year-old who had yet again narrowly escaped death. He earned more than £7,500 in those six weeks, at a time when the Prime Minister earned £5,000 a year.[55]

'Peace-loving, kind-hearted, pussy-footed people have been so busy disarming the English-speaking peoples that they have developed a new naval power in the Far East,' Churchill told the Union League Club in Chicago on 2 February. 'If the United States wishes to build a new ship I would say, "Build it and God bless you."'[56] Clearly, his attitude towards a powerful US Navy had completely changed since 1927. Between 28 January and 10 March 1932, he undertook a marathon, fifteen-state, twenty-eight-city, forty-one-day, 11,700-mile lecture tour. The northernmost city visited was Toronto, the easternmost Boston, the westernmost Minneapolis and the southernmost New Orleans, once again underlining how much better travelled he was on the American continent than any other British politician of the era. At Gettysburg, one of those present noted that 'he startled the guide by correcting him as to the disposition of troops and guns. When a check-up was later made, Mr Churchill was proved to have been completely right.'[57]

On 9 March, Churchill was interviewed by CBS Radio in New York. 'I think in most people's lives good and bad luck even out pretty well,' he said. 'Sometimes, what looks like bad luck may turn out to be good luck and vice versa . . . I've done a lot of foolish things that turned out well, and a lot of wise things that have turned out badly. The misfortune of today may lead to the success of tomorrow.'[58] That was all true in his own case, but he then made a terrible prediction: 'I don't believe we shall see another great war in our time. War, today, is bare – bare of profit and stripped of all its glamour. The old pomp and circumstance are gone. War is now nothing but toil, blood, death, squalor and lying propaganda.* Besides, as long as the French keep a strong army, and Great Britain and the United States have good navies, no great war is likely to occur.'[59] Of the English-speaking peoples, Churchill argued, 'There must be some organizing force at the summit of human affairs, some chairmanship in the Council of Nations, strong enough to lead them out of their present confusion, back to prosperity.' World prosperity and world peace, he said, would come from 'the two world creditor nations acting together', and he added, 'My confidence in the British Empire is unshakeable.'[60] He also had confidence in the United States. 'If the whole world except the United States sank under the ocean that community could get its living. They

* A variation on this language would form part of one of his most famous speeches in May 1940.

carved it out of the prairie and the forests. They are going to have a strong national resurgence in the near future.'[61]

On arriving at Paddington station from Southampton on 18 March, Churchill was presented with a magnificent £2,000 Daimler limousine, given by 140 of his friends, organized by Bracken, with Sinclair as treasurer, to celebrate his escape from death. The contributors were a Who's Who of Churchill's closest friends, and included Beaverbrook, Boothby, Camrose, Carson, Chaplin, Duff and Diana Cooper, Grey, Horne, Keynes, Macmillan, Londonderry, Moyne, Lutyens, Riddell, Spears, Lord Weir, Esmond Harmsworth, the Duke of Westminster and the Prince of Wales.[62] Of those asked, only the Lyttons were unable to find the £15 contribution.[63] 'I cannot tell you what pleasure the gift of this lovely motor car has been to me,' Churchill told Ian Hamilton, another contributor, 'most of all for the friendship which inspired it.'[64]

His Wilderness Years may have been lonely politically, but they never were socially. Many of the Daimler contributors were Other Club members, who were joined that year by Bracken, Sir John Lavery, Sir Edward Grigg and Eddie Marsh, among others. In March, wagers were taken there as to who would succeed MacDonald as prime minister, with the names of Neville Chamberlain, Stanley Baldwin, Robert Horne (who was present and bet that he would not), Walter Runciman, Sir John Simon and Herbert Samuel, all being mentioned, but not the 'pious founder' of the Club himself.[65]

On 13 March 1932, while Churchill was in mid-Atlantic returning home on board the *Majestic*, Adolf Hitler had won eleven million votes in the German elections, against the eighty-four-year-old Paul von Hindenburg's eighteen million. In the second round of voting on 10 April, in which Hindenburg was re-elected president with nineteen million votes, Hitler increased his vote to thirteen million. On 11 July, Churchill made his first public reference to Hitler. Ramsay MacDonald had returned from the Lausanne Conference, at which the Versailles reparations clauses against Germany had been hugely reduced by France and Britain, despite the fact that the United States had not lifted the British or French war debts owed to them. 'Of course, anything which removes friction between Germany and France is to the good,' Churchill acknowledged in the Commons.

> True, there are three thousand million marks which are to be payable by Germany, but I notice that Herr Hitler, who is the moving impulse behind the German Government and may be more than that very soon, took occasion to state yesterday that within a few months that amount would not be

> worth three marks. That is an appalling statement to be made while the ink is yet damp upon the parchment of the Treaty. Therefore I say that Germany has been virtually freed from all reparations. There has been no Carthaginian peace.* Neither has there been any bleeding of Germany white by the conquerors. The exact opposite has taken place. The loans which Britain and the United States particularly, and also other countries, have poured into the lap of Germany since the firing stopped, far exceed the sum of reparations which she has paid; indeed, they have been nearly double. If the plight of Germany is hard – and the plight of every country is hard at the present time – it is not because there has been any drain of her life's blood or of valuable commodities from Germany to the victors.[66]

That truth did not prevent the Nazis becoming the largest party in the Reichstag elections only twenty days later.

Churchill had been to Germany just twice in his life, and then only briefly for the Army manoeuvres before the war. He was not well versed in German culture, and years before had said, 'I'll never learn the beastly language until the Kaiser marches on London!'[67] In August 1932 he toured Marlborough's Danubian battlefields, including Blenheim itself, with his pretty seventeen-year-old schoolgirl daughter Sarah, the military historian Colonel (later Major-General) Ridley Pakenham-Walsh, who had served at Gallipoli, and Lindemann (who picked up the bills at the Hotel Continental). The group found artillery and bullet marks on a barn at Ramillies and recognizable trenches at Schellenberg. 'I was able to re-people them with ghostly but glittering armies,' Churchill reported to the Oxford historian Keith Feiling.[68] He had told George Harrap, the publisher of his coming Marlborough biography, 'I am happiest in the eighteenth century.'[69]

In late August he almost met Hitler in Munich, when the Nazi Party publicist, Harvard-educated Ernst 'Putzi' Hanfstaengl, tried to arrange an encounter between the two men.[70] 'Herr Hitler,' Hanfstaengl said to his leader in his apartment, 'don't you realize the Churchills are sitting in the restaurant? . . . They are expecting you for coffee and will think this a deliberate insult.' Hitler was unshaven and had too much to do. 'What on earth would I talk to him about?' he asked.[71] It probably would not have been a very fruitful conversation, as Churchill sent an oral message via Hanfstaengl: 'Tell your boss from me that anti-Semitism may be a good starter, but it is a bad sticker.'† 'Why is your chief so violent about the Jews?' Churchill asked Hanfstaengl. 'I can quite understand being angry with Jews who have done wrong or are against the country, and I

* A harsh peace like the one Rome imposed on Carthage in 146 BC.

† In relating this incident, Churchill later modified this to 'bad stayer' (*CIHOW* p. 12).

understand resisting them if they try to monopolize power in any walk of life; but what is the sense of being against a man simply because of his birth? How can any man help how he is born?' He concluded his account of the near-meeting with the joke, 'Thus Hitler lost his only chance of meeting me.'[72] Hanfstaengl claimed that Churchill asked, 'How does your chief feel about an alliance between your country, France and England?' This would have been in accord with Churchill's interest in an anti-Soviet bloc, but it would have to be at the price of Hitler changing the essential nature of his regime. In any case, Churchill was in no position to offer anything at the time. It turned out to be fortunate that Churchill did not meet Hitler, as the encounter proved an embarrassment to several of those Britons, such as Lloyd George, the Duke of Windsor and Churchill's cousin Lord Londonderry, who did.

In his war memoirs published sixteen years later, Churchill wrote, 'I had no national prejudices against Hitler at this time. I knew little of his doctrine or record and nothing of his character. I admire men who stand up for their country in defeat, even though I am on the other side. He had a perfect right to be a patriotic German if he chose.'[73] On 23 November 1932, two months before Hitler came to power, Churchill made his first major speech about German rearmament. He spoke of how much the borders of Poland, Romania, Czechoslovakia and Yugoslavia all depended on the Versailles Treaty being upheld, and made reference to the Hitler Youth:

> I have respect and admiration for the Germans, and desire that we should live on terms of good feeling and fruitful relations with them, but we must look at the fact that every concession . . . has been followed immediately by a fresh demand . . . Now the demand is that Germany should be allowed to rearm. Do not delude yourselves. Do not let His Majesty's Government believe . . . that all that Germany is asking for is equal status . . . That is not what Germany is seeking. All these bands of sturdy Teutonic youths, marching through the streets and roads of Germany, with the light of desire in their eyes to suffer for their Fatherland, are not looking for status. They are looking for weapons, and, when they have the weapons, believe me they will then ask for the return of lost territories and lost colonies, and when that demand is made it cannot fail to shake and possibly shatter to their foundations every one of the countries I have mentioned, and some other countries I have not mentioned.[74]

The speech caused hardly a ripple in British politics or the press. The difficulty was that people had heard this kind of thing from him before, for several decades. Since he had prescribed extravagances as an important part of oratory in 1897 he had been producing them persistently. The

British people recalled – with varying degrees of accuracy – how he had predicted civil war in Ireland, Bolshevism in Poland and Germany, war against Kemalist Turkey, bloodshed in the General Strike and the collapse of law and order across northern India, most of which had so far happened. So by the time the greatest threat to civilization in the twentieth century genuinely did arrive, the public were inured to Churchill acting the part of Cassandra and did not believe him. Worse, many MPs who did not trust his judgement and despised his ambition were convinced that his warnings stemmed from self-interest rather than genuine concern. 'Winston is making by far the best speeches in this parliament,' noted Robert Bernays, a National Liberal MP, in December, 'and yet *The Times* continually pretends that they are in bad taste and against the public interest.'[75] Bernays, too, was doubtful of Churchill's sincerity. In February 1933 he described a ten-minute attack on Neville Chamberlain over unemployment as 'the most scorching indictment of the government I have heard this parliament. Winston was really moved, although it may have been the emotion of the actress who works herself up into such a passion that she doesn't get over it even in her dressing room.'[76]

On 30 January 1933, President von Hindenburg appointed Hitler chancellor of Germany. A few weeks later, Churchill told the House of Commons, 'Thank God for the French Army,' which he considered the best in the world, and the most reliable bulwark against German revanchism.[77] He was to make many predictions and pronouncements that turned out to be wrong over the next six years, as he had over the past thirty, but the fact remains that he was the first, most eloquent, best-informed and for a very long time the only senior British politician to warn of the threat that Hitler was increasingly posing to peace, civilization and the British Empire. Furthermore, as we shall see, he offered practical responses and solutions – which is why when Roosevelt asked him in 1943 what the conflict should be called, Churchill replied, 'The Unnecessary War'.[78]

Churchill soon started to receive visits at Chartwell from experts in their fields who brought warnings about German military strength and plans, and also about British military weakness. These were often coordinated through Desmond Morton, his chief intelligence adviser and a former MI5 agent and currently a member of the CID sub-committee on economic warfare, who lived near by. Visitors included Sir Robert Vansittart and Ralph Wigram of the Foreign Office, Heinrich Brüning, the anti-Nazi Chancellor of Germany from 1930 to 1932, the RAF officers Wing Commander Tor Anderson and Group Captain Lachlan Maclean, and the French Popular Front politicians Pierre Cot and Léon Blum. These brave men provided Churchill with facts, figures, arguments and insights, sometimes endangering their careers by doing so, helping him to build up a comprehensive picture of the Nazi threat, and the British Government's inadequate response to it.

Churchill also made contact with the leading proponents of offensive tank warfare, the journalist Basil Liddell Hart and the military historian Major-General J. F. C. Fuller, corresponding with and meeting them during the Wilderness Years, at least until Fuller's Fascist tendencies became apparent. 'A point was made about the length of a mechanized division,' Churchill wrote to Liddell Hart in mid-February after one of their meetings. 'But surely the true test is their speed in passing a given point.'[79] As ever, he was keeping as up to date as he possibly could with technical developments in warfare. By the mid-1930s, no leading politician in Britain was as well informed about the capacities and limitations of both Britain's armed forces and Germany's.

On 9 February 1933, the Oxford Union debating society passed the motion 'That this House will in no circumstances fight for King and Country' by 275 votes to 152. Churchill described it as 'an abject, squalid, shameless avowal'.[80] Randolph returned to his alma mater to try to get the motion overturned in a rowdy debate three weeks later, but was defeated by 750 votes to 138. 'Nothing is so piercing as the hostility of a thousand of your own contemporaries,' Churchill wrote proudly to Hugh Cecil of his son, 'and he was by no means crushed under it.'[81] Eight days afterwards, in a speech to the Anti-Socialist and Anti-Communist Union in London, Churchill called the Oxford vote 'a very disquieting and disgusting symptom. One can almost feel the curl of contempt upon the lips of the manhood of Germany, Italy, and France when they read the message sent out by Oxford University in the name of Young England.'[82] It was in this speech that Churchill referred to Mussolini as 'The greatest lawgiver among men'.[83] He made almost equally unfortunate remarks about Japan, which in 1931 had invaded Manchuria: 'I hope we shall try in England to understand a little the position of Japan, an ancient State, with the highest state sense of national honour and patriotism and with a teeming population and a remarkable energy. On the one side they see the dark menace of Soviet Russia. On the other the chaos of China, four or five provinces of which are now being tortured under Communist rule.'[84] As with Mussolini, he allowed his anti-Communism to blur his judgement.

On 27 February, the Reichstag burned down in mysterious circumstances, increasing the sense of crisis in Germany. Six days later the Nazis won seventeen million votes, or 44 per cent of the popular vote. Churchill responded in March with his first Commons speech on the vital need massively to increase the size of the RAF as soon as possible, perhaps his most important message to Britain over the next six years. 'The whole speech,' concluded Bernays, 'though a plea for realism, was really the resurrection of the war mentality.'[85] Within that seeming contradiction lay Churchill's great problem in a country and empire that had suffered so grievously in the Great War.

'When we read about Germany,' he said on 24 March, on the day an Enabling Act gave Hitler full dictatorial powers, 'when we watch with surprise and distress the tumultuous insurgency of ferocity and war spirit, the pitiless ill-treatment of minorities, the denial of the normal protections of civilized society to large numbers of individuals solely on the ground of race . . . one cannot help feeling glad that the fierce passions that are raging in Germany have not found, as yet, any other outlet but upon Germans.'[86]

On 1 April, the persecution of the Jews in Germany began in earnest with a Government-orchestrated national boycott of all Jewish businesses and professions, enforced by Brownshirt thugs on the streets who sadistically assaulted and humiliated Jews at every opportunity. Churchill's philo-Semitism, so rare on the Tory benches, was invaluable in allowing him to see sooner than anyone else the true nature of the Nazi regime. 'I remember the tears pouring down his cheeks one day before the war in the House of Commons,' Attlee recalled many years later, 'when he was telling me what was being done to the Jews in Germany.'[87] On 13 April, Churchill condemned Hitler's 'most grim dictatorship. You have these martial or pugnacious manifestations, and also this persecution of the Jews . . . when I see the temper displayed there and read the speeches of the leading ministers, I cannot help rejoicing that the Germans have not got the heavy cannon, the thousands of military aeroplanes and the tanks of various sizes for which they have been pressing in order that their status may be equal to that of other countries.'[88] He warned that 'As Germany acquires full military equality with her neighbours while her own grievances are still unredressed and while she is in the temper which we have unhappily seen, so surely should we see ourselves within a measurable distance of the renewal of general European war.'[89]

It was natural for people to dislike hearing such grim forebodings, especially those who had lost fathers, sons, husbands and brothers in the last war. Pacificism was rife at the time – 11.6 million Britons signed the League of Nations' 'Peace Ballot' in 1934–5 – and it was far easier psychologically for people to portray Churchill as a warmonger than to face the terrible fact that the three-quarters of a million British Empire soldiers who had perished in 1914–18 might not have fought 'the war to end war' after all. Churchill meanwhile defended Versailles and the other post-war treaties, on the basis that they 'were founded upon the strongest principle alive in the world today, the principle of nationalism, or, as President Wilson called it, self-determination . . . It should be the first rule of British foreign policy to emphasize respect for these great Treaties, and to make those nations whose national existence depends upon and arises from the Treaties feel that no challenge is levelled at their security.'[90] Many people in Britain now felt that the Versailles Treaty had been too harsh on Germany, and that Hitler merely wanted to revise it.

Speaking to the Royal Society of St George in April, Churchill observed,

> All down the centuries, one peculiarity of the English people has cost them dear. We have always thrown away after a victory the greater part of the advantages we gained in the struggle. The worst difficulties from which we suffer do not come from without. They come from within . . . from the mood of unwarrantable self-abasement into which we have been cast by a powerful section of our own intellectuals. They come from the acceptance of defeatist doctrines by a large proportion of our politicians . . . Nothing can save England if she will not save herself. If we lose faith in ourselves, in our capacity to guide and govern, if we lose our will to live, then indeed our story is told.[91]

This was not what people wanted to hear either, though it became a refrain to which Churchill was often to revert. While many assumed that, given the terrible losses incurred in the First World War, Germany should be given every kind of accommodation so that a second should be avoided, Churchill crucially differed. For him, it was precisely *because* the losses were so terrible that Hitler must not be permitted to dishonour their sacrifice by achieving European domination, the aim of an earlier German regime which they had given their lives to prevent.

'It may well be that the most glorious chapters of our history are yet to be written,' he told the Society. 'Indeed, the very problems and dangers that encompass us and our country ought to make English men and women of this generation glad to be here at such a time. We ought to rejoice at the responsibilities with which destiny has honoured us, and be proud that we are guardians of our country in an age when her life is at stake.'[92] Hitler had by that stage not invaded anywhere, and would not for nearly three years. The speech was also notable for Churchill's views on Englishness. 'I am a great admirer of the Scots,' he said. 'I am quite friendly with the Welsh, especially one of them,' he added, meaning Lloyd George.

> I must confess to some sentiment about Old Ireland, in spite of the ugly mask she tries to wear. But this is not their night. On this one night in the whole

> year we are allowed to use a forgotten, almost a forbidden word. We are allowed to mention the name of our own country, to speak of ourselves as 'Englishmen', and we may even raise the slogan 'St. George for Merrie England' . . . There are a few things I will venture to mention about England. They are spoken in no invidious sense. Here it would hardly occur to anyone that the banks would close their doors against their depositors. Here no one questions the fairness of the courts of law and justice. Here no one thinks of persecuting a man on account of his religion or his race. Here everyone, except the criminals, looks on the policeman as a friend and servant of the public. Here we provide for poverty and misfortune with more compassion, in spite of all our burdens, than any other country. Here we can assert the rights of the citizen against the State, or criticize the Government of the day, without failing in our duty to the Crown or in our loyalty to the King.[93]

The superiority of the English ways of doing things over the Nazi was instinctive in him, and in August he joked in the Commons Smoking Room that 'It was now quite consistent with progressive thought to speak of the bloody Hun.'[94]

In May the Marquess of Linlithgow, a former Conservative Party chairman who was now chairman of the Select Committee on Indian Constitutional Reform, accused Churchill of wanting 'to recreate the India of 1900'. Churchill's letter to him in response was a powerful response as the war clouds gathered, unnoticed by everyone else but increasingly obvious to him. In it, he connected the liberals' view on India with the coming war against the Nazis. 'You assume the future is a mere extension of the past,' he wrote,

> whereas I find history full of unexpected turns and retrogressions. The mild and vague liberalism of the early years of the twentieth century, the surge of fantastic hopes and illusions that followed the armistice of the Great War, have already been superseded by a violent reaction against parliamentary and electioneering procedure and by the establishment of dictatorships real or veiled in almost every country . . . All the time you and your friends go on mouthing the bland platitudes of an easy safe triumphant age which has passed away, whereas the tide has turned and you will be engulfed by it. In my view England is now beginning a new period of struggle and fighting for its life . . . As long as we are sure that we press no claim on India which is not in their real interest we are justified in using our undoubted power for their welfare and for our own. Your schemes are twenty years behind the times.[95]

At the Other Club's twenty-first birthday banquet in July, with forty-nine people present, Jan Smuts, who had been prime minister of South Africa from 1919 to 1924, made a speech in which he said that Birkenhead and Churchill should have been prime ministers of Britain. 'Let me say this – if my old friend is careful, he will get there yet. He is still unsinkable, but he will have to be careful.'[96] In reply, Churchill said, 'I differ . . . about the inexpressible delights which, with some knowledge, he still believes reside in the office of Prime Minister!'[97] It must be doubted that a single person around the table believed him. He then spoke movingly of the Club members who had died. 'I am going to read you a list, because it will recall the faces of vanished friends, the echo of dearly loved laughter, the sparkle of an eye that carries with it conviviality, friendship and encouragement. Sir Henry Wilson perished under the bullet of an assassin,' Churchill said. 'Lord Kitchener was drowned at the hands of the enemy. Lord Lucas was killed fighting thousands of feet up in the high air. Tommy Robartes and Neil Primrose were killed in France and Palestine.' He recalled two other members, Sir John Cowans and Sir Laming Worthington-Evans, who had died at fifty-nine and sixty-two, due to the strain of their war work, and added, 'It is difficult to believe that they are gone, and only to think of them is to have renewed hope, and to feel that somewhere and somehow all the real unities of friendship will find their reincarnation. I cannot feel they have been unhappy in their death.'[98] Lloyd George made a rare appearance at the dinner and recalled the rancorous, partisan tempers and epithets of 1911: 'The things that were said about Winston on some occasions I could not repeat in this highly respectable club.'[99]*

Churchill's chauffeur, Sam Howes, remembered that Churchill 'always enjoyed himself there, always coming out around 2am, give or take an hour, in a very happy frame of mind'.[100] On one occasion he serenaded the upper windows of the Savoy with the whole verse and chorus of 'A Policeman's Lot is Not a Happy One', a song from Gilbert and Sullivan's *Pirates of Penzance* – appropriately enough, considering he had just been dining in the Pinafore Room – until the doorman complained that the former Chancellor was 'making a nuisance of himself'.[101] On one journey home at 1.30 a.m., Churchill pointed out the constellation of Orion to Howes, explaining to him how, back in the Egyptian desert in 1898, 'That group of stars saved my life.'

In early October, Churchill published the first volume of *Marlborough: His Life and Times*. The one-million-word book, published in four volumes

* They are unlikely to have been as unpleasant as what he himself told his mistress about Churchill the following February: 'He would make a drum out of the skin of his own mother to sound his own praises' (ed. Taylor, *Lloyd George Diary* p. 253).

between 1933 and 1938, took him as long to research and write as it took Marlborough to fight the War of Spanish Succession. He told the story of his ancestor in beautiful Augustan prose, but also discovered new sources, corrected earlier historians' errors, mastered foreign language documents and generally produced an outstanding work of history and of literature, one that appealed to a scholarly as well as to a popular audience.[102] (This was all from someone whose father had said, 'he has little [claim] to cleverness, to knowledge or any capacity for settled work.')[103] Churchill got Marlborough's birthplace wrong – it was Great Trill in Devon, not Ashe House a mile away – but otherwise his time devouring every book published on his illustrious ancestor meant that his account was remarkably accurate.[104]

When Harold Macmillan delivered Churchill's eulogy to the Other Club in February 1965, he argued that 'his ten years out of office, when he was writing the life of his great ancestor, Marlborough, laid the basis for his greatness.'[105] Churchill's primary researcher, the young Oxford historian Maurice Ashley, wrote that Churchill's own experiences to that date had been vital to the book because 'He could perceive how the minds of statesmen and commanders moved in those far-off times.'[106]

Churchill vigorously defended his ancestor's reputation against the 'sneers, calumnies and grave accusations' of historians such as Thomas Babington Macaulay, going so far as to state, 'We can only hope that Truth will follow swiftly enough to fasten the label "Liar" to his genteel coat-tails.'[107] Macaulay's main charge was that Marlborough was solely self-serving, one constantly made against Churchill throughout his life.

The writing of *Marlborough* also advanced Churchill's strategic views, already profoundly affected by the Great War, as he considered how his ancestor had approached coalition warfare. 'It was a war of the circumference against the centre,' he wrote of the War of Spanish Succession.[108] Until 1710, Marlborough was captain-general of the Army, and a leader of the coalition of nations that opposed French hegemony. Churchill admired him for the way he created a single strategy above the 'intrigues, cross-purposes, and half-measures of a vast unwieldy coalition trying to make war'.[109] Politically he regarded Marlborough as 'the greatest servant, who remained a servant, of any sovereign in history'.[110] In a neat sideswipe against the dictators, he wrote of Marlborough, 'not for him the prizes of Napoleon, or in later times of cheaper types.'[111] All this was ideal intellectual preparation for the role he was himself later to play.

Churchill also criticized 'our latter-day generals', for whom 'There are no physical disturbances: there is no danger: there is no hurry . . . There is nearly always leisure for a conference even in the gravest crisis.'

Marlborough, by contrast, was 'often in the hottest fire, holding in his mind the positions and fortunes of every unit in his army from minute to minute and giving his orders aloud'.[112] There were many fine epigrams in the book, such as when the young Marlborough cheekily slept with the King's powerful mistress, the Duchess of Cleveland: 'Desire walked with opportunity, and neither was denied.'[113] Or his description of Marlborough's love for his wife Sarah: 'It lasted for ever; neither of them thenceforward loved anyone else in their whole lives, though Sarah hated many.'[114] Marlborough so perfected 'the art of conquest' by his magnanimity in victory that it made 'the vanquished grateful for his praise'.[115]

Churchill presented Marlborough's meanness – it was said that he did not dot his 'i's so as to save money on ink – as commendable thrift, and depicted his treachery to James II in 1688 as an act of profound principle that helped alter Britain's geopolitical trajectory away from a pro-French Catholic tyranny, propelling 'the rise of Britain to the summit of Europe, curbing and breaking . . . the overweening power of France'.[116] Louis XIV held undisputed sway over continental Europe, but Churchill presented Marlborough as 'advancing at the head of the armies to the destruction of that proud dominion. He may even have seen at this early time the building up upon the ruins of the French splendour of a British greatness which should spread far and wide throughout the world and set its stamp upon the future.'[117]

What others such as Macaulay* saw as Marlborough's squalid betrayal of his own side Churchill recast as the start of a glorious period of national ascendancy. Yet he was under no illusions about his ancestor's readiness to compromise. 'What a downy bird he was,' he wrote to Clementine in 1935. 'He will always stoop to conquer. His long apprenticeship as a courtier had taught him to bow and scrape and to put up with the second or third best if he could get no better.' He summed him up as 'this valiant, proud, benignant, patient, and if necessary grovelling, daredevil and hero'.[118] Churchill was impatient and did not grovel, but otherwise Marlborough was, with Clemenceau, his role model.

Churchill related how Marlborough had reconstituted the English armed forces, making great strides in their training and discipline and winning victories. He then fell out of favour with King William III and was incarcerated in the Tower of London at one point. 'Ten years when the chances of a lifetime seemed finally to die . . . were to pass before he was again to exercise a military command,' Churchill wrote.[119] 'As he brooded on

* Who used words such as 'guilt and dishonour', 'turpitude' and 'arch-deceiver' (Macaulay, *History of England* vol. II ch. IX).

these wasted opportunities,' he added, 'as he no doubt felt how surely and how swiftly he could reshape the scene, and yet how carefully trammelled he was, can we wonder at the anger that possessed his soul? There was no prophetic spirit at his side to whisper, "Patience! The opportunity will yet be yours." His patience is almost proverbial. He had need for it all.'[120]

'You really are an amazing man!' Baldwin wrote to say. 'I look sometimes at that row of volumes in my little library, and I cannot think how you can have found the mere time to have gone through the physical labour alone of writing them. This last book would mean years of work even for a man whose sole occupation was writing history.'[121] For Churchill, writing history was a natural adjunct to making it. Like all his works, *Marlborough* tells us about the author as well as the subject.[122] He wrote of how during the early 1690s Marlborough 'had sunk now to the minor and unpleasant position of being a critic of mishandled affairs with whose main intention he agreed'.[123]

Churchill published the second volume of *Marlborough* in October 1934. This was about political friendship and the creation of alliances, particularly the vital relationship between Marlborough and Prince Eugene of Savoy. For someone who has been accused of gratuitous Anglo-centricity, Churchill was remarkably even-handed in allowing Eugene to share the glory with his ancestor. They started with a purely epistolary friendship in 1701 and didn't meet until 1704 but when they did, Churchill wrote, 'Then at once began that glorious brotherhood in arms that neither victory nor misfortune could disturb, before which jealousy and misunderstanding were powerless, and of which the history of war furnishes no equal example.'[124] At least until Churchill's own equally vital affinity with President Roosevelt 240 years later.

Leo Strauss, the American political scientist, considered *Marlborough* to be the greatest historical work of the twentieth century. A modern historian has perceptively described it as 'the capstone of [Churchill's] own political education'.[125] The breadth of Churchill's hinterland – his many and varied interests beyond politics – meant that he could regard politics with more detachment than most professional politicians, and thus not make the compromises others did in order to gain, or remain in, office.

*Marlborough* might have been the reason that Franklin Roosevelt, who had been elected president in November 1932, started to warm to Churchill, long before they met a second time.* Hearing that the President's son James was in England, Churchill invited him to Chartwell on 8 October, where after dinner he asked each guest to name their fondest wish. When

* See p. 261.

his turn came, Churchill said, 'I wish to be Prime Minister and in close and daily communication with the President of the United States. There is nothing we could not do if we were together.'[126] He then took a sheet of paper and drew an intertwined pound and dollar sign, which he referred to as 'the Sterling-Dollar', saying, 'Pray bear this to your father from me. Tell him this must be the currency of the future.' What if, James replied, his father preferred to call it the Dollar-Sterling? Churchill beamed, 'It's all the same, we are together.'[127] He handed James a copy of *Marlborough* to give to his father, with an inscription about the New Deal: 'To Franklin D. Roosevelt from Winston S. Churchill. With earnest best wishes for the success of the greatest crusade of modern times.' He heard via a third party two months later that the President was reading it 'with real pleasure'.[128]

# 16

# Sounding the Alarm
# October 1933–March 1936

*Where a band of ferocious men rise from depths to dictatorships there is no guarantee for life, or for law, or for liberty.*

Churchill speech to his Wanstead constituents, 7 July 1934[1]

*When the British sunlight fades, the jungle stirs with powerful creatures seeking their prey.*

Churchill's election leaflet, November 1935[2]

Germany walked out of the Geneva Disarmament Conference on 14 October 1933, and a week later turned its back on the League of Nations too. Eleven days after that, a pacifist Labour candidate won the Fulham East by-election with a 29.3 per cent swing, after the Labour leader, George Lansbury, had told voters, 'I would close every recruiting station, disband the army and dismiss the air force. I would abolish the whole dreadful equipment of war and say to the world "Do your worst." '[3] When Lansbury suggested that the Labour Party would never consent to Hitler rearming, Churchill reacted sarcastically in the Commons: 'is the right honourable Gentleman quite sure that the Germans will come and ask him for his consent before they rearm? Does he not think that they might omit that formality and go ahead without even taking a card vote of the Trades Union Congress?'[4]

Baldwin feared, probably rightly, that any open move towards large-scale rearmament would wreck the National Government at the polls. Churchill privately predicted after Fulham that 'Labour is likely to sweep the next election.'[5] A few days later he told a dinner party that he had come round to the League of Nations as the only hope of establishing a 'collective front to Germany'. When Robert Cecil asked why he had not supported sanctions against Japan after her invasion of Manchuria, he replied that China was too far away, and the League stood or fell 'by the attitude of Europe. War is a beastly thing now. All the glamour has gone out of it. Just a question of a clerk pulling a lever.'[6]

A month after Germany's withdrawal, Churchill criticized the Government's attempts to revive the World Disarmament Conference that had been conducted at Geneva since 1932, declaring that the Dutch, Danes and Swiss were all rearming because 'They all live around Germany, the most formidable people in the world, and now the most dangerous, a people who inculcate a form of blood-lust in their children, and lay down the doctrine that every frontier must be the starting point for invasion.'[7] In Whitehall, a new Defence Requirements Committee made up of senior forces officers and civil servants contemplated the problem of having to fight Japan and Germany simultaneously, and determined that, although the threat from Japan was more imminent, Germany was the 'ultimate enemy'. They concluded (with remarkable prescience) that large-scale rearmament was needed over the rest of the 1930s if the country was to be ready for war by the end of the decade.[8] But Neville Chamberlain, who was concerned that the cost of rearmament would threaten precarious post-Depression growth, refused to countenance the spending necessary.

On 7 February 1934, Churchill urged his fellow MPs to confront Britain's woeful unpreparedness in the air. His central argument was that the country needed to begin reorganizing civilian factories so that they could be turned over rapidly to wartime purposes:

> All over Europe that is being done, and to an extraordinary extent . . . What have we done? There is not an hour to lose. Those things cannot be done in a moment . . . This cursed, hellish invention and development of war from the air has revolutionized our position. We are not the same kind of country we used to be when we were an island, only twenty years ago . . . It is a question of safety and independence. That is what is involved now as never before.[9]

'A new situation has been created,' he insisted, 'largely in the last few years, partly in the last three or four years, largely, I fear, by rubbing this sore of the Disarmament Conference until it has become a cancer, and also by the sudden uprush of Nazi-ism* in Germany, with the tremendous

* The way he pronounced 'Narzees' and 'Narzism' was very different from the way we pronounce them today. 'When he spoke of the "Narzis",' wrote Leslie Hore-Belisha after the war, 'the very lengthening of the vowel carried with it his message of contempt. By these means he can, when he wishes, make not only every phrase but every word significant' (ed. Eade, *Contemporaries* p. 395). The writer Peter Fleming commended Churchill for his 'staunch refusal to give foreign words like "Nazi" any save the most insular pronunciation' (Fleming, *Invasion* p. 141).

covert armaments which are proceeding there to-day.' In that February speech, Churchill depicted the nightmare of being presented with an ultimatum by Germany of 'a very few hours; and if that answer is not satisfactory, within the next few hours the crash of bombs exploding in London and cataracts of masonry and fire and smoke will apprise us of any inadequacy which has been permitted in our aerial defences. We are vulnerable as we have never been before.'[10] He called for the building of 'an Air Force at least as strong as that of any Power that can get at us'.[11] Bernays, who supported disarmament and had heard some of the speech being practised in the Smoking Room beforehand, and noticed Churchill's rubbing an imaginary sore on his finger during the cancer analogy, wrote, 'Winston was superb . . . I couldn't help thinking in spite of myself that there might be something in it.'[12]

Few others agreed with him, however. When later in February Churchill told the Oxford University Conservative Association that rearmament was necessary 'for us to be safe in our Island home', there was only derisive laughter.[13] He continued to urge the need for stronger air defences in the Commons in March with the words 'All history has proved the peril of being dependent upon a foreign State for home defence instead of upon one's own right arm . . . I dread the day when the means of threatening the heart of the British Empire should pass into the hands of the present rulers of Germany . . . This terrible new fact has occurred. Germany is arming; she is rapidly arming and no one will stop her.'[14] Bernays recorded how Churchill 'wanders in and out, stirs uneasily in his seat and is in a fever of impatience to be up. He is like a pugilist waiting for the command "seconds out" in the ring.'[15]

In April 1934 Churchill discovered that the previous November Lord Derby and Samuel Hoare had illegally manipulated the evidence given by Manchester Chamber of Commerce (MCC) to the Commons Select Committee on India, by putting pressure on members of the MCC to change their statements about the impact that Indian self-government would have on trade. He decided to take the matter to the Commons Committee of Privileges. Since the views of the Lancashire cotton manufacturers were central to his argument about the ill-effect of Indian self-government on British trade, the next day he sensationally accused Derby and Hoare of a 'high crime' in a speech in the Commons.[16] Churchill had no more than hearsay and conjecture; none of the members of the MCC were willing to say on the record that Derby or Hoare had directly pressured them to change their statements, watering down the malign effects that Indian self-government was likely to have on the Manchester textile industry. As Derby's and Hoare's reputations and careers were on the line, the issue became extremely fraught, even though the Conservatives had an in-built majority on both committees.[17]

In his memoirs, Hoare described the charges that he and Derby had tampered with the evidence of the MCC as 'so groundless and irresponsible that they could be quickly laughed out of court'.[18] When the Committee of Privileges was convened, only one member out of the ten, Lord Hugh Cecil (Churchill's best man and close friend), supported Churchill. Several others, including Baldwin, MacDonald, Thomas Inskip, Clement Attlee, Sir Herbert Samuel and the senior Labour politician Arthur Greenwood, were leading proponents of the India Bill, which would have been badly disrupted had Hoare, the Secretary for India, been forced to resign. The Committee met sixteen times, heard testimony from fifteen members of the MCC, and, since Churchill could not prove his allegations with enough material evidence, completely cleared Hoare and Derby of any wrongdoing.

Yet the chairman of the India section of the MCC admitted that influence had been brought to bear. A letter from Derby to an MCC member stated, 'You will quite understand that the part I must play is [that of an] innocent observer who knows nothing about the matter,' and the Prime Minister offered Churchill a job if he would drop the issue. The Government refused to publish the full evidence, and whipped the vote on the Committee's report.[19] Churchill did no better in the Commons debate on the subject in June. Replying to him, Leo Amery said, 'At all costs he [Churchill] had to be faithful to his chosen motto: *fiat justitia ruat caelum*.'* 'Translate it,' demanded Churchill. 'I will translate it into the vernacular,' replied Amery. ' "If I can trip up Sam, the Government's bust." ' The House roared with laughter.[20] 'I ought not to have done that,' Churchill ruefully admitted in the Smoking Room afterwards, 'it was a first class blunder.'[21] 'Winston Churchill's stock never stood so low,' reported Lady Willingdon, the wife of the Viceroy of India, to Sir Miles Lampson, the High Commissioner in Egypt, on 13 August, 'largely as a result of his idiotic action in trying to impeach Derby over India.'[22]

Churchill told Cyril Asquith that he had 'sustained a very evil impression of the treatment I received and some day I hope to nail this bad behaviour upon a board, as stoats and weasels are nailed up by gamekeepers'.[23] It was only in the 1970s, years after Churchill's death, that Martin Gilbert, Churchill's official biographer, discovered a top-secret letter in the India Office archive from Hoare to Lord Willingdon, dated 3 November 1933. 'Derby has been exceedingly good with the Manchester Chamber

* 'Let justice be done even if the heavens fall' (the motto of Ferdinand I of Austria).

of Commerce,' it stated. 'He has induced them to withdraw a dangerous and aggressive memorandum that they had sent in to the Committee and fortunately I had prevented from being circulated. They have now substituted a very harmless document.'[24] Churchill never knew it, but he had been right all along. The short-term effect, however, was to lessen his standing in Parliament and to undermine his ability to convince his fellow MPs of the seriousness of what was happening in Germany.

On 30 June 1934, in a purge that became known as the Night of the Long Knives, Hitler ordered the arrest and execution without trial of several hundred people whom he considered to be actual or potential political opponents. 'Herr Hitler, whatever one may think of his methods,' opined *The Times*, 'is genuinely trying to transform revolutionary fervour into moderate and constructive effort and to impose a high standard of public service on National-Socialist officials.'[25] By contrast, Churchill told his Wanstead constituents a week later that:

> Minds are oppressed by the grisly events which occurred in Germany . . . It seems difficult to realize that a great and highly educated and scientific nation, with all its treasures of literature, learning, and music behind it, should present itself to the world in such an awful guise. We are in the presence of a tyranny maintained by press and broadcast propaganda and the ruthless murder of political opponents.[26]

He called for the doubling of the size of the RAF, and for a larger vote of credit 'as soon as possible to redouble the Air Force' once again. For this he was ridiculed by Herbert Samuel, and likened to 'a Malay running amok'.[27]

That same day, 30 June, Sunny, the 9th Duke of Marlborough, died. He was succeeded by the eldest of his two sons, but if he had died without a son, Churchill would have inherited the peerage, losing his seat in the Commons and almost certainly the chance of becoming prime minister, as it was not possible to renounce peerages until 1958. He could survive a school stabbing, a 30-foot fall, pneumonia, a Swiss lake, Cuban bullets, Pathan tribesmen, Dervish spears, Boer artillery and sentries, tsetse flies, a house fire, two plane and three car crashes, German high-explosive shells and snipers and latterly a New York motorist, but such was the British constitution that he also required a duke and duchess to produce boys rather than girls to allow him to continue his Commons career.

Although Parliament approved some RAF expansion in July, it came at the price of cuts in the Army and Navy budgets. Chamberlain meanwhile wanted to reduce defence expenditure by one-third, through a treaty with Germany that would confine the German Navy to one-third the size of the Royal Navy, and by scaling down any commitment to provide a BEF in France in the event of war.[28] Britain therefore did start rearming in 1934, but in a grudging, piecemeal, Treasury-led way that was given minimum publicity so as not to 'provoke' Hitler or, just as importantly, the British public. Churchill's role in prodding and demanding more was not yet resented by the Government. His sources of information were not prosecuted under the Official Secrets Act, despite the fact that several of them were known to MI5, who bugged his telephone.[29]

In mid-July, Churchill and Austen Chamberlain – who opposed the appeasement of Germany – announced themselves in favour of befriending the USSR and admitting it into the League of Nations.[30] This was a major step for so doctrinaire an anti-Communist as Churchill, and was easily presented by his enemies as yet another volte-face, but it was a measure of how necessary he considered the building of collective security against Hitler to be. Churchill met Ivan Maisky, the Soviet Ambassador to London, in 1935, and told him that the rise of the Nazis threatened to reduce Britain to 'a toy in the hands of German imperialism'. He suspended his anti-Russian stance, telling Maisky that he did not believe that the Soviet Union would pose a threat to Britain for at least ten years.[31] This time his prediction was remarkably accurate: his Iron Curtain speech came eleven years later. On 2 August 1934, President von Hindenburg died. Seventeen days later a plebiscite approved, by 38.4 million votes to 4.3 million, Hitler's appointment as Führer, with sole executive power. The Nazis now had unfettered power to turn Germany into a vicious totalitarian dictatorship, which they proceeded to do at the fastest pace possible. 'I was glad that so many had the courage to vote against making that gangster autocrat for life,' Churchill told Clementine, thinking of the brave 4.3 million.[32]

Later in August, Churchill, Lindemann and Randolph went to stay at the Château de l'Horizon at Golfe-Juan near Cannes, the large art deco seaside house* built by the American actress and Society hostess Maxine Elliott, who entertained lavishly. Born Jessie Dermott in 1868† in Rockland, Maine, the beautiful and witty daughter of an immigrant Irish sea captain, she acted in successful popular musicals, had a baby at fifteen with a man ten years her senior, became J. P. Morgan's mistress and was at least twice divorced (from an alcoholic Irish politician and an equally alcoholic comedian). She also made a lot of money in business and did relief work for Belgian refugees in the Great War, in which her much younger lover

* It is today owned by the King of Saudi Arabia.

† Or thereabouts; rather magnificently she lied about her date of birth even on her tombstone.

had been killed in battle. She had thus led just the kind of life that would amuse and impress Churchill, who had known her since 1905, when she had lived at Hartsbourne Manor in Hertfordshire and entertained Edwardian notables. 'She was lovable, fat, oh so fat, witty and gracious,' the Tory MP Henry 'Chips' Channon wrote when she died in 1940, listing Edward VII and Lord Curzon among her former lovers.[33]

Holidays at the Château de l'Horizon were fun: playing charades, Churchill once impersonated a bear under a rug.[34] One of the guests remembered Maxine lying on a chaise-longue, 'shading her ravaged beauty with a parasol, and she was addressing sharp words to a young English footman, tall and tanned, who was blinking nervously before her. "You *must* remember, Robert, to put sugar on the monkey's strawberries. Look! She's not eaten a thing."'[35] Clementine disliked the Riviera and came only once, for a short period. 'God, it's a ghastly place!' she supposedly said. 'I expect it's all right if you're a flower-shop owner or a waiter.'[36] Her husband spent the holiday painting and working on the proofs of the second volume of *Marlborough*. On the way back he travelled the Route Napoléon from Golfe-Juan to Grenoble. 'It was an amazing episode,' he told Clementine. 'I really must try to write a Napoleon before I die. But the work piles up and I wonder whether I shall have the time and strength.'[37] Regrettably, he never did. Churchill, Randolph and Lindemann stopped at Aix-les-Bains, where Baldwin was taking one of his six-week holidays, to urge him to set up an air research committee to prevent German bombers from getting through to London, as he had warned the House of Commons they 'always' would. Afterwards, Baldwin remarked that Churchill 'had never seen Mont Blanc, so he was going there, letting the mountains have a peek at him'.[38]

Churchill had been a sportsman, but in his late fifties he started to slow down and put on weight. He did not like tennis – which Clementine loved – as his weak shoulder precluded strong serves, and did not enjoy her other sport of skiing either. He had played polo until his fifties and still occasionally rode to hounds into his seventies, but he played golf only because it gave him the opportunity to spend long periods of time with Asquith and Lloyd George, and stopped once they had fallen from power. (In 1915 he described golf as 'Like chasing a quinine pill around a cow pasture.')[39] He swam in the heated pool at Chartwell – which Diana Cooper called 'Winston's delightful toy' – and shot, fished and went boar-hunting. None of these were things he could enjoy with Clementine, any more than his big-game hunting in Africa or big-game fishing in California had been. At the end of September 1934, Churchill and Clementine managed a rare holiday together for nearly a month. They cruised on Lord

Moyne's yacht *Rosaura*, a former passenger ferry, for nearly a month, sailing from Marseilles to Naples, Greece, Alexandria, Beirut, Syria and Palestine, only returning on 21 October. Moyne, who had been wounded and mentioned in dispatches in the Boer War and won a DSO and bar having fought in Gallipoli and at Passchendaele, joined the Other Club. This was made mildly awkward by the fact that another member, Oswald Mosley, a member since 1931, was sleeping with his wife, Diana. Extraordinarily, Mosley continued to attend until May 1935, despite his openly avowed Fascism. He was only formally expelled in 1945.

In November, Churchill conducted a parliamentary guerrilla war against the India Bill, with procedural motions, amendments and an effective filibuster supported by about thirty MPs. 'It is difficult to think that Mr Churchill has once been Chancellor of the Exchequer,' fumed the 'livid' Captain David Margesson, the National Government Chief Whip, who Bernays noted 'harangued' any Tory MPs who supported the rebellion.[40] The National Government's whipping operation was extremely effective, and no one was tougher or more ruthless than the hatchet-faced Margesson, although he recognized that there was no point whatever in attempting to bully or cajole Churchill. (Margesson was a bête noire to Clementine, and Mary thought he looked like Mephistopheles.)[41]

On 16 November, John Reith finally allowed Churchill on to the airwaves with a BBC radio broadcast entitled 'The Causes of War', in which Churchill starkly warned that Britain was 'in mortal danger'.[42] He argued that the nations of Europe faced 'the old grim choice our forebears had to face, namely, whether we shall submit to the will of a stronger nation or whether we shall prepare to defend our rights, our liberties and indeed our lives'. No one, he said, 'outside a madhouse' would want to start another war, but 'There is a nation which has abandoned all its liberties in order to augment its collective might. There is a nation which with all its strength and virtues is in the grip of a group of ruthless men preaching a gospel of intolerance and racial pride, unrestrained by law, by Parliament or by public opinion.'[43] It was as stark a warning as Churchill could make, but it had little or no effect on a nation that did not want to listen, or contemplate the consequences of his being right.

On 28 November, he made one of the most important speeches of his Wilderness Years, when he warned that Germany would achieve air parity with Britain during 1935. He sent the speech to Baldwin five days beforehand, as proof of his desire to be constructive.[44] He described bombing as 'the only form of war that we have seen in the world in which complete predominance gives no opportunity of recovery'.[45] He believed that 30,000 or 40,000 Londoners would be killed or maimed in a week of bombing. 'It is just as well to confront those facts while time remains to take proper measures to cope with them.'[46]

'To urge the preparation of defence is not to assert the imminence of war,' he said. 'On the contrary, if war were imminent, preparations for defence would be too late.' But he reiterated his central message: 'What is the great new fact which has broken in upon us during the last eighteen months? Germany is rearming. That is the great new fact which rivets the attention of every country in Europe, indeed in all the world, and which throws almost all other issues into the background.'[47] He appreciated that he was in a tiny minority in Parliament, but argued, 'What was the use of going to a division? You might walk a majority round and round the lobbies for a year, and not alter the facts by which we are confronted.'[48]

To celebrate his sixtieth birthday two days later, Venetia Montagu – one of his many female friends – threw a dinner in his honour. A number of worldly Society beauties were invited, such as Lady Castlerosse and Phyllis de Janzé. 'This is the sort of company I should like to find in heaven,' he said, thanking Venetia afterwards. 'Stained perhaps – stained but positive. Not those flaccid sea anemones of virtue who can hardly wobble an antenna in the turgid waters of negativity.'[49]

On 18 December, the forty-nine-year-old Clementine left on a four-month journey to the Dutch East Indies (present-day Indonesia) with Lord Moyne in *Rosaura*, on an expedition to bring living Komodo dragon giant lizards to Britain for the first time. They sailed through the Suez Canal, across the Indian Ocean and into the Pacific via (present-day) India, Burma, Thailand, Malaysia, Indonesia, Borneo, Papua New Guinea, Australia and New Zealand. In the event they caught two Komodo dragons, one of which, 6 feet long, lived at London Zoo until 1946. For all the lizards they were chasing in Indonesia, there was also one on board, in the shape of the lounge-lizard Terence Philip. Philip was a suave, handsome, debonair and cultivated bachelor art dealer, forty-two years old, who spoke fluent Russian and was much prized by London hostesses as a 'spare' man for dinner parties. 'During the months of this voyage, not surprisingly, she fell romantically in love with him,' wrote Mary Soames of her mother. 'It was a classic holiday romance.'[50]

Clementine acknowledged that Philip had not really been 'in love' with her but, she added, 'he made me like him'. She summed up their liaison wryly 'with a saying which seems to breathe the Edwardian world of her youth: *C'était une vraie connaissance de ville d'eau*'.[51] 'Altho' I like what I have seen of Mr Philip,' she wrote to her husband at the beginning of the trip, 'I don't know him at all well, and ten days tête-à-tête with a stranger is more trying (I expect, for I have never tried it) than complete solitude.'[52] 'I miss you very much and feel very unprotected,' he replied. 'But I did not feel I ought to try to do you out of a wonderful trip on which you had evidently set your heart.'[53] Philip visited Chartwell a few times after their return, but by then Clementine had returned to real life.[54] Both the physical extent of the romance and Churchill's inkling of it are to this day wrapped in even more impenetrable mystery than the membership of the Other Club's executive committee.

While worrying about Clementine catching malaria in Ceylon (modern Sri Lanka) Churchill was also able to tell her that their finances were strengthening for the first time since the Crash. Since September, he had written several film scripts for Alexander Korda, and 'We ought to be in a good position by this time next year. This would be important for you if anything happened to me or to my earning power.'[55] Had he accompanied her, he might have noticed the weakness of the landward defences of Singapore when the *Rosaura* moored there in January; instead he had to rely on her description of the dockyards.

Whether or not illicit sex was taking place in the South Seas, incest was certainly under way at Chartwell. 'All the black swans are mating,' Churchill told his wife, 'not only the father and mother, but both brothers and both sisters have paired off. The Ptolemys always did this and Cleopatra was the result. At any rate I have not thought it my duty to interfere.'[56] He wrote her passionate letters all the time she was away, but they were dictated. 'I have almost lost the art of thinking with a pen in my hand,' he told her.[57] At the same time he was writing in the *News of the World* that his marriage 'was much the most fortunate and joyous event which happened to me in the whole of my life, for what can be more glorious than to be united in one's walk through life with a being incapable of an ignoble thought?'[58]

One of the fruits of this happy union was causing Churchill consternation, however. Randolph had decided to stand in the Liverpool Wavertree by-election as an Independent against the official Tory candidate, with opposition to the Government of India Bill as his cause. 'This is a most rash and unconsidered plunge,' Churchill told Clementine. He was deeply embarrassed by the move politically, as it threatened to split the Tory vote and give a normally Conservative seat to Labour – which was precisely what happened.[59] 'I am vexed and worried about it,' Churchill said, but Randolph would not listen to advice.[60] Churchill nonetheless gave £200 to the campaign, one-sixth of the permitted total, with the Duke of Westminster giving £500, but he was in a quandary about whether to go to Liverpool to support his son, as Sarah and Diana did. Of course blood won out in the end over the threat of the withdrawal of the Tory whip, and he went up just before polling day, privately saying that Randolph's candidature was a 'spirited adventure'.[61]

When Clementine returned on 2 May 1935, she brought back a pink-beige dove from Bali, where she told her husband she had spent 'two entrancing days' the previous month.[62] When it died, she buried it under the sundial in the walled garden at Chartwell, beneath some engraved lines from the poet W. P. Ker that had been suggested to her by the travel writer Freya Stark:

> Here Lies the Bali Dove.
> It does not do to wander
> Too far from sober men,
> But there's an island yonder,
> I think of it again.

This has been interpreted by some as a reference to her months with Terence Philip, though the choice of 'sober men' hardly seems the ideal way of describing the husband from whom she had briefly wandered.

It has been alleged that in 1933 the fifty-eight-year-old Churchill began a four-year affair with the thirty-two-year-old Doris, Lady Castlerosse (née De le Vingne).* Lady Castlerosse was separated from her husband Viscount Castlerosse (later the 6th Earl of Kenmare) and had had an affair with Randolph in 1932.[63] Although Jock Colville claimed in 1985 that the rumours were true, half a century after the alleged affair, he did not become Churchill's private secretary until 1940, several years after it supposedly took place. In the same interview, the septuagenarian Colville also stated that 'Winston Churchill was . . . not a highly sexual man at all . . . He never ran after women.'[64] Lady Castlerosse herself told her sister and niece that she had been Churchill's lover.

The letters and telegrams exchanged between Churchill and Lady Castlerosse, who was another habitué of the louche Château de l'Horizon, are perfectly consistent with a friendship rather than an affair, not least because she asked Clementine as well as Churchill to dinners, and because, in a letter to Clementine, Churchill mentioned Doris as being present at Maxine Elliott's house.[65] (In one letter from 1937, Lady Castlerosse asks Churchill to telephone her and gives him her four-digit number, which had she been his mistress for four years he would presumably have already known.) Churchill liked the vivacious Doris and much has been made of

* Great-aunt of the supermodel Cara Delevingne, which partly explains the coverage that newspapers give the story.

the fact that he painted her four times, yet he also painted several other women, including Walter Sickert's wife Thérèse, Arthur Balfour's niece Blanche Dugdale, Sir John Lavery's wife Hazel, his own sister-in-law Lady Gwendeline Churchill, his secretary Cecily Gemmell, his wife's cousin Maryott Whyte and Lady Kitty Somerset. There is no suggestion he was sleeping with any of them. He painted Clementine three times. (The Churchills were so famously uxorious that *Punch* magazine nicknamed them 'the Birdikins'.)[66]

Although it is notoriously difficult to prove a negative, especially at a distance of more than eight decades, it is impossible to believe that Churchill genuinely had an affair with Lady Castlerosse, or anyone else.[67] He still loved Clementine passionately; she was his emotional rock, closest adviser, mother of his five children and greatest supporter through every conceivable reverse in life, as well as the recipient of several hundred heartfelt love-letters, one of which, from the Chateau de l'Horizon in September 1936 while Doris was staying there, ends, 'Tender love my sweet Clemmie, Always your devoted loving husband Winston'.[68]

Quite apart from the emotional reasons against there having been an affair, there were a host of practical ones too. Churchill still believed he was going to be prime minister; Lord Castlerosse worked for Beaverbrook and was an impoverished, alcoholic and occasionally violent gossip columnist; Randolph had slept with her in 1932 (occasioning a near-fight with Castlerosse); no love-letters exist; there were always other guests – including writers and journalists – and large numbers of servants present at the Château, as well as the extremely gossipy Maxine herself. Maxine's nephew-in-law, the writer Vincent Sheean, described Lady Castlerosse as an 'unrivaled nitwit' obsessed with her appearance, who, 'scratching the inside of her shapely bare legs, inquired in a piercing nasal voice, "Winston, why is it they always seem to go to *Geneva* for their meetings?"' Churchill replied, 'Because, my dear, Geneva happens to be the seat of the League of Nations. You have heard of it, no doubt?'[69]

Her ignorance was matched only by the semi-literate nature of her letters, just one of which might be open to a doubtful interpretation. In July 1937 she wrote to Churchill, 'I should so like to see you. I am not at all dangerous any more. I return on Tuesday, do ring me some time, Mayfair 3731. My love, Doris.'[70] The most likely interpretation is that she had given up flirting with him, further indication that they did not have any physical relationship.[71] She claimed one, a Churchill biographer has suggested, because 'She relied on attracting wealthy lovers to fund her extravagance, and she may well have tried to add to her allure as a *femme fatale* by whispering that the notably monogamous Churchill was one of her conquests.'[72] Churchill had plenty of good female friends with whom he did not have sexual relationships, among whom were Violet Bonham Carter, Venetia Montagu (née Stanley), Ava Waverley, Wendy Reves, Ettie Desborough, Maxine Elliott, Pamela Lytton, Daisy Fellowes and Muriel Wilson. Doris Castlerosse – who died of an overdose of barbiturates in the Dorchester Hotel in December 1942, while under police investigation for illegally selling diamonds – should be added to that list.[73] Churchill himself provides the best prism through which to view these flimsy and circumstantial allegations against him, when he wrote in his Clemenceau chapter of *Great Contemporaries*, 'The Muse of History must not be fastidious. She must see everything, touch everything, and, if possible, smell everything. She need not be afraid that these intimate details will rob her of romance and hero-worship. Recorded trifles and tittle-tattle may – and indeed ought – to wipe out small people. They can have no permanent effect upon those who have held with honour the foremost stations in the greatest storms.'[74]

On 4 March 1935, the Government published its Defence White Paper, intended to brace the public for a £10 million increase in arms spending. Chamberlain toned down its references to Germany, and was supported by Baldwin who told Sir Robert Vansittart, the strongly anti-Nazi Permanent Under-Secretary at the Foreign Office, that he did not think 'it was wise to indict Germany alone, since she was not the only power rearming'.[75] That was true, but the others were rearming because of Germany. In the debate on the White Paper, Clement Attlee said, 'We deny the proposition that an increased British air force will make for the peace of the world, and we reject altogether the plan of parity.' Another prominent Labour figure, Stafford Cripps, said, 'The Government has had its hands forced by the wild men like Mr Churchill.' The next year Cripps was to say that he did not 'believe it would be a bad thing for the British working class if Germany defeated us'.[76] Archie Sinclair, who was by then leader of the Liberal Party, denounced 'the folly, danger and wastefulness of this steady accumulation of armaments'.[77] With an election looming against such a background of abject pacificism, Baldwin's commendation of his own White Paper was lukewarm, as he argued, 'It is not a question in international affairs of doing what is ideally best, but a question of doing what is best under the circumstances.'[78]

'The Government tardily, timidly and inadequately have at last woken up to the rapidly increasing German peril,' Churchill told Clementine. But had it?[79] On 16 March, Hitler repudiated the disarmament clauses of Versailles and announced the creation of the Luftwaffe, which was banned by the Treaty, as well as the development of a conscripted army of half a million men when the Treaty stipulated an upper limit of 100,000. From his private information on the rate of German rearmament being provided by his informants, Churchill was able to tell the Commons three days later that:

> Enormous sums of money are being spent on German aviation and upon other armaments . . . From being the least vulnerable of all nations we have, through developments in the air, become the most vulnerable, and yet, even now, we are not taking the measures which would be in true proportion to our needs. The Government have proposed these increases. They must face the storm. They will have to encounter every form of unfair attack. Their motives will be misrepresented. They will be calumniated and called war-mongers. Every kind of attack will be made upon them by many powerful, numerous and extremely vocal forces in this country. They are going to get it anyway. Why, then, not fight for something that will give us safety?[80]

The House listened politely, but there was no response. 'As for Winston, he makes a good many speeches, considerably fortified by cocktails and old brandies,' Chamberlain wrote to his sister Hilda. 'Some of them are very good speeches in the old style, but they no longer convince.'[81]

Churchill sensed he was speaking into a void, and years later he wrote of that debate, 'I felt a sensation of despair. To be so entirely convinced and vindicated in a matter of life and death to one's country, and not to be able to make Parliament and the nation heed the warning, or bow to the proof by taking action, was an experience most painful.'[82] During the debate he was reminded of some lines of verse from *Punch* magazine which referred to a Victorian railway accident in Hampshire that he had learned as a teenager:

> Who is in charge of the clattering train?
> The axles creak, and the couplings strain,
> And the pace is hot, and the points are near,
> And Sleep has deadened the driver's ear;
> And signals flash through the night in vain,
> For Death is in charge of the clattering train.[83]

He did not recite it during the debate, but he often did during the Blitz.[84]

Churchill's stance on air rearmament appeared to be almost immediately vindicated when on 25 March Hitler told Anthony Eden that the Luftwaffe had now achieved parity with the RAF. This was in fact untrue, but it lent credence to what Churchill had been saying.[85] Baldwin's claim in the Commons the previous November that Germany had attained only half of Britain's front-line strength now seemed certainly wrong. Churchill told Clementine that it was a 'political sensation . . . This completely stultifies everything that Baldwin has said and incidentally vindicates all the assertions that I have made.'[86] Between 10 and 14 April, the Government attempted to negotiate a common front with France and Italy against Germany at Stresa on Lake Maggiore in Italy, which Churchill supported as a means of splitting the Fascist governments.

In April, Churchill decided he should try to alter his speaking style, to make it less sonorous and Victorian, to avoid sounding pompous to younger listeners. At sixty, he was an old dog to be learning new oratorical tricks, but as he told Clementine he would now 'talk to the House of Commons in garrulous unpremeditated flow'.[87] He tried it out once or twice, and 'They seem delighted. But what a mystery this art of public speaking is! It all consists in my (mature) judgment of selecting three or four absolutely sound arguments and putting these in the most conversational manner possible. There is apparently absolutely nothing in the literary effect I have sought for forty years!'[88] The declamatory style of Gladstone and Morley, and indeed his father, would be replaced by a much more genuine-sounding rhetoric, such as he was able to deploy during the Second World War.

'There is nothing new in the story,' Churchill told the Commons in May about Britain's failure to rearm. 'It is as old as the Sibylline Books.* It falls into that long, dismal catalogue of the fruitlessness of experience and the confirmed unteachability of Mankind. Want of foresight, unwillingness to act when action would be simple and effective, lack of clear thinking, confusion of counsel until the emergency comes, until self-preservation strikes its jarring gong – these are the features which constitute the endless repetition of history.'[89] The history he had in mind was Britain's 400-year-old foreign policy of forming European coalitions to face the strongest power on the continent, whether it be Spain, France or Germany. 'I have no doubt who it is now,' he added. 'It is thus through the centuries we have kept our liberties and maintained our life and power.'[90]

Churchill was answered sneeringly by Lieutenant-Colonel Thomas Moore, the Conservative MP for Ayr: 'Although one hates to criticize anyone in the evening of his days, nothing can excuse the right honourable Member for Epping for having permeated his entire speech with the atmosphere that Germany is arming for war.'[91] He went on, 'surely it is impossible

* Oracles bought from a sibyl, or fortune-teller, by King Tarquin of Rome.

to visualize a situation in which either the losers or the victors will ever again, at least in our lifetime, embark on such a disastrous conflict.'

On 22 May, Baldwin admitted to the Commons that he had been 'completely wrong . . . completely misled' in preparing his estimate of future German aircraft construction the previous November. In that debate, Churchill predicted that on current trends 'by the end of this year' the Luftwaffe 'will be possibly three, and even four, times our strength'.[92] Despite the dire nature of his warning, he was still able to joke about the Baldwin of 1930: 'In those days the Lord President was wiser than he is now; he used frequently to take my advice.' Churchill's central message was that 'It is very much better sometimes to have a panic feeling beforehand, and then to be quite calm when things happen, than to be extremely calm beforehand and to get into a panic when things happen.'

Churchill saw British history as a continuum, in which Britain's duty was to keep the balance of power in Europe. After Hitler had written to Rothermere in early May to assert that an Anglo-German alliance would protect 'the interests of the white race', Churchill reminded Rothermere of the fable of the tiger and jackal who went out hunting together, only for the tiger to eat the jackal afterwards, implying that if Hitler's offering was to be taken up he would sooner or later betray his British ally. And he gave Rothermere a history lesson.[93] 'If his proposal means that we should come to an understanding with Germany to dominate Europe, I think this would be contrary to the whole of our history,' Churchill told Britain's foremost press baron. 'We have on all occasions been the friend of the second strongest power in Europe and have never yielded ourselves to the strongest power. Thus Elizabeth resisted Philip II of Spain,' he reiterated. 'Thus William III and Marlborough resisted Louis XIV. Thus Pitt resisted Napoleon, and thus we all resisted William II of Germany. Only by taking this path and effort have we preserved ourselves and our liberties, and reached our present position. I see no reason myself to change from this traditional view.'[94]

Lord Crawford was present at a dinner of the parliamentary dining club Grillions at the Grosvenor House Hotel at this time, and noticed that the Cabinet ministers William Ormsby-Gore and Lord Eustace Percy (nicknamed by Churchill Lord 'Useless' Percy) deliberately sat at the far end of the table from Churchill, who was 'declaiming at the top of his voice and occupying the conversation without intermission. Besides he is bellicose on just those matters which ministers do not want to discuss in mixed company [that is, with those who did not support the Government] at the dinner table; but he is most entertaining if you surrender yourself to his domination.'[95]

On 5 June the long and bruising struggle over the Government of India Bill finally ended with the passing of the third reading by 386 to 122, giving the Indian provincial governments wide measures of self-government under an overall British aegis. There were about forty Labour MPs who voted against it because they thought it did not go far enough. After the Bill's passage Churchill invited one of Gandhi's Indian friends, G. D. Birla, to Chartwell. 'Tell Mr Gandhi to use the powers that are offered to make the thing a success,' he told him. 'I am genuinely sympathetic towards India. I have got real fears about the future . . . But you have got the things now; make it a success and if you do I will advocate your getting much more.'[96] When Birla duly relayed Churchill's words, Gandhi said, 'I have got a good recollection of Mr Churchill when he was in the Colonial Office and somehow or other since then I have held the opinion that I can always rely on his sympathy and goodwill.' That was going much too far, although Churchill did say that his esteem for Gandhi had risen since Gandhi had 'stood up for the Untouchables'.[97]

With the India Act passed, the ill, tired and sixty-nine-year-old Ramsay MacDonald resigned the premiership on 7 June 1935, in favour of Stanley Baldwin, who did not invite Churchill into the Government in the consequent reshuffle. When they disagreed so sharply about the scale and speed of rearmament, it is hard to see how he could have done, especially with a general election in the offing in which that critical issue would feature prominently. Eleven days later, the Government announced the terms of an Anglo-German Naval Agreement signed without French approval, which set German navy tonnage at 35 per cent of the Royal Navy's, much larger than that allowed by the Versailles Treaty, which Britain was therefore complicit in breaking. The Agreement, which Churchill described in Parliament as 'the acme of gullibility', was soon broken by the Germans, but it served to make the National Government look serious about arms reduction before the election on 14 November.[98]

'The League of Nations has been weakened by our action,' Churchill said in the debate on the Naval Agreement, 'the principle of collective security has been impaired . . . British influence has to some extent been dissipated, and our moral position, or at any rate our logical position, has been to some extent obscured. You could not have had a more complete and perfect example of how not to do it.'[99] He nonetheless voted with the Government, hoping that after the election he might be invited to join it, not least as a warning to Hitler that Britain was serious about stopping his drive for European hegemony. He did point out that the Germans had been able to convert the 10,000-ton ships permitted under Versailles into 26,000-ton warships 'by a concealment which the Admiralty were utterly unable to penetrate'.[100]

As long ago as April 1925, Hankey had invited Lindemann on to the new Air Defence Research Sub-Committee of the Committee of Imperial Defence. Baldwin had suspended the Committee in November 1928, and it was not to be revived until after Hitler had come to power. Baldwin asked Churchill to join the reconstituted Sub-Committee in July 1935, which later became known as the Tizard Committee after its new chairman, the chemist and inventor Sir Henry Tizard. It was to be the scene for a series of clashes between Tizard and Lindemann over how best to stop German bombers getting through, which have been described as 'perhaps the most notorious scientific feud of modern times'.[101] Churchill invariably supported Lindemann in these clashes, even though today we know that Tizard was more often correct in his scientific evaluations. Lindemann nonetheless is on record writing to Churchill in February 1936 'commending the successful work of [Robert] Watson-Watt on detection' – by which he meant radar – declaring himself 'an enthusiastic believer'.[102] By the outbreak of war, there were twenty radar stations between Portsmouth and Scapa Flow, which could detect aircraft from 50 to 120 miles away, flying above 10,000 feet. In Churchill's and Lindemann's view the Tizard Committee was not carrying out enough experiments on increasing the effective duration of shell bursts, or on kite-balloons, or on infra-red methods of homing in on enemy aeroplanes. Not all of these areas proved practicable, but at least they were trying to think constructively outside normal parameters.[103]

When the Government announced on 24 August that if Italy invaded Abyssinia (present-day Ethiopia) Britain would stand by her League of Nations obligations, Churchill did not want to antagonize Italy with the threat of sanctions.[104] He believed that an oil embargo would destroy the fragile Stresa Front (of Britain, France and Italy against Germany) and force Mussolini into Hitler's camp, all to stop Italy from taking a part of East Africa that no other European Power wanted. His attitude here was one of Realpolitik rather than ideology, which sat ill with the principles of human rights, democracy, self-determination and the rights of small countries that he was later to invoke.

On 2 October 1935, Mussolini did invade Abyssinia, whereupon the League of Nations imposed economic sanctions on Italy, in which Germany, Austria and Hungary did not join. Britain did not impose the sanctions that mattered most, those on oil, causing Labour and the Liberals to say the League was being sold out so as not to offend Italy, which was indeed the case. 'We cannot afford to see Nazidom in its present phase of cruelty and intolerance, with all its hatreds and all its gleaming weapons, paramount in Europe at the present time,' Churchill told the Commons on 24 October, significantly not calling for the sanctions on Italy to be extended to oil.[105] 'I venture to submit to the House that we cannot have any anxieties comparable to the anxiety caused by German rearmament,' he added.[106] Arthur Greenwood accused Churchill of 'trying to have it both ways. I have no doubt that he has perhaps succeeded in justifying his appointment to high office if the worst happens, and the National Government is returned.'[107]

During the election campaign, Baldwin told the British people, 'I give you my word there will be no great armaments.' In his election leaflet, Churchill lauded the past 'four years of steady and stable government' and argued, 'Last time you voted for National Solvency. Now it is National Safety which is at stake . . . We have fallen grievously behind in the Air, and we now have to make an intense effort to have as strong and good an Air Force as that of any country that can get at us.'[108] Of the dictatorships, he wrote, 'The world is divided between governments who own the peoples and peoples who own the governments. Free Parliaments and Democracy have been trampled down in most of the great countries of Europe. They have reverted to despotism and dictatorships; and all the apparatus of science and Civilization can be perverted to the propaganda of tyranny.'[109]*

The National Government won another landslide victory on 14 November 1935, with 432 seats to Labour's 154 and the Liberals' 20. Overall, the National Government supporters (mainly Conservatives) won 11.81 million votes, Labour 8.32 million and the Liberals 1.42 million. Duncan Sandys, Diana's Old Etonian, Oxford-educated former diplomat husband, was re-elected for Norwood, and Churchill was returned for Epping with a larger majority. Having toned down his criticisms of the Government he hoped to be given a ministerial job coordinating Britain's defences. But once again Baldwin did not call. At the time Churchill was profoundly disappointed, but later he wrote, 'Now I can see how lucky I was. Over me beat the invisible wings.'[110] It turns out those wings belonged to none other than Baldwin himself, who told Davidson, 'If there is going to be war – and no one can say that there is not – we must keep him fresh to be our war Prime Minister.'[111]

In an article entitled 'The Truth about Hitler' in the *Strand Magazine* in November 1935, Churchill attempted to be as even-handed as possible about the Führer. 'Those who have met Herr Hitler face to face in public business or on social terms have found a highly competent, cool,

* The concept of perverted science was a potent one, and was to reappear in a key speech in 1940.

well-informed functionary with an agreeable manner, a disarming smile, and few have been unaffected by a subtle personal magnetism,' Churchill wrote, in words that were long held against him – even though 'functionary' was hardly an encomium. 'Thus the world lives on hopes that the worst is over, and that we may yet live to see Hitler a gentler figure in a happier age. Meanwhile, he makes speeches to the nations, which are sometimes characterized by candour and moderation.'[112] The key word there was 'sometimes'. Churchill's detractors also rarely quote the other parts of the article, in which he wrote, 'Recently he has offered many words of reassurance, eagerly lapped up by those who have been so tragically wrong about Germany in the past. Only time can show, but, meanwhile, the great wheels revolve; the rifles, the cannon, the tanks, the shot and shell, the air-bombs, the poison-gas cylinders, the aeroplanes, the submarines, and now the beginnings of a fleet, flow in ever-broadening streams from the already largely war-mobilized arsenals and factories of Germany.'[113] Like his other articles on Hitler, Churchill submitted this in advance to the Foreign Office, which asked him to tone it down. He did, a little. When they still complained of its toughness, he published it anyway.

On 19 December, the Foreign Secretary, Samuel Hoare, was forced to resign over a pact he had signed with his French opposite number, Pierre Laval, which made concessions to Italy in Abyssinia that were decried by Parliament. His place was taken by the Lord President of the Council, Anthony Eden. There was no hint at this stage of what was to become an extremely close alliance: 'Eden's appointment does not inspire me with confidence,' Churchill wrote to Clementine. 'I expect the greatness of his office will find him out.'[114] A little later he told her, 'I think you will now see what a lightweight Eden is.'[115] He nevertheless asked Randolph not to write articles attacking Eden, adding, 'If not, I shall not be able to feel confidence in your loyalty and affection for me. Your loving father, Winston S. Churchill.'[116]

Randolph had been defeated in Liverpool West Toxteth in the general election, and now made more trouble for his father, standing in a by-election for the Scottish seat of Ross and Cromarty against the National Labour candidate, Malcolm MacDonald, son of Ramsay. 'You can see how unfortunate and inconvenient such a fight is to me,' Churchill told Clementine. 'It would seem very difficult for Baldwin to invite me to take the Admiralty or the co-ordinating job.'[117] His relations with Randolph were stormy; during one family row – which often ended in shouting matches and one or the other of them stomping off – Churchill said exasperatedly to his son, 'Randolph, do not interrupt me while I'm interrupting.'[118] Randolph received no reward for his absence of filial devotion, coming third in Ross and Cromarty with 2,427 votes to Malcolm MacDonald's 8,949.

Churchill was on holiday at the Hotel Mamounia in Marrakesh with Lord Rothermere,* playing his favourite card game bezique, working on the next volume of *Marlborough* and painting the Atlas Mountains, when a story broke in the press about his twenty-one-year-old daughter Sarah. She had taken up acting and was dancing in the comic revue *Follow the Sun* in Manchester when she fell in love with its star, the thirty-seven-year-old, divorced Austrian-born Jewish comedian Vic Oliver (né Victor Oliver von Samek).[119] Oliver was variously described as a comic, a violinist, a pianist, a contortionist, a trampoline expert and even a banjo-player.[120] The first three were true, but not the last three. Just as the 7th Duke of Marlborough had sent agents to learn more about Leonard Jerome before Lord Randolph Churchill married Jennie, so Churchill sent a lawyer to Vienna to discover what he could about Vic Oliver's background. 'Please write to Sarah – (but not severely),' Clementine asked her husband. 'But more important than writing is to get . . . Mr Vic Oliver's dossier.'[121] When Churchill met him in February, he reported to Clementine that 'He did not impress me with being a bad man; but common as dirt . . . A horrible mouth: a foul Austro-Yankee drawl. I did not offer to shake hands: but put him through a long examination.'[122] He extracted a promise to postpone the engagement for a year, during which the couple would not see each other, which Churchill said Oliver agreed to, 'not without dignity'.[123]

'I should think that any question of my joining the Government was closed by the hostility which Randolph's campaign must excite,' Churchill told Clementine on 15 January 1936. 'Kismet! [Fate!]'[124] In fact Baldwin had no intention of taking Churchill back under any conditions short of a world war. Less than a week later, the death of King George V on 20 January forced Churchill to cut short his holiday. His letter to the new monarch, his friend King Edward VIII, was oleaginous even by the exaggerated standards of Churchill's romantic monarchism. 'Your Majesty's name will shine in history as the bravest and best beloved of all the sovereigns who have won the Island Crown,' he wrote.[125]

In February 1936, the Cabinet approved building seven new battleships

* As 1935 ended, Churchill told his wife that Rothermere had made him two offers, of £2,000 if he went teetotal for the whole of the following year – 'I refused as I think life would not be worth living' – and £600 not to drink any brandy or undiluted spirits in 1936. He accepted the latter, and won (ed. Soames, *Speaking* p. 405).

and four aircraft carriers between 1937 and 1942, and expanding the RAF to 1,500 planes, with the possibility of more if the Luftwaffe continued to expand.[126] Defence spending for 1935–6 grew to £137 million, the highest as a proportion of GDP since before Churchill's chancellorship. Yet actual deliveries of aircraft ordered by the Air Ministry dropped in 1936 because of procurement bottlenecks. A central coordinating agency was badly needed, and Churchill wanted to run it.

On Saturday, 7 March 1936, the German Army suddenly and without warning entered the demilitarized zone of the Rhineland, in a blatant breach of the Versailles and Locarno treaties. Hitler was on the march.

# 17
# Apotheosis of Appeasement March 1936–October 1938

*How few men are strong enough to stand against the prevailing currents of opinion!*

Churchill, *London to Ladysmith via Pretoria*[1]

*Let us free the world from the approach of a catastrophe, carrying with it calamity and tribulation, beyond the tongue of man to tell.*

Churchill, House of Commons, April 1936[2]

On Saturday, 7 March 1936, the day that his troops entered the Rhineland, Adolf Hitler declared, 'The struggle for German equal rights can be regarded as closed . . . We have no territorial claims to make in Europe.'[3] It was a calculated sop to British and French opinion, in the hope that there would be no military retaliation for his flagrant breach of the Versailles settlement. After his speech, he dissolved the Reichstag. He had given orders to his generals to withdraw in the face of any active opposition from the French Army, but despite Churchill's pleas to Pierre Flandin, the French Foreign Minister, there was none. Even if Baldwin and Eden had been prepared to risk war, which they told Flandin they were not, there was nothing they could have done without the French.[4]

'Wars do not always wait until all the combatants are ready,' Churchill remarked in a debate on rearmament three days after the remilitarization of the Rhineland. 'Sometimes they come before any are ready, sometimes when one nation thinks itself less unready than another, or when one nation thinks it is likely to become, not stronger, but weaker as time passes. I fear, indeed, that there may be a culminating point in the history of Europe . . . I cannot tell when it will be reached. It will certainly be reached in the lifetime of the present Parliament.'[5] That Parliament was due to come to an end in the autumn of 1940.

At a meeting of the Commons Foreign Affairs Committee, Churchill called for a 'coordinated plan', spearheaded by the League of Nations, to persuade France to stand up to Germany. He was told that the main members of the League were 'totally unprepared from a military point of view', which was taken as a good argument for doing nothing.[6] In fact at that point France was far more heavily armed than Germany, Italy was still at least theoretically in the anti-German camp established at the Stresa Conference, and the Royal Navy was supreme – but nothing was done, in the hope that Hitler was telling the truth.[7]

Churchill warned the Commons on 10 March that Germany was spending £1.5 billion 'upon warlike preparations directly or indirectly . . . These figures are stupendous. Nothing like them has ever been seen in time of peace.'[8] He acknowledged that the British Government had started to rearm, but said that the effort was not enough. 'Germany will be outstripping us more and more even if our new programmes are accepted,' he said, 'and we shall be worse off at the end of this year than we are now, in spite of all our exertions.'[9] His warnings were not of the slightest use. Flandin told him that Baldwin did not even want the League Council to be convened to discuss sanctions against Germany.[10] The press, Opposition and Empire prime ministers all opposed action over the Rhineland, so Churchill did not bother pressing an already lost cause.

He was nonetheless profoundly disappointed when Baldwin announced on 12 March not the new ministries of Defence and Supply which he had long been advocating, but merely a new minister for the coordination of defence, a primarily advisory rather than executive role, who was going to be the profoundly uncharismatic functionary Sir Thomas Inskip, the Attorney-General. Baldwin told Davidson 'he didn't want to have a Minister of Defence who was going to set the Thames on fire,' which, as things turned out, was an unfortunate turn of phrase. Davidson himself thought Inskip 'somewhat ponderous, and not very active in decision-making' and having 'a certain rigidity of outlook'.[11] Ten days earlier, Churchill had told Clementine, 'I do not mean to break my heart whatever happens. Destiny plays her part. If I get it, I will work faithfully before God and man for Peace, and not allow pride or excitement to sway my spirit.'[12] Of the nine men Churchill had thought might get the job, Inskip had not figured at all.

He saw Inskip's appointment as another missed opportunity to warn the Nazis of British resolve, writing later, 'It was certainly obvious that Hitler would not like my appointment.'[13] Neville Chamberlain noted that Inskip's appointment might not excite enthusiasm, but at least 'he would involve us in no fresh perplexities.' He wrote to his sister Ida, who lived with Hilda, 'I am thankful in the circumstances we have not got Winston as a colleague. He is in his usual excited condition that comes on him when he smells war, and if he were in the Cabinet we should be spending all our time in holding him down instead of getting on with our business.'[14]

Later that month, Harold Nicolson noted in his diary, 'Winston gathered a group together in the smoking-room and talked about funk versus national honour and our duty to generations yet unborn.'[15] In the debate on Germany on 26 March, Churchill again called for the League to take action, but he was privately growing contemptuous of it, and the Rhineland crisis encouraged him to think more in terms of a collective security pact that could surround and contain the Third Reich and which therefore must include the USSR.[16] 'We would be complete idiots were we to deny help to the Soviet Union at present,' he told Ivan Maisky on 8 April, 'out of a hypothetical danger of Socialism which might threaten our children and grandchildren.'[17] Because of this changed stance, Churchill was no longer seen as an enemy in Russia and his effigy was discreetly taken down from the shooting gallery in Moscow's Park of Culture and Rest.[18]

Churchill did not believe Hitler's protestations. 'This Rhineland business is but a step, is but a stage, is but an incident in this process,' he warned the Commons.[19] He said he was in favour of negotiating with Hitler, but only from a position of strength: 'Do not let us have it out as if we were a rabble flying before forces we dare not resist.' As ever he based his arguments on the experiences of the past. 'The whole history of the world is summed up in the fact that when nations are strong they are not always just, and when they wish to be just they are often no longer strong,' he said. 'I desire to see the collective forces of the world invested with overwhelming power. If you are going to run this thing on a narrow margin . . . you are going to have war.'[20] One of the reasons why Churchill became prime minister in 1940 was that, although few had heeded his speeches, many others remembered that he had made them.

Churchill was not ideologically opposed to redressing Germany's grievances over Versailles. He was prepared to consider the return of her West African colonies, an aspect of his policy not covered in the first volume of his war memoirs, *The Gathering Storm*, but plainly found in the official parliamentary record, Hansard.[21] 'I hold that the time is coming for a final and lasting friendly settlement with Germany,' he said in early April. 'The time available is short.' He proposed discussions about restoring Germany's colonial possessions even as late as December 1937 as part of an agreement on collective security and Western rearmament. 'I believe we still have a year to combine and marshal superior forces in defence of the League and its Covenant,' he told the League's foremost champion in Britain, Lord Cecil of Chelwood, in April 1936.[22] He invited Cecil to Chartwell to discuss lifting the League sanctions on Italy (and offered 'to show you my swimming pool: it is limpid and tepid').[23] While they were all at Chartwell *en famille*, Churchill would startle his children with statements ringing out across the lawn such as 'In twenty short minutes the enemy, on leaving the coast of France, can be overhead, menacing, in a way never before contemplated, the security of our Island!'[24]

Churchill was now constantly musing about strategies to overawe Hitler, however outlandish. The same month that he invited Robert Cecil to Chartwell, he sent Inskip a version of Fisher's old plan of dispatching a Royal Navy squadron to a Russian base in the Baltic.[25] Hankey complained to Inskip that it was a 'fantastic' idea (in this case not a term of approbation). Churchill told Wallis Simpson, the King's mistress, at a lunch of Sibyl Colefax's, that in the Mediterranean 'Our communications cannot be left at the mercy of so unreliable a thing as Italian friendship. We must retain that command of the Mediterranean which Marlborough, my illustrious ancestor, first established.'[26] His warnings to the Commons continued unabated. On 23 April he spoke of 'an explosion and a catastrophe the course of which no imagination can measure, and beyond which no human eye can see'.[27] On 3 April Eden had promised Parliament that no 'military plans' would be put into operation – even if Germany refused so much as to discuss the Rhineland coup.[28]

In May at Grillions, Crawford thought Churchill 'very noisy and too glib in denouncing the Government'.[29] Yet he did not publicly attack Baldwin, adopting a chiding public tone rather than embracing outright opposition. 'Winston is angling to be made Minister of Munitions,' Chips Channon wrote speculatively, 'but Baldwin hates him so much that I doubt if he will succeed.'[30] In the Commons on 21 May, Churchill said that the Great War had taught the importance of depriving the Secretary for War of responsibility for his munitions supply, adding that ultimately Kitchener had been thankful to cede control. 'This is one of the lessons which we all had to learn with blood and tears. Have we really got to learn them all over again now?'[31] Of the arguments put by the appeasers that high defence spending might damage British trade, he said, 'How thin and paltry these arguments will sound if we are caught a year or two hence, fat, opulent, free-spoken – and defenceless.'[32]

The most damaging of all the criticisms of Churchill continued to be the general accusation that he lacked judgement. 'One of these days I'll make a few casual remarks about Winston,' Baldwin told Tom Jones, his private secretary, on 22 May. 'I've got it all ready. I am going to say that when Winston was born, lots of fairies swooped down on his cradle [with] gifts – imagination, eloquence, industry, ability – and then came a fairy who said: "No one person has a right to so many gifts," picked him up and gave him such a shake and twist that with all these gifts he was denied judgment and wisdom. And that is why while we delight to listen to him in this House we do not take his advice.'[33]*

Baldwin never made that speech, but it was the main line of attack by the National Government's whips, and had the advantage of a narrative that encompassed Sidney Street, Tonypandy, Antwerp, Gallipoli, the Gold Standard, Indian self-government and, shortly, Churchill's egregious self-harm in the Abdication Crisis. It amounted to a formidable indictment sheet. What it ignored, of course, was the truth about Tonypandy and Antwerp, the triviality of Sidney Street, the sincerity of his stance on India and the fact that the decision on the Gold Standard had been wholeheartedly supported by Baldwin, Chamberlain and the Government whips of the day.

Four days later, Churchill made his own views on Baldwin similarly plain. 'He will never retire of his own accord!' he told Maisky, whom he saw frequently at this time in pursuit of Soviet help in creating a cordon sanitaire around Germany. 'He wants to stay not only until the Coronation but afterwards too if he can. Baldwin must be *kicked out* – that is the only way to get rid of him.'[34] He likened the Prime Minister to 'a man who has held on to the gondola of a rising balloon. If he lets go when the balloon is only five or six metres† above the ground, he will fall, but he won't break his bones. The longer he hangs on, the surer he is to die when he does inevitably fall.' It was an imaginative analogy, but a bad prediction.‡ It reminded Maisky of Churchill's response to his earlier question about why Baldwin had delayed the appointment of Inskip for so long: 'Why, Baldwin is looking for a man smaller than himself as Defence Minister, and such a man is not easy to find.'[35]

Another criticism levelled at Churchill at the time was that he was too bound up with recriminations over previous Government blunders. When in a defence debate on 29 May Inskip pointedly asked him what use there was in dwelling on the past, Churchill retorted, 'I will tell the House the use of recriminating about the past. It is to enforce effective action at the present.'[36] He was particularly frustrated by the lack of progress made by the Sub-Committee for the Scientific Survey of Air Defence (the successor to the Air Defence Research Sub-Committee) in researching anti-bomber

* It was not an original thought, but a telling one lifted from Birkenhead's book *Contemporary Personalities* (1924), which Birkenhead had put in a kinder way.

† Churchill almost certainly said yards but the Soviets used the metric system.

‡ At the Other Club in late May, Churchill wagered 'Crinks' Johnstone £25 that 'Mr Baldwin will not be P.M. on July 2, 1938'.

ideas. Spectacular breakthroughs were being made in the field of radar, but on 22 June Churchill told Lord Swinton, the Air Minister, that these were not enough, a situation made worse by Tizard's vendetta against Lindemann (which was fully reciprocated). 'What surprises and grieves me is your attitude, and that you should be apparently contented with the way this work is going. During the ten months I have sat on the Committee I have been shocked at the slowness with which every investigation proceeds,' he complained. 'The experiments are neither large nor expensive, but they must be numerous, and can only advance by repeated trial and error.'[37] The Committee met only once a month and he told Swinton he was 'certain that nothing will result before the period of maximum danger for Europe and our country has come', which Swinton doubtless thought typical Churchillian hyperbole.[38] On 3 September, Swinton dissolved the Committee after receiving three resignations, including Tizard's.[39] Two months later it was reconstituted, again under Tizard's chairmanship, with precisely the same membership except Lindemann, who was dropped.

At a lunch at the Savoy Grill honouring the German anti-Nazi ex-diplomat Albrecht von Bernstorff* in June, with Duff Cooper, Bob Boothby and Harold Nicolson present, Churchill asked Bernstorff how to prevent a second German war. 'Overwhelming encirclement,' he replied.[40] Churchill agreed. In a speech to the Commons Foreign Affairs Committee in July, he argued that Britain had to defend both her Empire and the Rhine frontier, 'a gigantic task', but if she let Hitler do what he liked in the East, Germany, 'in a single year, would become dominant from Hamburg to the Black Sea, and we should be faced by a confederacy such as had never been seen since Napoleon'.[41] He was still ignored in Parliament, although that month Eleanor Rathbone, an Independent MP for the Combined English Universities, told a left-wing political summer school, 'Watch that man carefully. You may feel distrustful. So did I. I'm not certain yet. But I ask you to dispel prejudice and consider the facts. Churchill for three years has pointed out extensive German rearmaments. Later facts have justified his estimates.'[42]

On 17 July 1936, a section of the Spanish Army revolted against the Popular Front Government in Madrid, whereupon a full-scale civil war broke out. Churchill's antipathy towards the Spanish Republicans was partly explained by his personal fondness for the ex-King Alfonso XIII, whom they had overthrown in 1931. He had met Alfonso in 1914, liked him and was to write about him sympathetically in *Great Contemporaries*, in which he blamed his fall in part on 'the propaganda of Moscow'.[43]

* Bernstorff was murdered by the Nazis in 1945.

21. Winston Churchill by his friend Walter Sickert in 1927, painted when Churchill was chancellor of the Exchequer.

22. Arthur Balfour in 1912. He suffered Churchill's jibes for five years, but later they became friends.

23. Field Marshal Lord Kitchener in 1915. He made a better poster than a Secretary for War.

24. Lord Curzon in 1921. The Churchill family nicknamed him 'All-Highest' for his sense of superiority.

25. The Tory statesman and barrister F. E. Smith, Churchill's best friend and one of his few superiors in witty repartee.

26–7. Churchill took up painting at the lowest point in his life, after the Dardanelles disaster. Here, he and Clementine were staying at Hartsbourne Manor in Hertfordshire, the home of the American actress Maxine Elliott.

28. Churchill sent his family around Chartwell to collect the materials for this painting, *Bottlescape*, in 1926.

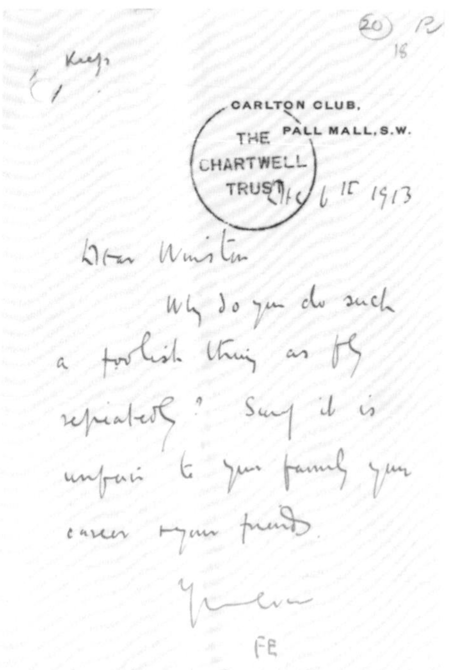

CARLTON CLUB,
PALL MALL, S.W.

THE CHARTWELL TRUST

Dear Winston

Why do you do such a foolish thing as fly repeatedly? Surely it is unfair to your family your career & your friends.

Yours ever

FE

29. F. E. Smith admonished Churchill in December 1913 for continually risking his life by learning to fly.

30. Churchill arrived at Hilsea in Hampshire by air with pilot Major Gerard in 1915.

31. Lieutenant-Colonel Churchill of the 6th Battalion, The Royal Scots Fusiliers, in the lines behind Ploegsteert in Belgium. To the left of him is his second-in-command, friend and future Liberal Party leader Major Archie Sinclair.

32. Churchill wore a French *poilu*'s steel helmet in the trenches and in this portrait by Sir John Lavery in 1916.

33. Churchill visited the Pyramids during the Cairo Conference on 20 March 1921. The first five figures on camelback are (*left to right*) Clementine Churchill, Churchill, Gertrude Bell, Lawrence of Arabia, Detective Constable Walter Thompson.

34. Churchill playing polo with his cousin the Marquess of Londonderry, later a leading appeaser, at Roehampton Polo Club in May 1921.

35. Chartwell Manor in Kent, which Churchill bought in 1922 and loved passionately thereafter.

PLEASE PASS ON THIS COPY OR DISPLAY IT

# The British Gazette

Published by His Majesty's Stationery Office.

No. 8 LONDON, THURSDAY, MAY 13, 1926 ONE PENNY

## GENERAL STRIKE OFF

### UNCONDITIONAL WITHDRAWAL OF NOTICES BY T.U.C.

### Men To Return Forthwith.

### SURRENDER RECEIVED BY PREMIER IN DOWNING STREET.

### Negotiations To Be Resumed In The Coal Dispute.

**The General Strike, which began at midnight on Monday, May 3, ended yesterday in an unconditional withdrawal of the strike notices by the General Council of the Trades Union Congress. The news of the settlement was conveyed to the public in the following official communiqué :—**

WHITEHALL, May 12.

It was intimated to the Prime Minister that the Trades Union Council desired to come and see him at Downing-street, and they arrived soon after 12 noon. Mr. Pugh made a statement, in which he stated that the Trades Union Council had decided to call off the strike notices forthwith.

The Prime Minister then spoke briefly. He stated that he was very glad to hear what Mr. Pugh had said, and he would report it to his colleagues in the Cabinet.

As regards the coal industry, the Prime Minister said that negotiations would be resumed, and the Government would consider as to what steps should be taken.

The whole proceedings lasted a very few minutes.

#### THE DECISION OF THE T.U.C.

#### NO RESUMPTION BY MINERS.

Mr. Cook And End Of The General Strike.

"Nothing To Do With Us."

#### THE KING TO THE NATION.

Appeal For Lasting Peace.

DIFFICULTIES STILL AHEAD.

"Let Us Forget Elements of Bitterness."

The King last night issued the following message from Buckingham Palace :—

TO MY PEOPLE.

The Nation has just passed through a period of extreme anxiety. It was to-day announced that the General Strike had been brought to an end.

At such a moment it is supremely important to bring together all my people to confront the difficult situation which still remains. This task requires the co-operation of all able and well-disposed men in the country. Even with such help it will be difficult, but it will not be impossible.

Let us forget whatever elements of bitterness the events of the past few days may have created, only remembering how steady and how orderly the country has remained, though severely tested, and forthwith address ourselves to the task of bringing into being a peace which will be lasting because, forgetting the past, it looks only to the future with the hopefulness of a united people. GEORGE R.I.

#### REINSTATEMENT. No Obligations Incurred.

#### CIVIC SERVICE.

Home Secretary And Volunteer Labour.

#### POSTAL SERVICES.

Delivery Of Parcels To Be Resumed.

#### APRIL TRADE RESULTS.

#### VOLUNTARY SERVICES.

#### MR. BALDWIN ON THE FINISH.

Victory Of Common Sense.

STATEMENT IN PARLIAMENT.

*Westminster, Wednesday.*

NATURE OF THE PEACE.

#### THE NEWS IN PARIS.

Profound Relief In British Circles.

#### RESUMPTION OF RACING.

#### "British Gazette" Circulation.

| | |
|---|---|
| May 5 | 232,000 |
| May 6 | 507,000 |
| May 7 | 655,000 |
| May 8 | 836,000 |
| May 10 | 1,127,600 |
| May 11 | 1,801,400 |
| May 12 | 2,209,000 |

#### THE BIRTH AND LIFE OF THE "BRITISH GAZETTE"

An Unexampled Achievement In Journalism.

HOW AN IMPROVISED NEWSPAPER REACHED A CIRCULATION OF 2,209,000.

A FAMOUS LETTER.

THE GOVERNMENT ARRIVE.

A CRUCIAL TEST.

(Continued on Page 2.)



36. The eighth and final issue of the *British Gazette*, which Churchill edited throughout the General Strike of 1926.

37. Tea at Chartwell in August 1927 (*left to right*): Thérèse Sickert, Diana Mitford (later Mosley), Eddie Marsh, Churchill, Professor Frederick Lindemann, Randolph Churchill, Diana Churchill, Clementine and Walter Sickert.

EPPING DIVISION OF ESSEX.
PARLIAMENTARY ELECTION, MAY, 1929.


38. Churchill wearing an astrakhan coat for his general election address in 1929.

39. Churchill was elected chancellor of Bristol University in 1929. He wore his father's Chancellor of the Exchequer robes to ceremonies.

40. The Other Club has dined in the Pinafore Room at the Savoy Hotel from 1911, when Churchill and F. E. Smith founded it, to the present day.

41–2. Sir Alfred Munnings, an Other Club member, drew these sketches in July 1929 and at Christmas 1934.

In an article in the *Evening Standard* entitled 'The Spanish Tragedy' on 10 August, Churchill wrote of his fear of a 'Communist Spain spreading its snaky tentacles through Portugal and France'.[44] It was his continuing anti-Communism and romantic monarchism that led Churchill initially to sympathize with the Nationalists in the early part of the war, when it seemed like an uprising of aristocrats, Catholics, monarchists, conservatives and soldiers. He slowly distanced himself in 1937 once it became clear that it was actually a Falangist-Fascist movement that was supported by Hitler and Mussolini, including militarily. Churchill backed the unheroic but pragmatic non-interventionist policy of the Chamberlain Government, which was based on not imperilling Gibraltar and the all-important straits through which the Royal Navy sailed in and out of the Mediterranean Sea.

Over the summer, he became ever more publicly critical of the defence apparatus and particularly of Inskip. 'He has allowed himself to become the innocent victim of responsibilities so strangely, so inharmoniously, so perversely grouped,' he told MPs on 20 July, 'endowed with powers so cribbed and restricted, that no one, not even Napoleon himself, would be able to discharge them with satisfaction.'[45] An argument used by Inskip (and many historians since) that, if Britain had rearmed earlier, the RAF would have built inferior aircraft to those it constructed later, was torn apart by Churchill in that debate:

> If our aircraft factories had been set to work three years ago, albeit on the old type of machines, that would not have prevented the substitution of the new type for the old at the same date which is now operative . . . If the factories had been thrown into activity, if apprentices had been engaged, if plant and staff had been extended and developed, they would have been all the more capable of taking the new types, the transference would have been made with far better facilities and the deliveries would have flowed out in far greater volume at an earlier date.[46]

Furthermore, the older aircraft could have been used for training new pilots. Churchill estimated that Germany spent £800 million on preparations for war in 1935, and perhaps £900 million in 1936. 'I would endure with patience the roar of exultation that would go up when I was proved wrong,' he told the House about these figures, 'because it would lift a load off my heart and off the hearts of many members. What does it matter who gets exposed or discomfited? If the country is safe, who cares for individual politicians, in or out of office?'[47] In gaining the Rhineland without a shot being fired, he said, 'An enormous triumph has been gained by the Nazi regime.'[48]

On 5 August, Churchill invited William S. Griffin, the isolationist editor of William Randolph Hearst's *New York Enquirer*, to Morpeth Mansions. According to Griffin, Churchill said, 'America should have minded her own business and stayed out of the World War.'[49] When in 1939 Churchill heard that Griffin had claimed this, and that it was being repeated in Congress and on the German radio, he stated that it was 'a vicious lie', whereupon Griffin sued him for $1 million in damages and asked the US courts to direct Churchill's American earnings from his books against the settlement. The case was not heard until October 1942, when it was dismissed, not least because Churchill was by then prime minister and America's ally, whereas Griffin was under house arrest for sedition.

The Churchill family was plunged into a very public and embarrassing crisis on 14 October when the twenty-two-year-old Sarah eloped to New York to marry Vic Oliver, whom they disapproved of and had asked her not to see for twelve months. 'Darling Mummie,' she wrote after she had left, 'I can offer no excuse but things didn't seem to be working out so well . . . I'm very very sorry to do it this way. I don't like "backing out" but I think it is the best solution. The blessing and "consent" we were going to get in January were going to be very hollow – how could they be otherwise when both your hearts and minds are so set against it.'[50] The postscript read, 'Please make Papa understand that I did not just wait till he was out of the country – it was a last minute decision. I just have to go – I'm sorry.'* Randolph took the next liner to New York amid a flurry of press speculation – there were one hundred reporters covering the story at one point – but he could not persuade Sarah to change her mind.

Sarah's next letter to her mother, from the Lombardy Hotel in New York, said how hard it was 'To be in love and to . . . realize . . . that the man is despised by those who say they love you – to continually and perpetually have him insulted and treated as a low adventurer – to be made to feel you have committed an error of taste, and finally even to have your sincerity questioned . . . I had a feeling that Papa was not playing quite straight with us.'[51] It was true; Churchill had hired lawyers in Austria and America to ascertain that Oliver was not about to commit bigamy.[52] After the couple married on Christmas Day, both the press speculation and Churchill and Clementine's opposition subsided.

Churchill's task of warning the British people about the threat posed by Hitler was made all the harder by the many prominent Britons publicly

* She asked her mother to have all her letters burned. They were carefully preserved and are to be found at the Churchill Archives Centre in Cambridge.

fawning over the German leader. In September, Lloyd George wrote to the German Ambassador to London, Joachim von Ribbentrop, to say that even before he met Hitler 'I had the greatest admiration for your wonderful Führer,' but that since then 'that admiration had been deepened and intensified. He is the greatest piece of luck that has come to your country since Bismarck, and personally, I would say since Frederick the Great.'[53] To Lord Londonderry, who had praised Hitler publicly and privately, Churchill wrote in October 1937 that Britain could not 'agree to [the Germans] having a free hand so far as we are concerned in Central and Southern Europe. This means that they would devour Austria and Czechoslovakia as a preliminary to making a gigantic middle-Europe bloc. It would certainly not be in our interest to connive at such policies of aggression.'[54] He had spotted Hitler's next two targets, but no one would listen.

While unveiling a monument to T. E. Lawrence in Oxford on 6 October 1936, Churchill was asked at a dinner at All Souls whether there was going to be a war. 'Certainly,' he replied, 'a very terrible war in which London will be bombed and Buckingham Palace will be razed to the ground, and the lions and tigers will escape from the Zoo and roam through the streets of London attacking people.'[55]* Lawrence, another good friend of Churchill's to die young, had been killed in a motorbike accident near his bungalow in Dorset, on 19 May 1935, aged only forty-seven. 'He was indeed a dweller upon the mountain tops where the air is cold, crisp and rarefied, and where the view on clear cold days commands all the Kingdoms of the world and the glory of them,' Churchill wrote in his obituary. 'Just as an aeroplane only flies by speed and pressure against the air, so he flew best and easiest in the hurricane. He was not in complete harmony with the normal. The fury of the Great War raised the pitch of life to the Lawrence standard. The multitudes were swept forward until their pace was the same as his. In this heroic period he found himself in perfect relation both to men and events.'[56] As so often with his writing about others, Churchill's eulogy struck more than a passing note of self-reference. Twenty years after the eulogy, he said of Lawrence, once the inventions and exaggerations of *Seven Pillars of Wisdom* and the revelations of his masochistic homosexuality – about the latter of which Churchill 'expressed strong distaste' – had been exposed, 'He had the art of backing uneasily into the limelight. He was a very remarkable character, and very careful of that fact.'[57]

* Buckingham Palace was indeed bombed, though not razed to the ground. London Zoo in fact stayed open, although the poisonous reptiles and dangerous animals were put down, the big cats were moved to Whipsnade Zoo, and the only escapee during the Blitz was of a zebra and her foal, which were rounded up on their way to Camden Town.

When in 1937 the actor Leslie Howard was chosen by Alexander Korda to play Lawrence, Churchill had a number of conversations with him, which Howard said helped him considerably.[58] Churchill had been working for Korda's studio since September 1934, on a number of film ideas such as 'Will Monarchies Return?', 'The Rise of Japan', 'Marriage Laws and Customs' and King George V's Silver Jubilee. He asked for £2,000 for working on the Lawrence of Arabia script, but didn't complain when he got £250 instead.[59] One of the minor changes he suggested to *Lawrence of Arabia* was that 'You can hardly talk of arousing the Arabs to a Crusade, which were things instituted to do them in. Jehad is the real word.'[60] Churchill was keen that Lawrence's heroism and willingness to ignore military convention were emphasized to the full. 'Surely you should blow up half a dozen trains in different ways!' Churchill wrote to Korda. 'The approach in the distance; the scene in the railway carriage; the tense excitement of the ambush; the terrible explosion; the wreck of the locomotive, etc, and the fact of the sole communications of an army being cut off – all very pretty!'[61] One criticism was that 'We have vague galloperaverings [gallopings] of horsemen doing impossible charges, in the style of some of the absurdities of *Bengal Lancer*.'[62] One person for whom the 1935 British imperial epic movie *Lives of a Bengal Lancer* was not absurd was Adolf Hitler, whose favourite film it was.

'There is no greater mistake than to suppose that platitudes, smooth words, timid policies, offer today a path to safety,' Churchill said in a Commons debate on collective security on 12 November 1936. 'Only by a firm adherence to righteous principles . . . can the dangers which close in so steadily upon us and upon the peace of Europe be warded off and overcome.'[63] He demanded a parliamentary inquiry into the state of British defences, a demand which was easily brushed aside by the huge Government majority, as he knew it would be. In that speech, while criticizing Soviet intervention in the Spanish Civil War, he ended by describing 'another Russia, which only wishes to be left alone in peace'. He hoped, through collective security, that the Soviet Union might play a part in preserving peace, although he was not yet prepared to call for an all-out alliance, sensing that public opinion was not yet ready.[64] His views on what role Russia might play in collective security oscillated, because drawing in the Soviet Union involved alienating countries like Poland, as well as British Roman Catholics and many Conservatives.[65] He was not altogether consistent in his arguments about how to stave off war in other respects too. In November 1936 he repudiated what he had said six months earlier about redressing German grievances, although in December 1937 he returned to it, stating that 'war conquests' could be ceded to Germany as part of a general settlement. He did not advocate a formal Franco-Anglo-Russian alliance until just before the Czechoslovakia crisis in the autumn of 1938.* His stances in the second half of the 1930s were far more varied than he recorded in *The Gathering Storm*, in which he presented himself as having seen through Fascism immediately and having opposed its appeasement unswervingly. Nevertheless, he remained by far the most formidable opponent of Nazi Germany and its appeasement in British politics.

In the collective security debate, Churchill quoted Samuel Hoare, by then the First Lord of the Admiralty, saying of a future Ministry of Supply, 'We are always reviewing the position.' 'The Government simply cannot make up their minds,' he pronounced in one of his most spirited sallies,

> or they cannot get the Prime Minister to make up his mind. So they go on in strange paradox, decided only to be undecided, resolved to be irresolute, adamant for drift, solid for fluidity, all-powerful to be impotent. So we go on preparing more months and years – precious, perhaps vital, to the greatness of Britain – for the locusts to eat. They will say to me 'A Minister of Supply is not necessary, for all is going well.' I deny it. 'The position is satisfactory.' It is not true. 'All is proceeding according to plan.' We know what that means.[66]

Searchlight crews were training without searchlights, the Tank Corps was not getting the latest tanks, and 'Unless the House resolves to find out the truth for itself it will have committed an act of abdication of duty without parallel in its long history.'[67] He had honed some of his phrases during a 'violent altercation' at the Other Club with Alfred Munnings over Hitler's claims to have achieved air parity.[68] 'The era of procrastination, of half-measures, of soothing and baffling expedients, of delays, is coming to its close,' Churchill said in his peroration. 'In its place we are entering a period of consequences.'[69] Baldwin's reply was trenchant:

> I put before the whole House my own views with appalling frankness . . . Supposing I had gone to the country and . . . said that Germany was rearming and that we must rearm, does anyone think that this pacific democracy would have rallied to that cry? I cannot think of anything that would have made the loss of the Election from my point of view more certain.[70]

* Nor was it clear how useful Russia would be as an ally. At the Other Club in November 1937, the financier Norman Holden wagered Brendan Bracken £100 that 'in the event of war between Russia and Germany, Russia will be the first to ask for an armistice' (Other Club Betting Book). The same wager was taken up by the journalist Colin Coote, Bob Boothby and Earl De La Warr, with the 'Final decision to be given by the Chairman of the Club at the first meeting after armistice'. Many years later, 'Mr Winston Churchill, as the said Chairman, decided that Mr Norman Holden had lost the bet.'

Writing to Sir Archibald Boyd-Carpenter, an old schoolfriend, the next day, Churchill said, 'I have never heard such a squalid confession from a public man as Baldwin offered us yesterday.'[71] As we have seen, after the war Churchill exacted a concealed revenge for this appalling frankness: in the index of *The Gathering Storm* under 'Baldwin' he put 'confesses putting party before country'.[72] This was deeply unfair. Through selective quotation – possibly by Randolph, who edited that section – Churchill made it appear that Baldwin was speaking about the actual election of 1935, whereas he was really referring to a conjectural 1934 election that never happened. In the 1935 election, Baldwin did advocate larger defence spending, though nothing like as much as Churchill wanted and (it turned out) that Britain needed.

'Why do you not have Winston Churchill in your British Cabinet,' Germany's Deputy Führer Rudolf Hess asked Lord Londonderry's eldest son Lord Castlereagh at this time, 'then we should know you meant business?'[73] He could not know that the Baldwin Government was about to be greatly strengthened, and Churchill correspondingly badly weakened, by a crisis that emerged from, of all unlikely places, a sermon by the Bishop of Bradford. In his speech of 12 November, Churchill had spoken of Parliament abdicating responsibility, yet tragically, just as he was landing some hard punches on Baldwin's Government, people started to concentrate on another abdication altogether.

Shortly after Bishop Blunt had mentioned the King's 'need for grace' in a sermon on 1 December 1936, the story of Edward VIII's relationship with the married American Wallis Simpson, who had been twice divorced, became public. Churchill, who had known for some time about the affair, had been thinking of ways around the problem, and came up with a plan to allow the King to contract a morganatic marriage with Mrs Simpson, who would become the non-royal Duchess of Cornwall, on the model of some European royal marriages such as that of Archduke Franz Ferdinand of Austria. 'Max rang me up to say that he had seen the gent,' Churchill cryptically wrote to Clementine on 27 November, 'and told him the Cornwall plan was my idea. The gent was definitely for it. It now turns on what the Cabinet will say. I don't see any other way through.'[74] In fact the Cornwall plan stood no chance of success, but Churchill's romantic monarchism and long-standing friendship with the King led him to champion Edward VIII's cause, ultimately disastrously. These were his genuine motives, rather than a cynical hope to use the crisis to overthrow Baldwin with the formation of a 'King's Party', as his detractors assumed. (Lord Crawford, for example, wrote of Churchill's seeing 'the fruits of office temptingly close before his eyes. His judgement is nearly always wrong however resonant his prose – he is an evil counsellor.')[75]

Churchill had misread the importance of Wallis Simpson to the King from the outset. 'Women play only a transient part in his life,' he had confidently informed the novelist Marie Belloc Lowndes. 'He falls constantly in and out of love. His present attachment will follow the course of all the others.'[76] He also misread his own relationship with the King, making his stance in defending him during the crisis all the more ludicrous. As Sir Alan 'Tommy' Lascelles, the King's assistant private secretary, wrote in his diary years later, 'Winston's sentimental loyalty to the D[uke] of W[indsor] was based on a tragic false premise – viz, that he really *knew* the D. of W. – which he never did.'[77] This sentimental loyalty was epitomized when he told Duff Cooper that 'The hereditary principle must not be left to the mercy of politicians trimming their doctrines "to the varying hour".' 'What crime has the king committed?' he later asked, and of the Privy Council meeting on his accession 'Have we not sworn allegiance to him? Are we not bound by that oath?'[78]

Churchill's idea of a morganatic marriage, whereby Mrs Simpson would not become queen nor her children inherit the throne, was a concept unknown to British law, where wives automatically assumed the rank and status of their husbands, and would never have been accepted by the Commons, Lords or Church. It was an imaginative but ultimately unworkable solution to a knotty problem, and Churchill continued to push it in December until he had used up all his political capital. Later in life, when asked whether he had really been willing to accept Wallis Simpson as queen of England, he replied, 'Never for one moment did I contemplate such a dreadful possibility.'[79] It was true, though it did not look that way to many people at the time.

Although recent research has established that there were millions of ordinary Britons who thought the King should indeed to be allowed to marry Mrs Simpson, the Establishment was unanimous in its opposition, led by *The Times*, the Archbishop of Canterbury, the Dominion premiers and the entire Cabinet except Duff Cooper. The King was supported only by the Beaverbrook and Rothermere press, the Communist Party, Sir Oswald Mosley's British Union of Fascists and Churchill.[80]

Churchill's advice to the King was to delay until after the Coronation (intended for 1937) and fight it out, knowing how difficult it would be constitutionally for Baldwin to force a reigning king off the throne against his wishes. But as Beaverbrook was to tell Churchill, 'Our cock won't fight.'[81] By then, however, Churchill had made it clear that he himself would indeed fight.

*The Gathering Storm* is not a helpful guide to this period; Churchill claimed that he had made a statement on the royal issue at an 'Arms and the Covenant' meeting at the Royal Albert Hall on 3 December 1936, but he did not.[82] He did speak at Prime Minister's Questions the next day, however, and Chips Channon noted that he had 'got up, his voice breaking, and with tears in his eyes, said he hoped nothing irrevocable would be done before reflection, or words to that effect, and the din of cheering was impressive'.[83] In fact he had merely asked for Parliament to be kept informed of events, and if Churchill himself mistook the cheering for support, he was soon to be sorely disabused. The next day, he put out a public statement urging 'time and patience', but the King had run out of the former and the Government of the latter. Still, he wrote to the King from Morpeth Mansions that evening:

> Sir, News from all fronts! No pistol to be held at the King's head. No doubt this request for time will be granted. Therefore – no final decision or Bill till Christmas – probably February or March. *On no account must the King leave the country.* Windsor Castle is his *poste de commandement* [battle station]. When so much is at stake, no minor indiscretions can be indulged . . . Max . . . is a tiger to fight. I gave him the King's message – but *please* telephone or write – better telephone . . . A *devoted* tiger! Very scarce breed . . . Summary. Good advances on all points giving prospects of gaining good positions and assembling large forces behind them.[84]

Churchill's excited conviction, complete with French military terms, that he was about to keep the King on his throne is palpable.

Opinion had in fact already moved decisively against the King. The Establishment, as Lascelles put it, 'would not tolerate their monarch taking as his wife, and their Queen, a shop-soiled American, with two living husbands and a voice like a rusty saw'.[85] James Stuart, a Tory whip, put the changed mood in the House down to the 123 Lancashire and Yorkshire MPs who had returned from the weekend in their constituencies 'adamant against the King's marriage'.[86] The respectable tendency in the British Establishment was now in full-throated cry against delaying the Abdication. Churchill had completely misjudged the situation. On the afternoon of Monday, 7 December, during Prime Minister's Questions in the Commons, he tried to plead for the King to be given more time, but was shouted down.

In *My Early Life* Churchill had written that the House of Commons 'is always indulgent to those who are proud to be its servants'.[87] It certainly was not indulgent to him that Monday. Hansard records shouts of 'Order' and 'No' at him while others present remember yells of 'Drop it!' and

'Twister!'[88] The Speaker ruled him out of order, even though he was trying to ask a question. Lord Winterton described the incident as 'one of the angriest manifestations I have ever heard directed against any man in the House of Commons'.[89] Churchill stalked out of the Chamber, shouting out to Baldwin, 'You won't be satisfied until you've broken him, will you?'[90] He went to the ticker-tape machine in a corridor off the lobby, and read it with Davidson. 'He said that his political career was finished,' Davidson recorded. 'I have sometimes wondered whether it was his half-American background that made him so insensitive to what the British really felt in their bones about such matters.'[91] Harold Nicolson noted that 'Winston collapsed utterly in the House . . . He has undone in five minutes all the patient reconstruction work of two years.'[92]

Since the King had by then effectively decided to bow to the will of the Government and Establishment and abdicate, it was all the more tragic for Churchill to have expended political capital in the way he did, breaking his lance in such a totally lost cause. Nevertheless, at 6 p.m. that evening in Committee Room 14, Churchill spoke on defence matters to 150 members of the Tory backbench 1922 Committee, the largest attendance that year. He mentioned – five years to the day before the attack on Pearl Harbor – 'our weakness in the face of Japan in Far Eastern waters', and laid stress in particular on the importance of the base at Singapore.[93] He detailed British military weakness, taking questions from several MPs. After over an hour, the record notes, 'Mr Churchill was thanked for his address.' He was not thanked 'cordially' or 'most cordially', as the minutes record of almost every other speaker that year. He was, however, cheered loudly by MPs three days later, once the Abdication Bill had passed, when he effected a graceful withdrawal. 'We must obey the exhortations of the Prime Minister to look forward,' he said, only now prepared to admit defeat.[94] After it was all over he told Bernard Baruch, 'I should not have acted otherwise. As you know in politics I always prefer to accept the guidance of my heart to calculations of public feeling.'[95]

Churchill lunched with the King at Fort Belvedere on 11 December, the day of the Abdication. He inserted at least two phrases into his last broadcast as king – 'bred in the constitutional tradition by my Father', and 'one matchless blessing, enjoyed by so many of you and not bestowed on me, a happy home with his wife and children'.[96] In his memoirs, the Duke of Windsor recalled that during that lunch 'I ceased to be King.' When he said goodbye to Churchill, he recorded, 'there were tears in his eyes. I can still see him standing at the door; his hat in one hand, stick in the other. Something must have stirred in his mind; tapping out the solemn measure with his walking stock, he began to recite, as if to himself: "He nothing common did or mean / Upon that memorable scene." His resonant voice seemed to give especial poignancy to those lines from the ode written by Andrew Marvell on the beheading of Charles I.'[97] That evening, Churchill told Wing Commander Anderson, 'Poor little lamb, he was treated worse than any air mechanic, and he took it lying down.'[98]

Clementine joked that her husband was the last believer in the Divine Right of Kings, but by December 1936 it was no longer funny: the Abdication Crisis vitiated his position in the far more consequential struggle over rearmament.[99] It was immediately added to the long list of Churchill's supposed misjudgements, thus undermining the public perception of his stance on Hitler. Even in July 1940 Churchill's three private secretaries agreed that his 'excessive loyalty to his friends and a natural disinclination to hurt anybody's feelings . . . has already cost him much in leading him to support King Edward VIII: by doing so he forfeited the confidence of the House of Commons and of the country.'[100] The Churchills stayed loyal to their friends the Windsors, who had gone to live in France. Three months after the Abdication, when Lord Granard criticized Mrs Simpson at a dinner party, Clementine turned to him and asked crushingly, 'If you feel that way, why did you invite Mrs Simpson to your house and put her on your right?' Chips Channon recorded that 'A long and embarrassed pause followed.'[101]

The Abdication Crisis also damaged Churchill's relationship with Bob Boothby, who wrote to him after the scene in the Commons on the 7th to say, 'What happened this afternoon makes me feel that it is almost impossible for those who are most devoted to you personally to follow you blindly (as they would like to do) in politics. Because they cannot be sure where the Hell they are going to be landed next.'[102] Churchill took five days to reply, and their intimacy was never quite the same again. Boothby later claimed that the 7 December humiliation was the only time he had ever seen Churchill the worse for drink in public, but by then he was deeply embittered and frankly untrustworthy as a witness.[103] Churchill's following in Parliament now consisted of only three people: Freddie Guest, Duncan Sandys and Brendan Bracken, two of whom were family.[104]

Although the Duchess of Windsor was denied the honour of being styled a royal highness, which she and her husband greatly resented, Churchill neck-bowed and Clementine curtsied to her easily enough when they met, though it was only four or five times over the rest of their lives.[105] Churchill told the Duke the day after the Abdication that he would 'watch over your interests so far as Parliament and the Cabinet are concerned', which he was not called upon to do.[106] By April he was writing with what dignity he could muster to the new King, George VI, to say, 'I have served Your Majesty's grandfather, father and brother for very many years, and I earnestly hope that your Majesty's reign will be blessed by Providence and will add new strength and lustre to our ancient Monarchy.'[107]

This very public triumph of forbidden love was followed a fortnight later by Sarah's marriage to Vic Oliver in New York. The Churchills sent them no congratulations. 'It was a rather quiet Christmas and New Year at Chartwell,' Mary recalled. The mood was further darkened by the death of the forty-six-year-old Ralph Wigram on New Year's Eve, from lung cancer.* Along with Michael Creswell, Wigram had given Churchill inside information from the Foreign Office about what the appeasers were planning, and he had become a friend.[108] 'I admired so much his courage, integrity of purpose, high comprehending vision,' Churchill wrote to his widow, Ava. 'He was one of those – how few – who guard the life of Britain. Now he is gone – and on the eve of this fateful year. Indeed it is a blow to England and to all that England means.'[109] To Clementine he described Wigram as 'A bright steady flame burning in a broken lamp, which guided us towards safety and honour.'[110]

Despite the initial froideur, Sarah and her new husband were invited to stay at Chartwell in January 1937. Churchill called his new son-in-law into his study and asked him about his music-hall engagements, to ascertain how much he was earning. 'A great thing, work,' he said. 'See that you keep it up.'[111] In time he was to call him Victor, and introduced him to the black swans Pluto and Persephone and the white ones Juno and Jupiter, to a goat that butted him and to enormous goldfish that rose to the surface of the pond when Churchill called out, 'Hike! Hike!'[112] Oliver was astonished at Churchill's ability to quote proverbs or poems or sayings from statesmen, writers and actors, along with their sources and dates. In his memoirs, he recalled that, although he was introduced to many eminent men and women at Chartwell and Chequers over the years, 'there was never a hint of snobbery or discrimination as far as their son-in-law was concerned.'[113] Churchill even gave him a signed four-volume set of *Marlborough*. 'When he spoke of family or country with special feeling,' Oliver recalled, 'there would be tears, unashamed, in his eyes.'[114] During the war, Oliver would play Churchill's favourite songs on the piano at Chequers, such as 'Daisy, Daisy' and 'Lily of Laguna' while Churchill would sing along 'in a hoarse, off-key voice'.[115]

Although Churchill was to earn £15,000 (approximately £780,000 in today's money) in 1937, and was by then paid the vast sum of £400 per

* Not suicide, as has been alleged; the coroner's report is conclusive.

article by newspapers, by early February the costs of running Chartwell were so high that he told Clementine, who was skiing at Zürs, that if he received an offer of £25,000 for the house he would accept it, 'having regard to the fact that our children are almost flown, and my life is probably in its closing decade'.[116]

In his life of Marlborough, Churchill had accused the notorious 2nd Earl of Sunderland of being 'one of those dangerous beings who, with many gifts of mind, have no principle of action; who do not care what is done, so long as they are at the centre of it; to whom bustle, excitement, intrigue, are the breath of life; and whose dance from one delirium to another seems almost necessary to their sanity.'[117] As 1937 dawned, that was how many, indeed perhaps most, Britons thought of Churchill himself. His campaign against German air rearmament seemed, in light of the campaign against Indian self-government, the Abdication Crisis and much else, just another way to try to undermine the Baldwin Government and to thrust himself forward.

'Baldwin flourishes like the green bay tree,' Churchill complained to Sir Percy Grigg on 25 January. 'He has risen somewhat like the Phoenix ... from the pyre on which the late monarch committed suttee.'[118] Concentrating his fire now on defence matters, Churchill attacked Inskip in the Commons for having promised that 100 of the 124 squadrons projected for air defence would be ready by the end of March 1937, only to admit that just twenty-two would be, the rest not until late July.[119] 'Even if the full programme of 124 had been completed by 31 March, it would still not have given us parity with the German strength at that date, or anything like it,' Churchill said. 'We have been most solemnly promised parity. We have not got parity ... Nor shall we get it during the whole of 1937, and I doubt whether we shall have it or anything approaching it during 1938.'[120]

As well as opposing the Nazis themselves, Churchill also wanted to help their victims. The British Government had been increasingly concerned since the late 1920s that large-scale Jewish immigration into Palestine was destabilizing the Mandate territory it had been given to administer. In May 1936 it had established a Royal Commission chaired by Lord Peel to consider both that issue and the partitioning of the Holy Land between the Arabs and Jews. Giving evidence to the Commission in March 1937, Churchill made it clear that the Palestinian Arabs' decision to take up arms for their imperial masters the Turks and refusal to participate in the Arab Revolt had destroyed any sympathy he might have had for them. 'These Arabs were a poor people, conquered, living under the Turks fairly well,' he told the Commission.

> they lived fairly easily in a flat squalor typical of pre-war Turkish Empire provinces, and then when the war came they became our enemies and they filled the armies against us and fired their rifles and shot our men ... But our armies advanced and they were conquered ... They were beaten then and at our disposition. Mercy may impose many restraints ... They were defeated in the open field. It is not a question of creeping conquest. They were beaten out of the place. Not a dog could bark. And then we decided in the process of the conquest of these people to make certain pledges to the Jews.[121]

Churchill was coldly uncompromising in his conclusion: 'I do not admit that the dog in the manger has the final right to the manger, even though he may have lain there for a very long time.'[122] His next comment offends modern sensibilities, but was perfectly orthodox thinking at the time:

> I do not admit, for instance, that a great wrong has been done to the Red Indians of America, or the black people of Australia. I do not admit that a wrong has been done to those people by the fact that a stronger race,* a higher grade race, or, at any rate, a more worldly-wise race, to put it that way, has come in and taken their place. I do not admit it. I do not think the Red Indians had any right to say, 'The American Continent belongs to us and we are not going to have any of these European settlers coming in here.' They had not the right, nor had they the power.

Among Churchill's papers is an anti-Semitic article written in 1937 by Adam Marshall Diston, who sometimes ghost-wrote early drafts of his pieces, entitled 'How the Jews Can Combat Persecution'. It was written for publication under Churchill's name. From the lack of Churchill's red-lined annotations, and the fact that it was never published, indeed that Churchill prevented its publication when it was suggested to him three years later, it can safely be assumed that Churchill had not read it initially and disapproved of it when he finally did. Yet detractors continue to point to it as evidence that he was a closet anti-Semite.[123]

'I have tried very sincerely to adopt a neutral attitude of mind in the Spanish quarrel,' he told the Commons. 'I refuse to become the partisan of either side. I will not pretend that, if I had to choose between Communism and Nazi-ism, I would choose Communism. I hope not to be called upon to survive in the world under a Government of either of those dispensations.'[124] All too often, the last sentence goes unquoted.[125] In a *Sunday Chronicle* article soon afterwards, entitled 'The Creeds of the Devil', he indulged his genius for metaphor to the full, writing of how

* Churchill used the word 'races' in the way that today we use 'peoples'.

Communism and Fascism reminded him 'of the North Pole and South Pole. They are at the opposite ends of the earth, but if you woke up at either Pole tomorrow you could not tell which one it was. Perhaps there might be more penguins at one, or more Polar bears at the other, but all around would be ice and snow and the blast of a biting wind.'[126] Churchill was one of the first to recognize that the Fascism and Communism had much more in common than what divided them, and in their totalitarianism were in fact sister-creeds.

'We seem to be moving, drifting, steadily, against our will, against the will of every race and every people and every class, towards some hideous catastrophe,' he further elaborated in his Commons speech in April. 'Everybody wishes to stop it but they do not know how.'[127] 'Winston Churchill made a terrific speech,' Channon noted, 'brilliant, convincing, unanswerable and his "stock" has soared, and people today are . . . saying once more that he ought to be in the Government.'[128] Churchill certainly needed his stock to rise: on 28 April his group of parliamentary supporters shrank to two with the death from cancer of his cousin Freddie Guest at the age of sixty-one. He had played backgammon with him as he was dying. 'I have never known anyone show such a complete contempt of death and make so little fuss of it,' he told Marsh.[129] There was nothing in the world that he admired more than that.

Although he had lost one ally, the next month he gained another. Taking advantage of his connection as the son of one of Churchill's colonels of the 4th Hussars, Rear Admiral Bertram Ramsay had an 'absolutely frank' interview with Churchill in May. He warned him about the Admiralty's complacency as well as 'antiquated administration, customs and views which handicap us most unduly with efficient nations like the Germans'.[130] He described Lord Chatfield, who had taken over from Inskip as minister for the coordination of defence in January, as 'an absolute disaster', a view Churchill was beginning to share.[131] Churchill told Ramsay there was very little he could do so long as he was out of office, and Ramsay retired from the Navy the following year. When war broke out, Ramsay was brought out of retirement: Churchill told him that he had been absolutely right, and put him in several key roles such as overseeing the Dunkirk evacuation and the naval part of the D-Day landings.

King George VI's Coronation took place on 12 May 1937. At the moment when the Queen Consort Elizabeth was crowned, Churchill, with tears in his eyes, turned to Clementine and said, 'You were right; I see now that the other one [Mrs Simpson] wouldn't have done.'[132] He told the Duke of Windsor himself that the ceremony had been 'a brilliant success'.[133] (The

Duke had listened to the Coronation service on the radio in France, while knitting a blue sweater for his fiancée.) When the Windsors married in France the following month, the Churchills sent a wedding present – wishing 'Your Royal Highness and your bride [a neat way of avoiding having to describe the Duchess as a royal highness] many days of mellow sunlight in the land you love' – but they did not attend.[134] In October he advised the Windsors, who had visited Hitler earlier that month, that if they crossed the Atlantic on the German liner *Bremen* rather than the French *Normandie* they risked offending millions of Jews.[135] The Windsors chose the *Bremen*.

Churchill embarked in mid-May on a libel action against Geoffrey Dennis, a League of Nations employee who in his book *Coronation Commentary* had described him as 'an unstable ambitious politician, flitting from party to party, extreme reactionary, himself the first-fruit of the first famous snob-dollar marriage; "half an alien and wholly undesirable" as long ago was said'.[136] In his defence, Dennis argued that the half-alien quote was from the *National Review* in 1905, which he said had been bandied about a lot during the Abdication Crisis. It took two years, but Churchill eventually won the case.

With the Coronation a success, Baldwin retired in his seventieth year and – very unusually for British premiers – entirely at a time of his own choosing. In 1929, Churchill had mused to Clementine that he might take up ranching in Canada if Neville Chamberlain ever became prime minister.[137] Yet on 31 May 1937, it was he who formally seconded the motion for Chamberlain's election as Conservative leader, and thus premier, at a special meeting of the entire Party hierarchy at Caxton Hall, Westminster. 'There is no rivalry, there are no competing claims,' Churchill said. 'Mr. Chamberlain stands forth alone as the one man to whom at this juncture this high and grave function should be confided.' He went on to speak of Chamberlain's 'credentials of memorable achievement'.[138] The election was approved by acclamation. 'If I take him into the Cabinet he will dominate it,' Chamberlain now said of Churchill. 'He won't give others a chance of even talking.'[139] So even though Churchill had had a prominent role in his election, no call came from Chamberlain either. (A few weeks earlier he had privately quoted Lord Haldane's remark that arguing with Churchill 'is like arguing with a brass band'.)[140] This was the moment when Clementine finally gave up her belief that her sixty-three-year-old husband would ever get into government again, though she did not tell him so.[141] When Churchill spotted Baldwin in the Smoking Room shortly afterwards, he jibed, 'Well, the light is at last out of that old turnip.'[142]

Churchill was now free to denounce the Government, and not just over the pace and scale of rearmament. Saying that he felt 'an avuncular interest' in the new Government, he nonetheless attacked a proposed Excess Profits Duty, which the Treasury had acknowledged would not raise much money. 'The most healthy tax is one whose sole purpose is revenue,' Churchill said. 'Taxation to give effect to some political purpose, or even to inculcate some moral principle, is usually found to fall short of the highest standard of financial economy.'[143] To be even-handed, Churchill also said, 'I know that it is the Socialist idea that making profits is a vice, and that making large profits is something of which a man ought to be ashamed. I hold the other view. I consider that the real vice is making losses.'[144] Chamberlain withdrew the duty.

Churchill's parliamentary duties now took up three days a week. He was also working on no fewer than three books: writing the fourth volume of *Marlborough*, reading for a history of the English-speaking peoples, for which he had signed a £20,000 contract back in 1932, and correcting the proofs of *Great Contemporaries*. 'I really don't know how I find all that I need, but the well flows freely,' he reported to Clementine, then at an Austrian spa, on 25 July: 'only the time is needed to draw the water from it.'[145] He dictated 20,000 words of *Marlborough* in a single week that month, and drew her a picture of a pig carrying a 10-ton weight on its back. His working method was to read all the primary resources that his research assistants, who by then included the Oxford-educated William Deakin, provided for him, and then dictate to a secretary in his study at Chartwell.

*Great Contemporaries* was published on 4 October to overwhelmingly positive reviews and large sales. It was essentially a reprint (though with considerable editing in some cases) of essays, articles and eulogies originally published elsewhere, and was full of aperçus about twenty-one statesmen and soldiers he had known. Asquith's mind 'opened and shut like the breech of a gun', Lawrence of Arabia was 'one of Nature's greatest princes', and 'It might be said that Lord Rosebery outlived his future by ten years and his past by more than twenty.' Of Lord Curzon's life he wrote, 'The morning had been golden; the noontide was bronze; and the evening lead. But all were solid, and each was polished till it shone after its fashion.'[146] All the Britons he wrote of were dead, and the book's theme was of friendship which transcends generations and political parties, particularly his own with Birkenhead and Lawrence, and his father's with Lord Rosebery and Joseph Chamberlain.[147] The essay on Chamberlain was almost hagiographic; he obviously did not want to close the door on serving under his son.

'Whatever one may think about democratic government,' Churchill said in his portrait of Lord Rosebery, who had never been in the Commons, 'it is just as well to have practical experience of its rough and slatternly foundations. No part of the education of a politician is more indispensable than the fighting of elections.'[148] He portrayed Arthur Balfour as 'a being high-lifted above the common run'.[149] The ex-Kaiser was described as 'a very ordinary, vain, but on the whole well-meaning man' with 'no grandeur of mind or spirit' who nonetheless had thought of himself as 'far above ordinary mortals'.[150] Here too Churchill had a contemporary note to strike: that the German people 'worship Power, and let themselves be led by the nose'.[151]

Churchill included a sharp attack on George Bernard Shaw in *Great Contemporaries* – the only non-soldier or statesman in the book – for his apologist stance towards Stalinist Russia. 'Here we have a state . . . nearly half a million of whose citizens,' he said, 'reduced to servitude for their political opinions, are rotting and freezing through the Arctic night; toiling to death in forests, mines and quarries, many for no more than indulging in that freedom of thought which has gradually raised man above the beast.'[152] This was written over twenty years before Alexander Solzhenitsyn started writing *The Gulag Archipelago*.

Four more chapters were added in the second edition a year later, including one on Franklin Roosevelt. Churchill had clearly forgotten he had ever met him, although he knew Roosevelt had enjoyed reading *Marlborough*. 'A single man whom accident, destiny, or Providence, has placed at the head of one hundred and twenty millions . . .' he wrote of the President, 'has set out upon this momentous expedition,' and prophesied that 'his success could not fail to lift the whole world forward into the sunlight of an easier and more genial age.'[153] It was as much a love-letter as objective analysis, although there were occasional barbs; in one sentence he suggested that 'the policies of President Roosevelt are conceived in many respects from a narrow view of American self-interest.' As so often in Churchill's writing there was an element of self-reference, as in his description of a man 'trained to public affairs, connected with . . . history by a famous name . . . he contested elections: he harangued the multitude . . . He sought, gained and discharged offices of the utmost labour and of the highest consequence.'

Above all, what Churchill saw and admired in Roosevelt was his courage. At forty-two, the age at which Churchill had been serving in the trenches, Roosevelt was, in Churchill's words, 'struck down with infantile paralysis. His lower limbs refused their office. Crutches or assistance were needed for the smallest movement from place to place.' Churchill also admired his luck, and claimed (wrongly, in fact) that his winning of the Democratic nomination in 1932 had at one moment turned 'upon as little as the spin of a coin'. This led Churchill to reach for one of his most unrestrained extravagances: 'Fortune came along, not only as a friend or even as a lover, but as an idolator.' He made no effort to conceal his admiration for Roosevelt's forceful, whirlwind imposition of the New Deal, writing, 'Although Dictatorship is veiled by constitutional forms, it is none the less effective. Great things have been done, and greater attempted.' His breathless description of 'the renaissance of creative effort with which the name of Roosevelt will always be associated' stood him in good stead two years later, when the President opened a personal correspondence with him.

Churchill controversially included a portrait of Hitler in his book, which he softened on the imploring of the Foreign Office. 'I have on more than one occasion made my appeal in public that the Führer of Germany should now become the Hitler of peace,' he wrote. 'Success should bring a mellow, genial air and, by altering the mood to suit the new circumstances, preserve and consolidate in tolerance and goodwill what has been gained by conflict.'[154] It was naive perhaps, but it was also strategic, and the essay included criticism of Hitler's 'ferocious' persecution of the Jews. Hindenburg, meanwhile, was excused for 'opening the floodgates of evil upon German, and perhaps upon European, civilization' because he had been senile.[155]

When the *News of the World* serialized the Hitler chapter the week after publication, Churchill slipped in two lines from an article he had published in the *Strand* in 1935, saying it was Hitler's choice 'whether he will rank in Valhalla with Pericles, with Augustus and with Washington, or welter in the inferno of human scorn with Attila and Tamerlane'.[156] All Britain and France had to do, he argued in an *Evening Standard* article in October entitled 'War is Not Imminent', was to make it clear to Hitler that further alterations to the map of Europe in contravention of the Versailles Treaty were unacceptable. But when Lord Halifax (formerly Lord Irwin, who had succeeded to his father's viscountcy), who was lord president of the Council, leader of the House of Lords and an influential voice in foreign affairs because of his closeness to Chamberlain, visited Hitler the next month at the Berghof, his Bavarian Alpine home at Berchtesgaden, no such lines were drawn.

As late as October 1937, Churchill had not fully accepted that the Soviet Union, whose regime he loathed, would need to be a formal part of any collective security system to encircle Germany. He was remarkably consistent in his appraisal of the true nature of Hitler's regime, and of the need to rearm, during the Wilderness Years, but in considering how best to stop Hitler his ideas evolved over the extent to which the League of Nations or the Soviets could be appealed to, and how to deal with Mussolini and the Spanish Fascist dictator General Francisco Franco. It was not until the Czech crisis of 1938 that he unequivocally opposed all appeasement and openly embraced the need for a Russian alliance.

On Remembrance Day 1937, Churchill published an article in the *Evening Standard*. 'Dictators ride to and fro on tigers from which they dare not dismount,' he wrote. 'And the tigers are getting hungry.'[157] That year he wrote sixty-four articles, just over half of them for the *Evening Standard*, but his views had diverged so significantly from those of Beaverbrook over appeasement that his contract was not renewed. People did not want to read his Cassandra-like warnings, any more than MPs wanted to listen to them. Some now left the Chamber when he got up to speak rather than flooding into it, as they had done as recently as 1935. That Christmas, Churchill gave Lord Blandford, his eleven-year-old godson and the future 11th Duke of Marlborough, a gold watch, with the advice, 'Never confuse leadership with popularity.'[158]

December also saw Lord Cranborne, the Under-Secretary at the Foreign Office and later 5th Marquis of Salisbury, and grandson of the Prime Minister who had destroyed Lord Randolph Churchill, elected to the Other Club. 'I never remember a dull one,' he said of the dinners, 'from the moment when one arrived to the moment when, late in the evening, one had reluctantly to decide to go home.'[159] Churchill, he recalled, 'would arrive, beaming, benevolent, very pink and white in his dinner jacket. The conversation flowed very freely . . . No subject was barred – least of all politics . . . I have very seldom seen tempers lost, even in discussion on highly controversial subjects.'[160] The previous month the strongly pro-appeasement Lord Mottistone had wagered Churchill, Duff Cooper and Boothby £100 to £10 that 'no hostile bomb would be dropped on the soil of Great Britain for twenty years'.[161] At that point the whole of the rest of the table of twenty-one people, with only Walter Elliot, Munnings and Holden refusing, took on the bet. War was in the air.

Churchill made his last suggestion for buying off the Nazis with the restoration of their colonies – and only if all the rest of the Great War's victorious Allies joined in – on 21 December 1937. 'It would have to be part of a general settlement,' he said, which would involve Hitler disarming to some extent and giving up any future territorial demands.[162] 'Although there are a large number of people in this country who would be willing to make sacrifices to meet German wishes about the colonies if they could be assured that it meant genuine lasting peace to Europe,' Churchill told MPs, 'none of them would yield one scrap of territory just to keep the Nazi kettle boiling.' With its control of the Atlantic, he calculated, the Royal Navy could have supervised the reconquest of these mainly West African colonies if necessary.

Churchill had been avid for an increase in British air power now for five years, but his prediction, made in an article on 7 January 1938, that 'The air menace against properly armed and protected ships at sea will not be of a decisive character' was ill judged.[163] Yet that same month Chamberlain made a far worse error in turning down President Roosevelt's offer to hold an international conference in Washington to help resolve European disagreements. Even had it failed, such a conference might have drawn the United States into European affairs and publicly exposed Hitler's unreasonableness, especially if he had refused to participate. 'That Mr. Chamberlain, with his limited outlook and inexperience of the European scene,' Churchill wrote ten years later, 'should have possessed the self-sufficiency to wave away the proffered hand stretched out across the Atlantic leaves one, even at this date, breathless with amazement.'[164]

Churchill left for the Château de l'Horizon for twelve days' holiday in January 1938. As his secretary Violet Pearman told Lindemann on his return, 'Contrary to our expectations he has not lost a thing on his journeyings alone, and is very pleased.'[165] His hostess, Maxine Elliott, threw a dinner for him, the Duke and Duchess of Windsor and Lloyd George. Churchill said to her, 'You have a strange party tonight, my dear. It consists entirely of the *ci-devant*. Ex-kings, ex-prime ministers, ex-politicians.'[166] Vincent Sheean recalled the occasion as 'a strange, surréaliste evening', where the discussion at dinner revolved around the issue of compulsory showers at South Welsh coalmine pitheads. 'In the exquisite little room, gleaming with glass and silver, over the flowers and champagne . . . what did they have to speak of but dirt on a miner's neck?'[167]

'The W[indsor]s are very pathetic, but also very happy,' Churchill reported to Clementine. 'She made an excellent impression on me, and it looks as if it would be a most happy marriage.'[168] He was hard at work shortening the fourth volume of *Marlborough* from 750 to 650 pages for his publishers, which he understandably likened to 'cutting off your own fingers and toes'.[169] (Most readers today wish he had ignored them.) Having lost £18,000 on the American stock market since the Crash, Churchill badly needed the book sales. Chartwell had to be put on the market once again, though not for long and fortunately without attracting enquiries.

On 20 February 1938, Anthony Eden resigned as foreign secretary, in protest at Chamberlain's private overtures to Mussolini and the refusal of Roosevelt's conference offer. 'From midnight till dawn I lay in bed consumed by emotions of sorrow and fear,' Churchill wrote in *The Gathering*

*Storm*. 'There seemed one strong young figure standing up against long, dismal, drawling tides of drift and surrender, of wrong measurements and feeble impulses . . . Now he was gone. I watched the daylight slowly creep in through the windows, and saw before me in mental gaze the vision of Death.'[170] If this account is true, it must have been one of his lowest points during his Wilderness Years. Yet there was little Eden had done in his foreign secretaryship to deserve such an encomium, which only appeared a decade later, when Eden had been his deputy for eight years. On 18 March, Churchill's was the fourth name on a round-robin letter of 150 Tory MPs congratulating Chamberlain on his sixty-ninth birthday and assuring him 'of their wholehearted confidence'.[171] Although Eden had resigned over the appeasement of Italy rather than Germany, there was no doubt that he was also frustrated and irritated by the pro-Germans in Chamberlain's Cabinet, such as the Health Minister Sir Kingsley Wood, who, Eden wrote, 'was always complaining that I did not succeed in making friends with Hitler'.[172] In 1941, Churchill admonished Eden for not having 'chosen a bigger issue for resignation, but admitted . . . that the Foreign Secretary is not a free agent in these matters'.[173]

In May 1937, Churchill had told a lunch of Lady Colefax's that 'he was really the Leader of the Opposition as the Labour people are so ineffectual, weak and uneducated.'[174] Now that position was about to be usurped by the forty-year-old Eden, who seemed to represent the vigorous future as much as Churchill did the encumbered past. Eden's supporters in Parliament far outnumbered Churchill's. Derisively nicknamed 'the Glamour Boys' by the whips, the Eden Group stayed aloof from Churchill.[175] In March, Eden again refused to join the Other Club. 'We decided that we should not advertise ourselves as a group,' wrote Harold Nicolson of Eden's supporters, 'or even call ourselves a group.'[176] Their meetings were held at the house of the rich, American-born Conservative MP Ronald Tree in Queen Anne's Gate, and Eden ensured that no minutes were kept and there was no formal agenda. Among those attending were the National Government MPs Leo Amery, Ronald Cartland, Duff Cooper, Anthony Crossley, Hubert Duggan, Paul Emrys-Evans, Sir Derrick Gunston, Richard Law, Harold Macmillan and Louis Spears, but in the debate on Eden's resignation, when Churchill supported Eden, only twenty-five Tories abstained, and the rest supported the Government. In private, Churchill was coming to despise the bulk of the Tory Party. Writing to Marsh that month about his revisions to the last volume of *Marlborough*, in which his ancestor was brought down by cowardly, worthless back-stabbers, he said, 'I hope it will bring home to modern readers the life and drama of that great age. How like their forerunners the modern Tories are!'[177]

On 12 March 1938, German troops crossed the Austrian border and the following day Hitler proclaimed Anschluss (the incorporation of Austria into the German Reich). The gravity of these events could not be exaggerated, Churchill told the Commons on the 14th. 'Europe is confronted with a programme of aggression, nicely calculated and timed, unfolding stage by stage, and there is only one choice open, not only to us, but to other countries who are unfortunately concerned – either to submit, like Austria, or else to take effective measures while time remains to ward off the danger, and, if it cannot be warded off, to cope with it.'[178] He predicted that by 1940 the Wehrmacht 'will certainly be much larger than the French Army . . . Why be edged and pushed farther down the slope in a disorderly expostulating crowd of embarrassed States? Why not make a stand while there is still a good company of united, very powerful countries that share our dangers and aspirations?'

Churchill attempted to educate legislators about the country that he had long suspected would be Hitler's next target. 'To English ears, the name of Czechoslovakia sounds outlandish,' he said. 'No doubt they are only a small democratic State, no doubt they have an army only two or three times as large as ours, no doubt they have a munitions supply only three times as great as that of Italy, but still they are a virile people; they have their treaty rights, they have a line of fortresses, and they have a strongly manifested will to live freely.'[179] France had a defensive alliance with Czechoslovakia but Britain did not, so Churchill proposed what he now called 'a Grand Alliance' comprising Britain, France, the USSR and the Little Entente countries of Czechoslovakia, Romania and Yugoslavia – with that, 'you might even now arrest this approaching war.'[180] (Poland had to be excluded from the Grand Alliance because it refused to coalesce with Russia and claimed Czech territory.)

Dining at Pratt's Club in St James's on 16 March, Churchill told Nicolson he had some sympathy for Chamberlain's position, placing the blame for Britain's weakness on Baldwin and saying the situation was now materially worse than in 1914. 'Yet if we take strong action,' he had to admit, 'London will be a shambles in half-an-hour.'[181] A week later, he saw Maisky for lunch in Randolph's flat, possibly because he wanted the meeting to be secret. It was not impossible that MI5 were watching their own founder's flat in Morpeth Terrace, as well as bugging his telephone.[182]

Maisky found Churchill 'greatly agitated' by the liquidation by Stalin of over three-quarters of the Red Army High Command, right down to the level of colonel. 'Could you, please, tell me what is going on in your country?' Churchill began. He said that Russia needed to join the Grand

Alliance, but that the latest purges meant that 'Russia, broadly speaking, has ceased to exist as a serious factor in foreign politics.'[183] When Maisky denied that, Churchill continued with what Maisky called 'a crafty grin', 'Of course, you are ambassador and your words have to be taken *cum grano salis* [with a pinch of salt].'[184] When Maisky asked what was happening in Britain, Churchill admitted that 'Over the last five or six years, the leading group of the party had indeed displayed cowardice and short-sightedness on a scale with few, if any, precedents in history.'[185] As for himself, Churchill 'remarked venomously [that] it is far more pleasant to read books or write articles than to try to convince ministerial nonentities that twice two is four'.[186] Although not everything Maisky wrote can be believed, there is no reason to doubt that Churchill told him, as he reported, that Eden would not clash with the Conservative Party as he had 'already grown used to power and his high standing. This can spoil a man.'[187] Churchill predicted that ultimately Hitler would invade the USSR, 'with its vast territories and immeasurable resources'. By then he had read *Mein Kampf* (in translation) where Hitler laid out Germany's need for *Lebensraum* in the east.

Churchill spoke plainly to Maisky:

> Today, the greatest menace to the British Empire is German Nazism, with its idea of Berlin's global hegemony. That is why, at the present time, I spare no effort in the struggle against Hitler. If, one fine day, the German Fascist threat to the Empire disappears and the Communist menace rears its head again, then – I tell you frankly – I would raise the banner of the struggle against you once more. However, I don't anticipate the possibility of this happening in the near future, or at least within my lifetime.[188]

It was instructive that, although almost the only part of the British Empire within immediate range of German bombers was the British Isles, it was the Empire Churchill nonetheless said was under threat.

On Thursday, 24 March 1938, Churchill delivered one of the most powerful orations of his life, on the threat the Nazis posed to Czechoslovakia. The Treaty of Versailles had left 3.5 million ethnic Germans within the borders of the newly created Czechoslovakia, most of them in the Sudetenland, and Hitler was demanding that they be incorporated into the Third Reich. This would leave Czechoslovakia strategically indefensible. Chamberlain had warned that if war broke out between Germany and Czechoslovakia, 'it would be quite impossible to say where it might end and what Governments might become involved.'[189] In the debate, Churchill called for ministries of supply and defence to be created:

> I have set the issue before the House in terms which do not shirk realities. It has been said by almost all speakers that, if we do not stand up to the dictators now, we shall only prepare the day when we shall have to stand up to them under far more adverse conditions. Two years ago it was safe, three years ago it was easy, and four years ago a mere dispatch might have rectified the position. But where shall we be a year hence? Where shall we be in 1940?[190]

His imagery was vivid and his words well chosen: 'I have watched this famous Island descending, incontinently, fecklessly, the stairway which leads to a dark gulf. It is a fine broad stairway at the beginning, but after a bit the carpet ends. A little further on there are only flagstones. And a little further on still these break beneath your feet.'[191] 'You can imagine that delivered in a packed and sombre House,' Robert Bernays wrote to his sister. 'It was like our drawing room clock emitting the strokes of doom.'[192]

Churchill continued:

> Look back upon the last five years since, that is to say, Germany began to rearm in earnest and openly to seek revenge. If we study the history of Rome and Carthage, we can understand what happened and why. It is not difficult to form an intelligent view about the three Punic Wars; but if mortal catastrophe should overtake the British Nation and the British Empire, historians a thousand years hence will still be baffled by the mystery of our affairs. They will never understand how it was that a victorious nation, with everything in hand, suffered themselves to be brought low, and to cast away all that they had gained by measureless sacrifice and absolute victory – gone with the wind!* Now the victors are the vanquished, and those who threw down their arms in the field and sued for an armistice are striding on to world mastery. That is the position – that is the terrible transformation that has taken place bit by bit . . . Now is the time at last to rouse the nation. Perhaps it is the last time it can be roused with a chance of preventing war, or with a chance of coming through to victory should our efforts to prevent war fail. We should lay aside every hindrance and endeavour by uniting the whole force and spirit of our people to raise again a great British nation standing up before all the world; for such a nation, rising in its ancient vigour, can even at this hour save Civilization.[193]

Chamberlain wrote to his sister that Churchill had told him before the debate that he was no longer looking for office for himself, and would

* Margaret Mitchell's novel, published in 1936, was in the process of being made into an Oscar-winning movie, starring Clark Gable, Churchill's favourite actress Vivien Leigh and his friend Leslie Howard.

continue his 'avuncular' attitude towards his Government. 'I can't help liking Winston although I think him nearly always wrong and impossible as a colleague. Everyone in the House enjoys listening to him and is ready to cheer and laugh at his sallies but he has no following of any importance.'[194] It was a wholly inadequate reaction. Churchill was explaining eloquently and precisely what Hitler was doing, and begging for Britain to take timely action to stop him, but he was being flippantly dismissed.

In May the Chamberlain Government, partly in order to show Germany that it was prepared to revise treaties, unilaterally gave up the United Kingdom's rights over the three Irish ports – Berehaven, Queenstown and Lough Swilly – awarded to them by the Treaty negotiated by Churchill in 1921. Churchill bitterly denounced the move, which he called 'this improvident example of appeasement', and pointed out that it would profoundly worsen the Royal Navy's strategic position in the eastern Atlantic in the event of a war with Germany should the Irish Free State choose neutrality. He accused the Government of 'casting away real and important means of security and survival for shadows and for ease'.[195] The ports were essential places from which to hunt enemy submarines and protect convoys, he said, calling them 'the sentinel towers of the western approaches by which the forty-five million people on this island so enormously depend on foreign food for their daily bread'.

Years later, Churchill recalled 'the looks of incredulity, the mockery, derision and laughter I had to encounter on every side, when I said that Mr. de Valera might declare Ireland neutral'.[196] 'Winston is even against the Irish Treaty,' Chips Channon noted in his diary of the revised agreement. 'Is Winston, that fat, brilliant, unbalanced, illogical orator, more than just that?'[197] Churchill was almost the only person to oppose it, and was attacked for doing so by Leo Amery, among several others. The Admiralty was later to compute that ceding the Treaty ports – for which Britain received nothing in return, beyond some dubious goodwill – led directly to the loss of 368 Allied ships and 5,070 lives during the Second World War.[198] As Amery had to admit in his autobiography, 'Churchill's immediate apprehensions were amply justified.'[199] After Churchill's abstention in that vote, he started to abstain consistently in votes on foreign policy. He did not vote against the Government, because it had a majority of over 200: he might well have had the Tory whip withdrawn and been deselected at the next election. That month he wagered Duff Cooper £6 to £4 that one would take place before the end of February 1939.[200]

'We repudiate all ideas of abject or slothful defeatism,' Churchill told a Manchester audience in May. 'We wish to make our country safe and strong – she can only be safe if she is strong – and we wish her to play her part with other parliamentary democracies on both sides of the Atlantic Ocean in warding off from Civilization, while time yet remains, the devastating and obliterating horrors of another world war.'[201] That same day he set out his views on the subject of European confederation, hoping to breathe fresh life into an idea that might help collective security. Using a biblical reference, from II Kings chapter 4, in a *News of the World* article entitled 'The United States of Europe', he wrote of Britain: 'We are with Europe, but not of it. We are linked, but not compromised. We are interested and associated, but not absorbed. And should European statesmen address us in the words which were used of old, "Wouldst thou be spoken for to the king, or the captain of the host?" we should reply, with the Shunamite woman: "I dwell among my own people."'[202]

As he explained six days later in another *News of the World* article, 'It is the English-speaking peoples who, almost alone, keep alight the torch of freedom. These things are a powerful incentive to collaboration. With nations, as with individuals, if you care deeply for the same things, and these things are threatened, it is natural to work together to preserve them.'[203] He then dilated upon the power of words in discussing how, among the English-speaking peoples, as the name suggests, 'The greatest tie of all is language . . . Words are the only things that last forever. The most tremendous monuments or prodigies of engineering crumble under the hand of time. The Pyramids moulder, the bridges rust, the canals fill up, grass covers the railway track; but words spoken two or three thousand years ago remain with us now, not as mere relics of the past, but with all their pristine vital force.'[204] Sadly we do not have the words he used when, later that month, at the request of the Foreign Office the England football team gave the Nazi salute as the German national anthem was played in the Olympic Stadium in Berlin.

On 25 May 1938, Chamberlain formally rejected Labour's and Churchill's call for an inquiry into air defences and the creation of a ministry of supply. 'Why does my right honourable Friend resist this plan so obdurately?' Churchill asked the Prime Minister, likening him to St Anthony the Hermit, who 'was much condemned by the Fathers of the Church because he refused to do right when the Devil told him to. My right honourable Friend should free himself from this irrational inhibition, for we are only at the beginning of our anxieties.'[205] He asked, 'Why is it, if all is going well, there are so many deficiencies? Why, for instance, are the Guards drilling with flags instead of machine guns?' He wanted to know why it was impossible to equip the Territorial Army simultaneously with the Regular Army, and closed with fighting words: 'I assert that the Air Ministry and the War

Office are absolutely incompetent to produce the great flow of weapons now required from British industry.'[206] (Once asked which department he hated more, the Foreign Office or the Treasury, he replied, 'The War Office.')[207]

In mid-June Duncan Sandys sent a draft parliamentary question to Leslie Hore-Belisha, the Secretary for War, about London's air defences, one that could only have been based on secret information. He was threatened with prosecution when he refused to disclose his informant, but was upheld by the Commons Privileges Committee. Churchill's comment on the Attorney-General's attempt to try Sandys under the Official Secrets Act was that since it was devised to protect national defence, it should not be used to shield ministers who had neglected national defence.[208] 'Of course Sandys was only a dummy,' Chamberlain told his sister. 'Winston was the real mover and he saw or thought he saw an opportunity of giving the Government a good shake. People who have spent weekends at country house parties where he has been a guest tell me that he has bored the whole company by monopolizing the conversation and denouncing the Government all day long . . . I don't think his enmity is personal to me; it is just his restless ambition that keeps him incessantly criticizing any Administration of which he is not a member.'[209] The idea that Churchill might be genuinely motivated by conviction seems not to have occurred to Chamberlain, who tended to see politics in intensely personal terms, a trait that was ultimately to lead to his downfall.

Churchill tried to alert Sir Maurice Hankey, the Cabinet Secretary, to what he and Sandys had been told about Britain's air defences, but Hankey merely upbraided him for two hours about soliciting secret information, and for telling the Sub-Committee for the Scientific Survey of Air Defence that he had 'never in the past known anything so slow as the work of this committee'.[210] Hankey told Churchill that his behaviour was 'wrong', 'infectious', 'embarrassing' and 'subversive to discipline'. Churchill, staggered by his attitude, responded in a letter. 'My dear Maurice,' he wrote, 'I certainly did not expect to receive from you a lengthy lecture when I went out of my way to give you, in strict confidence, information in the public interest. I thank you for sending me the papers back, and you may be sure I shall not trouble you again in such matters.'[211] Years afterwards he told Eden that Hankey's later attempt at friendship was like 'the caress of a worm'.[212]

*Arms and the Covenant*, Churchill's book of speeches on rearmament published on 24 June, sold only 4,000 copies, despite good reviews, an indication of how little the subject interested the public. As the Sudeten situation worsened, Churchill wrote to Lloyd George: 'I think we shall have to choose in the next few weeks between war and shame, and I have very little doubt what the decision will be.'[213] That month the anti-Nazi German Ewald von Kleist visited Chartwell and assured Churchill that at least half of the Wehrmacht High Command 'were convinced that an attack on Czechoslovakia would involve Germany in war with France and Britain and that Germany could not last three months'.[214] Churchill passed this on to Halifax, but it merely prompted Chamberlain's closest adviser, the arch-appeaser Sir Horace Wilson, to note that Churchill was being 'mischievous'.[215]

Churchill certainly continued to make plenty of mistakes and incorrect predictions – on 1 September, for example, he wrote an article that included a phrase about 'the undoubted obsolescence of the submarine as a decisive war weapon' – yet overall his conviction that Hitler craved European hegemony, a conviction based on intelligence gleaned from many sources such as Bernstorff, Kleist, the Sudeten leader Konrad Henlein (whom he had met in May but failed to persuade to stop agitating for unification with the Reich), and from his informants in the armed forces and civil service, far more closely approximated to the truth than what Chamberlain and Halifax believed, despite their having the whole secret intelligence apparatus at their disposal.[216]

Hitler's increasingly belligerent pronouncements about the Sudetenland were clearly now opening the prospect of armed conflict. On 15 September 1938, Chamberlain flew to Germany to meet the Führer at Berchtesgaden. On his return, he told his sisters that Hitler was 'a man who could be relied upon when he had given his word'.[217] With the Chiefs of Staff advising him that Britain could do nothing to prevent the destruction of Czechoslovakia if she chose to fight, and that if Britain went to war with Germany, then Italy and Japan might join in to dismember the British Empire, and with no appetite for war among the French, the press,* the City, the Government, Parliament or the public, Chamberlain decided to put pressure on Edward Beneš, the Czech President, to accede to Hitler's demands. The Dominion premiers were no more keen to go to war with Germany in September 1938 than they had been to go to war with Turkey in September 1922.

On Chamberlain's return on 17 September, he told the Cabinet, according to Inskip's diary notes, that Hitler was 'the commonest little dog he had ever seen', that at Berchtesgaden 'There were very many pictures of women with nothing on,' and that he 'came to the conclusion that – though Hitler was determined, his objectives were strictly limited . . . The P.M. said more than

* *The Times* had argued in a leader on 7 September that the Sudetenland should be absorbed by the Reich – precisely Hitler's demand.

once to us that he was just in time.'[218] Apart from his snobbery and prudery, it was clear that Chamberlain believed Hitler's assurances that, after the Rhineland, Austria and now the Sudetenland, he had no more territorial claims to make in Europe. Two days later he remarked to his sisters, 'I am the most popular man in Germany!'[219] In fact, as a result of his exertions, there was one man who was about to be much more popular, once he had pulled off the coup – in the form of the Munich Agreement – of incorporating 3.5 million Sudeten Germans into the Reich without a shot being fired.

It has been argued by Chamberlain's supporters and Churchill's detractors that as the British armed forces were now so weak relative to the German it was irresponsible of Churchill to decry the Munich Agreement, and that Chamberlain was right to buy a year's breathing space in which Britain could rearm before the Second World War broke out. Against that, it must be recalled that Chamberlain genuinely believed he had delivered peace, that he was not just buying time, and whereas Russia and Czechoslovakia (with her strong fortifications, 1.5 million-man army and Skoda armaments factories) were opposed to Germany in 1938, neither was in 1939. By late September the French Army was partly mobilized, and the British Navy entirely so, prompting Hitler to remark to Göring, 'The English fleet might shoot after all,' and to postpone German mobilization.[220]

A forceful and energetic British prime minister determined to stop Hitler from bullying small Slavic countries might have been able to push a reluctant France to go further in honouring her Treaty commitment. The extra year that Munich 'bought' for peace was put to good use by Germany; one-third of the tanks used in the invasion of France were of Czech manufacture. In this there are good arguments on both sides, therefore, but there is no doubt that had Churchill been heeded in his many detailed and eloquent warnings about the true nature of the German threat over six years, the British armed forces would not have been in the parlous state they were. That evaluation needs to be made from the moment when Hitler came to power, not just when he threatened war over the Sudetenland five years later.

On 22 September, Chamberlain flew to Bad Godesberg for further negotiations with Hitler over the geographical extent of the absorption of the strategically vital Sudetenland into the Reich. Churchill told Bob Boothby that the Government was 'unfit to conduct either a peace or war'.[221] On 27 September Chamberlain broadcast to the British people: 'How horrible, fantastic, incredible it is that we should be digging trenches and trying on gas-masks here because of a quarrel in a faraway country between people of whom we know nothing.' Britain had been a leading signatory to the Treaty that had brought Czechoslovakia into existence at

Versailles, and she knew a lot about the people on the other side of the quarrel. As for the trenches dug in London parks as rudimentary air-raid shelters and for use against German glider landings, it was pointed out that they had quickly filled with water, and the public had to be protected from falling into them.

The next day, 28 September, Chamberlain was speaking in the House of Commons when an aide passed him Hitler's invitation to meet at Munich on the 29th. Triumphantly, he said he would go, and the House gave him a standing ovation. Only Eden, Amery, Nicolson and Churchill stayed seated, as MPs around them shouted, 'Get up! Get up!' When Chamberlain left the Chamber, Churchill rose, shook his hand and wished him 'God speed'.[222] Another version goes: 'I congratulate you on your good fortune. You were very lucky.'[223] When Anthony Crossley told Churchill that Tory MPs in a London club were accusing him of 'disreputable intrigues', he replied with suitably aristocratic insouciance, 'Many thanks for your letter. I am entirely indifferent to such opinions as you mention. The last word has not been spoken yet.'[224]

On 29 September, Chamberlain flew to meet Hitler, Mussolini and the French premier Édouard Daladier – but not Beneš, who was not invited – at Munich. Almost the whole Cabinet, including Duff Cooper, went along to Heston Aerodrome to wave him off. A lunch held in the Mikado Room at the Savoy that day, organized by an anti-appeasement pressure group called Focus, which worked closely with Churchill, brought a total of twenty-three people together, including Liddell Hart, Violet Bonham Carter, Louis Spears, Megan Lloyd George, Archie Sinclair, Arthur Henderson, Harold Nicolson, Lord (George) Lloyd, Lord Cecil of Chelwood and Clementine.[225] 'Winston's face was dark with foreboding,' Bonham Carter recalled years later. 'I could see that he feared the worst, as I did.'[226] At the lunch, Churchill tried to organize a joint telegram from senior parliamentarians to be sent to Chamberlain in Munich 'abjuring him to make no further concessions at the expense of the Czechs'. Although Lloyd, Cecil of Chelwood and Sinclair agreed to sign it, when they telephoned other leaders Eden did not want to be seen as pursuing a vendetta against Chamberlain, and Attlee felt he could not sign without the approval of the National Executive of the Labour Party.

'The telegram was not dispatched and one by one our friends went out – defeated,' wrote Violet Bonham Carter years later.

> Winston remained, sitting in his chair immobile, frozen, like a man of stone. I saw the tears in his eyes. I could feel the iron entering his soul. His last attempt to salvage what was left of honour and good faith had failed. I spoke

with bitterness of those who had refused even to put their names to principles and policies which they professed. Then he spoke: 'What are they made of? The day is not far off when it won't be signatures we'll have to give but lives – the lives of millions. Can we survive? Do we deserve to do so when there's no courage anywhere?'[227]

In May he had written a *News of the World* article in which he had said, 'The shores of History are strewn with the wrecks of empires. They perished because they were found unworthy. We would court – and deserve – the same fate if, in the coming years, we so denied our destiny and our duty.'[228] Destiny and Duty were at the forefront of Churchill's mind throughout the Sudetenland Crisis, and never more so than on 29 September.

That evening, thirty-two members of the Other Club dined in the Savoy's Pinafore Room a few doors down the corridor from where Churchill had had lunch. There were two Cabinet ministers, Duff Cooper and Walter Elliot, as well as several MPs and distinguished non-politicians such as Trenchard, Munnings, Gordon Selfridge, Donald Somervell, H. G. Wells and Edwin Lutyens. Churchill's friends Moyne, Lloyd, Marsh, Keyes, Bracken, Lindemann and Boothby were also there, as was Jack Churchill, but so were the pro-appeasers Garvin and Mottistone and the newspapermen Astor and Rothermere. 'Churchill was in a towering rage and a deepening gloom,' recalled Colin Coote, who went out to get a late edition of a newspaper in the Strand which carried the outline of the Munich Agreement.[229] It stated that Chamberlain had agreed that the Sudeten areas of Czechoslovakia, which were geographically and ethnically interpreted greatly to Germany's advantage, would pass into the Reich's hands almost immediately, thereby leaving Czechoslovakia completely defenceless against Hitler, and the Versailles Treaty so much waste paper. 'Winston ranted and raved,' according to Lord Moyne's diary, 'venting his spleen on the two Government ministers present and demanding to know how they could support a policy that was "sordid, squalid, sub-human and suicidal".'[230]

Duff Cooper seized the newspaper from Coote and read out the terms, 'with obvious anger and disgust. There was a silence as if all had been stricken dumb. Duff rose, and exited without a word.'[231] In his autobiography *Old Men Forget*, Duff Cooper wrote that as the details of the Agreement arrived 'The more voluble members of the company condemned them and I listened with increasing gloom. Argument grew fierce and heated. A very distinguished elderly publicist [almost certainly the septuagenarian Garvin] declared that he had been insulted and left the building.

I was still a member of the Government and felt myself in loyalty bound to defend their policy. I did so for the last time.'[232] Churchill left soon after Duff Cooper, stopping with Richard Law outside the door of one of the rooms to listen to the sound of loud laughter as a clown performed at a birthday party. 'As we turned away,' Law recalled, 'he muttered, "Those poor people! They little know what they will have to face."'[233]

Chamberlain returned from Munich the next day, 30 September 1938, waving a piece of paper at Heston Aerodrome on which he and Hitler had recorded their mutual desire for their peoples never to go to war again. 'PEACE' read the *Daily Express* headline that day beneath the strapline 'The Daily Express declares that Britain will not be involved in a European war this year, or next year either'. In the car driving to London, Lord Halifax tried to persuade Chamberlain to widen the Government by bringing in the Labour and Liberal parties, but the Prime Minister could not see any advantage to that, as he had convinced himself that he had genuinely brought peace. The King, with blithe disregard for the monarch's constitutional impartiality – the Agreement was opposed by both opposition parties and there was still to be a debate and vote in Parliament – invited Chamberlain on to the balcony of Buckingham Palace to wave to the cheering crowds alongside the Queen and himself. Chamberlain then drove through the celebrating populace to Downing Street, where he announced from an upper window to the packed throng below, 'This is the second time in our history that there has come back from Germany to Downing Street peace with honour. I believe it is peace for our time.'[234] (The first time had been when Disraeli and Lord Salisbury had returned from the Congress of Berlin with a genuine peace with honour in 1878.) Churchill could not join in the celebrations, believing the Czechs to have been betrayed in a grubby deal of which Britons would shortly be ashamed.

On 2 October, Duff Cooper resigned as first lord of the Admiralty, giving his reasons the next day at the start of a four-day debate on the Agreement. 'The Prime Minister has believed in addressing Herr Hitler through the language of sweet reasonableness,' he said. 'I have believed that he was more open to the language of the mailed fist.' He said he did not trust Hitler's promises in the way that Chamberlain did, and ended: 'I have ruined, perhaps, my political career. But that is a little matter; I have retained something which is to me of great value – I can still walk about the world with my head erect.'[235] 'My dear Duff,' Churchill wrote to him, 'Your speech was one of the finest Parliamentary performances I have ever heard. It was admirable in form, massive in argument and shone with courage and public spirit.'[236]

But this view was far from unanimous. In the debate in the House of Lords the following day, Baldwin said of Hitler's invitation to Chamberlain to meet in Munich, 'It was just as though the finger of God had drawn the rainbow once more across the sky and ratified again His Covenant with the children of men.'[237] Lord Ponsonby, a pillar of the Establishment whose father had been Queen Victoria's private secretary, said, 'I have got the greatest possible admiration for Mr. Churchill's Parliamentary powers, his literary powers, and his artistic powers, but I have always felt that in a crisis he is one of the first people who ought to be interned.'[238]

On Wednesday, 5 October 1938, the third day of the debate in the Commons, Churchill spoke, just after hearing the news that Beneš had resigned and gone into exile. A series of Tory MPs had praised Chamberlain's 'courage, sincerity and skilful leadership'. One had gone so far as to say, 'our leader will go down to history as the greatest European statesman of this or any other time.' A Liberal MP had even asked, 'What is Czechoslovakia?' In front of a hostile House which barracked him loudly, Churchill gave the greatest speech of his life thus far. He and his Party had long parted ways; friends like Jack Mottistone, Ian Hamilton, the Duke of Windsor, Charlie Londonderry, Bendor Westminster and David Lloyd George had all praised appeasement, and some even the Führer himself. Churchill had not held office for nine years and had been passed over for it on four occasions, and he was speaking to a House that was about to vote in favour of the Munich Agreement by 366 to 144. Yet still he produced something sublime.

'If I do not begin this afternoon by paying the usual, and indeed almost invariable, tributes to the Prime Minister for his handling of this crisis, it is certainly not from any lack of personal regard,' he started. 'But I am sure it is much better to say exactly what we think about public affairs, and this is certainly not the time when it is worth anyone's while to court political popularity.' He praised the speeches of Duff Cooper and Richard Law, saying of the former that 'He showed that firmness of character which is utterly unmoved by currents of opinion, however swift and violent they may be.'[239] Disdaining a slow build-up in which he attempted to get his audience's sympathy and support, Churchill instead said, 'I will, therefore, begin by saying the most unpopular and most unwelcome thing. I will begin by saying what everybody would like to ignore or forget but which must nevertheless be stated, namely, that we have sustained a total and unmitigated defeat, and that France has suffered even more than we have.' 'Nonsense!' shouted Nancy Astor. 'When the Noble Lady cries "Nonsense",' Churchill said, 'she could not have heard the Chancellor of the Exchequer admit in his illuminating and comprehensive speech just now that Herr Hitler had gained in this particular leap forward in substance all he set out to gain.'* He continued, 'The utmost my right honourable Friend the Prime Minister has been able to secure by all his immense exertions . . . the utmost he has been able to gain—' but was interrupted by a number of MPs shouting, 'Is peace!' When he was finally allowed to finish his sentence, he said, 'has been that the German dictator, instead of snatching his victuals from the table, has been content to have them served to him course by course.'[240]

In trying to explain the difference between the terms Chamberlain got at Berchtesgaden, at Godesberg and at Munich, Churchill varied the metaphor. '£1 was demanded at the pistol's point. When it was given, £2 were demanded at the pistol's point. Finally, the dictator consented to take £1 17s. 6d. [that is, 93.75 per cent of £2] and the rest in promises of good will for the future.'[241] Of the country at the heart of this crisis, he said, 'All is over. Silent, mournful, abandoned, broken, Czechoslovakia recedes into the darkness. She has suffered in every respect by her association with the Western democracies and with the League of Nations, of which she has always been an obedient servant.'[242] Only days after hordes had thronged the streets of London to celebrate the Agreement, he said:

> We are in the presence of a disaster of the first magnitude which has befallen Great Britain and France. Do not let us blind ourselves to that. It must now be accepted that all the countries of Central and Eastern Europe will make the best terms they can with the triumphant Nazi Power. The system of alliances in Central Europe upon which France has relied for her safety has been swept away, and I can see no means by which it can be reconstituted.[243]

He had earlier prophesied that in 'a period of time which may be measured by years, but may be measured only by months, Czechoslovakia will be engulfed in the Nazi régime'.[244] It was an extraordinary thing to say; and virtually none of his listeners thought it likely.

When Churchill criticized Chamberlain for describing Czechoslovakia as a faraway country of which we knew nothing, Nancy Astor shouted out, 'Rude!', which prompted Churchill to retort, to much laughter, 'She must very recently have been receiving her finishing course in manners.'[245] He also attacked the National Government for squandering a series of opportunities since 1933 for 'arresting the growth of the Nazi power', allowing Germany to rearm while not rearming Britain, quarrelling with

* It was true; John Simon had admitted what he called 'the fact that the Reich is now acquiring the territory which he [Hitler] demanded, not indeed by invasion or war, but by cession – cession which the French and British pressed the Czechs to make' (Hansard vol. 339 col. 340).

Italy without helping Ethiopia, discrediting the League of Nations, neglecting to build alliances, with the result that 'they left us in the hour of trial without adequate national defence or effective international security.'[246]

'There can never be friendship between the British democracy and the Nazi Power,' he continued,

> that Power which spurns Christian ethics, which cheers its onward course by a barbarous paganism, which vaunts the spirit of aggression and conquest, which derives strength and perverted pleasure from persecution, and uses, as we have seen, with pitiless brutality the threat of murderous force. That Power cannot ever be the trusted friend of the British democracy. What I find unendurable is the sense of our country falling into the power, into the orbit and influence of Nazi Germany.[247]

He well understood the 'natural, spontaneous outburst of joy and relief' shown by the British people that week:

> but they should know the truth. They should know that there has been gross neglect and deficiency in our defences; they should know that we have sustained a defeat without a war, the consequences of which will travel far with us along our road; they should know that we have passed an awful milestone in our history, when the whole equilibrium of Europe has been deranged, and that the terrible words have for the time being been pronounced against the Western democracies: 'Thou art weighed in the balance and found wanting.' And do not suppose that this is the end. This is only the beginning of the reckoning. This is only the first sip, the first foretaste of a bitter cup which will be proffered to us year by year unless by a supreme recovery of moral health and martial vigour, we arise again and take our stand for freedom as in the olden time.[248]

Four decades earlier, he had written of oratory, 'Abandoned by his party, betrayed by his friends, stripped of his offices, whoever can command this power is still formidable.' Now he had personified that truth. Even detractors such as Amery were 'really impressed' with the speech and Channon admitted that it 'discomfited the Front Bench', but a leading constituent and former supporter, Sir Harry Goschen, told Sir James Hawkey, the chairman of the Epping Conservative Association, 'It was rather a pity that he broke up the harmony of the House by the speech he made . . . I think it would have been a great deal better if he had kept quiet and not made a speech at all.'[249] Thirty Conservatives besides Churchill abstained, including Eden, Duff Cooper, Amery, Macmillan and Sandys, thirteen of whom remained seated as an additional statement of disapproval to the whips.[250]

Churchill's abstention caused fury in the Epping Constituency Association. The Chigwell branch chairman described the speech as 'a mockery and a shame' and another branch chairman called Churchill 'a menace in Parliament'.[251] At the end of October, the Buckhurst Hill branch stated, 'We feel increasingly uneasy at Mr Churchill's growing hostility to the Government and the Prime Minister in particular.'[252] The Harlow branch felt the same way. With a general election less than two years away, the whips started exploring whether Churchill could be deselected.

'I must say that I found the four days' debate in the House a pretty trying ordeal,' Chamberlain complained to his sisters on 9 October, 'especially as I had to fight all the time against the defection of weaker brethren and Winston was carrying on a regular conspiracy against me with the aid of [Jan] Masaryk, the Czech Minister. They, of course, are totally unaware of my knowledge of their proceedings. I had continual knowledge of their doings and sayings which for the nth time demonstrated how completely Winston can deceive himself when he wants to.'[253] MI5's decision to spy on the perfectly legitimate dealings of an MP with the Ambassador of a friendly, would-be allied country underlines just how hard it was for Churchill to steal any kind of march on the Government.

In his essay on Clemenceau in *Great Contemporaries*, Churchill had commended the way the Frenchman was 'fighting, fighting all the way' through life.[254] Over the next five months Churchill had to fight the Government whips, the Prime Minister, the press (especially *The Times*), Conservative Central Office, his backbench colleagues, the Security Services and his own constituency association. In some parliamentary divisions he led a party of three, and sometimes two. Yet in that same desolate period he showed the greatest moral courage of his life, and laid the foundations of his future wartime leadership.

# 18
# Vindication
# October 1938–September 1939

*Stripped of his offices, he was the target of every calumny which a furious faction could hurl or an envious aristocracy applaud; when all that he had done was belittled and his victories contemned or written off.*

Churchill on the 1st Duke of Marlborough[1]

*Are we going to make a supreme additional effort to remain a Great Power, or are we going to slide away into what seem to be easier, softer, less strenuous, less harassing courses, with all the tremendous renunciations which that decision implies?*

Churchill, House of Commons, 17 November 1938[2]

On 16 October 1938, Churchill was allowed to broadcast to the United States. Because Sir John Reith, Director-General of the BBC, who hated him, deliberately kept him off the airwaves as much as possible in the 1930s, his mastery of radio broadcasting was not the result of practice. He had a natural affinity with the microphone, easily making the necessary leap between the expansiveness of a public speech and the intimate, almost conversational style of a radio address. He used the opportunity to tell Americans that 'Dictatorship – the fetish worship of one man – is a passing phase. A state of society where men may not speak their minds, where children denounce their parents to the police, where a businessman or small shopkeeper ruins his competitor by telling tales about his private opinions – such a state of society cannot long endure if brought into contact with the healthy outside world.'[3] It was not in dictators' power 'to cramp and fetter the forward march of human destiny. The preponderant world forces are upon our side; they have but to be combined to be obeyed. We must arm. Britain must arm. America must arm.'[4]

Reaching back into history, as he so often did in his speeches, Churchill said, 'Alexander the Great remarked that the people of Asia were slaves because they had not learned to pronounce the word "No". Let that not be the epitaph of the English-speaking peoples or of Parliamentary democracy, or of France, or of the many surviving liberal states of Europe.'[5] He argued that, for all the totalitarians' pomp and seeming power, 'in their hearts there is unspoken fear. They are afraid of words and thoughts: words spoken abroad, thoughts stirring at home – all the more powerful because forbidden – terrify them.'[6] He challenged Americans, 'will you wait until British freedom and independence have succumbed, and then take up the cause when it is three-quarters ruined, yourselves alone?'[7]

Although Churchill had been regularly described as a warmonger in Britain, it was not until 6 November that Adolf Hitler called him that, in a speech at a rally.[8] Churchill replied in the Commons in words that have often been quoted only in part to suggest that he still admired Hitler. 'I am surprised that the head of a great State should set himself to attack British Members of Parliament who hold no official position and who are not even the leaders of parties,' Churchill said.

> I have always said that if Great Britain were defeated in war I hoped we should find a Hitler to lead us back to our rightful position among the nations. I am sorry, however, that he has not been mellowed by the great success that has attended him. The whole world would rejoice to see the Hitler of peace and tolerance, and nothing would adorn his name in world history so much as acts of magnanimity and of mercy and of pity to the forlorn and friendless, to the weak and poor.[9]

This was no more than he had already written in *Great Contemporaries* and in newspaper articles, but now he went on, 'Let this great man search his own heart and conscience before he accuses anyone of being a warmonger. The whole peoples of the British Empire and the French Republic earnestly desire to dwell in peace side by side with the German nation. But they are also resolved to put themselves in a position to defend their rights and long-established civilizations. They do not mean to be in anybody's power.'[10] Seen in context, Churchill's references to Britain finding a Hitler to lead her and to 'this great man' were only part of a wider message of defiance to him.

Two days later Hitler responded: 'Churchill may have fourteen thousand, twenty thousand or thirty thousand votes behind him – I am not so well informed about that – but I have forty million votes behind me . . . If these English solicitors of world democracy argue that in one year we have destroyed two democracies, I can only ask – Good gracious, after all, what is democracy? Who defines it? Has the Almighty perhaps handed the key to democracy to such people as Churchill?'[11] He later said that Churchill 'appears to live on the moon'.[12] It was remarkable that Hitler should choose to attack a British MP who held no ministerial office and whose influence on the Government at this time was negligible.

It did Churchill's standing in Britain no harm to be criticized by name by Hitler, as it refuted the feeling among many in the political class, and the media, that he was now an irrelevant has-been. On 9 November, Harold Nicolson wrote to his wife, Vita Sackville-West, to tell her about a 'hush-hush meeting' of the Edenites. He was at pains to point out that they were 'distinct from the Churchill group', as they were keen not 'to do anything rash or violent', and they 'do not give the impression (as Winston does) of being more bitter than determined, and more out for a fight than for reform'.[13] That evening at Grillions Club, Churchill said he thought that the attack on him in the German press and by other Nazi ministers 'must be some *arrière-pensée* – as though this were the prelude to some fresh campaign against us'.[14]

In fact the campaign the Nazis unleashed that very night – known to history as Kristallnacht – was against the Jews. Eight thousand Jewish shops and 1,688 synagogues were ransacked, 267 synagogues were burned down, nearly a hundred Jews murdered, thousands beaten up and 30,000 sent to concentration camps. This was supposedly a spontaneous retaliation for the murder of a German diplomat, Ernst vom Rath, by a German-born Polish Jewish refugee in Paris.[15] Over the following days, the Nazi press tried to link Churchill, Duff Cooper and Clement Attlee to vom Rath's assassination, complete with photographs captioned 'Jewish murderers and their instigators!'[16] For all the public jubilation in Britain over Munich, the nature of the Nazi regime had not altered one jot.

Churchill was still a member of the CID's Sub-Committee for the Scientific Survey of Air Defence, and on 14 November, prompted by Lindemann, he proposed investigating the possibility of a 'necklace' of barrage balloons at an altitude of 35,000 feet, with explosive cables hanging from them and 'strung out as a curtain round the coast from the Isle of Wight to the Tyne at intervals of approximately 170 yards'.[17] This was completely impractical, of course, and would have been hideously expensive, but it showed that he was thinking about these problems.

When Churchill asked for fifty Tory MPs to join him in the division lobby to oppose the Government's plans to make the War and Air ministries responsible for their own munitions production, rather than create a single ministry of supply, only Bracken and Macmillan actually did so. Boothby abstained, and the Government had a majority of 196. It was the first time Churchill had voted against the National Government since the India Bill in 1935. On 17 November he blamed the Tory backbenchers for the state of Britain's armaments, telling them frankly that:

> pledged, loyal, faithful supporters on all occasions of His Majesty's Government must not imagine that they can throw their burden wholly on the Ministers of the Crown. Much power has rested with them. One healthy growl from those benches three years ago and how different to-day would be the whole lay-out of our armaments production! Alas, that service was not forthcoming. We have drifted on in general good-natured acquiescence for three whole years . . . three whole years with the facts glaring us full in the face.[18]

Chamberlain took the opportunity to mock Churchill in his reply. 'If I were asked whether judgment is the first of my right honourable Friend's many admirable qualities I should have to ask the House of Commons not to press me too far,' he said. This was greeted with loud laughter at Churchill's expense.[19] Churchill replied in his constituency a few days later: 'I will gladly submit my judgment about foreign affairs and national defence during the last five years in comparison with his own.'[20] He then quoted the Prime Minister's statement in February that European tensions had greatly relaxed, whereupon:

> a few weeks later Nazi Germany seized Austria. I predicted that he would repeat this statement as soon as the shock of the rape of Austria passed away. He did so in the very same words at the end of July. By the middle of August Germany was mobilizing for those bogus manoeuvres which, after bringing us all to the verge of a world war, ended in the complete destruction and absorption of the republic of Czechoslovakia. At the Lord Mayor's Banquet in November at the Guildhall, he told us that Europe was settling down to a more peaceful state. The words were hardly out of his mouth before the Nazi atrocities upon the Jewish population resounded throughout the civilized world.

Chamberlain wrote to his sister Hilda: 'I see that Winston has been making a long and bitter attack on me. That shows that I got under his skin as I meant to do when I suggested that he lacked judgment. He knows it is true and can't bear to hear it said.'[21] Of Churchill's specific points he had nothing to say.

Randolph chose this fraught moment to engage in a full-scale row with his father. 'You always treat me with great suspicion and often when others are present allow it to be seen how little confidence you have in my discretion,' he complained. 'In future I will endeavor to hide my feelings and to bear your violent rebukes in silence.'[22] Churchill replied the next day, 'I was so much surprised when in the midst of my explaining to you the details of a private business transaction, you suddenly suggested opening it up in the Londoner's Diary,' Churchill wrote of the *Evening Standard*'s gossip column. 'I begged you not to do so in excessive vehemence . . . but you got angry – which is infectious.' He continued, 'You are quite wrong in thinking that I do you harm with strangers. I always on the contrary say "You can talk to R with perfect confidence, as long as you mark clearly what is or is not for publication." ' He signed off 'Always your loving father', adding the postscript, 'I think I have given many proofs of my confidence in you.'[23] Randolph wrote back the same day with thanks 'for your nice letter. I know you did not mean to be unkind to me, and silly of me to have got upset.'[24] The relationship between father and son was hardly ever less than stormy, and painful for Churchill, as it became clear that they were not going to have the close working relationship that he had longed for with his own father. In another letter, ironically enough written on Valentine's Day, Churchill wrote, 'My dear Randolph, In your letter I don't see why you did not, as soon as you saw I was offended, say you were sorry. But all the same I forgive you. Your loving father, Winston S. Churchill.'[25]

After the Duchess of Atholl, a Tory MP, had given up the Tory whip in April 1938 and then criticized the Munich Agreement, her Kinross and Western Perthshire Conservative Association deselected her, so she resigned the seat and stood in the ensuing by-election as an Independent. Could Churchill support her, or would that lay him open to deselection, an ever-present danger for him in Epping? The open letter he sent her, published in *The Times*, couched his support in terms of constitutional precedent. 'This is the course I have always proposed to follow myself should circumstances require it,' he wrote. 'I therefore feel the fullest sympathy with you at the present juncture.'[26] He went on to say that her defeat would be 'relished by the enemies of Britain and freedom' and would be 'widely accepted as another sign that Great Britain . . . no longer has the spirit and willpower to confront the tyrannies and cruel persecutions which have darkened the age.' She nonetheless lost to the official Tory candidate by 10,495 to 11,808.

On 15 December, Leo Amery took a committee room in the House of Commons to set up another mainly Tory pressure group, the Policy Study Group, which for all its anodyne title was to attract around forty MPs, although only fifteen turned up to its first meeting.[27] The list of National Government MPs connected with the Group was a Who's Who of anti-appeasers that included Vyvyan Adams, Harold Nicolson, Duff Cooper,

Lord Cranborne, Louis Spears, Ronald Cartland, Godfrey Nicholson, Paul Emrys-Evans, Harold Macmillan and Roger Keyes. Churchill's supporters were represented by Brendan Bracken, Bob Boothby and the Group's secretary, Duncan Sandys. Churchill was not invited himself, as even anti-appeasers thought his presence would give ammunition to the Government whips. The Group held meetings in the Commons, wrote policy papers, tried to encourage the Government to be tougher on Germany and Italy, and advocated rearming to the maximum extent that the economy could withstand, while bringing America and Russia into European affairs. Among Sandys's papers is a list of those who abstained from various Commons votes, featuring Churchill, Eden, Lord Wolmer, Macmillan, Nicolson, Keyes and others, and adjacent to it a list of 'Rats', including Sir Edward Grigg, A. P. Herbert and Ronald Tree, who had failed to do so.[28]

As 1938 closed, Churchill was laying the bricks for Orchard Cottage at the bottom of the Chartwell orchard, which Mary recalled was 'intended to be a "retreat" from the big house in time of crisis' (that is, it would double as a bomb-shelter).[29] He was also dictating 1,500 words a day for his history of the English-speaking peoples,* as well as attending parliamentary debates, while nursing his constituency in an effort not to get deselected. 'I do not think war is imminent for *us*,' he told Clementine, who was on holiday on Lord Moyne's yacht in the Caribbean. 'Only further humiliations, in which I rejoice to have no share.'[30] He asked whether the sea and rest were 'recharging your batteries. That is what I want to know: and even more – Do you love me?'[31]

The death at sixty-eight of Sidney Peel, to whom Clementine had been twice secretly engaged when she was eighteen, led Churchill to commiserate. 'Many are dying now that I knew when we were young,' he wrote. 'It is quite astonishing to reach the end of life and feel just as you did fifty years before. One must always hope for a sudden end, before faculties decay.'[32] During the Wilderness Years, Churchill had lost Lord Birkenhead aged fifty-eight in 1930, T. E. Lawrence aged forty-six in 1935, Ralph Wigram also aged forty-six in 1936, and Freddie Guest aged sixty-one in 1937, on top of all of those who had died in the Boer War, Great War and the 1920s. So in writing on Boxing Day to Lord Craigavon (the former Sir James Craig), who had also been captured by the Boers in 1900 and was now prime minister of Northern Ireland, as well as an Other Club

* He had reached the medieval period, and told Clementine on the subject of Joan of Arc, 'I think she is the winner in the whole of French history. The leading women of those days were more remarkable and forceful than the men' (ed. Soames, *Speaking* pp. 443–4).

member since 1916, he undoubtedly meant it when he said, 'You are one of the few who have it in their power to bestow judgments which I respect.'[33] Another was Reggie (by then Major-General Sir Reginald) Barnes, who wrote to Churchill in December 1938, 'Well dear old pal, this is to send my love, and to assure you that I myself – and many others – perhaps not so stupid! – believe in you.'[34] By the dawn of 1939, Churchill had narrowed down the number of people – never very considerable – whose opinion he gave a damn about. This was a prerequisite for continuing on his way in the face of so many who opposed him. He cared more for the approval of the shades of his father and friends, both alive and dead, than for what he had contemptuously described as 'currents of opinion, however swift and violent they may be'.[35]

By 1939 too, most of those who had blighted Churchill's career, and those friends who had been serious rivals – including Bonar Law, Curzon, MacDonald, Balfour, Carson, Fisher, Kitchener and Austen Chamberlain – were dead. Baldwin had retired and Lloyd George was friendly, at least in public. Churchill was in the limbo between out-of-office politician and elder statesman, but crucially he had not given up his hopes for the premiership, however unlikely it must have seemed, with his following in the Commons amounting to fewer than the fingers of one hand. Of course there were plenty of powerful people who considered it their duty to stymie his future prospects, but Chamberlain, Simon, Halifax and Hoare were not big beasts of the calibre he had grown up fighting for and against. (Chamberlain was still so proud of the Munich Agreement that his Christmas card that year featured the twin-engined Lockheed Electra aeroplane in which he had flown to Germany.)

There is a fascinating dichotomy in that, although the appeasement movement was intended to prevent another war breaking out, most of its leaders had not seen action in the Great War, whereas most of the anti-appeasers had. Ramsay MacDonald, Stanley Baldwin, Neville Chamberlain, Samuel Hoare, Kingsley Wood and R. A. 'Rab' Butler had not served in the Great War, whereas the leading anti-appeasers, such as Churchill, Anthony Eden MC, Alfred Duff Cooper DSO, Roger Keyes KCB, DSO, Louis Spears MC, George Lloyd DSO and the much wounded Harold Macmillan all had.

On 30 December, Churchill wrote a *Daily Telegraph* article entitled 'The Spanish Ulcer', the name Napoleon had given the Peninsular War of 1808–14. In it, he argued that 'If Franco won, his Nazi backers would drive him to the same kind of brutal suppressions as are practised in the totalitarian states.' Franco did not need Hitler's encouragement to massacre up to 100,000 of his Republican enemies when he duly won in

March 1939. Churchill sent the article to Halifax, opining, 'Our interests are plainly served by a Franco defeat.'[36] It was a late conversion but a sincere one.

On 7 January 1939, Kingsley Martin, the editor of the *New Statesman*, published an interview with Churchill. 'I see no reason why democracies should not be able to defend themselves without sacrificing fundamental values,' Churchill declared.[37] He did not think full-scale conscription was necessary, but would not hesitate to enlarge the Territorial Army by ballot. He argued that the National Government's 'leaders failed to appreciate the need [to rearm] and to warn the people, or were afraid to do their duty . . . War is horrible, but slavery is worse, and you may be sure that the British people would rather go down fighting than live in servitude.'[38] It was a refrain he was to reprise regularly over the next six years, supported by his deep reading of history, but at the beginning of 1939 the British people were showing precious little of the willingness to fight that he had ascribed to them. Over the next six years, Churchill constantly averred that he was merely articulating the deep pride and bellicosity in the British people, but much of that spirit actually came from their visceral response to his vision, rather than originating from them.

In January 1939 Churchill left with Lindemann for the sunshine of the Château de l'Horizon, where he painted and worked on his history of the English-speaking peoples. He hoped that he could transform his financial fortunes by publishing it before the end of 1939, assuming nothing significant happened before then. 'It is a formidable grind,' he told Clementine, who was still in the Caribbean, 'but will put things on a very satisfactory basis.'[39] He lunched with Paul Reynaud, the French Minister of Finance, in Paris en route, and also met the three-times Prime Minister Léon Blum and the former Foreign Minister Yvon Delbos, who came down 'deshabillé' as he lived in Blum's apartment block. Delbos claimed that Generals Maurice Gamelin and Alphonse Georges would have broken through the German line on the fifteenth day if France had gone to war for her ally Czechoslovakia.

'I do not think it would be much fun to go and take these burdens and neglects upon my shoulders,' Churchill told Clementine on 8 January in reference to the lack of air-raid precautions, 'certainly not without powers such as they [the Government] have not dreamed of according.'[40] If he were ever to become prime minister, he then mused, it would have to be with very enhanced powers in the field of defence. Meanwhile, Chamberlain told his sisters that he had received a letter from a mechanical engineer called Neville Gwynne asking him not to visit Rome, but instead to make a wide alliance of European powers against Hitler. 'In other words better abandon my policy and adopt Winston's! Fortunately my nature is, as Ll G says, extremely "obstinate", and I refuse to change.'[41]

Chamberlain and Halifax visited Mussolini on 11 January 1939, but were unable to draw him away from Hitler's orbit. The Anschluss had brought the Reich to Italy's northern border. 'Chamberlain's visit to Rome did no harm,' was Churchill's view to Clementine. 'That is the most we can say of it.'[42] When Molly, Duchess of Buccleuch told him that Chamberlain was coming to address the local Tories at Drumlanrig Castle and wondered where best to put the podium, he replied, 'It doesn't matter where you put it, as long as he has the sun in his eyes and the wind in his teeth.'[43]

Churchill dined with the Duke and Duchess of Windsor in Antibes in January. The Duke, wearing a kilt of the Stuart tartan, argued vigorously against Churchill's recent articles opposing Franco and in favour of a Russian alliance. 'We sat by the fireplace,' recalled Maxine Elliott's nephew-in-law Vincent Sheean, 'Mr Churchill frowning with intentness at the floor in front of him, mincing no words . . . declaring flatly that the nation stood in the gravest danger of its long history.' The Duke was 'eagerly interrupting whenever he could, contesting every point, but receiving – in terms of the utmost politeness so far as the words went – an object lesson in political wisdom and public spirit. The rest of us sat in silence: there was something dramatically final, irrevocable about this dispute.'[44] Churchill had discovered beyond doubt how fundamentally unsound the ex-King was about the Nazis. He remained respectful throughout this 'prolonged argument', but did point out to him that 'When our kings are in conflict with our constitution, we change our kings.'[45] Five days later, at another dinner party across the Atlantic on Barbados, Lord Moyne's mistress, Vera, Lady Broughton,* and others expressed their approval of a BBC broadcast that had attacked the anti-appeasers. Clementine promptly booked herself on the SS *Cuba* and sailed the next day for Britain to take up her place beside her husband.

On 30 January in the Reichstag, Hitler described Churchill, Duff Cooper and Eden as 'apostles of war'.[46] He also openly promised 'the destruction of the Jewish race in Europe' should war break out. Churchill continued to be concerned with the pace of rearmament in Britain, which finally increased even though Chamberlain was still convinced that he had secured peace in his time. The monthly production of Hurricanes rose

* The estranged wife of Sir Delves Broughton, who was to kill the Earl of Erroll in Kenya in 1941 and himself in 1942.

from twenty-six in October 1938 to forty-four in September 1939 and of Spitfires from thirteen to thirty-two, while the monthly output of anti-aircraft guns increased from fifty-six to eighty-five. The number of squadrons with these new fighter models increased from six to twenty-six. All this is sometimes held to justify the Munich Agreement, but it ignores what was happening in Germany. While Britain concentrated on bolstering her air defences, the German Army grew exponentially vis-à-vis the British, even after Britain introduced conscription in April 1939. The War Office estimated the German Army to number 690,000 in fifty-one divisions at the time of Munich. A year later, it had grown to 2,820,000 in 106 fully equipped divisions. The British Army, in the meantime, grew from only two fully equipped divisions to five adequately equipped ones.

On 2 March 1939, Eden's friend Jim Thomas wrote to his closest ally in politics, 'Bobbety', Lord Cranborne, to say that David Margesson had floated 'the idea of Halifax as the next P.M. – either de-bag* him of the Lords for that period or keep him there provided there is someone big enough and whom he knew and trusted to run the Commons. A[nthony] is obviously the person . . . Halifax's stock is on the rise and his firmer foreign policy draws more of A[nthony]'s followers to him both in the House and in the country.'[47] Eden's relatively sotto voce critique of the Government in early 1939 becomes more explicable in these circumstances. It was not the only scheme pursued by the Tory Establishment to silence the anti-appeasement voice.

Between November 1938 and mid-March 1939, Conservative Central Office made a coordinated and sophisticated attempt to deselect Churchill as the Conservative candidate for Epping. Colin Thornton-Kemsley, the thirty-five-year-old honorary treasurer of the Essex and Middlesex Provincial Area of the National Union of Conservative and Unionist Associations, led a move to take over key branch committees of the Epping constituency. His ultimate object was to get a majority on its Central Council to deselect Churchill for the general election due the following year.[48] 'It was made clear to me that the growing revolt in the Epping Division was welcomed in high places,' Thornton-Kemsley said later.[49] As the Duchess of Atholl's fate showed, this could have meant Churchill's leaving Parliament at precisely the moment he was most needed. He is often accused of opposing appeasement because he had nothing to lose by it, but in fact he came close to losing something he prized greatly: his seat in the House of Commons.

* A schoolboy expression meaning take his trousers off, but in this case meaning divesting him of his peerage.

There were twenty-six branches in the constituency, and Thornton-Kemsley and his confederates recruited new members to the Association in those branches which were over-represented on the constituency's Central Council. Suddenly small towns and villages in Essex became battlegrounds between the pro- and anti-Churchill forces. The parish of Matching, for example, with only 384 electors, sent five representatives to the Council. At places like Theydon Bois and Chigwell, large numbers of people with no need to prove they were Conservatives started to enrol, gain voting rights and then outvoting long-standing pro-Churchill constituency officers. Churchill reacted by threatening to form separate branch committees, but that violated the Association's constitution. Thornton-Kemsley meanwhile wrote letters to the local press demanding that Churchill resign the Conservative whip and stand as an Independent because of his opposition to the Munich Agreement.

In his memoirs, written in 1974, Thornton-Kemsley understandably sought to downplay his attempts to silence Churchill, dismissing them as 'very childish and impertinent' and a 'futile insurrection', but at the time they were much more serious than that. He acknowledged that 'a strong Conservative candidate backed by the Party machine might have let the Liberal in on a split vote,' which was doubtless what the pro-appeasement Party authorities were hoping for. Of the local branches, Waltham Abbey and Nazeing were 'known to be against the Member', Thornton-Kemsley recalled. Added to Theydon Bois, Chigwell and Epping itself, where his supporters had ousted Churchill's, 'it looked as if the Council meeting might . . . prove to be "a damned close-run thing".'[50]

Thornton-Kemsley worked tirelessly. On 25 January, he got himself elected chairman of the Chigwell branch, due, as the local paper announced, to a 'strong feeling in Chigwell in favour of Mr Chamberlain's appeasement policy and unsympathetic to Mr Churchill's attitude'.[51] In a press statement, he condemned what he called 'Mr Churchill's unhelpful attitude towards the man at the helm'.[52] Afterwards the Loughton branch passed a motion requesting that Churchill support the Prime Minister, and Theydon Bois proclaimed itself 'overwhelmingly' in support of Chamberlain.[53] The Chigwell branch had voted by fourteen members to four against Churchill, and the Loughton branch by thirty-one to fourteen.

The opposition came to a head at a dinner of the Nazeing Unionist Association on 4 March, where Epping constituency officials denounced the absent Churchill, and Thornton-Kemsley said that he 'ought no longer to shelter under the goodwill' of the Conservative Party. A Captain Jones came up with the old saw, 'I admire his brains and mental capacity but I decry his judgement,' and a Major Bury said he had 'come to the end of my patience' with him. One speaker said that 'Mr Chamberlain is one of the greatest premiers England has ever had' and opined that Munich was 'one of the greatest acts in history'.[54] Someone used the word 'expulsion' in reference to Churchill and no one spoke up against it.[55]

Churchill had already made it clear in his public letter to the Duchess of Atholl that the only honourable course after deselection would be to resign and refight the seat as an Independent. No other winnable Conservative constituency would have taken him after Munich, and he would have been unlikely to win as an Independent Conservative in that political environment. Almost any other politician, faced with a revolt on such a scale in his constituency within a few months of a general election, would have made compromises or toned down his speeches to head off a potentially disastrous outcome. Instead, Churchill went straight to Thornton-Kemsley's own branch of Chigwell only six days after the Nazeing meeting and told them, of his speech denouncing the Munich Agreement the previous October, 'I do not withdraw a single word,' and added, 'I read it again only this afternoon, and was astonished to find how terribly true it had all come.'[56] 'Many people at the time of the September crisis thought they were only giving away the interests of Czechoslovakia,' he told another branch, Waltham Abbey, on 14 March, 'but with every month that passes you will see that they were also giving away the interests of Britain, and the interests of peace and justice.'[57] He asked, apropos of the deselection efforts:

> What is the use of Parliament if it is not the place where true statements can be brought before the people? What is the use of sending Members to the House of Commons who say just the popular things of the moment, and merely endeavour to give satisfaction to the Government Whips by cheering loudly every Ministerial platitude, and by walking through the Lobbies oblivious of the criticisms they hear? People talk about our Parliamentary institutions and Parliamentary democracy; but if these are to survive, it will not be because the Constituencies return tame, docile, subservient Members, and try to stamp out every form of independent judgment.[58]

At dawn the next morning, the entire geopolitical landscape changed when Germany invaded the rump of Czechoslovakia. Hitler proclaimed the establishment of a new 'Protectorate of Bohemia and Moravia' from Prague Castle the next day. All the years of protestations about how Hitler wished only to incorporate ethnic Germans into the Third Reich were revealed overnight to have been lies, and those appeasers who believed him to have been his dupes – well meaning, perhaps, but dupes all the same.

The only senior political figures who had not been duped were Churchill and, to a lesser and later extent, Eden, Leo Amery, Duff Cooper and Lord Lloyd. That day, Churchill lunched with Maisky at Randolph Churchill's apartment, where he 'expressed his view that Hitler's move against Czechoslovakia by no means signified a turn towards the East. Before striking a serious blow to the West, Hitler simply had to secure his rear.'[59] It was another brilliantly counter-intuitive piece of analysis and prediction.

On 31 March, Chamberlain guaranteed Poland's and Romania's independence. Britain and France could do nothing militarily to defend them, but the promise was intended to serve as a tripwire for Hitler if he made further attempts to dominate Europe. The Government also announced a doubling of the size of the Territorial Army, as Churchill had been demanding for months. He, meanwhile, called publicly for 'the maximum co-operation possible' with the Soviet Union.[60] On 3 April he once again delved into history to warn that 'Nothing with which Napoleon threatened England is half as intimate or direct as the destruction and ordeal which would fall upon this country should we be involved in a modern war.'[61] At no point did he try to minimize the horrors that would be unleashed in the event of a future conflict.

Harold Macmillan was lunching at Chartwell on Good Friday, 7 April 1939, when the news came through that Mussolini had invaded Albania. 'It was a scene that gave me my first picture of Churchill at work,' he recalled. 'Maps were brought out; secretaries were marshalled; telephones began to ring. "Where was the British fleet?" That was the most urgent question.' Macmillan wrote, 'I shall always have a picture of that spring day and the sense of power and energy, the great flow of action, which came from Churchill, although he then held no public office. He alone seemed to be in command, when everyone else was dazed and hesitating.'[62] Chamberlain complained to Ida two days later about being 'badgered' for a meeting of Parliament by the opposition parties, and by 'Winston who is the worst of the lot, telephoning almost every hour of the day.'[63] He in fact called twice, and sent one messenger with suggestions about the Royal Navy's dispositions in the Mediterranean, including making a British naval and air base out of the (neutral) Greek island of Corfu.

On 13 April, Churchill supported the reintroduction of conscription. 'When we aspire to lead all Europe back from the verge of the abyss on to the uplands of law and peace,' he said, 'we must ourselves set the highest example. We must keep nothing back.'[64] After the debate, he invited David Margesson to dinner, and 'informed him bluntly of his strong desire to join the Government'.[65] Chamberlain readily admitted that Churchill 'would certainly help on the Treasury bench in the Commons', but, apropos of the Corfu suggestion, 'Would he wear me out resisting rash suggestions of this kind?'[66]

A week later, Chamberlain confirmed that a ministry of supply would be set up, but then he played with the House by pausing before announcing the name of the minister to run it. Channon noted that the House was 'expecting, half hoping, half fearing, that it would be Winston'.[67] Instead, Chamberlain said, 'With the approval of the King, I am able to announce that the Minister in charge of the new Department will be my right honourable Friend the present Minister of Transport.'[68] Leslie Burgin was as entirely unremarkable as Thomas Inskip, Lord Swinton and Lord Chatfield; yet another chance to send Hitler and Mussolini an unmistakable message had been wilfully squandered. Of a debate on conscription on 27 April, Channon wrote that 'the speech of the afternoon was doubtless Winston's, a magnificent effort'. Chamberlain was seen writing copious notes on House of Commons paper during the debate. It turned out that he was jotting down observations about salmon fishing for the Tory MP Anthony Crossley, who was writing a book on the subject.[69]

In a *Daily Telegraph* article entitled 'The Russian Counterpoise' on 4 May, Churchill tackled Poland's understandable reluctance to join forces with Russia, a country that had invaded and partitioned her territory several times, and her resulting opposition to a Grand Alliance. 'It must be vividly impressed upon the Government of Poland', he wrote, that Russia 'may be decisive in preventing war, and will in any case be necessary for ultimate success . . . From the moment when the Nazi malignity is plain, a definite association between Poland and Russia becomes indispensable.'[70] Unfortunately, the British Government approached the concept of a Russian alliance slowly and doubtfully, and dithered for too long. The Foreign Office took weeks to send a junior official to Moscow. Stalin, fearful of Hitler's long-term intentions, nonetheless made a tentative offer of a triple alliance with Britain and France in order to contain Germany.

By this time no more was being heard about Thornton-Kemsley's attempted coup in Epping. (He was given a Scottish seat by Central Office, and remained an MP until 1964.) The extent to which Hitler's seizure of the rump of Czechoslovakia had altered the public perception of Churchill can be seen by a Gallup Poll in May 1939, which asked whether respondents were in favour of Churchill returning to the Cabinet: 56 per cent said yes, 26 per cent no and 18 per cent were undecided.[71] Yet he was still seen by Chamberlainites as the enemy within. 'All the tricks of publicity and of persuasion', wrote Davidson, 'are being used by Winston and his friends, and should there be another Munich over Poland to give us a breathing space, an attack will develop on the P.M.'[72] The idea that Poland could be abandoned and dismembered just as Czechoslovakia had been was less shocking to Davidson than the fact that 'The press appears to be completely open to Winston and the critics; to put it quite frankly, the situation could not be worse.'[73] (Unless, of course, one were a Pole.) Churchill's speeches made a similar impression on George VI, who told William Lyon Mackenzie King, the Canadian Prime Minister, that 'He would never wish to appoint Churchill to any office unless it was absolutely necessary in time of war.'[74] Mackenzie King noted in his diary, 'I must say that I was glad to hear him say that because I think Churchill is one of the most dangerous men I have ever known.'

On 9 May, when it looked as if Chamberlain and Halifax were not only doubtful about Russia's offer of a triple alliance with Britain and France but actually about to turn it down, preferring to stay close to Poland, Churchill exploded in the Commons:

> If His Majesty's Government, having neglected our defences for a long time, having thrown away Czechoslovakia with all that Czechoslovakia meant in military power, having committed us without examination of the technical aspects to the defence of Poland and Rumania, now reject and cast away the indispensable aid of Russia, and so lead us in the worst of all ways into the worst of all wars, they will have ill-deserved the confidence and, I will add, the generosity with which they have been treated by their fellow-countrymen.[75]

Churchill then went up to the Corn Exchange in Cambridge to make a speech reminding people of what they might shortly be fighting against. 'They cannot pursue their course of aggression without bringing about a general war of measureless devastation,' he said of Hitler and Mussolini. 'To submit to their encroachments would be to condemn a large portion of Mankind to their rule; to resist them, either in peace or in war, will be dangerous, painful and hard. There is no use at this stage in concealing these blunt facts from anyone. No one should go forward in this business without realizing plainly both what the cost may be, and what are the issues at stake.'[76] Demonstrating his ability to throw in jokes even in the most serious moments, he said that after the occupation of Prague 'This damnable outrage opened the eyes of the blind, made the deaf hear, and even in some cases the dumb spoke.'[77]

While Churchill was pushing for the Government to conclude an alliance that could keep the peace by threatening Hitler with a war on two fronts – the central reason for Germany's eventual defeat in the Great War – he was also thinking of what might happen in the event of catastrophe in the West. In June he attended a dinner party given by Kenneth

Clark, Director of the National Gallery, attended by Walter Lippmann, the influential American columnist, and the biologist Julian Huxley. Lippmann said that Joseph P. Kennedy, the American Ambassador to London, had told him that war was inevitable and Britain would be beaten.[78] Churchill replied,

> Supposing (as I do not for one moment suppose) that Mr Kennedy were correct in his most tragic utterance, then I for one would willingly lay down my life in combat, rather than, in fear of defeat, surrender to the menaces of these most sinister men. It will then be for you, for the Americans, to preserve and to maintain the great heritage of the English-speaking peoples. It will be for you to think imperially, which means always to think of something higher and more vast than one's own national interests. Nor should I die happy in the great struggle which I see before me, were I not convinced that if we in this dear dear island succumb to the ferocity and might of our enemies, over there in your distant and immune continent the torch of liberty will burn untarnished and (I trust and hope) undismayed.[79]

It was merely a dinner party, but Churchill was clearly already beginning to summon up the ideas and phrases of the great speeches of the coming years.*

In July, having published *Step by Step*, a collection of speeches about foreign affairs, Churchill stayed at Chartwell, reaching 480,000 words of the projected 530,000 words of his history of the English-speaking peoples, and building his cottage/air-raid shelter. Kathleen Hill, who was hired as a typist in 1937 but became his personal secretary during the war, recalled that, while he was bricklaying, 'We used to take our notebooks and mount the ladder – even there he could dictate . . . Often we would dash up to the House of Commons, he dictating as we drove, and then we would type it out in the Commons. Sometimes we would pass the sheets in as he was speaking.'[80]

That summer, a gigantic poster appeared in the Strand in London, bearing only the words 'What Price Churchill?' It was paid for by an advertising agent, J. M. Beable, who told the *Advertisers' Weekly*, 'I was more anxious to get people thinking of the reinstatement of Churchill than necessarily to advocate that policy.'[81] Even though the cause of Churchill's reinstatement was taken up by the *Daily Telegraph*, *Star*, *Sunday Graphic*, *Observer*, *Yorkshire Post Mirror*, *Evening News*, *Daily Mail* and even the Communist

* It was not all geopolitics at this time. After meeting at dinner, Huxley took Churchill to see the giant panda at the London Zoo. 'It has exceeded all my expectations,' Churchill said, shaking his head approvingly, 'and they were very high.' (Addison, 'Three Careers' p. 199.)

*Daily Worker* that month, and 375 members of the staffs from every British university appealed to Chamberlain, nothing short of war would persuade the Prime Minister to have such a disruptive force back in the Cabinet. Maisky recorded Anne Chamberlain's advice to her husband: 'an invitation to Churchill to enter the Cabinet would be tantamount to your political suicide.'[82] Chamberlain himself told his sister Ida, 'The longer the war is put off the less likely it is to come at all . . . That is what Winston & Co never seem to realize.'[83] He invited Lord Camrose, the owner of the *Daily Telegraph*, to No. 10 and told him that, although he himself had 'quite cordial' personal relations with him, Churchill 'was liable to lose his temper in argument and a number of his colleagues had found it the easier way not to oppose him'.[84] He further told Camrose of Churchill's Corfu suggestion, claiming that, when Mussolini had invaded Albania, Churchill 'was on the doorstep all day'.[85] On 27 July, Camrose's brother Lord Kemsley, editor-in-chief of the *Sunday Times*, visited Hitler at the annual Wagner festival at Bayreuth in northern Bavaria, and when the Führer spoke of the danger that Churchill's powers of expression posed to the Chamberlain Government, Kemsley reassured him that 'Mr Churchill had been unfortunate in his campaigns on at least four occasions in the past,' so the Führer really had nothing to worry about.[86]

In a debate on 2 August 1939, Churchill argued that Parliament should reassemble on 21 August, rather than the Government's preferred date of 3 October, because he believed that Hitler was preparing to invade Poland. 'All along the Polish frontier from Danzig to Cracow there are heavy massings of troops,' he warned MPs, 'and every preparation is being made for a speedy advance.' There were five German divisions in a high state of mobility around Breslau, he said, and public buildings in Bohemia were being cleared for the accommodation of the wounded.[87] Few believed him. When Chamberlain turned the vote into a motion of confidence in himself, which he won by 116 votes, the House of Commons went on holiday. 'His are summer storms,' Chamberlain wrote to Ida, 'violent but of short duration and often followed by sunshine. But they make him uncommonly difficult to work with.'[88] Eden seemed to agree, asking his lieutenants Lord Cranborne and Richard Law what they should do in the election that they all assumed was coming in November, 'Would we stand as Independent Conservatives? Would we seek to create a new party? What should our relations be with Winston?'[89]

Churchill spoke with sarcastic humour in his broadcast to America on 8 August, saying of the announcement that two million Germans were going 'on manoeuvres' in September, 'After all, the Dictators must train their soldiers. They could scarcely do less in common prudence, when the Danes, the Dutch, the Swiss, the Albanians and of course the Jews may leap out upon them at any moment and rob them of their living-space.'[90] As August progressed, Stalin turned away from the alliance that he had proposed but that Chamberlain had only half-heartedly begun to negotiate, and instead invited the Reich's Foreign Minister Joachim von Ribbentrop to Moscow to negotiate a pact with his Soviet opposite number V. I. Molotov that would soon give the USSR the Baltic States and the eastern half of Poland and ensure a war between Germany and the capitalist powers Britain and France from which Russia could stand aloof.

While Chamberlain went fishing in Scotland during the long parliamentary recess he had insisted upon, Churchill and Louis Spears visited the Maginot Line defensive fortifications, where they talked far into the night with General Gamelin, the Commander-in-Chief of the French Army, about the use of artificial fog and the possibilities of disrupting Rhine traffic with fluvial mines.[91] At one meal at Malmedy with General Georges, the Commander of the French Field Army, Churchill's 'face had ceased smiling', Spears recalled, 'and the shake of his head was ominous when he observed . . . that it would be very unwise to think the Ardennes were impassable to strong forces . . . "Remember," he said, "that we are faced with a new weapon, armour in great strength, on which the Germans are no doubt concentrating, and that forests will be particularly tempting to such forces since they will offer concealment from the air."'[92] The French disbelief that any such attack was possible reminded Spears of an occasion in 1915 when Churchill had tried to explain his theory of 'land cruisers' (that is, tanks) to a French general, who found it absurd, and who, after he had left, said to Spears, 'Your politicians are even funnier than ours.'[93]

'Nothing will happen till . . . early or mid-September,' Churchill predicted to Clementine on 14 August, writing from the Ritz Hotel in Paris, 'which would still leave Hitler two months to deal with Poland, before the mud season in that country.'[94] His working holiday was cut short on 23 August with the announcement of the Nazi–Soviet pact. He immediately returned to London, recognizing that Russia's alliance with Germany meant that war was now only a matter of days away. 'So far as strategy, policy, foresight, competence are arbiters,' he later wrote, 'Stalin and his commissars showed themselves at this moment the most completely outwitted bunglers.'[95] Parliament was recalled for 24 August.

Churchill was met at Croydon Aerodrome by his former bodyguard, Detective Inspector Walter Thompson, who had guarded him on and off between 1921 and 1932. Thompson had retired from Special Branch in 1936 and become a grocer, but Churchill brought him back in a private capacity at £5 a week after a French politician told him his life might be in danger.[96] 'The Germans believe I am one of their most formidable enemies,' Churchill told Thompson. 'They will not stop short of assassination.'[97] A tall, strong and trim forty-eight-year-old, Thompson stayed with Churchill for the next six years. 'If the Old Man wanted me again,' Thompson wrote later, 'that was good enough.'[98] Of Churchill's return at Croydon he recalled, 'He was looking fit and full of energy as usual, but his expression was grim.'[99] When they reached Chartwell, Churchill gave him a Colt automatic pistol. 'He is a first-class shot,' Thompson recalled, 'and takes a jealous pride in the care of his personal armoury.'[100] Once war broke out, Thompson was paid by the Government, and carried the standard-issue Webley .32 revolver. Churchill insisted that those around him be armed on journeys abroad, and once upbraided a private secretary for not bringing a revolver with him. Years afterwards, Thompson recalled of his boss, who was sixteen years older than him, 'The impulsiveness and tireless energy of Mr Churchill always made it difficult for me to do my job. I could not keep him from heading straight into danger – no one on earth could do that – but I did have to fight to keep up with him.'[101]

When Parliament reassembled, Eleanor Rathbone told MPs what they knew to be true, though none had so far stated openly, namely that Churchill 'all along has prophesied that these things would happen, but his advice was neglected'.[102] A week later, on Friday, 1 September 1939, Hitler invaded Poland. Chamberlain drew up a list for a War Cabinet of six, which included Churchill as minister without portfolio. He did not, however, declare war, as he had bound Britain to do in March.

On Saturday, 2 September, Britain had still not declared war, possibly because Sir Nevile Henderson, the British Ambassador in Berlin, had warned that an air attack on London was planned to follow immediately afterwards. The evacuation of 1.2 million urban children to the countryside was well under way. The French wanted to delay any declaration out of fear of immediate bombing, and Chamberlain told Inskip about 'the hundreds of thousands of children in France that would be killed if war came'.[103] He invited Churchill to No. 10 to offer him a place in the War Cabinet, which Churchill accepted at once, expecting an imminent declaration.[104]

At 7.45 p.m., however, in his first public address since the invasion of Poland, Chamberlain told the Commons, 'If the German Government should agree to withdraw their forces then His Majesty's Government would be willing to regard the position as being the same as it was before the German forces crossed the Polish frontier.' As Arthur Greenwood, Deputy Leader of the Labour Party since 1935, rose from the Opposition front bench to reply for Labour, Leo Amery called out, 'Speak for England, Arthur!' 'An act of aggression took place thirty-eight hours ago,' Greenwood said. 'I wonder how long we are prepared to vacillate at a time when Britain, and all that Britain stands for, and human civilization are in peril.'[105] It was the speech of his life, and were he not headed for the Cabinet Churchill would no doubt have echoed him.

That night, Churchill was visited at Morpeth Mansions by Eden, Boothby, Bracken, Sandys and Duff Cooper, all in a state of what Cooper described in his diary as 'bewildered rage' at Chamberlain's inaction. Boothby wanted Churchill to attack Chamberlain the next day 'and take his place',which Churchill sensibly rejected, knowing that the great mass of the Conservative Party still supported Chamberlain.[106]

Instead he wrote to Chamberlain after midnight to urge that a further effort should be made to bring the Liberals into the Government, even if Labour was 'estranged'. He was ignored. That night he also telephoned Charles Corbin, the French Ambassador, to say that if France betrayed the Poles as she had the Czechs, he, a convinced lifelong Francophile, would be completely indifferent to the fate of France. When Corbin tried to speak of 'technical difficulties' in declaring war, Churchill retorted, 'I suppose you would call it a technical difficulty for a Pole if a German bomb fell on his head!'[107]

At 11.15 a.m. on Sunday, 3 September, a two-hour ultimatum having expired that morning, Neville Chamberlain broadcast the news that Britain was at war. Air-raid sirens sounded over London, a noise Churchill was later to describe as 'those banshee howlings'.[108] Walter Thompson recalled that 'Mr Churchill stalked to the entrance of the flats and stared up into the sky like a warhorse scenting battle. It took some time to persuade him to go to the air raid shelter. He would not have moved only he realized that he ought to set an example.' As Churchill put it later, 'we made our way to the shelter assigned to us, armed with a bottle of brandy and other appropriate medical comforts.'[109] Once there, 'he prowled about like a caged animal,' wrote his bodyguard, 'yet I could see that he was relishing this moment. As soon as the All Clear sounded, Mr Churchill was off like a shot, back down the street and straight up to the roof of the flats, where he scanned the sky for aircraft.'[110] He then took his Daimler to the Commons where he received a note from Chamberlain asking to see him after the statements by the party leaders and others.

In his opening statement, Chamberlain said he hoped to see the destruction of Hitlerism. Arthur Greenwood then expressed his relief that 'The intolerable agony of suspense . . . is over.' Even though Churchill had been out of office for a decade, and spoke for no one besides himself, the Speaker turned to him immediately after Archie Sinclair, the Leader of the Liberal Party. Churchill generously praised Chamberlain's work to stave off war. 'In this solemn hour it is a consolation to recall and to dwell upon our repeated efforts for peace,' he said.

> All have been ill-starred, but all have been faithful and sincere. This is of the highest moral value – and not only moral value, but practical value – at the present time because the wholehearted concurrence of scores of millions of men and women, whose co-operation is indispensable and whose comradeship and brotherhood are indispensable, is the only foundation upon which the trial and tribulation of modern war can be endured and surmounted.[111]

He then placed the struggle on a higher plane:

> This is not a question of fighting for Danzig [modern-day Gdansk] or fighting for Poland. We are fighting to save the whole world from the pestilence of Nazi tyranny and in defence of all that is most sacred to man. This is no war of domination or imperial aggrandizement or material gain; no war to shut any country out of its sunlight and means of progress. It is a war, viewed in its inherent quality, to establish, on impregnable rocks, the rights of the individual, and it is a war to establish and revive the stature of Man.[112]

Both Boothby and Amery observed that this had been the speech of a true war leader, whereas Chamberlain's had not, a distinction that was to be noted by many more people over the next eight months. A week into the war, Chamberlain wrote to Ida from Chequers, 'What I hope for is not a military victory – I very much doubt the possibility of that – but a collapse of the German home front.'[113] It was hardly the right mentality for the man who was leading Britain into war.

After the final speeches on 3 September, Churchill visited Chamberlain in his room behind the Speaker's Chair. Someone, possibly David Margesson, had pointed out to Chamberlain that Churchill 'would be a very dangerous member of the Cabinet if he were left to roam over policy [that is, as a minister without portfolio], and it would be much safer to give him a job of work'.[114] So Chamberlain offered him the position of first lord of the Admiralty with a seat in the War Cabinet, which Churchill said he was 'very glad' to accept. Despite the Dardanelles, his period at the Admiralty made it the obvious post for him, not least because the 7th Earl Stanhope, who was also leader of the House of Lords, had been there for less than a year and was easier to replace than Leslie Hore-Belisha at the War Office or Sir Kingsley Wood at Air. Stanhope was made lord president of the Council to make way for Churchill.

Churchill of course did not know anything of these calculations behind his appointment. 'I felt a serenity of mind and was conscious of uplifted detachment from human and personal affairs,' he later wrote. 'The glory of Old England, peace-loving and ill-prepared as she was, but instant and fearless at the call of honour, thrilled my being and seemed to lift our fate to those spheres far removed from earthly facts and physical sensation.'[115] When he got back to the car he told Clementine, 'It's the Admiralty, that's a lot better than I thought!'[116] Winston and Clementine went to lunch with Vic and Sarah Oliver and Duncan and Diana Sandys at the Olivers' flat in Marsham Street, Westminster, where they toasted 'Victory' over a bottle of champagne.[117] 'No one would listen to my warnings,' Churchill told Vic, who thought him 'sadder than I have ever known him' – all his dire predictions having come true.[118] He told the Admiralty that he would be arriving later in the afternoon to take up his office, whereupon the Board signalled to the Fleet: 'WINSTON IS BACK'. Some captains, such as Lord Louis Mountbatten commanding the destroyer HMS *Kelly*, found the message inspirational, while others took it more in the nature of a warning that a ball of energy was about to burst upon them.*

After lunch Churchill calmly took his afternoon nap, on the Olivers' bed, and at 5 p.m. he attended the first meeting of the newly constituted War Cabinet, comprising Chamberlain, Halifax (Foreign Secretary), Sir John Simon (Chancellor of the Exchequer), Sir Kingsley Wood (Secretary for Air), Samuel Hoare (Lord Privy Seal), Lord Chatfield (Minister of Defence Coordination), Lord Hankey (Minister without Portfolio), Leslie Hore-Belisha (Secretary for War) and himself. Instead of a tight War Cabinet of six, there were no fewer than nine, with an average age of sixty-four – Churchill's own age. They had all been prominent appeasers except for Churchill, and none, except possibly Hore-Belisha, had the kind of hunger for the offensive that would be necessary in a major war. Lord Crawford told Inskip of the 'amount of critical remarks about Churchill's getting the Admiralty' that were already circulating in the Carlton Club and House of Lords.[119] That the majority of Conservatives had been proved so spectacularly wrong about Hitler was not going to lessen their antagonism towards him; indeed it might have made it worse.

After the War Cabinet meeting, Churchill went to the Admiralty at 6 p.m. A *Life* magazine photographer caught the First Lord just before he

* The message has not been found in the Admiralty's signals book, but its informality implies it was sent unofficially.

entered the front door. Carrying a cigar, newspaper and walking stick, two red boxes and his gas mask at his feet, he had a long key chain dropping almost to his knees on which he kept the keys to his red boxes.[120] (These were never mislaid because, in another of his personal inventions, he had a long silver chain which went around his back and, threaded through the sides of his braces, allowed bunches of keys to rest in both trouser pockets.)[121] He was smiling. 'So it was that I came again to the room I had quitted in pain and sorrow almost a quarter of a century before,' Churchill later wrote. 'Once again we must fight for life and honour against all the might and fury of the valiant, disciplined, and ruthless German race. Once again! So be it.'[122] He remained at the Admiralty until the early hours of the following morning familiarizing himself with Fleet positions, and had charts brought in of the North Sea, of which he said, 'I used these last time.'[123] He also asked for an octagonal table he used to have, which was produced by the office-keeper.

A few days later, Churchill received a letter from Colin Thornton-Kemsley MP, written from his Army camp. 'I have opposed you as hard as I knew how,' it read. 'I want to say only this. You warned us repeatedly about the German danger and you were right . . . Please don't think of replying – you are in all conscience busy enough in an office which we are all glad that you hold in this time of Britain's danger.'[124] Churchill of course did reply, accepting the apology and adding, 'I certainly think that Englishmen ought to stand fair with each other from the outset in so grievous a struggle, and so far as I am concerned the past is dead.'[125]

# 19

# 'Winston is Back'
# September 1939–May 1940

*Men and kings must be judged in the testing moments of their lives. Courage is rightly esteemed the first of human qualities because . . . it is the quality which guarantees the others.*

Churchill on King Alfonso XIII of Spain in *Great Contemporaries*[1]

*Of course I am an egotist. What do you get if you aren't?*

Churchill to Attlee, undated[2]

When Churchill became first lord of the Admiralty on Sunday, 3 September 1939, the Royal Navy was the largest in the world, comprising twelve battleships, six aircraft carriers, fifty-six light and heavy cruisers and over 180 destroyers.[3] But the nature of naval warfare had changed dramatically in the twenty-four years since he had last occupied the office. 'For the first time in history,' Admiral William James, Deputy Chief of the Naval Staff, later wrote, 'there would be no great fleets staring at one another across the narrow seas and moving majestically into battle, but instead encounters between high-speed vessels whose freedom would be severely restricted by the aeroplane.'[4] Submarines would harass Britain's oceanic lifelines even more than in the Great War – indeed on that very night of 3 September the passenger liner *Athenia*, on her way from Glasgow to Montreal, was torpedoed by a German U-boat, drowning 112 passengers, including twenty-eight Americans, only hours after the declaration of American neutrality.

Churchill also returned to a very different Admiralty than the one he had left in 1915. The War Staff he had instituted now had large Operations and Planning divisions, manned by officers who had been long preparing for this war. Admiral James was impressed by Churchill's remarkable grasp of sea-warfare, and in particular the numerous minutes he wrote on matters such as forming search units to hunt German raiders in the oceans, the design of ships to combat submarines, the laying of a mine barrage between Scotland and Norway, modifying the convoy system, and much else.[5]

Churchill immediately withdrew authorization for the construction of all cruisers being built in accordance with the Anglo-German Naval Agreement, as new armaments could now be installed on existing ships capable of taking on the German 8-inch-gun cruisers. A few days later he suspended work on all battleships scheduled to be launched before 1942, so that the shipyards could concentrate on building destroyers to fight the U-boat menace that he saw developing from the spring of 1940. He pressed for a reduction in the tonnage of destroyers in order to keep them nimble, ordered all ships to have radar installed and, as in the Great War, called for all merchantmen to be armed.[6] He also changed routines in order to give destroyer crews more rest, and cancelled the regulation regarding compulsory courts martial every time ships were damaged, which he thought discouraged initiative.

As in 1911–15, Churchill interested himself in every aspect of the Navy, however minor. His minutes covered subjects as diverse as the destruction of confidential information, the provision of emergency candles in air raids, decorations for minesweeper personnel, the 'lamentable' number of heavy woollen 'duffle-coats' per ship, whether sailors should play backgammon or cards (he preferred backgammon as the games took longer) and the removal of rubbish that might block the ventilators of the 'Citadel' annexe on the corner of Horse Guards Parade which housed the Operational Intelligence Centre. He insisted on all ranks having the opportunity to rise to officer status in every area of the Service, for, as he put it with a nod to Hitler's unlikely early career, 'If a telegraphist may rise, why not a painter? Apparently there is no difficulty about painters rising in Germany.'[7]

It was by no means inevitable that Churchill would get on with the First Sea Lord, Admiral Sir Dudley Pound, who had been Lord Fisher's additional naval assistant in the Great War. Churchill had privately criticized Pound's disposition of the Mediterranean Fleet during the Albanian crisis in June, and Pound had seen Churchill up close during the Dardanelles debacle. Yet they quickly established a mutual regard which developed into a powerful bond of affection. Pound nevertheless retained the authority regularly to turn down Churchill's proposals, but only once he was fully in control of his facts. He always called Churchill 'Sir' rather than 'First Lord', or later 'Prime Minister'.[8] As one of those who worked closely with them recalled, 'Pound's temperament, calm and deaf as required – never getting into heated argument – made for peace.'[9] Churchill, who had by then learned from the Dardanelles, appreciated Pound's level-headedness and strength of character. 'Pound [has] the best brain in the Navy,' he was to say, 'though the most cautious.'[10] With a first lord with natural instincts for bold offensives, a cautious first sea lord was no bad thing. 'The First Sea Lord normally would agree with what Winston proposed,' Admiral Sir Guy Grantham recalled of their working method. 'After leaving the Map Room, Pound would work out with the Naval Staff what could be done, and would signal the necessary operation orders. He would always be ready to face afterwards any complaint of Winston's that changes had been made.'[11] It was a system of civilian–military relations that worked remarkably well, but depended entirely on the mutual respect between Churchill and Pound. Four months after they had started working together, despite Churchill's interventions both large and small, the First Sea Lord wrote to the Commander-in-Chief Home Fleet, Admiral Sir Charles Forbes, 'I have the greatest admiration for W.S.C., and his good qualities are such, and his desire to hit the enemy so overwhelming, that I feel we must hesitate in turning down any of his proposals.'[12]

Churchill was not content with a War Plan based on protecting convoys and maintaining a tight blockade of Germany, but was always looking for ways of taking the fight to the enemy. Only three days into the conflict he proposed Operation Catherine, a plan 'to force a passage into the Baltic and to maintain there a naval force'.[13] This was intended to cut off Swedish iron-ore supplies to Germany, and perhaps influence the policy of neutral Russia. He wanted to convert older battleships for service in the narrow waters of the Skagerrak by giving them large anti-torpedo bulges, stronger armoured decks and more anti-aircraft guns.

Pound did not oppose the extraordinarily risky plan immediately or outright, but instead asked Admiral the Earl of Cork and Orrery to make a full appreciation of it with the Naval Staff. He then undercut the plan by stages, insisting that Russia not be involved, demanding 'active cooperation' from Sweden (which he knew would never be forthcoming) and pointing out the danger from winter ice and how a German invasion of Denmark might cut off the fleet in the Baltic. He also reminded Churchill how much destroyers were needed for convoy protection.[14]

'I could never be responsible for a naval strategy which excluded the offensive principle and relegated us to keeping open the lines of communication and maintaining the blockade,' Churchill wrote to Pound on 11 December, but Operation Catherine provided a template for how Pound was to use careful professional analysis to wean Churchill off impractical plans without ever needing to employ the word 'no'.[15] After four months of discussion,

Churchill finally agreed to shelve it. He claimed in his memoirs that various senior Admiralty figures such as Tom Phillips, the Deputy Chief of the Naval Staff, and Bruce Fraser, the Third Sea Lord, had shown 'strong support' for it, whereas in fact they had been just as opposed as Pound, as was Rear Admiral John Godfrey, the Director of Naval Intelligence.[16]

When that first day Pound directed Captain Richard Pim to organize Churchill's Map Room he admitted, 'It won't be easy.'[17] Sure enough, on 4 September, Churchill gave the tall, shrewd Ulsterman only forty-eight hours to get it all fully operational. He did it, and thereafter Pim and his team plotted the position of every significant British, Allied, Axis or neutral ship, submarine and aircraft squadron across the globe using coloured pins on giant charts and maps attached to boards all around the First Lord's Old Library overlooking Horse Guards Parade. 'Very good, very good,' Churchill said when he saw the room for the first time, 'but the maps will have to be replaced. When you know me better, you will know that I only paint in pastel shades. These strong colours under the lamps would give you and me severe headaches.'[18] New maps were acquired, along with special lighting and extra telephone lines. Wherever there was spare wall-space, Churchill hung his own paintings.

One chart showed the position, speed, composition and destination of every convoy. Churchill also wanted to know the names of all the escort commanders and the weather they were facing. When a gale warning was received, a cardboard dolphin would go up on the board.[19] The map included convoys' dates of sailing and details of lading. Sir John Gilmour, Minister of Shipping, was once telephoned in the middle of the night by Churchill with the comment, 'It seems to me that those ships loading in the River Plate should have sailed by now. Please let me have a report.'[20] When he saw a ship crossing the Atlantic with 7,000 tons of eggs he had Pim ask the Ministry of Agriculture how many eggs there were per ton, and exclaimed, when told the answer, 'Do you realize that cargo represents one egg for every second person in the British Isles?'[21]

Churchill visited the Map Room in his dressing gown at seven o'clock each morning for a summary of the overnight reports. He would often return during the day and hold meetings there, especially during crises, and would visit again before going to bed. When he once found Pim on his hands and knees working on a big map on the floor, with his naval cap upside down beside him, Churchill took a sixpence out of his pocket and dropped it in.[22]

The Churchills gave up their lease on Morpeth Mansions and moved into the top two floors of Admiralty House in September, where they had lived from 1911 to 1915. A private secretary noted 'the lovely drawing room with its curious ugly dolphin furniture' and an inner room with Churchill's desk and a nearby table 'laden with bottles of whisky, etc'. On it were toothpicks, gold medals which he used as paperweights, 'innumerable pills and powders' and special cuffs to save his coat-sleeves from becoming dirty, rather like those worn by footmen while polishing silver.[23] Brendan Bracken became Churchill's parliamentary private secretary, his eyes and ears at Westminster, a job at which he excelled. 'Prof' Lindemann became an unpaid 'Personal Adviser to the First Lord on Scientific Development', and took rooms at the nearby Carlton Hotel so that he could join Churchill after dinner and work and talk late into the night with him.[24] He set up his own Statistics Section in the Admiralty that supplied Churchill with his own data, independent of other departments.

Every Tuesday night while he was at the Admiralty, Churchill threw dinner parties for fourteen people. They began with a Swedish milk punch which was, according to one of his aides, 'a great success as a "party-starter"'.[25] These brought together ministers, senior civil servants and members of the Army Council, Air Council and Admiralty Board in an atmosphere of easy informality.

Lieutenant-Commander C. R. 'Tommy' Thompson, Flag Lieutenant to the Board of Admiralty, had been introduced to Churchill by Bracken, whom he had known from the *Enchantress* when Duff Cooper was first lord. Thompson was forty-five, and due to retire from the active list in a few weeks. He had commanded submarines for thirteen years, but was not promoted because he had run the *Oberon* on to a sandbank for a few hours in the early 1930s in dense fog in the Thames. He later said he considered this 'the luckiest thing that ever happened to me' because it meant that he was asked to work with Churchill as his personal assistant throughout the war. He gave no policy advice, but was in charge of organizing Churchill's everyday life and especially the logistics for his many overseas journeys. Those trips often therefore included Tommy Thompson as organizer and Walter Thompson as protection officer.

Returning to government gave Churchill an opportunity to mend damaged relationships and make valuable new contacts. 'Winston Churchill came to see me,' the King noted in his diary on 5 September. 'Very pleased to be back in harness again. Wanted more destroyers. Liked the Board of Admiralty.'[26] Churchill's relations with the King, who had distrusted him during the Abdication Crisis and because of his attacks on appeasement, a policy which the King had wholeheartedly supported, improved steadily. This was helped by Churchill's monarchism; even in private and informal conversations Churchill referred to him as 'our noble King'.[27] The King had joined the Navy in 1909 and had served at the Battle of Jutland and so they had the Service in common and started tentatively to form a bond that was eventually to become as strong as any Churchill enjoyed in public life. In the first year of the war, the King was nonetheless closer in temperament as well as political outlook to Lord Halifax, and Lady Halifax was one of the Queen's ladies-in-waiting.

As soon as he assumed office, Churchill began to write regular letters to Chamberlain, thirteen in the first six weeks, covering every aspect of the war, which as a member of the War Cabinet he had every right to do. Chamberlain complained of their length, and said, 'Of course I realize that the letters are for the purpose of quotation in the book that he will write hereafter.'[28] He might not have been entirely wrong, but that was certainly not their primary purpose. On 18 September, to take one example among dozens, he wrote to Chamberlain about the number of civilians it would take to produce 2,000 warplanes a month, to point out that the Army should reach fifty-five divisions in two years (against ninety in 1918) and to demonstrate how through 'clever dovetailing' it was possible to ensure that the provision of explosives and steel should not compete with aeroplane production.[29]

The most important new relationship Churchill forged as first lord, however, was not initiated by him. On 11 September 1939, President Franklin Roosevelt inaugurated a correspondence with Churchill that was to have world-historical significance, and that opened up a second line of communication to the British Government independent of Chamberlain, though with his knowledge. 'My dear Churchill,' the President began, 'It is because you and I occupied similar positions in the [First] World War that I want you to know how glad I am that you are back again in the Admiralty . . . What I want you and the Prime Minister to know is that I shall at all times welcome it if you will keep me in touch personally with anything you want me to know about.'[30] He closed with a personal note, 'I am glad you did the Marlboro volumes before this thing started – and I much enjoyed reading them.' Churchill grasped the opportunity eagerly, choosing 'Naval Person' as his hardly impenetrable codename. (When he became prime minister he changed it to 'Former Naval Person'.) Over the next five years he sent 1,161 messages to Roosevelt and received 788 in reply, averaging one exchange every two or three days for the rest of Roosevelt's life. Nearly two years of this epistolary friendship prepared them both for their historic meeting in August 1941.

At the Other Club on 11 September, Churchill and Chatfield proposed a toast to Lord Gort, a Club member who had won the Victoria Cross in the Battle of the Canal du Nord in 1918 and was going out to France to command the British Expeditionary Force (BEF) that was dispatched to France on the outbreak of war. They also sent a telegram congratulating another member, General Jan Smuts, for the parliamentary vote of eighty to sixty-seven that had brought South Africa into the war on the Allied side, as a result of which he had also become prime minister again. Had South Africa not joined the Allies – or worse, had she joined the Axis as some Afrikaner nationalists wanted – the all-important resupply of India and Egypt might have become impossible.[31]

That night Lord Trenchard proposed to his fellow Club members that the RAF should be bombing Germany from its French bases. The head of Bomber Command, Air Chief Marshal Sir Edgar Ludlow-Hewitt, took part in the discussion, as did Admiral of the Fleet Sir Roger Keyes. Churchill had a group around his dinner table at the Savoy with as much military experience and seniority in service as Chamberlain had on the Chiefs of Staff Committee itself, if not more. Throughout the war, these dinners at the Other Club furnished Churchill with ideas, arguments and statistics that he put to good use.

In the War Cabinet, Churchill invariably took the most aggressive stance. When early in the conflict it opposed initiating the bombing of Germany, he said he 'didn't see why the disgusting stentorian slumber of the Boche should remain undisturbed'.[32] Once the discussion got around to the optimum bomb-size to use, he wanted the biggest bombs possible, otherwise, as he put it, the RAF 'might as well drop roasted chestnuts'.[33] The height of absurdity in what was called the Phoney War – the eight-month period after the war started but before any fighting began between the British and Germans on land – came when the RAF was prevented from bombing targets in the Black Forest because so much of it was private property.[34] 'Up to the present I can't say that I think W.C. has been particularly helpful,' was Chamberlain's assessment on 17 September, 'though certainly he would have been a most troublesome thorn in our flesh if he had been outside.'[35] Two days later, Churchill first brought up the possibility of buying twenty elderly destroyers from the Americans and demanding back the port of Berehaven from de Valera for the duration of the war. He also wanted to stop the flow of iron ore from Narvik to Germany by infringing neutral Norway's sovereignty and laying minefields that would compel the German ships to leave Norwegian territorial waters and head out into the open sea. Cabinet and Foreign Office opposition meant that the mines were not laid off Norway until April 1940, no destroyers came from the Americans until September 1940 and Berehaven was never used to save the lives of British sailors.[36]

By 14 September, Chips Channon was noting in his diary, 'I am told that Winston is already driving the Admiralty to distraction by his interference and energy.'[37] Churchill attached three gradations of label to minutes and memoranda leaving his office. One demanded 'Action this day', another 'Report within three days', another 'Report as soon as possible'.[38] Tommy Thompson noted that the second and third were rarely used, and soon fell out of circulation. The 'Action this day' label, which was coloured red, produced noticeable activity in its recipients. When Sir James Lithgow, Controller of Merchant Shipbuilding, smuggled a few of the labels out of Churchill's office he was 'highly elated with the results they produced', but was soon caught and made to hand the rest back.[39] On the morning of 18 October, Churchill's junior minister at the Admiralty, Sir Geoffrey Shakespeare, arrived in his office to find a minute on his desk, with an 'Action this day' label attached, saying, 'I am concerned about the shortage of fish . . . We must have a policy of "utmost fish". Parliamentary Secretary will report to me by midnight with his proposals. W.S.C.'[40]

Shakespeare arranged with the Ministry of Agriculture to call a conference of trawler-owners from Hull, Grimsby and elsewhere, with representatives of the Navy present to explain how they would be protected from U-boats. A new Fishing Promotion Council was created, and Ernest Bevin, the powerful General Secretary of the Transport and General Workers' Union, was invited to the Admiralty to help foster the policy of 'utmost fish'. He was told by Churchill, 'We must fight for this part of our food supply as hard as we do against the U-boats.'[41] In January, Churchill asked Bevin for a copy of a speech he had given to the Institute of Transport which argued for a single transport authority for the duration of the war. Churchill and Bevin came from totally different backgrounds, had different interests and of course had been on opposite sides during the General Strike, but their admiration was immediate, mutual and genuine.

Churchill was fortunate to be in charge of the only Service that was at full-scale war from the moment hostilities commenced on 3 September. The Army was stationed on the Franco-Belgian border, while the RAF was busy dropping propaganda leaflets over Germany. The eight months after September 1939 may have been nicknamed the 'Phoney War' and the 'Bore War', but there was nothing phoney or boring about the war at sea.

The first transatlantic convoy sailed on 6 September. Churchill and the Admiralty had learned the lesson of the Great War: that merchantmen sailing together protected by a screen of warships provided the safest way of transporting supplies. Warships engaged in 'hunting groups' on search-and-destroy missions against U-boats might have been better employed in these convoy escorts. Nevertheless, escort protection was never a guarantee of survival: on 17 September, one of Britain's six aircraft carriers,

HMS *Courageous*, carrying fifty-two aeroplanes, was sunk by a U-boat to the west of Ireland, despite her escort of four destroyers. Churchill had made the mistake of thinking that the invention of sonar would neutralize the U-boat menace.[42] Yet he was a quick learner, and was soon telling colleagues that as a result of information gleaned from the survivors of one U-boat 'we are increasing the depth of our depth charges.'[43]

Churchill's energy was indeed formidable. On a single day taken almost at random from this period – Thursday, 21 September 1939 – Churchill persuaded the War Cabinet to approve the building of a further 200,000 tons of shipping, 'with the idea of maintaining an annual output of at least 1.1 million tons gross', contributed to its discussion on air defence, visited naval establishments in and around Portsmouth and wrote eleven letters, including one to Chamberlain about the War Cabinet, one to Pound about improving aircraft carriers and torpedo nets, one to Phillips about mine-laying in strong currents and about magnetic mines dropped from the air, one to Admiral Little about a cinema ship at Scapa Flow, one to Rear Admiral Geoffrey Arbuthnot, the Fourth Sea Lord, about the underground storage of oil, one to Sir Archibald Carter, the Permanent Secretary at the Admiralty, about the sinking of the *Athenia*, and to others about ships in harbour firing at German raiders.[44] Most days produced similar numbers of ideas and what Channon had called 'interference'.

On 26 September, Churchill made his first speech from the dispatch box in a decade. Chamberlain preceded him, and Harold Nicolson recorded that, as the Prime Minister spoke, 'One feels the confidence and spirits of the House dropping inch by inch. When he sits down there is scarcely any applause. During the whole speech, Winston Churchill had sat hunched beside him looking like the Chinese god of plenty suffering from acute indigestion. He just sits there, lowering, hunched and circular, and then he gets up. He is greeted by a loud cheer from all the benches and he starts to tell us about the naval position.' He started with a joke* about how it was strange to find himself in the same room at the Admiralty with the same charts fighting the same enemy and dealing with the same problems. Grinning, and glancing down at Chamberlain, he then said, 'I have no conception how this curious change in my fortunes occurred.'[45] Nicolson noted that 'The whole House roared with laughter and Chamberlain had not the decency even to raise a sickly smile. He just looked sulky.'[46]† As well he might have, as this was the first of a long series of

* Unrecorded in Hansard.

† Not for nothing did Bracken nickname Chamberlain 'the Coroner'. The industrialist Baldwin was 'the Ironmonger'.

almost pitch-perfect parliamentary performances in which Churchill showed his mettle as Chamberlain's prospective successor.

Nicolson was of course a partisan anti-Chamberlainite, but even one of Chamberlain's greatest supporters, Chips Channon, expressed admiration for Churchill's speech. 'The PM made his usual dignified statement: unfortunately, he was followed by Winston, who executed a tour-de-force, a brilliant bit of acting and exposition, in describing in detail the work of the Admiralty. He amused and impressed the House . . . he must have taken endless trouble with his speech, and it was a great contrast, which was noticed, to the PM's colourless statement.'[47] Lord Crawford, Churchill's critic of over forty years, noticed that at Grillions Club, where during the Wilderness Years ministers had moved away from Churchill, now 'all applauded Churchill's spirited speech describing the naval situation – helpful, hopeful, determined; the very tonic the House of Commons wanted, and a real foil to Chamberlain's stiff summary without light or shade. Churchill wiped Chamberlain's eye, and I expect he did so with gusto.'[48] Churchill had indeed taken great trouble with his speech, but then he did with all of them, with many rewrites and endless practice.

Churchill gave a narrative account of the various engagements, and described the U-boat war already under way as 'hard, widespread and bitter, a war of groping and drowning, a war of ambuscade and stratagem, a war of science and seamanship'.[49] As Nicolson noted,

> His delivery was really amazing and he sounded every note from deep pre-occupation to flippancy, from resolution to sheer boyishness. One could feel the spirits of the House rising with every word. It was quite obvious afterwards that the Prime Minister's inadequacy and lack of inspiration had been demonstrated even to his warmest supporters. In those twenty minutes Churchill had brought himself nearer the post of Prime Minister than he has ever been before. In the Lobbies afterwards even Chamberlainites were saying, 'We have now found our leader.' Old Parliamentary hands confessed that never in their experience had they seen a single speech so change the temper of the House.[50]

Before Churchill could become prime minister he had to look like one, and in a series of such speeches over the next eight months he did just that. His chief rival for the succession, Lord Halifax, was not in the Commons, and was no orator. If, as many suspected, Margesson had insisted that Churchill be given the Admiralty because 'he must be "nobbled" by having a department which would occupy all his time,' it had spectacularly back-fired. Churchill had the freedom now to make uplifting speeches on life-and-death issues, ones that regularly put any other rivals in the shade with their sense of purpose and humour.[51] (He cut out one quip from his September speech as just too flippant: he had been going to say, 'Our destroyers then engaged that particular submarine, and all that thereafter was seen of the vessel was a large spot of oil and a door which floated up to the surface bearing my initials.')[52]

John Reith left the BBC in late 1938, so nothing now could prevent Churchill from broadcasting. In his first broadcast of the war, on 1 October, Churchill said, 'The heroic defence of Warsaw shows that the soul of Poland is indestructible, and that she will rise again like a rock, which may for a spell be submerged by a tidal wave, but which remains a rock.'[53] 'Russia has pursued a cold policy of self-interest,' Churchill said, and he freely admitted, 'I cannot forecast to you the action of Russia. It is a riddle wrapped in a mystery inside an enigma: but perhaps there is a key. That key is Russian national interest. It cannot be in accordance with the interest or the safety of Russia that Germany should plant itself upon the shores of the Black Sea, or that it should overrun the Balkan States and subjugate the Slavonic peoples of South-Eastern Europe. That would be contrary to the historic life-interests of Russia.'[54] He promised that the war would last as long as Hitler 'and his group of wicked men, whose hands are stained with blood and soiled with corruption, can keep their grip upon the docile, unhappy German people'. Afterwards, his old friend Ettie, Lady Desborough wrote to him to say his broadcast was 'a touchstone lifting up our hearts. You made me feel that all that matters most is unconquerable, serenely sheltered somewhere – to hold us all together.'[55] She had lost two sons in the Great War, but Churchill's words strengthened her, as they did millions of Britons when at 9 p.m. the radio news was turned on in pubs and homes and he filled his listeners with a warlike spirit that Chamberlain's worthy but unheroic phraseology simply could not.

The next evening the King complimented Churchill on his broadcast. As he recorded in his diary, 'In answer to my question as to whether we should not have to help Germany to stop Bolshevism coming into Germany, he said Naziism and Bolshevism were as bad as each other and there was very little to choose between them.'[56] It seems extraordinary that, when Britain was actually at war with Nazi Germany, Churchill should have to explain to the King that Bolshevism was not the greater threat. Nor was this to be the only discussion they would have on the subject. At first sight Churchill's own attitude towards Russia seems completely inconsistent.[57] He started out with trying to support Russia through the Dardanelles in 1915, then proclaimed a profound enmity of the Bolsheviks, then by the late 1930s advocated an alliance with them, then in 1939–40 supported Finland in her war against them, then in 1941 he allied Britain with them overnight, then in 1946 denounced them, only in the 1950s to seek détente with them. He ratted and re-ratted on his parties in the House of Commons, but his stance towards the USSR he changed no fewer than six times. The explanation was not so much a lack of consistency, as is often alleged, but a consideration of what was in the 'historic life-interests' of the British Empire at each stage.

At an Eden Group dinner at the Carlton Club on 3 October, Waldorf Astor said that it was essential that Churchill become prime minister. Harold Nicolson then suggested that, after Chamberlain had turned down Hitler's expected peace offer, 'when the war really begins, there will be such an outburst of public indignation that a Coalition will have to be formed. It is evident that none of the Opposition leaders will enter a Cabinet which contains Chamberlain, Simon and Hoare, and that therefore the removal of these three will take place almost automatically.'[58] Duff Cooper and Leo Amery added that there was no time to lose.

Discussions like this one among MPs and other influential figures undermine the notion that the anti-appeasers had no plan in May 1940, and that Churchill's premiership emerged out of some magical combination of luck and circumstance.[59] In fact, the Tory and National Government rebels had been discussing precisely the scenario that eventually unfolded for a full seven months before it did. Even at an Edenite gathering, Churchill's name came to the fore rather than that of their own leader, who had not thus far made inspiring speeches in his minor post of dominion secretary.

The twenty-eight-year-old Randolph, who had joined the 4th Hussars on the outbreak of war, married Pamela Digby, the 11th Baron Digby's pretty and outgoing daughter, at St John's Smith Square on 4 October 1939. The wedding was followed by a buffet lunch for sixty at Admiralty House. When it was suggested that Randolph didn't have enough money to marry, Churchill shot back, 'What do they need? Cigars, champagne and a double bed.'[60] The congregation cheered the bridegroom's father when he arrived in the church, which is not the British custom at all, but he had made his rousing broadcast only three days previously. According to one of the guests, Maud Russell, Churchill 'cried a lot during the service'.[61] She also maliciously recorded of Randolph, 'I haven't the slightest doubt that he's marrying because he thinks it's time and right that Winston must have a grandson. He has proposed to four or five women in the last few months.' Randolph made a mistake in marrying the nineteen-year-old Pamela just before he left for long tours of duty abroad. He might have been ready to settle down, but she most certainly was not.

Two days later, Maisky was asked to appear at the Admiralty for a meeting at 10 p.m. 'Not exactly the ordinary hour for receiving ambassadors in England, but the present situation is far from ordinary, and the man who invited me is also far from ordinary!'[62] He noted that the walls of Churchill's office were covered with a collection of the most varied maps of every corner of the world, thickly overlaid with sea routes. 'A lamp with a broad, dark shade hangs from the ceiling, giving a very pleasant soft light.'[63]* Churchill said he would 'be happy to philosophize about the peculiar romance of my returning to this room after a quarter of a century, were it not for the devilish task at hand of destroying ships and human lives'.[64]

They discussed the peace terms that Hitler had (as the Eden Group had anticipated) announced in the Reichstag that day, in which he mentioned Churchill by name three times – 'If, however, the opinions of Messrs. Churchill and his followers should prevail,' the Führer had said at one point, 'this statement will have been my last' – and Chamberlain not at all. Hitler had offered peace on the basis that he be allowed to keep Poland and Czechoslovakia and that Germany's colonies be returned, whereupon Britain would be permitted to retain her Empire. When Maisky mentioned the terms, Churchill 'sprang to his feet and quite abruptly began pacing the room', saying 'Personally, I find them absolutely unacceptable. They are the terms of a conqueror! But we are not yet conquered! No, no, we are not yet conquered! . . . Some of my Conservative friends advise peace. They fear that Germany will turn Bolshevik during the war. But I'm all for war to the end. Hitler must be destroyed. Nazism must be crushed once and for all. Let Germany become Bolshevik. That doesn't scare me. Better Communism than Nazism.'[65]

Churchill continued to make his antipathy to Communism plain, even in such circumstances and to the Soviet Ambassador, but he was also prepared to be hard and practical, telling Maisky that British and Soviet interests 'do not collide anywhere'.[66] The Soviet Union had compelled the three hitherto independent Baltic States of Lithuania, Latvia and Estonia to accept Red Army bases on their territory in October 1939, and was to occupy and annex them the following May and June. 'In essence,' Churchill said, 'the Soviet Government's latest actions in the Baltic correspond to British interests, for they diminish Hitler's potential *Lebensraum*. If the Baltic countries have to lose their independence, it is better for them to be brought into the Soviet state system rather than the German one.'[67] He could not know that the Baltic States were thereafter to remain within

* It was the one that had been there in 1911–15, was subsequently removed and then replaced when Churchill returned.

the Soviet maw for half a century. But this extravagant embrace of Russia was a temporary expediency born of war. He made sure Britain never recognized the annexations, safeguarded Baltic gold in London and continued to allow the annexed countries diplomatic recognition.

On 9 October the King recorded a tired, yawning Churchill 'busy making drafts of the reply [by Chamberlain] to Hitler. He wanted a much sterner reply [than the Foreign Office proposed], but I said do leave the door open at this stage. Hitler can't be having it all his own way at home. Winston is difficult to talk to but in time I shall get the right technique I hope.'[68] Since Churchill was trying to ensure that the War Cabinet slammed the door shut to any peace offer from Hitler, despite Halifax thinking 'negotiation not impossible', it was small wonder the King found conversation difficult.[69]

Despite the best efforts of Rab Butler, the Under-Secretary at the Foreign Office, to do all he could 'in keeping the door slightly ajar', on 12 October Chamberlain finally announced an outright rejection of Hitler's peace offer.[70] Channon, who was Butler's parliamentary private secretary and close friend, noted that Churchill 'sitting opposite him (there was no room on the Government bench for his baroque bottom) joined in the cheering'.[71] That same day, anticipating redoubled German aggression, Churchill wrote a minute to Pound warning, 'These next few days are full of danger.' Sure enough, at 12.58 on the morning of 14 October the battleship HMS *Royal Oak* was torpedoed at anchor inside the Royal Navy's base at Scapa Flow in the Orkney Isles, drowning 833 men. Churchill blamed the poor defences there on Treasury miserliness, just as he put the paucity of destroyers down to Sir John Simon's parsimony as chancellor of the Exchequer.[72]

'It was like a body blow to Winston,' recalled Detective Inspector Thompson. 'Not for the first time in those grim days I heard him mutter "If only they had taken notice of me a few years ago, this would not have happened."'[73] Only the previous day, Churchill had written a communiqué saying that Friday the 13th would be unlucky for German submarines, which now looked absurdly hubristic.[74] (He was very superstitious, and attached 'great importance' to the fact that the battleship had been sunk on a day, as he told an aide, when he 'had mistakenly put on a black tie instead of his usual spotted one'.)[75] 'Poor fellows, poor fellows,' Churchill told the officer who brought him the news of the *Royal Oak*, 'trapped in those black depths.' Mary recalled that her father 'felt the loss of life very much. He realized what it all meant, the loss of the great ships, the loss of the men.'[76] It was almost a month – during which HMS *Belfast** and

* Now moored on the River Thames.

*Nelson* were mined – before Churchill was able to persuade the Admiralty to sink the blockships (still in position today), install the anti-aircraft guns and lay new anti-torpedo netting necessary to improve the defences at Scapa Flow. (On one visit there, he arranged to have food thrown from the dummy battleship and aircraft carrier so that seagulls would fly around them to lend verisimilitude for any German reconnaissance.)[77] 'Always see for yourself,' Churchill advised Hore-Belisha. 'Once you have seen a thing working, you know how it works.'[78]

For Chamberlain, the fate of the *Royal Oak* brought a sudden, overdue, though swiftly dispelled moment of self-realization. 'How I hate and loathe this war,' he told Ida on 15 October. 'I was never meant to be a War Minister and the thought of all those homes wrecked with the *Royal Oak* makes me want to hand over my responsibilities to someone else.'[79] The 'someone else' he was thinking of was Lord Halifax, one of the few members of the Government even less martially inclined than himself, and it was Churchill who continued to urge action in the War Cabinet. In late October, he warned its members, 'Decisive actions are likely to begin' in the spring, and argued for as many troops as possible to be in the line before then.[80] He also wanted 'to survey the possibilities of a German landing, especially now the nights are getting longer'. This left Inskip complaining that he was 'always fertile in imagination'.[81] In November Churchill promoted Operation Royal Marine, a plan to float thousands of fluvial mines down the Moselle and other French tributaries into the Rhine, which he hoped would result in German bridges being destroyed and river traffic halted.[82] Other floating bombs would be dropped by plane into the Ruhr. (When discussing this with Air Commodore John Slessor, Churchill said, 'This is one of those rare and happy occasions when respectable people like you and me can enjoy pleasures normally reserved to the Irish Republican Army.')[83] The idea faced stiff resistance in the Foreign Office, and it 'appalled' Daladier and Gamelin, who feared that it might draw German reprisals on France.[84] This was the moment that Lloyd George chose to make a speech in favour of peace negotiations. 'I do not know what [Lloyd] George is thinking about,' an exasperated Churchill told the journalist W. P. Crozier. 'For God's sake no weakness now; it would mean our total absolute defeat.'[85]

On 13 November Maisky lunched with Churchill and Bracken at Bracken's house, 8 Lord North Street, in Westminster. 'From the outside, a very plain, small house,' recorded the Ambassador, 'on the inside, a superbly furnished modern apartment fit for a representative of the bourgeois intelligentsia.'[86] Churchill arrived late from a War Cabinet meeting, but was 'in fine fettle: fresh, younger, full of energy, with a spring in his step'.

Pulling on his cigar, he told Maisky, 'Your non-aggression pact with Germany triggered the war, but I bear you no grudge. I'm even glad. For a long time now I've felt that a war with Germany was *necessary*. Without your pact, we would have hesitated and drawn things out, until we procrastinated to the point when we could no longer win the war. But we will win it, even though it will cost us dearly.'[87] Summarizing Churchill's remarks, Maisky concluded, 'In peacetime the British often look like pampered, gluttonous sybarites, but in times of war and extremity they turn into vicious bulldogs, trapping their prey in a death grip.'[88]

On 23 November, Churchill was thrilled by an important breakthrough in the war against magnetic mines. A German plane had dropped one on to the mudflats off Shoeburyness, just north of the Thames Estuary, which had not exploded but was clearly visible at low tide. Coming back from dinner at the Other Club, he called an immediate meeting of every official serving in the Admiralty and between eighty and one hundred of the directors of every division and department, to hear the whole story from Lieutenant-Commander Roger Lewis, who had earlier that day defused the mine with a hammer, screwdriver and his penknife while the tide was coming in. 'We have got our prize,' Churchill told his delighted audience. The knowledge gained meant that the Navy could 'de-gausse' or demagnetize its ships by placing a coil of copper cable around them.[89] When Lewis was asked 'Were you frightened?', Pound interjected that the question was unworthy of being posed to an officer of the Royal Navy, 'Frightened? Of course he wasn't frightened!'

On 13 December, Lieutenant-Commander Edward Bickford, captain of the submarine HMS *Salmon*, torpedoed two German cruisers, the *Nürnberg* and *Leipzig*, on the same day, for which Churchill awarded him an immediate DSO and promoted him to commander. They became friends, and Churchill often invited the thirty-year-old sailor to his Admiralty flat for dinner when he was on leave. When Churchill's family noticed how tired and drawn the handsome, newly wedded Bickford had become during the first half of 1940, Churchill tried to get him to take a break from active operations, but Bickford said he could not desert his shipmates.[90] On 9 July 1940, HMS *Salmon* was lost with all hands in a German minefield off south-west Norway. Yet another young Paladin was dead. 'I find it difficult to realise he no longer exists,' Mary wrote in her diary, 'and that somewhere his dead body is being dashed and mouldered by the cold sea waves.'[91]

On 17 September, Russia invaded Poland from the east, in accordance with the secret clauses of the Molotov–Ribbentrop Pact, and swiftly crushed any resistance, taking large numbers of Polish soldiers into captivity. By the middle of the following month, there was still no military activity in the West, so the major action was taking place at sea, as the Royal Navy tried to sink German raiders attacking Allied shipping in the Atlantic. During the Battle of the River Plate in mid-December 1939, as Commodore Henry Harwood's three cruisers HMS *Ajax*, *Achilles* and *Exeter* engaged the German pocket battleship *Graf Spee* (which Churchill pronounced 'Schpeee' instead of 'Schpay'), Churchill hardly left the Map Room, and listened to an American eyewitness radio account of its scuttling off Montevideo ('Monty-viddy-oh'), the capital of Uruguay, on 17 December. He had wanted to send Harwood orders based on the account he was hearing over the radio, rather than waiting up to six hours to receive signals that were being relayed over a network of stations in the Falklands, Sierra Leone, Gibraltar and finally decoded in Whitehall. He was firmly told by Pound that he could not order the dispositions of Royal Navy vessels on the basis of an American wireless broadcast and must leave decisions to the man on the spot.[92] Once the *Graf Spee* had been scuttled, Churchill promoted Harwood to rear admiral and gave him a knighthood.

The homecoming of HMS *Exeter* offered Churchill a splendid opportunity to place its exploits in the grand continuum of British history. He went down to Plymouth to tell the crew,

> When you came up the river this morning, when you entered the harbour and saw the crowds cheering on the banks, one may almost think that there were other spectators in the great shades of the past, carrying us back to the days of Drake and Raleigh, to the great sea dogs of the olden times. If their spirits brooded on this scene you would be able to say to them 'We, your descendants, still make war and have not forgotten the lessons you taught.'[93]

One of the Harrow School Songs is entitled 'When Raleigh Rose'.

Churchill too undoubtedly saw himself being watched by 'the great shades of the past'. A lunch was given at the Guildhall the following February for the crews of HMS *Exeter* and *Ajax* (HMS *Achilles* was still at sea). There he continued the historical theme: 'The warrior heroes of the past may look down, as Nelson's monument looks down upon us now, without any feeling that the island race has lost its daring or that the examples they set in bygone centuries have faded as the generations have succeeded one another.'[94] During his attack, Harwood had flown 'England expects that every man will do his duty', Nelson's signal at the Battle of Trafalgar. 'Neither the new occasion, nor the conduct of all ranks and ratings, nor the final result, were found unworthy,' Churchill pronounced.[95] Afterwards, Walter Thompson worried about the scores of sailors who mobbed him, writing, 'The boys who did get near Winston were pumping his arms and hammering him on the back with wholehearted clumps. Mr Churchill is tough, but he was no longer a youngster and some of the boys put real beef into their pats! I saw him wince once or twice, but he took it all in the best of spirits, grinning hugely.'[96]

Russia attacked Finland on 30 November. This prompted Churchill once again to press for Britain and France to cut Germany off from her iron-ore supply by occupying the massive Gällivare iron-ore field in Sweden and the Norwegian port of Narvik, from which the ore was exported to Germany in the winter months when the Gulf of Bothnia was frozen. At the very least, he urged, the Navy must be allowed to mine the waters around Narvik. The Cabinet, guided by Halifax, decided on 16 December against such a violation of two neutrals' sovereignty. Churchill replied with an appeal to morality over legality. 'The final tribunal is our own conscience,' he said.

> We are fighting to re-establish the reign of law and to protect the liberties of small countries. Our defeat would mean an age of barbaric violence, and would be fatal not only to ourselves, but to the independent life of every small country in Europe . . . Small nations must not tie our hands when we are fighting for their rights and freedom. The letter of the law must not in supreme emergency obstruct those who are charged with its protection and enforcement . . . Humanity, rather than legality, must be our guide.[97]

The Cabinet turned him down again.

Yet Churchill was never defeated by such setbacks in Cabinet. Leslie Hore-Belisha later claimed that part of his success in politics came from the fact that he approached meetings completely differently from other politicians. 'He knows when he enters a Cabinet or committee meeting what he wants done. He has a scheme, a plan, a solution. Not for him the patient hearing while others sort out their views. He takes the initiative with a proposal of his own for others to support or, if they are so inclined, attack.'[98] Churchill always tried to ensure that policy discussions were framed around his own agenda and proposals. He also made powerful use of graphs, statistical tables and maps to appeal to his audience's visual imagination. 'If he cannot win his way in an argument he will probably propose the adjournment of the meeting to another day,' Hore-Belisha noted, 'when he will appear again, reinforced with new and weightier evidence, facts and information, and renew the attack.'[99] Meetings were intended to promote his agenda and confound those of his rivals, not to reach objective conclusions after due consideration of all the alternatives.

On 16 January, the King told the Prime Minister that Churchill's plan to prevent iron ore from leaving Narvik 'savoured too much of a second Dardanelles and he agreed'.[100] Four days later, however, the Supreme War Council, which had been set up in September 1939 to coordinate Anglo-French military action and included the French High Command, executed a complete volte-face and agreed to land a force at Narvik on 20 March, which would then seize the Gällivare orefields and move east to aid Finland against Russia. Swedish and Norwegian agreement would simply have to be obtained by *force majeure*. Despite continuing misgivings in the highest circles in London, Churchill's plan was back on track.

That evening he made a deeply controversial broadcast to the neutral countries that was very unpopular in some areas of the Government and Whitehall, especially the Foreign Office. He did not believe that the Baltic States could in practice stand up to Russia, for reasons of geography, whereas Finland could. He praised the Finnish resistance to the USSR: 'Only Finland – superb, nay, sublime – in the jaws of peril – Finland shows what free men can do. The service rendered by Finland to Mankind is magnificent ... Everyone can see how Communism rots the soul of a nation; how it makes it abject and hungry in peace, and proves it base and abominable in war.'[101] Finland's resistance clearly changed the view he had expressed to Maisky about the alignment of British and Soviet interests. As for the neutrals, whom Churchill always treated somewhere between malingerers and outright cowards, he said, 'Each one hopes that if he feeds the crocodile enough, the crocodile will eat him last. All of them hope that the storm will pass before their time comes to be devoured. But I fear – I fear greatly – the storm will not pass. It will rage and it will roar, ever more loudly, ever more widely.'[102]

Halifax was furious, telling Chamberlain that it had set back relations with the neutrals three months and had done 'incalculable harm'.[103] He sent Churchill a note about it in Cabinet, only to receive the reply, 'Asking me not to make a speech is like asking a centipede to get along and not put a foot on the ground.'[104] Chamberlain forced Churchill to apologize to Halifax as the offensive 'crocodile' line had not been cleared by No. 10 or the Cabinet. 'It is a heavy price that we have to pay for our Winston,' the Prime Minister told Ida, 'and the groundlings whose ears are so tickled by his broadcasts do not stop to consider whether their satisfaction that the things we all feel and say in private should be said in public, is not too dearly gained.'[105] Of course what could not be quantified was how many Swiss, Irish, Belgians or Swedes, on hearing the broadcast, resolved to support the Allies. 'Papa's broadcast magnificent,' Mary wrote in her diary. 'It makes me at once proud and humble to have such a great father.'[106]

For all the complaints that the neutrals had been offended, this was another one of the speeches that showed Churchill's attitude to the war so clearly to the British people. 'Certainly it is true that we are facing numerical odds,' he readily admitted, 'but that is no new thing in our history. Very few wars have been won by mere numbers alone. Quality, willpower, geographical advantages, natural and financial resources, the command of the sea, and, above all, a cause which rouses the spontaneous surgings of the human spirit in millions of hearts – these have proved to be the decisive factors in the human story.'[107] He continued with a vision of the war's eventual outcome. 'Let the great cities of Warsaw, of Prague, of Vienna banish despair even in the midst of their agony. Their liberation is sure. The day will come when the joy-bells will ring again throughout Europe, and when victorious nations, masters not only of their foes but of themselves, will plan and build in justice, in tradition, and in freedom a house of many mansions where there will be room for all.'[108] In those cities and later across Occupied Europe, listening to Churchill's broadcasts over the radio became punishable by death, yet still people listened, because he could provide that one thing these tortured populations needed more than anything else: hope.

Churchill also spoke of 'the first U-boat campaign for the first time being utterly broken, with the mining menace in good control, with our shipping virtually undiminished'.[109] Lord Halifax told Lady Alexandra 'Baba' Metcalfe, Lord Curzon's daughter and his close friend, 'It is incredible that a man in his position should make such gaffes. His bragging about the war at sea is followed every time by some appalling losses.' Churchill said in the broadcast that 'It seems pretty certain tonight that half the U-boats with which Germany began the war have been sunk, and that their new building has fallen far behind what we expected.'[110] In fact only nine out of fifty-seven had been sunk, that is 15 per cent, as his own Naval Intelligence Department estimated. Churchill had reached his 50 per cent figure by adding sixteen 'probably sunk' to the nine 'known sunk', and an extra eight that Lindemann's Statistics Section had somehow spirited up. When Captain A. G. Talbot, director of the Anti-Submarine Warfare Division of the Admiralty, pointed out that the sinkings had been nothing like the number mentioned in the broadcast, Churchill responded with a minute on 22 January: 'Thirty-five is the lowest figure that can be accepted' for the number of U-boats sunk and damaged, 'and is practically admitted by the Germans themselves,' which it certainly had not been.[111] 'There are two people who sink U-boats in this war, Talbot,' he said. 'You sink them in the Atlantic and I sink them in the House of Commons. The trouble is that you are sinking them at exactly half the rate I am.'[112] In a similar spirit, Churchill told Captain Pim, 'Our submarines are, unfortunately, sometimes sunk, but please remember that U-boats are *destroyed*.'[113]

In early April 1940, Talbot estimated that nineteen had been destroyed (the correct figure was indeed nineteen), forty-three were at large and two under repair. The comprehensive list of U-boat losses compiled in 2014 from German Navy and other official sources supports Talbot and Godfrey's analysis of the numbers, and undermines Churchill, Pound and Lindemann's. Only three U-boats were actually sunk in September 1939, four in October, one in November and one in December. Early 1940 was not much better, with two in January, five in February, three in March, four in April and one at the end of May, a total of twenty-three while Churchill was first lord. Of these, ten were sunk by ships, five by unknown causes, three by mines, one by ships together with shore-based aircraft, one by shore-based aircraft alone, one by ship-based aircraft, one by another submarine and one by collision.[114]

It is no denigration of the great courage shown by the Royal Navy to point out that the numbers of U-boats that Churchill claimed to have been sunk on his watch bore no relation to the twenty-three that genuinely were sunk. Once methods of destruction improved, the numbers rose dramatically – only twenty-four were sunk in 1940 but 37 in 1941, 89 in 1942, 272 in 1943, 291 in 1944, and 141 before the beginning of May 1945 when the vast majority of the 355 remaining U-boats were scuttled.[115] Talbot's unwillingness to go along with the First Lord's wildly exaggerated claims meant that on 25 April Churchill had to write to Pound to say, 'It might be a good thing if Captain Talbot went to sea as soon as possible.'[116] Talbot did so and had a distinguished career commanding the aircraft carrier HMS *Furious* and becoming a rear admiral, but he never returned to a post at the Admiralty.

'His preference for pursuing ideas of his own devising is, after all, an attribute of great men,' Admiral Godfrey (himself the model for 'M' in his assistant Ian Fleming's James Bond novels) wrote of Churchill in his draft memoirs.

> In Churchill, it led to a ruthlessness in his opposition to the ideas of others that he felt stood in the way. To get his own way he used every device, and brought the whole battery of his ingenious, tireless and highly political mind to the point at issue. His battery of weapons included persuasion, real or simulated anger, mockery, vituperation, tantrums, ridicule, derision, abuse and tears, which he would aim at anyone who opposed him or expressed a view contrary to the one he had already formed, sometimes on quite trivial questions.[117]

It was true, and was key to Churchill's war-fighting, and the reason that Chamberlain had kept him out of the Government for as long as he possibly could. Godfrey was never reconciled to the First Lord's methods.

Critics have accused Churchill of lying about the U-boat sinkings in order to promote his prime ministerial ambitions, but the buoying up of morale, which of course was what Churchill was trying to do, is an essential part of waging war. 'Is everything you tell us true?' a young rating asked Churchill on board a battleship in 1940. 'Young man,' Churchill replied, 'I have told many lies for my country and will tell many more.'[118] He was regularly to exaggerate successes for propaganda purposes long after he had got to Downing Street too.

In a speech in Manchester on 27 January, Churchill called for a million women to help the war effort in the munitions factories, freeing up men for the fighting services.[119] He understood that people did not mind being asked to make sacrifices if they knew them to be necessary. 'This is no time for ease and comfort,' he said in reference to the extension of rationing. 'It is the time to dare and endure. That is why we are rationing ourselves, even while our resources are expanding. That is why we mean to regulate every ton that is carried across the sea and make sure that it is carried solely for the purpose of victory.'[120] Churchill appreciated that people would not accept the deaths of merchant seamen for the importing of non-essential luxuries. He also spoke of the way Poles were being tortured, shot in numbered batches and terrorized. He told the story of a Pole dragged out of a chemist's shop in order to make up the total the Nazi officer had demanded for a mass execution.

'Come then,' Churchill said, 'let us to the task, to the battle, to the toil – each to our part, each to our station. Fill the armies, rule the air, pour out the munitions, strangle the U-boats, sweep the mines, plough the land, build the ships, guard the streets, succour the wounded, uplift the downcast, and honour the brave. Let us go forward together in all parts of the Empire, in all parts of the Island. There is not a week, nor a day, nor an hour to lose.' One listener wrote later, 'Nobody in that hall that day could fail to be thrilled by the historic phrases which surged through the free world like a clarion call.'[121] Randolph and Mary had accompanied him, and at a family dinner party on the train returning to London, Tommy Thompson noted that 'he was happier and more at ease than they had seen him for some time.'[122] Lord Crawford wrote on 26 January that 'If Chamberlain broke his leg, Churchill would be driven to Downing Street by public opinion.'[123]

Churchill was a loyal member of the Government, neither undermining Chamberlain nor permitting Bracken to do so. On 4 February he attended a meeting in Paris of the Supreme War Council. On the train from Charing Cross to board a destroyer at Dover with the Prime Minister, Halifax and Sir Alec Cadogan, who had taken over from Vansittart as the permanent under-secretary at the Foreign Office, Chamberlain 'rather tentatively' showed Churchill the telegrams exchanged with Washington over the unwelcome prospect of a peace mission to Europe by Sumner Welles, the American Under-Secretary of State, which ruled out direct peace talks with Hitler. Cadogan noted that 'Winston – after a second sherry – read them through and, with tears in his eyes, said "I'm proud to follow you!"'[124]

On 16 February, on Churchill's orders, a party from HMS *Cossack* boarded the *Graf Spee*'s supply vessel *Altmark* in the Jösing Fjord in Norway, freeing 299 captured British merchant seamen. The words 'The Navy's here!' called out to the prisoners became a proud national catchphrase. The Norwegians impeded the operation, protested about the violation of their neutrality and allowed the *Altmark* to return to Germany, undermining any hope that they might acquiesce in the occupation of Narvik. Halifax had not opposed the *Cossack* operation, however. 'That was *big* of Halifax,' Churchill said afterwards.[125]

Returning from Clydeside after the launching of HMS *Duke of York* that month, Churchill complained to the King about how often Admiralty ministers and civil servants told him he was wrong and that projects could not be carried out. 'Perhaps they're sometimes right,' observed the King, smiling. 'Nine times out of ten,' replied an unabashed Churchill.[126] That was correct, and Pound and his team had become expert in finding the one idea that was good while winnowing out the other nine. 'We were to find out that Mr Churchill needed a diet consisting of the carcasses of abortive and wild-cat operations,' wrote Admiral Godfrey in his disapproving draft memoirs, yet, as with Churchill's plan to capture the island of Pantelleria later that year, he could be dissuaded.[127] Similarly, when it was discovered that Hitler's minister without portfolio and former Reichsbank President Dr Hjalmar Schacht was on board an Italian ocean liner docked at Gibraltar, Churchill wanted him taken off the ship and arrested. Halifax did not want to antagonize the still-neutral Mussolini, however, so nothing was done.[128]

After a Cabinet meeting in late February, at which Chamberlain said that the Americans and neutrals would disapprove of Churchill's plan to mine Norwegian waters, Churchill attended a jocular lunch in his honour given by parliamentary journalists in the Victoria Hotel with Chamberlain present. He told them, 'I am – and I say it with becoming modesty – a constant ingredient – almost an indispensable ingredient – in the whole of that constitutional process that you gentlemen discharge.'[129] Of his Wilderness Years he said, indicating Chamberlain, 'I have passed under what might be called the Frown of Power.'[130] After speaking about himself for forty minutes, he 'pledged himself loyally to serve the "Captain" for the duration of the voyage', at which the Prime Minister bowed his acknowledgement.[131]

'People say Churchill is tactless,' Lord Crawford wrote three days after the Guildhall lunch for the crews *Exeter* and *Ajax*,

> that his judgements are erratic, that he flies off at a tangent, that he has a burning desire to trespass upon the domain of the naval strategist – all this may be more or less true but he remains the only figure in the Cabinet with the virtue of constant uncompromising aggressive quest of victory. He delivers the massive killing blow, encourages the country, inspires the fleet – the more I see and hear of him the more confident I am that he represents the party of complete . . . victory![132]

If anything explains how Churchill became prime minister, it is an encomium such as this from an old antagonist. The 27th Earl of Crawford (created 1398) and 10th Earl of Balcarres (created 1651) was a pillar of the Establishment. He attended Eton and Oxford, had a good Great War, was reputed to have turned down the viceroyalty of India, had been Bonar Law's chief whip in the Commons and had sat in the same Cabinet as Churchill from 1916 to 1922. 'Bal' Crawford had called Churchill 'a born cad' of Indo-Mexican blood who was prone to lunacy, and had spread every vicious rumour about him from the so-called Ulster Pogrom onwards. Yet his view had begun to change after Churchill's Commons speech the previous September, and by late February 1940 he saw him as the only figure in the Cabinet who could deliver complete victory. This was the last diary note Crawford was to write, as he died soon afterwards and never saw Churchill enter No. 10 to fulfil his prediction.

Crawford's diary shows that attitudes to Churchill were starting to change on the Conservative benches in February and March, although he was still distrusted there. Archie Sinclair made it clear how much the Liberal Party could be relied upon to support Churchill should circumstances change when he told the Commons on 6 March, 'We are all resolved to win this war. We are all sure we can win it. It is only when I look down that Front Bench in the absence of the First Lord of the Admiralty that doubt chills me.'[133] The years of friendship since Churchill had appointed Sinclair his trusted second-in-command in the trenches, where they had messed together and risked death daily, were about to pay off spectacularly.

Finland signed an armistice with Russia on 13 March, ending the excuse that Britain and France planned to use to violate Norwegian and Swedish sovereignty. Yet Churchill still wanted to go ahead with the Narvik operation, in the face of united War Cabinet opposition. 'I am very deeply concerned about the way the war is going,' he wrote to Halifax the next day. It was costing the Treasury £6 million a day in a 'money-drain'. 'There is no effective intimacy with the French,' 'the Germans are the masters of the North', so he concluded, 'Faithful discharge of duty is no excuse for ministers: we have to contrive and compel victory.'[134] Three days later, at lunch with Eden, Halifax said he was 'prepared to face' having Churchill as minister of defence, representing all three Services in the Cabinet. 'There were only three men in the Cabinet itself who [have] support in the country,' Eden told him – Churchill, Chamberlain and Halifax himself – as 'the rest were civil servants and more or less discredited politicians.'[135] Eden probably disqualified himself as simply too young – he was only forty-two.

On 28 March in London, after Paul Reynaud had replaced Daladier as French premier, the sixth Supreme War Council finally approved Churchill's plan to flood the Rhine with fluvial mines, although the French Cabinet overruled Reynaud three days later.[136] The Council did however put out a joint communiqué promising 'Both Governments mutually undertake that during the present war they will neither negotiate nor conclude an armistice or treaty of peace except by mutual agreement.'[137] The next day, Churchill vented his frustrations to Crozier. He said he needed fifty or sixty more destroyers, and explained that he would have liked to interdict the Swedish iron ore, 'but there are always so many people to persuade in these matters'.[138] Churchill told Crozier that he got on well with Chamberlain. 'I have no desire at all myself to be Prime Minister,' he said, 'and any suspicions that he used to have that I might be dangerous to him have now disappeared. I determined – obviously I must – that I must work well with him and I do, and I believe that he now likes me.'[139] The last part of this at least was true: Chamberlain and Churchill got along well in person, whatever they said about each other privately. Such was the collegiate atmosphere of British politics in that period, especially in wartime, and Churchill's lifelong capacity not to allow 'the rancour and asperity of politics' to damage personal relations.

Although there was no activity on the Western Front, Churchill did not believe it could last for long. 'More than a million German soldiers, including all their active divisions and armoured divisions, are drawn up ready to attack, at a few hours' notice, all along the frontiers of Luxembourg, of Belgium and of Holland,' Churchill said in a broadcast on 30 March. 'At any moment these neutral countries may be subjected to an avalanche of steel and fire; and the decision rests in the hands of a haunted, morbid being, who, to their eternal shame, the German peoples in their bewilderment have worshipped as a god.'[140] He then demanded of the strong pacifist movement in Britain, 'Although the fate of Poland stares them in the face, there are thoughtless dilettanti or purblind worldlings who sometimes ask us, "What is it that Britain and France are fighting for?" To this I answer: "If we left off fighting you would soon find out."'[141] Four days later, 1,500 pacifists, Fascists, Independent Labour Party members and Communists cheered at a mass meeting in Kingsway Hall in Holborn when they heard Churchill denounced by the Marquess of Tavistock for trying to 'whip up war' against Germany, and Hitler praised for what he had done for the German working class.[142]

Churchill was not consulted about the Cabinet reshuffle of 3 April, in which Samuel Hoare and Kingsley Wood swapped places and the Ministry for Coordination of Defence was abolished. Churchill was, in Eden's words, 'saddened and disgusted' at the lack of warning and the fact that the slippery Sam Hoare got the Air Ministry and the unimpressive Oliver Stanley stayed in place at the War Office, which Churchill hoped would go to Eden, who stayed as dominions secretary. Eden said that Chamberlain 'had only accepted W and me because he could not avoid it', whereupon 'Winston maintained that there would be more chances, many more on this rough voyage and sought to hearten himself in this strain, and no doubt me too. But he was worried and depressed, which is not wonderful.'[143] Churchill, while remaining at the Admiralty, did however also become chairman of a new Military Coordination Committee, consisting of the three Service chiefs and their ministers, which met daily. This guaranteed friction with Stanley and Hoare, as he was not formally senior to then, and gave him no official power of direction or input, even over what the Chiefs of Staff were planning. 'The office,' as the Labour MP Colonel Josiah Wedgwood put it to Bracken, 'if one can use such a word, adds to his responsibilities but gives him no real powers.'[144] It would, however, put Churchill even more directly in the firing line should things go wrong.

One positive aspect of the reshuffle was that Churchill inherited the fifty-three-year-old Major-General Hastings Ismay as his personal chief of staff. After Sandhurst and a posting in India, 'Pug' Ismay had served in Somaliland, been military secretary to the Viceroy of India and secretary to the Committee of Imperial Defence (succeeding Hankey) in 1938. Maud Russell called him 'a nice goggle-eyed, swarthy soldier', but he was very much more than that.[145] He was a frank admirer of Churchill (he could quote whole passages from *The World Crisis*) but he knew precisely where his duty lay in liaising between the military Chiefs of Staff and Churchill. Early on in the job, after Ismay had attempted to interpret a paper from the Chiefs of Staff that Churchill did not like, Churchill asked Ismay what he '*really*' thought of it. 'Do you wish me to be of value to you or not?' asked Ismay. 'Naturally,' Churchill replied, 'of course I do.' 'Then,' said Ismay, 'you will never ask me that question again.'[146] Churchill quickly established an exceptionally close working relationship with him, and the Chiefs of Staff trusted him implicitly too. He would soon stand them both in very good stead.

On 4 April, Chamberlain made a speech about the war situation in which he limply said of Hitler, 'One thing is certain; he has missed the bus.'[147] In Paris the next day, Churchill told the French that Britain would go ahead with the mining of Narvik, and that Operation Wilfred, as it was code-named, was scheduled for the night of 8 April. As it turned out, that was only a matter of hours before Hitler launched Operation Weserübung, the invasion of Denmark and Norway, at dawn on 9 April, in accordance with a long-prepared plan. It was brilliantly executed: the Germans swiftly occupied Oslo, Stavanger, Bergen, Trondheim and Narvik, securing all the major ports and airfields. The brave but small Norwegian Army was taken by surprise. Oslo was captured by only six companies of German paratroops, before Junkers 52 transport aircraft brought in 29,000 soldiers in 3,000 sorties.[148] Hitler had clearly not missed the bus.

Almost everything that could go wrong in the eight-week-long Norway Campaign did, and much of it must be laid at Churchill's door, since he was first lord of the Admiralty and it was a largely naval-led campaign, with half the Home Fleet involved. At 6.30 a.m. on 9 April, before the Cabinet knew about the fall of Narvik to the Germans, he told them, 'Our hands [are] now free and we [can] apply our overwhelming sea power on the Norwegian coast. We could liquidate these landings in a week or two.'[149] He did not believe the Germans were even necessarily heading towards Narvik.[150] He has been accused, with some validity, of pushing a reluctant Chamberlain into an unwinnable campaign in a way that showed that he had learned little from the past.[151]

One major problem was the lack of central direction. In Admiral James's words, the campaign 'was to a great extent conducted separately by the three services without guidance or direction by the Prime Minister or an effective representative of supreme executive power'. That was Chamberlain's fault, and a lesson Churchill certainly did learn.[152] Had the Military Coordination Committee been given teeth to do what its title implied, Churchill might have been able to get a grip on the campaign, but Hoare and Stanley, correctly in constitutional terms, thought of themselves as independent agents.

The catalogue of errors was humiliating.[153] Major-General Mackesy did not capture Narvik because he did not have the same orders from the War Office that the naval commander, Admiral Lord Cork, had from the Admiralty.[154] ('If this officer appears to be spreading a bad spirit through the higher ranks of the land forces,' Churchill told Cork at one point, 'do not hesitate to relieve him or place him under arrest.')[155] By the time the Chiefs of Staff gave definite orders to take both Narvik and Trondheim, the Germans had air superiority in both places. 'The Chiefs of Staff', Churchill later complained, 'worked as a separate and largely independent body without guidance or direction from the Prime Minister,' let alone from himself.[156] Admiral Roger Keyes wanted to command a special force to take Trondheim, but Pound opposed the Trondheim attack (Operation Hammer), and Churchill changed his mind about it more than once. Churchill also sent Cork orders without informing Admiral Forbes, under whom Cork served.

Narvik was finally captured on 13 April, but could only be held long enough to destroy the port installations. Supply ships had been loaded in such a way that, although guns could be disembarked, their ammunition was in different vessels; the British Army had too few 25-pounder guns and anti-tank guns, while German reconnaissance planes had the benefit of twenty hours of daylight per day. In the final evacuation, the battlecruiser HMS *Glorious* and her destroyers were sunk by the battleship *Scharnhorst*. Small wonder that Churchill later called it 'this ramshackle campaign'.[157]

The Germans took the initiative in the Norway Campaign and never really lost it, and they made virtually no serious errors, while the British and French made many.[158] There were shortcomings in British naval intelligence and, once Denmark had fallen in a single day on 9 April, Luftwaffe bombers closed the Skagerrak straits connecting the North Sea and the Baltic, allowing the Germans to supply their forces in Norway with ease. When the British captured the two ports of Namsos and Åndalsnes on 14 April, Stuka dive-bombers were able to flatten both. The campaign was only one day old before Churchill fell out with the new Air Minister. 'Winston', Eden noted in his diary on 10 April, 'is indignant with Sam H[oare] whom he suspects of being eager to score off him, and whom he regards as unsuited to inspire the Air Force at a time like this. "A snake" and some stronger epithets.'[159]

Churchill's 'promotion' had inspired envy and resentment. Inskip (another snake, who resented Churchill taking the job he had once failed in) complained bitterly that he 'now becomes almost equal in power to the PM', which was a ridiculous claim.[160] In a debate on Norway on 11 April, Churchill used a woeful historical analogy, telling the Commons, 'I consider that Hitler's action in invading Scandinavia is as great a strategic and political error as that which was committed by Napoleon in 1807, when he invaded Spain* . . . We shall take all we want of this Norwegian coast now, with an enormous increase in the facility and in the efficiency of our blockade.'[161] It was almost as bad as saying that Hitler had missed the bus. Maisky, who was present, wrote in his diary, 'I had never seen him in such a state. He clearly hadn't slept for several nights. He was pale, couldn't find the right words, stumbled and kept getting mixed up. There was not a trace of his usual parliamentary brilliance . . . Churchill produced rather lame arguments to explain the German breakthrough: bad weather, the vastness of the sea, the impossibility of controlling it all, and so on.'[162]

Churchill complained to the King that with the Coordination Committee, War Cabinet, Commons debates and thirty or forty important naval messages coming in daily, 'which have to be sifted and carefully gone through, before sending out new instructions to the Fleet off Norway', he found it hard to get on with his Admiralty work.[163] He could, however, still find time to see the King, and somehow, too, he was able to continue working at night on the manuscript of his *History of the English-Speaking Peoples*.† Even in the midst of the Norway Campaign, at eleven o'clock one evening in late April, Churchill was able to discuss with William Deakin and Freddie Birkenhead the Norman invasion of England in 1066. Deakin recalled that, despite naval signals being brought in by admirals as the battle progressed,

> talk ranged round the spreading shadows of the Norman invasion and the figure of Edward the Confessor who, as Churchill wrote, 'comes down to us faint, misty, frail'. I can still see the map on the wall, with the dispositions of the British fleet off Norway, and hear the voice of the First Lord as he grasped with his usual insight the strategic position in 1066. But this was no lack of attention to current business. It was the measure of the man with the supreme historical eye. The distant episodes were as close and real as the mighty events on hand.[164]

By 20 April, the atmosphere in the Coordination Committee had become so acrimonious that Churchill asked Chamberlain to chair it, saying 'They'll take from you what they won't take from me.'[165] The Prime Minister told Hilda that there was 'a general conviction that Winston has smashed the machine we had so carefully built up to ensure that all projects should be

* A rare historical error: Napoleon was invited to march through Spain on his way to Portugal in 1807; he invaded Spain in 1808.

† Anticipating a drop of three-quarters of his income on returning to office, Churchill officially retired as an author for tax purposes again in September 1939, just as he had when he was at the Treasury.

thought out and examined . . . he puts intenser pressure on his staff than he realizes. The result is that they are apt to be bullied into a sulky silence.' Once Chamberlain had taken over, however, 'The result was magical. We are always unanimous.'[166] Unanimous, perhaps, but not victorious.

In mid-September 1939, Clement Davies, a Welsh Liberal MP who had resigned the whip, set up the All-Party Action Group (also known as the Vigilantes), a small group that met every Thursday at the Reform Club, with Boothby as its secretary. In April 1940 the 4th Marquess of Salisbury inaugurated what he called the Watching Committee of Tory members of both Houses, which met at his house in Arlington Street in St James's. Although the membership of these loose, informal organizations – Focus, the Policy Study Group, the Glamour Boys, the All-Party Action Group and the Watching Committee – overlapped a good deal, they were all critical of Chamberlain to a greater or lesser degree, though by no means all pro-Churchill.

Churchill told Lord Salisbury on 23 April that 'The press had much exaggerated his role as Coordinator of Defence . . . He had no right to initiate suggestions or make decisions.'[167] When Salisbury told him the names of his new Watching Committee, which would watch the Government and keep up pressure on it to pursue the war aggressively, 'he purred like a pleased cat.' The next day he complained to the King that in Norway 'Nothing goes right for us. We have not the air supremacy, and it is difficult to find places for our aircraft owing to snow.'[168] At the Other Club two days later he disclosed to Camrose that 'he was afraid there would be more bad news from Norway and was very pessimistic about our chances in the South of that country.'[169] It was probably more than he should have vouchsafed to a newspaperman, but Camrose was a personal friend and no one ever leaked anything said at the Club. One of its recent members, Churchill's son-in-law Duncan Sandys, was wounded while serving with the Norwegian Expeditionary Force, giving him a permanent limp.

By late April, Chamberlain was considering making Churchill the scapegoat for what was clearly a coming defeat in Norway. Lord Dunglass, his parliamentary private secretary (later Sir Alec Douglas Home, Prime Minister), asked Chips Channon, 'Did I think that Winston should be deflated . . . Ought he to leave the Admiralty?' Channon concluded, 'Evidently these thoughts are in Neville's head. Of course he ought to go, but who could we replace him with?'[170] Had Churchill been humiliatingly demoted or dismissed for his lack of grip on the campaign, it is hard to envisage how he could have become prime minister two weeks later.

On 26 April, the Military Coordination Committee, and later the War Cabinet, agreed to prepare for the evacuation of all forces from Norway, to Reynaud's fury, contradicting a plan to fight on there that had been agreed with the Supreme War Council only three days before. 'Winston's attitude was most difficult,' Chamberlain noted, 'challenging everything the Chiefs of Staff suggested and generally behaving like a spoiled and sulky child.'[171] After the Committee meeting at 6 p.m., Churchill asked Chamberlain to make him minister of defence.

'The Whips are putting it about that it is all the fault of Winston,' recorded Harold Nicolson on 30 April, the day after the evacuation from Åndalsnes, 'who has made another forlorn failure.'[172] The King's diary entry for 30 April also suggests that Churchill was being set up to take the blame for Norway, to protect Chamberlain at a time when Lloyd George was increasingly being discussed as a national saviour, as he had been in 1916. 'Winston still seems to be causing a good deal of trouble according to the P.M.,' the King noted after Chamberlain's weekly audience with him.

> I asked whether Winston was to blame for the change of plan when the [Operation] Hammer force did not attack Trondheim. The P.M. told me yes. W was frightened that we might lose some big ships, and so were his advisers in the Admiralty, and on this fact he made the Chiefs of Staff agree with him. Hence the delay in landing more troops at Namsos and Andalsnes. The P.M. is having another talk with W tonight, laying down what he can and cannot do without the War Cabinet's sanction.[173]

In fact Churchill was in no position to 'make' the Chiefs of Staff agree with him over anything.

In the event, Chamberlain came down on Churchill's side, deciding to make him minister of defence in all but name. When Hoare and Stanley threatened to resign sooner than formally report to Churchill, Chamberlain threatened to resign himself 'and let W.C. be Prime Minister as well as Defence Minister . . . they said that would be too great a disaster and they would do what I asked them'.[174] Chamberlain drew up a letter delineating the new arrangements, which gave Churchill what was effectively the post for which he had first asked Lloyd George in the early 1920s, and had urged should be created since the mid-1930s.

Churchill accepted immediately, on 30 April, circulating a memorandum to the War Cabinet stating that he 'will be responsible on behalf of the [Military Coordination] Committee for giving guidance and directions to the Chiefs of Staff Committee and for this purpose it will be open to him to summon that Committee for personal consultation at any time when he considers it necessary'.[175] Despite the Norway defeat, for which he had been partly responsible, Churchill had accrued more power to himself. In the Commons, which knew little of what was happening,

Channon reported that 'there is more talk of a cabal against poor Neville. "They" are saying it is like 1915 all over again, that Winston should be Prime Minister as he has more vigour and the country behind him.'[176]

The evacuation of Namsos began on 1 May and continued for forty-eight hours. As a sudden downpour drenched Horse Guards Parade, Churchill quipped to Jock Colville, then Chamberlain's private secretary, 'If I were the first of May, I should be ashamed of myself.' Colville, who at this time admired Chamberlain and was sceptical about Churchill, acidly recorded in his diary, 'Personally I think he ought to be ashamed of himself in any case.'[177] Channon was equally unimpressed after seeing Churchill joking and drinking in the Smoking Room with Labour's A. V. Alexander and Archie Sinclair, whom he called 'the new Shadow Cabinet'. 'David Margesson says we are on the eve of the greatest political crisis since 1931,' recorded Channon.[178] 'To gain time he [Chamberlain] has given Winston more rope.'[179]

Chamberlain was running out of rope to give. The evacuation from Trondheim on 2 May made it clear to all that Britain had been defeated in a major campaign: for something as serious as that, the Prime Minister has to take ultimate responsibility. Lord Lloyd told his son David, who was stationed in Palestine, 'The public seem to realize the full naked results of our past unpreparedness, of which I think you have heard me speak a good deal in the last seven or eight years.'[180] If the public put the Norway debacle down to general unpreparedness over years, rather than to operational decisions taken during the campaign, the blame would fall on Chamberlain rather than Churchill.

Despite the litany of errors, there were some consolations from the Norway campaign. Whereas the Royal Navy had lost an aircraft carrier, two cruisers, a sloop and nine destroyers, Germany had lost three cruisers, and ten of her twenty-two destroyers and her only two operational battle-ships were damaged, much greater losses proportionately to the size of her navy than Britain's.[181] An intact German Navy fighting off Dunkirk the following month could have been a decisive force, but in early May the Germans had only one large cruiser, two light cruisers and seven destroyers ready for immediate service, not enough even to come out of port.

Chamberlain told Hilda on 3 May that 'Winston changed his mind four times over Trondheim . . . I don't blame W.C. for these very natural alter-nations . . . Only they don't square with the picture the gutter press and W.C.'s "Friends" try to paint of the supreme War Lord.'[182] He ended, 'It's a vile world, but I don't think my enemies will get me down this time.'[183]

# 20

# Seizing the Premiership May 1940

*The men of destiny do not wait to be sent for; they come when they feel their time has come. They do not ask to be recognized, they declare themselves; they come like fate; they are inevitable.*

Alexander MacCallum Scott, *Winston Spencer Churchill in Peace and War*[1]

*He had that ruthless side without which great affairs cannot be handled.*

Churchill on H. H. Asquith in *Great Contemporaries*[2]

The Norway Debate of Tuesday, 7 May and Wednesday, 8 May 1940 in the House of Commons was described by one of its participants, Sir Stafford Cripps, as 'the most momentous that has ever taken place in the history of Parliament'.[3] Although the official motion for debate was merely 'That this House do now adjourn' – that is, end its session – it turned into a vote of confidence in the Chamberlain Government, covering far more than just the recent campaign. Churchill had to show perfect loyalty to the man under whom he was serving, as did Brendan Bracken, who would under normal circumstances have dearly loved to vote to bring Chamberlain down. Just before the debate, misjudging events completely, Chamberlain told Lord Halifax that he doubted it would all 'amount to much'.[4]

Although as a senior member of the Cabinet, Churchill was committed to supporting Chamberlain in the debate, several of those who landed the heaviest blows against the Government were known to be his closest friends, so suspicion was rife among Chamberlainites that Churchill was secretly encouraging the rebellion. All that can be said for certain as he sat beside Chamberlain is that he stayed outwardly absolutely loyal, whatever was going through his mind and happening in his heart. If he was merely acting, it was the performance of a lifetime.

A backbench Tory MP, John Moore-Brabazon, surreptitiously took photographs during the debate with his tiny Minox camera, breaking the Commons' rules. From these we can see that when Chamberlain rose to defend the performance of his ministry, the Chamber and galleries were packed. He gave an uninspiring recitation of events in Norway, in which he said, somewhat self-pityingly, 'Ministers, of course, must be expected to be blamed for everything,' whereupon Labour MPs shouted, 'They missed the bus!' The Speaker had to intervene to quieten the Chamber. Chamberlain soldiered on through a long, self-exculpatory and uninspiring defence of his Government and himself. 'I do not think that the people of this country yet realize the extent or the imminence of the threat which is impending against us,' he said, whereupon one MP called out, 'We said that five years ago!'[5]

The debate was as much about appeasement as about Norway, about the past as about the future, further complicating Churchill's position. Chamberlain announced that he had given Churchill enhanced powers chairing the Military Coordination Committee, but not until the campaign was nearly over. 'The change would have been made in any case,' he claimed. Describing his position as war leader, he could only come up with the lacklustre line, 'For my part I try to steer a middle course.'[6]

Speaking next, Clement Attlee, Leader of the Labour Party, said that both Chamberlain and Churchill had been far too optimistic over Norway. He took the Commons through the setbacks and disasters of the campaign, quoting Chamberlain's speeches against him, saying of Churchill's dual job at the Admiralty and the Military Coordination Committee, 'The First Lord of the Admiralty has great abilities, but it is not fair to him that he should be put into an impossible position like that.'[7] Attlee attacked Chamberlain for not having the 'energy, intensity, drive and resolution' necessary, adding of the appeasers, 'They missed all the peace buses but caught the war bus.' In closing, he said explicitly that 'to win the war, we want different people at the helm from those who have led us into it.' Attlee's speech laid the ground for other speakers' attacks on the Government over supply, munitions production, rationing, recruitment, industrial policy, military and civilian organization and other vital aspects of the war about which Churchill had been highly critical of the Government for many years. Attlee's colleague Arthur Greenwood later echoed his conclusion, declaring, 'Wars are not won on masterly evacuations,' and 'more foresight and energy, and stronger and more ruthless will to victory, are required in the supreme direction of our war effort.'[8]

After Sir Henry Page Croft had supported Chamberlain and Colonel Josiah Wedgwood had attacked him aggressively, Admiral Sir Roger

Keyes, MP for Portsmouth North, wearing his Admiral of the Fleet uniform, complete with six rows of medal ribbons, stood up. Almost all of the many contemporaneous accounts of that day refer to Keyes's indictment of Chamberlain over Norway, which he called 'a shocking story of ineptitude'. He quoted from a speech of Chamberlain's the previous week about the strategic importance of capturing Trondheim, and contrasted it with the debacle that took place there. Even though Keyes had been prevented by Churchill from commanding the attack on Trondheim, he lauded him, describing Gallipoli as 'a brilliant conception of the First Lord of the Admiralty to circumvent the deadlock in France and Belgium' and blaming its defeat entirely on Fisher.[9] 'I am longing to see proper use made of his great abilities,' Keyes said. 'He has the confidence of the Navy, and indeed of the whole country, which is looking to him to help win the war.'[10] It was the only time in the whole debate that it was suggested Churchill should take over from Chamberlain, and even then it was veiled, for fear of provoking a reaction from Chamberlainites. Certainly, no one mentioned Churchill when, later on, a National Liberal MP, George Lambert, said, 'I ask honourable Members whom they suggest as Prime Minister, other than my right honourable Friend the present Prime Minister.'

Leo Amery made the most electrifying speech of the debate, despite his reputation as a generally dull speaker. He questioned the timing of Churchill's promotion in a way that reflected well on Churchill and badly on Chamberlain, and ended a powerful indictment of the Prime Minister's war leadership with Oliver Cromwell's famous words to the Rump Parliament in 1653: 'You have sat too long here for any good you have been doing. Depart, I say, and let us have done with you. In the name of God, go.'[11] Although they were the words of a military dictator dismissing an elected Parliament, the effect was dramatic. Two Chamberlainite backbenchers then spoke, but because Churchill was a loyal minister they could not attack him. Then Lord Winterton, who like Attlee and Josiah Wedgwood had fought at Gallipoli, castigated the Government for not asking for greater sacrifices from the nation, adding, 'I wish expressly to exclude from my condemnation the First Lord of the Admiralty.'[12]

Oliver Stanley, the Secretary for War, tried his best to rescue the situation, and a couple of backbench National Government supporters came to Chamberlain's defence, but by the end of the first day's debate it was clear that it was not just the handling of the Norway campaign that was on trial, but the Government itself. On the second day, Wednesday, 8 May, the senior Labour figure Herbert Morrison complained that Churchill was going to be the last speaker in the debate, 'when there can be no comments upon his evidence', likening it to 'the chief witness who refuses to go into the box'.[13] He asked a series of questions of Churchill about machine guns being sent to Norway without spare barrels, troops not having snow shoes, anti-aircraft guns arriving a week late and so on, which struck the first serious note of criticism of Churchill in the debate so far. 'Finally,' he asked, 'is it the case that the right honourable Gentleman the First Lord of the Admiralty is being used as a sort of shield by the Prime Minister when he finds it convenient to do so?' He announced that the Labour Party intended to divide the House at the end of the debate that night – theoretically on the adjournment, but in fact on Chamberlain's premiership. Chamberlain received what *The Times* called 'a great roar of cheers' when he replied, 'I say this to my friends in the House – and I have friends in the House . . . I accept the challenge. I welcome it indeed . . . and I call on my friends to support us in the Lobby tonight.'[14] This was soon characterized as a blatant appeal to narrow party and personal loyalty at a time of national peril, and it backfired disastrously.

Sir Samuel Hoare, the Air Minister and the arch-appeaser of the 1930s, spoke next and was badly mauled by a series of interventions from Admiral Keyes, Labour's Hugh Dalton and no fewer than seven other MPs. He was reduced to admitting that the RAF was 'not nearly big enough', a damaging remark from a minister of a government that had been in office for almost the whole of the previous decade. Lloyd George then delivered a devastating speech against the Prime Minister, whom he had hated ever since Chamberlain had helped bring him down in 1922. 'Strategically, we are infinitely worse off' than in 1914, he said, a sobering analysis from the Great War premier.[15] He pointed out that Churchill had been right in the 1930s about German rearmament. When he then said, 'I do not think that the First Lord was entirely responsible for all the things that happened there [that is, Norway],' Churchill rose to interrupt: 'I take complete responsibility for everything that has been done by the Admiralty, and I take my full share of the burden.' Lloyd George continued with the crushing sally, 'The right honourable Gentleman must not allow himself to be converted into an air-raid shelter to keep the splinters from hitting his colleagues.'[16] Lady Alexandra Metcalfe reported to Halifax that Lloyd George's joke left Churchill 'like a fat baby swinging his legs on the front bench trying not to laugh'.[17] Then Lloyd George turned on Chamberlain. 'It is not a question of who are the Prime Minister's friends. It is a far bigger issue . . . I say solemnly that the Prime Minister should give an example of sacrifice, because there is nothing which can contribute more to victory in this war than that he should sacrifice the seals of office.'[18] He sat down, having waited eighteen years for that succulent piece of revenge.

Duff Cooper picked up the theme of Churchill being used to protect

Chamberlain. 'He will be defending with his eloquence those who have so long refused to listen to his counsel,' he said, 'who treated his warnings with contempt and who refused to take him into their own confidence . . . I will beseech my fellow Members not to allow the charm of his eloquence and the power of his personality to carry them away tonight.'[19] Duff Cooper was the first Conservative MP to say that he would be voting against the Government. That morning, Lord Salisbury had urged the Watching Committee not to do that, as he did not think they had the numbers necessary, but as it became clear that as many as thirty National Government MPs might do so, and that even more would abstain, his view changed.[20]

Churchill's problem was well summed up by Harold Nicolson, who wrote, 'On the one hand he has to defend the Services; on the other, he has to be loyal to the Prime Minister. One felt it would be impossible to do this after the debate without losing some of his own prestige, but he manages with extraordinary force of personality to do both things with absolute loyalty and apparent sincerity, while demonstrating by his brilliance that he really has nothing to do with this confused and timid gang.'[21] 'The doubt was in everybody's mind,' recorded Channon, 'would Winston be loyal? He finally rose, and one saw at once that he was in bellicose mood, alive and enjoying himself, relishing the ironical position in which he found himself, i.e. that of defending his enemies, and a cause in which he did not believe . . . How much of the fire was real, how much ersatz, we shall never know.'[22]

By that time, Churchill's friends had effectively insulated the House from what he was going to say. It was not one of his vintage performances. He offered a workmanlike defence of the Government and the Norway Campaign, but a bad-tempered exchange broke out when the Labour MP Emanuel Shinwell interrupted him. Churchill said, 'He skulks in a corner,' a comment he refused to withdraw. A question was then asked whether 'skulks' was parliamentary language, and a drunken Glaswegian Labour MP, Neil Maclean, said he thought Churchill had said 'skunks' rather than 'skulks'.[23] It put Churchill off his stride, in a way that had not happened in the Munich debate, when he had been arguing for a cause in which he passionately believed.

'All day long we have had abuse,' Churchill said in his forty-five minute speech, 'and now honourable Members opposite will not even listen.'[24] When the House calmed down slightly, he argued that German air superiority had been the primary problem in Norway. 'Exception has been taken because the Prime Minister said he appealed to his friends,' Churchill said. 'He thought he had some friends, and I hope he has some friends.

He certainly had a good many when things were going well. I think it would be most ungenerous and unworthy of the British character, and the Conservative Party, to turn in a moment of difficulty without all the processes of grave debate which should be taken.'[25] Churchill's final plea was to 'Let pre-war feuds die, let personal quarrels be forgotten, and let us keep our hatreds for the common enemy.'

'It was interesting and brilliant, but unconvincing,' thought Maisky, who was watching from the gallery.[26] John Reith, who was now minister of information and an MP, was predictably harsher: 'I felt throughout that Churchill was such a hypocrite as he was loving the criticisms against the Government knowing that it was all helping to put him in power. Sickening.'[27] But not all were so damning. Attlee in his draft memoirs wrote of 'a very loyal effort by Churchill to turn the tide'.[28] Leo Amery recalled that 'What really mattered was that it strengthened Churchill's position with the defenders of the Government without weakening it in the eyes of those who saw in him the obvious successor to Chamberlain.'[29] The King was of course not present but was told that 'Winston wound up and made a very good speech, which stopped the rot.'[30] But it had not.

Clementine and Mary were in the gallery. 'The House was in a most uncertain, unpleasant and sensitive and restless mood,' Mary wrote in her diary. 'There were frequent interruptions – also quite a lot of cheering. Papa's handling of the actual matter and of the House was nothing short of *superb*. I listened breathless with pride, apprehension and desire. A storm of interruptions [from Shinwell, Maclean and others] arose making Papa sit down and the speech ended amid catcalls from both sides of the House. There was a spirit of criticism and ferocity to be felt most strongly. Bitter opposition to Chamberlain and many members of the Cabinet even within the ranks of the Tory party.'[31]

Apart from the furore at the end, the debate could hardly have gone better for Churchill. Chamberlain had referred to his 'friends in the House', but six of the seven most powerful interventions in the debate – those from Sinclair, Wedgwood, Keyes, Winterton, Lloyd George and Duff Cooper – were made by members of the Other Club, all of them close friends of Churchill's, some for decades.* The seventh and most powerful speech of all, from Amery, was certainly not hostile to Churchill. The Labour Party had been generally respectful and the Tory backbenchers had not sought to pass the blame for Norway from the Prime Minister on

* As recently as April 1939, Harold Nicolson had noted, 'It is curious that little way that Winston has when he speaks to Lloyd George of calling him "my dear"' (ed. Nicolson, *Diary and Letters* I p. 394).

to him. Indeed throughout the two long days of debate no one placed the blame for a primarily naval campaign on the minister responsible for the Navy. As Morrison had pointed out, Churchill had spoken last and therefore his assertions could not be challenged. It was exceptionally ironic that, although it was Chamberlain who was most criticized for the defeat in Norway, the person who was more directly responsible for it – Churchill – was to benefit most.

When MPs started walking through the voting lobbies, Maisky felt that 'the Chamber buzzed like a disturbed bee-hive.'[32] The division was 'Ayes' 281, 'Noes' 200. A Government majority of only 81, given its technical majority of over 200, was a serious moral defeat for Chamberlain. 'Triumphant roars erupted like a storm from the Opposition benches' when Margesson read out the numbers, wrote Maisky. 'Chamberlain sat in his place, white as chalk.'[33] Some forty-one National Government MPs had voted against him, and, just as importantly, around fifty had abstained. The rebels had included Lady Astor, Bob Boothby, Harold Macmillan, Quintin Hogg, Duff Cooper, John Profumo, Louis Spears, Lord Wolmer, Harold Nicolson, Leslie Hore-Belisha and of course Leo Amery and Admiral Keyes. There were rowdy scenes as Harold Macmillan and Lord Winterton tried to sing 'Rule, Britannia', until they were silenced by furious Tories. Labour MPs shouted, 'You've missed the bus!' at Chamberlain and 'Go, go, go, go!'[34] Chamberlainites shouted back 'Quislings!'* and 'Rats!' at the rebels, who shouted 'Yes-men!' back at them.[35] Channon wrote, 'It was like bedlam.'

Seven months later, Churchill told Jock Colville that the debate had been 'a wonderful opportunity for him: the stars in their courses had fought on his side. He had been able to defend his chief to the utmost and only to win esteem and support in so doing. No one could say he had been disloyal or had intrigued against Chamberlain.'[36]

That night Bracken, who had been told by Attlee that Labour would serve in a Halifax Government, made Churchill promise not to speak first when he and Chamberlain discussed the situation at No. 10 the next day.[37] Beaverbrook, who was prone to self-mythologizing, told the historian John Grigg that the meeting between Bracken and Churchill had been in his flat at Stornoway House on Green Park, and that Churchill 'was inclined to put duty above personal considerations' and serve as minister of defence under Halifax, but that 'It was Bracken who had the decisive influence on Churchill.'[38] Labour Party members were about to leave for

* After the Norwegian traitor Vidkun Quisling, whose Fascist followers had helped the Germans.

their annual party conference in Bournemouth, and Rab Butler had conversations with both Hugh Dalton and Herbert Morrison, who unofficially told him that Labour would enter a Halifax-led government, Dalton adding that 'Churchill must stick to the war.'[39] Butler quickly passed the information on to Halifax.

Thursday, 9 May 1940 was a fine, dry day, with twelve hours of sunshine and a temperature of 65 degrees Fahrenheit. The Government's business managers, led by Lord Dunglass at No. 10 and David Margesson in the Whips Office, tried to ascertain exactly how dangerous the vote had been for the Prime Minister, hoping to limit the damage and allow him to continue in office. 'I can tell you this, you utterly contemptible little shit,' Margesson told John Profumo, a twenty-five-year-old soldier who had been elected to Parliament only two months earlier, 'on every morning that you wake up for the rest of your life you will be ashamed of what you did last night.'[40] By contrast, Alec Dunglass and Sir Horace Wilson emolliently invited leading Tory backbenchers into Downing Street to hear their grievances and tell them that the unpopular Sir John Simon and Sir Samuel Hoare could be dropped from the Government (something Simon and Hoare were not told). At 9 a.m., Chamberlain offered Amery any job in the Government except the premiership. Amery refused, telling the Prime Minister he must resign. The time-honoured practice of throwing loyal colleagues to the wolves having failed, Chamberlain called Halifax over to No. 10 at 10.15 a.m., without telling him that Amery had been offered his job.

Churchill meanwhile had won the allegiance of someone who had hitherto been somewhat aloof, but who now rallied to him. Anthony Eden went over to the Admiralty at 9.30 a.m. and found him shaving. Churchill told him 'He thought that Neville would not be able to bring in Labour and that a National Government must be formed.'[41] At lunch that day, Churchill and Sir Kingsley Wood, the squat Lord Privy Seal and formerly loyal Chamberlainite, told Eden that 'Neville had decided to go. Kingsley thought W should succeed and urged that if asked he should make plain his willingness.' Wood, who Eden thought was 'shrewd, friendly and limited', had either resented being demoted from air minister on 3 April or was simply acting out of opportunism, or both, but his intervention the next day was to prove crucial. Before the war, Wood had been the most pro-German minister in Chamberlain's Government; now he was ready to try to make Churchill prime minister.[42]

When Chamberlain and Halifax met at 10.15 a.m., they agreed that the Labour and Liberal parties had to be brought into the Government, something Halifax had been advocating ever since the car journey back from Heston Aerodrome after Munich. In the very likely event that Labour would refuse to come in under Chamberlain, the Prime Minister asked the Foreign Secretary whether he would form a government, in which he pledged to serve under him. 'I put all the arguments that I could think of against myself,' Halifax wrote in his diary, primarily that of the 'difficult position of a P.M. unable to make contact with the centre of gravity in the House of Commons'.[43] Chamberlain made the obvious point that, because it would be a coalition, little opposition could be expected in the Commons anyhow.

The conversation had a psychosomatic effect on Halifax, giving him a stomach ache. When he returned to the Foreign Office, he told Rab Butler that 'he felt he could do the job. He also felt that Churchill needed a restraining influence. Could that restraint be better exercised if he himself became Prime Minister or as a Minister in Churchill's government? Even if he chose the former role, Churchill's qualities and experience would surely mean that he would be "running the war anyway" and Halifax's own position would speedily turn into a sort of honorary Prime Minister, living in a kind of twilight just outside the things that really mattered.'[44] He knew that his lack of expertise in military matters was unacceptable in a wartime premier. What everyone from Dalton to Halifax now seems to have taken for granted was that, despite Norway, Churchill would soon be in complete control of Britain's war-fighting as an all-powerful minister for the coordination of defence.

With the support of the King, the outgoing Prime Minister, the Labour leadership and enough Conservative MPs to constitute a commanding majority in the Commons, the premiership was theoretically Halifax's for the taking, had he insisted upon it, or had he put personal ambition before the national interest. Chamberlain had not consulted Churchill over the last reshuffle in April, and had he similarly simply gone to the Palace on the morning of 9 May and recommended that the King appoint Halifax, there was nothing Churchill could have done other than promise to serve loyally. As late as March 1940, Chamberlain had written, 'I would rather have Halifax succeed me than Winston.'[45] Churchill certainly could not have refused to serve in wartime simply because he knew he would make a better war leader. He acknowledged as much when he told W. P. Crozier on 26 July, while scooping the ice out of his whisky and soda and throwing it in the coal bucket, 'I owe something to Chamberlain, you know. When he resigned he could have advised the King to send for Halifax and he didn't.'[46] In many ways the meeting between Chamberlain and Halifax alone on the morning of 9 May, where Halifax did not immediately insist on taking the premiership should Labour decline to come into the government under Chamberlain, was more important than the one at which Churchill was present that afternoon.

After his lunch with Wood and Eden, Churchill went to No. 10 to join Chamberlain and Halifax in asking Attlee and Arthur Greenwood to persuade Labour's National Executive Committee in Bournemouth to join a coalition government. Arriving straight from a lunch given at the Reform Club by the extremely anti-Chamberlain Clement Davies, who had warned them that the Prime Minister was hoping to cling on to power, Attlee and Greenwood entered the Cabinet Room and sat at the table across from Chamberlain, who was flanked by Churchill and Halifax.[47] 'Chamberlain pressed us strongly to join his Government and was vigorously supported by Winston,' Attlee later wrote.[48] When Churchill tried to tell them what a charming colleague Chamberlain was, Greenwood cut him off with the words 'We haven't come here to listen to you orating, Winston.'[49]

Attlee and Greenwood agreed to go to Bournemouth to put two questions to the National Executive, which strangely Attlee needed to note down, namely '(1) Would they enter a Government under the present Prime Minister? (2) Would they come in under someone else?' Attlee would telephone the answers to No. 10 the next day.[50] They warned Chamberlain that they thought Labour would be very unlikely to be willing to serve under him – hardly a surprise as Attlee's speech in the Norway Debate had called for 'different people at the helm'.

The King sympathized with his Prime Minister. 'It is most unfair on Chamberlain to be treated like this after all his good work,' he wrote in his diary. 'The Conservative rebels like Duff Cooper and others ought to be ashamed of themselves for deserting him at this moment.'[51] (Duff Cooper had, perhaps not coincidentally, been Edward VIII's only Cabinet supporter during the Abdication Crisis.)

With relatively few MPs in Parliament, Labour did not have the power to choose which Conservative should take over, which considering the pro-Halifax views expressed the previous night by Attlee, Morrison and Dalton was just as well for Churchill. (Despite being an hereditary viscount who had been born in a castle, Halifax had promoted Dominion status for India, and got on well personally with the Labour leadership.) Once Attlee and Greenwood had left, Chamberlain brought in Margesson to discuss with Churchill and Halifax who should become prime minister if Labour refused to join the Government under himself.

What was said at the unminuted meeting between the four men at 4.30 p.m. on 9 May must be pieced together from several different sources of differing levels of trustworthiness. The most plausible account is to be found in the diary of Alec Cadogan, whom Halifax saw immediately afterwards. 'P.M., Winston and I discussed possibilities,' Halifax told him.

> P.M. said I was the man mentioned as the most acceptable. I said it would be a hopeless position. If I was not in charge of the war (operations) and if I didn't lead in the House, I should be a cypher. I thought Winston was a better choice. Winston did *not* demur. Was very kind and polite but showed he thought this [the] right solution. Chief Whip and others think feeling in the House has been veering towards him. If N.C. remains – as he is ready to do – his advice and judgement would steady Winston.[52]

Halifax had been viceroy of India and the close confidant of two prime ministers. In peacetime he could have kept Churchill more or less in order in much the way Lloyd George and Baldwin had, but – as he had admitted to Butler the previous day – he knew that in wartime he would have swiftly been thrown into the shade. Halifax's self-abnegation was therefore well judged.

Churchill's account of the interview was written eight years after the event, got both the date and the time of the interview wrong and omitted Margesson's presence altogether. 'I have had many important interviews in my public life,' he wrote, 'and this was certainly the most important. Usually I talk a great deal, but on this occasion I was silent.'[53] Churchill claimed that only after a 'very long pause', which seemed even longer than the two minutes' silence on Armistice Day, did Halifax, almost out of embarrassment, blurt out the claim that his peerage disqualified him from the premiership, whereupon, Churchill added, 'It was clear that the duty would fall on me – had in fact fallen on me.' In this version, Churchill did not do anything at all except stay silent in order to become prime minister. Margesson, when proofreading a friend's book about 1940 long after the war, did not amend a sentence that read: 'According to Margesson, the silence was in fact a short one, broken almost immediately by Halifax urging Churchill's greater fitness for leadership in war.'[54]

Margesson's role is referred to in a handwritten but undated account by Beaverbrook of a meeting at which he was of course not present, but of which he seems to have been given an inside account by someone, probably Churchill. 'Margesson was called in,' it reads. 'The question was asked in the form of a statement by C denigrating Ch's standing with the Labour Party. Then the Great Silence.'[55] Beaverbrook later wrote, 'It was Margesson's finding that most Tory MPs wanted Halifax as Prime Minister.'[56] This contradicted what Halifax told Cadogan. Even if true, it would not have unduly discomfited Churchill, who knew perfectly well that he was less popular than Halifax with the MPs of both major parties. Churchill – the terror of Tonypandy in Labour mythology – had bad blood with the Labour Party going back to before the General Strike, which had re-emerged in the contretemps with Shinwell only the previous night.

Eden's diary records the information, presumably also gleaned from Churchill, that at the meeting Churchill 'had made it plain' that he hoped Chamberlain would become leader of the House of Commons and continue to lead the Conservative Party, while Churchill became prime minister and minister of defence.[57] This was shrewd: Churchill did not want Tory MPs, bitter about their leader's downfall, feeling free to attack his Government. However unpopular Chamberlain was starting to become over appeasement in the country, he still held great sway over the Tory backbenchers in Parliament.

So did the premiership fall into Churchill's lap, or was it handed to him by Halifax, or did he grasp the opportunity the moment he saw his chance? In 2001, an edition of Joseph P. Kennedy's private papers cast fresh light on events. On 19 October 1940, Neville Chamberlain, by then knowing he was dying of cancer, which had not been diagnosed at the time of the debate, invited Kennedy to his country home to say farewell. The conversation came round to that crucial May meeting, and Chamberlain told Kennedy that after the Labour Party leaders had left 'He then wanted to make Halifax P.M. and said that he would serve under him. Edward, as [is] his way, started saying, "Perhaps I can't handle it being in the H[ouse] of Lords" and Finally Winston said, "I don't think you could." And he wouldn't come and that settled it.'[58] Under this formulation – the only account from Chamberlain about what had happened five months earlier – there is no elongated silence from Halifax as in Churchill's account written eight years later, since the 'Finally' (with a capital 'F') came after Halifax's admission, not before.

It is worth considering alternative accounts that emerged over the years, with the obvious proviso that the tale grew greatly in the telling. In March 1942 in Washington, after discussing the meeting with Beaverbrook, Halifax noted in his diary, 'Winston had no doubt that it ought to be him, and was very much concerned as to what were his best tactics when we all talked it over. These he apparently concluded had better be those of complete silence. I remember him following very much that sort of line at the time.'[59] Also in 1942, Cadogan gave a slightly different version of the story to Sir Miles Lampson in Cairo, in which Halifax's gentlemanly diffidence was taken advantage of by Churchill. In this account, Lampson noted that Chamberlain had said Halifax 'had the best claim. Halifax who really wanted the job . . . replied with his usual and becoming modesty that while he was greatly flattered he wasn't sure whether perhaps Winston had the better qualifications. On this, Neville turned to Winston who at once and much to Halifax's bewilderment replied that he certainly thought he had better qualifications and should be offered the job!'[60]

Churchill remained consistent in this account. In 1947, he told his doctor, Lord Moran, 'I could see from what the Prime Minister said that he wanted Halifax to succeed him. He looked across the table at me, but I said nothing, and there was a very long pause. Then Halifax said that it would be very difficult if the Prime Minister was a peer. I could tell that he had thrown in his hand.'[61] That was very much the version he published the following year in his war memoirs. In the 1950s, Churchill told his Chief Whip, 'For once I did not even have to argue my own case.'[62] When Tommy Thompson's recollections of the war were published in 1963, he claimed that Churchill told him immediately after the interview, 'It was the only time in my life when I have kept my mouth shut.'[63] Of the six relatively contemporaneous accounts of the interview – that is, Halifax's contemporaneous diary entry, Halifax's contemporaneous report to Cadogan, Chamberlain's report to Kennedy, Halifax's report to Cadogan reported to Lampson, Churchill's account to Moran and Churchill's memoirs – in all but the last two (from the late 1940s) Churchill took the premiership rather than waiting for it to be awarded to him.*

It seems extraordinary that the Prime Minister and Foreign Secretary in a wartime emergency saw it as an insuperable constitutional issue that a peer who became prime minister could not sit in the House of Commons, and allowed an arcane constitutional point to decide who should be Britain's war leader at such a perilous time. If Parliament could pass an Act of Attainder condemning Lord Strafford to death by name in 1641, it could also have passed a single-clause Act of Parliament allowing Halifax

* There is another version of the meeting, put out by Jock Colville when he published his diaries, *The Fringes of Power*, in 1985: 'Winston told me several times that when Chamberlain had summoned Lord Halifax and himself to the Cabinet Room he looked at him sharply and said, "Can you see any reason, Winston, why in these days a Peer should not be Prime Minister?" Winston saw a trap in this question. It would be difficult to say yes without saying frankly that he himself should be the choice. If he said no, or hedged, he felt sure that Mr Chamberlain would turn to Lord Halifax and say, "Well, since Winston agrees I am sure that if the King asks me I should suggest his sending for you." Therefore Winston turned his back and gazed out on the Horse Guards Parade without giving any reply. There was an awkward pause, after which Halifax himself volunteered the suggestion that if the King were to ask Mr Chamberlain's opinion about his successor, he should propose Mr Churchill' (Colville, *Fringes* p. 123). In this (much later) version, Chamberlain was presented as trying to trick Churchill, who won the premiership largely out of Lord Halifax's social embarrassment. This might have been a story Churchill told Colville 'several times', but anecdotes do not become truer the more often they are told; if anything the reverse is true.

to speak in the Commons 300 years later. The King, who was meant to be the guardian of the constitution, asked Chamberlain whether Halifax's peerage could not simply be put into what he called 'abeyance'.[64] Here was another perfect opportunity – a suggestion from the guardian of Britain's unwritten constitution – for Chamberlain to stymie Churchill had he wanted to take it.

It might be that everyone was using the peerage as a convenient excuse to get over the fact that Halifax truly did not want the premiership – at least at that time, because he knew he would be quickly and possibly humiliatingly overshadowed by Churchill. It was evident to all the principal actors that the time had come for leadership from the one man who had got Hitler and the Nazis right from the beginning, not sermons from someone who, despite being a godly and decent man, had got him wrong until almost the very end. Although Halifax's speeches at the time were thoughtful and high-minded, they had none of the fire and poetry of Churchill's.

In stating baldly that he did not think Halifax could handle the premiership from the Lords, whether he said it immediately or after a silence (or even a Great Silence), it is clear that Churchill *did* seize the premiership rather than having it handed to him, as he preferred to make out in his memoirs. This would have been completely in accordance with the way he had behaved throughout his life. He had always thrust himself into the arena, and felt no guilt or embarrassment about demanding what he saw as his due. His journey to the Sudan without regimental permission in 1898, his prison-break from Pretoria in 1899, his visit to Sidney Street in 1911, his mobilization of the Grand Fleet without Cabinet authorization in July 1914, his commandeering of the Turkish warships in August 1914, his defence of Antwerp in October 1914, his order to attack Kotlas without Government permission in 1919, his peace-making with Michael Collins in 1921 regardless of the Tory backbenchers, his buying Chartwell in 1922 without agreeing it with Clementine, and his order for the *Cossack* to board the *Altmark* in February 1940 – all these were opportunities grasped, of acting first and leaving the consequences to take care of themselves. His hero Napoleon believed that success was its own justification. In the idiom of the day, Churchill had 'form' in pushing for office going back thirty years, so why should it be any different with the highest office, which he had coveted for even longer?

Churchill had been thrusting in a way that was considered almost unBritish, and was deeply at odds with the cult of the inspired amateur that had been inculcated into so many of his contemporaries by which the prizes of life were meant to drop into one's lap unbidden. Completely rejecting this latter attitude, Churchill had refused Campbell-Bannerman's offer of financial secretary to the Treasury in order to represent the Colonial Office in the Commons, and he had refused Asquith's offer of the chief secretaryship of Ireland, holding out for the home secretaryship instead. He had proposed himself as first lord of the Admiralty to Asquith in 1911 and minister of defence to Lloyd George in 1919, to whom he also forcibly expressed his displeasure at not being made chancellor of the Exchequer in 1921. He had made his desire to be minister of supply obvious to both Baldwin and Chamberlain, and in April 1939 he had taken Margesson out to dinner to inform him 'bluntly of his strong desire to join the Government'.[65] In 1940 he had pushed to be minister of defence de facto if not de jure. Now that the premiership was palpably within his grasp for the first but also possibly the last time, he was not about to defer to a hesitant and to his mind militarily unqualified appeaser. Furthermore, Churchill genuinely believed that his own leadership was more likely to preserve Britain and her Empire than that of Halifax.

For although Clementine had finally given up hope in June 1937 of her husband ever becoming prime minister, he himself never had. That hope had animated him and driven him even when there seemed no likely path leading him to Downing Street. 'In the high position I shall occupy, it will fall to me to save the capital and save the Empire,' he had told Murland Evans when he was sixteen.[66] At the time of Eden's resignation, he had described himself as the unofficial leader of the Opposition, and until the last eight months he had, perhaps ill-advisedly, never bothered to hide his driving ambition. He was fortunate that such was the paucity of talent in British politics that once it was recognized Chamberlain had to go there was virtually no one other than Halifax to contend for the post. Eden, Cranborne and Duff Cooper were the only ministers to have resigned over appeasement, and none was of enough heft to be considered prime ministerial material at the time, and nor were Leo Amery, John Anderson or Lord Chatfield. At forty-four Oliver Stanley was too young. Lloyd George was seventy-seven, pro-peace and even more unpopular with the Establishment than Churchill. He had also hailed Hitler as the German 'Unknown Warrior come to life'. Furthermore, none of these showed anything of Churchill's fascination for war and grand strategy – nor Churchill's hunger for the office. Churchill was also both an insider who had been chancellor and home secretary, and an outsider who had been out of office for all but the final four months of the 1930s. His age, sixty-five, was not held against him as he exuded energy, and was replacing the septuagenarian Chamberlain.

The 4.30 p.m. meeting therefore ended with agreement that Chamberlain would advise the King to send for Churchill if Labour called the next day refusing to serve under Chamberlain. Churchill and Halifax then sat in the garden of No. 10 together for a while. Bob Boothby, who had been in the Commons all day, wrote to Churchill that evening identifying those who would oppose Halifax. 'It is quite a powerful group,' he wrote, not knowing that Halifax was no longer in the running.[67] In fact the fourteen MPs he named were a small, disparate band, mostly obscure backbenchers – anything but a powerful group.

There was not enough time for a concerted public call to be made for Churchill to succeed Chamberlain. It was down to Churchill to take the prize through sheer force of personality, and the momentum that came from having been right about Hitler. At dinner at 8.30 that evening with Eden and Sinclair, Churchill, who Eden thought was 'quiet and calm', reported that, assuming that Labour refused to serve under Chamberlain, the Prime Minister 'would advise the King to send for him. Edward [Halifax] did not wish to succeed. Parliamentary position too difficult.'[68] He offered Eden the War Ministry, which was gratefully accepted.

It might be unpalatable in our more egalitarian era to admit it, but Churchill became prime minister by a process that was far from democratic. He was chosen not by a Cabinet vote, nor by a national election, nor even by an elected committee or caucus of MPs, but by the smallest self-selecting electorate imaginable: Chamberlain, Churchill, Halifax and Margesson. All four men were privately educated: two at Harrow (Churchill and Margesson), one at Rugby (Chamberlain) and one at Eton (Halifax). Three of these four late-middle-aged Englishmen hailed from the upper classes (Margesson was the nephew of an earl) and Chamberlain's father, one of the greatest statesmen of Victorian Britain, would undoubtedly have become a viscount or earl had he survived his stroke. Not only were the Labour and Liberal parties not asked for their opinion, but the sole person required to affirm the choice made by this tiny cabal, completely unrepresentative of the British people, was their unelected hereditary monarch, King George VI. If virtually any other, larger political body had been consulted – the Cabinet, the Privy Council, the Conservative Party, the House of Lords – Halifax would probably have been chosen, especially if the views of the City of London, the BBC, *The Times*, the Church of England and so on had been taken into account. Churchill had made himself eligible through his speeches and broadcasts, through his early appreciation of the Nazi threat and through his persistence in urging his countrymen to readiness, but in May 1940 his judgement was still distrusted by large swathes of the British Establishment.

At dawn the next day, Friday, 10 May 1940, Hitler invaded Luxembourg, Holland and Belgium. The attack that Churchill had correctly anticipated for the spring was now unleashed, though none could have predicted that it would come in the middle of a full-scale British political crisis. The Cabinet met at 8 a.m. and heard of the German attempt to outflank France's Maginot Line. Churchill came up with a proposal to try to sow dissension in Germany by offering the ex-Kaiser, who was living in exile in Holland, asylum in Britain.[69] (In fact Wilhelm II was delighted with Hitler's conquests.) At the meeting, Chamberlain made no mention of his intention to resign, and by 11.30 a.m. had concluded that the military situation was so serious that it justified his postponing his resignation altogether. He asked Attlee for a statement supporting the Government, but when the announcement was made it referred only to the war effort, and made no mention of support for the Government in general or of him in particular.

Sir Horace Wilson, the Permanent Secretary to the Treasury and Head of the Home Civil Service, whom Chamberlain had sent to meet Hitler during the Munich Crisis, was 'especially indignant' about Labour's position. But Kingsley Wood told the Cabinet unequivocally that Hitler's attack now meant that the pressure on Chamberlain to step down immediately had increased rather than decreased. Hoare supported the Prime Minister, but as he later noted, 'No one said anything in the Cabinet except me. Edward [Halifax] quite heartless.'[70] Eden might have written Wood off as 'A useful family solicitor type', but it was this short, squat political nonentity who effectively ended Chamberlain's premiership.[71] He would soon be rewarded with the chancellorship of the Exchequer, just as Margesson's swift footwork at the 4.30 p.m. meeting the previous day ensured that he too was rewarded with high office.

Attlee met the National Executive Committee of the Labour Party in Bournemouth at 3.40 p.m., which unanimously agreed that the Party should enter the Government, but not under Chamberlain.[72] Attlee and Greenwood found a hotel telephone booth from which to telephone the news to No. 10 at 4.45 p.m. and they then caught the 5.15 p.m. to London's Waterloo station.

That afternoon, loyalists around the Prime Minister made yet another effort to persuade Halifax to change his mind. Chamberlain's parliamentary private secretary, Lord Dunglass, telephoned Chips Channon at the Foreign Office to have him ask Rab Butler to talk Halifax round. 'I persuaded Rab to go along to Halifax's room for one last final try,' Channon wrote in his diary; 'he found Halifax had slipped out to go to the dentist's without Rab seeing him – and [Halifax's private secretary] Valentine

Lawford . . . who neglected to tell Halifax that Rab was waiting, may well have played a decisively negative role in history.'[73] Channon 'sat numb with misery'.[74] Had he had any real interest in becoming prime minister at that stage, it seems unlikely that Halifax would have gone to the dentist.

Chamberlain now made his way to Buckingham Palace. 'I saw the PM after tea,' the King recorded in his diary.

> He . . . told me he wished to resign so as to make it possible for a new Prime Minister to form a Government. I accepted his resignation, and told him how grossly unfairly I thought he'd been treated, and that I was terribly sorry that all this controversy had happened. We then had an informal talk about his successor.* I, of course, suggested Halifax, but he told me that H was not enthusiastic, as being in the Lords he could only act as a shadow or a ghost in the Commons, where all the real work took place. I was disappointed over that statement as I thought H was the obvious man, and that his peerage could be placed in abeyance for the time being. Then I knew there was only one person who I could send for to form a government who had the confidence of the country, and that was Winston. I asked Chamberlain his advice, and he told me Winston was the man to send for.[75]

From this account, Chamberlain did not even have to suggest Churchill to the King, who despite all his reservations had already divined him to be the only alternative.

So it was Churchill who was sent for, at six o'clock that evening. 'His Majesty received me most graciously and bade me sit down,' Churchill later wrote. 'He looked at me searchingly and quizzically for some moments, and then said, "I suppose you don't know why I have sent for you?" Adopting his mood, I replied: "Sir, I simply couldn't imagine why." He laughed and said, "I want to ask you to form a Government." I said I would certainly do so.'[76] This charming anecdote, in which the King makes a light joke of the profound importance of appointing a wartime premier while the Germans were attacking, has always been accepted as just that. However, it is clear from the King's own diary account that he genuinely thought Churchill did not know why he had been sent for, and took seriously Churchill's reply to what Churchill had thought was a joke. 'I sent for Winston and asked him to form a Government,' the King wrote in his diary. 'This he accepted and told me that he had not thought this was the reason for my having sent for him. He had thought it possible of

* It is hard to think what would constitute a formal talk, if not a discussion between the King and his outgoing Prime Minister about who should be the next prime minister during a world war.

course, and gave me some of the names of people he would ask to join his Government. He was full of fire and determination to carry out the duties of Prime Minister.'[77]

Back at the Admiralty – Chamberlain would take some time to move out of No. 10 – Detective Inspector Thompson congratulated Churchill, saying that his task was enormous. 'God alone knows how great it is,' the new Prime Minister replied, with tears in his eyes. 'All I hope is that it is not too late. I am very much afraid it is. We can only do our best.'[78] When Attlee and Greenwood reached the Admiralty from Waterloo station, they did not press Churchill over the number of portfolios that Labour were to get in the coalition. Churchill was anyway generous to them, appointing both Attlee and Greenwood to the five-man War Cabinet that was also to include Chamberlain and Halifax.

'He was anxious to get the [news about] the War Cabinet and the Service Ministers out as soon as possible,' Attlee recalled. 'We also discussed other appointments and pretty well settled things on Saturday at one or two meetings.'[79] Churchill admired Attlee's authority, helpfulness, dispatch and lack of opportunism; he remembered it for years and it sealed the respect he had for him. A few days later, the Labour Party Conference endorsed the National Executive's decision to enter the Government by 2,413,000 votes to 170,000.

Churchill was fortunate that Chamberlain was prepared to join his Government, although such was the opposition among Labour MPs and anti-appeasement Tories to the ex-premier becoming leader of the House of Commons that he became lord president of the Council instead. That evening Churchill wrote to him, 'To a large extent I am in your hands,' and asked him to continue as leader of the Conservative Party. Many Tories were furious that they had won the Norway Debate by eighty-one votes but had nevertheless lost their Prime Minister. Chamberlain could have proved a dangerously disruptive colleague, but he and Churchill worked well together, as Churchill showed him regard and even affection at every opportunity. That did not mean that the diehard Chamberlainites showed any regard, let alone affection, for Churchill. At 7.15 p.m., Alec Dunglass and Jock Colville went from No. 10 to the Foreign Office to see Rab Butler and Chips Channon. 'We drank in champagne the health of the "King over the water" (not King Leopold,* but Mr Chamberlain),' wrote Colville.[80] This Jacobite toast from the 1715 Rebellion enjoined loyalty to the Old Pretender, King James II's son, and secret opposition to the new Hanoverian regime. Churchill would have to work hard to win

* King Leopold III of the Belgians, then fighting against the German invasion.

over these three Chamberlainite Tory MPs and his own new assistant private secretary Colville.

At that doleful drinks party, Rab Butler said:

> The good clean tradition of English politics, that of [William] Pitt [the Younger] as opposed to [Charles James] Fox, had been sold to the greatest adventurer of modern political history. He had tried earnestly and long to persuade Halifax to accept the Premiership, but he had failed. He believed this sudden coup of Winston and his rabble was a serious disaster and an unnecessary one: the 'pass had been sold' – by Chamberlain, Halifax and Oliver Stanley. They had weakly surrendered to a half-breed American whose main support was that of inefficient but talkative people of a similar type, American dissidents like Lady Astor and Ronnie Tree.[81]*

This anti-Americanism was not confined to Churchill's political enemies; when he heard his former friend was to become prime minister, Hilaire Belloc asked, 'Are we going to be ruled by that Yankee careerist?'[82]

For Channon, an American himself, 10 May 1940 was 'Perhaps the darkest day in English history', not because Hitler was devastating neutral countries and about to attack France, but because of the fall of his hero Neville Chamberlain.[83] 'We were all sad, angry and felt cheated and outwitted,' he wrote.[84] Halifax told Butler that day, 'The gangsters will shortly be in complete control.'[85]

Hitler's attack turned Churchill's perceived weaknesses into priceless assets almost overnight. His obvious interest in warfare was no longer warmongering, it was invaluable. His oratorical style, which many had derided as ham-acting, was sublime now that the situation matched his rhetoric. His obsession with the Empire would help to bind its peoples together as it came under unimaginable stress, and his chauvinism left him certain that, if they could get through the present crisis, the British would prevail over the Germans. Even his inability to fit comfortably into any political party was invaluable in the leader of a government of national unity.

At 9 p.m. Chamberlain announced his resignation in a broadcast to the nation, and urged everyone to support his successor. Princess Elizabeth, then aged fourteen, told her mother that it had moved her to tears. That night, Margot Asquith went to commiserate with Chamberlain at No. 10. 'He said that no one could have been nicer than Winston,' she recorded, 'that nothing just now mattered in any way about *him* – or about *any*

* Although Nancy Astor had voted No after the Norway Debate, she was no supporter of Churchill's, and Tree was an Edenite.

individual – all that mattered was that they should be *united*.' Lady Asquith could not of course resist a tart remark, writing, 'I looked at his spare frame and keen eye and could not help comparing it with Winston's self-indulgent rotundity.'[86]

Churchill worked into the night constructing his first Government. 'I was conscious of a profound sense of relief,' he later wrote. 'At last I had the authority to give direction over the whole scene. I felt as if I were walking with destiny, and that all my past life had been but a preparation for this hour and for this trial . . . I thought I knew a good deal about it all, and I was sure I should not fail. Therefore, although impatient for the morning, I slept soundly and had no need for cheering dreams. Facts are better than dreams.'[87] He expressed the determination and anxiety of that momentous day when he spoke to Lord Moran in 1947, rather more colloquially than he did in his memoirs: 'I could discipline the bloody business at last. I had no feeling of personal inadequacy, or anything of that sort. I went to bed at three o'clock, and in the morning I said to Clemmie, "There is only one man who can turn me out and that is Hitler."'[88]

# PART TWO
# The Trial

# 21
# The Fall of France May–June 1940

*When a country undergoes so frightful a catastrophe as France, every other evil swarms down upon her like carrion crows.*

Churchill to Clementine, January 1943[1]

*I displayed the smiling countenance and confident air which are thought suitable when things are very bad.*

Churchill writing of June 1940, *Their Finest Hour*[2]

Churchill certainly did know 'a good deal about it all' by the time he became prime minister, having held every great office of state except the Foreign Office. Aged sixty-five, he was superbly prepared – in experience, psychology and foresight – for the coming hour and trial. At twenty-three, he had identified the five aspects of rhetoric that moved the human heart, and over the following four decades he had perfected them. At twenty-five, he had written that if Britain were ever invaded 'there would be some – even in these modern days – who would not care to accustom themselves to a new order of things and tamely survive the disaster,' and in October 1912 he started to think where the Germans might land an invasion force.[3] As early as May 1901 he had warned that a European war would be 'a cruel, heart-rending struggle, which, if we are ever to enjoy the bitter fruits of victory, must demand, perhaps for several years, the whole manhood of the nation, the entire suspension of peaceful industries, and the concentrating to one end of every vital energy in the community'.[4]

In the debate on the Finance Bill of 1903, Churchill had said that 'He had always thought that it ought to be the main end of English statecraft over a long period of years to cultivate good relations with the United States,' asking 'in times of war what greater security could they have for the food supply across the Atlantic'?[5] In 1907 he had visited East Africa, where between June 1940 and November 1941 Britain was to enjoy her first strategic land victory of the war. In 1909 he had urged his colleagues in government to contact Orville Wright to 'avail ourselves of his knowledge'.[6] In March 1913, in a debate on the Navy Estimates, he envisaged the House of Commons being bombed from the air, and only a year later foresaw how 'The war aeroplane flying in its own country, unhampered . . . and close to its base, must be a far more efficient fighting instrument than any similar craft that could come across the seas.'[7] The Battle of Britain and the Blitz were to find him mentally prepared. Of his lifelong interest in aerial warfare, he was accurately to write in his war memoirs, 'Although I have never tried to be learned in technical matters, this mental field was well lit for me.'[8]

Churchill's fascination with science and new weaponry – of which the aeroplane and the tank were only the most prominent – was another key preparation for his premiership, as was his demand in August 1917 that a report on tank production be sent him 'on a single sheet of paper'.[9] Churchill had gained a good deal of his scientific knowledge from Professor Lindemann, and back in September 1924 he had written an article about nuclear bombs in the *Pall Mall Gazette*, anticipating by fifteen years Albert Einstein's letter to President Roosevelt about the possibility of producing one. 'Might not a bomb no bigger than an orange be found to possess a secret power', Churchill had asked, 'to blast a township at a stroke?' He had also foreseen the V-1 and V-2 missiles, wondering, 'Could not explosives, even of the existing type, be guided automatically in flying machines by wireless or other rays, without a human pilot, in ceaseless procession upon a hostile city, arsenal, camp or dockyard?'[10]

Churchill's creation of the code-breaking unit Room 40 at the Admiralty in the Great War, the first such agency in seventy years, had taught him the value of receiving raw, unprocessed intelligence data, rather than having it passed through committees. This stood him in excellent stead in the Second World War, and he had also learned from observing Sir Douglas Haig's Intelligence Department that 'The temptation to tell a chief in a great position the things he most likes to hear is one of the commonest explanations of mistaken policy. Thus the outlook of the leader on whose decisions fateful events depend is usually far more sanguine than the brutal facts admit.'[11]

As minister of munitions in the Great War, Churchill had run what he had accurately described as 'the biggest purchasing business and industrial employer in the world'.[12] His frequent visits to the front and to the headquarters of the BEF presaged the way that he familiarized himself with the situation in the subsequent conflict. 'The war will be long and sombre,' he had warned the National Liberal Club in September 1914, not believing in sugaring the pill.[13] 'Trust the people' had been his father's motto, and in November 1914 he considered the possibility of fighting on if France fell, telling the House of Commons, 'even if we were single-handed, as we were in the days of the Napoleonic wars, we should have no reason to despair of our capacity . . . to go on indefinitely.'[14] As early as 1932, even before Hitler came to power, Churchill had told the Commons, 'Tell the truth to the British people. They are a tough people, a robust people. They may be a bit offended at the moment, but if you have told them exactly what is going on you have insured yourself against complaints and reproaches which are very unpleasant when they come home on the morrow of some disillusion.'[15] His attitudes and convictions during the Second World War had deep roots.

The Great War strategy of encircling, blockading, battering and simply outnumbering the enemy had been explained by Churchill in a speech of May 1916, when he said, 'If the Germans are to be beaten decisively, they will be beaten like Napoleon was beaten and like the Confederates were beaten – that is to say, by being opposed by superior numbers along fronts so extensive that they cannot maintain them or replace the losses incurred along them.'[16] He was to say much the same thing pursuing his African, Mediterranean and Balkan strategies at Allied conferences in 1943 and 1944. 'It was a war of the circumference against the centre,' he had written of Marlborough's strategy, and so would the Western Allies' strategy be 240 years later.[17] Similarly, Churchill's extraordinary memorandum of April 1918 suggesting that Lenin be persuaded to re-enter the war – 'Let us never forget that Lenin and Trotsky are fighting with ropes around their necks' – meant that he was not left hesitating when he needed to ally himself with Stalin once Hitler had betrayed the Nazi–Soviet Pact.[18]

As first lord of the Admiralty before the Great War Churchill had kept Asquith informed of events and his thoughts with regular letters, which have rightly been described as 'lengthy, cogent, well-argued and informative documents'.[19] He was the master of the departmental minute, a preparation that was to put him in good stead in his wartime correspondence with President Roosevelt. That crucial relationship was all the stronger for his writing of *Marlborough*, in which he lauded his great ancestor for the way he pursued his ends despite all the 'intrigues, cross-purposes, and half-measures of a vast unwieldy coalition trying to make war'.[20]

Churchill was about to enter by far the most strenuous half-decade of his life, but he did it fortified by sixty-five years of conscious or unconscious preparation. He had told the Royal Society of St George in April 1933, with rhetoric that was to be characteristic of his wartime oratory, that 'It may well be that the most glorious chapters of our history are yet to be written. Indeed, the very problems and dangers that encompass us and our country ought to make English men and women of this generation glad to be here at such a time. We ought to rejoice at the responsibilities with which destiny has honoured us, and be proud that we are guardians of our country in an age when her life is at stake.'[21]

By May 1940, Churchill's personality had been shaped by his experiences so completely that it was not to change perceptibly for the rest of his life. The singleness of purpose was there, of course, which merged into an undeniable ruthlessness when the occasion demanded – which it was now often to do. Yet allied to that was a calmness under pressure and a sense of humour that allowed him to crack jokes however bad the situation got. His experiences under fire on battlefields as far afield as Spion Kop in the Boer War and the Western Front in the Great War had left him with no very high opinion of military experts, which was also to prove useful in the series of defeats that were about to befall British arms. He had made many catastrophic errors in his long career, but, as we shall see, he had learned from them.

One of the pieces of advice that Churchill had given Georges Clemenceau during the Great War had been 'to forget old quarrels . . . In England we . . . make many muddles, but we always keep more or less together.'[22] On Saturday, 11 May 1940, Churchill started appointing the rest of his Government, a delicate balancing act between the three major parties and the factions within them. He would have to offset the competing expectations of his friends and supporters with those of the bitter Chamberlainites who formed the majority in the Commons. Clement Attlee was given the non-portfolio post of lord privy seal but also became deputy leader of the House of Commons, while Neville Chamberlain was made chairman of various important Cabinet committees that dealt with the home front. Arthur Greenwood, the Deputy Leader of the Labour Party, became minister without portfolio, with a seat in the War Cabinet. 'I did not like having unharnessed ministers around me,' Churchill wrote later. 'I preferred to deal with chiefs of organizations rather than counsellors. Everyone should do a good day's work and be accountable for some definite task, and then they do not make trouble for trouble's sake or to cut a figure.'[23]

Sir John Anderson, who was always more an extremely competent civil servant than a politician, remained as home secretary and Kingsley Wood was appointed chancellor of the Exchequer. The Service ministers were calibrated carefully between the parties, with the Conservative Anthony Eden becoming secretary for war, the Liberal Party leader Archie Sinclair becoming air minister and Labour's A. V. Alexander succeeding Churchill as first lord of the Admiralty. Although Halifax could not be moved from the Foreign Office, the other leading appeasers were carefully prised away from positions of power. Hoare was given a post where his propensity for appeasing Fascist dictators could do his country some good: as ambassador to Franco's Spain. Simon was 'kicked upstairs' to the lord chancellorship for the rest of the war, and Hankey was moved out of the War Cabinet to the chancellorship of the Duchy of Lancaster, the ministerial backwater Churchill himself had so despised in 1915.

'I must say that Winston has been most handsome in his appreciation of my willingness to help and my ability to do so,' Chamberlain wrote to Ida on 11 May. 'I know that he relies on Halifax and me.'[24] It was true, but that did not mean that Churchill's myrmidons had to respect Chamberlain's. That morning, Sir Horace Wilson, Chamberlain's closest adviser, whom Churchill magnanimously allowed to retain both of his high-ranking jobs in the Civil Service, despite having been a leading appeaser, turned up for work at No. 10 as usual. Churchill ordered him to empty his desk and leave Downing Street by 2 p.m. At lunchtime Wilson sent a message asking for extra time, whereupon Churchill told Bracken, 'Tell that man if that room is not cleared by 2 p.m. I will make him Minister to Iceland.'[25] (Britain had occupied Iceland the day before, to deny it to the Germans.) When Wilson returned from lunch he found Bracken sitting at his desk and Randolph on his sofa, both smoking large cigars.[26] His belongings were piled up in the corridor. Wilson left without a word, and his career ended as soon as he reached the earliest Civil Service retirement age of sixty in 1942.

Lord Beaverbrook's appointment as minister of aircraft production drove the King to write a handwritten note of protest, but despite his romantic monarchism Churchill firmly insisted on his right to appoint the man who was during the Battle of Britain to have the most important job in the Government after his own.[27] Similarly, when Churchill asked for Bracken to join the Privy Council, complaints arose from Buckingham Palace because of his murky background. Relations between Churchill and the King were good, and were about to become excellent, but there were still occasional crinks, and this might have proved one. 'Mr Bracken is a Member of Parliament of distinguished standing and exceptional ability,' Churchill to wrote to Sir Alec Hardinge, the King's private secretary. 'He has sometimes been almost my sole supporter in the years when I have been striving to get this country properly defended, especially from the air. He suffered as I have done every form of official hostility. Had he joined the ranks of the time-servers and careerists who were assuring the public that our air force was larger than that of Germany, I have no doubt that he would long ago have attained high office.'[28] Bracken was appointed to the Privy Council forthwith, a sign of political success even though the body was largely honorific.

Beaverbrook was an erratic ally, but constantly energetic and galvanizing. The previous November, Maisky had noted that Beaverbrook on one day 'might praise [Churchill] as Britain's greatest statesman, on another he might call him a "swindler", "turncoat" or "political prostitute"'.[29] The new minister lunched with Churchill at the Admiralty on 10, 11 and 12 May. He was so pleased to be back in the Churchillian fold that, as the Tory MP Beverley Baxter said, 'he is like the town tart who has finally married the Mayor!'[30] Moran correctly spotted that because Beaverbrook was 'almost the last of those who had lived with him through the shocks and strains of the First World War . . . it comforted the P.M. to talk to [him], and to compare their troubles with those they had had to overcome in the First World War'.[31]* Beaverbrook stimulated Churchill – 'Some people take drugs,' he once said; 'I take Max.'[32] Churchill reckoned that he would fling himself into the vital task of turning out the maximum number of fighter planes in the months ahead. He would be proved right.[33]

When Randolph complained that David Margesson had retained his job as chief whip, despite having orchestrated opposition to his father, Churchill replied, 'I do not think there is anyone who could advise me better about all those elements in the Tory party who were so hostile to us in recent years. I have to think of unity, and I need all the help I can get.'[34] Speaking to Eden he 'consoled himself with [the] reflection that M would whip with as much energy for us as against us!'[35] Bracken wrote Churchill a note warning that Margesson (whom he nicknamed 'the Parachutist', possibly because, like the Germans in Norway, he had successfully dropped into enemy territory) 'disliked a number of our friends', but this did not prevent the Prime Minister from inviting Margesson to help fill the junior Government posts, something he had no time to do himself. Margesson served his new master with commendable loyalty, becoming secretary for war before the year was out.

Duff Cooper became minister of information, taking over from Sir John Reith, who confided to his diary, 'How filthy this treatment – and what a *rotten* government.'[36] Reith was nonetheless quick to accept the Ministry of Transport from Churchill, who had little inkling of the depths of Reith's contempt for him. Ernest Bevin was found a seat in Parliament and was appointed minister of labour, a vital post controlling the country's

* The others were Smuts, Spears and Keyes, though none was as close to Churchill as Beaverbrook at this time.

manpower resources and industrial relations, which he held throughout the war.

Oliver Stanley, who had fallen out with Churchill during the Norway campaign, turned down the Dominions Office because he did not like Churchill's tone of voice in offering it.[37] (Churchill nonetheless gave him another chance when he appointed him colonial secretary in November 1942.) Hore-Belisha refused both the Ministry of Information and the Board of Trade, whereupon Churchill growled, 'If you attack me I shall strike back and remember, while you have a 3.7-inch gun I have a 12-inch gun.'[38]

Churchill brought people in from outside the Commons, as Lloyd George had done in the Great War. As well as Reith and Beaverbrook, he gave ministries to businessmen: Sir Andrew Duncan at the Board of Trade and Lord Woolton as minister for food, and, later, Oliver Lyttelton, a banker who became minister for war production. Woolton's junior minister, Bob Boothby, was dissatisfied with his lowly position. When Clement Davies got no post at all, despite his role in bringing down Chamberlain, Boothby said it showed Churchill 'did not treat his friends well'.[39] That was certainly not true. Churchill could not fit everyone into his government, and his nurturing of friendships through the years of adversity meant that by 1940 he was in a position to appoint trusted people to key positions. Boothby just was not one of them. Lindemann became the Government's chief scientific adviser (though his role extended far beyond that), Lord Lloyd took over as colonial secretary and Lord Cranborne as paymaster-general, while Lord Moyne and Harold Macmillan became parliamentary secretaries at respectively Agriculture and the Ministry of Supply. Later in the war, Churchill found junior places for his son-in-law Duncan Sandys and his friend James de Rothschild.

The most important of all of Churchill's appointments, however, was of himself to the new position of minister of defence. 'The Minister of Defence represents the Service Ministers in the War Cabinet,' he explained to the Commons, 'and he, in the name of the War Cabinet and subject to its accord, directs the conduct of the war. The Minister of Defence is also Prime Minister, and he can therefore exercise his general function of superintendence and direction without impinging upon the constitutional responsibilities of the Service Ministers.'[40] Churchill had proposed a ministry of defence to Lloyd George in July 1919, but it was misinterpreted as a power-grab.[41] The Ministry itself did not come into existence until 1964, but the post of minister of defence in May 1940 was a clear statement about who was in charge. Churchill had run huge departments before, so he knew how the machinery of government worked. The Admiralty, War Office and Treasury were among the largest ministries in Whitehall, and as minister of munitions he had overseen 2½ million workers. In each case, except at the ultra-conservative Treasury, he had instituted new organizational structures, energizing the departments. He did the same thing as prime minister, placing himself unequivocally at the centre of the Government, ready to amalgamate ministries or create new ones if necessary.

Churchill immediately created a powerful Defence Committee (Operations) of the Cabinet, which he chaired and through which the Chiefs of Staff Committee's recommendations were funnelled to the War Cabinet. He or Attlee would chair the meetings comprised of the three Service ministers, the three Chiefs of Staff, the Foreign Secretary and any other ministers deemed necessary on an ad hoc basis. 'It was the politicians who ran the war,' Averell Harriman, Roosevelt's envoy, succinctly put it in his memoirs.[42] Diehard Chamberlainites disapproved. 'Churchill being defence minister as well as P.M.,' noted Reith. 'Heaven help us.'[43]

The new arrangements were the culmination of a lifetime's thought about civil–military relations. 'I was ruined for the time being in 1915 over the Dardanelles,' Churchill explained in his war memoirs, 'and a supreme enterprise was cast away, through my trying to carry out a major and cardinal operation of war from a subordinate position. Men are ill-advised to try such ventures. This lesson had sunk into my nature.'[44] 'It took Armageddon to make me Prime Minister,' he told Boothby. 'But now I am determined that power shall be in no other hands but my own. There will be no more Kitcheners, Fishers or Haigs.'[45] Fortunately Clement Attlee, who admired Churchill as a strategist, approved of this approach. 'My own experience of the First World War, and my readings in history,' he was later to write, 'had convinced me that the Prime Minister should be a man who knew what war meant, in terms of the personal suffering of the man in the line, in terms of high strategy, and in terms of that crucial issue – how the generals got on with their civilian bosses.'[46] The two men quickly established a relaxed and trusting working relationship.*

The military assistant secretary to the War Cabinet, Colonel Ian Jacob (son of the Other Club member Field Marshal Sir Claud Jacob), became a key figure in the disciplined, good-natured, intelligent and ferociously efficient entourage that Churchill built around him. Jacob worked directly under Ismay, and described the impact of the new arrangements. 'Previously we had seen this dynamo threshing around unharnessed and uncentred, dislocating and disrupting, even destroying from time to time,' he wrote. 'Now, with the dynamo in the right place, it was a different

* When Attlee fell over a bench in the Commons Chamber, Churchill joked, 'Get up, get up, Lord Privy Seal! This is no time for levity' (*CIHOW* p. 321).

story . . . Once the Prime Minister had been more or less harnessed to the machinery, the effects were terrific. Things began to hum, and they hummed till the end of the war. It is impossible to put into words the change that we felt. His power seemed to be turned on all the time.'[47] Although Chamberlain had tried to fight the war by delegation, Churchill would not. 'It hardly seems necessary to emphasize', Jacob added afterwards, 'that the P.M. cannot delegate his activities to a Minister of Defence or other Ministers. The task of conducting the war in both its civil and military aspects must be carried out by the Prime Minister.'[48]

This accretion of power did not mean that Churchill had become a dictator, as his detractors then and subsequently tried to make out. He needed to secure the agreement of the Chiefs of Staff and vice versa, and crucially he never once rejected their unanimous professional advice on an operational matter in the entire course of the war. 'I cannot say that we never differed among ourselves,' he said in a truly glorious understatement in his memoirs, 'but a kind of understanding grew up between me and the British Chiefs of Staff that we should convince and persuade rather than try to overrule each other. This was of course helped by the fact that we spoke the same technical language, and possessed a large common body of military doctrine and war experience . . . There was no division, as in the previous war, between politicians and soldiers, between the "Frocks" and the "Brass Hats" – odious terms which darkened counsel.'[49]

The British constitution was full of powers that existed, often for historical reasons, but were never used. Monarchs could theoretically refuse to sign Bills into law, for example, or declare war without the sanction of Parliament, but long before George VI's time they did neither. Churchill's ability as minister of defence to overrule the Chiefs of Staff, a prerogative he never exercised, was one of these. There were plenty of fraught meetings over the next five years, so tense that one can see where Churchill's signet ring dug a groove into the arm of his chair in the Central War Rooms when he rubbed and thumped it, but they did not go beyond the bounds of acceptable disagreements among gentlemen (although the handsets of telephones regularly had to be changed as Churchill banged them on the desk when he got bad connections).

'I spent the day in a bright blue new suit from the Fifty-Shilling Tailors,' wrote Jock Colville on 13 May, 'cheap and sensational looking, which I felt was appropriate to the new Government.'[50] The Churchills were initially as doubtful of Colville as he was of them. Mary described how at first 'I suspected him – rightly, on both counts! – of being a "Chamberlainite" and a "Municheer".'[51] Yet Colville was already admitting to his diary that with Eden, Duff Cooper, Lord Lloyd and Morrison in the

Government it 'should be able to get things done. Moreover the Government has the complete confidence of the country.' Colville soon became a convinced Churchillian, which he remained for life, and was one of the principal witnesses of much of what Churchill said and did during the Second World War.

Beginning on 10 May, the French Army and the British Expeditionary Force (BEF) had moved north to the River Dyle in central Belgium to meet the German attack through neutral Holland and Belgium. But General Erich von Manstein executed a 'sickle-cut' manoeuvre behind them, and on 12 May fast-moving German armoured columns supported by Stuka dive-bombers suddenly emerged from the heavily forested and mountainous Ardennes, which had previously been thought impassable, and made straight for the Channel coast. 'Poor people,' Churchill told Ismay as they walked from the Admiralty to Downing Street that day, as the news came in of the surprise German attack. 'They trust me, and I can give them nothing but disaster for quite a long time.'[52]

The next afternoon, at 2.45 on Monday, 13 May, Churchill made his first speech as prime minister. The Commons was still in ferment over the new Government, whose membership was still being announced. Channon recorded that Ernest Brown, a National Liberal MP demoted from minister of labour to minister for Scotland, despite his being English, 'inveighed against Winston; others did likewise'.[53] When Chamberlain entered the Chamber, MPs rose to their feet, cheered, waved their order papers and gave him what one of them described as 'a terrific reception'. It showed how right Churchill had been to include him in the Government.[54] Churchill's own entry moments later was far more muted, as he and others were to remark several times over the coming months.[55] The Labour benches gave what Maisky described as 'relatively feeble applause', while 'most Tories remained silent. But Churchill didn't seem to mind.'[56] In the House of Lords the announcement of the new Government by Lord Halifax was received in dead silence.[57] 'I don't think Winston will be a very good P.M.,' Halifax wrote in his diary that day, 'though I think the country will think he gives them a fillip.'[58]

Churchill's speech lasted only seven minutes, but it was one of the greatest ever made in the House of Commons, and one of the triumphs of his oratory:

> I would say to the House, as I said to those who have joined this Government: 'I have nothing to offer but blood, toil, tears and sweat.' We have before us an ordeal of the most grievous kind. We have before us many, many long

months of struggle and of suffering. You ask, what is our policy? I will say: It is to wage war, by sea, land and air, with all our might and with all the strength that God can give us; to wage war against a monstrous tyranny never surpassed in the dark, lamentable catalogue of human crime. That is our policy. You ask, what is our aim? I can answer in one word: It is victory, victory at all costs, victory in spite of all terror, victory, however long and hard the road may be; for without victory, there is no survival. Let that be realized; no survival for the British Empire, no survival for all that the British Empire has stood for, no survival for the urge and impulse of the ages, that Mankind will move forward towards its goal. But I take up my task with buoyancy and hope. I feel sure that our cause will not be suffered to fail among men. At this time I feel entitled to claim the aid of all, and I say, 'Come then, let us go forward together with our united strength.'[59]

These were the notes that Churchill would strike repeatedly over the coming months and years: gravely defiant, evoking the Empire, never minimizing the dangers and difficulties ahead, seeking to inspire courage, while holding out the ultimate prospect of victory over Hitler. To a population craving direction at a bewildering time, when there was a strong peace movement as well as a vacuum of leadership at the top of politics, Churchill's words were a clarion call to which they responded immediately and overwhelmingly positively.*

After he had sat down, Lloyd George made a speech in support of Churchill, in which he spoke of their friendship, during which Nicolson observed, 'Winston cries slightly and mops his eyes.'[60] As he left the Chamber, Churchill said to Desmond Morton, 'That got the sods, didn't it?'[61] But it had not. 'The new PM spoke well, even dramatically,' wrote Channon, 'but he was not well received.'[62] Two Tory MPs expressed their anger and regret that Chamberlain had lost the premiership. Sir Stafford Cripps somewhat ominously said, 'I do not desire to make any criticism of the right honourable Gentleman or his Government, favourable or otherwise.'[63] The vote on whether 'This House welcomes the formation of a Government representing the united and inflexible resolve of the nation

* The most memorable phrase of the speech had had a long and elaborate genesis. A correspondence in the *Manchester Guardian* pointed out that Livy, Cicero and Pizarro had written of blood, sweat and toil – though tears were a characteristic Churchillian addition. In 1611 John Donne had rhapsodized about 'tears, or sweat, or blood' in one of his religious sonnets, however, and A. E. Housman's sequence of poems *A Shropshire Lad* contains 'Tears . . . sweat . . . blood'. (Weidhorn, *Rhetoric* p. 134 n. 22.) The phrase 'blood and sweat and tears' appeared in one of Theodore Roosevelt's speeches in 1897, and Churchill had used 'blood and sweat' in *London to Ladysmith*. He had also mentioned 'blood, sweat and tears' in a *Daily Telegraph* article on General Franco. (*CIHOW* pp. 4, 33.)

to prosecute the war with Germany to a victorious conclusion' was won by 381 to nil, but the absence of real enthusiasm was unmistakable.

After the debate, Churchill offered Lloyd George the Ministry of Agriculture, an offer which he repeated several times that month; Lloyd George refused it each time, ostensibly on the grounds that he could not sit at the Cabinet table with Chamberlain, but really because he was already calculating his chances of succeeding Churchill should he fail. In October, he told A. J. Sylvester, his private secretary, 'I shall wait until Winston is bust.'[64] Over the course of the war he grew increasingly bitter. 'Lloyd George is in an irritable, carping mood,' Maisky wrote after visiting him at Churt in May 1943. 'Especially when it comes to Churchill. Lloyd George finds something dark and sinister in whatever Churchill does. Might it be because the old man has been twiddling his thumbs during this war, and is now taking it out on Churchill?'[65]

On the evening of the next day, 14 May, news arrived that the Germans were about to break through the French Army's defensive positions at Sedan in the Ardennes, just south of the Franco-Belgian border. At 7 p.m. the War Cabinet met to consider Paul Reynaud's urgent request for more RAF fighter squadrons to be sent to France immediately. 'Very gloomy and unpleasant meeting,' noted Cadogan.[66] The RAF had scored some outstanding successes on the first day of the attack, when the Allies shot down 353 German planes, one-sixth of their total, but in the first four days of fighting they themselves had lost 260 planes out of a front-line operational force of 474 planes.[67] 'We should hesitate before we denude still further the heart of the Empire' was Churchill's initial response.[68]

Like all his colleagues and the Allied commanders, Churchill was surprised by the sheer speed with which the German Blitzkrieg – a new type of warfare that closely coordinated air and ground power – sliced through the French Army and the BEF. In January 1939 he had written that, although tanks had made a 'glorious' contribution to victory in 1918, he doubted they would 'play as decisive part in the next war . . . nowadays, the anti-tank rifle and the anti-tank gun have made such great strides that the poor tank cannot carry a thick enough skin to stand up to them'.[69] He had also misjudged the role of air power, writing, 'So far as fighting troops are concerned, it would seem that aircraft are an additional complication rather than a decisive weapon.'[70] He was wrong on both counts – but once again he would learn quickly.

At 7.30 the next morning, Reynaud telephoned Churchill to say that the German panzers had now comprehensively broken through at Sedan, that the road to Paris lay open and that France desperately needed RAF fighter squadrons to save the capital, as well as for bombing raids on the Ruhr.

Later that morning, Holland surrendered. Air Chief Marshal Sir Hugh 'Stuffy' Dowding, head of Fighter Command, made a special request to attend the Defence Committee meeting at 10.15 a.m., at which Beaverbrook, Air Marshal Charles Portal, head of Bomber Command, and Air Chief Marshal Sir Cyril Newall, the Chief of the Air Staff, were also present. Dowding showed them a graph depicting the losses his fighter squadrons were suffering. He now had only thirty-six squadrons instead of the fifty-six he had been promised when the war broke out and the fifty-eight which the Air Council had estimated was the minimum necessary to defend Britain.[71] Even that had been based on the assumption that Britain would be attacked from Germany rather than from France.

'If the present rate of wastage continues for another fortnight,' Dowding told the Defence Committee, 'we shall not have a single Hurricane left in France or in this country.'[72] He laid particular emphasis on the last four words. Complete silence followed his report. Beaverbrook later claimed that Dowding had thrown down his pencil in exasperation and threatened to resign, although no one else recalled that. Accounts also differ over figures Dowding gave of the remaining squadrons – Churchill claimed in his memoirs that he had said twenty-five, not thirty-six – and whether the key moment came at the Defence Committee at 10.15 a.m. or the War Cabinet at 11.30 a.m.[73] What is indisputable, however, is that Churchill and his advisers had to decide how many aircraft they should allocate to France and to Britain, and they were in no doubt about Dowding's views on the matter.[74]

Dowding wrote a letter to Harold Balfour, the Under-Secretary of State for Air, immediately after the meeting summing up what he had told the Defence Committee: that within the last few days, the equivalent of ten squadrons had been sent to France and the Hurricane squadrons remaining in Britain were seriously depleted, leaving only twenty-five in the whole country. 'I must therefore request that as a matter of paramount urgency', he wrote, 'the Air Ministry will consider and decide what level of strength is to be left to the Fighter Command for the defences of this country, and will assure me that when this level is reached, no fighter will be sent across the Channel however urgent and insistent the appeals for help may be . . . If the Home Defence Force is drained away in desperate attempts to remedy the situation in France, defeat in France will involve the final, complete and irremediable defeat of this country.'[75]

Despite Dowding's warning, at 11.30 a.m. the War Cabinet agreed to dispatch an extra four squadrons to France immediately. Preparations were also made for two more to be made available at short notice, although the French would be informed only about the four.[76] It was also agreed that Bomber Command should attack railways and oil refineries in the Ruhr and other military objectives east of the Rhine, in raids of up to one hundred bombers. Cadogan wrote in his diary, 'Now the Total War begins!'[77]

'As you are no doubt aware,' Churchill telegraphed to President Roosevelt that day, 'the scene has darkened swiftly. The enemy has a marked preponderance in the air, and their new technique is making a deep impression upon the French.'[78] Of course the Blitzkrieg had made a deep impression on the British as well, but Churchill was not going to admit that yet. 'The small countries are simply smashed up, one by one, like matchwood,' he continued, adding that soon Mussolini 'will hurry in to share the loot of Civilization. We expect to be attacked here ourselves, both from the air and by parachute and airborne troops in the near future, and are getting ready for them. If necessary, we shall continue the war alone, and we are not afraid of that. But I trust you realize, Mr President, that the voice and force of the United States may count for nothing if they are withheld too long. You may have a completely subjugated Nazified Europe established with astonishing swiftness, and the weight may be more than we can bear.'[79]

He urged that the United States help arm the United Kingdom, in particular asking for 'the loan of forty or fifty of your older destroyers to bridge the gap between what we have now and the large new construction we put in hand at the beginning of the war'.[80] He also wanted 'several hundred of the latest types of aircraft', which he said 'can be repaid by those now being constructed in the United States for us. Thirdly, anti-aircraft equipment and ammunition, of which again there will be plenty next year, if we are alive to see it.' He wanted to buy steel, as the ore supply from Sweden, Africa and Spain had been 'compromised'. 'We shall go on paying dollars for as long as we can, but I should like to feel reasonably sure that when we can pay no more, you will give us the stuff all the same.' He wanted an American naval squadron to make a prolonged visit to Northern Ireland to dissuade German parachute attacks there, and 'Sixthly, I am looking to you to keep that Japanese dog quiet in the Pacific.'[81] It was a very tall order. Roosevelt only agreed straight away to the anti-aircraft guns and steel, although he added in his reply that to fulfil the last request the US Fleet was being concentrated at Pearl Harbor in Hawaii.

On 16 May, the King noted in his diary that instead of coming to see him Churchill had flown to Paris 'to "hold" Reynaud's hand'.[82]* It was

* Although Buckingham Palace courtiers complained that Churchill would occasionally change the times of his audiences with the King, or cancel them altogether at short notice, his monthly

the first of five flights Churchill would make to France between 16 May and 13 June, none without danger. 'Winston arrived full of fire and fury,' wrote Oliver Harvey, a senior diplomat at the British Embassy in Paris, 'saying the French were lily-livered and must fight.'[83] 'After conference with Paul Reynaud,' noted Harvey, 'he took a graver view.' He found male Embassy staff busily burning archives and the females preparing to leave for Le Havre.* Churchill told Lady Campbell, the Ambassador's wife, 'consolingly' that 'This place will shortly become a charnel house.' 'Outside in the garden of the Quai d'Orsay,' he recalled in his war memoirs, speaking of the French Foreign Ministry, 'clouds of smoke arose from large bonfires, and I saw from the window venerable officials pushing wheel-barrows of archives on to them.'[84]

Churchill assumed that the French would fight for their capital city. He had taken with him Sir John Dill, the Vice-Chief of the Imperial General Staff, and Ismay, and in Paris they met his liaison officer with the French Government, Louis Spears. 'While this meeting was indeed rather crucial,' recalled Lieutenant-Colonel Sir Harold Redman of the War Office, 'and although it has been dignified with the title of Supreme War Council, it was in fact just a hurried get-together of principals, called at the instigation of an over-optimistic Prime Minister, rightly determined to go and find out for himself, at the chief danger point, the exact state of affairs.'[85] Any optimism Churchill might have felt was completely expunged when General Gamelin explained that German armour had broken through on a 40-mile-wide front in the Hirson–Montcornet–Neufchâtel area, only 110 miles from central Paris. When Churchill asked 'Ou est la masse de manoeuvre?' ('Where are your reserves?'), Gamelin said 'Aucune' ('None'). When he asked Gamelin his plans for a counter-attack, the commander of French forces simply shrugged his shoulders.[86] Spears wrote that 'Churchill's mind simply could not grasp it at first, it sounded so incredible, but, when it did penetrate, was like a cold hand placed on his heart.'[87] All his strategic assumptions since 1918 had vanished with a single gesture.

Gamelin said that the Germans had 'supériorité de nombres, supériorité d'armes, supériorité de méthodes' ('superiority in numbers, equipment, tactics').[88] It was untrue: the Wehrmacht were inferior in both numbers and armaments to the French Army in May 1940, though they were far superior in terms of strategy and tactics. To explain the rapid rout of the

engagement cards show that he generally changed them by only half an hour and hardly ever cancelled them. Churchill went to Buckingham Palace as tradition dictated, despite the fact that he was of course by far the busier of the two men.

* Which Churchill pronounced to rhyme with 'carver'.

massive French Ninth Army, one of Gamelin's staff officers pointed out that the figures given for 'mobilized' men had included large numbers of postmen, railway workers and municipal employees who had been carrying on their civilian duties and had been mobilized only on paper, leaving Churchill further aghast.[89]

Nevertheless, the French promised a counter-attack from the south, though the Britons present did not set much store by it. At 9 p.m. Churchill telegraphed from Paris to instruct the War Cabinet in London to convene immediately. 'Situation grave in the last degree.' He had asked Chamberlain to 'mind the shop' and now requested the release of six further RAF squadrons, on top of the four already on their way. 'The French Higher Direction of the war is within measurable distance of being beaten,' Dill reported to the War Cabinet.[90] 'We must remember that the B.E.F. might have to undertake a most difficult and hazardous operation: that of withdrawal in the face of the enemy.'[91] Newall reported that seven fighter squadrons were then in northern France and three in the south. 'There remained in the United Kingdom only six complete Hurricane squadrons,' he said. These were being moved to Kent.[92] It was ironic that the agonized debate over how to allocate the all too scarce RAF squadrons – commit them to the Battle of France or preserve them for a possible Battle of Britain – should have been chaired by the man who could have prevented this dilemma in the first place, had he not so seriously underfunded defence for half a decade during his chancellorship and premiership.

By midnight the War Cabinet had agreed to Churchill's request for six squadrons to be made available as soon as possible 'for operations in France' but would not let them be stationed there. The four squadrons that had already been promised would be stationed in France and the extra six would be based in southern England, protected by radar but subject to greatly reduced engagement times as they would have to cross the Channel and back. Three would fly in the mornings, three in the afternoons, only in daylight, and three would effectively cover the BEF as much as the French Army. Brigadier Arthur Cornwall-Jones of the Cabinet Office used Hindi to communicate this qualified approval to Ismay, in order to confuse any German eavesdroppers.* Fighter Command had clawed back as much protection as it could, but was still left with only twenty-five squadrons based in Britain. 'If we send the fighters and lose them,' noted Tom Phillips at the Admiralty, 'then this country will be left at the mercy of concentrated German air attack and can hardly avoid destruction.'[93]

Churchill's message, which mentioned 'the mortal gravity of the hour',

* The Chief of the Air Staff was called 'CAS Sahib'.

had left civil servants unimpressed. Chamberlain's private secretary, Arthur Rucker, said, 'He is still thinking of his books,' and even Eric Seal, Churchill's own principal private secretary, spoke of Churchill's 'blasted rhetoric'.[94] In one sense Churchill did have an eye on history. The ten squadrons were needed, he told the War Cabinet, 'to give the last chance to the French Army to rally its bravery and strength. It would not be good historically if their requests were denied and their ruin resulted.'[95]

When Churchill returned to Hendon Aerodrome the next day, Colville thought he 'looked quite cheerful, having slept and breakfasted well at the Embassy'.[96] The Prime Minister said that the French needed to fight 'under a clean sky', but they 'are crumpling up as completely as did the Poles'.[97] To the would-be saviour of Antwerp in 1914, the situation in Belgium came as less of a surprise than the collapse of France. 'Our forces in Belgium will inevitably have to withdraw in order to maintain contact with the French,' he told Colville. 'There is, of course, the risk that the B.E.F. may be cut off if the French do not rally in time.'[98]

He ordered the Admiralty and Shipping Ministry to start planning a rescue fleet should the BEF need to be evacuated from Boulogne, Calais or Dunkirk. The Admiralty had a register of hundreds of civilian craft of every kind, and Churchill knew the area well: Château Verchocq, where he had spent much of the Great War, was in the Pas-de-Calais.[99] He also asked the Chiefs of Staff to report on how they would plan to continue the war in what was euphemistically termed 'A Certain Eventuality', meaning the capitulation of France.

'The French are evidently cracking, and the situation is awful,' Churchill told the War Cabinet on his return.[100] One piece of seemingly good news was that Gamelin had been replaced as French commander-in-chief by the more vigorous General Maxime Weygand, but in fact it made no difference.[101] Throughout this extraordinarily tense period, Churchill somehow found time to telephone his friend Harold Nicolson to invite him to become a junior minister. 'Harold, I think it would be very nice if you joined the Government and helped Duff at the Ministry of Information,' he said. 'There is nothing that I should like better,' replied Nicolson. 'Well,' said Churchill, 'fall in tomorrow.'[102]

Chamberlain was impressed. 'I must say Winston has shown up well so far,' he told Hilda.[103] He then added, 'There has been much resentment among those who are personally devoted to me, both at my treatment and the way that the "Treachery Bench"* has been given office. This would

* The Government front bench was officially called the 'Treasury Bench'; the pun was intended to describe the MPs who had voted against Chamberlain in the Norway Debate.

certainly have broken out if there had been any change in the [Conservative Party] Leadership.'[104]

Churchill asked Chamberlain if he minded sitting in the same Cabinet as Lloyd George, whom he was still trying to appoint minister of agriculture with wide powers to increase food production, while admitting 'that he himself distrusted Ll.G.'. When Chamberlain said he would sooner retire, Churchill backed off and stopped asking Lloyd George. He acknowledged that Chamberlain was giving him 'splendid help' and said he did not want his Government 'knocked about'.[105] At 10.30 p.m. he saw the King for their weekly audience. The King noted with some bathos, 'The situation was serious, and he is afraid that some of the French troops had not fought as well as they might have done.' Then he added, 'The French Army is not beaten as it has not yet fought.'[106] The swift demoralization of the French Army, with all too few notable exceptions, was the most shocking of all the surprises to Churchill of May and June 1940, as he had set such store by it in the inter-war years. He had not appreciated the extent to which the losses of the Great War and the social and political crises of the 1930s had sapped military morale.

At 5.30 p.m. on 18 May, the War Cabinet agreed that in the event of an invasion of Britain the Government would declare a state of emergency and assume drastic powers over property, business, labour and services, and planned legislation accordingly. When A. V. Alexander suggested sending forces to the Greek island of Crete, which had excellent harbours, and airfields from which the RAF could bomb Romanian oilfields, Churchill turned it down. 'Our hands were too full elsewhere.'[107] It was also feared that it might provoke Italy to declare war. 'I declare I have never been the enemy of Italian greatness nor at heart the foe of the Italian law-giver,' Churchill had somewhat oleaginously written to Mussolini on the 16th, but, as he told Roosevelt, he thought it only a matter of time before Italy declared war.[108] That night in the Upper War Room at Admiralty House, Colville recorded, 'Winston was in excellent humour,' because he 'is full of fight and thrives on crisis and adversity'.[109]

On 19 May the Germans drove north-west to try to cut through to Abbeville on the Channel coast and get between the BEF, which was still engaged with German forces to the north, and the bulk of the French Army further south. 'French army not fighting,' noted Cadogan, echoing what Churchill had said to the King. 'B.E.F. threatened with extinction. Cabinet instructed General Lord Gort, the commander-in-chief of the B.E.F., to try to fight his way southwards along the coast.'[110] Sir Edmund Ironside, the Chief of the Imperial General Staff (CIGS), ordered Gort to move back along his supply line to Amiens. Gort refused, telling General Henry Pownall at the War Office, 'that the French First Army on his right had faded away and that he proposed to base himself on Dunkirk, hold a semi-circular line . . . and fight it out with his back to the sea'.[111] Colville, who only the previous day had been criticizing Churchill's 'love of rash and spectacular action' in his diary, now admitted, 'It is refreshing to work with somebody who refuses to be depressed even by the most formidable danger that has ever threatened this country.'[112]

That morning, Trinity Sunday, Clementine walked out of the service at St Martin-in-the-Fields in Trafalgar Square in revulsion at the pacifist sermon. 'You ought to have cried "Shame", desecrating the House of God with lies!' her husband said approvingly. He asked Colville to inform Duff Cooper, the Minister of Information, 'with a view to having the man pilloried'. After lunch came the news that the French forces south of the BEF had simply melted away, opening up a vast gap on its right flank. Churchill was summoned back from Chartwell, where he had gone to write his first broadcast as prime minister, to consider Gort's urgent demand to retire to the sea and form a bridgehead around Dunkirk.[113] The Cabinet met at 4.30 p.m. and decided that the BEF must continue to fight southwards towards Amiens, to try to regain contact with the rest of the French Army.

That evening, Churchill made his broadcast:

> This is one of the most awe-striking periods in the long history of France and Britain. It is also beyond doubt the most sublime. Side by side, unaided except by their kith and kin in the great Dominions and by the wide Empires which rest beneath their shield – side by side, the British and French peoples have advanced to rescue not only Europe but Mankind from the foulest and most soul-destroying tyranny which has ever darkened and stained the pages of history. Behind them, behind us – behind the Armies and Fleets of Britain and France – gather a group of shattered States and bludgeoned races: the Czechs, the Poles, the Norwegians, the Danes, the Dutch, the Belgians, upon all of whom the long night of barbarism will descend, unbroken even by a star of hope, unless we conquer, as conquer we must, as conquer we shall. Today is Trinity Sunday. Centuries ago words were written to be a call and a spur to the faithful servants of Truth and Justice: 'Arm yourselves, and be ye men of valour, and be in readiness for the conflict; for it is better for us to perish in battle than to look upon the outrage of our nation and our altar. As the Will of God is in Heaven, even so let it be.'[114]*

* A paraphrase of I Maccabees 3: 58–60 (verses that in the King James Version begin 'And Judas said, arm yourselves, and be valiant men').

The nation knew it was being led, and vigorously, and liked the fact. It was unimaginable that Chamberlain, Halifax or virtually anyone else would have employed such stirring language as Churchill did in these almost poetic broadcasts, which sounded far more formidable, with their growls and pregnant pauses, than is evident from the printed page. The Home Intelligence Department of Duff Cooper's Ministry of Information compiled daily reports on the morale of the nation, collected from a wide range of people and organizations. The Mass-Observation movement eavesdropped on people's conversations in places such as cinemas and food queues, while the semi-official Wartime Social Survey unit (soon nicknamed 'Cooper's Snoopers') undertook a primitive form of polling. The daily reports were also based on Scotland Yard's Special Branch reports, mail intercepts, BBC *Listener* magazine surveys, military censors' reports and questionnaires filled in by W. H. Smith & Son, the London Passenger Transport Board and the Citizens' Advice Bureaux. 'All comments were favourable,' it reported people saying of Churchill's broadcast, 'a good fighting speech', 'makes you feel you're taken into his confidence', 'he's not hiding things'.[115]

'Another glorious day,' mused Cadogan on 20 May. 'Only man is vile.'[116] Ambassador Kennedy's messages to Roosevelt that Britain was finished might have been what prompted the President on 20 May to send for Lord Lothian, the British Ambassador to Washington, and tell him that domestic political considerations made it impossible in the short term to sell Britain the fifty destroyers. 'I understand your difficulties,' Churchill told the President on receipt of the news, 'but I am very sorry about the destroyers. If they were here in six weeks they would play an invaluable part. The battle in France is full of danger to both sides. Though we have taken heavy toll of enemy in the air and are clawing down two or three to one of their planes, they have still a formidable numerical superiority. Our most vital need is, therefore, the delivery at the earliest possible date of the largest possible number of Curtiss P40 fighters now in course of delivery to your Army.'[117]

Churchill then wrote about a potential German invasion of Britain in a way that was to concentrate Roosevelt's mind in the coming months. 'Members of the present Administration would likely go down during this process should it result adversely,' he said, 'but in no conceivable circumstances will we consent to surrender.'[118] He then added,

> If members of the present Administration were finished and others came in to parley amid the ruins, you must not be blind to the fact that the sole remaining bargaining counter with Germany would be the Fleet, and, if this country

> were left by the United States to its fate, no one would have the right to blame those responsible if they made the best terms they could for the surviving inhabitants. Excuse me, Mr President, putting this nightmare bluntly. Evidently I could not answer for my successors, who in utter despair and helplessness might well have to accommodate themselves to the German will.[119]

Churchill knew that it was vital for Roosevelt to understand the imminence and immensity of the danger and its capacity to bring the problem to his own shores. The Royal Navy was the largest in the world and, were it ever allied to the German Navy, and possibly the French and Italian navies too, would dwarf the American Navy and be able to destroy the cities all along the eastern seaboard of the United States. 'Considering the soothing words he always uses to America,' noted Colville, 'and in particular to the President, I was somewhat taken aback when he said to me, "Here's a telegram for those bloody Yankees. Send it off tonight."'[120]

Once German columns reached Amiens on 21 May and were on their way to Boulogne, Ironside warned Churchill that the BEF's lines of communication were in serious danger. Any possibility of sending further RAF squadrons to help the French Army, 'thus denuding our defences at home', was over.[121] The British High Command was staggered that France should have 'so far put up less resistance to invasion than did Poland, Norway or Holland'.[122] 'In all the history of war,' Churchill said to Colville as he tried to get Reynaud on the telephone, 'I have never seen such mismanagement.'[123]

Churchill flew to Paris at 8.30 a.m. on 22 May to try to encourage Reynaud and Weygand to counter-attack. 'He started in blinding rain and the clouds were low,' Clementine wrote to Beaverbrook after seeing him off.[124] He initially thought Weygand 'magnificent', but reports of French fighting spirit were bad. 'Will the French fight?' Cadogan wondered. 'Our fellows will probably fight – as it is their only chance of getting out!'[125] Ismay feared that the French would use Britain's refusal to send more infantry divisions, let alone the fifteen fighter squadrons they were now requesting, as an excuse to accept generous peace terms from the Germans.

The same day, on the basis of a report to the War Cabinet on the 'Fifth Column Menace', which detailed ways in which Norwegian, Belgian and Dutch Fascists had assisted in the German invasions of their countries, the House of Commons approved Regulation 18B (1A), an amendment to the Defence of the Realm Act, which permitted the arrest and internment without trial of 'enemy aliens and suspect persons'. The Government's case was aided by the arrest two days earlier, with US support, of Tyler Kent, an American Embassy cipher clerk who had copied at least six telegrams between Roosevelt and Churchill, and sent at least one of them to the Italian Embassy with the help of British Fascists. As soon as the Regulation had been passed, large roundups of foreign nationals and British Fascists began, with the internment without trial of the military historian J. F. C Fuller, George Pitt-Rivers, one of Britain's richest men, Archibald Maule Ramsay, a Conservative MP, Sir Oswald Mosley, the leader of the British Union of Fascists, followed by his wife Diana, who, like Pitt-Rivers, was a cousin of Clementine's. This was, as Colville recalled, 'a fact which piqued Winston and caused much merriment among his children!'[126] Churchill said such measures were 'in the highest degree odious', but a justifiable emergency measure when Britain was under imminent threat of invasion.[127] Over the next two months, 753 Fascists and 28,000 Germans and Austrians were interned, at first in prisons and then in a series of makeshift camps around the country, even though the vast majority of the latter had no sympathy for Hitler. The camp at Ascot was housed in the winter quarters of the Bertram Mills Circus, while several others were set up on the Isle of Man.[128]*

Also that same day – 22 May 1940 – the Allied cryptographers at Bletchley Park in Buckinghamshire broke the Luftwaffe code for the Enigma cipher machine. They would break the German naval code in June 1941 and the Wehrmacht code three months later.[129] For much of the war this stream of decrypts, known by its special security classification Ultra, allowed the Allies to read many of the communications sent and received between the German High Command, Army High Command, Wehrmacht, Luftwaffe, Kriegsmarine, SS, Abwehr (intelligence) and the Reichsbahn (railways). All told, several million communications were intercepted and decoded from the correspondence of the Führer himself right down to that of the harbour-master of Olbia in Sardinia (when Italian ciphers were broken in July 1941). The Bletchley code-breakers – as many as 10,000 men and women by the end of the war – were, as Churchill put it, 'the geese who laid the golden eggs' and who, just as importantly, 'never cackled'. Such was the seriousness with which those at Bletchley took their obligation to silence that many of them refused to speak about what they had done there, even after the existence of Ultra became public knowledge in the early 1970s.

Churchill had always been fascinated by every aspect of secret intelligence. As home secretary and first lord of the Admiralty he had been

* Once the immediate threat was over, Churchill was in the vanguard of his colleagues in pressing for the internments to be eased. By the end of 1941 only 200 British Union of Fascists members were still in detention; the Mosleys were released in 1943.

instrumental in setting up MI5, MI6 and Room 40 before the Great War, and he now immediately recognized the vital importance of the Ultra material. He authorized the Joint Intelligence Committee (JIC) to contact him at any hour of the day or night on the basis of information received from Bletchley.[130] In September 1940, he ordered Sir Stewart Menzies, the Chief of the Secret Intelligence Service, known as 'C', to send him 'daily all Enigma messages', so that he could read them in their raw decrypted form, even prior to their being evaluated by the JIC.[131] These were delivered in buff-coloured boxes to which Churchill had the only key in Whitehall. He codenamed the information Boniface, so that if news of it ever leaked the enemy would think that it all came from a single highly placed agent, and he ensured that only thirty-one people on the Allied side knew that Britain had a high-level source of information. The King knew, but the Free French and Russians were never told, and nor was President Roosevelt until just before America entered the war. Even then, he complained that 'this vast congregation who are invited to study these matters' was too large.[132]

Yet the events in France in the summer of 1940 were so fast moving that Ultra was of no practical use. By 23 May, with no sign of the promised French counter-attack from the south, German armour was being reported around Étaples, Montreuil, Boulogne and Calais. The BEF was now cut off from its supplies, and could no longer break through southwards to rejoin the French.[133] At 6 p.m. Churchill spoke to Weygand, who said that his plans needed more time to bear fruit. Ironside and Dill were inclined to encourage Weygand to continue his operations around Amiens, Albert and Péronne, not least because they believed that if the BEF retired to the Channel ports, no more than a small proportion could be brought home.[134]

Weygand claimed that the French had recaptured Amiens and Péronne, which it later transpired they had not. At the War Cabinet meeting at 7 p.m., Churchill said he had been giving consideration to an observation Attlee had made a few days earlier about the danger of falling between two stools, and why it might be best for the BEF to retreat towards Dunkirk. Captain Pim later recalled a meeting of the Defence Committee in the Upper War Room of the Admiralty, in which 'The P.M. got to his feet and, with his hand stuffed in the back of his trousers, paced to and fro: "We cannot leave our Army to be slaughtered or to surrender. No, never that! We must get them out."'[135] If the whole Regular Army and half of its equipment were lost, he said, 'We would replace the latter, but if we lose the men then we lose the war. Our men must battle through to Dunkirk. When they get there, the Navy will get them out.'[136]

'The Prime Minister came at 10.30 p.m.,' noted the King that night.

'He told me that . . . he would have to order the B.E.F. back to England. This operation would mean the loss of all guns, tanks, ammunition, and all stores in France. The question was whether we could get the troops back from Calais and Dunkirk. The very thought of having to order this movement is appalling, as the loss of life will probably be immense.'[137]

'I cannot understand the situation around Calais,' Churchill told Ismay on 24 May.

> Why does not Lord Gort attack them in the rear at the same time that we make a sortie from Calais? . . . Here is a General with nine divisions about to be starved out, and yet he cannot send a force to clear his communications. What else can be as important as this? . . . Apparently the Germans can go anywhere and do anything, and their tanks can act in twos and threes all over our rear, and even when they are located they are not attacked. Also our tanks recoil before their field guns, but our field guns do not like to take on their tanks . . . Of course if one side fights and the other does not, the war is apt to become somewhat unequal.[138]

Churchill's anger and bewilderment were palpable. It was the start of a secret suspicion, subsequently borne out by events but of course impossible to articulate publicly, that British leadership and battlefield tactics were initially not as bold and efficient as German. 'I was shocked by the utter failure to grapple with the German armour,' he wrote in his war memoirs, 'which, with a few thousand vehicles, was encompassing the entire destruction of mighty armies.'[139]

Thus, on the 24th, the Germans reached the outskirts of Calais. Brigadier Claude Nicholson was ordered to form his 30th Brigade into an inner line of defence and to 'fight it out in the town and endeavour to engage the Germans in street fighting, which they would be very anxious to avoid if possible'.[140] Churchill told Nicholson, 'The eyes of the Empire are upon the defence of Calais, and His Majesty's Government are confident that you and your gallant regiment will perform an exploit worthy of the British name.'[141] On the 25th Churchill, Ironside and Eden instructed Nicholson, 'Have greatest possible admiration for your splendid stand. Evacuation will not (*repeat* not) take place, and craft required for above purpose are to return to Dover.' Churchill later recalled, 'One has to eat and drink in war, but I could not help feeling physically sick as we afterwards sat silent at the table.'[142] It was even harder for Eden, whose old regiment formed part of the brigade. For the next three days, Nicholson refused repeated German invitations to surrender and survive. He fought on until all resistance collapsed and what was left of his command was captured. He later died in captivity. In August, Churchill said of 30th

Brigade, 'The men of Calais were the bit of grit that saved us by stopping them, as Sidney Smith stopped Napoleon at Acre.'[143]

What Churchill could not know was that at noon that same day Hitler had personally issued an order for German tanks to halt outside Dunkirk for various operational reasons, a command that was not rescinded until 1.30 p.m. on 26 May. This gave Gort the vital breathing space necessary to throw up a perimeter defence around the town and organize a full-scale evacuation of the BEF back across the Channel. While flying over Dunkirk in September 1944, Churchill told a Belgian diplomat, 'I shall never understand why the German Army did not finish the British Army at Dunkirk.'[144]

On 25 May, Churchill replaced Ironside with Dill, Ironside taking over Home Forces. He represented it as Ironside's own 'spirited and selfless offer', but this is unlikely to have been the case: he was to move many generals during the war, impatient with anyone he thought of as underperforming. That day the Chiefs of Staff produced the top-secret briefing paper Churchill had requested, entitled 'British Strategy in a Certain Eventuality'. It predicted that the Germans would try to subdue Britain through 'unrestricted air attack aimed at breaking public morale, starvation of the country by attacks on shipping and ports and occupation by invasion', and concluded, ominously, 'It is impossible to say whether the U.K. could hold out in all circumstances.' Ultimate victory depended on American economic and financial succour, 'without which we do not think we could continue this war with any chance of success'.[145]

The Foreign Office had been approached by the Italian press attaché, Gabriele Paresci, to discuss terms under which Italy would remain neutral. Churchill and the War Cabinet 'saw no objection to an approach of the character suggested', so long as it was kept secret. As Cadogan's diary made clear, the discussions were to be about Italy's 'reasonable' claims that might be considered at any future peace conference.[146] On the afternoon of 25 May, Halifax met Giuseppe Bastianini, the 'well-mannered, conciliatory' Italian Ambassador, at the Foreign Office, and turned the conversation away from Italian neutrality and towards the much more serious question of whether Mussolini might mediate a cease-fire with Germany. That was not what Churchill and the War Cabinet had authorized at all.

On 26 May, Paul Reynaud flew to London for lunch with Churchill, who reported to the Cabinet afterwards that although the French premier had not said that France would capitulate 'all his conversation goes to show that he sees no alternative.'[147] As Cadogan recorded, Churchill 'seemed to think we might be almost better off if France *did* pull out and we could concentrate on defence here', which was certainly the view of

Dowding and others.[148] He also recorded that Churchill was 'against making [a] final appeal, which Reynaud wants, to Musso'.[149] If Italy could be persuaded to remain neutral, Reynaud thought, the French could bring up to ten divisions presently guarding southern France to take part in the struggle against the Germans. This seemed to make sound strategic sense.

Churchill was about to enter a murky area of discussions that would eventually be used to try to blacken his reputation. In the War Cabinet that afternoon, Halifax asked Churchill 'whether, if he was satisfied that matters vital to the independence of this country were unaffected, he would be prepared to discuss terms'. In reply to this hypothetical question, Churchill said 'that he would be thankful to get out of our present difficulties on such terms, provided we retained the essentials and the elements of our vital strength, even at the cost of some territory'.[150] Chamberlain had Churchill putting things more colloquially, and specifically saying, 'If we could get out of this jam by giving up Malta and Gibraltar and some African colonies he would jump at it.'[151] This remark, as recorded in the Cabinet minutes and noted by Chamberlain in his diary, is regularly used by Churchill's detractors to suggest that he did not want to fight on in 1940. Yet they do not take into account either the political context – Churchill did not wish to seem completely unpersuadable and obdurate to his colleagues – or the vital following line, 'But the only safe way was to convince Hitler he couldn't beat us.'[152] The only way of doing that was to fight on, which he proposed to do, and which is what happened. Attlee and Greenwood supported him in that policy, and Chamberlain ultimately did too.[153]

Churchill did not believe Hitler would offer peace terms that could be acceptable to Britain, but as importantly he understood that the very act of trying to discover them, via Mussolini or anyone else, would be so demoralizing to Britons if the news got out (and it would have been in the Nazis' interest to publicize them) that it was not worth the attempt. In his war memoirs nine years later, he wrote, 'Future generations may deem it noteworthy that the supreme question of whether we should fight on alone never found a place on the War Cabinet agenda. It was taken for granted and as a matter of course by these men of all parties of the State, and we were much too busy to waste time upon such unreal, academic issues.'[154] It was to protect the reputation of Britain (and to a lesser extent probably also that of Lord Halifax) that he made that blatantly untrue statement. In fact the subject was discussed no fewer than eight times at Cabinet meetings over four days, as an increasingly frustrated Halifax was brought to the brink of resignation by an utterly inflexible Churchill, who would not agree to put out peace feelers. In the course of these discussions,

Halifax spoke of 'certain rather profound differences of points of view which he would like to make clear'.[155] He would not have needed to do so had Churchill been in any way willing to countenance his pursuit of peace.

The French premier returned to his London Embassy at 4 a.m. on 27 May, having failed to persuade the British to engage with the Italians or to let France make a separate peace with Germany. 'He told us that Halifax was the only one to have shown some understanding,' his aide, Lieutenant-Colonel Paul de Villelume, recorded in his diary. 'Churchill a prisoner of the swashbuckling attitude he always takes in front of his ministers was decidedly negative.'[156]

Later that day in Cabinet, Halifax quoted Churchill as having said 'that he would be thankful to get out of our present difficulties on such terms, provided we retained the essentials and the elements of our vital strength, even at the cost of some territory'. But he then complained, 'The Prime Minister seemed to suggest that under no conditions would we contemplate any course except fighting to a finish.'[157] This was in fact always Churchill's line, which is clear if all four days' discussions are read together, and the crucial sentence from Chamberlain's diary too. At the War Cabinet meeting at 4 p.m. on 27 May, Churchill broke precedent and invited Archie Sinclair to join the deliberations, in his capacity as leader of the Liberal Party. Sinclair also supported him.

On 26 May, HMS *Curlew*, a light cruiser, was sunk by German bombers in Ofotfjord on the way into Narvik. *Curlew* had been sailing at 15 knots in very confined waters with little room for evasive manoeuvre, but she had radar and anti-aircraft guns. Her sinking should have sent shockwaves through No. 10 and the Admiralty, but it did not, perhaps because only nine crewmen were killed. It had long been assumed by Churchill and many others that thick deck armour and anti-aircraft guns meant that aircraft could not sink ships, yet *Curlew* showed that direct hits from medium-sized Stuka bombs could pierce decks, and anti-aircraft fire was sometimes ineffectual. It was surprising that such an early and convinced advocate of air power as Churchill should have clung for so long to the belief that modern warships were almost invulnerable from the air. As was confirmed that same day at Dunkirk, they certainly were not.

Operation Dynamo, Vice-Admiral Bertram Ramsay's plan for evacuating the BEF and as many French and Belgian troops as possible from the beaches of Dunkirk on what Churchill later called a marine 'magic carpet', began at seven o'clock that evening. On the first day, Cadogan articulated the views of many when he wrote, 'Position of the B.E.F. quite awful, and I see no hope for more than a tiny fraction of them now that Belgium has capitulated.'[158]

Although it suited Churchill politically to blame the thirty-eight-year-old King Leopold III of the Belgians for the disastrous timing of the capitulation, Leopold had warned Admiral Keyes, his liaison officer, as early as 20 May that this might happen, and had told King George VI on the 25th that he could no longer hold out, both of whom passed the message on.[159]

Reynaud blamed Leopold bitterly for the gap that had opened up in the Allied line on 28 May, but on 30 May King George wrote in his diary, 'The real reason for the press tirade against [Leopold] is to bolster up French morale. The French must have an outside scapegoat.'[160] He refused to strip King Leopold of his British colonelcy or to remove his Garter banner from the Chapel Royal at Windsor (although the Belgian King was not invited to Princess Elizabeth's wedding in 1947). On 1 July Colville conceded in his diary, 'Leopold was the scapegoat,' as Churchill also admitted to Archduke Otto von Habsburg after the war.[161]

In Cabinet on 27 May Halifax threatened to resign if he were not allowed to pursue peace negotiations. Churchill took much the same position as two days earlier, saying 'that he thought the issue which the War Cabinet was called upon to settle was difficult enough without getting involved in the discussion of an issue which was quite unreal and was most unlikely to arise. If Herr Hitler was prepared to make peace on the terms of the restoration of German colonies and the overlordship of Central Europe, that was one thing. But it was quite unlikely that he would make any such offer.'[162] Nor would he let Halifax solicit one.

Colville, who did not attend Cabinet meetings and got his information from Churchill, wrote in his diary that day, 'The Cabinet are feverishly considering our ability to carry on the war alone in such circumstances, and there are signs that Halifax is being defeatist. He says that our aim can no longer be to crush Germany but rather to preserve our own integrity and independence.'[163] Halifax told Cadogan that, after the Cabinet, Churchill had been 'very affectionate!'[164] Cadogan advised Halifax not to resign, saying that he too was 'bored' by Churchill's 'rodomontades'.

Later that day, Churchill received a telegram from Lothian saying that Roosevelt had suggested that, if the British Isles were successfully invaded by Germany, the Royal Navy should sail to Canada and the future British seat of government should be Bermuda not Ottawa, as monarchy could not return to the American continent.[165] It was an extraordinary statement to have made at such a moment, and Churchill would certainly not concede that the King had no right to reside in his own Dominion if he so chose. He did not reply to Roosevelt. 'Pour me out a whisky and soda, very weak, there's a good boy,' Churchill said to Colville before going to bed at midnight.[166]

On 28 May the situation at Dunkirk was still desperate, but the evacuation had begun successfully. Much depended on whether German dive-bombers could destroy the single jetty which stretched out far into the sea and was used by the Navy to ferry men off the beaches; it miraculously survived the next six days. Admiral Keyes nonetheless arrived in London in the morning to say that Gort did not rate the chances of saving the BEF very high. Churchill braced the Commons for 'hard and heavy tidings'.[167] 'The idea of losing Gort and his band, all the flower and youth of our country, the Army's backbone, in officers and men is truly tragic,' wrote the King after Churchill's audience with him.[168] When Halifax returned to the subject of peace negotiations in the Cabinet that day, Churchill made his stance even clearer than before. 'Signor Mussolini, if he came in as mediator, would take his whack out of us,' the Cabinet minutes record him saying.

> It was impossible to imagine that Herr Hitler would be so foolish as to let us continue our rearmament. In effect, his terms would put us completely at his mercy. We should get no worse terms if we went on fighting, even if we were beaten, than were open to us now. If, however, we continued the war and Germany attacked us, no doubt we should suffer some damage, but they would also suffer severe losses. Their oil supplies might be reduced. A time might come when we felt we had to put an end to the struggle, but the terms would not then be more mortal than those offered to us now.[169]

As with his earlier statements, this was an attempt to seem reasonable, yet also to outmanoeuvre Halifax, which he succeeded in doing. No official vote was taken, but Chamberlain and the two Labour members supported Churchill's stance. Halifax stated that they could not know what Hitler's terms might be unless they asked for them. Churchill instead drew on his deep historical knowledge to say that 'Nations which went down fighting rose again, but those which tamely surrendered were finished.'[170] On 26 May, Cadogan had found Churchill 'too rambling and romantic and sentimental and temperamental', concluding, 'Old Neville still the best of the lot.'[171] Yet it was precisely that temperament that was to prevent Britain from going down the path of peace negotiations with Hitler. Had Halifax become prime minister sixteen days earlier, peace negotiations would almost certainly have begun.

Churchill was probably wrong to assume that Hitler's terms would have been overly harsh; they would probably have been quite reasonable, judging by those he offered in October 1939 and again in August 1940. He saw his historic task as destroying Communism, Judaism and the Slavs, and establishing *Lebensraum* in the East for the Aryan people. For this he needed to fight a single-front war against the USSR. He had no great ideological animus against the Anglo-Saxons or the British Empire, at least until it looked like they were stymieing his plans. His assault on Russia would have been enormously helped had he not needed to invade Britain's allies, Yugoslavia and Greece, in April 1941: it would have given him two more months outside Moscow before the weather turned that autumn.

That afternoon, Churchill sent a minute to all Cabinet ministers and senior officials saying,

> In these dark days the Prime Minister would be grateful if all his colleagues ... would maintain a high morale in their circles; not minimizing the gravity of events, but showing confidence in our ability and inflexible resolve to continue the war until we have broken the will of the enemy to bring all Europe under his domination. No tolerance should be given to the idea that France will make a separate peace; but whatever may happen on the Continent, we cannot doubt our duty and we shall certainly use all our power to defend the Island, the Empire and our Cause.[172]

During the militarily disastrous Black Week in the Boer War, Queen Victoria had said, 'We are not interested in the possibilities of defeat; they do not exist.' Churchill had three copies of that quotation made, which he now placed along the Cabinet table.[173]

The war aim of breaking the will of the enemy to conquer all of Europe was something short of the 'Victory at all costs' of his speech of 13 May, but since then the Allies had suffered a mounting catastrophe – although, for the moment, France was still fighting.[174] If Britain could survive the coming months, Churchill reasoned, she could consider how to win the war afterwards.

On the fourth day of Halifax's demands for peace negotiations, Churchill called together the wider Cabinet – excluding the War Cabinet – and delivered a speech that, very unusually for him, he did not sketch out or practise beforehand. As it was an informal meeting it went unminuted, but Hugh Dalton, the Minister of Economic Warfare, a socialist who had agreed with Churchill on nothing in peacetime, noted what was said in his diary. Churchill started by giving 'a full, frank, and completely calm account of events in France', and concluded by saying,

> I have thought carefully in these last days whether it was part of my duty to consider entering into negotiations with That Man. But it was idle to think that, if we tried to make peace now, we should get better terms than if we fought it out. The Germans would demand our fleet – that would be called

> 'disarmament' – our naval bases, and much else. We should become a slave state, though a British Government which would be Hitler's puppet would be set up under Mosley or some such person. And where should we be at the end of all that? On the other hand, we had immense reserves and advantages. And I am convinced that every man of you would rise up and tear me down from my place if I were for one moment to contemplate parley or surrender. If this long island story of ours is to end at last, let it end only when each one of us lies choking in his own blood upon the ground.[175]

This was no mere bravado. Churchill had seen plenty of people die choking in their own blood upon the ground and knew what he was offering his ministers, just as he had effectively ordered Nicholson to fight to the death in Calais. As his bodyguard Walter Thompson put it, 'He did not practise shooting on the range of Chequers just for the fun of the thing.'[176] He arranged to have a Bren gun put in his government car so that he could fight back if it was attacked, and when travelling by sea he ordered that his lifeboat should carry one to enable him to fight any U-boat that sank his ship. He also carried his revolver on his journeys to France, telling Thompson, 'One never knows; I do not intend to be taken alive.'[177] When asked in old age if he had ever contemplated suicide, he said, 'No. Well, only philosophically.' What if he had lost the war and faced capture? 'Certainly not!' came the reply.[178] When the War Office produced a speech for him to use in the event of invasion, Churchill dismissed it, for 'using conventional adjectives, attached to conventional nouns, merely for the sake of effect'. He said that if he did ever have to make such a speech, it would end with the words: 'The hour has come; kill the Hun.'[179] He also intended to use the phrase, 'You can always take one with you.'[180] There were plans in place in Whitehall for the Royal Family to follow Britain's gold reserves to Canada to continue the resistance from there. No such plans existed for Churchill. When he told his ministers he intended to fight to the death, therefore, it was not one of his oratorical extravagances.

His ministerial colleagues, most of whom had fought in the trenches and seen death close at hand, knew the stakes and the consequences too. Nonetheless, at the end of his speech, they rose to applaud and cheer him, walking around the Cabinet table to shake his hand and slap him on the back. 'He was quite magnificent,' recorded Dalton. 'The man, and the only man we have, for this hour.' Recounting the incident in his memoirs, Churchill said he believed that the ministers that day 'represented the House of Commons and almost all the people. It fell to me in these coming days and months to express their sentiments on suitable occasions. This I was able to do because they were mine also. There was a white glow, overpowering, sublime, which ran through our Island from end to end.'[181] 'Almost all the people' – but not Halifax. When Churchill reported the meeting to the War Cabinet, the Foreign Secretary knew he had been comprehensively outmanoeuvred.*

Late that evening, Captain Pim, who had been continuously on duty for thirty-six hours, asked Churchill for five days' leave so that he could command a flotilla of small boats in Operation Dynamo. 'God bless you,' Churchill said. 'I wish I was going myself.'[182] Pim's twenty vessels took around 3,500 men from the beaches to the destroyers, under almost continuous artillery and aerial bombardment. When he returned on 2 June, Churchill said gruffly, 'So you're back again to do some work.'[183] Pim saw the twinkle in his eye. He had joined the Paladins.

On 29 May, Churchill telegraphed Reynaud and Weygand to let them know that 50,000 troops had been evacuated from Dunkirk successfully and he hoped for another 30,000 out that night. He made it clear that the operation was precarious in the extreme. 'Front may be beaten in at any time or piers, beaches and shipping rendered unusable by air attack and also by artillery fire from south-west,' he said. 'No one can tell how long present good flow will last, or how much we can save for the future.'[184] The ships were taking as many French and Belgian troops as possible, with equal priority to British, and there were plans to send a Second BEF to Saint-Nazaire to continue the fight. He also assured Reynaud that regular forces were being recalled from India, Palestine, Australia and Canada to join the struggle in France. That same day he asked Ismay whether German guns taken as trophies in the Great War could be reconditioned for use, and whether wax could be supplied to troops to deaden the din of battle.[185] On 30 May, he told Gort that once no further organized resistance was possible at Dunkirk he was ordered to 'capitulate formally and to avoid useless slaughter'.[186] The fear that the French might suddenly capitulate caused Churchill, Attlee, Dill and Ismay to fly to Paris on 31 May, arriving late because the plane had to take a wide detour to avoid the Luftwaffe already patrolling the skies north of the city. Over lunch at the British Embassy, Churchill heard that 150,000 men had been taken off the Dunkirk beaches, 15,000 of whom were French. 'P.M. said he would be content with nothing less than two hundred thousand,' noted Harvey.[187] 'His sole

* When on 30 May Desmond Morton discovered that Stanley Bruce, the Australian High Commissioner in London, had written a formal memorandum proposing an international conference 'to formulate a peace settlement', because 'the further shedding of blood and the continuance of hideous suffering is unnecessary', Churchill wrote the word 'Rot' on Morton's report (OB VI p. 436).

topic of conversation was of the possibility of substantial numbers of troops being got off the beaches,' recalled Walter Thompson. 'For once, his face, grave and strained, showed the anxiety that he felt.'[188]

The Supreme War Council met at the French War Ministry that afternoon. Weygand told Churchill that large numbers of troops were being pulled off the now redundant Maginot Line to defend Paris, but he said that unless Britain could pour RAF squadrons into the fighting taking place south of the Somme the situation was hopeless. Churchill told Spears after the meeting that the French considered themselves beaten.[189] Commander Tommy Thompson described the Great War hero, Marshal Philippe Pétain, as 'an impassive, remote spectator, showing not a flicker of interest or enthusiasm as Churchill outlined British plans'.[190]

On Saturday, 1 June the number of evacuees from Dunkirk rose to 200,000 as Churchill had hoped. 'Winston very encouraged by this,' noted Harvey, 'and says he may be able to do more for the French on the Somme.'[191] Churchill made it back to London in time to hold a Cabinet meeting at 1.20 p.m. The whole Cabinet rose to applaud Gort, the commander of the BEF when he returned from Dunkirk. Gort reported that, apart from two divisions there under General Bênoit de La Laurencie, the French had been 'worse than useless'.[192]

When Morton passed on the Foreign Office's plans to evacuate the Royal Family and parts of the Government in the event of invasion, Churchill said, 'I believe we shall make them rue the day they try to invade our island. No such discussion can be permitted.'[193] Similarly, to a request from Sir Kenneth Clark, the Director of the National Gallery, that Britain's art treasures should be sent to Canada, the Prime Minister replied, 'No, bury them in caves and cellars. None must go. We are going to beat them.'[194] The masterpieces were duly sent to a disused slate mine at Manod Mawr in Wales. In time, part of Britain's gold reserves were moved from under the Bank of England to a vault in Toronto, in a nerve-wracking operation during which a few U-boats in the mid-Atlantic could have nearly bankrupted Britain.

On 2 June, Churchill started to try to form a Second BEF to send to Brittany as soon as possible, not, as he made clear to the Chiefs of Staff, because he thought it might turn the tide of the fighting, but as a desperate attempt to keep France in the war. 'We must have plans worked out which will show the French that there is a way through if they will only be steadfast.'[195] 'How wonderful it would be', Churchill wrote to Ismay, 'if the Germans could be made to wonder where they were going to be struck next instead of forcing us to try to wall in the Island and roof it over. An effort must be made to shake off the mental and moral prostration to the will and initiative of the enemy from which we suffer.'[196] The Second BEF, initially comprising a brigade of the 52nd Lowland Division, landed in Normandy on 7 June, under the command of General Alan Brooke, with plans for the Canadian 1st Division to join them.

At the 11.30 a.m. War Cabinet on 3 June, Dowding, who had only 331 fighter aircraft left, urged that the RAF should not be sent to fight above the Somme, and his advice was finally taken. The next day, the last British soldier came off the beaches of Dunkirk: General Harold Alexander. He had been preceded by no fewer than 338,225 men of the BEF and the French and Belgian armies. The BEF had lost over 40,000 men killed, wounded or captured in the campaign, and the same number of French troops were taken into captivity when Dunkirk fell. The RAF had flown 2,739 sorties in nine days protecting the Army, losing 116 pilots, Bomber Command alone losing seventy-six aircraft. Overall, since 10 May the RAF had lost 1,067 aircraft and 1,127 pilots and aircrew.[197] A total of 933 British ships took part in Operation Dynamo, of which 236 were lost and a further 61 put out of action. The BEF destroyed as much of its equipment as it could, but it was devastating to lose 60,000 vehicles, 2,000 field guns, 90,000 rifles, 600,000 tons of fuel, several hundred tanks and 400 anti-aircraft guns.[198] In early June 1940, the sole unit in the British Isles with all its weaponry intact was the 1st Canadian Division at Aldershot. If an invasion had taken place, that would have been the only organized and equipped body of regular troops between the south coast beaches and London. When Pound brought the list of all the Royal Navy ships damaged and out of action, Churchill joked, 'As far as I can see, we have only the *Victoria & Albert* left.'[199] (The *Victoria & Albert* was the Royal Yacht.)

On 4 June, Churchill had the exceptionally difficult task of explaining to the Commons what had happened. He produced a speech which ranks alongside those of Pericles and Abraham Lincoln as one of the greatest addresses of history. He started by calmly and factually telling the story of the German breakthrough, the severing of the BEF's lines of communication through Amiens and Abbeville, and the nature of Blitzkrieg, behind which 'plodded comparatively slowly the dull brute mass of the ordinary German Army'.[200] He then ruthlessly, and perhaps reprehensibly, repeated Reynaud's accusation against King Leopold. 'Suddenly,' Churchill said, 'without prior consultation, with the least possible notice, without the advice of his ministers and upon his own personal act, he sent a plenipotentiary to the German Command, surrendered his Army, and exposed our whole flank and means of retreat.'[201] Churchill called it a 'pitiful episode', but tellingly that phrase did not find its way into his memoirs. When questioned about it after the war, he said he had been reporting the situation as he believed it to be at the time, which (because he had had Keyes's and the King's warnings) was only partly true.

'A miracle of deliverance, achieved by valour, by perseverance, by perfect discipline, by faultless service, by resource, by skill, by unconquerable fidelity, is manifest to us all,' Churchill then said.[202] Echoing Arthur Greenwood's remark in the Norway Debate, that 'Wars are not won on masterly evacuations,' Churchill said: 'We must be very careful not to assign to this deliverance the attributes of a victory. Wars are not won by evacuations. But there was a victory inside this deliverance, which should be noted.'[203] That was the victory of the RAF, of which he said:

> There never has been, I suppose, in all the world, in all the history of war, such an opportunity for youth . . . These young men, going forth every morn to guard their native land and all that we stand for, holding in their hands these instruments of colossal and shattering power, of whom it may be said that 'Every morn brought forth a noble chance / And every chance brought forth a noble knight,'* deserve our gratitude, as do all the brave men who, in so many ways and on so many occasions, are ready, and continue ready, to give life and all for their native land. Nevertheless, our thankfulness at the escape of our Army and so many men, whose loved ones have passed through an agonizing week, must not blind us to the fact that what has happened in France and Belgium is a colossal military disaster . . . We must expect another blow to be struck almost immediately at us or at France. We are told that Herr Hitler has a plan for invading the British Isles. This has often been thought of before. When Napoleon lay at Boulogne for a year with his flat-bottomed boats and his Grand Army, he was told by someone, 'There are bitter weeds in England.' There are certainly a great many more of them since the British Expeditionary Force returned.[204]

After warning that Hitler would use 'the originality of malice, the ingenuity of aggression', to invade Britain, he went on:

> I have, myself, full confidence that if all do their duty, if nothing is neglected, and if the best arrangements are made, as they are being made, we shall prove ourselves once again able to defend our Island home, to ride out the storm of war, and to outlive the menace of tyranny, if necessary for years, if necessary alone. At any rate, that is what we are going to try to do. That is the resolve of His Majesty's Government – every man of them. That is the will

* From Tennyson's 'Morte d'Arthur'.

> of Parliament and the nation . . . Even though huge tracts of Europe and many old and famous States have fallen or may fall into the grip of the Gestapo and all the odious apparatus of Nazi rule, we shall not flag or fail.

He then delivered his peroration:

> We shall go on to the end, we shall fight in France, we shall fight on the seas and oceans, we shall fight with growing confidence and growing strength in the air. We shall defend our Island, whatever the cost may be. We shall fight on the beaches, we shall fight on the landing grounds, we shall fight in the fields and in the streets, we shall fight in the hills. We shall never surrender. And even if – which I do not for a moment believe – this Island or a large part of it were subjugated and starving, then our Empire beyond the seas, armed and guarded by the British Fleet, would carry on the struggle, until, in God's good time, the New World, with all its power and might, steps forth to the rescue and the liberation of the Old.[205]*

Chips Channon, who was sitting directly behind Churchill, recorded in his diary, 'He was eloquent, and oratorical, and used magnificent English; several Labour members cried.'[206] Harold Nicolson wrote to his wife Vita Sackville-West, 'This afternoon Winston made the finest speech that I have ever heard. The House was deeply moved.'[207] She replied, 'It sent shivers (not of fear) down my spine. I think that one of the reasons why one is stirred by his Elizabethan phrases is that one feels the whole massive backing of power and resolve behind them, like a great fortress: they are never words for words' sake.'[208]† Churchill's post-war bodyguard, Ron Golding, who was an RAF squadron leader in 1940, recalled, 'After those speeches, we *wanted* the Germans to come.'[209]

Over the next two weeks in June 1940, the French inundated Churchill with demands for more air support, even though there were 144 British fighters in action over France on 6 June and similar numbers every day until France capitulated. 'Reynaud howling for all our fighters' was how Cadogan put it.[210] Newall and Dowding were adamantly opposed to sending more fighter squadrons to France to take part in what the Cabinet,

* An echo of the nineteenth-century British Foreign Secretary George Canning's boast to the House of Commons in 1826: 'I called the New World into existence, to redress the balance of the Old.'

† Almost all of his 141-word peroration was made up of monosyllable or short words, and almost all were derived from Old English, although 'confidence' comes from Latin and 'surrender' from French. It has been alleged that the actor Norman Shelley impersonated Churchill in delivering the speech on the radio at nine o'clock that evening. In fact the announcer read out long verbatim extracts of it as part of an extended parliamentary report. The speech itself was not recorded at the time: what we hear today is Churchill's voice recorded for Decca Records at Chartwell in 1949.

Chiefs of Staff and civil servants were all increasingly coming to see was a losing battle.

Nevertheless, Churchill wanted to use small batches of troops to attack the Germans along the European coastline in Denmark, Holland and Belgium. 'Enterprises must be prepared,' he told Ismay on 5 June, 'with specially trained troops of the hunter class who can develop a reign of terror down these coasts, first on the "butcher and bolt" policy, but later on . . . we should surprise Calais or Boulogne, kill and capture the Hun garrisons and hold the place until all the preparations to reduce it by siege or storm have been made, and then away.'[211] He also wanted light armoured units to 'crawl ashore, do a deep raid inland cutting a vital communication, and then back leaving a trail of German corpses behind them'.[212] Despite the reverses of the last seven weeks, his instinct for attack was undiminished. As early as 6 June, only two days after the last troops had left Dunkirk, he asked the War Office planners for 'proposals for transporting and landing tanks on the beach'. It was precisely four years before D-Day. On 20 June he suggested the formation of 'a Corps of at least five thousand parachute troops'.[213]

Mussolini declared war on Britain and France on 10 June. When Colville woke Churchill from his afternoon nap to give him the news, the Prime Minister growled, 'People who go to Italy to look at ruins won't have to go as far as Naples and Pompeii in future.'[214] The new threat in the Mediterranean required some repositioning of ships, but the news had been expected for months, especially after Churchill had refused to negotiate peace in late May. The British Army crossed the border into Libya to start offensive operations on 11 June, which lasted for two months before the Italians forced them back into Egypt. Between 5 and 19 August, the Italians also forced the British to evacuate British Somaliland, much to Churchill's chagrin. The day the Anglo-Italian war began, he approved a proposal to remove the Order of the Garter from King Victor Emmanuel III of Italy, who had not stood up to Mussolini's drift to war, saying, 'I think there should be the utmost ignominy and publicity in the case of this miserable puppet.'[215]

That same day, he was forced to postpone his visit to France when the French Government fled Paris for Briare, 60 miles south-east of Orleans, on their way south to Tours. Churchill was in fact encouraged by this, as it seemed to show that they intended to fight on. He flew to Briare at 3 p.m. on 11 June in an Imperial Airways Flamingo aircraft, escorted by nine Spitfires, the most that Group Captain Stephen Beaumont's 609 Squadron could muster at short notice. Weygand's headquarters in the Château de Muguet at Briare could only accommodate Churchill: Eden, Dill, Ismay and Spears had to sleep in a train near by. At the chateau there was only one ancient telephone fixed to the wall in the butler's pantry, connected to the village post office, which was not manned throughout the day.[216] In a two-hour Supreme War Council meeting on the 11th and then for several hours on the 12th, Churchill met Reynaud, Pétain, Weygand, General Alphonse Georges, the Commander-in-Chief of the north-east front, and the new Minister for War, the forty-nine-year-old General Charles de Gaulle, a 6 foot 5 inch hero of the Great War.

Paris was about to fall at any moment, and the two delegations discussed every aspect of the war. Churchill told them that the 1st Canadian Division would be landing in France to bring up the number of divisions ready to fight in the Second BEF to four, with a fifth on its way to form a defensive redoubt in Brittany that the Germans would not be able to pierce. He also emphasized how vulnerable the long German lines of communication now were to air attack. Dill offered Weygand the overall command of British troops, to use however he saw fit. Weygand's only response was to say that the collapse of France was now to be measured in hours rather than days.[217]

General Georges told the meeting that the Allies had lost thirty-five of their 103 divisions. He privately also informed Spears that the French Government were secretly preparing to ask Hitler for an armistice and, as Churchill later put it, that 'we should take our steps accordingly.'[218] Churchill spoke of 'the Breton Redoubt' at the meeting, but the French pointed out that since 70 per cent of their industrial plant was located in the Paris area, that was no long-term solution to France's predicament. When Churchill argued that it would buy time for the Americans to enter the war, Pétain, in one of his few interventions, said it would also mean the destruction of France. Pétain then spoke openly of the need for an armistice.[219] De Gaulle, by total contrast, said he was ready to fight a 'war of columns', pitting mobile units against the German tanks. None of the other Frenchmen expressed any enthusiasm about either that or continuing the war from French North Africa.[220]

Churchill had to urge Reynaud 'vehemently' to permit RAF Wellington bomber raids on Turin and Milan to go ahead. (Reynaud feared Italian reprisals on southern France.) In the event they had to be abandoned as the French Air Force leaked the plans to the locals at Salon-de-Provence, who dragged farm carts and other obstructions on to the airfield to prevent the British planes taking off.[221] Admiral François Darlan, the French Naval Minister, promised that if there were an armistice the powerful French Fleet – which if allied to the German Navy might overwhelm the Royal Navy – would not fall into German hands, but would instead sail to Canada.[222]

Weygand outlined the plight of the French Army. 'Here is the decisive point,' he said. 'Now is the decisive moment. The British ought not to keep a single fighter in England. They should all be sent to France.'[223] At this there was a long pause, provoking the anxiety of Churchill's advisers, who feared that his generosity, lifelong Francophilia, courage and optimism would lead him to promise more air support, despite the warnings of Newall and Dowding. Speaking very slowly, Churchill replied, 'This is not the decisive point. This is not the decisive moment. The decisive moment will come when Hitler hurls his Luftwaffe against Britain. If we can keep the command of the air over our Island – that is all I ask – then we will win it all back for you . . . Whatever happens here, we are resolved to fight on for ever and ever and ever.'[224] This decision not to commit the remainder of British air forces to France, despite overweening pressure from his ally and his own Francophilia, was one of the most critical judgements he ever made.

When Reynaud asked what would happen when the Germans attempted to invade Britain, Churchill replied, 'I haven't thought that out very carefully, but, broadly speaking, I should propose to drown as many as possible of them on the way over, and then "*frapper sur la tête*" [knock on the head] anyone who managed to crawl ashore.'[225] To maintain a sense of humour and optimism even in such an appalling situation was completely characteristic. Fortunately, he had left the conference when Weygand predicted to Reynaud that within a month Britain would have 'her neck wrung like a chicken'.[226] On the way back, his plane had to fly at 100 feet, just above sea level, to avoid two German fighters firing at fishing boats.[227]

During the journey home, Ismay suggested that, as the divisions earmarked for the Second BEF would have to be evacuated almost immediately, their deployment should be unobtrusively delayed. 'Certainly not,' replied Churchill. 'It would look very bad in history if we were to do any such thing.'[228] At this point he should not have had an eye to history and should have been guided by purely military considerations. Against Dill's and Ismay's better judgement, though not their outright opposition, further units of the Second BEF were sent to France. Their commander General Brooke privately denounced the plan to Eden and Dill as a futile political gesture, which it was. When Ismay then said that he was pleased Britain would be fighting on alone as 'we'll win the Battle of Britain,' Churchill gave him a look and replied, 'You and I will be dead in three months' time.'[229] For all his seemingly constant and complete certainty of victory and unwavering defiance in public, with the French, in Cabinet, in the Commons, to the press and over the airwaves, he could sometimes admit to his colleagues that it might not be thus. Later, Churchill said he wished he had stayed in France for ten days 'and left Neville to carry on at home', but it is unlikely he could have kept an utterly demoralized France in the war for a moment longer.[230] Now, as he told the King on his return on the 12th, 'The invasion of this country comes next in the German programme.'[231]

Shortly after midnight Reynaud asked Churchill to come back to France. This time they were to meet at the Tours prefecture at 3.45 p.m. on the 13th. Churchill thought the summons 'ominous', as Reynaud had promised to consult him in person before France surrendered and he was furious that Reynaud had mentioned the time and place of the meeting over an open telephone line.[232] He left early in the morning on 13 June, with Halifax, Beaverbrook, Cadogan and Ismay, protected by twelve Spitfires of Beaumont's 609 Squadron. They took off not knowing exactly where they would land. 'We were actually flying blind waiting for instructions as to where we could find the French Cabinet,' Walter Thompson recalled.[233] Churchill had asked him to bring along his Colt .45 revolver, saying, 'If we are attacked on the way I may be able to kill at least one German.'[234]*

There was a thunderstorm and heavy rain as they flew over the Channel Islands and landed at the Tours aerodrome, pockmarked with bomb craters that no one had filled in for ten days. In his unpublished autobiography, Group Captain Beaumont recorded that 'The airfield at Tours must have been a good example of the disintegration into which France had sunk. Here we were, with the Prime Minister of Britain. No one initially was there to meet him. Tours airfield with its long, uncut grass, shabby buildings resembling a bankrupt flying club . . . was totally unlike our spruce R.A.F. stations.'[235]

Commander Tommy Thompson eventually found two French Air Force officers eating sandwiches. 'They seemed surprised to see us,' he recalled. 'Everyone had gone to lunch. They offered to drive us to Tours in two very small cars of their own. We squeezed in with some difficulty.' Thompson found himself sitting on Lord Beaverbrook's lap.[236] 'Complete chaos,' recalled Cadogan. They drove past long lines of refugees streaming south. Once they had reached Tours, they went to the Hôtel Grande Bretagne, found Paul Baudouin, the Under-Secretary of State to the Prime Minister, and managed to have what Cadogan noted was a 'Very good lunch and W.S.C. in very good form.'[237]

As they ate, Baudouin, who had opposed the declaration of war against

* General Brooke noted that 'He would certainly have sold his life dearly if it ever came to it' (Bryant, *Turn of the Tide* p. 263).

Germany, attempted to persuade Churchill to release France from the promise made on 28 March not to agree to a separate peace. In the words of Commander Thompson, 'Mr Churchill gave him no encouragement whatever.'[238] All the while, Thompson wrote, the refugees were 'rattling at the doors and staring enviously through the windows'. The British party had entered the hotel by a back entrance, but Churchill insisted on leaving by the main doorway 'so that the crowds in the streets could see that their allies had not deserted them'.[239] Many of the unending line of escaping vehicles driving through the town, with personal belongings strapped to their roofs, had smashed windscreens and bodywork riddled with machine-gun fire.[240]

Weygand and Pétain refused to attend the meeting at the Prefecture, on the grounds that further resistance to the Germans was futile. Reynaud and Baudouin, whom Cadogan described as 'a wet blanket', asked Churchill either to enter into peace negotiations with the Germans or to release France from her obligation not to agree to a separate peace. Churchill (Spears translating when his highly Anglicized French proved unintelligible) tried to persuade the French to make another appeal to Washington, and urged them to continue the war. 'I know the British people,' Churchill told the French leaders,

> their endless capacity for enduring and persisting and for striking back. And they will strike until the foe is beaten. You must give us time. We ask you to fight on as long as possible, if not in Paris, at least behind Paris, in the provinces, down to the sea, then, if need be, in North Africa. The alternative is the destruction of France . . . France must fight on. She still has her fine navy, her great empire. With what remains of her army she can pursue guerrilla warfare on a grand scale and wage war on the enemy's communications.[241]

He went on to say that 'This was certainly the darkest hour for the Allied cause. Nevertheless his confidence that Hitlerism would be smashed and that Nazidom could and would not overrule Europe remained absolutely unshaken.'[242] Churchill was seated opposite Reynaud in an armchair, 'gripping the arms and speaking with such passion as to move all those who heard him to the deepest emotion'.[243] Beaverbrook later recalled it as 'the most impressive of all his speeches'.[244] But only de Gaulle responded supportively to his exhortation. Churchill gratefully and prophetically described him, to his face, as '*L'homme du destin*'.[245]

Churchill refused to release the French from their pledge. To add to the drama of the day, the Comtesse Hélène de Portes, Reynaud's mistress, made repeated attempts to enter the final Supreme War Council meeting, until a French naval officer shouted at Baudouin, 'Get that woman out of here, for the dignity of France!'[246] The following year Clementine said that her husband 'was all but attacked by Mme de Portes who wanted to scratch his face . . . She screamed and was hysterical and demanded to be admitted.'[247] The French Government was disintegrating, and Churchill had tears in his eyes when he said goodbye to Reynaud at the entrance of the Prefecture.[248]

On 14 June, the Germans entered Paris. Weygand informed Alan Brooke, the commander of the Second BEF in Brittany, that all organized resistance would soon be over. Churchill called Brooke at his headquarters at Le Mans and over a bad phone line told him, in Brooke's words, 'I had been sent to France to make the French feel that we were supporting them. I replied that it was impossible to make a corpse feel, and that the French army was, to all intents and purposes, dead, and certainly incapable of registering what had been done for it.'[249] It was the first time the two men had conversed. Brooke had to persuade the Prime Minister that his force could do no good, that it was running severe risks of capture every hour it remained. After half an hour's difficult discussion, Churchill gave his permission to evacuate the Second BEF back to Britain. Its duty to history had been done, even if no one had much noticed.[250]

The Simons finally moved out of 11 Downing Street on 14 June and Chamberlain was able to move in, thus allowing the Churchills to install themselves at No. 10. Churchill had already moved out of Admiralty House to make way for A. V. Alexander, so he and his family had been living temporarily at the Carlton Hotel at the bottom of Haymarket. The Churchills took with them the Admiralty's ferocious black tomcat Nelson, which quickly fell out with the Downing Street cat known as the 'Munich Mouser'.[251] (It is not difficult to guess which animal Churchill supported in the ensuing struggles. 'Nelson is the bravest cat I ever knew,' he said. 'I once saw him chase a huge dog out of the Admiralty.')[252] After Goonie died in 1941, Jack Churchill, who was always on good and close terms with his brother, also came to live at No. 10, taking his meals with the private secretaries and going on several tours of inspection with him.

On 15 June, Australia and New Zealand reiterated to Britain their unqualified support, come what may. By contrast, Cadogan noted that day, the 'United States look pretty useless. Well, we must die without them.'[253] That evening Churchill told Colville at Chequers, 'The war is bound to become a bloody one for us now . . . what a tragedy that our victory in the last war should have been snatched from us by a lot of softies!'[254] After dinner he went walking with Duncan Sandys among the roses in the garden. When Colville brought out yet more bad news from France, he replied, 'Tell them that if they let us have their fleet we shall never forget, but that if they surrender without consulting us we shall never forgive. We shall blacken their names for a thousand years!' Then, half afraid that Colville would take him literally, he added, 'Don't, of course, do that just yet.'[255] Despite the news from France, Colville said Churchill was 'in high spirits, repeating poetry, dilating on the drama of the present situation, maintaining that he and Hitler only had one thing in common – a horror of whistling – offering everybody cigars, and spasmodically murmuring, "Bang, Bang, Bang, goes the farmer's gun, run rabbit, run rabbit, run, run, run."'[256]* He took a telephone call from Ambassador Kennedy, and told him that America 'would be a laughing-stock on the stage of history' if she only offered Britain economic and no military aid, and at 1 a.m. he lay on the sofa of the Great Hall, puffed on his cigar, discussed how to increase the RAF's front-line fighter strength and then – very unusually for him – 'told one or two dirty stories', before saying, 'Good-night, my children' and going to bed.[257]

At 7.30 a.m. on Sunday, 16 June, Colville knocked on Churchill's bedroom door at Chequers to tell him that Reynaud was about to be replaced by Marshal Pétain. He found him 'looking like a rather nice pig, clad in a silk vest'.[258] Churchill called a Cabinet meeting for 10.15 a.m. and after breakfast was driven to London, disregarding traffic lights and speeding down the Mall to arrive just as it assembled. During the meeting they learned that Pétain had ordered the French Army to lay down its arms. 'After the Cabinet, the P.M. paced backwards and forwards in the garden, alone,' wrote Colville, 'his head bowed, his hands behind his back. He, I am sure, will remain undaunted.'[259]

At another Cabinet meeting at 3 p.m. a plan was presented for a Declaration of Union by which Britain and France would fuse together into one country. The idea had been conceived by the French diplomat René Pleven to justify the wholesale evacuation of the French Army to Britain, and worked on by Robert Vansittart, Jean Monnet the head of the Inter-Allied Commission, Sir Arthur Salter the civil servant, Lord Lloyd and Charles de Gaulle, who was in London for a twenty-four-hour visit. 'I had very little to do with this,' Churchill was to say later. 'It was a wave of

* Churchill's dislike of whistling was provoked that summer: he was walking down King Charles Street in Whitehall when he came across an adolescent boy, hands in pockets, whistling loudly and cheerfully, walking in the other direction. 'Stop that whistling,' Churchill said sternly. 'Why should I?' replied the boy. 'Because I don't like it and it's a horrible noise.' Without breaking step the lad said, 'Well, you can shut your ears, can't you?' and walked on past, continuing to whistle. Churchill found this very funny, and repeated, 'You can shut your ears, can't you?' as he crossed Foreign Office Yard, chuckling to himself. (Thompson, *Shadow* p. 40.) It was a silly incident, hardly worth noting – except that one cannot imagine it being replicated in Berlin if a young boy had irritated the head of the German Government in the same way.

Cabinet emotion.'[260] Chamberlain went to update the King on 'what is being done to his Empire', and the tricolour was flown over Westminster Abbey for the only time in history. 'Who knows,' Colville joked, 'we may yet see the "fleurs de lys" restored to the Royal Standard!'[261]* He thought the new country might be called 'Frangland'.

When Pétain was told of the idea he ridiculed it as 'fusion with a corpse' (strikingly, the same metaphor used by Brooke two days earlier). At the time, however, Colville wrote, 'Everybody has been slapping de Gaulle on the back and telling him that he shall be Commander in Chief (Winston muttering "*Je l'arrangerai*").'[262] The fact that such senior figures were willing to entertain such an outlandish proposal was a sign of how desperate the British were not to allow the fourth largest fleet in the world to fall into German hands. De Gaulle flew back to Bordeaux that evening, only to find on landing that he had been dismissed.

On the morning of Monday, 17 June, news arrived that Marshal Pétain, the new head of the French Government, was preparing to sign an armistice with the Germans. The unmentionable 'Certain Eventuality' was now a certainty. Churchill telegraphed Pétain to say that he could not believe that he and Weygand 'will injure their ally by delivering over to the enemy the fine French fleet. Such an act would scarify† their names for a thousand years of history.'[263] Baudouin, the new Foreign Minister, confirmed that the Fleet would sail from Toulon to the French colony of Algeria to keep it out of German hands. Having made arrangements for meetings in France that afternoon, in order to fool any Pétainists watching him, de Gaulle accompanied Spears to Bordeaux airport and, just as the plane was taking off, jumped aboard and flew to London, with only the uniform he was wearing. His wife and children left the next day from Brest. He was not to set foot on the soil of mainland France for another four years.

That day, the Cunard liner *Lancastria*, filled with troops from the Second BEF and civilians returning to Britain, was sunk in the Loire Estuary by the Luftwaffe. Four thousand people drowned, more than in the *Titanic* and *Lusitania* combined; it remains the largest single-ship loss of life in British maritime history. The Second BEF was not making the kind of history Churchill had intended. He tried to keep the news secret through the use of a press-gagging 'D' Notice, but it leaked out via the United States and by late July was known in Britain.‡

* The kings of England had claimed the throne of France until the reign of George III.

† 'pain by severe criticism' (*Shorter Oxford Dictionary*).

‡ Occasionally serious losses of life were kept out of the newspapers for reasons of morale, such as the Bethnal Green tube disaster which cost 173 lives in March 1943, and the Slapton Sands debacle that cost 800 lives in April 1944.

Rab Butler met Björn Prytz, the Swedish Ambassador, by chance in St James's Park on 17 June. They went back to the Foreign Office together where Butler gave Prytz a message from Lord Halifax, that 'Common sense and not bravado would dictate the British Government's policy.'[264] Prytz sent the message to the Swedish Foreign Ministry in English, just as he had taken it down, and added that MPs were telling him, 'if and when the prospect of [peace] negotiations arises . . . Halifax may succeed Churchill.'[265] The phrase about common sense was a clear insinuation that, should the military situation deteriorate further, a new, Halifax-led government would entertain peace offers from Germany. When Churchill read the message nine days later, thanks to surveillance of Swedish diplomatic traffic by British intelligence, he asked for an explanation. Halifax claimed that Butler's message had been badly misinterpreted by Prytz. (That was unlikely, since the half-British Prytz, an Anglophile educated at Dulwich College, spoke fluent English and had written the message down in English.) Butler was a charming and intelligent man with a gift for friendship who later in the war reformed the British education system, but in the greatest crisis of his country's life his judgement was found woefully wanting. With magnanimity, Churchill did not destroy his career over what he termed his 'odd language', and allowed him to stay in his post for another thirteen months. Halifax was not to last so long. Churchill still had his critics on the Tory benches. Even after his inspiring 'We shall fight on the beaches' speech, Euan Wallace, Minister of Transport under Chamberlain, noted that there was 'some controversy in the Smoking Room afterwards about his double reference to fighting alone', and Walter Elliot, Chamberlain's former Health Minister, concluded that the Government's honeymoon period was coming to an end.[266]

'The P.M. gave me such a kind and human goodnight when he went up to bed at one o'clock this morning,' John Martin, one of Churchill's private secretaries, told his parents on 17 June, 'put his hand on my arm and said he was sorry that there had been no time in all the rush of these days to get to know me.'[267] The 'rush' of that day had seen France drop out of the war, with all the perils that implied. Yet there were those who preferred it that way. In the previous ten days, Fighter Command had lost 250 fighters over France, and when Dowding heard of the French surrender he fell to his knees and thanked God that no more could be sent. 'It will almost be a relief when we are left alone to fight the Devil,' Cadogan wrote in his diary, 'and win or die.'[268] John Martin wrote in his, 'Our turn will come now.'[269]

# 22

# The Battle of Britain June–September 1940

*Hitler could do anything he liked where there was no salt water to cross, but it would avail him nothing if he reached the Great Wall of China and this Island remained undefeated.*

Churchill, July 1940[1]

*Into his speeches he telescopes the history of a race and makes it present-day history ... Thus he redeems the aristocratic tradition and restores aristocratic leadership.*

Dorothy Thompson in the *Washington Post*, September 1940[2]

On Tuesday, 18 June 1940, Charles de Gaulle broadcast an appeal over the BBC for his countrymen to come to London and join the Free French. 'I say to you that nothing is lost for France,' he said. 'The same means that overcame us can bring us to a day of victory.' Churchill now championed de Gaulle leading a Free French movement to rally resistance to the German occupation, and ensured that he had access to the airwaves. When he was asked after the war by his Chief Whip, James Stuart, why he had been such an ardent Francophile, he replied, 'On account of the need of French manpower against Germany.'[3] His Francophilia had been genuine and emotional, and nothing like as cynical as this implies, but it was true that in June 1940 French manpower could no longer be used against Germany. Churchill admired de Gaulle's bravery in escaping from France, and through all the coming vicissitudes in their extremely stormy relationship he never abandoned the belief that he was the greatest Frenchman since his personal hero, Clemenceau. 'He had to be rude to the British in order to prove to French eyes that he was not a British puppet,' he wrote. 'He certainly carried out this policy with perseverance. He even one day explained this technique to me ... I always admired his massive strength.'[4] Recognizing de Gaulle's determination to keep fighting Germany, the

Ministry of Works gave the new 'Free French' who were rallying to him offices in Trafalgar House at 11 Waterloo Place.[5]

Churchill also spoke on 18 June, delivering a speech in the Commons (repeated in a broadcast) which became one of his most celebrated. He started by condemning those who were persecuting Chamberlain and the appeasers: 'If we open a quarrel between the past and the present, we shall find that we have lost the future.'[6] He then discussed the likelihood of an airborne invasion of Britain, and gave hope that 'the winter will impose a strain upon the Nazi regime'. It was hardly a plan for victory, but he reminded his listeners that in the Great War 'We repeatedly asked ourselves the question: How are we going to win? and no one was able ever to answer it with much precision, until at the end, quite suddenly, quite unexpectedly, our terrible foe collapsed before us. And we were so glutted with victory that in our folly we threw it away.'[7]

The Italian Navy had performed badly in the Great War, allowing Churchill to joke that 'There is a general curiosity in the British Fleet to find out whether the Italians are up to the level they were in the last war or whether they have fallen off at all.'[8] It was extraordinary that he made jokes even in so important a speech about so serious a subject, but it was something he had always done. The writer Peter Fleming, analysing the reasons why this line went down so well with Parliament and the public, suggested, 'If he had ended "or whether they are even worse", he would have scored a hit and pleased the groundlings; by employing a subtler twist of denigration he gave to the passage that characteristic lilt of gaiety and evoked in his hearers the agreeable sensation of being made privy to a personal code of humour.'[9]

Churchill's peroration will be remembered as long as the English language is spoken. 'What General Weygand called the Battle of France is over,' he said.

> I expect that the Battle of Britain is about to begin. Upon this battle depends the survival of Christian Civilization. Upon it depends our own British life, and the long continuity of our institutions and our Empire. The whole fury and might of the enemy must very soon be turned on us. Hitler knows that he will have to break us in this Island or lose the war. If we can stand up to him, all Europe may be free and the life of the world may move forward into broad, sunlit uplands. But if we fail, then the whole world, including the United States, including all that we have known and cared for, will sink into the abyss of a new Dark Age made more sinister, and perhaps more protracted, by the lights of perverted Science. Let us therefore brace ourselves to our duties, and so bear ourselves that, if the British Empire and its

> Commonwealth last for a thousand years, men will still say 'This was their finest hour.'[10]*

When he conjured up the dystopia of a Nazi era 'protracted by the lights of perverted Science', he was probably referring to new explosives, advanced submarines and poison gas more than the veiled reference we infer today to the military use of nuclear fission, which he knew German scientists were researching in Berlin. The reference to the United States was also deliberate. Churchill was very conscious in 1940 and 1941 of addressing an American as well as a British audience, for only when the United States entered the war could Britain really hope to win, rather than just survive.

'Today's speech by Churchill has lifted morale,' Maisky noted. 'His firm statement . . . was met with loud applause from all the benches.'[11] When Harold Nicolson at the Ministry of Information 'bullied' Churchill into reprising the speech that evening in a radio broadcast, which Churchill did not want to do as he was so busy, Nicolson recorded, 'he just sulked and read his House of Commons speech over again. Now, as delivered in the House of Commons, that speech was magnificent, especially the concluding sentences. But it sounded ghastly on the wireless. All the great vigour he put in it seemed to evaporate.'[12] Perhaps Nicolson was right and it was less powerful than the original delivery, but that is certainly not the impression one gets hearing those sublime words on the recorded wireless version today.

After the speech, Churchill had an audience at Buckingham Palace. 'He looked tired and was depressed over France,' the King noted in his diary. 'But he was full of fight over this country. I talked to him about E[lizabeth] and M[argaret] R[ose] being a liability in case of invasion. He said "No."'[13] He felt that sending the princesses to Canada would be damaging to morale. That evening, as Colville took the Prime Minister a telegram while he was dressing for dinner, Churchill said, 'Another bloody country gone west, I'll bet.'[14] When Colville asked him what time he wished to see the Polish leader General Władysław Sikorski the next day, he said noon, 'and

* Churchill had used the construct of a 'thousand years' in 1907, 1909, 1911, 1920, 1934, 1937 and 1939 to describe the length of time Britain had been building free institutions safe from invasion – ever since she had 'seen the camp fires of an invader', as he had put it on one memorable occasion. In 1922 he predicted that the Arabs would not irrigate and electrify Palestine in a thousand years, a period of time that appealed to his historical sensibility. (It was also of course used by Hitler to describe his 'thousand-year Reich'.) In fact, the British Empire was not long to outlast Hitler's Nazi one. The word 'British' was dropped from the title of the Commonwealth in April 1949, so 'the British Empire and its Commonwealth' lasted less than a decade after the speech.

then went on to quote some entirely bogus quotation about that time of day, which he pretended was spoken by the nurse in *Romeo and Juliet*'.[15] Inventing cod-Shakespeare was an indication of how well he really knew the real thing. He continued to be playful even in desperate circumstances.

On 21 June, Halifax suggested that Gibraltar should be offered to Spain after the war in exchange for neutrality. 'Spaniards will know that, if we win, discussion would not be fruitful; and if we lose, they would not be necessary,' Churchill replied. 'It only shows weakness and lack of confidence in our victory, which will encourage them the more.'[16] Instead, he authorized a secret agent, Captain Alan Hillgarth, to slip a £100,000 bribe in cash (approximately £5.2 million in today's money) to one of Franco's generals on the golf links. When more was demanded he minuted in red ink, 'Yes. Indeed. W.S.C.'[17]

The same day, as Britain braced herself for the German bombing campaign that would inevitably precede an invasion, Churchill summoned a twenty-eight-year-old scientist, Dr R. V. Jones, a former pupil of Lindemann's at Oxford and now Deputy Director of Intelligence Research at the Air Ministry, to No. 10 to explain his plan to counter the enemy's development of *Knickebein* (curtsey) and *X-Gerät* radar beams. These could guide German bombers 'like an invisible searchlight', as Churchill put it, even in fog and cloud where RAF fighters could not locate them.[18] Jones had discovered a way to twist the beams to send them off-kilter. When he received the summons to No. 10, he initially assumed it was a practical joke, but there was nothing funny about the meeting that ensued, which Churchill later told Jones came at 'one of the blackest moments of the war'.[19] 'From our encounter,' Jones wrote later,

> I of course felt the elation of a young man at being noticed by the Prime Minister, but somehow it was much more. It was the same whenever we met in the war – I had the feeling of being recharged by contact with a source of living power. Here was strength, resolution, humour, readiness to listen, to ask the searching question and, when convinced, to act. He was rarely complimentary at the time, handsome though his compliments could be afterwards, for he had been brought up in sterner days. In 1940 it was compliment enough to be called up by him in a crisis; but to stand up to his questioning attack and then to convince him was the greatest exhilaration of all.[20]

Jones's counter-measures bent the German radar beams well enough to save Derby on one occasion, where the Rolls-Royce factory built the Merlin engines for Hurricanes and Spitfires.[21] Churchill brought him back to No. 10 whenever the Germans developed a new threat (such as the V-1 and V-2 terror weapons in 1943 and 1944) and gave him the responsibility for developing 'Window' (or 'Chaff') to protect Bomber Command against German radar detection.

In his war memoirs Churchill called the measures and counter-measures taken as each side tried to outwit the other 'the battle of the beams'. These included X-apparatus (a form of radar that was installed in British bombers), Gee (a British version of *Knickebein*), a navigational instrument called H2S, Starfish decoy fires to confuse German bombers, and the 'unrotated projectile', a small anti-aircraft rocket. Lindemann was involved in all these projects and was the co-inventor of the proximity fuse which was eventually responsible for destroying one in six of the V-1 'doodlebug' flying bombs before they reached London.[22] Another German beam was codenamed the Headache by the British, and Churchill dubbed a new British technique for intercepting bombers by night the Smeller.[23] He took a close, scientifically informed interest in every one of these developments.

Marshal Pétain formally signed the Armistice with Germany on 22 June. France was partitioned between his Government based at Vichy, which ruled the south-east and much of the centre of the country, and Germany which ruled the north, the Paris area, part of the centre and the whole western seaboard. Article 8 of the Agreement stated that the French Fleet would be demobilized under German or Italian control. Churchill expressed his grief and amazement at the terms in an official statement that day, adding, 'Neither patience nor resolution will be lacking in any measures [the British Government] may think it right to take for the safety of the Empire.'[24] He was already contemplating one of the most ruthless attacks on an erstwhile ally in the history of modern warfare. 'I think he is the right man at the moment,' Baldwin privately conceded that day, followed by the predictable patronizing criticism: 'I always did feel that war would be his opportunity. He thrives in that environment.'[25] Eric Seal, Churchill's principal private secretary, told Colville over lunch how much Churchill had changed since becoming prime minister. 'He has sobered down, become less violent, less wild, less impetuous.'[26] He was still exceptionally demanding on all of those around him, however, expecting them to be ready to do anything he asked of them immediately, day and night, and capable of curtness or even rudeness if it was not done.

Shortly afterwards, Churchill had a long audience with the King and Queen. He told them that the *Richelieu*, France's newest battleship, had put to sea from Dakar, and 'her destination would either be Plymouth or

Davy Jones's Locker.' 'He is furious with France,' the King recorded. 'Why should we be polite to her after her behaviour to us? Broken her word and her alliance and her Fleet all over the place. We are now alone in the world waiting. A critical three months and then the winter . . . He said the War Cabinet represented all three parties and were as one, all in favour of fighting.'[27]

They then discussed the Duke of Windsor, who had gone with his wife from Paris to the south of France, en route to Spain. Churchill saw this as a potentially calamitous decision, putting the Duke in danger of capture by the Germans.[28] If he returned to Britain, he added, the Duke would 'have no following here'. 'We must guard against his becoming champion of the disgruntled,' the King noted in his diary. 'We told him we could not meet "her",' by which he meant the Duchess. The King and his Prime Minister also discussed the princesses again. 'Winston was not in favour of evacuation now, and I said but do make arrangements now in case they are needed.'[29]*

At 1.10 on the morning of 26 June, an air-raid siren went off during a War Cabinet meeting and Attlee, Greenwood and Sir John Anderson joined the Churchill family in the No. 10 air-raid shelter. 'We all bundled down into the shelter,' noted Mary Churchill in her diary, 'except of course Papa and some of the staff who stayed and worked.'[30] The next morning, Colville went to Churchill's bedroom at about ten o'clock to find him sitting in bed in a red dressing-gown (most of Churchill's large array of silk Chinese dressing-gowns featured dragons), smoking a cigar, dictating to Kathleen Hill who sat at a typewriter at the foot of the bed. By his side was a 3-foot-tall chrome ashtray. 'His black cat Nelson . . . sprawled at the foot of the bed and every now and then Winston would gaze at it affectionately and say "Cat, darling."'[31]

Churchill was not nearly so affectionate to his staff. That day Clementine wrote her only letter of 1940 to her husband. It said:

> One of the men in your entourage (a devoted friend) has been to me and told me that there is a danger of your being generally disliked by your colleagues and subordinates because of your rough, sarcastic and overbearing manner. It seems that your Private Secretaries have agreed to behave like schoolboys and 'take what is coming to them' and then escape out of your presence shrugging their shoulders . . . I must confess that I have noticed a deterioration in your manner, and you are not so kind as you used to be. It

* In early July, the King noted that Ironside was 'planning a mobile column for E[lizabeth, the Queen] and me in this country and that the other plan was for further away' (that is, Canada).

> is for you to give the orders and if they are bungled – except for the King, the Archbishop of Canterbury and the Speaker – you can sack anyone and everyone. Therefore with this terrific power you must combine urbanity, kindness and if possible Olympic calm. You used to quote 'On ne règne sur les âmes que par le calme'.* I cannot bear that those who serve the country and yourself should not love you as well as admire and respect you.[32]

She included a sketch of a cat. She had written the letter at Chequers the previous weekend, ripped it up and then rewritten and delivered it, even though they lived in the same house. There is no reply on record.

Colville did not see the letter, but he agreed with its sentiments. In his own assessment, written after the war, he added some essential notes of redemption:

> Never normally considerate, except to those in pain or in trouble, he was more than normally inconsiderate and demanding during the last months of 1940. He complained of delays when there were none; he changed carefully laid plans at the last minute; he cancelled meetings and appointments without caring for anyone's inconvenience but his own . . . The sound of hammering, often on account of building activities he himself had set in train, caused outbursts of fury . . . If, however, he had been unjustly angry, he seldom failed to make amends, not indeed by saying he was sorry but by praising the injured party generously for some entirely disassociated virtue . . . Churchill's ill-tempered phase was a passing one, nor was it constant. What was constant was the respect, admiration and affection that almost all those with whom he was in touch felt for him despite his engaging but sometimes infuriating idiosyncrasies.[33]

He also noted that he never saw Churchill drunk.

There is something rather wonderful about the fact that, at a particularly perilous point in a war for the continued independent existence of the nation, the British Prime Minister could be upbraided by his wife for being short tempered; we can be fairly certain that no one was saying this to Churchill's opposite number in the Reich Chancellery. The day Clementine delivered that letter, the Cabinet had been informed that the French authorities in Syria and Algeria would remain loyal to the Pétain Government. 'This is tragic news as it delivers North Africa, with its vast supplies, into the hands of the enemy,' Colville wrote, 'and our lifeline in the Near East is threatened.'[34] For all the complaints behind his back, not one of Churchill's entourage would have wanted to be anywhere else – there were

* 'One can reign over hearts only by keeping one's composure.'

no requests for transfers. His rages were summer squalls that disappeared as quickly as they came. Colville elsewhere wrote of Churchill, 'When he was at No. 10 there was always laughter in the corridors, even in the darkest and most difficult times.'[35]

For all her insight and moderating tendencies, Clementine could sometimes be very tart herself. Colville observed that she 'considers it one of her missions in life to put people in their place and prides herself on being outspoken'.[36] Ten days before writing her letter she had been very rude to David Margesson at lunch at No. 10, accusing him of having put the interests of the Tory Party before those of the country during the appeasement period. According to Violet Bonham Carter, 'Winston kept intervening saying "Clemmie, you really can't say that,"' but she did, and when Margesson offered to leave, Churchill suggested that Clemmie finish her lunch next door in the small dining room, whereupon 'Clemmie got up magnificently and said "In the small dining room? Certainly not. We are going to the Ritz."'[37] She then left the table with Mary. Clementine later wrote to Margesson to apologize: 'I expect you know how terribly I feel about the past; but I ought not to have behaved as I did.'[38] In 1946, she told Halifax that if he had been prime minister instead of her husband, Britain would have lost the war. That time she did not apologize.

On 21 June, Churchill had asked Ismay for a list of all the military supplies that had landed in Britain from the United States. Ismay replied, 'Nil.'[39] Nor was anything expected for two weeks. The Americans' response to an urgent request to buy 250,000 rifles seemed to have stalled. 'Up til April they were so sure the Allies would win that they did not think help necessary,' Churchill told Lothian in Washington. 'Now they are so sure we shall lose that they do not think it possible . . . We have really not had any help worth speaking of from the Unites States so far. We know [the] President is our friend, but it is no use trying to dance attendance upon Republican and Democratic conventions . . . Your mood should be bland and phlegmatic.'[40] In a paraphrase of another remark of Queen Victoria's in Black Week during in the Boer War, he ended, 'No one is downhearted here.' Despite all the setbacks of recent days, his determination was unaffected. When Eliot Crawshay-Williams, a former assistant private secretary, suggested to Churchill on 28 June that Britain should use her 'nuisance value' to get 'the best peace terms possible' from Hitler, he replied, 'Dear Eliot, I am ashamed of you for writing such a letter. I return it to you – to burn and forget.'[41]

The French capitulation extinguished any hope that Germany could be starved through a naval blockade as she had been in the Great War, so

Churchill's thoughts turned to overwhelming air attack instead, encouraged by Lindemann who had always been a powerful advocate of strategic bombing. 'When I look round to see how we can win the war I see that there is only one sure path,' Churchill wrote to Beaverbrook on 8 July.

> We have no Continental Army which can defeat the enemy's military power – the blockade is broken and Hitler has Asia and probably Africa to draw from. Should he be repulsed here or not try invasion, he will recoil eastward, and we have nothing to stop him. But there is one thing that will bring him back and bring him down, and that is an absolutely devastating attack by very heavy bombers from this country upon the Nazi homeland. We must be able to overwhelm them by this means, without which I do not see a way through.[42]

The Germans began daylight bombing in early July, initially targeting aircraft production and munitions factories and other facilities on the south coast but also in places as far afield as Norwich, Newcastle and Newport. On 29 June, warned that bombers might be passing close to Chequers, Churchill said, 'I'll bet you a monkey to a mousetrap [slang for £500 to a sovereign, or £1] they don't hit the house,' and hurried excitedly outside to see if he could catch sight of anything, while shouting at a bemused sentry, 'Friend – Tofrek* – Prime Minister!'[43] When the next day he was told that six people had died of heart failure during the air-raid warnings, he said that he himself was more likely to die of overeating, but he hoped not to 'when so many interesting things were happening'.[44]

At lunch the next day, Randolph said that he thought Chamberlain and the leading appeasers should be 'punished', prompting Churchill to reply, 'We don't want to punish anyone now – except the enemy.'[45]† After lunch, General Sir Andrew Thorne, who commanded XII Corps in Kent, told Churchill that he thought the Germans would land 80,000 men between Thanet and Pevensey on England's south coast. (Julius Caesar had landed at Pevensey in 55 BC.) Churchill said the Navy 'will have much to say to this', but did not think it possible to hold 'the whole expanse of beaches' across the entire southern coast.[46] Thorne argued that, even if the

* Tofrek – a British victory over Mahdist forces in the Sudan in 1885 – was the password of the day.

† Churchill never criticized the loyal, cancer-stricken Chamberlain, but when told that the Germans had bombed the Baldwin family's factory in South Wales, he remarked, 'Very ungrateful of them' (Colville, *Fringes* p. 179). Nonetheless, when in February 1943 Churchill heard that Baldwin was being insulted in public and that stones had been thrown at his car, he publicly invited him to lunch at No. 10. 'The furnace of the war has smelted out all base metals from him,' Baldwin said of Churchill afterwards. (ed. Nicolson, *Diaries and Letters* II p. 307.)

Germans' left flank could be held down in Ashdown Forest in East Sussex, their right could still advance through Canterbury to London, especially if his 3rd Division was sent to Ulster for training. Churchill gave orders to prevent that from happening.[47]

By contrast, the Admiralty refused Churchill's request to station capital ships south of the Wash on England's east coast. As had already been made clear in Norway and Dunkirk, aircraft posed a far greater danger to ships than had been appreciated, and Admirals Pound and Forbes were right to keep the Navy at Scapa Flow. No amount of prime ministerial scorn could induce them to change their dispositions. Pound was rightly guarding his forces until the actual hour of the invasion came.

On 1 July, Churchill asked Ismay to investigate 'drenching' the beaches with mustard gas in the event of an invasion. 'I have no scruples,' he wrote, 'except not to do anything dishonourable.'[48] He certainly did not think gassing invaders qualified as dishonourable, especially as he had heard from Maisky that the Germans intended to use gas themselves. When someone in the Cabinet questioned the policy, Churchill expostulated, 'Can't we do what we like with our own beaches?'[49] Intelligence reports meanwhile came in from Norway that there would be diversionary attacks on the east coast, while the real assault would come across the Channel. That month and the next, Churchill visited almost every stretch of coastline where an invasion was possible. His staff briefed him on which troops, guns and equipment were stationed at each, so that when he arrived he could ask probing questions. On these morale-boosting tours of inspection he displayed no outward signs of the anxiety he felt about the state of Britain's defences after the BEF had left all its heavy weaponry behind at Dunkirk.[50] These were confined to his meetings with the Chiefs of Staff and individual commanders.

On one of these forays, he met Major-General Bernard Montgomery at his headquarters in Sussex, who complained that, although he was in command of one of the few fully equipped divisions in England, it needed buses to make it mobile.[51] Churchill was impressed by Montgomery's forthrightness, and quickly provided them.* On a visit to the 3rd Battalion

* The following February, Churchill was less impressed when he heard that General Montgomery was making his entire staff go on regular 7-mile runs, with only those officers over fifty being excused. 'Does he run the seven miles himself?' Churchill minuted the Secretary for War. 'If so, he may be more useful for football than for war. Could Napoleon have run seven miles across country at Austerlitz? Perhaps it was the other fellow he made run . . . In my experience, based on many years' observation, officers with high athletic qualifications are not usually successful in the higher ranks.' (WSC, *TSSW* III p. 647.) A few days later he told General Sikorski, 'The only exception might be in the Italian army, where a general might find it useful to be a good runner' (Kennedy, *Business* p. 79).

of the Grenadier Guards at Louth, the Brigade Major apologized to him for being late for lunch, saying he had had to arrest a soldier for talking on parade. Churchill asked what had been said. The Brigade Major replied, 'Just after you'd passed down the line this man was clearly heard to remark "Pugnacious old bugger, ain't he?"' Needless to say, Churchill was delighted.[52] Such approbation was widespread; in July 1940, he received a job-approval rating from the Gallup organization of 88 per cent with only 7 per cent disapproving.[53] He told his dinner guests that 'he could not quite see why he appeared to be so popular. After all since he came into power, everything had gone wrong and he had had nothing but disasters to announce.'[54] Yet that popularity continued; throughout 1940 it stayed in the high 80s, and remained in the 80s until July 1942, when it dipped to 78 per cent.[55]

On 2 July, General Wilhelm Keitel, Chief of the Armed Forces High Command, issued an order entitled 'The War against England'. 'The Führer and Supreme Commander', it began, 'has decided that a landing in England is possible, provided that air superiority can be attained and certain other necessary conditions fulfilled.'[56] At the Berghof in the Bavarian Alps, Hitler had approved the plan of Keitel's deputy, General Alfred Jodl, for the Luftwaffe to destroy the RAF and British aircraft-production factories, while air and sea attacks destroyed British shipping. British cities would then be bombed to create maximum terror, culminating in an invasion in August or September, once British morale had collapsed.[57] Hermann Göring, who commanded the Luftwaffe, assured the Führer that RAF Fighter Command could be defeated in less than a week.

It was at this perilous moment that the Duke and Duchess of Windsor decided to set preconditions before they deigned to return to Britain from Madrid. They demanded a meeting with the King and Queen to signal their social acceptability, and compensation from the Government if they were to lose the tax-free status they had enjoyed in France. As the King and Queen didn't want them back in Britain, Churchill offered the Duke the governorship of the Bahamas, reminding him that as a serving officer he would have to obey orders and warning him never to express any views 'about the war, or about Germany, or about Hitlerism, which is different to that adopted by the British nation and Parliament'.[58] In the Cabinet Room on the night he made the offer, he asked Beaverbrook, 'Do you think he will take it?' 'Sure he will,' Beaverbrook replied, 'and he'll find it a great relief.' 'Not half as much as his brother will,' said Churchill, methodically pushing each of the chairs around the Cabinet table into place with his stomach.[59]

The Duke accepted the job, as Beaverbrook had predicted, although there were occasional flare-ups, and one ill-judged interview with an American magazine in March 1941 that Churchill rightly complained was 'defeatist and pro-Nazi' and could 'only bear the meaning of contemplating a negotiated peace with Hitler'.[60] The Duke replied that it was hard for him 'to believe that you are still the friend you used to be'.[61] In fact, Churchill had been a far better friend than the Duke deserved, protecting his reputation and constantly (though unsuccessfully) promoting a family reconciliation. The King was relieved by his brother's appointment, but wrote in his diary, 'I don't think the Bahaman ladies will be best pleased!' The Queen suggested to the Colonial Secretary Lord Lloyd that they would think the Duchess was 'the lowest of the low'.[62]

Two of the world's most powerful warships, the French battlecruisers *Dunkerque* and *Strasbourg*, were stationed at Mers-el-Kébir in late June, the large anchorage off Oran in Algeria, accompanied by two battleships, *Provence* and *Bretagne*, several light cruisers, destroyers and submarines. Vice Admiral Sir James Somerville was ordered to proceed there with Force H, an even more powerful fleet, which included HMS *Hood*, *Valiant*, *Resolution* and *Ark Royal*, and to give the French admiral, Marcel Gensoul, four options. Gensoul could sail his fleet to a British port and serve with the British; he could sail to a British port and be repatriated to France; he could demilitarize his ships at Mers-el-Kébir and then sail to the French West Indies; or he could scuttle the fleet.

While Gensoul was securing instructions from Admiral Darlan at Vichy, the Admiralty intercepted an order from Admiral Maurice Le Luc, the French naval Chief of Staff, instructing all French warships in the western Mediterranean to sail to Gensoul's aid. Tragically, the Admiralty did not also intercept Darlan's orders telling Gensoul not to allow the fleet to fall into German hands, but instead to sail to the United States or to scuttle; nor did it pick up a statement made by Vichy but unverified to the effect that the Germans had agreed to the demilitarization of the French fleet in North Africa.[63] Gensoul told Somerville's emissary about both of these messages, but a breakdown in telegraphic communications meant that Somerville's report was not received by the Admiralty in an intelligible state.

By the evening of 1 July, Churchill felt he could not take any risk regarding the French fleet. 'It was two o'clock in the morning before [Churchill] came to his decision,' Beaverbrook recalled that night. 'He had to stand alone. He could not seek support – and he did not . . . Immediately after reaching it he went out of the Cabinet room into the garden at No 10, Downing Street. He marched up and down the lawn and a high wind was blowing – a very high wind. The night was dark. There were no lights anywhere and he found his way up and down the lawn because he knew the ground so thoroughly . . . He was terribly disturbed and only recovered after a few minutes of vigorous exercise.'[64]

'You are charged with one of the most disagreeable and difficult tasks that a British admiral has ever been faced with,' Churchill telegraphed Somerville on 2 July, 'but we have complete confidence in you and rely on you to carry it out relentlessly.'[65] Churchill later described his order to sink the French fleet at Oran and to seize French ships at Portsmouth as a 'hateful decision, the most unnatural and painful in which I have ever been concerned'.[66] Operation Catapult on 3 July 1940 resulted in the sinking of the *Bretagne*, and the damaging and running aground of the *Provence* and *Dunkerque*, with three French destroyers damaged and one run aground. The *Strasbourg* escaped to Toulon. In all, 1,297 French sailors were killed, and two Britons. At a Chiefs of Staff meeting during the action, Churchill observed sardonically that 'The French were now fighting with all their vigour for the first time since the war broke out.'[67] He said he could not see how full-scale war with France could now be avoided. 'It is so terrible that we should be forced to fire on our own erstwhile allies,' Mary noted in her diary. 'Papa is *shocked* and deeply grieved that such action has been necessary.'[68]

Churchill's speech to the Commons on 4 July explaining the 'sad duty' he had felt compelled to undertake induced audible gasps of surprise.[69] 'It was a very sad day for Papa,' wrote Mary. 'His statement was sorrowful, sombre, but resolved and encouraging. He explained the situation and the Government's action to a gloomy, crowded, attentive House. When, after nearly an hour, the House began to cheer – the cheering grew and grew, until the House was on its feet – Tories – Liberals – Labour (except ILPs).'[70]* This was the same House of Commons that had shouted Churchill down during the Abdication Crisis. 'The grand finale ends in an ovation,' recorded Nicolson, 'with Winston sitting there with tears pouring down his cheeks.'[71] As the cheering continued, the great Francophile told Leslie Hore-Belisha, 'This is heartbreaking for me.'[72]

At the same time as he showed such resolution over the French fleet, Churchill was forced to appease Japan by closing the Burma Road that connected the British colony to the Chinese border, thereby cutting supplies of war materiel off from the Chinese Nationalist forces under Chiang Kai-shek who were fighting against the Japanese.[73] Without diplomatic support

* The three Independent Labour Party MPs.

from the United States, Churchill thought, it was impossible to do anything else without risking a war with Japan. 'We are short of everything,' he told Lord Lloyd, 'except enemies.'[74] He did not want, as Cadogan put it in a neat understatement, 'all the inconvenience of war with Japan', and anyway the rainy season was about to make the road impassable.[75] The Government, though not Churchill personally, was starting to come in for criticism, and not just for kowtowing to Japan. When on 5 July Boothby, Under-Secretary for Food, sent him a memorandum complaining that 'We were not getting on with the war, especially conscription of labour,' Churchill exploded and 'told him if he did not mind his own business he would perhaps have no business to mind!'[76] He was not about to allow junior ministers to interfere in other departments, in the manner that he himself had done for decades.

Between 9 and 31 July, under a cash-and-carry agreement with President Roosevelt, huge American munitions convoys finally arrived in a range of British ports, with half a million rifles and their ammunition and over three hundred 75mm field guns. Churchill ensured that special trains were waiting to transport the cargoes to the Local Defence Volunteers (later the Home Guard) and the Army, starting with the coastal units, which stayed up through the night to receive them and then, as Churchill recalled, 'Men and women worked night and day making them fit for use. By the end of July we were an armed nation, so far as parachute or airborne landings were concerned. We had become a "hornet's nest".'[77]

There was now much speculation about which particular day the invasion would fall on, so the American munitioning could not have come at a better time. 'The invasion and great attack is now said to be on Thursday,' Colville wrote in his diary on Tuesday, 9 July.[78] On the 10th, the King recorded Churchill as being 'in very good form and much more cheerful than of late. He was not afraid of invasion, we should put up a stout resistance all round.'[79]

Hitler had 2,670 bombers and fighters deployed in the Western theatre, not enough for a full-scale invasion of Britain unless he could win air superiority quickly and decisively, and then attack the Royal Navy from the air, which, as had already been shown, could be an effective strategy. Although there were constant overlaps between them, the Battle of Britain can be divided into four general phases, as Jodl's plan was put into operation. The period from 26 June to 16 July saw scattered, generally small-scale air raids against specified targets, especially in the period after 4 July when daylight attacks were made against British shipping. Then from 17 July until 12 August attacks increased on southern coast ports and airfields, with heavy night raids on aircraft factories. Operation Adlerangriff (Eagle

Attack) began on 13 August, a massive daylight assault intended to destroy the RAF in dogfights across southern England, and accompanied by the bombing and strafing of aerodromes and runways. This was supported after 19 August by the night bombing of ports and cities, including of London docklands and suburbs after 25 August. After 7 September, London became the main target of what became known as the Blitz. These were the months of which Mary would later declare that, although there were other anxious times after 1940, 'Never again, I think, did one feel one could scarcely breathe. We got through the days living from news bulletin to news bulletin, and dreading what each one might bring.'[80] John Martin agreed: 'It may have been "the finest hour",' he wrote later, 'but when we were living through it, it was a time of agony piled on agony . . . At the time no solid grounds for confidence were visible.'[81]

German radio was confidently predicting the coming invasion – codenamed Operation Sealion – from late June. Joseph Goebbels, Hitler's Propaganda Minister, alleged that Churchill was being bribed by the Jews to continue the war but that a fifth column would soon remove him from power. He encouraged Britons to write chain letters for peace, to hiss and boo Churchill's appearance on the cinema newsreels and to horsewhip him whenever he appeared in public.[82]

On 11 July, during his tour of the coastal defences, concrete pillboxes and troops along the south-east coast from Dover to Whitstable, Churchill went deep inside the subterranean tunnels under Dover Castle. He also inspected a 14-inch gun that he wanted to use to bombard the French coast. The military dismissed this as 'a pure stunt', but he knew it would at least give the impression that they were fighting back.[83] He saw the coast of France and patrols of Spitfires 'glinting in the sun ten thousand feet above us', but Churchill was disappointed because, as Colville recorded, 'the whole object of his journey had really been to see an air raid!'[84]

'The P.M. was his brave confident self,' noted Duff Cooper's wife, the Society beauty Lady Diana Cooper, after they had lunched together on 12 July, 'and said that production was splendid and with America's help – and it was coming over in mass – we won't be beaten and we'll save the world yet.'[85] That evening, wearing the uniform of an honorary air commodore, he watched twelve Hurricanes take off for a patrol at Kenley in Surrey in the pouring rain. 'I never hated the Germans in the last war,' he told General Sir Bernard Paget, Commander-in-Chief of South-Eastern Command, and General Sir Claude Auchinleck, Commander-in-Chief of Southern Command, at dinner that night, 'but now I hate them like . . . well, like an earwig.'[86] He told them he could not see victory coming much before 1942, by which time he hoped to have a fifty-five-division army, but the next three months would simply be about holding out until the weather in the Channel became too bad for the Germans to risk an invasion. The coming winter would be terrible for the peoples of Occupied Europe, he said, as 'Hitler will take the other children's candy' – that is, confiscate their food supplies.[87]

Paget and Auchinleck both believed that the Norwegian fishing fleet might be commandeered by the Germans for a diversion on the east coast, while glider-borne troops and parachutists would seize a port on the south coast for the real attack. Britons would not necessarily have had to 'fight them on the beaches', because Churchill planned to concentrate troops in mobile divisions further inland, ready to converge once it was clear where the Germans had landed in force. Yet Ultra decrypts and aerial reconnaissance indicated that they were not as yet making the energetic preparations necessary if they were truly bent on invading the United Kingdom in the short term. 'He emphasized that the great invasion scare . . . is serving a most useful purpose,' Colville recorded: 'it is well on the way to providing us with the finest offensive army we have ever possessed and it is keeping every man and woman tuned to a high pitch of readiness. He does not wish the scare to abate therefore, and although personally he doubts whether invasion is a serious menace he intends to give that impression, and to talk about long and dangerous vigils, etc., when he broadcasts on Sunday.'[88]

Should the populace be encouraged to fight? Paget believed that they would be massacred if they did, and that the general public should therefore be ordered to stay at home. Churchill disagreed, and was 'sufficiently ruthless to point out that in war quarter is given, not on grounds of compassion but in order to discourage the enemy fighting to the bitter end', noted Colville. 'But here we want every citizen to fight desperately and they will do so the more if they know that the alternative is massacre. The Local Defence Volunteers must be armed and prepared . . . and even women must, if they wish, be enrolled as combatants.'[89]

On 13 July, although he had been prime minister for only nine weeks, Churchill told Colville that 'it gave him confidence to be able to see clearly how this war could and should be won . . . This week-end he felt more cheerful than at any time since he took office.'[90] For 'Even if "that man" (as he always calls Hitler) were at the Caspian – and there was nothing to stop him going there – we should bring him back "to find a fire in his own backyard and we will make Germany a desert, yes a desert."'[91] Churchill assumed that Hitler would turn on the USSR long before Ultra decrypts started to hint at it, but also that the Germans would crush the Russians in the opening stages of the attack. The next day, reflecting on Britain's strategic situation he said, 'Hitler must invade or fail. If he fails he is bound to go East, and fail he will.'[92]

That evening – Bastille Day – Churchill delivered a broadcast that was heard by nearly two-thirds of the adult population of the United Kingdom.[93] 'Our painful task is now complete,' he said of Oran, predicting confidently that 'a liberated France will once again rejoice in her greatness and her glory.'[94] Now,

> We are fighting by ourselves alone; but we are not fighting for ourselves alone. Here in this strong city of refuge which enshrines the title-deeds of human progress and is of deep consequence to Christian Civilization; here, girt about by the seas and oceans where the Navy reigns; shielded from above by the prowess and devotion of our airmen – we await undismayed the impending assault. Perhaps it will come tonight. Perhaps it will come next week. Perhaps it will never come. We must show ourselves equally capable of meeting a sudden violent shock or – what is perhaps a harder test – a prolonged vigil. But be the ordeal sharp or long, or both, we shall seek no terms, we shall tolerate no parley; we may show mercy – we shall ask for none.

He added, 'Hitler has not yet been withstood by a great nation with a willpower the equal of his own.'[95]

'Should the invader come to Britain,' he continued,

> there will be no placid lying down of the people in submission before him, as we have seen, alas, in other countries. We shall defend every village, every town, and every city. The vast mass of London itself, fought street by street, could easily devour an entire hostile army; and we would rather see London laid in ruins and ashes than that it should be tamely and abjectly enslaved. I am bound to state these facts, because it is necessary to inform our people of our intentions, and thus to reassure them.[96]

Home Intelligence reported universal approval across all regions of the country for the speech. The assurance that there would be no peace discussions was found 'welcome and heartening'. A typical comment, from Bristol, was 'That's the sort of thing we want and he's the fellow we can follow.'[97] Harold Nicolson wrote to his wife quoting Horace's *Odes*: 'What a speech! *Si fractus illabatur orbis, / Impavidum ferient ruinae.** Thank God for him.'[98]

* 'If the whole world were to crack and collapse about him, / Its ruins would find him unafraid' (the translation provided by his son – ed. Nicolson, *Diaries and Letters*, II p. 102).

'I feel better,' Churchill told Beaverbrook over the telephone on 16 July, just as the RAF had survived the first phase of the German attack and punished the Luftwaffe accordingly. 'The air boys have done it. We live on their wings.'[99] Always an admirer of courage and youth, the combination of them that he found in the pilots thrilled him. 'It is a very remarkable thing that the young should be so much braver than the old,' Churchill told Mary that October, 'for they have so much more to lose – but it is so.'[100] But it was far too early to celebrate victory in mid-July – daylight raids were just beginning in earnest and dogfights were to be fought over southern England for another two months. As Colville reported, Dowding was warning that 'each side must sooner or later begin a race for the destruction of the other's aircraft production industry, and this, of course, will imply bombing the civilian population. Then the real test will begin: have we or the Germans the sterner civilian morale?'[101]

Lunching on 17 July with Edgar Mowrer, the Pulitzer Prize-winning journalist from the *Chicago Daily News*, Churchill resuscitated his vision of a dystopian future for America in the aftermath of a successful German invasion of Britain. 'I myself shall never make peace with [the] Germans,' he said; 'that is not at all what I am here for.'[102] But if Oswald Mosley were to hand over the Fleet, the United States Navy would then face the combined German, Italian, British and what was left of the French fleets, 'massed in one armada'. 'Make no mistake: if he got us down he would go for you at once.' The best way to prevent this 'dire jeopardy', he argued, was to sell Britain 'your destroyers – the obsolete ones', as well as to allow 'your adventurous young men to enlist with us, if they cared to', for 'What more glorious thing can a spirited young man experience than meeting an opponent at four hundred miles an hour, with twelve or fifteen hundred horse power in his hands and unlimited offensive power?'[103] 'Sometimes I wish they would come at once,' he said of the Germans. 'We have reached a high level of expectancy and it is rather a shame to let any of our fire subside.'[104] When Bracken saw a draft of the piece, he declared it 'awful', horrified by its reference to a Mosley premiership. He persuaded Mowrer to delete that, denying that Churchill had ever suggested such an eventuality.

Hitler made what he called his 'last appeal to reason' on 19 July, saying that he had never planned to 'destroy or even damage' the British Empire. 'Churchill has said that he will fight on,' he said, adding of Londoners, 'Awful vengeance will be brought on them. Not, of course, on Churchill, who will run away to Canada, but on the people themselves. I shall speak a great prophecy. A great empire will be destroyed, an empire which I had never intended to destroy.'[105] The Delphic Oracle itself could not have produced a finer irony. 'I do not propose to say anything in reply to Herr Hitler's speech,' Churchill told Robert Vansittart at the Foreign Office, 'not being on speaking terms with him.'[106] When the Luftwaffe dropped leaflets over Britain featuring Hitler's speech, Churchill's popularity only increased.

On 22 July, Churchill changed the name of the Local Defence Volunteers to the 'Home Guard', against the advice of the War Office and many of its senior officers, but Eden recorded, 'He was insistent.'[107] He later changed the 'Communal Feeding Centres', which he thought 'suggestive of Communism and the workhouse', to 'British Restaurants', telling Woolton, 'Everybody associates the word "restaurant" with a good meal, and they may as well have the name if they cannot get anything else.'[108] General Alexander recalled that when he used the term 'Hitler's European Fortress' Churchill 'turned on me in anger and said, "Never use that term again. Never use that term again." Winston had a very acute sense of the meaning of words.'[109] His acute sense was not just of their meaning, but of their emotional impact. In the spring of 1941, he complained to Duff Cooper about the message 'Stay put' which would be sent out by the Ministry of Information in the event of a German invasion. 'First of all, it is American slang; secondly, it does not express the fact. The people have not been "put" anywhere. What is the matter with "Stand fast", or "Stand firm"? Of the two I prefer the latter. This is an English expression, and it says exactly what is meant.'[110]

The same day that he coined the name Home Guard, 22 July, the Cabinet set up the Special Operations Executive, or SOE, after weeks of inter-departmental wrangling, 'to coordinate all action, by way of subversion and sabotage, against the enemy'. 'And now,' Churchill told Hugh Dalton, its first director, 'go and set Europe ablaze!'[111] Churchill disliked Dalton personally, but thought him effective, and approvingly dubbed him 'the Minister for Ungentlemanly Warfare'.[112] Over the coming years, Dalton, and his successor Lord Selborne (an Other Club member), scored some notable successes, though at a high cost to SOE's brave personnel. The Executive was formed from two different bodies. MI(R) were the 'boffins' (scientific experts) and bomb-makers, nicknamed 'Churchill's Toyshop', who invented weapons such as the limpet mine and two anti-tank weapons, the Blacker Bombard and the PIAT. Meanwhile, Section D infiltrated agents into Nazi-occupied Europe. Its initial driving spirit, Colonel Colin Gubbins, claimed to have picked up useful tips from Al Capone in what he called 'hitherto unthinkable methods of warfare'.[113]

Powerful forces in Whitehall that profoundly disapproved of SOE – which was often called 'the mob' or 'the racket' – included MI6, the

Foreign Office and the RAF. Charles Portal thought 'the dropping of men dressed in civilian clothes for the purpose of attempting to kill members of the opposing forces is not an operation with which the Royal Air Force should be associated'.[114] But Churchill felt that this was no time for niceties. The most important and successful SOE exploit was Operation Gunnerside in February 1943, in which Norwegian SOE-trained explosives experts destroyed the Norsk Hydro heavy-water plant at Rjukan, which helped deny Germany the atomic bomb. That operation alone justifies SOE's creation.[115] Other successes included destroying the Pessac power station near Bordeaux and the Peugeot plant at Sochaux, capturing an Italian liner, blowing up a strategic Greek viaduct and several Albanian bridges, carrying out a bribery operation in Spain, escorting the Emperor Haile Selassie back to his throne in Addis Ababa, kidnapping General Kreipe on Crete, arranging the assassination of Reinhard Heydrich and organizing the sabotage of roads and railways in June 1944 that meant that the Das Reich panzer division took seventeen days to get to Normandy after D-Day.[116] SOE delivered 10,000 tons of weapons into France by clandestine means during the war, and 18,000 into Occupied Yugoslavia, where the partisans used them to hold down several German divisions in 1944. Unorthodox warfare appealed to Churchill, who believed that Britain should undertake direct, full-scale, expensive continental military engagements only once the Germans were severely weakened, and although local populations suffered terribly in Nazi reprisals, SOE did keep alight the flame of resistance in Europe.

Churchill brought Beaverbrook into the War Cabinet on 2 August. As minister of aircraft production, Beaverbrook had been constantly involved in inter-departmental feuding – with Ambassador Sir Stafford Cripps in Moscow, with Bevin over manpower, with Sinclair over pilot training, and so on. But he had increased fighter-plane production, if occasionally by piratical means, and Churchill saw the man he called 'the Bottle Imp' as a political ally.[117] He did not care that Beaverbrook was hated by many for the way his newspapers had for years championed anti-Establishment causes such as Imperial Preference, and Edward VIII during the Abdication Crisis. 'I was revolted by his having monkey-like hands as they stretched out to grab ice cubes out of the bowl,' General Brooke wrote during a weekend at Chequers that month. 'The more I saw of him throughout the war, the more I disliked and mistrusted him. An evil genius who exercised the very worst of influence on Winston.'[118] To Eden, Halifax 'expressed anxiety as to Winston's judgment' in appointing Beaverbrook.[119] Clementine had no such qualms. 'I rejoice that you are coming in to the War

Cabinet,' she wrote. 'Winston badly needs your help.'[120] That was not to say that Churchill always supported Beaverbrook over others in the Cabinet – certainly not over Bevin, whom Churchill admired.*

On 3 August the Home Intelligence Department Reports arrived from fourteen regions of the country. One might have expected as the bombing got worse that morale would deflate, but extraordinarily the opposite was true. 'No nervousness at invasion threats,' reads a typical response. 'Enemy troops may land, but Hitler will be sorry he sent them.'[121] During one Cabinet meeting a rumour was heard that German parachutists had actually landed in England. 'The Prime Minister got very excited about this and suggested that a £1,000 reward should be given to anyone apprehending a German parachutist,' recalled Lawrence Burgis, the Cabinet stenographer. This sum was whittled down to £100, and Churchill sent John Anderson out to discover what was happening. As he passed behind the Prime Minister's chair, Churchill said, 'We'll give you a hundred pounds if you get one.'[122] The humourless Anderson replied that he didn't need a monetary reward to do his duty.

Charles de Gaulle claimed in his memoirs that in August 1940 he found Churchill at Chequers shaking his fists at the sky and crying, 'So they won't come!' When he asked his host why he wanted to bring on the bombing of British cities, Churchill replied, 'You see, the bombing of Oxford, Coventry, Canterbury, will cause such a wave of indignation in the United States that they'll come into the war![123] Yet he was wrong: for all their indignation, Americans watched the bombing of British cities for sixteen months before Hitler entirely unnecessarily declared war on them. On the night of 9 August, a German bomber flew over Chequers and everyone rushed out into the garden to take a look. When Pound stumbled down two sets of stairs in the dark, Churchill teased him, saying: 'Try and remember you are an Admiral of the Fleet and not a Midshipman!'[124]

The taciturn, thoughtful General Sir Archibald Wavell, Commander-in-Chief in the Middle East, was also staying that night. Churchill was unimpressed with his understated personality. 'Winston maintains that he is a good average colonel,' Eden noted, 'and would make a good chairman of a Tory association.'[125] Wavell was facing the prospect of the Germans and Italians preparing to attack – as Churchill had warned the King in mid-July – Egypt, Kenya, Somaliland, Palestine and Iraq, where

* When Bevin came to stay at Chequers that month – shocking Colville by the way he ate honey off his knife – Churchill said that 'Bevin was a good old thing and had "the right stuff in him" – no defeatist tendencies' (Colville, *Fringes* p. 220).

they might have as many as half a million men, five times the number of Commonwealth troops.[126] So in August 154 tanks were sent to Wavell in Egypt, at Churchill's insistence, a huge risk that he would not have taken if he had genuinely expected an invasion of Britain. He believed that A. V. Alexander and Pound were being 'confoundedly cautious' in sending the tanks around the Cape rather than trying to 'dash' through the (Italian submarine-infested) Mediterranean.[127] It is impossible to know what would have happened had they made the 'dash', but it was indicative of Churchill's impatient, offensive spirit that he wanted them to.

During tea at Chequers on 11 August, private secretaries were constantly sent off to telephone Fighter Command to discover 'the latest score' in planes being shot down. Churchill went off to a nearby rifle range after that to fire his Mannlicher M1895 bolt-action rifle at one, two and three hundred yards. 'He also fired his revolver, still smoking a cigar, with commendable accuracy,' recalled Colville. 'Despite his age, size and lack of practice, he acquitted himself well. The whole time he talked of the best method of killing Huns. Soft-nose bullets were the thing to use and he must get some.' When Randolph pointed out that dum-dum bullets had been banned under the Hague Convention, his father said that 'the Germans would make short work of him if they caught him, and so he didn't see why he should have any mercy on them. He always seemed to visualize the possibility of having to defend himself against German troops!'[128] (The SS indeed had Chartwell on their *Sonderfahndungsliste* (Special Search List), though Churchill would probably not have been waiting for them when they came to call.)

The 13th of August was the Germans' *Adlertag* (Eagle Day). No fewer than 1,485 sorties were made against Fighter Command's airfields and infrastructure in southern England. 'What a slender thread the greatest of things can hang by!' Churchill said, echoing a phrase of Napoleon's.[129] On the third day of Operation Eagle Attack, a massive air battle took place. Churchill, 'consumed with excitement', drove to Fighter Command headquarters at RAF Bentley Priory in Stanmore in north-west London.[130] 'The daring exploits of the fighter pilots in the Battle of Britain aroused in him a latent schoolboy instinct of hero-worship,' Colville recalled. 'When I myself went off to train as a pilot [in 1944], he said to me with emotion that I was joining "the cavalry of modern war".'[131] The man who had charged at Omdurman was never far below the surface.* On his

* 'You know why I hate the Nazis?' Churchill said to the war correspondent Quentin Reynolds. 'I hate them because they frown when they fight. They are grim and sullen. Now, take our magnificent Air Force lads – they grin when they fight. I like a man who grins when he fights.' (Reynolds, *All About* p. 152.)

return from Stanmore, Churchill asked that Chamberlain be informed that over a hundred German planes had been shot down. 'It is typical of W to do a small thing like that which could give such great pleasure,' Colville noted.[132] Churchill described it to Colville as 'one of the greatest days in history', with 161 confirmed German losses to thirty-four RAF that day, at least according to official British sources.[133] Radar early warning, the Spitfire's tight turning circle, well-trained and brave pilots fighting above their own soil and help from Polish, Commonwealth and other pilots were among the factors contributing to victory.* Mary was shopping in Harrods when the air-raid sirens went off at 12.30 p.m. the next day. 'I wish Hitler could have seen the complete calm of the great crowd assembled on the ground floor,' she wrote in her diary.[134] Three days later at Chequers, Churchill was 'irritable, worrying about Mrs Churchill, left behind in London, where air raids were threatened', his private secretary John Martin noted. 'In the end he decided to return to London after dinner and we drove back in the dark.'[135] Journeys such as this, in the Prime Minister's Humber car with a bell attached, could be exhilarating for Churchill's entourage. 'It is fun driving in the P.M.'s cortège,' wrote Colville: 'no attention is paid to traffic lights or speed limits.'[136]

Victory in the Battle of Britain was by no means assured by Tuesday, 20 August 1940, when Churchill made one of his greatest speeches of the war. 'If after tales of the panic-stricken British crushed in their holes cursing the plutocratic Parliament which has led them to such a plight – if after all this his whole air onslaught were forced after a while tamely to peter out, the Führer's reputation for veracity of statement might be seriously impugned,' he declared.[137] He promised the British people that the bombing of Germany's military industries and communications and her air bases and storage depots 'will continue upon an ever-increasing scale until the end of the war' as this was 'one at least of the most certain, if not the shortest, of all the roads to victory'.[138] He also praised the heroic efforts of the pilots of Fighter Command: 'The gratitude of every home in our Island, in our Empire, and indeed throughout the world, except in the abodes of the guilty, goes out to the British airmen who, undaunted by odds, unwearied in their constant challenge and mortal danger, are turning the tide of the World War by their prowess and by

* One by-product of the Battle of Britain was a renewed admiration for the Poles, who served in large numbers in the RAF having escaped the German invasion via Romania. 'When we have abolished Germany,' Churchill told Gort and Dowding in September, 'we will certainly establish Poland – and make them a permanent thing in Europe.' He suggested that one Pole was worth three Frenchmen: Gort and Dowding suggested ten. (Colville, *Fringes* pp. 245–6.)

their devotion. Never in the field of human conflict was so much owed by so many to so few.'[139]*

Churchill also paid tribute to the men of Bomber Command, and to de Gaulle, who since his escape had been condemned to death *in absentia* for treason by the Vichy Government. Then he turned again to America, arguing that her fate and that of the Commonwealth nations were inevitably interlinked. 'These two great organizations of the English-speaking democracies, the British Empire and the United States, will have to be somewhat mixed up together in some of their affairs for mutual and general advantage . . . I could not stop it if I wished; no one can stop it. Like the Mississippi, it just keeps rolling along.† Let it roll. Let it roll on full flood, inexorable, irresistible, benignant, to broader lands and better days.'[140]

Lines that thrilled ordinary people listening at 9 p.m. in pubs across the nation and that have become some of the most famous in our language did not always stir others in the political class, especially people who had opposed Churchill ideologically for years. Chips Channon was 'unimpressed'. Ivan Maisky thought 'Churchill was not at his best today.'[141] 'I am sure that today he is wholly intoxicated by the war,' sneered Lloyd George's daughter Megan, also an MP. 'He thinks only of that, is interested only in that.'[142]

'The secret of his great speeches was that he himself dictated all he was going to say,' explained Leslie Rowan, his private secretary, after the war. 'He did not accept, even in technical matters, the official texts which had to be submitted to him.'[143] Yet there were also technical reasons why they worked so well during the Second World War, besides the extraordinary amount of practice he had had at public speaking over the past four decades. Back in September 1904, he had adopted a stylistic device that he was often to reprise: the use of four consecutive alliterative adjectives before a noun. Speaking of efficient local government being refused funds by an incompetent Whitehall, he had told the Reform Club of Manchester, 'Like Oliver Twist, they ask for more; and Bumbledom and Beadledum can

* The most famous phrase of the speech had been playing in Churchill's mind for some time – not always in the context of such a noble cause. In 1936 he wrote, referring to the RMS *Queen Mary* in a *Strand Magazine* article, 'Never in the whole history of Atlantic travel has so lavish provision been made for those who travel "tourist"' (WSC, *CE* p. 332). Sir John Moore said of his campaign in Corsica in 1793, 'never was so much work done by so few men.'

† The phrase about the Mississippi 'rolling along' came from the song 'Ol' Man River' from *Show Boat*, the hit Broadway musical of 1927, with lyrics by Oscar Hammerstein II, which Churchill sang (out of tune) in the car on the short journey back to Downing Street.

only stare, and answer with a sullen, senseless, solid, stupid "No."'[144] His speaking technique adopted several other such deliberate techniques too. When Charles Eade congratulated him on the climax of his Manchester speech of 27 January 1940, he pointed out, wordsmith to wordsmith, 'that he had used nearly all words of one syllable'.[145]

'Short words are the best and the old words when short are the best of all,' Churchill said after the war.[146] He also made full use of anaphora, the repetition of the same words or phrases in successive sentences – 'We shall fight . . . we shall fight . . . we shall fight' – a proven oratorical formula dating back to Demosthenes. In *Kim*, by Rudyard Kipling, one of Churchill's favourite authors, there was a scene where seal pups are 'fighting on the beaches, fighting in the surf'. (By total contrast with Churchill, Hitler virtually stopped making broadcasts once the war started going badly. During the whole of 1944, for example, he spoke on German radio only once.)

The choice of 'benignant' in his 20 August 1940 speech, which comes from Old French, rather than the more common 'benign', was another example of Churchill's deliberate use of obscure and archaic words to strengthen his message. After Churchill's speeches had been delivered, his private secretaries would correct Hansard's official report where the stenographers had taken the words down wrongly, and they altered the text in some places to improve its style and grammar. As Colville explained, 'the P.M.'s speeches are essentially oratorical masterpieces and in speaking he inserts much that sounds well and reads badly.'[147] This explains why the printed texts of Churchill's speeches often do not tally precisely with what his listeners believed they had heard.

After dinner on 21 August, Churchill told Eden he was receiving 'little help from Cabinet colleagues . . . He and I and Max have to carry the Government . . . Sometimes he felt tired and he had never felt so lonely.'[148] Churchill's friend Ian Hamilton had written about 'the arctic loneliness of command', and Churchill felt it powerfully. He sounded out Eden about taking the Foreign Office, sensing that Halifax had little support in the country. Chamberlain was clearly now dying of cancer, and although Churchill said he would have resigned under the circumstances, he felt he could not ask him to do so.[149]

By that stage in the war, Britain's financial situation was dire. The Johnson Debt Default Act passed by Congress in 1934 prohibited foreign nations in default on their First World War war debts (as Britain was) from marketing bond issues in the United States. The Neutrality Act of 1939 further instituted a strict 'cash-and-carry' basis for arms purchases. Taken together, these meant that Britain had run out of dollars and gold with which to buy the munitions she needed to survive. 'Our reserves of gold and foreign currencies are desperately low and we can only carry on a few months longer,' Colville reported. Churchill nonetheless persuaded the Cabinet to go on placing orders for armaments in the United States, in the belief that after the election in November Roosevelt might display more generosity. In the last resort there was a scheme to requisition wedding rings and jewellery 'in order to shame the US', although it was estimated this would raise only some £20 million.[150]

'If the military position should unexpectedly deteriorate,' Churchill told the Cabinet, 'we should have to pledge everything we had for the sake of victory, giving the United States, if necessary, a lien on any and every part of British industry.'[151] His five years at the Treasury, and the debacle over the Gold Standard which he – and many economists and experts – had got so badly wrong, stood him in good stead now and gave him the strength to stand up to the officials who wanted him to cut back on armaments orders from America. 'If we go down under Germany's onslaughts,' he told the King, 'our reserves will be of no use to us, but if we can withstand them, the United States must come to our aid.'[152] The Roosevelt Administration assumed that the wily British were exaggerating their poverty in order to get the two laws repealed so that they could buy munitions on credit; Britain was indeed hiding the true extent of her penury but the purpose was not to influence US legislation; rather it was to prevent her weakness from becoming so apparent that there would be a run on sterling.

In mid-August the Cabinet was told that Britain would run out of dollars by Christmas. Unless Americans could be convinced to repeal or amend those two laws, national bankruptcy seemed a genuine possibility. Beaverbrook complained to Churchill that the American Government 'is asking for the moon and appears unwilling to pay sixpence', and J. M. Keynes used the phrase 'beggar my neighbour' to describe its attitude.[153] Under heavy pressure from Roosevelt, the British Government took out a $300 million loan from the Belgian Government-in-exile, which had large African assets, and his Administration would soon be shipping British gold from Simonstown in South Africa to New York in return for munitions, as well as taking it from the bank where it was being kept in Toronto.[154] When Sir Kingsley Wood suggested that Britain could be recompensed for the financial support she gave to Holland by changing the present 60/40 Dutch–British ownership of Royal Dutch Shell to 50/50, Churchill said he never again wanted to hear any proposal for taking advantage of an Allied country's misfortunes.[155] Although Britain was in dire straits financially, Churchill had no wish to plunder the assets of countries suffering under Nazi occupation. (The Dutch and Belgian merchant fleets had sailed to Britain at the time of Dunkirk.) Instead, he hoped that the Roosevelt Administration would repeal the legislation that prevented it from lending money to Britain with which to buy munitions.

Between 24 August and 6 September, more than a thousand German sorties were made over Britain every twenty-four hours in an attempt to destroy the RAF's command and control stations. During one ten-day period, the RAF lost 154 pilots and 213 aircraft, and only sixty-three newly trained pilots and fewer than 150 fighter aircraft arrived to replace them. In one respect, the British had a considerable advantage: German pilots who baled out over Britain were interned for the rest of the war, whereas RAF pilots who did the same could be back up in the air that same day.[156] Nonetheless, by early September attacks by General Kesselring's Luftflotte 2 on Air Vice Marshal Keith Park's 11 Fighter Group threatened to break the RAF's command and control system in the south of England.

'Now that they have begun to molest the capital, I want you to hit them hard,' Churchill told Air Chief Marshal Newall, 'and Berlin is the place to hit them.'[157] On the night of 25 August, the RAF bombed armament factories in Berlin and at the city's Tempelhof Airport. Later that month he said, 'Let 'em have it. Remember this. Never maltreat the enemy by halves.'[158] At that stage of the war, and for some time afterwards, the RAF bombed military and industrial targets rather than city centres. In mid-October, when an MP told him that the public demanded all-out bombing of German civilians, especially in Berlin, Churchill replied, 'My dear sir, this is a military and not a civilian war. You and others may desire to kill women and children. We desire (and have succeeded in our desire) to destroy German military objectives. I quite appreciate your point. But my motto is "Business before pleasure."'[159]

While directing which cities to bomb, and working to avert a full-scale financial crisis in late August, Churchill was also inspecting the defences of the south-east. At night he returned to No. 10 to sleep in the air-raid shelter there with Clementine and the family.[160] At 9.30 p.m. on the 27th when the sirens were sounding, 'Winston, to his obvious regret, refused brandy and demanded iced soda-water, saying he was ashamed of the easy life he led and had never before lived in such luxury.'[161]

At Chequers on 30 August, fortified by 1911 vintage champagne – the soda-water puritanism had lasted a full three days – Churchill announced that 'only three things worried him': the proportions of air losses were too high; shipping losses in the North-Western Approaches of the Atlantic 'might be mortal'; and the gun batteries at Gris Nez at the Pas-de-Calais could close the Channel and leave Dover 'in ashes'.[162] All three were eventually addressed successfully. 'My object is to preserve the maximum initiative energy,' Churchill said. 'Every night I try myself by court-martial to see if I have done anything effective during the day. I don't mean just pawing the ground – anyone can go through the motions – but something really effective.'[163] He brought the Joint Planning Staff down to Chequers to discuss possible future actions such as the recapture of Oslo, an amphibious invasion of Italy, raiding the Channel Islands, seizing Casablanca and Dakar, cutting off the Cherbourg Peninsula, landing in the Low Countries and seizing the Ruhr, with forces of 100,000 to 120,000 men involved in some of these putative operations.[164] All of these plans were far beyond current British capabilities, and became possible only once America had entered the war.

On Saturday, 31 August, Fighter Command lost thirty-nine planes and fourteen pilots killed, but the Luftwaffe was suffering far heavier losses. The Germans also grossly overestimated the damage they were inflicting on the RAF. Churchill visited the fighter pilots of No. 11 Group headquarters at RAF Uxbridge (which can still be visited today) and watched an air battle in progress. The operations room 50 feet underground, with its Women's Auxiliary Air Force personnel moving squadrons around on vast maps, its coloured lights and its real-time updates, was the perfect place to watch the Battle of Britain unfold.[165] Pouring himself a glass of brandy at Chequers at lunchtime just before the Uxbridge trip, 'and eyeing us all benevolently', as Colville put it, Churchill remarked that 'It was curious, but in this war he had had no success but had received nothing but praise, whereas in the last war he had done several things which he thought were good and had got nothing but abuse for them.'[166] He then allowed himself a private dig at the Americans, saying that 'their morale was very good – in applauding the valiant deeds done by others!'[167]

Churchill got into an argument with Dowding over dinner, over whether it was acceptable to shoot enemy pilots landing by parachute, 'Dowding maintaining it should be done and the P.M. saying that an escaping pilot was like a drowning sailor'. Except for this wish not to exterminate unarmed pilots, Colville recorded, the Prime Minister 'was in a very ruthless frame of mind'.[168] After dinner, Pound called from the Admiralty to report that from the look of enemy ship movements 'the invasion may be pending'. That would have triggered Operation Cromwell, with the hitherto silenced church bells rung across southern England as a signal for the Home Guard to go into action.

'It is terrible – terrible – that the British Empire should have been gambled on this,' Churchill said of the appeasement of Hitler when he was back at Uxbridge the following day.[169] On his return to Chequers he was told that a brand-new cruiser, HMS *Fiji*, had been torpedoed in the North-Western Approaches. Three major ships had now been lost there – including one full of children being evacuated to New York, which had 'distressed him particularly'. 'The Admiralty is now the weak spot,' Churchill said, 'the air is all right.'[170] At dinner, he told two Coldstream Guards officers who were on duty at Chequers (one of whom, John Sparrow, was later warden of All Souls, Oxford), 'that we could not hope to pile up sufficient men and munitions to outmatch the Germans. This was a war of science, a war that would be won with new weapons.'[171]*

Since August, Churchill had been negotiating a deal to get fifty destroyers from the United States in exchange for ninety-nine-year leases for American bases on British possessions in Newfoundland, Bermuda, the Bahamas, several West Indian Islands and British Guiana. To critics concerned by the loss of sovereignty, Churchill pointed out that the deal was as much about boosting morale and enticing America towards war as gaining the materiel itself. 'If the proposal went through,' he told the Cabinet, 'the United States would have made a long step towards coming into the war on our side. To sell destroyers to a belligerent nation [is] certainly not a neutral act.'[172] Churchill asked Ambassador Kennedy to tell Roosevelt, 'In the long history of the world, this is a thing to do now.' He himself told the President, 'Every destroyer you can spare us is measured in rubies.'[173]

On the first anniversary of the outbreak of war, Churchill announced the destroyers-for-bases deal. Although he knew that some of the fifty American destroyers were all but obsolete, they took over the patrol duties of other destroyers that could now be used in battle, at a time when Britain was dangerously short of escort vessels. The propaganda value of any American support was immense.[174] 'After a year of war,' the King reported of Churchill, 'he felt more confident about our position today. In the Battle for Britain in the air, he thought Germany were using a larger percentage of their air force than we were. We are using one-third of our fighter force.'[175] Two weeks later Churchill told the Cabinet, repeating his vision of the way ahead, 'The fighters are our salvation . . . but the bombers alone provide the means of victory . . . In no other way at present visible can we hope to overcome the immense military power of Germany.'[176]

* An amused Colville noted that Clementine 'does nothing but profess democratic and radical sentiments', but at the same time put off inviting any of the officers at Chequers to dinner, 'until the guard consisted of the Coldstream' (Colville, *Fringes* p. 238).

On 4 September, Hitler spoke at the Berlin Sportpalast. He announced that because 'Herr Churchill' had promised to increase attacks on German cities, 'we will erase their cities from the earth.'[177] Churchill spoke in the Commons that same day, reporting that 1,075 civilians had been killed in air raids during August, and 800 homes destroyed. 'Our sympathy goes out to the wounded and to those who are bereaved,' he said, 'but no one can pretend that out of forty-five million people these are losses which, even if multiplied as they may be two or three times, would be serious compared to the majestic world issues which are at stake.'[178] They were to be multiplied fifty times by the end of the war, but the sentiment still held true.

That night at the Other Club, Churchill was presented with a silver snuffbox inscribed with the words 'This box, which once was Nelson's, we now confide to you, Winston Churchill.'[179] He sat next to Keynes, who told his mother that he had found him 'in absolutely perfect condition, extremely well, serene, full of normal human feelings and completely uninflated. Perhaps this moment is the height of his power and glory, but I have never seen anyone less infected with dictatorial airs or hubris. There was not the faintest trace of the insolence which Lloyd George, for example, so quickly acquired.'[180]

# 23
# The Blitz
# September 1940–January 1941

*Nothing surpasses 1940.*

Churchill, *Their Finest Hour*[1]

*This was a time when it was equally good to live or die.*

Churchill, *Their Finest Hour*[2]

It was just as well that Churchill was in 'perfect condition': within forty-eight hours he was to be tested as never before in his long and eventful life. On Saturday, 7 September 1940, three days after Hitler's speech at the Berlin Sportpalast, the London Blitz began with a raid of 200 bombers which killed 300 Londoners. The Luftwaffe was to assault the capital for four terrifying months, and initially the bombers returned for fifty-seven consecutive nights. Searchlights, sirens and bomb-blasts were to stalk the daily lives of millions of Londoners. In 1934, Churchill had predicted chaos when 'under the pressure of continuous attack upon London, three or four million people would be driven out into the open country around the metropolis'.[3] In the event, three million people, the quarter of the city's population who were non-essential for the war effort, had already been calmly and safely evacuated all over the country, and there was no panic in the capital.

Switching the Luftwaffe from carrying out daylight raids on RAF installations in southern England to undertaking night raids on London was a major strategic blunder, because it allowed Fighter Command to repair its runways, hangars and command and control stations. 'At first we could do little but take our punishment,' recalled Ismay, but Churchill then set up the Night Air Defence Committee, which brought together anti-aircraft gunners, scientists and airmen to discuss how to combat the danger from the Luftwaffe. 'Soon the number of aircraft destroyed increased, and the altitude at which they flew increased too, lessening their accuracy.' A few days into the Blitz, Churchill visited the docklands in the East End of London. 'Fires were still raging all over the place,' wrote Ismay, 'some of the larger buildings were mere skeletons, and many of the smaller houses had been reduced to rubble. The sight of tiny paper Union Jacks which had already been planted on two or three of these pathetic heaps brought a lump to one's throat.'[4]

Their first stop was an air-raid shelter where forty people had been killed and many more wounded by a direct hit the previous night. There, Ismay remembered,

> we found a big crowd, male and female, young and old, but all seemingly very poor. One might have expected them to be resentful against the authorities responsible for their protection; but, as Churchill got out of the car, they literally mobbed him. 'Good old Winnie,' they cried. 'We thought you'd come and see us. We can take it. Give it 'em back.' Churchill broke down, and as I was struggling to get to him through the crowd, I heard an old woman say 'You see, he really cares: he's crying.'[5]

Whereas Hitler never once visited a bomb-site, driving past such scenes with the curtains of his Mercedes-Benz drawn, Churchill went constantly to the East End during the Blitz to boost morale. On these inspection visits, he covered miles of ground at a remarkably fast pace, despite generally engaging in no exercise and often being driven even the very short distance from Downing Street to the House of Commons. (Walter Thompson lost two stone in weight having to keep up with him.) These visits to bomb-sites proved extraordinarily good for public morale. In his memoirs, Churchill wrote of a visit to Peckham in south London, where the crowd shouted, 'Let them have it too!' He wrote, 'I undertook forthwith to see their wishes were carried out; and this promise was certainly kept.'[6] On a couple of occasions there were angry shouts directed against Churchill for the devastation wrought, against the hundreds of times when he was cheered; similarly some people looted neighbours' empty, bombed-out houses and businesses, but these instances of opportunism were few and in no way overshadowed the many thousands of daily acts of heroism, selflessness and communal solidarity.[7]* Having watched many air battles,

* Even during the Battle of Britain and the Blitz, with so many other things on his mind, the traumatic events of 1886 were never far from it. Lord Cranborne (who become the 5th Marquess of Salisbury in 1947) recalled that in September 1940, during dinner, 'Churchill, as he sometimes did, sank into a silent and sombre reverie. Then he suddenly turned to me and said, apropos of nothing, "I always consider that your grandfather treated my father disgracefully."' Cranborne, who was paymaster-general, was taken aback and murmured some emollient comment in reply. 'The conversation trickled into the sand,' he said, 'and the dinner party reverted

and been, in Colville's words, 'much affected by the plight of those whose houses have been destroyed or badly damaged by raids', Churchill tried to get the compensation for destroyed homes raised to £1,000 (approximately £52,000 in today's money).[8]

As well as housing, Churchill paid very close attention to rationing throughout the war, recognizing how closely related food was to morale. He inundated the Food Minister Lord Woolton with questions and suggestions about every aspect of rationing, opposing any rules that he thought unnecessary.[9] 'Almost all the food-faddists I have ever known, nut-eaters and the like, have died young after a long period of senile decay,' he wrote to Woolton in mid-July, for example. 'The British soldier is more likely to be right than the scientists. All he cares about is beef . . . The way to lose the war is to try to force the British people into a diet of milk, oatmeal, potatoes, etc, washed down on gala occasions with a little lime juice.'[10] Churchill presided over meetings to ensure that cooking stoves and other amenities were provided in air-raid shelters.[11]

He attended the first of what became regular Tuesday lunches with the King on 10 September. Because of the sensitivity of the matters discussed, they served themselves from a sideboard so that no servants needed to be present. Churchill entrusted the King with every wartime secret, including the Ultra and atomic ones, knowing there would be no leaks, and that this was one person who was not secretly after his job. Typically seeing their relationship in the perspective of history (and overlooking the claims of Queen Victoria and Benjamin Disraeli), Churchill said that there had been no precedent for 'the gracious intimacy' between monarch and Prime Minister 'since the days of Queen Anne and Marlborough during his years of power'.[12] He was the only one of the King's four premiers to be addressed by his Christian name.[13] As the King and Queen travelled widely around the country, Churchill was able to gain insights from them about conditions and morale too.

On Wednesday, 11 September 1940, Churchill reminded the British people in a radio address that they had been in a position of mortal peril often before, and had first survived and then triumphed in every case. 'We must regard the next week or so as a very important period in our history,' he told them.

> It ranks with the days when the Spanish Armada was approaching the Channel, and Drake was finishing his game of bowls; or when Nelson stood

---

to the rather more important questions of bombers and fighters, and Hitler and Goering.' (Blake, 'Conservative' p. 2.) His ancestry did not affect Cranborne's career, however; he was promoted to dominions secretary the following month.

> between us and Napoleon's Grand Army at Boulogne. We have read all about this in the history books; but what is happening now is on a far greater scale and of far more consequence to the life and future of the world and its Civilization than these brave old days of the past. Every man and woman will therefore prepare himself to do his duty, whatever it may be, with special pride and care.[14]

'These cruel, wanton, indiscriminate bombings of London are, of course, a part of Hitler's invasion plans,' he said.

> He hopes, by killing large numbers of civilians, and women and children, that he will terrorize and cow the people of this mighty imperial city, and make them a burden and an anxiety to the Government and thus distract our attention unduly from the ferocious onslaught he is preparing. Little does he know the spirit of the British nation, or the tough fibre of the Londoners, whose forebears played a leading part in the establishment of Parliamentary institutions and who have been bred to value freedom far above their lives. This wicked man, the repository and embodiment of many forms of soul-destroying hatred, this monstrous product of former wrongs and shame, has now resolved to try to break our famous Island race by a process of indiscriminate slaughter and destruction. What he has done is to kindle a fire in British hearts, here and all over the world, which will glow long after all traces of the conflagration he has caused in London have been removed. He has lighted a fire which will burn with a steady and consuming flame until the last vestiges of Nazi tyranny have been burnt out of Europe, and until the Old World and the New can join hands to rebuild the temples of Man's freedom and Man's honour, upon foundations which will not soon or easily be overthrown.[15]

The Canadian diplomat Charles Ritchie noted in his diary, 'He makes them feel they are living their history.'[16] Churchill could do this because the battles and struggles of the Elizabethan and Napoleonic wars were then taught in schools, so the stories of Drake and Nelson were well known to his listeners. The Russian Ambassador noted the effect that Churchill's oratory and leadership had on the British people. 'It's precisely the resolute and definite character of the British Government's stance which has done so much to help the masses overcome their initial fright,' wrote Maisky. 'There is no panic in the country and Churchill intends to fight tooth and nail.'[17] Churchill repeatedly said both during the war and after that all he did was to reflect and articulate the British people's determination to fight on until victory, but he did much to create, sustain and direct it too.

For the moment, however, Churchill's sole strategy was to try to get through the German attack from day to day, and to keep Britain in the war until a plan for eventual victory could be formulated once survival was sure. Sunday, 15 September 1940 saw the last mass daylight air attack on Britain. Kesselring sent over 400 fighters to escort a hundred bombers. A gigantic air battle broke out over south-eastern England which turned out to be one of the most decisive battles of the war. Churchill watched it from RAF Uxbridge and left a memorable account of the battle:

> One after another signals came in, '40 plus', '60 plus'; there was even an '80 plus' . . . Presently the red bulbs showed that the majority of our squadrons were engaged . . . I became conscious of the anxiety of the Commander, who now stood still behind his subordinate's chair. Hitherto I had watched in silence. I now asked: 'What other reserves have we?' 'There are none,' said Air Vice-Marshal Park.* In an account which he wrote about it afterwards he said that at this I 'looked grave'. Well I might. What losses should we not suffer if our refuelling planes were caught on the ground by further raids of '40 plus' or '50 plus'! The odds were great; our margins small; the stakes infinite.[18]

'It was not until later in the day, at Chequers,' wrote John Martin, 'that we realized the magnitude of the British victory.'[19] At the time the RAF believed (or at least claimed) that 186 German planes had been shot down, although today we know the true number was fifty-six. Martin could wake Churchill up from his afternoon nap with the words, 'All is redeemed by the air.'[20] Two days later, Hitler postponed Operation Sealion, and on 12 October the invasion was formally called off, as Hitler put it, 'until the following spring'.[21]

Churchill was not to know that immediately; and on 17 September he called a secret session of the House of Commons to inform Members of the measures being taken to repel the expected invasion. No visitors or journalists were allowed. Just as he was about to speak, the Air Raid Precaution spotters on the roof blew their whistles to warn that bombers were on their way, so the MPs went down to the shelters until it was safe to re-emerge. When they returned to their benches, Churchill warned that the bombing would get worse, that the Palace of Westminster was 'the easiest of all targets' and that the Germans had enough shipping ready for half a million men to cross the Channel. 'We should, of course, expect to

* Park meant that there were no reserves at that moment in No. 11 Group. There were more than 350 fighter planes elsewhere in the United Kingdom, but they were defending other vital areas.

drown a great many on the way over,' he said by way of qualification, 'and to destroy a large proportion of their vessels.'[22] He added that with German exploitation of real fog or the deployment of artificial fog along the British coastline, 'One must expect many lodgments or attempted lodgments to be made on our island simultaneously.'[23] Harold Nicolson wrote in his diary, 'I must say that he does not try to cheer us up with vain promises.'[24]

As Colville walked back to No. 10 afterwards, there was 'a vast explosion. I met the P.M. who swore that he had seen, from his bedroom window, a bomb hit Buckingham Palace. Everybody was packed off to the shelter.'[25] Buckingham Palace was hit nine times during the war, on that occasion by a time-bomb dropped in its gardens. Churchill told the Commons shortly afterwards,

> The deliberate and repeated attacks upon Buckingham Palace and upon the persons of our beloved King and Queen are also intended, apart from their general barbarity, to have an unsettling effect upon public opinion. They have, of course, the opposite effect. They unite the King and Queen to their people by new and sacred bonds of common danger, and they steel the hearts of all to the stern and unrelenting prosecution of the war against so foul a foe.[26]

The next day, 18 September, a parachute land-mine shattered windows at No. 10 and the Foreign Office, and embedded a piece of shrapnel firmly into the panelling of the private secretaries' office next to Churchill's, which Martin saw as 'a reminder to treat seriously our alarm bell'.[27] Churchill was meanwhile writing to Alexander saying, 'First Lord, Surely you can run to a new Admiralty flag. It grieves me to see the present dingy object every morning. W.S.C.'[28] Suggestions that he was stooping to trivialities with such continuous small orders miss the point that he understood morale to be a vital aspect of war.

Despite postponing the invasion, Hitler continued to bomb Britain intensively, both in the hope of breaking civilian morale so that a renewed invasion attempt could be made in the future, and for revenge against the bombing of Berlin and other cities, which he and Göring had told the German people was a military impossibility. Over the next four months, Churchill visited more than sixty towns and aerodromes that had been subjected to heavy bombing. The defiance he had heard on his trips to Peckham and the docklands in the early stages grew stronger as the bombing became fiercer. 'We can take it, we can take it,' was the cry Walter Thompson recorded, 'but give it to them back.'[29] Churchill replied, 'We will give it back tenfold, but first we must turn out the planes. Give us a little more time and I promise you repayment – repayment with compound interest.'[30] On 19 September he ordered Portal at Bomber Command to hit Berlin as soon as the weather permitted, adding, 'as the Germans were dropping these parachute mines indiscriminately, we must say that we would drop two for every one of theirs.'[31] Ultimately over half a million Germans died from aerial bombardment during the war, to Britain's 58,000. After seeing the devastation caused by a land-mine parachuted on to Wandsworth in south London in early October, Colville recorded that Churchill was 'becoming less and less benevolent towards the Germans, and talks about castrating the lot. He says there will be no nonsense about a "just peace".'[32] That night he described the Boer War as 'the last enjoyable war'.[33]

On 20 September, Ultra intelligence led Churchill to tell Colville, without revealing the source, that he thought it 'doubtful whether invasion will be tried in the near future'.[34] He nonetheless worried about the thick fog from the North Foreland to Dungeness which would prevent early warning being given to the Home Guard, and regularly rang the Admiralty to ask about the weather in the Channel.[35] As it took a few days to decrypt Enigma messages at that time, and there was in any case a time-lag between Hitler's decision to postpone Operation Sealion and any perceptible reduction in forces on the Channel coast, Churchill cannot really be accused of misleading Parliament about the likelihood of an invasion, and in any case he wanted Britons to continue to believe they were under imminent threat, as a spur to unity and productivity. One invasion scare in late September was triggered by Roosevelt, who claimed to have information from a 'most reliable source' in Berlin that it was imminent.[36] Overall, however, Churchill believed that the Germans had missed their opportunity. 'Hitler could and should have invaded this country after Dunkirk,' he told the King on 1 October, 'leaving the advance into Paris until later. The French could not have prevented Germany from doing so.'[37]

On 23 September, as the Germans expanded their attacks to Coventry, Birmingham and Liverpool, the Free French suffered a serious reverse at Dakar when they attempted to wrest Senegal from Vichy.[38] Churchill had initially supported the operation, codenamed Menace, despite the Chiefs of Staff being highly doubtful about it. 'Let 'em have it,' he had said. 'Once the battle is joined, let 'em have it.'[39] It had involved the Royal Navy transporting General de Gaulle and his small Free French force to Dakar, but unfortunately the Pétainist forces were fully prepared for the attack and repulsed it easily. De Gaulle had hoped that sheer *force majeure* would win over the local population, but he had not wanted Frenchmen to fight Frenchmen, a preference which lowered him in Churchill's estimation. Vichy then bombed Gibraltar in retaliation. Churchill, who had overruled de Gaulle and Vice Admiral Sir John Cunningham and insisted on the operation going ahead, decided that no explanation should initially be offered to Parliament or the nation, but his silence undermined confidence in his Government. The *Daily Mirror* ran an article entitled 'The Gallipoli Touch?' 'Feeling at the Carlton Club is running high against him,' recorded Channon.[40] Commenting on the absence of a reprimand for Cunningham, who commanded the Royal Navy element of the operation, Churchill wrote in his memoirs, 'It was one of my rules that *errors towards the enemy* must be lightly judged.'[41] 'There was no dash,'[42] Churchill told the King of the Dakar expedition. 'It is very depressing that we cannot have a success anywhere.'[43] It was not wholly true; the RAF had carried out a 120-bomber raid on Berlin the previous night. 'We only bomb military objectives, of course,' Churchill said, 'but if the enemy persist in indiscriminate bombing of civilian dwellings we shall have to do the same.'[44]

On 27 September 1940, Germany, Italy and Japan signed a ten-year Tripartite Pact. All three Fascist powers were now formally allied, recognizing a 'New Order' in Europe and the Far East. Churchill looked 'pensive' when he heard the news but not down-hearted, as closer cooperation between the Axis powers had been expected and, as he put it, one of the clauses was 'aimed plum at the United States'.[45]

Chamberlain was now in the terminal phase of his cancer. 'I can't bear to think of Neville being under this continual bombardment in London,' Churchill had written to Chamberlain's wife Anne on 20 September. 'He must give himself a decent chance to recover full efficiency. I have been very much worried about you both during these last ten days.'[46] When it was clear that would not happen, Chamberlain resigned on 1 October, turning down Churchill's offers of a peerage and the Order of the Garter, saying, 'I prefer to die plain Mr Chamberlain, like my father before me, unadorned by any title.'[47] Churchill offered Eden the choice of either the 'entirely domestic' job of lord president of the Council within the War Cabinet, chairing committees concerning the home front, or continuing outside it as secretary for war, with responsibility for the Army, because he could not have the ministers for the Navy and RAF inside it too. Eden opted for the latter. Churchill would have liked to move Eden to the Foreign Office, but he could not risk having Halifax leave the Government at the same time as Chamberlain.[48] 'He reiterated that he was now an old man,' Eden told his diary, 'that he would not make LG's mistake of carrying on after the war, that the succession must be mine – John Anderson could clearly not be in the way in this respect.'[49] It was the first of fifteen years of such promises to Eden, of which the kindest thing that can said was that he meant them at the time.

In the Cabinet reshuffle three days later, which Churchill admitted to Chamberlain was partly designed to distract attention from the Dakar fiasco, Anderson became lord president of the Council and Herbert Morrison took over as home secretary, while Ernest Bevin and Kingsley Wood entered the War Cabinet in their present posts of minister of labour and chancellor of the Exchequer.[50] 'The people are not ready to take heed of good counsel,' Lloyd George wrote to Frances Stevenson. 'They still cherish illusions of "complete victory". Maybe Hitler is not ready to agree to the only peace which a British Government can accept.'[51]

At the same time as the Cabinet reshuffle, Churchill shook up the Services. Sir Charles Portal had impressed Churchill and became chief of the Air Staff, at the age of only forty-seven, in place of Sir Cyril Newall. There were changes in the upper echelons of the Admiralty – Churchill had long wanted to promote the fighting admirals Phillips, Harwood and Tovey, though Pound stayed on as first sea lord, and General John Kennedy became director of operations at the War Office. 'He is extraordinarily obstinate,' Kennedy was soon writing of the Prime Minister. 'He is like a child that has set his mind on some forbidden toy. It is no good explaining that it will cut his fingers or burn him. The more you explain, the more fixed he becomes in his idea.'[52] Kennedy never really understood that Churchill liked to bounce impossible ideas off the Planning Staff in order to work out in his own mind the few which were practicable, or might be so in the months or years to come. It was exhausting and frustrating for the planners, of course, but that was ultimately what they were there for. 'To cope with the situation adequately,' Kennedy wrote, 'it would almost have been worthwhile to have two staffs: one to deal with the P.M., the other with the war.'[53]

Wavell kept his job as commander-in-chief in the Middle East, despite Churchill's lack of enthusiasm for him. At a Defence Committee meeting in late September, Churchill had severely criticized Wavell's Egyptian dispositions. Eden strongly defended the general by pointing out that he was hampered by a lack of equipment, especially planes. Afterwards, Churchill said that Eden 'ought not to be so violent with him', but Eden merely replied that the Prime Minister was forever attacking the Army unjustly. 'He retorted that he was far harder on the Navy,' which was hardly an excuse.[54] When Churchill described Dill as 'just a pleasant old gentleman', Eden came to his defence too. On 22 September at Chequers, Churchill said that he expected Wavell to be victorious over the Italians in Egypt, 'unless, of course, our men fight like skunks* and the Italians like heroes', but he thought the opposite more likely to be the case.[55]

Churchill was unreceptive when in December Wavell complained that Jewish refugees had managed to land in Palestine, at a time when they were being refused entry permits by the British authorities there, effectively a death-sentence for those attempting to flee Nazi-occupied Europe. Churchill had eloquently denounced the notorious 1939 White Paper that had severely restricted Jewish immigration into Palestine. 'Now, there is the breach,' he had told Parliament, 'there is the violation of the pledge; there is the abandonment of the Balfour Declaration; there is the end of the vision, of the hope, of the dream . . . What will those who have been stirring up these Arab agitators think? Will they not be encouraged by our confession of recoil? Will they not be tempted to say: "They're on the run again. This is another Munich."'[56] Now, as prime minister, he found himself equally powerless to help the Jews. Eden recorded in his diary Churchill's 'vehement telephone call denouncing Wavell and all in the Middle East as Jew-baiters. "Why cannot W[avell] mind his own business?"' Eden retorted that it would indeed become Wavell's business 'if the Arabs caused trouble over the migrants'. Churchill replied, 'Nothing would induce me to modify my view.'[57] Yet such was the political and bureaucratic opposition within Westminster and Whitehall that Churchill could not get the Zionist view adopted by the British authorities in Palestine. It was a further indication that, powerful though he was, he still had to convince colleagues, and was far from the omnipotent British dictator some of his detractors were to depict.

If he had been authoritarian, he would certainly not have tolerated the press criticism to which he was subjected almost throughout the war. In October, he launched into a tirade in Cabinet against the left-wing *Daily Mirror*, saying he wanted it suspended. 'Winston frightfully excited about it,' Halifax wrote in his diary, 'seeing in its tone clear evidence of Fifth Column activity.' Yet Churchill quickly changed his mind, and freedom of speech and of the press survived the war remarkably well. The next day he told the Commons, 'Our people do not mind being told the worst.' The previous week, 180 Londoners had been killed by 250 tons of bombs. He extrapolated that statistic to say that at that rate it would take ten years to demolish half the houses of London, and that 'Quite a lot of things are going to happen to Herr Hitler and the Nazi regime before ten years are

* The use of the word 'skunk' makes one wonder what he had in fact said about Shinwell in the Norway Debate four months earlier. See p. 498.

up. And even Signor Mussolini has some experiences ahead of him which he had not foreseen at the time when he thought it safe and profitable to stab the stricken and prostrate French Republic in the back. Neither by material damage nor by slaughter will the people of the British Empire be turned from their solemn and inexorable purpose.'[58] 'Winston made one of his best speeches in the House,' Eden wrote in his diary. 'A very remarkable performance even for him. For the moment criticism of Dakar is silenced.'[59]

It was an emotional moment for Churchill on 8 October when he introduced Randolph, who had been elected MP for Preston unopposed, to the House. There was much applause, which was, as Colville was at pains to point out, for the father rather than the son. 'We have a deep animal love for one another,' Churchill said of his relationship with Randolph, 'but every time we meet we have a bloody row.'[60] Randolph delivered his maiden speech in the Commons in November. His proud father was present, but in sharp contrast to Churchill's policy of never attacking the Tory former appeasers in public – they still made up the majority of the Conservative parliamentary party – Randolph said, 'Looking around this House – I say this with all deference – one can see a number of honourable and right honourable Gentlemen who in a greater or lesser degree bear some responsibility for the state of our Forces and any shortage of equipment which might perhaps handicap those who plan our strategy. I have no wish to recriminate about the past.'[61] The claims to deference and absence of recrimination can safely be discounted, but his main point was as true as it was self-indulgent and unhelpful to his father. Randolph's military service in Africa and Yugoslavia meant that he made only three parliamentary speeches in his career, which was probably just as well.

Chamberlain's illness forced him to resign from the leadership of the Conservative Party as well as from his Cabinet post. Churchill was invited to succeed him. Clementine and some others thought he should not take on the job, but, remembering the way the Tories had brought Lloyd George down in 1922, when he was prime minister but not a party leader, he decided to accept. 'I should have found it impossible to conduct the war', he stated in his memoirs, 'if I had had to procure the agreement . . . not only of the Leaders of the two minority parties but of the Leader of the Conservative majority . . . I do not feel I could have borne such a trial successfully in war.'[62] Halifax proposed him at the Party meeting at Caxton Hall in Westminster on 9 October, although he privately commented how hard it was for him 'avoiding a comparison between Neville and Winston while managing to say nice things about each'. He still regarded Chamberlain as much the better prime minister, not least because of his more crisp and efficient chairing of Cabinet meetings, at which Churchill tended to expound, reminisce and joke.

As Churchill had been a Conservative for only sixteen years, and in his Liberal days had denounced the Tory Party with all the zeal of a convert, he had to choose his words of acceptance carefully. 'I shall attempt no justification,' he said; 'it springs most deeply from the convictions of my heart, that at all times according to my lights and throughout the changing scenes through which we are all hurried I have always faithfully served two public causes which I think stand supreme – the maintenance of the enduring greatness of Britain and her Empire and the historical continuity of our Island life.'[63] He thus accepted the leadership 'solemnly but also buoyantly', admitting, 'I have a tendency against which I should, perhaps, be on my guard, to swim against the stream.' It was just as well he had not posted the letter he had written to Hugh Cecil thirty-seven years earlier, in which he stated, 'I hate the Tory party, their men, their words and their methods. I feel no sort of sympathy with them.'[64] Considering the sheer fury that he had aroused so often on the Tory benches in the past it was a tribute to his present stature, as well as to his perseverance and his message, that he was now unanimously elected as the Party's leader.

The next day at Chequers Pamela Churchill gave birth to a son, whom she and Randolph christened Winston, a fine compliment. The grandfather visited Chequers the next day. 'Probably they don't think I am so foolish as to come here,' he said of the Germans; 'but I stand to lose a lot, three generations at a swoop.'[65]* That weekend, smoking an immense cigar at lunchtime, he expressed his belief that air raids produced 'the sort of war which would suit the English people once they were used to it. They would prefer all to be in the front line, taking part in the Battle of London, than to look on helplessly at mass slaughters like Passchendaele.'[66] At dinner with Attlee and Randolph, swapping election stories, he said 'he had learned one great lesson from his father: never to be afraid of British democracy.'[67] He quipped to Attlee the next day, 'A Hun alive is a war in prospect.'[68]

Pound, Portal and Dowding were staying at Chequers on 13 October

* Churchill provided entertaining company for the young Winston. When he was three and a half, the child was given a model railway set. 'My grandfather got down on the bedroom floor with me and, together, we assembled the circular track,' he recalled. 'To his huge delight, he saw there were two clockwork locomotives. Giving one to me and keeping the other for himself he exclaimed: "You wind one up, Winston – I'll wind up the other! Let's put them back-to-back. Let's have a crash!"' (ed. Langworth, *Dream* p. 56.) Churchill enjoyed playing with children's toys; during the Great War he and his nine-year-old nephew Johnnie made a cantilever crane 15 feet long and 8 feet high out of Meccano, in the dining room at 41 Cromwell Road. 'The servants were forbidden to move it,' recalled Johnnie, 'and my uncle gazed fondly at his creation during meals.' (Churchill, *Crowded Canvas* p. 33.)

and as Churchill said goodnight 'He told them he was sure we were going to win the war, but he confessed he did not see clearly how it was going to be achieved.'[69] He wanted a large army in the Middle East by January, and mobile divisions for amphibious operations, though these were not really blueprints for victory over a Nazi-controlled Europe. 'Bombing of military objectives seems at present to be our main road home,' he wrote to Halifax.[70] Part of Churchill's genius in 1940 was not only keeping Britain in the war, but infusing the country with a belief in ultimate victory while having no convincing rationale – apart from a general belief in bombing – for how it would come about. Although he liked and admired Dowding personally, he acquiesced in his replacement as head of Fighter Command by Sholto Douglas the next month, because Portal and Sinclair both felt that Dowding was not getting to grips with the German night attacks and opposed the new 'Big Wing' formations that the Air Ministry wanted to employ to counter the German threat. It was another example of Churchill not allowing personal considerations to affect policy.

Back at No. 10 on 14 October, he was halfway through dinner in the steel-shuttered basement when he had what he later called 'a providential impulse'.[71] He got up and went to the kitchen to tell Georgina Landemare, his cook, as well as the butler and kitchen-maid, to leave the food on the hot-plates and go to the air-raid shelter immediately. He then returned to the table. Three minutes later, a bomb landed between No. 10 and the Treasury, causing 'a really very loud crash, close at hand, and a violent shock showed that the house had been struck'.[72] Walter Thompson came in to check that the Prime Minister was unharmed and to inform his guests – Archie Sinclair, John Moore-Brabazon (the new Transport Minister), Oliver Lyttelton (the new President of the Board of Trade) and Sir Stewart Menzies, the head of MI6 – that considerable damage had been done. 'The mess in the house was indescribable,' John Martin told his parents, 'windows smashed in all directions, everything covered with grime, doors off hinges and curtains and furniture tossed about in a confused mass . . . The hut of the soldiers who guard Downing Street was completely demolished: fortunately they had taken refuge elsewhere.'[73] Churchill told Thompson, 'A pity it didn't fall a little closer in order to test our defences.'[74] In fact it was just as well it had not, since the bomb-blast had devastated the kitchen and pantry as the large plate-glass window blew in.[75] Nonetheless, Churchill and his colleagues continued their dinner, and later went up on to the Air Ministry roof to watch the raid. Lord Lloyd, who at the Colonial Office was quite close to the explosion, wrote to his son later that night to say, 'Winston is all right, having a very good dinner and very cheery.'[76]

The next day at lunch, Churchill told the King 'that he had saved his cook and those in the kitchen'.[77] As we have seen, Churchill could be thoughtless and curt towards his staff sometimes, but that evening his natural sense of *noblesse oblige*, and what he believed to be the 'invisible wings' that flapped over him, had saved at least three lives. The King, who had been told about the Air Ministry roof escapade, appealed to him not to take such risks, reflecting in his diary, 'I cannot afford to lose him nor can the country at this moment.'[78]*

On another occasion Churchill's private secretary John Peck saved Downing Street by putting out an incendiary bomb that had entered diagonally through an upper window and ignited some bedding.[79] Despite the immediacy of these dangers, Churchill disliked using the shelter at No. 10. Peck had to stand on his authority as a Downing Street air-raid warden to order him into it. 'I'm not going,' Churchill said. 'I'm sorry, Sir,' replied Peck, 'I'm in command here. You really must go too. All the rest of us have got to go in.'[80] Churchill, 'rather amused but still grumbling', did what he was told. When nothing happened, he said, 'This is ridiculous,' and left with the rest of the staff following him.† It was not that he underestimated the dangers; Churchill often thought about his own death in 1940, telling Colville that he did not 'much believe in personal survival after death, at least not of the memory'.[81]

On 15 October, in one of the heaviest attacks of the war, 400 tons of high explosive and thousands of incendiary bombs were dropped on London. Churchill took the King's advice and spent the night in 'the Barn', the disused Down Street underground station in Mayfair where the Railway Executive had a suite of offices. He hated it: as Tommy Thompson recalled, 'he felt restless and out of touch with events.'[82] On the 17th another bomb fell 40 yards from No. 10, killing four people in the Treasury basement.[83] When, on 18 October, an unexploded mine was found in St James's Park, Churchill refused to leave No. 10, 'and was chiefly worried about the fate of "those poor little birds"' on the lake.[84] (It was successfully defused.)

Ignoring these dangers, Churchill would often walk around Whitehall at night. At 4.30 one morning in October, after a long meeting discussing air-raid damage, he accompanied the commander of Britain's anti-aircraft

* The Carlton Club in Pall Mall was destroyed on 14 October, and when Churchill visited its ruins the next day he found a smashed marble bust of Pitt the Younger and the Chief Whip's bedroom slippers (Martin, *Downing Street* p. 31).

† Churchill knew that Peck was the only one of the four private secretaries who had a wife doing war work in London, and that they had been married only a year, so he took him to Chequers far less often than the other three, and was 'genuinely and kindly concerned' (Peck, *Dublin from Downing Street* p. 70).

defences, General Sir Frederick Pile, from the War Office back to No. 10 looking for Bovril* and sardines. He rapped on the famous black door with his walking stick, shouting, 'Goering and Goebbels coming to report,' adding to the doorman who opened it for them, 'I am *not* Goebbels.'[85]

The degree to which those around Churchill expected him to be demanding and idiosyncratic is highlighted by a practical joke of John Peck's around this time. He drew up a spoof minute on Downing Street writing paper which gave instructions that special offices be set up for the Prime Minister at Selfridge's department store, in the Archbishop of Canterbury's home at Lambeth Palace, at RAF Stanmore, at the London Palladium Theatre and in the London suburbs of Tooting Bec and Mile End Road, each with enough accommodation for Mrs Churchill, two shorthand typists, three secretaries and Nelson the cat, 'and a place for me to watch air-raids from the roof'.[86] Office hours were to be between 7 a.m. and 3 a.m., and everything had to be ready in three days' time. Peck then forged Churchill's initials at the bottom and attached one of the red 'Action this day' labels, ensuring that it circulated quickly around the office. The spoof completely convinced Desmond Morton, Ian Jacob, Eric Seal and Pug Ismay.

Alternatives to No. 10 were, however, genuinely necessary. No major structural alterations had been made to the building since Robert Walpole's time two centuries earlier, and it was hardly robust. On one occasion, in order to reassure some Cabinet ministers, Churchill had prodded one of the low ceilings with his stick and 'To everyone's amazement it went straight through to the Treasury passage above. Only three inches of crumbling lath and plaster covered the room they were in.'[87] There was a small air-raid shelter in the corner of the garden next to the Treasury wall, but it had become obvious that it would not be enough for a full-scale attack.[88] With the Admiralty, Home Office, Colonial Office and Treasury all hit by bombs in mid-October, and Whitehall and Trafalgar Square now full of bomb-craters, on 19 October the Churchills moved from Downing Street into the 'No. 10 Annexe', a flat on the ground floor of what was then the Office of Works (now the Treasury) at Storey's Gate facing St James's Park. Thirty to forty members of the War Cabinet and Planning staffs were housed in the Central War Rooms, and on the floor above theirs were Morton's and Lindemann's offices.

Below the Annexe (where the Churchill War Rooms are today) was a bunker covered by thick concrete, installed specially for the purpose in 1938, complete with a water-pumping system as it was lower than the

* The first syllable of which he pronounced as in 'Hove'.

nearby Thames.* Churchill slept in the bunker only three times out of the 1,562 nights of the war, preferring to trust to the strong stone building above and its sliding steel shutters over the windows.† Naval anti-collision matting was originally hung over them, but he took a strong dislike to it and it was soon replaced.[89] 'It is sad to leave the old building,' Churchill said of No. 10, 'especially as I fear it will not survive the Battle of London.'[90] During the daytime, he spent as much time as he could at Downing Street. At night, Clementine insisted on taking her turn doing fire-watching duties on the Annexe roof.[91]

Nothing anyone, even the King, could say would stop Churchill from going on to the Annexe roof during air raids, wearing his steel helmet, siren suit and RAF greatcoat, and, as Walter Thompson recalled, 'smoking a cigar and watching intently as explosions and fires lit up the battered city'.[92] In response to Thompson's and Clementine's protestations, Churchill merely said, 'When my time is due, it will come.'[93] He used to quote Raymond Poincaré, the French President during the Great War: 'I take refuge beneath the impenetrable arch of probability.'[94] Thompson had a sandbag shelter built on the roof, in which Churchill would take sanctuary only 'when he heard the shrapnel splattering down on the leads'. On one occasion, Churchill was standing in the doorway of the Annexe, watching the shell bursts and following the searchlights when Thompson suddenly flung himself on to the Prime Minister. '"Don't do that," he roared at me,' Thompson recalled. 'It may have been lucky that I did for some of the shrapnel flew through the open doorway, and a colleague of mine in the rear of the party was hit . . . That was only one of the many incidents I remember of Winston Churchill taking deliberate risks during the Blitz. He insisted on seeing for himself what was going on.'[95] Churchill would not leave No. 10 to go back to the Central War Rooms bunker until the anti-aircraft guns had actually started firing. On one occasion, a 1,000-pound bomb landed on the spot where he had been standing one minute earlier.[96] 'He would often return to No. 10 before daylight, while the raid was still on,' recalled Thompson.[97]

Churchill asked Captain Pim to set up a Map Room in the Annexe complex, with a huge map of the Atlantic Ocean on one wall, and later a map of the Russian front on the wall opposite, and later still a map of the Far East. The pins used were red for British, brown for French, yellow for Dutch, white for German and so on. The coloured phones for the different

* Churchill's hobby as a bricklayer proved useful when he spoke knowledgeably to the builders who were working on the Central War Rooms, and others who were installing Morrison air-raid shelters for Londoners.

† It is still possible to see where the shutters were attached to the stone.

Services were nicknamed 'the beauty chorus'. A staircase connected Churchill's private rooms in the Annexe to the Map Room. VIPs who were escorted there by Churchill over the coming years included the King, Charles de Gaulle, Robert Menzies the Australian premier, King Haakon of Norway, the Russian general Filipp Golikov, Wendell Willkie and Averell Harriman, President Roosevelt's special envoy. John Peck recalled that 'Expeditions up to the roof over the Annexe became a feature of the Churchills' entertaining.'[98]

Churchill insisted that the Government stayed in Whitehall throughout the Blitz. 'Mr Churchill took the view', recorded Thompson, 'that it was essential that they took at least the same chances as the remainder of the population of London.'[99] In the event of invasion, the Government would have decamped 7 miles away to the Paddock, the codename given to a forty-room underground bunker in Brook Road, in the north-west London suburb of Dollis Hill, to conduct the resistance. In those circumstances, Churchill said, ministers 'must get used to being troglodytes', or as he called them, 'trogs'.[100] Although the Royal Family would by then have moved to Canada, Churchill intended to fight it out in Dollis Hill. The long story of Britain as a Great Power would have ended in a bloody *Götterdämmerung* in the unlikely location of the London Borough of Brent.

The War Cabinet met 919 times between Churchill's becoming prime minister and the end of the Coalition on 28 May 1945, averaging once every two days, but it met 193 times in the permanent crisis between May and December 1940, more than in any subsequent calendar year. Usually it met at No. 10 or in the Central War Rooms, but on rare occasions it was convened in the Down Street underground station, the Rotunda bunker in Horseferry Road, Church House in Westminster and once in the Paddock (to test it) on 3 October 1940.

'When he took over from Neville Chamberlain he put a bomb under Whitehall,' recalled Air Marshal Sir Charles Portal. 'From then till the end of the war he was constantly urging, driving, probing, restless in his search for new ways for getting at the enemy. He would ring you up at all times of the day or night and you had to be continually on your toes, always searching into your own mind for the means of improving the job you were set to do.'[101] Chamberlain had a single telephone at Chequers, and that was in the kitchen. Churchill installed a whole battery in his office there, which Portal recalled were 'in constant use'.[102] 'The P.M.'s confidence and energy are amazing,' agreed his private secretary, John Martin, who told his parents during the Battle of Britain, '"Nobody left his presence without feeling a braver man" was said of Pitt [the Elder]; but it is no less true of him.'[103]

Having worked for both prime ministers, Colville noted that 'Chamberlain had drive, but he had not Winston's probing and restless mind: he expected his subordinates to work with the same tirelessness and efficiency that he showed himself, but never questioned their ability to do so. Winston, on the other hand, is always looking for shortcomings and inspires others to be as zealous ferrets as himself.'[104]

'A sense of urgency was created in a very few days and respectable civil servants were actually to be seen running in the corridors,' Colville later recalled. 'No delays were condoned; telephone switchboards quadrupled their efficiency; the Chiefs of Staff and the Joint Planning Staff were in almost constant session; regular office hours ceased to exist, and weekends disappeared with them.'[105] War Cabinet meetings were convened on Bank Holidays, and during crises sometimes took place as late as 1.45 a.m. Ismay, Jacob and the third member of the War Cabinet Secretariat, Colonel Leslie Hollis, worked fifteen-hour days, seven days a week, and when the Prime Minister was preparing an important speech, the duty secretary would often be kept up until nearly 6 a.m., and was expected to be back at her desk again by ten o'clock that morning.[106] They did not complain about these hours; they knew they were at the very centre of world-historical events.

Norman Brook, who joined the Cabinet Secretariat in 1941, described how 'Everything he wanted had to be done at once: all demands, however exacting and unreasonable, had to be met . . . the work was heavy, and the pace was hot.'[107] James Stuart, a Tory whip, recalled that Churchill 'was not an easy man to work with or to serve: far from it. He was argumentative; he wanted his own way . . . and he was a bit of a bully.'[108] Among other things, Churchill's secretaries were expected to know how many words he had dictated per page. They had to be able to take down precisely what he was saying when he was growling with a cigar in his mouth and walking away with his back to them. They also had to get used to his idiosyncratic ways and vocabulary. 'I think being shouted at was one of the worst things to get over,' said Grace Hamblin, who nonetheless, like almost all his secretaries, grew to adore him. 'I came from a quiet family. I had never been shouted at.'[109] She recalled the time he had commanded Kathleen Hill, 'Fetch me Klop.' Hill proudly struggled back some time later bearing Professor Onno Klopp's fourteen volumes of *Der Fall des Hauses Stuart und die Succession des Hauses Hannover* (1875–88). 'God Almighty!' Churchill roared. He had meant her to bring his hole-puncher, which he nicknamed 'Klop' for reasons of onomatopoeia. (He despised staples and paperclips; sheaves of paper had to be 'klopped' and then fastened together with metal-and-thread Treasury tags.) Once

Churchill realized that he had hurt Mrs Hill's feelings, however, he complimented her on her handwriting. His secretaries had to gauge his emotions at any particular moment. 'A sudden passage of pathos or a mention of disaster while dictating a speech would bring the tears to his eyes,' recalled Mary Shearburn; 'sometimes he would be almost sobbing, with tears running down his cheeks at the end of an affecting period.'[110]

Churchill's dictated minutes were nicknamed 'prayers' by his staff, because they often began 'Pray explain' or 'Pray let me have your views'. This synonym for 'please' had already become obsolete by then (like 'prithee') and Churchill used it deliberately. The aesthete Sir Harold Acton noted that nobody used the word 'foe' to mean 'enemy' either, except Churchill. Attempting to persuade the British people to look back hundreds of years to similar moments of national peril, Churchill found it helpful to adopt deliberately archaic language. Old-fashioned, but not rambling. He always insisted on concision in official documents, believing there was no issue so complex that its essentials could not be condensed into a few pages, and very often he ordered that it be summarized on only one.* 'It is sheer laziness not compressing thought into a reasonable space,' he said.[111] Ever a stickler for linguistic clarity and precision, Churchill sent a minute to Sinclair in May 1940 complaining that some enemy planes were reported 'out of action' and others 'destroyed', asking 'Is there any real difference between the two, or is it simply to avoid tautology? If so, this is not in accordance with the best authorities on English. Sense should not be sacrificed to sound.'[112] As Colville later put it, 'Nothing irritated him more than over-complication of issues or the use of obscure language by those who thought they were being clever by making themselves incomprehensible to ordinary people.'[113]

Churchill's wartime daily schedule varied, but in general he was woken at 8 a.m. and brought newspapers, which he would read for twenty minutes, followed by a substantial breakfast during which he would read the official news bulletins. After breakfast, sitting in bed, propped up with pillows and wearing his elbow pads, he would light a cigar and begin work, reading, dictating and speaking on the telephone until shortly before 1 p.m. Service chiefs would occasionally be received in his bedroom. He would then rise and go to the bathroom for a hot bath,† to gargle and sniff a saline solution nasal douche to clear his nostrils. He was a pioneer

* Nor was it just wartime exigencies that demanded brevity. 'This Treasury paper, by its very length,' he wrote on one in the 1950s, 'defends itself against the risk of being read' (Moran, *Struggle* p. 746).

† He would only get into the bath when it was two-thirds full and 98 degrees. It was then brought up to 104 degrees and almost overflowing.

of electric razors, which had not been mass-produced until 1937. He was also pleased with what he called 'the excellence of his teeth-cleaning apparatus, an electrical appliance which spurts water at a high velocity into his mouth and removes the taste of cigars'.[114] Then he would dress with the aid of his valet, Frank Sawyers, and have lunch, followed by an hour-long sleep in his bed. His daily afternoon naps continued throughout the war, extending his working day from 9 a.m. to 1 a.m. or 2 a.m.[115] 'You must sleep some time between lunch and dinner,' he said, 'and no half-way measures. Take off your clothes and get into bed. Don't think you will be doing less work because you sleep during the day. That's a foolish notion held by people who have no imagination. You will be able to accomplish more. You get two days in one – well, at least one and a half, I'm sure.'[116] Churchill had starting sleeping for an hour in the afternoon when he was at the Admiralty during the Great War, as 'I found I could add nearly two hours to my working effort by going to bed for an hour after luncheon.'[117] To facilitate his naps when travelling, Walter Thompson carried a black satin eye-bandage wherever they went, as well as a special pillow.[118] After his nap he often took a second bath, otherwise, in Thompson's words, 'there was the Dickens to pay.' (When he was in Egypt in 1921 and there was no water for his bath on his train, he had it stopped and the water was heated from the locomotive's boiler.)[119] Dinner would normally be taken at 8 p.m., and afterwards he would work long into the night. Churchill slept well throughout the war: 'In its darkest times I never had any trouble sleeping,' he recalled. 'I could always flop into bed and go to sleep after the day's work is done . . . I slept sound and awoke refreshed, and had no feeling except appetite to grapple with whatever the next morning's boxes might bring.'[120]

At Chequers that September, Churchill first wore a pair of overalls of his own invention, initially made from different fabrics including velvet by Turnbull & Asser, the Jermyn Street tailors, which he called a 'siren suit', although everyone else referred to them as his 'rompers'. They had breast and side pockets, were generously cut and had fold-over cuffs, and came in various colours, including burgundy, blue and bottle-green.[121] 'The P.M. was clad in his air-force blue, zip-fastened cloth overall which he straps tightly round his stomach and in which he looks like an Eskimo,' recorded Colville.[122] Like his electric razor and 3-foot key-chain, it was a labour-saving device, as were the shoes he sometimes wore with zip fasteners instead of laces.[123] Time spent dressing and undressing was theoretically less time spent on the war, although he tended to talk to private secretaries or dictate to his secretaries while dressing, undressing, shaving and even sometimes bathing. 'Normally the private secretary stood in the PM's bedroom while he stripped, scratched himself between the shoulder blades with a long-handled hairbrush, and put on his sleeping garment,' recalled Peck years later, 'a vest of approximately the same length as the miniest of mini-dresses.'[124]

These remarkably open domestic arrangements were apparent in other ways too. Chequers and No. 10 enjoyed surprisingly haphazard security against assassination and terrorism. John Martin recalled that there was a competition in the Foreign Office to see who could get into Downing Street with the least adequate credentials. A railway season ticket and golf club membership card were runners-up, but 'finally the prize went to a man who walked confidently through the entrance holding out a slice of cake.'[125] One major, sent to test the security at Chequers, managed to get upstairs, where a housemaid directed him to the Prime Minister's bedroom, and he got back to the front door undetected.

Churchill broadcast to France on 21 October (somewhat tactlessly, Trafalgar Day) first in French – 'Français! c'est moi, Churchill, qui vous parle' – and subsequently in English. After what had happened at Oran, he had much to do to persuade the French that he was a Francophile, but he did not want worse relations with Vichy France than was absolutely necessary. 'For more than thirty years in peace and war I have marched with you, and I am marching still along the same road,' he said. 'Herr Hitler is not thinking only of stealing other people's territories, or flinging gobbets of them to his little confederate [Mussolini]. I tell you truly what you must believe when I say this evil man, this monstrous abortion of hatred and defeat, is resolved on nothing less than the complete wiping out of the French nation, and the disintegration of its whole life and future.'[126] Jacques Duchesne, the head of the BBC French section, helped Churchill practise this broadcast, which took place while bombs were falling. For technical reasons they had to record from No. 10 rather than the War Rooms, and when Duchesne pointed out how little protection there was, Churchill laughed and replied, 'Si une bombe tombe sur la maison, nous mourons ensemble comme deux braves gens!' (If a bomb lands on this house, we'll die together like two brave men!)[127] The Prime Minister had already made a gaffe on entering the room, when he asked, 'Where is my frog speech?'[128] Duchesne looked pained. Hitler was about to meet Pétain at Montoire in central France, prompting Churchill to remark of the Vichy regime, 'Owing to our unexpected resistance, they have been able to market their treachery at a slightly higher rate than would otherwise have been possible.'[129] He nonetheless stopped the MI6 attempts to bribe Pierre Laval, the Vichy premier, to leave France, saying 'He is no longer worth buying.'[130]

The day after Churchill's broadcast a corruption scandal brought down a firm friend and supporter of his. 'Political systems can to some extent be appraised by the test of whether their leading representatives are or are not capable of taking decisions on great matters on their merits,' he had written in 1929, 'in defiance of their interests and often of their best friends.'[131] Bob Boothby, Churchill's private secretary at the Treasury in the 1920s and an anti-appeaser in the 1930s, and an Other Club member, was forced to resign from his parliamentary secretaryship at the Ministry of Food on 22 October as a result of a financial scandal. He had publicly advocated the unfreezing of £240,000 of Czech assets that belonged to the wife of a Czech business associate without informing the Commons that, if it were to happen, he would receive 10 per cent. Boothby assumed that Churchill would protect him, but he was never to hold ministerial office again. 'He has been one of my personal friends,' Churchill told the Commons, 'often a supporter at lonely and difficult moments, and I have always entertained a warm personal regard for him. If it is painful to us, it is also a loss to all. It is a loss to His Majesty's Government.'[132] He was not, however, about to risk his Government's reputation at such a perilous time by permitting him to stay in office. He privately remarked that Boothby 'should join a bomb disposal squad as the best way of rehabilitating himself in the eyes of his fellow men. After all, the bombs might not go off.'[133] It sounded cruel, but that is much what he himself had done in 1915, when the six-week average life-expectancy for new officers on the Western Front was not dissimilar to that of bomb-disposal squads in the Second World War. He told Colville, however, about those persecuting Boothby, 'If there was one thing in the world he found odious, it was a man-hunt.'[134] There, too, was a reflection of 1915.

In late October, Churchill took his special train up to Scotland to inspect General Sikorski's forces and the dockyards at Rosyth.* 'A lot of people talked a lot of nonsense when they said wars never settled anything,' Churchill said on the way north; 'nothing in history was ever settled except by wars.'[135] He also said he believed that every prospective Army officer should read Plutarch's *Lives*. On his return to London, while being cheered by a crowd en route to Downing Street, he told Colville, 'I represent to them something which they wholeheartedly support: the determination

* The train had been donated by the London, Midland & Scottish Railway Company and had two saloon cars, bedrooms, bathrooms, offices, VIP compartments, a dining car and luggage van. It was a comfortable way to travel and could fit in secretaries, bodyguards and photographers. Wherever it stopped, the Prime Minister's coach was connected to the nearest telephone line and when the operator asked for 'Rapid Falls 8833', Churchill was put through to No. 10.

to win. For a year or two they will cheer me.'[136] He recognized that his time to produce victories was finite.

Italy invaded Greece on 28 October and the Greek Prime Minister, Ioannis Metaxas, immediately appealed to Churchill for help, saying, 'The war we confront today is thus solely a war for honour.'[137] It was hard to see how British strategic interests were served by aiding Greece, but on being informed that Athens had been bombed Churchill replied without hesitation, 'Then we must bomb Rome.'[138] ('Rome will not be unbuilt in a day,' he told a Tory MP.)[139] As early as 2 November, British troops started arriving in Greece from Egypt. 'One salient fact leaped upon us,' Churchill wrote in his memoirs. 'Crete! The Italians must not have it.'[140] His last words to Dill as he drove away from Chequers at teatime were 'Don't forget – the maximum possible for Greece.'[141] The deployment to Greece was supported by the Defence Committee, including Eden and Dill, but it was primarily Churchill's initiative. Like the Norway campaign, it was a costly mistake, taking enough from Wavell to weaken him just as he was about to attack the Italians at Mersa Matruh in Egypt, but not sending enough to Greece to be able to affect the outcome there.

Churchill eagerly awaited the result of the American presidential election in November, confident that America would enter the war after Roosevelt had beaten his Republican opponent Wendell Willkie. In the meantime, he told Colville, 'He quite understood the exasperation which so many English people feel with the American attitude of criticism combined with ineffective assistance; but we must be patient and we must conceal our irritation.'[142] (He said this alongside bursts of singing 'Under the Spreading Chestnut Tree'.) In Boston on 30 October, President Roosevelt told his countrymen, 'I shall say it again and again and again: Your boys are not going to be sent into any foreign wars.'[143] However dispiriting those words were for Britons, it was a prerequisite for Roosevelt's re-election: despite overwhelming sympathy for the Allies, comparatively small numbers of Americans wanted to join the fight.

No fewer than 1,733 Luftwaffe planes were shot down over England between 10 July and 31 October 1940, at the cost of 915 RAF fighters. Churchill's estimate to Roosevelt in May of ratios of 'two or three to one' had almost been borne out.[144] 'Only about thirty per cent of the R.A.F. pilots came from Public Schools,' he told the new Home Secretary, Labour's Herbert Morrison, who had left school to become an errand boy at fourteen, 'the remainder being products of the Elementary Schools and professional classes. It is striking that none of the aristocracy chose the R.A.F. – they left it to the lower-middle class.' Colville's account of the conversation continued, 'The P.M. then waxed eloquent on the disappearance of the aristocracy from the stage and their replacement by these excellent sons of the lower-middle classes. He paid a tribute to what they had done for England.'[145] Churchill had not abandoned his class entirely, however, offering a peerage in December to his old friend Lord Hugh Cecil, Provost of Eton College and the youngest son of the 3rd Marquess of Salisbury, telling him that 'It would be good to have you in the House of Lords . . . to sustain the aristocratic morale and to chide the Bishops when they err . . . Now that I read in the newspapers that the Eton flogging block is destroyed by enemy action, you may have more leisure and strength.'[146]

On 4 November, London had its first night free of air raids for eight weeks. The Luftwaffe had decided to extend its raids to industrial centres and ports around the country. London continued to be hit regularly thereafter, but not continuously. When Italian planes took part in the bombing, Churchill said that he would bomb Rome as soon as there were enough Wellingtons stationed at Malta, from where bombing runs against Naples were already taking off. When Colville said he hoped they would spare the Colosseum, he said it wouldn't hurt it 'to have a few more bricks knocked off it', and quoted Byron's lines from *Childe Harold's Pilgrimage*, 'While stands the Coliseum Rome shall stand / When falls the Coliseum Rome shall fall.'[147] In the event, however, his love of history protected central Rome from the devastation that could easily have been unleashed upon it. 'We must be careful not to bomb the Pope,' he said to Sir Richard Peirse, the new Commander-in-Chief of Bomber Command; 'he has a lot of influential friends!'[148] Later that month, when told that eight Italian planes had been shot down in one raid over London, he gave a whoop of joy.[149]

In the Commons on 5 November, he delivered a speech that he had dictated in the Hawtrey Room at Chequers, to the accompaniment of Strauss waltzes on Mary's gramophone. 'The Greek King, his Government and the Greek people have resolved to fight for life and honour, lest the world should be too easily led in chains,' he proclaimed.[150] Nicolson observed that Churchill 'rubs the palms of his hands with five fingers extended up and down the front of his coat, searching for the right phrase, indicating cautious selection, conveying almost medicinal poise'. After the speech, he 'slouches into the smoking-room and reads the *Evening News* intently, as if it were the only source of information available to him'.[151]

The news Churchill desperately wanted to hear came later that day: Roosevelt beat Willkie by 449 electoral votes to 82. He had carried thirty-eight states to ten, and became the first president ever to be elected to a third term. The margin in total votes was slimmer than his electoral victory made it seem: he had received 27.2 million votes to Willkie's 22.3 million. Churchill felt 'indescribable relief'. Willkie was not an isolationist, but Mary summed up the feeling in the Churchill household when she wrote in her diary, '*Glory Hallelujah!!* A delicious poke in the snoot for Hitler.'[152] With Roosevelt safely re-elected, Churchill sent him a telegram on 16 November that he later described as 'one of the most important I ever wrote', asking for arms to be lent or leased to Britain under a programme whereby Britain would repay the United States over the very long term.[153] (Even he would probably not have guessed that the final instalment of the loan, of $83.25 million, would only be repaid in 2006.) Harry Hopkins, Roosevelt's closest confidant, later told Churchill that the President 'read and re-read this letter as he sat alone in his deck-chair' while cruising in the Caribbean on board an American warship, the *Tuscaloosa*, and 'for two days he did not seem to have reached any clear conclusion'.[154] An extraordinary idea was forming in the President's mind, however.

In November, for the first time, the Commons met at Church House in Westminster, because it was considered safer than the Palace of Westminster. In his last appearance in the Commons before the move, Churchill was able to announce, to great cheers, the Mediterranean Fleet's decisive victory over the Italian Navy at the Battle of Taranto on the night of the 11th. 'We've got some sugar for the birds this time,' he told Channon, smiling.[155] It was the first time the Commons had sat anywhere else since the fire of 1834, and Channon noted that 'Winston watched the confusion with amusement.'[156] 'Members are complaining openly that Winston trades on his position,' Channon added, 'on his immense following in the country, though his popularity is on the decline: but it is still high.'[157] This was wishful thinking on Channon's part; among the public Churchill's popularity was as high as ever, but many Conservative backbenchers were still not reconciled to him. When the seventy-one-year-old Chamberlain died on 9 November, therefore, Churchill had to tread a careful line in his panegyric in Westminster Abbey.

Most politicians would have temporized in their eulogy of a predecessor whose central policy they had resolutely opposed for years, whom they had replaced in a controversial coup and whose still-unreconciled supporters formed a majority of the House of Commons. Churchill, however, used the pulpit at Chamberlain's funeral on 14 November in the freezing cold Abbey – its stained-glass windows had been removed for safe keeping and the gaps imperfectly boarded up – as an opportunity for a magnificent oration.

'In paying a tribute of respect and of regard to an eminent man who has been taken from us,' Churchill told a packed congregation, 'no one is obliged to alter the opinions which he has formed or expressed upon issues which have become a part of history; but at the lychgate we may all pass our own conduct and our own judgments under a searching review. It is not given to human beings, happily for them, for otherwise life would be intolerable, to foresee or to predict to any large extent the unfolding course of events. In one phase men seem to have been right, in another they seem to have been wrong.' Chamberlain had been wrong about appeasing Hitler, but he had, as Churchill said, the 'benevolent instincts of the human heart . . . even at great peril, and certainly to the utter disdain of popularity or clamour', striving 'to the utmost of his capacity and authority, which were powerful, to save the world from the awful, devastating struggle in which we are now engaged'.[158]

'History, with its flickering lamp,' Churchill continued,

> stumbles along the trail of the past, trying to reconstruct its scenes, to revive its echoes, and kindle with pale gleams the passion of former days. What is the worth of all this? The only guide to a man is his conscience; the only shield to his memory is the rectitude and sincerity of his actions. It is very imprudent to walk through life without this shield, because we are so often mocked by the failure of our hopes and the upsetting of our calculations: but with this shield, however the fates may play, we march always in the ranks of honour.[159]

Channon, who sat alongside Rab Butler in the second pew, noted that 'Winston had the decency to cry as he stood by the coffin.'[160]

Churchill reprised this speech before the Commons in Church House for Hansard, his first time speaking there. Colville 'did not think the P.M.'s delivery was equal to the magnificence of his language', not least because of the small Chamber, the coughing of MPs and the creak of the dais when people stepped on to it.[161] When Kathleen Hill complimented him on the speech Churchill said, 'Well, of course I could have done it the other way around.'[162] He had not changed his opinion of appeasement, after all. To Nicolson he said that the funeral oration 'was not an insuperable task, since I admired many of Neville's great qualities. But I pray to God in his infinite mercy that I shall not have to deliver a similar oration on Baldwin. That indeed would be difficult to do.'[163] (He was spared.) To James Stuart, a Chamberlainite MP, Churchill said, 'What shall I do without poor Neville? I was relying on him to look after the home front for me.'[164] He now had to rely on Attlee, Morrison and Anderson, who did not have the same political assumptions as Churchill at all.

The Tory MP Ronnie Tree asked Churchill if he would like to stay at his country house, Ditchley Park in Oxfordshire, during full moons, after German reconnaissance planes had flown over Chequers, bombs had been dropped near by and the Air Staff became alarmed that there might be a heavy attack.[165] 'While I am always prepared for martyrdom,' he explained, 'there is no point in tempting Providence.'[166] He thought the Government's alternative accommodation offered in Worcestershire was too far away, whereas Ditchley was only 75 miles from Whitehall.* Tree and his wife Nancy (later Nancy Lancaster) entertained with 'the standards and atmosphere of a pre-war house-party', wrote Martin.[167] 'It is without exception the most beautiful house I have ever seen,' noted Mary, and Churchill regularly held meetings with generals and admirals in the Chinese Room there.[168] On the afternoon of Chamberlain's funeral, as Churchill set out for Ditchley, John Martin handed him his buff-coloured box of Enigma decrypts. On reaching Kensington Gardens, only a few minutes into the journey, Churchill ordered the driver to turn around and return to Downing Street. From the decrypts he had learned that a major raid, codenamed Moonlight Sonata, was about to take place, and although Bletchley Park could not identify where it was headed, the setting of the *X-Gerät* beams suggested that the target was London.[169] As Martin put it, Churchill 'was not going to sleep quietly in the country while London was under what was expected to be a heavy attack'.[170] Bracken sent the Prime Minister's female staff home and to the Dollis Hill bunker. Churchill's natural courage and his desire to be at the centre of the action meant that he headed to the Air Ministry roof with his binoculars.[171]

In fact, the raid that night was on the city of Coventry, in the Midlands, where 544 people were killed and 420 injured, and only one of the 515 German aircraft was shot down.[172] A myth developed that Churchill knew that Coventry was going to be bombed and allowed it to happen in order to protect the secrecy of Ultra; but in fact it was not named as the target.[173] Heavy raids on Birmingham between 19 and 22 November, and on Southampton on the 23rd and Bristol on the 24th, left Churchill commenting on the 'Complete failure of all our methods'. Hurricanes and anti-aircraft guns had been sent to the Midlands after the Coventry raid, yet still the Luftwaffe came on, though they were now mainly bombing at night, and thus less accurately.[174]

Yet even the air threat was, as Churchill said on 22 November, 'as nothing to that of the submarines'.[175] He returned to the question of the

* The title of Tree's memoir of the war years, *When the Moon was High*, implies that Churchill went there every time the full moon fell at a weekend, but in fact, as the Chequers visitors' books attest, the Churchills stayed at Chequers on eleven full-moon nights during the war, and invited dozens of distinguished guests to join them.

Irish Treaty ports, and complained to Lord Cranborne, the Dominions Secretary, that Sir John Maffey, the British Ambassador in Dublin, 'should not be encouraged to think that his only task is to mollify de Valera and make everything, including our ruin, pass off pleasantly'.[176] In early December he wondered whether the Irish Free State might be coerced by sanctions into changing its stance. Yet nothing would move the Taoiseach, de Valera, to allow the Royal Navy to use the ports in the struggle against Fascism.

On 30 November, his sixty-sixth birthday, Churchill wrote Roosevelt a fifteen-page letter summarizing the strategic situation and once more pressing him for support. It went through several revisions and was not dispatched until 7 December. 'The decision for 1941 lies upon the seas,' it read;

> unless we can establish our ability to feed this Island, to import munitions of all kinds which we need, unless we can move our armies to the various theatres where Hitler and his confederate Mussolini must be met, and maintain them there . . . we may fall by the way and the time needed by the United States to complete her defensive preparations may not therefore be forthcoming. It is therefore in shipping and in the power to transport across the oceans, particularly the Atlantic Ocean, that in 1941 the crunch of the whole war will be found.[177]

He asked for more shipping, more destroyers, pressure on de Valera to provide Irish bases, and US warships to convoy American merchant vessels. He ended: 'If . . . you are convinced, Mr President, that defeat of the Nazi and Fascist tyranny is a matter of high consequence to the people of the United States and to the Western Hemisphere, you will regard this letter not as an appeal for aid, but as a statement of the minimum action necessary to achieve our common purpose.' In discussing how to pay for all this, he had declared earlier in the letter, 'I should not myself be willing, even in the height of this struggle, to divest Great Britain of every conceivable saleable asset, so that after the victory was won with our blood and sweat, and civilization saved and the time gained for the United States to be fully armed against all eventualities, we should be stripped to the bone.'[178] Yet it was hard to see how that could be avoided.

Churchill wrote to Sinclair and Portal in December asking for a paper of 'not more than two or three sheets' estimating what the size of the Luftwaffe would be between the end of March and June 1941. The statistics he received from the Air Ministry, the Ministry of Economic Warfare, the Ministry of Aircraft Production and his own Statistical Office were sometimes wildly divergent. He tried to impose Lindemann's organization on the other ministries, but they were loath to give up independent statistics-gathering and presentation. So Churchill 'let the argument rip healthily between the departments', as he later wrote. 'This is a good way of finding out the truth.'[179] At the end of the year Sinclair and Portal concluded that the German preponderance was now approximately four to three, whereas during the Battle of France it had been two to one, and by April the proportion would be even better. Churchill recognized that the darkest days of the Battle of Britain and the immediate invasion threat were now behind them. In December, Eden noted in his diary, 'Winston was tired but cheerful. We spoke of the dark days of the summer. I told him that Portal and I had confessed to each other that in our hearts we had both despaired at one time. He said, "Yes, normally I wake up buoyant to face the new day. Then I awoke with dread in my heart."'[180] Yet nothing any of those men did or said in public, to the press, in Parliament or to their own staffs, or even to their wives, let slip for one minute that they had the slightest doubt in ultimate victory. It was the quintessence of leadership.

In early December Churchill was intensely frustrated. As well as the stubbornness of de Valera, he was angry that Admiral Keyes's plan for Operation Workshop, the seizure of the small island of Pantelleria, had been blocked by the Chiefs of Staff. Yet the problems involved in holding and supplying the tiny island only 63 miles south-west of Sicily, with its poor harbour and inadequate airfield, far outweighed the benefits, and the Chiefs of Staff had been right to veto the operation. Admiral Sir Andrew Cunningham, the Commander-in-Chief, Mediterranean, had so vigorously opposed it that Churchill had said, 'Surely no such feelings should exist between old comrades.'[181] Keyes had meanwhile condemned Churchill's 'craven-hearted advisers' so aggressively that Churchill, unwilling as ever to overrule the Chiefs, had been forced to tell him, 'You and your Commandos will have to obey orders like other people and that is all there is to be said about it.'[182]

Churchill also thought Wavell was tardy in launching Operation Compass against the Italians in Egypt, and although the Italians were being beaten back by fierce Greek resistance in the Balkans, on 3 December Dill asked, 'What is Germany doing?' – a question he should have been answering, not asking – whereupon Churchill replied, 'They are preparing something terrible.'[183] After a Defence Committee meeting on 5 December, Churchill proposed to Eden that he take over Wavell's command, using the precedent of the Duke of Wellington having been an MP before he fought the Peninsular War. 'I declined, very firmly!' noted Eden.[184] Wavell launched Operation Compass in the Western Desert on 9 December. Over the next six weeks he advanced 200 miles and captured 113,000 prisoners. At lunch with the King on the 10th, 'Winston kept on repeating we must have a success,' but now it was finally happening and the next day he was able to telephone the King to announce the first land victory since the war began.[185] Churchill told Lindemann that 'he had been living on hopes of it for five weeks and had been terrified some sandstorm would give the men on the spot a chance to back out' – an indication of how much he doubted the generals' fighting spirit.[186] Within three months of Operation Compass, Churchill had given Wavell five more campaigns to fight, in Greece, Syria, Iraq, Ethiopia and Eritrea, but not the massive reinforcements necessary for victory in any but the most minor ones.

The day Operation Compass was launched, the fourteenth-century St Stephen's Cloister in the Palace of Westminster was badly hit in an air raid, fully justifying Churchill's decision to move Parliament to Church House. Channon found the Members' cloakroom 'a scene of devastation; confusion, wreckage, broken glass everywhere, and the loveliest, oldest part of the vast building a shambles. Suddenly I came upon Winston Churchill wearing a fur-collared coat, and smoking a cigar . . . "It's horrible," he remarked to me without removing his cigar; and I saw that he was much moved, for he loves Westminster . . . "Where Cromwell signed King Charles's death warrant," he grunted.'[187]

On 12 December, Lord Lothian died in Washington from uremic poisoning after five days' illness, aged only fifty-eight.* Churchill's eulogy to Lothian at Westminster was once again partly self-referential. 'I cannot help feeling that to die at the height of a man's career,' he told his fellow MPs, 'the highest moment of his effort here in this world, universally honoured and admired, to die while great issues are still commanding the whole of his interest, to be taken from us at a moment when he could already see ultimate success in view, is not the most unenviable of fates.'[188] Later in the war, once Russia and America were in the conflict and victory was certain, he was often to say that if he himself died during the war it would be an enviable death.

Churchill initially considered appointing Lloyd George to succeed Lothian as ambassador to Washington, but he was uncertain whether he

* A course of antibiotics would have cured Lothian had he not, as a Christian Scientist, refused to consult a doctor. The next day at dinner Churchill asked if anyone around the table was a Christian Scientist. 'Well,' said Lindemann, 'I am if you divide the two words – a Christian and a Scientist.' Churchill then said, 'I am willing to admit you may have some claim to be the latter.' 'Which is the only one of the two on which you have any qualifications to judge,' Lindemann retorted. (Colville, *Fringes* p. 312.)

could be trusted. He finally did make the offer, but it was turned down on health grounds. Cripps could not be moved from Moscow as 'He is a lunatic in a country of lunatics, and it would be a pity to move him.'[189] Lords Cranborne and Vansittart were considered, before Churchill eventually decided on Halifax, thus opening the way for Eden to go back to the Foreign Office. In October he had said, 'What is wanted in that department is a substantial application of the boot,' which he thought Eden could administer.[190] It would, moreover, remove Halifax, whom he saw as a restraining influence at best, and at worst a possible supporter once again of peace negotiations if the war were to go badly. Churchill used foreign postings cannily to remove potential opponents and replace them with supporters; as well as Halifax, Hoare and Malcolm MacDonald (who was sent to Canada as high commissioner), he sent five other Chamberlainite former ministers abroad as the governors of Burma and Bombay, as minister resident in West Africa and as the high commissioners to Australia and South Africa. Several others were removed from the Commons through the time-honoured expedient of ennobling them.

Churchill told Jock Colville on 12 December that after victory had been won 'He did not wish to lead a party struggle or a class struggle against the Labour leaders who were now serving him so well.' Instead he would 'retire to Chartwell and write a book on the war, which he already had mapped out in his mind chapter by chapter'.[191] That he was already seeing the struggle in terms of its literary potential in part explains why every order and minute had to be put in writing. More importantly, Churchill refused to take responsibility for anything unless it was written down, something that became a key aspect of Whitehall lore.*

In any discussion of Britain's war aims during the Battle of Britain, Churchill was adamantly clear. 'There was only one aim,' he said: 'to destroy Hitler.' He believed that after the war was won 'There would be a United States of Europe, and this Island would be the link connecting this Federation with the New World and able to hold the balance between the two.' When asked whether that meant a new balance of power, he said, 'No, the balance of virtue.'[192] Talking about what he called that

* The Churchill family knew that Colville was keeping a diary: did Churchill deliberately use him as his Boswell, giving him his best bons mots and allowing him to attend events he knew would be historic? Colville himself might have suspected as much, writing that when he told Churchill that he would not be allowed by the British people to retire, 'This was not just Boswellian; there was not at present any man of the right calibre' (Colville, *Fringes* p. 310). On 1 January 1941, Churchill wrote a minute forbidding officials from keeping diaries which left Colville 'rather conscience-stricken'. Fortunately for historians, he and everyone else around the Prime Minister chose to ignore it.

'boob' Thomas Inskip, he added, 'We shall win, but we don't deserve to; at least, we do deserve it because of our virtues, but not because of our intelligence.'[193] By mid-December, he was already turning his thoughts to the post-war world. He told Colville there would be four confederations – the Northern, Mitteleuropean, Danubian and Balkan (including Turkey) – which would meet in a Council of Europe. 'The English-speaking world would be apart from this,' he said, 'but closely connected with it.'[194] In general, however, he avoided conversations about post-war reconstruction and 'war aims'. 'Do not let spacious plans for a new world divert your energies from saving what is left of the old,' he told Lord Reith, the Minister of Works and Buildings.[195] It was a good metaphor for his overall view.

Although Churchill took only eight days' actual holiday between the outbreak of war and Germany's surrender,* he could sometimes escape for the odd hour. After lunch at Ditchley on 15 December, for example, he went to Blenheim. 'We spent quite a long time on our hands and knees on the library floor,' a member of his secretariat recalled, 'while he reconstructed the battle of Blenheim for us with tin soldiers.'[196] That evening he watched *Gone with the Wind*, which left him 'pulverised by the strength of their feelings and emotions' and gave him a lifelong *tendresse* for Vivien Leigh, to whom he later presented a painting.[197] That night at 3 a.m., throwing himself on a chair in his bedroom, he collapsed between the chair and a stool, in Colville's words, 'ending in a most absurd position on the floor with his feet in the air. Having no false dignity, he treated it as a complete joke and repeated several times, "A real Charlie Chaplin!"'[198]

A few days later Churchill took four ministers, as well as Colville and his brother Jack, to their old school to hear the Harrow School Songs and to speak to the pupils.† An extra verse had been inserted into 'Stet Fortuna Domus' in his honour. 'He sang lustily, as did we all, and seemed to remember most of the words without referring to the book,' recalled Colville. 'We have sung of "the wonderful giants of old",' Churchill told the boys,

> but can anyone doubt that this generation is as good and as noble as any the nation has ever produced, and that its men and women can stand against all

* Two days in Pompano, Florida, 10 and 11 January 1942, and even then he had cables delivered on both days; and six days fishing in Canada after the 1943 Quebec Conference.

† Earlier that year, on being asked how the public schools were faring in the war, Churchill had quipped, 'Much as usual: Harrow has Amery, Gort and myself, Eton has the King of the Belgians and Captain Ramsay, and Winchester has Oswald Mosley to their credit' (ed. Rose, *Baffy* p. 174). It was a good joke – the last two were in prison for Fascism – and underlines how little he blamed Lord Gort for the defeat on the continent.

> tests? . . . Hitler, in one of his recent discourses, declared that the fight was between those who have been through the Adolf Hitler Schools and those who have been at Eton. Hitler has forgotten Harrow, and he has also overlooked the vast majority of the youth of this country who have never had the advantage of attending such schools, but who have by their skill and prowess won the admiration of the whole world.

Thinking perhaps of the 70 per cent of RAF fighter pilots who had gone to state schools, he added, 'When the war is won by this nation, as it surely will be, it must be one of our aims to work to establish a state of society where the advantages and privileges which hitherto have been enjoyed only by the few shall be far more widely shared by the many and the youth of the nation as a whole.'[199] After his speech the senior pupils clustered around him. 'They'd lose all shyness,' Colville remembered of such occasions, 'and he'd talk to them absolutely as an equal.'[200] Churchill got on well with young people, be they Harrow schoolboys, naval midshipmen, his children's friends, the guards at Chequers or his own grandchildren.

As Christmas approached, Churchill told Halifax that he was sending him to Washington as ambassador, strengthened by Home Intelligence surveys which showed that Halifax had inherited some of the late Neville Chamberlain's unpopularity with the public over appeasement. When Halifax protested, Churchill told him he 'would never live down the reputation for appeasement which he and the Foreign Office had won themselves here. On the other hand he had a glorious opportunity in America, because unless the United States came into the war we could not win, or at least we could not win a really satisfactory peace.'[201] It was true, but nonetheless a considerable admission to make, even privately. Halifax threatened to resign from politics altogether, and Lady Halifax upbraided Churchill for exiling them. But in the end he went, the King softening the blow of departure by telling him that 'if anything happened to Winston . . . he could always be recalled.'[202] As part of his brief, Churchill sent Halifax a minute on 20 December saying, 'We have not had anything from the U.S. that we have not paid for and what we have had has not played an essential part in our resistance.'[203] Halifax's primary duty was to ensure that Congress passed legislation as soon as possible that would allow Britain to buy weapons she did not have to pay for immediately.

Halifax's reluctant acquiescence meant that Churchill could finally tell Eden that 'he much wanted' him back at the Foreign Office.[204] Eden was twenty-three years younger than Churchill and in many ways the son he wished he had had. After the war, Colville wrote of the 'almost paternal affection' Churchill felt for Eden, contrasting it with the frustrated fatherly feelings he found it impossible wholly to confer on Randolph.[205] Churchill had never been able to fulfil what he had called 'his dearest wish' of working closely with his own father, but now he could with this almost surrogate son (though there were occasional blazing rows with him too). The next month he told Eden that his jump from war secretary to foreign secretary compared to moving from the fourth form at school to the sixth* – further evidence, perhaps, of exceptional favour, and of Churchill's paternal attitude.[206] Churchill asked Margesson to take Eden's place as secretary for war, and James Stuart to take Margesson's as chief whip. Though both had been enthusiastic *Munichois*, they were completely loyal to Churchill. The Prime Minister told Stuart that part of his job would be to protect Beaverbrook from the backbenchers.†

When Eric Seal, his principal private secretary, asked for a week off at Christmas for the Downing Street staff, Churchill replied from Chequers that the request 'surprises me. No holidays can be given at Christmas, but every endeavour should be made to allow members of staff to attend Divine Service on Christmas Day, either in the morning or afternoon. My own plans will be to work either here or in London continuously, and I hope that the Recess may be used not only for overtaking arrears, but for tackling new problems in greater detail.'[207] He later wished his staff 'A busy Christmas and a frantic New Year'.[208] As he told Colville, 'Continuity of work never harmed anyone.'[209]

At Chequers the Churchill family had the largest turkey John Martin had ever seen, a posthumous present from Lord Rothermere, who had died a month earlier. Afterwards they all listened to the King's speech on the wireless and later had sing-songs till midnight during which 'the P.M. sang lustily, if not always in tune, and when Vic [Oliver] played Viennese waltzes he danced a remarkably frisky measure of his own in the middle of the room'.[210] 'This was one of the happiest Christmasses I can remember,' Mary wrote in her diary. 'Despite all the terrible events going on around us. It was not happy in a *flamboyant* way. But I've never before seen the family look so happy, so united, so sweet. I wonder if we will all be together next Christmas? I pray we may.'[211] Rather eccentrically,

* In American terms, moving from sophomore to senior year in high school.

† On receipt of one of Beaverbrook's regular resignation threats, over his bad relations with the Air Ministry, Churchill told him in December, 'It is more in the public interest that there should be sharp criticism and counter-criticism between the two departments than that they should be handing each other out ceremonious bouquets' (Colville, *Fringes* p. 317). His reply to another resignation threat ended by his invoking the courage of the radical French revolutionary: 'Danton, no weakness' (ibid. p. 330).

Churchill gave the King a siren suit for Christmas, and the Queen a copy of Fowler's *Modern English Usage*.[212]

On New Year's Day 1941, inspecting girders above the War Rooms using only the torch in the handle of his walking-stick, Churchill stepped up to his ankles in liquid cement. When Colville joked that he had met his Waterloo, Churchill shot back, 'How dare you! Anyhow, Blenheim, not Waterloo.'[213] That night, Wood and Eden spoke to Churchill about the country's dire financial condition. A Lend-Lease Bill was making its way through Congress that would allow Britain to buy munitions but not pay for them until after the war. The fear was, however, as Colville summarized Churchill's view, that 'the Americans' love of doing good business may lead them to denude us of all our realizable resources before they show any inclination to be the Good Samaritan.'[214]

Militarily, the situation in Libya continued to go well against the Italians, with the town of Bardia falling on 4 January. Churchill was in a fine mood two days later when he wrote to the King, 'Your Majesties are more beloved by all classes and conditions than any of the princes of the past. I am indeed proud that it should have fallen to my lot and duty to stand at Your Majesty's side as First Minister in such a climax of the British story.'[215] With his extraordinary memory for anniversaries, he also wrote that day to Ian Hamilton forty-one years after his victory over the Boers: 'I am thinking of you and [the Battle of] Waggon Hill when another January 6th brings news of a fine feat of arms.'[216]

At the end of 1940, Enigma intercepts had revealed that German forces were concentrating in the Balkans, especially Bulgaria, indicating that Hitler intended to invade neutral Yugoslavia and also go to war against Greece, which had so far been doing well in her struggle against Italy.[217] 'Nothing would suit our interest better than that any German advance into the Balkans should be delayed till the Spring,' Churchill told the Chiefs of Staff on 6 January. 'For this very reason one must appreciate that it will begin earlier.'[218] The War Office thought the attack would take place in March, but Churchill leaped on one decrypt that ordered rear detachments to be ready by 20 January, and on the strength of that alone he persuaded the Defence Committee that Wavell, who was then pursuing the Italians hard in North Africa with considerable success, should fly to Athens to offer immediate assistance. Hitler had only intended to seize Greek territory as far south as Salonica in order to guard his right flank during his planned invasion of Russia that summer, but the arrival of British forces persuaded him to take the whole country.[219] Churchill wanted to be a good ally to Greece, but also hoped to increase British prestige in the eyes of the

Bulgarians, Turks and perhaps even the Russians (whose non-aggression pact with the Germans still held) and the Americans.[220]

At a lunch given by the Anglo-American Pilgrims Society in Halifax's honour on 9 January, prior to his departure for Washington, Churchill expressed his belief that:

> The identity of purpose and persistence of resolve prevailing throughout the English-speaking world will, more than any other single fact, determine the way of life which will be open to the generations, and perhaps to the centuries, which follow our own . . . I have always taken the view that the fortunes of Mankind in its tremendous journey are principally decided for good or ill – but mainly for good, for the path is upward – by its greatest men and its greatest episodes. I therefore hail it as a most fortunate occurrence that at this awe-striking climax in world affairs there should stand at the head of the American Republic a famous statesman, long versed and experienced in the work of government and administration, in whose heart there burns the fire of resistance to aggression and oppression, and whose sympathies and nature make him the sincere and undoubted champion of justice and of freedom, and of the victims of wrongdoing wherever they may dwell.[221]

The next day, with that encomium printed in the newspapers, Churchill met Harry Hopkins, Roosevelt's personal envoy, who was to become crucial in smoothing the path between Prime Minister and President. The forty-nine-year-old Hopkins had administered several New Deal relief agencies and had been US commerce secretary from 1938 to 1940; Churchill affectionately nicknamed him 'Sancho Panza' for his loyalty to Roosevelt, and Hopkins's directness in conversation led Churchill to joke that he would ennoble him as 'Lord Root of the Matter'.[222] Their first lunch, on 10 January, went on until 4 p.m., even though three-quarters of Hopkins's stomach had been removed in 1939 as a result of cancer. Churchill did everything possible not only to charm Hopkins but to impress him both with the robust state of British morale and with the desperate need for immediate American aid. 'The President is determined that we shall win the war together' was Hopkins's oral message to Churchill. 'Make no mistake about it. He has sent me here to tell you that at all costs and by all means he will carry you through, no matter what happens to him – there is nothing he will not do so long as he has human power.'[223] Commander Thompson recorded Churchill as being 'deeply moved' by this (which probably means tearful).[224] Hopkins also brought for his host a verse from a Longfellow poem of 1849, 'The Building of the Ship', which the President had written out.

Hopkins travelled with Churchill to Ditchley the next day, and in the entirely candle-lit dining room there that evening he told those present that

Roosevelt had had a radio brought in during a Cabinet meeting so they could listen to Churchill's speech. This left the Prime Minister 'touched and gratified'.[225] Churchill said he could hardly remember what he had said the previous summer, but just that 'it would be better for us to be destroyed than to see the triumph of such an imposter.'[226] 'Socialism is bad,' he said, 'jingoism is worse, and the two combined in a kind of debased Italian Fascism is the worst creed ever designed by man.'[227] That weekend, Hopkins noted that Churchill 'always seemed to be at his command-post on the precarious beachhead and the guns were continually blazing in his conversation; wherever he was, there was a battlefront – and he was involved in the battles not only of the current war but of the whole past from Cannae to Gallipoli'.[228] It seems surprising that Churchill should have brought up the latter while trying to impress this crucially important visitor, but he did.

A hint of Churchill's irritation with the United States might be noticeable from his only half-joking question to Hopkins at dinner the following night. He 'asked what the Americans would do when they had accumulated all the gold in the world and the other countries decided that gold was of no value except for filling teeth'.[229] 'Well,' replied the frail but urbane Hopkins, 'we shall be able to make use of our unemployed in guarding it!'[230] That evening, puffing on 'a phenomenally large cigar', Churchill gave Hopkins a general overview of the war. 'Germany had sixty millions on whom she could count; the remainder [that is, the Italians and the Romanians] were at least a drag and potentially a danger,' he said.

> The British Empire had more white inhabitants than that and if the U.S. were with us – as he seemed in this discourse to assume they actively would be – there would be another 120 millions . . . He did not believe the Japanese would come in . . . and he thought it more than probable that the Germans would be obliged to occupy the whole of France, thus driving the French to take up arms again in North Africa . . . He believed that Oran had been the turning-point in our fortunes: it made the world realize that we were in earnest in our intentions to carry on.

Colville wrote, 'I think Hopkins must have been impressed.'[231] But while watching the movie *Night Train to Munich* with Hopkins at Chequers that night, Churchill was handed the news that the light cruiser HMS *Southampton* had been sunk off Malta by Luftwaffe dive-bombers. He blamed it on the aborted Operation Workshop, saying, 'I flinched, and now I have cause to regret it.'[232]

On 14 January 1941, Churchill took Hopkins, Clementine, Ismay, Martin and his doctor Sir Charles Wilson (later Lord Moran) to Scapa Flow to see off Lord and Lady Halifax, who were leaving on the newly launched battleship HMS *King George V*. On hearing that Prince Regent Paul of Yugoslavia was opposed to the British setting up a front in Salonica out of fear that it would encourage the Germans to attack his country, Churchill told the Chiefs of Staff, 'Prince Paul's attitude looks like that of an unfortunate man in a cage with a tiger, hoping not to provoke him while steadily dinner-time approaches.'[233] It was not long before Paul, whom Churchill nicknamed 'Prince Palsy', was proved right.

On 16 January, after dining and sleeping aboard HMS *Nelson* the previous night, Churchill and his party attended a trial of new rockets fired from the battleship's turret, a multiple-projector that hurled bombs and wire into the sky to counter dive-bombing. Unfortunately, not enough allowance had been made for the wind and 'One of the projectiles got entangled in the rigging,' wrote Martin. 'There was a loud explosion and a jam-jar-like object flew towards the bridge, where we were standing. Everyone ducked and there was a loud bang, but no serious damage was done.'[234] After getting to his feet, Churchill observed drily, 'I think there is something not quite right about the way you are using this new weapon.'[235]

Churchill then took Hopkins and the party to visit the Rosyth naval base, the dockyards at Inverkeithing ('where the P.M. was received with immense enthusiasm') and the civil defence sites in Glasgow.[236] At a large municipal dinner in Glasgow that evening Harry Hopkins made a short speech that was all the more impressive for its gentle delivery. He gave the audience a sense of the enormous help which would soon be coming from across the Atlantic as soon as the Lend-Lease Bill passed Congress. He concluded with words from the Book of Ruth, 'Whither thou goest, I will go; and where thou lodgest, I will lodge. Thy people shall be my people, and thy God, my God.' Hopkins then added quietly, 'Even to the end.'[237] Churchill wept.

# 24
# 'Keep Buggering On'
# January–June 1941

*Most wars are mainly tales of muddle.*

Churchill, *Marlborough*[1]

*Napoleon could order, but Marlborough could never do more than persuade or cajole. It is hard to win battles on that basis.*

Churchill to General Edmonds, 1934[2]

On 22 January 1941, when the strategically important Libyan port of Tobruk fell to Wavell, Churchill had some good news to tell the Commons. 'I am sure there are an awful lot of things which could be done better,' he said, 'and I do not at all resent criticism, even when, for the sake of emphasis, it for a time parts company with reality.'[3] When he used the Latin expression *primus inter pares* (first among equals), Labour MPs shouted out, 'Translate!' 'Certainly I shall translate,' Churchill said, 'for the benefit of any Old Etonians who may be present.'[4] Colville noted that 'The House was entertained by his quips and his mastery of the art of anti-climax.'[5] He also took the opportunity to praise Beaverbrook as 'an old sea raider, which is a euphemistic method of describing a pirate', describing him as 'a man of altogether exceptional force and genius, who is at his very best when things are at their very worst'.[6]

That same day, Churchill wrote to Eden of his outrage that the tax burden in Egypt was falling disproportionately heavily on the *fellaheen* (peasantry), rather than 'the rich pashas and landowners and other pretended nationalists', adding, 'A little of the radical democratic sledge-hammer is needed in the [Nile] Delta, where so many fat, insolent class and party interests have grown up under our tolerant protection.'[7] This went to the heart of what he felt the British Empire was about – the protection of the poorest from the rapacity of their own countrymen – although it was hardly the ideal time to alienate anyone in Egypt. For many people, Churchill personified the Empire he loved. As they inspected the Dover battery together, Hopkins overheard a workman say, 'There goes the bloody British Empire.'[8] When Hopkins told him, 'Winston's face wreathed itself in smiles and, turning to [Colville], he lisped "*Very* nice."' Churchill now knew that a German invasion was unlikely. He said that he woke up in the mornings, 'as he nearly always had, feeling as if he had a bottle of champagne inside him and glad that another day had come'.[9] The British people, who unlike the Prime Minister had no access to Ultra decrypts, still believed an invasion was likely; that month 62 per cent of them told the Gallup organization that they thought the Germans would indeed attempt one. When asked who would win the war, however, 82 per cent thought it would be Britain, 10 per cent thought there would be a stalemate, 8 per cent had no opinion and 0 per cent said Germany.[10]

When Jack asked Churchill how Britain was going to recapture British Somaliland, which had been invaded by the Italians, Churchill pointed out that Libya needed to be liberated first, according to Napoleon's maxim 'Frappez la masse et le reste vient par surcroît' (Strike the main body and the rest will follow).[11] He drafted a telegram to Wavell asking why, of the 300,000 servicemen in North Africa, only 45,000 were actually in the field. It was a regular complaint of his throughout the war. When Dill requested that he not send it, Churchill said that 'plain speaking was necessary in war and he didn't see why Wavell should want still more Y.M.C.A.s etc. behind the lines.'[12] Nonetheless, the telegram was not sent.

Churchill understood that the visits of Harry Hopkins, Roosevelt's friend, were his best opportunity to entice the United States towards active involvement in the war. If Britain had negotiated peace with Hitler in 1940, he told Hopkins, it would only have meant the 'spring of the tiger' in a few years' time. 'Never give in, and you will never regret it,' he said.[13] The unrelenting charm offensive worked. 'Your Former Naval Person is not only the Prime Minister,' Hopkins reported to Roosevelt. 'He is also the directing force behind the strategy and conduct of the war in all its essentials. He has an amazing hold on the British people of all classes . . . The spirit of this people and their determination to resist invasion is beyond praise. No matter how fierce the attack may be you can be sure that they will resist it, and effectively.'[14] Joseph Kennedy, who had resigned his ambassadorship after Roosevelt's re-election in November, had told the President that Churchill was anti-American and disliked Roosevelt himself, a fiction completely dispelled by Hopkins's visit.[15]

On Sunday, 26 January, standing in front of the Great Hall fireplace at Chequers, Churchill expounded some of his wide-ranging views on modern history to Hopkins, Portal, Lindemann, Jack and Colville. He denounced Joseph Chamberlain for fomenting the Boer War, which he claimed had stimulated Germany to build her High Seas Fleet and criticized Baldwin for having 'made possible the resurgence of Germany and the decay of our own strength'.[16] He pointed out that, while the Versailles Treaty had extracted £1 billion in reparations from Germany, Britain and America had then lent her twice that. Once the war had been won, in about twenty months' time, he predicted, there would 'once more be those who wished to help Germany on to her feet. "Only one thing in history is certain: that Mankind is unteachable."'[17] He added that 'He hated nobody and didn't feel he had any enemies – except the Huns, and that was professional!'[18]

After peace had been won, Churchill believed, the world would have a brief 'opportunity to establish a few basic principles'. He thought future international relations could be based more on Christian ethics, 'and the more closely we follow the Sermon on the Mount, the more likely we are to succeed in our endeavours'. But such an approach was 'absurd' in wartime, and he denounced the Cabinet committee on the subject of war aims, which he said had so far only come up with 'a vague paper, four-fifths of which was from the Sermon on the Mount and the remainder an election address'.[19] When Hopkins predicted that Japan would bring America into the war, Churchill was quick to say that 'The advantage of America as an ally to the disadvantage of Japan as an enemy was as ten to one.' Their respective steel-production figures proved it, for 'modern war is waged with steel.'[20] He speculated that the Japanese must have been shocked by the fate of the Italian Navy, attacked from the air at Taranto. 'Fate holds terrible forfeits for those who gamble on certainties,' he mused.[21] In fact, Japan had learned a good deal from that attack.

Hopkins reassured his host that Roosevelt 'would lead American opinion not follow it'. He said the President 'was convinced that if England lost, America, too, would be encircled and beaten ... He did not want war ... but he would not shrink from war.'[22] At last Churchill was receiving assurance that Britain would not be left to fend for herself. Colville found him 'most communicative and benign' before he went to bed that night, explaining the dangers the Germans would have faced if they had invaded Britain without air superiority, especially if their lines of communication had been cut by the Royal Navy. Churchill went to bed to read Boswell's *Tour of the Hebrides* and, 'smiling sweetly', wished his own Boswell goodnight.[23]

On 29 January, Roosevelt took the encouraging step of authorizing top-secret Anglo-American staff talks in Washington, to examine various war scenarios by which the two countries could defeat the Axis Powers.[24] These were called the ABC-1 talks, and they formed the basis for future Allied plans for the war and for friendly mutual interactions between decision-makers from both countries. Churchill did not discount the possibility that Germany could attack Tunis and Bizerta from Sicily 'and try her invasion of the U.K. at the same time', probably accompanied by gas attacks on the aerodromes. He believed that the RAF's 'more efficient pilots should destroy and disperse any mass air attack they can put up, except if they use gas'. On 30 January, major air raids started again, for the first time in weeks. When Churchill heard a stick of bombs land on Horse Guards Parade shortly after Captain Pim had left in that direction, he telephoned the Admiralty to check that Pim was unharmed, which he was.[25]

In North Africa, Wavell, who had advanced 500 miles against the Italians at the cost of only 2,000 killed and wounded, warned that he could not mount an attack on Benghazi before the end of February. Churchill started to think that Britain's main effort should be diverted to Greece instead.[26]*

The situation there was complicated by the death of the seventy-year-old Metaxas through a throat infection on 29 January, which the Germans (groundlessly) claimed had been the result of an assassination ordered by Churchill. On 4 February, Churchill told the King that 'Germany will go into Bulgaria and mess up the Balkans,' that 'Hitler must bolster up Italy' against the Greeks and that 'We shall have a bad time here in the way of bombing,' but there were now 1,200 fighter aircraft in Britain.[27] The death from leukaemia of Lord Lloyd aged only sixty-one that day meant the loss of a friend, Other Club member and colleague who had called for rearmament against Germany even earlier than Churchill and who had fought staunchly against Indian self-government alongside him. 'Lord Lloyd and I have been friends for many years and close political associates during the last twelve years,' Churchill said in his Commons eulogy.

> We championed several causes together which did not command the applause of large majorities; but it is just in that kind of cause, where one is swimming against the stream, that one learns the worth and quality of a comrade and friend . . . It is sometimes said that good men are scarce. It is perhaps because the spate of events with which we attempt to cope and which we strive to

* To a general who had spoken too loosely to reporters about the coming attack on Benghazi, Churchill said, 'These gentlemen of the press were listening carefully to every word you said – all eagerly anxious for a tiny morsel of cheese which they could publish. And you go and give them a whole ruddy Stilton!' (ed. Eade, *Contemporaries* pp. 147–8).

> control have far exceeded, in this modern age, the old bounds, that they have been swollen up to giant proportions, while, all the time, the stature and intellect of man remain unchanged.[28]

Churchill had expressed this thought in his essay 'Fifty Years Hence' back in 1931, and he was to do so several times again, including in his Nobel Prize acceptance address. The way that human intellect and decency were not keeping pace with scientific breakthroughs was also to concentrate Churchill's mind as the atomic bomb was developed.

Lloyd's death necessitated a reshuffle. Among other changes, Lord Moyne was moved from Agriculture to Lloyd's place as colonial secretary. Churchill wanted a duke in the Government, so Moyne's place at the Ministry of Agriculture was taken by the 16th Duke of Norfolk, who was helped in his advancement by the fact that four other dukes – Buccleuch, Westminster, Bedford and Manchester – had opposed the war at its outbreak. When Eden commiserated with him over the time and trouble involved in the reshuffle, Churchill said he enjoyed Cabinet-making.[29]

Just as Hopkins visited Chequers to say goodbye to Churchill on 9 February, word arrived that the House of Representatives had approved the Lend-Lease Bill by 260 to 165. Once it had been approved by the Senate and signed into law by the President, Britain would be able to buy £3 billion worth of arms from the United States, and make repayments over many decades. The next day Churchill's evening broadcast was, in Colville's words, 'addressed very largely to American ears'.[30] He mocked Mussolini: 'One of the two dictators – the crafty, cold-blooded, black-hearted Italian, who had thought to gain an empire on the cheap by stabbing fallen France in the back – got into trouble.'[31] He described Wavell with his customary quadruple adjectives as 'a master of war: sage, painstaking, daring, and tireless'.[32] Most memorably, he quoted from Henry Longfellow's poem 'The Building of the Ship'. 'President Roosevelt', he said,

> wrote out a verse, in his own handwriting, from Longfellow, which he said, 'applies to you people as it does to us'. Here is the verse:
>
> Sail on, O Ship of State!
> Sail on, O Union, strong and great!
> Humanity with all its fears,
> With all the hopes of future years,
> Is hanging breathless on thy fate!
>
> What is the answer that I shall give, in your name, to this great man, the thrice-chosen head of a nation of a hundred and thirty millions? Here is the

> answer which I will give to President Roosevelt: Put your confidence in us. Give us your faith and your blessing, and, under Providence, all will be well. We shall not fail or falter; we shall not weaken or tire. Neither the sudden shock of battle, nor the long-drawn trials of vigilance and exertion will wear us down. Give us the tools, and we will finish the job.[33]

Benghazi fell to Wavell on 6 February. Dill initially wanted him to be allowed to pursue the Italians to Tripoli, and thus to expel them from North Africa, but Churchill believed there was now an opportunity for British forces to get to northern Greece in time to counter the German thrust, and that this was a higher priority. He told the King that the capture of Benghazi three weeks ahead of schedule meant that many more men and much more materiel could be sent to Greece, 'as the Greeks have done so well'.[34] At a Cabinet meeting on 11 February, just before Eden and Dill left for Cairo to discuss the Greek expedition with Wavell, it was reported that 'Special Intelligence' (that is, Ultra) indicated that Germany would invade Greece in mid-March and was expected to take Athens with ten divisions by mid-April.

The Greek adventure was later defended by Churchill as an act of chivalry demanded by considerations of honour, but in fact he had concrete strategic grounds for deploying no fewer than 55,000 men there: he wanted to shore up the 'Balkan bloc' of Yugoslavia, Romania, Bulgaria, Greece and Turkey, much the same bloc he had had in his sights at the time of the Dardanelles expedition in 1915. Yet Turkey was now solidly neutral, and it was unlikely that Romania or Bulgaria would alter their stance as a result of the appearance of a British Expeditionary Force in Greece. Crucially, the situation in North Africa was entirely altered by the arrival in Tripoli on 12 February of General Erwin Rommel at the head of German divisions of the newly formed Afrika Korps. The British should have withdrawn the troops they had committed to Greece so as to concentrate on this potent new threat to Egypt and the Suez Canal, the lifeline to India and Britain's Far Eastern possessions.

On 20 February Churchill cabled Eden and Dill in Cairo, 'Do not consider yourself obligated to a Greek enterprise if in your hearts you feel it will only be another Norwegian fiasco. If no good plan can be made please say so. But of course you know how valuable success would be.'[35] The three commanders-in-chief in the Middle East also recommended the Greek expedition, even after Admiral Sir Andrew Cunningham had said he could no longer promise he could capture Rhodes as the main air base. In what is today called groupthink, a dangerous unanimity emerged in support of the Greek adventure. Proponents now included Churchill,

Eden, Dill and the Chiefs of Staff, the local commanders-in-chief and, at least initially, Wavell.

Churchill agreed with the Polish commander General Sikorski that the Turks would enter the war only when they had decided their national interest dictated it, but he argued, albeit hopefully, that the Americans were 'moving into the war by sentiment'.[36] 'Do you play poker?' Churchill asked Sikorski at Ditchley on 16 February. 'Here is the hand that is going to win the war: a royal flush – Great Britain, the Sea, the Air, the Middle East, American aid.'[37] He therefore deprecated the need for a major continental commitment, let alone a march on Berlin. Lady Diana Cooper left a charming account of that weekend at Ditchley, writing to her son John Julius, 'We had two lovely films after dinner – one was called *Escape* and the other was a very light comedy called *Quiet Wedding*. There were also several short reels from Papa's ministry. Winston managed to cry through all of them, including the comedy.'[38] She told Churchill that the greatest thing he had done was to give the British people courage. 'I never gave them courage,' he replied. 'I was able to focus theirs.'[39]

With Eden in Cairo evaluating the Greek expedition alongside Dill and Wavell, it fell to Churchill himself to conduct an interview with the Japanese Ambassador Mamoru Shigemitsu on 24 February, after which he was asked to supply a record of the conversation to the Foreign Office. He had to admit, 'he could remember his own remarks, but found it difficult to recall the other side of the conversation.'[40] Maisky, who was not present, said to Lloyd George that he had heard that Churchill had tears in his eyes when he told Shigemitsu that Britain was going to prevail over Germany. 'Yes, that happens to Winston,' replied Lloyd George. 'He is a very emotional man. So what? Now he has tears because he wants to crush Hitler. Within a year he may have tears because of the shock of the horrors of war . . . Things change.'[41] One thing that had not changed was Lloyd George's cynicism and enmity.

'Both Winston and Eden know that fighting on the mainland of Europe against Germany is a gamble,' the King wrote in his diary after seeing Churchill on 25 February, 'but Greece has fought so well, and Turkey and Yugoslavia may be fortified by the thought and knowledge that British troops will be fighting in the Balkans.'[42] There were not enough, however. Many Australians, New Zealanders, South Africans and Poles who were about to be sent to Greece later complained that not enough Britons were being committed to the operation, over which the Commonwealth governments were not even consulted. Churchill knew that grand strategy could not be decided upon by a Commonwealth committee, but he could have been much more adept at managing sensibilities over issues such as this, particularly where the Australians were concerned, who would soon be under threat from Japan at home, would lose thousands of men at Singapore and were widely extended in Africa and now Europe.

'We are prepared to run the risk of failure,' Eden telegraphed from Cairo, 'thinking it better to suffer with the Greeks than to make no attempt to help them.' That night the news came through that a transatlantic convoy had been very badly mauled. Bracken suggested to Colville that he not tell the Prime Minister until the next day, in case it affected his sleep. When at 3 a.m. Churchill asked if there was any Admiralty news, Colville felt he had to tell him, whereupon he became 'very pensive'. Colville remarked that it was very distressing news. 'Distressing!' Churchill replied. 'It is terrifying. If it goes on it will be the end of us.'[43]

Despite these struggles for the life of the nation, MPs insisted on 27 February that Churchill debate the arcane constitutional issue of the House of Commons Disqualification (Temporary Provisions) Bill, about whether they should be allowed to retain their seats in Parliament while serving abroad. Churchill concluded that 'Five or ten years' experience as a member of this House is as fine an all-round education in public affairs as any man can obtain,' and argued that they should be able to retain their seats (thereby making it easier for him to continue sending Chamberlainites to honorific posts around the Empire).[44] He then dined at the Other Club where David Margesson, the Secretary for War, was now a member, demonstrating again Churchill's disinclination to pursue vendettas.*

Just as the British Commonwealth troops were embarking for Greece in large numbers, Margesson decided he disliked the venture. He said he had gone along with it because 'the P.M. felt that our prestige in France, in Spain and in the U.S. could not stand our desertion of Greece.'[45] Political prestige was given precedence over strategic imperatives. Eden merely said it was 'as tough a proposition as ever I have known.'[46] Cunningham repeated that his resources were badly overstretched, and now Dill was opposed too. All this left Churchill sneering, 'The poor Chiefs of Staff will get very out of breath in their desire to run away.'[47] On 6 March, Colville reported that 'The P.M. harangued the Chiefs of Staff at No. 10

* More than twenty Other Club members served in the Churchill Government during the Second World War; indeed in July 1945 over a quarter of the entire Government were members of the Club. In moulding it since its rebirth in 1925 to include talented people whom he could get to know socially, Churchill had in effect been grooming a government-in-waiting, without his or their suspecting it. Attending its dinners could be dangerous during the Blitz; in April 1941 a bomb exploded outside the south-west corner of the Savoy Hotel, damaging the two rooms to the immediate left of the Pinafore Room. Yet during the war dinners were better attended than ever before. 'There is no record that the Club ever had to take shelter or wanted to,' recorded one member, the newspaperman Colin Coote. (Gilbert, *Other Club* p. 173.)

continuously from 11.30 to 1.30 [p.m.].'[48] Yet as events were soon to show, they were right – at least in the more recent manifestation of their views – and Churchill wrong. The shadows of Gallipoli, when Churchill had also harangued wavering Service Chiefs to get his way on a risky Balkan adventure, were lengthening.

Lunch that day was with Clementine, Lindemann, the Countess of Portarlington (a distant cousin of Churchill's), the journalist Charles Eade and James B. Conant, the President of Harvard and chairman of the US National Defense Research Committee, down in the basement of No. 10, now strengthened by steel girders.[49] They ate a fish patty, steak tournedos with mushrooms, braised celery, peaches and cheese, and had sherry before lunch, white wine, port, brandy and coffee, as well as cigarettes and cigars. Churchill spoke 'with considerable satisfaction' about a Commando raid on the Lofoten Islands near Narvik two days earlier, which had destroyed 800,000 gallons of fish oil destined for German vitamins, but he naturally did not mention that the raiders had also captured the rotor wheels and codebook of an Enigma machine, which were already being pored over at Bletchley Park. Of air raids, Churchill said, 'Although it was always good to take a chance, you should never offer a "sitter" [sitting duck].'[50] When the conversation turned to reports that Englishwomen had been giving cups of tea to German pilots who had been shot down, Clementine commented on the inability of the English to hate their enemies. 'Before this war is over,' Churchill said, 'we should be hating our enemies alright.'[51]

Lady Portarlington said she sympathized with American isolationists who were saying that nothing was worse than war. 'Slavery is worse than war,' Churchill interrupted. 'Dishonour is worse than war.'[52] Smoking a cigar that he relit at least ten times, and drinking 'quite a lot of port and brandy', he pointed out that the Germans had rejected Hitler twice in free elections, the second time by a bigger majority than the first. Eade was impressed by the informality of the lunch. When Churchill finished his main course, he took his own plate to the sideboard. Discussing scientific matters, probably for Conant's benefit, Churchill asked the Prof why, if it 'is constantly halving itself, is there any uranium left on earth?'[53] He then put forward a curious science-based argument for the existence of God, saying that 'The Sun is much hotter than the Earth, which shows that the Earth must have been separately heated at a date much later than the Sun.'[54] The lunch, which lasted from 1.35 to 3.20 p.m., was joined by Bracken, who surprised Eade by calling the Prime Minister 'Winston'.

When on 4 March the King questioned the rights that the Americans would have over their bases in the British West Indies, over which Churchill was negotiating with John G. 'Gil' Winant, the charming and handsome fifty-one-year-old new American Ambassador, the Prime Minister told him 'that the Lease & Lend Bill would have to be passed first as without it we should be unable to carry on and win the war'.[55] Four days later the Lend-Lease Bill passed the Senate by sixty votes to thirty-one. The fifth card of the royal flush had fallen into place. In his Mansion House speech that November, Churchill lauded the Lend-Lease Act, saying that £3 billion had been made available 'to the cause of world freedom without – mark this, for it is unique – the setting up of any account in money. Never again let us hear the taunt that money is the ruling thought or power in the hearts of the American democracy. The Lend and Lease Bill must be regarded without question as the most unsordid act in the whole of recorded history.'[56]

The first large units of British Commonwealth troops disembarked in Greece on 9 March. Although Dill had concluded that the risks had increased after German troops had entered Bulgaria, which had joined the Axis on 1 March, Wavell (initially), Cunningham (with reservations), Air Chief Marshal Arthur Longmore, the Commander-in-Chief of the RAF in the Middle East, Cadogan and now also General Smuts were all in favour of the expedition, as was the War Cabinet, especially Eden. The coming Greek debacle cannot therefore all be blamed on Churchill, although as prime minister and cheerleader he must take the ultimate responsibility (and indeed never sought to evade it).

That weekend, General Sir Alan Brooke, the flinty, no-nonsense Commander-in-Chief of Home Forces, a scion of Ulster's 'Fighting Brookes' family, came to dine and sleep at Chequers. 'He was in great form,' the general wrote of Churchill in his diary, 'and after dinner sent for his rifle to give a demonstration of the "long port", which he wanted to substitute for the "slope".* He followed this up with some bayonet exercise! . . . Luckily PM decided to go to bed early and by midnight I was comfortably tucked away in an Elizabethan four-poster bed dated 1550!' After the war, Brooke wrote, 'This evening remains very vivid in my mind, as it was one of the first occasions on which I had seen Winston in one of his really lighthearted moods. I was convulsed watching him give this exhibition of bayonet exercises, dressed up in his romper suit and standing in the ancestral hall of Chequers. I remember wondering what Hitler would have made of this demonstration of skill at arms.'[57] (A more jaundiced Brooke would later describe Churchill's late-night meetings as 'the Midnight Follies', after a popular dance troupe.)

* The slope has the rifle on the left shoulder, inclined at 45 degrees; the port has the rifle held much more tiringly in front of the body at 45 degrees.

At their Tuesday lunch the following week, Churchill told the King 'he felt the responsibility greatly at having acquiesced in sending help to the Greeks, when all the disadvantages were uppermost, and that anything might happen before we got there.'[58] That day, he had a victory to celebrate when Lend-Lease was signed into law by President Roosevelt. Over $30 billion worth of American-produced war materiel would be sent to Britain over the next four years, far more than she could ever pay for. One price for this was that Britain was forced to abandon the Imperial Preference system, which since 1932 had put tariffs on goods and produce from outside the British Empire. Cadogan considered this to be 'rather impertinent blackmail' by the Americans. Churchill had his eyes on the far greater goals of staving off national bankruptcy and acquiring the weapons needed to fight the war effectively.[59] Britain had reached the very end of her dollar reserves before Congress passed the Bill. The first appropriations were made only thirteen days later.[60] In the Commons, Churchill described Lend-Lease as a second Magna Carta. During Operation Compass, some American Congressmen had been invited to lunch at Chequers, one of whom asked, 'What will happen if the Germans gain a foothold in this country and you are overrun?' Churchill replied, 'With dying hands we will pass on the torch to you,' adding that the Royal Navy would continue the fight from new bases overseas.[61] The implied threat that the fleet might be handed over to the Germans by a Mosley government no longer needed to be made, now that Lend-Lease arms were flowing across the Atlantic.*

On 18 March, Cadogan described Churchill walking around the site of the fortress being built on Whitehall Gardens to protect the War Office, 'with his cigar, up and down ladders, puddling through half-set concrete, talking to workmen about their private affairs, putting to any sufficient audience the question "Are we downhearted?" and really enjoying himself thoroughly'.[62] 'To work for Mr Churchill was to be harnessed to a miniature whirlwind,' wrote an Admiralty aide.[63] Walter Thompson, who never went to bed before him, agreed, noting that his master regularly worked 120 hours a week. Churchill's hearing was keen and his optician said his eyesight was that of a man ten years younger.[64] He was overweight,

* Churchill tried to stay closely informed about American politics, and in February 1944 wanted to invite Isaiah Berlin, the Oxford don who wrote insightful reports on the subject from the Washington Embassy, to No. 10. However, he confused him with the American singer-songwriter Irving Berlin, who was in Britain to raise money for Service charities. Over lunch, Churchill plied the composer of 'White Christmas' and 'Alexander's Ragtime Band' with questions such as 'When do you think the war will end, Mr Berlin?' The entertainer answered as well as he could, and it was not until later that the mistake was recognized. (Colville, *Fringes* p. 472.)

but otherwise in good shape. 'I was amazed at the speed with which this man of sixty-five walked along passages and up steep staircases,' said Charles Eade, a remark that was echoed by many others.[65]

The day after his visit to the War Office fortress, Churchill met Averell Harriman, Roosevelt's representative on shipping and supply. An international polo-player, New Deal administrator and the heir to his family's Union Pacific Railroad Company, Harriman was American aristocracy and Churchill immediately got on very well with him, taking him up to the roof of the Air Ministry during an air raid that night 'to watch the fun', and quoting to him 'Tennyson's prescient lines about aerial warfare'.[66]* 'Mr Harriman was tall, dark and handsome,' recalled an aide, 'with a gentle modest manner, yet always impressive.'[67] Very soon after he had met Pamela (whom he thought 'delicious'), Harriman began an affair with her in his suite at the Dorchester Hotel, while Randolph was serving in North Africa and arguing with his wife over money. (He was by no means her only sexual partner during the war.) In the spring of 1942, Winston Churchill told Pamela that he had been hearing 'quite a lot' about her and Harriman, but Pamela 'laughed it off', and they seem not to have discussed it again.[68]

Clementine seems to have known about the affair, but did nothing to discourage it. The Chequers visitors' books show that the couple – who married in 1971 after the death of Harriman's second wife – stayed regularly at Chequers with Winston and Clementine, along with Harriman's daughter Kathleen, who also knew. The Churchills have been accused of putting the good of Anglo-American relations before the survival of their son's marriage, by at worst facilitating and at best turning a blind eye to the affair taking place under their own roof. Randolph himself learned of it when he came home on leave in November 1942.

Sarah's marriage to Vic Oliver had also collapsed by the autumn of 1941, although it is unclear whether she had begun her affair with Gil Winant, the American Ambassador, by then, and she did not obtain a divorce until 1945. As she recorded the conversation with her father when she asked for a military posting, Churchill said, 'I hope he is going to be a gentleman and give you a divorce.' 'Of course not,' Sarah replied. 'I am leaving him.' 'You cheeky bitch,' Churchill joked, 'I would let you leave me!'[69] She joined the Women's Auxiliary Air Force, where she was

* From 'Locksley Hall':

> Saw the heavens fill with commerce, argosies of magic sails,
> Pilots of the purple twilight, dropping down with costly bales;
>
> Heard the heavens fill with shouting, and there rain'd a ghastly dew
> From the nations' airy navies grappling in the central blue.

stationed at RAF Medmenham, halfway between Chequers and London, interpreting aerial photographs.[70]

There was a sense in early 1941 of events simply taking place one after another, with little unifying theme besides simple survival, of Britain hanging on in the war for as long as possible until something showed up to turn the tide against Germany, although at that stage there was little to suggest what that might be. Churchill's own hopes for the United States to declare war, or for Hitler to overreach himself by attacking Russia, or for a decisive British victory in North Africa, or for an uprising across Occupied Europe, all seemed far-fetched to varying degrees at the time, and British strategic policy at the time might best be described in his own maxim 'Keep Buggering On'. He had spent 28 February presiding over the Import Executive, which was trying to tackle the shipping crisis brought on by sinkings very heavily outweighing purchases and new building. In the calendar year 1940, some 2.73 million tons of British shipping had been lost, and 0.82 million tons of Allied shipping, with only 221,935 tons of major new warships being built. 'We have got to lift this business to the highest plane, over everything else,' he told Pound.[71] Six months earlier, he had overcome Admiralty objections and established a Western Approaches command at Liverpool, which now proved extremely helpful in the anti-U-boat war. In early March he set up the Battle of the Atlantic Committee to coordinate ministers, civil servants, shipbuilders, scientific advisers and the Services. 'The Battle of the Atlantic has begun,' he announced. 'We must take the offensive against the U-boat and the Focke-Wulf* wherever we can and whenever we can. The U-boat at sea must be hunted, the U-boat in the building yard or in the dock must be bombed. The Focke-Wulf and other bombers employed against our shipping must be attacked in the air and in their nests.'[72] He initiated the arming of all merchant ships with improved anti-aircraft guns and had catapults installed on larger vessels to launch Hurricanes from their decks. He wrote in his war memoirs that 'The only thing that ever really frightened me during the war was the U-boat peril . . . I was even more anxious about this battle than I had been about the glorious air fight called the Battle of Britain.'[73]

When the Battle of the Atlantic Committee met for the first time on 19 March, sinkings were averaging 10 per cent per convoy. As Britain depended on imports for half her food and most of her raw materials, her situation would soon become extremely grave. 'I'm not afraid of the air, I'm not afraid of invasion, I'm less afraid of the Balkans,' Churchill told

* The FW 200 Condor aircraft.

the Cabinet the next day, 'but I am anxious about the Atlantic.'[74] In twelve weeks the U-boat wolfpacks had accounted for 142 Allied vessels, while two German battleships in the Atlantic, the *Scharnhorst* and *Gneisenau*, sank or captured 80,000 tons of Allied shipping in mid-March.[75] There were also 2.63 million tons of shipping in British ports needing repair, at docks which became ever more congested as damage exceeded the resources needed. 'How willingly would I have exchanged a full-scale attempt at invasion', Churchill wrote after the war, 'for this shapeless, measureless peril, expressed in charts, curves and statistics!'[76]

Events in Yugoslavia moved very quickly after Prince Regent Paul signed a pact with Hitler in Berlin on 25 March. The next day Churchill wrote to Sir Ronald Campbell, the British Ambassador in Belgrade. 'Continue to pester, nag, and bite. Demand audiences. Don't take No for an answer,' he urged. 'This is no time for reproaches or dignified farewells.'[77] The next day Paul was overthrown in a British-backed coup d'état by his seventeen-year-old nephew, King Peter. In a speech two weeks later Churchill said, 'A boa constrictor who had already covered his prey with his foul saliva and then had it suddenly wrested from his coils, would be in an amiable mood compared with Hitler, Goering, Ribbentrop and the rest of the Nazi gang when they experienced this bitter disappointment.'[78]

'The P.M. is overjoyed,' Colville recorded of the coup. 'The whole country is in ecstasies.'[79] In one speech that day, Churchill said, 'Early this morning the Yugoslav nation found its soul.'[80] In a second speech, at a lunch in honour of Winant, he said that the American Ambassador 'gives us the feeling that all President Roosevelt's men give me, that they would be shot stone dead rather than see this cause let down'.[81] Speculating aloud about how Britain might win the war, Churchill reminisced about his time at the Ministry of Munitions, when he was 'told that we were running short of this and that, that we were running out of bauxite and steel, and so forth; but we went on, and in the end the only thing we ran short of was Huns'.[82]

The Battle of Cape Matapan on 28 and 29 March saw Admiral Sir Andrew Cunningham's fleet sink three Italian heavy cruisers and two destroyers. Some 2,300 enemy sailors were killed, at the cost of four light cruisers damaged and three sailors killed.[83] The news 'was greeted with yells of delight' at Chequers. Churchill described the assault as 'The tearing up of the paper fleet of Italy'.[84] Overall, he thought, 'people were very much happier in the war than might have been expected.' Colville reported that even Rab Butler 'has, somewhat reluctantly, come to admire the P.M.'.[85] Churchill sent a telegram warning the French that if they continued to bomb Gibraltar, which they had been doing sporadically for some months, 'We bomb Vichy, and pursue them everywhere.' He then told Mussolini that if he scuttled ships in Massowah (modern-day Massawa in Eritrea), thus blocking the harbours, 'we won't feed an Italian in Africa'.[86] (Some ships were scuttled there much later on, but Italian prisoners-of-war continued to be fed.)

When Churchill discovered that General Brooke had been war-gaming the effects of five German divisions landing on the Norfolk coast and fighting their way inland, he sent him fourteen questions such as 'What naval escort did they have?', 'Was the landing at this point protected by superior enemy daylight fighter formations?' and 'How many men and vehicles were assumed to have landed in the first twelve hours, what percentage of loss were they debited with?' He concluded by saying, 'I should be very glad if the same officers would work out a scheme for our landing an exactly similar force on the French coast at the same range of our fighter protection, and assuming that the Germans have naval superiority in the Channel.'[87] Brooke replied a week later giving all the figures required, saying that 10 per cent losses had been assumed in crossing and a further 5 to 10 per cent on landing. He then entered into a five-week correspondence with Churchill on matters such as how the Germans would be able to find fuel and food in Britain.[88]

Rommel launched his assault on Wavell's positions in the Western Desert on 31 March. In only ten days he reached Tobruk, which he besieged. 'The German advance has taken us by surprise and an armoured brigade has been cut up,' noted Colville, adding, 'The P.M. confided to me that he thought Wavell, etc., had been very silly in North Africa and should have been prepared to meet an attack there.'[89] He ordered Wavell to hold Tobruk at all costs and Admiral Cunningham to block Tripoli Harbour. Cunningham considered this suicidal, although he did shell the harbour and sink several enemy vessels there.[90] Cunningham was also told to resupply the strategically vital island of Malta, which was effectively under siege from the air, and to cut Axis communications between Italy and Africa.

Wavell was meanwhile ordered to use the forces that had recaptured British Somaliland to invade Ethiopia, pressing home the advantage there. He was later to complain that Churchill left him constantly overstretched, which was true, and that the Prime Minister 'never realized the necessity for full equipment before committing troops to battle'. He remembered him 'arguing that because a comparatively small number of mounted Boers had held up a British division in 1899 or 1900, it was unnecessary for the South African Brigade to have much more equipment than rifles before taking the field'.[91] On 2 April, Churchill sent Wavell an Enigma decrypt showing that Rommel had been refused air support by Berlin due to the needs of other theatres, and had been ordered not to move further east into Egypt for the time being.[92] Nonetheless, the next day Benghazi had to be evacuated by Wavell, who had been severely weakened by the hiving off of large numbers of troops to the Greek expedition. 'The P.M. is greatly worried,' noted Colville.[93] A visit to Liverpool and Manchester was cancelled on the news.

That same day, Churchill passed on to Cripps, for forwarding to Stalin, information from Ultra – claiming it came from 'a trusted agent' in the German High Command – that three German armoured divisions had been ordered to move from the Balkans to Kraków in Poland in late March, an order that had been countermanded after the Belgrade coup. Unlike the Chiefs of Staff and most of the intelligence services, Churchill suspected this meant that Hitler was planning to invade Russia as soon as his southern flank had been secured in Yugoslavia and Greece. Stalin dismissed the warning as mere 'English provocation', just as he had ignored Churchill's similar warning in June 1940 that Germany would turn east. Stalin did not receive the warning immediately, as Cripps could only get a meeting with a junior Politburo member weeks later, so little credibility did the Soviets give the British vis-à-vis the Germans at that time.[94]

Yugoslavia was invaded by the German Army on 6 April. Her territory was attacked from three sides simultaneously and Belgrade smashed by bombing. Greece was attacked that day too. 'We had had to help Greece, but by doing so we had let loose the dogs of war in the Balkans,' Churchill told the King. 'We hoped to be able to help both Greece and Yugoslavia, but the German war machine once it started was a very hard one to stop.' Then he mused, 'We have done very well against Italy, but Germany is the enemy.'[95] He ended by turning back to the theatre that was most on his mind at the time: 'The Battle of the Atlantic is the only one that matters,' he told the King, 'and America is on our side.'

The news that the Germans had entered Salonica on 9 April led to 'a silent wince of pain throughout the House', Harold Nicolson recorded.[96] Churchill lightened the mood three days later by announcing that 'Ten United States Revenue cutters, fast vessels of about two thousand tons displacement, with a fine armament and a very wide range of endurance, have already been placed at our disposal by the United States Government and will soon be in action. These vessels, originally designed to enforce Prohibition, will now serve an even higher purpose.'[97] He likewise showed good humour two days after that when taking Winant and Harriman around Swansea, where he was so mobbed by several hundred dockers that he put his distinctive, square-crown bowler hat on to his cane and waved it around for those at the back of the crowd who could not see him. That night he slept on his train in a siding near the Severn Tunnel, from where his party could see a heavy bombing raid taking place on Bristol.

Churchill had been elected chancellor of Bristol University in June 1929. He took his responsibilities seriously, giving out degrees and occasionally delivering important speeches, and was to become the longest-serving chancellor of any British university.[98] 'I always enjoy coming here,' he told his doctor, not least because it gave him the chance to wear his father's chancellor of the Exchequer robes again. His powers were limited though; in the late 1930s he wrote to the Vice Chancellor asking for a place at the University to be given to a Jewish dental student whose parents wanted him to escape Nazi Germany. The Vice Chancellor refused. (The student survived, and went to live in the American Midwest.)[99] When Churchill went to Bristol to confer honorary degrees on Winant and Robert Menzies, the Australian Prime Minister, in mid-April, air raids had killed or wounded several hundred people in the city. In Colville's words, Churchill and his party 'walked and motored through devastation such as I had never thought possible'.[100] Yet the bombed-out houses had Union Jacks flying in the ruins, and when the crowds gathered round Churchill they waved and cheered. 'He kept murmuring to himself "Wonderful people . . . wonderful people."'[101] (When he waved, he told Tommy Thompson on a different occasion, he 'tried to catch a person's eye as this gave a direct communication with the individual'.)[102] Some buildings close to the Wills Tower, where the ceremony took place, were still on fire, and several of the dons wore their academic robes over their dirty Civil Defence uniforms, having worked through the night to pull people from the rubble. 'Throughout the ceremony,' recalled Thompson, 'the acrid smell of burning kept drifting through the broken windows of the hall.'[103] Churchill was proud that the University conducted the ceremony 'with faultless ritual and appropriate decorum' and that no part of it was omitted.[104]

'That you should gather in this way is a mark of fortitude and phlegm,' Churchill told his audience,

> of a courage and detachment from material affairs worthy of all that we have learned to believe of ancient Rome or of modern Greece. I go about the country whenever I can escape for a few hours or for a day from my duty at headquarters, and I see the damage done by the enemy attacks; but I also see side by side with the devastation and amid the ruins, quiet, confident, bright, and smiling eyes, beaming with a consciousness of being associated with a cause far higher and wider than any human or personal issue. I see the spirit of an unconquerable people. I see a spirit bred in freedom, nursed

> in a tradition which has come down to us through the centuries, and which will surely at this moment, this turning-point in the history of the world, enable us to bear our part in such a way that none of our race who come after us will have any reason to cast reproach upon their sires.[105]

Afterwards, Tom Harrisson of the Mass-Observation movement saw 'great tears of angry sorrow in his eyes. He was so visibly moved by the suffering that he saw, yet so visibly determined to see that it spelt not defeat, but victory.'[106] As his train pulled out of Bristol station, Churchill, still tearful, said to Commander Thompson, 'They have such faith – it is a grave responsibility.'[107] That night, Roosevelt announced that, even without a state of war existing between his country and Germany, the US Navy would extend its anti-U-boat patrols from 300 miles from the American coast, which it had been patrolling since October 1939, as far east as the 25th Meridian, which extends through Greenland and the Cape Verde Islands, thereby freeing up more Royal Navy vessels to fight U-boats closer to home waters. The Defence Committee meanwhile decided to undertake the hugely risky Operation Tiger, by which 238 tanks would be sent to Alexandria via the Mediterranean, rather than by the Cape route. Churchill argued strongly for the risk to be taken, but at the end of the hard-fought meeting he said, 'If anyone's good at praying, now's the time.'[108] It turned out to be the right decision, with only one transport ship sunk.

This was indeed a 'turning-point in the history of the world', but it was by no means clear at the time which way history would turn. Rommel took Bardia on 13 April. The Iraqi politician Rashid Ali al-Gaylani's 'Golden Square Coup' in Baghdad threatened to turn his country over to the Axis, and Yugoslav opposition to Germany collapsed on 18 April. That week, in the heaviest raids of the war, 2,000 Londoners and 3,000 Liverpudlians were killed. London's West End, Piccadilly, St James's Street, Pall Mall, Lower Regent Street and the Admiralty were all hit hard. Of the last, Churchill observed that 'this gave him a better view of Nelson's Column' from his seat at the Cabinet table.[109]

On 18 April, Alexandros Koryzis, the new Greek Prime Minister, shot himself. After the Greek armies that had been fighting the Italians in Albania since October 1940 had capitulated on 20 April, and Germany had established total air superiority over Greece, the Defence Committee took the decision to evacuate the country. It was Gallipoli, Namsos, Narvik, Dunkirk and Dakar all over again, with people joking that 'BEF' stood for 'Back Every Friday'. Nonetheless, the King recorded after their weekly lunch, 'P.M. was in good form and not depressed over the situation in Greece . . . evacuation is being arranged.'[110]

Greece capitulated on 24 April. 'The House of Commons is restive and the Government's popularity is declining,' Channon noted, 'but the Prime Minister's position seems secure.'[111] Although Churchill's support for the Yugoslav coup and intervention in Greece looked like a fiasco at the time, it later seemed inspired, though not for any reason connected with British arms. By August 1941, the Prime Minister was telling Colville that the Yugoslav coup 'might well have played a vital part in the war' in that it had caused Hitler 'to bring back his Panzer divisions from the north and postponed for six weeks the attack on Russia'.[112] He was supported in this assertion after the war by the senior German staff officer General Günther Blumentritt, who stated that 'the Balkan incident postponed the opening of the [Russian] campaign by five-and-a-half weeks', while another senior strategist, General Siegfried Westphal, put it at six.[113] As a result, the Germans were unable to reach Moscow until the autumn, when Russia's rainy season turned to a winter so cold that petrol froze. The Wehrmacht stalled outside Moscow, giving the Russians an opportunity for a forceful counter-attack in December, recapturing Kaluga on 30 December. The iron law of unintended consequences had once again acted in Churchill's favour.

In his broadcast of 27 April, Churchill presented the British Empire's support of the Greeks as a moral rather than strategic issue. 'By solemn guarantee given before the war, Great Britain had promised them her help,' he said.

> They declared they would fight for their native soil even if neither of their neighbours made common cause with them, and even if we left them to their fate. But we could not do that. There are rules against that kind of thing; and to break those rules would be fatal to the honour of the British Empire, without which we could neither hope nor deserve to win this hard war. Military defeat or miscalculation can be redeemed. The fortunes of war are fickle and changing. But an act of shame would deprive us of the respect which we now enjoy throughout the world, and this would sap the vitals of our strength.[114]*

Churchill openly admitted the 'gravity ... of the war situation' in his speech, but said that to leave Whitehall 'to go out to the front, by which I mean the streets and wharves of London or Liverpool, Manchester, Cardiff, Swansea or Bristol, is like going out of a hothouse on to the bridge of a fighting ship. It is a tonic which I should recommend any who are

* Of course, Britain had not helped Poland militarily, despite having given a similarly solemn guarantee before the war.

suffering from fretfulness to take in strong doses when they have need of it.'[115] After arguing that the air-raid wardens, members of the Home Guard and factory workers were 'proud to feel that they stand in the line together with our fighting men', he added, 'This is indeed the grand heroic period of our history, and the light of glory shines on all.'[116]

A staple of Churchill's speeches by then was a contemptuous sideswipe at Mussolini, and he did not disappoint: 'This whipped jackal, Mussolini,' he said, 'who to save his own skin has made all Italy a vassal state of Hitler's Empire, comes frisking up at the side of the German tiger with yelpings not only of appetite – that can be understood – but even of triumph.'[117] Yet neither Hitler nor Mussolini would ultimately triumph, he assured his listeners, partly because 'There are less than seventy million malignant Huns – some of whom are curable and others killable – many of whom are already engaged in holding down Austrians, Czechs, Poles, French, and the many other ancient races they now bully and pillage.'[118] In hailing the effect that Lend-Lease was already having in rearming Britain, Churchill ended with lines from Arthur Hugh Clough's poem 'Say Not the Struggle Naught Availeth':

> And not by eastern windows only,
> When daylight comes, comes in the light;
> In front the sun climbs slow, how slowly!
> But westward, look, the land is bright.[119]

With Rommel at the gates of Tobruk, less than 250 miles from the Egyptian border, Churchill on 28 April wrote a War Cabinet directive entitled 'The Defence of Egypt', ordering that all plans for the evacuation of the country and blocking of the Suez Canal were to be kept under the strict control of Cairo headquarters. 'No whisper of such plans is to be allowed.' He added that no surrenders of units would be permitted unless 'at least 50 per cent casualties had been suffered', adding, 'According to Napoleon's maxim, "When a man is caught alone and unarmed, a surrender may be made." But Generals and Staff officers surprised by the enemy are to use their pistols in self-defence. The honour of a wounded man is safe. Anyone who can kill a Hun or even an Italian has rendered a good service. The Army of the Nile is to fight with no thought of retreat or withdrawal.'[120]

This was fighting talk. Less impressive was Churchill's prediction, in the same directive, that 'Japan is unlikely to come into the war unless the Germans make a successful invasion of Great Britain.' He concluded from this that 'There is no need at the present time to make any further dispositions for the defence of Malaya and Singapore beyond the modest arrangements which are in progress.'[121] Because any attack by Japan in the Far East would provoke American intervention, there was to his mind no need to make a priority of fortifying either Singapore or Hong Kong.

In May, Leslie Rowan joined what Churchill called his 'Secret Circle', the inner entourage allowed to see everything except the dates of operations and the contents of his buff boxes containing Ultra decrypts.[122] At his very brief interview for the job of private secretary, Churchill asked Rowan whether his current job at the Treasury had involved trying to cut naval expenditure. 'Yes, sir,' Rowan replied, 'I do my best.' It was a test; for, as Rowan later wrote, Churchill 'hated above most things what he called "the official grimace", by which he meant civil servants' polite but insincere remarks designed to please'.[123] Rowan effectively got the job by honestly admitting that he had been engaged in cutting back Churchill's beloved 'Senior Service'. 'He was quite often inconsiderate,' Rowan recalled of Churchill as a boss. 'But we all felt, rightly, that we were serving a real leader; such a person as is only produced once in a century, even if that often.'[124] When at Chequers Rowan tried to excuse himself from dinner because it was Clementine's birthday, thinking the Churchills might like to dine alone, he was told, 'You will do no such thing; Clemmie and I should like you to dine with us.'[125] Churchill recognized no frontier between his office and his quarters. 'We might find ourselves working with Churchill in his study or in his bedroom,' recalled Edward Bridges, the Cabinet Secretary, 'or be called to take some urgent orders while he was having a meal with his family. Before long he had us all feeling that we had in some sense become honorary members of his family.'[126]

Every moment of the war, Churchill had at least one of his four private secretaries capable of being physically present by his desk or at his bedside within a couple of minutes. On one occasion in 1943 he growled at John Peck, 'Gimme the moon,' and it was some time before Peck divined that he was being asked for the dates in the summer months of 1944 when there would be a full moon for the Normandy invasion.[127]

On 15 February 1941, Beaverbrook had yet again threatened to resign, this time over his disagreements with Ernest Bevin about various aspects of the Production Executive. 'Whole performance lasts hour and half,' noted a weary Eden in his diary.[128] On 1 May, Churchill finally moved Beaverbrook out of the Ministry of Aircraft Production, replacing him with John Moore-Brabazon, although 'the Beaver' stayed in the War Cabinet as minister of state, a new title invented especially for him. With no specific departmental duties, his main task was to advise the Prime Minister, and not become an opponent of the Government. Churchill also appointed Frederick Leathers minister of war transport. He soon introduced a standing joke that Leathers, who had been chairman or director of more than fifty companies, would get a step in the peerage for every additional million tons of supplies he brought into the country. When Leathers arrived with a good monthly report, Churchill would say, 'At this rate you'll soon be an earl – perhaps a duke by the end of the year,' whereas bad reports would prompt him to say, 'If this goes on I shall have to reduce you to a baronet.' Leathers did not find the conceit quite so funny, and merely replied, 'Just as you please, Prime Minister.'[129]*

In early May Lady Astor showed Churchill and Harriman around her Plymouth constituency, which had been smashed in five raids over nine days. They saw a bus that had been blown on to the roof of a building 150 yards away, and heard the hammering of nails into coffins in the room next door to where 'some forty slightly injured' men lay.[130] 'I've never seen the like,' Churchill kept repeating. Colville wrote that the Prime Minister was in 'worse gloom than I have ever seen him'. Largely for Harriman's benefit, Churchill imagined a world in which Germany was victorious throughout the Middle East, saying, 'Hitler's robot new order would receive the inspiration which might give it real life.'[131] He hoped that Tobruk might be 'playing the same part as Acre did against Napoleon'. In 1799, the Anglo-Turkish defence of the city (modern-day Akko) had forced Napoleon to abandon his Syrian Campaign. 'It was a speck of sand in the desert which might ruin all Hitler's calculations,' he said.[132] But if not, with Hitler in control of Iraqi oil, and Ukrainian wheat already being supplied to him by the Russians, even the staunch resolve they had encountered in Plymouth would not 'shorten the ordeal'.[133] The next day Churchill was morose for a different reason, having discovered that Clementine had used some of his favourite Queensland honey to sweeten her rhubarb.[134]

It was during this period that Churchill made a trip to Chartwell, where he sometimes went if he had an important speech to write. Over lunch in the cottage he had built, he rehearsed under his breath the speech he was planning to deliver to the Polish people, while telling Jock the marmalade cat, 'Dear cat, it's so sad in wartime I can't give you any cream.'[135] On 3 May, he broadcast the speech:

> All over Europe, races and States whose culture and history made them a part of the general life of Christendom in centuries when the Prussians were no better than a barbarous tribe, and the German Empire no more than an agglomeration of pumpernickel principalities, are now prostrate under the dark, cruel yoke of Hitler and his Nazi gang. Every week his firing parties

* He nonetheless did receive his promotion, starting the war a baron and ending it a viscount.

> are busy in a dozen lands. Monday he shoots Dutchmen: Tuesday, Norwegians; Wednesday, French or Belgians stand against the wall; Thursday it is the Czechs who must suffer. And now there are the Serbs and the Greeks to fill his repulsive bill of executions. But always, all the days, there are the Poles. The atrocities committed by Hitler upon the Poles, the ravaging of their country, the scattering of their homes, the affronts to their religion, the enslavement of their manpower, exceed in severity and in scale the villainies perpetrated by Hitler in any other conquered land.[136]

He was right; the destruction of Poland at the hands of both the Nazis and Soviets was cataclysmic. Between 1939 and 1945 the population of Poland declined by 17.2 per cent, more than that of any other European country.

Hitler replied the next day, saying Churchill's speech 'was symptomatic of a paralytic disease, or the ravings of a drunkard'. Over the next two years he was to refer to Churchill as a 'lunatic', 'gabbler', 'drunkard', 'madman', 'unscrupulous politician', 'criminal', 'bloodthirsty amateur strategist', 'warmonger', 'hypocritical fellow' and – weirdly – 'lazybones'.[137] Hitler's secretary, Christa Schroeder, recalled that 'emotion would take over' when he dictated to her about three subjects – Roosevelt, Churchill and Bolshevism. 'His voice often skipped over bits' as a result. 'Then his choice of words would not be so fussy,' she wrote.

> For my part if he mentioned the 'whisky-guzzler' . . . too often, I would simply omit some of the references. Interestingly enough, when reading through the draft he would never notice these cuts, a sign of how worked up he had been. In these situations, his voice would increase to maximum volume, over-pitch so to speak, and he would make lively gestures with his hands. His face would become florid and the anger would shine in his eyes. He would stand rooted to the spot as though confronting the particular enemy he was imagining.[138]

Churchill would have been delighted to know the effect he was having on the Führer.

Wavell was already being ordered to fight at Tobruk, in Greece and in Ethiopia. In early May Churchill also insisted on new interventions in both Iraq and Syria, albeit with skeleton forces. He knew the geography of Iraq well, having created the country as colonial secretary and then arranged for its policing from the air. When Wavell suggested a 'settlement' in Iraq rather than the expulsion of Rashid Ali, Churchill told the King that Wavell 'was getting tired and might want a rest', and that General Auchinleck might replace him.[139] The King contrasted Wavell with

Churchill, noting, 'There has been some criticism that Winston does things too much himself but he has to, and is full of energy and initiative. I wish we had more people of his calibre.'[140] Ultimately, the British operations carried out against Vichy in Syria and Rashid Ali in Iraq were cheap, important and successful.[141]

On Wednesday, 7 May 1941, Churchill was forced to justify the Greek debacle in a vote of confidence in the House of Commons demanded by Lloyd George and Hore-Belisha. The wording of the motion, moved by Eden, was 'That this House approves the policy of His Majesty's Government in sending help to Greece and declares its confidence that our operations in the Middle East and in all other theatres of war will be pursued by the Government with the utmost vigour.' Lloyd George accused Churchill of being surrounded by 'yes-men' and said that talk of invading Europe one day was 'fatuous'. In his reply, Churchill said this was 'not the sort of speech which one would have expected from the great war leader of former days . . . It was the sort of speech with which, I imagine, the illustrious and venerable Marshal Pétain might well have enlivened the closing days of M. Reynaud's Cabinet.'[142] It was a low blow, but well deserved. Turning to Hore-Belisha's insistence that the intelligence apparatus should give a full and accurate account of the enemy's likely intentions, Churchill retorted, 'That is one of those glimpses of the obvious and of the obsolete with which his powerful speech abounded.'[143] As so often, Churchill sought to put Britain's present predicament into its historical context. 'Some have compared Hitler's conquests with those of Napoleon,' he said.

> It may be that Spain and Russia will shortly furnish new chapters to that theme. It must be remembered, however, that Napoleon's armies carried with them the fierce, liberating and equalitarian winds of the French Revolution, whereas Hitler's Empire has nothing behind it but racial self-assertion, espionage, pillage, corruption, and the Prussian boot. Yet Napoleon's Empire, with all its faults, and all its glories, fell, and flashed away like snow at Easter till nothing remained but His Majesty's Ship *Bellerophon*, which awaited its suppliant refugee.[144]

He was at pains to draw a distinction between two distinct types of military mistakes: 'There is the mistake which comes through daring, what I call a mistake towards the enemy, in which you must always sustain your commanders, by sea, land or air. There are mistakes from the safety-first principle, mistakes of turning away from the enemy; and they require a far more acid consideration.'[145] Norway, Dakar and Greece – and, by implication perhaps, Gallipoli – were in that first category. 'When I look back on the perils which have been overcome,' he said in conclusion, 'upon the great mountain waves through which the gallant ship has driven, when I remember all that has gone wrong, and remember also all that has gone right, I feel sure we have no need to fear the tempest. Let it roar, and let it rage. We shall come through.'[146] He won the vote by 447 to 3, and as he walked out of the Chamber there was a spontaneous burst of cheering which was then taken up in the Members' lobby beyond. Colville noted that 'He went to bed elated by his forensic success.'[147]

Churchill's maxim for soldiering through situations – 'Keep Buggering On' – provides a useful summation of his military strategy in the period between Dunkirk and Russia's entry into the war a year later. To Björn Prytz, the Swedish Ambassador, he also used an invented mock-Aesop fable in early May:

> There lived two frogs, an optimist and a pessimist. One evening they were jumping over some grass and detected the wonderful smell of fresh milk emanating from a nearby dairy. The frogs were tempted and jumped into the dairy through an open window. They miscalculated and flopped into a large jar of milk. What to do? . . . The pessimist looked around and, seeing that the walls of the jar were high and sheer and that it was not possible to climb up, fell into despair. He turned on his back, folded his legs and sank to the bottom. The optimist did not want to perish so disgracefully. He also saw the high and sheer walls, but decided to flounder while he could. All night long he swam, beat the milk energetically with his legs, and displayed various forms of activity . . . By the time morning came, the optimistic frog had, quite unawares, churned a big knob of butter out of the milk and thereby saved his life. The same will happen to the British Empire.[148]

Confident from Ultra decrypts that it would soon come, Churchill told Prytz that the knob of butter was 'the impending clash between the U.S.S.R. and Germany'. In that event, he said, 'To crush Germany I am prepared to enter into an alliance with anyone, even the Devil!'[149]

The Chamber of the old House of Commons was destroyed in a massive air raid three days later, on 10 May 1941, the first anniversary of Churchill's coming to power. Two thousand fires were started that night, and 3,000 Londoners killed or wounded.[150] The face of the Big Ben clock-tower was pocked and scarred when a bomb went through it. Churchill gave William Brimson, the Commons' head doorkeeper, an engraved silver snuffbox to replace the one that was lost in the subsequent fire.

That night, the Duke of Hamilton telephoned Valentine Lawford, Anthony Eden's private secretary, with the news that Rudolf Hess, the Deputy Führer of Germany, had parachuted on to his Scottish estate, in search of 'friendly elements' with whom to discuss an armistice, despite not having Hitler's authority for any such offer. Lawford told Colville, who telephoned Churchill at Ditchley. The Prime Minister was watching a Marx Brothers movie and initially said, 'Tell that to the Marx brothers!' before it was calmly explained to him that the story was true. Churchill gave orders that Hamilton was to be flown immediately to Northolt Aerodrome and then brought to Ditchley, but only after Colville had established that 'it really was the Duke and not a lunatic.'[151] Before putting the phone down he said, 'Hess or no Hess, I'm going to watch the Marx Brothers.'[152]

Once Hess had been positively identified by Ivone Kirkpatrick, the former First Secretary in Berlin, Churchill allowed only Eden, Attlee and Beaverbrook to see the transcript of the Kirkpatrick–Hess interview (itself an insight into his view of the senior governmental structure at the time). 'It is clear that Hess is no traitor but genuinely believes he can persuade us that we cannot win and that a compromise peace is obtainable' was the gist of it. 'His essential prerequisite is the fall of the Churchill Government.'[153] Churchill was amused when Hamilton, who had never before met Hess, told him that Hess had chosen to fly to him because he was lord steward of His Majesty's Household, which the Deputy Führer took to be a real rather than honorific title, and therefore would be able to urge his ideas upon the King. 'I suppose he thinks that the Duke carves the chicken,' Churchill suggested, 'and consults the King as to whether he likes breast or leg!'[154] The consequences were not so humorous, of course: Churchill did not want anyone in Britain, America or Russia suspecting that he or his Government was interested in peace negotiations. He therefore told the public the truth: that it had been the deranged act of a man close to a mental breakdown; and indeed Hess attempted to commit suicide on 16 June.[155] After extensive debriefing in the Tower of London, Hess spent much of the rest of the war at a camp near Abergavenny in Wales.

'My Lord Steward, Hamilton, has only been appointed for a year,' the King noted in his diary. 'I had to ask Walter [the 8th Duke of] Buccleuch, his predecessor, to leave owing to his sympathy with the Nazis. Perhaps the post of Lord Steward is bewitched or is it Germanised.'[156] At lunch, Churchill joked to the King that 'He would be very angry if Beaverbrook or Anthony Eden suddenly left here and flew off to Germany without warning.'[157] He reported Hess's peace offer – 'Hitler to have a free hand in Europe, but he could not negotiate with the present British Government' – and teasingly asked the King whether he 'was sure I did not wish him to resign just when things looked brighter for us'.[158]

'It looks as if Hitler is massing against Russia,' Churchill told General

Smuts on 16 May. 'A ceaseless movement of troops, armoured forces and aircraft northwards from the Balkans and eastwards from France is in progress.'[159] He had warned Stalin twice and been ignored both times. Churchill read Hitler's mind better than the Chiefs of Staff, who did not believe until 31 May that Germany was going to attack Russia.

On 20 May, the German XI Air Corps attacked the Commonwealth troops on Crete under the New Zealand general Bernard Freyberg, capturing the vital airfield at Maleme. After eight days' fierce fighting, the island had to be evacuated by the Allied forces, largely for lack of air support. The Mediterranean Fleet lost three cruisers and six destroyers evacuating 16,000 of the 26,000 soldiers on the island.[160] After the operation, the fleet was reduced to two battleships, three cruisers and seventeen destroyers.[161] Colville had expressed dismay about the losses of HMS *Gloucester* and *Fiji* in the battle off Crete. 'What do you think we build the ships for?' Churchill retorted, deprecating the Navy's way of 'treating ships as if they were too precious to risk'.[162]

Churchill blamed Wavell for not sending enough tanks to Crete, although he and the Chiefs of Staff persisted in believing that the German assault on the island was a deception to mask an actual attack on Syria or Cyprus. On the night of 10 May Churchill had informally discussed replacing Wavell with General Claude Auchinleck, but had received support only from Beaverbrook, while Eden, Attlee and Margesson were all opposed.[163] He later told his entourage – shades of Antwerp – that if only he could be put in command in the Middle East he would 'gladly lay down his present office – yes, and even renounce cigars and alcohol!'[164]

On 21 May, Coastal Command reported that the German battleship *Bismarck* – the most powerful warship afloat, with a crew of 2,200 – and her escort cruiser *Prinz Eugen* had been sighted in the Denmark Strait between Iceland and Greenland, making for the Atlantic. Part of Admiral Sir John Tovey's Home Fleet, including HMS *Hood*, the largest battlecruiser in the Royal Navy, with a crew of 1,418, was sent to intercept them. When Churchill awoke on the morning of Saturday, 24 May at Chequers, he was told that the *Hood* had been sunk by the *Bismarck* – with the loss, as it later turned out, of all but three of her crew. Fourteen years later, the recollection of it could still bring tears to his eyes.[165]

After the catastrophic loss of the *Hood*, a 1,700-mile chase ensued, in high winds, high seas and a blizzard, as the Home Fleet led by the battleship *King George V* tried to exact vengeance. Churchill spent the weekend in 'agonizing suspense' at Chequers, fearful that the *Bismarck* might intercept a large Allied troop convoy to the south escorted only by destroyers, or escape altogether to a French Atlantic port such as Brest.[166] He stayed glued to the constantly updated charts in the Hawtrey Room as, in Commander Thompson's reminiscence, 'Time and again sighting reports were followed by signals that the shadowing cruisers had lost the *Bismarck* once more.'[167] Vic Oliver remembered his father-in-law that weekend 'looking inexpressibly grim', and at one point shouting at him as he played the piano, 'Stop! Don't play that! Nobody plays the Dead March in my house.'[168] (In fact it had been Beethoven's 'Appassionata'.)

The next day, a Sunday, was also spent in 'fearful gloom'. Churchill could not understand why HMS *Prince of Wales* had not pressed home an attack, and kept saying 'it is the worst thing since Troubridge turned away from the *Goeben* in 1914'.[169] He later considered court-martialling her captain, but was prevented from doing so by Tovey, who threatened to appear for the defence. Before he went to bed, Churchill opined that the last three days had been the worst of the war so far – especially if the *Bismarck* were to reach safety at Brest 700 miles away. 'Poor Winston very gloomy,' Cadogan noted after Cabinet in London on the 26th, 'due of course to *Hood* and Crete.' He described the discussions there as 'tiresome and most acrimonious'.[170] Eden agreed. 'A most gloomy day – *Bismarck* appears to have been lost,' he wrote in his diary. 'The worst Cabinet we have yet had this evening – Winston was nervy and unreasonable and everyone else on edge.'[171] Very unusually for Cabinet meetings, there were long periods of complete silence.

Churchill spent most of that night in the No. 10 Annexe Map Room. 'Under these brilliant lights shining on all the maps around the room where the plotting continued hour by hour,' recalled Captain Pim, 'phases of the great sea battle were recorded.'[172] At one point, Churchill and Pound signalled to Tovey that although HMS *King George V* was running out of fuel the chase must not be abandoned, and the flagship could be towed home if necessary. This was an exceptionally dangerous thing even to contemplate in an ocean full of U-boats. That night, Swordfish aircraft from the carrier HMS *Ark Royal* crippled the *Bismarck* in torpedo attacks, and before midnight she was rudderless. She stayed afloat for ten hours as HMS *Rodney* and *King George V* shelled her.

Churchill had just sat down after making a statement on Crete in the cramped Church House the next morning when Bracken handed him a piece of paper. 'I crave your indulgence, Mr Speaker,' Churchill said, interrupting a Labour MP. 'I have just received news that the *Bismarck* has been sunk.' Torpedoes from the cruiser HMS *Dorsetshire* and scuttling by her captain had finally destroyed her at 10.40 a.m. Only 114 of her crew survived. Nicolson reported 'wild cheers' on Churchill's announcement, and John Martin 'Great jubilation'.[173] When Churchill lunched with the King 'he was delighted with the sinking of the *Bismarck* as it makes our Atlantic position better, in that we only have the *Tirpitz* to deal with now . . . The *Bismarck* was certainly unsinkable by gunfire.'[174]

On 2 June the Churchills went to Chartwell, theoretically for some rest, and indeed at one point the Prime Minister lay down prostrate on the dining-room floor while Clementine played backgammon with Colville, but then he stayed up until 1.30 a.m. dictating and went back to London the next day. 'There is a storm of criticism over Crete, and I am being pressed for explanations on many points,' he wrote to Wavell. 'Do not worry about this at all now. Simply keep your eye on Exporter [the Syrian campaign], and, above all, on Bruiser [the relief of Tobruk]. These alone can supply the answers to criticisms just or unjust . . . As Napoleon said: "La bataille répondra [The battle is the reply]."'[175] Three days later the King noted of his Prime Minister, 'He has high hopes for Libya, as we have the troops, tanks and the aircraft all ready for the thrust. He wants Wavell to wage a ruthless advance against the Germans and really press them hard giving them no time for rest or sleep.'[176] Over Greece, Churchill told the King, 'Our leaving there is not a major disaster. It is a battle fought in a campaign, and should be treated as such.' Nevertheless, he was fortunate that the confidence motion had taken place three weeks before the evacuation, rather than during or after it.

'On all sides one hears increasing criticism of Churchill,' noted Channon on 6 June. 'He is undergoing a noticeable slump in popularity and many of his enemies, long silenced by his personal popularity, are once more vocal. Crete has been a great blow to him.'[177] Churchill was nonetheless able to make light of this in his next Cabinet meeting. 'People criticize this Government,' he said, 'but its great strength – and I dare say it in this company – is that there's no alternative! I don't think it's a bad Government. Come to think of it, it's a very good one. I have complete confidence in it. In fact there has never been a government to which I have felt such sincere and whole-hearted loyalty!'[178]

Churchill defended the Greek expedition and the evacuation of Crete in a ninety-minute speech to the Commons four days later, despite telling the King that day that he 'considered it a bad system to allow a debate every time things went wrong for us'.[179] During his speech, he said of the British people, 'They are the only people who like to be told how bad things are, who like to be told the worst, and like to be told that they are very likely to get much worse in the future and must prepare themselves for further reverses.' About Crete, he said, 'Defeat is bitter. There is no use in trying to explain defeat. People do not like defeat, and they do not

43. *Winston is Back*: David Jagger painted this supremely Churchillian portrait at the Admiralty in 1939.

The P.M. is represented as having saved us
from horrors of war, which glared upon
us in such a hideous form.

There was never any danger of Gt. Britain
or France being involved in war w G.
at this juncture,
if they were ready to sacrifice
CZ.

The terms which P.M. brought back fr Munich
cd hv bn easily agreed thro ordinary
channels of diplomacy, at any time
during the summer.

There was no need for all this tremendous
perturbation.

There was never any danger of a fight
if all the time one side meant to give way completely.

When one reads the Munich terms,
& sees what is happening from hour to hour
in CZ.,
when one is assured tt Parliament
supports it all,
it is impossible not to ask -
what was all the fuss about?

The resolve taken & the course followed
may hv bn wise or unwise,
prudent or short-sighted,
but there was certainly no reason
to call all this formidable
apparatus into play, if
in their hearts they were
ready to abandon the whole
contention,



44. A page from Churchill's Munich Speech of 5 October 1938, showing the 'psalm' format he adopted in his speech notes.

45. In July 1939 this giant poster appeared in the Strand in London, asking what it would take to bring Churchill back into the Government in the face of the Nazi threat.

46. Churchill returned to the Admiralty as first lord on the evening war was declared, on 3 September 1939, with his cigar, gloves, newspaper, walking stick, two red boxes, gas mask and a long chain on which he kept the keys to his red boxes.

47. The senior members of Chamberlain's Government on 4 September 1939 under the portraits of William Gladstone and Lord Salisbury. *Standing left to right*: Sir John Anderson, Maurice Hankey, Leslie Hore-Belisha, Winston Churchill, Sir Kingsley Wood, Anthony Eden and Sir Edward Bridges. *Seated left to right*: Lord Halifax, Sir John Simon, Neville Chamberlain, Sir Samuel Hoare and Lord Chatfield.

48. Churchill with King George VI and Queen Elizabeth while cheerfully inspecting the bomb damage to Buckingham Palace in September 1940.

To Andrew Roberts from Nancy Lancaster

49. A weekend 'when the moon was high' at Ditchley Park in December 1940. *Left to right*: Brendan Bracken, Lord Cranborne, Richard Law, Winston Churchill, Clementine Churchill, Lady Cranborne, Ronald Tree (obscured), Nancy Tree (later Lancaster).

50. Churchill made many morale-boosting visits to bomb-damaged areas during the Blitz. Here he is outside a shop in Ramsgate in 1940.

51. Churchill attached these labels to important memoranda that he wished his ministers to deal with immediately.

52. A desk in the Map Room of the No. 10 Annexe, where Churchill moved during the Blitz.

53. Churchill's War Cabinet of October 1941, photographed in the garden of 10 Downing Street. *Seated left to right*: Sir John Anderson, Winston Churchill, Clement Attlee, Anthony Eden. *Standing left to right*: Arthur Greenwood, Ernest Bevin, Lord Beaverbrook, Sir Kingsley Wood.

54. Churchill and President Franklin Roosevelt at a press conference at the White House on 23 December 1941. Churchill was wearing a cigar band as a ring and Roosevelt wore a black armband in memory of his mother Sara, who had died in September.

55. A 'visit to the Ogre in his den': Churchill went to meet Marshal Joseph Stalin in the Kremlin in August 1942.

56. At the British Embassy in Cairo on 5 August 1942, seated with his friend and close adviser Field Marshal Jan Christian Smuts. Air Chief Marshal Sir Arthur Tedder (*left*) and General Sir Alan Brooke (*right*) are standing behind them.

57. On board the *Queen Mary* with Admiral of the Fleet Sir Dudley Pound, First Sea Lord, on the way to the Trident Conference in May 1943.

CARD

ENGAGEMENTS.

# JANUARY, 1943.

| | | |
|---|---|---|
| | Tues. 12 | Sat. 23 |
| | Wed. 13 | SUN. 24 |
| | Thur. 14 | Mon. 25 |
| | Fri. 15 | Tues. 26 |
| | Sat. 16 | Wed. 27 |
| | SUN. 17 | Thur. 28 |
| | Mon. 18 | Fri. 29 |
| | Tues. 19 | Sat. 30 |
| | Wed. 20 | SUN. 31 |
| | Thur. 21 | |
| | Fri. 22 | |

H.M. STATIONERY OFFICE. CODE 66-11-0.

58. Churchill had engagement cards covering every month of the war. This one features the Casablanca Conference, where President Roosevelt is codenamed 'Don Q', based on the Churchill family's nickname for him of 'Don Quixote'.

WAR OF NERVES

59. A cartoon by Vicky (Victor Weisz) of the *News Chronicle* in February 1943 depicts Hitler being driven mad by Churchill's ubiquity.

60. Churchill showed Roosevelt this scene at Marrakesh, and then gave his rendition of it – his only wartime painting before VE Day, entitled *The Tower of Katoubia Mosque* – to the President.

61. Churchill gives his by now famous V-for-Victory sign to cheering sailors on disembarking from the *Queen Mary* at New York in May 1943.

like the explanations, however elaborate or plausible, which are given of them. For defeat there is only one answer. The only answer to defeat is victory.'[180] Two days later, he admitted in a broadcast, 'We cannot yet see how deliverance will come, or when it will come, but nothing is more certain than that every trace of Hitler's footsteps, every stain of his infected and corroding fingers will be sponged and purged and, if need be, blasted from the surface of the earth.'[181] The key element of that deliverance was now only ten days away. Yet even if Germany were to invade the Soviet Union, many assumed the Wehrmacht would continue its long series of victories, now against a Red Army so weakened by purges against its High Command in the late 1930s that it had barely been able to subdue Finland the previous year. On 16 June, everybody around the Annexe's mess table except Bracken and Tommy Thompson 'thought that Russia would give way to Germany without a fight'.[182]

Churchill had been encouraging Wavell to attack Rommel ever since 9 May, on the basis of Enigma decrypts that seemed to show that the German Army in that theatre was exhausted and unable to take the offensive until the arrival of the 15th Panzer Division anticipated later that month.[183] It is possible that he underestimated Rommel's strength by reading too much into the constant demands sent to Berlin for more troops, aircraft and supplies. Wavell launched Operation Battleaxe (formerly codenamed Bruiser) on 15 June. This was the first time in the war that British troops had met German without air inferiority. But by the end of the second day of the offensive little progress had been made, partly because Wavell still depended on 2-pounder tank guns. Churchill found Wavell's inability to break through Rommel's line on the second day 'almost unbearable'.[184] Wavell lost more than a hundred tanks, and Cadogan wrote, 'Our great offensive in Libya has ended in a bloody nose – for us.'[185] 'Winston rang me up,' recorded Eden on 18 June, 'very sad.'[186]

As neither of the Other Club's joint secretaries, Brendan Bracken and the Liberal MP Harcourt 'Crinks' Johnstone, was able to reach the Savoy on the night of 19 June due to unexploded bombs and road closures, Churchill and H. G. Wells formed themselves into a Committee of Public Safety and decided that Braken and Johnstone should pay for the dinner of the eighteen members who did make it, as an 'unforeseen obligation'.[187] Churchill went to Chequers two days later, and Winant, Eden and Bridges came to dine and sleep. At dinner he predicted that 'a German attack on Russia is certain and Russia will assuredly be defeated'.[188] He added that he would nonetheless 'go all out to help Russia'. Walking on the lawn after dinner, he told Colville 'that he had only one single purpose – the destruction of Hitler – and his life is much simplified thereby'.[189]

When Operation Barbarossa, Hitler's 161-division, three-million-man invasion of the Soviet Union, was launched just before dawn on Sunday, 22 June 1941 – unanticipated by Stalin, despite many warnings – Churchill was primed with Britain's response, broadcast at 9 p.m. that day. The news of the invasion brought 'a smile of satisfaction on the faces of the P.M., Eden and Winant', recorded Colville.[190] For even if the Germans won militarily, as most people, including the Chiefs of Staff, assumed they would, they would have vast tracts of territory to hold down and occupy against a large and recalcitrant population. The Russians went overnight from helping the Germans with food and oil to fighting them to the death.*

The broadcast was only ready twenty minutes before he delivered it, perhaps deliberately as it meant that Eden and Cadogan could not vet it. 'At four o'clock this morning Hitler attacked and invaded Russia,' Churchill began.

> All his usual formalities of perfidy were observed with scrupulous technique ... Hitler is a monster of wickedness, insatiable in his lust for blood and plunder. Not content with having all Europe under his heel, or else terrorized into various forms of abject submission, he must now carry his work of butchery and desolation among the vast multitudes of Russia and of Asia. The terrible military machine, which we and the rest of the civilized world so foolishly, so supinely, so insensately allowed the Nazi gangsters to build up year by year from almost nothing, cannot stand idle lest it rust or fall to pieces. It must be in continual motion, grinding up human lives and trampling down the homes and the rights of hundreds of millions ... So now this bloodthirsty guttersnipe must launch his mechanized armies upon new fields of slaughter, pillage and devastation ... I see also the dull, drilled, docile, brutish masses of Hun soldiery plodding on like a swarm of crawling locusts.[191]

The last sentence was a good example of his use of four adjectives – even if locusts hop and fly rather than crawl.

In now advocating a full-scale alliance with Russia, Churchill performed another swift volte-face after a lifetime of being the most vocal

* On 29 March, Churchill had given his lunchtime listeners at Chequers a short lecture on the various invaders of Russia down the ages, especially King Charles XII of Sweden, whose invasion had come to grief at the Battle of Poltava a century before Napoleon's 1812 campaign. Churchill recognized the enormity of what Hitler had undertaken, and described it as 'the fourth climacteric' of the war, the first three being the Fall of France, the Battle of Britain and the passing of Lend-Lease. 'Trust him to find a word no one else had ever heard of,' wrote Elizabeth Layton (later Nel), a secretary who had started working for him that April (Nel, *Personal Secretary* p. 71).

anti-Bolshevik in British politics. 'No one has been a more consistent opponent of Communism than I have for the last twenty-five years,' he conceded. 'I will unsay no word that I have spoken about it. But all this fades away before the spectacle which is now unfolding. The past with its crimes, its follies and its tragedies, flashes away.'[192]* Looking to the future, he said, 'We have but one aim and one single irrevocable purpose. We are resolved to destroy Hitler and every vestige of the Nazi regime . . . Any man or state who fights on against Nazidom will have our aid. Any man or state who marches with Hitler is our foe.'[193] There was an appeal to Western self-interest, too. Hitler's 'invasion of Russia is no more than a prelude to an attempted invasion of the British Isles', he said. 'The Russian danger is therefore our danger, and the danger of the United States, just as the cause of any Russian fighting for his hearth and home is the cause of free men and free peoples in every quarter of the globe.'[194]

Churchill announced this full-scale alliance with Soviet Russia after minimal consultation with his colleagues. Even Eden had precious little input into the decision. Nor had he consulted the Russians themselves. Over dinner at Chequers that evening Eden and Cranborne argued from the Tory point of view that the alliance 'should be confined to the purely military aspect, as politically Russia was as bad as Germany and half the country would object to being associated with her too closely'. Yet Churchill's view 'was that Russia was now at war; innocent peasants were being slaughtered; and we should forget about Soviet systems or the Comintern and extend our hand to fellow human beings in distress'. Colville recalled that this argument 'was extremely vehement'.[195] Churchill once again saw the larger context; he was leader of the Conservative Party but had not spent a lifetime in it, unlike Eden and Cranborne.

The vehemence of the discussion then extended to appeasement, as Churchill denounced Lord Chatfield, who as first sea lord had not opposed the cession of the Irish Treaty ports in 1938, and other appeasers whose desire for 'absurd self-abasement had brought us to the verge of annihilation'. For the first time since the war began, he also criticized Chamberlain, whom he called 'the narrowest, most ignorant, most ungenerous of men'. It was a far cry from his eulogy the previous November, but probably closer to what he now felt. Going to bed that night, Churchill 'kept on repeating how wonderful it is that Russia had come in against Germany when she might so easily have been with her'.[196] The next day he ordered the Chiefs of Staff to investigate the possibilities of large raids across the

* Almost certainly a conscious echo of Gibbon's description of history as 'little more than the register of the crimes, follies, and misfortunes of Mankind'.

Channel. 'Now the enemy is busy in Russia is the time to "Make hell while the sun shines."'[197]

Churchill immediately started looking at ways to ship supplies to Russia around northern Norway, and by rail from the Persian Gulf to the Caspian Sea. He came up with a colourful analogy to describe the nerve-wracking prospect of having Soviet Russia as an ally, telling Eddie Marsh, 'In his native forests, the gorilla is an object of awe and terror: in our Zoological Gardens he inspires vulgar curiosity: in our wife's bed, he is a cause of *potential* embarrassment and anxiety.'[198] When Stafford Cripps, the Ambassador to the Soviet Union, Peter Fraser, the Prime Minister of New Zealand, and Lords Cranborne and Beaverbrook came over for lunch on the 22nd, Churchill teased the left-wing Cripps, saying that the Russians were barbarians and that 'not even the slenderest thread connected Communists to the very basest type of humanity'.[199] Yet they were going to be Britain's allies for the next four years, and for every five German soldiers killed in combat during the Second World War, four were to die on the Eastern Front.

# 25
# 'Being Met Together'
# June 1941–January 1942

*He was fighting all the time, whether he had armies to launch or only thoughts.*

Churchill on Marshal Foch in *Great Contemporaries*[1]

*The more they talked over what they had to do, the better they understood and liked one another.*

Churchill, in *Marlborough*, on the Duke's meeting with Prince Eugene of Savoy in 1704[2]

Two days after Hitler had unleashed Operation Barbarossa on Russia, Churchill said to the King, 'What a chance for the U.S.A. to come into the war now; a heaven-sent opportunity.' He also said that he was going to replace General Wavell with General Auchinleck as commander-in chief, Middle East. 'I find that when Winston has made up his mind about somebody or something, nothing will change his opinion,' the King noted. 'Personal feelings are nothing to him, though he has a very sentimental side to his character. He looks to one goal and one goal only: winning the war. No half measures.'[3]

Chips Channon described the transfer of his friend Wavell to commander-in-chief of the Indian Army as 'a sacrifice to Winston's personal dislike. No General in all history has had so difficult a role, fighting on five fronts and harassed daily by contradictory cables.'[4] Although Dill disapproved of the change, he knew there was no point in continuing to defend Wavell in view of the Prime Minister's obvious loss of confidence in him. The next day, Churchill sent Oliver Lyttelton to be minister resident in the Middle East, appointed Beaverbrook to the powerful role of minister of supply and brought in the businessman Sir Andrew Duncan to become president of the Board of Trade.

That evening, Churchill told a secret session of the Commons, which had moved from Church House to the House of Lords Chamber, that as 4.6 million tons of shipping had been lost in the past year the figures could no longer be published. It was not that he had doubted the ability of his countrymen to take bad news, but, as he told the House, 'We cannot afford to give any advantages to the enemy in naval information,' he said, 'nor can we afford to paint our affairs in the darkest colours before the eyes of neutrals and to discourage our friends and encourage our foes all over the world.'[5] He spoke of the terrible challenges they faced, saying that nothing in the Great War 'was comparable to the dangers and difficulties which now beset us'. 'Every high authority that I know of, if asked in cold blood a year ago how we should get through, would have found it impossible to give a favourable answer.'[6] He acknowledged his own role in constantly prodding and pestering his ministers, saying that far from being 'a mutual-admiration society', as Lloyd George had suggested, in fact he was more critical of them even than the Government's opponents – 'In fact, I wonder that a great many of my colleagues are on speaking terms with me.' Nonetheless, 'It is the duty of the Prime Minister to use the power which Parliament and the nation have given him to drive others, and in a war like this that power has to be used irrespective of anyone's feelings. If we win, nobody will care. If we lose, there will be nobody to care.'[7]

In March 1940, the Austrian-born nuclear physicist Otto Frisch and his German-born colleague Rudolph Peierls, both British citizens and refugees from Nazism, wrote a top-secret memorandum for the Government about the possible construction of 'super-bombs' based on a nuclear chain reaction of uranium, which contrary to most physicists in the field they argued was feasible. (Niels Bohr, Enrico Fermi and the late Sir Ernest Rutherford had all discounted the possibility.) Frisch and Peierls's paper led Sir Henry Tizard, chairman of the Whitehall effort to apply science to warfare, to set up the (acronymically meaningless) MAUD Committee of scientists to investigate, spurred on by an article in *The Times* in early May suggesting that the Germans were working on a similar project.[8] Far more than any other prominent politician of the day, except Sir John Anderson, who had written a thesis on the chemistry of uranium at Leipzig University, Churchill was well placed to consider the strategic possibilities thrown up by nuclear fission. He had read and re-read all of H. G. Wells's science fiction, had predicted the creation of a powerful bomb 'no bigger than an orange' as early as September 1924, had read a book on quantum theory in 1926, had written about the prospect of nuclear fission during the 1930s and had discussed it with Lindemann a good deal.[9] It was one of the great coincidences of history that just as science made possible a world-changing and ultimately war-winning device, the most scientifically literate of all the contenders was knocking at the door of 10 Downing Street.

In July 1941 the MAUD Committee of scientists reported both that it was theoretically possible to build an atomic bomb of potentially massive force and that it could be combat-ready in two years; if so, it was likely to be decisive. It recommended close cooperation with the Americans, and warned that Germany was almost certainly working on its own version.[10] Despite its momentousness, the report was in danger of being stillborn. MAUD's chairman Sir Henry Tizard worried that such a 'big and highly speculative industrial undertaking' would cut off funding to other military technology projects, while the director of scientific research at the Ministry of Aircraft Production thought that it would take a decade, not two years, to construct the bomb. He was echoed by one of the Committee members, Patrick Blackett of Oxford University. It took Lindemann to ignite the Tube Alloys project – a codename chosen for its maximum boringness – and excite Churchill about its prospects.

There are many justifiable criticisms of the Prof – his combativeness, Teutonophobia, egomania and so on – but it was fortuitous that he had the ear of Britain's scientifically minded Prime Minister. Churchill's articles and conversations around the Chartwell table with Lindemann about physics were to prove more relevant than either man could have guessed at the time. In August, Churchill wrote to the Chiefs of Staff saying he agreed with the arguments put forward by Lindemann that the United Kingdom should start building her own nuclear bomb. Lindemann did not minimize the expense or difficulty of the process, but he wrote, 'It would be unforgivable if we let the Germans develop a process ahead of us by means of which they could defeat us in war, or reverse the verdict after they had been defeated . . . Whoever possesses such a plant should be able to dictate terms to the rest of the world.'[11] Churchill appointed Anderson, Lord President of the Council, to head the new Directorate of Tube Alloys, effectively making him minister for the Bomb. Anderson was a dependable if uninspiring Scottish former senior civil servant who had been governor of Bengal in the mid-1930s.

When Auchinleck took up command of the Middle Eastern theatre on 30 June, the Axis held all of Cyrenaica except for besieged Tobruk, although the surrender of Italian remnants in East Africa had opened the Red Sea to American shipping. Auchinleck was hardly in place before arguments began over the timing of Operation Crusader, his big offensive intended to relieve the siege. Auchinleck wanted four to five months to prepare, whereas Churchill was keen that it should come much earlier, so as to capitalize on Germany's preoccupation with the Eastern Front.[12] Auchinleck insisted that he could not launch Crusader until the British Eighth Army had had time to regroup, re-equip, reorganize, improve supply and train its armoured forces. Churchill was impressed by the 6 foot 2 Auchinleck's demeanour and personality, but by now he was not convinced of his military skill, despite having appointed him to replace Wavell.*

When Jock Colville asked for permission to join the RAF in early July, Churchill acceded, saying that a fighter pilot 'had greater excitement than a polo-player, big game shot and hunting-man rolled into one'.[13] (He had been all three, so he knew.) Archie Sinclair was staying at Chequers, and Churchill said that after victory 'There should be an end to all bloodshed, though he should like to see Mussolini, the bogus mimic of Ancient Rome, strangled like Vercingetorix in old Roman fashion.'[14] Hitler and the leading Nazis would be sent to a remote island, though not St Helena, as that would 'desecrate' Napoleon's memory. He also inveighed against defeatism and said, 'It would be better to make this island a sea of blood than to surrender if invasion came.'[15]

After a review of Civil Defence units in Hyde Park on 14 July, Churchill gave a speech in County Hall, recalling the Blitz of the previous winter. 'When at that moment the doleful wail of the siren betokened the approach of the German bombers,' he said, 'I confess to you that my heart bled for London and the Londoners.'[16] He said the rest of Britain had borne up just as well as London, and predicted that in the coming Luftwaffe campaign:

> London will be ready. London will not flinch, London can take it again. We ask no favours of the enemy. We seek from them no compunction. On the contrary, if tonight the people of London were asked to cast their vote whether a convention should be entered into to stop the bombing of all cities, the overwhelming majority would cry, 'No, we will mete out to the Germans the measure, and more than the measure, that they have meted out to us . . . We will have no truce or parley with you or the grisly gang who work your wicked will. You do your worst and we will do our best.' Perhaps it may be our turn soon; perhaps it may be our turn now.[17]

The alliteration of 'grisly gang who work your wicked will' almost sounded like a music-hall turn, but it worked.

* Of his own skill at warfare, however, Churchill joked to Eden at this time, 'Remember that on my breast are the medals of the Dardanelles, Antwerp, Dakar and Greece' – to which he could have added Norway (Keegan, *Second World War* p. 312).

On 18 July Stalin made an urgent appeal to Churchill to open what became popularly known as a Second Front in north-west France to take pressure off Russia.* Churchill replied that he would do 'Anything sensible and effective' to help the Russians that he could, but 'To attempt a landing in force would be to encounter a bloody repulse, and petty raids would only lead to fiascos doing far more harm than good to both of us.'[18] He nonetheless promised to consider aerial and naval operations in the Arctic. (It was noted by his secretaries that Churchill used the word 'Russians' when he wished to confer approbation, but 'Soviets' when being pejorative.) Maisky visited Chequers on 19 July. 'We shall bomb Germany mercilessly,' Churchill told him. 'Day after day, week after week, month after month! . . . In the end we will overwhelm Germany with bombs. We will break the morale of the population.'[19] Harry Hopkins then entered the room, and promised to smooth the supply issues that they had been having.† Maisky left with the view that 'The entire burden of fighting against the war machine rests upon our shoulders.'

Churchill carried out a major Government reshuffle the next day. It was a painful one for him because he had to demote Alfred Duff Cooper, a friend and Other Club member who had resigned over Munich and had been a key supporter in the Norway Debate. He had known for some time that he had not been a successful information minister, telling Bracken, in his presence, 'You should never harness a thoroughbred to a dung-cart.'[20]‡ The campaign against Cooper's Snoopers had also weakened him, and Churchill could not allow him to be a drag on his Government. He gave Cooper Hankey's place as chancellor of the Duchy of Lancaster, while Brendan Bracken became minister of information and proved a great success.

* The phrase Second Front was a term of Soviet propaganda, since Britain had already been fighting Germany on at least five fronts before the Soviets were forced by invasion to drop their pro-German neutrality: in northern France, the air, the Atlantic, North Africa and the Mediterranean.

† Harry Hopkins had returned to Britain that day, laden with hard-to-obtain ham, cheese and cigars for Churchill. In a potent symbol of Anglo-American amity, he was invited to attend the Cabinet. 'We had to get rid of him before the end on the excuse that we were going to discuss home affairs,' Cadogan recorded, 'and then discussed America and the Far East!' (ed. Dilks, *Cadogan* p. 393).

‡ Duff Cooper had not been helped by the appointment of Frank Pick, the former chairman of the London Passenger Transport Board, as director-general at the Ministry of Information in August 1940. Hearing that Pick had a moral objection to publishing a clandestine newspaper for subversion purposes, as he considered it unethical to lie, Churchill grasped Attlee's hand and cried, 'Shake him by the hand! Shake him by the hand! You can say to St Peter you have met the perfect man.' Pick was sacked after four months in the job, after which Churchill said, 'Never let that impeccable bus conductor darken my doorstep again.' (Halle, *Irrepressible* pp. 175–6.)

Churchill appointed Brigadier George Harvie-Watt to Bracken's place as his parliamentary private secretary, his eyes and ears in the Commons. Harvie-Watt did an excellent job, sending detailed reports about any potential ructions on the backbenches. These reports could sometimes be caustic. He informed the Prime Minister that a speech by Attlee on civil aviation had been 'dreary' and that Wavell had been 'rather dull' when speaking to MPs. Occasionally, Churchill wrote on them 'Mrs C[hurchill] to see', even some that had no obvious connection to her, to keep her fully informed of events. Harvie-Watt investigated what went on in meetings between Labour MPs and trade unionists and kept an eye on pressure groups being set up by Tory MPs.[21] Churchill had seen the effect on the Chamberlain Government of the various Tory groups before the Norway Debate and did not want to fall victim to the same phenomenon. When Harvie-Watt told Churchill that Sir Douglas Hacking, the Conservative Party chairman, 'is not nearly strong enough to deal with modern political problems', he was soon replaced (earning for Churchill Hacking's 'intense dislike' for the rest of the war).[22]

Rab Butler was moved out of the Foreign Office, and promoted to president of the Board of Education, where he abolished fees for state secondary schools with a landmark Act in 1944. In his place as under-secretary for foreign affairs, Churchill had wanted to put his son-in-law Duncan Sandys, but Eden wanted the job to go to Richard Law instead, so Sandys became financial secretary at the War Office. With accusations of nepotism abounding, John Peck offered Colville £5 if he dared suggest to Churchill that the best choice for minister of information would be Vic Oliver, but was not taken up on it.[23]

Churchill's occasional practice of holding his fingers up in a V-sign, to signify the word Victory, had been picked up in Occupied Europe, where 'V' was being chalked and painted on to walls as a sign of defiance. The Government now launched an official propaganda campaign on 20 July, as Churchill broadcast that 'The V-sign is the symbol of the unconquerable will of the Occupied territories, and a portent of the fate awaiting the Nazi tyranny. So long as the peoples of Europe continue to refuse all collaboration with the invader, it is sure that his cause will perish, and that Europe will be liberated.'[24] Churchill's use of the sign came naturally to a politician from the Victorian era who understood the power of symbols. His cigars, bow-ties, square-crown bowlers and canes were powerful images which he used consciously, and which made him instantly recognizable in cartoons and newspaper illustrations. His father had worn high collars and a handlebar moustache, and Joseph Chamberlain a monocle and orchid, for much the same reason. One problem with the V-sign was that it was only the turn of a wrist away from a rude gesture, and Churchill did not always remember that. More seriously, the Russians somehow interpreted it as meaning that he was about to open a Second Front.[25]

Watching the movie *Citizen Kane* on the evening of the reshuffle, Churchill 'was so bored that he walked out towards the end', although it might have been because it slandered his friend and erstwhile host William Randolph Hearst.[26] He stayed up until three o'clock that morning, when finally Attlee and Harriman were yawning so much that Hopkins insisted that the Prime Minister, who was still 'in irrepressible spirits', go to bed.[27] 'I'm not surprised they all leave you, the way you go on,' Hopkins teased Churchill, referring to Colville's decision to join the RAF and Seal's to take up a post in America.* (Seal's place as principal private secretary had been taken by John Martin.)

At lunch in the Annexe shortly afterwards, Churchill said that seeing how the Vichy French were putting up a stout resistance against Auchinleck's forces in Syria, 'it was a pity they had not fought with the same courage and spirit against the Germans in France.'[28] He believed the 'best and noblest blood' of France had been drained away in the Great War. When Lady Wimborne suggested – presumably as a joke – that they exterminate all German babies once the war had been won, Charles Eade recorded that 'Winston got a laugh by saying "Need we wait as long as that?"'[29] He described Barbarossa as a 'windfall' and said he thought the Russians would still be fighting in twelve months' time, which would at the very least delay any invasion attempt on Britain. The appeaser Geoffrey Dawson had recently left the editorship of *The Times*. Churchill cruelly remarked that it was 'the last flick of a Quisling', but added that 'Anger is a waste of energy. Steam which is used to blow off a safety valve would be better used to drive an engine.'[30] Dawson was replaced by another former appeaser and critic of Churchill, Robert Barrington-Ward.

Hopkins had brought with him the important news that Roosevelt would like to meet Churchill, a major advance in the Prime Minister's project to get America more closely bound up with the war. Before that, Hopkins was going to meet Stalin. The night he left, he and Churchill

* When Colville told the Prime Minister about the maths and other intelligence tests he had been forced to take before being allowed to join the RAF, Churchill 'said that if that was the standard, Nelson and Napoleon would have been considered unsuitable. What, he wanted to know, was the use of catering for a lot of "chess-players who would die young of epilepsy"?' (Colville, *Fringes* p. 428). (In fact, both Nelson and Napoleon were proficient mathematicians who would probably have excelled at such tests.)

walked up and down the back lawn of Chequers and Churchill asked him 'to assure Stalin that Britain would give him all possible support'.[31] Churchill was already thinking of an eventual cross-Channel attack and in July urged Roosevelt to begin building landing craft for tanks, almost three years before D-Day – even though the United States was not yet a belligerent.

At the end of July, the King noted in his diary that the Prime Minister 'does not think Japan will go to war with us or the U.S.A. Our combined freezing of assets and breaking commercial treaties have come as a shock to Japan.'[32] On 17 August he added that Churchill had 'told Menzies not to worry about Japan. Roosevelt is sending Japan a strong note and we shall back him up.' Even as late as 12 September, Churchill was still saying that the Japanese would climb down in the face of the Western oil embargo, whereas in fact it might have been the need for oil that drove the bellicose elements in the Japanese Government to put the Empire on the road to all-out war.

There had long been widespread calls for a new position of minister of production, with a seat in the War Cabinet and powers to exercise control over the three supply sections of the Admiralty, War Office and Air Ministry. To counter this clear assault on his own authority, Churchill worked on a speech throughout the weekend at Chequers, staying up until 4.50 one morning to get it right. 'Where is the super-personality', he asked sarcastically in the Commons on 29 July,

> who, as one of the members of the War Cabinet, will dominate the vast, entrenched, established, embattled organization of the Admiralty to whose successful exertions we owe our lives? Where is the War Cabinet Minister who is going to teach the present Minister of Aircraft Production how to make aircraft quicker and better than they are being made now? . . . When you have decided on the man, let me know his name, because I should be very glad to serve under him, provided that I were satisfied that he possessed all the Napoleonic and Christian qualities attributed to him.[33]

The next afternoon the Soviet–Polish Treaty was signed at the Foreign Office, fifteen minutes late because Churchill's nap had gone on longer than the usual one hour. Eden had mediated the hard-fought negotiations between the Russians and Poles, who hated one another. Maisky noted that 'Churchill really had just got out of bed' for the ceremony. 'This could be seen from his sagging face, his red, somewhat watery eyes, and his generally sleepy appearance.'[34] The Prime Minister nonetheless 'inspected the room with a furtive smile'. The Treaty allowed 78,000 prisoners-of-war out of the USSR, who went on to form the bulk of the Polish II Corps, which fought with great distinction in Italy in 1944 and 1945. To the Poles' indignation, however, it left the post-war frontier unsettled. If the Poles had known that the Russians had executed more than 14,000 Polish officers in cold blood in the Katyń Forest the previous year, there could have been no treaty, but at that stage neither they nor the British Government had yet been apprised of that horrific truth.

The prospect of meeting Roosevelt off the coast of Newfoundland left the Prime Minister, in Colville's words, 'as excited as a schoolboy on the last day of term'.[35] The two men had been exchanging telegrams at a growing pace, but their first face-to-face meeting since 1918 was bound to be a climactic moment, for good or ill. The importance of the trip to Churchill was underlined by the number of people he took with him, including Dill, Pound, Lindemann, Cadogan, Vice Chief of the Air Staff Sir Wilfrid Freeman, Tommy Thompson and John Martin. 'The P.M. set out for the north with a retinue that Cardinal Wolsey might have envied,' noted Colville.[36]

On the 12.30 p.m. train from Marylebone railway station on 3 August, dressed in his air-force blue siren suit and yachting cap, Churchill 'deplored the rash of modern houses' in the suburbs outside London. Cadogan pointed out 'that one might view them as the encampment of the anti-Bolshevik host', which placated him.[37] Over the past forty-eight years, he estimated, he had consumed half a bottle of champagne a day and wanted to know how far up the carriage that would come.[38] The Prof, with the help of the slide rule he always carried with him, estimated that it would reach up to less than half the height of the dining saloon, which left the Prime Minister unimpressed.[39]

On Monday, 4 August, the party boarded the battleship HMS *Prince of Wales* at Scapa Flow, where they found an exhausted Harry Hopkins just back from Moscow. Hopkins had brought 'ample supplies' of caviar from Stalin, and Churchill observed, 'It was very good to have such caviar even though it meant fighting with the Russians to get it.'[40] He planned all the details of the entertainment that followed, ordering grouse, turtle soup and a band. His original quarters were above the propellers but in gales the stern shuddered, so he moved to the Admiral's sea cabin on the bridge.[41] 'We are just off,' Churchill cabled Roosevelt later that day. 'It is twenty-seven years ago today that Huns began their last war. We must make a good job of it this time. Twice ought to be enough. Look forward so much to our meeting. Kindest regards.'[42] That night, Churchill and his entourage visited the Map Room, at which point, for the only time on the whole voyage, all the lights fused.[43]

Over the following days as they walked up and down the cold and blustery deck, Churchill and Cadogan went through all the likely discussion points – a declaration of Anglo-American post-war aspirations, closer staff cooperation, specific munitions needed under Lend-Lease and so on – with Cadogan playing the role of Roosevelt.[44] This allowed Churchill to practise arguments and be ready with responses to the President's replies to them. He read C. S. Forester's novel *Captain Hornblower*, set in the Napoleonic Wars, and the party watched movies every night in the Wardroom, such as Donald Duck's *Foxhunting* and Laurel and Hardy's *Saps at Sea* – which 'delighted' Churchill – and, of course, *That Hamilton Woman*, which, as Commander Thompson recalled, 'never failed to move him, although he had seen it many times before'.[45] 'Gentlemen,' Churchill told his entourage, 'I thought this film would interest you, showing great events similar to those in which you have been taking part.'[46] It was one of the few films that his staff did not think was abysmal, and it made Churchill cry. There is a scene in which Admiral Nelson, played by Laurence Olivier, tells the Board of Admiralty, 'Gentlemen, you will never make peace with Napoleon! Napoleon cannot be master of the world until he has smashed us up, and believe me, gentlemen, he means to be master of the world! You cannot make peace with dictators. You have to destroy them, wipe them out!' Churchill also watched 'one particularly banal film about love in a New York department store with evident enjoyment'. The Laurel and Hardy film *Swiss Miss* he pronounced 'A bright if inconsequential performance'.[47] While the reels were being changed, he asked for Noël Coward's 'Mad Dogs and Englishmen' and a popular dance tune, 'Franklin D. Roosevelt Jones', to be played on the gramophone. He knew every verse of both songs by heart.

The ship observed radio silence throughout the six-day journey, so for the first time in almost two years Churchill found himself isolated from direct responsibility for the daily course of events, and could send no signals, though he wrote letters that were dispatched once they had berthed in Newfoundland. On the second day they had to leave their destroyer escort behind as a result of heavy seas. Later, a drastic change of course was necessitated when a U-boat was sighted. The sea was so rough on 5 August that breakfast was cancelled, prompting Churchill – an heroic breakfaster on the Edwardian model – to declare, 'Tout au contraire [All is against us].'[48] In the rough weather Churchill spent most of his time in his quarters or on the bridge. 'All this ozone is making me lazy,' he remarked. 'I used to want to see red boxes all the time. Now I have difficulty in driving myself to two hours' work a day.'[49] When challenged to a game of backgammon, Hopkins warned Churchill that he played well. 'That's alright,' Churchill replied. 'I play low.'[50] The next day, when

Hopkins refused a second brandy at lunchtime, the Prime Minister said, 'I hope that, as we approach the United States, you are not going to get more temperate.'[51] The *Prince of Wales* picked up another destroyer escort on 6 August, and the night before they reached Newfoundland they watched *That Hamilton Woman* yet again, the fifth time Churchill had seen it in a month.[52] Hopkins then took seven guineas (some £380 in today's money) off him at backgammon.

When dawn rose on Saturday, 9 August 1941, the ship was close to Naval Station Argentia, near the Newfoundland shore. 'On the starboard beam they could see densely wooded valleys filled with grey mist,' recalled Thompson.[53] At 9 a.m. they entered Placentia Bay and anchored alongside the cruiser USS *Augusta*, the presidential flagship. Roosevelt had also brought along the battleship *Arkansas* and cruiser *Tuscaloosa*. The band of the *Prince of Wales* played 'The Star-Spangled Banner' and from across the waves could be heard 'God Save the King'. At 11 a.m. President Roosevelt stood at the head of the gangway on USS *Augusta*, leaning on the arm of his son Elliott, and shook hands with Churchill, Pound, Dill, Cadogan, Lindemann and Martin, welcoming them aboard for the first meeting of the Conference codenamed Riviera. He was accompanied by General George C. Marshall, Chief of Staff of the US Army, Admiral Harold Stark of the Navy, General Henry 'Hap' Arnold of the Army Air Force, Sumner Welles, the Under-Secretary of State, and one of the President's other sons, Franklin Roosevelt Jr. Churchill handed the President a letter from the King, though the dignity of the occasion was somewhat undermined by the attendant film crew insisting on his doing it twice more, for the benefit of the cameras.

The first social interaction between President and Prime Minister was an unfortunate one. Roosevelt said he had met Churchill before, during the Great War, of which he had 'treasured recollections', to which his guest had to admit 'frankly that it had slipped his memory!'[54] (Roosevelt was being diplomatic; at the time he had thought Churchill 'a stinker'.)* Although Churchill had told the Dominion premiers before leaving for Newfoundland that he had never met Roosevelt, in *The Gathering Storm* he was to write, 'I had met him only once in the previous war. It was at a dinner at Gray's Inn, and I had been struck by his magnificent presence in all his youth and strength.'[55] His flattery in *Great Contemporaries* and in recent speeches had expunged the poor impression made in Gray's Inn back in 1918. Later that day Roosevelt wrote to Margaret 'Daisy' Suckley, his distant cousin and close friend, 'He is a tremendously vital person and

* See p. 261.

in many ways is an English Mayor LaGuardia!* Don't say I said so! I like him – and lunching alone broke the ice both ways.'[56] In total, Churchill and Roosevelt were to spend no fewer than 113 days together during the Second World War on nine separate occasions.

'No one can comprehend the movements leading up to the battle of Blenheim unless he realizes that Eugene and Marlborough were working like two lobes of the same brain,' Churchill had written in *Marlborough*. 'They were in constant touch with one another.'[57] Many of Churchill's political friendships had not ended well, such as those with Asquith, Baldwin and now Lloyd George, but this had to be different. He therefore spared no effort to get on well with Roosevelt, recognizing in him a fellow aristocrat, democrat and social reformer. He was to declare that 'No lover ever studied every whim of his mistress as I did those of President Roosevelt.'[58] Lunch that first day was spent getting to know each other, but there were of course many concrete things both leaders wanted from the Placentia Bay meeting. These included further and deeper staff talks, a public declaration to deter Japanese aggression, agreement over American naval patrols around British-controlled Iceland, fast-tracked supply requests under Lend-Lease and a joint declaration of universal principles that would encourage both the English-speaking peoples and neutrals to recognize that the war was being fought for values wholly superior to those of the Nazis.

Such was Churchill's capacity for compartmentalizing his mind that in the period back on the *Prince of Wales* between lunch and dinner he sent off a telegram to Sir John Anderson complaining that motorists who received extra petrol ration coupons were being required to account for every journey to the authorities: 'To create and multiply offences which are not condemned by public opinion, which are difficult to detect and can only be punished in a capricious manner, is impolitic.'[59] At dinner that night aboard the *Augusta*, this time with Cadogan, Marshall and others present, the discussion turned to the profitability and problems of Roosevelt growing Christmas trees at his country estate of Hyde Park in upstate New York. 'Later, of course,' Cadogan noted, 'the party got down to some business.'[60]

Early the next morning, with Churchill 'storming around the deck', Cadogan was asked to draft a declaration of joint principles that was to form the basis of what became the Atlantic Charter. Roosevelt then came aboard the *Prince of Wales* with several hundred American Navy servicemen and Marines for a Sunday service on the quarterdeck. Churchill chose

* Fiorello LaGuardia was the 5 foot 2 inch, obese but highly energetic Mayor of New York City.

the hymns: 'For Those in Peril on the Sea', 'Onward Christian Soldiers' and 'O God our Help in Ages Past'. 'Every word seemed to stir the heart,' he later wrote. 'It was a great hour to live.'[61] He choreographed the service so that it was, as he put it, 'fully choral and fully photographic'.[62] The Union Jack and the Stars and Stripes were draped side by side on the altar; the American and British chaplains shared in the readings from the King James Bible; sailors from both nations were intermingled. He also took the opportunity to give Roosevelt the draft joint declaration for discussion with his advisers. Roosevelt ordered that every sailor present be given 200 cigarettes each, as well as some fruit and cheese.

Churchill had asked for a dozen brace of grouse to be brought on the voyage, and these were eaten for lunch with the British and American Chiefs of Staff. After the President had left that afternoon, Churchill went on to the beach, where Cadogan recorded him 'enjoying himself like a schoolboy on holiday, insisting on rolling boulders down a steep cliff'.[63] Martin saw him collecting a fistful of flowers. That night, Churchill and his entourage had dinner on the *Augusta* with eight Americans and the President's Scottish terrier, Fala. 'I think it was felt by everyone present', Captain Pim wrote later, 'that [upon] the reaction of these two great leaders, perhaps the greatest for many generations, to each other, and the wisdom of their counsels, the freedom of the world might well depend.'[64]

The next day, 11 August, saw the first serious discussions, conducted without a fixed agenda in an atmosphere Thompson described as 'easy informality'.[65] They were wide-ranging and included using the Azores as an Allied base in the event of a German move into the Iberian Peninsula, and a future Allied landing in Europe, codenamed Roundup. Future detailed staff conversations in Washington were agreed upon. The next day, Beaverbrook flew in, and Lend-Lease was added to the mix. Above all, agreement was reached on the text of the Atlantic Charter, as well as a joint message to Stalin and a communiqué about the talks. There were no disagreements on any matters of substance, and all of Churchill's objectives were achieved at the Conference, as well as friendly relationships being established between the British and American staffs, primarily between Dill and Marshall.

'The President of the United States and the Prime Minister, Mr Churchill, being met together,' the Charter began, 'deem it right to make known certain common principles in the national policies of their respective countries on which they base their hopes for a better future for the world.' The first was 'Their countries seek no aggrandizement, territorial or other.' The second, 'They desire to see no territorial changes that do not accord with the freely expressed wishes of the people concerned,' and thirdly,

'They respect the right of all peoples to choose the form of government under which they will live; and they wish to see sovereign rights and self-government restored to those who have been forcibly deprived of them.' Although the United States was not about to declare war on Germany, as some in Britain had unrealistically hoped she might, the sixth article of the Charter, which began, 'After the final destruction of the Nazi tyranny . . .', represented unequivocal language from a neutral power.

There then followed principles regarding the access of all states to trade and raw materials on equal terms, the fullest economic cooperation of all nations, freedom from want and fear in all lands, the traversing of the high seas and oceans without hindrance, and general disarmament and abandonment of the use of force. The Charter was subsequently signed by the governments-in-exile of Belgium, Czechoslovakia, Free France, Greece, Luxembourg, Holland, Norway, Poland and Yugoslavia – and, somewhat cynically, by the USSR. It was astonishing that so committed an imperialist as Churchill could have put his name to Article Three, but such was the imperative of establishing common purpose with the United States. The Atlantic Charter was announced on 14 August, which was the first moment the world knew that Roosevelt and Churchill had met, and that they were in total accord about the underlying principles for the world they wanted to build after the extirpation of Nazism. It provided a potent rallying cry for the forces of freedom, so that people could feel they had something inspiring to fight for, and not just something evil to fight against.

At 5 p.m. on 12 August, the *Prince of Wales* sailed away with her escort of destroyers to Iceland. On the afterdeck, Churchill stood waving his cap to each American ship in turn, remaining on deck until they were almost out of sight. Two days later the battleship had to alter course owing to U-boats spotted in the area. The next day, they joined a homebound convoy of seventy-two ships in all, some of which had aircraft visible on their decks, which Churchill called 'a delectable sight'.[66]* The convoy was formed of twelve columns 500 yards apart, and the *Prince of Wales* was able to make two runs through it. The men lining the decks on each ship cheered wildly when they spotted Churchill on the bridge, giving the V-sign.

The next day he met the Icelandic Prime Minister in Reykjavik, and on 18 August, following a full gale that reduced visibility (and thus danger from enemy U-boats and aircraft), the *Prince of Wales* arrived at Scapa Flow in brilliant sunshine at 9 a.m. On the train back to London,

* During this period there were around fifteen convoys at sea in the Atlantic at any one time.

Churchill asked for a Benedictine liqueur, and ten minutes later for a brandy. Reminded by the attendant that he had already had a Benedictine, he said, 'I know; I want some brandy to clear it up.'[67]

The next morning, Churchill had lunch with the King and shared his thoughts about Roosevelt. 'W. was greatly taken by him,' the King recorded, 'and has come back feeling that he knows him. He had several talks with him alone, when W put our position to him very bluntly. If by spring, Russia was down and out, and Germany was renewing her Blitzkrieg here, all our hopes of victory and help from the U.S.A. would be dashed if America had not by then sent us masses of planes, etc, or had not entered the war. F.D.R. has got £3,000,000,000 to spend on us here . . . He thought Japan would remain quiet.'[68]

Despite his broad grin at King's Cross that morning, and the undoubted success of the meeting with Roosevelt, Churchill continued to feel that the situation was very grim. The Germans were moving fast towards Moscow and Leningrad; war production was encountering problems, including bottlenecks and – shockingly – strikes.[69] But on 21 August, against his generals' advice, Hitler decided to slow the advance eastwards and to send a large part of his armour southwards towards Kiev in order to seize Ukraine's agricultural resources. It was a monumental blunder, fatally weakening the all-important thrust against Moscow – which had it succeeded would have forced Stalin and the Soviet Government back beyond the Urals.

That same day, the first Arctic convoy arrived in north Russia, carrying two Hurricane squadrons. Tanks followed, despite the detriment to Britain's position in the Western Desert. By the end of the war, Britain had sent 720 ships to the Soviet Union in forty convoys, and had delivered over four million tons of supplies, 5,000 tanks and 7,000 aircraft. These convoys diverted fleets that would otherwise have been used to protect home waters or Atlantic convoys.[70] Appalling weather and encroaching deck-ice in winter, almost perpetual daylight in summer, the close proximity of Luftwaffe airfields, and well-hidden fjords where their raiders lurked, all gave the Germans huge advantages over the north Norwegian convoys. Yet Churchill hardly received a word of thanks from Stalin, only bitter complaints that not enough was being sent. In his speech on the twenty-fourth anniversary of the October Revolution, Stalin told his audience, 'Our country is waging a war of liberation single-handed, without military help from anyone.' Moreover, British sailors were ill treated in Murmansk and Archangel.

For all Stalin's ingratitude, Churchill was horrified by what was happening to his people. 'As his armies advance,' Churchill said of Hitler in a broadcast on 24 August focusing on the Atlantic Charter, but also touching on the terrible massacres taking place in Russia of civilians, especially Jews and Communists,

> whole districts are being exterminated. Scores of thousands – literally scores of thousands – of executions in cold blood are being perpetrated by the German police-troops upon the Russian patriots who defend their native soil. Since the Mongol invasions of Europe in the sixteenth century there has never been methodical, merciless butchery on such a scale, or approaching such a scale. And this is but the beginning. Famine and pestilence have yet to follow in the bloody ruts of Hitler's tanks. We are in the presence of a crime without a name.[71]

As German *Einsatzgruppen* (murder squads) sent reports back to Berlin via their Enigma machines filled with enormous but mysterious figures, it had dawned on Bletchley that these were the numbers of people being massacred.[72] Churchill was not believed by many neutrals, who thought he was merely spouting Allied propaganda. Some, such as the *New York Times*, tucked the news away in only a few column inches on their inside pages.

'Do not despair,' Churchill said, addressing the peoples of Occupied Europe, 'your land shall be cleansed . . . Keep your souls clean from all contact with the Nazis; make them feel even in their fleeting hour of brutish triumph that they are the moral outcasts of Mankind. Help is coming; mighty forces are arming in your behalf. Have faith. Have hope. Deliverance is sure.'[73] Thousands of people who lived under Nazi occupation during the war testified that Churchill's speeches gave them hope when little else did. They listened to him illegally on secret radio sets, even though doing so could be a capital offence. In his message to the *Jewish Chronicle* on its centenary in November, Churchill wrote, 'None has suffered more cruelly than the Jew the unspeakable evils wrought on the bodies and spirit of men by Hitler and his vile regime. The Jew bore the brunt of the Nazis' first onslaught upon the citadels of freedom and human dignity . . . Once again, at the appointed time, he will see vindicated those principles of righteousness which it was the glory of his fathers to proclaim to the world.'[74]

On 25 August, with the Germans outside Kiev, Britain and Russia jointly invaded Iran with a small force. They were victorious in three days, and the Shah's son was installed in his father's place on the Peacock Throne. Britain was now able to supply Russia by land, and to protect the Anglo-Iranian Oil Company's Abadan oilfields. 'We had been doing something for which we had justification but no right,' Churchill admitted privately.[75]

Churchill made an impassioned plea to Winant over brandy at the end of dinner at Chequers five days later, with Halifax and Eden in attendance. He argued that after signing the Atlantic Charter 'America could not honourably stay out. She could not fight with mercenaries . . . If she came in, the conviction of an Allied victory would be founded in a dozen countries . . . We must have an American declaration of war, or else, though we cannot now be defeated, the war might drag on for another four or five years, and civilization and culture would be wiped out.' If America did come in, however, 'Her belligerency might mean victory in 1943.'[76] Winant suggested that the United States might join the war by March, but this gave the Prime Minister 'little satisfaction', not least because it was pure guesswork.[77] To lighten the mood after that, he gave 'an interesting account of the love life of the duck-billed platypus'.[78] (It is polygynous.)

Churchill went to the Dorchester Hotel on 4 September for a farewell dinner for the now nineteen-year-old Mary as she left to serve in an anti-aircraft battery near Enfield as a member of the Auxiliary Territorial Service, the women's branch of the British Army. He was applauded right through the hotel from the front door to his seat in the restaurant. He had to be back at No. 10 by 10 p.m., however, to receive a letter from Stalin, delivered by Maisky. Stalin was demanding a Second Front in France or the Balkans, to draw thirty or forty German divisions off the Eastern Front. He also wanted 30,000 tons of aluminium, and at least 400 planes and 500 tanks per month. Without it, he warned, Russia might be knocked out of the war.

'I have no doubt that Hitler still wishes to pursue his old policy of beating his enemies one by one,' Maisky quoted Churchill as saying. 'I would be ready to sacrifice fifty thousand English lives if, in so doing, I could draw even just twenty German divisions from your front!'[79] But, he then added, just as the English Channel 'prevents Germany from jumping over into England, it likewise prevents England from jumping into Occupied France'. Nor were there the troops, aircraft or shipping tonnage for a Balkans campaign. Churchill pointed out that it had taken seven weeks to transfer four British divisions from Egypt to Greece, which was a friendly country, and concluded, 'No! No! We can't walk into certain defeat either in France or in the Balkans!'[80]

On the question of supplies, Churchill told Maisky, 'We, too, are short of arms. More than a million British soldiers are still unarmed!' He pointed out that Britain's entire tank production did not amount to 500 a month. 'In 1942, the situation will change,' Maisky recorded him saying. 'Both we and the Americans will be able to give you a lot in 1942. But for now . . . Only God, in whom you don't believe, can help you in the next six to seven weeks.'[81] When Maisky asked for his plan for the future, the Prime Minister replied that it was to prevent invasion of the mother country; hold the Nile Valley and Middle East; win back Libya; secure supplies to the USSR via Iran and other routes; 'draw Turkey onto our side'; 'bomb Germany incessantly'; conduct a relentless submarine war; increase the number of troops in the Middle East from 600,000 to 750,000 by the end of 1941 and to a million by the spring of 1942.[82] Maisky sensibly did not report back to Moscow Churchill's response to the 'underlying air of menace' in Maisky's appeal: that after the Nazi–Soviet Pact, 'Whatever happens and whatever you do, you of all people have no right to make reproaches to us.'[83] In the light of Stalin's letter, Churchill cancelled a trip to Dover. Colville concluded, 'We look like being faced with a decision of the same kind as that in the closing stages of the Battle of France: throw in everything to save our Allies or reserve our strength in case the worst happens. Fortunately in this case our cupboard is not so bare.'[84] Meanwhile in Moscow Cripps was still being ignored by Molotov and wanted to come home. 'The resting bosom of Sir Stafford must be wounded and chilled,' Churchill told his staff. 'Well, I'm afraid he will have to pig it like the rest of us.'[85] He called Cadogan to say that Cripps 'must be stopped' from returning, adding that he did not want the message to come from him.[86]

Eden reported that Churchill was 'in great spirits' as they lunched alone that day. The Prime Minister told Eden that although he could help the Tory Party electorally in the post-war world, 'he felt no enthusiasm for post-war problems'. Eden replied that they needed new young candidates, since 'No one would vote for the men of Munich.' 'Winston was as usual full of fight,' Eden reported.[87] Once again, Churchill had given Eden cause to believe that he might take over the Tory leadership once the war was won. He was never a cruel man, but his treatment of Eden's ambitions for the premiership was heartless.

That evening, after agreeing a package of 30,000 tons of aid with Maisky, Churchill took Beaverbrook and Eden to the Ritz for a dinner of oysters, partridge and nostalgia. 'Winston said that he would like best to have F.E. back to help him,' Eden noted. Not the F. E. Smith of his 'last sodden years' but the one of 1914 or 1915. After him, he would like to have Balfour. When Beaverbrook said that 'if he had played [his] cards well when he was at the Admiralty early in the last war, especially with [the] Tory Party, he could have been P.M. instead of [Lloyd] George,' Churchill agreed. Churchill then described the moment when he learned that Lloyd George had not intended to include him in his Cabinet in

December 1916 as the 'toughest moment of his life'.[88] He then worked until 3 a.m. on his reply to Stalin, postponing his departure for Ditchley. 'I feel the world vibrant again,' he told Martin.[89] It had taken Hitler's great blunder to make it so.

On 11 September, the King 'found Winston much more optimistic and for the first time he told me that he thought that Germany might at some time crumple from within'.[90] That was a strange prediction, when Kiev was about to fall, but Churchill also thought Hitler's generals might prevent him from using gas on the battlefield if they thought they were losing. Desmond Morton had told him that he believed Stalin had given orders to British Communists to overthrow him when the time was ripe.[91] Speculation and rumour were running rife.

On 18 September, the day Kiev fell, Churchill acceded to the Australian Government's demands that their troops be withdrawn from Auchinleck's command. It was frustrating, but Churchill saw the wider political picture, telling the War Cabinet that 'Allowances must be made for a Government with a majority of one faced by a bitter Opposition, part of which at least are isolationist in outlook. It is imperative that no public dispute should arise between Great Britain and Australia. All personal feelings must therefore be subordinated to the appearance of unity. Trouble has largely arisen through our not having had any British infantry divisions in the various actions, thus causing the world to suppose that we are fighting our battles with Dominion troops only.'[92] Having learned the lesson of Gallipoli, he assured Canberra, 'At whatever cost your orders about your own troops will be obeyed.'[93]

Churchill ensured that the Dominion governments received weekly reports from the General Staff (daily in the case of ongoing operations) as well as Cabinet summaries, and he sent many personal telegrams.[94] Whenever Dominion prime ministers visited Britain they were invited to War Cabinet meetings. Yet he prevented an Imperial War Cabinet from being set up, and did not go into details about impending operations. When, in late May 1944, Mackenzie King asked when D-Day would be taking place, Churchill told him it might be as late as 21 June, when it was in fact intended for 5 June.[95] Considering the extraordinary contribution the Dominions and colonies made to the war – in the Army alone, twenty-one of the fifty-five divisions that Churchill planned were going to be non-British – and given that Churchill believed in the Empire, it is extraordinary what little say he gave them in the creation of grand strategy.

Churchill sent Beaverbrook to Moscow on 22 September to negotiate plans for supplying Russia. While he was there, Beaverbrook became such an advocate of the Second Front that he started to undermine Churchill politically. Even before he left, his newspapers were regularly criticizing members of the Government of which he was a prominent member. 'Altogether he is a pleasant, easy and loyal colleague!' Eden noted with heavy sarcasm in his diary that month.[96]

As a special sign of his approbation, the King appointed Churchill to the ancient and prestigious post of lord warden of the Cinque Ports on 23 September. Churchill was attracted by the historical connections – Pitt the Younger, Wellington and Palmerston had all held the post, which had been created in the twelfth century – but he was daunted by the cost of the upkeep of Walmer Castle, built by Henry VIII. Lord Reading, who had held the post in the mid-1930s, had employed fourteen servants and five gardeners there.[97] The Lord Warden did have the right to all whales washed ashore within the limits of his jurisdiction, which in olden times might have been a boon, but this was now actually a liability, as they also had to be buried at his expense. When the lord warden's flag arrived at Chartwell after the war it was flown with pride, and Churchill responded with a slight paraphrasing of 'The Jabberwocky': 'Calloo! Callay! O frabjous day! And so he chortled in his joy.'[98] He had a miniature version of the flag made to fly on the front of his official car.* When the Churchills visited Walmer Castle two days after his appointment, Clementine thought it 'gloomy and unwieldy'.[99] 'I very much doubt whether it will ever be possible for me to live at Walmer Castle,' he told the Minister of Works, 'or indeed whether anybody will be able to live in such fine houses after the war.'[100]

The next day the Churchills went from Walmer to Coventry by train. The notoriously unpunctual Prime Minister was not dressed when it arrived at the platform, where the Midlands Regional Commissioner, the Earl of Dudley, and the Mayor and a welcoming committee were waiting. This was because, although he believed he could bathe, shave and dress in fifteen minutes, in fact it took him twenty. 'Consequently he is late for everything,' noted Colville, and 'Mrs C. seethed with anger.'[101] The Churchills were taken around the city, the bombed-out Cathedral, and the communal graveyard where the victims of the November 1940 air raid were buried. At the Armstrong Siddeley aircraft and torpedo factory, the men in each workshop clanged their hammers in an enthusiastic but deafening welcome. Similarly, at the Whitley bomber factory, which was a hotbed of Communism, Churchill's appearance with cigar and square-crown hat 'quite captivated the workforce who gave him vociferous applause'. Churchill flourished the V-sign, despite, as Colville put it, 'the

* Now in the possession of the author.

representations repeatedly made to him that this gesture has quite another significance'.[102]

In Birmingham the next day, where a Spitfire flew upside down over the Churchills' heads only 40 feet above the ground, they drove through the city for several miles past packed, cheering crowds to the railway station. 'I have seen the P.M. have many enthusiastic receptions,' Colville wrote, 'but never one to equal this.'[103] On the way home, Tommy Thompson asked him how he could have made three or four long speeches in succession without repeating himself, using what Churchill called his 'Speechform' of notes with subject headings. 'It isn't nearly as difficult as you think,' the Prime Minister replied. 'I just start my mouth off talking and leave it.'[104]

While dressing for dinner on 28 September, Churchill told Colville that 'So far the Government had only made one error of judgment: Greece.'[105] He now blamed that campaign on Sir John Dill. Colville knew that the Greek campaign had in fact been Churchill's idea and that Dill had initially opposed it, but the Prime Minister 'has now got his knife right into Dill and frequently disparages him'.[106] (Dill presumably reciprocated the lack of regard: his views on Churchill were excised from Reith's draft memoirs before publication at the request of the Cabinet Office.)[107] An earlier disagreement between the Prime Minister and CIGS illustrates the gulf between their personalities. Among General Sir John Dill's papers is a letter from Churchill dated 19 October 1940 with a red 'Action this day' label, supporting the appointment of Major-General Sir Percy 'Hobo' Hobart (pronounced Hubbard) to train the 11th Armoured Division. Dill had vigorously opposed this on the grounds that Hobart, who had been retired by Wavell and was now serving as a lance-corporal in the Home Guard, was 'difficult to serve with ... his judgements were impetuous and inconsistent ... unwilling to listen to the opinion of others ... unsympathetic ... he had too jealous a regard for the interests of his own formation ... self-opinionated, lacked stability, and would not carry out the instructions of his superiors ... his personality did not make for harmonious working, and ... he showed little consideration for others'.[108] Before he sent his memorandum to the Prime Minister, Dill presumably had not considered that it read like a summary of many of the criticisms made of Churchill himself. Nonetheless, Dill had to acknowledge that Hobart was also 'an excellent trainer and had first-rate knowledge of the organization, armament and maintenance of tank formations'.

'Such prejudices attach frequently to persons of strong personality and original view,' Churchill wrote back.

> We are now at war, fighting for our lives, and we cannot afford to confine Army appointments to persons who have excited no hostile comments in their career . . . Cromwell, Wolfe, Clive, Gordon, and in a different sphere [T. E.] Lawrence, all had very close resemblance to the characteristics. They had other qualities as well and so I am led to believe has General Hobart. This is a time to try men of force and vision and not to be exclusively confined to those who are judged safe by conventional standards.[109]

By then, he had come to see Dill as personifying the latter. After dinner with Lord Rosebery, son of the late Prime Minister, and the regional commissioner for Scotland, at Dalmeny House on the Firth of Forth soon afterwards, Churchill upbraided Dill over his reluctance to employ Hobart. 'Remember, it isn't only the good boys who win the wars; it is the sneaks and the stinkers as well.'[110] Hobart was appointed, and his contrarian, maverick ideas produced new weapon after weapon – nicknamed 'Hobart's Funnies' – that proved invaluable on D-Day.

On 28 September 1941, Colville noted that Churchill thought that an early Second Front on the continent 'could only have one outcome. The War Office would not do the job properly; indeed it was unfair to ask them to pit themselves against German organization, experience and resources. They had neither the means nor the intelligence.'[111] It was almost an admission that the Germans were better than the British at warfare, an exceptionally dangerous concept to float even privately, but one to which he would sometimes return, and which was shared by several other senior military and diplomatic figures – at least in the first half of the war.

In a speech on 30 September, Churchill joked about politicians who cared too much about public opinion to show proper leadership. 'Nothing is more dangerous in wartime than to live in the temperamental atmosphere of a Gallup Poll,' he said, 'always feeling one's pulse and taking one's temperature. I see that a speaker at the weekend said that this was a time when leaders should keep their ears to the ground. All I can say is that the British nation will find it very hard to look up to leaders who are detected in that somewhat ungainly posture.'[112]

On 4 October Churchill had to sack a third old friend and Other Club member (after Boothby and Duff Cooper), writing to Admiral Roger Keyes, the Director of Combined Operations, 'I have to consider my first duty to the State, which ranks above personal friendship. In all the circumstances I have no choice but to arrange for your relief.'[113] Churchill had appointed the sixty-eight-year-old in July, but it was one of his worst personnel decisions since Fisher. In the battle for resources, Keyes managed repeatedly to antagonize all three Chiefs of Staff, which was disastrous for someone whose job was to combine them for offensive operations. He questioned the judgement of everyone else, and acted as though he was the only one who had any offensive spirit. Churchill admired Keyes, and owed him much for starting the avalanche against Chamberlain in the Norway Debate, but he was the wrong man for the job. He would probably have been dismissed sooner but, in Martin's words, the 'constant attacks on him only aroused the PM's loyalty'.[114] In Keyes's place, Churchill appointed the King's cousin Lord Louis Mountbatten, a captain with only four years' seniority, and upgraded his title to chief of combined operations.

On 7 October, the King noted that Churchill was 'worried over the Russian situation, which is serious, as the Germans have started another advance in the central sector'.[115] The Wehrmacht had reached Moscow's subway stations, and winter could not come soon enough for the Russians. Stalin now insisted that thirty British divisions be landed at Archangel, another completely impossible request, as he must have known. Churchill had other worries that day too when John Curtin of the Australian Labor Party became prime minister and proved uncompromising about Canberra's control over its troops in the Middle East, regardless of the danger it might pose for the Crusader offensive for the relief of Tobruk, dangers that Churchill pointed out as eloquently as he could, but to no avail.[116]

When Auchinleck signalled that he wanted to postpone Operation Crusader another fortnight, and the Chiefs of Staff opposed Churchill's plans for attacking either Trondheim or Sicily, he remarked bitterly, 'I sometimes think some of my generals do not want to fight the Germans.'[117] He sent Auchinleck three Ultra decrypts that month showing Rommel's relative unpreparedness.[118] On 7 October, Roosevelt stated publicly that the Atlantic meeting had not brought the United States closer to war.

Despite these anxieties, Eden had 'A most enjoyable evening' with Churchill the next day at Chequers. Discussing Conservative Party matters, Churchill said that 'In time all the Munich men would be driven out. Neville was lucky to have died when he did. Edward [Halifax] could not have stayed at the Foreign Office. The public that had forgotten its own errors would only remember its former leaders', and would take vengeance.'[119] Eden defended Dill as an excellent staff officer who had made good appointments, as if that were enough in a global conflict. The next day, Churchill personally lit the fire in Eden's bedroom, prompting the Foreign Secretary to write in his diary, 'I know no one with such perfect manners as a host, especially when he feels like it!'[120] Beaverbrook, who had recently returned from Russia, came to stay at Chequers and told Churchill and Eden that Stalin would fight on and hated Hitler 'with cold fury'.[121] In front of Eden, he brought up the subject of who would become prime minister 'if anything befell Winston'. Churchill said it would be Eden, but Beaverbrook suggested the Chamberlainites would want David Margesson. Churchill 'dissented strongly at this. Said he hadn't the brain, nor grasp, nor any of qualifications needed . . . John Anderson would have more chance.' Eden himself said Beaverbrook would also be in the running, and Churchill agreed.[122] They then ate the caviar Beaverbrook had brought back from Russia, and went to bed at 3 a.m.

Roosevelt wrote Churchill an important letter on 11 October, which was hand-delivered by Frederick Hovde, the head of the London office of the US National Defense Research Committee. 'It appears desirable that we should correspond or converse concerning the subject which is under study by your MAUD committee, and by Dr Bush's organization in this country,' Roosevelt suggested, referring to Vannevar Bush's Uranium Committee, 'in order that any extended efforts may be coordinated or even jointly conducted.'[123] This cooperation offered benefits to both countries, because, although Britain was further ahead with the science at that stage, America had far more resources, finance and laboratories, thousands of miles away from the Luftwaffe's furthest reach.[124] Yet Churchill responded warily, and only several weeks later, concerned that giving the United States nuclear secrets might not be wise while she remained neutral. He only really engaged over nuclear issues with Roosevelt in June 1942, at a meeting at Hyde Park. Throughout the war, he kept everything to do with the Bomb as his private fiefdom, separate from the Cabinet: only he, Lindemann and Anderson knew every aspect of what was going on.[125] As he was later to put it, 'Scientists should be on tap, but not on top,' and in nuclear matters he felt the same way about his ministers.[126]

By mid-October Churchill was urging Operation Jupiter on the Chiefs of Staff, a landing in northern Norway to secure northern convoy routes to the USSR.[127] It would have been open to German counter-attack and very hard to resupply, and was to become a running sore between him and the Chiefs of Staff for many months, further undermining his confidence in Dill. 'Winston had never been fond of Dill,' Alan Brooke wrote after the war. 'They were entirely different types of characters, and types that could never have worked harmoniously together. Dill was the essence of straight forwardness, blessed with the highest of principles and an unassailable integrity of character. I do not believe that any of these characteristics appealed to Winston, on the contrary, I think he disliked them as they accentuated his own shortcomings in this respect.'[128] Brooke wrote of Dill that 'Winston's methods were frequently repulsive to him.' (Brooke felt contempt for most politicians, Churchill included, and excepting only Stalin and Smuts, whom he rated highly.)

On 21 October, four senior cryptographers from Bletchley Park, including Alan Turing and Gordon Welchman, wrote directly to Churchill to complain about staffing bottlenecks that were dangerously affecting the production of 'bombes', the electrical devices needed for their computing machines. The letter was handed personally to Brigadier Harvie-Watt at No. 10 by Stuart Milner-Barry of the legendary Hut 6, where much of the cryptographers' best work was done. Churchill immediately wrote an 'Action this day' minute to Ismay, ordering that the cryptographers at Bletchley should receive everything they needed 'on extreme priority' and asking him to report when it was done.[129] Within days, the cryptographers had been supplied, and the War Office bureaucracy understood the pull that they had with the Prime Minister, making further allocations easier.

A movement to push Churchill to adopt a Second Front gathered momentum by late October, led by Beaverbrook and Cripps. Both men eyed the possibility of succeeding Churchill if the opportunity arose. There were letters in the press, public meetings and poster campaigns to suggest that Britain was fighting the war 'to the last drop of Russian blood'. Maisky coordinated the campaign, complaining to Harold Nicolson that Churchill would not give Russia more aid because he 'was dominated by the idea that the war would last six or seven years'.[130] When Churchill was shown a Communist Party leaflet alleging that 'In Britain we . . . still believe that others will do the fighting and dying while we draw the profits' and 'It is time to open a Second Front' he told Harvie-Watt 'the answer was "Balls".'[131]

To Randolph, then serving in Cairo, he wrote on 30 October, 'Things are pretty hard here now that the asthma season has come on and Max [who was asthmatic] fights everybody and resigns every day. The Communists are posing as the only patriots in the country. The admirals, generals and air marshals chant their stately hymn of "Safety First". The Shinwells, Wintertons and Hore-Belishas do their best to keep us up to the mark. In the midst of all this I have to restrain my natural pugnacity by sitting on my own head. How bloody!'[132]

Churchill went back to the Harrow School Songs at the end of the month, and heard the new verse added to 'Stet Fortuna Domus', which began, 'Nor less we praise in darker days / The leader of our nation / And Churchill's name shall win acclaim / From each new generation.' In his speech he said of the year 1941, 'This is the lesson: never give in. Never give in. Never, never, never, never – in nothing, great or small, large or petty. Never give in except to convictions of honour and good sense. Never yield to force; never yield to the apparently overwhelming might of the enemy.'[133] He then announced that he would like to alter a word in the verse dedicated to him: 'I have obtained the Head Master's permission to alter "darker" to "sterner" . . . Do not let us speak of darker days; let us speak rather of sterner days. These are not dark days: these are great days – the greatest days our country has ever lived – and we must all thank God that we have been allowed, each of us according to our stations, to play a part in making these days memorable in the history of our race.'[134]

Churchill's repeated references to history throughout his wartime oratory underline how central the past was to all his thinking. As a practising historian, he saw everything that was happening to Britain through the lens of an heroic past that he believed she had experienced for over a thousand years, and which he had already begun to write about in his history of the English-speaking peoples in 1939. 'The longer you can look back, the farther you can look forward,' he told the Royal College of Physicians in March 1944. 'This is not a philosophical or political argument – any oculist will tell you this is true.'[135] Of course it was indeed a philosophical-political argument, as was clear from what he said next: 'The wider the span, the longer the continuity, the greater is the sense of duty in individual men and women, each contributing their brief life's work to the preservation and progress of the land in which they live.' Churchill used the Second World War to remind the British people about their history, and he did so while telling them that they were writing the most glorious pages of it.

In November, Churchill awarded a peerage to Lindemann, who became Lord Cherwell. This ignited false rumours in the Commons about his having German parentage, and he was nicknamed 'Baron Berlin'. When a Tory Member* asked Churchill a question about Lindemann's job, salary and number of assistants, the Prime Minister answered it respectfully and factually, but later turned on the MP in the Smoking Room, 'bellowing at him like an infuriated bull'. 'Why the hell did you ask that question?' he roared. 'Don't you know that he is one of my oldest and greatest friends?' Channon recorded that 'It was an extraordinary scene,' but concluded, 'Winston's almost blind loyalty to his friends is one of his most endearing qualities.'[136] Churchill's loyalty to his friends was not blind – as Boothby, Duff Cooper and Keyes had discovered – but it was fierce when, as in Lindemann's case, they had done no wrong. The following day Churchill made light of the criticisms, telling his fellow MPs, 'There was

* Channon said it was Sir Waldron Smithers, but Hansard records Sir George Broadbridge.

a custom in Imperial China that anyone who wished to criticize the Government had the right to . . . and, provided he followed that up by committing suicide, very great respect was paid to his words, and no ulterior motive was assigned. That seems to me to have been, from many points of view, a wise custom, but I certainly would be the last to suggest that it should be made retrospective.'[137]

On 16 November Churchill finally replaced Dill, whom he had taken to calling 'Dilly-Dally', with Sir Alan Brooke as chief of the Imperial General Staff (CIGS). As early as July 1940 he had complained to Eden that Dill 'strikes me as being very tired, disheartened and over-impressed with the might of Germany'.[138] Far from appointing a yes-man to take his place, as other politicians might have done, Churchill chose someone who he knew would not back down, except to overwhelmingly convincing argument. 'When I thump the table and push my face towards him, what does he do?' Churchill said of Brooke. 'Thumps the table harder and glares back at me. I know these Brookes – stiff-necked Ulstermen and there's no one worse to deal with than that!'[139]

The 'Fighting Brookes' of Colebrooke and Fermanagh had served in the British Army since the English Civil War: no fewer than twenty-six of them had fought in the Great War and twenty-seven would fight in the Second World War. Churchill had been friendly with Alan Brooke's eldest brother Victor when they were cavalry subalterns in the mid-1890s, and had served as assistant adjutant in the South Africa Light Horse under another brother, Ronnie. The first husband of Alan Brooke's wife had died of wounds sustained at Gallipoli, so Brooke was well aware of Churchill's strengths and weaknesses long before their first conversation over the telephone line from Le Mans in June 1940.

As we have seen, one of the most useful insights Churchill gained from the Great War was the phenomenon he had seen in Haig's Intelligence Department. 'The temptation to tell a chief in a great position the things he most likes to hear is one of the commonest explanations of mistaken policy,' he had written. 'Thus the outlook of the leader on whose decisions fateful events depend is usually far more sanguine than the brutal facts admit.'[140] Churchill therefore appointed men like Brooke and Admiral Sir Andrew Cunningham, who told him exactly what they thought he needed to hear. Brooke did not seek out confrontation with the Prime Minister, but neither did he shy away from it. He tended to choose his battles carefully, not opposing him over trivial matters. He was to tell Moran that 'every month' of working with Churchill 'is a year off my life'.[141] Earlier in 1941, Lord Vansittart had told the newspaper editor W. P. Crozier that 'Churchill needs people beside him who can say quite firmly "No", when he wants to do something wrong and insist that he must not do it.'[142] Such a man was Brooke, whom Churchill respected and whom he knew would not allow him to repeat errors such as Gallipoli or Greece.

What Churchill could not know was the strength of criticism Brooke nightly vouchsafed to his diary – published in 1957, greatly hurting Churchill – about his lack of strategic sense. Churchill and Brooke never became friends; he was not invited to join the Other Club, for example, although Portal was already a member by the time Brooke became CIGS. The Chartwell visitors' book, which records the names of all those who came to stay there after 1922, does not include Brooke's.[143] Their clashes could be titanic. Brooke would sit across the Cabinet table from Churchill refusing to budge on points of military policy, occasionally snapping pencils in half, and Churchill could be extremely rude to him on occasion. 'Those damned planners of yours plan nothing but difficulties,' he once said, calling the Joint Planning Staff 'psalm-singing defeatists'.[144] The underlying problem was that Churchill believed that the Chiefs of Staff were institutionally risk-averse. 'You may take the most gallant sailor, the most intrepid airman, or the most audacious soldier,' he told Harold Macmillan in November 1943, 'but put them at a table together – what do you get? *The sum total of their fears!*'[145]* It was not true – Brooke was a master-strategist – but the constant creative tension between a prime minister bent on aggression and a CIGS equally intent on waiting for the right moment to strike in fact worked remarkably well, however wearing it was for the latter.

Auchinleck launched Operation Crusader in the Western Desert at dawn on 18 November, in the wake of a violent storm that had kept enemy reconnaissance planes on the flooded airfields. 'Battle in Libya began,' noted Martin. 'P.M. very impatient at absence of news of its progress.'[146] The objective was to recapture Cyrenaica and destroy Axis armour. Commonwealth strength matched Rommel's on the ground, and 'the Auk' had overwhelming air superiority. General Sir Alan Cunningham's Eighth Army benefited from a tactical surprise, but by the afternoon of 19 November fierce armoured fighting at Sidi Rezegh slowed down the advance. Auchinleck flew from Cairo to take personal control of the battle. 'This intense fighting cannot go on indefinitely,' Churchill told the Cabinet on 24 November; 'if we can keep them moving they can't stick it out.' He nonetheless acknowledged that the 'Germans fight with courage & skill'.[147] By 27 November, Rommel had contained the thrust, but in mid-December he was forced to retreat, having lost 33,000 men (mainly

* Macmillan noted that he said this 'with frightful sibilant emphasis'.

captured) and 300 tanks, for which the RAF under Air Marshal Arthur Tedder deserved much of the credit.

Churchill followed the battle closely, but even at its height was able to enjoy lunch with old friends in the basement of No. 10. General Sir Reginald Barnes came on 19 November. Charles Eade was surprised to hear Churchill call him 'Reggie', while Barnes called Churchill 'old dear'.[148] Churchill was amused that an American bishop he had briefly met had been accused of burning down his own church for the insurance money.[149] The conversation turned to the Japanese Navy. 'So far as their aeroplanes were concerned,' Churchill said, 'we were of the opinion that they were not good.' It was another bad underestimation of the Japanese capability; the Mitsubishi A6M Zero was at the time the best carrier-based fighter aircraft in the world.[150] When Eade suggested that the British purchasing agents in America were buying munitions for which the United States would not be paid, Churchill 'with a flash of vigour' said, 'They will be paid. They will be paid with victory.'[151] Using a simile that was curious even for him, he then 'likened himself to a dead cat, floating on the sea, but which would eventually be washed up on the shores of victory'.[152] (He agreed with Eade that he would not want anyone else saying that of him.)

On 30 November, Churchill's sixty-seventh birthday, he had to break the news to Clementine that Esmond Romilly, her sister Nellie's twenty-three-year-old son, was missing in action in a Royal Canadian Air Force bombing run over Germany. It later transpired that he had been shot down returning over the North Sea. The number of close friends, family and colleagues of the Churchills who lost children in the Second World War was eventually to be just as high as in the First, constantly and literally bringing the horror of the conflict home to them.

At a Defence Committee meeting at 10 p.m. on 4 December, with Eden about to go to Moscow and hoping to offer Stalin ten squadrons of aircraft, Churchill exploded at the Chiefs of Staff who did not want Eden to make it too definite. Brooke wrote of Churchill's 'most awful outburst of temper, we were told that we did nothing but obstruct his intentions, we had no ideas of our own, and whenever he produced ideas we produced nothing but objections, etc. etc! Attlee pacified him once, but he broke out again, then Anthony Eden soothed him temporarily, but to no avail. Finally he looked at his papers for some five minutes, then slammed them together, closed the meeting and walked out of the room!'[153] With Dill such behaviour might have worked, but not with Brooke. 'It was pathetic and entirely unnecessary,' he noted. 'We were only trying to save him from making definite promises which he might find hard to keep later on. It is all the result of overworking himself and keeping too late hours. Such a pity. God knows where we would be without him, but God knows where we shall go with him!'

On Sunday, 7 December 1941, the Japanese attacked the US Navy base at Pearl Harbor in Hawaii, sinking or seriously damaging seven of the eight battleships stationed in the port. Over the coming days, Japan launched invasions of Malaya, the Philippines, Borneo, Thailand, Hong Kong and the Dutch East Indies. Churchill was at Chequers giving a dinner to celebrate Kathleen Harriman's twenty-fourth birthday. As they were finishing, a radio was brought into the dining room by Frank Sawyers so that Churchill and his guests could listen to the BBC nine o'clock news, a regular practice. In a spectacularly bad piece of news editing, the fact that the Japanese had attacked American ships in Hawaii came towards the end of the broadcast. Churchill immediately went to his study with Winant to telephone Roosevelt. 'Mr President, what's this about Japan?' he asked. 'They have attacked us at Pearl Harbor,' Roosevelt replied. 'We are all in the same boat now.'[154]

In his annual Mansion House Speech back on 10 November, Churchill had renewed in public the promise he had privately given Hopkins at Ditchley in January. 'Should the United States become involved in war with Japan,' he said, 'the British declaration will follow within the hour.'[155] So on the same night that he spoke to Roosevelt after the attack on Pearl Harbor, at 1 a.m. on 8 December, Churchill wrote to the Japanese Chargé d'Affaires in London declaring war. He ended the letter, 'I have the honour to be, with high consideration, Sir, Your obedient servant, Winston S. Churchill.'[156] After the war he observed, 'Some people did not like this ceremonial style. But after all, when you have to kill a man it costs nothing to be polite.'[157] He also told Eade years later that the Japanese should have been 'received at Hong Kong by an Englishman in formal morning dress with a top hat who would say to them, "By landing on this island, you have committed an act of war against the British Empire, and nobody has ever done that and survived"'.[158]

Although Germany and the United States were not yet at war, Churchill wrote in his war memoirs of his euphoria that evening:

> No American will think it wrong of me if I proclaim that to have the United States at our side was to me the greatest joy . . . So we had won after all! Yes, after Dunkirk; after the fall of France; after the horrible episode of Oran; after the threat of invasion . . . We had won the war. England would live; Britain would live; the Commonwealth of Nations and the Empire would live . . . Once again in our long Island history we should emerge, however

> mauled or mutilated, safe and victorious. We should not be wiped out. Our history would not come to an end . . . I thought of a remark which Edward Grey had made to me more than thirty years before – that the United States is like "a gigantic boiler. Once the fire is lighted under it there is no limit to the power it can generate." Being saturated and satiated with emotion and sensation, I went to bed and slept the sleep of the saved and thankful.[159]

Of the American people themselves, he wrote, 'Some said they were soft, others that they would never be united. They would fool around at a distance. They would never come to grips. They would never stand blood-letting. Their democracy and system of frequent elections would paralyse their war effort. They would be just a vague blur on the horizon to friend or foe. Now we should see the weakness of this numerous but remote, wealthy, and talkative people. But I had studied the American Civil War, fought out to the last desperate inch.'[160] He had also, unlike Hitler, Mussolini or General Hideki Tojo, the Japanese Prime Minister, visited the United States many times, crossing the country from the West Coast to the East, and had visited twenty-eight of the forty-eight states of the Union, so he knew what an angry and motivated America could do.

The morning after the attack, Churchill returned to London for an emergency Cabinet meeting. Only the previous week, he had privately predicted to the American journalist John Gunther that in the event of war the Japanese would 'fold up like the Italians', because they were 'the wops of the Far East'.[161] Once again, recourse to racial stereotyping had led him badly to underestimate a determined enemy. Fortunately Gunther did not use the quotation he had been given. Churchill effectively admitted he had been wrong when on 15 February 1942 he said in a broadcast, 'No one must underrate any more the gravity and efficiency of the Japanese war machine. Whether in the air or upon the sea, or man to man on land, they have already proved themselves to be formidable, deadly, and, I am sorry to say, barbarous antagonists.'[162] With ten operational Japanese battleships in the Pacific to America's two after Pearl Harbor, Churchill now recognized that there was 'a serious danger that the United States might pursue the war against Japan in the Pacific and leave us to fight Germany and Italy in Europe, Africa, and in the Middle East'.[163]

The US War Department threatened to suspend Lend-Lease shipments to the Middle East immediately after Pearl Harbor, and Beaverbrook had to work hard to make sure that was avoided. Churchill became convinced that his personal presence was needed in Washington as soon as possible to ensure that what became known as the 'Germany First' policy – by which the most powerful of the Axis powers was to be defeated before

Japan – remained as the Roosevelt Administration's strategic priority, even though Japan had attacked the United States and Germany had not. In fact he need not have worried, because Germany First had been the War Department's policy since long before Pearl Harbor, recognized as central to winning the war by such American strategists as General Marshall and a then fairly junior planner, General Dwight D. Eisenhower.

On 9 December, Churchill wrote to Roosevelt suggesting a visit to Washington to 'review the whole war plan in the light of reality and new facts, as well as the problems of production and distribution'.[164] In those days, the Prime Minister needed the Sovereign's permission to leave the country. 'We have to be careful', Churchill told the King in his letter requesting leave to go to the United States, 'that our share of munitions and other aid which we are receiving from the United States does not suffer more than is, I fear, inevitable.'[165] He added that he was expecting Germany and Italy to declare war on America 'as they have bound themselves by treaty to do so. I shall defer progressing my visit to the President until this situation is more clear.'[166] Churchill had misinterpreted the terms of the Axis Pact – Germany was under no obligation to declare war – but clearly a personal meeting with the President was now of the first importance.

Churchill made a formal statement to the Commons two days after the attack on Pearl Harbor. 'Winston enters the Chamber with bowed shoulders and an expression of grim determination on his face,' recorded Nicolson. 'The House had expected jubilation at the entry of America into the war and are a trifle disconcerted. He makes a dull matter-of-fact speech.'[167] Churchill could hardly have been expected to express jubilation at the deaths of nearly 3,000 Americans. Some Chamberlainite MPs saw the military disaster in the Pacific primarily in terms of British politics. Geoffrey Lloyd whispered to Chips Channon 'how lucky Winston was. Now Libya will be forgotten. Russia saved the Government in July; now Japan will do likewise.'[168]*

At lunch with the King that day, Churchill was critical of the dispositions Admiral Stark had adopted for the battleships at Pearl Harbor. 'There are only two effective U.S. ships in the Pacific,' he said, 'which means that the U.S.A. has already lost command of the sea in the Pacific. A very serious situation for our ships the *Prince of Wales* and *Repulse*

* Churchill and Roosevelt have been accused by conspiracy theorists of knowing about the attack on Pearl Harbor in advance and doing nothing to prevent it, but serious historians universally agree there is no credible evidence to support any such claim, and that it would have gone against every aspect of the President's and Prime Minister's patriotism and sense of honour.

which are out there. The reaction of Americans will probably be an attack on F.D.R.'s Administration for not being prepared, not even the Fleet. Fancy the U.S. Fleet being in harbour when the authorities must have known that Japan was already on a war footing.'[169] The following January he was still critical; in a letter to the King discussing the possibility of a Japanese invasion of Australia he wrote, 'The U.S. fleet would have prevented this from happening had her Fleet been on the high seas instead of at the bottom of Pearl Harbor where it is.'[170] This established a recurring theme of criticism of America that Churchill pursued in his private audiences with the King, saying things about Roosevelt and the alliance that he could not possibly express to anyone else other than Clementine, and which he knew would never leak. Churchill's occasional irritation and even anger with his new ally and partner are clear from the King's diary records of the Tuesday lunches. Churchill used these as a way of venting his frustrations with American policy in much the same way that Alan Brooke used his diary to vent his frustration with the Prime Minister.

On 10 December 1941, the battleship HMS *Prince of Wales*, which had taken Churchill to Placentia Bay, and the cruiser HMS *Repulse* were sunk by Japanese bombers and torpedo-aircraft off Malaya. Churchill knew the commander of the Force Z flotilla, Vice Admiral Sir Tom Phillips, as he had been vice chief of the Naval Staff when Churchill had been first lord, and had greatly admired him. Now Phillips and 840 sailors were dead.[171] Churchill has been criticized for the losses, but it was Phillips, not Churchill, who had opted to sortie from Singapore without air cover, hoping to disrupt Japanese landings on Malaya. Modern scholarship has largely absolved the Prime Minister of responsibility for the disaster.

The naval situation was now critical. The aircraft carrier HMS *Ark Royal* and the battleship HMS *Barham* had been sunk by U-boats in November 1941 in the Mediterranean; the light cruiser HMS *Neptune* was sunk by a mine off Tripoli on 19 December, when the cruisers *Penelope* and *Aurora* were also damaged; the light cruiser HMS *Galatea* was sunk off Alexandria by a U-boat on 14 December, and the battleships HMS *Valiant* and *Queen Elizabeth* were badly damaged by Italian frogmen in Alexandria Harbour on 19 December. By Christmas 1941, all that remained of Admiral Cunningham's Mediterranean Fleet was three cruisers and a few destroyers. There were no Royal Navy capital ships in the whole of the Far Eastern theatre.

Nonetheless, Churchill expected Singapore to hold out for six months. The garrison of 130,000 British, Indian and Australian troops under Lieutenant-General Arthur Percival looked strong enough to deal with any Japanese incursions. After the humiliating surrender of the garrison two months later, Churchill conceded that he had had very little knowledge of the city's landward defences. 'It had never entered my head that no circle of detached forts of a permanent character protected the rear of the famous fortress,' Churchill later wrote in his war memoirs. 'I cannot understand how it was I did not know this . . . My advisers ought to have known and I ought to have been told, and I ought to have asked.'[172]

On 11 December, the House heard the Prime Minister's statement on the attack on Force Z 'in gloomy silence'.[173] Churchill described himself as 'honoured to have established personal friendship' with Vice Admiral Phillips, and declared, 'In my whole experience I do not remember any naval blow so heavy or so painful as the sinking of the *Prince of Wales* and the *Repulse* . . . These two vast, powerful ships constituted an essential feature in our plans for meeting the new Japanese danger as it loomed against us in the last few months.'[174] Afterwards he made the same speech as a broadcast. A few days later Harvie-Watt informed him that MPs 'generally felt that you had been ill-advised to undertake that task, as it appeared to Members – and they had received similar expressions of opinion from constituents – that you were very tired, and in consequence your speech might not have had the full effect it might have'.[175] Churchill circled the words 'very tired' in red, adding 'Yes', and 'Well, who forced me? And why am I not allowed a gramophone record of a statement in the House?'[176] Commons tradition prevented the Prime Minister's speech from being broadcast from the Chamber, or even recorded in the Chamber for later broadcast.

Later that day, the long-anticipated news arrived that Germany and Italy had declared war on the United States (the only country Hitler ever formally declared war against). When Churchill heard the news, he told John Martin, 'The stars in their courses are fighting for us.'[177] He telegraphed Roosevelt to say, 'The accession of the United States makes amends for all, and with time and patience will give certain victory.'[178] For Hitler it was a literally suicidal decision.

On 12 December, Churchill lunched with the King, who recorded him saying of himself and Roosevelt, 'Together they must make a plan for the future as they are the only two people who can.'[179] Later that day, he left London by train for the Clyde with Beaverbrook, Pound, Harriman, Moran, Brigadier Hollis, Colonel Jacob, Commander Thompson and John Martin. Dill also came, as he was going to be the British liaison officer with the American Joint Chiefs of Staff. Events in the Far East were moving so quickly that Churchill decided to leave Brooke in London to oversee them. At 12.30 p.m. on 13 December, the party left on board the new

45,000-ton battleship HMS *Duke of York*, the sister ship to the *Prince of Wales*, for what was codenamed the Arcadia Conference.

With gale-force winds in the Atlantic, it was an uncomfortable journey, and a dangerous one. 'The enormous vessel rolled and heaved,' recalled Sub-Lieutenant Vivian Cox, one of Pim's Map Room assistants, 'and so did most of the passengers.'[180] 'For thirty-six hours we were within five or six hundred miles of Brest,' Churchill wrote to Clementine, 'with its bomber squadrons, and it was very fortunate that no Focke Wulf spotted us through the gaps in the clouds.'[181] Clementine had become chairman of the Red Cross Aid to Russia Fund in October, and had raised a million pounds for it. As part of the disinformation campaign over Arcadia, the newspapers showed Churchill buying an Aid to Russia badge from his wife on 16 December in London, when he was actually at sea. 'It is a horrible world at the moment,' Clementine wrote to her husband, 'Europe overrun by the Nazi hogs, and the Far East by the yellow Japanese lice.'[182]

For much of the journey, HMS *Duke of York* could not sail at much more than 6 knots for fear of losing her three-destroyer escort. They finally took the decision to leave HMS *Faulknor*, *Foresight* and *Matabele* behind on the afternoon of the 17th. In order to minimize detection by U-boats, the ship ran obliquely across the waves, making her roll heavily. 'However, once you get used to the motion,' Churchill wrote, 'you don't care a damn.'[183] There was a stifling atmosphere below decks, with no ventilation once the watertight doors were closed. Beaverbrook joked that he had never travelled in such a large submarine.[184] U-boats were constantly reported in the vicinity, and Churchill 'spoke hopefully of ramming one'.[185]

Churchill did not suffer from seasickness, which he put down to taking a double dose of Mothersill's Remedy on the first day. 'The P.M. was in constant high spirits and never turned a hair,' Cox wrote in his diary. 'He was ubiquitous . . . He must have walked miles during the voyage, and all this with a beaming face and a complexion as pink and white as any preparatory school boy.'[186] He watched a movie every night; his favourite was the Tyrone Power film *Blood and Sand*, about bullfighting. 'The cinema is a wonderful form of entertainment, and takes the mind away from other things,' he wrote.[187] He kept up a running commentary on the movies whether they were Westerns or historical dramas. 'In the wardroom movie show there was no question that Winston Churchill was every bit as entertaining as most of the films,' recorded Cox.[188] He read two novels on the journey, C. S. Forester's *Brown on Resolution* (1929) and Frederick Britten Austin's account of Napoleon in Egypt, *Forty Centuries Look Down*

(1936), and – now that Oliver Lyttelton had introduced clothes rationing – wrote to Clementine promising to buy her a few pairs of stockings.

The four memoranda that Churchill wrote for the Chiefs of Staff on board HMS *Duke of York* between 16 and 20 December, covering 7,000 words, broadly set out the strategy that the Western Allies were to follow in the next phase of the war. From not having a plan beyond mere survival, he could now, with the Russians and Americans in the war, see the way ahead clearly. The Germans had been stopped at the gates of Moscow earlier that month, and had run out of momentum there, even if they were still surging forward further south and had captured Kiev in October. 'Hitler's failure and losses in Russia are the prime fact in the war at this time,' began the first memorandum, entitled 'The Atlantic Front'. 'Neither Great Britain nor the United States have any part to play in this event, except to make sure that we send, without fail and punctually, the supplies we have promised. In this way alone we shall hold our influence over Stalin and be able to weave the mighty Russian effort into the general texture of the war.'[189] Although Hitler had by no means 'failed' up to that point, Churchill recognized that by not taking Moscow he had suffered a major strategic reverse, and the two countries' disparity in population meant that German losses could not be sustained in the same way that Russian ones could be. He nonetheless correctly predicted that the Germans might take Crimea.

For the Western Allies, Churchill said that if Vichy did not cooperate in Morocco, Algeria and Tunisia 'A campaign must be fought in 1942 to gain possession of, or conquer, the whole of the North African shore, including the Atlantic ports of Morocco.' He mentioned 'convenient landing-places in Algeria and Tunis'. He also foresaw the day that 'the Germans would take over the whole of France and rule it as Occupied territory', which eventually happened in November 1942.[190] He wanted three US divisions and one armoured division sent to Northern Ireland as 'a powerful additional deterrent against an attempt at an invasion by Germany', as well as twenty 'American bomber squadrons to come into action from the British Isles against Germany', producing 'ever more severe and more accurate bombing of their cities and harbours'.[191] He added, 'It seems probable that the Spaniards will not give the Germans a free passage through Spain to attack Gibraltar and invade North Africa.'[192]

In his second memorandum, 'The Pacific Front', Churchill predicted that the Japanese 'would strike at Burma and the Burma Road, thus isolating China. No relief is possible for Hong Kong.* The Japanese must be

* Which was lightly defended and fell in a fortnight.

expected to establish themselves on both sides of the Straits of Malacca.'[193] In the third memorandum, entitled '1943', he predicted that by early 1943 the whole North African shore and Levant 'would be in Anglo-American hands'.[194] (It happened in May of that year.) Later in 1943, 'The Russian position would be strongly established,' and 'It might be that a footing would already have been established in Sicily and Italy, with reactions inside Italy which might be highly favourable. But all this would fall short of bringing the war to an end.'[195] That could be achieved only by 'the liberation of the captive countries of Western and Southern Europe by the landing at suitable points, successively or simultaneously, of British and American armies strong enough to enable the conquered populations to revolt'.

Churchill went on to mention 'the French Channel coasts and the French Atlantic coasts' as places where that might happen during the summer of 1943.[196] In principle, he wrote, 'the landings should be made . . . disembarking not at ports but on beaches, either by landing-craft or from ocean-going ships specially adapted.' In his last memorandum, 'Notes on the Pacific', he predicted, 'We must expect to be deprived one by one of our possessions and strongpoints in the Pacific,' but the objective of the Western Allies should be to have 'a definitely superior battle fleet in the Pacific, and we must aim at May as the date when this will be achieved'.[197] (The Battle of Midway took place in June 1942.)

Although he made some incorrect predictions in these memoranda – he thought Singapore would not fall for six months, for example, and that the war could be won in 1944 – together they constitute a masterpiece of foresight and clear strategic thinking. In some of his predictions, he was only a month or two away from what actually took place. Churchill is correctly credited with showing prescience about Nazism in the 1930s and Stalinism in the 1940s, but he also deserves great credit for mapping out the course of the Second World War with extraordinary accuracy while crossing the storm-tossed Atlantic in December 1941. Although Brooke castigated Churchill in his diaries, this route to victory – from North Africa to Tripoli to Sicily to mainland Italy to the beaches of the French coast – was precisely the one he wanted to adopt too. The drawing down of German strength into Africa and the Mediterranean before the great blow was landed in Normandy was Churchill's strategy, fully supported by Brooke and the whole of the General Staff. On individual operations Brooke often opposed Churchill; over the grand strategic concept of the war in Europe, they agreed wholeheartedly.

Just before reaching the Virginia coast, Churchill told Captain Cecil Harcourt that he would like to see the *Duke of York* sail at full speed, scornful of the objection that the water was shallow and it would send up an immense wash. At 28 knots, a massive stern wave was created which, because someone had left the scuttles open, flooded several rooms between decks, including the Admiral's cabin that Churchill used, and he had to shave with his trousers rolled above his knees, 'humming a little tune to himself', Vivian Cox recalled. 'He knew he had really been rather naughty.'[198] At 2.15 p.m. on 22 December, the ship docked at Hampton Roads, Virginia. Churchill and his entourage were driven to the Norfolk aerodrome and fifty minutes later they were being greeted by President Roosevelt at Washington's National Airport, an unusual and unmistakable mark of respect. After three years of the London blackout, Churchill found it strange to see Christmas decorations illuminating the streets. He checked the beds in various rooms for comfort, and chose the Rose Bedroom (today the Queen's Bedroom) on the second floor of the White House, the same floor as the President and across the hall from what is now called the Lincoln Bedroom, where Harry Hopkins had been living since May 1940.[199]

Churchill lived in the White House for three weeks. The nearby Monroe Room was set aside as his Map Room. Once it had been announced that he was in Washington, huge numbers of presents started to arrive from American well-wishers, including hundreds of boxes of cigars. These were X-rayed by the Secret Service and only those given by people cleared by security were allowed through.* One tribute which found its way into the Prime Minister's bedroom was a 6-foot high V-sign made from lilies, carnations and irises.

Although Churchill breakfasted alone, as he always did, he lunched and dined with Roosevelt and Hopkins most days. They quickly got on first-name terms, and spent long hours together in the Map Room talking strategy. It was there that Churchill secured the movement of over 60,000 American troops to garrison Northern Ireland, after which he told Cox of Roosevelt, 'It is a great blessing for Mankind that he was called to his high office at this moment of history.'[200] The President mixed gin-based martinis in the evenings, though not for his guest who found them 'filthy'.[201] Churchill pushed Roosevelt in his wheelchair down to the elevator to take him to dinner, which he likened to Sir Walter Raleigh laying out his cloak for Queen Elizabeth I.[202] They even wandered in and out of each other's bedrooms and bathrooms, and Patrick Kinna, Churchill's stenographer, witnessed a 'naked and unashamed' Churchill joking to

* In England, the Secret Service's Lord Rothschild checked the gifts of cigars by smoking one per box.

Roosevelt, as he had his towel passed to him after a bath, 'The Prime Minister of Great Britain has nothing to conceal from the President of the United States.'[203] Yet on occasion he had; Churchill did not, for example, reveal to Roosevelt that HMS *Queen Elizabeth* and *Valiant* had been badly damaged by Italian frogmen in Alexandria Harbour on 19 December.

The first of eight major conversations between Churchill, Roosevelt, the British Chiefs of Staff and the US Joint Chiefs of Staff took place on 23 December. Churchill reacquainted himself with General George C. Marshall, the most powerful of the three US Chiefs of Staff, and effectively, though never formally, their chairman. 'I have always had a great respect for his really outstanding qualities,' Churchill was to write to Clementine in 1947, 'if not as a strategist, as an organizer of armies, a statesman, and above all a man.'[204] The low opinion he came to have of Marshall as a strategist matched the one Brooke had of both of them.

On Christmas Eve, the giant National Christmas Tree was illuminated on the White House lawn, and several thousand people gathered for speeches and carol-singing. 'I spend this anniversary and festival far from my country, far from my family, yet I cannot truthfully say that I feel far from home,' Churchill told them in his speech, which was broadcast live.

> Whether it be the ties of blood on my mother's side, or the friendships I have developed here over many years of active life, or the commanding sentiment of comradeship in the common cause of great peoples who speak the same language . . . I cannot feel myself a stranger here in the centre and at the summit of the United States . . . This is a strange Christmas Eve. Almost the whole world is locked in deadly struggle, and, with the most terrible weapons which science can devise, the nations advance upon each other . . . Let the children have their night of fun and laughter. Let the gifts of Father Christmas delight their play. Let us grown-ups share to the full in their unstinted pleasures before we turn again to the stern task and the formidable years that lie before us, resolved that, by our sacrifice and daring, these same children shall not be robbed of their inheritance or denied their right to live in a free and decent world. And so, in God's mercy, a happy Christmas to you all.[205]

Hong Kong surrendered to the Japanese on Christmas Day, as the British and American Chiefs of Staff sat together looking at ways of reinforcing the Far East by diverting convoys. When Lord Halifax, the British Ambassador to Washington, visited Churchill that evening he found him sitting in his dressing-gown preparing his speech for a Joint Meeting of Congress, 'surrounded by cigars, whiskies and sodas and secretaries!'[206] (Roosevelt's daughter Anna Boettiger described how Churchill's sneezes after his liberal use of snuff 'rock the foundations of the house and he then blows his nose about three times like a foghorn'.)[207] There had only been two Joint Meetings of Congress before in America's history, in 1874 and 1934, so this was a tremendous honour.

Churchill started his speech on 26 December with a joke: 'I cannot help reflecting that if my father had been American and my mother British, instead of the other way around, I might have got here on my own.'[208]* There was laughter and an immediate standing ovation, even from isolationists. 'I am a child of the House of Commons,' he continued.

> I was brought up in my father's house to believe in democracy. 'Trust the people' – that was his message. I used to see him cheered at meetings and in the streets by crowds of working men way back in those aristocratic Victorian days when, as Disraeli said, the world was for the few, and for the very few. Therefore I have been in full harmony all my life with the tides which have flowed on both sides of the Atlantic against privilege and monopoly, and I have steered confidently towards the Gettysburg ideal of 'government of the people, by the people, for the people' . . . In my country, as in yours, public men are proud to be the servants of the State and would be ashamed to be its masters.[209]

Churchill went on to say, 'To me the best tidings of all is that the United States, united as never before, have drawn the sword for freedom and cast away the scabbard.'[210] He spoke of how, considering the relative resources of the United Kingdom and United States, 'It becomes still more difficult to reconcile Japanese action with prudence or even with sanity. What kind of a people do they think we are?' This earned him another standing ovation, with cheers. 'Is it possible they do not realize that we shall never cease to persevere against them until they have been taught a lesson which they and the world will never forget?'[211]

That evening, while using 'considerable force' to open a stiff sash window in his bedroom, Churchill felt a pain over his heart and down his left arm, and became short of breath. 'His symptoms were those of a coronary insufficiency,' his doctor, Charles Moran, recorded. 'The textbook treatment for this was at least six weeks in bed. That would mean publishing to the world . . . that the P.M. was an invalid with a crippled heart and a doubtful future.'[212] Moran therefore 'adopted a policy of "watchful waiting"'. Although he believed that Churchill had suffered a myocardial

* Churchill always thought he would have done well in American politics. 'I could swim in those waters alright,' he told Charles Eade (CAC EADE 2/2).

infarction – essentially a heart attack – he informed neither Churchill nor his American colleagues of this. Instead, he gave him advice that it was impossible for him to follow, that he 'must try to ease up a little on his work'. On his eventual return to London, Moran got a second opinion from Dr John Parkinson, who assured Churchill that he had not had a heart attack. Modern medical analysis suggests that he may have had a muscle strain or a strain of the bony and cartilaginous chest wall.[213] Nonetheless, it was a concern for someone who still believed he would not see old age.

The Arcadia Conference concluded on 14 January 1942. It was agreed that American troops should be sent to Northern Ireland to train, and to deter invasion. Joint committees on munitions production and shipping were set up. Cooperation in intelligence-gathering was agreed upon. Joint commands were established in the north-west Europe, south-east Asia and the Mediterranean theatres of the war.[214] The south-east Asian command was called ABDA – American–British–Dutch–Australian – and placed under General Wavell. Hopkins and Beaverbrook were appointed to head the new Joint Munitions Assignment Board. The Germany First strategy was explicitly reaffirmed in writing.[215] Churchill explained the thinking behind this strategy in his statement to Congress the following year: 'It was evident that, while the defeat of Japan would not mean the defeat of Germany, the defeat of Germany would infallibly mean the ruin of Japan.'[216]

The other great achievement of the Arcadia Conference was to inaugurate a Combined Chiefs of Staff Committee (CCS) in Washington, with ultimate direction over the grand strategy of the war. Such an integrated Allied command was unprecedented and indeed revolutionary. In the Great War, planning and execution had been left up to individual armies in individual sectors, albeit under the overall command of Marshal Foch, for whom there was to be no equivalent in the Second World War. 'War,' Churchill had written in *The World Crisis*, 'which knows no rigid divisions between French, Russian and British Allies, between Land, Sea and Air, between gaining victories and alliances, between supplies and fighting men, between propaganda and machinery, which is, in fact, simply the sum of all forces and pressures operative at a given period, was dealt with piecemeal. And years of cruel teaching were necessary before even imperfect unifications of study, thought, command and action were achieved.'[217] The CCS, with its unified control over all theatres, was in large part the product of Churchill's long-held views on these matters, going back to the Great War, and was pushed through despite the suspicions of the absent Brooke, who jealously guarded British independence in strategy-making.

Marshall's close friendship with Dill, who stayed in Washington as the liaison between the CCS and the British Chiefs of Staff, helped ensure that friction was kept to a minimum. Since the British and American Chiefs met only at conferences, British independence was safeguarded in practice, and the stationing of the CCS apparatus in Washington did not affect it.

On 27 December, the Australian Prime Minister John Curtin announced that 'Australia looks to America, free of any pangs as to our traditional links or kinship with the United Kingdom.'[218] Churchill was furious. Moran claimed that Churchill said the Australians came from 'bad stock', although the remark – clearly a reference to the convict fleets – cannot be verified because Moran's diary entries were not all written contemporaneously, and his notes often do not correspond with the version of the diary he published in 1966, which was itself denounced as false by many of Churchill's entourage.[219] Nonetheless, Curtin's statement did mark the beginning of the movement of Australia from the orbit of Britain, which could not protect her effectively, to the United States, which soon could.

By the end of 1941, Britain was spending more than half her Gross Domestic Product on the war, but that was soon to be dwarfed by the American contribution. In 1940, the United States produced less than half the amount of munitions produced by the United Kingdom, in 1941 it was two-thirds, in 1942 twice as much, in 1943 nearly thrice and in 1944 almost four times the amount. Whereas in 1942 one-tenth of Britain's munitions came from America, by 1943–4 this was over a quarter and in certain important areas up to half.[220] It meant that, as time went on, the American voice in strategic counsels grew stronger, and the British consequently and proportionately weaker. Australia had chosen the stronger protector, and there was little Churchill could do about it.

On 28 December, Churchill left for Ottawa, where he stayed with the Earl of Athlone, the Governor-General of Canada, and two days later spoke to the Canadian Parliament. He left the writing of the speech so late that the last typed page had to be slipped into his hand by his private secretary after he had started speaking.[221] 'We have not journeyed across the centuries, across the oceans, across the mountains, across the prairies, because we are made of sugar candy,' he told Canadian MPs.[222] 'We shall never descend to the German and Japanese level, but if anybody likes to play rough we can play rough too. Hitler and his Nazi gang have sown the wind; let them reap the whirlwind.'

Of the Reynaud Cabinet, he said, 'When I warned them that Britain would fight on alone whatever they did, their generals told their Prime Minister and his divided Cabinet, "In three weeks England will have her neck wrung like a chicken." Some chicken! Some neck!'[223] Colin Coote later called this joke a vulgarism, and A. P. Herbert a music-hall gag, but it got a hearty laugh from the parliamentarians.[224]

Immediately after the speech, Churchill was led into the Speaker's chamber by Mackenzie King, where the young Armenian-Canadian photographer Yousuf Karsh was waiting to take his picture. He seemed reluctant as he had not been warned this would happen, but conceded that Karsh could take one photograph. 'I offered him an ash-tray for his cigar but he pointedly ignored it, his eyes boring into mine,' Karsh recalled. 'At the camera, I made sure everything was in focus, closed the lens and stood up, my hand ready to close the shutter release, when something made me hesitate.' Karsh then said, 'Forgive me, sir,' and without permission removed the cigar from Churchill's mouth. 'His jaw tightened in belligerence; his eyes blazed. I clicked the shutter.'[225] The result was the greatest of all the thousands of images of Churchill, capturing his resolution, defiance and solidity, and, as Karsh noted, also his capacity for belligerence. It was not the only photo of Churchill taken by Karsh that day – he was allowed to take at least eight others, and one with Mackenzie King after Churchill had 'assumed a more benign attitude' – but it is the one that fully deserves the overworked adjective 'iconic'. It was the cover of *Life* magazine in May 1945 and became the defining image of him, and can be seen on the dust jacket of this book.

That evening, Churchill met the Canadian flying ace Air Vice Marshal Billy Bishop, VC, CB, DSO and Bar, MC, DFC, at a dinner given by Mackenzie King. Bishop had shot down seventy-two enemy aircraft in the Great War, and Churchill's customary fascination with Paladins caused consternation among his security detail when he got into Bishop's car rather than his own at the end of the evening, swapping war stories with him on the way to Bishop's home for a nightcap, rather than returning to Government House.[226] Before leaving for Washington in the President's special train on New Year's Eve, Churchill was presented with a British Columbia sealskin wedge cap. He told a press conference that it was 'A very odd thing that when I woke up very early this morning, I thought what a pity I hadn't got one of those lovely Canadian hats . . . It fits beautifully, and is large enough to allow for any swelling that may take place.'[227]

On New Year's Day 1942, Churchill, Roosevelt, Maxim Litvinov, the Russian Ambassador to Washington, and the Chinese Ambassador signed the Joint Declaration of the United Nations, which committed Russia and China to the principles of the Atlantic Charter. This was then countersigned by twenty-two other nations the next day. They also all pledged not to make separate peace treaties with the Axis powers. Roosevelt chose the title 'United Nations' because he feared the word 'Alliance' might cause constitutional difficulties with Senate isolationists, and Churchill thought 'Associated Powers' sounded 'flat'. In support of the President's choice, Churchill showed him Byron's lines from *Childe Harold*: 'Here, where the sword United Nations drew / Our countrymen were warring on that day!'[228] It was yet another occasion that his phenomenal memory for poetry allowed him to produce the perfectly apposite wording for what was needed.

Churchill had enjoyed a good relationship with the North American press corps ever since coming back from Cuba in 1895. Although they knew he would never give away operational details – and they would not have printed them even if he had – he always supplied good copy. During the conference he gave them several memorable quips and phrases, such as 'Signor Mussolini's position is indeed unenviable; the organ grinder still has hold of the monkey's collar.'[229] Asked why Canada had not expelled the Vichy Ambassador, he replied, 'A courtyard likes to have a window.' Of Rudolf Hess he said, 'He tells us that Hitler loves England and that his heart would bleed for us if Germany had to invade Great Britain.' He played it carefully when asked whether it was vital to the war effort that Roosevelt remained president, saying, 'After a long experience of public life I have come to the conclusion that very few understand the politics of their own country – and none the politics of other countries.'[230]

On 10 January 1942, Churchill travelled to Pompano, Florida, 30 miles south of Palm Beach, to spend two days resting at a secluded villa owned by Edward R. Stettinius, the Lend-Lease administrator and later US Secretary of State. He used the alias 'Mr Lobb' (the name almost certainly chosen after Lobb's, his St James's Street cobbler) who was 'an invalid requiring quiet' with John Martin as his English butler.[231] He worked before lunch – pouches were sent daily from Washington by plane – and swam in the sea naked every day, 'rolling and plunging in the warm water like a contented dolphin'.[232] Roosevelt's principal Secret Service bodyguard, who had been assigned to Churchill, told the President afterwards that on one occasion the Prime Minister had been 'rolled by rough seas. He had then got up and shaken his fist at the sea, and been rolled again, and reduced to a state of great indignation.'[233]

In the evenings, Churchill sat on the verandah watching ships. In the spirit of the rationing in force in Britain, for breakfast he ate left-over steak from the night before. Confusion was caused in the kitchen when he refused his clam chowder and asked instead for Bovril. On 11 January, telling Roosevelt about his return journey over the telephone, he said,

'I mustn't tell you on an open line how we shall be travelling, but we shall be coming by puff-puff.'[234]

Churchill left Washington after dinner on 14 January, and Roosevelt went to the railway station to see him off. Afterwards, Hopkins 'confessed' to Dean Acheson, the Assistant Secretary of State, 'that to have Winston here more than twice a year would be very exhausting', because 'days would end at 2 a.m. or 3 a.m. and at 6.45 a.m. Churchill would open the door, slipperless, and ask if he'd done anything about what they had been discussing the previous night.'[235]

The original idea had been to travel back in HMS *Duke of York* from Bermuda, but bad news from Malaya and the stirrings of political opposition in London meant that he needed to return quickly, so he took his first flight across the Atlantic instead, on board the Boeing 314A Clipper flying boat *Berwick*, painted in olive-drab camouflage.[236] First he went to Bermuda and spoke to the House of Assembly in Hamilton, joking about the 'rough and slatternly foundations' of democracy but reaffirming his faith in it. Then he flew back home, a flight of eighteen hours and twenty-three minutes. 'I adhered to my rule in these long flights that meals should be regulated by stomach-time,' he later wrote. (He also called it 'tummy-time'.) 'When one wakes up after daylight, one should breakfast; five hours after that, luncheon. Six hours after luncheon, dinner. Thus one becomes independent of the sun, which otherwise meddles too much in one's affairs and upsets the routine of work.'[237]

He arrived at Plymouth at 9.45 a.m. on 17 January 1942. It had been a long but extremely productive journey. There had been no major disagreements with the Americans, who after months of unofficial staff talks seemed to see the overall grand strategy of the war in much the same way as the British, and proved helpful in every other respect too. Moreover, Hitler's declaration of war and Roosevelt and Marshall's commitment to Germany First meant that Churchill was no longer the supplicant he had been in 1940 and 1941. In reply to advice recommending that Churchill continue to use cautious language in dealing with the United States, he replied, 'Oh! That is the way we talked to her while we were wooing her; now that she is in the harem, we talk to her quite differently!'[238]

# 26

# Disaster
# January–June 1942

*I did not suffer from any desire to be relieved of my responsibilities. All I wanted was compliance with my wishes after reasonable discussion.*

Churchill of February 1942[1]

*When things are going well, he is good; when things are going badly, he is superb; but when things are going half-well, he is hell on earth.*

Ismay on Churchill, August 1942[2]

On 18 January 1942, Churchill reported to the War Cabinet – which now consisted of Anderson, Attlee, Wood, Eden, Morrison, Beaverbrook, Bevin, Greenwood and Lyttelton – on the outcome of the Arcadia Conference. According to the shorthand notes made by Lawrence Burgis, its stenographer, he disclosed that the 'last thing' the President had said when he 'came to see me off' was 'To the bitter end – trust me.'[3] He added that the United States was 'setting about the war with great vigour' and had 'jumped right into it', displaying her 'sense of resolve to fight it out'. The Americans understood that 'Hitler is the enemy.' They would 'do what they can re Japan – But . . . nothing would get in the way of defeating Hitler.' Although they were 'Anxious to get into combat with the enemy', there was 'Olympian calm at the White House'.[4] Pausing to reminisce about his flight back – 'I drove the plane for a bit . . . Engines purred like happy kittens' – he then gave an overview of the war. He said that Britain 'Should not have got through but for Russia', and advocated sending Russia everything possible. British aircraft and tanks should be 'all disposed of to the best of our ability' wherever they were most needed. Much therefore needed to be sent to the Eastern Front. He said that Roosevelt had approved of attacks on the North African coast, and that victory over

Germany would come, 'if we do it well . . . in '43 – if clumsily '44 or '45. Supplies of materiel and manpower are overwhelming.'[5] It was Brooke who made the worst prediction of the meeting, saying, when asked about the reinforcement of Singapore, 'If we can go on putting stuff in, it ought to be all right.'[6]

'Winston told me in private he was confident now of ultimate victory,' the King noted in his diary the following day, 'as the United States of America were longing to get to grips with the enemy and were starting out on a full-out output of men and material. The U.K. and U.S.A. are now "married" after many months of "walking out".'[7] That same day the Japanese invaded Burma, a country Churchill's father had annexed to the Empire in 1886. It was another blow. Before long Sir William Beveridge, the Liberal social reformer, was calling for Churchill to lead 'a different government'. The *Manchester Guardian* stated that 'The public disquiet about our lamentable failures in the East and about the pace of our war production needs to be met with frankness and without respect of persons,' and criticism from backbench Chamberlainites grew louder and harsher, with ever more demands that Churchill give up being minister of defence and appoint a minister of production with powers approaching his own.[8] When John Curtin, the Australian Prime Minister, said publicly that the evacuation of Singapore would be 'an inexcusable betrayal', Churchill, in Cadogan's words, 'finally lost his temper' in the War Cabinet, in the presence of the former Prime Minister of Australia, Earle Page.[9] He stayed civil by telegram, however, passing on Wavell's hope that 'a counter-stroke will be possible in February'.[10] One fillip at that difficult time was the postscript to an otherwise businesslike telegram from Roosevelt on 30 January, which read, 'It is fun to be in the same decade as you.'[11]*

Entering the Commons for the first time in three weeks, Churchill was given a civil rather than enthusiastic reception. 'He looked fat and cross,' noted the reliably malicious Chips Channon; 'it was obvious that he was disappointed by his reception.'[12] Randolph, home on leave, complained that it was 'Nothing like the reception Chamberlain got when he returned from Munich.'[13] Churchill's woes greatly increased when Rommel launched a new offensive on 21 January, which led to the evacuation of Benghazi on the 28th and Derna on 3 February, and drove the Eighth Army back to the Gazala Line that defended Tobruk. In addition Churchill had to tell the Defence Committee, 'It was apparent that we could not consider Singapore a fortress, for it seemed that no proper landward

* Often misunderstood as referring to the 1940s; in fact Roosevelt was celebrating his sixtieth birthday that day.

defences had been prepared . . . Taking the widest view, Burma was more important than Singapore. It was the terminus of our communications with China which it was essential to keep open.' As for reinforcing Malaya, 'We did not wish to throw good men after bad.'[14] By now Brooke agreed.

Eden noted that Churchill appeared tired and depressed and had a cold. 'He is inclined to be fatalistic about the House,' he observed, 'maintained that the bulk of Tories hated him, that he has done all he could and would be only too happy to yield to another, that Malaya, the Australian Government's intransigence and "nagging" in the House was more than any man could be expected to endure.'[15] Churchill was further frustrated when MPs rejected his motion to allow his speeches to be recorded in the Commons, thus forcing him to repeat them verbatim over the radio, which he found exhausting. 'The loyalties which centre upon Number One are enormous,' Churchill later wrote of prime ministers. 'If he trips he must be sustained. If he makes mistakes they must be covered. If he sleeps he must not be wantonly disturbed. If he is no good he must be pole-axed. But this last extreme process cannot be carried out every day; and certainly not in the days just after he has been chosen.'[16] In the face of the opposition he was now confronting, Churchill decided to make the next debate on the war into a motion of confidence in his Government. Harvie-Watt reported on 23 January that only 'a handful' of MPs would vote against the Government, 'though some, a larger number', might abstain.[17] Since abstentions had brought down Chamberlain, the decision was not without risk.

'It is because things have gone badly, and worse is to come, that I demand a vote of confidence,' Churchill said at the start of the three-day debate on 27 January, which was so crowded that MPs had to sit on the steps of the throne (the Commons were now sitting in the House of Lords).[18] Watching from the gallery were Clementine – 'her hair grey now', Channon noted – Diana, Pamela, Jack and his daughter Clarissa. Churchill was disarmingly honest, admitting that 'While facing Germany and Italy here and in the Nile Valley, we have never had any power to provide effectively for the defence of the Far East.'[19] 'No one need be mealy-mouthed in debate,' he declared, 'and no one should be chicken-hearted in voting. I have voted against Governments I have been elected to support, and, looking back, I have sometimes felt very glad that I did so. Everyone in these rough times must do what he thinks is his duty.'

A large number of MPs spoke in the debate, and the greatest criticisms of Churchill came from the Chamberlainite Tories, one of whom, Sir Archibald Southby, harked back to the Norway Debate, asking, 'What was the origin of the Government?' Sir Alexander Erskine-Hill spoke of 'anxiety' about the war situation; Herbert Williams said that 'There have been too many mistakes' and that Churchill should not be minister of defence; Sir James Henderson Stuart spoke of a 'deep, general uneasiness' in the nation, and Thomas Sexton said, 'The people of this country are bewildered,' while Stephen Davies accused the Government of having a 'criminal' attitude towards India and several MPs called for a new ministry of production to be set up.[20] Yet, although some threatened it, none was about to vote to bring Churchill down. 'In two and a half years of fighting we have only just managed to keep our heads above water,' Churchill admitted. 'When I was called upon to be Prime Minister, now nearly two years ago, there were not many applicants for the job. Since then, perhaps, the market has improved. In spite of the shameful negligence, gross muddles, blatant incompetence, complacency, and lack of organising power which are daily attributed to us – and from which chidings we endeavour to profit – we are beginning to see our way through. It looks as if we were in for a very bad time, but provided we all stand together, and provided we throw in the last spasm of our strength, it also looks, more than it ever did before, as if we were going to win.'[21] He added, without naming Curtin or Australia, that 'To hear some people talk, one would think that the way to win the war is to make sure that every Power contributing armed forces and every branch of these armed forces is represented on all the councils and organisations which have to be set up, and that everybody is fully consulted before anything is done. That is in fact the most sure way to lose a war.[22]

He turned to the grand strategy in North Africa. 'We have a very daring and skilful opponent against us,' he said of Rommel, 'and, may I say across the havoc of war, a great general.'[23] He was much criticized for that encomium, but he republished it in his war memoirs; it was reminiscent of his maiden speech praising the Boers and his admiring remarks about Dervish bravery in *The River War*. Churchill's code as a soldier had taught him to admire his enemy if he thought him deserving, though that in no way diminished his determination to destroy him. His main point of argument in the debate was that the strategic and political decisions to aid Russia, to go on the offensive in Libya and to accept the weakness of the Far East as a consequence 'will be found to have played a useful part in the general course of the War', despite what he called 'the unexpected naval misfortunes and the heavy forfeits which we have paid, and shall have to pay, in the Far East'.[24]

As Churchill had explained in his opening speech, it was important that those who criticized his Government should receive an answer:

> I feel entitled to come to the House of Commons, whose servant I am, and ask them . . . to give me their encouragement and to give me their aid. I have never ventured to predict the future. I stand by my original programme, blood, toil, tears and sweat, which is all I have ever offered, to which I added, five months later, 'many shortcomings, mistakes and disappointments'. But it is because I see the light gleaming behind the clouds and broadening on our path, that I make so bold now as to demand a declaration of confidence of the House of Commons as an additional weapon in the armoury of the United Nations.[25]

Churchill won by 464 votes to one – the Independent Labour MP Jimmy Maxton. During the debate Sir Archibald Southby, the Tory MP for Epsom, had referred to Randolph as 'my honourable and gallant Friend – honourable because of the circumstances of the war which brought him into this House completely uncontested, and perhaps of a military rank—' before he was shut up by the Speaker.* Afterwards Southby approached the Prime Minister to ask him to congratulate Randolph on his rapid promotion. 'Winston shook his fist in his face,' recalled a spectator. '"Do not speak to me," he shouted. "You called my son a coward. You are my enemy. Do not speak to me."'[26] Churchill was able to take most criticism of himself with equanimity, but attacks on his family or friends always brought out the tiger in him.

Churchill was fortunate in the timing of the vote. As it was being taken, the news arrived that the Germans had captured Benghazi. The Japanese were now within 18 miles of Singapore, and after the debate a statement was finally released disclosing that the battleship HMS *Barham* had been sunk off Egypt in November with the loss of 862 lives. (The news of the damage to HMS *Queen Elizabeth* and *Valiant* by Italian frogmen in Alexandria Harbour in December remained embargoed.) It was now twenty months since Churchill had been chosen to lead the country, and then by less than a handful of people. By early 1942, with the whole of Western Cyrenaica in Axis hands, he was highly conscious of the pressing political as well as military need for an unequivocal victory in the Desert.

On 1 February, the Germans added a fourth rotor wheel to their U-boats' Enigma coding machines. This plunged the Ultra decrypts for German naval 'Shark' codes into gobbledygook for almost a year, until Bletchley was able to break back into the code in December. Shipping losses escalated alarmingly as a result, because the U-boat wolfpacks could

* MPs traditionally refer to one another as 'honourable' Members, and 'gallant' is added where the Member was or had been in the armed forces. Southby's sneer lay in his purporting to explain what, uttered by any other MP, was a simple courtesy.

not be located, and any hope for a cross-Channel attack had to be postponed until the Battle of the Atlantic had been won. In January, a total of 419,907 tons of British, Allied and neutral shipping was sunk, but in February it was 679,532 tons and in March 834,164 tons. In the calendar year 1942 nearly eight million tons was lost.[27] 'Poor Winston very desperate', noted Cadogan.[28]

Brooke informed the Cabinet in early February that the remaining Commonwealth forces in Malaya had withdrawn inside Singapore, where they had four months' supply of food and water. Churchill said that it was the 'Will of the Cabinet to defend it to the last'.[29] He cabled Wavell, 'There must at this stage be no thought of saving the troops or sparing the population. The battle must be fought to the bitter end at all costs.'[30] 'The PM is worried and angry over events in the Far East,' the King noted on 3 February. 'Singapore has not been fortified from the landward side even with tank traps and pill-boxes hidden in the jungle. These could have been done by the troops themselves. 15" guns pointing out to sea are no form of defence.'[31]

On 5 February, Churchill proposed to the Cabinet that he personally go to India to make an offer to the Congress Party of post-war independence if they would suspend their campaign of civil disobedience adopted in October 1940 and instead cooperate with the British and help defend India from the Japanese. Cadogan thought the plan 'brilliantly imaginative and bold', but with the situation in Malaya 'he must remain here to take the bump' should Singapore, on its southern tip, fall.[32] 'We must fight the Japanese for the honour of our race, the Empire and the Army without thought of saving our troops or sparing the population of seven hundred thousand,' Churchill told the King at lunch on 10 February. 'When the Japs land we must kill them in the swamps, and in the jungle. We cannot allow our country's reputation and our race to fall while the Russians are fighting back hard and the U.S. troops at Luzon in the Philippines are putting up a stubborn defence.' Yet he acknowledged that he had few reserves to put into the fight, and that the situation was perilous. 'Winston is prepared for a series of misfortunes in the Far East if Singapore falls, as we cannot get reinforcements there in a moment,' noted the King, 'and we don't know where to put them.'[33]

As anxiety about Singapore rose, the Germans pulled off the humiliating Operation Cerberus, which became known to Britons as the 'Channel Dash'. Between 11 and 13 February, the *Scharnhorst*, *Gneisenau* and *Prinz Eugen* sailed from Brest up the English Channel without the Admiralty being able to do anything about it: they had no capital ships off the south coast with which to engage them. 'I'm afraid, sir,' Pound telephoned an incredulous and dismayed Churchill, 'I must report that the enemy battlecruisers should by now have reached the safety of their home waters.' Churchill went quiet, then asked, 'Why?' He put the phone down before Pound had a chance to go through the litany of errors that had taken place.[34] Cadogan described it as 'The blackest day, yet, of the war.'[35] Attacks by the RAF, Fleet Air Arm,* Royal Navy and coastal artillery had failed to do more than scratch the enemy vessels. Harold Nicolson thought people were more distressed about the escape of the *Scharnhorst* and *Gneisenau* than by the prospective loss of Singapore: 'They cannot bear the thought that the Germans sailed past our front door.'[36]

Beaverbrook, whom Churchill had recently appointed to the new position of minister of war production, had soon clashed badly with Bevin and others in the Government, and his newspapers were openly promoting the Second Front and undermining key ministers. Churchill rowed with Clementine over the appointment. 'My Own Darling,' she wrote when Beaverbrook was just eight days in the job, 'I am ashamed that by my violent attitude I should just now have added to your agonising anxieties – Please forgive me. I do beg of you to reflect whether it would not be best to leave Lord Beaverbrook entirely out of your Reconstruction . . . Is not hostility without better than intrigue and treachery and rattledom† within? . . . The temper & behaviour you describe (in Lord B) is caused I think by the prospect of a new personality equal perhaps in power to him and certainly in intellect. My darling, try ridding yourself of this microbe which some people fear is in your blood. Exorcise this bottle Imp and see if the air is not clearer and purer.'[37] The 'new personality' was Sir Stafford Cripps, who had finally returned from Moscow and was immensely popular as he was identified with the Red Army's great sacrifices. Outside the Government, he was the focus for all the hopes of those, especially on the left, who felt they had no voice because Labour was in the coalition. He refused Churchill's offer of the Ministry of Supply, preferring to wait and see if he might be in a position to take Churchill's own place instead. Nor was he the only candidate. 'Everyone is in a rage against the Prime Minister,' Chips Channon wrote of the Channel Dash. 'Rage; frustration. This is not the post-Dunkirk feeling, but ANGER . . . were Londoners Latins there would be rioting. I have never known so violent an outburst . . . there is some talk about the formation of a so-called "Centre Party" composed of Liberals, disgruntled Conservatives, etc., with Beaverbrook at its head.'[38]

* Founded in 1924, the Fleet Air Arm was a revival of the Royal Naval Air Service that Churchill had created in 1914.

† That is, the behaviour of a rattlesnake.

The next day, Churchill ordered the new chief of Bomber Command, Sir Arthur 'Bert' or 'Bomber' Harris, to destroy German civilian morale, a task that Harris set about with relish. Large, four-engined bombers were coming into production in early 1942, but Lindemann had ascertained that the night bombing had been doing little damage to specified targets compared to the much more accurate but expensive daylight bombing. Churchill wanted to show Stalin that Britain was actively helping draw German resources away from the Eastern Front and show the British people that they were hitting back, so the criteria for what constituted a legitimate target were widened. Factories, railway yards, port facilities and industrial areas were all now included. There was little debate, at least at this stage in the war, about whether 'de-housing' the enemy by bombing workers' homes should be considered a war crime. Defending Germany against Harris's bombers tied up vast amounts of German resources, Luftwaffe planes and manpower, and although German arms production continued to increase until the late spring of 1943, it did not do so at anything like the rate it would have otherwise.[39]

At 4 p.m. on Sunday, 15 February 1942, the news arrived at the War Office that General Percival had surrendered Singapore to the Japanese. More than 80,000 Commonwealth troops, including many Australians, were taken prisoner. 'India is naked,' noted General John Kennedy. 'Ceylon, the main fleet base, very bare. Fighting is going on near Rangoon . . . Australia (and the base at Port Darwin) is also comparatively defenceless.'[40] In his broadcast to the nation at 9 p.m., Churchill made no attempt to minimize the catastrophe. 'I speak to you all under the shadow of a heavy and far-reaching military defeat,' he said. 'It is a British and Imperial defeat. Singapore has fallen. All the Malay Peninsula has been overrun.'[41] He nonetheless celebrated the fact that America was now in the war:

> That is what I have dreamed of, aimed at and worked for, and now it has come to pass. But there is another fact, in some ways more immediately effective. The Russian armies have not been defeated, they have not been torn to pieces. The Russian people have not been conquered or destroyed. Leningrad and Moscow have not been taken. The Russian armies are in the field . . . Here, then, are two tremendous fundamental facts which will in the end dominate the world situation and make victory possible in a form never possible before.[42]

There was an implied admission that Britain could not have won otherwise.

'To-night the Japanese are triumphant,' he continued. 'They shout their exultation round the world. We suffer. We are taken aback. We are hard pressed. But I am sure even in this dark hour that "criminal madness" will be the verdict which history will pronounce upon the authors of Japanese aggression, after the events of 1942 and 1943 have been inscribed upon its sombre pages.'[43] 'No one must underrate any more the gravity and efficiency of the Japanese war machine,' he said, which he himself had undoubtedly done.[44] In closing he tried to reinvigorate the Blitz spirit of 1940–41. 'This, therefore, is one of those moments when the British race and nation can show their quality and their genius . . . when it can draw from the heart of misfortune the vital impulses of victory. Here is the moment to display that calm and poise combined with grim determination which not so long ago brought us out of the very jaws of death.'[45]

'His broadcast', thought Nicolson, 'was not well liked. The country is too nervous and irritable to be fobbed off with fine phrases. Yet what else could he have said?'[46] In the House of Lords, Hankey and Chatfield attacked Churchill for concentrating power too much in his own hands. 'It is wrong to depend so much on one man who is so temperamental,' General Kennedy wrote after listening to Churchill's speech, 'so lacking in strategical knowledge and in judgment despite his other great qualities.'[47] The Prime Minister had woefully underestimated the Japanese, and had done very little to protect the Empire he loved, but did this mean he would be ousted? Goebbels was noting in his diary at the time, 'England has nobody to put in his place.'[48] That wasn't quite true. Cripps and Beaverbrook were clearly manoeuvring for the job, but neither was poised to strike so soon after the last confidence motion.

Despite the almost unanimous vote at the end of the parliamentary debate, the endless criticism finally got to Churchill. Commander Thompson noticed 'an increasing sense of frustration and depression. To some of those closest to him he hinted that he was seriously thinking of handing over his responsibilities.'[49] He told Captain Pim that he was 'tired of it all', saying that he was thinking of resigning. 'By God, sir,' Pim exclaimed. 'You cannot do that!'[50] Yet he was unrepentant about the priorities he had set. Had the 450 aircraft shipped by Britain to Russia by September 1941 gone instead to Singapore, Kennedy had argued, they might have slowed down the Japanese advance.[51] 'If the Malay Peninsula has been starved for the sake of Libya and Russia,' Churchill nonetheless told Attlee, 'no one is more responsible than I, and I would do exactly the same again.'[52] He was capable of differentiating the important but ultimately peripheral from the strategically vital, and keeping Russia in the war was very much the latter. At the Other Club, H. G. Wells wagered Lord Camrose £100 'that the British will not recover Singapore in three years'.[53] They did not, but whether they did or not did not matter compared to the vital importance of helping the Soviets fight the Nazis.

Churchill expressed his frustration to the King at the criticisms of his leadership. 'He was very angry over all this,' the King noted, 'and compares it to hunting the tiger with angry wasps around him.'[54] Little did the Prime Minister know that the King himself was a bit of a wasp. After the fall of Singapore and the Channel Dash, he had told Sir Alec Hardinge, his private secretary, to 'find out what is in people's minds over all of this, to give me a line to go on when I see the PM'. Hardinge saw Eden and Cranborne. 'Both are agreed and so is everyone else that Winston is the right, and indeed the only, person to lead the country through the war,' Hardinge reported. 'But there is a growing feeling that owing to his innumerable preoccupations, there may well be aspects of Defence which do not get all the attention that they should. This feeling is developing into one of exasperation, as our reverses continue . . . The extension of the war to the Pacific is imposing too great a burden for any one individual to carry.'[55]

Churchill was received in silence when he entered the Chamber on 17 February to announce the fall of Singapore and explain the Channel Dash. 'MPs were caustic and sniffy,' Maisky reported. 'They gave Churchill a bad reception and send-off. I've never seen anything like it.'[56] Channon agreed. 'Never have I known the House growl at a Prime Minister. Can he ever recover his waning prestige? . . . Certainly nothing he has ever touched – Dardanelles, Abdication, India Bill – has come off well.'[57] The Dardanelles expedition had taken place twenty-seven years before, yet whenever Churchill was perceived to have made an error, it immediately reappeared in the roll of shame. 'However tempting it might be to some when much trouble lies ahead', Churchill told the Commons, 'to step aside adroitly and put someone else up to take the blows, the heavy and repeated blows, which are coming, I do not intend to adopt that cowardly course, but, on the contrary, to stand to my post and persevere in accordance with my duty as I see it.'[58] At lunch the next month he said to Robert Barrington-Ward, the editor of *The Times*, 'I am an old man. Not like Lloyd George, coming out of the last war at fifty-six or so. I may be seventy before this war ends . . . No man my age has had to bear such disasters as I have.'[59] Barrington-Ward noted that he did not sound old when he said it.

To placate opinion, keep his post of minister of defence and perhaps also to distract attention from the cascade of recent bad news, Churchill instituted another wide-ranging Government reshuffle on 19 February. Cripps was persuaded to join the Government as lord privy seal and leader of the House of Commons. Beaverbrook, preparing to be the Government's candid critic and, he hoped, prime minister-in-waiting, resigned from the Ministry of Production 'on health grounds' after only fifteen days in the job, and was replaced by the businessman Oliver Lyttelton. 'People don't resign in war,' Churchill had told Beaverbrook. 'You either die or are sacked!'[60] But Beaverbrook did resign, just as Churchill had himself resigned in November 1915. The Cabinet Secretary Edward Bridges later spoke of how 'he had rarely in his life been so shocked as he was by the final interview between the Beaver and Winston . . . they abused each other like a pair of fishwives'.[61] As Ian Jacob observed, however, 'Churchill could afford to lose Beaverbrook, but he couldn't afford to lose Bevin.'[62] Nonetheless Churchill offered Beaverbrook the ambassadorship to Washington the next month – without telling Halifax. It was refused.

As secretary for war during the disasters, Margesson had to take responsibility for them. Churchill's letter to him was a model of its kind. 'My dear David,' he wrote, 'I am very sorry to tell you that the reconstruction of the Government which the pressure of events and opinion has rendered necessary, makes me wish to have the War Office at my disposal . . . I think you have done extremely well . . . I hope you will keep in touch with me, and let me have the benefit of your advice from time to time.'[63] Margesson replied equally graciously: 'I hope that my going will make things easier for you and to some extent lighten your almost unbearable burden. I hate leaving the War Office; but what do personal feelings matter in days like these.'[64] The highly competent Sir James Grigg replaced him, and stayed in the post for the rest of the war.

Attlee was given the newly created position of deputy prime minister and also became dominions secretary. This meant he would now chair all Cabinet meetings when Churchill was away. The Ministry of Economic Warfare was taken from Dalton and given to Lord Wolmer (who inherited the Earldom of Selborne a week later) and Lord Cranborne became colonial secretary and leader of the House of Lords, two moves that Nicolson described as 'the reinstatement of the upper class'.[65] With Greenwood retiring and Kingsley Wood leaving the War Cabinet, that body was reduced from nine to seven: Churchill, Attlee, Eden, Cripps, Anderson, Bevin and Lyttelton. Reith left the Government altogether, happy to escape what in his diary he called 'Churchill and his rotten gang'.[66]

'He was gloomy about the future,' the King noted after his lunch with Churchill on 24 February, 'as he cannot see how we can reinforce any part of the world sufficiently. The shipping position prevents us moving more than three divisions in the year, we would like to move ten . . . Burma, Ceylon, Calcutta and Madras in India and part of Australia may fall into enemy hands. Can we stick together in the face of all this adversity? We must somehow. Winston is feeling the strain I can see . . . I told him the country was behind him. He thought because there was no one else.'[67]

In early March Churchill appointed Brooke to take Pound's place as chairman of the Chiefs of Staff Committee. Pound had performed badly over the Channel Dash and was starting to suffer from narcolepsy, though he was not removed from the post of first sea lord.[68] Churchill found a way of breaking the news gently. 'You are in a different position from the other two Chiefs of Staff because you are conducting the naval war over its whole spread in direct contact with the enemy and are in fact a Super Commander-in-Chief,' he wrote. 'You know I have the greatest confidence in your judgment and in your handling of the Fleet.'[69]

'Poor old PM in a sour mood and a bad way,' Cadogan noted on 4 March. 'I don't think he's well and I hear he's played out.'[70] The next day he added, 'Poor old Winston, feeling deeply the present situation and the attack on him, is losing his grip I fear.' At dinner at Claridge's Hotel that evening, General Kennedy, Robert Skelton, the managing editor of the *Daily Telegraph*, and Sir Archibald Rowlands, Permanent Under-Secretary at the Ministry of Aircraft Production, all agreed that 'Winston was finished.' Skelton unpatriotically added, 'He almost wished for another big disaster because it would finish Winston.'[71] Hankey, on his last day in government, told Kennedy, 'Everybody felt that Winston was a gambler whose gambles did not come off.'[72] Churchill was aware of the precariousness of his position, telling Malcolm MacDonald, the son of the former Prime Minister, 'I am like a bomber pilot. I go out night after night, and I know that one night I shall not return.'[73]

Thus it is wrong to think that the British Establishment wholeheartedly supported Churchill's premiership in the darkest days of the Second World War: it tolerated him for the lack of a viable alternative and because he was still popular with the public. It also refused to acknowledge that many of the defeats for which he was being blamed were directly attributable to the failure to heed his warnings and adopt his rearmament proposals in the 1930s. At a deeper level, he could not be forgiven for having been proved right about their flagship policy of those years: appeasement.

On 7 March Rangoon fell and the Japanese threat to India became very serious. Australia, which had lost a large number of troops in Singapore, refused to commit any more to Burma, and demanded the return of the rest from the Middle East, fearing a direct threat to her mainland after the northern port of Darwin had been heavily bombed on 19 February. It now seemed that Malta could not possibly hold out much longer under the sustained Axis bombing campaign. Auchinleck continued to refuse Churchill's calls for an early renewal of the desert offensive, there was a desperate shortage of shipping, and Roosevelt seemed to question the Germany First policy in his cables and was doubting the wisdom of Churchill's proposed attack on French North Africa codenamed Operation Gymnast.

It was at this moment that the British Prime Minister chose to publish an article in the *Sunday Dispatch* entitled 'Are There Men on the Moon?' which he had written before the war. It predicted 'journeys through space in vessels carrying supplies of food and oxygen to the moon and the nearer planets'. Churchill wrote that he was not 'so immensely impressed by the success we are making of our civilization here that I am prepared to think we are the only spot in this immense universe which contains living, thinking creatures, or that we are the highest type of mental and physical development which has ever appeared in the vast compass of space and time'.[74] No one seems to have asked why, at this critical juncture of the war, Churchill was publishing articles about extra-solar planets and whether there was intelligent life elsewhere in the universe. He was in many respects a profoundly eccentric and unpredictable person.

Churchill was so concerned about 'people sending messages causing despair, alarm and confusion' that in March 1942 he considered imposing some form of domestic censorship, starting with the *Daily Mirror*, whose speculation about future operations came close to damaging national security. 'Got to face this,' Churchill told his colleagues. 'Censorship dealing with expressions of opinion damaging to the national morale . . . Parliament must give us more powers – very few would vote against it. We are now being disintegrated [*sic*] in morale.'[75] Cripps agreed and Grigg said that there ought to be censorship of messages liable to damage Army morale, but Brooke said he would look at any such proposals 'with the greatest alarm' as it might alienate the press.[76] Churchill added that he wanted 'More effective control over the Press' and of 'messages in and out of the country'. Nothing came of it, but it was indicative of Churchill's deep anxiety about the fragility of national morale at the time.

Churchill soon realized he could not himself go to India to persuade the Congress Party to drop its anti-British campaign and concentrate on helping to defend the sub-continent against the Japanese. Instead, Cripps was sent out to conduct talks with Mohandas Gandhi. Congress rejected any proposal that would give Britain even a partial continuing measure of constitutional connection with India, and by 9 August Gandhi and the Congress leaders had to be jailed, as the British and Indian armies struggled to hold the Japanese back from the gates of India. The King had never been to India, but he was deeply concerned about the situation there. 'It is like a three legged stool,' Churchill explained. 'Hindustan, Pakistan and Princestan. The latter two legs, being minorities, will remain under our rule.'[77] That was not Gandhi's plan. On 24 May he said, 'Leave India in God's hands, in modern parlance, to anarchy, and that anarchy may lead to internecine warfare for a time, or to unrestricted dacoities [gang-robberies]. From these a true India will arise in place of the false one we see.'[78] Churchill was not about to condemn the sub-continent to Gandhi's outlandish prescription. Neither had he been in accord with Gandhi's advice to Britons during the London Blitz: 'Invite Hitler and Mussolini to take what they want of the countries you call your possessions. Let them take possession of your beautiful island with its many beautiful buildings. You will give all this, but neither your minds nor your souls.'[79]

If Britons felt disinclined to go along with the Mahatma's proposal, they may have recognized that it was at least consistent with his earlier suggestions to Ethiopians to 'allow themselves to be slaughtered' by the Italians, since, 'after all, Mussolini didn't want a desert', and his proposition to German Jews after the Kristallnacht atrocity that if they would only adopt his philosophy of non-violent action 'what has today become a degrading man-hunt can be turned into a calm and determined stand offered by unarmed men and women possessing the strength of suffering given to them by Jehovah', as that would convert the SS 'to an appreciation of human dignity'.[80] In May 1940 Gandhi told a friend, 'I do not consider Hitler to be as bad as he is depicted. He is showing an ability that is amazing and seems to be gaining his victories without much bloodshed.'[81] In his last letter to Hitler, on December 1941, Gandhi praised the Führer's 'bravery [and] devotion to your Fatherland . . . Nor do we believe that you are the monster described by your opponents.'[82] Gandhi was fortunate that it was the Viceroy who ruled India rather than Hitler; the Führer's advice to Lord Halifax when they met at Berchtesgaden in 1937 had been 'Shoot Gandhi.'[83]

The King recorded Churchill's delight on 10 March that the Americans were sending divisions to Australia and New Zealand 'as soon as can be, so that existing Australian and New Zealand divisions can remain in the Middle East, and thus save shipping. This is a great move on the part of the USA.'[84] Of General Douglas MacArthur's appointment in Australia, Churchill added, 'We can now leave that part of the Pacific area to USA while we concentrate on the Indian Ocean and Ceylon area . . . The most important thing to remember is that we and USA must not fall out over details of strategy.'[85]

On 15 March, Churchill invited Maisky to Chequers for Sunday lunch so that he could receive a message from Stalin saying that 1942 should be the decisive year of the war. 'The PM, dressed in his habitual siren suit, greeted me in jovial, friendly fashion and apologized for his domestic appearance,' Maisky wrote. 'Having undergone a minor operation* today, he had been unable to return to the city and was obliged to receive me at home.'[86] Eden was present, and together they discussed the Baltic States in the light of America's refusal to recognize their annexation by the USSR. When Maisky asked what he thought of Stalin's statement about 1942, 'Churchill's countenance darkened immediately. He shrugged his shoulders and uttered with slight irritation: "I don't see how 1942 can become the decisive year."'[87] He pointed out that whereas Russia felt stronger in 1942 than in 1941, 'I feel weaker. Last year we had to fight against two major powers, this year – against three.' He then brought up issues of press, Parliament and production. 'There followed a long, animated, and at times even heated' exchange of opinions about opening up the Second Front, in which 'the Prime Minister resolutely avoided making any specific commitments.'[88]

When the conversation returned to India, Maisky wrote that his host:

> responded with considerable anger and irritation. 'Cripps won't be able to do anything there,' he uttered curtly . . . 'In general, the Indians are not a historic nation. Who has not conquered them? Whoever came to India from the north became her master. Throughout their history the Indians have barely ever enjoyed true independence . . . I'm prepared to leave India this very moment . . . But what would happen then? . . . If we leave, fighting will break out everywhere, there'll be a civil war. Eventually, the Muslims will become masters, because they are the warriors, while the Hindus are windbags. Yes, windbags!'[89]

Maisky thought Churchill seemed in 'a twilight mood', and recorded him saying, 'I'm not long for this world . . . I'll be ashes soon.'[90]

Maisky also told Churchill that Russia expected that gas would be used by the Germans in their next offensive. In response, the Prime Minister told the War Cabinet that he thought Britain should 'treat the use of gas against Russia as against us – we would retaliate against Germany – we make common cause with Russia over that and would . . . consider we could deter Germany by making an announcement – if . . . Stalin wanted us to do so we need plenty of warning. Go into gas mask situation. Furbish them up and good thing to use them every day.'[91] Brooke thought they

* Cadogan mentioned a 'small operation' and Oliver Harvey a 'mysterious minor operation' in their diaries on that day too. We do not know what it was.

had to 'Work out carefully what our reserves are. Must go 100% out if we start.' In fact Britain never made the threat, and gas was never used on the battlefields of the Second World War.

'Here is a thought from this amateur strategist,' Roosevelt cabled Churchill on 18 March. 'There is no use giving a single further thought to Singapore or the Dutch East Indies. They are gone. Australia must be held and . . . we are willing to undertake that. India must be held and you must do that . . . and I think you can hold Ceylon . . . You must hold Egypt, the Canal, Syria, Iran and the route to the Caucasus.'[92] In effect, Roosevelt wanted Churchill to agree in principle to the British taking responsibility for all that lay west of Singapore, 'the Gibraltar of the East' as it had once been called, while the United States would concentrate on the Pacific.[93] 'I know you will not mind my being brutally frank with you when I tell you that I think that I can personally handle Stalin better than either your Foreign Office or my State Department,' he continued. 'Stalin hates the guts of all your top people. He thinks he likes me better, and I hope he will continue to do so.'[94] In fact, Stalin saw both capitalist leaders in much the same light.

'Just now I am having a very rough time,' Churchill told Smuts, 'but we must remember how much better things are than a year ago, when we were all alone. We must not lose our faculty to dare, particularly in dark days.'[95] That day starving Malta, which had endured her thousandth air raid the previous December, was finally reached by two merchantmen, the *Talabot* and the *Pampas*, which escaped German bombers and provided supplies that allowed the island to fight on, although the 5,000 tons that arrived was only a fraction of the 26,000 tons that had left Egypt. 'The reward justified the price exacted,' Churchill wrote in his war memoirs. 'Revictualled and replenished with ammunition and vital stores, the strength of Malta revived, regaining the dominating position in the Central Mediterranean.'[96]

Brooke told the War Cabinet on 30 March that the German invasion of Russia could result in two million German casualties. 'It came from God – we did nothing about it,' Churchill said. 'The war can't end in 1942 – optimistically 1943.'[97] Churchill was never short of critics in the War Office, but they often held contradictory opinions over the precise nature of his supposed strategic incompetence. Brooke confided to his diary on 1 April his 'growing conviction that we are going to lose this war unless we control it very differently and fight it with more determination'.[98] The blame lay in the fact that all politicians were bad strategists, and having 'a government with only one big man in it, and that one man a grave danger in many respects', made matters worse. General John Kennedy criticized Churchill for reinforcing Singapore instead of Rangoon, and wrote that 'All our troubles in the Mediterranean now would have been avoided if we had gone to Tripoli instead of Greece.' Yet five days later he was noting that Rangoon could not be defended in the absence of naval cover and that 'Greece may have delayed the German operations in Russia sufficiently to tip the scale against them last autumn.'[99]

At lunch with Eden, Harriman and Ismay on 2 April, someone suggested to Churchill that he give up the Ministry of Defence on health grounds. 'Winston made it plain' that he would not, Eden recorded, because 'He sees himself in Roosevelt's position as sole director of war.'[100] Eden privately noted, 'It is not what the country wants, nor does it produce good results.' If even those three staunch supporters were discussing the possibility of his renouncing the supreme direction of Britain's war-fighting, the political threat was clearly serious. 'There is no day-to-day direction of the war except by Chiefs of Staff and Winston,' Eden wrote in his diary, 'the Chiefs of Staff are only too ready to compromise where issues should be decided and Winston's unchecked judgement is by no means infallible.' This was unfair; the Chiefs of Staff regularly checked Churchill's more ill-judged ideas, but Eden considered caballing with Lyttelton and Cripps when the latter returned from India. He wanted to try to force Churchill to be more collegiate in decision-making, but accepted that the 'difficulty is Winston is probably constitutionally incapable of working any other way'.[101]

Eden was Churchill's lieutenant, closest ally and political heir, but it is evident that even he was greatly frustrated by the extent to which the Prime Minister failed to delegate power. 'The truth is, I am much troubled about the present methods of conducting the war, and am in some doubt what I should do,' Eden complained to Cranborne, his closest friend in politics.

> There is no real improvement, no greater order since the change. Winston continues to keep the military side entirely in his hands in contact with the Chiefs of Staff. One would not boggle at that if the results were good, but they're not! . . . What troubles me is that I, and I suppose other members of the War Cabinet, are regarded by the public as those running this war, and we don't one little bit. Even the Defence Committee doesn't . . . I still believe that the right way to run this war is by a small Cabinet of four or five that meets daily, but I don't believe that Winston would ever accept that. Altogether I am most unhappy . . . But my colleagues seem perfectly content and anyway I didn't want to talk to them about this before I have spoken to Winston, which I propose to do next week. I really feel that I would much rather be out of the Government than continually accepting responsibility for decisions of which I know nothing.[102]

Thus even Eden was actively considering turning himself into a candid critic outside the Government, so inoculating himself against blame for further defeats, and keeping himself among the front-runners for the premiership should Churchill fall.

In March and April, Churchill used the information he gleaned from Ultra decrypts provided by Bletchley Park, which was still able to read German non-naval codes, to try to persuade Auchinleck that Rommel had far fewer tanks than his intelligence staff were telling him he had. But he had been misreading the decrypts – the numbers referred to tanks in certain areas, not overall – and by the end of April he admitted as much to Auchinleck.[103] Seemingly chastened, Churchill made no attempt to use decrypts in the Western Desert for the next seven months, yet the experience did not encourage him to revise his declining view of Auchinleck as a strategist, however much he admired him as a person. He had begun to consider replacing him with General Harold Alexander, a fellow aristocrat, Old Harrovian and amateur painter, who had won gallantry awards in the Great War and had distinguished himself in the Dunkirk and Burma campaigns.

On 9 April, 35,000 American troops had been captured on the Bataan Peninsula in the Philippines, the largest surrender in American history. Major reverses of this kind worried Churchill lest it persuade the Americans to ditch the Germany First policy and concentrate instead upon defeating Japan. George Marshall and Harry Hopkins arrived in London the next day, bringing what became known as the Marshall Memorandum. Far from stepping away from Germany First, this contained proposals for Operation Roundup, the major Anglo-American cross-Channel assault prepared for some time in 1943 (which ultimately became Operation Overlord, launched on D-Day in 1944), and Operation Sledgehammer, a smaller, mainly British landing in north-west France – seizing Cherbourg or Brest – in 1942, to be launched as an emergency if Russia looked to be on the verge of capitulating. There was also Operation Bolero, whereby a large American force would be sent to Britain as a prerequisite for either.

Churchill and Brooke had serious reservations about the advisability of Sledgehammer, as they believed that any attack on the Cherbourg Peninsula could be too easily bottled up and would not draw off the number of divisions from Russia that the Americans hoped and the Russians needed. Churchill wanted instead to undertake Operation Jupiter in Norway or Gymnast in North Africa. Yet the British could not simply turn down Marshall's ideas because they were eager for the Americans to send men to protect the United Kingdom under Bolero, and had to protect the

Germany First policy. Churchill and Brooke did want to undertake Roundup until a much later stage. Delicate negotiations were therefore needed. Western strategy was ultimately to be made through the interaction of the political masters, Roosevelt and Churchill, and their two most senior staff officers, Marshall and Brooke, and much of it can be viewed through the prism of the way these four men worked with one another, especially in relation to their shifting views over the timing of the decisive cross-Channel attack. At present, Churchill and Brooke knew that, although Marshall wanted this grand assault to take place earlier rather than later, Roosevelt did not.[104]

Hopkins was invited to Chequers for the weekend of 11–12 April. A telegram arrived there from Roosevelt at three o'clock on Sunday morning which criticized the breakdown of the Cripps–Gandhi talks: 'The deadlock has been caused by the unwillingness of the British Government to concede to the Indians the right to self-government . . . during the war.'[105] Roosevelt suggested that Churchill should immediately 'set up a nationalist government similar in essence to our own form of government under the Articles of Confederation' of 1781. Churchill resented this as an unwarranted American interference in British Empire matters. According to Hopkins's scribbled notes, 'Churchill refused to be responsible for a policy which would throw the whole subcontinent of India into utter confusion while the Japanese invader was at its gates.'[106] Instead, he offered to resign, 'if that would do any good in assuaging American public opinion'. It is doubtful he meant it seriously, although he did later state that if the Cabinet had not supported him over India, the centrepiece of the Empire, 'I would not have hesitated to lay down my personal burden, which at times seemed more than a man could bear.'[107]

Churchill chose his words carefully in composing his reply. 'You know the weight which I attach to everything you say to me,' he began. 'Anything like a serious difference between you and me would break my heart, and would surely deeply injure both our countries at the height of this terrible trouble.'[108] (His rather different post-war judgement was that 'States which have no overseas colonies or possessions are capable of rising to moods of great elevation and detachment about the affairs of those who have.')[109] He then turned to the military strategy for Roundup, continuing,

> I am in entire agreement in principle with all you propose, and so are the Chiefs of Staff. We must of course meet day-to-day emergencies in the east and west while preparing for the main stroke . . . I have no doubt that I shall be able to send you our complete agreement. I may say that I thought the

> proposals made for an interim operation in certain contingencies this year met the difficulties and uncertainties in an absolutely sound manner. If, as our experts believe, we can carry this whole plan through successfully, it will be one of the grand events in all the history of the war.[110]

This too was disingenuous; Churchill knew from the minutes of a Chiefs of Staff meeting on 9 April that his own experts did not believe in Sledgehammer any more than he himself did. It turned out once more that the Prime Minister of Great Britain did indeed have something to conceal from the President of the United States.

Churchill opened the key Defence Committee meeting to discuss the Marshall Memorandum on 14 April, attended by Hopkins and Marshall, by saying that it was:

> a momentous proposal, which had now been fully discussed and examined by the Staffs. For himself, he had no hesitation in cordially adopting the plan. The conception underlying it accorded with the classic principles of war – namely, concentration against the main enemy. One broad reservation must however be made – it was essential to carry on the defence of India and the Middle East. We could not possibly face the loss of an army of six hundred thousand men and the whole manpower of India. Furthermore, Australia and the island bases connecting that country with the United States must not be allowed to fall, as this would inevitably prolong the war. This meant that we could not entirely lay aside everything in furtherance of the main object proposed by General Marshall.[111]

Marshall then spoke at length about the possibility of launching Sledgehammer before the autumn of 1942, admitting that the American contribution would have to be 'a modest one' because of shipping constraints over the next five months.[112] Sledgehammer had been conceived as a way of taking pressure off Russia, and although Moscow had survived the invasion, the Soviets were still under immense pressure, especially further south. Marshall now saw Sledgehammer as being desirable in itself as early as possible. Brooke remarked that if Britain were 'forced to undertake an operation on the Continent, it could only be on a small scale'.[113] Several others spoke at the meeting, including Hopkins, Attlee, Eden and Mountbatten, all along similar lines. Churchill summed up, saying that although details of the cross-Channel plan still needed to be worked out, 'It was clear that there was complete unanimity on the framework,' but he would request help in the Indian Ocean, 'without which the whole plan would be fatally compromised'. He was confident, however, that 'It would gradually be known that the English-speaking peoples were resolved on a great campaign for the liberation of Europe,' and he promised Marshall 'that nothing would be left undone on the part of the British Government and people which could contribute to the success of the great enterprise on which they were about to embark'.[114]

The very extravagance of Churchill's language, with no dates given and no indication of whether he was referring to Sledgehammer, Bolero or Roundup, ought to have given Marshall pause for thought.[115] Churchill and Brooke certainly wanted a cross-Channel attack, but not until the Middle East and India were safe. The truth was that Churchill only ever saw Sledgehammer as a risky feint, much preferring Gymnast, which later became Operation Torch, in North Africa. 'But I had to work by influence and diplomacy in order to secure agreed and harmonious action with our cherished ally,' as he admitted in his war memoirs, 'without whose help nothing but ruin faced the world. I did not therefore open any of these alternatives at our meeting on the 14th.'[116] The British needed large numbers of American troops to be stationed in Britain, not least for protection against the possibility of a German invasion should Hitler emerge victorious in Russia. In order to secure Bolero, therefore, Churchill glided over his reservations about Sledgehammer, saying that the technical details relating to 'landing craft and all that' could be worked out by the staffs.

'Everyone was enthusiastic,' Ismay recalled of the 14 April meeting, 'everyone seemed to agree with the American proposals in their entirety. No doubts were expressed . . . Perhaps it would have obviated future misunderstandings if the British had expressed their views more frankly . . . The Defence Committee accepted the proposals in principle,' and 'our American friends went happily homewards under the mistaken impression that we had committed ourselves to both Roundup and Sledgehammer.' With his characteristic penchant for understatement, Ismay added, 'This misunderstanding was destined to have unfortunate results.'[117]

Marshall later became convinced that Churchill and Brooke had deliberately misled him, and that their opposition to Sledgehammer which emerged that summer also extended to any form of Roundup, which it did not. It seems that Churchill and Brooke said less than they might have so as to lead the Americans to believe they would support an early Second Front in 1942. They needed to persuade them to commit troops and resources to Germany First that might otherwise have gone east to avenge defeats like Bataan.[118]

'A momentous meeting at which we accepted their proposals for offensive action in 1942 perhaps and in 1943 for certain,' Brooke wrote in his diary, employing Churchill's adjective. 'They have not begun to recognize all the difficulties of this plan and all the difficulties that lie ahead of us!

The fear I have is that they should concentrate on this offensive at the expense of all else! We have therefore been pressing on them the importance of providing American assistance in the Indian Ocean and Middle East.'[119] This was an accurate summation of the double act that Churchill and Brooke had put on for Marshall's and Hopkins's benefit. In a later analysis, Brooke explained,

> With the situation prevailing at the time, it was not possible to take Marshall's 'castles in the air' too seriously! It must be remembered that we were at that time literally hanging on by our eyelids! Australia and India were threatened by the Japanese, we had temporarily lost control of the Indian Ocean, the Germans were threatening Persia and our oil, Auchinleck was in precarious straits in the desert, and the submarine sinkings were heavy ... We were desperately short of shipping and could stage no large-scale operations without additional shipping.[120]

On 15 April, Brooke tested Marshall by asking, 'Do we go east, south or west after landing [in France]? He had not begun to think of it!!'[121]

Hopkins and Marshall remained in Britain until 17 April, and Churchill invited Hopkins to several meetings of the War Cabinet, at which the discussions were limited to issues the British wanted the Americans to know about.[122] He also insisted on taking Marshall to see a demonstration of low-level strafing near Warminster, despite the fact that a Spitfire pilot had killed several spectators in a practice run the previous day.[123] Churchill cabled Roosevelt to say, 'We wholeheartedly agree with your conception of concentration against the main enemy, and we cordially accept your plan with one broad qualification': it was 'essential that we should prevent a junction of the Germans and Japanese'.[124] This could have been a qualification so broad it might have wrecked Roundup, since the hinge between the Middle East and the Indian Ocean was as large as it was vulnerable. Churchill sought to reassure Roosevelt by adding, 'Marshall felt confident that we could together provide what was necessary for the Indian Ocean and other theatres, and yet go right ahead with your main project.'[125] He had outlined a plan that was at best a red herring and at worst deliberately misleading. 'The campaign of 1943 is straightforward, and we are starting joint plans and preparations at once,' he cabled. 'We may, however, feel compelled to act this year ... Broadly speaking, our agreed programme is a crescendo of activity on the Continent, starting with an ever-increasing air offensive both by day and night and more frequent and large-scale raids, in which the United States troops will take part.'[126] This sounded like nothing less than an endorsement of Sledgehammer in five months' time, or even 'before then', if United States troops started flooding into Britain.

When Churchill entered the Commons on 23 April for the fourth of the five secret sessions of the war, he was received with a noticeably weaker cheer than Cripps had been on his return from India.[127] The Prime Minister adopted what Nicolson called 'his solid, obstinate, ploughman manner' as he took the House through all of the disasters since Pearl Harbor, including, five months after it had taken place, the attack in Alexandria Harbour that had been kept secret until then. Churchill promised that there would be a full public inquiry into the fall of Singapore as soon as circumstances allowed. (They never did.) He also had to 'admit that the violence, fury, skill and might of Japan has far exceeded anything which we had been led to expect'.[128] Considering that Japan had been fighting in China for over ten years by then, displaying all those elements, he should not have been so surprised. He read out an Admiralty paper from earlier in the year predicting that the *Gneisenau* and *Scharnhorst*, then stationed at Brest, might sail through the Channel in broad daylight to safety, 'because I am anxious that Members should realize that our affairs are not conducted entirely by simpletons and dunderheads as the comic papers try to depict'.

'Any featherhead can have confidence in times of victory, but the test is to have faith when things are going wrong for the time being,' he told the House, 'and when things happen which cannot be explained in public.'[129] The nearest he got to criticizing the Army was when he said that its conduct in Singapore in surrendering 100,000 men to a Japanese army of 30,000, 'does not seem to have been in harmony with the past or present spirit of our forces'.[130] He ended without rhetoric but with a statement on the United States' war materiel production, and the House gave him a fine ovation.[131] Even Channon described the ninety-minute speech as 'a tour de force . . . We left the Chamber confident that the war would, after all, be won, thanks chiefly to the stupendous American production.'[132]

To add to all Churchill's other anxieties, that month Randolph joined a parachute detachment of the Special Air Service (SAS) formed by Major David Stirling to fight behind enemy lines in the Western Desert. Stressing that Randolph had a young wife and baby, not to mention a father bearing a terrible burden, Clementine wrote to her husband, 'I think his action is selfish and unjust to you both, and as regards Pamela one might imagine she had betrayed him or left him.'[133] Churchill and Clementine had warmed to the vivacious, aristocratic Pamela, who lived at No. 10 and Chequers for much of the early part of the war when Randolph was serving abroad. On the rare occasions when they used the Annexe air-raid shelter, Pamela slept on the top bunk and Churchill, snoring so powerfully it made the metal bunk-bed shake, slept on the bottom, while Clementine sensibly stayed in her own room. Clementine's letter indicates that they did not know at that stage that she was having an affair with Averell Harriman. Of course the Prime Minister could not have his son withdrawn from a position of danger, but Clementine suggested she might write to Randolph to ask him to rejoin the 4th Hussars, adding something that no mother could have easily written, 'He might listen to me, as though he does not care for me, I know he respects me.'[134] Clementine rang Pamela, who 'seems so calm and sensible and *she* feels all is for the best'.[135] (Of course Pamela's willingness to have her cuckolded husband join one of the highest-risk units of the Army may be open to a cynical interpretation, especially as she was now having an affair with the American journalist Edward R. Murrow, as well as with Harriman.) On 20 May, returning from a raid in the desert with David Stirling and Fitzroy Maclean, Randolph's car overturned twice, killing one passenger and injuring others, including Randolph, who spent several weeks in a Cairo hospital. He then developed pneumonia in one lung as a result of the contusions on his chest, and his injured vertebrae forced him to wear an iron support for several months.[136]

Another family drama ensued the following month, when the eighteen-year-old Mary Churchill became engaged to the twenty-nine-year-old Eric, Viscount Duncannon, the future 10th Earl of Bessborough. 'I have persuaded Winston to be firm and say they must wait six months,' Clementine told Beaverbrook, whom she seems to have trusted in personal if not political matters; 'they do not know each other at all. Please keep my doubts and fears to yourself.'[137] Clementine's doubts might have stemmed from the fact that Duncannon's father had once wooed her.[138] The engagement was eventually called off by Mary at her parents' request. Clementine might have been a bit of a snob, but she was not about to sacrifice her daughter's future happiness for the prospect of her becoming a countess.

In one area of his private affairs at this time, Churchill was spared the danger of personal embarrassment. Anthony Moir, his solicitor at Fladgate & Co., was shown into the Cabinet Room in mid-May 1942 to discuss whether Churchill could appeal against an Inland Revenue assessment that the sale to a newspaper of serial rights to an old work at a fixed sum for each instalment was a taxable royalty rather than an untaxable outright sale, even though he had given up his status as an author when he joined the Government on the outbreak of war. 'If I appeal, will it be entirely private; can anyone get to know about it?' Churchill wanted to know. 'Is it right for me, in my position, to appeal; I am also First Lord of the Treasury?'[139] The appeal was heard in September, and after half an hour's deliberation the General Commissioners quashed the assessment.

On 27 April, Charles Portal gave to the Defence Committee details of major raids on Germany over four consecutive days. Lawrence Burgis recorded Churchill saying, 'Don't make too much of this in Press – we're hitting them three times as hard ... Communiqué a bit too sensational. Tone down, and keep in proportion. Don't give out photos.'[140] He did not want liberal and Church circles to denounce Harris's bombing offensive, although both groups were to launch their critiques in earnest six months later. At the same meeting, Churchill denounced the elderly 'R' class battleships as 'Floating coffins. Unsafe to face any modern vessels or air attack.' Although none of these remarks made it into the official minutes, Burgis's verbatim notes make it clear that much plain-speaking was done there.

From No. 10 Churchill would deluge Brooke in the War Office with an endless barrage of pointed remarks and questions. On 5 May, he wrote of a report from Libya, 'What is the meaning of the expression "Failed to silence machine-gun posts"? It seems an odd description of an action. Evidently what happened was merely a skirmish. Surely the way to silence machine-guns is to bring up some guns and shell them.'[141] Brooke, a Royal Artilleryman and acknowledged expert, who was one of the officers credited with inventing the 'creeping barrage' in the Great War, did not appreciate being lectured on such matters, not least because he knew Churchill knew that it was impractical always to call up artillery to deal with a troublesome machine gun. Two days later, as British troops successfully invaded Madagascar, Churchill rang Brooke again and again to ask how the operation was going. 'If Churchill fell down in an apoplectic fit we should get on perfectly well without him,' General Kennedy wrote that day. 'But to shaft him while he is *compos mentis* is quite a different proposition, for, with all his faults, he towers above the other politicians.'[142]

Churchill marked his second anniversary as prime minister on 10 May by broadcasting on the war situation. He told his countrymen with almost flippant playfulness that Hitler had made a 'grand blunder. He forgot about the winter. There is a winter, you know, in Russia. For a good many months the temperature is apt to fall very low. There is snow, there is frost, and all that. Hitler forgot about this Russian winter. He must have been very loosely educated. We all heard about it at school; but he forgot it. I have never made such a bad mistake as that.'[143] Of the bombing offensive against Germany, he said that the civilian population had 'an easy way to escape from these severities. All they have to do is to leave the cities where munitions work is being carried on. Abandon their work, and go out into the fields, and watch their home fires burning from a distance. In this way they may find time for meditation and repentance.'[144] On a trip to Leeds six days later, he spoke to a crowd of over 20,000 people from the Town Hall steps. 'We have reached a period in the war when it would be premature to say that we have topped the ridge, but now we see the ridge ahead,' he told them. 'Whatever we have got to take we will take, and we will give it back in even greater measure.'[145] Nor was this just rhetoric; the first thousand-bomber raid was unleashed that month on Cologne.

The King noted that Churchill 'was in very bad form' at their Tuesday lunch on 19 May, when he said, 'Nothing is going right for us, and our ships sank at once when bombed by the Japanese.' Churchill suggested 'that he should go to Washington himself soon . . . to try to get some sense into Admiral King . . . [who] wants his ships to fight Japan, General Marshall wants his Army to fight Germany, and General Arnold cannot supply both with aircraft'. The King tried to argue him out of his idea of appointing Beaverbrook as ambassador to Washington. 'I feel Winston is frightened of Beaverbrook and wants him away,' he suggested. 'I found it was no use arguing with him in the state he was in.'[146]

On 20 May, the same day as Randolph's accident, Vyacheslav Molotov, the Soviet Foreign Minister, flew to Britain on his way to Washington, to demand a Second Front in 1942. He also wanted to advance negotiations on the Anglo-Soviet Treaty, which had become badly stuck over the post-war Russo-Polish border and recognition of the annexations of the Baltic States. Churchill invited the Russian party to stay at Chequers, where the housekeeper was disconcerted to find a loaded revolver on Molotov's bed. At one of their dinners, Churchill complained about the dry, tasteless, long-refrigerated quail being served, saying, 'These miserable mice should never have been removed from Tutankhamen's tomb!'[147] – which must have tested the interpreters.

At their strategy meeting, Churchill told Molotov that it was 'the earnest resolve of the British Government to see what could be done this year to give the much needed support to the valiant Russian armies'. He then added, 'It was unlikely that any move we could make in 1942, even if it were successful, would draw off large numbers of enemy land forces from the Eastern Front.'[148] Molotov reported to Stalin that he found Churchill 'manifestly unsympathetic'.[149] The antipathy was mutual. 'I have never seen a human being who more perfectly represented the modern conception of a robot,' Churchill later wrote of Molotov.[150] Churchill disliked the pending Treaty, feeling it betrayed the Poles and Balts and was contrary to the Atlantic Charter. 'We must remember that this is a *bad* thing,' he told Cadogan. 'We oughtn't to do it, and I shan't be sorry if we don't.'[151] Days of further negotiations produced deadlock, until Churchill, according to the King, 'told Molotov frankly why we were fighting Germany, to uphold the rights of smaller nations.'[152] Eden suggested that the territorial questions could be left in abeyance and on 26 May a twenty-year treaty of friendship was signed instead.

At dawn the next day, Rommel started the Battle of Gazala, his massive southerly tank offensive in the Western Desert, driving a wedge into Auchinleck's positions. He managed to reach the high ground between El Adem and a desert position the Army dubbed Knightsbridge, from where he could menace Tobruk, the key to a wider German attack on Egypt. Auchinleck was left under no illusions by Churchill about the importance of holding the port, which he told him he could do. On the second day of the offensive, Churchill sent Roosevelt two telegrams setting out his and Brooke's doubts about a cross-Channel attack in 1942, and his own arguments for Operation Jupiter. 'We must never let Gymnast pass from our minds,' he added, still insistent on American support in the Middle East. 'All other preparations would help if need be towards that.'[153] The two greatest problems with an early Sledgehammer or Roundup, Churchill explained, were that the Luftwaffe commanded the air above the landing sites and the Allies did not have enough landing craft – only 383 were expected to be ready by August and 566 by September. Furthermore, American troops would not be ready until early 1943.

Despite this, after Roosevelt had met Molotov in Washington between 29 May and 1 June, the President issued a communiqué stating, 'Full understanding was reached with regard to the urgent tasks of creating a Second Front in Europe in 1942.'[154] The Americans were promising the Russians something they knew the British did not want and could not deliver. Because Churchill certainly did want Roundup to take place eventually, on 30 May he resuscitated an idea he had originally proposed to Lloyd George in 1917: to build and transport an artificial harbour to the invasion beaches. 'They *must* float up and down with the tide,' Churchill wrote to Mountbatten, the head of Combined Operations, of these Mulberry harbours. 'The anchor problem must be mastered. The ships must have a side-flap cut in them, and a drawbridge long enough to overreach the moorings of the piers. Let me have the best solution worked out. Don't argue the matter. The difficulties will argue for themselves.'[155]

Two years and one week later, two gigantic concrete harbours, each the size of Dover's docks, designed and constructed in such a way that they could be assembled in Britain and then towed across the Channel, were put in place on the Normandy shore. At the same time, in order to ensure that the invasion was properly fuelled, 30-mile-long 'Pipe-Line Underwater Transport of Oil' (PLUTO) pipelines were laid. If Churchill was genuinely uninterested in Operation Overlord, as he is often accused of being, he would not have urged these and many other initiatives in the way he did, years before D-Day.

Churchill told the King that he wanted to visit Auchinleck, as 'He feels that people out there may be contemplating surrender, instead of enthusing everybody to fight to the last man like they would have here, and in the same way as the Russians are fighting in their own country.'[156] For the moment Brooke dissuaded him.

Over the last weekend in May, the RAF launched a large raid over the Ruhr. Fifty-one bombers were shot down out of 1,137 that took off. With the Ukrainian front stabilized and the Battle of Gazala still in the balance, Churchill told Cadogan, 'We've had worse weekends.'[157] At the War Cabinet meeting on 1 June, however, Pound had to report that a convoy from Iceland to Russia had been very heavily mauled. Of its thirty-five ships, six had been sunk by bombers and one by a U-boat, with the overall loss of 147 tanks, thirty-seven aircraft and 770 vehicles. Churchill wanted the next convoy postponed, but Eden pointed out the bad effect that would have on Stalin, so it was not. A week later Churchill called Eden at his country home, Binderton House in Sussex, to tell him about the 'disappointing' reports from Libya, where Rommel was retaining the initiative, which depressed them both. 'I fear we have not very good generals,' Churchill said.[158] He was also depressed by the continuing opposition of the Chiefs of Staff to Operation Jupiter, guided in part by the experience of the last convoy. 'The politicians are much abused, but they get little help or inspiration from their Service advisers,' Churchill told Eden, who wrote in his diary, 'It can hardly be denied.'

In June, the King raised the issue of Churchill's successor in the event of his death. They agreed on Eden, but the King insisted that something should be in writing, which he himself helped to draft. (When Churchill claimed in his war memoirs that the initiative had come from him, he was reminded by the King that it had not.)[159] Churchill duly wrote the letter, and sealed the envelope with red wax bearing the imprint of a sphinx and a phoenix. 'In case of my death on this journey I am about to take,' it stated, 'I avail myself of Your Majesty's gracious permission, to advise that you entrust the formation of a new Government to Mr Anthony Eden, who is in my view the outstanding minister of the largest political party in the House of Commons and in the National Government over which I have the honour to preside.'[160] In the event of both Churchill and Eden being killed, Churchill suggested the King send for Sir John Anderson.

The journey Churchill mentioned in his letter was to Washington, where he hoped to persuade Roosevelt to undertake Operation Gymnast, the joint Anglo-American invasion of French North Africa, and to postpone any early cross-Channel attack. He also wanted to minimize the concentration of American forces in the Pacific until Germany was defeated, and to discuss a future partnership in nuclear research. If possible, he hoped to do this over the heads of Marshall and the Joint Chiefs of Staff, appealing directly to their Commander-in-Chief. Churchill took great heart from the American victory at Midway on 4 June, which resulted in the sinking of four Japanese aircraft carriers. 'Losses at sea would produce signs of fear on part of the Japs,' he told the War Cabinet, saying it was a 'chance for us to get teeth into her tail'.[161] He then asked for a report from Wavell, opining that 'The further removed from danger and fighting, the more dangers and responsibilities seem to weigh with officers.'[162]

On 10 June there was a hard-fought War Cabinet over how best to respond to the terrible news from Lidice in Czechoslovakia, where the SS had executed 173 people in a reprisal for the assassination of Obergruppenführer Reinhard Heydrich by two SOE-trained Czech operatives. Churchill had told President Beneš that the RAF would wipe out three German villages in response, suggesting that one hundred bombers would be required to drop incendiaries from low levels in bright moonlight, with the reason announced afterwards. If it was 'thought worthwhile', Churchill told his colleagues, the RAF could 'fit it in when they can'.[163]

Archie Sinclair said he did not think the lives of RAF crews should be risked on a vengeance mission. Attlee doubted whether 'it is useful to enter into competition in frightfulness with the Germans'. Morrison said there would be reprisals on British villages, and Anderson also opposed it. Eden liked the 'deterrent element', and Bevin argued that 'Germany responds to brute force and nothing else.' Bracken and Cranborne were opposed. As usual, Churchill was bellicose. 'My instinct is strongly the other way,' he said. Amery asked, 'Why a village? Why not a residential town?', but Cripps said that the operational argument against it was 'very strong'. Churchill concluded by saying, 'I submit (unwillingly) to the view of the Cabinet against.'[164]

At a Chiefs of Staff meeting that evening, Churchill told Brooke that he had doubts about Auchinleck's offensive spirit. 'I don't know what we can do for that Army,' he kept repeating, 'all our efforts to help them seem to be in vain.' He then added mercilessly that the troops defending Egypt 'all come up for their rations but not to fight'. Before going to bed, Brooke told Barney Charlesworth, his aide-de-camp, 'Well, that is one of the bloodiest days I have had for a long time.'[165] After the war, Brooke complained of the way Churchill would say things like 'Pray explain, C.I.G.S., how is it that in the Middle East seven hundred and fifty thousand men always turn up for their pay and rations, but when it comes to fighting only one hundred thousand turn up?! Explain to us now exactly how the remaining six hundred and fifty thousand are occupied!'[166] On 14 June, Churchill telegraphed Auchinleck to say that he presumed 'there is no serious question in any case of giving up Tobruk. As long as Tobruk is held, no serious enemy advance into Egypt is possible.'[167] Auchinleck reiterated that he had 'no intention of giving up Tobruk'.[168]

Three days later, Churchill left London by special train, and by 11.30 p.m. had reached Stranraer on Loch Ryan in Scotland. There he walked along the pier singing the Great War song 'We're Here Because We're Here'. He then took off in a Bristol flying boat with Brooke, Ismay, Brigadier G. M. Stewart, the Director of Plans of the War Office, Charles Moran his doctor, Commander Thompson, Patrick Kinna his stenographer, John Martin and Frank Sawyers his valet, for the twenty-seven-hour, 3,000-mile flight over Newfoundland, landing on the Potomac River at Washington at 8 p.m. local time on the 18th, prior to having dinner with Halifax at the British Embassy. It was to be his only wartime transatlantic round trip by air. During the journey, he worked on his papers, went forward from time to time to talk to the crew and 'ate a hearty meal' according to the dictates of tummy-time.[169]

The next day, Churchill flew up to Roosevelt's family estate, Hyde Park, on the banks of the Hudson River in upstate New York. The President came out to meet him at New Hackensack airfield in his Ford V8 convertible car, whose foot controls had been adapted to operation by hand, allowing him to drive – precariously, Churchill recalled – back to Hyde Park. Churchill added a complete collection of his own books, bound in red leather, to the fine library there. 'We spent two days at Hyde Park,' recalled John Martin, 'the P.M. in constant conference with the President, driving out in the afternoons to tea.'[170] In their discussions on the Bomb, with only Hopkins present, the two men agreed, in Churchill's words, that 'We should at once pool all our information, work together on equal terms, and share the results, if any, equally between us.'[171] Churchill claimed in his memoirs that by the end of June 1942 the details of the full atomic merger had been orally agreed, witnessed by Hopkins.

One leading historian has correctly described Churchill's account of this crucial discussion, which was written nearly a decade later with no notes to guide him, as full of 'serious factual errors'.[172] Although Churchill went into great detail in his memoirs about where the meeting took place, 'after luncheon' and in the 'intense heat' of the day, and how they had 'settled the basis of an agreement', the official historian of the British atomic project could find no evidence of Churchill having been briefed on Tube Alloys before he left for Washington, let alone any evidence of an agreement.[173] Churchill most probably had a short, unminuted conversation about the general desirability of nuclear cooperation, but he later conflated his June 1942 meeting in his mind with the far more important, and substantial, discussions that took place in September 1944, which did indeed lead to a formal understanding known as the Hyde Park Agreement. The best construction that can be put on it all is that Churchill's memories in 1950 were confused.[174] Roosevelt did confirm at the time to Dr Vannevar Bush that he was 'in complete accord' with Churchill on atomic matters, but otherwise we know next to nothing about what precisely was agreed.[175] By not pinning down Roosevelt on areas such as electro-magnetic separation and plutonium-breeding, where the Americans were far advanced, the unbriefed Churchill left them with a significant advantage.[176] The omission supports the likelihood that nothing significant was agreed in June 1942, as Churchill used regularly to say that 'Nothing counts unless it is in writing.'[177]

It was at Hyde Park that Churchill made clear his profound reservations about Sledgehammer and an early Roundup, and put the case strongly for Operation Torch (formerly Gymnast). Roosevelt wanted American troops to be fighting the Germans by the time of the mid-term elections in early November. If the British would not agree to an offensive in France in 1942, he recognized it would have to be in North Africa, despite Marshall and the Joint Chiefs' opposition to what they called a 'strategy of dispersion'.

Churchill and Roosevelt returned to Washington in the President's special train on 21 June, and Churchill once again stayed at the White House. It was there, during a meeting in the Oval Office with Marshall and Brooke present, that Roosevelt handed Churchill a note saying that Tobruk had fallen. 'Defeat is one thing,' Churchill wrote of this devastating moment, 'disgrace is another.'[178] Over 33,000 Commonwealth troops had been taken prisoner by an Axis force half its size. Tobruk's enormous fuel and ammunition dumps had not been destroyed: they were now in German hands. Admiral Harwood, who had taken over from Cunningham, had to move the fleet south of the Suez Canal; for the first time in centuries the Royal Navy had been chased out of the Mediterranean Sea. 'I am the most miserable Englishman in America since Burgoyne,'* Churchill said.[179]

* General John Burgoyne surrendered at the Battle of Saratoga in 1777.

'What can we do to help?'[180] Roosevelt immediately asked. 'Give us as many Sherman tanks as you can spare, and ship them to the Middle East as quickly as possible,' Churchill replied. The Americans stripped 300 Sherman tanks and 100 self-propelled guns from their 1st Armoured Division which was being deployed to Northern Ireland and shipped them to the British Army in Egypt instead. When one of the ships carrying scores of the tanks was torpedoed, they were immediately replaced without the British having to ask. It was a magnificent response, for which Churchill was always grateful. Roosevelt was less solicitous in private. When his cousin Daisy Suckley asked him where the blame lay for the Egyptian situation, 'He said partly Churchill, mostly the bad generals.' Suckley noted that the President 'was depressed over the situation. If Egypt is taken, it means Arabia, Syria, Afghanistan, etc., i.e. the Japs and Germans control everything across from the Atlantic to the Pacific – that means all the oil wells, etc., of those regions.' When she asked whether victory was certain, he replied, 'Not necessarily.'[181]

# 27
# Desert Victory June–November 1942

*I undertook the office of Prime Minister and Minister of Defence, after defending my predecessor to the best of my ability, in times when the life of the Empire hung upon a thread.*

Churchill, 2 July 1942[1]

*Great battles, won or lost, change the entire course of events, create new standards of values, new moods, new atmospheres, in armies and in nations, to which all must conform.*

Churchill, *Marlborough*[2]

June 1942 was the worst month of the war so far for Allied and neutral shipping losses, with 173 ships – comprising 834,196 tons – sunk, 83 per cent by U-boats, and 60 per cent in the Caribbean and Gulf of Mexico. An attempt to resupply Malta resulted in only two merchant ships out of seventeen getting through. 'There were no such black moments as the Dardanelles in the Second War,' Clementine recalled after the war. 'When he became Prime Minister, he was quite sure that God had created him for that purpose.' She was emphatic that throughout the conflict, 'even at bad moments, we never had a doubt of victory or a moment of despair.'[3] In fact there were several moments that certainly approached despair – Singapore and Tobruk were two of them and there would be more. Any other response would have been strangely inhuman. Churchill could be deeply saddened by individual pieces of news, and temporarily extremely gloomy, but never what we would now call depressed, and his general outlook was positive and combative. The earlier crises of his life had given him the mental and moral toughness to see him through these moments; it would have been impossible for a genuine depressive to have carried himself, those around him and the country itself through such crises.*

On 23 June he was given further unwelcome news. Sir John Wardlaw-Milne, a senior Conservative MP, had put down a motion of no confidence in Churchill's Government, to be debated on 1 July. 'The House was electrified and cheered,' wrote Channon. 'The lobbies soon hummed, and everyone I saw was suddenly as excited as an aged virgin being led to her seducer's bed.'[4] He noted that 'Everyone agreed that Winston should cease to be Minister of Defence.' Hore-Belisha, who along with Roger Keyes supported the motion, said to Channon, 'When your doctor is killing you, the first thing to do is get rid of him.' Ernest Brown, the Minister of Health, added that it was 'extremely difficult' for Government ministers to be loyal to Churchill, leading Channon to lament, 'If only Mr Chamberlain was alive. Many a Member who voted against him would willingly now withdraw his vote.' For all the leadership that Churchill was giving the country, the military and naval reverses and disappointments were making Chamberlainites intensely critical of him. His Gallup approval rating had fallen to 78 per cent in July, down from 88 per cent in July 1940. It was a noticeable drop, and the lowest he registered during the war.[5] A by-election in the normally very safe Tory seat of Maldon in Essex was won by the Independent Labour Party on 25 June, with a drop in the Conservative vote from 53.5 to 31.3 per cent. In one of his characteristically candid assessments, Brigadier Harvie-Watt warned, 'It would be a mistake to think that there is not grave anxiety in the House,' although he still believed that fewer than twenty MPs would actually vote against the Government in the confidence motion.[6]

On 22 June, Churchill, who was still in Washington, met General Dwight D. Eisenhower, the cheery, intelligent War Department planner, for the first time, and they discussed the technicalities of the cross-Channel operations, as they also did in White House meetings the next day, making it clear that they did want a large joint amphibious landing in France at some stage. Churchill watched a mass parachute drop at Fort Jackson in South Carolina on 24 June, commanded by General Mark Clark. There followed a live-firing exercise performed by what Churchill called 'the mass-produced American divisions'. When Ismay said, 'To put these troops against German troops would be murder,' Churchill said, 'You're wrong. They are wonderful material and will learn very quickly.'[7] He was

* Jock, the marmalade cat at Chartwell, died on the same day that Tobruk fell, but it was decided not to inform Churchill until he returned from Washington (Pawle, *Warden* p. 119).

'much impressed by the American Generals Eisenhower and Clark', Pamela reported to Randolph the next month, 'particularly the latter whom Winston describes as the American Eagle'.[8] As the party at Fort Jackson embarked on to the plane for the flight back to Washington, Sawyers, who Brooke noticed had been 'absorbing refreshments . . . fairly efficiently' all day, 'and was distinctly affected by what he had consumed', blocked the Prime Minister's way and refused to let him pass until he had turned down the brim of his panama hat. 'Winston, rather red and looking angry, turned the brim down,' recorded an amused Brooke. 'Thereupon Sawyers stood to one side, muttering to himself, "That's much, much better, much better."'[9]

The next day, the Eighth Army was forced to retreat to Mersa Matruh. It had lost over 230 tanks since Rommel's offensive began. 'We have suffered one of the most decisive defeats ever inflicted,' wrote Cadogan.[10] Three days later the Eighth Army was forced to retreat even further, to El Alamein, the last defensive position before the Nile Delta itself, only 66 miles from Alexandria and 160 miles from Cairo. The desert narrows there to a 35-mile front between the sea and the Qattara Depression, an impassable marsh stretching far to the south.

Having achieved all he had wanted in America, but facing serious political danger back home, Churchill flew back from Washington on 25 June via Baltimore and Botwood in Newfoundland, landing at Stranraer on the 27th. At lunch with Clementine, Eddie Marsh, Ronnie Tree and Pamela, he said how wonderful it was that the country was united behind him 'when I'm admittedly the biggest defeat-merchant in English history'.[11] However much the country as a whole was behind him – with over three-quarters of those polled by Gallup still supporting him – he still had to face a very testing time from MPs.

On 1 July 1942, Wardlaw-Milne moved his censure motion in the Commons. He had offered to withdraw it the day before but Churchill said that it was 'imperative that the matter should go forward to an immediate issue'.[12] In the two-day debate, which on the first day started before lunch and ended after midnight, Wardlaw-Milne built up a case for a 'strong and independent man' to take command of the armed forces, arguing that the Prime Minister should attend to matters on the Home Front. He then wrecked his own argument by saying that the new supremo should be the Duke of Gloucester, an affable member of the Royal Family, but by no estimation a strategic genius. 'The House roared with disrespectful laughter,' recorded Channon, 'and I at once saw Winston's face light up, as if a lamp had been lit within him and he smiled genially. He knew now that he was saved, and poor Wardlaw-Milne never quite regained the hearing of the House.'[13] Attacks were made by other speakers on the Ministry of Information, the Ministry of Supply, the War Office and the Air Ministry, while various Government ministers were described as 'nincompoops', 'incompetents' and 'the greatest friend Hitler ever had'. Churchill escaped personally, although Lord Winterton did say, 'No one dares to put the blame where it should be put constitutionally – on the Prime Minister.'* On the second day of the debate, Aneurin Bevan, a high-living left-wing Labour MP for whom Bracken coined the phrase 'Bollinger Bolshevik', woundingly remarked, 'The Prime Minister wins debate after debate, and loses battle after battle. The country is beginning to say that he fights debates like a war, and the war like a debate.'[14] The losses to U-boats, the retreat in Libya and the fact that British tanks were being outgunned were all brought up.

Churchill's ninety-minute reply was frank and masterly. He took the House through the defeats, admitting that Rommel's 400-mile advance was a grave blow. 'We are at this moment in the presence of a recession of our hopes and prospects in the Middle East and in the Mediterranean unequalled since the fall of France. If there are any would-be profiteers of disaster who feel able to paint the picture in darker colours, they are certainly at liberty to do so.'[15] Yet he defended his conduct in the face of these setbacks. 'Some people assume too readily that, because a Government keeps cool and has steady nerves under reverses, its members do not feel the public misfortunes as keenly as do independent critics,' he said. 'On the contrary, I doubt whether anyone feels greater sorrow or pain than those who are responsible for the general conduct of our affairs.'[16]

'I have never made any predictions, except things like saying that Singapore would hold out,' he said. When the laughter had died down, he pointed out, 'What a fool and a knave I should have been to say that it would fall!'[17] He said that he asked no special favours:

> I am your servant, and you have the right to dismiss me when you please. What you have no right to do is to ask me to bear responsibilities without the power of effective action, to bear the responsibilities of Prime Minister but clamped on each side . . . If today, or at any future time, the House were to exercise its undoubted right, I could walk out with a good conscience and the feeling that I have done my duty according to such light as has been granted to me. There

* Churchill had his revenge three years later, when he said of Winterton, 'Unless in the future his sagacity and knowledge of the House are found to be markedly superior to what he has exhibited today, I must warn him that he will run a very grave risk of falling into senility before he is overtaken by old age' (*CS* VII p. 7127).

> is only one thing I would ask of you in that event. It would be to give my successor the modest powers which would have been denied to me.[18]

The Government won the vote by 475 to 25, with thirty MPs abstaining, including Winterton, Shinwell, Southby, Nancy Astor and Megan Lloyd-George. Among those who voted against him were Bevan, Hore-Belisha, Wardlaw-Milne and Clement Davies. Churchill then rose, smiled up at Clementine in the Speaker's Gallery and left. Cadogan recorded him later talking to a Frenchman about 'Les vingt-cinq canailles qui ont voté contre moi [The twenty-five villains who voted against me].'[19] 'Such victories are not the hardest things in our life,' Churchill told Maisky the next day. The King noted, 'He was glad to have disposed of what he called "the weaker brethren" in the House of Commons.'[20]

Clementine was not so confident, saying, 'If the situation at the Front does not improve, who knows what may happen?'[21] Churchill had to tell Maisky that, with American troops still numbering fewer than 80,000 in Britain, there was no possibility of an early Second Front. 'One has to deceive one's enemy,' he said, 'one can sometimes deceive the general public for its own good but one must never deceive one's ally.'[22] Asked to explain the British defeats in North Africa, he said bluntly, 'The Germans wage war better than we do. Especially tank wars. Also, we lack the "Russian spirit": die but don't surrender!'[23] He blamed the Tobruk defeat on the South African general Hendrik Klopper, who he said 'got cold feet and waved the white flag twenty-four hours after the German attack began'. When Maisky said the Russians would have shot a general like that on the spot, Churchill replied, 'I'd have done the same. But just you try!'[24]

Churchill took notice of the substantive, as opposed to personal, criticisms in the debate, and reconfigured Whitehall with brand-new ministries, such as Food, Light and Power in July 1942, Reconstruction in November 1943 and minister residencies for the Middle East, West Africa, Washington (for Supply) and North-West Africa. He had once again been fortunate in the timing of the censure motion, because only two days later disaster overtook the PQ17 convoy to Murmansk. Back in February, the Germans had redeployed much of their heavy surface fleet and a large number of U-boats to northern Norway. As a result, the Allied Arctic convoys suffered much heavier losses, but since the Cape route via Iran was 14,500 miles long, also very dangerous and took seventy-six days Churchill and Roosevelt, under pressure from Stalin, continued to use the northern Norwegian route, despite opposition from the Admiralty and the US Navy Department. On 18 May, Churchill had told the War Cabinet that it was 'our duty to fight these convoys through, whatever the cost'.[25] Yet at 21.36 hours on 4 July Admiral Pound, in the belief that the *Tirpitz*, then the largest battleship in the Atlantic, was on its way towards the Anglo-American PQ17 convoy, ordered its thirty-five ships to scatter. Pound feared that otherwise *Tirpitz* 'would have sunk every single vessel within an hour or so'.[26] Yet the intelligence was wrong, and the *Tirpitz* was not in the area, whereas German bombers and U-boats were. No fewer than twenty-three vessels, comprising 118,000 out of the convoy's 200,000 tons of shipping, were sunk. Four hundred tanks and 210 planes went to the bottom of the sea.

Losses of up to half was the same casualty rate for which Churchill had denounced Haig on the first day of the Somme, with the added dimension that there were more killed and fewer wounded when a ship sank than when a battalion was massacred in no man's land. 'There's no sense in sending tanks and planes to certain ruin,' Churchill told Maisky. 'We might as well sink them in the Thames.'[27] The Defence Committee cancelled the August convoy, but the September one lost twelve ships out of forty. For the next two years, convoys ran only during the winter months, resulting in fewer losses.[28]

On 8 July, complaining to the Chiefs of Staff about their opposition to all his strategic concepts, Churchill said sarcastically, 'We'd better put an advertisement in the papers, asking for ideas.'[29] The next day he was furious with a decision taken in his absence about rationing continuing into peacetime. 'Are we to tell the British soldier returning from the war', he asked the Cabinet rhetorically, 'that he is to tighten his belt and starve, in order that Roumanians may batten on the fat of the land? I've never heard of such a thing.'[30] Cadogan wrote of the heated discussion that then took place, 'Winston enjoyed it more than anyone.'

Marshall, Hopkins and the rebarbative, Anglophobic Admiral Ernest J. King, Chief of Staff of the US Navy, arrived in Britain for further strategy discussions on 18 July. Roosevelt wanted Americans fighting in the Western theatre soon, and this was the Joint Chiefs' last attempt to persuade the British to agree to a cross-Channel attack in 1942, rather than an invasion of North Africa. The discussions were not going to be easy, because the Joint Chiefs thought, not without reason, that back in April the British had pronounced themselves in favour of an attack in France, albeit with certain caveats. Now, Churchill had changed his mind and suborned their President in favour of a North African assault far from the centre of events. Admiral King and American generals such as Albert Wedemeyer believed that this was to prop up the British Empire in the Middle East, rather than to destroy Hitler as soon as possible. They also believed that Churchill's and Brooke's experiences in the trenches in the Great War meant that they did not want to face the Germans on land until the Russians had so weakened the Reich that the fighting would be easier. Admiral King did not even believe in Germany First, and would have preferred a concentration against Japan, a campaign that would be dominated by the Navy he led.

In the talks that started on 20 July, Brooke refused to undertake Sledgehammer, which he told the Americans 'could only lead to the loss of some six divisions without achieving any results!'[31] The British position was that, as Ian Jacob of the War Cabinet Secretariat condensed it, 'The Battle of the Atlantic must be won, the Mediterranean must be opened to shipping, Italy should be knocked out, and Germany should be subjected to an ever-increasing bombardment from the air. These measures, together with the attrition on the Russian front, might soften up the German hold on North-West Europe and enable an assault landing to succeed.' It is remarkable – despite Brooke treating Churchill in his diaries as a strategic idiot – how closely this plan mirrors what Churchill had written in his four memoranda when crossing the Atlantic in 1941. Meanwhile, Jacob added, 'Churchill liked to keep all options open, a phrase he often employed.'[32] To clear the Mediterranean, the Axis forces needed to be expelled from Africa, which Operation Torch was intended to achieve, hence Cadogan's note of 22 July, saying that Churchill was 'wildly keen' about the North African strategy.[33]

Three strategic considerations were uppermost in Churchill's thinking at this time. The first was that a serious rift with Roosevelt was unthinkable; the second was his enthusiasm for action on the largest scale possible as soon as it was safe to undertake it, and the third was what Jacob called 'a haunting fear in Churchill's mind of an invasion that would result in a static stalemate, a stabilizing of the line, and thus a creation of another Western Front'.[34] To that extent, Wedemeyer and others were right to think that the Great War had influenced Churchill's thinking. Much more influential, however, was the British Army's experience at Dunkirk in 1940, in terms of both the Germans' capacity to manoeuvre and the BEF's inability to stop them. Churchill would not commit Britain to either Sledgehammer or Roundup until he was reasonably certain of its success. To his mind this required decisive prior victories in the Mediterranean and the Atlantic.

Once Marshall had established that Roosevelt would not support his threatening the British with a Japan First policy if they did not agree to undertake Sledgehammer or Roundup in 1942, the Joint Chiefs accepted that the focus for the rest of the year would instead be on North Africa with Operation Torch, to be launched before the end of October, with Eisenhower as its commander-in-chief. Once North Africa was cleared of Axis forces and thus Egypt and the route to India were safe, the Allies could then undertake a Mediterranean strategy against Italy and choose a path into Occupied Europe that went through either southern France or the Balkans or both, which would draw off German forces from the cross-Channel attack. Churchill was made by both the British and American staffs to appreciate that Operation Jupiter in northern Norway was not going to happen. The Joint Chiefs flew back home unhappy, but utterly committed to making the North African invasion work. The King noted, 'Winston looked very tired after his strenuous week convincing the Americans we are right.'[35]

By August Churchill's approval rating as measured by Gallup was up to 82 per cent and in November 1942 it reached the low 90s where it stayed until January 1944; it then dipped to the high 80s, and remained there with occasional movements upwards throughout the year. These were remarkably high numbers rarely seen before or since for any other prime minister. Even in April 1945 he was still approved of as prime minister by 91 per cent of those polled.[36]

After a month of indecisive fighting on the North African front, Churchill suggested that he and Brooke should fly to Cairo. The journey soon turned into an even more ambitious expedition when a message was received from Archie Clark Kerr, the British Ambassador to Russia, saying that Stalin wanted to meet Churchill in Moscow. Churchill recognized that Stalin would not see Operation Torch as the Second Front he needed, indeed that he would be furious, and felt that someone needed to tell him face to face. Ultimately it had to be him. 'To start on these missions and then to fail in either would have been disastrous both for our cause and for Churchill as a political leader,' his private secretary Leslie Rowan wrote after the war. 'Much better never to have started at all. Such a thought never entered Churchill's head; he saw where the course of duty led, and that was enough for him.'[37] When Eden suggested that if he went to Cairo he would just get in the way, Churchill replied, 'You mean like a great blue-bottle buzzing over a huge cowpat!'[38] Yet all his instincts told him he needed to see the situation on the ground for himself.

'I am shocked by Auchinleck's latest wire,' Churchill told the King on 1 August. The Commander-in-Chief in the Middle East had informed him that he intended to remain on the defensive until mid-September. 'How strong will the enemy be by then! In Russia, too, the materials for a joyous meeting are meagre indeed. Still, I may perhaps make the situation less edged.'[39] The next day, Churchill and Brooke took off from RAF Lyneham heading for Gibraltar. Others would join them, including Wavell, Tedder and Cadogan.

They flew in the first plane to be specifically assigned to Churchill, an American-built, four-engined, Consolidated LB-30A based on the B-24 Liberator bomber and named *Commando*. William J. Vanderkloot, an American who had volunteered for the RAF before Pearl Harbor, was Churchill's personal pilot. The plane was bitterly cold and deafeningly noisy. Food was cooked on a gas stove, although Churchill ate cold beef sandwiches on the flight. 'The bread must be wafer thin,' he ordered; 'it is nothing more than a vehicle to convey the filling to the stomach.'[40] With no cabin pressurization, the plane rarely went above 8,000 feet, yet Churchill still wore an oxygen mask when he slept on the mattresses laid on the freezing steel deck of the bomb bay.

The flight involved crossing Spanish territory. Vanderkloot said this could be done at night, as Spanish fighter planes had not shown any interest hitherto.[41] Churchill liked the plan, and Moran did not want to give him the inoculations necessary for the alternative 7,000-mile, three-day route via Lagos and Khartoum. Once he had landed at Gibraltar, Churchill 'lay on the bed in his underwear and held forth to us', Cadogan recorded. 'He seemed none the worse for the journey.'[42] The next day they flew on to Cairo. From the front of the plane Churchill saw the great River Nile, on which he had taken a paddle-steamer as a young subaltern exactly forty-four years earlier.

Churchill met Auchinleck at 5.30 p.m. on 3 August. He had not at that stage decided to relieve him of his command. He wanted to discuss the possibility with Smuts, whose disinterested views he always respected and who had come from South Africa to meet him. 'Smuts was magnificent in counsel,' Churchill wrote to Clementine. 'He fortified me where I am inclined to be tender-hearted, namely in using severe measures against people I like.'[43] With everything at stake in both domestic politics and the alliance, Churchill wanted to see plans for a decisive offensive at an early opportunity, to avenge the series of defeats the Eighth Army had suffered, silence the critics back home and create a pincer movement that would crush Rommel once Operation Torch was unleashed in the west.[44] It became clear that Auchinleck could not provide them.

Churchill stayed at the British Embassy with Sir Miles Lampson, occupying both of the two air-conditioned rooms there. He had himself photographed with Auchinleck on 5 August, which he might not have done had he already decided to sack him. Cadogan tried to get him to meet Panayotis Canellopoulos, the Greek Minister of State, that same day.

Cadogan had to go to Churchill's bathroom, where he 'found the Prime Minister wallowing about like a porpoise, and throwing his sponge up and down to the chant of "Canellopoulos! Can'tellopoulos! Canellopoulos . . ."'[45] (He did eventually see the Greek minister.) Churchill later, in the sweltering heat, visited Auchinleck's headquarters at El Alamein, which he described as 'full of flies and important military personages'.[46]

The next day, back in Cairo, Churchill had an audience with the twenty-two-year-old King Farouk of Egypt. Standing next to Lampson's map of North Africa, the King put his hand over the whole of Cyrenaica, portentously stating that it had once all belonged to Egypt. 'Winston at once replied that he could not remember when,' Lampson recorded in his diary. 'To the best of his belief it had belonged to Turkey before the Italians took it. This rather stumped King Farouk.'[47] Churchill was right; in the thirteenth century BC it had been the Cyrenaican tribes who had made incursions into Egypt, rather than the other way around. During the meeting, Farouk had lolled back in his chair, starting sentences with 'You know, Churchill . . .', which the Prime Minister later told Lampson had been 'cheeky' – and it had certainly been foolish to try to bandy history with a professional historian.[48]

That evening, Churchill, Brooke and Smuts agreed that Auchinleck needed to be replaced by General Sir Harold Alexander as commander-in-chief in the Middle East, while Lieutenant-General William 'Strafer' Gott would take over the Eighth Army, which had also been directly commanded by Auchinleck since June. Churchill found inadequate staff work at Cairo, undertaken by large numbers of officers whom he called 'the Gabardene swine' after the gabardine trench coat worn by officers.

Churchill sacked Auchinleck at his El Alamein headquarters; the Auk took it with what the Prime Minister described as 'soldierly dignity'.[49] To General Alexander he later likened the experience to killing a magnificent stag.[50] 'It was a terrible thing to have to do,' Churchill told Harold Nicolson later. 'It was a terrible thing. It is difficult to remove a bad General at the height of a campaign. It is atrocious to remove a good General. We must use Auchinleck again.'[51] (Auchinleck became commander-in-chief in India in 1943.) But morale in the Eighth Army was low and an exceptional commander was needed to defeat Erwin Rommel in the Western Desert. 'I saw that Army,' Churchill told Nicolson. 'It was a broken, baffled Army, a miserable Army . . . I made my decision. I telegraphed to the Cabinet. I then took off all my clothes and rolled in the surf. Never have I had such bathing.'[52]

Insofar as there was a common thread in Churchill's dismissals or reassignments of Ironside, Gort, Dill, Dowding, Wavell and Auchinleck, it was that they were on the verge of sixty, and were tired, in some cases exhausted, by the stressful commands they had held since 1939. Some of Auchinleck's key appointments had left Churchill and Brooke underwhelmed; they had also become convinced that Auchinleck simply did not have the charisma and offensive spirit necessary to reinvigorate the Eighth Army. Churchill had also been frustrated to learn that the more than 300 Sherman tanks sent to Egypt after the fall of Tobruk had not been employed as 'a mass of manoeuvre', to use a Napoleonic phrase, but instead parcelled out in small numbers to existing formations. 'Everyone who knew Auchinleck was sad at what happened,' recalled Rowan, but 'less courage on the part of Churchill in . . . taking responsibility for this unpleasant decision, or less capacity in him to see the simple truth that Auchinleck had to be replaced, could have changed the course of the war'.[53]

Churchill informed the Cabinet only after he and Brooke had reached the decision. 'Now for a short spell I became "the man on the spot",' he later wrote. 'Instead of sitting at home waiting for the news from the front I could send it myself. This was exhilarating.'[54] 'Your prime duty will be to take or destroy at the earliest opportunity the German-Italian Army commanded by Field Marshal Rommel, together with all its supplies and establishments in Egypt and Libya,' Churchill wrote to General Alexander.[55] On 7 August 'Strafer' Gott was shot down flying to Cairo to take up his command, on the same route that Churchill had flown only a few days previously. 'So poor Winston sat speechless and desperate during dinner and had hardly recovered before the small hours,' Cadogan recorded.[56] 'Imagine my grief when even while the Cabinet was sitting in London,' Churchill wrote to Clementine, 'I had to telegraph that he had been killed.'[57]

Gott's death meant that General Bernard Montgomery, a protégé of Brooke's, took over the Eighth Army instead. Montgomery had a reputation for abrasiveness, but as Churchill told his wife, 'In Montgomery we have a highly competent daring and energetic soldier . . . If he is disagreeable to those about him, he is also disagreeable to the enemy.'[58] In *Marlborough*, Churchill had written that military genius was 'much rarer than the largest and purest diamonds . . . But when from time to time it flashes upon the scene, order and design with a sense of almost infallibility draw out from hazard and confusion.'[59] Modern estimations are that Montgomery was too cautious a commander to be considered a military genius, but what Churchill desperately needed now was an unambiguous victory, however it was achieved, and he saw in Montgomery someone who could bring order and optimism to an army that looked chaotic and demoralized.*

On 8 August, on his second visit to the front, Churchill made seven speeches to four armoured brigades in six hours.[60] Back in Cairo for dinner at the Embassy with the two SAS heroes David Stirling and Fitzroy Maclean, he challenged Smuts to see who could recite the most Shakespeare. After a quarter of an hour Smuts lost, as Churchill churned on. A few minutes later, Smuts realized that his opponent was once again producing cod-Shakespeare verses that owed nothing to the Bard and everything to the Prime Minister's imagination. As they were walking around the garden afterwards, Churchill teased Maclean that he had become an MP in order to avoid the regulations that banned diplomats from joining the Services. 'Here is the young man', he said to Smuts and Stirling, 'who has used the Mother of Parliaments as a public convenience.'[61]

After being briefed by Stirling on an impending attack on Benghazi, and the way that the SAS represented 'a new form of warfare' which had 'awesome potential', Churchill quoted to Smuts the lines from Byron's *Don Juan*: 'He was the mildest-mannered man / That ever scuttled ship or cut a throat.' The next day, he summoned Stirling to the Embassy to discuss greatly expanding the SAS. With Churchill's support, vehicles, weapons, ammunition and permissions were found far easier to obtain from the Cairo military authorities than hitherto. Churchill nicknamed Stirling the 'Scarlet Pimpernel' for his combination of overt gentlemanliness and covert lethality, admiring the way he took his unit on daring long-range penetrations sometimes hundreds of miles behind enemy lines.

On 10 August, Churchill set off on the second part of his mission: the visit to Stalin. Clementine characterized this as the 'visit to the Ogre in his den'; Churchill described his mission as 'like carrying a large lump of ice to the North Pole'.[62] He flew from Cairo to Teheran in the company of Averell Harriman, whose advice he wanted on how to deal with Stalin. His party also included Brooke, Wavell, Tedder and Cadogan. They stayed in the British Summer Legation at Gulhek, high in the hills outside the capital, to avoid the noise and potential assassins in the city. At 5.30 a.m. on Wednesday, 12 August, 'a lovely summer morning', he took off for

* Churchill's sense of humour did not desert him during this taxing period. When Smuts accused him of not appealing enough to religious motives in politics, he replied, 'I have made more bishops than anyone since St Augustine' (Moran, *Struggle* p. 57). It might seem insensitive to joke on the very day Gott died, but, as he wrote years later, 'Who in war will not have his laugh amid the skulls?' (WSC, *TSWW* V p. 81).

Moscow.[63] 'Soon we were flying north towards a gap in the mountains bordering the Caspian Sea,' recalled Tommy Thompson. 'Away to the east we could see the snow-capped peak of Mount Demavend, looking staggeringly majestic in the morning sun.' On the journey, Churchill awarded Thompson 'ten demerits' for not having ensured that the Embassy put mustard on his ham sandwiches.[64] (These demerits were more than erased on the return flight by champagne and caviar.)

They landed at Moscow in the early evening and were met by Stalin (wearing a khaki shirt, blue trousers and half-length boots), Molotov and a large assembly of Politburo members, commissars and generals, after which they were driven to State Villa No. 7, some 8 miles outside Moscow.[65] Tedder was so suspicious that the villa was bugged that he sensibly wrote 'Méfiez-vous [Watch out!]' on a scrap of paper and passed it to Churchill when the Prime Minister started being indiscreet.[66]

The first strategy meeting with Stalin took place that night. After being driven the twenty minutes to the Kremlin in a car with 2-inch-thick bullet-proof windows, Churchill noticed – but did not mention – that Stalin's office was 'furnished in the faded scarlet and gold magnificence of Czarist days'.[67] Churchill, Harriman, Ambassador Sir Archibald Clark Kerr and their interpreter John Dunlop were met by Stalin, Molotov, Marshal Kliment Voroshilov of the State Defence Committee and their interpreter Pavlov. 'I would not have come to Moscow unless I felt sure I would be able to discuss realities,' Churchill began. He told Stalin that a Second Front in Europe was impossible in the near term, whereupon 'Stalin's face crumpled up into a frown,' Dunlop noted.[68] 'Stalin kept getting up and walking across the big room to a writing table in which he delved for cigarettes,' Clark Kerr reported to Eden. 'These he tore to bits and stuffed into his absurd curly pipe. In his turn, the P.M. when he had shot his bolt got up and had a walk, pulling from his heated buttocks the seat of his trousers which had clearly stuck to them. It was indeed a warm night. There was something about this dumpy figure, plucking at his backside, which suggested immense strength but little distinction.'[69]

When Churchill's language got so far ahead of Pavlov that the translator could not tell Stalin exactly what was being said, Stalin remarked, 'I did not understand, but I like the spirit.'[70] The Wehrmacht had reached the River Volga – the Battle of Stalingrad began only ten days later – and with many Russian, Belorussian and Ukrainian cities in German hands the Red Army was stretched almost to breaking point. But the Soviet leader quickly grasped the potential of Operation Torch, and seemed almost friendly, at least initially. Cadogan recorded Churchill telling him that the meeting 'had gone very well. The P.M. had hoped to soften the impact of the "No

Second Front in 1942" by explaining our plans for Torch . . . which he had done in some detail. The P.M. said Stalin had taken this unexpectedly well and had even said the equivalent of "God prosper your enterprise."'[71] The meeting ended at 10.40 p.m. on that positive note.

The next day, Thursday, 13 August, was a different matter altogether. Arriving at the Kremlin, Churchill was handed one of Stalin's characteristically tough memoranda attacking the lack of a Second Front in 1942, which ignored Torch altogether. It was as though the previous day's discussions had not taken place at all. When Churchill explained that the losses in the PQ17 convoy had been too high to launch another convoy in August, Stalin said, 'This is the first time in history that the British Navy turned back from a battle,' an implication of cowardice designed to provoke Churchill.[72] Stalin told Churchill that he had broken his word, that the Germans were not invincible and that 'If the British would only fight they would find that the Germans were not supermen.'[73] Harriman recalled that an incensed Churchill kept his temper and did not mention 'what must have been uppermost in his mind', namely that it had been the Ribbentrop–Molotov Pact that made the German attack in the West possible in the first place. In his unpublished memoirs, Cadogan at one point likened Churchill under Stalin's and Molotov's needling attacks to 'a bull in the ring maddened by the pricks of the picadors'.[74] The British changed interpreters, using Major Arthur Birse in place of Dunlop, who Churchill complained had introduced his own feelings into statements, 'like a hairdresser'.[75]

Churchill's self-control was all the more remarkable as Clark Kerr believed him to have been in a bad mood from a hangover.[76] At one point in the discussions, Churchill drew Stalin a sketch to explain that the Anglo-American strategy was 'to attack the soft underbelly of the crocodile as the Russians attacked the hard snout'.[77] It is surprising Churchill thought this analogy would have appealed to Stalin, but he also used a globe in Stalin's office to explain the geographical advantages of expelling the Axis from the Mediterranean.

The first full day of discussions ended at 2 a.m. with Stalin declaring 'he was bound to say that he did not agree with Mr Churchill's arguments'.[78] Clark Kerr was impressed by Churchill's 'ability to transform his face from the rosiest, happiest, the most laughing, dimpled and mischievous baby's bottom into the face of an angry and outraged bullfrog!'[79] Harriman recalled that the talks 'turned out to have moments of agreement and moments of violent argument'.[80] Churchill cabled to Roosevelt and the War Cabinet to say he had had a 'most unpleasant discussion' in which Stalin had said 'a great many insulting things'.

Patrick Kinna, who was at the State Villa when Churchill stormed back there, remembered him saying, 'I have just had a most terrible meeting with this terrible man Stalin . . . evil and dreadful.' Whereupon Clark Kerr said, 'May I remind you, Prime Minister, that all these rooms have been wired and Stalin will hear every word you said.'[81] Clark Kerr played a key role in calming Churchill down after Stalin's aggressive rebuff. Walking around the villa's grounds the next morning, with Churchill wearing a 'preposterous ten gallon hat' in the bright sunshine, the tall, urbane veteran diplomat spoke very frankly to the Prime Minister.[82] He told him that his approach to Stalin was all wrong and failed to use his gift for charm. Furthermore, 'He was an aristocrat and a man of the world and he expected these people to be like him. They weren't. They came straight from the plough or the lathe. They were rough and inexperienced.'[83] 'But that man insulted me,' Churchill replied. 'I represent a great country and I am not submissive by nature.'[84] Clark Kerr recorded Churchill saying this 'sulkily over his hunched shoulders'. He advised that the Prime Minister should not break off relations simply because he had been 'offended by a peasant who didn't know any better'.[85]

Stalin's mood was to change several more times in the course of the four days of talks. At one point Churchill had to suggest he would go back to London without anything being agreed. But eventually the two men came to an understanding.[86] Stalin needed British aid, and Churchill needed the Russians to continue fighting. The threat to leave Moscow 'was not bad temper', Rowan recalled, 'it was a calculated response to a calculated move, and it succeeded.'[87] At another point in the negotiations, the British were told they could not see Stalin for several hours because, his staff said, he was 'out walking'.[88] There were several marathon late-night eating and drinking sessions, with twenty-course meals and long patriotic toasts that went on until 3 a.m. This was another trial for which Churchill had had a lifetime's preparation, though it tested the constitutions of several of his entourage.

The discussions, often over tables 'groaning with food and drink', were not confined to the war. At one point Churchill asked Stalin what had been his most anxious moment in his career, to which Stalin replied the collectivization of Soviet agriculture. 'What happened to the kulaks?' Churchill then asked, of the millions of richer peasants who had been killed during that process. 'There was not even the flicker of an eyelid,' Cadogan recalled. 'He [Stalin] turned and with a nonchalant wave of the hand said, "Oh! They went away."'[89]

After the final session of talks on 15 August, there was a 'long and convivial' dinner in Stalin's flat in the Kremlin, where Churchill met Stalin's daughter Svetlana, ate suckling pig (which Stalin ate with his fingers), drank a good deal of vodka, swapped jokes with the Soviet leader and discussed with him the relative merits of Marlborough and Wellington (on Napoleon's birthday), with the result that the two men finally got on well after denouncing each other in public for two decades.[90] When he returned to the villa early the next morning, Churchill called Stalin 'that great man', and not solely for the benefit of the listening devices. The next morning, as he flew back to Cairo via Teheran, he had to 'breakfast off aspirins'.[91]

If Churchill had any doubts about the wisdom of his opposition to Operation Sledgehammer, they were laid to rest three days later by Operation Jubilee, Lord Louis Mountbatten's disastrous Combined Operations raid on Dieppe, which had been intended to placate the Russians, test German defences, draw forces to the west and boost morale. It turned out to be a complete fiasco, in which 68 per cent of the mainly Canadian troops who took part were killed, wounded or captured. Five days later, Churchill asked Ismay to 'ascertain the facts' about the planning of the raid, in particular whose idea it had been 'to attack the strongly fortified town front without first securing the cliffs on either side, and to use our tanks in frontal assault off the beaches'.[92] Ismay replied eight days afterwards, enclosing Mountbatten's report, which blamed Montgomery, who was then in charge of South-Eastern Command. Occupied by many other things, Churchill took it no further, but when he came to write his memoirs in 1950 'he smelled a rat and was determined to find it' the truth behind the raid.[93]

Churchill discovered that there had in fact been two plans to attack Dieppe: Montgomery's, codenamed Operation Rutter, had been abandoned and replaced with Jubilee, Mountbatten's concept and the one put into operation on 19 August 1942. Churchill then asked whether the Chiefs of Staff or Defence Committee or War Cabinet had ever formally approved Jubilee, 'or was it all pushed through by Dickie Mountbatten on his own without reference to higher authority?'[94] When Ismay investigated it became clear that the latter was the correct explanation, whereupon Mountbatten became seriously agitated.[95] He sent pages of tendentious corrections to Churchill's draft memoirs, suggested that Ismay refuse to give Churchill copyright permission for his report and argued that the 68 per cent casualty figure was 'not one which our side should stress'. Mountbatten effectively begged Ismay – who had been his chief of staff when he was viceroy of India three years earlier – not to expose him as the person behind the planning of Jubilee.[96]

Mountbatten's cover-up went so far as to assert that the naval commander for the raid, Admiral James Hughes-Hallett, had discussed it with

Churchill beforehand. (Hughes-Hallett told Ismay that he could not remember whether the conversation had taken place before or afterwards.) Mountbatten also stated that the reason the Chiefs of Staff had no record of discussing the Jubilee plan was for reasons of security, even though plenty of equally sensitive operations were routinely recorded in the Chiefs of Staff Committee minutes. Under time pressure from his American publishers, Churchill simply accepted all of Mountbatten's revisions and amendments, which, as the historian David Reynolds points out, 'passed responsibility back to Churchill and the Chiefs, played down the Canadian losses and played up the benefits of the operation', which were actually somewhere between minimal and non-existent.[97]

On 24 August 1942, Churchill reached Gibraltar on his way home. Because of the security implications of his being recognized there, he was confined to Government House, although he discussed with Brooke 'disguising himself as an Egyptian demi-mondaine or an Armenian suffering from toothache so as to be allowed out'.[98] Later that day, he reached Lyneham Aerodrome, where Clementine came out to meet him. 'A flight of ten thousand miles through hostile and foreign skies may be the duty of young pilots,' the American General Douglas MacArthur, himself a Medal of Honor holder, was to say of Churchill's London–Moscow journey, 'but for a statesman burdened with the world's cares it is an act of inspiring gallantry and valor.'[99]

John Martin thought Churchill 'seemed remarkably fit' as he alighted from the plane.[100] Back in London, the Prime Minister boasted to James Stuart, 'As for all this talk about Russian drinking – there is nothing in it. I drank twice as much as they.'[101] Six weeks later he told Eade that 'although he regarded him as an uncouth and bear-like individual, he nevertheless rather liked Stalin and that he had many things in common. At the same time, he was quite plain that Russia had no sort of gratitude towards us for all we had done to help them.'[102] He added that although he would rather be president of the USA than prime minister of Britain, 'he did not want to be Stalin, with the authority to say, "Take away that man and shoot him."'[103]

'The greatest goodwill prevailed, and for the first time we got on to easy and friendly terms,' Churchill reported to the War Cabinet. 'I feel that I have established a personal relationship which will be helpful . . . Now they know the worst, and having made their protest are entirely friendly; this in spite of the fact that this is their most anxious and agonising time.' It turned out this was appallingly naive. Stalin told Maisky in October, 'All of us in Moscow have gained the impression that Churchill is aiming at the defeat of the U.S.S.R., in order then to come to terms with the Germany of Hitler or [ex-Chancellor Heinrich] Brüning at the expense of our country.'[104] Stalin did not trust Churchill, because he did not trust anyone (except, for two years, Adolf Hitler).

Yet Churchill could not discover Stalin's true views about him because after June 1941 Britain's intelligence services were ordered not to spy on Britain's new Soviet ally, a mistaken policy that was certainly not reciprocated.[105] Soon after his return, Churchill flattered Stalin egregiously, saying in the Commons, 'Above all, he is a man with that saving sense of humour which is of high importance to all men and all nations, but particularly to great men and great nations. Stalin also left upon me the impression of a deep, cool wisdom and a complete absence of illusions of any kind.'[106]* To the King, Churchill described Stalin as 'a cold, uncouth man, but with an understanding mind . . . In private both he and Molotov smiled and even laughed at Winston's answers to their somewhat pertinent questions to the past. Stalin knows nothing of the rest of the world.'[107]

On 25 August, the King's younger brother, the Duke of Kent, was killed in a plane crash in Scotland while on active duty with the RAF. 'Nothing can fill the awful gap,' Churchill said in his eulogy in the Commons. 'Nothing can assuage or comfort the loneliness and deprivation which fall upon wife and children when the prop and centre of their home is suddenly snatched away. Only the faith in a life after death in a brighter world where dear ones will meet again – only that and the measured tramp of time can give consolation.'[108] It was the only occasion on which Churchill expressed a belief in any kind of life after death. His words were presumably primarily designed to help assuage the grief of the Duke's widow, Marina, whom he had once described as the most beautiful woman he had ever seen.[109]

On 9 September Churchill was informed that the Indian Congress Party would offer only passive resistance should the Japanese invade the subcontinent, and would not help the British to defend it. 'I hate Indians,' Churchill apparently told Amery. 'They are a beastly people with a beastly religion.'[110] Churchill has rightly been castigated for remarks such as these, but the many encomia he paid to the Indian Army – at 2.5 million, the largest all-volunteer army in history – have tended to be ignored, along with the fact that he did continue to protect India with British Army divisions that could have been put to very good use elsewhere. 'The unsurpassed

* In December 1929 Churchill had referred to Stalin as Trotsky's 'subordinate in revolutionary rank, his inferior in wit, though not perhaps in crime' (WSC, *GC* pp. 123–5). He cut that chapter out of wartime editions of the book.

bravery of Indian soldiers and officers, Moslem and Hindu alike,' he said, and their 'glorious heroism' in campaigns from Abyssinia and North Africa to Burma and Italy, 'shine forever in the annals of war'.[111] Such considered remarks are far more meaningful than the tasteless racial jibes he sometimes made, often from exasperation or to provoke his colleagues, rather than because he meant them. 'The fact should sometimes be noted', Churchill said at the Guildhall in September 1944, 'that under British rule in the last eighty years incomparably fewer people have perished by steel or firearms in India than in any similar area or community on the globe.'[112] He saw it as Britain's duty to continue to make sacrifices to see that this continued. 'The Japs breed like vermin and die like heroes,' he also told a small lunch party in Downing Street.[113]

In late September, six weeks into the five-month pivotal Battle of Stalingrad, Churchill expressed his 'confidence in continued Russian resistance'. Every night the RAF dropped on to German cities the equivalent of three and a half times the weight of bombs that had destroyed Coventry, halting the increase in the Third Reich's arms production and starting the process of demoralization of the German people. At this singularly inauspicious moment, a further political crisis developed in London as Cripps threatened resignation, saying he was 'not satisfied with the conduct of the war'.[114] He wanted a War Planning Directorate set up, which would clip Churchill's powers.[115] In the continued absence of a victory in the Western Desert, Churchill was still politically vulnerable and Harold Nicolson wondered whether Cripps was about to 'create an alternative Government and take Winston's place'.[116]

Ever since his return from Moscow in January, Cripps had found himself immensely popular. Churchill believed that his time as ambassador had gone to his head, remarking, 'There, but for the grace of God, goes God.'[117] As if to underline his messiah status, Cripps would eat frugal breakfasts at Lyons corner houses alongside local office workers. A foolproof indication of when politicians are 'on manoeuvres' for the premiership is when they tramp around the country making speeches far outside their portfolios. When the Gallup polling organization asked, 'If anything should happen to Mr Churchill whom would you like to succeed him as prime minister?', 34 per cent replied Eden, but 28 per cent replied Cripps, and no one else got more than 3 per cent.[118] That summer, Cripps had begun a series of speeches all over Britain on issues unconnected with his ministerial duties, on matters as diverse as social security, slums, universal education, civil aviation, housing, National Savings, 'the extremes of wealth or poverty' and how to 'get rid of unemployment'.[119] He sent a message to China on United Nations Day, and spoke on the BBC about obeying God's purpose.

Cripps was easily the most active member of the War Cabinet besides Churchill himself, and a potential challenger for the premiership if anything were to go wrong with Montgomery's forthcoming offensive at El Alamein, planned for late October. Cripps went so far as to make some thinly veiled criticisms of Churchill in public. 'I have felt in this country since my return a lack of urgency,' he said. 'I feel that we are not "all out" in our effort and determination.'[120] In the event, on 21 September, Churchill, Attlee and Eden managed to persuade Cripps not to resign before Montgomery's offensive. Churchill privately dismissed the War Planning Directorate idea as a 'disembodied Brains Trust', after the popular radio programme of that name.[121] 'We shall lose the war if Churchill stays,' Aneurin Bevan told Nicolson, but failed to persuade him. 'I still see Winston as the God of War,' Nicolson noted.[122]* After the war, Churchill claimed that September and October 1942 had been the most anxious months of the entire struggle for him, and it is easy to see why. Although the chances of invasion were now low, Allied shipping losses were the heaviest of the war (in November, 800,000 tons); the Germans had taken central Stalingrad; Montgomery had made no advance from El Alamein; Cripps and Beaverbrook were circling and preparing to strike; Japan had overrun one-eighth of the world's surface and now threatened both India and Australia.[123] Even in the extremely unlikely event of a German collapse, there was the spectre of a resurgent Russia marching across a devastated continent. 'It would be a measureless disaster', Churchill told Eden, 'if Russian barbarism overlaid the culture and independence of the ancient States of Europe.'[124]

Beaverbrook was still campaigning for a Second Front outside the government, hopeful of an opportunity to replace Churchill as prime minister if he stumbled, but he seems to have been a healing influence within the Churchill family at this time. 'I am so grateful to you for being the mediator between Randolph and Pamela *and* between Randolph and Winston,' Clementine wrote to him on 8 October. 'I hope that now, until he returns to Egypt, Randolph may see his father constantly. He truly loves Winston and this estrangement has been a sorrow and has weighed on both of them.'[125]

Receiving the Freedom of the City of Edinburgh on 12 October, Churchill burnished his Scottish credentials. 'First of all, I decided to be born on St Andrew's Day,' he declared, before pointing out that both his

* That day, asked to give the House a 'categorical denunciation' of the Vichy premier, Pierre Laval, Churchill joked, 'I am afraid I have rather exhausted the possibilities of the English language' (WSC, *End* p. 186).

wife and his Great War regiment were Scottish, and 'I sat for fifteen years as the representative of "Bonnie Dundee", and I might be sitting for it still if the matter had rested entirely with me.'[126] He spoke of Commando raids along the French coast, and of how 'there comes out of the sea from time to time a hand of steel which plucks the German sentries from their posts with growing efficiency, amid the joy of the whole countryside.'[127] With the music-hall entertainer Sir Harry Lauder in the audience, he added, 'Let me use to you the words of your famous minstrel – he is here today – words which have given comfort and renewed strength to many a burdened heart: Keep right on to the end of the road, Keep right on to the end.'[128]

The next day, when the imposition of the colour bar by the American Army on British restaurants was discussed in the Cabinet, Lord Cranborne said that one of his black officials in the Colonial Office could no longer go to a restaurant because American officers had imposed a whites-only policy there. 'That's alright,' Churchill said, 'if he takes a banjo with him, they'll think he's one of the band!'[129] Having made this insensitive joke, Churchill went on to address the situation with the seriousness it deserved, and the Cabinet concluded that the US Army 'must not expect our authorities, civil or military, to assist them in enforcing a policy of segregation. It was clear that, so far as concerned admission to canteens, public houses, theatres, cinemas, and so forth, there would, and must, be no restriction of the facilities hitherto extended to coloured persons as a result of the arrival of United States troops in this country.'[130]

On Friday, 23 October 1942, Montgomery launched his offensive at El Alamein, which lasted for twelve days and nights and which Churchill wanted to dub the 'Battle of Egypt'. That night, Churchill attended a dinner the King and Queen were giving at Buckingham Palace in honour of Eleanor Roosevelt, the President's wife. Afterwards, everyone watched Noël Coward's thinly veiled encomium to Louis Mountbatten in the splendid propaganda movie *In Which We Serve*. Churchill kept asking for information about how the battle was progressing, until nothing would content him but telephoning the War Office himself. He returned singing 'Roll Out the Barrel' 'with gusto', Tommy Lascelles noted, 'but with little evidence of musical talent'.[131]

By 29 October, both Churchill and Eden were showing signs of irritation with Montgomery for not yet having broken through Rommel's line, but Brooke calmed them, convinced that positive results were about to show. Sure enough, on 3 November, Operation Supercharge, the strongest of Montgomery's attacks so far, spearheaded by General Bernard Freyberg's 2nd New Zealand Division, broke through the German defences in the fourth phase of the battle, forcing Rommel to start his retreat to Fuka. 'P.M. in London in a state of over-excitement,' observed Cadogan that day.[132] It was on 3 November, at his Tuesday lunch with the King, that Churchill could finally say with certainty, 'I bring you victory.'[133] 'We thought he had gone mad,' the Queen remarked later. 'We had not heard the word since the war began.'[134] Churchill was particularly pleased with two Ultra telegrams in which Rommel gave Hitler 'a very depressing account' of the battle.[135]

At a Cabinet discussion on a Foreign Office paper about European federalism in the post-war world, Cadogan noted, 'P.M. of course excited by Egyptian news, and his excitement took the not unexpected form of "Damn Europe: we'll be strong enough to go our own way."'[136] By 4 November, Rommel was in full retreat. Montgomery's army had captured 30,000 Axis troops, and that evening Montgomery dined with the German General Ritter von Thoma in his desert caravan. Napoleon and Marlborough used to dine with defeated generals in their tents after battles, so when an MP complained privately about Montgomery's actions Churchill replied gravely, 'Poor von Thoma. I, too, have dined with Montgomery.'[137] (He was later privately to say of the highly egotistical Monty, 'In defeat unbeatable: in victory unbearable.')[138]

Churchill ordered the nation's church bells to be rung on Sunday, 15 November, once there was no possibility of a successful German counter-attack. When it was pointed out that the bells had probably rusted up and the bell-ringers were serving in the forces, his response was that 'That didn't matter.'[139] Nor did it; the joyful popular response on hearing the church bells rung for a genuine victory is recorded in many of the diaries and letters of the day.

'We are not celebrating final victory,' Churchill told those around him. 'The war will still be long. When we have beaten Germany, it will take us two more years to beat Japan. Nor is that a bad thing. It will keep America and ourselves together while we are making peace in Europe. If I am still alive, I shall fling all we have into the Pacific.'[140] His public estimation of the significance of El Alamein was expressed in his speech at the Mansion House on 10 November, when he proclaimed, in an epigram that would have made Edward Gibbon proud, 'Now, this is not the end. It is not even the beginning of the end. But it is, perhaps, the end of the beginning.'[141]

# 28
# 'One Continent Redeemed'
# November 1942–September 1943

*The problems of victory are more agreeable than those of defeat, but they are no less difficult.*

Churchill, House of Commons, November 1942[1]

*Basically, I am Commander-in-Chief here. Naturally enough, I can't always carry out what I want, but I can always prevent that which I don't want.*

Churchill to Ivan Maisky, April 1943[2]

On Sunday, 8 November 1942, over 100,000 troops of the United States and British armies stormed ashore in north-west Africa at three places along the Moroccan coast, and also at Oran and Algiers. There was some resistance by Vichy forces, which cost the lives of 850 Allied soldiers, but when it quickly became clear that Operation Torch was an overwhelming assault Admiral Darlan, the Vichy Commander-in-Chief in North Africa, negotiated a ceasefire with Eisenhower under which he was allowed to retain a wide measure of administrative control.

'Winston revelled over our success!' wrote Brooke the next day.[3]* After a triumphant drive along the Strand to St Paul's Cathedral, Churchill delivered the Mansion House Speech at the Lord Mayor's Luncheon on 10 November. 'We have victory,' he told his audience, 'a remarkable and definite victory. The bright gleam has caught the helmets of our soldiers, and warmed and cheered all our hearts . . . The Germans have been

* Years later Brooke added, 'I think this is the only occasion on which he expressed publicly any appreciation or thanks for work I had done during the whole of the period I worked for him' (eds. Danchev and Todman, *War Diaries* p. 340). While that was not literally true – Churchill called Brooke 'that great officer' in a speech after D-Day, mentioned him in his Victory Day speech in 1945 and awarded him a viscountcy – it was indeed noticeable how little Churchill mentioned the other great British master-strategist of the war (*CS* VII p. 6976).

outmatched and outfought with the very kind of weapons with which they had beaten down so many small peoples.' Although Vichy forces had fought against the Allies during Operation Torch, he continued to believe that the French would ultimately contribute to the defeat of Nazi Germany: 'I declare to you here, on this considerable occasion, even now when misguided or suborned Frenchmen are firing upon their rescuers, I declare to you my faith that France will rise again.'[4] He then added an unambiguous reference to the Far East and India:

> We have not entered this war for profit or expansion, but only for honour and to do our duty in defending the right. Let me, however, make this clear, in case there should be any mistake about it in any quarter. We mean to hold our own. I have not become the King's First Minister in order to preside over the liquidation of the British Empire. For that task, if ever it were prescribed, someone else would have to be found.[5]

It was a clear message not just to the Japanese and the Indian National Congress, but also to the Americans, that Churchill did not believe the Empire's days were numbered. Indeed, he saw the war as being fought as much for the Empire as for Britain, and the Empire had responded magnificently, providing men, money and materiel in huge amounts, without being called upon. In return, Britain helped protect India from a Japanese invasion which, had it been as murderous as Japan's occupation of the Philippines, would have left fifty million Indians dead. Churchill's lifelong belief in the Empire was profoundly to affect both the grand strategy Britain was to adopt and her relations with the Americans later in the conflict.

'This noble Desert Army, which has never doubted its power to beat the enemy,' Churchill later said of Montgomery's men and their victory at El Alamein, 'and whose pride had suffered cruelly from retreats and disasters which they could not understand, regained in a week its ardour and self-confidence. Historians may explain Tobruk. The Eighth Army has done better: it has avenged it.'[6] (Tobruk itself would be retaken on 13 November.) He then cleverly ascribed the concept of Operation Torch to Roosevelt, even though it had originally been his idea. 'On my first visit to Washington after the United States was attacked by Japan, Germany and Italy,' he said, 'President Roosevelt favoured the idea that French North Africa was specially suitable for American intervention in the Western theatre. This view was fully shared by us.'[7] The sleight of hand was spotted by Lascelles, Ismay and some others, but he hoped to encourage the Americans to take credit for an operation that the Joint Chiefs of Staff had actually opposed until the very end of July.

Hitler responded to the assault on North Africa by occupying the whole of France in November, whereupon the French scuttled their fleet at Toulon, an action that would have saved 1,300 lives had they taken it at Oran two years earlier. When, on 11 November, a sacred day for the Great War generation, Churchill entered the Commons to announce that there had been 59,000 Axis casualties at El Alamein to the Commonwealth's 13,600, he was received with prolonged cheers. 'I am certainly not one of those who need to be prodded,' he said. 'In fact, if anything, I am a prod. My difficulties rather lie in finding the patience and self-restraint to wait through many anxious weeks for the results to be achieved.'[8] In explaining the strategic situation, he spoke of 'the exposure of the underbelly of the Axis, especially Italy, to heavy attack'.[9] Although he did not use the adjective 'soft' to describe that underbelly, as he had with Stalin and again with General Mark Clark and on other occasions, the implication was that an Italian campaign might be easy.

From mid-November, Churchill began to use Ultra decrypts again, for the first time since he had admitted to misreading them in April. Frustrated by what he saw as the sluggishness of Montgomery's pursuit of Rommel, he quoted to Alexander the serial numbers of the decrypts showing 'a condition of weakness and counter-order among the enemy of a very remarkable character'.[10] Alexander and Montgomery were rightly conscious of the Wehrmacht's capacity for counter-attack, however, and did not allow Churchill's interventions to alter the pace of their methodical and successful advance. It turned out to be the last significant time that Churchill used the Ultra decrypts to support his arguments in operational decisions.[11] For the rest of the war, he retained his enthusiasm for reading German decrypts, but after this there were so many of them being produced that the Joint Intelligence Committee had to choose which ones he should see. He left no one in any doubt about their importance, however, telling Major Alexander Standish, General Omar Bradley's chief Ultra officer, in August 1944 'that he would sacrifice three divisions rather than have this information revealed and if any man did reveal it, intentionally or unintentionally, he would be summarily court martialed and shot'.[12]

Churchill could now turn his attention to Cripps. 'Now that there are successes and the Government policy vindicated,' the King recorded, 'Winston calls him the War Cabinet Unexploded Bomb.'[13] In a quick reshuffle, Cripps was made minister for aircraft production, a position no longer in the War Cabinet, where he stayed for the rest of the war. Eden took on Cripps's post as leader of the House of Commons while also remaining foreign secretary, and Lord Cranborne performed Cripps's other role as lord privy seal. Lindemann replaced Cranborne as paymaster-general, bringing another close friend and supporter into the Cabinet.

Churchill's sights were now on Italy. 'When a nation is thoroughly beaten in war it does all sorts of things which no one can imagine beforehand,' he told the War Cabinet on 22 November.[14] The Combined Chiefs of Staff were not yet thinking in terms of an Italian mainland campaign, but Churchill was, and had been since his four memoranda of the previous year. He saw it as a way of drawing German resources away from the beaches of north-west France.*

In the fifth and last secret session in the Commons, on 10 December, Churchill defended Eisenhower's deal with Darlan, by which the Vichy authorities continued to govern Tunisia and Algeria. Explaining why there were so few Free French and so many collaborationists, he said, 'The Almighty in His infinite wisdom did not see fit to create Frenchmen in the image of Englishmen.'[15] The French general Henri Giraud had escaped from prison and reached Algeria, only to clash with de Gaulle over who would chair the French Committee of National Liberation (FCNL), which was intended to coordinate all French anti-Vichy forces both in France and abroad. Churchill commented, 'We all thought General Giraud was the man for the job, and that his arrival would be electrical. In this opinion, General Giraud emphatically agreed.'[16] Churchill described Marshal Pétain – which he pronounced 'Peatayne' – as 'that antique defeatist', and when he sat down he received a great cheer.

Roosevelt had grown to loathe de Gaulle for his French chauvinism, his habit of constantly giving priority to French interests over Allied ones and his attempts to sabotage US–Vichy relations. 'De Gaulle is out to achieve one-man government in France,' the President told his son Elliott. 'I can't imagine a man I would distrust more.'[17] He wrongly suspected de Gaulle of being Churchill's puppet, because he had been given refuge by the British Government, which also sustained the Free French forces. 'I am no more enamoured of him than you are,' Churchill protested in a telegram on the same day as the secret session, 'but I would rather have him on the Committee than strutting about as a combination of Joan of Arc and Clemenceau.'[18] When, on another occasion, Bracken said that de Gaulle regarded himself as a reincarnation of St Joan, Churchill growled, 'Yes, but *my* bishops won't burn him!'[19] Churchill was enormously frustrated

* On a Sunday afternoon in early December, while staying at Dorneywood, the Buckinghamshire house of the industrialist Sir Courtauld Thomson, Churchill found much-needed relaxation playing Corinthian Bagatelle, an early form of pinball with a wooden board, ball and metal pins. He reached the impressive score of 1,015, after playing for three hours. Scores of over a thousand are recorded in Dorneywood's 'Golden Book', and his was witnessed by Mountbatten, Lindemann and Harriman. (The author also appears, having achieved a four-figure score early in the twenty-first century.)

and irritated by de Gaulle, but – although sorely tempted, and sometimes on the verge of doing so – he never withdrew his support from him. Darlan he genuinely detested, describing him in November as 'a bloody swine'.[20] Darlan's assassination by a French monarchist on Christmas Eve 1942 has been blamed on Churchill, but without much evidence.

It was not just over relations with de Gaulle that Churchill had to tread carefully with the Americans. Their demands for an end to Imperial Preference led him to remark to Herbert Morrison, who was about to give a speech on post-war colonial policy, 'Considering that for seventy or eighty years we kept our colonies absolutely open to the trade of the world without claiming the slightest preference or imposing any taxation except for revenue, and that it was the Americans by their high tariff policy who led the world astray, it is pretty good cheek of them now coming to schoolmarm us into proper behaviour. However I am not suggesting you should use that particular sentence.'[21] On New Year's Day, Churchill told the King about future military strategy: 'We have to collaborate with the Americans over these matters as we cannot do them without their help. They are so slow in training their army and getting it over here.'[22]

Churchill, Roosevelt and the American and British Chiefs of Staff agreed to meet at the US Army's Anfa Camp, a former tourist hotel outside Casablanca, to decide where the next Anglo-American blow should fall after the Axis had been completely expelled from North Africa. Churchill took off for the Conference, codenamed Symbol, from RAF Lyneham in his Liberator plane *Commando** on 12 January 1943. The King recorded him that day as admitting that 'He will have to be much firmer with FDR than before, as he must make him understand that we cannot carry on without the help he has already promised us.'[23] He took Portal, Harriman, Moran, Pim, Commander Tommy Thompson, Detective Inspector Walter Thompson,† John Martin and Sawyers. It was to be the first of four long journeys he made in 1943, taking him outside Britain for nearly four months. When he landed, Churchill was supposed to go immediately into an armoured car to hide his identity from the people working in the fields near by, but he decided to stay to welcome General Ismay's plane, maintaining that there was no real danger of being recognized as he was in uniform under his codename Air Commodore Frankland. This fooled nobody. 'In spite of Churchill's uniform there could be no mistaking his

* The plane was lost over the Atlantic in 1945.

† Walter Thompson's son, Fred, who was one of the first pilots in the heroic target-marking Pathfinder squadrons of Bomber Command and had won the DFC flying forty-three missions over enemy territory, was shortly to be killed in action, adding to the long list of people Churchill knew personally whose sons had died in the war.

contour,' Harriman recalled.[24] Ismay later observed that he had looked more like an air commodore disguised as the Prime Minister than the other way around.

Once established in the comfortable Villa Mirador in the grounds of the luxury hotel, some 200 yards from Roosevelt's much plusher villa, and Captain Pim having set up a Map Room, Churchill invited Generals George Marshall and Mark Clark to lunch and Admiral King, Harriman and others to a convivial dinner.* Roosevelt arrived on 14 January, and over the course of the next nine days the Combined Chiefs decided on the allocation of materiel to the various theatres of war. The Americans had still to be persuaded to embrace a Mediterranean strategy for 1943 rather than a cross-Channel one. The Anglophobic General Albert Wedemeyer later complained that they had been 'led up the garden path' by Churchill at Casablanca. 'They may say I lead them up the garden path,' Churchill retorted the following year, 'but at every stage of the garden they have found delectable fruit and wholesome vegetables.'[25] It was agreed at Casablanca that the next target would be Sicily. 'I absolutely refuse to be fobbed off with a sardine,' Churchill said when Sardinia was suggested.[26] It was also decided that Alexander would become Eisenhower's deputy commander-in-chief for the Tunisian campaign, 'with the real direction and planning of the main operation', Churchill told Clementine, while General Henry 'Jumbo' Maitland Wilson would succeed Alexander as commander-in-chief in the Middle East.

At the end of the Conference, Churchill assented to Roosevelt's proposal that the Allies demand Germany's unconditional surrender, thereby closing off the possibility of a negotiated peace with any Nazi successor to Hitler. Critics have alleged that this helped the Nazis to persuade the German people to fight on even once they knew they would lose, but Churchill publicly stated that it imposed clear duties on the victors. 'It does not mean that they are entitled to behave in a barbarous manner, nor that they wish to blot out Germany from among the nations of Europe,' he reported to the Commons on his return. 'If we are bound, we are bound by our own consciences to civilization.'[27] The demand was believed to raise Allied morale, and anything less would certainly have increased

* At one point during the Conference, Hopkins walked in on Churchill drinking wine at breakfast. The Prime Minister explained that he had 'a profound distaste on the one hand for skimmed milk, and no deep-rooted prejudice about wine' (ed. Sherwood, *Hopkins* II p. 685). 'I saw Winston drink a bottle of white wine for breakfast in Cairo,' Ian Jacob told the author (interview with General Sir Ian Jacob, 28 October 1988). The novelist C. P. Snow once said that Churchill could not have been an alcoholic, because no alcoholic could have drunk that much.

Stalin's suspicions that the Western Allies would be prepared to do a deal with the Germans in the closing stages of the war, but Churchill was never happy with it, and did not feel Roosevelt had given him enough warning of so important a departure.

Early in the Conference, Churchill said to Clementine of 'Don Quixote' – their private name for Roosevelt – that 'I have a very strong sense of the friendship which prevails between us.'[28] The Prime Minister and President ate most meals together and stayed up late, and Churchill rightly viewed the results of the Casablanca Conference as a great success. The Mediterranean strategy of attacking Sicily first and then Italy had been agreed by the Americans; escorts and landing craft were promised for an eventual reconquest of Burma in 1944; aid to Russia was to be increased; de Gaulle and Giraud had (however briefly) shaken hands for the cameras; global dispositions of forces and their overall commanders had been agreed. Churchill was a central figure, along with Roosevelt, Marshall and Brooke, in all of these agreements, and was delighted by their outcome. 'It is in every respect as I wished and proposed,' he told Clementine.[29]

After the final press conference on 24 January – 'We charmed them all right,' Churchill assured the President – he and Roosevelt drove to Marrakesh. They reached the beautiful villa of the American Vice Consul Moses Taylor in the late afternoon.[30] Churchill wrote in his war memoirs of 'the gay life of the city, including fortune-tellers, snake-charmers, masses of food and drink, and on the whole the largest and most elaborately organized brothels in the African continent. All these institutions were of long and ancient repute.'[31] He painted his only picture of the years between 1939 and VE Day, from the roof of the villa, a landscape of a portion of the city dominated by a shrine. He gave the painting, entitled *The Tower of Katoubia Mosque*, to Roosevelt.*

Roosevelt left Marrakesh on the morning of 26 January. That evening, Churchill flew to Cairo, where he ordered the British commanders-in-chief assembled there to plan for Operation Accolade, the capture of the Dodecanese Islands, with the utmost 'ingenuity and resource'.[32] Brooke considered it a distraction from the Italian campaign, but Churchill hoped that if Britain could reoccupy Crete and capture the Dodecanese she could restrict enemy movement in the eastern Mediterranean, open up the Bosporus and even the Balkans, and inspire Turkey to enter the war, so permitting the use of Turkish air bases to hit Axis targets in Greece,

* It required effort, since he had been suffering from painful 'Housemaid's Elbow', not an affliction one would immediately associate with Winston Churchill. Although it was now clearing up, he wore special elbow pads to protect against it. The painting is now in the possession of the actress Angelina Jolie.

Romania and Bulgaria.[33] The operation had obvious echoes of Gallipoli, and Roosevelt and Marshall opposed it outright, refusing to participate. Three days later, one of the men who could have stymied Accolade, Brigadier Vivian Dykes, Director of Plans at the War Office, died in a plane crash. On 31 January, Churchill flew to Adana to meet President Ismet Inönü of Turkey in his special train near Yenidje. 'Please do not worry about my personal safety,' he wrote in response to a concerned telegram from the War Cabinet asking him not to run the risk of assassination by going to Turkey, 'as I can take care of myself and am very quick to see where danger lies.'[34] Just before he took off, contemplating Dykes's death but also his own, Churchill told Ian Jacob, 'I think it's a pretty straight run now; even the Cabinet could manage it.'[35]

Churchill told President Inönü that as the Allies were now certainly going to win the war, Turkey should ensure that she profited from the coming victory by abandoning her neutrality. He later told the War Cabinet that he had 'made friends at once' with Inönü, and that the Turks 'longed for our victory'.[36] He flew to Nicosia the next day. The press was later told that Churchill, who was travelling under the soubriquet 'Mr Bullfinch', had stopped off in Cyprus to inspect the 4th Hussars, but in fact he was scouting it out as an appropriate place for meeting Stalin and Roosevelt that autumn. 'The island is perfect,' he told Maisky. 'Easily cut off from everywhere. Nobody will know a thing.'[37]

He was in Cairo on 2 February when Field Marshal Friedrich Paulus surrendered over 200,000 Axis troops at Stalingrad. He wrote to congratulate Stalin, making the terrible prediction that Turkey would enter the war before the end of 1943. 'I told them that in my experience the U.S.S.R. had never broken an engagement or treaty,' he told Stalin, a disingenuous remark that would have surprised the Churchill of the 1920s.[38] He also told Roosevelt that he thought Stalin should be told about their plans for Italy, saying that 'no one can keep secrets better.'[39] He suggested that they also inform Stalin that 'We are aiming at August for a heavy operation across the Channel, for which between seventeen and twenty British and United States divisions will be available.'[40] But he added that weather, shipping and landing craft would be limiting factors, and that it could not happen if they encountered stiff German resistance in Sicily and mainland Italy.

On 5 February, he left Cairo for the Western Desert to witness the formal entry of the Eighth Army into Tripoli and inspect the massed parades of 40,000 troops. 'After the war when a man is asked what he did it will be quite sufficient for him to say, "I marched and fought with the Desert Army," ' he told them. 'And when history is written and all the facts are known, your feats will gleam and glow and will be a source of song and story long after we who are gathered here have passed away.'[41] Brooke noted that when the 51st Highland Division marched past, 'with the wild music of the pipes in my ears . . . I looked round at Winston and saw several tears on his face'.[42]

On 7 February, despite the fact that his plane had developed engine trouble on a stopover in Algiers, Churchill flew up the Bristol Channel and landed at RAF Lyneham at 11 a.m. Sawyers had said to him on the flight, 'You are sitting on your hot-water bottle. That isn't at all a good idea.' 'Idea?' replied the Prime Minister. 'It isn't an idea, it's a coincidence.'[43] Churchill went to Eden's country house, Binderton, where they watched the recently released movie *Casablanca*, and, according to Eden's diary, 'Winston fulminated against de Gaulle' for his behaviour at the Symbol Conference.[44] He was also angry that the War Cabinet had tried to dissuade him from going to Turkey, and Eden recorded him saying that 'He must be allowed to go where he liked when he was abroad . . . Anyway, if he had been killed, it would have been a good way to die and I should only have come into my inheritance sooner.'

Beaverbrook had not yet given up his hopes of becoming prime minister, and was now hoping to replace Churchill with a triumvirate of himself, Eden and Bevin. His plan was stillborn, not least because Bevin, who disliked and distrusted him, immediately told Churchill. When asked how Churchill could remain on good personal terms with Beaverbrook after this, Bevin explained, 'Well, you see, it's like this: it's as if the old man had married an 'ore. He knows what she is, but he loves her.'[45] Beaverbrook had a twenty-three-page document drawn up by one of his researchers, entitled 'Winston Churchill's False Prophecies and Some Economic Consequencies [*sic*]' – a list of all of Churchill's supposed errors of judgement, including the Dardanelles, the Gold Standard, articles from the 1930s, the Abdication Crisis (in which he himself had been Churchill's principal ally), the speech to the neutrals of January 1940, predictions of victory in Crete and Tobruk, and much more.[46] It was all supported with references and annotations, largely from Hansard and Beaverbrook's own newspapers. The paper was never used, but Beaverbrook was primed just in case his old friend were to show signs of political vulnerability.

On 9 February Churchill entered the Commons for the first time since his return from Casablanca to a resounding cheer. 'We have to make the enemy burn and bleed in every way that is physically and reasonably possible,' he told MPs, 'in the same way as he is being made to burn and bleed along the vast Russian front from the White Sea to the Black Sea.'[47] Then he added, 'When I look at all that Russia is doing and the vast achievements of the Soviet Armies, I should feel myself below the level of events if I were not sure in my heart and conscience that everything in human power is being done and will be done to bring British and American Forces into action against the enemy with the utmost speed and energy and on the largest scale.'[48] Churchill went on to pay tribute to 'this vehement and formidable General Montgomery, a Cromwellian figure, austere, severe, accomplished, tireless, his life given to the study of war, who has attracted to himself in an extraordinary measure the confidence and the devotion of his Army'.[49] He then read out a message he had received from General Alexander following his defeat of Rommel: 'His Majesty's enemies, together with their impedimenta, have been completely eliminated from Egypt, Cyrenaica, Libya and Tripolitania. I now await your further instructions.' He paused, and then added, with perfect understatement, 'Well, obviously, we shall have to think of something else.'[50] After his speech, he gathered MPs around him in the Smoking Room. 'What seems to have impressed him most was the reception given him by the Italian population in Libya,' Nicolson recorded. '"They cheered me," he said, "and clapped their hands like this," and at that he stuck his cigar in his mouth and clapped his hands, saying 'Eeveever".'[51]*

On 16 February, Churchill contracted pneumonia with an inflammation of the base of his lung. Moran prescribed the new sulphonamide antibiotic known as M & B (after its makers, May & Baker Ltd), but for the next six days the Prime Minister was incapacitated. Once again he was lucky in his timing; M & B was the first chemical treatment for pneumonia to be invented. When he felt well enough he read *Moll Flanders* and on the 22nd he wrote to the King, who came to visit him convalescing at Chequers. 'De Gaulle is hostile to this country, and I put far more confidence in Giraud than in him,' he insisted, albeit allowing that his 'insolence . . . may be founded on stupidity rather than malice . . . He now wishes to go on a tour round his dominion, *mes fiefs* as he calls them. I have vetoed this, as he would simply make mischief and spread Anglophobia wherever he went.'[52]† Churchill prevented de Gaulle from going

* That is, *Evviva* (Hurrah).

† When this letter was published in Churchill's memoirs in 1951, the first sentence was omitted entirely, as was the phrase about de Gaulle's stupidity, and 'insolence' was altered to 'roughness' (WSC, *TSSW* IV p. 657). Also cut was a remark about the Eighth Army: 'The enemy make a great mistake if they think that all the troops we have there are in the same green state as our United States friends.' Similarly excised was a comment on Gandhi's hunger strike: 'The old humbug Gandhi is lasting much longer than we were assured was possible, and one wonders whether his fast is *bona fide*.' (RA PS/PSO/GVI/C/069/29.)

to Syria, to which the general replied, 'Alors, je suis prisonnier,' and returned to his Government-lent home in Hampstead. Churchill called de Gaulle's Foreign Office liaison and said, 'I hold you responsible that the Monster of Hampstead does not escape.'[53]

'I tried to persuade him to take some Ovaltine at night,' Churchill's nurse, Doris Miles, reported to her husband Roger, 'but he declared he hates "pap" – can't stand milk or porridge, kind of "Steak and beer" for breakfast type.'[54] From Downing Street on 23 February she wrote, 'One thing that might amuse you is his fluid intake chart. It goes something like this: Champagne 10oz; Brandy 2oz; Orange juice 8oz; whisky and soda 8oz. Doesn't that make your tongue hang out?!'[55] By 1 March, Churchill was feeling much improved, though still weak, and Doris noted that 'He sings a lot, rather tunelessly, and at the top of his voice.' A Great War song that he liked to sing while being given bed-baths went:

> Wash me in the whitewash on the wall,
> Don't wash me in the water
> You wash your dirty daughter,
> Wash me in the whitewash on the wall.[56]

When he was able to have proper baths, Nurse Miles noted that he was proud of being able to turn off the taps at Chequers with his toes. In early March he was able to work, with 'a couple of secretaries and several whiskies' until after midnight, with much laughter audible through the doors, and by 15 March he had recovered.

Rommel made four major counter-attacks in Tunisia in early March, but they were all rebuffed by Eisenhower and Montgomery. On 9 March the 'Desert Fox' was invalided back to Germany for medical treatment, but really to escape capture. Yet, for all the good news in Africa, Britain was still being bombed regularly by the Luftwaffe. On the night of 3 March, 173 civilians were killed in Bethnal Green tube station, many as they fell down the steps and were crushed in the panic. Churchill wanted the news censored, stating that he was 'Against giving such limelight to this incident', not least because 'We said earlier "no panic": this makes it clear there *was* panic.'[57]

On 21 March Churchill gave his first broadcast about the challenges Britain would face after the war, an indication of his growing confidence that victory was in sight. Although he had been too ill to attend the debate on the Beveridge Report on 18 February, the speech was a masterly analysis, but also an attempt to contest the middle ground of politics with Labour. He praised the work of Sir William Beveridge, 'You must rank me and my colleagues as strong partisans of national compulsory insurance for all classes for all purposes from the cradle to the grave,' and added that everyone must work, 'whether they come from the ancient aristocracy or the modern plutocracy, or the ordinary type of pub-crawler'.[58] He had no compunction in saying, 'We must establish on broad and solid foundations a National Health Service. Here let me say that there is no finer investment for any community than putting milk into babies. Healthy citizens are the greatest asset any country can have.' Just as radically, Churchill promised, 'No one who can take advantage of a higher education should be denied this chance. You cannot conduct a modern community except with an adequate supply of persons upon whose education, whether humane, technical, or scientific, much time and money have been spent.'[59] This was all classic Tory Democrat language, with references to his father and quotes from Disraeli. He also spoke of the employment that would arise from 'the replanning and rebuilding of our cities and towns', and made no attempt to hide the fact that 'We must expect taxation after the war to be heavier than it was before the war, but we do not intend to shape our plans or levy taxation in a way which, by removing personal incentive, would destroy initiative and enterprise.'[60] He spoke of a 'Four Years' Plan' for the economy, demobilization, the creation of a Council of Europe that would 'harmonise with the high permanent interests of Britain, the United States and Russia', and even the coming of television. His peroration was personal. 'I have tried to learn from events,' he said,

> and also from my own mistakes, and I will tell you my solemn belief, which is that if we act with comradeship and loyalty to our country and to one another, and if we can make State enterprise and free enterprise both serve national interests and pull the national wagon side by side, then there is no need for us to run into that horrible, devastating slump or into that squalid epoch of bickering and confusion which mocked and squandered the hard-won victory we gained a quarter of a century ago.[61]

'You know you must never be frightened of me when I snap,' Churchill told his new secretary, Marian Holmes, on 24 March, 'with a cherubic smile'. 'I'm not snapping at you but thinking of the work.'[62] Holmes quickly became one of his favourite secretaries. He took her to several conferences and prized her for her efficiency, courage and good looks. That same March Jock Colville also reported back for duty in Downing Street, after serving eighteen months with the RAF. He found Churchill's 'mind as vigorous, his heart as staunch as ever, but thought his physical appearance showed signs of wear and tear'.[63]

On Friday, 26 March, after Montgomery had been besieging the Mareth

Line for a week and just before he broke through it into southern Tunisia, Brooke was sent for by Churchill. 'By the time I had reached him in the Annexe he was in his bath!'[64] recalled the conservative-minded Ulsterman. 'However he received me as soon as he came out, looking like a Roman centurion with nothing on except a large bath towel draped around him! He shook me warmly by the hand in this get up and told me to sit down while he dressed.' Brooke found this 'a most interesting procedure', as the Prime Minister put on his white silk vest, then white silk drawers, and 'walked up and down the room in this kit, looking rather like "Humpty Dumpty", with a large body and small thin legs!' When the collar of his white shirt failed to close around his neck, Churchill simply left it open and used his bow tie to keep it together, 'rather as Oliver Hardy might'. Brooke continued to watch, as 'the hair (what there is of it!) took much attention', and a handkerchief was sprayed with scent and then rubbed over his head. 'The few hairs were then brushed, and finally sprayed direct!' As he put on his trousers, waistcoat and coat, Churchill 'rippled on the whole time about Monty's battle and our proposed visit to North Africa'. For all the criticisms of Churchill in Brooke's diaries and the rows between them, on this occasion 'the main thing he wanted to say was that he thought I looked tired last night at the meeting we had and that I was to take a long weekend!'[65]

Brooke was nonetheless back in London on Monday to tell the War Cabinet about Rommel's defeat. The advance into Tunisia continued throughout April as the Eighth Army met American armies coming from the west before an attack on Tunis itself. April 1943 also saw a major increase in U-boat sinkings due in part to longer-range bombers, and there was a consequent reduction in Allied shipping losses. In all, 793 German U-boats were destroyed or captured in the Second World War; of the nearly 40,000 men who served on them, three-quarters died at sea. 'Up to the end of March there was a real danger of the enemy severing our sea-lines of communication,' Admiral James recalled, 'but after that the defence forces slowly but steadily acquired dominance over the U-boats.'[66] In the summer of 1943, the Mediterranean could finally be reopened to Allied shipping, almost a year after the fall of Tobruk.

When on 8 April Eisenhower intimated that the arrival of German reinforcements in Sicily might rule out Operation Husky, the Allied invasion of the island set for July, Churchill was predictably acerbic. 'If the presence of two German divisions is held to be decisive against any operation of an offensive or amphibious character open to the million men now in North Africa,' he wrote to the Chiefs of Staff, 'it is difficult to see how the war can be carried on. Months of preparation, sea power and air power in abundance, and yet two German divisions are sufficient to knock it all on the head . . . I trust the Chiefs of Staff will not accept these pusillanimous and defeatist doctrines, from whomever they came . . . What Stalin would think of this, when he has 185 German divisions on his front I cannot imagine.'[67] It was a rare underestimation; Stalin in fact faced slightly more than that. Husky stayed on track.

On 18 April 1943, Germany announced the discovery of the mass graves of over 14,000 Polish officers in the forest of Katyń. The Soviet Union denied responsibility, a lie it was to continue to tell until 1990, but the truth quickly became clear when the Poles and Red Cross came to investigate. At the end of May, Owen O'Malley, the British liaison Ambassador to the exiled Polish Government in London, sent Eden a powerful document explaining in ghastly detail the way the Russians had cold-bloodedly massacred the Polish officers in March 1940.[68] Churchill read the report but decided that wartime exigency required silence from him and the Foreign Office. The nonchalance with which Stalin had dismissed the 'disappearance' of the kulaks at their meeting in Moscow meant that, however much Churchill may have been shocked, he could not have been entirely surprised. 'The atrocities by Lenin and Trotsky are incomparably more hideous, on a larger scale, and more numerous than any for which the Kaiser himself is responsible,' Churchill had written back in 1919. But now their equally brutal successor was a vital ally.[69]

Harold Nicolson recorded in his diary that when he asked Churchill about Katyń, 'he grins grimly: "The less said about that the better."'[70] 'Even if the German statements were to prove to be true,' Churchill told Maisky at Chequers on 23 April, 'my attitude towards you would not change. You are a brave people, Stalin is a great warrior, and at the moment I approach everything primarily as a soldier who is interested in defeating the common enemy as quickly as possible.'[71] 'Everything can happen in war,' he added, the lower-rank commanders are capable of 'doing terrible things' when acting on their own initiative.[72] Both men knew that such a large-scale massacre could not possibly have taken place except on the Politburo's direct orders. Morally, Churchill's stance was insupportable, but politically it was unavoidable. It was one of the occasions in his career when Realpolitik trumped morality, and even decency, in the pursuit of the greater cause.

By mid-April Churchill was convinced that a new viceroy was needed to break the political deadlock with the Indian National Congress, which was still refusing to aid the war effort undertaken for India's protection from the Japanese. After considering Attlee, Sinclair, Cranborne and

Lampson, he decided it should be Anthony Eden, who recorded him as saying, after dinner on 21 April, 'what a calamity it would be to win this war and lose India [and] that he was convinced that only I could save India. That I was his chief lieutenant and only really intimate friend among his colleagues and that though he would hate to lose me, etc., etc.'[73] Four days later, Sir Alec Hardinge called Eden and urged him to stay in London in order 'to have some influence on Winston', and suggested that Churchill, 'even unconsciously', wanted 'a freer hand at home'. Hardinge also wrote to the King, saying that Eden 'is the only person who talks to the P.M. as an equal and can argue with him without it being a "row"! Whom would the P.M. get hold of to confide in and to discuss matters with – at all the hours of the day and night? One dreads to think that it might be Beaverbrook.'[74] That prospect being too awful, the next day the King wrote to Churchill subtly putting the argument that Eden could not be spared.

It was only on 8 June that Churchill finally had to accept, after a 'very frank' discussion with Eden, that he would not be able to persuade him to become viceroy of India. A week later he told Eden's wife Beatrice that she had missed her opportunity of riding on elephants.[75] Anderson was rejected in part because courtiers thought his vivacious wife Ava would not be a suitable vicereine (though Churchill liked her), and Sinclair could not go because then the appeaser Sir Herbert Samuel would lead the Liberals. So, even though no one, least of all Churchill, was very enthusiastic, the post went to Wavell. Wavell was a brave, charming, sincere and cultivated soldier, but a diplomat-politician such as Eden would have been able to negotiate with Gandhi and the other nationalist leaders far more effectively.

Just as the Axis powers were about to be expelled from North Africa, and on the eve of the Italian campaign, Admiral King again called into question the Germany First policy in discussions among the US Joint Chiefs of Staff. When this got back to London, Churchill concluded that another major conference in Washington was needed, telling the King that if British commanders-in-chief accepted the invitations currently being extended to go there, they would need 'political backing on the higher levels necessary to prevent them being overweighted by the "Pacific First" school'.[76] He wanted to commit the Americans to Operation Avalanche, the invasion of mainland Italy, as soon as Sicily had fallen, to set a date for the cross-Channel attack in 1944 and to discuss nuclear issues.

Looming victory in the Battle of the Atlantic meant that one significant objection to the launch of an early amphibious attack on France – namely that expeditionary forces might not be resupplied owing to U-boat action – was fast disappearing. In May 1943 the so-called Air Gap – the waters south of Greenland where convoys could not be covered by land-based planes – was finally closed by the use of Very Long Range (VLR) aircraft such as Liberator bombers, with ranges of up to 700 miles. That month Admiral Karl Dönitz, the commander of the German Navy, had to withdraw his forces from the mid-Atlantic entirely.

Churchill has sometimes been criticized for misallocating scarce bomber squadrons in 1942 and the first half of 1943, preferring Bomber Command over Coastal Command.[77] In fact, the problem was within Coastal Command, which until the autumn of 1942 used most of the planes needed to close the Air Gap to hunt U-boats in the Bay of Biscay rather than to provide convoy support in the mid-Atlantic.[78] At the first meeting of the Anti-U-Boat Warfare Committee which Churchill set up and chaired in November 1942, both land-based and carrier-borne solutions were considered for closing the Air Gap, and land-based aircraft were identified as the best solution. Even though the Casablanca Conference had allocated eighty VLR aircraft to close the Gap, the process of modifying Coastal Command's Liberator III bombers to VLR status took time – it was all done by a single firm based in Prestwick on the west coast of Scotland – and after four months only two Liberators had been adapted.[79] Once the Air Gap started to be closed in the spring of 1943, fifteen U-boats were sunk in March, another fifteen in April and forty-one in May, out of an operational fleet of 200.[80]

On 5 May, travelling this time as Air Commodore Spencer (doubtless reflecting his pride in one of his surnames), Churchill, accompanied by Wavell and Brooke, embarked on the *Queen Mary*, the 80,000-ton luxury flagship of the Cunard Line, which had won the Blue Riband for the fastest Atlantic crossing, now converted into a troopship and painted a naval grey.[81] She was carrying 5,000 German POWs who were being transferred to internment in America. Six days later the ship anchored off Staten Island and Churchill took a special train to Washington where they were welcomed by the Roosevelts that same evening.

The Trident Conference began the next day and lasted until 25 May. It reached several momentous decisions. After the presumed success of Husky, which would be launched in July, all Mediterranean forces would be made available to invade Italy, except for four American and three British divisions which would be withdrawn and held in readiness for Operation Roundup, which would take place on 1 May 1944. In the Pacific theatre, British forces had been obliged to withdraw to the line on the Arakan coast of Burma from which they had set out nearly six months earlier. It was agreed in Washington that an Allied combined operation would be undertaken against Japanese forces there after Italy had surrendered. All this planning was given immediacy on 13 May when

Churchill received a telegram from Alexander. 'Sir,' it stated, 'it is my duty to report that the Tunisian campaign is over. All enemy resistance has ceased. We are masters of the North African shores.'[82] On the 7th, the Americans had captured Bizerta and the British Army entered Tunis. Church bells were rung again all over Britain for the first time since El Alamein.

While Churchill was staying at Roosevelt's mountain retreat in Maryland, known as Shangri-La (present-day Camp David), Clementine wrote that Randolph was attempting a rapprochement with Pamela, despite his drinking and debts and the painful discovery of her affair with Harriman. 'How I wish that could happen,' Clementine wrote. 'Perhaps it will.'[83] The next day, still at Shangri-La, Churchill learned of the success of the 'Dambusters Raid' against the Möhne, Sorpe and Eder dams of the Ruhr in an extremely difficult operation requiring extraordinary skill and courage, which flooded 50 square miles of industrial plant. 'The conduct of the operations demonstrated the fiery, gallant spirit which animated your aircrews,' he told 'Bomber' Harris, 'and the high sense of duty of all ranks under your command.'[84] Air losses at that time were so high that it was statistically almost impossible for bomber crews to complete a twenty-five-mission tour.

Churchill delivered his second speech to a Joint Meeting of Congress on 19 May. 'The experiences of a long life and the promptings of my blood have wrought in me the conviction that there is nothing more important for the future of the world than the fraternal association of our two peoples in righteous work both in war and peace,' he said.[85] He assessed the recent campaign in North Africa, revealing that 'The African excursions of the two dictators' had cost them 950,000 soldiers, 2.4 million tons of shipping, nearly 8,000 aircraft, 6,200 guns, 2,550 tanks and 70,000 trucks, and quoted the saying, 'The Hun is always either at your throat or at your feet.' He finished by declaring that having arrived 'at this milestone in the war: we can say, "One Continent redeemed".'[86] Churchill did not of course include in his address any of the complaints that he was regularly making about both the British and American armies at this time. He had gone so far as to tell General Kennedy that the Americans were 'like a peacock – nearly all tail'.[87] He was less circumspect than he should have been, telling Maisky in early February that American divisions each had over 18,000 soldiers, 'But fifty thousand if you count the entire attending personnel.'[88] He then 'with blatant sarcasm in his voice, started enumerating . . . two laundry battalions, one battalion of milk sterilizers, one battalion of hairdressers, one battalion of tailors, one battalion for the uplift of the troops and what-not'.[89] He did have a point – when the

US Army landed in North Africa, it set up three complete Coca-Cola bottling plants – but he criticized the British Army almost equally. 'We've sent nearly half a million combatants to North Africa,' he said. 'But it actually amounts to a mere ten to eleven divisions.'

When the Trident Conference had concluded, Churchill, Brooke and Marshall flew to Algiers via Botwood in Newfoundland and Gibraltar, to oversee the planning for the invasion of Sicily. Over the Atlantic, their Bristol flying boat was struck by lightning. 'All at once there was a sudden shock and bump,' Churchill recalled. 'I awoke. Something had happened. There were no consequences, which after all are what is important in air journeys . . . To a groundsman it would seem quite a dangerous thing. Afterwards I learned that there had been a good deal of anxiety.'[90] Lightning strikes were more dangerous for 1940s aircraft than they are for today's. Electrical generators could fail, causing loss of instrumentation, and compasses could also be affected. On the next stage of the journey, Churchill travelled in an Avro York, a British, four-engined high-wing passenger plane, which had a bar, tables with ashtrays, windows, books, newspapers and an electronically heated lavatory seat. (Churchill complained that it was too hot, so it was disconnected.)[91]

In Algiers from 28 May, Churchill stayed in Admiral Cunningham's villa, where he enjoyed the cool breeze coming up from the sea, and was in a fine mood.[92] Marshall and Eisenhower were ready for Operation Husky. 'No people respond more spontaneously to fair play,' Churchill told Attlee. 'If you treat Americans well they always want to treat you better.'[93] He was pleased to have Randolph with him; their son had lost weight, he told Clementine, and 'looks the picture of health'.[94] Churchill was due to meet de Gaulle in Algiers, and he reported to Clementine that he expected to have serious disagreements with him, because the general 'will do his utmost to make a row and assert his personal ambition'.[95] Yet there was a reasonable degree of agreement over future operations and zones of influence, at least in the short term. The Russians were behaving well, too. When asked by an American reporter what he thought of Stalin's decision to abolish the Comintern, the organization dedicated to promoting global revolution, Churchill merely said, 'I like it.'[96]

A highlight of the trip had been his address to over 3,000 British troops in the Roman amphitheatre at Carthage, where the acoustics were so good that no loudspeakers were necessary. He told them that the Tunisian victory meant a shortening of 'this obstinate war and a long step forward towards peace, home and honour'.[97] He ended with 'God bless you all' and cheerily waved his pith helmet atop his walking stick. 'I was speaking where the cries of Christian virgins rent the air whilst roaring lions devoured them,' he told Ismay, Brooke, Eden and Randolph afterwards, 'and yet I am no lion and certainly not a virgin!!'[98] Eden later recalled that day and the next as being the happiest of the war for him, riding with Churchill at informal parades and between lanes of cheering troops, who 'were relaxed and happy in their victory, as they had every right to be'.[99] On its front page, the American service newspaper *Stars and Stripes* contrasted the way 'the Tommies roared their approval [of Churchill], the sounds echoing sharply through the ruins of the massive bowl which symbolized the once-great Roman Empire' with the scrapheaps of Axis planes at nearby Tunis airport, 'ruins of the once extensive Mussolini Empire'.[100] 'The P.M. was in very good form,' Martin noted when he arrived back in Britain on 5 June, 'and had thoroughly enjoyed his "expedition".'[101]

In mid-June Churchill very prematurely offered Brooke the post of supreme commander for Operation Roundup. 'He said many nice things about having full confidence in me, etc.,' Brooke wrote at the time, adding later, 'This news gave me one of my greatest thrills during the war. I felt that it would be the perfect climax to all my struggles.'[102] Yet both of them should have recognized that the decision over who would command Roundup – later renamed Operation Overlord – would not ultimately be up to the British, as they would be junior partners in the enterprise. Of the 1.452 million troops who were to land in France by 25 July 1944, some 56 per cent were from the United States and 44 per cent from Britain, Canada and the other contributing countries. As the Americans were providing the most men for the operation, it could only be expected that its commander was going to be an American. In that calendar year, whereas Britain produced 28,000 warplanes and Germany and Russia 40,000 each, the United States produced 98,000 thousand. America's military-industrial might was formidable and dramatically transformed the calculus of the war. One of the reasons that Churchill wanted an Imperial Conference in July 1943, the King noted after a lunch in early April, was 'so as to discuss the question of putting up a united British Commonwealth and Empire front to show the world and USA that we are one unity. The Americans are always saying they are going to lead the post-war world.'[103]

A year after the first thousand-bomber raid, on Cologne, Churchill was starting to have doubts about the saturation-bombing policy. He was shown a film at Chequers in late June made by the RAF of the bombing of Wuppertal in Westphalia and asked afterwards, 'Are we beasts? Are we taking this too far?'[104] He commissioned a judge, Sir John Singleton, to produce a report on the bombing policy, which eventually called for more of an emphasis on strategic bombing rather than the carpet-bombing of cities.[105] German cities continued to be smashed night after night, however, a campaign that severely restricted the increase in the war-materiel production of the Third Reich, at the total cost of over 55,000 Bomber Command airmen.[106] 'Even when most ill,' Doris Miles wrote to her husband of Churchill, 'he would ring up Bomber Command in the early hours of the morning to find out how many casualties we had (not how many bombs had been dropped) and how many planes had got back safely.'[107]

If Churchill had doubts over saturation bombing, he largely kept them to himself. On 25 July Hamburg was devastated by a high-explosives firestorm, with the planes protected by the first use of the Window anti-radar device. Churchill had denounced 'These cruel, wanton, indiscriminate bombings of London' in September 1940, and was now carrying out his promise to Londoners of full retaliatory vengeance. He has been criticized for allowing Bomber Command too many scarce resources, especially metals that were in short supply and much needed for tanks and ships.

British war materiel was suffering for other reasons too. By May 1943 the defects in the Crusader tank were so obvious that production had to be halted. Even so, the Ministry of Supply could not do so as quickly as they wished. When General Sir Ronald Weeks, the Deputy CIGS, suggested that all the new but defective tanks might be used without their turrets as 17-pounder anti-tank guns instead, Churchill shook his head and, borrowing a joke from his 1929 Budget speech, said slowly, 'General, you remind me of a man who gets out of the bed in the morning, removes a box of biscuits and wanders round the streets of London trying to find a dog or dogs to give them to.'[108] He took intense personal interest in every aspect of war-materiel production, constantly prodding and urging.*

Churchill found himself in a minority of one on 2 July, when the Cabinet discussed the subject of Palestine. In December 1942, the House of Commons had stood in silence as an act of respect for Jews who were being exterminated by *Einsatzgruppen* murder squads in eastern Europe. Yet seven months later in Cabinet, Oliver Stanley, the Colonial Secretary, accused the Jews of Palestine of being 'totalitarian, aggressive and expansionist' in the

* This not only extended to tanks, ships and aircraft. 'I am told that in spite of contributions from civilian supplies there is at present a shortage of playing-cards for use by the forces and workers in industry,' he wrote to Hugh Dalton, the President of the Board of Trade, in July 1943. 'The importance of providing amusement for the forces in their leisure hours and in long periods of waiting and monotony in out-of-the-way places, and for the sailors penned up in their ships for months together, cannot be overstated. Nothing is more handy, more portable, or more capable of prolonged usage than a pack of cards.' (WSC, *TSSW* V p. 578.)

way that they were 'wedded to . . . the adoption of a Jewish State. They are trying to run a state within a state much on Nazi lines.'[109] 'I'm committed to the creation of a Jewish national home in Palestine,' Churchill replied. 'Let us get on with that; and at the end of the war we shall have plenty of force with which to compel the Arabs to acquiesce in our designs. Don't shirk our duties because of difficulties.'[110]

Attlee wanted to press ahead with the formulation of a post-war policy on Palestine, but Churchill thought this inopportune, knowing it would be anti-Zionist. Stanley emphasized 'the difference between a Jewish National home and a Jewish state, which the extremists now demand'. Eden said he could not support 'a Jewish national state for all Palestine', and thought 'the extremists' should be warned off that line soon by a joint Anglo-American declaration. Churchill reported that he had brought up the idea with Roosevelt of establishing Jewish colonies in Cyrenaica and Tripolitania, but the President had thought that Jews who had escaped the Nazis would return after the war 'to European countries of origin'. One unnamed minister even said he feared that 'Violence in Palestine may cause renewed persecution of Jews all over the world.'

Eden characterized the Jewish position as 'You clear out and we'll settle with the Arabs.' Amery added that the Government 'Can't be stampeded by Jewish extremists.' Cranborne argued that the 'Jews and Arabs were both playing off against us.' Wavell's view was that 'From the point of view of security of the British Empire, the present aspirations of Jews in Palestine are a real menace to our position in the Middle East and subsequently in India.' 'Remember that when the percentage of Jews in any one European state goes above a certain level,' said Herbert Morrison, 'there's bound to be anti-Semitism.'[111] (The percentage of Jews in the Cabinet was nil.) After further interjections from Amery and Lyttelton, Churchill ended the discussion by disagreeing with the whole of the rest of his Cabinet, saying that he 'Would prefer to leave them [the Jews] with arms to fight it out!' He then added, 'These Jewish arms would be turned in *our* favour.'[112] A Cabinet committee was appointed to consider long-term policy, a classic manoeuvre of Churchill's when he was heavily outnumbered to ensure nothing was done.

Two days later, on 4 July, General Sikorski died in a plane crash at Gibraltar. 'Soldiers must die,' Churchill said in a broadcast to Polish troops about their leader, whom he had come to like and admire greatly, 'but by their death they nourish the nation which gave them birth.'[113]*

* The conspiracy theory that Churchill was responsible for assassinating Sikorski in order to weaken the Poles relative to the Russians is entirely groundless.

The next day, Germany launched its massive Kursk Offensive near Orel, which was first blunted by the well-defended Russians and later decisively turned back in the largest tank battle in history. In the calendar year 1943, when 70,000 Western servicemen, including bomber crews, died fighting Germany, two million Russian soldiers were killed, nearly thirty times the number.

Churchill's policy of doing everything possible to keep the Soviet Union supplied, even at the inadvertent cost of Singapore, had clearly been the correct one. Yet, as Ian Jacob pointed out in a lecture to the Royal United Services Institute after the war, 'There was little or no communication of facts or ideas and we had no real idea of Russian military thinking. The fundamental Russian distrust of the West, which was temporarily allayed by the German attack on Russia and our immediate response to it, very soon re-established itself and prevailed throughout. Fortunately, the almost complete geographical separation of the Russian theatre of war mitigated these disadvantages.'[114] Instead of any attempt at real engagement, Stalin sent Churchill cables full of accusations that the Western Allies were contemplating betraying Russia. 'He told me he was very annoyed with Stalin over his series of rude telegrams,' the King noted after their lunch on 29 June. 'Though neither he, Eden nor the Foreign Office thought that Stalin was contemplating making a separate peace with Germany.'[115]

On the same day that the Battle of Kursk was launched, Churchill, ever capable of traversing seamlessly from the sublime to the ridiculous and back, thanked Dr Herbert Evatt, the Australian Foreign Minister, for giving him Splash, a stuffed duck-billed platypus, 'and the very informative book on the life and habits of the Platypus which accompanied it'.[116] Churchill placed Splash in the lobby at No. 10 and occasionally regaled people with information about its love-life, on which he had become an authority. Another quadrupedal gift that year, though this time living, was Rota, a fully grown lion, given by a Mr and Mrs Thompson, which Churchill gave to the London Zoo. 'If there are any shortcomings in your work I shall send you to him,' he said to one of his humourless civil servants. 'Meat is very short now.'[117] (The man took him seriously and reported that the Prime Minister was 'in a delirium'.) When Churchill visited Rota at the zoo in August 1943, he also went inside the swan enclosure, telling the swans, 'I suppose you would like to feed me.'[118]

Operation Husky was launched on 9 July: 160,000 Allied troops charged ashore on beaches in southern Sicily under total air cover and with some 3,000 vessels in support, a number that could not have been assembled before the Battle of the Atlantic had been won and the North

African coast cleared of Axis troops.[119] In July 1943, the Germans had twelve divisions in Italy and the Balkans, which by the end of the year had grown to more than thirty.[120] To prevent the Allies from hitting southern German targets from Italian airfields, they were forced to contest Italy with resources they would have preferred to have used at Kursk and to repulse the cross-Channel attack, so Churchill and Brooke's plans were vindicated. 'The P.M. was in bubbling form,' Marian Holmes wrote in her diary the next day.[121] Although he was committed to Overlord, and was not about to renege on the agreements made in Washington, Churchill naturally had occasional fears for the success of what would be an extraordinarily difficult operation. He told the US War Secretary Henry L. Stimson in mid-July that he could see 'the Channel being full of corpses of defeated allies'.[122]

In contrast to these gloomy thoughts, the romantic in Churchill was evident when the Foreign Office objected that month to the twenty-year-old King Peter II of Yugoslavia marrying his twenty-two-year-old third cousin, Princess Alexandra of Greece and Denmark,* on the grounds that Royals should not marry in wartime. They claimed that the principle was originally Serbian, but Churchill said he did not believe that a martial race like the Serbs would deny a king 'a chance of perpetuating his dynasty, and anyhow of giving effect to those primary instincts to which the humblest of human beings have a right ... *Prima facie* this would seem to condone extra-marital relations.'[123] He told Eden that 'We might be back in the refinements of Louis XIV instead of the lusty squalor of the 20th century ... My advice to the King ... will be to go to the nearest Registry Office and take a chance. So what?'[124] They married the next year.

By 12 July Churchill wanted to break with de Gaulle over his obdurate refusal to put Allied considerations over purely French ones, but Eden wanted to support him as leader of the Free French. In a row that continued from after dinner to 2 a.m., Churchill said 'he would fight vigorously, to the death' to replace de Gaulle with someone less chauvinistic about French interests.[125] In May, when Giraud and de Gaulle had formed separate factions in the French Committee of National Liberation, Eden and the Cabinet prevented Churchill from ending British material support for de Gaulle, although official recognition of the Free French as the provisional government of France did not come till October 1944, four months after D-Day. 'I, of course, am exceedingly pro-French,' Churchill asserted; 'unfortunately the French are exceedingly pro-voking.'[126] In a face-to-face row with de Gaulle, Churchill had said in his inimitable

* The paternal aunt of HRH Prince Philip, Duke of Edinburgh.

Franglais, 'Si vous m'obstaclerez, je vous liquiderai!'[127] (Another witness recorded it as 'Et, marquez mes mots, mon ami – si vous me double-crosserez, je vous liquiderai.')[128]

Not wanting to end the night quarrelling, Churchill turned the discussion to a subject upon which he and Eden saw eye to eye: 'We discussed the Tory Party and both agreed how little we liked it and how little it liked us.' (These were of course the two people who led the party between 1940 and 1957.) 'On which harmonious note we parted.'[129] They had another late-night, hour-long shouting match on 2 August over Operation Lifebelt, an attack on the Azores that Churchill wanted and Eden opposed, at the end of which Churchill apologized for being obstreperous. 'I feared that I had been obstreperous too,' Eden wrote in his diary. 'Oh you,' Churchill shot back, 'you were bloody.'[130] A few days later, Churchill told Eden that being foreign secretary and leader of the House of Commons was 'wonderful training' for the premiership.[131]

At lunch on 19 July with Sir Alan 'Tommy' Lascelles, who had become the King's new principal private secretary after Hardinge resigned earlier that month, and Sir Arcot Ramasamy Mudaliar, who occasionally attended War Cabinet meetings representing India, Churchill held forth on one of his favourite subjects, the many benefits of the British Empire for its native peoples. 'It was only thanks to the beneficence and wisdom of British rule in India, free from any hint of war for a longer period than almost any other country in the world,' he said, that India 'had been able to increase and multiply to this astonishing extent'.[132] He nonetheless thought that 'This vast and improvident efflorescence of humanity must stop,' and told Mudaliar, 'Your people must practise birth control.' Lascelles noted, 'Winston said that the old idea that the Indian was in any way inferior to the white man must go.' Instead, he said, 'We must all be pals together. I want to see a great shining India, of which we can be as proud as we are of a great Canada or a great Australia.'[133]

Churchill had previously long instanced the astonishing population growth in India in the first four decades of the twentieth century as a mark of the success of the Empire and in November 1942 he was still boasting to the Spanish Ambassador, the Duke of Alba, 'Since the English occupation of India the native population has increased by a hundred million. Since the American War of Independence, the Red Indian population has practically died out.'[134] Yet by taking Churchill's occasional anti-Indian remarks wildly out of context, some of his detractors maintain that he used the terrible Bengal Famine of 1943–4 – in which according to official estimates 1.5 million people died, though some commentators put the figure at double that, or even more – to commit what they describe as 'genocide' on the Bengalis.[135] The truth could not be more different.

On 16 October 1942 a cyclone hit Bengal and Orissa, destroying the rice harvest. The Muslim-dominated local administration, elected under the terms of the India Act of 1935, dealt with the problem corruptly and negligently, and Lord Linlithgow, the Viceroy, and other British Raj officials also failed to get a grip on the situation early enough.[136] Indian merchants, especially rice and grain wholesalers and retailers, saw prices soar and, anticipating further rises, they hoarded supplies. 'There is much graft and knavery,' wrote Wavell, who became viceroy in October 1943, to Leo Amery, Secretary of State for India, describing the activities of 'unscrupulous dealers'.[137] Churchill stated in Cabinet on 7 October that one of Wavell's first duties as viceroy was to see to it 'that famine and food difficulties were dealt with'.[138] The next day he wrote to Wavell about what he called the 'actual famine' in India. 'The hard pressures of world-war have for the first time for many years brought conditions of scarcity,' he told him, 'verging in some localities into actual famine, upon India. Every effort must be made, even by the diversion of shipping urgently needed for war purposes, to deal with local shortages.'[139] Unfortunately, as Lord Leathers, the Minister for War Transport, was to point out shortly afterwards, 'It was clearly quite impossible to provide shipping to meet the demand of 1½ million tons of grain made by the Government of India.'[140] Much has been made of Churchill's refusal of an offer from the Canadian government of 100,000 tons of wheat in November 1943, on the grounds that it would take two months to reach India and that 'in the present circumstances it would be unjustifiable to impose any additional strain on our shipping resources (especially if that involved seeking further assistance from the Americans)', yet his detractors do not quote the decision taken by that same War Cabinet that it would instead consider 'at an early meeting, the question of sending further supplies of food grains to India, possibly from Australia' – which is what happened.[141]

In earlier famines, shortfalls were partly made up by Burmese and other south-east Asian rice crops, but the Japanese now controlled Burma, Thailand, Vietnam, Malaya and the Philippines; indeed their troops were actually inside India itself, at Kohima in Nagaland and Imphal in Manipur. The Japanese had maintained a large fleet in the Bay of Bengal since April 1942, and had bombed eastern Indian cities. The military situation was made all the more difficult by Gandhi's campaign to force the British to quit India, which he did not end despite the imminent Japanese threat. To make matters worse, the cyclone had disrupted the winter harvest in the northern parts of India that had helped with famines in the past, and washed away railway lines needed to transport food to stricken areas. Indian provincial governments with food surpluses such as the Punjab refused to part with them, and hoarding was made worse by the Government's policy of 'Indianisation' which discouraged the Viceroy from issuing direct instructions from Delhi.[142] When the famine was at its height in June 1943, Sir Chhotu Ram, the Revenue Minister of Punjab, instructed farmers not to sell their grain to the central Government under a certain price.[143]

On 4 August 1943, Churchill agreed that 150,000 tons of Iraqi barley and Australian wheat should be sent to Bengal, insisting on 24 September that 'Something must be done'; he was also 'very strong on the point that Indians are not the only people who are starving in this war'.[144] These words, and others like them recorded by Amery in his diary, sound harsh today but reflected reality, and after uttering them Churchill agreed to the dispatch of an extra 50,000 tons of food. If food had been available and easily transportable, Churchill would have sent it, which does not constitute a desire to commit genocide, any more than politically incorrect remarks about Indians constitute a motive for it. Almost all of the remarks Amery ascribed to Churchill were paraphrases rather than direct quotations, and should be seen in light of what one of the Prime Minister's private secretaries called his 'provocative humour'.[145] These racially charged jokes, which would be regarded as totally unacceptable today, were then, as one historian puts it, 'part of the bedrock of contemporary British humour and were regular features of *Punch* during the inter-war years and after'.[146] They certainly had no effect whatever on British policy towards the famine, which was to send whatever could be spared whenever possible, while taking into account the threat from Japanese submarines.

Wavell's request to London for 1.5 million tons of food grains in early February 1944 was turned down by the Cabinet in London, which replied that the Government in Delhi needed to impose effective rationing across the sub-continent, raise taxes and above all impose commodity price controls in the face of rising inflation. The Cabinet also suspected that the shortages were 'partly political in character, caused by Marwari [Hindu] supporters of Congress [Party] in an effort to embarrass the existing Muslim Government of Bengal'.[147] The Cabinet wanted the Viceroy to be much tougher on the Government in Calcutta. If the cyclone had struck in peacetime, the Raj would probably have prevented the famine with the competence with which it had managed previous natural disasters since the mid-nineteenth century. But there was war raging on many fronts, there were food shortages in Britain and there was a severe lack of available shipping. Bengalis started to starve in large numbers in 1943, even though the Churchill Cabinet ensured that by January 1944 a total of 130,000 tons of barley had been shipped from Iraq, 80,000 from Australia, 10,000 from Canada and a further 100,000 from Australia.[148]

'I will certainly help you all I can,' Churchill telegraphed Wavell in February 1944, 'but you must not ask the impossible.'[149] Leo Amery, the Secretary of State for India, told the Viceroy the same month that Churchill 'was not unsympathetic' to the appalling situation, but simply could not spare the shipping as a result of the large numbers of ongoing military operations. To reduce the desperately difficult moral decisions that Churchill and many others had to take to the level of accusations of deliberate genocide is biased and unhistorical. If men such as Wavell, Amery and Claude Auchinleck, the Commander-in-Chief in India, had for a moment suspected that Churchill wanted Bengalis to die, they would not have continued to serve in their posts.

The awful truth about the famine is that the toll on shipping since the start of the war meant that the Allies were stretched to breaking point in 1943–4, and the Cabinet placed the Russian and transatlantic convoys, and the military shipping necessities of operations against Germany in Sicily and mainland Italy, and for amphibious attacks such as Salerno and Anzio, above the pressing need to feed the millions of starving Bengalis – even assuming that the ships could have negotiated the Bay of Bengal safely. Dire food shortages in liberated southern Italy and Greece and in Holland after D-Day, where severe malnutrition was common in the population, also had to be taken into consideration. Lord Leathers's view was that the Government in Delhi needed to solve its own mishandling of food distribution. Wavell was using the Army to get food to the worst-hit areas but it was nothing like enough.

'The Prime Minister said that it was clear that His Majesty's Government could only provide further relief for the Indian situation at the cost of incurring grave difficulties in other directions,' the Cabinet minutes record for 24 April 1944. 'At the same time his sympathy was great for the sufferings of the people of India.'[150] A few days later he asked Roosevelt for enough shipping to make up the shortfall, saying he was 'seriously concerned' about the famine and explaining that Wavell still needed a million extra tons, but that although the wheat was in Australia the ships were lacking; he was refused on the grounds of the need for ships to supply the Pacific and D-Day operations.[151] By the end of 1944, one million tons of grain had been secured from Australia and the South-East Asia Command, which has led some to conclude that without Churchill the Bengal Famine would actually have been worse.[152] One historian of the famine has concluded that 'Far from seeking to starve India, Churchill and his

Cabinet sought every way to alleviate the suffering without undermining the war effort.'[153]

When told on 19 July that the bombing of the Roman railway marshalling yards had begun, Churchill said, 'Good. And have we hit the Pope? Have we made a hole in his tiara?'[154] This was classic Churchillian mischief-making: he knew perfectly well that Rome's marshalling yards were nearly 3½ miles from St Peter's, on the other side of the Tiber. Lunch that day lasted until 3.15 p.m., because Churchill wanted to upbraid Bracken about 'Your pansies in the B.B.C. who talk about "Syr-a-cusa", rather than Syracuse'.[155]

The next day, Chamberlain's black cat at No. 10, the Munich Mouser, was found dead in the Foreign Office. 'Winston says he died of remorse and chose his deathbed accordingly,' recorded Eden. When the Prime Minister said that he feared the cat had been thrown on the ash heap, when he would readily have given him a burial in the garden of No. 10, Eden replied, 'Yes, "R.I.P. Munich Mouser" would have looked well there! We laughed a good deal about the poor cat.'[156] Churchill later told Rab Butler that the Mouser's antagonist, Churchill's own cat Nelson, contributed more to the war effort than Butler himself, because 'he acts as a hot water bottle and saves fuel and power'.[157]

On the evening of 25 July, while Churchill was watching *Sous les toits de Paris*, a musical comedy released in 1930, the BBC Monitoring Service rang Chequers with the news that the success of Operation Husky had emboldened King Victor Emmanuel and Marshal Badoglio to overthrow Mussolini and have him arrested. 'The film was stopped,' Marian Holmes recalled, 'the lights went on, and the P.M. announced the good news. Everyone clapped.'[158] Churchill telephoned Eden at 11.30 p.m. and 'After some jubilation and reminiscences of the humiliation of Neville and Edward [Halifax]'s visit to Rome, we discussed next moves.' The first was to try to bring the Italians over to the Allied side. 'We were in the presence of an event of utmost consequence,' Churchill said.[159] When he entered the Chamber of the Commons two days later, he was given a fine reception. 'We should let the Italians,' he said, 'to use a homely phrase, stew in their own juice for a bit, and hot up the fire to the utmost in order to accelerate the process.'[160] The BBC was instructed that the Italian translation should use the word 'minestrone', so that it did not translate as 'boil in her own oil'.[161]

Churchill worried that Stalin 'would be infuriated' that he was going to meet Roosevelt again without him at the Quadrant Conference in Quebec in August, despite Stalin's refusal to travel. 'If we could persuade the Americans to help us form a line in the valley of the Po this year and thus open a real Second Front,' he told Eden, 'Joe might become more amenable again.'[162] He and Eden set sail on the *Queen Mary* from the

Clyde at 6 p.m. on 5 August, reaching Halifax, Nova Scotia, in five days and five hours. Their entourage included Clementine, Mary, Averell Harriman and his daughter Kathleen, Ismay, Pound, Brooke, Portal, Martin, Leathers and Mountbatten, the last of whom Churchill described as 'young, enthusiastic and triphibious'.[163] On the journey, he indulged his love of meeting brave men by listening to Squadron Leader Guy Gibson describe the Dambusters Raid, and to Brigadier Orde Wingate, founder of the Chindits, describe fighting deep behind Japanese lines in Burma. When, before they left the Clyde, Wingate had said he was going to miss his wife Lorna, as he had only a limited amount of leave before he would have to return to the jungle, Churchill had had her taken off her south-bound train at Edinburgh and brought on board the ship to Canada.

While crossing the Atlantic, Churchill wrote a memorandum on code-words. 'Operations in which large numbers of men may lose their lives ought not to be described by codewords which imply a boastful and over-confident sentiment,' he began,

> such as 'Triumphant', or, conversely, which are calculated to invest the plan with an air of despondency, such as 'Woebetide', 'Massacre', 'Jumble', 'Trouble', 'Fidget', 'Flimsy', 'Pathetic', and 'Jaundice' . . . Names of living people – ministers or commanders – should be avoided; e.g., 'Bracken' . . . Intelligent thought will readily supply an unlimited number of well-sounding names which do not suggest the character of the operation or disparage it in any way and do not enable some widow or mother to say that her son was killed in an operation called 'Bunnyhug' or 'Ballyhoo'. Proper names are good in this field. The heroes of antiquity, figures from Greek and Roman mythology, the constellations and stars, famous racehorses, names of British and American war heroes could be used, provided they fall within the rules above. An efficient and a successful administration manifests itself equally in small as in great matters.[164]

Arriving at Halifax at 4 p.m. on 9 August, Churchill took the personal train of the president of the Canadian National Railways to Quebec. Crowds collected at every stop to wave at and cheer the Prime Minister as he gave his V-sign.[165] He stayed at the Citadel in Quebec, the Governor-General's summer residence on the heights overlooking the St Lawrence River, where the Conference took place. Churchill told Mackenzie King 'that he was quite different than he had been in earlier years. [He] had learned a great deal. He had made many mistakes in the first war. He was making fewer in this war because of those he had made earlier . . . Above all, he had learned to consider very carefully matters and to be cautious.'[166] (It is unlikely that the Chiefs of Staff, who were trying to dissuade him from proposed attacks on Malaya and northern Sumatra at the time, would have agreed.) Later that day, on the way to Roosevelt's residence at Hyde Park, Churchill and Mary visited Niagara Falls, which he had last seen in 1900. When a journalist asked, 'Do they look the same?', Churchill replied, 'Well, the principle seems the same. The water still keeps falling over.'[167]

In their two days together at Hyde Park, Churchill and Roosevelt agreed that Britain and the United States would exchange nuclear information with each other but with no other Power, and that nuclear weapons would not be used by either without the other's approval. Once again, nothing was put down on paper. British scientists started to work at the Los Alamos nuclear facility in New Mexico shortly afterwards. Churchill also gave Roosevelt the secret O'Malley report on the Katyń Massacre, which he called 'a grim, well-written story', adding that he would like it back once the President had read it, 'as we are not circulating it officially in any way'.[168]

When Harry Hopkins pressed for the job of supreme commander of Operation Overlord to go to General Marshall rather than Brooke, Churchill acquiesced. Once he had broken the news to Brooke on his return to Quebec from Hyde Park, the CIGS, in his own words, was 'swamped by a dark cloud of despair', writing later, 'Not for one moment did he realize what this meant to me. He offered no sympathy, no regrets at having had to change his mind, and dealt with the matter as if it were one of minor importance!'[169] Part of Brooke's animus against Churchill can be put down to that dream-smashing moment of utter disappointment, although there had been plenty of previous criticisms too.

By the time Roosevelt arrived in Quebec for the Quadrant Conference on 17 August, the whole of Sicily was in Allied hands and German forces were in retreat along the southern Russian front. Ian Jacob recalled the Conference, which took place over the next eight days, as the time when:

> the increasing strength of America began to exert the prepondering effect on Allied decisions that grew steadily as the years 1943 and 1944 unfolded . . . They [the Americans] were not prepared to discuss future plans in the Pacific in the same way as they discussed those in Europe or the Indian Ocean. They would not allow anyone to have a hand in discussing allocations of equipment to the Pacific . . . They would not allow [Mountbatten, who became the supreme commander in south-east Asia at the Conference] control over U.S. Air Forces engaging in supplying China "over The Hump" [a dangerous air route over the Himalayas] . . . The surprising fact is that so great a degree of harmony and combined working was achieved.[170]

There was little harmony between Churchill and Brooke, who disagreed over whether the main British strategy against Japan should now concentrate on liberating British colonies around the Bay of Bengal, which Churchill wanted, or helping the United States in the Pacific, which the Chiefs of Staff preferred to do. During the conference, Brooke ranted in his diary about 'a peevish temperamental prima donna of a Prime Minister, suspicious to the very limits of imagination, always fearing a military combination of effort against political dominance . . . He has been more unreasonable and trying than ever this time . . . I wonder whether any historian of the future will ever be able to paint Winston in his true colours?'[171] As soon as the Conference ended, Churchill, Brooke and Portal went fishing on the Lac des Neiges for six days, living in log cabins with hot baths and blazing fires, guarded by scarlet-coated Mounties. 'Everything here has gone off well,' Churchill cabled Attlee in London before they left. 'Stalin has of course studiously ignored our offer to make a further long and hazardous journey in order to bring about our tripartite meeting. In spite of all this I do not think his manifestations of ill-temper and bad manners are preparatory to a separate peace with Germany, as the hatreds between the two races have now become a sanitary cordon in themselves.'[172] Churchill felt emotional as Eden and he were soon to part. 'I don't know what I should do if I lost you all,' he told him. 'I'd have to cut my throat. It isn't just love, though there is much of that in it, but that you are my war machine. Brookie, Portal, you and Dickie. I simply couldn't replace you.'[173] Churchill might not have praised 'Brookie' much in public, or even to his face, but he was appreciative and even affectionate about him behind his back.

Churchill was staying in the White House on 3 September when the Allies successfully launched Operation Avalanche, crossing the Straits of Messina to land on mainland Italy. That day the Italians, led by King Victor Emmanuel III and the former commander in Africa, Marshal Pietro Badoglio, signed the Armistice of Cassibile with the Allies, which was announced five days later, taking Italy out of the war and paving the way for a formal surrender, although the Germans made it clear that they would continue to contest every inch of the peninsula. Ever alive to semantics and the political ramification of words, Churchill wrote to Eden later on to encourage the Foreign Office to standardize terms:

> 1. We 'invade' all countries with whom we are at war.
>
> 2. We 'enter' all subjugated Allied lands we wish to 'liberate'.
>
> 3. With regard to a country like Italy with whose Government we have signed an Armistice, we 'invaded' in the first instance but, in view of the Italian cooperation, we must consider all further advances by us in Italy to be in the nature of 'liberation'.[174]

'The P.M.'s sleeping arrangements have now become quite promiscuous,' Cadogan wrote to his wife on 4 September. 'He talks with the President until 2 a.m. and consequently spends a large part of the day hurling himself violently in and out of bed, bathing at unsuitable moments and rushing up and down corridors in his dressing gown.'[175] After lunch at the White House on 5 September, sitting on the South Portico, Mrs Ogden Reid, whose husband was the publisher of the *New York Herald Tribune*, a long-standing proponent of Indian independence, asked Churchill, 'What do you intend to do about those wretched Indians?' 'Madam,' Churchill replied, 'to which Indians do you refer? Do you by any chance refer to the second greatest nation on earth which under benign and beneficent British rule has multiplied and prospered exceedingly, or do you mean the unfortunate Indians of the North American continent which under your administration are practically extinct?'[176] Roosevelt, who had seated her next to Churchill hoping for such an eruption, was convulsed with laughter.*

Churchill stayed in Washington for eleven days, longer than originally planned, but he wanted to be with the President when Italy formally surrendered and was determined not to be caught in the mid-Atlantic when what he called 'the Italian climax' occurred.[177] While waiting for news from Rome, he drove out to the National Naval Medical Center at Bethesda in Maryland to visit Captain Pim who had ruptured a disc in his back. He also appointed Fitzroy Maclean to the role of liaison officer with Marshal Tito, the Yugoslav Communist resistance leader, whose partisan army Britain had been aiding since May.† He went on to offer Windsor Castle as the venue of a 'Big Three' meeting between Stalin, Roosevelt and himself (without warning the King).[178] But Stalin remained adamant that he would not go far from Russia, while Eden noted Roosevelt's 'determination not to agree to a London meeting for any purpose, which he says is for electoral reasons'.[179] Eden thought this 'almost insulting' considering that Churchill had visited Roosevelt four times already.

During this hiatus, on 6 September Churchill was awarded an honorary degree at Harvard University in Cambridge, Massachusetts. Wearing an Oxford DCL cap and gown hastily borrowed in New York, which John Martin thought made him look like 'a genial Henry VIII', he made one

* Overall, Churchill thought highly of Mrs Reid, however, having told Mary in August 1940 that she was running 'the most majestic campaign in the history of journalism' by supporting active American participation in the war (CAC MCHL 1/1/2).

† When a Yugoslavian general asked to be parachuted into the Balkans, Churchill said, 'I'm not sure I should make a good landing by parachute. I'd break like an egg.'

of the central addresses of his life, conveying his vision for the future of the English-speaking peoples.[180] 'Twice in my lifetime the long arm of destiny has searched across the oceans and involved the entire life and manhood of the United States in a deadly struggle,' he said. 'There was no use in saying "We don't want it; we won't have it; our forebears left Europe to avoid these quarrels; we have founded a new world which has no contact with the old." There was no use in that. The long arm reaches out remorselessly, and everyone's existence, environment, and outlook undergo a swift and irresistible change.'[181]

Addressing himself to the youth of Britain and America, he said,

> There is no halting-place at this point. We have now reached a stage in the journey where there can be no pause. We must go on. It must be world anarchy or world order. Throughout all this ordeal and struggle which is characteristic of our age, you will find in the British Commonwealth and Empire good comrades to whom you are united by other ties besides those of State policy and public need. To a large extent, they are the ties of blood and history. Naturally, I, a child of both worlds, am conscious of these.

In an oblique acknowledgement that the days of the Western empires were numbered, or perhaps a nod to America's tradition of anti-imperialism, Churchill said, 'The empires of the future are the empires of the mind.'[182] There was more than an echo in that declaration of his hero Napoleon's statement that 'The only victories which leave no regret are those which are gained over ignorance.'*

Churchill defined what connected the English-speaking peoples as 'Law, language, literature – these are considerable factors. Common conceptions of what is right and decent, a marked regard for fair play, especially to the weak and poor, a stern sentiment of impartial justice, and above all the love of personal freedom.'[183] There were overtones in

* One part of the Harvard speech was rather strangely devoted to a new language called Basic English. Invented by Charles Kay Ogden in 1930, it had only 650 nouns and 200 verbs, and Churchill had somehow convinced himself that 'The widespread use of this would be a gain to us far more durable and fruitful than the annexation of great provinces' (WSC, *TSWW* V p. 571). He also discussed it with Roosevelt at the Quadrant Conference, since it fitted in with his developing views about the English-speaking peoples. 'Propagate our language all over the world is the best method,' he told the Cabinet in July 1945. 'This will be the English-speaking century. It can be learned in two to four weeks' ('Diaries of Cabinet Secretary Sir Norman Brook', *New York Times* 22 January 2006). The paucity of the actual vocabulary of Basic English left Roosevelt unconvinced. 'I wonder what the course of history would have been', he told Churchill, 'if in May 1940 you had been able to offer the British people only "Blood, work, eye water, and face water" which I understand is the best Basic English can do with five famous words' (ed. Kimball, *Complete Correspondence* III p. 154).

this of his description in *My Early Life* of the Religion of Healthy-Mindedness of the 4th Hussars mess in the 1890s. To those isolationists who believed the United States should not have gone to war, he said,

> The price of greatness is responsibility. If the people of the United States had continued in a mediocre station, struggling with the wilderness, absorbed in their own affairs, and a factor of no consequence in the movement of the world, they might have remained forgotten and undisturbed beyond their protecting oceans: but one cannot rise to be in many ways the leading community in the civilized world without being involved in its problems, without being convulsed by its agonies and inspired by its causes.[184]

Churchill had signed the contract for his *History of the English-Speaking Peoples* as long ago as 1932, and had been making speeches on the subject of Anglo-American unity of purpose since the earliest years of the century. Now he crystallized his thoughts by saying, 'The gift of a common tongue is a priceless inheritance and it may well someday become the foundation of a common citizenship. I like to think of British and Americans moving about freely over each other's wide estates with hardly a sense of being foreigners to one another.'[185] Despite his irritation with the United States over the debt and cruiser-building in the 1920s, and not passing over enough war materiel in 1940, he had long understood that Britain's future largely depended on strong ties with the United States. 'If we are together nothing is impossible. If we are divided all will fail. I therefore preach continually the doctrine of the fraternal association of our two peoples . . . for the sake of service to mankind and for the honour that comes to those who faithfully serve great causes.'[186] It was to be a doctrine that he continued to proclaim for the rest of his life.

Finally, on 8 September 1943, Italy surrendered. For a brief moment, the garden path looked as if it was lined with delectable fruits. Churchill did not venture to guess at this time how long the Germans would continue to fight on, but when a Cabinet minister complained that they would follow anybody, like sheep, he replied, 'Oh it is far worse than that; they are *carnivorous* sheep!'[187]

# 29
# The Hard Underbelly
## September 1943–June 1944

*There is only one thing worse than fighting with allies, and that is fighting without them!*

Churchill at Chequers, April 1945[1]

*Don't worry, it doesn't matter if I die now; the plans of victory have been laid, it is only a matter of time.*

Churchill to Sarah, Carthage, December 1943[2]

Churchill was staying at Hyde Park on 12 September 1943 when the dismaying news arrived that Mussolini had been freed in a daring raid on his hilltop prison by German paratroops. He was later installed as dictator of a rump Republic of Salò, based on Lake Garda. Mary's diary makes it clear that this did not spoil her parents' thirty-fifth wedding anniversary. Churchill told Clementine that 'he loved her more and more every year.'[3] Returning to Britain, Churchill and his entourage took the presidential train from Hyde Park to Halifax, Nova Scotia. John Martin wrote, 'We pass a splash of autumn colouring, almost unbelievably red and gold, the Hudson Valley looking at its best.'[4] The British party left Halifax in the ageing battlecruiser HMS *Renown* at 3 p.m. on 14 September. Captain Edward Parry celebrated Mary's twenty-first birthday with gunnery practice the next day, and Churchill played a good deal of bezique and poker on the journey. When they arrived in Britain on the 19th, Eden noted, 'He looked pretty well and seems in good spirits.'[5]

Two days later, Churchill entered the House of Commons after six weeks away, to loud cheers. He gave a two-hour speech, divided in half by lunch. 'When I hear people talking in an airy way of throwing modern armies ashore here and there as if they were bales of goods to be dumped on a beach and forgotten,' he said, 'I really marvel at the lack of knowledge which still prevails of the conditions of modern war.'[6] The line could have come from one of Brooke's diary entries about him. The press had been hard on the Government in recent weeks, mainly over trivialities compared to the victories that had now put Sicily, southern Italy, Sardinia, Corsica (liberated that month) and the Italian Fleet in Allied hands. Churchill laughed this criticism off by suggesting it was like the story of a 'sailor who jumped into a dock, I think it was at Plymouth, to rescue a small boy from drowning. About a week later this sailor was accosted by a woman who asked, "Are you the man who picked my son out of the dock the other night?" The sailor replied modestly, "That is true, Ma'am." "Ah," said the woman, "you are the man I am looking for. Where is his cap?" '[7]

'Nazi tyranny and Prussian militarism are the two main elements in German life which must be absolutely destroyed,' Churchill proclaimed. 'They must be absolutely rooted out if Europe and the world are to be spared a third and still more frightful conflict.'[8] Of Italy he said, 'We must not add needlessly to the weight of our task or the burden that our soldiers bear. Satellite states, suborned or overawed, may perhaps, if they can help to shorten the war, be allowed to work their passage home.'[9] Nicolson noted how on the phrase 'suborned and overawed' Churchill had 'raised his arm as if about to deliver the most terrific thunderbolt from his rich armoury of rhetoric', only to drop his arm suddenly and remove his spectacles, before continuing with a grin, 'may perhaps be allowed to work their passage home'. Nicolson believed that 'It is in this that one finds his mastery of the House. It is the combination of great flights of oratory with sudden swoops into the intimate and conversational. Of all his devices it is the one that never fails.'[10] 'Winston's speech was a masterpiece, even for him,' wrote Eden, 'and he devastated the critics in advance.'[11]

'He was looking very well,' the King recorded after lunch with Churchill that day, 'and was pleased with what he had accomplished at Quebec, and during his stay with FDR in Washington. He was sure he and FDR trusted one another and that the Combined Chiefs of Staff Committee were in complete agreement as to future strategy.' Churchill nonetheless told the King, 'The Americans had originally thought of going to Sardinia only!!'[12]

Sir Kingsley Wood got out of bed in the morning of 21 September and fell down dead. He had done a solid job as chancellor of the Exchequer in dangerous times for the British economy. Even though he had helped Churchill replace Chamberlain in May 1940, Churchill had never warmed to him because he had been the most pro-German of the appeasers. His death allowed Churchill to move Sir John Anderson to the Treasury, Attlee to lord president of the Council and Cranborne to his old job of dominions secretary. This permitted Beaverbrook to return to the Government as lord privy seal, and once again become intimate with Churchill, further evidence of the

Prime Minister's magnanimity in victory. He no longer had reason to fear Beaverbrook's intriguing for his job now that the war was going well.

Attlee's Lord President's Committee took over responsibilities for many aspects of the home front, much as Chamberlain had done before his death. In all there were no fewer than 400 Cabinet committees and sub-committees formed during the war, which held 8,000 meetings examining every area of national life, emerging and then disappearing as the need came and went. The Reconstruction Committee, for example, met only four times in 1941 but over a hundred times in 1944. When the war ended, the Cabinet Office had a staff of 576 people, having had fewer than fifty before the war.[13]

In October, the Luftwaffe started bombing London again. Mary's Hyde Park battery saw a good deal of action. Wearing his steel helmet, Churchill would sometimes visit his daughter unannounced to talk with her comrades, bringing his dinner guests with him, including on one occasion Brooke. 'Sometimes I go to Maria's battery,' Churchill wrote to Randolph, using her family nickname, 'and hear the child ordering the guns to fire.'[14] His paternal pride was palpable. With Diana volunteering as an air-raid warden, Clementine doing fire-watching duty, Sarah in the WAAF identifying enemy positions from aerial reconnaissance photographs, and Randolph parachuting into Occupied Yugoslavia in January 1944, the Spencer-Churchill family's reputation for personal courage and public service was a proud one.

Churchill's failure to persuade the Americans to take part in Operation Accolade, the forthcoming attack on Rhodes and the Dodecanese Islands, left him frustrated. 'The difficulty is not winning the war,' he told his secretary Marian Holmes on 7 October, 'it is in persuading people to let you win it – persuading fools.'[15] 'He seemed distressed and said he felt "almost like chucking it in",' she wrote in her diary. The Americans rightly thought that Churchill hankered after a campaign in the Balkans to head off the Russians. Brooke believed that Churchill was on the verge of 'endangering his relations with the President and with the Americans, and also the whole future of the Italian campaign', for the sake of capturing Rhodes. 'I am slowly becoming convinced that in his old age Winston is becoming less and less well balanced! I can control him no more.'[16]

It is not true that after the Trident Conference Churchill wanted to postpone, still less cancel, Operation Overlord from its original launch date of 1 May 1944, as has sometimes been alleged.[17] When, on 14 October 1943, the King wrote to him to suggest that the Mediterranean was the place to fight rather than northern France, Churchill replied that 'There is no possibility of going back on what is agreed. Both the U.S. Staff and Stalin would violently disagree with us. It must be remembered that this country is the only one from which our Metropolitan Fighter Air

Force can make its weight tell. I think there are resources for both theatres.'[18] But there also needed to be limits to the Americans' domination of strategy. Five days later Churchill told the King that the United States 'cannot have Supreme Commanders both here (Marshall) and in the Mediterranean (Eisenhower) and we must not allow it. The Mediterranean is our affair and we have won the campaigns there.'[19]

Churchill was naturally extremely concerned about the risks Overlord would undoubtedly involve, not least because his record of amphibious attacks since 1915 had been very patchy. He openly told Roosevelt later that month, 'I am more anxious about the campaign of 1944 than about any other in which I have been involved.'[20] Yet there is a vast difference between worrying over the success of an operation and wanting to postpone or cancel it. 'There is of course no question of abandoning "Overlord" which will remain our principal operation for 1944,' Churchill wrote to Eden at the end of October. 'The retention of landing craft in the Mediterranean in order not to lose the battle of Rome may cause a slight delay, perhaps till July.' This technical problem regarding landing craft did indeed put Overlord back to early June 1944.[21]

At lunch with Charles Eade on 14 October, Churchill firmly rejected the first course of macaroni and cheese, saying, 'The main position is Irish stew and we should not be weakened by attacking these barbed wire entanglements.'[22] Several times during the luncheon he slipped his hands through his waistcoat armholes and leaned back in his chair saying, 'What a year it has been! What a magnificent year!'[23] Eade was about to go to the Far East as press adviser to Mountbatten, and Churchill told him that in his view the less news there was of the south-east Asian war in the near future the better. 'He did not want this war written up and publicised at the moment,' Eade noted. 'It would be better if it were forgotten.'[24] The men of the Fourteenth Army, which was then struggling in Burma, had dubbed themselves 'the Forgotten Army', and it seems that they had good reason. Churchill wanted the Americans not to withdraw the four US and three British divisions from Italy in 1943 to prepare for Operation Overlord. Any publicity about progress being made needed to be directed towards Italy. He believed it would be possible to undertake Operation Overlord and attacks in northern Italy simultaneously, although not also an attack in the south of France, which he had always opposed.

On 21 October, Pound died. He had suffered a stroke on the last day of the Quebec Conference, and although for a time he thought he could pass it off, by 8 September he had to tell Churchill that he was no longer fit for duty. Churchill had visited Pound just before he died, having secured for him the Order of Merit. 'His face was set,' Churchill recalled. 'He could not speak. But he took my hand. He died on Trafalgar Day. Death is the greatest gift that God has made to us.'[25] Pound's best friend, Vice Admiral Geoffrey Blake, recorded, 'The PM was, as I knew he would be, greatly affected, and came out of his sick room weeping.'[26] Churchill said that Pound had been one of the four men from whom he had gained the greatest benefit in discussions on the general conduct of the war, the others being Beaverbrook, Smuts and Bracken.[27] This was hard on Brooke, Eden and Portal, but probably true. Pound's successor as first sea lord and chief of the Naval Staff, Admiral Sir Andrew Cunningham, also kept a diary, and was just as acerbic about Churchill as Brooke.

In a debate on 28 October about the form the House of Commons should take when it was rebuilt after the war, Churchill argued strongly that it should be an exact replica of the one destroyed. 'We shape our buildings,' he said, 'and afterwards our buildings shape us. Having dwelt and served for more than forty years in the late Chamber, and having derived very great pleasure and advantage therefrom, I, naturally, should like to see it restored in all essentials to its old form, convenience, and dignity.'[28] He believed that the party system was 'much favoured by the oblong form of the chamber. It is easy for an individual to move through those insensible gradations from Left to Right, but the act of crossing the floor requires serious consideration. I am well informed on this matter.'[29] Churchill was also of the view that the Chamber should be capable of fitting only two-thirds of its members, because 'If the House is big enough to contain all its Members, nine-tenths of its debates will be conducted in the depressing atmosphere of an almost empty or half-empty Chamber. The essence of good House of Commons speaking is the conversational style, the facility for quick, informal interruptions and interchanges.'[30] Elsewhere he said of MPs, 'They must have to crowd to get to their seats. And when it is a great occasion they must stand in the passages, and in the gangways. There must be an air of excitement. Why, even a nightclub can't succeed if you have a place where everybody could sit or dance.'[31]

On 30 October 1943, Churchill was bequeathed £20,000 (over £800,000 in today's money) on the death of his friend the South African miner and financier Sir Henry Strakosch.* The next day, Marian Holmes's diary records that Churchill was understandably 'in high spirits. He began, but did not finish, the jingle "There was a young lady of Crewe." '[32] (This was probably just as well, as it was a lewd limerick unfit for the ears of his young secretary.) With the Eighth Army taking Isernia, 90 miles from Rome, on 4 November, Kiev retaken by the Russians two days later

* Thereby rather exploding the myth that rich Jews backed Churchill in the hope of future gain.

and the weather finally allowing the Murmansk convoys to resume in relative safety, Churchill had every reason to feel positive. He amused the King when telling him about his efforts to coerce Turkey into entering the war, saying, 'The Foreign Secretary asks me "What shall I say to Turkey?" I say to him, "Tell them that Christmas is coming." '[33]

In October 1943, a European Advisory Commission had been set up by the foreign ministries of the United States, the USSR and Britain, which split Germany and Austria into zones of occupation and delineated how far each army could march in liberating Europe. The zones would be run by AMGOT, which stood for Allied Military Government for Occupied Territories.* Berlin, Prague and other important central European cities were to be captured by the Red Army for the obvious operational reason that they were much closer, but also because as far as Eisenhower was concerned it was capable of accepting and absorbing far more casualties than the Western democracies. For all that important central European cities would fall inside the Soviet sphere of influence, AMGOT did mean that Denmark, the Benelux countries and the western part of Germany liberated by Anglo-American forces would be administered by the Western Powers, and crucially that there would be no clashes between Soviet and Western forces over territory in the closing stages of the war.

By November 1943, major differences had arisen between Churchill and the Chiefs of Staff over the best strategy to adopt in fighting Japan. Whereas the Chiefs broadly believed victory would come from supporting American attacks on the Japanese-held islands in the Pacific Ocean, Churchill wanted to concentrate on recapturing the former British territories of Burma, Malaya and Hong Kong, thereby restoring the imperial prestige so badly lost in December 1941. He wanted to undertake Operation Culverin against northern Sumatra, for example, and to make use of British bases in the Middle East, Ceylon and India. This Bay of Bengal strategy therefore fundamentally clashed with the Chiefs' preference for a quicker victory in the central and south-west Pacific. Ismay believed that the 'waffling that there has been for nearly nine months over the basic question of our strategy in the Far East will be one of the blackest spots in the record of the British higher direction of the war which has, on the whole, been pretty good'.[34]

* Soon afterwards, Churchill asked Alec Cadogan whether 'Amgot' meant camel dung in Turkish. Cadogan put the question to the Foreign Office linguists and replied that 'It does not correspond to any single Turkish word. There are, however, two Turkish words, "Ahm" and "Kot", which an English scholar would, not incorrectly, translate as "Cunt" and "Arse"' (*TCD* 19 pp. 651 and n. 2). On learning this, 'The Prime Minister was put in a good frame of mind for the rest of the day' (ed. Russell, *Constant* p. 229).

In order to establish priorities globally, the Big Three prepared to meet in Teheran in late November, a destination that would not take Stalin far from the USSR. Before then, Churchill wanted to confer with the Middle Eastern command in Cairo. He had a heavy cold and was slightly feverish from inoculations against typhoid when he boarded HMS *Renown* at Plymouth at sunset on 12 November, lovingly nursed on the journey by his temporary aide-de-camp, his daughter Sarah. When Moran suffered a fall getting into the ship's tender, Churchill enjoyed pretending to be his doctor. 'Charles when ill refuses his own drugs with a sad air of inside knowledge,' he said.[35]

Arriving in Malta on 17 November, Churchill stayed with Lord Gort, the Governor, at his residence, the San Anton Palace, where he had meetings with Eisenhower, Alexander, the British Chiefs of Staff and Tedder. Gort was a stickler for eating no more than the meagre rations allowed to the embattled Maltese, but, as Lawrence Burgis recalled Ismay telling him, such 'lofty Spartanism did not appeal in practice very much to the Prime Minister. Rather pathetically he drew Ismay to one side and beseeched: "If you are going back to our lovely ship do get them to send me up a pound of butter."'[36] Churchill read a book on William Pitt the Younger that Clementine had sent him, which, according to Sarah, 'kept him happy for hours'.[37]

It was while he was at Malta that Churchill learned of the British defeat in the Dodecanese, the first really serious reverse since Tobruk. He had pressed for the pro-Allied Italians holding the islands to be reinforced with British troops in a scaled-down version of Operation Accolade, which they had been on 15 September. This prompted heavy bombing after 26 September from the Germans, who also meanwhile captured Rhodes. The Germans invaded Leros and the rest of the Dodecanese on 12 November, forcing the British Army to evacuate four days later, with the loss of 600 killed, a hundred wounded and 3,200 taken prisoner, three destroyers sunk and 115 RAF planes based at Cyprus lost. It was not a defeat on anything like the scale of Tobruk, but if Churchill had listened to the Americans – or perhaps if the Americans had not taken their air force from Cyprus in late October to fight in Italy, as they had every right to do and had warned they would – it might not have happened. General Kennedy blamed Churchill, who had 'pressed the whole scheme most ardently', and claimed that General Jumbo Wilson 'lacked either the judgment or the courage to tell the P.M. that the project had become unsound and dangerous'.[38] Nonetheless, Kennedy admitted, 'The P.M. on paper has full professional backing for all that has been done. According to the documents he cannot be blamed. This is a good illustration however of the price we have to pay occasionally for his ignorance of military affairs combined with his confidence in his own military judgement.'[39]

Churchill, now codenamed Colonel Warden,* telegraphed Clementine, 'Am still grieving over Leros, etc. It is terrible fighting with both hands tied behind one's back.'[40] Sarah wrote in her diary that 'Leros made him very unhappy – but at intervals enjoyed himself and played a lot of bezique with Randolph who has been sweet.'[41] Randolph did not stay sweet for long. 'Papa was a little unhappy again about Randolph,' she reported to Clementine the next day as they sailed for Alexandria, 'and Randolph about himself and Papa.' Then she added cryptically, 'I wonder if a lot of people talking and explaining something about which none of us knows the complete story really helps.'[42]

Churchill reached Alexandria on 21 November, and flew on to Cairo in a C-47 Dakota, a military transport aircraft. That day he wrote to Herbert Morrison, the Home Secretary, asking him to support the highly controversial decision to release Oswald Mosley, the leader of the British Union of Fascists, from prison now that the threat of invasion had lifted. Mosley had been held without trial under Section 18B since May 1940. 'The power of the Executive to cast a man into prison without formulating any charge known to the law,' Churchill said, 'and particularly to deny him judgment by his peers for an indefinite period, is in the highest degree odious, and is the foundation of all totalitarian Governments, whether Nazi or Communist . . . Nothing can be more abhorrent to democracy than to imprison a person or keep him in prison because he is unpopular. This is really the test of civilization.'[43] He later said of the Cabinet's decision to support Morrison in the face of angry demonstrations in Trafalgar Square, 'People who are not prepared to do unpopular things and to defy clamour are not fit to be Ministers in times of stress.'[44]

The five-day Cairo Conference, codenamed Sextant, with Roosevelt and the Chinese Generalissimo Chiang Kai-shek, was held at the Mena House Hotel, not far from the Pyramids. Churchill stayed at the palatial villa of Richard Casey, Minister Resident in the Middle East. On 23 November, he asked Sarah to find out if a car could get Roosevelt to the Sphinx. When she discovered that it could, 'my father bounded into the room and said, "Mr President, you simply must come to see the Sphinx and the Pyramids. I've arranged it all." '[45] It would be, as Churchill is credited with saying, 'the two most talkative people in the world meeting the most silent'.[46] When Roosevelt leaned forward on the arms of his chair and tried to rise, only to sink back again, Churchill turned away and said, 'We'll wait for you in

* A nod to his lord wardenship of the Cinque Ports.

the car.' Outside in the shimmering sunshine, Sarah 'saw that his eyes were bright with tears. "I love that man," he said simply.'[47]

Madame Chiang came to meetings with her husband. 'Papa was impressed by her,' Sarah observed, 'and there is no doubt that she is far and away the best interpreter.'[48] Brooke recalled that 'at one critical moment her closely clinging black dress of black satin with yellow chrysanthemums displayed a slit which extended to her hip bone and exposed one of the most shapely of legs. This caused a rustle amongst those attending the conference and I even thought I heard a suppressed neigh come from a group of some of the younger members!'[49] Sarah told Clementine that Madame Chiang was 'exotic, sinister, smooth, a trifle phoney? Perish the thought!'[50] Churchill and Brooke thought the Americans were over-impressed by the Chinese, and that they had done little to justify the central post-war position Roosevelt planned for them. This was another unfair racial assumption. The Chinese lost fifteen million people fighting the Japanese for fourteen years between 1931 and 1945, and deserved recognition for it.

On 25 November, Roosevelt threw a grand Thanksgiving dinner for twenty people, complete with an immense turkey and an Army band playing in the background. The President carved the turkey and, as Sarah told her mother, 'Both Papa and he made little speeches afterwards. Papa with tears flowing down his cheeks.' They then sang 'Home on the Range'. Sarah told Clementine that her father had 'wanted to send planes to get you!'[51] That evening might be seen as the high-water mark of the Roosevelt–Churchill friendship. 'Nothing could exceed the amicable relations between me and Admiral Q [the codename for Roosevelt] and indeed throughout all our large parties of British and Americans,' Churchill told Clementine. 'Thus differences of outlook may be reconciled by agreements which also spell action.'[52] These differences included American opposition to action in the eastern Mediterranean, aiding Tito to any degree that might open up a Balkan campaign and putting pressure on Turkey to enter the war. Nor, alarmingly, did Roosevelt want to discuss how to approach Stalin when they got to Teheran.[53]

'Now for the high jump,' Churchill told his entourage as they flew on the RAF York for the five-and-a-half-hour journey to Teheran. 'We shall be crossing four great rivers, the Tigris, the Euphrates, Jordan, and Nile, and the wilderness and the mountains,' he added. 'There will be nowhere, should we feel tired, that we could put our feet down to rest.'[54] On the desert part of the journey, Sarah's artist's eye noticed that it was 'for the most part sepia coloured, but every now and then slashed with a red or aquamarine seam of colour'.[55] Perhaps recalling the advice he gave his officers in January 1916 as they went into the trenches, Churchill told Sarah, 'War is a game played with a smiling face, but do you think there is laughter in my heart? We travel in style and round us there is great luxury and seeming security, but I never forget the man at the front, the bitter struggles, and the fact that men are dying in the air, on the land, and at sea.'[56] When they arrived in the Iranian capital the security arrangements were not at all good, and the cars crawled through the jammed streets. 'Anyone could have shot my father at point blank range or just dropped a nice little grenade into our laps,' recalled Sarah.[57] At one point, the car was totally stationary for three minutes with crowds milling around. Churchill suggested to Sir Reader Bullard, the British Minister in Teheran, that in future the jeep full of soldiers behind them should be an open one. 'Not of course that they could do anything to save us, but at least it would save them from the embarrassment of doing nothing at all.'[58] Arriving at the British Legation, Churchill read *Oliver Twist* till midnight.

The Teheran Conference (codenamed Eureka) marked the first time Stalin met Roosevelt face to face, and both were determined to make a success of it. Roosevelt even agreed to move from the American Legation to the Russian Embassy, on security grounds.[59] Churchill did not miss the significance of this, and the effect a close Russo-American relationship might have on British prestige and influence. 'I realised at Teheran for the first time what a small nation we are,' Churchill told Violet Bonham Carter eight months later. Moran was more blunt, noting that 'The P.M. is appalled by his own impotence.'[60]

To this day we do not know to what extent Stalin was goading Churchill when he proposed at Teheran that 50,000 German officers should be shot once victory was won, in order to extirpate German military might. When Roosevelt said the number should be 49,000, Churchill assumed it was all a joke, until Elliott Roosevelt made a serious speech agreeing with Stalin's proposal. 'At this intrusion I got up and left the table,' Churchill wrote in his memoirs, 'walking off into the next room, which was in semi-darkness. I had not been there a minute before hands were clapped upon my shoulders from behind, and there was Stalin, with Molotov at his side, both grinning broadly, and eagerly declaring that they were only playing, and that nothing of a serious character had entered their heads.'[61] What Stalin, Molotov and Elliott Roosevelt did not know – though the President did – was that Churchill had read Owen O'Malley's report on Katyń, and knew that Stalin was perfectly capable of carrying out such a crime without a blush.

'Stalin indulged in a great deal of "teasing" of me,' Churchill wrote later, 'which I did not at all resent.' In not responding with his own devastating wit and irony, which he could easily have done but which would have soured relations, Churchill showed admirable self-restraint. 'Atmosphere most cordial but triangular problems difficult' was how Churchill summed up the conference to Clementine.[62] It was not true that Roosevelt sided with Stalin against Churchill at Teheran, although he did laugh at some of Stalin's sallies. Roosevelt also 'cautioned Stalin against bringing up the problems of India with Churchill, and Stalin agreed that this was undoubtedly a sore subject', but Churchill's love of the Raj was hardly a secret.[63]

Overall the Eureka Conference was a success. Stalin gave his first indication that, after Germany had been beaten, 'We shall be able by our common front to beat Japan,' as he put it.[64] He not unreasonably insisted that the Western Allies decide who would command Operation Overlord, and would not believe the operation would happen until they did.[65] When Stalin approved of issuing fake invasion plans for Overlord, Churchill said, to Stalin's vast amusement, 'In wartime, Truth is so precious that she should always be attended by a bodyguard of lies.'[66] There was an embarrassing moment when the splendid, Sheffield-made Sword of Stalingrad, a present from King George VI, was presented by Churchill to Stalin, who handed it to Marshal Voroshilov, who promptly let it slip out of its scabbard and drop on the ground.

Although Roosevelt has been accused of caballing with Stalin against Churchill at Teheran, the Foreign Office record of a conversation at the Soviet Embassy on 30 November shows that, if anything, Churchill attempted to cabal with Stalin. 'The Prime Minister said that he was half-American and he had a great affection for the American people,' it reads. 'What he was going to say was not to be understood as anything disparaging of the Americans and he would be perfectly loyal towards them, but there were things which it was better to say between two persons.'[67] He then pointed out that there were thirteen to fourteen Allied divisions in Italy of which nine or ten were British. 'The choice had been represented as keeping to the date of Overlord or pressing on with the operations in the Mediterranean,' he said. 'But that was not the whole story.'

The Americans wanted to undertake Operation Buccaneer, an amphibious assault to recapture the Andaman Islands in the Bay of Bengal in March. Churchill told Stalin he was not keen on it. 'The Americans had pinned us down to a date for Overlord, and operations in the Mediterranean had suffered in the last two months,' he explained. 'Our army was somewhat disheartened by the removal of the seven divisions. We had sent home our three divisions and the Americans were sending theirs, all in preparation for Overlord. That was the reason for not taking full advantage of the Italian collapse. But it also proved the earnestness of our preparations for Overlord.'[68] Churchill did not want Stalin to believe that Britain was not pulling her weight, or that he was compromising on the date for Overlord. 'If my shirt were taken off now,' Churchill said to Lascelles and Cunningham after dinner the following February, 'it would be seen that my belly is sore from crawling to that man. I do it for the good of the country, and for no other reason.'[69] He felt the humiliation, and was widely criticized for it, especially when he shortly had to bully Britain's brave Polish allies over their post-war frontiers with Russia, but Britain needed the Soviet Union to continue to win huge victories before Operation Overlord was launched in June.

Churchill's sixty-ninth birthday fell at the end of the Conference, and he invited Roosevelt, Stalin and their senior staffs to the British Legation for a grand dinner.[70] Sarah thought that Stalin, 'a frightening figure with his slit, bear eyes, was in jovial mood'.[71] She believed he had 'a great sense of humour as darting and swift as Papa's' and thought he made the best joke of the evening. 'When Papa during one of the many toasts remarked "England is getting pinker," Joe interjected, "It is a sign of good health."'[72] Sarah was disappointed that Randolph failed to propose a toast to his father's birthday. 'I couldn't help thinking how a few years ago he would never have been off his feet!' she told their mother. 'There is a big change in him.'[73] Nonetheless, a great many toasts were proposed and drunk throughout the night, including one to 'The Proletarian Masses' by Churchill, in response to which Stalin proposed one to the Conservative Party.[74] Sarah's health was proposed by Roosevelt, at which point Stalin rose and came around the table to clink glasses with her. 'Everyone most kind,' Churchill cabled Clementine on the last day of the conference. 'Things have taken a very good turn.'[75]

At 9.30 a.m. on 2 December, Churchill flew back to Cairo, drinking champagne and taking turtle soup over Baghdad. He looked 'very fit and pleased with the Teheran meeting' when Lampson met him later that day.[76] The Turkish delegation arrived two days later, led by President Inönü. As Sarah tucked Churchill into his mosquito net that night, she found him giggling to himself and asked why. 'The President of Turkey kissed me – twice,' he told her. 'The trouble with me is that I'm irresistible.'[77] He then added, 'But don't tell Anthony, he's jealous.'[78] The talks with the Turks, whom Churchill wanted to declare war against Hitler, continued to be unproductive, but it was at Cairo that Roosevelt, under the prompting he had received from Stalin at Teheran, chose Eisenhower to be the commander of Overlord, as he felt he could not be without Marshall in Washington.

On 8 December, Churchill dined at the Cairo Embassy with Randolph, Fitzroy Maclean and Julian Amery, Leo Amery's son, who, like Randolph, was soon to parachute into Occupied Yugoslavia. When asked about his future plans in politics, Churchill said, 'I am the victim of caprice and travel on the wings of fancy,' which ought to have left Eden, who was also present, highly concerned. When Maclean made a critical reference to Tito's Communism, Churchill said, 'Do you intend to make your home in Yugoslavia after the war?' Maclean replied no. 'Neither do I,' said Churchill. 'That being so, don't you think we should leave it to the Yugoslavs to work out their own form of government? What concerns us most now is who is doing the most damage to the Germans.'[79] It was harsh, even cynical, but also realistic. Churchill took the decision to support Tito in Yugoslavia in the belief that the partisans were killing more Germans than the Chetnik Royalists.

Smuts was also present that night, and the next morning took Brooke aside to say that 'He was not at all happy about the condition of the P.M. He considered he worked far too hard, exhausted himself, and then had to rely on drink to stimulate him again. He said he was beginning to doubt whether he would stay the course, that he was noticing changes in him.'[80] Churchill flew from Cairo to Tunis on 11 November, intending to stay with Eisenhower for a few days before going on to visit Alexander in Italy. Instead, he caught another serious bout of pneumonia, with inflammation of the lungs that required Moran immediately to summon a team of six doctors from Cairo under Brigadier R. J. V. Pulvertaft, as well as two nurses and an X-ray machine. John Martin said there were so many medics around that he could not get into his office. Churchill was put on more M & B, and Moran administered digitalis to strengthen the heart. He kept his sense of humour throughout: asked for a blood sample by Pulvertaft, he said, 'You can use my finger, or my ear, and, of course, I have an almost infinite expanse of arse.'[81]

'I am tired out in body, spirit and soul,' Churchill told Walter Thompson. 'All is planned and ready, in what better place could I die than here – in the ruins of Carthage.'[82] Clementine flew out immediately, wearing a padded flying suit in an unheated Liberator that took off in fog. In Tunis, Sarah read *Pride and Prejudice* aloud to Churchill and watched him sleep. In his war memoirs, Churchill claimed, 'I did not at any time relinquish my part in the direction of affairs, and there was not the slightest delay in giving the decisions which were required from me.'[83] Martin wrote that this was 'rather an exaggeration', and in fact 'for several days [he] was seriously ill'.[84] The public was told that he had a neuralgic sore throat. 'He is very naughty,' Sarah wrote to her lover, Gil Winant, on 22 December; 'his power of recovery and his indomitable vitality plus a healthy dislike of being managed are all well alive.'[85] That day, Churchill starting dictating his doctors' bulletins about the progress of his health, and smoking cigars, despite the patch that had been found on his lung.[86]

On Christmas Eve, a large number of senior commanders, including five commanders-in-chief – Wilson, Tedder, Eisenhower, Cunningham and Alexander – arrived to discuss Operation Shingle, an amphibious landing at Anzio, north of Naples, which Churchill hoped would deliver a decisive result in Italy and even lead to the fall of Rome before Overlord was launched. He held a conference in the dining room wearing his silk dressing-gown of blue and gold dragons.[87] Christmas lunch was the first meal he was able to take outside his room. 'The P.M. was up for it,' noted Martin, 'proposing a whole series of toasts.'[88] When he was served a custard while everyone else was eating Christmas pudding he said enviously, 'Any vehicle which conveys brandy to the stomach is to be commended.'[89] On Boxing Day, he received the splendid news of the *Scharnhorst* being sunk in the Battle of the North Cape.

As well as agreement to launch Shingle in January 1944, important personnel moves were undertaken once Churchill had recovered, with Jumbo Wilson becoming commander-in-chief in the Mediterranean, Alexander overall commander in Italy, and Tedder deputy supreme Allied commander for Overlord: three Britons in key roles. Churchill flew to Marrakesh on 27 December (taking oxygen at 12,000 feet) to convalesce at the Villa Taylor, with its excellent French chef.[90] From there he sent to Cairo for a major-general's insignia so that it could be wrapped up in Leslie Hollis's napkin as the first notification that he was being promoted.[91] Churchill also decorated Beaverbrook's son Max Aitken, a fighter ace, with the 1939–43 Star which had been hastily cut off Jock Colville's second tunic. Gestures such as these to those around him, and there were many more of them, such as ensuring the fire did not go out in rooms his secretaries had to wait in at Chequers, must be set against the similar number of instances of Churchill's selfishness and monomania.

'Winston sitting in Marrakesh is now full of beans,' noted Brooke back in London. 'As a result a three-cornered flow of telegrams is gradually resulting in utter confusion. I wish to God that he would come home and get under control.'[92] Churchill had been in Britain for only five weeks of the previous five months. At a dinner in honour of President Beneš – who was on his way from Moscow to London – on 5 January 1944, Churchill asked everyone around the table whether they thought that Hitler would still be in power on 3 September, the fifth anniversary of the declaration of war. Churchill, Beaverbrook and Colville thought he would; Beneš, Smuts, Moran, Tommy Thompson, Martin, Hollis and Sarah thought he would not.[93]

Beneš had been trying to reconcile the Poles to the Curzon Line* post-war

* First drawn up by Lord Curzon in 1919 to demarcate a future Polish–Russian border, and then substantially used in the Nazi–Soviet Pact for the Russian–German border of 1939–41. Areas to its west contained an overall ethnically Polish majority, and it is roughly the border between Poland, Ukraine and Belarus today.

border with Russia, and he hardened Churchill's heart against the London Poles, who were under pressure from Stalin to have their post-war state moved hundreds of miles to the west after the war to accommodate Russia and punish Germany. 'Russia, after two wars which have cost her between twenty and thirty millions of Russian lives,' Churchill cabled Eden on 7 January, 'has a right to the inexpungible security of her Western frontiers . . . Poland is now assigned a position as a great independent nation in the heart of Europe with a fine seaboard and better territory than she had before. If she does not accept this, Britain has discharged to the full her obligations and the Poles can make their own arrangements with the Soviets.'[94]

The next day, Randolph drunkenly attacked the absent Eden's qualities as foreign secretary, while Churchill stood up for him. Maclean, who was about to take Randolph away to liaise with Tito, assured everyone afterwards 'that all will be well in Yugoslavia owing to the absence of whisky and a diet of cabbage soup'.[95]

'The party is a circus,' Lady Diana Cooper wrote to her son John Julius on 10 January, having flown over from Algiers, where her husband was the British representative to the FCNL. 'It's lodged in a millionaire's pleasure dome, all marble and orange trees, fountains and tiles, in the richest Mohammedan style. There was our old baby in his rompers, ten-gallon cowboy hat and very ragged oriental dressing gown, health, vigour and excellent spirits. Never have I seen him spin more fantastic stuff, the woof of English and the warp of slang.'[96] She was right about slang; Churchill would occasionally descend into bouts of cockney, telling Leslie Rowan, 'Come on – stop muckin' me about!', and Marian Holmes, 'I ain't seen you for a long time,' or, when he accidentally lit the wrong end of his cigar, 'Oh lor'. Look what I've done!'[97]

The invitation to de Gaulle to lunch at Marrakesh on 12 January had twice nearly been rescinded when de Gaulle ordered the Free French general Jean de Lattre de Tassigny not to visit Churchill without himself being present, and later had Churchill's friend the former Prime Minister of France Pierre-Étienne Flandin arrested in Algiers. Nonetheless, it took place because Churchill wished to be as conciliatory as possible with Overlord now scheduled for later that year, for all his personal doubts about de Gaulle. 'Look here! I am the leader of a strong, unbeaten nation,' Churchill told him. 'Yet every morning when I wake my first thought is how I can please President Roosevelt, and my second thought is how I can conciliate Marshal Stalin. Your situation is very different. Why then should your first waking thought be how you can snap your fingers at the British and Americans?'[98] It had no effect on de Gaulle. To Martin, Churchill joked, 'Now that the General speaks English so well he understands my French perfectly.'[99]

That night, Churchill allowed Colville to rejoin his squadron. 'You seem to think that this war is being fought for your personal amusement,' Churchill told him, and after a pause, 'However, if I were your age I should feel the same, so you can have two months' fighting leave. But no more holidays this year.'[100] On 14 January, Churchill flew to Gibraltar for another conference on Operation Shingle and from there sailed for Plymouth on board HMS *King George V*. On the voyage he spent an hour in the gunroom answering questions from the midshipmen whom he encouraged to ask him whatever they liked about the war and about politics. 'They quite forgot he was the Prime Minister,' recalled Colville, 'and it was really marvellous to listen to him.'[101]

On the morning of 18 January, Churchill turned up unannounced in the Commons, after two months away. Harold Nicolson saw:

> a gasp of astonishment pass over the faces of the Labour Party opposite. Suddenly they jumped to their feet and started shouting, waving their [order] papers in the air. We also jumped up and the whole House broke into cheer after cheer while Winston, very pink, rather shy, beaming with mischief, crept along the front bench and flung himself into his accustomed seat. He was flushed with pleasure and emotion, and hardly had he sat down when two large tears began to trickle down his cheeks. He mopped at them clumsily with a huge white handkerchief.[102]

When, during Prime Minister's Questions, one MP fawningly suggested that the House should toast 'Death to all Dictators and Long Life to All Liberators, among whom the Prime Minister is the first', Churchill phlegmatically replied, 'It is very early in the morning.'[103]

'He was looking well and rested,' the King noted that day, 'though still rather weak on his legs, and he seems to have lost some of the fire in his eyes for the time being ... Thanks to the Americans we have lost our opportunity to capture Rhodes, and Rome is not yet ours. But at last we have control of the Mediterranean.'[104]

On 22 January, the Anzio landings began on the western Italian coast, an operation that Captain Harry C. Butcher, Eisenhower's naval aide, rightly described as 'the Prime Minister's pet military project'.[105] A British and an American division, totalling 36,000 men, with 3,000 vehicles landed behind the German lines ahead of General Clark's Fifth Army, virtually unopposed. Churchill told Alexander, 'Am very glad you are pegging out claims rather than digging in beach-heads.'[106] Very soon, however, it became clear that General John P. Lucas, the commander, was far too indecisive and slow to take advantage of the situation. 'I had hoped we were hurling a wildcat on to the shore,' Churchill complained after ten days, 'but all we had got was a stranded whale.'[107] It brought back horrible memories of Stopford's disastrous inertia and caution at Suvla Bay during the Gallipoli campaign.[108]

'The Germans are fighting magnificently,' Churchill told Colin Coote at an Other Club dinner on 27 January. 'Never imagine they are crashing. Their staff work is brilliantly flexible. They improvise units out of unrested remnants and those units fight just as well as the fresh ones.'[109] He considered flying out to the Anzio beachhead, but was persuaded not to.[110]

On 4 February Allied troops reached the medieval monastery of Monte Cassino which dominates the Liri Valley and the road to Rome, but found it impossible to break through the dogged German resistance across the peninsula. When Bevin suggested in the War Cabinet that Churchill should send Alexander a message of encouragement, the Prime Minister said, 'I'll think about it' – hardly an endorsement.[111] The monastery was razed by bombing in mid-February – it was a great cultural loss but the local commanders considered it tactically important. Yet it did not seem to do any good, and the breakthrough did not finally take place for another three months.

Churchill told Roosevelt on 11 February that peace overtures coming from the Bulgarian Government should not lighten the bombing of that country; indeed, 'If the medicine has done good, let them have more of it.'[112] Since Cairo there had been more and more issues where Churchill and Roosevelt diverged. The Americans showed no interest in prolonging the Italian monarchy, and other disagreements had emerged over issues as diverse as Argentine beef (which Roosevelt wanted to boycott to punish the Argentine Government for its Fascist sympathies but which Britain needed to buy), post-war civil aviation rights, Middle Eastern oil, imperial trading arrangements and other non-military topics in which Churchill felt the now far mightier United States was impinging upon the rights of the British Empire.[113] On 25 February Churchill even spoke to Brooke about 'The President's unpleasant attitude lately'.[114] His remonstrations were not always even answered, at least in full, and rarely by the President himself. There were 373 more messages sent by Churchill to Roosevelt during the war than were sent by Roosevelt to Churchill.

In some of the heaviest bombing raids of the war since May 1941, No. 10 was damaged on 20 February. All the windows and window frames were blown in and pieces of plaster fell down from the drawing-room ceiling, leaving great holes. 'Downing Street was carpeted with glass, and a bomb landing at the corner of the Treasury burst a large water main,' noted Colville.[115] Churchill, who had migrated back to No. 10 for meetings and meals, was forced to return to the Annexe for much of the time. In a broadcast from there he said, 'It was with great pleasure that I heard from Marshal Stalin that he, too, was resolved upon the creation and maintenance of a strong integral independent Poland as one of the leading Powers in Europe. He has several times repeated these declarations in public, and I am convinced that they represent the settled policy of the Soviet Union.'[116] He was not nearly as convinced of Soviet trustworthiness as his public pronouncements suggested. In early March, in a 'benevolent but sombre mood', he admitted to his guests at Chequers that he was disturbed by Stalin's attitude over Poland, saying that he felt like telling the Russians, 'Personally I fight tyranny whatever uniform it wears or slogans it utters.'[117]

In the Great Hall after watching a movie while smoking Turkish cigarettes, saying that they were the only thing he had ever got out of the Turks, the Prime Minister kept reverting to the point that he had not got long to live. With the gramophone playing the 'Marseillaise' and 'Le Régiment de Sambre et Meuse',* he told his guests, who included Ismay and Macmillan, that 'Far more important than India or the Colonies or solvency is *the Air*. We live in a world of wolves – and *bears*.'[118] He meant that only air superiority could fend off the coming Russian threat – this was exactly two years and one day before he made his Iron Curtain speech at Fulton, Missouri. Yet he was not sombre for long; a few days later, when asked by journalists who would defend the Government in a forthcoming debate, Churchill replied, 'If the worst came to the worst, I may have a shot at it myself.'[119]

Churchill was in a sombre mood, however, during lunch with the King on 7 March and complained about Roosevelt's 'unfortunate statement' at a press conference that he was prepared to give one-third of the Italian Fleet to Russia.

> This, the Russian attitude towards the Polish Government here over the Curzon Line, and the new wide Russian advance toward Tarnopol [Ternopol in western Ukraine] made Winston say that with a Bear drunken with victory in the east, and an Elephant lurching about in the west, we the United Kingdom were like a donkey in between them which was the only one who knew the way home. He told me the War Cabinet were very much alive to the dangerous attitude of Stalin and what a powerful Russia could do in the way of harm to the world. We don't want to have to fight Russia after the defeat of Germany.[120]

'I am hardening very much on this operation as the time approaches,' Churchill wrote to Marshall about Operation Overlord on 13 March, 'in

* A military march from Napoleon III's Second Empire.

the sense of wishing to strike if humanly possible even if the limiting conditions we laid down at Moscow are not exactly fulfilled.'[121] Those conditions had included there only being fifteen German divisions in northern France, whereas intelligence was now suggesting that there would be several more. Churchill's use of the phrase 'I am hardening' was taken by Eisenhower, when he repeated it to him on 15 May, to mean that Churchill had not been committed to Overlord before, but the letter to Marshall shows that that was far from the case.

The lowest point in relations between Churchill and the Chiefs of Staff was reached in late March 1944 over strategy in the Pacific. The Chiefs were reluctant to commit resources to Churchill's preferred Bay of Bengal strategy, and Churchill believed they had gone behind his back while he was in Marrakesh by making tentative draft plans for a Pacific strategy instead. 'I very much regret that the Chiefs of Staff should have proceeded so far in this matter and reached such settled conclusions upon it without in any way endeavouring to ascertain and carry the views of the civil power under which they are serving,' he wrote in an abrasive five-page memorandum. 'They certainly have the duty of informing me as Minister of Defence, and making sure I understand the importance they attach to the issue.'[122] To lecture Chiefs, who in Portal's case had been in the job five years, on their constitutional duties was as unnecessary as it was (probably deliberately) rude, but it was also a reminder of who held ultimate sanction.

He then changed tack on to the personal, writing, 'Considering the intimacy and friendship with which we have worked for a long time in so many difficult situations, I never imagined that the Chiefs of Staff would get into a great matter like this of long-term strategy into which so many political and other non-military considerations enter without trying to carry me along with them, so that we could have formed our opinions together.' Here, all in one sentence, was an appeal to comradeship, an accusation that they were trespassing into areas in which they had no authority to interfere, a lament that Churchill was effectively being cut out of the loop, a hint that he could have been persuaded anyway and lastly a warning that they needed to speak with one voice to the Dominions and the Americans. 'The Bay of Bengal will remain,' Churchill concluded defiantly and unequivocally, 'until the summer of 1945, the centre of gravity for the British and imperial war against Japan.'[123] In an early draft of his memoirs, Churchill ended the relevant chapter by saying that his 'rulings were accepted and the subject dropped', but since that was so patently untrue his researchers had to propose alternative endings. The paragraph accusing the Chiefs of Staff of reaching 'settled conclusions' without trying 'to ascertain and carry the views of the civil power' was considered so inflammatory that it was excised at the very last moment before publication, leaving a large gap on the page.[124]

'We discussed . . . how best to deal with Winston's last impossible document,' Brooke noted the next day. 'It is full of false statements, false deductions and defective strategy. We cannot accept it as it stands, and it would be better if we all three resigned rather than accept his solution.'[125] A reply was drawn up listing five errors of fact in Churchill's paper, and proposing that the Chiefs should 'discuss the subject with the P.M. and . . . suggest to him that his action is precipitate, is taken without full knowledge of all the factors and is, in any case, quite unnecessary at this stage'.[126] From Brooke's papers it is clear that Ismay was allowed to comment on the Chiefs' response before it was submitted, and he made no alterations to it. Churchill was therefore almost certainly forewarned of it, a sensible step.

The Chiefs of Staff's 'Private and Top Secret' reply to Churchill was delivered on 28 March. After a seemingly aquiescent opening paragraph – 'We feel sure that there is still some misunderstanding as to our views and proposals, and we welcome the opportunity of a further discussion with you on the whole subject' – the document categorically rejected all of Churchill's accusations.[127] 'We cannot accept the charge that you make,' the three Service chiefs wrote, 'that we have in any way committed His Majesty's Government to any particular line of policy without consulting you. We did our best to explain our views on long-term strategy for the war against Japan to you before Sextant,* but your other preoccupations, both before and after the Conference, precluded this. We were therefore at pains to ensure that the conclusions of the Combined Chiefs of Staff were couched in the most non-committal terms.'[128] In the event, as the key decisions did not need to be taken until after D-Day, the mass resignations were avoided and the temperature lowered, except in Brooke's and Cunningham's sulphurous diaries, and in Brooke's letters to Dill, which were full of contemptuous references to Churchill's ignorance of basic strategic concepts.[129]

'We can now say, not only with hope but with reason,' Churchill told the nation on 26 March, 'that we shall reach the end of our journey in good order, and that the tragedy which threatened the whole world and might have put out all its lights and left our children and descendants in darkness and bondage – perhaps for centuries – that tragedy will not come to pass.'[130] Of the forthcoming invasion of mainland Europe he said, 'when the signal is given, the whole circle of avenging nations will hurl themselves upon the foe and batter out the life of the cruellest tyranny which has ever sought to bar

* The Second Cairo Conference of December 1943.

the progress of mankind.'[131] A disgruntled Tommy Lascelles complained that 'It was the speech of an old man.'[132] One person who clearly did not agree was Anne Frank, who wrote in her diary from her secret attic in Amsterdam of her delight at 'A speech by our beloved Winston Churchill'.[133]

To Churchill's surprise, on 28 March the Government was defeated by one vote – 117 to 116 – on Clause 82 of Butler's Education Bill, relating to equal pay for male and female teachers. 'If only the Chancellor of the Exchequer could have been induced to break into a gentle trot,' Churchill remarked teasingly of Anderson, who had missed the vote, 'the Government would have been saved.'[134] It was the first actual defeat of the Government in the war. The Cabinet was unanimously in favour of turning the issue into a confidence vote, which the Government won soon afterwards by 425 to 23. 'I am not going to tumble around my cage like a wounded canary,' Churchill told an MP. 'You knocked me off my perch. You have now got to put me back on my perch. Otherwise I won't sing.' Nicolson noted, 'Everybody was ruffled and annoyed' by the Cabinet's decision to treat a minor domestic vote as one of no confidence. 'The only person who really enjoyed it was Winston himself. He grinned all over.'[135] Churchill did, however, complain to the King, who recorded, 'The House of Commons is a worry to him as it is a perpetual critic of the Government. Winston has enough things to think about already and suggests that he is not getting the support he deserves, for what he has done, and is doing, in running the war.'[136]

In April 1944, the Allies dropped 80,000 tons of bombs on Normandy. Churchill insisted on a careful review of this policy because of the effects on civilians. 'There was a limit to the slaughter and resulting anger it would arouse among Frenchmen beyond which we could not go,' he told the War Cabinet.[137] As with the Second BEF, the Greek expedition of 1941 and currently the Bay of Bengal strategy to recapture Britain's Far Eastern possessions before the Americans defeated Japan, Churchill was putting political considerations ahead of purely military ones.[138] But as he himself wrote in *The World Crisis*, 'At the summit, true politics and strategy are one.'[139]

'P.M. aged, tired, and failing to really grasp matters,' Brooke noted in his diary on 3 April. 'It is a depressing sight to see him gradually deteriorating. I wonder how long he will last, not long enough to see the war through I fear.'[140] That was just wishful thinking, as nothing was escaping Churchill's notice, and he was still in the forefront of British politics a decade later, long after Brooke, who was nine years younger, had retired. The day after Brooke wrote those lines, Churchill took over the Foreign Office while Eden was on holiday, and also asked the Home Secretary to 'Let me have a report on why the Witchcraft Act 1735 was used in a modern court of justice. What was the cost of this trial to the State?'[141] He wanted to know why judges were being 'kept busy with all this obsolete tomfoolery, to the detriment of necessary work in the courts'.[142] In a similar vein, he wrote to the Minister of Transport, 'I was delayed on my journey to Chequers owing to some new road works. Are you not aware that there is a war on? Pray cease this foolishness.'[143]

Marian Holmes enjoyed Churchill's caustic remarks about people, recording that in early April he referred to one general as 'a bladder with a name on it'.[144] At one point Leslie Rowan had to leave the room as he was laughing so much at Churchill's jokes. The Prime Minister was still regularly staying up until 3.30 a.m., which might have explained Brooke's double-edged concern. 'He drives himself far too hard,' Holmes wrote of Churchill two days before D-Day, 'and he nearly fell asleep over his papers.'[145] While it was undoubtedly true that Churchill was now tiring more easily in the fifth year of his war premiership, he was still capable of extraordinary acts of sustained stamina, not least because of his daily hour-long, reinvigorating naps. If he was asleep, with his black bandage over his eyes, when his car arrived at Chequers, it stayed parked outside the front door until he woke up.[146]

In mid-April 1944, Churchill began a campaign against Operation Dragoon (formerly Anvil) – the attack on the south of France that was intended to stop the Germans from withdrawing troops to counter Overlord. He told Marshall on 16 April that his support for Anvil at Teheran had come before the Allied advance on Rome had been checked at Monte Cassino. The Germans were now committing to Italy the very divisions that Anvil had been designed to draw away from Overlord. 'We must throw our hearts into this battle,' he wrote, 'and make Overlord an all out conquer or die.'[147] He no longer believed Anvil would help in that.[148] Anything that sounded critical of Overlord – such as his comment on a Foreign Office minute that 'This battle has been forced upon us by the Russians and the United States military authorities' – was excised from his war memoirs.[149] It is hard to escape the conclusion that he was deliberately leaving a secret paper trail of doubt and criticism, just in case the operation turned into a debacle similar to so many of the amphibious assaults that he had sponsored earlier in his career.

On 21 April, Churchill gave an impassioned defence of the British Empire in the House of Commons. 'What is this miracle, for it is nothing less, that called men from the uttermost ends of the earth,' he asked,

> some riding twenty days before they could reach their recruiting centres, some armies having to sail fourteen thousand miles across the seas before they reached

> the battlefield? What is this force, this miracle which makes Governments, as proud and sovereign as any that have ever existed, immediately cast aside all their fears, and immediately set themselves to aid a good cause and beat the common foe? You must look very deep into the heart of man, and then you will not find the answer unless you look with the eye of the spirit. Then it is that you learn that human beings are not dominated by material things, but by ideas for which they are willing to give their lives or their life's work.[150]

Yet five days later he made what Colville called a 'fiasco' of Prime Minister's Questions, losing his place, answering the wrong question and forgetting the names of important maharajahs.[151] He did have some bad days, but they were still far outnumbered by his good ones, and his powers of recuperation were extraordinary.

Harold Nicolson told Maud Russell that month that Churchill's 'voice sounded dull and rather tired, but whenever there was an interruption all his old speed, fire and brilliance returned in a flash'.[152] James Stuart told Eric Miéville, the King's assistant private secretary, 'that he could not make out what was in Winston's mind – he kept talking as if he were about to die'.[153] Churchill said to Brooke at this time that 'he no longer jumped out of bed the way he used to, and felt as if he would be quite content to spend the whole day in bed', comments that were only natural in a man his age under that amount of strain.[154]

On 15 May, the entire Allied top brass met for a briefing on Operation Overlord at Montgomery's 21st Army Group Headquarters which was located at his old school, St Paul's in Hammersmith. The King and Churchill were given armchairs; everyone else sat on the pupils' benches (although unlike schoolboys they were allowed to smoke). Eisenhower gave his assessment of what he hoped would take place in Normandy three weeks later, then Churchill spoke for half an hour and, although his words were not recorded, one of those present, Major-General Kennedy, wrote in his diary that the Prime Minister spoke 'in a robust and even humorous style, and concluded with a moving expression of his hopes and good wishes. He . . . spoke with great vigour, urging offensive leadership and stressing the ardour for battle which he believed the men felt.'[155]

Monte Cassino finally fell on 18 May and Rome might therefore be captured before D-Day, which was scheduled for 5 June. With British Commonwealth, American, French and Polish armies all engaged on the assault on the Italian capital, Churchill wanted the British contribution to be regularly mentioned in the press. Otherwise, as he told the War Cabinet, it 'looks as if the British were laggards in the show'.[156]

At lunch with the King in late May, Churchill said he was going to be on one of the warships bombarding Normandy on D-Day. The King was not surprised by this, and suggested that he would like to go too, to which Churchill 'reacted well'.[157] The Queen supported the idea, but Lascelles, Ismay, Eisenhower and crucially Admiral Ramsay, the overall commander of the naval side of Overlord, were all adamantly opposed to either of them going, especially on Churchill's choice of HMS *Belfast*, which would be shelling the French coast and thus could be exposed to Luftwaffe counter-attack. At lunch at the Annexe on 1 June, there was an extraordinary series of exchanges between the King, his private secretary and the Prime Minister. In light of the advice of Ramsay and the others, the King said that neither of them should go. Churchill countered that he could not recommend to the Cabinet that the King should go, but that he himself was certainly going. When Lascelles told Churchill that the King would find it hard to find a new prime minister in the midst of a major invasion of France, Churchill replied, 'Oh, that's all arranged for,' presumably referring to the sealed letter that he and the King had written proposing Eden as his successor.[158] Lascelles then argued that constitutionally Churchill could not leave the country without the King's consent, to which Churchill argued that as he would be on a British ship he would not actually be abroad. Lascelles pointed out that the ship would be outside British territorial waters, so in fact he would be.

'I am very worried over the P.M.'s seemingly selfish way of looking at the matter,' the King wrote in his diary that day. 'He doesn't seem to care about the future, or how much depends on him.'[159] The next morning he wrote to him:

> I want to make one more appeal to you not to go to sea on D-Day. Please consider my own position. I am a younger man than you, I am a sailor, and as King I am the head of all these Services. There is nothing I would like better than to go to sea, but I have agreed to stay at home; is it fair then that you should do exactly what I should have liked to do myself? You said yesterday that it would be a fine thing for the King to lead his troops into battle, as in old days;* if the King cannot do this, it does not seem to be right that his Prime Minister should take his place. Then there is your own position; you will see very little, you will run a considerable risk, you will be inaccessible at a critical time when vital decisions might have to be taken; and however unobtrusive you may be, your mere presence on board is bound to be a very heavy additional responsibility to the Admiral and Captain . . .

* Churchill's regiment, the 4th Hussars, had fought at the Battle of Dettingen in 1743, when King George II had been the last British sovereign to lead his troops into battle.

> I ask you most earnestly to consider the whole question again, and not let your personal wishes, which I very well understand, lead you to depart from your own very high standard of duty to the State.[160]

No immediate reply was received from Churchill, who was on his way to Portsmouth, so Lascelles called Churchill's train and elicited a 'rather ungracious' acceptance that he would not go.[161] Profoundly disappointed, Churchill then wrote a somewhat petulant letter to the King on 3 June:

> As Prime Minister and Minister of Defence, I ought to be allowed to go where I consider it necessary to the discharge of my duty ... I rely on my own judgement, invoked in many serious matters, as to what are the proper limits of risk which a person who discharges my duties is entitled to run. I must most earnestly ask Your Majesty that no principle shall be laid down which inhibits my freedom of movement when I judge it necessary to acquaint myself with conditions in the various theatres of war. Since Your Majesty does me the honour to be so much concerned about my personal safety on this occasion, I must defer to Your Majesty's wishes and indeed commands.[162]

The King wrote in his diary that day, 'I was not raising any constitutional point. I asked him as a friend not to endanger his life and so put me and everyone else in a difficult position.'[163]

'Personally I believe it was all bluff and that he never really meant to go,' Cunningham wrote in his diary, but it is clear from this correspondence – as well as from everything else we know about Churchill's lifelong love of being on the spot – that Cunningham was wrong.[164] Churchill had set his heart on attending the D-Day operations, and was angry enough after being stymied to write a letter to the King that verged, despite his fervent monarchism, on *lèse-majesté*. Churchill and Smuts boarded a motor launch and went down to Southampton Water, across the Solent to Cowes, and finally went ashore at a jetty in Portsmouth having seen the vast armada of vessels about to take part in the attack.

Rome fell on 4 June, only hours before D-Day was due to be launched. De Gaulle, who had finally been told of the impending liberation of his country, came to lunch with Churchill on the prime ministerial train. Valentine Lawford, Eden's private secretary, who was there, recorded in his diary that the lunch was 'long and not genial ... de Gaulle had no small talk, couldn't address a word to Bevin (on his left) and declined to respond to Winston's badinage. At one moment Winston bent slightly forward in his seat, turned his face round and up towards the general, and gave an entrancing childish grin. De Gaulle ... smiled a faded smile and looked as if someone had made him an improper proposal. Those two will never be happy together.'[165] He was right. In a row about the administration of post-Overlord France soon afterwards, de Gaulle called Churchill 'a gangster' and Churchill called de Gaulle 'a traitor'.[166] De Gaulle feared that Anglo-American military preponderance in France over the coming weeks and months would somehow impinge upon French independence. His truculence stemmed not only from his proud and spiky personality, but from four years of being the supplicant of Churchill and Roosevelt, dependent on them in ways he found humiliating to his highly developed sense of *amour propre*.

Eisenhower had proposed that on D-Day de Gaulle should broadcast to the French people that their day of liberation had arrived, asking them to cooperate fully with the Allied forces. Reporting on their discussion on the train to the War Cabinet the next day, Churchill said that, having seen the suggested text, 'De Gaulle refuses to broadcast. I told Eisenhower not to worry. If he won't he won't . . . I'm nearly at the end of my tether – it doesn't make the slightest difference to the outcome.'[167] Eden tried to explain de Gaulle's objections about French sovereignty in the face of American military might, but Churchill dismissed them and described de Gaulle's refusal as an 'odious example of his malice . . . no regard for common causes – may have to exhibit him in his true light – false and puffed up personality . . . If he does not broadcast now I'm through with him. Nothing will prevent me from talking.' Later in the discussion, Churchill repeated, 'I'm not going to quarrel with Roosevelt for the sake of de Gaulle.'[168] It seems extraordinary, but even on the eve of D-Day, four years after de Gaulle had set up the Free French in London, the leaders of both Britain and the United States felt such distrust of him. But they detested his French chauvinism and genuinely feared that he might try to turn France into an anti-Western Gaullist dictatorship after the war.

On Monday, 5 June, with all the ships and hands at the ready, the attack had to be postponed for twenty-four hours due to bad weather. This only increased the atmosphere of tension aboard Churchill's train. 'The P.M. looked anxious but he was amiable,' wrote Marian Holmes.[169] 'My Darling,' Clementine wrote to her husband, 'I feel so much for you at this agonizing moment – so full of suspense, which prevents me from rejoicing over Rome!'[170] At the Cabinet, Amery felt, 'Winston was evidently greatly stirred and at the end of his tether nervously, and no wonder. It is the most anxious moment of the whole war.'[171] Churchill announced the occupation of Rome and said he had expressed to Alexander the Cabinet's congratulations on his 'administrative skill, judgement, tenacity, and moral courage – our great debt to him. His victory – not anyone else's.'[172] (He did not want the credit to go to Mark Clark, who had in fact taken the city.) Amery also noted that 'Winston expressed himself very disappointed that Brooke could not assure him that we could overtake and destroy' all the Germans retreating from Rome.[173] Of Overlord itself he said the 'Danger of this operation is very great during the next thirty or forty days.' But he did 'Think we will get ashore and establish bridgehead.' It was an optimistic forecast for the benefit of the Cabinet. Sir Andrew Cunningham, the First Sea Lord, wrote in his diary, 'A good lunch and as usual lots of wine. P.M. very worked up about Overlord and really in almost a hysterical state. Much conversation. He really is an incorrigible optimist. I always thought I was unduly so but he easily outstrips me.'[174]

That same day at his dacha outside Moscow, Stalin made his true attitude towards both Roosevelt and Churchill abundantly clear to the Yugoslav Communist leader Milovan Djilas. 'Perhaps you think that just because we are allies of the English we have forgotten who they are and who Churchill is,' he said. 'There's nothing they like better than to trick their allies . . . And Churchill? Churchill is the kind of man who will pick your pocket of a kopeck, if you didn't watch him. Yes, pick your pocket of a kopeck! By God, pick your pocket of a kopeck! And Roosevelt? Roosevelt is not like that. He dips in his hand only for bigger coins. But Churchill? Churchill – will do it for a kopeck.'[175] Stalin's impression of Churchill's street-urchin capacities probably dated back to his intervention in the Russian Civil War. As for D-Day, of which he had been informed that night, Stalin said that it would be called off if there was any fog in the Channel. 'Maybe they'll meet with some Germans!' he continued, once again accusing the Allies of cowardice.

Churchill had prevented Operation Overlord from taking place any earlier by his refusal to agree to Sledgehammer or Roundup in 1942 and his promotion of the Mediterranean strategy at Casablanca in 1943. 'No one but he,' Harold Macmillan wrote in his diary in November 1943, 'and that only with extraordinary patience and skill, could have enticed the Americans into the European war at all.'[176] Yet now, with the Battle of the Atlantic won in the summer of 1943, and air superiority in early 1944, the Mulberry harbours and PLUTO, and a 6,000-vessel Allied fleet now at the ready, with the Germans weakened by the continued assault in Italy, and very much more so by the Russians, this great, nerve-wracking endeavour was finally under way. Back at the No. 10 Annexe, Churchill visited the Map Room three times during the night.[177] Before going to sleep, he said to Clementine, 'Do you realise that by the time you wake up in the morning twenty thousand men may have been killed?'[178] It was a moment of supreme anxiety, but his optimism had not been a pose or a fraud: it was the outcome of preparation, judgement, determination and pure leadership.

# 30
# Liberation
# June 1944–January 1945

*There is no reason to suppose that the war will stop when the final result has become obvious. The Battle of Gettysburg proclaimed the ultimate victory of the North, but far more blood was shed after the Battle of Gettysburg than before.*

Churchill to the House of Commons, 30 June 1942[1]

*We did not enter the war for any gain, but neither did we propose to lose anything through it.*

Churchill to Jock Colville, September 1944[2]

At noon on Tuesday, 6 June 1944 – D-Day – Churchill announced the fall of Rome to the Commons. He then said, 'I have also to announce to the House that during the night and the early hours of this morning, the first of a series of landings upon the European Continent has taken place.'[3] The atmosphere in the Chamber was described as one of 'hushed awe'.[4] Churchill then lunched with the King at Buckingham Palace and went with him to Air Chief Marshal Trafford Leigh-Mallory's Allied Air Headquarters at Stanmore, and then on to Eisenhower's Supreme Headquarters Allied Expeditionary Force headquarters at Bushey on the outskirts of London, where they were shown the progress of the battle on large maps. No mention was made of the recent contretemps over where Churchill would have preferred to be.

Churchill's primary worry was over the weather, and especially what he later described as the 'stormy waters, swift currents, and eighteen-foot rise and fall of the tide', which he feared might wreck the amphibious side of the assault. 'That was the element,' he added, 'this possible change in the weather, which certainly hung like a vulture poised in the sky over the thoughts of the most sanguine.'[5] In his memoirs he pointed out that 'The fools or knaves who had chalked "Second Front Now" on our walls for the past two years had not had their minds burdened by such problems. I had long pondered upon them.'[6] On D-Day the rain had stopped but high winds caused fast, high waves, which out in the Channel sank several landing craft carrying tanks, but not enough of them to stop D-Day from succeeding. Over 160,000 men landed in Normandy in twenty-four hours, parachuted from planes and landing on the five invasion beaches code-named Omaha and Utah (Americans), Sword and Gold (Britain) and Juno (Canadian). Although there were over 9,000 casualties that day, including 3,000 dead, this was at the lowest end of the spectrum of what had been feared.[7] Yet in all the anxiety of these days Churchill never lost his sense of humour. When an MP asked him on 8 June to ensure that the same mistakes over reparations were not made after victory that had been made after the Great War, the Prime Minister assured him that 'That is most fully in our minds. I am sure that the mistakes of that time will not be repeated. We shall probably make another set of mistakes.'[8]

On 12 June, Churchill embarked in the destroyer HMS *Kelvin* for Normandy. He took Brooke and Smuts with him, but not de Gaulle, with whom he was engaged in another furious row over the personnel in the new French Provisional Government, describing him to Eden as 'another Hitler'.[9] Churchill persuaded the *Kelvin*'s captain to take 'a plug at the Hun', firing at German targets such as gun emplacements at a range of only 6,000 yards, while Flying Fortresses, Liberators and other bombers swarmed overhead.[10] The party went ashore in a DUKW, a 2½-ton, six-wheeled amphibious truck, which landed at Courseulles. Montgomery was there to meet them with jeeps and they drove to his headquarters at Creully, past the damaged seafront, crashed planes, burned-out cars, signs for minefields and ripening crops. 'We are surrounded by fat cattle lying in luscious pastures with their paws crossed!' Churchill said to Brooke. Neither of them had expected to see horses, chickens and a well-kept countryside after five years of war.[11] Martin noted a burst of anti-aircraft fire as a German bomber came overhead, and 'the larger barks of the bigger guns (mainly naval) had been going on all the time.'[12] The Prime Minister was in his element.

Churchill was mobbed by all the soldiers who caught sight of him. He cruised up and down the coast from Arromanches on the River Orne aboard a launch, watching the ships disembarking troops, tanks, ammunition and equipment in immense quantities. 'As far as the eye could see the water seemed to be covered with a stupendous mass of rafts of all sizes for miles to the horizon on both sides,' wrote Martin.[13] They were near enough to see the smoke of battle over Caen, where the Germans were putting up a fierce resistance. 'P.M. looking a bit exuberant from his trip to the beachhead,' Cunningham noted after a Defence Committee meeting back in London the next day, 'was a bit childish at times.'[14] Churchill told the King that 'In one week more than 3½ times more men and stores have been landed in France than were landed in four months in 1939–40 with the help of the French and their ports. This is a most astonishing fact and revolutionises further expeditions.'[15]

When on 15 June a Tory MP criticized Churchill for visiting the front, suggesting that it was self-indulgent and dangerous, Bracken rounded on him in the Commons, and at the end of a witty and impassioned speech said, 'Neither the honourable and gallant Member nor anyone else can persuade the Prime Minister to wrap himself in cotton wool. He is the enemy of flocculence in thought, word or deed. Most humbly do I aver that, in years to come, a grateful and affectionate people will say that Winston Churchill was raised to leadership by destiny. Men of destiny have never counted risks.'[16]

On 19 June, General Alexander told Churchill that if his forces were left intact he could break into the Po Valley and 'finally eliminate [General Albert] Kesselring's two armies. There will be nothing to stop us marching straight to Vienna.'[17] This plan greatly appealed to Churchill, but not to Brooke or Marshall. Brooke told Churchill that with the topography of the Alps and the winter weather, 'even on Alex's optimistic reckoning . . . we should have three enemies instead of one'.[18] Marshall agreed, arguing that the Germans would merely withdraw from north Italy to the Alps, which could be held easily with far fewer divisions than the Allies had.

Despite its name, the Ljubljana Gap would in all likelihood have proved a trap, and Churchill's and Alexander's dream of British and Commonwealth forces reaching Vienna ahead of the Russians was only ever that. To have achieved it, Anvil – the attack in the south of France in mid-August that Roosevelt had promised Stalin at Teheran – would have had to be cancelled. Yet Roosevelt and Marshall were intent on honouring that commitment. Churchill nonetheless expended great energy, effort and political capital with the Chiefs of Staff and Roosevelt trying to get Alexander's plan adopted, deluging the President with telegrams on the matter and returning to it in Defence Committee meetings again and again.

The first of 9,521 V-1* rockets started to land on Britain on 13 June. Nicknamed 'doodlebugs' and 'buzz-bombs', they forced Churchill back into the Annexe again. On 8 September, the first of around 1,500 V-2 rocket-bombs landed on southern England, continuing until March 1945.

* For *Vergeltungswaffe* or vengeance weapon.

Flying at 3,580mph, the V-2 struck without warning with a one-ton payload that could destroy entire streets. Together, the V-1 and V-2 killed 8,938 British civilians and 2,917 servicemen, seriously injured 25,000 people and destroyed 107,000 homes in London and the south-east.[19] When Harvie-Watt noted that many people were being rendered homeless, Churchill circled the word 'homeless' and wrote in red pen, 'Why? They will have to crowd into other people's where one fire will suffice for cooking!'[20] When Herbert Morrison pressed for Allied strategy in France to be altered, to divert forces to capture the V-weapon launching-sites along the Channel coast before other, more important strategic objectives, Churchill refused. He could not allow the V-weapons to change strategy. 'This form of attack is, no doubt, of a trying character, a worrisome character,' he told the Commons on 6 July, referring to the V-1s, 'because of its being spread out throughout the whole of the twenty-four hours, but people have just got to get used to that.'[21] In mid-June, Captain Pim arranged for red and green lights to be installed in the Map Room of the Annexe to give warnings of approaching V-1s, although the only action that could be taken was to close the steel shutters and warn guests.[22]

Since there was no defence against the V-2 once launched, Churchill had to consider the additional possibility that the Germans might add chemical or biological weapons to the warheads. 'If the bombardment of London really became a serious nuisance and great rockets with far-reaching and devastating effect fell on many centres of Government and labour,' Churchill wrote to the Chiefs of Staff in July,

> I should be prepared to do anything that would hit the enemy in a murderous place. I may certainly have to ask you to support me in using poison gas. We could drench the cities of the Ruhr and many other cities in Germany in such a way that most of the population would be requiring constant medical attention. We could stop all work at the flying bomb starting points. I do not see why we should always have all the disadvantages of being the gentlemen while they have all the advantages of being the cad. There are times when this may be so but not now.[23]

The Chiefs of Staff firmly rejected the idea. Aware that Allied armies risked being confined in their beachheads and unable to break out into the wider French hinterland, Churchill also asked the Chiefs to consider whether mustard gas might be used 'to gain more ground in Normandy so as not to be cooped up in a small area'.[24] He argued that since 'nearly everyone recovers, it is useless to pretend that an equal amount of High Explosives will not inflict greater cruelties and suffering', and likened it to the bombing of cities, which was regarded as unacceptable in the Great

War, but 'now everybody does it as a matter of course. It is simply a question of fashion changing as she does between long and short skirts for women.'[25] The Chiefs rejected that idea too, and on 28 July Churchill reluctantly dropped the matter, grumbling, 'Clearly I cannot make headway against the parsons and the warriors at the same time.'[26]

On 18 June the Guards Chapel in Birdcage Walk, next to Buckingham Palace, took a direct hit from a V-1, just as Lord Edward Hay, whom Churchill had befriended at the Cairo Conference, was walking up to read the lesson. No fewer than 121 people were killed in that attack, including Hay. Churchill visited the site soon afterwards. One of the young Welsh Guardsmen present, the future historian Kenneth Rose, remembered 'the arc-lights shining on the scene and illuminating Winston Churchill, who stood on the rubble, weeping'.[27] The next day Parliament was moved back to Church House, which was thought to be of stouter construction than the Palace of Westminster. This seemed sensible; nevertheless, after the King had awarded medals at a ceremony in a basement room at Buckingham Palace near an air-raid shelter on 4 July, Churchill told Lascelles he thought this set a bad example when Government policy was to continue 'business as usual' regardless of the sirens, and that henceforth all investitures must be conducted above ground.[28]

When V-1s started flying over in the early morning of 22 June, Churchill asked Marian Holmes, to whom he was dictating, if she felt frightened. She said no, and later noted in her diary, 'How can one feel frightened in his company?'[29] She also recorded how tired Churchill got at this time; on 28 June he nearly fell asleep while Sawyers was putting drops in his ears to cure a bout of earache. Churchill did not drink heavily but he did he drink steadily, imbibing small amounts of whisky or brandy mixed with large amounts of soda for hours on end. 'At one point in the evening the P.M. accused me of neglecting him as I'd let his glass go dry,' Holmes recorded.[30] 'That's a damn pretty girl,' he said to John Peck afterwards. 'Lovely. The sort of girl who'd rather die than have secrets torn out of her.'[31] From him, there was no higher praise.

In June 1944 there was what Churchill was to call in his memoirs 'the first important divergence on high strategy between ourselves and our American friends'.[32] (He had diplomatically forgotten the Operation Torch controversy of 1942.) His campaign to ditch Operation Anvil and concentrate on the Italian campaign was long, hard fought and occasionally bitter, but was fully supported by the British Chiefs of Staff. Yet it came up against the combined refusal of Roosevelt and Marshall to depart from what had been agreed at Teheran. 'I find I must completely concur in the stand of the U.S. Chiefs of Staff,' Roosevelt wrote to Churchill on 28 June.

'General Wilson's proposal for continued use of practically all the Mediterranean resources to advance into Northern Italy and from there to the northeast is not acceptable to me, and I really believe we should consolidate our operations and not scatter them.'[33] Churchill saw Anvil itself as a scattering of resources, which it was.

The British used Ultra decrypts to show the Joint Chiefs that Hitler had ordered General Kesselring to prevent the Allies from breaking into the Po Valley at all costs, in order to protect Austria. It had no effect. 'We are deeply grieved by your telegram,' Churchill wrote to Roosevelt.

> The splitting up of the campaign in the Mediterranean into two operations neither of which can do anything decisive is, in my humble and respectful opinion, the first major strategic and political error for which we two have to be responsible . . . Our first wish is to help General Eisenhower in the most speedy and efficient manner. But we do not think this necessarily involves the complete ruin of all our great affairs in the Mediterranean, and we take it hard that this should be demanded of us . . . I think the tone of the American Chiefs of Staff is arbitrary, and I certainly see no prospect of agreement on the present lines. What is to happen then?[34]

Churchill had not mentioned the Balkans in his cable, but Roosevelt knew that he wanted to go on to Trieste after the Po. 'My interest and hopes center on defeating the Germans in front of Eisenhower, and driving on into Germany,' he replied. 'For purely political considerations here, I could never survive even a slight setback to "Overlord" if it were known that fairly large forces had been diverted to the Balkans.'[35] 'He was definitely annoyed at FDR's reply,' the King noted, 'and put out that all our well thought-out plans had been ignored by him and his Chiefs of Staff.'[36] Churchill did not take Roosevelt's no for an answer. Many of the more ill-tempered telegrams that followed were not published in his memoirs; there were many others which Ismay persuaded him not to send and which were then destroyed.[37] 'I hope you realize that an intense impression must be made upon the Americans that we have been ill-treated and are furious,' Churchill wrote to the Chiefs of Staff. 'If we take everything lying down, there will be no end to what will be put upon us.' Then, referring to the three American Joint Chiefs of Staff, he added, 'The Arnold–King–Marshall combination is one of the stupidest strategic teams ever seen.'[38]

Churchill reproduced part of his memorandum in his war memoirs, but not the last sentence. 'Winston is very bitter about it,' Lascelles noted on 6 July of the Anvil decision, 'and not so sure that he really likes F.D.R.'[39] In fact, neither Anvil nor the Balkans were of the greatest strategic significance, and Vienna would not have fallen quickly. Once the Allies were ashore in north-west France in June 1944, neither the south of France nor northern Italy mattered as much as crossing the Rhine and taking the Ruhr. Yet Churchill was also looking to the politics of a post-war Europe, where Romania, Bulgaria, Yugoslavia, Poland and Hungary – and possibly even Austria – would be in the Soviet sphere of influence if there were no Allied troops in any of those countries when the Germans surrendered. At the summit once again, true politics and strategy were one.

On 4 July, a report reached the Foreign Office that the 'unknown destination in the East' where so many of the Jewish deportations from Hungary had been reported going to earlier that year was the SS-run camp of Auschwitz-Birkenau in Poland.[40] It summarized another report from four Jewish escapees about exterminations at the camp, and estimated that Hungarian Jews were being killed there at the almost unbelievable rate of 12,000 per day.[41] The Jewish leader Chaim Weizmann met Eden two days later and asked him to bomb the Budapest–Auschwitz railway line. 'Is there any reason to raise this matter with the Cabinet?' Churchill replied to Eden the next day. 'Get anything out of the Air Force you can, and invoke me if necessary.'[42] Three days later Admiral Horthy, the Hungarian Regent, ended the deportations due to an entirely coincidental American daylight raid on Budapest that had hit the homes of several people involved in them, which the Hungarian Government fortunately misinterpreted as a warning.[43] Yet Auschwitz and its railway lines still needed to be destroyed, as hundreds of thousands of Jews from elsewhere in Europe were being transported there for extermination, and Horthy could change his mind at any time.

Churchill supported the Jewish Agency's requests for public exposure of the deportations. 'I am entirely in accord with making the biggest outcry possible,' he told Eden.[44] Radio broadcasts were made about Auschwitz, and Hungarian railway workers were warned in Hungarian that they were committing war crimes and would be punished.[45] The warnings were repeated by the BBC in October: 'If these plans are carried out, those guilty of such murderous acts will be brought to justice and will pay the penalty for their heinous crimes.'[46] However, the long-range bombing of Auschwitz and its railway lines needed to be done in daylight, and the USAAF, which undertook daylight raids, refused Churchill's request on 26 June and on several subsequent occasions.[47]

'There is no doubt that this is probably the greatest and most horrible crime ever committed in the whole history of the world,' Churchill wrote to Eden on 11 July 1944, long before the death camps were liberated the following January and February, 'and it has been done by scientific machinery by nominally civilized men in the name of a great State and one of the leading races in Europe. It is quite clear that all concerned in this crime who may fall into our hands, including the people who only obeyed orders by carrying out the butcheries, should be put to death after their association with the murders has been proved.'[48] Although Churchill wanted to relax the 1939 White Paper policy against Jewish immigration into Palestine, and to bomb Auschwitz, and to put pressure on General Franco, Marshal Tito and others to give Jews refuge from the Nazis, he was not all powerful in the British Government. He had little or no support from the Cabinet, Foreign Office, military or Civil Service, much of which had no sympathy for Jews (or worse). His efforts were consistently frustrated by those around him.[49] 'Unfortunately A E is immovable on the subject of Palestine,' Anthony Eden's private secretary Oliver Harvey wrote in his diary in April 1943, for example. 'He loves Arabs and hates Jews.'[50] In the House of Commons on 1 August 1946, Churchill declared, 'I must say that I had no idea, when the war came to an end, of the horrible massacres which had occurred; the millions and millions that have been slaughtered. That dawned on us gradually after the struggle was over.'[51] His comment to Eden of two years earlier shows that he had more than an inkling of the true extent of the Holocaust, but for all his lifelong philo-Semitism was unable to prevent it. He did what he could, much more than other politicians, but it was nothing like enough.

On Thursday, 6 July, Churchill got drunk. 'He was very tired as a result of his speech in the House concerning the flying bombs,' Brooke recorded after what he called the worst Defence Committee meeting of the entire war; 'he had tried to recuperate with drink. As a result he was in a maudlin, bad tempered, drunken mood, ready to take offence at anything, suspicious of everybody, and in a highly vindictive mood against the Americans. In fact, so vindictive that his whole outlook on strategy was warped.'[52] He abused Montgomery, whom Brooke defended, as well as other generals, and the row went on for four hours until 2 a.m., with further sideswipes at those aspects of the Chiefs' Middle Eastern and Far Eastern strategies that did not coincide with his own. When Attlee, Eden and Lyttelton supported the Chiefs, 'This infuriated him more than ever and he became ruder and ruder,' ending up with 'a real good row' with Attlee over the future of India.[53] Cunningham also wrote that 'The P.M. was in no state to discuss anything. Very tired and too much alcohol . . . he was in a terrible mood. Rude and sarcastic.'[54] Eden wrote of 'a really ghastly Defence Committee meeting nominally on Far Eastern strategy. Winston hadn't read the paper and was perhaps rather tight . . . Altogether a deplorable evening which couldn't have happened a year ago. There is certainly a deterioration.'[55]

The unimaginable pressures of his job had clearly got to Churchill, and on that occasion – a single one of the 2,194 days of the war – he cracked. Fortunately, no decisions were taken and there were no other accusations of drunkenness against Churchill at any other meeting of the war. The major bone of contention had been Alexander's strategy in Italy, which Churchill argued could have made more imaginative use of flanking manoeuvres instead of simply attacking Monte Cassino again and again over three months. Many military historians today support Churchill's drunken arguments over Brooke's sober ones. But Brooke was right in his regular complaint that Churchill constantly criticized senior officers. A couple of nights later at Chequers, the Prime Minister described a general to Marian Holmes as 'A useless puff-stick, puffing and blowing. He should be swatting flies in his wife's boudoir. I've turned the other cheek so often I ain't got no more cheeks to turn.'[56]

Caen finally fell on 9 July, after holding out for over a month. The next day, Churchill reported to the War Cabinet that the 'daily discharge' into France came to 25,000 men, 7,000 vehicles and 30,000 tons of stores. He was concerned about German soldiers who were being captured shortly after setting delayed-action mines, which went off after they surrendered. He wanted them to be 'held responsible'. By that stage, twenty-nine Allied divisions (fifteen American, fourteen British and Commonwealth) were engaging twenty-three German divisions in France.

Churchill had privately complained that one of the most striking aspects of the age was 'the lamentable lack of Charlotte Cordays', referring to the young woman who assassinated the French revolutionary Jean-Paul Marat in his bath in 1793.[57] Yet on 20 July 1944 a small group of German generals tried to kill Hitler in his East Prussian headquarters, the *Wolfsschanze*, although they succeeded only in shredding his trousers. Churchill has been criticized for showing no interest in contacting anti-Hitler elements in Germany during the war, but any attempt by British intelligence to approach political or military opposition elements in Germany would have aroused Stalin's suspicions that the Western Allies were planning to make a separate peace.[58] 'When Herr Hitler escaped his bomb on July 20th, he described his survival as providential,' Churchill told the Commons with high irony in September. 'I think that from a purely military point of view we can all agree with him, for certainly it would be most unfortunate if the Allies were to be deprived, in the closing phases of the struggle, of that form of warlike genius by which Corporal Schicklgruber* has so notably contributed to our victory.'[59] He later suggested that 'Even military idiots find it difficult not

* Hitler's paternal grandmother had been Maria Schicklgruber, and Hitler's father Alois had the name too until he legally changed it.

to see some faults in some of his actions . . . Altogether I think it is much better to let officers rise up in the proper way.' He said that the Bomb Plot had shown that 'The highest personalities in the German Reich are murdering each other, or trying to, while the avenging armies of the Allies close upon the doomed and ever-narrowing circle of their power.'[60]

The day after the Bomb Plot had failed, Churchill visited Montgomery's headquarters near Blay, in the Calvados department of Normandy. He inspected a hospital and a field bakery (he had long been insistent that the troops should get fresh bread, rather than 'compo' rations, whenever possible). He saw artillery in action near Tilly, and at one point was only 4,000 yards from the front. He also visited Arromanches, Bayeux and shattered Caen, which Martin recorded was 'very badly knocked about'.[61] On his return he told the War Cabinet that he had 'never seen such a happy army – magnificent looking army'.[62]

Moscow set up a Polish Committee for National Liberation at Lublin in late July, a puppet government in direct opposition to the legitimate Polish Government-in-exile in London. Two days later, the Poles of the Warsaw Home Army, who were loyal to the London Government-in-exile, staged an uprising in the Polish capital against the Wehrmacht garrison, a desperate, sixty-three-day struggle for liberation. By the end, the men were virtually wiped out and the women and children were taken to extermination camps. Stalin halted his forces outside Warsaw to allow the Germans to destroy the Home Army, denouncing the Uprising's leaders as 'criminal adventurers' and refusing to allow Allied aircraft landing rights to resupply them. Churchill contemplated suspending aid convoys to Murmansk in protest, but decided against it. 'Terrible and even humbling submissions must at times be made to the general aim,' he later wrote.[63]

Nothing could alter the central fact that Stalin was now in a commanding position in relation to eastern Europe. The success of Operation Bagration in July, in which the Red Army killed, wounded or captured 510,000 German troops of Army Group Centre in Belorussia, dwarfed even what had happened after D-Day. 'It is the Russian armies who have done the main work in tearing the guts out of the Germany army,' Churchill readily acknowledged to the House of Commons on 2 August. 'I salute Marshal Stalin, the great champion, and I firmly believe that our twenty years' treaty with Russia will prove one of the most lasting and durable factors in preserving the peace and the good order and the progress of Europe.'[64] The Russian armies, he said, 'bring the liberation of Poland in their hands. They offer freedom, sovereignty and independence' – even though by then he knew this was more of a hope than a real likelihood.[65]

Eight days later, Churchill flew from RAF Northolt to Algiers en route to a morale-boosting tour of Alexander's Fifth Army in Italy. While there, he visited Randolph in hospital. On 16 July, the Dakota plane in which Randolph was flying to Yugoslavia from Bari in Italy had stalled at a hundred feet and crashed. Ten of the nineteen passengers on board were killed; Randolph and his friend the novelist Evelyn Waugh were injured. Randolph was taken to hospital in Bari, and then on to convalesce in Algiers. 'No reference was made by either of us to family matters,' Churchill reported to Clementine. She had given him a letter to hand to Randolph, asking that the three-year-old Winston, who had been removed from Chequers during the marital breakdown, be allowed to return there. Churchill did not pass on the letter. 'I am sure he would have been profoundly upset and all his pent up feelings would have found a vent on me,' he wrote to her. 'Please forgive me for not doing as you wished. Where words are useless, silence is best.'[66] Baby Winston nonetheless did return to Chequers with his nanny by the end of the month.

De Gaulle – who apart from a twenty-four-hour visit to Bayeux on 13 June did not return to France until 20 August – refused to see Churchill while he was in Algiers, which left Churchill 'considerably affronted' according to his private secretaries, and 'justly incensed' according to the Foreign Office official Pierson Dixon.[67] De Gaulle was furious that the British and Americans had not yet recognized his Provisional Government,* while Churchill feared that the future Government of France would be the most anti-British in half a century.[68]

Churchill then flew to Naples, where on 12 August he met Marshal Tito at Queen Victoria's summer villa. He had aided the partisans heavily, and wanted to persuade Tito to ally himself with the West rather than with the Soviets after victory had been won. He told Tito expansively that he was sorry that he was so advanced in years that he could not land by parachute, otherwise he would have liked to have fought in Yugoslavia himself. 'But you have sent your son,' Tito replied, which brought tears to Churchill's eyes.[69] Seeing Tito's two formidable bodyguards, Boško and Prlja, he played a risky practical joke. Firmly grasping a large oblong gold cigar case that F. E. Smith's family had given him, Churchill 'marched towards them. Arriving within two yards, I drew it from my pocket as if it were a pistol. Luckily they grinned with delight and we made friends. But I do not recommend such procedure in similar cases.' Fitzroy Maclean recalled that 'for a split second I saw their trigger fingers tighten.'[70] As they sat down to dinner soon afterwards, Maclean took out a large

* Earlier that month in Washington de Gaulle had been given the seventeen-gun salute of a senior general rather than the twenty-one-gun salute of a head of state.

handkerchief and wiped the cold sweat off his brow. Although personal relations between Churchill and the Yugoslavian dictator were good, in the event Tito carried out a delicate balancing act between the West and the USSR after victory had been won, playing each off against the other until his death in 1980.

On 14 August, Churchill flew to Ajaccio in Corsica, where he recalled visiting Napoleon's childhood home there on holiday with Clementine in 1910. He watched Operation Anvil, now rechristened Dragoon, from the bridge of the destroyer HMS *Kimberley* the next day. The enemy guns were silenced by 8 a.m. 'This rendered the proceedings rather dull,' he told Clementine. 'We saw it all from a long way off . . . I could have gone with perfect safety very much nearer to the actual beaches.'[71] He continued disdainfully, 'One of my reasons for making public my visit was to associate myself with this well-conducted but irrelevant and unrelated operation,' and told her he had got sunburned. He congratulated Roosevelt on its success, but was never reconciled to the need for it and continued to maintain in his memoirs that with 'half of what had been taken from us . . . we could have broken into the valley of the Po, with all the gleaming possibilities and prizes which lay open towards Vienna'.[72]

Churchill picnicked with General Sir Henry 'Jumbo' Wilson, the Supreme Allied Commander in the Mediterranean, at Monte Cassino two days later, where he said the terrain reminded him of the North-West Frontier of his youth. All the time he was receiving reports of how the Allies were defeating the German Seventh Army in the Falaise Gap, the crucial bottleneck area that they had to force in order to fan out across France. He now proposed to Roosevelt that a new conference needed to be held in Quebec, where, as he told Clementine, the 'various differences that exist between the Staffs, and also between me and the American Chiefs of Staff, must be brought to a decision'.[73] He put his opinions bluntly to Clementine, saying that, of the three British armies in the field, Eisenhower commanded the one in France, General Alexander's 'is relegated to a secondary and frustrating situation' in Italy, and the third, in Burma, was 'fighting in the most unhealthy country in the world under the worst possible conditions to guard the American air line over the Himalayas into their very over-rated China. Thus two-thirds of our forces are being mis-employed for American convenience, and the other third is under American Command.'[74] To underline his frustration, he added that of the 40,000 casualties suffered in Burma for the six months of 1944, the majority were from disease.

After visiting Alexander's headquarters near Florence, Churchill met Pope Pius XII in Rome, and was in Siena when Paris began to be liberated on 24 August. He remained in Italy to watch the Eighth Army attack northwards across the enemy's defensive Gothic Line, living in a comfortable caravan furnished with two 'liberated' Louis Seize chairs. His ever-present historical sense came to the fore when he had what he called 'a magnificent view from the ramparts of bygone centuries', as they reached the River Metauro. 'Here Hasdrubal's defeat* had sealed the fate of Carthage,' he later wrote, 'so I suggested we should go across too.'[75] German artillery had stopped firing only a quarter of an hour earlier, and Churchill and Alexander could see tanks moving forward and firing and machine guns in action only a few hundred yards ahead. 'There were quite a lot of shells flying about, and land mines all over the place,' Alexander later recalled. 'He absolutely loved it. It fascinated him – a real warrior at heart.'[76]

Churchill returned to Northolt on 29 August with a temperature of 103 degrees (Martin said 104) and his third case of pneumonia in four years. The X-ray showed another small patch on his lung.[77] 'It would be a tragedy if anything were to happen to him now,' Cunningham wrote in his diary, completely contradicting everything else he had recently been writing about Churchill. 'With all his faults (and he is the most infuriating man) he has done a great job for this country, and besides there is no one else.'[78] No public mention was made of the illness. When the King came to visit Churchill in his bedroom at the Annexe two days later, he signed Montgomery's promotion to field marshal on Churchill's pillow.

Three days later his temperature had returned to normal and he was back, in Colville's words, 'in tearing form'.[79] He emptied his red ministerial box of work, finding time, apropos of the old legend that Britain would lose Gibraltar when the apes left the Rock, to tell the Colonial Secretary that 'The establishment of the apes on Gibraltar should be twenty-four and every effort should be made to reach this number as soon as possible and maintain it thereafter.'[80] In a conversation with Colville, he was already anticipating the criticism that would be made of his postponement of Overlord until the time was ripe, saying 'there may be an undistinguished minority who proclaim we ought to have invaded in 1943,' but they were wrong. When Cunningham said that the verdict of the Dragoon operation would depend on who wrote the history, Churchill replied 'that he intended to have a hand in that'.[81] It was a joke that he was often to make afterwards, but the way *The World Crisis* had influenced the public perception of the Great War left him in no doubt about how important his war memoirs would be in doing the same for the Second.

* The Battle of the Metaurus (207 BC) was a decisive moment of the Second Punic War.

In early September 1944 the British and Canadians captured Antwerp and destroyed V-weapon sites in the Pas-de-Calais and elsewhere. By then, Churchill was starting to consider holding a general election the following February. 'We should only lose by delay while the glamour wears off,' he told Eden.[82] On 5 September – only four days after recovering from his pneumonia – he left on the *Queen Mary* for the Octagon Conference in Quebec. He took a large entourage with him, including Clementine and Sarah, Moran, Brooke, Portal, Cunningham, Cherwell, Leathers, Ismay, Hollis, Colville, Martin and Brigadier Lionel Whitby, an expert in blood transfusion. Over oysters and champagne at dinner on the first evening aboard, he said that if there was a large Labour majority at the next election, 'Let it be so. What is good enough for the English people, is good enough for me.'[83] On the journey he read Trollope's political novels *Phineas Finn* and *The Duke's Children*.

With the Gulf Stream bringing temperatures into the mid-70s, the effect of the anti-malarial tablets Churchill had taken in Italy and the M & B from his pneumonia, he was, in Sarah's words to Mary, 'in low spirits and not very well'.[84] He was also rowing badly with the Chiefs of Staff over the Italian campaign, which he wanted reinforced but which they, by then rightly, saw (in Cunningham's description) as 'a secondary front'.[85] At every earlier Anglo-American summit, Churchill and the Chiefs of Staff had presented a united British stance, but this time they did not see eye to eye on either European or Pacific strategy. 'He was in his worst mood,' Cunningham recorded, 'accusing the Chiefs of Staff of ganging up against him and keeping papers from him and so on.'[86] Churchill also thought the Joint Planners were too optimistic about an early victory, and put it at 'even money that the Germans would still be fighting at Christmas'.[87]

Brooke wondered 'how much longer he will last. The tragedy is that in his present condition he may well do untold harm!'[88] Even the loyal Colville observed that the Prime Minister was 'highly irascible'.[89] The next day, after another difficult meeting, Brooke wrote, 'I find it hard to remain civil. And the wonderful thing is that three-quarters of the population of the world imagine that Winston Churchill is one of the Strategists of History, a second Marlborough, and the other quarter have no conception what a public menace he is and has been throughout this war! It is far better that the world should never know, and never suspect the feet of clay of that otherwise superhuman being. Without him England was lost for a certainty, with him England has been on the verge of disaster time and again . . . Never have I admired and despised a man simultaneously to the same extent.'[90] It is worth remembering that Brooke himself had fully supported Churchill's policy, as laid out in his four papers on grand strategy written on his journey to Washington in December 1941, of delaying the cross-Channel attack until after the Mediterranean strategy that later became Torch and Husky and Avalanche had borne fruit, which cleared the Axis out of North Africa and took the Italians – if not geographical Italy itself – out of the war. Brooke's animus blinded him to the extent to which Churchill had been responsible for delivering it politically.

The *Queen Mary* berthed at Halifax, Nova Scotia, after lunch on 10 September. A crowd had gathered, cheering and singing 'It's a Long Way to Tipperary', 'Pack Up your Troubles' and 'God Save the King', in which Churchill and Clementine joined enthusiastically.[91] The party took the train to Quebec, during which Churchill's temperature rose again and he was put to bed with an aspirin. Franklin and Eleanor Roosevelt were waiting for them at Quebec railway station the following morning, to take them to the Citadel. The President was not looking well, and had clearly lost a good deal of weight since their last meeting. Churchill told Colville that he feared the President was now 'very frail'.[92] There is no indication, however, that Roosevelt's failing health in any way affected the decisions he took either at Quebec or subsequently at Yalta; mentally he was as robust as ever.

American troops crossed the German frontier at Trier that same day. At lunch at the Citadel with the Roosevelts and Mackenzie King, Churchill brought up the subject of American military predominance. According to Mackenzie King's diary, 'Churchill remarked to the President that he was the head of the strongest military power today, speaking of air, sea and land. The President said that it was hard for him to realize that, as he did not like it himself. He could not feel that way.'[93] In order to balance the relative weights of their overall wartime contribution, which in materiel had become heavily skewed towards the United States, and maintain British influence, Churchill added, 'If Britain had not fought as she did at the start, while others were getting under way . . . America would have had to fight for her existence. If Hitler had got into Britain and some Quisling government had given them possession of the British navy, along with what they had of the French fleet, nothing would have saved this continent and with Japan ready to strike. The President was inclined to agree with him they could not have got ready in time.'[94] Churchill's message was clear, and was not disputed by a good-natured and emollient Roosevelt: whereas the United States was providing the lion's share of the men and materiel today, in 1940–41 Britain (and by implication Canada) had provided the equally crucial factor of time.

At the first plenary meeting of the Octagon Conference, which started at 11.45 a.m. on 13 September in the Citadel, Churchill opened proceedings with an overview of events since the Cairo Conference in December. The imperialist in him was once again to the fore when he confirmed that 'He had always advocated an advance across the Bay of Bengal and operations to recover Singapore, the loss of which had been a grievous and shameful blow to British prestige which must be avenged. It would not be good enough for Singapore to be returned to us at the peace table. We should recover it in battle.' He even congratulated the Americans on the success of Dragoon, 'which had produced the most gratifying results', something he simply did not believe.[95] Indeed, Churchill was generally exuberant, observing that 'Everything we had touched had turned to gold, and during the last seven weeks there had been an unbroken run of military success.'[96]

The most important questions to be discussed were the role Britain should play in the Pacific after the defeat of Germany, the future of the Italian campaign now that Paris had fallen and the Germans were on the retreat in eastern France, the scale of continued Lend-Lease shipments, the overall military strategy to be adopted when entering Germany, which parts of the country Britain and France should occupy, and a plan of the US Treasury Secretary, Henry Morgenthau, to deindustrialize Germany to prevent her launching a third world war in the twentieth century. They were major issues, but they were all settled after only four days of plenary sessions, in each of which Churchill was constantly to the fore.

He offered the British Fleet for operations against Japan in the central Pacific, even under an American commander, but Admiral King wanted to undertake the entire operation there solely with the US Navy, and effectively said as much. 'The offer has been made,' said Churchill. 'Is it accepted?' 'It is,' replied the President, overriding what he knew to be the Admiral's wishes.[97] Cunningham was surprised at this, as it seemed to contradict Churchill's Bay of Bengal strategy and his eagerness for the liberation of Singapore and of Britain's Far Eastern possessions. The explanation lay in the lack of a time-frame to Churchill's offer. The Americans agreed that Alexander could carry on fighting in Italy in order to hold down Kesselring's divisions, a concession that has been described as the 'last remnant of the peripheral strategy'.[98]

Churchill tried to warn Roosevelt about 'the rapid encroachment of the Russians into the Balkans and the consequent dangerous spread of Russian influence in the area', but the Americans scotched his plan to put an army into Istria as a staging-post into the Balkans by refusing the necessary landing craft, which they said were needed elsewhere. Churchill tried to argue that they had been part of a 'common pool' of production, and that

Britain had concentrated on other areas, but he failed to win the argument. 'Even if the war comes to a sudden end,' he had told Smuts in late August, 'there is no reason why our armour should not slip through and reach [Vienna].'[99] In fact there were two major reasons: lack of American support, and the German capacity for defending mountain passes, as had effectively been demonstrated at the Liri Valley below Monte Cassino. Such was the lack of American response that the official minutes merely stated, 'Balkans: Operations of our air forces and commando-type operations continue.'[100] To Roosevelt and Marshall the Balkans did not appear to be worth the healthy bones of a single American paratrooper. Strategically, at that stage of the war, this was right: it was essential for the Allies to concentrate on Germany. Yet it meant that much of the Balkans were to fall under Soviet control during the Cold War, as Churchill feared.

At the end of one Chiefs of Staff meeting at Quebec, Churchill told Portal he would have to discuss the anticipated zones of occupation in Germany. Colville knew he had not read the briefing notes, so he read them out to the Prime Minister in his bath. 'This bizarre procedure was accepted,' wrote Colville, 'but the difficulties were accentuated by his inclination to submerge himself entirely from time to time and thus become deaf to certain passages.'[101] Nonetheless, the deal was done whereby the Americans and British swapped the northern and southern occupation zones of Germany, which made good geographical sense.

Personal relations between Churchill and Roosevelt had recovered from their low point over Anvil/Dragoon. Wide-ranging discussions over strategy were of course interspersed with social occasions. Clementine had to shake hands with 700 people at a reception. 'I thought my arm would drop off,' she told Sarah.[102] 'The P.M. and President have their meals together and can have constant conversations without any fuss about arranging meetings,' recorded Martin.[103] One idea of the President's, or at least of Morgenthau's which Roosevelt supported enough to bring up at a formal meeting, was to eliminate 'the war-making industries in the Ruhr and in the Saar', thus turning Germany 'into a country primarily agricultural and pastoral in its character'.[104] Churchill even went so far as to initial a memorandum on the Morgenthau Plan on 15 September, persuaded by the profoundly Teutonophobic Lindemann, but he quickly changed his mind when Brooke pointed out that a populous Germany would be needed as a future ally against Russia. He thereafter denounced the Plan, on moral grounds among others, and little more was heard of it. Eisenhower's idea to mount a major northern effort encircling the Ruhr, with secondary attacks towards Bonn and Strasbourg, was approved. This satisfied neither Montgomery, who wanted to go straight into the Ruhr, nor General George S. Patton, commanding the US Third Army, who wanted to go to Berlin, but it was the correct strategy to adopt against an enemy with such a well-developed capacity for counter-attack.

After the final plenary session at noon on 16 September, Churchill and Roosevelt held a joint press conference on the sun-roof of the Citadel, wearing the academic robes of their McGill University honorary degrees. Churchill told journalists that the decisions made at the First Quebec Conference 'are now engraved upon the monuments of history', including Overlord, which had liberated 'the dear and beautiful land of France, so long held under the corroding heel of the Hun'. Of the war against Japan, Churchill told the Americans, 'You can't have all the good things to yourselves. You must share.'[105]

The next day, Operation Market Garden (hardly a title that fitted into Churchill's criteria for heroic or classical codenames), Montgomery's ambitious plan to capture a series of Dutch bridges around Eindhoven, Nijmegen and Arnhem, was launched, with catastrophic consequences for the British 1st Airborne Division, which lost over 7,000 men killed, wounded or captured.[106] This strengthened the argument for Eisenhower's 'broad front' strategy for invading Germany and encircling the Ruhr, over Montgomery and Patton's 'narrow thrust' approach of going deeper and faster towards Berlin. For all of his fascination with strategy, however, Churchill had remarkably little input into decision-making in the European theatre once the Allies had gone ashore at D-Day. By March 1945, Rowan thought that the Prime Minister was even 'losing interest in the war, because he no longer has control of military affairs. Up till Overlord he saw himself as Marlborough, the supreme authority to whom all military decisions were referred. Now, in all but questions of wide and long-term strategy, he is by force of circumstance little more than a spectator.'[107] He had not been deliberately sidelined, and he could have caused a good deal of trouble if he fundamentally disagreed with the overall approach, but Eisenhower was the supreme Allied commander and did not require Churchill's input on issues even as fundamental as whether to adopt a 'broad front' strategy for invading Germany or a 'narrow thrust' one.

On 18 September Churchill stayed at Hyde Park, where the Duke and Duchess of Windsor came for a purely social lunch. He had asked the King for a fraternal greeting he could pass on, but all he received was a telegram saying, 'In any discussion as to his future, perhaps you would put forward my conviction, which you already know, namely that his happiness will be best promoted by making his home in the U.S.A. Repeat U.S.A.'[108] Churchill dictated 'rather a crushing answer' to this to Colville, but, as was so often the case, he then destroyed it.[109] For all their mutual respect and affection, the emotions raised by the Abdication Crisis had obviously not entirely died in either man. In the end, Churchill replied in a conciliatory fashion, saying that he had not passed on the message in case it made the Windsors do the precise opposite.

It was at Hyde Park that Roosevelt and Churchill initialled a nuclear cooperation agreement that firmly rejected international control over the technology, as advocated by Sir John Anderson and Niels Bohr, the nuclear physicist. Lindemann had taken Bohr to meet Churchill after Bohr's escape from Denmark earlier that year, but the meeting had been a failure as Churchill abhorred Bohr's view that the whole world should share all nuclear knowledge, which he thought dangerously naive. He even briefly considered having Bohr interned, in case he gave nuclear secrets to the Soviets. This agreement was to be the basis for Anglo-American nuclear cooperation until the Americans suddenly and virtually without warning ended it with the McMahon Act of August 1946.

The Churchills boarded the *Queen Mary* in New York at 9.15 a.m. on 20 September. Over soft-shell crabs and large steaks, Churchill 'seemed well and pleased with himself', saying that Eisenhower believed 'a German collapse was not far off'.[110] His good humour clouded over only when he spoke of de Gaulle to Leathers, Cunningham and Ismay, to whom he said that in recent years 'my illusions about the French have been greatly corroded.'[111] De Gaulle's ingratitude was evident in the speech he made at the Hôtel de Ville in Paris the previous month in which he had said that the capital had been 'Liberated by itself, liberated by its people with the help of the armies of France, with the support and help of the whole of France, of France that is fighting, of France alone.'[112] De Gaulle was also giving direct orders to Leclerc's Free French division, despite its being in the corps commanded by the American general Leonard Gerow.

A U-boat in the Atlantic necessitated a southern diversion, much to Churchill's annoyance, as he wanted to be in the Commons before the end of the parliamentary recess. They went at 30 knots and he made it just in time, although it meant that their escort vessel, HMS *Berwick*, could keep up only by not taking the anti-U-boat precaution of zig-zagging. Colville noted that Churchill was reminiscing even more than he used to.

Churchill's speech in the Commons on 28 September put the best possible gloss on the disaster at Arnhem. '"Not in vain" may be the pride of those who have survived and the epitaph of those who fell,' he said.[113] For anyone who thought Montgomery had botched it – which he had – Churchill added, 'We must not forget that we owe a great debt to the blunders – the extraordinary blunders – of the Germans. I always hate to compare Napoleon with Hitler, as it seems an insult to the great Emperor and warrior to connect him in any way with a squalid caucus boss and butcher. But there is one respect in which I must draw a parallel. Both these men were temperamentally unable to give up the tiniest scrap of any territory to which the high-water mark of their hectic fortunes had carried them.'[114] He then gave several examples of Napoleon's strategy in 1813–14, likening it to the way that 'Hitler had successfully scattered the German armies all over Europe, and by obstination at every point from Stalingrad and Tunis down to the present moment, he has stripped himself of the power to concentrate in main strength for the final struggle.'[115] Harvie-Watt pronounced the speech 'excellent' but added that some MPs thought he had looked tired, and that his 'voice was not so good after the lunch interval'.[116]

As the Germans were forced out of Romania in September, Yugoslavia in October and Hungary in December 1944, attention turned to what form of government would take their place. De Gaulle's FCNL was finally recognized by the Allies as the legitimate government of France that month, but it became clear that only pro-Moscow puppet governments would be permitted in those eastern countries taken by Russia. Churchill's hope that Marshal Badoglio might retain power in Italy was not shared by Roosevelt, who faced a presidential election the following month and did not want to seem to prefer monarchists to progressives in liberated countries.

The final crushing of the Warsaw Uprising on 2 October boded ill for democracy in Poland. Churchill described the Poles to the Cabinet as 'These heroic people dogged by their maladroitness in political affairs for three hundred years'.[117] Even if they had been brilliantly adroit, it is hard to see how they could have regained their independence with over a million Red Army soldiers now stationed on their soil. Further south, the EAM, the political wing of the Greek Communist partisans, and the ELAS, their military wing, were preparing to seize power in Greece and prevent the return of King George II of the Hellenes and his Government-in-exile under the Liberal Prime Minister Georgios Papandreou.*

Churchill told the King there was a pressing need for another conference with Stalin in Moscow, to discuss Poland, the Balkans and especially Greece, explaining that it was important that Stalin understood 'that it is not a question of Roosevelt and me on one side and the Russians on the other'.[118] This was a futile hope: Stalin assumed that the capitalist powers

* With all these great issues at stake, Churchill somehow also found time to ensure that the No. 10 washroom got new hairbrushes, prompting Colville to observe, 'Being a great man, his approach to trivial matters is often an unusual one' (Colville, *Fringes* p. 522).

were in cahoots, and another personal meeting in Moscow was not about to disabuse him of this long-held view. But as Churchill had told the Octagon press conference, telegrams were 'simply dead, blank walls compared to personal contacts'.[119] He said to Lascelles, 'Next time, we must get Joe Stalin to meet *us* somewhere – perhaps at The Hague – though he is always miaowing about his health, and pretending that he is too sick to travel.'[120] Churchill left Northolt at midnight on 8 October and, after stopovers in Naples and Cairo – 'We flew down past Vesuvius,' noted John Martin, 'with a long black stream of lava from the latest eruption still smouldering' – they arrived in Moscow at noon on the 9th. The Conference was given the hardly impenetrable codename Tolstoy.

At the end of their first meeting in the Kremlin, Churchill leaned across the table and handed Stalin a half-sheet of paper, what he called a 'naughty document'.[121] In his own handwriting, it set out the influence that he suggested that Russia and the Western Allies should exert in eastern Europe after the war. It read:

> Roumania: Russia 90% the others 10%.
> Greece: Great Britain in accord with U.S.A. 90%:
> ~~The Others~~ Russia 10%.
> Yugoslavia: 50/50%.
> Hungary: 50/50%.
> Bulgaria: Russia 75% the others 25%.[122]

The crossed-out words and the hastily added 'in accord with U.S.A.' on the original document show how much Churchill initially regarded Greece as almost a British protectorate, since Roosevelt wanted no part in the coming struggle against the EAM/ELAS alliance. Stalin made no comment, but took a blue pencil and put a large tick on the paper, next to 'Roumania' but clearly endorsing the whole document.

'After this there was a long silence,' Churchill recalled. 'The pencilled paper lay in the centre of the table. At length I said, "Might it not be thought rather cynical if it seemed we had disposed of these issues, so fateful to millions of people, in such an offhand manner? Let us burn the paper." "No, you keep it," said Stalin.'[123] Stalin did not care whether he seemed cynical; he had got what he wanted and the real chances of Hungary and Yugoslavia experiencing equal control between the Soviet Union and the West after the war were nil. Churchill was pleased to get the document back, and the incident was not recorded in the official British record.[124]

Considering the overall geopolitical situation in mid-October 1944, when the Russians were already in complete control of Bulgaria and

Romania, Hungary was about to fall to them and Tito seemed to be being drawn into the pro-Moscow camp while Greece was under threat from a Communist insurgency that Stalin could have armed, directed and financed with ease, the so-called 'Percentages Agreement' represented a good deal for Britain and the West.[125] It was largely down to Churchill that Greece did not disappear behind the Iron Curtain in 1945. With no Americans present – Harriman played bezique with Churchill almost nightly, but did not attend the bilateral meetings with Stalin – Churchill was acutely conscious of needing Roosevelt to be informed at every step. 'I have to keep the President in constant touch and this is the delicate side,' he told Clementine, addressing her as 'Mrs Kent' and signing off 'Colonel Kent'.[126] Yet when he wrote to Roosevelt he did not mention the 'naughty document'. 'I have had very nice talks with the Old Bear,' he told Clementine of Stalin. 'I like him the more I see him. *Now* they respect us here and I am sure they wish to work with us.'[127] On 16 October, three days before he left Moscow, Churchill was sufficiently confident that Stalin would abide by the Percentages Agreement to order Lieutenant-General Richard Scobie to occupy Athens with British troops, and to fire on ELAS partisans if necessary.

The country conspicuously absent from the Percentages Agreement was, of course, Poland. Churchill believed that to maintain the Russo-Polish border roughly at the Curzon Line represented a fair deal for Poland, or at least one the Poles were in no real position to improve upon. Stanisław Mikołajczyk, the Prime Minister of the Polish Government-in-exile in London, told Churchill on 14 October in Moscow that the Curzon Line was unacceptable as it left too many major ethnically Polish cities in Russia, but Churchill replied, in what the Polish minutes of the conversation describe as 'a very violent manner', 'You are callous people who want to wreck Europe. I shall leave you to your own troubles. You have no sense of responsibility when you want to abandon your people at home, to whose sufferings you are indifferent.'[128] He added, 'You are absolutely incapable of facing facts. Never in my life have I seen such people . . . you hate the Russians.'[129] He was certainly right about that last. He was clearly being naive (again) or perhaps duplicitous in arguing that the nature of the Soviet Union had 'changed': in warning Mikołajczyk that he and his people would be 'liquidated' by the Russians if they did not accept the new borders, he was tacitly acknowledging that Stalin's regime had not changed in the least. When in 1953 Moran asked him whether the Polish account of what he had said was fair, Churchill admitted, 'You see, we were both very angry.'[130]

The Russians were in a position of overwhelming military strength across eastern Europe and had now established a puppet Polish 'Government' in Lublin purporting to speak for all Poles. 'Our lot from London are, as Your Majesty knows, a decent but feeble lot of fools,' Churchill wrote to the King of the Polish Government-in-exile, 'but the delegates from Lublin seem to be the greatest villains imaginable.' A settlement between the London and the Lublin Poles would be hard to achieve without the active support of the Roosevelt Administration, but it was such a sensitive subject in American politics given the millions of Polish-American voters that an early accord was unlikely, in which case 'We shall have to hush the matter up and spin it out until after the presidential election.'[131] That is exactly what happened.

At the Tolstoy Conference, Brooke explained Eisenhower's strategy in Europe to the Russian High Command, and John R. Deane, an American general, reported on the island-hopping strategy in the Pacific. When Deane said that the Japanese soldiers on islands that had been bypassed would be 'forced to subsist on coconuts and fish until the rising sun sets', Churchill added, 'They'll rot, they'll rot.'[132] (This was also the attitude he adopted towards the German garrison on the Channel Islands, which were not liberated until May 1945 as he did not want to be responsible for feeding all 28,000 German soldiers there.)[133]

The Conference participants underwent six-hour, fourteen-course banquets with endless toasts – at one feast John Martin stopped counting them when he got to twenty – and firework displays celebrating Red Army victories. At the Bolshoi Theatre, Churchill received a fifteen-minute standing ovation. 'Churchill loved it and revived the applause whenever it seemed to lag by well-timed finger signals of the V for Victory,' noted a spectator. 'Stalin retired from the box as soon as the lights had gone on but returned after ten minutes to take the applause with Churchill.'[134] Stalin saw him off from Moscow airport at 10.45 a.m. on the 19th, which was an almost unprecedented honour in the Soviet Union.[135] 'He was looking well and not too tired,' the King noted on the 24th. (In fact he had suffered another feverishly high temperature towards the end of the Moscow trip, which subsided only just before he came home.) 'He told me he . . . had lost 5lbs in weight, despite the feasts and late hours in Moscow. He said he found Stalin more ready to talk and was not quite so suspicious.'[136]*

* On his return from discussing global strategy with one of the giants of the era, Churchill was immediately brought back to mundane domestic politics when he found the Conservative Party in revolt against the Town and Country Planning Bill. During a 'violent discussion, though very good natured' with Bracken, Churchill threatened to resign the Party leadership if a majority of Conservative MPs voted against the Government, which in the event they did not (Colville, *Fringes* p. 526).

On 27 October, Churchill told the House of Commons how much better negotiations with the Russians and Yugoslavians went in person than by cable: 'Face to face, difficulties which appear really insuperable at a distance are very often removed altogether from our path.'[137] He was, Harold Nicolson noted, 'Cherubic, pink, solid and vociferous.'* Four days later, he asked for Parliament to prolong itself for another year, but said that he thought it might actually end sooner, when the German war was won. He told the House that he would not call an election in the immediate aftermath of victory. 'At the bottom of all the tributes paid to democracy is the little man,' Churchill said, 'walking into the little booth, with a little pencil, making a little cross on a little bit of paper – no amount of rhetoric or voluminous discussion can possibly diminish the overwhelming importance of that point.'[138] He had now decided against an early poll to exploit what he had described to Eden as 'the glamour' of victory. In announcing his refusal to call a 'khaki' election, as Salisbury had in 1900 and Lloyd George in 1918, Churchill won plaudits. 'I have never admired Winston's moral attitude more than I did this morning,' wrote Nicolson.[139]

On 4 November, Churchill invited Chaim Weizmann to lunch at Chequers. He said that the war would probably continue for another three to six months and although he could make no pronouncements about a Jewish state in Palestine because of Conservative Party opposition, if the Jews could get 'the whole of Palestine, it would be a good thing'.[140] He added that his friend Walter Guinness, now Lord Moyne, the Minister Resident in the Middle East, had come round to this thinking, and that Weizmann ought to visit him in Cairo.[141] Two days later, Moyne was shot dead in his car outside his Residence there by the Lehi, a Zionist terrorist organization. Churchill was incensed: Moyne had been a member of the Other Club, had hosted Clementine on his yacht and his son Bryan Guinness had been a close friend of Randolph's since the late 1920s. 'If our dreams for Zionism are to end in the smoke of assassins' pistols and our labours for its future to produce only a new set of gangsters worthy of Nazi Germany,' he told the Commons on 17 November, 'many like myself will have to reconsider the position we have maintained so consistently and so long in the past.'[142]

Yet despite this outrage he turned down a Colonial Office proposal in the wake of the killing to curb Jewish immigration to Palestine, and refused to appoint as Moyne's successor either of two senior Conservatives

* 'Collins,' Churchill told the Commons barman after his speech, 'I should like a whisky and soda – single.' He sat down but immediately got up and walked back to the bar to say, 'Collins, delete the word "single" and insert the word "double".' (ed. Nicolson, *Diaries and Letters* II p. 409.)

whom he knew were opposed to Zionism. Though not naturally vengeful, when he learned that the Egyptian Government was planning to postpone the assassins' executions, he telegraphed Lampson in late January to warn that this would 'cause a marked breach between Great Britain and Egypt'.[143] They were hanged in March.

On 7 November 1944, President Roosevelt was re-elected for an unprecedented fourth term with 432 electoral votes, thirty-six states and 25.6 million in the popular vote, against 99 electoral votes, twelve states and 22.0 million votes for Thomas E. Dewey, the Republican candidate. Churchill was delighted and relieved. Three days later, he flew to Paris for the Armistice Day procession, where he was invited to stay at the Quai d'Orsay. The last time he had been there, four years before, they had been burning documents in the courtyard prior to the arrival of the Wehrmacht. He walked down the Champs-Élysées with Charles de Gaulle on 11 November – their differences seemingly forgotten – past immense, wildly enthusiastic crowds who could be kept back from mobbing them only with the greatest difficulty. Ismay later told Maud Russell that the Paris trip had been 'very dangerous' for Churchill, who 'should never have been allowed to go but no one can ever stop him. Nothing would have been easier than to shoot him from any one of many hundred windows.'[144] Ismay was close behind him and was ready, if shooting started, to trip him up and bring him to the ground. 'He said the P.M., who is very emotional and cries equally from pleasure or from sadness, cried and sobbed from the moment he set foot in France.' When they landed at an airfield he had not visited before, where they were met by de Gaulle, Ismay thought he would be interested in it and ask a number of questions, 'but he was too busy crying. As they walked through the streets of Paris tears poured down his face.'[145]

Valentine Lawford, Eden's private secretary, noted in his diary, 'The crowd screamed untiringly for de Gaulle and Churchill, and I never remember seeing such happy faces as there were all around us, and on the balconies on either side of the avenue.'[146] Churchill laid a wreath at Clemenceau's statue on the corner of the Champs-Élysées and Avenue Nicolas II (today's Avenue Winston Churchill), said a few words to Clemenceau's daughter and then drove to Les Invalides to do the same at the tomb of Marshal Foch, close to that of Napoleon, and to meet Foch's widow. 'Not for one moment did Winston stop crying,' Eden told Nicolson, 'and he could have filled buckets by the time he received the Freedom of [the City of] Paris . . . They really yelled for Churchill in a way that he has never heard any crowd yell before.'[147]

The next day, Churchill spoke to a vast crowd at the Hôtel de Ville. 'I am going to give you a warning; be on your guard,' he started, 'because I am going to speak, or try to speak, in French, a formidable undertaking and one which will put great demands on your friendship for Great Britain.'[148] After the fifteen-minute speech, delivered in fluent but totally ungrammatical French, part of it in tears, he left with de Gaulle on the presidential train to visit the French Army headquarters at Maîche. Heavy snow curtailed part of the programme, and at one point aides had to get out and push their car when it got stuck in a snowdrift. Churchill insisted on inspecting some French Army detachments in the snow with de Gaulle, which made for some splendid propaganda photographs but worried his entourage because of his recent bouts of pneumonia. 'I think it was absolutely criminal on De G's part to take W for that *awful* drive in the snow,' Charles Portal wrote to Pamela Churchill, with whom he was now having an affair, unbeknown to either Randolph, Harriman or Churchill. 'We shall be lucky if it doesn't kill him.'[149] After visiting Eisenhower's advance headquarters near Rheims, Churchill returned to Northolt by air. That day he received the news that the *Tirpitz*, Germany's last remaining battleship, had been sunk in a Norwegian fjord by Lancaster bombers.

Back in London, he continued to issue instructions on matters small as well as large. A large matter was to try to help Eisenhower's advance by sending him the 12-, 13.5- and even 15-inch heavy guns presently at Dover, which could be placed on railway mountings in France. But he also wrote to Sir James Grigg, the Secretary for War, to say, 'Press on. Make sure that the beer – four pints a week – goes to the troops under fire . . . before any of the parties in the rear get a drop.'[150] He was less worried than he had been earlier about the V-2 rocket attacks, which although they were still taking place seemed to be killing far fewer people than he had originally feared. 'Although we should all be prepared to meet our Maker,' Cunningham noted Churchill as saying, 'we should remember that the chance of it happening was six hundred thousand to one!!'[151] Three days later those odds shortened drastically in south-east London when a single V-2 hit a Woolworths supermarket in Deptford and killed 168 people.

Until the spring of 1944, the British Empire had between a quarter and a third more divisions fighting the Axis globally than the United States, but by January 1945 the Americans had 60 per cent more.[152] This growing preponderance of American power led Churchill to write frankly to Roosevelt in November, 'You will have the greatest navy in the world. You will have, I hope, the greatest air force. You will have the greatest trade. You will have all the gold. But these things do not oppress my mind with fear because I'm sure the American people under your re-acclaimed leadership will not give themselves over to vainglorious ambitions, and that justice and fair-play will be the lights that guide them.'[153] The truth was that Churchill was more hopeful than certain at that stage that Roosevelt would be there to guide post-war America. It was not a letter he reprinted in his war memoirs.

By then, despite their continuing personal regard, there were even more policy areas over which the two leaders diverged. The Americans were willing to destabilize General Franco's regime in Spain, for example, but Churchill was opposed. He felt that although Franco was a Fascist he was also anti-Communist, and had remained commendably neutral in the perilous 1940–42 period. Similarly, a note of gentle reproach might be spotted in Churchill's telegram to Roosevelt of 22 November, when he said, 'I remain set where you put me on unconditional surrender.'[154] One telegram from Roosevelt over future civil aviation rights seemed to be accompanied by a threat of what Colville described as 'pure blackmail' as it was linked to continued Lend-Lease supplies. Gil Winant was so embarrassed by it that he didn't want to stay for lunch at Chequers, but Churchill cheerily insisted that 'even a declaration of war should not prevent them having a good lunch.'[155]

'It's hell being seventy,' Churchill told Lascelles on his birthday, on 30 November, excusing himself from the opening of Parliament in order to work on his speech on the Government's programme, which he wanted to do from bed.[156] Clementine meanwhile worried about whether to spend six shillings a head on roses for his birthday dinner. Among the huge numbers of letters and telegrams he received were ones from the Shah of Persia, the entertainer Harry Lauder, Queen Mary and Rosa Lewis, the legendary owner of the Cavendish Hotel, testament to the breadth of his acquaintance.* The following March, on hearing that Conservative Central Office had ordained that no one over seventy would be accepted as a candidate at the next election, Churchill wrote to Ralph Assheton, the chairman of the Conservative Party, 'I naturally wish to know at the earliest moment whether this ban applies to me.'[157]

A full-scale Communist revolt broke out in Greece on 3 December, with street-fighting in Athens. British troops defended the Greek Provisional Government against the Communist EAM political movement and its

* He kept the cards, as he did with almost all his correspondence throughout his life, knowing that his biographers would need material. There is even an undated note in his archive from a private secretary saying nothing more than 'The C.I.G.S. is very anxious to see you for ten minutes tomorrow. 1 p.m. would seem to be a suitable time' (CAC CHAR 20/139B/174).

ELAS paramilitary units. Monarchists wanted King George to return from London, though many Greeks preferred the Orthodox Archbishop Damaskinos to be made regent, at least for the moment. Churchill's and General Scobie's actions were unpopular on the left in Britain, because the Greek Communist partisans had resisted the Germans bravely. Even Clementine urged her husband not to denounce the Greek Communists publicly, given the courage they had shown. The Roosevelt Administration out of republican principle was opposed to the monarchist factions in both Italy and Greece, and did not support direct Allied intervention in either country.

Churchill saw the greater goal, that of a democratic Greece. In one telegram to Scobie he wrote, 'Treat Athens as a conquered city' – that is, he should temporarily impose British rule. Colville forgot to write the word 'Guard' on the telegram, the Foreign Office codeword that would have prevented it from being shared with the Americans, so it was also sent to the US headquarters at Caserta in Italy. From there it was sent on to the State Department and White House, where it was promptly leaked to the Anglophobic columnist Drew Pearson of the *Washington Post*, inflaming an American and British press that was already opposed to Churchill's stance. When Colville confessed his error, Churchill gracefully said it had been his own fault for keeping Colville up so late.[158] It was an integral part of Churchill's leadership code never to scapegoat subordinates.

There was a sense of unfinished business about Churchill's policy towards Greece. He was unable to help the Poles, for whom Britain had gone to war in 1939, but he was determined to save the Greeks, whom he had failed to protect successfully in 1941. On 5 December he therefore sent Scobie further orders, which he underlined in the telegram and italicized in his memoirs, saying, '*We have to hold and dominate Athens. It would be a great thing for you to succeed in this without bloodshed if possible, but also with bloodshed if necessary.*'[159] Scobie helped forestall a seizure of power by EAM/ELAS by intervening decisively in what was almost turning into a civil war.

Nevertheless, Churchill was not optimistic about the outcome. 'If, as is likely, the powers of evil prevail in Greece, we must look forward to a quasi-Bolshevised Russian-led Balkan peninsula and this may spread to Hungary and Italy,' he told Smuts later that month. 'I therefore see great danger in the world in these quarters, but I have not the power, without causing great stresses in the Government and quarrelling with the United States, to do anything effective.'[160] On 8 December, Churchill was on withering form in another no-confidence debate, attacking those who questioned his commitment to democracy in Italy and Greece. 'Democracy is no harlot to be picked up in the street by a man with a tommy gun,' he said. 'I trust the people, the mass of the people, in almost any country, but I like to make sure that it is the people and not a gang of bandits from the mountains or from the countryside who think that by violence they can overturn constituted authority, in some cases ancient Parliaments, Governments and States.'[161] In reply to one of the speeches of Aneurin Bevan, who led the pro-EAM group in the Commons, Churchill said, 'I should think it was hardly possible to state the opposite of the truth with more precision . . . He need not get so angry because the House laughs at him; he ought to be pleased when they only laugh at him.'[162] Of Emanuel Shinwell he added, 'I do not challenge the honourable Gentleman when the truth leaks out of him by accident from time to time.'[163] He won the debate by 279 votes to 30. On receiving a Labour deputation on Greece, Churchill asked them to be seated in the Cabinet Room before he came upstairs from lunch solely so that he could avoid shaking hands with Bevan.

On 15 December, the King offered Churchill the Order of the Garter. He 'became all blubby', the King noted in his diary, but nonetheless refused the honour because the war in Europe was not yet won.[164] This was amply demonstrated on 16 December with the launch of the Ardennes Offensive, Hitler's thirty-nine-division German counter-attack that precipitated the so-called Battle of the Bulge.

At 5.30 p.m. on Christmas Eve, Churchill and Eden decided they needed to fly to Athens, although they were unsure exactly what to expect. They did not ask the permission of the War Cabinet or warn the Americans, and Mary recalled that 'My mother – so stoical, and so used to stern priorities – was deeply upset, and wept.'[165] The Prime Minister and Foreign Secretary took off at 1 a.m. on Christmas Day. On the way from Athens airport, they passed a checkpoint which ELAS had mortared that very morning. Reaching the Greek capital, they stayed on HMS *Ajax*, anchored in Piraeus Harbour. The captain told him that he hoped he would not have to open fire, but might if required to support the Army. Churchill 'seemed delighted at the prospect', and replied, 'Pray remember, Captain, that I come here as a cooing dove of peace, bearing a spring of mistletoe in my beak – but far be it from me to stand in the way of military necessity.'[166]

In a planning meeting aboard *Ajax*, the British contingent – which included General Scobie, Field Marshal Alexander, Harold Macmillan, the Minister Resident at Allied Force Headquarters, and Sir Reginald

Leeper, the British Ambassador to Greece – had to decide how best to approach the monarchist Prime Minister Georgios Papandreou, the would-be Regent Archbishop Damaskinos and the republican anti-Communist General Nikolaos Plastiras. (A contingent from ELAS was to be invited to a meeting on 26 December despite the ongoing fighting against them.) 'Well, gentlemen,' Churchill said, 'it seems to me that we can't do better than put our money on General Plaster-arse, and hope that his feet are not made of clay.'[167]* Churchill later referred to the black-bearded Damaskinos as 'a scheming medieval prelate' and a 'pestilent priest from the Middle Ages', but he was persuaded that the Archbishop's involvement was needed to forestall all-out civil war, keep the Communists at bay and prepare for democratic elections. Sailors who were celebrating Christmas in fancy-dress on *Ajax* took the black-clad, bearded Damaskinos, who in his mitre stood nearly 7 feet tall, for one of their number, almost causing an embarrassing international incident.[168]

Going out on to *Ajax*'s quarterdeck on the morning of 26 December, Churchill could see the smoke of battle west of Piraeus Harbour, and hear shell and machine-gun fire. He watched RAF Beaufighters as they strafed an ELAS stronghold on the side of one of the hills surrounding Athens.[169] Churchill was dictating to Marian Holmes on board *Ajax* later that day when a shell rocked the ship. 'There,' he cried. 'You bloody well missed us! Come on – try again!'[170] As he was being taken to the shore on a launch, another shell landed fairly close by, and the ship had to be relocated a mile away thanks to trench-mortar fire.[171] Churchill went to the British Embassy to thank the staff, and then at 4 p.m. made his way to the Greek Foreign Ministry for a meeting of all the parties. The electricity had been cut off and the conference was held by the light of hurricane lamps.

After the Conference had started, three ELAS representatives, described by Colville as 'shabby desperadoes', entered the meeting, having been strip-searched for concealed weaponry. Churchill's natural reaction was to shake their hands, but he was prevented from doing so by Alexander's 'bodily intervention'.[172] He nonetheless did so later on, telling Clementine, 'They certainly look a much better lot than the Lublin illegitimates.'[173] The ELAS fighters paid tribute to Churchill, calling him 'our great ally', although not everything could be heard perfectly because of the Beaufighters overhead. The meetings went on all that day and the next, but without any sign of an agreement. By the end, however, Churchill and Eden decided to switch British support from King George and Papandreou

* Tommy Lascelles later told a friend, 'I would rather have said that than written Gray's *Elegy*' (ed. Hart-Davis, *King's Counsellor* p. 282 n. 1).

to Damaskinos and Plastiras. In the short term at least, this turned out to be the best way of saving Greece from Communism.

Before lunch on 27 December, Churchill again came under fire when a burst of long-range machine-gun fire hit a wall 30 feet above his head, and a woman in the street was killed. (When Churchill tried to get the Order of the British Empire for all the female staff at the Athens Embassy, Lascelles turned it down on the grounds that everyone in Britain was showing equal bravery.)[174] Having done all they usefully could, Churchill and Eden left Athens for Naples on 28 December. 'The hatreds between these Greeks are terrible,' he wrote to Clementine. 'When one side [ELAS] have all the weapons we gave them to fight the Germans with and the other, tho' many times as numerous, have none, it is evident that a frightful massacre would take place if we withdrew.'[175] When they returned to London, Churchill and Eden tried to persuade King George of Greece to accept Damaskinos's regency, which he adamantly refused to do. After a 'stormy' all-night meeting, Churchill rose from his seat, smiling, and put his hand on the King's shoulder, saying, 'Sir, we ought not to be talking to you like this. Have some more brandy.'[176] Churchill installed Damaskinos as regent, who appointed himself prime minister in October 1945 and recalled the King the following September.

'During the whole Greek episode, Churchill felt more lonely than at any other time in the war,' recalled Ian Jacob, 'yet he never gave up, and never doubted his own judgement.'[177] The fact that Britain did not withdraw, and that under the Percentages Agreement the Soviets did not support the Greek Communists, meant that ELAS surrendered on 11 January 1945, and Greece stayed on the democratic path. 'What is now clear', wrote Leslie Rowan a quarter of a century later, 'is that Greece would not have been a free country had it not been for Churchill's courage and grasp of the essential.'[178]

Churchill received an extraordinary amount of abuse in both Britain and America for supporting monarchists, clerics and 'reactionaries' over Communists and 'progressives'. H. G. Wells put his Other Club comradeship to one side and publicly denounced Churchill as a 'would-be British Führer', one of the stupider remarks of an otherwise highly intelligent man.[179]* On New Year's Day 1945, *The Times* attacked the Government's Greek policy. Churchill composed a crushing letter to the paper, but, as so often, decided not to send it. A year later, he was nonetheless able to tell Clementine, quoting Zechariah, 'All the cabinets of Central, Eastern

* Despite this abuse, Churchill said he had 'a high regard and respect' for Wells when he contributed to a memorial on his death in 1946 (Cherwell Papers K69/11).

and Southern Europe are in Soviet control, excepting only Athens. This brand I snatched from the burning on Christmas Day.'[180]*

Churchill said of the Germans' Ardennes counter-offensive, which almost reached the River Meuse, that he 'preferred a tortoise with its head out even if it looked like biting him'.[181] In January 1945, Montgomery launched a northern counter-attack which, along with a heroic defence of Bastogne by the Americans and another thrust by General Patton, forced the Germans back beyond their frontier by the end of the month. The battle had exacted a high cost: over 60,000 Americans were killed or wounded. That month, the Russians took Warsaw and were in almost complete possession of East Prussia, as General MacArthur invaded Luzon, and General William Slim crossed the Irrawaddy in Burma and liberated Akyab (Sittwe). All this persuaded Churchill that another Big Three conference was now needed, the first since 1943. When Roosevelt said he could only spend five or six days there, Churchill told Colville he was 'disgusted'. He wrote to Roosevelt, 'I do not see any . . . way of realizing our hopes about World Organization in five or six days. Even the Almighty took seven.'[182] Two days earlier he had remarked, 'This may well be a fateful conference, coming at a moment when the great allies are so divided and the shadow of the war lengthens out before us. At the present time I think the end of this war may well prove to be more disappointing than was the last.'[183] Roosevelt remarked to Joseph E. Davies, a former US ambassador to Moscow, that Churchill was 'becoming more and more mid-Victorian and slipping farther and farther back into last-century thinking'.[184] That was untrue, but he was certainly starting to ramble on in Cabinet meetings, which were now taking up to four and a half hours, as was noted by Eden, Attlee, Cadogan and several others. It got so bad that Attlee personally – for security reasons – typed out a very blunt letter to Churchill criticizing his 'lengthy disquisitions in Cabinet', often about discussion papers he had clearly not read. He also complained that the views of Beaverbrook and Bracken would often trump those of the relevant Cabinet committee. Churchill was furious, and drafted and redrafted a sarcastic reply, but then calmed down and sent a polite acknowledgement.

As so often, just when some people were starting to write Churchill off, he was able to draw on his lifetime of oratorical preparation to produce a superb performance that showed him to be in complete control. On 15 January, Marian Holmes found herself wiping whisky and soda off Churchill's false teeth after he sent a glass flying over the bedclothes, but

* Amos 4: 11 and Zechariah 3: 2.

three days later he mesmerized the Commons for two hours, at over 12,000 words one of his longest speeches of the whole war, despite having a cold and a sore throat, trouncing all his critics, such as Bevan and the Communist MP Willie Gallacher. 'Military victory may be distant, it will certainly be costly, but it is no longer in doubt,' he said. 'The physical and scientific force which our foes hurled upon us in the early years has changed sides, and the British Commonwealth, the United States and the Soviet Union undoubtedly possess the power to beat down to the ground in dust and ashes the prodigious might of the war-making nations and the conspiracies which assailed us.'[185] With Barrington-Ward present in the gallery of the Commons, he decided the time had come to go on the offensive against *The Times*. 'There is no case in my experience, certainly no case in my wartime experience, when a British Government has been so maligned and its motives so traduced in our own country by important organs of the press,' he said, and asked how the British could complain about American newspapers 'when we have, in this country, witnessed such a melancholy exhibition as that provided by some of our most time-honoured and responsible journals and others to which such epithets would hardly apply'.[186] There were loud and prolonged cheers, which according to the official history of *The Times* provided 'The first heavy shock Barrington-Ward suffered during his time as editor'.[187]

'We have sacrificed everything in this war,' Churchill said. 'We shall emerge from it, for the time being, more stricken and impoverished than any other victorious country. The United Kingdom and the British Commonwealth are the only unbroken force which declared war on Germany of its own free will.'[188] With an eye on American support, Churchill borrowed from the Gettysburg Address, saying that what he planned for Greece was 'Government of the people, by the people, for the people, set up on a basis of free and universal suffrage elections, with secrecy of the ballot and no intimidation'.[189] If the State Department could not support that, he implied, then it was not being true to American principles. Two nights later, Churchill invited all the typists, drivers and servants into No. 10 to watch a Bette Davis, Humphrey Bogart and Ronald Reagan movie, *Dark Victory*. Churchill would of course never know that one of the stars of that movie would be instrumental in destroying the Soviet tyranny which he hated as much as the Nazi.

On 24 January 1945, Churchill told Colville that it was half a century since his father's death. Colville wondered what Lord Randolph, his son Winston and his grandson Randolph all had in common, and decided it was their undeniable 'capacity for being utterly unreasonable'.[190]

# 31
# Victory and Defeat January–July 1945

*Here must be the end of the long war, and rest and glory after toil. All should be staked. Nothing should be neglected, and nothing should be withheld.*

Churchill, *Marlborough*[1]

*The English people always turned on those whom they thought had served them well in hard times.*

Churchill to John Colville, December 1944[2]

On Monday, 29 January 1945, the Battle of the Bulge having ended in victory only the previous week, Churchill flew from RAF Northolt in his C-54 Skymaster. He took Sarah as his aide-de-camp to a short conference (codenamed Cricket) with Roosevelt in Malta, before they both proceeded to Yalta in the Crimea for the Big Three conference (codenamed Argonaut). 'If only I could dine with Stalin once a week, there would be no trouble at all,' Churchill had told Colin Coote a year earlier. 'We get on like a house on fire.'[3] When they landed at 4.30 a.m. on 30 January (they were now able to fly across France, cutting the journey time significantly), Churchill was running a temperature of 102.5 degrees, so he stayed on board the plane, only transferring to the cruiser HMS *Orion* six hours later.[4] Moran almost summoned the haematologist Lionel Whitby from Bristol in the meantime. 'The Prime Minister gave us all rather a fright,' Martin wrote to Colville.[5]

The next day Churchill was well enough to hold useful conversations with Field Marshal Alexander, General Marshall, Admiral King, Harry Hopkins and Edward Stettinius, the US Secretary of State, although he spent much of the Cricket Conference in bed.[6] Hopkins, Eden, Harriman and Cadogan were also there, and Churchill reported to Clementine that 'All the conversations at the Conferences have been most friendly and agreeable.'[7] This was true even of those with Randolph, who had flown in from Bari where he was still convalescing from his plane crash injuries.*

On 1 February, another plane on its way to the Conference crashed off Lampedusa, killing the senior diplomat Peter Loxley, Brooke's aide-de-camp Major Barney Charlesworth, a member of Captain Pim's Map Room team Lieutenant-Colonel Bill Newey, Eden's doctor and one of his detectives. If John Martin had not dissuaded Churchill from bringing a second private secretary to the Conference, Jock Colville would have been on the plane too. Even with the Luftwaffe cleared from the Mediterranean, these long flights were not without risk. The plane was the same type that Churchill had flown in to North Africa, Italy, Teheran and Moscow.

Churchill had been reading a recently published book called *Verdict on India*, by the former pacifist and later Fascist-sympathizer Beverley Nichols, a fellow guest at the Château de l'Horizon in the mid-1930s. 'It certainly shows the Hindu in his true character and the sorry plight to which we have reduced ourselves by losing confidence in our mission,' Churchill reported to Clementine.

> Reading about India has depressed me for I see such ugly storms looming up there which . . . may overtake us. I have had for some time a feeling of despair about the British connections with India, and still more about what will happen if it is suddenly broken. Meanwhile we are holding on to this vast Empire, from which we get nothing, amid the increasing abuse and criticism of the world, and our own people, and increasing hatred of the Indian population, who receive constant and deadly propaganda to which we can make no reply. However out of my shadows has come a renewed resolve to go fighting on as long as possible and to make sure the Flag is not let down while I am at the wheel. I agree with the book and also with its conclusion – Pakistan.[8]

Nichols argued that only a Muslim-majority state in the north-western part of the Indian sub-continent could protect Muslim minority rights if and when the British left.

Roosevelt arrived in Valletta Harbour on 2 February, on board the heavy cruiser USS *Quincy*. 'The harbour made a perfect setting for the rather spectacular scene as the President's ship moved slowly past to its berth ahead of us,' John Martin wrote, 'the guards of honour standing to attention and the music of the "Star-Spangled Banner" sounding across

* Randolph was furious about not being invited on to Yalta, but to his father's relief took it out on Eden.

the water.'[9] The sailors of both the *Quincy* and *Orion* lined the rails, and everyone turned out on deck. The President, seated on the bridge, waved to Churchill, who waved back, as the Maltese thronged the harbour's rooftops. Sawyers was spotted by Sarah continually bowing and waving 'gracefully in acknowledgement', as though the cheers were meant for him, while everyone else stood to attention.

'My friend has arrived in best of health and spirits,' Churchill reported to Clementine.[10] This was untrue and inexplicable; almost everyone else who left memoirs or contemporaneous notes of the Malta and Yalta conferences commented on how ill Roosevelt looked. In March 1944 he had been diagnosed with high blood pressure and coronary artery disease, which had got much worse over the ensuing year. The British diplomat Gladwyn Jebb spoke for many when he recalled that he had been 'much distressed by his appearance which was, frankly, terrible'.[11] Sarah had to hide her shock later that day at how much Roosevelt had changed since Teheran. 'It was quite obvious that he was a very sick man,' she wrote, 'the bright charm and the brave, expansive heart were there, but his appearance gravely distressed my father and, indeed, everyone.'[12] Roosevelt's collapsing health – he was dead within ten weeks – could not but affect the tenor of the Conference. 'My father and all the British party felt a withdrawing of the former easy understanding which, in spite of many disagreements, had existed between the two leaders,' Sarah recalled.[13] However, this did not extend to serious discussions; Churchill complained to Hopkins that nothing of substance was discussed between him and Roosevelt, who had arrived only on the day before they were due to leave for Yalta and who showed little interest in formulating a joint Anglo-American approach to the coming meeting with Stalin.

The journey from Malta to Yalta was an exhausting one: seven hours by plane and an equally long drive over the mountains, although it did involve a break on the shores of the Black Sea, where, Martin recalled, 'the table groaned with caviar and the pop of champagne bottles went on all the time like machine-gun fire'.[14]* On the car journey, wearing the uniform of an honorary colonel of the 4th Hussars and a tall black fur hat, Churchill recited poetry, especially Byron's *Childe Harold*, for an hour, and slept for thirty minutes. When he reached the Vorontsov Palace where the British delegation was housed, which was modelled on a Scottish baronial hall, he went straight to bed.

* 'I could not live without champagne,' Churchill was to tell his friend Odette Pol-Roger in 1946. 'In victory I deserve it. In defeat I need it.' He described her house at 44 Avenue de Champagne, Épernay, as 'the world's most drinkable address'. (*CIHOW* p. 537.)

The British did not like the Palace, which had bugs of both the bed and electronic kind, as well as a disastrous combination of overcrowding and rudimentary plumbing. (It had been Field Marshal von Manstein's residence when the Germans occupied the Crimea, but had been badly damaged.) At one point, Sarah counted three field marshals queuing for one bucket. With omnipresent flies and midges, Churchill called Yalta 'the Riviera of Hades'.[15] None of that was mentioned when Stalin called on him on the afternoon of 4 February, however. 'He is greyer than I thought,' noted Valentine Lawford, 'and doesn't look into the eyes of those he is speaking to.'[16]

The Yalta Conference was easily the largest of the wartime conferences, with 750 accredited participants. It was held in the ballroom of the Livadia Palace at Yalta, the Americans' residence, which had the best wheelchair access for Roosevelt. It had been built in 1911 for the Romanov family the Bolsheviks had murdered in 1918. The children's nursery had been on the first floor, which for Lawford meant that there was 'an air of sorrow brooding over the place'.[17] Meetings were held around a large white round table in the former ballroom.[18] There were momentous questions to consider: the final destruction of Nazism; Russia's role in the Japanese war (the two countries had maintained an uneasy peace since 1939); a new 'United Nations Organization' to help keep future peace; what should happen to Yugoslavia; British responsibility for Greece; the zones of occupation for Berlin; the fate of non-German prisoners-of-war; the integrity and independence of Poland and other eastern European countries; the refugee problem, and the contours of the post-war financial structure.

The popular conception that Churchill and Roosevelt simply fell into a series of traps laid by Stalin, believed his lies and naively allowed him to get everything he wanted at Yalta is a myth. There were American officials in Roosevelt's entourage who were working for the Soviets, namely Alger Hiss of the US State Department and Assistant Treasury Secretary Harry Dexter White, but little indication that they significantly affected what was agreed. What happened there was much more complicated and subtle, with every part of the Agreement affecting every other. The central, ever-present fact lying behind everything was that Stalin had an army of more than six million men in eastern Europe, including by then in every region of Poland. The Western Allies thought they needed Russia to declare war against Japan once the German war was over, as they could not be certain that the atomic bomb – which for obvious reasons was not mentioned – actually worked.

Churchill and Roosevelt wanted the Russians to engage meaningfully in the work of the United Nations, which was intended as a global organization that would fulfil the Atlantic Charter's promise of 'the establishment of a wider and permanent system of general security'. Churchill promoted the concept of a Security Council where the Great Powers would ultimately be in control. Stalin agreed that Russia would be a founder member of the new organization, whose first general secretary was the British diplomat Gladwyn Jebb. When Roosevelt gave in to Russia's demands that its satellite states Ukraine and Belorussia should have separate representation (and thus votes) in the projected General Assembly of the United Nations, the British Foreign Office showed what Jebb called 'much indignation', but nothing could be done about it.[19] Accusations such as those made by Lawford that Roosevelt was 'a bit gaga and failing' were wide of the mark; his intellectual faculties were as powerful as ever; it was just his poor, pain-wracked body that was giving up.[20]

Poland was on the agenda for no fewer than seven of the eight plenary sessions at Yalta. Since the Russians were not going to accept anything less than the Curzon Line as their eastern frontier with Poland, in Jebb's view 'the proposal was hardly something that we could resist even if we had the power to do so.'[21] Churchill argued for more modest annexations from Germany, saying, 'It would be a great pity to stuff the Polish goose so full of German food that it died of indigestion,' but territory in the west that was ethnically and historically German was nonetheless added to Poland, and remains there to this day.[22] By 1950, between twelve and fourteen million Germans had moved from those historically German territories to lands behind the new German border, the largest movement of people in modern European history.

Another problem was the clear intention of the Russians to install the Lublin Poles in government in Warsaw. 'We can't go home without some sort of agreement that will guarantee the Poles free and unfettered elections,' noted Lawford.[23] On 11 February Churchill and Roosevelt persuaded Stalin to sign a Declaration on Liberated Europe, which promised 'the right of all peoples to choose the form of government under which they will live' and 'the restoration of sovereign rights and self-government to those people who have been forcibly deprived of them by the aggressor nations', while the Big Three would 'jointly assist' in the holding of 'free elections' under universal suffrage and the secret ballot.[24] Britain was not committed to accepting any specific western frontier for Poland, and undertook to recognize a new Polish government only if and when she was satisfied about its composition.

Eden was unhappy at the absence of an agreed Anglo-American agenda at Yalta, and complained to Lawford that 'he finds Winston (and Roosevelt, alas) waffling on without any idea of what we have come to discuss'. But this is belied by how much was achieved by Churchill and Roosevelt in that week.[25] Furthermore, it was thought the German war might extend into the autumn of 1945, and the war against Japan was expected to last a further eighteen months after victory had been won in Europe, perhaps until spring 1947.[26] It was therefore a great coup for Churchill and Roosevelt to get Stalin to promise that the USSR would declare war on Japan as soon as possible after the German surrender. It was also agreed that if France was to be allowed to pose as a victorious rather than defeated power, as de Gaulle was demanding, her zone of occupation of Germany would have to be taken out of the territory allotted to Britain and the United States, not Russia.

Churchill promised to keep up the saturation bombing of Germany, which was still firing V-2 rockets at Britain. On 5 February, the Russian General Staff requested a bombing raid against the German city of Dresden, a railway nodal point, to prevent Wehrmacht troops from being transferred from the Western Front to the Eastern. As a result, eight days later, Dresden was obliterated in an RAF raid, signed off by Attlee in London. The railway marshalling yards were a legitimate target, but the incompetent local Gauleiter had not provided shelters for more than a small minority of the city's population, and around 28,000 civilians were killed. The raid was not considered particularly unusual at the time, however, and Churchill never mentioned it to Colville, which he almost certainly would have had it been seen as anything out of the ordinary.

There was idealism at Yalta as well as Realpolitik, but there was also lethal decision-making. The fate of the tens of thousands of Russians, many of them Cossacks, who had fought for Hitler but had surrendered, or were in the process of surrendering, to General Alexander, was discussed on 10 February. The British did not want to keep these prisoners, whom they feared they could not feed, and considered they might hamper them militarily if relations with Tito's partisans turned sour. Churchill asked Stalin what he wanted done with them; Stalin replied that he 'hoped they could be sent to Russia as quickly as possible . . . The Soviet Government looked upon all of them as Soviet citizens . . . Those who had agreed to fight for Germany could be dealt with on their return to Russia.'[27] Churchill said the British 'were anxious that these prisoners should be repatriated'. Later that day, a Prisoners of War Agreement which put that wish into effect was signed by Eden and Molotov. Although Eden, Macmillan and Alexander were far more involved in its implementation, it was ultimately Churchill's responsibility, and another example of his occasional ruthlessness, as he could have been in little doubt about the prisoners' ultimate fate.

Between 18 May and 2 June 1945, the 1st Guards Brigade, part of the British V Corps that occupied Carinthia, the southern province of Austria, and several other British units handed over some 40,000 anti-Soviet Cossacks to the Red Army, including many who were not Soviet citizens and never had been. Similarly, though in this case there was no treaty obligation to do so, 30,000 Yugoslavs who had fought against Marshal Tito were sent to him. Most of these Cossacks and Yugoslavs were liquidated on arrival; the rest were incarcerated and cruelly punished for years. For the Foreign Office officials involved, suggests the historian of the British culpability for these events, 'The fate of the Russians whose return they enforced was an unfortunate but unavoidable sacrifice to the greater aim.'[28] Alas, that greater aim – good relations with the Soviets – was not attained either, and given Stalin's ideological views and paranoia probably never could have been. It was not Churchill's finest hour, though at the time Yalta was considered, as Clementine told him, 'a wonderful result equal to a major military victory or a whole victorious campaign'.[29]

'We have covered a great amount of ground,' he wrote to her, 'and I am very pleased with the decisions we have gained.'[30] A Reparations Commission was to be set up, which Churchill hoped would learn the lesson of the Great War and set a low figure, for as he told Roosevelt, 'If you want your horse to pull your wagon, you have to give him some hay.'[31] Greece was only mentioned insofar as Stalin said he 'did not wish to interfere' in the affairs of that country, whereupon Churchill replied that he was 'much obliged'.[32] Agreement was also reached on Yugoslavia, with Stalin promising that he would use his influence with Tito to hold free elections in which all the pre-war political parties could take part. Churchill said he knew he could 'rely on Marshal Stalin's goodwill' and Stalin replied 'that when he made a statement he would carry it out'.[33]

When Sarah said goodnight to her father on the evening of 7 February, Churchill said, 'I do not suppose that at any moment in history has the agony of the world been so great or widespread. Tonight the sun goes down on more suffering than ever before in the world.'[34] Yalta did not significantly lessen it, but that was not recognized at the time. Even the cynical Valentine Lawford, who had written (of the night Roosevelt and Stalin came to dinner at the Vorontsov Palace), 'Winston, of course, is always inclined to weep tears of brandy in gratitude for anything he interprets as a friendly gesture from his great compeer,' had to add, 'But it may really be that we are beginning to get on better terms with the Russians.'[35] Yet it was not to be. 'Our hopeful assumptions were soon to be falsified,' Churchill admitted in his war memoirs a decade later. 'Still, they were the only ones possible at the time'.[36] The Russian Army had been in Warsaw for three weeks and was now on the banks of the Oder; the empty promises Stalin made at Yalta were all based upon those solid, incontrovertible facts.

The Big Three had remade the world in eight days, but then at 4.30 p.m. on the 11th Churchill suddenly decided, while giving no reason, that he wanted to leave for Sevastopol (which he naturally insisted on calling Sebastopol) immediately, despite being scheduled to leave the next day. He gave his secretarial and household staff only one hour to pack everything up and be off, causing much consternation. Sawyers, who had last been seen 'dancing a minuet with some of the Russian servant-girls in the passage very early that morning', sat down on a trunk and let his 'curiously rose-coloured head' sink into his hands, wailing, 'He can't do this to me!'[37] Churchill spent three nights working in Sevastopol on the Cunard liner *Franconia*. On the way, he visited the battlefield of Balaclava, where the 4th Hussars had charged as part of the Light Brigade. 'Either they thought they had won the battle', he said of the Russians he met, 'or they had never heard of it.'[38] On board the *Franconia*, Sarah asked him if he was tired. 'Strangely enough, no,' he replied. 'Yet I have felt the weight of responsibility more than ever before and in my heart there is anxiety.'[39]

On 14 February, Churchill left Sevastopol after breakfast and drove three and a half hours to Saki airfield, from where he flew to Athens, over 'bleak, snow-covered country and past many sights of the war', including a wrecked train dangling from a high embankment in a gap left by a blown-up bridge.[40] Flying over the Dardanelles, the grave of his friend Rupert Brooke was pointed out to him – a speck of white on a hilltop on Skyros. As they landed, they saw the Acropolis, which that evening to mark his visit was floodlit for the first time since the German occupation.

Churchill drove in an open car with Regent-Archbishop Damaskinos* to Constitution Square, where they made short, impromptu speeches through amplifiers to a crowd estimated at between forty and fifty thousand people, exciting tremendous enthusiasm and repeated cheers.[41] 'I have never seen such a mass of people all jammed together,' he told the Cabinet later. 'If a by-election were held there between Aneurin Bevan and me he would not stand a chance.'[42]

The next day Churchill flew to Alexandria, where he went aboard USS *Quincy* for lunch with President Roosevelt. 'The President seemed placid

* Churchill correctly called him 'His Beatitude'. Damaskinos was in the habit of securing himself from interruption by hanging a notice on his door that read 'His Beatitude is at prayer,' prompting Churchill to remark, 'I'd like to try that at Downing Street, but I'm afraid no one would believe it' (Fishman, *Clementine* p. 100).

and frail. I felt that he had a slender contact with life,' he later wrote. 'We bade affectionate farewells.'[43] He suspected, rightly, that it would be the last time he would see him. He then flew on to Cairo, his fourth city in twenty-eight hours, and despite Randolph acting, as Lampson put it, 'as a deliberate foil to his father', Churchill's sallies 'were on many occasions indescribably apt and quick off the mark: more than ever he strikes me as a human dynamo'.[44]

Churchill spent the next two days near the Pyramids, and then at the Fayoum Oasis, meeting Emperor Haile Selassie, King Farouk I of Egypt, President Shukri al-Quwatli of Syria and King Ibn Saud of Saudi Arabia.[45] Among Ibn Saud's immense retinue were an astrologer, a food-taster, a chief server of ceremonial coffee and 'miscellaneous slaves, cooks, porters and scullions'.[46] They had come from Jeddah in a British destroyer, bringing sheep which they had slaughtered and eaten on the deck. Churchill described Ibn Saud as 'A splendid looking man . . . he boasts of his virility and how often he attends to his harem – he must keep a card index.'[47] The King urged Churchill to drink Mecca water. Despite the fact that he did not tend to drink much water on its own, Churchill said afterwards, 'I am not against it on an occasion like that.' When the royal chamberlain told him that smoking and drinking were banned in the King's presence owing to the Koran, Churchill replied that 'my religion prescribed as an absolute sacred ritual smoking cigars and drinking alcohol before, after, and if need be during, all meals and the intervals between them.'[48] All he noted of the chamberlain's response was 'Complete surrender.'[49]

There was no hint of surrender when Churchill asked for Ibn Saud's assistance in promoting 'a definite and lasting settlement between the Jews and Arabs', through a Middle Eastern Federation which he would head, of which Jewish Palestine would be an integral but self-governing part. The King turned the idea down flat. Driving back from the meeting, Churchill insisted on stopping and minutely inspecting the camels in his guard of honour. 'He remembered all about them from the River War,' wrote Lampson.[50] At dinner Churchill examined the presents that the King had given him. These included diamond rings, a jewelled sword and dagger, exotic scents and a trunkful of magnificent robes, worth a total of £3,500 (more than £120,000 today), all of which he had to hand over to the Treasury. In return, Churchill had been able to persuade the Treasury to give the King £100 worth of scent. Lampson then dressed him up in the robes, sword, rings, headdress and dagger, much to Churchill's amusement. 'He made an imposing figure,' recorded Lampson, but there is tragically no photograph.[51]

Churchill landed at RAF Lyneham in Wiltshire on 19 February after a fourteen-hour flight. 'He is marvellously well,' Clementine told Mary.[52] The whole Cabinet was waiting in the hallway at No. 10 to welcome him home, and followed him into the Cabinet Room to hear his account of the journey. 'All very enjoyable, I must say,' Churchill summed up his trip afterwards. 'I brought some goldfish from Moscow to swim in my pool, and we held our own against the bugs.'[53] Nevertheless, he asked to have his clothes fumigated, suspecting that they had acquired some 'unwelcome residents' at Yalta.[54] The next day he was received with cheers in the Commons. A small group of Tories, including Lord Dunglass, opposed the Yalta Agreement for failing to guarantee Polish independence and integrity, though they did not explain how that could actually have been achieved. Churchill later let Lady Diana Cooper and Venetia Montagu try on the splendid robes Ibn Saud had given him, with 'Lady Diana in purple and striking a dramatic pose'.[55]

'The P.M. was rather depressed,' Colville recorded that weekend at Chequers, 'thinking of the possibilities of Russia one day turning against us, saying that Chamberlain had trusted Hitler as he was now trusting Stalin (though he thought in different circumstances).'[56] Edward Bridges and Bomber Harris were staying too. Before dinner, when Colville asked Harris about the effect of the Dresden Raid, the head of Bomber Command replied, 'Dresden? There is no such place as Dresden.'[57] Once victory had been won and Germany destroyed, Churchill mused, 'What will lie between the white snows of Russia and the white cliffs of Dover?'[58] Perhaps the Russians might not want 'to sweep on to the Atlantic, or something might stop them as the accident of Genghis Khan's death had stopped the horsed archers of the Mongols, who retired and never came back'. When Harris asked if the Russians intended to dominate Europe, Churchill said 'Who knows? They might not want to. But there is an unspoken fear in many people's hearts.'[59] Listening to *The Mikado* on the gramophone that evening in the Great Hall, Churchill said it brought back the Victorian era for him, which he said 'will rank in our island history with the Antonine age' – the period of Roman peace and stability from AD *c.* 96 to 180.

He was in much the same mood when he reported to the King on his trip. 'Was Stalin's word to be trusted or not?' the King noted after their lunch. 'That remains to be proved but we must try it out.'[60] Churchill told Hugh Dalton around this time, 'Poor Neville Chamberlain believed he could trust Hitler. He was wrong, but I don't think I'm wrong about Stalin.'[61] Yet he clearly suspected it might have been the case, and was consequently on the lookout for Soviet backsliding on the promises made at Yalta, which was not slow in coming. Churchill's long anti-Communist past left him alert to the need to trust but verify. The simple fact is that Stalin lied to Churchill and Roosevelt at Yalta about Polish independence, free elections in eastern Europe and the influence he would wield there after the war. Neither could have known it for certain, however much they may have suspected it at the time, and there was little they could have done about it even if they had. The knowledge that he had been lied to, however, only added to Churchill's anger when he came to denounce the Soviets the following year.

In public, however, Churchill said that he trusted the Russians. 'The impression I brought back from the Crimea, and from all my other contacts,' he told a crowded House of Commons on 27 February, 'is that Marshal Stalin and the Soviet leaders wish to live in honourable friendship and equality with the Western democracies. I feel also that their word is their bond. I know of no Government which stands to its obligations . . . more solidly than the Russian Soviet Government. I decline absolutely to embark here on a discussion about Russian good faith. It is quite evident that these matters touch the whole future of the world.'[62] Churchill nonetheless separately offered British citizenship to any Pole who did not want to return home. As he told Harold Nicolson and Lord De La Warr, the Russian troops in Poland 'are on the spot; even the massed majesty of the British Empire would not avail to turn them off that spot'.[63] He also believed that because Stalin had not supported the Greek insurgency, his word might be trusted over Poland. The next day twenty-five mostly Conservative MPs voted against the Government in the debate on the Yalta Agreement and a number abstained, but 396 MPs voted in favour.

Between 2 and 6 March, Churchill toured the Western Front, entering Germany and visiting Montgomery's headquarters. He still worked on his boxes, however. 'On no account reduce the barley for whisky,' he was to tell the Agriculture Minister. 'This takes years to mature and is an invaluable export and dollar producer . . . It would be most improvident not to preserve this characteristic British element of ascendancy.'[64] When he reached the Siegfried Line, the German defensive fortifications also known as the West Wall, he halted his column of more than twenty cars and jeeps, got out and told the press photographers, 'This is one of the operations connected with this great war which must not be reproduced graphically.'[65] He then turned his back and urinated on Hitler's defences. 'I shall never forget the childish grin of intense satisfaction that spread all over his face as he looked down at the critical moment!' Brooke wrote. On that trip, Churchill also chalked the words 'Hitler, Personally' on a shell which was loaded into a gun whose lanyard he pulled to fire.[66] On the day after he returned to London from Eisenhower's headquarters at Rheims, the Americans crossed the Rhine at Remagen.

Between 23 and 26 March, Churchill visited the front again, this time to watch Operation Plunder, Montgomery's crossing of the Rhine near Wesel. When Colville returned to Montgomery's tactical headquarters with blood on his tunic after an 88mm shell landed 10 yards away and cut his jeep driver's artery, Montgomery criticized him for having gone up too close, but Churchill told his private secretary, 'I am jealous. You succeeded where I failed. Tomorrow nothing shall stop me.' Then he ended, poetically, 'Sleep soundly; you might have slept more soundly still.'[67]

On 25 March, two days after the Allied armies, Churchill crossed the Rhine in a landing craft at Büderich, 6 miles north of Eisenhower's headquarters at Rheinberg, where the river is about 400 yards wide. 'The PM has gone over to be with Montgomery at the commencement of the operations,' noted the King. 'He is very restless nowadays and cannot bear to be out of things.'[68] 'It was a relief to get Winston home safely,' Brooke recalled. 'I knew that he longed to get into the most exposed position possible. I honestly believe that he would really have liked to be killed on the front at this moment of success. He had often told me that the way to die is to pass out fighting when your blood is up and you feel nothing.'[69] Part of Churchill's admiration for Nelson was for his glorious death at the moment of victory. When his cousin Anita Leslie told Churchill that his insistence on standing on the most shelled part of the river bank 'to see better' had sent his staff frantic 'for fear something would happen to him', Churchill merely grinned and replied, 'Well, I'm an old man and I've worked hard. Why shouldn't I have a little fun?'[70]

Churchill told Colville that he thought the faces of the Germans he saw were 'very strained' which 'had moved and upset him'.[71] After almost six years of trying to bomb, crush and starve those same people, that might be considered hypocritical, but pity for the underdog was an instinctive part of his nature. If the Russians were as intent on European hegemony as Bomber Harris had suggested at Chequers, Churchill recognized that a deNazified Germany would need to be built up as soon as possible, and the country should not be dismembered, let alone pastoralized. Magnanimity in victory made good strategic as well as humanitarian sense to him, as always. 'The moment has come when the question of bombing of German cities simply for the sake of increasing the terror, though under other pretexts, should be reviewed,' Churchill told Ismay in a minute in late March, once protests had been made in Parliament and the liberal press about the Dresden Raid. 'Otherwise we shall come into control of an utterly ruined land . . . The destruction of Dresden remains a serious query against the conduct of Allied bombing.'[72] The raid provoked an attack on the Government's bombing policy in the Church of England and the House of Lords, and Churchill's minute proved so controversial in the Air Ministry that it had to be withdrawn and toned down, with all references to Dresden removed.

On 27 March, the day the last V-2 rocket fell on London, Churchill saw off Clementine, who was now president of the Red Cross Aid to Russia Fund, on a long journey to the Soviet Union. That same day, he learned that fourteen Polish leaders representing non-Communist political parties, including the heroic General Kazimierz Okulicki, one of the former commanders of the Home Army, had been arrested by the Red Army near Warsaw, despite written guarantees of safe conduct. After weeks of silence it transpired that they were going to be put on trial in Moscow.[73] If there was any one moment when Churchill was forced to recognize that Stalin had simply been lying to him at Yalta, and there was likely to be a rift with Russia after the German surrender, it was then. He described it in his memoirs as 'this sinister episode'.[74] Once Stalin had claimed on 5 May that Churchill's 'attitude excludes the possibility of an agreed solution to the Polish question', Churchill wrote to Washington the next day urging that 'we should hold firmly to the existing position obtained or being obtained by our armies in Yugoslavia, in Austria, in Czechoslovakia, on the main central United States front, and on the British front reaching up to Lübeck, including Denmark . . . I feel that we must most earnestly consider our attitude towards the Soviets and show them how much we have to offer or withhold.'[75] The Americans were not willing to join Churchill in this tough stance over the fourteen Poles, eleven of whom were sentenced to imprisonment for terms ranging between four months and ten years.

'Winston told me that he had to go slow over Poland,' the King noted after a conversation in mid-March, 'as he could not get the Americans to keep pace with him and we could not promise Poland anything without US backing.'[76] With Roosevelt now dying, that could not be expected in the short term. 'At the moment you are the one bright spot in Anglo-Russian relations,' Churchill told Clementine in Moscow on 2 April.[77] He felt that the chances of success for the United Nations Organization were very low now, because the Russians were being so 'utterly uncooperative about Poland'.[78]

David Lloyd George had died on 26 March. In his Commons eulogy, Churchill praised precisely those qualities that people most admired in Churchill himself. 'He imparted immediately a new surge of strength, of impulse, far stronger than anything that had been known up to that time,' he said of his war leadership in 1916, 'and extending over the whole field of wartime Government, every part of which was of equal interest to him.' Churchill spoke of Lloyd George's 'power to live in the present yet without taking short views; and secondly, his power of drawing from misfortune itself the means of future success. As a man of action, resource and creative energy he stood, when at his zenith, without a rival. His name is a household word throughout our Commonwealth of Nations.'[79] Churchill did not of course mention Lloyd George's visit to Hitler or, even more disreputably, his opposition to Britain fighting on in 1940. Two days later, he decided to have lunch in bed, but poured vinegar into his glass and whisky on to his sardines. 'I must be going dotty,' he said, as Sawyers dealt with it.[80]

Churchill knew about the European Advisory Commission's zones, of course, but nonetheless told Eisenhower, 'I deem it highly important that we should shake hands with the Russians as far to the east as possible.'[81] Since the Red Army incurred 200,000 casualties taking Berlin alone, Eisenhower was not about to rip up the agreements made with the Soviets at Yalta and earlier. A flash of resentment against the United States was evident in early April, when the State Department suggested that the Soviets be consulted over the rearming of Greece, prompting Churchill to note, 'This is the usual way in which the State Department, without taking the least responsibility for the outcome, makes comments of an entirely unhelpful character in a spirit of complete detachment.'[82]

Churchill warned the Dominions of the problems of Soviet bad faith in early April. At a War Cabinet attended by Smuts, Peter Fraser the Prime Minister of New Zealand, Sir Feroz Khan Noon of the Government of India, Wavell the Viceroy, and the Deputy Prime Minister of Australia, he said (according to Burgis's verbatim but fragmentary notes), 'Since Yalta great distresses . . . Since then spirit vanished. Stalin and Molotov not the masters they appear, it's the boys in the back room. Have altered their line – rude messages – hope get through this period . . . We're not biggest pebble on the beach – Russia and USA have overwhelming physical power – very serious reflection. Finland, Poland, Czechoslovakia – Germany beaten down – Austria, Hungary, the Balkans – cordon sanitaire – dominated by Soviets.'[83] Apart from the absurd notion that Stalin and Molotov might not be controlling Soviet policy, it was a clear warning of a looming rift, which Churchill argued could be overcome only through Commonwealth unity.

Diplomatic relations with Russia deteriorated still further when Stalin accused the British and Americans of conducting secret negotiations with the Germans at Berne in Switzerland, when in fact all Alexander had done was to inform Kesselring of how to go about surrendering unconditionally.[84] Stalin's distrust and paranoia were obvious. Roosevelt's tough response to Stalin on 4 April – 'Frankly I cannot avoid a feeling of bitter resentment towards your informants . . . for such vile misrepresentations of my actions' – explodes the myth that he was weak towards the Soviet Union in the last months of his life.[85] Churchill was delighted, but also acutely conscious of the United States' preponderance now in world affairs. 'Undoubtedly I feel much pain when I see our armies so much smaller than theirs,' he told Clementine. 'It has always been my wish to keep equal, but how can you do that against so mighty a nation and a population nearly three times your own?'[86] He stood in awe, telling Smuts at Chequers that weekend, as they dined off plovers' eggs and the finest South African brandy, that 'there was no greater exhibition of power in history than that of the American army fighting the battle of the Ardennes with its left hand, and advancing from island to island towards Japan with its right.'[87] (His relationship with Smuts was as close and confidential as ever. 'Smuts and I are like two old love-birds moulting together on a perch,' he told George Heaton Nicholls, the South African High Commissioner in London, 'but still able to peck.')[88]

'What is now Hitler's best course?' Churchill asked a lunch party at Chequers in early April, suggesting that the Führer might try to fly to Britain like Rudolf Hess and say, 'I am responsible; wreak your vengeance on me but spare my people.'[89] At this, the Duchess of Marlborough retorted that 'In such a case the only course would be to take him back and drop him by parachute over Germany.' In an attempt to use history as a guide to present action in Italy and Greece, Churchill told the Foreign Office that the war would never have come about had it not been for the way the Habsburgs and Hohenzollerns had been forced off their thrones 'under American and modernising pressure'. By 'making these vacuums we gave the opening for the Hitlerite monster to crawl out of its sewer on to the vacant thrones. No doubt these views are very unfashionable.'[90] They were indeed, but that did not necessarily make them wrong.

Churchill had hoped that his Coalition Government might continue until victory was won over Japan, but by 9 April he had to accept that Labour did not want to stay in it, and that despite his earlier promise to avoid one, there would have to be a general election after the German surrender. The return to party politics did not attract him, and Clementine urged him not to fight the election at all. 'You shouldn't use your great prestige to get them in again,' she said of the Tories. 'They don't deserve it.'[91] That was not in Churchill's fighting nature, and besides, for all the power he wielded, he had not won a personal mandate of his own for the premiership in a general election.

Franklin D. Roosevelt died at Warm Springs, Georgia, on Thursday, 12 April 1945. 'He was very distressed,' Colville wrote of Churchill. 'It is a bad moment for the removal of America's one great international figure.'[92] Churchill's grief was plain to see the next morning. 'I am much weakened in every way by this loss,' he told Captain Pim.[93] All the disagreements he had had with the President over the years were legitimate ones over strategy and policy, but their personal friendship was on a higher plane, and at key moments in the war – the quarter-million rifles in 1940, the mid-Atlantic patrols, the fifty destroyers, Lend-Lease, the post-Tobruk Sherman tanks, postponing Operation Roundup and championing Operation Torch, the Mediterranean strategy, among many others – Roosevelt had helped Britain enormously. 'He was a great friend to us,' Churchill told Walter Thompson. 'He gave us immeasurable help at a time when we most needed it.'[94]

'F.D.R.'s death is a terrible blow for us,' Eden wrote in his diary, 'Truman knows nothing and [the incoming Secretary of State James F.] Byrnes no more.'[95] Churchill had not met the new President, Harry S. Truman, and he later wrote of a 'deadly hiatus which existed between the fading of President Roosevelt's strength and the growth of President Truman's grip of the vast world problem. In this melancholy void, one President could not act and the other could not know.'[96] As the European war approached its end, large numbers of important decisions needed to be taken quickly, and with several important ministers out of the country the King and Lascelles persuaded Churchill not to fly over to New York for Roosevelt's funeral, however useful it might have been to make personal contact with Truman. Churchill made the decision to send Eden instead only three-quarters of an hour before his own scheduled departure. 'It would have been a great solace to me to be present at Franklin's funeral,' he wrote to Harry Hopkins, 'but everyone here thought my duty next week lay at home.'[97]

A memorial service was held at St Paul's Cathedral on 17 April. Chips Channon noted that Gil Winant* escorted Churchill, who was in tears, to the door. 'Turning back towards St Paul's,' Channon wrote, 'we saw Winston standing bare-headed, framed between two columns of the portico and he was sobbing as the shaft of sunlight fell on his face and the cameras clicked.'[98] In his emotional eulogy in the Commons afterwards,

* Winant was not long to outlive Roosevelt; he committed suicide while depressed and in debt in November 1947, aged only fifty-eight.

Churchill quoted Longfellow's lines 'Sail on, O ship of state,' and described Lend-Lease as 'the most unselfish and unsordid financial act of any country in all history'.[99] Perhaps with more self-reference, he added,

> What an enviable death was his! He had brought his country through the worst of its perils and the heaviest of its toils. Victory had cast its sure and steady beam upon him. In the days of peace he had broadened and stabilized the foundations of American life and union. In war he had raised the strength, might and glory of the great Republic to a height never attained by any nation in history . . . For us, it remains only to say that in Franklin Roosevelt there died the greatest American friend we have ever known, and the greatest champion of freedom who has ever brought help and comfort from the new world to the old.[100]

On 21 April, with his mortar board not quite on straight, Churchill conferred honorary degrees on Ernest Bevin and A. V. Alexander at Bristol University. He spoke of his faith in the British people, a faith that was an essential part of why he had always believed Britain would win the war, even if for the first two years he had not known precisely how. 'We have our mistakes, our weaknesses and failings,' he said, 'but in the fight which this Island race has made, had it not been the toughest of the tough, if the spirit of freedom which burns in the British breast had not been a pure, dazzling, inextinguishable flame, we might not yet have been near the end of this war.'[101] Martin noted that very unusually this speech was made impromptu. Despite entire streets being more or less destroyed in Bristol, Churchill could report to Clementine, a 'Terrific crowd and joyous reception.'[102] On St George's Day, the 23rd, he gave a speech about the English people in the Members' Dining Room of the Commons. 'Some people say that our extraordinary self-suppression, bashfulness, and reticence is the reason why we do not always figure in the forefront of triumphant declarations,' he said, 'but we nearly always get things settled the way we want.'[103] That same day he returned to his old hobby horse of the pronunciation of foreign place-names. 'I do not consider that names that have been familiar for generations in England should be altered to study the whims of foreigners living in those parts,' he minuted to the Foreign Office. 'Constantinople should never be abandoned, though for stupid people Istanbul may be written in brackets after it . . . Bad luck always pursues people who change the names of their cities . . . If we do not make a stand . . . the B.B.C. will be pronouncing Paris "Paree". Foreign names were made for Englishmen, not Englishmen for foreign names. I date this minute from St George's Day.'[104]

*

When the American and Russian armies met at Torgau on the Elbe on 25 April, Berlin was already surrounded by the Red Army, and reports and photographs of Buchenwald and Belsen concentration camps were horrifying the world. That day, a message arrived from Heinrich Himmler via Count Bernadotte, a cousin of the King of Sweden, offering to surrender all the troops in northern Germany to the Western Allies on terms short of unconditional surrender. It also stated that Hitler was 'moribund with cerebral haemorrhage', which he was not.[105] Churchill immediately summoned the Cabinet and Chiefs of Staff, declined the offer and informed Stalin. He nonetheless said that it showed 'They are done.'*

Mussolini was captured by partisans and shot on the shores of Lake Como on 28 April, and on 30 April Adolf Hitler committed suicide and his corpse was burned in the courtyard of the Reich Chancellery. When the German radio announced that Hitler had died 'fighting with his last breath against Bolshevism', Churchill said, 'Well, I must say I think he was perfectly right to die like that.'[106] Beaverbrook merely said 'he obviously did not'.

On the afternoon of 1 May, the Chamber of the House of Commons was full, expecting a victory announcement from Churchill, but all he did at that stage was to state, 'I have no special statement to make about the war position in Europe, except that it is definitely more satisfactory than it was this time five years ago.'[107] On 2 May, he could finally announce the unconditional surrender to Field Marshal Alexander of German forces in Italy, but other developments were looking ominous. The Soviets had unilaterally established a puppet government in Vienna, and pressure was expected to be exerted on Turkey. Yugoslav radio announced that Tito had taken Trieste from the Italians, supported by Russia (although this turned out to be false; Alexander had won the race there). The Americans were in de facto occupation of large parts of Germany, and Montgomery held Hamburg and Lübeck. Churchill asked Clementine to 'express to Stalin personally my cordial feelings and my resolve and confidence that a complete understanding between the English-speaking world and Russia will be achieved and maintained for many years, as this is the only hope of the world.'[108] When she presented Stalin with a gold fountain pen as a gift from Churchill, he ungraciously replied, 'I only write with a pencil.'[109]

'P.M. very tired, very busy, but in marvellous good-humoured form,'

* As so often, these great events were accompanied on the same day by something incredibly mundane, in this case his minute to Duncan Sandys, the Minister of Works, saying, 'Great harm is being caused to the grass in St James's Park by the failure of the great public to keep to the gravel paths,' and asking him to put up better notices (CAC CHUR 20/209).

Marian Holmes noted in her diary on 3 May. 'When saying goodnight to me, he grinned and said, "It's nice to be winning, isn't it?" '[110] The good news continued to flood in. All German forces in Holland surrendered to Montgomery on 4 May, and the Americans reached Linz on the 5th, as Eisenhower reported that all German troops were now on the verge of surrender. But as Churchill told Clementine that day, 'I need scarcely tell you that beneath these triumphs lie poisonous politics and deadly international rivalries.'[111] He asked her to come home, and not to delay beyond the 8th, now scheduled for the British and American Victory-in-Europe Day, though the Russians held theirs up until the next day.[112] There were rumours of a Russian parachute assault to liberate Denmark before Montgomery and capture the Kattegat, the key to the Baltic. They, too, were false – but an indication of how fast trust was disappearing.[113]

When Churchill awoke on Monday, 7 May, Captain Pim brought him news that Germany's overall formal surrender had been signed by the German general Alfred Jodl at 2.41 that morning at Eisenhower's headquarters. The war would officially end at midnight on Tuesday, 8 May. Churchill read the telegram, initialled it and handed it back, 'recalling that for three or four years Pim had generally brought him bad news but now he had redeemed himself by bringing the greatest and most welcome news of the war'.[114]

Tuesday, 8 May 1945 was declared a public holiday. Churchill worked in bed all morning. As he was about to leave No. 10 for the Palace, he spotted his cook, Georgina Landemare, who had come up from the kitchen to watch the celebrations. He broke away from his entourage milling around him, went over and shook her hand and thanked her for having looked after him so well through those years. After lunch with the King he returned to No. 10. Just as he was about to make the victory broadcast in the Cabinet Room at 3 p.m., he blew his nose with what Marian Holmes described as 'a terrific trumpet', and because it was a sunny day asked for the blinds to be pulled down.[115]

Churchill began the broadcast by telling the British people that Jodl had signed an unconditional surrender, and that 'The German war is therefore at an end.' The cheering in Trafalgar Square and Parliament Square could be heard in the Cabinet Room. He spoke of how after Russia and America had entered the conflict in 1941, 'Finally almost the whole world was combined against the evil-doers, who are now prostrate before us.' Harold Nicolson, who was in Parliament Square, noted that 'the crowd gasped' at the phrase. 'We may allow ourselves a brief period of rejoicing,' Churchill continued, 'but let us not forget for a moment the toil and efforts that lie ahead. Japan, with all her treachery and greed, remains unsubdued. The injury she has inflicted on Great Britain, the United States, and other countries, and her detestable cruelties, call for justice and retribution. We must now devote all our strength and resources to the completion of our task, both at home and abroad. Advance, Britannia! Long live the cause of freedom! God save the King!'[116] Watching him in the Cabinet Room, Holmes noticed that Churchill's voice broke slightly with emotion as he said the last line.

Churchill's open car could only just get from the back gate of Downing Street to the Houses of Parliament because of the huge crowd mobbing it all the way. The MPs in the Chamber were scarcely less excited than the crowd outside. Everyone (except for Ernest Millington, the new Common Wealth Party Member for Chelmsford) rose and cheered and waved handkerchiefs and order papers.[117] Churchill gave them the same speech, which most Members had already heard relayed in Parliament Square on loudspeaker vans. He then thanked the House for all its 'noble support' of him for the past five years – even though its support had in fact often been grudging, lukewarm and highly conditional.[118] He proposed that the House should go to St Margaret's Church across the road and give thanks for the victory, as it had after the Great War. There, the Speaker read out the names of the twenty-one MPs who had died during the war, including Churchill's friends Ronald Cartland and Victor Cazalet. Back in the Commons, a little boy dashed out from the crowd cheering in the Central Lobby and asked, 'Please, sir, may I have your autograph?' Churchill took a long time getting out his glasses and wiping them, then he signed the album, ruffled the boy's hair and said, 'That will remind you of a glorious day.'[119]

At 4.30 p.m. Churchill joined the Chiefs of Staff and the War Cabinet at Buckingham Palace. He went out on to the balcony with the King and Queen and the two princesses to be cheered by the vast populace that packed the Mall in one of eight separate appearances that the Royal Family made that day in response to demands from the crowds. Brooke pointed out in his diary, 'PM was very late as he insisted on coming in an open car!'[120] Churchill then made his way to the Home Office, where he went on to another balcony with the Chiefs of Staff and the War Cabinet, cheered by an enormous crowd stretching from the War Office to Parliament Square.[121] Later that evening, he spoke from the balcony of the Ministry of Health which overlooked Parliament Street and Whitehall. 'This is your victory,' he began, and the crowd roared back, 'No – it's yours!' He then said, 'It is the victory of the cause of freedom in every land. In all our long history we have never seen a greater day than this. Everyone, man or woman, has done their best. Everyone has tried. Neither the long years, nor the dangers, nor the fierce attacks of the enemy, have in any way weakened the independent resolve of the British nation. God bless you all.'[122]

After Churchill had dined at the Annexe with his family and Lord Camrose, the crowd in Parliament Street and Whitehall was demanding another speech from him, so at 10.30 p.m. he went back out on to the Ministry of Health balcony and, employing an almost pantomime manner, he reminded them of the long and perilous year between Dunkirk in 1940 and Hitler's invasion of Russia in 1941. 'There we stood, alone,' he said. 'Did anyone want to give in?' The crowd roared back 'No!' 'Were we downhearted?' 'No!' they cried in response. 'Now we have emerged from one deadly struggle – a terrible foe has been cast on the ground and awaits our judgement and our mercy.'[123]

The next day was another public holiday. Clementine – who was still touring Russia – urged Churchill to ensure that the public rejoicing continued on to Russia's V-E Day. After visiting the American, Soviet and French embassies, Churchill returned to the Ministry of Health balcony and led the communal singing of 'Rule, Britannia'. 'You never let the men at the front down,' he told the crowd.

> No one ever asked for peace because London was suffering. London, like a great rhinoceros, a great hippopotamus, saying: 'Let them do their worst. London can take it.' London could take anything. My heart goes out to the Cockneys. Any visitors we may happen to have here today – and many great nations are represented here, by all those who have borne arms with us in the struggle – they echo what I say when I say 'Good Old London!' . . . I return my hearty thanks to you for never having failed in the long, monotonous days and in the long nights black as hell. God bless you all. May you long remain as citizens of a great and splendid city . . . May you long remain as the heart of the British Empire.[124]

His thoughts at that moment of triumphal apogee, the greatest day of his long life, were of the Empire to which he had dedicated himself, the most powerful and constant love of his political career.

Churchill delivered another powerful victory broadcast on 13 May that gave his listeners an overview of the war, celebrating the bravery of the British people and their allies.* He did, however, want to hold up the irresponsible actions of the Irish Republic's leadership for public obloquy.

* Dictating an early draft of the broadcast, he put the lighted end of the cigar in his mouth. There followed 'an uproar of spitting and spluttering', but he assured those around him he had not burned his tongue. He was even more lachrymose than usual that day, reciting Tennyson 'with tears flowing down his face', and telling Holmes that 'Death was the only democratic institution – it comes to everyone.' (Marian Holmes's Diaries p. 12.)

'Owing to the actions of Mr de Valera,' Churchill said, 'the approaches which the Southern Irish ports and airfields could so easily have guarded were closed by the hostile aircraft and U-boats. This was, indeed, a deadly moment in our life and had it not been for the loyalty and friendship of Northern Ireland, we should have been forced to come to close quarters with Mr de Valera, or perish forever from the Earth.'[125] Instead of having to invade the Irish Republic, he said, 'We left the de Valera government to frolic with the Germans and later with the Japanese representatives to their hearts' content.' One of the worst examples of such 'frolicking' had come only days before Churchill's speech, when de Valera had crossed Dublin to visit the German Legation in order to sign the book of condolence on the death of Adolf Hitler, a truly extraordinary act in which, as the *New Statesman* wrote at the time, 'we can see the degradation of civilized beliefs and standards which made Hitler and his Nazi regime possible.' Churchill added, 'I can only pray that in years which I shall not see, the shame will be forgotten and the glories will endure, and that the people of the British Isles, as of the British Commonwealth of Nations, will walk together in mutual comprehension and forgiveness.'[126] He wept once again when dictating the words 'in years which I shall not see'.[127]*

The end of the war in Europe left Churchill exhausted. John Peck, the only one of his private secretaries to serve through the whole of his wartime premiership, noted years later, 'It is difficult to describe or imagine the loneliness of someone in Winston Churchill's position with the burden of responsibility that he carried and the knowledge that however much he shared or delegated it, the ultimate decisions were his.'[128] By May 1945, although he kept up a display of vigour in public, that weight of responsibility was visibly wearying him, and signs of exhaustion were evident to those closest to him.† 'The P.M. looks tired and has to fight for the energy to deal with the problems confronting him,' Colville noted. With huge amounts of correspondence needing his attention, almost more than in wartime, Churchill told Colville 'that he doubted if he had the strength to carry on'.[129] He particularly felt 'overpowered' at the prospect of another

* The speech was criticized for making no reference to Bomber Command, and, because his war memoirs did not cover the strategic bombing offensive in very great detail either, because Bomber Harris was the only senior commander not to receive a peerage and because no special medal was struck for the bombing campaign, it has been assumed that Churchill deliberately downplayed Bomber Command's role out of a sense of guilt for the destruction it had wrought on the Germans on his orders. Churchill did award Harris a baronetcy in 1953, but many thought that too little, too late.

† On 30 April, Peck had noticed that Churchill had dropped lighted cigar ash on to his bed-jacket, from which great puffs of smoke rose from the collar. 'Excuse me, sir,' said Peck, 'you are on fire. May I put you out?' 'Yes, do,' replied the Prime Minister. (Marian Holmes's Diaries p. 21.)

Big Three meeting, now scheduled for Potsdam in July, and 'weighed down by the responsibility and uncertainty'.[130] He told the other party leaders – Attlee, Sinclair and the National Liberal leader, Ernest Brown – that he would like them to stay in the Coalition until after Japan had been defeated, but if not there would have to be an election sooner rather than later, as the Government could not go on in 'an atmosphere of faction and quasi-electioneering'.

On 18 May, Attlee called from the Labour Party's Conference at Blackpool to say that the Coalition had to end forthwith. Churchill wrote a letter to the King 'for the archives' on 22 May, saying that he would need to form a purely Conservative government* until the general election now scheduled for 5 July.[131] Attlee had spotted how weak the Conservatives were in the country, despite the popularity of their leader. In January and February 1944 they had lost two by-elections to the Common Wealth and Independent Labour parties, which 'caused a pall of the blackest gloom to fall on the P.M. who is personally afflicted by this emphatic blow to the Government', recorded Colville.[132] Harold Nicolson – who thought Churchill might have become an electoral liability rather than an asset – found graffiti stating 'Winston Churchill is a bastard' in the railway station lavatory in Blackheath, and was told by an RAF wing commander, 'The tide has turned. We find it everywhere.' Nicolson put the phenomenon down to human nature. 'Once the open sea is reached,' he wrote, 'we forget how we clung to the pilot in the storm.'[133] In April 1945 the Conservatives suffered a smashing by-election defeat at Chelmsford, where the left-wing Common Wealth Party candidate again won and the Tory vote fell from over 70 per cent in the 1935 election to 42 per cent. Apart from Churchill himself the Tories had nothing genuinely popular to offer.

'An iron curtain is drawn down upon their front,' Churchill wrote to Truman of the Soviets on 12 May, in his first use of that phrase. 'We do not know what is going on behind.'[134] Were the United States to withdraw, he warned, 'a broad band of many hundreds of miles of Russian-occupied territory will isolate us from Poland ... it would be open to the Russians in a very short time to advance if they chose, to the waters of the North Sea and the Atlantic.' In fact the Russians abided by the terms that Molotov had agreed in the European Advisory Commission, which had delineated the limits of the Red Army's advance many months earlier. Churchill did not invent the term Iron Curtain, which had been around since 1918 and had appeared in a book Philip Snowden's wife Dame Ethel Snowden wrote

* Known as the Caretaker Government.

about Bolshevism in 1920, but he stored the evocative phrase away in his extraordinarily capacious memory for a quarter of a century, before deploying it to maximum effect in 1946.

On 22 May, Churchill received a memorandum marked Top Secret (in red, underlined capital letters) from the Joint Planning Staff of the War Cabinet. They concluded that if the United States were to remain completely concentrated on the Pacific War, the Soviets could seize western Europe with ease, and pose a threat to Britain – which would find herself in much the same situation as she had been in 1940, dependent on air and sea forces to repel an invasion, except this time the enemy would have more rockets than the Germans and even more men.[135] To protect against such an outcome, Churchill ordered the authors of the report (but not the Services ministry staff, as it was considered too sensitive) to compile a memorandum on what it thought might happen if the British Empire, the United States and the Polish and German armies had to go to war against a Russo-Japanese alliance in July 1945, in order to impose upon Russia 'a square deal for Poland'.[136]

The whole scenario – aptly codenamed Operation Unthinkable – was analysed in a detailed report on 8 June, complete with annexes including maps and opposing force sizes. It pointed out that the Russians outnumbered the Western Allies by three to one in Europe, and then examined the effect of war there, and in the Middle East, India and the Far East. The study concluded that it would be a 'long and costly' war, in which it was 'extremely doubtful whether we could achieve a limited and quick success'.[137] The Operation Unthinkable documents do not imply that Churchill was an inveterate anti-Communist warmonger, but show that he was preparing for every eventuality, however unlikely or unwelcome. They also underline how important it was for the West that the atomic bomb should actually work.

Churchill resigned as Coalition prime minister at noon on Wednesday, 23 May. He then went back to the Palace four hours later to be asked by the King to form a Conservative government. The reason that the 'last believer in the Divine Right of Kings', as Clementine described him, did not save himself the second journey was that he was anxious to demonstrate the somewhat arcane constitutional point that it was up to the King to choose for whom to send. The King used the second visit to offer Churchill the Order of the Garter again, which he refused again, this time on the grounds that there was now an election pending. At a victory party for all the Coalition ministers, tears poured down Churchill's cheeks as he told them that 'the light of history would shine on all their helmets'.[138] (Another deliberately atavistic military phrase; ministers wore hats.)

In his Caretaker Government, Churchill appointed Leslie Hore-Belisha, then an Independent MP, as minister of national insurance, despite Hore-Belisha's censure of him in 1942 – another prime example of Churchillian magnanimity. Bracken turned down the Board of Trade after a 'good old row' with Churchill over trade policy, and became first lord of the Admiralty instead. ('I loathe these scenes,' wrote Eden. 'They are a hideous waste of time and after my father's rages* these storms only bore me.')[139] The Tory MP Thelma Cazalet-Keir had led the rebellion over equal pay for women teachers in March 1944, almost the only Commons defeat the Government suffered in the whole war, but again magnanimously that did not prevent Churchill from offering her the post of parliamentary secretary to the Minister of Education. 'Thank you so much, darling,' she replied. 'That would be wonderful.'[140]

On 28 May, when Truman's special adviser Joseph Davies visited London to suggest to Eden that the President wanted to meet Stalin privately before the coming Potsdam Conference, Churchill set out succinctly the key differences between the United States' wartime allies and said it would be 'wounding' to Britain to be excluded from Truman's first meeting with Stalin. 'The Soviet Government have a different philosophy, namely Communism, and use to the full the methods of police government which they are applying in every State which has fallen a victim to their liberating arms,' he wrote.

> The Prime Minister cannot readily bring himself to accept the idea that the position of the United States is that Britain and Soviet Russia are just two foreign Powers, six of one and half a dozen of the other, with whom the troubles of the late war have to be adjusted. Except insofar as force is concerned, there is no equality between right and wrong. The great causes and principles for which Britain and the United States have suffered and triumphed are not mere matters of the balance of power. They in fact involve the salvation of the world.[141]

Although the Soviet Union suffered over 90 per cent of the casualties of the Big Three Powers, Churchill did not want the Americans to behave as if Stalin's totalitarian dictatorship had some sort of moral equivalency with the Western democracies. Truman nonetheless went ahead and met Stalin privately.

* Sir William Eden, the 7th Baronet, had once thrown a barometer down the front steps of his country house on a rainy day, when it had predicted fine weather for a hunt meet, shouting 'See for yourself, you fool!'

Churchill's preoccupation with the brutality of Stalin's new regimes in eastern Europe, and his habits in talking about the Nazis, spilled over unfortunately into his election rhetoric. Broadcasting from the small study at Chequers on 4 June, he told the country, 'No Socialist Government conducting the entire life and industry of the country could afford to allow free, sharp, or violently worded expressions of public discontent. They would have to fall back on some form of Gestapo, no doubt very humanely directed in the first instance. And this would nip opinion in the bud; it would stop criticism as it reared its head, and it would gather all the power to the supreme party and the party leaders, rising like stately pinnacles above their vast bureaucracies of Civil servants, no longer servants and no longer civil.'[142] Equating the mild-mannered Clement Attlee who had served Churchill loyally and well throughout the Coalition Government, for much of it as his deputy, to the Gestapo was clearly absurd, and it cost the Conservatives votes. People assumed that Beaverbrook or Bracken had had a hand in inserting the phrase, but they had not. The original copy of the speech, which Colville donated to Harrow School, was heavily altered by Churchill with lots of additions in the margin, but not the disastrous line about the Gestapo.[143] Clementine had asked him to cut the line, but he had recently read Friedrich von Hayek's book *The Road to Serfdom*, and he left it in.[144] Colville sat in the room during the speech, and 'was amused to note that his gestures to the microphone were as emphatic as those he uses in a political speech to a large audience and far more than those he employs in ordinary conversation . . . For the first time he was speaking against the clock which made him hurry unduly.'[145] Churchill told Charles Eade the next month that the time would come when the speech 'would be recognised as one of the greatest he had ever delivered', but that has not happened yet.[146]

Many historians today believe that the Gestapo remark made little difference to the outcome of the election, and that most Britons were perfectly capable of differentiating between Churchill the great wartime Prime Minister whom they mobbed at election meetings up and down the country, and Churchill the Tory Party leader against whom they voted with perfect equanimity. Marie Belloc Lowndes believed that working people would vote Labour for much the same reasons as in the past. To her mind it had nothing to do with Churchill and everything to do with 'bitterness at this Government's record as to housing, coal, and the very high cost of living'.[147]

Since his Epping constituency had been split into two, Woodford and Epping, Churchill stood as the Conservative and National candidate for Woodford. He told his constituents, 'I can say with heartfelt gratitude that, without your unswerving support during the eleven years I was in the political wilderness, I should not have been in a position to be called upon to assume the supreme responsibility for guiding our country at the moment of its mortal danger.'[148] The dangers posed by Thornton-Kemsley and his supporters in Chigwell, Nazeing and elsewhere were generously forgotten. 'I feel that my faculties and energies are as good as they have ever been,' he wrote. 'Therefore unless relieved by the nation, I cannot shrink from the tasks which have devolved upon me. The war itself is not finished.'[149]

At lunch with the King on 20 June, Churchill said he was convinced that 'all the young men and women in the Services will vote against him.'[150] He was largely right: the three-million-strong Service vote went solidly for Labour, in the hope of getting the welfare state that the Beveridge Report had promised in 1943. Labour offered national insurance, massive housebuilding, family allowances, nationalization and a chance to vote against the Chamberlainite MPs who had supported appeasement. At his birthday party in Teheran in 1943, in one of his toasts, Churchill had said 'England is getting pinker,' and it was true.[151] Labour was more in tune with the wartime ethos of equality and 'fair shares'. Its manifesto had wide appeal, and its electoral machinery was no longer inferior to the Tories'. Its leaders – such as Attlee, Bevin, Dalton, Cripps and Morrison – were also well known to the electorate from their important wartime roles, and were deservedly trusted by them.

Yet when Churchill spoke to large enthusiastic crowds at Leeds, Bradford, Preston, Glasgow and Edinburgh, he convinced himself that he would win, even though, as Colville sagely pointed out, it was a parliamentary rather than presidential contest. Beaverbrook, Conservative Central Office and most commentators were predicting a hundred-seat Tory majority. Only Bracken thought the Tories would lose. By 4 July, the day before polling, Churchill told Brooke that his electioneering tours had left him more tired than at any time since his prison escape in the Boer War.[152]

After the votes had been cast on 5 July, and at the start of a three-week process of collecting the Services' ballot papers from around the world, Churchill went for a painting holiday in the Pyrenees near Hendaye. 'The Prime Minister floated, like a benevolent hippo, in the middle of a large circle of protective French policemen who had duly donned bathing suits for the purpose,' wrote Colville.[153] That did not prevent a French countess who had been a notorious collaborator from trying to swim out to speak to him. (She was intercepted by swimming detectives.) Before Churchill left, he asked Truman to telegraph him the results of the plutonium atomic tests at Alamogordo in New Mexico: 'Let me know whether it is a flop or a plop.'[154] He had already given his consent to the Americans to use the atomic bomb against Japan if the tests proved successful. The following May he discussed the morality of the decision with William Mackenzie King, telling him 'that he would have to account to God as he had to his own conscience for the decision made which involved killing women and children and in such numbers'.[155] He pointed out that without the Bomb the war could have gone on another year, leading to even greater numbers being killed, and with 'a breaking down of civilization bit by bit'. In what he said was 'a universe governed by moral laws of justice and right', he believed he 'had done what was right'.

Churchill flew from Bordeaux to Berlin on 15 July for the Potsdam Conference (codenamed Terminal). Touring the ruins of Hitler's Reich Chancellery, he was recognized by a crowd of Germans. Except for one old man who shook his head disapprovingly, all the rest cheered him. 'My hate had died with their surrender and I was much moved by their demonstrations,' wrote Churchill later, 'and also by their haggard looks and threadbare clothes.'[156] He visited Hitler's office in the main building and the room in which the Führer had shot himself in the bunker below. On a table in Eva Braun's room there was still a vase with a branch in it that had until recently been a spray of blossom. In his war memoirs, Churchill wrote of how he 'went down to the bottom and saw the room in which he and his mistress* had committed suicide, and when we came up again they showed us the place where his body had been burned'.[157] He had finally tracked the beast to its lair.

On 17 July, Churchill learned that the Alamogordo test had been a resounding 'plop'. A month later he told MPs that 'The eagerly awaited news . . . could leave no doubt in the minds of the very few who were informed, that we were in the presence of a new factor in human affairs, and possessed of powers which were irresistible.'[158] 'What was gunpowder?' he asked Henry Stimson a few days later. 'Trivial. What was electricity? Meaningless. This Atomic Bomb is the Second Coming in Wrath.'[159] As the Potsdam Conference opened, Truman was able to tell Stalin officially about the existence of the Bomb. Stalin showed the requisite amount of surprise, not revealing that his spies had kept him fully informed and that he was already trying to build his own. Churchill was impressed on meeting Truman, describing him as 'A man of immense determination. He takes no notice of delicate ground, he just plants his foot down firmly upon it.'[160]

* A libel on Eva Braun, who died as Frau Hitler.

The Potsdam Conference lasted from 17 July to 2 August. Churchill was allocated a villa at 25 Ringstrasse, where mosquito nets were put up in his bedroom and the nights were hot. When Tommy Lascelles's son John complained indignantly to Rowan that Churchill was flying the Royal Standard from his car, he was assured that in fact it was the pennant of the Lord Warden of the Cinque Ports. Although both Eden and Cadogan criticized him heavily at Potsdam for not engaging more, Churchill knew that he was returning to Britain on 25 July for the election results and might not be prime minister for the second half of the Conference.[161] For that reason he had brought Attlee along with him, who would be replacing him in the event of a Labour victory.

Less explicable was his remark at Potsdam to Eden about Stalin – 'I like that man' – after the Russian dictator's unconscionable behaviour over the Nazi–Soviet Pact, Katyń Massacre, Warsaw Uprising, Okulicki arrest and so on. Where was the Churchill of 1931, who had denounced Stalin's 'morning's budget of death warrants'? Or of May 1945, who had lectured Joseph Davies about the lack of moral equivalency between Communist behaviour and Western? There is no accounting for personal attraction, and his feeling did not last long. At the time, Churchill had stronger complaints about the journalists covering the conference, writing to Clementine that he was 'besieged . . . by a host of reporters who are furious at not being able to overrun us. It is impossible to conduct grave affairs except in silence and secrecy.'[162]

Churchill was wearing his siren suit and sitting in the Map Room in the Annexe with Beaverbrook and Margesson as the election results started arriving at 10 a.m. on Thursday, 26 July. The results were put up on to a screen by Captain Pim, constituency by constituency, as soon as Central Office reported them and the ticker-tape machine confirmed them. After half an hour it was clear that things were not going well. Bracken lost Paddington North early on by a huge 6,500 votes. 'My father sat at the head of the table and acknowledged the news of each result with a nod of the head, and passed no comment,' Sarah recalled. 'As it became increasingly obvious that it was a tidal wave, his natural humour reasserted itself, superficially anyhow.'[163] By noon it was clear that there was going to be a Labour landslide. 'The most depressing atmosphere I could ever have imagined,' wrote Marian Holmes that day. 'Everyone at the office was completely stunned.'[164]

Duncan Sandys lost in Norwood and Harold Macmillan in Stockton. Other ministers who lost their seats included Leo Amery, Sir Percy Grigg, Richard Law, Sir Donald Somervell the Home Secretary and several more. 'To my dying day I shall never forget the courage and forbearance you showed at that most unhappy luncheon after defeat was known,' Margesson wrote to Churchill soon afterwards. 'It was a terrific example of how to take it on the chin without flinching.'[165] When Clementine said over lunch that it could be a blessing in disguise for him, Churchill replied, 'At the moment it seems quite effectively disguised.'[166] Leslie Rowan, who saw more of Churchill that day than any other official, noted, 'No single word of condemnation passed his lips.'[167] When Moran later spoke of the people's ingratitude, Churchill replied, 'Oh, no. I wouldn't call it that. They have had a very hard time.'[168] He was however shocked that the Independent who stood against him in Woodford had received 10,488 votes, even though he himself had won 27,688.

Labour won 393 seats, the Conservatives 213, the Liberals 12 (not including Sinclair, who lost Caithness), with other parties winning the remaining twenty-two. Labour had never had an overall majority before, let alone one of 146 seats. They polled 11.99 million votes, to the Conservatives' 9.99 million, the Liberals' 2.25 million and the Communist Party's 102,800. The Tory share of the popular vote, at 39.8 per cent, was nothing like as disastrous as the Party's small number of seats implied. At 4 p.m. Churchill saw Lascelles at the Annexe. 'He did not seem depressed,' Lascelles wrote, 'nor did he talk so. He attributed his defeat to the people's reaction to their sufferings of the past five years – they have endured all the horrors and discomforts of war, and, automatically, they have vented it on the government that has been in power throughout the period of their discomfort.'[169] When Lascelles gave him a message from the King saying how much he would miss him, Churchill became 'emotional'. He wrote to Attlee to say, 'I wish you all success in the heavy burden you are about to assume,' prompting the keen grammarian Lascelles to note that he meant 'success in the bearing of the heavy burden'.[170]

Churchill went to the Palace to resign that evening. 'I saw Winston at 7 p.m. and it was a very sad meeting,' the King noted. 'I told him I thought the people were very ungrateful after the way they had been led in the war. He was very calm and said that with the majority the socialists had over the other parties and with careful management they could remain in power for years.'[171] Churchill refused the King's third offer of the Order of the Garter, supposedly saying afterwards, 'Why should I accept the Order of the Garter from His Majesty when the people have just given me the order of the boot?'[172] When he got back to the Annexe, Churchill thanked everyone who had worked for him in the Map Room – Pim was to receive a knighthood in his resignation honours list – and he told Lawrence Burgis, 'I shall not be idle. I shall write, I shall speak on the wireless and I shall still be an MP, although I shall never return to Number Ten.'[173] The next day, as he prepared to move out of Downing Street, he told Anthony Eden in the Cabinet Room, 'Thirty years of my life have been passed in this room. I shall never sit in it again. You will, but I shall not.'[174]

'I must confess I found the event of Thursday rather odd and queer,' Churchill perceptively wrote to Hugh Cecil, now Lord Quickswood, three days after the defeat, 'especially after the wonderful welcomes I had received from all classes. There was something pent up in the British people after twenty years which required relief. It is like 1906 all over again.'[175] The election result came as a great shock to other people too, especially foreigners. One of Pamela Churchill's current lovers, Major-General Frederick Lewis Anderson, the commander of the US Eighth Air Force, wrote to her, 'I was so shocked by the news of Winston's defeat. My heart turned over and I felt a great injustice had been done to a very personal friend.'[176] When Averell Harriman tried to console Churchill by saying that under the proportional representation system he would still have been prime minister, of a Conservative–Liberal coalition, he indignantly rejected the idea, saying, 'I will fight against the evils of proportional representation with all my strength,' and explained that democracy could succeed only if the people knew which party was accountable and responsible for the decisions taken in government.[177]

On his last weekend at Chequers, Sarah noticed that Churchill's keys that opened the Government dispatch boxes, which had been on his watch chain since 1939, were no longer there. 'I miss the boxes,' he told her. In the Chequers visitors' book, at the bottom of the page for 30 July 1945, are the signatures 'Clementine S. Churchill' and 'Winston S. Churchill'. Below, in Churchill's handwriting, is the single word 'Finis'.

# 32
# Opposition August 1945–October 1951

*The misery of the whole world appals me and I fear increasingly that new struggles may arise out of those we are successfully ending.*

Churchill to Clementine, February 1945[1]

*Socialism is the philosophy of failure, the creed of ignorance, and the gospel of envy.*

Churchill, Perth, May 1948[2]

Churchill once asked his actress daughter Sarah, 'Do you mind when a show breaks up?' 'Oh yes, terribly,' she replied. 'So do I,' he said.[3] By 1945, he had fulfilled the task he had foreseen for himself at Harrow of saving London, but despite being seventy years old and out of office he could not bring himself to retire from politics. He had been rejected by the electorate in the only general election he had fought as Party leader and, however much he could explain it, it stung badly. He told Charles Eade that he 'could not desert the Conservative Party when it had suffered a defeat', but then he laughed and told the greater truth, that 'Politics was life blood to him.'[4] Many monuments were proposed to him after the war, and £50,000 was even raised for a 200-foot carving of his face in the White Cliffs of Dover, complete with a large cigar with a permanently lit end in red, for the safety of shipping.[5] But the monument he wanted most after the 1945 debacle was electoral victory, even if it meant disappointing Anthony Eden's hopes for another decade.

As a memento, Churchill had 136 bronze medallions of 4-inch diameter struck at his own expense by Spink & Son and gave one to each of the ministers who had served under him, as well as to the three Chiefs of Staff, Smuts, Mountbatten, Field Marshals Montgomery and Alexander, Edward

Bridges the Cabinet Secretary, Pug Ismay and William Mackenzie King,* as well as a posthumous one for Admiral Sir Dudley Pound that was given to his eldest son, a naval officer. Each medallion was engraved with the words 'Salute the Great Coalition 1940–1945'. 'It would make an excellent paperweight,' Churchill told the King, who also received one.[6]

In a way, defeat really was a blessing in disguise for Churchill. The issues now facing the Government, such as Indian independence and the retreat from Empire, demobilization, reconstruction and financial austerity, housing, and decommissioning the Sterling Area, were not ones that would have stimulated him or played to his strengths. 'The next two years will present administrative difficulties of an unprecedented character,' he told Hugh Cecil, 'and it may well be that a Labour administration will have a much better chance of solving this than we.'[7] He admitted the same thing to Marian Holmes, in a mutually tearful goodbye. 'Perhaps they can do better than me, especially on housing and coal,' he said, before thanking her for keeping secrets, flying to conferences and 'putting up with all my bad tempers'.[8]

There were other advantages to being out of office. Churchill could not have warned of the threat of Soviet Communism if he had also had to deal diplomatically with the USSR from day to day. Leaving No. 10 also allowed him to put his money worries behind him for the first time in his life. He would write *The Second World War*, his six volumes of memoirs comprising over 4,200 pages, for enormous advances, something he could never have had time to do as prime minister.

One reason that Churchill was not crushed by the election defeat was partly because he was an historian, and knew the many precedents well. His hero, Marlborough, had also been subjected to what the 1st Duke had called 'the base ingratitude of my countrymen' when Queen Anne turned to the Tories.[9] Another hero, Clemenceau, was not chosen as president in 1920, despite winning the Great War. 'When the victory was won,' Churchill had written of him in *Great Contemporaries*, 'France to foreign eyes seemed ungrateful.'[10] Back in August 1941, he had told Colville that he did 'not expect to retain his popularity if he wins the war for us: he has before him the examples of Wellington† and Disraeli‡ amongst others'.[11] The 1945 electoral defeat therefore fitted into a grand historical

* Probably for hosting the two Quebec conferences, as his Australian and New Zealand counterparts were not on the list.

† An election-losing prime minister despite having won the Battle of Waterloo.

‡ Who lost the 1880 general election despite having saved European peace at the Congress of Berlin two years earlier.

theme of successful heroic endeavour followed by expulsion from power by an ungrateful people.

Churchill also knew himself to be exhausted, although he could not publicly acknowledge it, and desperately in need of time to relax and regain his strength and energy. Over his 1,900 days as prime minister and minister of defence he had travelled 110,000 miles abroad by ship, train and plane, taking him to Cairo four times, Washington and Moscow thrice, Quebec twice, as well as Bermuda, Teheran, Casablanca, Italy, Normandy, Paris, Malta, Yalta, Athens, Belgium and Berlin. As early as August 1944 he had told Rowan, 'I've only half the life left in me these days,' and in November 1945 he admitted that had he won the election 'he might very likely have been a dead man by now.'[12] Throughout the coming years of opposition, Churchill built up his strength for another assault on the premiership, not least by taking month-long painting and writing semi-holidays in various warm climes far away from the British winters.*

Churchill undertook the duties of leader of the Opposition entirely on his own terms. 'Our leader did not often grace us with his presence,' recalled the Tory Chief Whip, James Stuart, 'but remained a law unto himself, taking part in such debates as he wished to.'[13] When Churchill was in Britain, he presided over the weekly business of the Shadow Cabinet, which was formally called the Leader's Consultative Committee and whose membership was amorphous and secret, and he also gave a fortnightly lunch to the Party leadership.[14] With a Labour majority of 146, there was little point in opposing for its own sake. To make up for not having the Civil Service to supply detailed expert knowledge, Rab Butler set up a very efficient research department at the Conservative Central Office, which featured Iain Macleod, Reginald Maudling, Enoch Powell

* The Churchills' first move out of No. 10 and Chequers was to Claridge's Hotel while they looked for a London residence. Waiting for his car to arrive one evening, he recited to the doorman a refrain from the old Tivoli Music Hall song:

> I've been to the North Pole,
> I've been to the South Pole,
> The East Pole, the West Pole,
> And every other kind of pole,
> The barber's pole,
> The greasy pole,
> And now I'm fairly up the pole,
> Since I got the sack
> From the Hotel Monopole.

(Churchill, *Tapestry* p. 88.) The 'greasy pole' was a reference to Disraeli's remark that to reach the premiership you had to climb to the top of the greasy pole of politics.

and others, who started to provide well-argued, factually accurate fresh thinking.

When Churchill entered the Commons, which still met in the Lords Chamber, for the first time since the election, all the Tory MPs stood up and sang 'For He's a Jolly Good Fellow'. At this, the far larger number of Labour MPs, so many that they overflowed on to the Opposition benches all the way up to the first gangway, leaped up and sang 'The Red Flag'. 'That was the first and last time that ridiculous anthem was sung in the Chamber of the House of Lords,' noted Woodrow Wyatt, a newly elected Labour MP, in his diary, 'where previously the only thing red had been the colour of the benches. All very exhilarating.'[15]

On 6 August 1945, an atomic bomb was dropped on Hiroshima in Japan, killing over 100,000 people. 'The revelations of the secrets of nature, long mercifully withheld from Man,' read the Attlee Government's statement, drafted by Churchill before his defeat, 'should arouse the most solemn reflections in the mind and conscience of every human being capable of comprehension. We must indeed pray that these awful agencies will be made to conduce to peace among the nations and that instead of wreaking measureless havoc upon the entire globe they may become a perennial fountain of world prosperity.'[16] Three days later, another Bomb was dropped on Nagasaki, killing more than 40,000 people and forcing Japan to surrender. Churchill told the Commons that the only alternative was to have 'sacrificed a million American, and a quarter of a million British, lives'.[17]

'The decision to use the atomic bomb was taken by President Truman and myself at Potsdam,' Churchill told the Commons on 16 August, 'and we approved the military plans to unchain the dread, pent-up forces.'[18] He had understood the power of nuclear fission since 1924, and after the amount of money, time, expertise and effort that had gone into building the Bomb, it would have been unacceptable for soldiers to have died in their hundreds of thousands to salve politicians' consciences about using it. It was approved overwhelmingly by the public, and especially by the armed forces, at the time.*

Churchill did reflect upon the morality of the decision to drop the Bomb several times in later life, and not only with Mackenzie King. In July 1946 he advanced the view that in his career 'the decision to release the Atom

* In that same speech, continuing his practice of lightening sombre moods, he told the new Parliament that 'A friend of mine, an officer, was in Zagreb when the results of the late General Election came in. An old lady said to him, "Poor Mr. Churchill! I suppose now he will be shot." My friend was able to reassure her. He said the sentence might be mitigated to one of the various forms of hard labour which are always open to His Majesty's subjects' (*CS* VII p. 7215).

Bomb was perhaps the only thing which history would have serious questions to ask about . . . I may even be asked by my Maker why I used it but I shall defend myself vigorously and shall say – "Why did you release this knowledge to us when mankind was raging in furious battles?" '[19] As he had also said in the debate of 16 August 1945, 'The bomb brought peace, but men alone can keep that peace, and henceforward they will keep it under penalties which threaten the survival not only of civilization but of humanity itself.'[20]

In the Commons in mid-August 1945, Churchill criticized the Attlee Government for giving too much of German Silesia to Poland in recompense for the Polish territory ceded to Russia up to the Curzon Line. 'There are few virtues that the Poles do not possess,' he quipped, 'and there are few mistakes they have ever avoided.'[21] It is very unlikely, of course, that Churchill himself could have negotiated any better deal for the Poles at Potsdam than Attlee did, but now he was leader of the Opposition it was incumbent on him to make party political capital where he could. He also used the phrase 'iron curtain' for the first time in public, about the expulsion of millions of Germans from the new Poland: 'It is not impossible that tragedy on a prodigious scale is unfolding itself behind the iron curtain which at the moment divides Europe in twain.'[22] It was entirely in keeping with Churchill's belief in magnanimity after victory that he should have expressed concern for the welfare of the millions of Germans who were being expelled from their homes with no more than what they could carry and load on to their handcarts. He was already also denouncing the tyrannical behaviour of the Communist governments of Poland, Hungary, Yugoslavia, Romania and Bulgaria, the night-time 'knock at the door' from the secret police of those countries, prior to the disappearance of citizens.[23]

On 2 September 1945, the day that Japan formally surrendered, Churchill flew to Lake Como in Italy in Field Marshal Alexander's Dakota for a painting holiday, taking Sarah, Moran, his secretary Elizabeth Layton, two detectives and Sawyers, to stay in the Villa La Rosa, which had once been owned by a supporter of Mussolini's. Clementine was meanwhile completing the purchase of 28 Hyde Park Gate, their London residence for the rest of Churchill's life. 'I am much better in myself,' he told her, 'and am not worried about anything . . . This is the first time for very many years that I have been completely out of the world.'[24] He might not have worried about it, but the truss he was now having to wear until a two-hour operation* in June 1947, as the result of a long-delayed

* Which left him with an 8-inch scar.

re-emergence of the hernia he had suffered jumping off the Wimbornes' bridge in 1893, was certainly inconvenient.[25]

Field Marshal Alexander was also a recreational painter, and occasionally he and Churchill would paint the same scene. 'Now come here, Alex, come here,' Churchill would say, standing in front of one of the hideous paintings on the walls of the Fascist's villa, 'now really look at this, we really paint better than the bastard who painted this one.'[26] On one warm evening, looking out across the serene waters of the lake, the silence broken only by the goat-bells in the distance, Churchill told the two junior Army officers who were with him, 'Out of a life of long and varied experience, the most valuable piece of advice I could hand on to you is to know how to command the moment to remain.' One of them replied, 'That is what I am trying to do now, sir.'[27]

Churchill was so relaxed in Italy that he even gave up his afternoon naps – as it turned out, for ever. Yet he did not consider giving up politics. Of his Shadow Cabinet he wrote to Clementine, 'There will be no lack of topics to discuss when we all come together again.'[28] Yet when he got back he found that relatively few aspects of politics engaged his genuine interest – the partitions of India and Palestine, the future of Burma and atomic relations with Russia among them – and he was generally content to leave everything else to Eden, Butler, Woolton, Lyttelton and Macmillan.

Churchill kept up a constant fire against socialism and the Labour Party in Parliament, mocking the Government's rationing regime as a 'Queuetopia'. 'The inherent vice of capitalism is the unequal sharing of blessings,' he said in a debate in October. 'The inherent virtue of Socialism is the equal sharing of miseries.'[29] Aneurin Bevan was a favoured target. 'I say today that unless the right honourable Gentleman changes his policy and methods and moves without the slightest delay,' he said in December of Bevan's attack on private housebuilders, 'he will be as great a curse to this country in time of peace, as he was a squalid nuisance in time of war.'[30] Asked by a reporter why Attlee did not go to Moscow to meet Stalin, Churchill replied, 'He dare not absent himself from his Cabinet at home. He knows full well that when the mouse is away the cats will play.'[31] When the Labour former Cabinet minister Wilfred Paling shouted, 'Dirty dog!' at Churchill, he received the reply, 'The right honourable Member should remember what dirty dogs do to palings.'[32] Describing Stafford Cripps, he spoke of 'that acuteness and energy of mind with which he devotes himself to so many topics injurious to the strength and welfare of the State'.[33] Constant sallies and quips such as these, as much as his stature as leader of the Opposition, meant that the Chamber always filled up whenever Churchill was on his feet.

Churchill's most celebrated witticism – especially as he (sadly) never made the remark about drinking Lady Astor's poisoned coffee were he her husband – was delivered when the Labour MP Bessie Braddock told him in 1946, 'Winston, you are drunk, and what's more you're disgustingly drunk,' and he had replied, 'Bessie my dear, you are ugly, and what's more you're disgustingly ugly. But tomorrow I shall be sober and you will still be disgustingly ugly.'[34] Mary Soames disbelieved that story on the basis that her father was never so ungallant towards women, and Churchill's detective on the evening in question confirmed that Churchill was not drunk, let alone disgustingly so, 'just tired and wobbly'.[35] Furthermore, the same joke can be found almost verbatim – swapping 'drunk' for 'crazy' – in a W. C. Fields movie, *It's a Gift*, of 1934. If it did happen, Braddock's remark was certainly a gift for Churchill, whose phonographic memory allowed him to make the most famous riposte in the entire canon.

Leaving Eden in charge of the Conservative Party, Churchill visited Cuba in February 1946, staying at the Hotel Nacional in Havana, and telling a press conference, 'In my country the people can do as they like, although it often happens that they don't like what they have done.'[36] He then went on to visit Eisenhower in Washington, where he stayed at the British Embassy, and on 26 February became a doctor of law at the University of Miami, one of sixteen such academic honours bestowed on him by universities around the world between 1926 and 1954. 'I am surprised that in my later life I should have become so experienced in taking degrees, when, as a school-boy, I was so bad at passing examinations,' he said at Miami. 'In fact one might almost say that no one ever passed so few examinations and received so many degrees.'[37] The central messages of his speech were that 'No boy or girl should ever be disheartened by lack of success in their youth, but should diligently and faithfully continue to persevere and make up for lost time,' and that 'Expert knowledge, however indispensable, is no substitute for a generous and comprehending outlook upon the human story, with all its sadness and with all its unquenchable hope.'[38]

Churchill had travelled to the United States because he had been offered an honorary degree from Westminster College in Fulton, Missouri, the President's home state. Truman's handwritten endorsement of the invitation, and the prospect of an extended journey in his company, persuaded Churchill to accept. Travelling with Truman to Jefferson City, Missouri, overnight in the *Ferdinand Magellan*, the presidential train, Churchill told Clark Clifford, one of Truman's aides, that 'There is one country where a man knows he has an unbounded future: the U.S.A., even though I deplore some of your customs . . . You stop drinking with your meals.'[39]

An indication of what it was like to work for Churchill is evident from a letter that his secretary Jo Sturdee (later the Countess of Onslow) sent to her parents from the train, saying that while she had been trying to type up his acceptance speech for the honorary degree at the Embassy, he was constantly bombarding her with 'Come along, come along. Where are all my telegrams? Hasn't anything come from England? Surely there is a newspaper I can look at. What have you done with my red pen? Tell the Ambassador I want to see him. Where's Sawyers! Haven't you opened the post yet?'[40]

Once it was typed up, Truman read the speech, and said he had no criticism or alteration to make. Instead, he said, 'Clement Attlee came to see me the other day. He struck me as a very modest man.' 'He has much to be modest about,' retorted Churchill.[41] He said it more because it was a quick and funny witticism against a political rival than because he truly meant it; in private Churchill usually deprecated criticism of Attlee, who had been instrumental in removing Chamberlain, and who had served so patriotically under him for so long. Indeed, when Freddie Birkenhead asked Churchill in March 1946 which of his former Labour colleagues he respected the most, fully expecting Churchill to say Bevin, 'Rather to my surprise, he unhesitatingly said "Attlee".'[42]

Churchill's speech at Fulton was officially entitled 'The Sinews of Peace', but was quickly called 'The Iron Curtain Speech'. 'The United States stands at this time at the pinnacle of world power,' he began, in Westminster College's large gymnasium. 'It is a solemn moment for the American Democracy. For with primacy in power is also joined an awe-inspiring accountability to the future. If you look around you, you must feel not only the sense of duty done but also you must feel anxiety lest you fall below the level of achievement.'[43] Of the United Nations, he said, 'We must make sure that its work is fruitful, that it is a reality and not a sham, that it is a force for action, and not merely a frothing of words, that it is a true temple of peace in which the shields of many nations can some day be hung up, and not merely a cockpit in a Tower of Babel.'[44] He then said he had 'come to the crux of what I have travelled here to say. Neither the sure prevention of war, nor the continuous rise of world organization will be gained without what I have called the fraternal association of the English-speaking peoples. This means a special relationship between the British Commonwealth and Empire and the United States.'[45] He wanted this to go so far as to involve 'the joint use of all Naval and Air Force bases in the possession of either country all over the world'.[46]

So far everything seemed positive, and little more than he had said at Harvard in September 1943. But then he delivered a warning just as grave, and just as prescient, as any that he made about the Nazis during the appeasement period. In words that were swiftly picked up around the globe, he came to the true crux of what he had come to say, which was more about Russia than about the English-speaking peoples. 'From Stettin in the Baltic to Trieste in the Adriatic,' he declared,

> an iron curtain has descended across the Continent. Behind that line lie all the capitals of the ancient states of Central and Eastern Europe: Warsaw, Berlin, Prague, Vienna, Budapest, Belgrade, Bucharest and Sofia, all these famous cities and the populations around them lie in what I must call the Soviet sphere, and all are subject in one form or another, not only to Soviet influence but to a very high and, in many cases, increasing measure of control from Moscow . . . The Communist parties, which were very small in all these Eastern States of Europe, have been raised to pre-eminence and power far beyond their numbers and are seeking everywhere to obtain totalitarian control. Police governments are prevailing in nearly every case, and so far, except in Czechoslovakia, there is no true democracy.[47]

'Last time I saw it all coming and cried aloud to my own fellow-countrymen and to the world, but no one paid any attention,' Churchill continued.

> Up till the year 1933 or even 1935, Germany might have been saved from the awful fate which has overtaken her and we might all have been spared the miseries Hitler let loose upon mankind. There never was a war in all history easier to prevent by timely action than the one which has just desolated such great areas of the globe. It could have been prevented in my belief without the firing of a single shot, and Germany might be powerful, prosperous and honoured to-day; but no one would listen and one by one we were all sucked into the awful whirlpool. We surely must not let that happen again.[48]

Churchill said that war was not imminent and that the Soviets did not want war, but 'What they desire is the fruits of war and the indefinite expansion of their power and doctrines.' The dangers would not be removed by appeasing Russia, he argued. 'From what I have seen of our Russian friends and Allies during the war, I am convinced that there is nothing they admire so much as strength, and there is nothing for which they have less respect than for weakness, especially military weakness.' He urged that therefore 'the old doctrine of a balance of power is unsound', and instead the United States and Britain needed to join in 'fraternal association' to defend freedom 'not only for us but for all, not only for our time, but for a century to come'.[49]

The reaction was immediate and almost unanimously denunciatory. Eleanor Roosevelt, the President's widow, pronounced herself outraged. Trygve Lie, the Secretary-General of the United Nations, told the British Ambassador to the UN that the speech had played into the hands of anti-Western elements in Moscow.[50] The Democrats in the US Congress were furious. The press, not just on the left, was overwhelmingly negative in both Britain and America, let alone elsewhere. More than a hundred Labour MPs signed a motion denouncing the speech. Eden tried to discourage Churchill from any 'further polemics with Stalin'.[51] Truman himself denied any foreknowledge of the speech, and Dean Acheson, his Under-Secretary of State, declined to attend a reception for Churchill, the invitation for which he had already accepted.[52]

Churchill was generally accused of being a reactionary warmonger who failed to appreciate the Russian sacrifices in the war, and the essentially benevolent nature of 'Uncle Joe'. Even today, revisionist historians still sometimes blame Churchill for launching the Cold War with the Iron Curtain speech, rather than pointing out that there was already one being fought, which the West was losing. Ernest Bevin, now foreign secretary, and Thomas Dewey, who was to become the Republican candidate for the presidency, were two of the very few not to repudiate Churchill, since they had reached much the same conclusions about Stalin's motives themselves.

Churchill did not mind the attacks on him, indeed while eating caviar at a *Time* magazine lunch a couple of days later he said that 'Uncle Joe' had sent him regular supplies since 1941, but that he did not expect to receive any more.[53] 'Suppose Churchill's vision had been proved wrong,' wrote Leslie Rowan in 1968, 'he might never have lived it down. But he had the courage of his convictions.'[54] As in the 1930s, the sheer level of abuse and condemnation only added to Churchill's sense of vindication when Soviet actions shortly proved him right, and his army of critics completely wrong. Unlike in the 1930s, he had much more of a reputation to lose, but that did not stop him.

Visiting Roosevelt's grave at Hyde Park on 12 March, Churchill turned away, 'eyes brimming', and as he walked from the graveside he was heard to say, 'Lord, how I loved that man' – much the same words he used to Sarah at the Pyramids during the war.[55] The difference between his old companion-in-arms and the new President was made evident on 1 August when Truman signed into law the McMahon Act, which ended access to American nuclear information by any other country, even the United

Kingdom and Canada, which had both taken part in the Manhattan Project. The nuclear partnership was over, and the Act was not amended till 1958. Churchill's failure to get either of the two Hyde Park Agreements in writing led to the massive expense of Britain having to build her own Bomb.

By August 1946, Eden was complaining to Lord Cranborne that Churchill's 'patent inclination is to go on with everything as long as he can . . . It is not so much that we disagree, though naturally we do that, as that our minds work now on quite different planes. It wasn't so in war, but it is so now.'[56] Eden's tragedy was that, for all Churchill's faults and absences and lack of preparation and often reactionary views, he was a world-historical figure and a giant on the international stage – and still a big vote-winner for the Conservative Party, which might well have been annihilated in 1945 without him. Eden was none of those things, and was also frequently seriously ill. (His ulcers were too bad to let him campaign in the 1945 general election, for example.) So although the long-time heir apparent, and most of the rest of the Tory hierarchy, wanted Churchill to retire in 1947, they could not insist upon it, and if it had become known that they were doing so, the situation would have been worse.[57] With his instinctive feel for power and prestige in politics, Churchill knew this, and seemed almost to enjoy it. When James Stuart finally did sound him out about retiring, 'He reacted violently, banging the floor with his stick.'[58] (He clearly did not appreciate that his reliance on a stick perhaps added substance to their argument.) Soon afterwards, he told his constituents that he would 'soldier on' until he had turned out the socialists.

In May, on receiving the Freedom of Westminster, Churchill had repeated his view from the 1930s that 'India is a continent as large as and more populous than Europe, and not less deeply divided by racial and religious differences than Europe. India has no more unity than Europe, except that superficial unity which has been created by our rule and guidance in the last hundred and fifty years.'[59] On 1 August he gave a public warning that Indian independence, to which the Labour Party was committed, would result in large loss of life, most probably in the north-western part of the sub-continent. He had robustly declared in November 1942 that he had 'not become the King's First Minister in order to preside over the liquidation of the British Empire', and now he could criticize from the sidelines. 'We declare ourselves ready to abandon the mighty Empire and Continent of India with all the work we have done in the last two hundred years, territory over which we possess unimpeachable sovereignty,' he told the Commons. 'The Government are, apparently, ready to leave the four hundred million Indians to fall into all the horrors of sanguinary civil war – civil war compared to which anything that could happen in Palestine would be microscopic. Wars of elephants compared with wars of mice.'[60]

'It was a cardinal mistake to entrust the government of India to the caste Hindu, Mr [Jawaharlal] Nehru,' Churchill added in the Commons in March 1947. 'He has good reason to be the most bitter enemy of any connection between India and the British Commonwealth.'[61]* Churchill had not set foot in India since Queen Victoria was on the throne, and had no alternative plan for the sub-continent beyond 'Keep Buggering On'. But he never really resiled from the words which summed up his feelings about what Labour was doing on the sub-continent, 'It is with deep grief I watch the clattering down of the British Empire with all its glories, and all the services it has rendered to mankind. I am sure that in the hour of our victory now not so long ago, we had the power to make a solution of our difficulties which would have been honourable and lasting. Many have defended Britain against her foes. None can defend her against herself.'[62]

In his Party Conference speech in October 1946, Churchill had seemed prescient about events in northern India too. The massive population transfers that took place as Britain handed over power to the successor states of India and Pakistan in August 1947 had led to the massacre of enormous numbers of Hindus, Muslims and Sikhs in the Punjab and North-West Frontier Province. He blamed the Labour Government. 'Indian unity created by British rule will swiftly perish,' he said, 'and no one can measure the misery and bloodshed which will overtake these enormous masses of humble helpless millions, or under what new power their future and destiny will lie. All this is happening every day, every hour. The great ship is sinking in the calm sea. Those who should have devoted their utmost efforts to keep her afloat have instead opened the sea-cocks.'[63] Historians still debate how many people perished during the partition of British India into India and Pakistan in late 1947: most estimate more than half a million but some think twice that, and at least sixteen million were permanently displaced.

* By 1955, he had turned 180 degrees, writing to Nehru, then prime minister of an India that had stayed in the Commonwealth, 'I hope that you will think of the phrase "The Light of Asia". It seems to me that you might be able to do what no other human being could in giving India the lead, at least in the realm of thought, throughout Asia, with the freedom and dignity of the individual as the ideal rather than the Communist Party drill book' (OB VIII p. 1094). Being Churchill, he even had a quip about such a comprehensive volte-face: 'In the course of my life I have often had to eat my words, and I must confess that I have always found it a wholesome diet' (ed. Wheeler-Bennett, *Action* p. 28).

Churchill did not propose a viable alternative, and if anything he toned his criticisms down because Pug Ismay was chief of staff to Mountbatten, the Viceroy, but he was right about the widespread misery and bloodshed that followed Mountbatten's ill-timed and under-policed partition plan. 'The slaughter of five hundred thousand human beings, and the misery of so many millions more is not an event which even the most callous and the most brutalized of beings should describe as a trifle or which should be compared to some hypothetical alternative,' Churchill said in late October 1947. 'It is not a trifle; it is a horror, which should raise grief and heart-searchings in all concerned.'[64] The next month Churchill found the appeal of the politician Sir Feroz Khan Noon, who begged the British Government for Pakistan to be allowed to buy arms to defend herself, a 'most moving document'.[65]

On 19 September 1946, Churchill made another momentous speech, this time from the splendid purple marble podium in the Great Hall of Zurich University. It picked up on a phrase from a speech of April 1944 in which he had mentioned a future United States of Europe.[66] Churchill recognized that the two greatest tragedies of his lifetime had both stemmed from Franco-German wars, and he pledged himself to building a new Franco-German amity that would be the essential first step along the road to European unity, and which he also hoped would be a counterpoise to Soviet Communism. At Zurich he used the phrase 'Let Europe arise!'[67] This was his Western European counterpart to the Fulton speech, a passionate statement in support of European unity, which still reads very well today. In his peroration, he as usual made it perfectly clear – as he always did whenever he spoke in public or private on the subject – that he did not intend Britain to join the United Europe herself: 'In all this urgent work, France and Germany must take the lead together. Great Britain, the British Commonwealth of Nations, mighty America, and I trust Soviet Russia, for then indeed all would be well, must be the friends and sponsors of the new Europe and must champion its right to live and shine.'[68]

Churchill made another emotional appeal for a united continent at an important meeting of the United Europe organization at the Albert Hall on 14 May 1947. Germany and France 'would form one major regional entity' in the new post-war world, he said. 'There is the United States with all its dependencies; there is the Soviet Union; there is the British Empire and Commonwealth; and there is Europe, with which Great Britain is profoundly blended. Here are the four main pillars of the world Temple of Peace.' He intended Britain to be, as he put it, a friend and sponsor and 'profoundly blended' with a United Europe, though not an integral part of it. He promoted the same message again when he opened the Congress of Europe at The Hague in May 1948. Gladwyn Jebb, the British representative at Brussels, realized early on that 'Churchill was himself clearly not a "European" at all. If he had had his way, Britain would have been "associated" with a Europe that would extend from Lisbon to Brest-Litovsk . . . but would never have formed part of it herself. Why the European federalists should have apparently thought at one time that he was thinking of British membership of a federal Europe I have never understood. He always made it quite clear that Britain, if he had anything to do with it, would stand aloof.'[69] Jebb was right, for as Churchill stated in a foreign policy debate on 10 December 1948,

> We are not seeking in the European movement . . . to usurp the functions of Government. I have tried to make this plain again and again to the heads of the Government. We ask for a European assembly without executive power. We hope that sentiment and culture, the forgetting of old feuds, the lowering and melting down of barriers of all kinds between countries, the growing sense of being 'a good European' – we hope that all these will be the final, eventual and irresistible solvents of the difficulties which now condemn Europe to misery. The structure of constitutions, the settlement of economic problems, the military aspects – these belong to governments. We do not trespass upon their sphere.[70]

Churchill was a constant advocate of friendship with the new, democratic Germany.* 'Where are the Germans?' he growled, glaring around the chamber of the Council of Europe Consultative Assembly in Strasbourg in 1949. (He knew perfectly well that they were about to be invited to the next meeting, but it made good theatre.) Richard Stokes, a Labour MP who had criticized him throughout the war and was now advocating friendship with Germany, asked him as they left the Smoking Room of the Commons if he had forgiven him. 'Of course I've forgiven you,' Churchill said. 'Indeed, I agree with very much that you are saying about the Germans. Very good. Such hatred that I have left in me – and it isn't much – I would rather reserve for the future than the past.' He then moved off, adding to his entourage, 'Hmm. A judicious and thrifty disposal of bile.'[71]

In a stupendous act of generosity and admiration, a small group of Churchill's closest and richest friends, led by Lord Camrose, clubbed together to

* The Nuremberg Trials of the twenty-two most prominent Nazis, which ended with the hanging of twelve of them in October 1946, led Churchill to say to Pug Ismay, 'It shows that if you get into a war, it is supremely important to win it. You and I would be in a pretty pickle if we had lost' (Ismay, *Memoirs* p. 157).

buy Chartwell for £85,000 in 1947 (around £2.55 million in today's money) and present it to the National Trust, with the proviso that Churchill and Clementine could reside there for the rest of their lives without charge. Churchill received £50,000 and the National Trust £35,000 for the property. In fact, Clementine moved out soon after Churchill's death, but it meant that his beloved house was safe, and moreover that he received a huge payment that he could spend on an increasingly aristocratic lifestyle, which already included splendid holidays and gambling at Monte Carlo, but was also soon to include horse racing. Churchill turned a summerhouse at Chartwell into a butterfly house soon after the war, stocking it with the larvae of Red Admiral, Peacock, Tortoise Shell, Clouded Yellow, Painted Lady and Vanessa butterflies. He would sit in it for hours and watch them emerge from their chrysalises, whereupon he enjoyed releasing them. 'There was a great resurgence of the butterfly population in that part of Kent,' recorded the lepidopterist Hugh Newman, 'thanks to Mr Churchill.'[72]

On 11 February 1947 Mary married Christopher Soames, an Old Etonian former Coldstream Guards officer who had won the Croix de Guerre when he was wounded in the Middle East on attachment to the Free French, and who had subsequently become assistant military attaché in Paris. It was to be a very happy marriage, but a mere twelve days after the wedding Jack Churchill died of heart disease. Churchill visited his younger brother daily during his illness, and was with him at the very end. 'I feel lonely now that he is not here,' he told Hugh Cecil, 'after sixty-seven years of brotherly love.'[73] He recalled his father telling him aged five that he had a brother, and how Jack had come to live with him in Downing Street during the war. 'He had no fear, and little pain,' Churchill told Hugh Cecil of Jack. 'Death seems very easy at the end of the road. Do you think we shall be allowed to sleep a long time? I hope so.' To Jack's son he said, 'Johnny, I will take your father's place. Come to me if you are in trouble. I will be your father.'[74] Fatherliness, its presence and absence, was always an important element in his makeup. Young Winston recalled that at Chartwell 'I would hand him the bricks while he mixed his "pug", as he called his sand and cement . . . I have little doubt that it was because of his less than happy relationship with his father that he indulged me with so much grandparental sunshine.'[75]

The Conservative Party's *Industrial Charter* pamphlet was published in May 1947, which reconciled the Tories to much of Labour's programme, including the welfare state and most of the nationalisation that had taken place. It sold 2.5 million copies, was adopted by the Party Conference in October and helped to make the Conservatives electable again. Churchill's initial reaction to the Charter was, as he told its principal author, Butler, 'I do not agree with a word of this,' yet he saw how important it was for the Party to avoid seeming reactionary.[76] Meanwhile, Lord Woolton forced through internal Party reforms designed to bring in young, able MPs in place of the elderly Chamberlainites from the 1935 intake.

'If I repeated the Fulton speech today,' Churchill told his constituents in September, 'it would be regarded as a stream of tepid platitudes.'[77] Stalin's judicial executions in the Soviet satellite states, brutal suppression of democratic parties, overturning of elections and constant aggressions were proving Churchill right, and the speech turned out to be a crucial moment in turning American public opinion towards embracing the robustly pro-democracy Truman Doctrine, backed up in the coming years by the Marshall Plan (massive US subsidies to restore economic health to western Europe), the Berlin Airlift and the creation of NATO. The Soviet subversion of Czechoslovakia into its sphere in 1948 merely added to the recognition that Churchill had been right all along.

Churchill's prescience about Communism had mirrored what he had said about Nazism, but this time he was able to halt the appeasement that might otherwise have once again become the West's default mechanism. Late in 1947, at one of Churchill's regular lunches at Hyde Park Gate for new Tory MPs, one of them asked about the atomic bomb. 'Well,' he replied, 'if the Russians did attack, I should let them come on, then I should drop some atom bombs behind – Plonk, plonk, plonk!' He jabbed his fingers on the table top hard enough to leave imprints in the cloth, adding: 'They'll never get back!'[78]

In a debate on 28 October 1947, Churchill clearly set out an almost libertarian Tory alternative to socialism, with yet another phrase that was to live on. 'Establish a basic standard for life and labour and provide the necessary basic foods for all,' he said. 'Once that is done, set the people free. Get out of the way, and let them all make the best of themselves, and win whatever prizes they can for their families and for their country . . . Only in this way will an active, independent, property-owning democracy be established.'[79] The phrase 'property-owning democracy' was thereafter used by every Tory premier from Anthony Eden to Margaret Thatcher. Fuelled by his reading of Friedrich von Hayek's book *The Road to Serfdom*, he seemed to be adopting a free-market alternative to his long-standing Tory Democrat paternalism.

On 5 November, Churchill attacked the Burma Independence Bill, and in particular the actions of U Aung San,* the Burmese nationalist leader

* Father of Aung San Suu Kyi.

who had supported the Japanese, and in Churchill's words 'raised what we might call a Quisling army to come in at the tail of the Japanese and help conquer the country for Japan. Great cruelties were perpetrated by his army. They were not very effective in fighting, but in the infliction of vengeance upon the loyal Burmese – the Burmese who were patriotically fighting with British and Indian troops to defend the soil of Burma from Japanese conquerors – great cruelties were perpetrated on those men, because they had helped us to resist the Japanese.'[80]

Replying to him was Woodrow Wyatt, who said, 'This afternoon we have had an excellent exposition from the right honourable Member for Woodford of what a genuine Tory faith in Empire really means. The Tory belief in Empire means, "Be dominated by us. If you don't like it, get out." ' After the debate, Churchill met Wyatt outside the Smoking Room. ' "That was a very good debating speech," he growled in that slow voice to which the world had thrilled during the war and which was now thrilling me,' recorded Wyatt. 'I mumbled something about hoping I had not been too rude. "I ask for no quarter," he paused. "And I bear no malice." How could one not love such a man?'[81]

'No one pretends that democracy is perfect or all-wise,' Churchill said at the second reading of the Parliament Bill on 11 November, which amended and strengthened the Commons' powers over the Lords. 'Indeed, it has been said that democracy is the worst form of Government except all those other forms that have been tried from time to time; but there is the broad feeling in our country that the people should rule, continuously rule, and that public opinion, expressed by all constitutional means, should shape, guide, and control the actions of Ministers who are their servants and not their masters.'[82] Then he obdurately reverted to the tenor of his 'Gestapo' election address, adding, 'As a free-born Englishman, what I hate is the sense of being at anybody's mercy or in anybody's power, be he Hitler or Attlee. We are approaching very near to dictatorship in this country, dictatorship that is to say – I will be quite candid with the House – without either its criminality or its efficiency.'[83] Churchill well knew, having appointed Attlee as his deputy prime minister, that that was ludicrous.

On 20 November, Princess Elizabeth married Prince Philip Mountbatten (formerly Prince Philip of Greece and Denmark) at Westminster Abbey. Churchill arrived characteristically late, which allowed him to receive a standing ovation as he walked down the nave, certainly not the only occasion at which he arrived late in order to make an entrance. At Fulton he had held up the entire motorcade until he could find a match to light his cigar, and he would even on occasion 'time' his cigar-smoking to ensure that the stubs were long enough for the photographers.[84] Such showmanship was always part of his politician's trade.

During a family dinner with Randolph and Sarah at Chartwell in late November, Sarah pointed to an empty chair at the table and asked her father, 'If you could seat anyone there, whom would it be?' She assumed he would say Marlborough, Caesar or Napoleon. 'Oh, my father, of course,' he immediately replied.[85] He told Randolph and Sarah that he had dreamed that his father had visited him in his studio, and they encouraged him to write about it. A few months later he dictated an article-cum-short-story entitled 'The Dream'.[86] It was first called 'Private Article', intended only for family distribution, and in his will he bequeathed it to Clementine.

'One foggy evening in November 1947 I was painting in my studio at the cottage down the hill at Chartwell,' it began.[87] He had been given a portrait of his father and was making a copy of it, 'though I am very shy of painting human faces'. He continued, 'I was just trying to give a twirl to his moustache when I suddenly found an odd sensation. I turned round with my palette in my hand, and there, sitting in my red leather upright armchair, was my father. He looked just as I had seen him in his prime, and as I had read about him in his brief year of triumph [1885–6]. He was small and slim, with the big moustache I was just painting, and all his bright, captivating, jaunty air. His eyes twinkled and shone. He was evidently in the best of tempers.'

Yet almost the first thing that the ghost says is that he didn't think his son 'could earn your living that way', that is by painting.[88] He might be in the best of tempers, but he was still putting his son in his place. 'I don't remember anything after ninety-four,' the ghost says of the year before he died, 'I was very confused that year,' an elliptical reference to Lord Randolph's illness. The ghost wanted to talk politics, and asked whether the monarchy had survived, allowing Churchill to say that it was 'stronger than in the days of Queen Victoria'. The ghost then asks about the Carlton Club, which Churchill says was being rebuilt, but because the ghost doesn't know there have been two world wars he assumes it was through dilapidation rather than because the vast Victorian stone building at 100 Pall Mall had been destroyed by German bombs on the night of 14 October 1940, and says, 'I thought it would have lasted longer; the structure seemed quite solid.'[89] Thus Winston creates the central conceit of the story – that his father never guesses that the son was a great statesman who had won the war, but assumes him to have been no better than he had thought him in 1894.

They go on to discuss horse racing, the Americanism 'OK', the Primrose League which has 'never had more members'. On looking at Winston's art, the ghost had 'that curious, quizzical smile of his, which at once disarmed and disconcerted'.[90] They discuss the Church of England, and Churchill reveals that 'We have a Socialist Government, with a very large majority,' but makes no mention of whom they won it from. Instead they talk of Arthur Balfour who Winston reports 'came an awful electoral cropper' without mentioning that he was himself in part responsible. Churchill adds of the Labour Party, 'You know, Papa, though stupid, they are quite respectable, and increasingly bourgeois. They are not nearly so fierce as the old Radicals.'[91] Of the female franchise he tells his astonished father that women 'are a strong prop to the Tories' and 'It did not turn out so badly as I thought.'[92]

Winston tells his father that he makes his living as a writer, and that Blenheim was still in the hands of their family, although most of it was occupied by MI5, a government department formed in the war. 'War, do you say? Has there been a war?' 'We have had nothing else but wars since democracy took charge,' says Churchill.[93] At that point, the ghost says of his son, 'I was not going to talk politics with a boy like you ever. Bottom of the school! Never passed any examinations, except into the Cavalry! Wrote me stilted letters. I could not see how you would make your living on the little I could leave you and Jack, and that only after your mother . . . But then of course you were very young, and I loved you dearly. Old people are always very impatient with young ones. Fathers always expect their sons to have their virtues without their faults.'[94]

He learns that Winston had become a major in the yeomanry – for some reason Churchill didn't tell him he had been a lieutenant-colonel in the trenches – 'He did not seem impressed.' Of the world wars, Winston explained that Britain had won all their wars and 'We even made them surrender unconditionally.' 'No one should be made to do that,' the ghost states. 'Great peoples forget sufferings, but not humiliations.' 'Well, that is the way it happened, Papa.'[95] Might there have been in that exchange a trace of criticism of the policy Roosevelt had bounced Churchill into at Casablanca, without adequate warning? Churchill has to explain to his father that Britain was no longer the foremost Great Power she had been in his day, and that it was now America. 'I don't mind that,' the ghost says. 'You are half American yourself.'[96] They then speak of the brotherhood of Canada, Australia and New Zealand, but when the ghost asks about India and Burma, Winston has to admit, 'Alas! They have gone down the drain,' at which his father 'gave a groan'.[97]

Asked about Russia, Churchill says that there was still a tsar but not a Romanov: 'He is much more powerful, and much more despotic.' He then told his father about the Holocaust during the war: 'In the last one seven million were murdered in cold blood, mainly by the Germans. They made human slaughter-pens like the Chicago stockyards.'[98] The ghost of his father then says, 'I never expected that you would develop so far and so fully. Of course you are too old now to think about such things, but when I hear you talk I really wonder you didn't go into politics . . . You might even have made a name for yourself.'[99] The apparition then lights a cigarette and, as the match flares, he vanishes. 'The illusion had passed . . . But so vivid had my fancy been that I felt too tired to go on. Also, my cigar had gone out, and the ash had fallen among all the paints.'[100]

The piece is funny and full of irony. 'The Labour men and the trade unions look upon the Monarchy not only as a national but a nationalized institution,' he wrote. 'They even go to the parties at Buckingham Palace. Those who have very extreme principles wear sweaters.'[101] The references to 'stupid' Labour, the blaming of democracy for wars, India going down the drain, 'despotic' Stalin, all meant that the 'Private Article' had to stay private, and was not published until the first anniversary of his death. Nevertheless the still-burning psychological need for Churchill to have his father's posthumous approval is evident: over half a century after Lord Randolph's death, he has him say, 'I never expected that you would develop so far and so fully' and 'I loved you dearly.'[102] When asked by friends whether 'The Dream' was fictional, he 'would smile and say, "Not entirely." '[103]

'The Dream' can also be read as a lament for the demise of British power and Victorian certainty, which certainly afflicted Churchill badly in the year that the jewel in the crown of the British Empire was lost, something that Churchill always saw as a tragedy. It is no coincidence that the idea was conceived in late November 1947, just as the massacres on the North-West Frontier and in the Punjab were reaching their zenith. The transfer of power in India was utterly traumatic for him, and 'The Dream' might almost be seen as therapy.

Overwhelmingly, though, the story was Churchill's belated, subtly stated response to his father's conviction that he would be a failure in life. For all Churchill's seeming modesty in not mentioning to his father the fact that he had been prime minister and one of the saviours of Western civilization, the reader nonetheless inevitably concludes that Churchill's achievements in the tumultuous twentieth century were far greater than his father's in the relatively quiet and peaceful nineteenth. The avoidance of saying so makes the point all the more powerfully. Underlying it is an acute psychological appraisal of a boy who only ever wanted his father's approval, but never received it.

*

In a stupendous deal negotiated by his literary agent, Emery Reves (whom he had known since the anti-appeasement struggle), the rights to *The Second World War* were sold for $1.4 million in the United States (approximately $16.1 million in today's money) and £555,000 (approximately £16.7 million) in the United Kingdom. Churchill wrote these volumes in his seventies, with a good deal of help with the initial drafts from literary assistants. 'Your task, my boy, is to make Cosmos out of Chaos,' he said to one of them, Denis Kelly, in the muniment room at Chartwell, to where he had moved his huge archive of wartime minutes and documents, which he treated as his private property despite many of them clearly stating they belonged to His Britannic Majesty's Government.[104] Norman Brook, the Cabinet Secretary, ordered civil servants to ensure that Churchill and his assistants 'should be given all possible facilities and assistance'.[105] This has been condemned as gross favouritism, but the book became excellent British propaganda in the United States and worldwide.

In mid-December 1947, Churchill went to Marrakesh to stay at the Mamounia Hotel for a month, courtesy of his American publishers. He took along William Deakin, another literary assistant, who had been parachuted into Occupied Yugoslavia to liaise with Tito, to work on the proofs of the first volume of *The Second World War*, which was to be entitled *The Gathering Storm*. These writing and painting holidays were attended by family, friends, secretaries, Sawyers, literary assistants and other miscellaneous staff. Mary counted over one hundred items of luggage on one holiday.[106] Even royalty now travelled less extravagantly.

On Christmas Eve, Churchill and Sarah visited a nightclub in Marrakesh, where he noticed a beautiful lady dining alone. 'The gentleman had to go back to his family,' Sarah explained. 'How do you know that?' he asked. 'Don't gentlemen usually go home to their families?' she replied.[107] So he rose to his feet and danced Sarah around the floor until they reached the 'forlorn but proud' lady on the other side of the room, to whom Churchill said, 'You are the Christmas fairy, may I have a dance?' They danced, and Churchill took his leave of her back at her table. The detectives were worried she might have been a spy. The next day he received a telegram stating, 'You will never know my name but I am proud to have danced with Winston Churchill.'

Walter Graebner, Churchill's American publisher, recalled that Churchill took a special delight in his picnic customs when they visited the Atlas Mountains, which 'he quickly elevated to the rank of formal ceremonies'.[108] One was the drinking of old Indian Army toasts. At the end of a picnic, everyone would rise to drink the toast of the day. On Sundays it was 'To Absent Friends', on Mondays 'To Men', on Tuesdays 'To Women', on Wednesdays 'To Religion', on Thursdays 'To our Swords', on Fridays 'To Ourselves' and on Saturdays 'To Wives and Sweethearts'. 'You know, most people are going to be very surprised when they get to Heaven,' Churchill told Graebner on this trip. 'They are looking forward to meeting fascinating people like Napoleon and Julius Caesar. But they'll probably never be able to find them, because there will be so many millions of other people there too – Indians and Chinamen and people like that. Everyone will have equal rights in Heaven. That will be the real Welfare State.'[109]

Although Churchill worked with Deakin most days in Morocco, he did it in the sunshine and clean air away from the London winter. 'I do not need rest,' he told Clementine, 'but change is a great refreshment.'[110] A bout of bronchitis had Moran and Clementine flying out in case it was renewed pneumonia, and there was a rumour that Churchill was about to die. Lascelles even wrote out a draft statement for the King in response to an announcement.[111] Jo Sturdee was amused by the way that scores of reporters from around the world flew into Marrakesh 'in special planes galore, hoping to be in at the death, only to find the Old Fox sitting in his usual place in the dining room looking as round and as well as ever'.[112]

*The Gathering Storm*, which covered the period between the end of the Great War and May 1940, was published by Houghton Mifflin in America in June 1948 and Cassell & Co. in October that same year. (The British editions always came out some months later for copyright-related reasons.) It was an immediate and huge bestseller, indeed Churchill's bestselling book by far. The initial edition sold twenty-five times more copies than *The World Crisis*, and far more quickly. It was serialized in eighty magazines worldwide, and appeared in fifty countries in twenty-six languages.

In a debate on foreign affairs in January 1948, Churchill had declared, 'For my part, I consider that it will be found much better by all parties to leave the past to history, especially as I propose to write that history myself.'[113] It got a good laugh, and his book was emphatically not intended to tell the story of the Second World War objectively. 'This is not history,' he was at pains to point out to Deakin and others, 'this is my case.'[114] Historians who complain that not enough emphasis was given to one or another aspect of the war that Churchill was not directly involved in have failed to appreciate that, despite the work's seemingly objective and over-arching title *The Second World War*, the six volumes were intended to be, as he said, Churchill's story, supported with documentation just as *The World Crisis* had been. It did this with overwhelming success, not just in terms of books sold but in the way that the strategy and course of that war is still popularly conceived today.

One of the few criticisms Churchill ever made of the 1st Duke of Marlborough was that he never wrote his memoirs: 'He seems to have felt sure that the facts would tell their tale.'[115] Churchill's own monument was not going to be made 'by piling great stones on one another', as he put it, but by these war memoirs. Much of the first draft was written by a talented literary team, which he nicknamed 'the Syndicate', and which included Kelly, Deakin, Pug Ismay, Lieutenant-General Sir Henry Pownall for the Army, Commodore Gordon Allen for the Navy and Air Chief Marshal Sir Guy Garrod for the RAF, and Maurice Ashley, an Oxford don. Turning early drafts into the finished product, once Churchill had extensively rewritten them, was a laborious process. Most chapters went through up to a dozen versions, the last five being 'Provisional Semi-Final', 'Provisional Final', 'Almost Final', 'Final' and 'Subject to Full Freedom of Proof Correction'.

In 1919, Churchill had been asked to provide the wording for a French war memorial; he suggested, 'In War: Fury. In Defeat: Defiance. In Victory: Magnanimity. In Peace: Goodwill.'[116] It had been rejected, so now he used it as the 'Moral of the Work' here, substituting 'Resolution' for 'Fury'. In the very month of publication, Stalin cut West Berlin off from the rest of Germany, so food and supplies had to be airlifted in, just as the Czech Communist Party staged a coup d'état in Prague. *The Gathering Storm* was thus also timely in its denunciation of creeping totalitarianism.

Not everyone was happy with it. 'I think that the Party resents his unimpaired criticisms of Munich,' noted Chips Channon.[117] Stanley Baldwin had died in December 1947, but his friends were outraged both by Churchill's description of him as little more than 'the greatest party manager the Conservatives had ever had' and by the allegation in the index that Baldwin had confessed to putting his Party before his country over rearmament in an imagined general election before the actual 1935 one.[118] Eden complained to Cranborne that Churchill had got his policy towards Mussolini wrong, but easily the most abusive were Emanuel Shinwell who dismissed the book as a 'novel' and the newly elected Labour MP Michael Foot* who wrote that, while the book was 'vastly more enjoyable and instructive' than Hitler's *Mein Kampf*, when it came to 'personal conceit and arrogance there is some likeness between the two'.[119] Though that was complete nonsense, the coverage of the Rhineland crisis in the book was misleading, and of course Churchill was presented as omniscient, which he had not been.[120]

In March 1949 Churchill published *Their Finest Hour*, the second

* Foot beat Randolph in Plymouth (Devonport), in Randolph's last attempt to enter Parliament.

volume of his war memoirs, covering the events of May 1940 to January 1941. (The French edition was entitled *L'Heure tragique.*)[121] There could be no mention of Ultra, of course, but otherwise the second volume was less controversial than the first had been and than subsequent ones were to be. 'When before, through all the centuries of this island's history, has such a theme matched such a pen?' asked the *Spectator*. In total, Churchill's six volumes of war memoirs numbered two million words and can still today be read as a work of literature as well as of history.

When on 4 July 1948 Aneurin Bevan, the Health Minister, described Conservatives as 'lower than vermin', it was clear that Churchill, who had long had a strong antipathy for him, would reply. Six days later at Woodford, he said, 'We speak of the Minister of Health, but ought we not rather to say the Minister of Disease, for is not morbid hatred a form of mental disease, moral disease, and indeed a highly infectious form? Indeed, I can think of no better step to signalize the inauguration of the National Health Service than that a person who so obviously needs psychiatric attention should be among the first of its patients.'[122] (On a later occasion, apropos of Bevan's hatred of the rich, Churchill said, 'Hate is a bad guide. I have never considered myself at all a good hater – though I recognize that from moment to moment it has added stimulus to pugnacity.')[123]

In Aix-en-Provence in August, looking for what he called 'paintacious' places, Churchill made it clear to Boothby that, in crises like the Berlin Airlift, had he been at No. 10, he would have made use of the Western nuclear monopoly. 'I would have it out with them now,' he said of the Soviets. 'If we do not, war might come. I would say to them, quite politely, "The day we quit Berlin, you will have to quit Moscow." I would not think it necessary to explain why.' He believed that the Americans were letting the Kremlin think they had forgone the nuclear option, but 'With me around they would not be so sure.'[124] This was not something he was willing to say in public, and whenever he did tiptoe towards it, both the left-wing press and even *The Times* were quick to denounce him as a warmonger.

At the Conservative Party Conference at Llandudno in Wales on 9 October, Churchill unveiled his idea of Britain being the link between 'the three great circles among the free nations and democracies' – the British Empire and Commonwealth, the United States and a United Europe – referring to the Soviets' 'aggressiveness and malignity' and saying, 'the only sure foundation of peace and the prevention of actual war rests upon strength.' He denounced the Czech coup, which had led to the probable murder of his friend Jan Masaryk, the Czech Foreign Minister: 'Stalin has perpetrated exactly the same act of aggression in 1948 as Hitler did when he marched into Prague in 1939, nine years ago . . . This is all set forth before our eyes as plainly as Hitler told us about his plans in his book *Mein Kampf*. I hope that the Western nations, and particularly our own country and the United States, will not fall into the same kind of deadly trap twice over.'[125] Shinwell replied to this the next day: 'Mr Churchill is a great war leader, of course he is. That's why he wants another war.'[126]

*Pravda* called Churchill 'the bison of British reaction', the *Daily Worker* said he was an 'atom gangster' and *The Times* described his views as 'dangerously simple'.[127] Churchill was not deflected and spoke unequivocally in a debate in January 1949: 'I think the day will come when it will be recognized without doubt, not only on one side of the House but throughout the civilized world, that the strangling of Bolshevism at its birth would have been an untold blessing to the human race.'[128] In private he kept on advocating the exploitation of the West's nuclear monopoly until the Soviets successfully tested their own Bomb in August 1949, when he rapidly reassessed the situation, recognizing that nuclear confrontation with them was now impossible. The only solution now could be a negotiated compromise to end the arms race, while ideological pressure was maintained in the hope that Communism would collapse internally.

Just before his seventy-fourth birthday in November 1948, Churchill showed his continued physical vitality by riding out with the Old Surrey and Burstow Hunt, which met at Chartwell Farm. 'It really was quite an achievement,' recalled Mary, 'but we were all deeply relieved when, having made his point, Winston did not make a habit of riding again.'[129] In 1949, encouraged by Christopher Soames, Churchill nevertheless took up horse racing, adopting his father's racing colours of pink with chocolate sleeves and cap. After buying Colonist II, a grey French colt, he invested in thirty-seven more racehorses over the following years. He would talk to his horses before races, and when Colonist II once came fourth he explained, 'I told him this is a very big race and that if he won he would never have to run again but spend the rest of his life in agreeable female company. Colonist II did not keep his mind on the race.'[130] When Colonist II beat Above Board, the King's horse, at Hurst Park in May 1950, he wrote to Princess Elizabeth, 'I wish indeed that we could both have been victorious – but that would be no foundation for the excitements and liveliness of the turf.'[131] By the time of his death he had won seventy races. It gave him excitement and pleasure, although Clementine never wholly approved. A few years after the victory at Hurst Park, when it was suggested that Colonist II be put out to stud, he remarked, 'And have it said that the Prime Minister of Great Britain is living off the immoral earnings of a horse?'[132]

*

The State of Israel was created in May 1948 and had been welcomed by Churchill. In January 1949 he described it to a sceptical House of Commons, and a Labour Government that had still not recognized it, as 'an event in world history to be viewed in the perspective, not of a generation or a century, but in the perspective of a thousand, two thousand or even three thousand years. That is a standard of temporal values or time values which seems very much out of accord with the perpetual click-clack of our rapidly changing moods and of the age in which we live.'[133] Two months later in the United States, where he had gone to meet President Truman and speak at the Massachusetts Institute of Technology, he told a largely Jewish audience in New York, 'Remember, I was for a free and independent Israel all through the dark years when many of my most distinguished countrymen took a different view. So do not imagine for a moment that I have the slightest idea of deserting you in your hour of glory.'[134]

At a dinner given by the Time-Life founder Henry Luce in New York on 25 March, Churchill said that the Soviet Politburo 'is quite as wicked but much more formidable than Hitler, because Hitler had only the *Herrenvolk* stuff and anti-Semitism . . . He had no theme.* But these fourteen men in the Kremlin have their hierarchy and a church of Communist adepts whose missionaries are in every country as a fifth column.'[135] He recalled the furore his Fulton speech had created, and said, 'I remember some words that my father spoke when I was an urchin – I remember that he said a man who can't take a knockdown blow isn't worth a damn. Well, I've always tried to live up to that and on the whole it's quite a healthy process.' But, he added, 'You don't want to knock a man down except to pick him up again in a better state of mind.'[136]

Churchill then asked who had created the changed world in the three years since Fulton, saying, 'No one could possibly have done it but Mr. Stalin. He is the one.'[137] There was no more 'I like that man,' as there had been at Potsdam. Now he said, 'I tell you it's no use arguing with a Communist. It's no good trying to convert a Communist, or persuade him.' Instead, the only thing to do was 'to convince the Soviet Government that you have superior force' and also that 'you are not restrained by any moral consideration if the case arose from using that force with complete material ruthlessness. And that is the greatest chance of peace, the surest road to peace.'[138]

'Little did we guess that what has been called The Century of the Common Man would witness as its outstanding feature more common men

* Churchill believed in themes. 'Take this pudding away!' he once told a waiter in the 1950s. 'It has no theme.' (Christopher Soames in *Finest Hour* no. 50 p. 16.)

killing each other with greater facilities than any other five centuries put together in the history of the world,' Churchill told the Massachusetts Institute of Technology* in Boston on 31 March.[139] Forty years before it happened in Europe, Churchill predicted the demise of Communism:

> Laws just or unjust may govern men's actions. Tyrannies may restrain or regulate their words. The machinery of propaganda may pack their minds with falsehood and deny them truth for many generations of time. But the soul of man thus held in trance or frozen in a long night can be awakened by a spark coming from God knows where, and in a moment the whole structure of lies and oppression is on trial for its life. Peoples in bondage need never despair.[140]

It was a positive message when Berlin was still under blockade, and the Airlift continuing. In January 1953 he predicted that Colville would live to see the defeat of Communism, and was almost right; Colville died in 1987, only two years before the fall of the Berlin Wall.[141]

On 24 August 1949, while on holiday in the south of France, Churchill suffered a minor stroke, one of a series over the coming years. He had been playing cards at 2 a.m. when he noticed a cramp in his right leg and right arm, which he still had when he woke up later that morning, as well as difficulty in writing. His speech was unaffected though, and Moran told him that 'A very small clot has blocked a very small artery.'[142] It was kept secret, but in retrospect it would have been a good time for Churchill to have left the Commons and handed over to the next generation. Five days afterwards, however, the Soviets successfully tested their own atomic bomb, which made him feel it was imperative to stay in front-line politics.

From early 1949, the Labour Government's popularity had been starting to wane, as austerity continued to bite and rationing showed no signs of being lifted. On being told by a Party worker that voting intentions in the Hammersmith South by-election that February were 'higgledy-piggledy', Churchill asked, 'What do you mean? How much higgledy, and how much piggledy?'[143] It turned that out the Tory added 5.2 per cent to the vote there, not enough for victory but a positive sign. Stafford Cripps's 31 per cent devaluation of sterling on 18 September, from $4.03 to $2.80, severely undermined the Labour Government's reputation for economic competence, however (though privately Churchill was forced to admit to Clementine by the following January that 'None of the evils of Devaluation have really manifested themselves yet and are only on the way').[144] Cripps, who had

* It was Churchill's positive experience of MIT that led him to ask for a scientific and technological college at Cambridge as his memorial.

been chancellor of the Exchequer since 1947, had nine times denied that he would devalue – which of course he had to in order to protect sterling – so earning Churchill's unfair rebuke that he had deceived Parliament. In response, Cripps accused Churchill of 'guttersnipe politics' and refused to accept a Bristol University honorary doctorate from him later on that year.

'Winston's childish side is ever engaging,' Chips Channon recorded on 28 September 1949.

> Today I saw him come into the Members' Lobby . . . [and ask] for snuff, which the attendant handed him from a silver box. Then, surprisingly, Winston looked at the [Sergeant-at-Arms'] Chair (which he must have known for forty years) as if he had never seen it before in his life, got into it, and sat there for fully five minutes, bowing and beaming at other Members . . . A boyish prank . . . A few minutes later, however, he was making what was to be one of his very greatest speeches [on the devaluation of sterling] to a crowded and anxious house.[145]

Churchill's refusal to abide by rules and conventions also extended to ignoring all 'No Smoking' signs, and continuing to tip the House of Commons staff despite all gratuities being banned by the Labour-controlled Kitchens Committee.

'Writing a book is an adventure,' Churchill said on receiving the *Times* Literary Prize that November. 'To begin with it is a toy, an amusement; then it becomes a mistress, and then a master, and then a tyrant, and then the last phase is that, just as one is about to be reconciled to one's servitude, one kills the monster.'[146] The quips kept coming on his seventy-fifth birthday party at Hyde Park Gate later that month; when the photographer expressed his hope that he would also shoot his hundredth birthday party, 'I don't see why not, young man,' Churchill replied. 'You look reasonably fit and healthy.'[147] Asked if he feared death, he said, 'I am ready to meet my Maker. Whether my Maker is prepared for the great ordeal of meeting me is another matter.'[148]

On 11 January 1950, Attlee suddenly dissolved Parliament for an election on 23 February, cutting short Churchill's holiday in Madeira. Churchill called the Party leadership together and in nine hours they thrashed out the election manifesto together, based largely on the Industrial Charter.* *This is the Road* pledged to 'maintain and improve the

* When he summoned the psephologist Dr David Butler of Princeton University for a four-hour discussion about the election, he was taken aback to discover that Butler was only twenty-five years old. 'Better hurry up, young man,' he told him. 'Napoleon was only twenty-six when he crossed the bridge of Lodi.' Butler recalled, 'I was quite in awe. I wasn't a Conservative supporter but I knew I was in the presence of the greatest man in the world.' (*Daily Telegraph* 7 April 2015.)

62. Churchill liked Sir Oswald Birley, who painted this portrait in 1951, because he had won the Military Cross in the Great War.

63. Churchill, wearing his 'siren' suit, with General Dwight D. Eisenhower near Hastings in Sussex in May 1944.

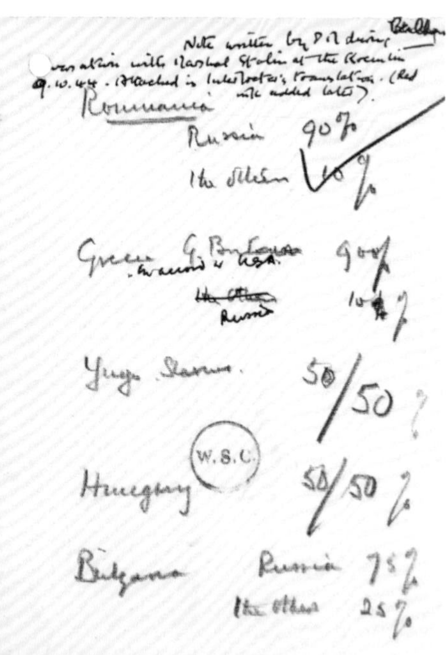

Note written by P.M. during conversation with Marshal Stalin at the Kremlin 9.10.44. Attached in Interpreter's translation. (Red tick added later).

Roumania

Russia 90%

The others 10%

Greece G. Britain 90%
(in accord with U.S.A.)

~~The others~~ Russia 10%

Yugo-Slavia 50/50%

W.S.C.

Hungary 50/50%

Bulgaria Russia 75%

The others 25%

64. The notorious percentages agreement of October 1944 which carries Stalin's large tick. Denounced for its cynicism, it in fact saved Greek democracy.

65. Churchill walking down the Champs-Élysées on Armistice Day 1944 in tears. *Left to right*: Inspector James Battley (Eden's detective), Alfred Duff Cooper (behind), Commander 'Tommy' Thompson, Eden, Churchill, de Gaulle.

66. Churchill, Roosevelt and Stalin share a moment of good humour at the Yalta Conference in the Crimea in February 1945.

67. Churchill crossed the River Rhine into Germany on 25 March 1945. Behind him leaving the landing craft can be seen Field Marshal Brooke and Eisenhower's mistress, Kay Summersby.

68. Churchill's private secretaries on the steps of the No. 10 garden in September 1941. *Left to right*: John 'Jock' Colville, Leslie Rowan, Churchill, John Peck, John Martin, Edith Watson, Commander Tommy Thompson, Anthony Bevir, Charles Barker.

69. The Chiefs of Staff in the garden of 10 Downing Street the day before VE Day in May 1945. *Seated left to right*: Marshal of the RAF Sir Charles Portal, Field Marshal Sir Alan Brooke, Winston Churchill, Admiral of the Fleet Sir Andrew Cunningham. *Standing left to right*: Major General Leslie Hollis; General Sir Hastings 'Pug' Ismay.

33.

From Stettin in the Baltic
to Trieste in the Adriatic,

an iron curtain has descended
across the Continent.

Behind that line
lie all the capitals of the ancient states
of Central and Eastern Europe.

Warsaw, Berlin, Prague, Vienna, Budapest,
Belgrade, Bucharest and Sofia,

all these famous cities and the populations
around them

lie in the Soviet sphere

and all are subject
in one form or another,

not only to Soviet influence
but to a very high and increasing
measure of control fr Moscow.

70. Churchill delivering his 'Sinews of Peace' speech at Westminster College, Fulton, Missouri, on 5 March 1946 in which he was the first to warn of a Soviet-dominated eastern Europe.

71. The page from his Fulton speech that warned that an 'iron curtain' had fallen across Europe.

72. Churchill with parrots at Miami Beach in 1946, alongside Clementine and Sarah Churchill.

73. Churchill, in tears, being applauded for his speech at the Congress of Europe meeting at The Hague in May 1948.

74. Churchill accepting a cigar with glee in 1951.

75. Churchill's successful speech at the Conservative Party Conference in Margate in October 1953 secured his continued premiership four months after he had suffered a stroke in Downing Street.

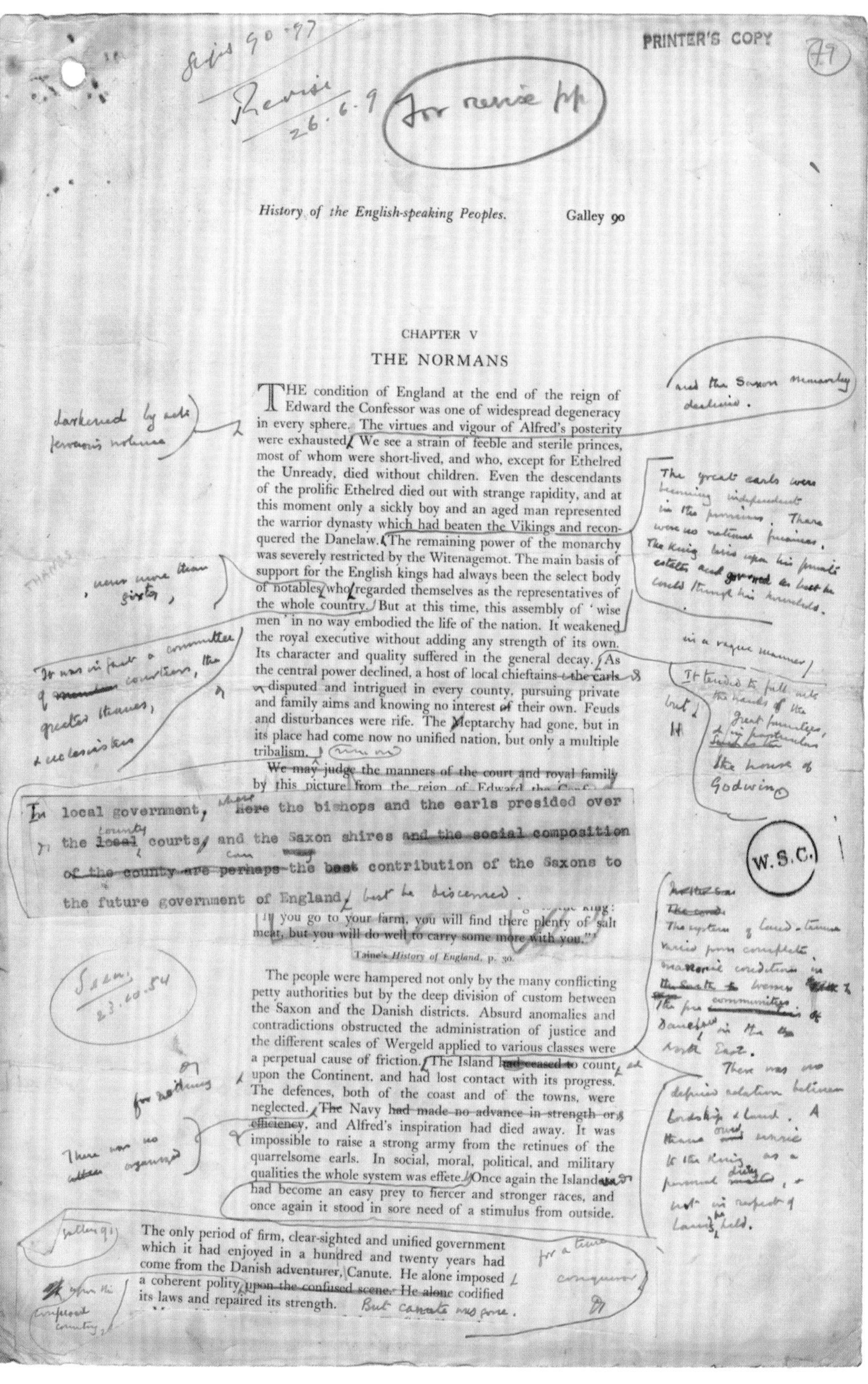

PRINTER'S COPY

*History of the English-speaking Peoples.* Galley 90

CHAPTER V

THE NORMANS

THE condition of England at the end of the reign of Edward the Confessor was one of widespread degeneracy in every sphere. The virtues and vigour of Alfred's posterity were exhausted. We see a strain of feeble and sterile princes, most of whom were short-lived, and who, except for Ethelred the Unready, died without children. Even the descendants of the prolific Ethelred died out with strange rapidity, and at this moment only a sickly boy and an aged man represented the warrior dynasty which had beaten the Vikings and reconquered the Danelaw. The remaining power of the monarchy was severely restricted by the Witenagemot. The main basis of support for the English kings had always been the select body of notables who regarded themselves as the representatives of the whole country. But at this time, this assembly of 'wise men' in no way embodied the life of the nation. It weakened the royal executive without adding any strength of its own. Its character and quality suffered in the general decay. As the central power declined, a host of local chieftains—the earls—disputed and intrigued in every county, pursuing private and family aims and knowing no interest of their own. Feuds and disturbances were rife. The Heptarchy had gone, but in its place had come now no unified nation, but only a multiple tribalism.

We may judge the manners of the court and royal family by this picture from the reign of Edward the Conf...

In local government, here the bishops and the earls presided over the local courts, and the Saxon shires and the social composition of the county are perhaps the best contribution of the Saxons to the future government of England.

...king: "If you go to your farm, you will find there plenty of salt meat, but you will do well to carry some more with you."[1]

Taine's *History of England*, p. 30.

The people were hampered not only by the many conflicting petty authorities but by the deep division of custom between the Saxon and the Danish districts. Absurd anomalies and contradictions obstructed the administration of justice and the different scales of Wergeld applied to various classes were a perpetual cause of friction. The Island had ceased to count upon the Continent, and had lost contact with its progress. The defences, both of the coast and of the towns, were neglected. The Navy had made no advance in strength or efficiency, and Alfred's inspiration had died away. It was impossible to raise a strong army from the retinues of the quarrelsome earls. In social, moral, political, and military qualities the whole system was effete. Once again the Island had become an easy prey to fiercer and stronger races, and once again it stood in sore need of a stimulus from outside.

The only period of firm, clear-sighted and unified government which it had enjoyed in a hundred and twenty years had come from the Danish adventurer, Canute. He alone imposed a coherent polity upon the confused scene. He alone codified its laws and repaired its strength.

W.S.C.

76. A corrected galley proof page of *A History of the English-Speaking Peoples* with Churchill's amendments in red. The blue crayon and black ink are from the hand of Denis Kelly and Eddie Marsh, respectively, and the proof-reader has responded in green.

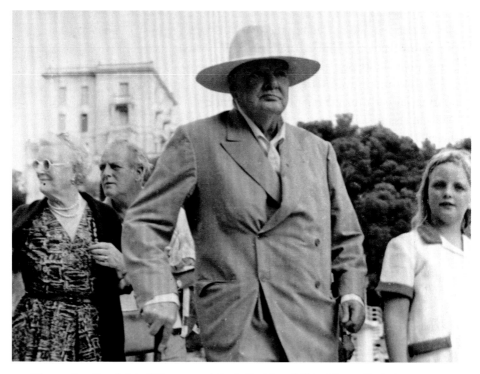

77. Clementine, Randolph, Winston and Arabella Churchill in Monte Carlo in 1958.

78. Sailing away: Churchill aboard Aristotle Onassis's yacht, the *Christina*, off Capri in July 1959.

Health Service' while freeing 'the productive energies of the nation from the trammels of overbearing state control and bureaucratic management'. 'I am much depressed about the country because for whoever wins there will be nothing but bitterness and strife,' he told Clementine, 'like men fighting savagely on a small raft which is breaking up.'[149] As for the result, 'All is in the unknown. However there would be no fun in life if we knew the end at the beginning.'[150]

Churchill threw himself into the campaign, attacking an early form of political correctness at a speech in Cardiff in early February.

> I hope you have all mastered the official Socialist jargon which our masters, as they call themselves, wish us to learn. You must not use the word 'poor'; they are described as the 'lower income group'. When it comes to a question of freezing a workman's wages, the Chancellor of the Exchequer speaks of 'arresting increases in personal income' . . . There is a lovely one about houses and homes. They are in future to be called 'accommodation units'. I don't know how we are to sing our old song 'Home Sweet Home'. 'Accommodation Unit, Sweet Accommodation Unit, There's no place like our Accommodation Unit.' I hope to live to see the British democracy spit all this rubbish from their lips.[151]

Equally jocularly, he told an Edinburgh audience six days later, 'I doubt if it gives very much pleasure to the average Socialist when he wakes up in the morning to say to himself, "Oho, I own the Bank of England, I own the railways, I own the coalmines." But if it does give him any actual pleasure, he is certainly dearly paying for it.'[152]

Knowing that he was likely to be accused of warmongering, and deeply mindful that Soviet Russia was now a nuclear power, Churchill coined a new phrase when he said of the Russians, 'The idea appeals to me of a supreme effort to bridge the gulf between the two worlds, so that each can live their life, if not in friendship at least without the hatreds of the Cold War. You must be careful to mark my words in these matters because I have not always been proved wrong. It is not easy to see how things could be worsened by a parley at the summit, if such a thing were possible.'[153] Labour dismissed the idea as a 'stunt', but such was Churchill's capacity for popularizing such phrases as 'business as usual' and 'iron curtain' that all such leader-to-leader meetings have since been called 'summits'.

Churchill and his party had a formidable hill to climb. The 1945–50 Parliament had passed no fewer than 347 Acts of Parliament, had implemented the Beveridge Report in full with the National Insurance Act of 1946 and the National Assistance Act of 1948, created the National Health Service, built over a million new houses, and raised the school-leaving age to fifteen. Labour had also nationalized the coalmines, the railways, gas, electricity, road haulage and the Bank of England. It had given India, Pakistan, Ceylon and Burma their independence, withdrawn from Palestine and helped found NATO. Many of these were genuine achievements, but the cost had been shortages, rationing, austerity, high taxation, Party splits, the devaluation of sterling and an utterly exhausted Cabinet: both Bevin and Cripps were to be dead within two years.

Refreshed by their time out of office, the Conservatives were able to field a strong front-bench team, including Anthony Eden, Harold Macmillan, Rab Butler, Oliver Stanley and Oliver Lyttelton. Churchill had been able to choose a Shadow Cabinet he liked and admired; six out of the twenty of them were holders of the Military Cross and eight of them members of the Other Club. Its minutes show how informal and collegiate, even chatty, their discussions were.[154]

On a voter turnout of 84 per cent, the highest since 1906 and never bettered since, Labour won 315 seats, the Conservatives 298, the Liberals 9 and others 3, giving Attlee, discounting the Speaker, an effective majority of five. The Conservatives had gained a massive eighty-five seats (virtually a 40 per cent increase). Labour had won 13.27 million votes, the Conservatives 12.5 million and the Liberals 2.62 million. 'Winston spoke today in the Defence debate for over an hour and seemed in the highest spirits,' Channon noted in mid-March. 'No extinct volcano he.'[155]

Churchill had been thinking deeply about the consequences of the Soviet Bomb, and the concept that came to be called mutually assured destruction, and he shared his thoughts in an Olympian speech in the Commons in late March. 'Moralists may find it a melancholy thought that peace can find no nobler foundations than mutual terror,' he said.[156] He reprised some thoughts from the Fulton speech, concluding that 'Man in this moment of his history has emerged in greater supremacy over the forces of nature than has ever been dreamed of before. He has it in his power to solve quite easily the problems of material existence. He has conquered the wild beasts, and he has even conquered the insects and the microbes. There lies before him, as he wishes, a golden age of peace and progress. All is in his hand. He has only to conquer his last and worst enemy – himself.'[157] As he put it five years later, he worried that 'The deterrent does not cover the case of lunatics or dictators in the mood of Hitler when he found himself in his final dug-out.'[158]

In April 1950, Churchill published *The Grand Alliance*, the third volume of *The Second World War*, covering the entry of the USSR and the USA into the war. Not surprisingly, given the theme and author, the book was now being likened by some reviewers to Julius Caesar's *Gallic Wars*.[159] 'I must justify myself before history,' Churchill openly admitted to a Conservative Party official who had been kept waiting at Chartwell as he worked.[160] The American serial rights alone brought in half a million dollars (roughly $5.25 million today) from *Life* magazine. 'I'm not writing a book,' he said. 'I'm developing a property.'[161]

In June Churchill somewhat hypocritically attacked Labour for boycotting a conference on the Schuman Plan which presaged the European Iron and Steel Community, and two months later at Strasbourg he supported the creation of a European Army, although Eden told Cranborne that 'It was probably useful as rallying French and Germans and Winston never intended it to go further.'[162] Yet that month, when pressed in the Commons, Churchill admitted that he could not 'at present' foresee Britain becoming 'an ordinary member of a Federal Union limited to Europe'.[163] He went on to explain that this was primarily because of Britain's position 'as the centre of the British Empire and Commonwealth', as well as 'our fraternal association with the United States in the English-speaking world'. It is of course the duty of an Opposition to oppose, but it soon turned out that he himself had no intention of doing in office what he was criticizing Labour for refusing to do.

'In our European Movement we have worked with federalists,' he told the Commons on the same occasion, 'and we have always made it clear that, though they are moving along the same road, we are not committed to their conclusions.'[164] British pro-Europeans despaired of him; Jebb complained that 'Churchill decided to have it both ways,' concluding once again that 'He was not really . . . in favour of joining anything like a supranational Europe.'[165] He was right, and on 12 August 1948 Churchill had told Violet Bonham Carter that the 'Federal solution' could not work because 'a Parliament of Europe [is] quite impracticable'.[166]

In late June 1950, Stalin encouraged the North Korean Communist leader Kim Il-Sung to invade South Korea, in order to test Western willpower. Truman and Attlee reacted robustly, going to South Korea's defence. 'The old man is very good to me,' Churchill said to Sir David Maxwell Fyfe, a lawyer MP and future home secretary. 'I could not have managed this situation had I been in Attlee's place. I should have been called a warmonger.'[167] Since Truman was ten years younger than Churchill, Maxwell Fyfe not unnaturally asked, 'What old man?' 'God, Sir Donald,' came the reply. We can only speculate why Churchill always called Sir David Sir Donald.

The death of the eighty-year-old Field Marshal Jan Smuts on 11 September led Churchill to continue his tradition of speaking about himself in his friends' eulogies, telling the Other Club that Smuts had been 'our greatest living member'.[168] He had met him half a century earlier, and admired him unreservedly, accepting advice from him that he would not have taken from anybody else besides Clementine.[169] A former enemy in the Boer War, he had become a close friend and trusted adviser, not least because Churchill knew that Smuts was not after his job. Now Beaverbrook was almost his only surviving connection to the Great War generation.

In November, *The Hinge of Fate*, the fourth volume of his war memoirs, was published, which covered the period from Japan's onslaught after Pearl Harbor through to the fall of Tunis. With the Cold War now heating up considerably, Churchill minimized his disagreements with the Americans over strategy in 1942. He was also generous to de Gaulle, who was to become president of France again in 1958: 'Always, even when he was behaving worst, he seemed to express the personality of France – a great nation, with all its pride, authority and ambition.'[170] Because George Marshall was the US Secretary of Defense and Eisenhower was thought to harbour presidential aspirations, while Churchill himself was only one electoral heave away from being back in Downing Street, he was conscious that he might have soon to work with all three men one day. This volume of his memoirs, though again beautifully written, does not dwell on the turbulent internal ructions of the Allies. It was also criticized for underplaying Auchinleck's defensive First Battle of El Alamein while overplaying Montgomery's offensive Second Battle there.[171]*

In a debate on the international situation in mid-December, Churchill took the unexpected stance of praising appeasement, at least in some situations. After Attlee had declared that there could be no appeasement of Russia, Churchill replied, 'Appeasement in itself may be good or bad according to the circumstances. Appeasement from weakness and fear is alike futile and fatal. Appeasement from strength is magnanimous and noble and might be the surest and perhaps the only path to world peace.'[172] He went on to condemn the growing movement for 'no first use' of nuclear weapons as meaning 'you must never fire until you have been shot dead. That seems to me undoubtedly a silly thing to say and a still more imprudent position to adopt. Moreover, such a resolve would undoubtedly bring war nearer.' Channon noted that when Churchill was booed by 'hundreds of enraged, roaring Socialists' in response to the remark, 'My impression was that he deliberately created it.'[173]

Churchill was back at the Mamounia Hotel for Christmas, and when

* One of Auchinleck's staff officers, Major-General Eric Dorman O'Gowan, even launched a libel action which forced Churchill to tone down criticisms of Auchinleck in subsequent editions.

he returned to London more rumours of his death circulated. 'I am informed from many quarters that a rumour has been put about that I died this morning,' Churchill stated in mid-February. 'This is quite untrue. It is however a good example of the whispering campaign which has been set on foot. It would have been more artistic to keep this one for polling day.'[174] Churchill's good-humoured, optimistic outlook contrasted well with the Government's obvious look of exhaustion, so he kept it up. When Stalin accused Attlee of being a warmonger over the Korean War and rearmament, Churchill said that Labour was intending to call him a warmonger in the next election, so, 'Stalin has therefore been guilty, not only of an untruth, but of infringement of copyright.'[175]

Although Bevan had indeed been 'a squalid nuisance' during the war, he was of great use to the Conservatives in April 1951 when he and two other ministers, including Harold Wilson, a future prime minister, resigned over the imposition of Health Service charges at a time of rearmament. Churchill told an audience at the Albert Hall that 'Mr. Attlee combines a limited outlook with strong qualities of resistance. He now resumes the direction and leadership of that cluster of lion-hearted limpets . . . who are united by their desire to hold on to office at all costs to their own reputations and their country's fortunes, and to put off by every means in their power to the last possible moment any contact with our democratic electorate.'[176] There were shades of his attacks on the Balfour Government in 1905 in these speeches. In Woodford in July, Churchill was guilty of another monstrous exaggeration, claiming that 'Six years of Socialist Government have hit us harder in our finance and economics than Hitler was able to do.'[177] It was completely untrue – the Second World War had cost Britain almost one-third of her net wealth – and for all that it was eye-catching it was hardly worthy of Churchill to claim it.

On 19 September, Attlee announced a general election for 25 October, hoping to increase his parliamentary majority from just five. The Shadow Cabinet adopted the slogan 'Britain Strong and Free', and promised to build 300,000 houses in three years. Churchill asked Violet Bonham Carter, then a Liberal MP, to give an election broadcast for the Tories, hoping that the two parties might even merge.[178]* The Liberals refused on her behalf, and after three days of attempted persuasion he gave up, but for a moment it seemed a serious prospect, and a sign that he was prioritizing the Tory Democrat element of his political thinking over his

* Because Churchill had performed badly in a television screen-test in 1949 – he disliked the medium immediately and intensely – the only Tory party political TV broadcast of the election was done by the much more telegenic Eden. 'Even though we have to sink to this level,' Churchill said of television, 'we always have to keep pace with modern improvements.' (*CIHOW* p. 474.)

short-lived libertarian beliefs. ('We were never Tories and we never will be!' a drunken Randolph had shouted at Woodrow Wyatt a few years earlier. 'We just make use of the Tory Party.')[179]

Churchill confronted the warmonger accusation on 6 October, telling an Essex audience that 'I am sure we do not want any fingers upon any trigger . . . I do not believe that a Third World War is inevitable. I even think that the danger of it is less than it was before the immense rearmament of the United States. But I must now tell you that in any case it will not be a British finger that will pull the trigger of a Third World War.'[180] Churchill backed this up in a radio broadcast two days later, saying, 'I do not hold that we should rearm in order to fight. I hold that we should rearm in order to parley.' He reiterated it in a speech at Plymouth: 'If I remain in public life at this juncture it is because [peace] . . . is the last prize I seek to win.'[181] Despite this, just before polling day, the Labour-supporting *Daily Mirror* published a picture of a revolver on the front page, with the headline 'Whose Finger on the Trigger?' Another Labour slogan in the election read, 'Vote for Churchill and reach for your rifle; vote Labour and reach old age.' Churchill, however, was able to portray Labour as weak for having allowed Mohammed Mossaddegh, the Prime Minister of Iran, to undermine the Shah of Persia and nationalize British-owned oil installations, including the Anglo-Iranian Oil Company's Abadan refinery, a major humiliation for Britain across the Middle East.[182]

On Thursday, 25 October 1951, the Conservatives won 321 seats, Labour 295, the Liberals 6 and others 3. Labour won 13.95 million votes, the Conservatives 13.72 million and the Liberals 730,000. The Conservatives therefore won the election with a small but workable majority of seventeen seats, despite getting fewer votes than Labour, the only such outcome in the entire post-war period to date. In 1945 most commentators believed Labour would stay in power for at least a decade, and some had predicted two, but they were out in only six years.[183] At the end of his novel *Savrola*, 'after the tumults had subsided, the hearts of the people turned again to the illustrious exile who had won them freedom and whom they had deserted in the hour of victory'.[184] Fifty-one years after its publication, Churchill's life was imitating his art.

# 33
# Indian Summer
# October 1951–April 1955

*Many people say I ought to have retired after the war, and have become some sort of elder statesman, but how could I? I have fought all my life and cannot give up fighting now!*

Churchill to R. V. Jones, 1946[1]

*He still dominated the Cabinet, now more Buddha than Achilles.*

John Colville on Churchill's second premiership[2]

Churchill was a month off his seventy-seventh birthday when he became prime minister again on Friday, 26 October 1951. Six years after his defeat in the 1945 election, he had returned for a full period of office after the tumultuous historic one, something that had not been achieved by any of his heroes: Marlborough, Wellington, Disraeli, Clemenceau or Lloyd George. As during the war, he also took the post of minister of defence himself, and Eden became foreign secretary. Although Eden wanted to be deputy prime minister, as Attlee and Morrison had been, Norman Brook, the Cabinet Secretary, and Sir Alan Lascelles argued that it would be an infringement of the Crown prerogative, and Churchill supported them despite these recent precedents. Jock Colville became Churchill's joint principal private secretary, and against their better judgement Lords Ismay and Cherwell (Prof Lindemann) agreed to join the Cabinet.

The Tory Democrat, 'One Nation' nature of the Government was underlined by the appointment of Rab Butler as chancellor of the Exchequer, the Keynesian Harold Macmillan at Housing and the lawyer Sir Walter Monckton as minister of labour, with a mandate to preserve industrial peace at any price. Baldwin's government had almost been derailed by the General Strike; this time the unions were going to be bought off, almost whatever the cost.[3] Although Walter Elliot wanted to be minister of health, he missed the call from No. 10 as he and his wife were out walking their dog.[4] Churchill had never much liked the former appeaser, so instead the job went to Harry Crookshank, who had served as postmaster-general during the war. Bracken had become an MP again, but his sinus problems were too bad for him to serve in the Cabinet; he soon received a peerage, but never took his seat in the Lords. Viscount De L'Isle seems to have been made an air minister largely on the basis of his having won the Victoria Cross.[5] Duncan Sandys went to the Ministry of Supply. Another Other Club member, David Lloyd George's son Gwilym, took the important post of minister of food, with orders to abolish rationing as soon as possible.

Still hoping to bring the Liberals into coalition, Churchill offered the Ministry of Education to their leader, Clement Davies (who had helped make him prime minister in 1940 but then voted against him in the confidence motion of July 1942). When Davies had to refuse it on political grounds, Churchill tearfully praised him for his self-abnegation.[6] The formation of the Government lasted a week: Churchill forgot what office he was supposed to be offering Nigel Birch (it was the under-secretaryship of air) and took an hour to offer John Boyd-Carpenter the post of financial secretary to the Treasury because he reminisced about his own time turning down the post in 1905.

Churchill himself thought of the idea of appointing ministers who would have oversight over coordinating the policies of more than one department, thus allowing him to have a smaller Cabinet.[7] Lord Woolton was appointed lord president of the Council, with oversight over the ministries of Agriculture and Fisheries and of Food, while Lord Leathers coordinated those of Transport, Civil Aviation, and Fuel and Power. Lindemann took over responsibility for scientific and atomic research, development and production, as well as overseeing Churchill's statistical office. These were posts that the three peers – swiftly nicknamed 'Overlords' – had excelled in during the war, but all three performed disappointingly in the very different peacetime political environment. There was confusion over whether their roles were executive or merely consultative, what their relations with the ministers in charge of the individual departments would be, and whether they were responsible constitutionally to Parliament or just to the Cabinet. They were not given enough staff for interventionist roles, even if they had wanted them, which Woolton at least did not. Furthermore, all three were peers, removed from the centre of legislative power in the Commons. The Opposition, Civil Service and departmental ministers all disliked the system intensely, and with his long experience of the way Westminster and Whitehall worked Churchill should have foreseen the problems of inventing an additional tier of government. It was finally abandoned in September 1953.

At Chequers on 23 March 1952, Churchill summed up the agenda for his ministry as 'Houses and meat and not being scuppered'.[8] The Government would eschew the radicalism of those Conservatives who believed that Britain would spend the 1950s slipping behind her global competitors such as Germany and Japan if she did not shake up her trading and industrial practices. Domestically, Churchill supported Macmillan against the Treasury over housebuilding and as a result 300,000 new houses were indeed built in three years, and a million by 1955. As far as the abolition of rationing was concerned, Churchill started off under a grave misconception about quite how bad the food situation had become. He asked Gwilym Lloyd George to make a model of the actual rations allowed to each British adult. So Lloyd George took a large tin dish to No. 10 with a painted piece of meat, a little heap of pretend sugar and so on. 'Not a bad meal,' Churchill said, with some satisfaction. 'But these are not rations for a meal or for a day,' said Lloyd George, 'they are for a week.' 'A week!' came the outraged reply. 'Then the people are starving. It must be remedied.'[9] Rationing persisted because of a balance of payments crisis, however, although Churchill fretted over it regularly and worked hard to alleviate it, highly conscious of how politically important it was. It was one of that Government's proudest achievements finally to abolish it altogether in July 1954. The steel and road haulage industries were denationalized, but otherwise the programme of the Attlee Government was left largely unaltered. Churchill did approve breaking the monopoly on broadcasting held by the BBC, which he had long regarded as institutionally left wing and which had also kept him off the airwaves in his struggle against appeasement in the 1930s. The commercial company ITV began broadcasting in September 1955.

Churchill found the problems of peace – the economy, road haulage, trade disputes, balance of payments and so on – far duller than those of the war. Except for 'houses and meat', he concentrated his energies largely on foreign policy, although his involvement in the Korean conflict was relatively limited, as it was very much an American-led operation, even if large numbers of British troops did fight bravely there. When it was suggested that China might be invaded, he rightly opined, 'That would be the greatest folly. It would be like flies invading fly-paper.'[10] His acute historical sense told him, correctly, that his Indian Summer premiership, as it became known, would not occupy one-hundredth of the interest, perhaps in publishing terms one-thousandth – of his wartime one, and he was prone to long bouts of nostalgia. His occasional reactionary remarks were made with good humour and at the time were greeted in the playful spirit in which most of them were intended, as when he said, 'I have always considered that the substitution of the internal combustion engine for the horse marked a very gloomy milestone in the progress of mankind.'[11]

Although his general health was good for man of his age, encroaching deafness was now a problem, and he eventually had to have a hearing-aid system with an amplifier put in front of him on the Cabinet table. 'He plugged in his earphones, put them on, switched on the amplifier, tapped it once or twice, and for a quarter of an hour he held forth,' recalled Lord Mountbatten of a visit he made to No. 10 as the commander of NATO forces in the Mediterranean.[12] Churchill only switched the amplifier off when it was Mountbatten's turn to reply. 'I watched Winston today, with his hand to his ear, listening to a fellow MP in the Division Lobby,' wrote Chips Channon at this time. 'He has this trick of pretending to be deafer than he is, when he wants to shed a bore, or protect himself from importunities.'[13] One reporter noted that, when Churchill first had to resort to hearing-aids in Opposition, he was reluctant to be seen using them in public, 'Since then, however, he has come to employ them as a weapon in debate, like his glasses.'[14]

Churchill's once-prodigious memory was also starting to let him down. Soon after appointing him, he forgot the name of an under-secretary in his Government, and it was impossible to expect him to remember those of his backbenchers. He could still make jokes about their names though; of Sir Alfred Bossom he told Eden, 'But that is ridiculous; that is neither one thing nor the other.'[15] To help himself he used nicknames; Sir Thomas Padmore was 'Potsdam' and General Sir Nevil Brownjohn 'Shorthorn', for example.[16] He could nevertheless occasionally stun the House with his memory, as when he was asked the name of his under-secretary for Welsh affairs, and, after answering correctly, he added in fluent Welsh 'Môr o gân yw Cymru i gyd' (All Wales is a sea of song).[17] He later explained that he had learned the phrase at an Eisteddfod he had attended with Lloyd George over thirty years earlier.

'Conscious that many people feel that he is too old to form a government,' Harold Macmillan observed at the start of the ministry, 'he has used these days to give a demonstration of energy and vitality. He has voted in every division; made a series of brilliant little speeches; shown all his qualities of humour and sarcasm, and crowned it all by a remarkable breakfast (at 7.30 a.m.) of eggs, bacon, sausages and coffee, followed by a large whisky and soda and a huge cigar. The latter feat commanded general admiration.'[18] Churchill said privately that he intended to be prime minister for only a year before handing over to Eden. 'He just wanted, he said, to have time to re-establish the intimate relationship with the United States . . .', Colville recorded, 'and to restore at home the liberties which had been eroded by war-time restrictions and post-war socialist measures.'[19] Since

Labour had nationalized one-fifth of the nation's Gross Domestic Product over the past six years, rescinding socialist measures was clearly going to take more than one year. Furthermore, his concentration on foreign policy would inevitably lead to clashes with Eden, whose courage, integrity and energy he respected, but not always his judgement. In his 'Indian Summer' premiership, Churchill tended to listen to Christopher Soames and Norman Brook, whom he elected to the Other Club, more than to Eden.

Another complication in Churchill's relationship with Eden was that Clarissa Churchill, Jack's beautiful and charming daughter, had been going out with the Foreign Secretary, who was by then divorced from his first wife Beatrice. Although Eden was twenty-three years older than Clarissa, they were married in August 1952, with the reception held at No. 10. Churchill used Clarissa as a conduit to send his future nephew-in-law messages, as in late November that year, when Eden's private secretary noted in his diary, 'P.M. has told Clarissa he wants to give up. She says he is looking for an opportunity and Anthony must be gentle with him.'[20] If indeed Churchill did say that to his niece one year into what turned out to be a three-and-a-half-year premiership, it was disingenuous. When the very next month at Chequers Eden asked him directly when he intended to go, Churchill replied, after a long silence, 'Often I think there are things I could say, speeches I could make more easily, if I were not Prime Minister.'[21] That was verging on deception.

Churchill had already abandoned the wartime practices of afternoon naps and late-night reading of the first editions of the next day's papers, but he smoked just as many cigars and, in Colville's recollection, 'although he was never inebriated (or, indeed, drank between meals anything but soda-water flavoured with whisky), he would still consume, without the smallest ill-effect, enough champagne and brandy at luncheon or dinner to incapacitate any lesser man'.[22] 'When I was younger I made it a rule never to take strong drink before lunch,' Churchill told the King in January 1952. 'It is now my rule never to do so before breakfast.'[23]

Churchill lost no time in also disappointing those who wanted Britain to join the project for European unity, including both his sons-in-law Duncan Sandys and Christopher Soames. On 29 November 1951, he wrote a minute on Robert Schuman's visionary plan for a European Iron and Steel Community – which was to form the basis for the later European Economic Community – that stated unequivocally,

> Our attitude towards further economic developments on the Schuman lines resembles that which we adopt about the European Army. We help, we

> dedicate, we play a part, but we are not merged with and do not forfeit our insular or Commonwealth character. Our first object is the unity and consolidation of the British Commonwealth ... Our second, 'the fraternal association' of the English-speaking world; and third, United Europe, to which we are a separate, closely- and specially-related ally and friend ... It is only when plans for uniting Europe take a federal form that we ourselves cannot take part, because we cannot subordinate ourselves or the control of British policy to federal authorities.[24]

'Where do we stand?' he asked the Commons eighteen months later.

> We are not members of the European Defence Community, nor do we intend to be merged in a Federal European system. We feel we have a special relation to both. This can be expressed by prepositions, by the preposition 'with' but not 'of' – we are with them, but not of them. We have our own Commonwealth and Empire ... We shall continue to play a full and active part in plans for the political, military and economic association of Western Europe with the North Atlantic Alliance.[25]

Soon after coming to power, Churchill reduced his own and his colleagues' ministerial salaries to set the nation an example of voluntary economy, which was denounced by Woodrow Wyatt as a 'cheap demagogic gesture', but which seemed to be appreciated by the country. 'I think the honourable Gentleman is a judge of cheap demagogic gestures,' he replied to Wyatt, 'but they do not often come off when he makes them.'[26] Another early act was to ensure that a pension provision was made for the heroic Polish general Tadeusz Bór-Komorowski, who had led the Warsaw Uprising but was by then living in England and working as an upholsterer. He also awarded a peerage to General Sir George 'Ma' Jeffreys, his commanding officer in the trenches.

While Churchill enjoyed scoring points off his opponents as much as any politician during his Indian Summer premiership, he generally eschewed naked partisanship. In a defence debate on 6 December 1951, he commended Attlee and even Shinwell for their patriotic efforts over conscription, the atomic bomb and rearmament. Macmillan recorded that there were 'tears in his eyes' when he did so.[27] Churchill even paid Aneurin Bevan a backhanded compliment in the same debate when he gave him 'an honourable mention for having, it appears by accident, perhaps not from the best of motives, happened to be right'.[28] This lack of ideological partisanship was most regularly seen in the approach he took to the trade unions. In December 1940 he had told Colville that after the war 'He did not wish to lead a party struggle or a class struggle against the Labour leaders who were now serving him so well.'[29] That sentiment endured into peacetime, and was fully taken advantage of by organized labour, whose demands increased in step with their appeasement. Tom O'Brien, the TUC President, would visit Churchill on holiday in the south of France, and the Government's determination to pursue industrial peace at almost any cost led to inflationary wage settlements, especially once public sector unions demanded pay comparability with private corporations and the Government failed to point out the differences between the two, not least in terms of job security. There was a series of what have been called 'industrial Munichs' during the Indian Summer ministry, such as when Churchill phoned Butler to boast that he had averted a threatened Christmas rail strike in 1954. Not unnaturally, the Chancellor of the Exchequer asked on whose terms the dispute had been settled? 'Theirs, old cock!' came the Prime Minister's breezy reply.[30]

It is doubtful that any of this would have been very different if Eden rather than Churchill had been prime minister. For all that the personnel made it look like a reprise of the glory days of the war, this was going to be, as Churchill had said of Baldwin's 1924–9 ministry, 'a capable, sedate government'.[31] The fading red 'Action this day' labels were left out on the Cabinet table on the day of Churchill's return to office, but since they were never used they were later put back in a drawer.

'We are resolved to make this Island solvent, able to earn its living and pay its way,' Churchill said in a broadcast in December, just prior to leaving for America for a summit meeting. 'We have no assurance that anyone else is going to keep the British lion as a pet.'[32] He boarded the *Queen Mary* at Southampton on New Year's Eve with an entourage reminiscent of the great wartime transatlantic journeys, including Eden, Ismay, Lindemann, Sir William Slim (the CIGS) and Colville. When it turned out that the anchor was fouled and they had to spend the night in port, Mountbatten came over from his nearby country house at Broadlands, but, according to Colville, 'talked arrant political nonsense . . . The P.M. laughed at him but did not, so Pug Ismay thought, snub him sufficiently.'[33]

During the crossing everyone worked hard on mountains of paperwork except Churchill, who said he was going to America 'to re-establish relations, not to transact business'.[34] In fact there was much more to it than that: Churchill wanted American support against Egyptian demands that Britain give up her bases in the Suez Canal Zone, and to establish new terms of formal nuclear cooperation between Britain and America that had been severed by the McMahon Act.

Churchill stayed at the British Embassy in Washington and the talks were held at the White House. President Truman was personally as friendly as ever, but he would not move on either Suez or the nuclear issue. On 10 January, Churchill took a train to Ottawa, where Colville had written a speech for him to deliver to both Houses of the Canadian Parliament. 'I may feel bound to use it,' Churchill told him, 'in which case it will be the first time in my career I have ever used somebody else's speech.'[35] In the end, he wrote his own. He had almost cancelled the trip upon learning that the Canadian Government had decided that 'Rule, Britannia' should no longer be played by the Canadian Navy or Air Force. He was persuaded not to by Clementine, who, according to Colville, threatened 'to close down Chartwell and move to a flat by the sea in Brighton' if he did.[36] When he disembarked from the sleeper in Ottawa, the Royal Canadian Air Force band struck up 'Rule, Britannia'. Needless to say, Churchill wept.

Back in Washington on 17 January, Churchill delivered his third and last speech to a Joint Meeting of Congress. (He had still been in bed in the Embassy working on the speech when he needed to leave and had arrived at the Capitol with only two minutes to spare.) 'It is my belief that by accumulating deterrents of all kinds against aggression we shall, in fact, ward off the fearful catastrophe,' he said, 'the fears of which darken the life and mar the progress of all the peoples of the globe.'[37] He added of the Korean War, 'Our two countries are agreed that if the truce we seek is reached, only to be broken, our response will be prompt, resolute and effective.'[38] That went down well in America, but at home he was criticized by the Labour Party for seeming to advocate a nuclear war against China. Churchill pointed out that there was no atomic implication to the words 'prompt, resolute and effective', and 'Certainly, if one is dealing in general terms, they are better than "tardy, timid and fatuous".'[39]

Over Suez, Churchill profoundly disagreed with Eden, who believed that Britain should cede the Canal Zone unilaterally to foster good relations with Egypt. This prompted Churchill's jibe to Colville that he 'never knew before that Munich was situated on the Nile'. He privately described Eden as a failure as foreign secretary, 'tired, sick and bound up in detail'.[40] It had long been a source of regret to him that he had held every great office except that of foreign secretary and he said to Colville that if Eden resigned over Suez he would take over the Foreign Office himself.

On 6 February 1952, King George VI died in his sleep at Sandringham, aged only fifty-six, yet another of Churchill's friends and Paladins – the King had fought at the Battle of Jutland – to die tragically young. Edward Ford, the King's assistant private secretary, found Churchill in bed at No. 10 at 9.15 a.m., with papers strewn all around him, and said, 'Prime Minister, I've got bad news for you,' and told him of the death. 'Bad news?'

replied Churchill. 'The worst.' Ford recalled that 'He slumped as a man in shock, clearly deeply affected. He then thrust his papers aside, saying "How unimportant these matters seem." '[41] Churchill phoned Eden to say, 'Anthony, imagine the worst thing that could possibly happen . . .'[42] Soon afterwards, Colville found Churchill sitting alone with tears in his eyes, looking straight in front of him and reading neither his official papers nor his newspapers. 'I had not realised how much the King had meant to him,' he recorded. 'I tried to cheer him up by saying how well he would get on with the new Queen, but all he could say was that he did not know her and that she was only a child.'[43]

'During these last months the King walked with death, as if death were a companion, an acquaintance, whom he recognized and did not fear,' Churchill said in a broadcast that same evening. 'In the end, death came as a friend; and after a happy day of sunshine and sport, and after saying goodnight to those who loved him best, he fell asleep as every man or woman who strives to fear God and nothing else in the world may hope to do.'[44]

As well as crying when he heard the news of the King's death, Churchill cried while dictating his eulogy to Jane Portal, his secretary and the air marshal's niece, then on rehearsing the broadcast, and then again on the way to Heathrow Airport to meet the new Queen, Elizabeth II, who was returning with the Duke of Edinburgh from Kenya, and then also at the King's funeral at Windsor Castle on 15 February.[45] Much more unusually, he refused a whisky and soda at the Deanery after the funeral.[46] On his note that was placed on top of the King's coffin, Churchill wrote the words 'For Valour', the rubric of the Victoria Cross.

Churchill had ended his broadcast on the death of the King on a more positive note, drawing on history as few others could: 'I, whose youth was passed in the august, unchallenged and tranquil glories of the Victorian era, may well feel a thrill in invoking, once more, the prayer and the anthem, "God Save the Queen!" ' Now, in the Commons on 11 February, he said of the young Queen, 'With the new reign we must all feel our contact with the future. A fair and youthful figure – princess, wife and mother – is the heir to all our traditions and glories never greater than in her father's days, and to all our perplexities and dangers never greater in peacetime than now. She is also heir to all our united strength and loyalty.'[47] The Queen was twenty-five, but Churchill had spotted early promise in her. In January 1944 he had proposed that when she became eighteen that April she should be given the title Elizabeth, Princess of Wales. The King had turned down the idea, but it showed the confidence Churchill had long had in her abilities. Churchill established an early and excellent rapport with the new monarch, with whom, as all his entourage immediately spotted, he became besotted.

'When Winston had his weekly audience in the Bow Room at Buckingham Palace,' Lascelles wrote in his diary, 'I, having shown him in, would sit next door till he came out, when we shared whiskies and soda for half an hour. I could not hear what they were talking about, but it was, more often than not, punctuated by peals of laughter, and Winston generally came out wiping his eyes. "She's *en grande beauté ce soir*," he said one evening in his schoolboy French.'[48] On another occasion he commented to Moran, 'All the film people in all the world, if they had scoured the globe, could not have found anyone so suited to the part.'[49]

When Churchill woke up on the morning of 21 February 1952, he found he had difficulty in finding the words for what he wanted to say. He had suffered another cerebral arterial spasm; as an historian of Churchill's health has put it, there was 'evidence of a more generalized insufficiency of the blood supplying a large area of the lateral portion of the left brain'.[50] Moran warned that it 'might be the precursor to an immediate stroke; if not, it was a plain warning that if the pressure were not relaxed, dire results would follow in six months or less'.[51] Churchill therefore handed over the Ministry of Defence to Field Marshal (now Earl) Alexander, but he showed no interest in Moran's advice that he give up the premiership, and crucially Clementine did not insist upon it.

Soon, as so often before, his remarkable powers of recuperation reasserted themselves. At a party at No. 10 later that month for Ismay, who was about to take up the post of secretary-general of NATO, Ismay said in his speech that he regretted leaving behind his herd of Jersey cows in Gloucestershire. 'Quite easy,' heckled Churchill. 'Milk the cows in the morning, fly to Paris, and milk the Americans in the afternoon!'[52] (Lascelles nervously checked there were no Americans present.) On the question of whether the Army should adopt Belgian, British or American automatic rifles, Sir William Slim said, 'I suppose we shall end up with some mongrel weapon, half-British and half-American.' 'Pray moderate your language, Field Marshal,' said Churchill. 'That's an exact description of me.'[53]

As lunchtime approached, Churchill did not like ministers leaving meetings before him, but when he got bored he himself would find ways of leaving early. At one Defence Committee meeting recalled by John Boyd-Carpenter, a junior Cabinet minister,

> He suddenly interrupted, pointing a finger at the window, and said in a loud voice, 'What's that bird?' Ministers, generals and others started giving quick

> identifications. 'I think it was a jay, Prime Minister,' said one. 'A big seagull, Prime Minister,' said another. In the confusion he got up from his chair and began to leave the Cabinet Room. On his way he passed me and I quite daringly said, 'I didn't see the bird, Prime Minister.' 'There wasn't one,' he said, with an immensely pleased grin, and stumped happily out of the room. He had obviously enjoyed seeing these eminent men making fools of themselves in attempting to please him.[54]

(This tactic wouldn't have worked in the war, as Brooke was an eminent ornithologist with no interest in pleasing him.)

Churchill's rhetoric sometimes spilled over from public meetings and Parliament into his everyday conversation. When Sir Steuart Mitchell, the Controller of Guided Weapons and Electronics at the Ministry of Supply, showed Churchill and Clementine a film of a guided missile in March 1952, Churchill said to her, 'This *contraption* seeks out the enemy. Smells him out. And devoid of human aid encompasses his destruction.'[55] His dry wit was on constant display at Prime Minister's Questions. When in 1952 a pompous Tory MP, Raymond Gower, called for a national day of prayer and asked, 'Will the Prime Minister assure the House that, while we have quite properly attended to the physical needs of defence and of our other problems, we should not neglect these spiritual resources which have inspired this country in the past and without which the noblest civilization would decay?' Churchill replied, 'I hardly think that that is my exclusive responsibility.'[56]

Labour MPs found it hard to score points off Churchill, even when he quite plainly contradicted himself. When James Callaghan, a future Labour prime minister, pointed out that he had said one thing in opposition about the post of Allied naval commander in the Mediterranean but quite another in government, Churchill merely smiled and said, 'My views are a harmonious process which keeps them in relation to the current movement of events.'[57] Churchill had several Labour MPs who constantly tried to trip him up, principally Bevan, Shinwell, Callaghan, Wyatt and Emrys Hughes, but such were his put-downs that by 1954 booklets were being published containing his best epithets against them. 'I can assure the right honourable Gentleman that the spectacle of a number of middle-aged gentlemen who are my political opponents being in a state of uproar and fury is really quite exhilarating to me,' he told Herbert Morrison.[58]

In April 1952, Montgomery, who was a regular visitor at Chartwell, asked Churchill to define 'a great man', asking whether Hitler, for example, had been great. 'No,' Churchill replied, 'he made too many mistakes.'[59] Whereupon Montgomery pressed him on Napoleon, whom he described as 'the Hitler of the nineteenth century'. Sadly Churchill's refutation of that canard was not recorded. 'And surely the great religious leaders were the real great men?' Montgomery continued. 'The P.M. said their greatness was indisputable, but it was of a different kind. Christ's story was unequalled and his death to save sinners unsurpassed; moreover the Sermon on the Mount was the last word in ethics.' Churchill was not exactly acknowledging Christ's divinity, but his statement that the Crucifixion saved sinners was the closest he ever came to it.

On 23 May, for the first time in his very long political career, Churchill delivered a speech that had been written by someone else. It was to a dinner of tax inspectors, and Colville, who had written it, saw that as 'a sign of advancing senility'.[60] Churchill was by no means yet approaching senility, though he was certainly able to make jokes about his old age. When a Labour MP said that the Prime Minister was giving the House less information than Gladstone had at the time of the Crimean War, he replied, 'I am afraid I have not got at my fingers' ends the exact part which Mr Gladstone took in the Crimean War; it was even before my time.'[61] He persistently deflected serious criticism by eliciting the laughter of the Commons, on both sides of the aisle.

By June, Churchill saw the possible election of Dwight Eisenhower in the presidential elections in November as a further reason to stay in office, in order to bring about another Big Three summit at which he could broker a lasting settlement with the Russians. Otherwise, as he told Colville, 'The zest is diminished.'[62] He had fish tanks installed in his working library at Chartwell and filled with brightly coloured tropical fish, the feeding of which, Colville complained, 'was a frequent diversion from serious work'.[63] In July, a lift was installed at Chartwell at Beaverbrook's expense, which went up one storey, from the ground floor to Churchill's bedroom and study on the first floor.

When in the summer of 1952, Hewlett Johnson, the 'Red Dean' of Canterbury, returned from the USSR and Communist China with what he claimed was 'cast iron evidence' that the Americans had been using germ warfare in Korea, Churchill refused all calls for him to face an inquiry, saying, 'Free speech carries with it the evil of all foolish, unpleasant and venomous things that are said, but on the whole we would rather lump them than do away with it.'[64] (The evidence turned out to have been falsified.) Churchill managed to persuade Truman to join him in sending Mohammed Mossaddegh a stern warning about his anti-Western stance in August. It was the first time since 1945 that the Americans had taken Britain's side against a third power. Eden, who was on honeymoon at the time, approved.

*Closing the Ring*, the fifth volume of Churchill's war memoirs, which took the account up to the eve of D-Day, was published in September, during the American presidential election campaign, and contained no strictures on Eisenhower, the Republican candidate. 'I want no criticism of America at my table,' Churchill said at a lunch at No. 10. 'The Americans criticize themselves more than enough.'[65] Surprisingly enough, Churchill privately wanted Adlai Stevenson, the Democratic candidate, to beat his old wartime comrade, because he believed that Eisenhower was 'violently Russophobe' and would not want the wide-ranging conference with the Soviets for which he was starting to hanker as the grand finale of his political career.[66] What Churchill failed to appreciate was that neither the USA nor the USSR was particularly interested in coming to terms at that time, and even if they had been they no longer needed him to facilitate it.

At 9.15 a.m. local time on 3 October 1952, Operation Hurricane turned Britain into the world's third nuclear power, when an atomic bomb exploded in the Monte Bello Islands in the Pacific with a force larger than those that had destroyed Hiroshima and Nagasaki put together. Churchill had prepared two telegrams for Sir William Penney, the Director of the Atomic Energy Research Establishment: 'Thank you, Dr Penney' if it were a failure, but 'Well done, Sir William' if a success.[67] Churchill was informed at Balmoral, where there is some film footage of him chatting to Prince Charles and waving a clublike piece of driftwood while out on a fishing expedition with the Royal Family. (Prince Charles later recalled Churchill had said he was 'waiting on the Loch Ness monster'.)[68] Soon nuclear technology made its quantum leap to the thermonuclear hydrogen bomb, which had a potential yield hundreds of times greater than Nagasaki and Hiroshima combined, and in June 1954 Churchill ordered that a British version should be built; one was successfully tested in 1957. He told Colville that 'we are now as far from the age of the atomic bomb as the atomic bomb itself from the bow and arrow.'[69]

Dwight Eisenhower was elected president on 4 November 1952. 'For your private ear,' Churchill told Colville, 'I am greatly disturbed. I think this makes war much more probable.'[70] Even before Eisenhower had been inaugurated, Churchill decided to repeat his Washington trip of the previous year. 'He is getting tired and visibly ageing,' Colville wrote. 'He finds it hard work to compose a speech and ideas no longer flow.'[71] Before Churchill left for America, however, he had to deal with a vote of no confidence in early December. 'I have today to deal with a motion of censure,' he said, 'and therefore I hope I shall be pardoned if I do not confine myself entirely to the uncontroversial methods which I usually practise.'[72] He could not let the opportunity go without a dig at Bevan, noting that he 'resumes his role of virtuous indignation reinforced with the abuse for which he is celebrated'. Bevan's demands for Churchill's resignation during the war and his remark about Tories being 'lower than vermin' more than justified the Prime Minister's regular, hard-hitting rebukes. Churchill even attacked Bevan when he wasn't directly involved in a particular issue: when recalling his own suggestion in 1949 that Communist China should be recognized, Churchill said, 'If you recognize anyone it does not mean that you like him. We all, for instance, recognize the right honourable Gentleman the Member for Ebbw Vale.'[73]

On 30 December, Churchill boarded the *Queen Mary* again, with Clementine, Mary and Christopher Soames to sail to New York, talking on the train to Southampton of the War of 1812 and the future of Pakistan. He wanted to have a broad *tour d'horizon* with the President-elect, which would include Mossaddegh, the European Army, the Korean War, Suez and the Mau Mau terrorism of the Kikuyu tribe against white farmers in British Kenya. He said he intended 'to preach to Eisenhower the vital importance of a common Anglo-American front "from Korea to Kikuyu and from Kikuyu to Calais" '.[74] Whether the President-elect was in a mood to continue to be preached at by Churchill was another matter.

On the journey, Churchill lamented to Colville that owing to Eisenhower's victory he would have to excise from *Triumph and Tragedy*, the sixth and concluding volume of his war memoirs, 'the story of how the United States gave away, to please Russia, vast tracts of Europe they had occupied and how suspicious they were of his pleas for caution'.[75] He claimed that the 1945 general election had occupied so much of his attention that he could not stem 'this fatal tide', and that had Roosevelt survived 'he would have seen the red light in time to check the American policy: Truman, after all, had only been a novice, bewildered by the march of events and by responsibilities which he had never expected.' This version of history was faulty. Both the European Advisory Commission and the Yalta Agreement had preceded Truman's presidency, and in 1945 Churchill had expressed great hope and conviction that Poland was going to retain its integrity and independence. The Allies could hardly have done any more for Poland with the Red Army in complete occupation of eastern Europe, and with the legitimate government in London unable to return to Warsaw under threat of incarceration, or worse. Churchill was attempting to revise history to his advantage and to Truman's disadvantage, although he must have known that Colville knew the truth, and so was thus merely venting his grievances.

After dinner in the Verandah Grill of the *Queen Mary*, Colville fired thirty questions at Churchill that he might be expected to be asked at his press conference on arrival in New York, such as:

Colville: 'What are your views, Mr Churchill, on the present stalemate in Korea?'

Churchill: 'Better a stalemate than a checkmate.'

Colville: 'How do you justify such a great expenditure on the Coronation of your Queen, when England is in such financial straits?'

Churchill: 'Everyone likes to wear a flower when he goes to see his girl.'

Colville: 'Is not British policy in Persia throwing Persia into the hands of the Communists?'

Churchill: 'If Britain and America refuse to be disunited, no ill can come.'[76]

The *Queen Mary* docked in New York on the morning of 5 January 1953, and the Churchills went to stay at Bernard Baruch's apartment on Fifth Avenue, where Eisenhower visited at 5 p.m., fifteen days before becoming president. 'Winston said that a protoplasm was sexless,' recorded Colville. 'Then it divided into two sexes which, in due course, united again in a different way to their common benefit and gratification. This should also be the story of England and America.'[77] Eisenhower's diary noted that Churchill 'is as charming and interesting as ever, but he is quite definitely showing the effects of the passing years'.[78] Of the importance of Britain enthusiastically joining the European Unity project, he wrote, 'It is almost frustrating to attempt to make Winston see how important it is [for Britain to show] leadership in bringing about this development . . . He has developed an almost childlike faith that all of the answers are to be found merely in British-American partnership . . . Winston is trying to relive the days of World War Two.' During the substantive talks the two men also disagreed on Indo-China, Iran, the Suez Canal Zone evacuation, Britain joining the proposed European Army and especially a nuclear non-proliferation deal with the Soviets. The sermons Churchill had promised to preach Eisenhower were indeed not appreciated, although the old wartime nostalgia was. Churchill also saw the Duke and Duchess of Windsor in New York on that trip, but only for half an hour. Their behaviour during the war had ended any lingering affection for them that Churchill had once had.

On 7 January 1953, at Eisenhower's suggestion, John Foster Dulles, who was about to be sworn in as secretary of state, told Churchill baldly that it was a 'most unfortunate' idea for him to visit Washington in early February, at the very start of Eisenhower's presidency, because Americans already thought Churchill had too much influence over American foreign policy. 'Whereupon W[inston] sat up and growled,' recorded Colville.[79] Before he went to bed, Churchill 'said some very harsh things about the Republican Party in general and Dulles in particular', which Soames and Colville thought 'both unjust and dangerous'. He said he wanted nothing more to do with Dulles, whose 'great slab of a face' he 'disliked and distrusted'.[80] Only a few days later, Churchill described Eisenhower as 'a real man of limited stature'.[81] Ever since the days of Bourke Cochran, and certainly since the 1920s, Churchill had sympathized with the Democrats in American politics.

On 8 January, Churchill had dinner at the British Embassy in Washington with President Truman, who had less than two weeks left in office. He made a pro-Zionist speech, which practically all the Americans present disliked, though they admitted to Colville 'that the large Jewish vote would prevent them disagreeing publicly'.[82] It was on that occasion that Churchill said to Truman, 'I hope you have your answer ready for that hour when you and I stand before St Peter and he says, "I understand you two are responsible for setting off those atomic bombs." '[83] Before Truman could reply, Robert Lovett, the US Defense Secretary, intervened: 'Are you sure, Prime Minister, that you are going to be in the same place as the President for that interrogation?' 'Lovett,' replied Churchill, 'my vast respect for the Creator of this universe and countless others gives me assurance that He would not condemn a man without a hearing.'

After the President had left, the Americans – Harriman, Acheson and General Walter Bedell Smith among them – ganged up on Churchill over the question of the proposed European Army, which they all supported but which, Colville reported, he described as ' "a sludgy amalgam" infinitely less effective than a Grand Alliance of national armies'.[84] They got nowhere with him over his opposition to fusing the European countries' armed forces into one outside NATO, which therefore never happened.

Churchill's remark about St Peter was typical of his thoughts at the time; while shaving on the morning of 24 January, he said to Colville, 'It's the day my father died. It's the day I shall die, too.'[85]

The death of Joseph Stalin in Moscow on 5 March 1953 meant that Churchill was the last of the Big Three left alive, and he had been the eldest. 'What is called the cold war – which is not a legal term – continues,' he said that day. 'What we are faced with is not a violent jerk, but a prolonged pull. We must create forces which can play a real part as a deterrent against aggression and also can afford some measure of defence should war come.'[86] When Stalin's death was announced the next day, he telegraphed Eisenhower urging him to take advantage of the new situation in Moscow, suggesting that he himself would be willing to make what he called a 'solitary pilgrimage' there, to see if the West and the USSR could write a new page in history, 'with something more coherent on it than a series of casual and dangerous incidents at the many points of contact between the two divisions of the world'.[87]

Eden was in Boston being treated for the effects of a botched gall-bladder operation in April, and was not back until the autumn. His illness was so serious that David Astor, editor of the *Observer*, tried to commission an obituary from Lord Cranborne (who had become the 5th Marquess of Salisbury in 1947).[88] Churchill seriously considered moving into the Foreign Office and working from there, as the 3rd Marquess had while prime minister. Without consulting the Cabinet or the Foreign Office, let alone Eisenhower and Dulles, in May Churchill took advantage of Eden's incapacity to make a sensational statement to the Commons. A 'conference on the highest level should take place between the leading Powers without long delay,' he announced, 'at the summit of the nations . . . At the worst the participants . . . would have established more intimate contacts. At the best we might have a generation of peace.'[89] Some in the Cabinet considered resignation over this unauthorized démarche, and to offset it Eisenhower hastily convened a meeting in Bermuda in June, to which, to Churchill's chagrin, he also invited the French. No one at the time knew it, but that was to be the last speech the Prime Minister was to deliver in Parliament for five months.

Churchill's final acceptance of the Order of the Garter in April 1953 allowed him to look magnificent in its mantle (which he wore over his uniform as lord warden of the Cinque Ports) at the Coronation two months later. He now became 'Sir Winston', and was able to joke, 'Now Clemmie will have to be a lady at last.'[90] At the investiture ceremony, he wore the same insignia as the 1st Duke of Marlborough in 1702. When Emrys Hughes asked in the Commons whether he would not now be going to 'another place' – meaning the House of Lords – Churchill replied, 'Provided the term "another place" is used in its strictly Parliamentary sense, I will gladly give the assurance required.'[91]

The Coronation of Queen Elizabeth II on 2 June 1953 seemed another good time for Churchill to retire, just as Baldwin had after the previous Coronation, but he could not because of Eden's absence, and he still wanted to pursue his dream of ending the Cold War. 'I'm glad I was wrong,' Churchill said of the Abdication at this time. 'We could not have had a better king. And now we have this splendid Queen.'[92]*

Shortly after the Coronation, an issue arose as to whether Princess Margaret, the Queen's younger sister, should be allowed to marry the divorcee Group Captain Peter Townsend, her late father's equerry. 'This

* To a young American student before a Coronation luncheon in Westminster Hall on 27 May, Churchill gave the extremely sage advice, 'Study history, study history. In history lie all the secrets of statecraft' (OB VIII p. 835).

is most important,' Churchill told Tommy Lascelles. 'One motor accident, and this young lady might be our queen.'[93] (In fact it would have had to have been an accident that also killed Prince Charles and Princess Anne.) Although emotionally Churchill liked the idea of a gallant and handsome Battle of Britain fighter pilot marrying a beautiful princess, once it was pointed out to him by Lascelles at Chartwell that some Commonwealth countries might not accept the child of a divorcee as their future monarch, he decided that Princess Margaret must renounce her right to the throne in order to marry Townsend.[94] The main thing, he emphasized, was to give the least possible pain and anxiety to the Queen. The relationship ended, and Princess Margaret blamed Lascelles for ruining her life. In fact it had been Churchill, in consultation with Lord Salisbury and Rab Butler, but not with the divorcee Eden, who was still in Boston.

On Tuesday, 23 June 1953, at the conclusion of a dinner at No. 10 for Alcide De Gasperi, the Prime Minister of Italy, Churchill, who had made a delightful impromptu speech about the Italian contribution to civilization, suffered a stroke.[95] 'He sat down and was almost unable to move,' wrote Colville. 'After the guests had left, he leant heavily on my arm but managed to walk to his bedroom.'[96] No one seemed alarmed by the Prime Minister's slurred speech and unsteadiness on his feet, one of the advantages of having a reputation for enjoying alcohol. Moran diagnosed a stroke, yet such was Churchill's extraordinary physical constitution that he was able to preside over the Cabinet the next morning, as he had not been mentally incapacitated by it.[97] The medical records of his neurologist, the appositely named Sir Russell (later Lord) Brain, show that Churchill made a steady and relatively quick recovery, although there were naturally serious concerns at the time.

'I certainly noticed nothing beyond the fact that he was very white,' Harold Macmillan recalled of the Cabinet meeting of the morning of 24 June. 'He spoke little, but quite distinctly.'[98] Butler agreed that nobody noticed anything strange except that the Prime Minister was quieter than usual.[99] Yet the minutes show that he spoke at least one paragraph on four of the five different subjects under discussion.[100]

Churchill was taken to Chartwell at noon the following day. 'I must tell you, with great sorrow, that the PM is seriously ill,' Colville wrote to Lindemann that afternoon.

> He had an arterial spasm, or possibly a clot, after the De Gasperi dinner on Tuesday. His articulation and his movements are seriously affected and unless – as is just possible – there is a miraculous recovery in the next forty eight hours . . . his office will have to be abandoned. His courage is beyond praise and Clemmie's too; but it is heart-rending to be here and to see the

> physical deterioration that has asserted itself. He finds great difficulty in speech and since this morning he has all but lost the use of his left arm.[101]

Moran feared he might not live through the weekend.

Lascelles (and thus the Queen), Eden, Norman Brook, Salisbury, Butler, Lindemann and Patrick Buchan-Hepburn, who had taken over as Tory chief whip in 1948, were all told about the stroke, on an almost wartime need-to-know basis, yet not a word about it was published until Churchill himself casually mentioned it in a speech in the Commons a year later.[102] Churchill's close and long friendships with almost all the major press barons, especially Beaverbrook, Bracken, Camrose and Esmond Rothermere, made this possible – another great trial for which he had inadvertently long prepared. His friends' code of *omertà* did the rest.

Over the next three weeks, when Churchill was incapacitated at Chartwell, several important subjects were to come before Cabinet, including the Korean War, East–West trade, British shipping in the China Seas, the European Defence Community, a treaty with Libya, food prices, a Regency Bill, the sheikhdoms of the Persian Gulf, televising the State Opening of Parliament, the appointment of a royal commission on the press, rail fares, the development of Gatwick Airport and the situation in Egypt.[103] With Eden undergoing another gall-bladder operation, Rab Butler presided at Cabinet the Monday after the stroke, saying that the Prime Minister 'was suffering from severe over-strain' and would 'lighten his duties for at least a month', but would 'continue to receive the more important official papers'.[104]

After a week, Churchill began to improve, though Colville noted that 'his powers of concentration appeared slight and he preferred Trollope's political novels to work'.[105] Christopher Soames helped carry on the business of government, seeing secret Cabinet documents not normally permitted to a mere parliamentary private secretary. (By then, in Colville's psychologically acute phrase, Soames 'held the place in Churchill's heart so long reserved for Randolph who had been incapable of filling it'.)[106] This unconstitutional state of affairs, in which the Prime Minister's son-in-law and an unelected private secretary (Jock Colville) held effective executive power in Britain via the equally unelected Cabinet Secretary – even if they did not use it – continued for several weeks until the end of July, by which time Churchill was sufficiently restored to take an active interest in affairs of state.[107]

Moran and Brain meanwhile signed an anodyne and misleading communiqué that did not mention the stroke but stated that Churchill was 'in need of a complete rest' because of the strain of the Coronation. Nor were the Americans told the truth about why the Bermuda Conference now needed to be postponed for a full six months. In retrospect, it seems extraordinary that Churchill could have continued in office for nearly two more years after suffering such a serious medical setback. Either Clementine or the Queen could have stepped in, but neither did so; nor did any Cabinet minister wish to be seen to conspire against him. Although Eden wrote to Salisbury on 14 July, 'I confess to being rather taken aback that he has come to no final decisions,' he lacked the ruthlessness, or heartlessness, to strike.[108]

Moran stated in his (not wholly reliable) diaries that thirteen days after the stroke Churchill was able to declaim the first thirty-four lines of Longfellow's poem 'King Robert of Sicily', getting only half a dozen words wrong out of more than 250.[109] Yet most of Churchill's entourage believed that Moran invented and exaggerated too much for his testimony to be worthwhile, and Lord Brain wrote to *The Times* in 1966 saying, 'I cannot accept the accuracy of all that Lord Moran says about the consultations which he reports.'[110] There were some things that Moran recorded that do ring true, however, such as Churchill saying on 2 July that he did 'not believe in another world; only in black velvet – eternal sleep'.[111] Churchill also noted that of the seventeen politicians in Sir James Guthrie's group portrait *Some Statesmen of the Great War*, he was the only one still alive.* The next day, Churchill spoke of his chronic lachrymosity, saying that he had even cried over *Phineas Finn*, 'though it is not at all a moving story'.[112] In April 1952, he had cried at Stafford Cripps's memorial service, despite disliking him.[113]

By 24 July 1953, Churchill was largely restored to physical health, but he complained that his memory had suffered. He intended to resign in October, but was still keen on the idea of 'bringing something off with the Russians and . . . the idea of meeting [Stalin's successor Georgy] Malenkov face to face'.[114] Despite the Korean War ending, at least with an armistice, Churchill still had a low estimation of the Eisenhower Administration, and regretted Adlai Stevenson's defeat the previous year. He told the Queen he would retire if he found he could not deliver the Leader's speech to the Conservative Party Conference in Margate in October. He was still capable of coining regular witticisms, however; when Soames said that Harry Mackeson should be removed as secretary for overseas trade, but didn't deserve a peerage, Churchill replied, 'No, but perhaps a disappearage.'[115] (He got a baronetcy.)

Eight weeks after his stroke, Churchill presided over a Cabinet meeting, on 18 August, which went well. The next day he decided that once he had finished *The Second World War*, the last volume of which would be published in November, he would start publishing his *History of the English-Speaking Peoples*, which he had suspended writing in 1939. 'I shall lay an egg a year,'

* William Hughes, the former Prime Minister of Australia, had died the previous year.

he said, 'a volume every twelve months should not mean much work.'[116] Even for a prime minister who had suffered a stroke. On 19 August, a CIA- and MI6-supported coup in Teheran overthrew the Mossaddegh Government of Iran and paved the way for the return of the Shah. This was to have profound international consequences, even to the present day. 'Young man,' he told the CIA operative who had organized it, who is believed to have been Kermit Roosevelt Jr, grandson of President Theodore Roosevelt, 'if I had been a few years younger, I would have liked nothing better than to have served under your command in this great venture.'[117] Churchill has been much criticized for this intervention in Iranian domestic politics, but it kept that country firmly in the Western camp for over a quarter of a century, beyond which no statesman can be expected to foresee.

Churchill delivered a fine, almost hour-long speech to the Party Conference at Margate on 10 October, attesting to his recovery and ending rumours about his retirement. He had taken an amphetamine pill beforehand which he nicknamed a 'Moran', asking afterwards, 'The pill was marvellous. What was in it?'[118] The answer was Benzedrine, but the dosage is unknown.[119] In his speech he said the previous few months had been 'the first time in my political life that I have kept quiet for so long' but did not explain why.[120] He welcomed Germany 'back among the Great Powers of the world', and said, 'If I stay on for the time being, bearing the burden of my age, it is not because of love for power or office. I have had an ample share of both. If I stay it is because I have the feeling that I may . . . have an influence on what I care about above all else, the building of a sure and lasting peace.'[121] Lord Moran meanwhile noted that while his other patients' sole concern after they had suffered strokes was in staying alive, by contrast Churchill 'never for a moment seems to give a thought to this'.[122]

On 15 October Churchill learned that he had been awarded the Nobel Prize. 'Is that you, Anthony?' he telephoned Eden in Paris. 'How are you? I thought you would like to know that I have just been awarded a Nobel Prize.' Then, after a pause and a chuckle, he added, 'But don't worry, dear, it's for Literature, not for Peace.'[123] Churchill had written thirty-seven books, of which seven were specifically cited by the Master of Ceremonies, namely *The River War*, *Lord Randolph Churchill*, *The World Crisis*, *Marlborough*, *Thoughts & Adventures*, *My Early Life* and *Great Contemporaries*. Unfortunately the award ceremony clashed with the rearranged Bermuda Conference in December, so Clementine went to Oslo to accept the Prize on his behalf. He chose in his acceptance speech to sound a tocsin about the condition of the world. 'Never in the field of action have events seemed so harshly to dwarf personalities,' she read to the Swedish Academy. 'Rarely in history have brutal facts so dominated thought or has such a widespread individual virtue found so dim a collective focus. The fearful question confronts us: Have our problems got beyond our control? Undoubtedly we are passing through a phase where this may be so.'[124] His prescription was 'tolerance, variety and calm.'

On 20 October Churchill took another 'Moran' pill before going to the House of Commons for his first Prime Minister's Questions in seventeen weeks. Woodrow Wyatt caught the mood of the Chamber when he said, 'May I first of all ask the Prime Minister whether he is aware . . . that the House of Commons is a duller place without him?'[125]

Churchill published *Triumph and Tragedy* on his seventy-ninth birthday on 30 November. He set out its theme after the title page, 'How the great democracies triumphed, and so were able to resume the follies which had so nearly cost them their life'. Back in August, Churchill and Montgomery had listed five 'capital mistakes' that they believed the Americans had made in the war, most of which had been Eisenhower's.[126]* Yet *Triumph and Tragedy* made no criticism of Eisenhower, whom Churchill flew out to Bermuda to meet the following day. Joseph Laniel, the French Prime Minister, was also going to be there. On his way out, Churchill was photographed carrying C. S. Forester's novel entitled *Death to the French*. (It was set in the Peninsular Wars, in which the 4th Hussars had fought with distinction.)

Arriving in Hamilton, the capital of Bermuda, where the Royal Welch Fusiliers paraded with their regimental mascot, Churchill telegraphed to Clementine in Stockholm, 'Excellent journey. All well. Goat splendid.'[127] When it was discovered that no black guests had been invited to the banquet at Government House, Churchill insisted that they should be.[128]

In Bermuda, Churchill completely failed to persuade Eisenhower and Dulles of the benefits of meeting Malenkov and the new Soviet leaders. At the first plenary session on 4 December, he spoke of 'easement' with the Soviet Union, which was not appeasement because it would take place from a position of strength. Yet Eisenhower responded with a statement that the Soviet Union was 'a woman of the streets and whether her dress was new, or just the old one patched, it was certainly the same whore underneath'.[129] At this, Colville noticed, there were 'Pained looks all

* '1. They had prevented Alexander getting to Tunis the first time, when he could easily have done so. 2. They had done at Anzio what Stopford did at Suvla Bay: clung to the beaches and failed to establish positions inland as they could well have done . . . 3. They had insisted on Operation Anvil, thereby preventing Alexander from taking Trieste and Vienna. 4. Eisenhower had refused to let Monty, in Overlord, concentrate his advance on the left flank. He had insisted on a broad advance, which could not be supported, and had thus allowed Rundstedt to counter-attack on the Ardennes and had prolonged the war, with dire political results, to the spring of 1945. 5. Eisenhower had let the Russians occupy Berlin, Prague and Vienna – all of which might have been entered by the Americans' (Colville, *Fringes* pp. 674–5).

round', but the French supported the Americans.[130] Before the session adjourned, Eden asked when the next meeting should be, to which Eisenhower replied, 'I don't know. Mine is with a whisky and soda.'[131]

Churchill and Eisenhower had earlier discussed what would happen if North Korea broke the armistice which had been signed on 27 July, and which had brought the fighting to an end without a peace treaty. When the Americans announced their inclination to use the atomic bomb if the Chinese supported the North Koreans again, Churchill and Eden were strongly opposed now that the Western powers no longer had an atomic monopoly.[132] Other discussions, on 5–8 December, on Egypt, which the Americans were threatening to supply with weapons, on Indo-China and on the European Army, were completely overshadowed by the nuclear issue. To appeals from Eisenhower that Britain should commit troops in support of France in Indo-China, Churchill replied that he had reached his eightieth year without ever having heard the word 'Cambodia' and did not intend to start worrying about the place now.[133]

After the end of a further session, on 7 December, at least according to Moran, Churchill said of Dulles, 'Ten years ago I could have dealt with him. Even as it is I have not been defeated by this bastard. I have been humiliated by my own decay.'[134] (Although Churchill did not tend to swear much, Mary Soames attested that 'He could be pretty earthy when occasion demanded it.')[135] Eisenhower left Bermuda before lunch the next day, without having been persuaded by Churchill to let Germany join NATO, any more than the President had persuaded him of the benefits of a European Army. 'I feel like an aeroplane at the end of its flight,' Churchill said to Butler shortly after his return, 'in the dusk, with the petrol running out, looking for a safe landing.'[136]

'Problems will arise if many coloured people settle here,' Churchill told the Cabinet on 3 February 1954. 'Are we to saddle ourselves with colour problems in the United Kingdom? They are attracted by the Welfare State. Public opinion in the United Kingdom won't tolerate it once it gets beyond certain limits.'[137] Churchill nonetheless thought that Commonwealth immigrants should be allowed to continue to enter Britain, and that time was needed for 'public opinion [to] develop a little more before taking action'.[138] At that time the foreign-born population of England numbered 60,000, out of 38.6 million. Although Churchill did not like the implosion of the Empire he had so loved and fought for, and denounced what he called 'the magpie society', he did not attempt to impose curbs on immigration, which were not introduced until the early 1960s. On the issue of West Indian immigration, on another occasion he told the Cabinet that a good slogan was 'Keep England white', indicating that his views on the matter of ethnicity had not materially changed since his adolescence.[139]

'Remember that we can't expect to put the whole world right with a majority of eighteen,' Churchill told Norman Brook, the Cabinet Secretary.[140] He seems to have been conscious not just of a lack of political zest. Standing next to Woodrow Wyatt in the Members' lavatory in the Commons in March 1954, he 'smiled sadly' and said, 'Poor little bird. It can't even hop out of its nest any more.'[141] By May 1954, Churchill was even taking amphetamine pills before addressing the Conservative Women's Conference in the Albert Hall.

Because a general election had to be called by October 1956, Eden was becoming more insistent on Churchill setting a firm date for his resignation and sticking to it, so that he could be in Downing Street long enough beforehand to establish himself. In June, Churchill told him he would resign in the autumn, but then it suddenly appeared that Eisenhower might have altered his opposition to holding talks with the Soviets and there emerged the possibility, at least in Churchill's own mind, that he could indeed become the bridge in the Cold War, at a time of rivalry between Western and Soviet proxies in Syria, Vietnam, Iran, Thailand, Hungary, British Guiana and Central Africa.

On 24 June he took off from Heathrow Airport for Washington with Eden, Lindemann, Moran, Colville and Soames to promote the idea of a 'summit', and also provide for, as Colville put it, 'an occasion for clearing the air and creating good feeling'.[142] The agenda would therefore also cover Indo-China, Germany and Egypt. This time Churchill was invited to stay at the White House, and on the first day of talks Eisenhower seemed to commit himself to a London conference between Britain, the United States and Germany to agree on a common line before holding further talks with the Russians. On 26 June, Churchill told congressional leaders, 'Meeting jaw to jaw is better than war' (which was later paraphrased as 'Jaw-jaw is better than war-war').[143]

Yet just as Churchill thought that there was a real breakthrough, on 27 June Dulles downgraded the London conference idea to the British simply holding bilateral talks with the Russians, to which the United States would not object.[144] Churchill privately said of Dulles, 'He is the only case of a bull I know who carries his china closet with him.'[145] (He later also made the declension, 'Dull, duller, Dulles.')[146] The British party returned from Washington without anything much to show for the journey.

Churchill reluctantly allowed withdrawal from the Suez bases in July 1954, but Egypt had never been a directly ruled imperial possession, and he fought a determined rearguard action against the Mau Mau insurgency in Kenya, and strongly supported General Sir Gerald Templer's struggle against Communist guerrillas during the Malayan Emergency. In Kenya it descended into a dirty war in which there were atrocities committed on both sides, and some 12,000 people lost their lives. Churchill could see the way the post-war mood was turning against colonialism. 'I could have defended the British Empire against anyone,' he told an aide later on, 'except the British people.'[147] He had kept his promise of 1942 not to preside over the liquidation of the British Empire, with no part of it becoming independent during his time as prime minister, but the year after he left office Sudan gained its independence, and then Ghana and Malaya (modern-day Malaysia) in 1957, and Kenya in 1964.

In early July, his Washington bid having failed, Churchill fixed the tentative date of 20 September 1954 for his handover to Eden, after a visit to Moscow in early August in which he would propose arms reductions and other measures designed to promote a general easement of the Cold War. The Cabinet – which privately now wanted Churchill to resign, was doubtful about appeasing the Russians and was more respectful of American leadership in the area – was collectively opposed to making an approach to Moscow, indeed Salisbury threatened to resign as lord president of the Council over the issue, with Churchill privately saying he 'didn't give a damn' if he did. 'Your grandfather hates me,' Churchill told the seven-year-old Robert Cecil (later 7th Marquess of Salisbury) on a visit to Hatfield. It was not true, though Salisbury did resent 'the way this policy was bounced on the Cabinet by Winston', as he put it to Eden.[148]

As Lord Randolph Churchill had said of Gladstone in 1886, so now it was Winston Churchill who was 'an old man in a hurry' and who admitted to Colville that he was 'prepared to adopt any methods to get a meeting with the Russians arranged'.[149] The crucial Cabinet meeting came on Friday, 23 July, when Salisbury (again) and Crookshank threatened to resign if Churchill asked the Russians for a meeting. The weekend was spent in suspense as to whether Churchill himself would resign and thus split the Cabinet and Party. On Sunday, 25 July the Russians themselves solved the problem by demanding a meeting of thirty-two foreign ministers to discuss a pan-European security plan. 'Foreign secretaries of the world unite,' quipped Churchill, 'you have nothing to lose but your jobs.'[150]*

The Monday Cabinet meeting therefore passed off without dispute, with Lord Salisbury 'smiling again' and Churchill 'feeling that he had at

* When Colville's Italian cook arrived at work very pregnant that month, the result of a liaison with a man in a street in Verona after dark, Churchill quipped, 'Obviously not one of the Two Gentlemen' (Colville, *Fringes* p. 701).

least made the effort'.[151] When an offer for a meeting was made through Eden rather than Churchill, the Russians did not receive it enthusiastically, so it sank into the background. 'This is a most delightful world, full of novelties,' Churchill told Lawrence Burgis sarcastically of the nuclear proliferation that he had been powerless to halt. 'Some of us who are about to pass on leave you our best wishes.'[152] As a result of his disappointment and irritation at having been outnumbered in Cabinet, in early August he changed his mind about handing over to Eden in the autumn. He enjoyed office, genuinely thought he could effect a diplomatic breakthrough with the post-Stalin Politburo and was increasingly suspicious that Eden would not be an effective successor. He knew, as Colville put it, 'how difficult it would be for them to *turn* him out without ruining their chances at the next election'.[153] At Chartwell he complained that never before had a prime minister been hounded from office 'merely because his second-in-command wanted the job'. He wrote Eden a letter that went through six drafts, saying that he had decided to remain as prime minister until a general election in November 1955. It emphasized how much better it would be for Eden to take over a new ministry, and even tried to make it sound as though he was doing Eden a favour. Churchill sent a copy to Clementine who he knew wanted him to retire much earlier than that, saying, 'I hope you will give me your love.'[154] 'Eden was dejected,' recorded Colville, 'but there was in fact nothing he could do about it.'[155] A measure of Churchill's continued popularity was the 30,000 cards and 900 presents he received on his eightieth birthday in November.

To mark the occasion, the two Houses of Parliament gave Churchill a portrait, painted by Graham Sutherland, which he, with deliberate ambiguity, described at a joint meeting of the Lords and Commons in Westminster Hall as 'a remarkable example of modern art. It certainly combines force and candour.'[156] He had been shown a photograph of it by Clementine after she had lunched with Sutherland, and 'almost shouted' at Anthony Moir, his solicitor, 'Is it or is it not a libel? I won't accept it. I won't go down in history looking like that.'[157] To his new, and last, private secretary, Anthony Montague Browne, he said, 'I look like a down-and-out drunk who has been picked out of the gutter in the Strand.'[158] In September 1944, while staying at Hyde Park, Clementine had found a painting of Churchill by Paul Maze, which she thought 'a horrible caricature'. As she reported to Sarah, 'I boldly told the President I did not like it and he said "Nor do I." So I said "May it come out?" and he said "Yes," and so now it is destroyed.'[159] Similarly, some time in 1955 or 1956 she, Grace Hamblin (now Clementine's secretary) and Grace's brother burned the Sutherland portrait at Chartwell. Since Clementine had promised

Churchill that 'it would never see the light of day', we can conclude that this auto-da-fé took place with his compliance.[160]

At the ceremony in Westminster Hall, Churchill repeated his view of the British people during the war that 'Their will was resolute and remorseless and, as it proved, unconquerable. It fell to me to express it, and if I found the right words you must remember that I have always earned my living by my pen and by my tongue. It was a nation and race dwelling all round the globe that had the lion heart. I had the luck to be called upon to give the roar.' Of his contribution to grand strategy he then added, 'I also hope that I sometimes suggested to the lion the right places to use his claws.'[161] In this speech and others, such as the El Alamein reunions of 10,000 veterans at which he spoke in 1949 and 1950, Churchill was careful to avoid the kind of vainglorious boasting and compulsive exaggeration that were to spoil the reputations of Montgomery and Mountbatten, among others.

Churchill's birthday party that night numbered 250 people at Downing Street. 'The State Rooms', recalled a guest, 'were looking at their best with all their valued possessions, wonderful flowers, and the women wearing lovely dresses and magnificent jewellery.'[162] Pug Ismay proposed Churchill's health at midnight, and in the course of his reply Churchill said, 'I should never have got nor remained here without the help of my dear Clemmie.'[163] It was an obvious moment for him to announce his resignation, and yet another that he passed up. By now Woodrow Wyatt was calling him 'an ancient monument in his own lifetime'; more delicately the name 'Churchill' was already gracing various varieties of chrysanthemum, daisy, fuchsia, gladiolus, hyacinth, sweet pea and rose.[164]

'Those hungry eyes, those hungry eyes!' Churchill joked to the sculptor Oscar Nemon about his would-be successor. 'I really should resign. One cannot expect Anthony to live forever.'[165] Chamberlain could of course have said the same of Churchill's hungry eyes in 1939 and 1940, although he had by no means been the natural successor. On 21 December 1954, Churchill had what Eden recorded as a 'grudging' conversation in which he offered to resign in June or July 1955. 'The old man feels bitterly towards me,' Eden noted, 'but this I cannot help. The colleagues are unanimous about drawling cabinets, the failure to take decisions, the general atmosphere of *après moi le déluge*, and someone has to give a heave.'[166] Of course the irony was that *après* Churchill, there was indeed a *déluge* due to Eden's mishandling of the Suez crisis of 1956. By contrast, Churchill's Indian Summer premiership had shown he was capable of mending bridges – welcoming former antagonists de Valera and Nehru to Downing Street and supporting the end of active warfare in Korea, as well as trying to shed his reputation as a class warrior by regularly caving in to trade union demands over pay and conditions.

On 1 February 1955, in yet another discussion about the handover date, Churchill told Eden that he would go on Tuesday, 5 April that year. In his last major speech, he told a packed House of Commons on 1 March, having ripped up the Foreign Office brief that he was given, that in nuclear terms 'Safety will be the sturdy child of terror, and survival the twin brother of annihilation.'[167] He added that 'We must also never allow, above all, I hold, the growing sense of unity and brotherhood between the United Kingdom and the United States and throughout the English-speaking world to be injured or retarded . . . The day may dawn when fair play, love for one's fellow-men, respect for justice and freedom, will enable tormented generations to march forth, serene and triumphant from the hideous epoch in which we have to dwell. Meanwhile, never flinch, never weary, never despair.'[168] This public acknowledgement of what was to become known as mutually assured destruction was his last major political intervention in public life, and it was an intensely sobering one.

When on Friday, 11 March Sir Roger Makins, the British Ambassador in Washington, reported that Eisenhower had suggested a meeting with Churchill and Adenauer in Paris in early May to discuss meeting the Russians, Churchill decided he needed to stay in office beyond 5 April, seeing it, as Colville noted, as another 'chance of escape from his increasingly unpalatable timetable'.[169] Eden was predictably infuriated and at Monday morning's Cabinet meeting he bluntly asked the Prime Minister when he intended to resign. Churchill coldly stated that 'It was not a matter on which he required guidance or on which Cabinet discussion was usual.'[170] Later that same day, it was established from Winthrop Aldrich, the American Ambassador to London, that Eisenhower was not in fact contemplating a meeting with the Russians at all. That, Churchill told Clementine, 'relieves me of my duty to continue, and enables me to feed the hungry'.[171] What Churchill did not know, and which Colville only discovered by accident later, was that there had been 'quiet talks' between Sir Ivone Kirkpatrick, Eden's Permanent Under-Secretary at the Foreign Office, and Aldrich.[172] So Eden did finally ease Churchill out of Downing Street, by going behind the Prime Minister's back to the Americans.

Churchill hated leaving office. 'It's the first death,' Clementine told Mary, 'and for him, a death in life.'[173] He formed what Colville called 'a cold hatred of Eden' and 'sought to persuade his intimate friends that he was being hounded from office'.[174] He also said that giving up politics after nearly sixty years was 'a terrible wrench'.[175] Even as late as 28 March he tried to wriggle out of having to go. When he learned that Nikolai Bulganin, Malenkov's successor, had spoken in favour of four-power talks, he told Colville that with a dock strike, a newspaper strike,* a Budget and the date of the election still to be decided, 'He could not possibly go at such a moment just to satisfy Anthony's personal hunger for power,' and threatened to hold a Party meeting on the issue.[176]

Again showing keen psychological insight, Colville advised Eden that 'Amiability must be the watchword,' because 'The Prime Minister thrived on opposition and showdowns; but amiability he could never resist.'[177] After the Churchills had dined with the Edens on 29 March, Churchill slept on the decision, and the next morning changed his mind a fourth time and agreed to leave office on 5 April. The decision left Churchill, in Colville's view, 'a sad old man'.[178] He had taunted the Attlee Government for being limpet-like in hanging on to power, but its tenacity paled beside that of the octogenarian Churchill.

The evening before he went, the Queen and Prince Philip came to dinner at No. 10, an unprecedented honour for a prime minister. Randolph got drunk and the Duchess of Westminster put her foot through Clarissa's train – 'That's torn it, in more than one sense,' joked the Duke of Edinburgh – but otherwise it was a great success.[179] That night, Churchill sat on his bed wearing his Garter and Order of Merit and knee-breeches. Then he suddenly said to Colville with vehemence, 'I don't believe Anthony can do it.'[180] It seemed a cruelly unfair thing to say of the person who had been his right-hand man for fifteen years – the longest-serving heir apparent in British political history – but it turned out to be accurate.

At his last Cabinet meeting, on Tuesday, 5 April 1955, wearing his frock-coat prior to going to Buckingham Palace to resign, Churchill made the philosophical point to his colleagues that 'Man is spirit.'[181] His also gave them the practical advice, 'Never be separated from the Americans.'[182] He bid adieu, saying, 'He trusted that they would be enabled to further the progress already made in rebuilding the domestic stability and economic strength of the United Kingdom and in weaving still more closely the threads which bound together the countries of the Commonwealth, or, as he still preferred to call it, the Empire.'[183]

It is striking how closely those words resembled the ones he had written when he had set out his political creed to his mother back in December 1897, aged only twenty-three: 'I shall devote my life to the preservation of this great Empire and to trying to maintain the progress of the English people.'[184] Churchill's Indian Summer premiership had seen the end of the Korean War, a million houses built, the abolition of rationing, the end of

* Meaning the resignation would not be covered in the press.

austerity and the beginning of a return to prosperity. Britain had become a nuclear power; no part of the British Empire had been liquidated; the Coronation had been a great success, and Mount Everest had been conquered.[185] In retrospect, and despite the appeasement of the trade unions, the first half of the 1950s were something of a golden age for Britain, and at least some of the credit for that must go to the Prime Minister of the day.

Abroad, he had tried to hinder the disintegration of the British Empire as much as he could for as long as possible. The Disraelian creed of *Imperium et Libertas* and his father's ideas of Tory Democracy ran through his career, and although he changed political parties, he never changed those.[186] It is rare for a politician to espouse the same guiding principles for fifty-eight years, and it was immensely fitting that the very last words he spoke to his Cabinet as prime minister were of the Empire.

The Queen offered him a dukedom, her private office having earlier ascertained from Churchill's that he would refuse it. He did not want to stymie Randolph's and his grandson Winston's political careers, and as he told Colville, 'Quite seriously, I wish to die in the House of Commons as Winston Churchill.'[187] There had been no non-royal dukedoms created since that of Westminster in the year of Churchill's birth, and they were not considered appropriate to the era of the Common Man, yet it is hard to imagine who would ever be more deserving of one than Winston Churchill. He enjoyed joking about what would have happened if he had accepted; having bought the 120-acre Bardogs Farm that lay adjacent to Chartwell, he said, 'Duke of Bardogs would sound well, and Randolph could be Marquis of Chartwell.'[188] He had told Colville, 'I should have to be Duke of Chartwell, and Randolph would be the Marquis of Toodledo.'[189] In fact he would probably have taken the dukedom of London, in commemoration of his defiance during the Blitz.

On the last weekend at Chequers before his resignation, Churchill had the gigantic Rubens painting *The Lion and the Mouse*, which depicted a scene from Aesop's Fables, taken down from the Great Hall. 'It always bothered Sir Winston,' recalled Grace Hamblin, 'because he could not see the mouse.'[190] So he took up his brush and painted in the mouse more clearly, in an attempt to improve the work of Peter Paul Rubens.[191] 'And if that is not courage,' Mountbatten said later, 'I do not know what is!'[192]

# 34
# 'Long Sunset'
# April 1955–January 1965

*It is foolish to waste lamentations upon the closing phase of human life. Noble spirits yield themselves willingly to the successively falling shades which carry them to a better world or to oblivion.*

Churchill on the death of the 1st Duke of Marlborough[1]

*'Vehement, high and daring' was his cast of mind. The life he lived was the only one he could ever live; he must go on to the end.*

Churchill, *Savrola*[2]

'I look forward to a leisure hour with pleasurable agitation,' Churchill told the art historian Sir John Rothenstein at Chartwell after his retirement from the premiership; 'it's so difficult to choose between writing, reading, painting, bricklaying and three or four other things I want to do.'[3] As well as his active life in Kent, whenever he attended the Commons MPs would crowd around him in the Smoking Room and bars, both to hear his remarks and so they could say that they had spoken to a living legend. The young Tory MP Angus Maude recalled him telling a group of them, for example, that 'The secret of drinking is to drink a little too much all the time.'[4]

It was a tribute to Churchill's stewardship that in the snap general election that Anthony Eden called for 26 May 1955, the Conservatives won 344 seats to Labour's 277 and the Liberals' 6, with 13.30 million Conservative votes to Labour's 12.40 million, giving Eden a fifty-nine-seat majority. Churchill was re-elected for Woodford with a majority of 15,808.

On 11 July, Dr A. L. Rowse, an Oxford don, visited Churchill at Chartwell, Churchill having sent his car to pick him up from All Souls, flying the pennant of the lord warden of the Cinque Ports. 'Fortunately, I wrote down everything he said to me,' noted Rowse. 'Looking back over it, I rather think he meant me to, himself so historically minded.'[5] Looking around the library, Rowse saw history, biography, political memoirs, Walter Scott, Macaulay, Samuel Johnson, Marlborough's and Lord Randolph Churchill's correspondence and a recent biography of Eden. A Labour supporter, Rowse was struck by how Churchill 'didn't speak as a party man at all; above all that. He spoke of the Conservative Party as "they".' Churchill sounded almost libertarian, saying of nationalization and taxation, 'You don't create wealth by just taking it away from other people. There should be minimum standards for people, and beyond that – free run.'[6] They drank Harvey's Bristol Cream sherry before lunch and a very good hock during it, and Churchill pressed port on him with the cheese* afterwards, settling on a Cointreau with his coffee.

After lunch, 'slightly sozzled', Rowse went up to Churchill's study to discuss King Charles I and to allow Churchill to read Rowse's manuscript for a book on the early Churchill family, the reason for the visit. Of James I's execution of Sir Walter Raleigh, Churchill said, 'I have always thought that one of the worst blots against that extravagant sodomite.' (He clearly didn't know about Rowse's own sexual orientation.) Of the 1st Duke of Marlborough's affair with Charles II's inamorata Lady Castlemaine, he commented, 'To have been seduced at sixteen [actually twenty-one] by the King's mistress must have been an interesting and valuable experience.'[7] He then fed the goldfish, which he called his 'darlings'. Showing him the Boer War reward poster, Churchill said, 'Twenty-five pounds; that is all I am worth.' Rowse remembered it ever afterwards as 'Quite the most wonderful day I have spent in my life.'[8]

Churchill enjoyed inviting visitors to Chartwell; on one occasion he offered a whisky and soda to a Mormon, who replied, 'May I have water, Sir Winston? Lions drink it.' 'Asses drink it too,' came the reply. Another Mormon present said, 'Strong drink rageth and stingeth like a serpent.' 'I have long been looking for a drink like that,' Churchill retorted. When Anthony Montague Browne, who remained his private secretary for the rest of his life, later congratulated him on those ripostes, he grinned and said, 'None of it was original. They just fed me the music hall chance.'[9] Teetotallers were staple butts of his humour. The death in October 1944 of Archbishop William Temple, whom Churchill had disliked for his left-wing views, had made him, in Colville's words, 'quite ribald'.[10] 'Look, only sixty-three, a teetotaller,' he said of the primate, 'and look at me, not a teetotaller, and seventy.'[11] As a drinker, smoker and carnivore, outliving

* 'Stilton and port are like man and wife,' Churchill said. 'They should never be separated.' (Graebner, *My Dear Mr Churchill* p. 61).

teetotallers and vegetarians never failed to give Churchill immense satisfaction.

By August 1955, when Montgomery visited him to reminisce about the war and Oscar Nemon sculpted him, Churchill had restarted writing his *History of the English-Speaking Peoples*. He had almost completed it at the Admiralty in late 1939, but since then had been busy with other things. When he had originally signed the contract (for £20,000) in October 1932, he had said that it would cover the English-speaking peoples' 'quarrels, their misfortunes and their reconciliation', and that its 'object was to lay stress upon the common heritage of the peoples of Great Britain and the United States as a means of enhancing their friendship'.[12] He concluded the work in late 1955, helped by Maurice Ashley, Bill Deakin and Denis Kelly. 'The American blood that flowed in his veins helped shape his book,' wrote Ashley, 'and his aristocratic habits never dimmed his democratic sympathies, even if he attributed the achievements of the past to great men rather than to the masses.'[13] It was an uplifting account, and even included as historical fact the legend of Alfred the Great burning the cakes. When Deakin pointed out that it was almost certainly untrue, Churchill told him, 'At times of crisis, myths have their historical importance' – a comment that was as much an insight into 1940 and 1941 as into the Viking Wars of King Alfred.[14] The fourth and final volume ended in 1901, with the death of Queen Victoria and the start of what Churchill was to call 'the century of storm and tragedy', which he had already comprehensively covered in *The World Crisis* and *The Second World War*. For all Churchill's admiration of Robert E. Lee and the Confederates as soldiers, Abraham Lincoln was the hero of the final volume, and he described the American Civil War as 'the noblest and least avoidable of all the great mass-conflicts of which till then there was record'.[15]

As well as writing, Churchill continued to read voraciously, the London Library providing him with Dickens, Kipling, Austen and Conrad, and the adventure stories of Forester, Stevenson, Fennimore Cooper and the Bulldog Drummond tales of H. C. McNeile ('Sapper'). He also very often turned to Shakespeare for relaxation.* Although he went for daily walks at Chartwell, and continued with his bricklaying, Churchill naturally slowed down physically in his mid-eighties. 'I get my exercise as a pall-bearer to my many friends who exercised all their lives,' he said.[16] He still went up to London regularly. Taken to Boodle's Club by Montague

* Richard Burton had not found it relaxing when Churchill came to watch him play *Hamlet* at the Old Vic in 1953, when he loudly recited the words along with Burton during the performance, and afterwards went backstage to ask, 'My Lord Hamlet, may I use your lavatory?' (*FH* no. 141 p. 29).

Browne, Churchill said, 'I do like this club; most of your members are decent country gentlemen.' When Browne pointed out that half the people there were stockbrokers, Churchill affected indignation, saying, 'You shouldn't say such things of your fellow-members! Really, my dear, you must avoid this penchant for pessimistic judgement.'[17]

In January 1956, Churchill made the first of many visits to Emery Reves and Wendy Russell's beautiful house La Pausa, in Roquebrune near Monte Carlo, originally built by Bendor Westminster for his mistress Coco Chanel. The Reveses did not marry until 1964, so Clementine did not care to meet them, calling their common-law marriage 'that unconventional and uneasy ménage', even though there was nothing uneasy about it, except for the way it made her feel.[18] Churchill had never been prudish about other people's relationships, and moreover enjoyed the sunshine, lavish hospitality, bezique and chance to entertain friends. On 6 February, he dined on board the *Christina*, the yacht owned by the fabulously rich Greek shipowner Aristotle Onassis. Clementine disapproved of her husband spending his time with such plutocrats, but Churchill felt that after his exertions he deserved some fun and luxury in his old age.

On 23 April, St George's Day, Churchill published *The Birth of Britain*, the first of four volumes of *A History of the English-Speaking Peoples*, which Clement Attlee suggested should really have been entitled, 'Things in History Which Have Interested Me'.[19] In his review in the *New York Times*, Harold Nicolson noted how for Churchill 'almost every critical turn of historic fortune has been due to the sudden apparition in an era of confusion and decay of one of the great figures of history', such as Alfred the Great, Queen Elizabeth I and Pitt the Younger.[20] Churchill wrote, 'Alfred had well defended the Island home,' he praised King Alfred's study of history, and stated that it was his 'sublime power to rise above the whole force of circumstances, to remain unbiased by the extremes of victory or defeat, to persevere in the teeth of disaster, to greet returning fortune with a cool eye, to have faith in men after repeated betrayals'.[21] Although the final volume closed on Queen Victoria's death, it was very obvious to his readers who was the last person in that heroic continuum. The book sold extremely well and has been translated into eleven languages. Thanking Churchill for the second volume in November, David Maxwell Fyfe, now Lord Kilmuir, perceptively wrote, 'I have always believed that a living sense of history is a *sine qua non* of a politician. Your volume not only confirms this but will create that sense in innumerable people.'[22]

In early June 1956, the last British troops left the Suez Canal Zone under the agreement Eden had negotiated during Churchill's premiership, and three weeks later Colonel Abdul Nasser was elected president of Egypt. Then, on 26 July, Nasser suddenly and without warning nationalized the Anglo-French-owned Canal, plunging its owners and users into a full-scale crisis. Churchill was initially in favour of acting 'with vigour, and if necessary with arms' to reverse the decision and overthrow Nasser, and told Eden so. He also told Clementine he feared that with Eisenhower fighting a re-election campaign, Eden might 'wait for America, who for the third time will arrive on the scene very late'.[23] In retrospect, that would have been the sensible thing for Eden to have done, and would also have been in accordance with Churchill's own final advice to the Cabinet, 'Never be separated from the Americans.'[24] Yet Eden disregarded the advice and during the summer and autumn built a coalition with France and Israel against Egypt without warning Eisenhower, who, as Churchill had appreciated, was in the midst of a presidential re-election campaign. On 20 October, Churchill suffered another small stroke and was flown home from La Pausa, three days before British and French troops seized the Suez Canal. Eisenhower was re-elected on 6 November, but his hostile stance towards the Anglo-French military action did not perceptibly soften once he was safely back in the White House.

It is hard not to detect a sense of *Schadenfreude* in Churchill's attitude towards Eden over Suez, whether or not he really said to Moran, 'It serves Anthony right. He has inherited what he let me in for.'[25] He certainly did say that the Suez operation was 'the most ill-conceived and ill-executed imaginable . . . I would never have dared; and if I had dared, I would certainly never have dared stop.'[26] Even before the last British troops had to quit Egypt in humiliation, victims of a perceived American threat to sterling if they persevered in the occupation of the Canal, Churchill was trying to rebuild the Special Relationship. 'There is not much left for me to do in this world and I have neither the wish nor the strength to involve myself in the present political stress and turmoil,' he wrote to Eisenhower in late November. 'But I do believe, with unfaltering conviction, that the theme of the Anglo-American alliance is more important today than at any time since the war.'[27]

Churchill's private feelings towards Eisenhower were as negative as ever, however. The following September, staying at La Capponcina, Beaverbrook's villa on the Cap d'Ail in the south of France, he spoke about Nevil Shute's newly published apocalyptic novel *On the Beach*, which was about the effects of a nuclear war. 'I think the earth will soon be destroyed,' Churchill said. 'And if I were the Almighty I would not recreate it in case they destroyed Him too the next time.'[28] He thought he might send a copy to Nikita Khrushchev, the new Soviet leader, but when asked about Eisenhower he said it would be 'a waste of money'.

'The Middle East is one of the hardest-hearted areas in the world,' Churchill told Montague Browne in 1958. 'It has always been fought over, and peace has only reigned when a major power has established firm influence and shown that it would maintain its will. Your friends must be supported with every vigour and if necessary they must be avenged. Force, or perhaps force and bribery, are the only things that will be respected. It is very sad, but we had all better recognise it. At present our friendship is not valued, and our enmity is not feared.'[29] The disaster in the Middle East brought about Eden's resignation on 9 January 1957, which was a tragedy involving family as well as politics for Churchill, because Clarissa was his niece. 'They bear their lot with courage,' Churchill told Clementine.[30] Eden was succeeded by Harold Macmillan, a sturdy anti-appeaser whom Churchill had always liked and promoted.

Frederick Lindemann, the Prof, Lord Cherwell, died in his sleep on 3 July 1957. After a friendship of thirty-six years, the closest of Churchill's life alongside F. E. Smith and Brendan Bracken, he attended his funeral at Christ Church, Oxford, and despite his infirmity he insisted on accompanying the coffin to the grave. 'He was a man individual in character, of great courage both moral and physical,' Churchill said at the Other Club.[31] The following month Anthony Beauchamp, Sarah's ex-husband, committed suicide, which affected her deeply and drove her to further alcoholism, at a time when Randolph was still drinking heavily and Diana was not at ease with herself either.[32] Of the four surviving Churchill siblings, Mary was alone undamaged by the undoubted strains of being the child of a great man.

In 1958, a fund was launched to set up Churchill College, Cambridge, which would concentrate on science and technology. When consulted on the idea of its bearing his name, Churchill said, 'After all, it does put me alongside the Trinity.'[33] He wanted the college to admit women on equal terms with men. 'When I think what women did in the war,' he said, 'I feel sure they deserve to be treated equally.'[34] It might also be seen as a belated apology for his short-sighted opposition to female suffrage forty years earlier.

In the first half of 1958 Churchill contracted pneumonia at La Pausa in February, suffered a relapse in March and then contracted pleurisy after a fall in April. Roy Howells became his full-time attendant. 'You were very rude to me, you know,' Churchill once told him. 'Yes, but you were rude too,' Howells replied, whereupon Churchill, 'with just the hint of a smile', said, 'Yes, but I *am* a great man.'[35]

Churchill visited Brendan Bracken, who was dying of oesophageal cancer, at the Westminster Hospital three times in early August 1958. He was staying with Beaverbrook on the French Riviera when he heard of Bracken's death on 8 August, aged only fifty-seven. 'Tell me one thing, Pat,' Churchill asked Sir Patrick Hennessy, Bracken's friend, who had been with him at the end. 'Did he die bravely?' When told that Bracken had died very bravely, all Churchill said, 'tears streaming down his face', was 'Poor, dear Brendan.'[36] Bracken had predicted of himself, 'I shall die young and be forgotten.' He did indeed die young, after a lifetime of heavy smoking, but Churchill's 'faithful chela' and most trusted political adviser, the man who stood by him through the Wilderness Years, the successful Minister of Information during the Second World War, the founder of the modern *Financial Times* and *History Today*, has not been forgotten. Churchill had lost his two best friends in little over a year. On 20 November, he told the Other Club, 'We have suffered a great, swingeing blow. Brendan has gone. We can all remember how, in dark times, his spirit, his charm and wit were able to rise superior to personal sorrow or grave events. He bore his illness with courage and patience. Now he is no more, and we all feel the poorer for his loss.'[37]

From 22 September to 10 October 1958, Churchill took the first of eight cruises on the *Christina* that he would enjoy over the next five years. His granddaughter Celia Sandys recalls them as 'extravagantly luxurious'.[38] He sailed in the Mediterranean, in the Caribbean and once to New York, although on that occasion he was too ill to disembark. Mary calculated that from 1956 to 1962 her father spent an average of seventeen weeks a year abroad, in sunny climes. 'The closing days or years of life are grey and dull,' Churchill told Clementine on 14 October 1958, 'but I am lucky to have you at my side.'[39] By the close of the 1950s, Churchill's memory was starting to fade; he had to ask who Herbert Morrison was, and although he could remember that he had been first lord of the Admiralty during the Battle of the River Plate, he could not recall in which war it was fought.[40] When he attended debates in the Commons, he sat in his corner seat below the gangway, where he had sat during the Wilderness Years, and in 1959 he became Father of the House, the member with the longest continuous service there, despite its being broken by the period he was out of Parliament in the early 1920s.

Churchill visited Nice, Monte Carlo, the Italian Riviera, the Greek islands and Istanbul (which of course he still called 'Constantinople') on the *Christina* in 1959. He took along Toby, a budgerigar given him by Duncan Sandys.[41] Onassis's girlfriend, the opera diva Maria Callas, was on board, and Celia Sandys remembers that, when Churchill sang his favourite music-hall tunes, 'There was something incongruous about Maria Callas pretending to enjoy singing along to "Daisy, Daisy".'[42] In sight of the Temple of Poseidon at Sounion – where Byron had carved his name on a column – Churchill recited from *Don Juan*. At Rhodes he of course loved the Valley of the Butterflies.

'From Smyrna we sailed through the Dardanelles at night,' Celia noted, 'in case they stirred up bad memories for the guest of honour.'[43] In fact, however, Churchill 'was quite aware of what was going on. He referred to the Dardanelles at dinner that night, but did not dwell on the subject, and neither did anyone else.'[44] The changing scenes as they cruised from one magnificent site to the next 'seemed visibly to stimulate him'. Nor had he lost his power to reprimand; one evening Daisy Fellowes, who had married Churchill's first cousin in 1919, was staying at the Cap d'Ail and said, near the seemingly asleep Churchill, 'What a pity that so great a man must spend his declining years in the company of Onassis and Wendy Reves,' only for a growl to be heard and then, 'Daisy, Wendy is three things you'll never be. She is young, she is beautiful, and she is kind.'[45]

Churchill painted in January and February 1959 on his last visit to Marrakesh. 'The weather has been wonderful,' Montague Browne wrote to Beaverbrook from the Mamounia Hotel on the last day of the holiday, 'but he is increasingly sunk in torpor and lassitude, though not precisely gloom, and takes less and less interest in what is going on.'[46] That month, Churchill published his last original piece of writing, an abridged one-volume edition of *The Second World War* with an epilogue on the period 1945–57. In March, a one-man show of his paintings at the Royal Academy was a great success, attracting nearly twice as many attendees as the Leonardo drawings the previous year.

Churchill suffered another slight stroke on 19 April 1959, which gave him some pain and difficulty in speaking.[47] Yet only three days later he attended the Other Club and a few days after that he addressed a crowded Woodford constituency meeting, announcing that he would stand for Parliament once again, to great cheers. The next month he was mobbed in New York, with people holding their children up in crowds so that later in life they could say that they had seen Winston Churchill.

He stayed at the White House for three nights, and took his first flight in a jet aircraft. He also magnanimously visited John Foster Dulles, who was dying of cancer, and George Marshall, who was unable to speak from a stroke, and who died that October. After Churchill had seen Eisenhower, the President said to his daughter-in-law sadly, 'I only wish you had known him in his prime.'[48] On the plane journey back home, Churchill noticed a throbbing pain in his right little finger, where it turned out that the blood supply had stopped, perhaps due to his signet ring acting as a tourniquet, and the tip of his finger had to be cut off due to dry gangrene.

Churchill made his last political speech on 29 September 1959, in the election campaign at Woodford. 'Among our Socialist opponents there is great confusion,' he said. 'Some of them regard private enterprise as a tiger to be shot. Others look on it as a cow they can milk.'[49] At that point he made the gesture of a cow's udders being pulled. 'Only a handful see it for what it really is – the strong and willing horse that pulls the whole cart along.' His election leaflet proclaimed, 'We must never forget our unique position as the heart and centre of the British Commonwealth and Empire, and a leading partner in the Atlantic Alliance.'[50] He was re-elected in his fifteenth and last election aged eighty-four, with a majority of almost 15,000 votes, as Macmillan and the Conservatives won a majority of a hundred seats. His last public speech came on 31 October, after unveiling a statue of himself at Woodford. His theme was the British people. 'By our courage, our endurance, and our brains we have made our way in the world to the lasting benefit of mankind,' he said. 'Let us not lose heart. Our future is one of high hope.'[51]

Churchill's own vision of the future during the 1960s was in fact one of dark despondency. 'I have worked very hard and achieved a great deal,' he often used to tell Montague Browne and others, 'only in the end to achieve nothing.'[52] He may perhaps have been referring to his inability to win a settlement of the Cold War, but it is more likely to have been a reflection of newfound British weakness in the world after Suez, and the unravelling of the British Empire that he had loved and sworn to protect. He made only one other intervention in international affairs post-Suez, when in 1961 he tried to persuade Macmillan to postpone the Queen's visit to Ghana on the grounds that its first prime minister, Kwame Nkrumah, was an Anglophobe authoritarian.[53] It went ahead and was a considerable success.

In January 1961, Toby the budgerigar flew out of the window of Churchill's room at the Hôtel de Paris in Monte Carlo, never to return. 'I do grieve for Toby,' he told Clementine. 'I keep hoping against hope that I shall hear that he has been recovered safe and well.'[54] He enjoyed gambling there, especially roulette, where other patrons would applaud on his arrival at the tables, in his detective Edmund Murray's recollection, 'spontaneously and respectfully, many with tears in their eyes'.[55] Arriving in New York on *Christina* on 19 April, he flew home two days later, having watched the *Queen Mary* leave the Cunard pier for its transatlantic voyage, just as she had on his historic wartime journeys of 1943 and 1944.

Churchill painted his last picture, *The Goldfish Pool at Chartwell*, in 1962, which he gave to Murray. On 28 June, he had a fall in his bedroom in the Hôtel de Paris and fractured his left hip and thigh. The X-ray showed the previous break of 1893 when he jumped from the Wimbornes' bridge, and he was flown home, for the last time. 'Remember, I want to die in England,' he told Montague Browne. 'Promise me that you will see to it.'[56] Against the French doctors' advice that he should not be moved, Harold Macmillan sent an RAF Comet air ambulance the next day. Churchill stayed in the Middlesex Hospital for fifty-five days, and when Montgomery went to visit him there he found him smoking cigars and 'protesting against Britain's proposed entry into the Common Market'.[57] The Churchill family rebuked Montgomery for telling the press this, and Montague Browne wrote what he later called a 'fence-sitting letter' to the press, but no one actually denied that Churchill had said it. Meanwhile, the cigar butts were taken from the dustbins by reporters.

The fall in Monaco was the last in a very long series of accidents – including falls from horses and down stairs, several car and plane crashes, a house-fire, a bridge-jump, a near-drowning and being run over among them – that had started with his fall from his tricycle aged five. When he fell downstairs in Jodhpur in 1899, he had joked to his mother, 'I trust the misfortune will propitiate the gods – offended perhaps at my success and luck elsewhere.'[58] The gods had certainly demanded a full share of propitiation, and the Monaco fall destabilized him so much that by September 1964 he could no longer recognize Montgomery.

Churchill had planted shrubs and bushes at Chartwell over the years especially to attract the many strains of butterflies he had introduced, and on sunny days he would sit in a chair, as Mary recalled, 'strategically placed before the opulently flowering buddleias, watching with rapt enjoyment the vivid, quivering splendour of the butterflies – the Red Admirals, the Peacocks, and the Painted Ladies – as they fluttered and feasted on the purple, honey-laden flowers'.[59] He had watched butterflies in Cuba, collected them in India, become fascinated by them in prison in South Africa, and written about them on his East African journey and in California; they were to be the last of the very many enthusiasms of his long life as his mind slowly slipped away.

In April 1963, he was proclaimed an honorary citizen of the United States by President Kennedy in Washington, and he watched Randolph read out his speech by closed-circuit television. On 19 October, Diana died from an overdose of sleeping pills; Churchill wrote to Clementine from Chartwell about their grief, but also of their love.[60] A month later he watched the television reports of the assassination of President Kennedy, whom he greatly admired, and wept.

Churchill made his last visit to Parliament on 27 July 1964, and the next day Sir Alec Douglas Home, the Prime Minister, and other senior politicians lunched at Hyde Park Gate to present him with a unanimous resolution of the House on his retirement after over sixty years as a member of Parliament. He celebrated his ninetieth birthday at Hyde Park Gate, and ten days later he attended the Other Club for the last time. 'It had become increasingly difficult to awaken the spark, formerly so vital,' recalled Montague Browne in his moving account of Churchill's last ten years, *Long Sunset*, 'and all that could be said was that he knew where he was and was happy to be there.'[61]

Later in December 1964, Churchill suffered a cerebral arterial spasm. His last coherent words, spoken to Christopher Soames, were 'I'm so bored with it all.'[62] On the night of 9 January 1965, he suffered a massive stroke, and thereafter never regained consciousness. He nonetheless stayed alive for fifteen days, lying in a bed brought into the drawing room at 28 Hyde Park Gate. His cat Jock lay there too, and there were flowers and candles in his room. Shortly after 8 a.m. on Sunday, 24 January 1965, the noble heart of Sir Winston Spencer-Churchill beat its last.

Churchill had told Jock Colville in 1953 that he would die on the anniversary of his father's death, and he did. Nor was that the last of his tributes: Churchill had originally intended to be buried under the croquet lawn at Chartwell, but having visited the graves of his father, mother and brother at St Martin's Church in Bladon, within view of Blenheim Palace, in the late 1950s he changed his mind and decided to rest with them. Lord Randolph Churchill's grave is today marked with a sign that says 'Father', so ironically he is memorialized through his relation to the son he so underestimated, indeed in many respects despised.

'Now Britain is no longer a Great Power,' murmured Charles de Gaulle, President of France since 1959, when he heard the news of Churchill's death.[63] It came at a time when the Labour Government was considering withdrawing all British troops from east of Suez, effectively closing down the British Empire. 'The day of giants is gone forever,' the historian Sir Arthur Bryant wrote in the *Illustrated London News*. The novelist V. S. Pritchett wrote, 'We were looking at a past utterly irrecoverable.'[64]

The Queen instructed the Duke of Norfolk, the Earl Marshal, that Churchill's funeral should be 'on a scale befitting his position in history', thus guaranteeing it would be the grandest non-royal funeral since the Duke of Wellington's in 1852, even overshadowing that of Gladstone in 1898. Years in the planning, the arrangements, codenamed Operation Hope Not, needed to be constantly updated due to Churchill's great longevity. Churchill himself had played relatively little part in planning the event, although he promised Harold Macmillan that there would be 'lively hymns', and said to Montague Browne, 'Remember, I want lots of military bands.' He got no fewer than nine.

Churchill's lying-in-state in Westminster Hall took three days and nights, his coffin draped with a Union Flag on which rested his insignia of the Order of the Garter. Over 320,000 people filed past the catafalque, which was guarded at each corner by members of the Services who stood statue-still, their heads bowed in respect and homage.[65] 'Two rivers run silently through London tonight,' wrote a spectator, 'and one is made of people. Dark and quiet as the night-time Thames itself, it flows through Westminster Hall, eddying about the foot of the rock called Churchill.' Even more people might have come had not the thermometer dipped below zero; indeed the day of the funeral itself was so cold there were casualties among the police horses. Across the country, flags flew at half-mast, newspapers printed lengthy obituaries, black armbands were worn, football matches were postponed, shops closed and the National Association of Schoolmasters even cancelled a strike.

'It is with profound sorrow that the Government and people of India have learnt of the passing away of the Rt. Hon. Sir Winston Churchill, the greatest Englishman we have known,' the President of India, Sarvepalli Radhakrishnan, wrote to the Queen. 'The magic of his personality and his mastery of words renewed faith in freedom in most difficult years of the Second World War. He left his imprint on the face of Europe and the world. His unforgettable services will be cherished for centuries. I convey to Your Majesty, the British Government and the people of Britain, our deepest sympathy in your great loss. It must be some comfort for you to know that your grief is shared by millions all over the world.'[66]

St Paul's Cathedral was the obvious place for the funeral; no fewer than twenty-eight bombs had fallen on it during the war, one of them a massive 500-pounder. Yet Sir Christopher Wren's masterpiece had miraculously survived. Moreover, Nelson's and Wellington's funerals had taken place there. A break with precedent was the decision of the Queen to attend personally, a special mark of royal favour as sovereigns did not attend non-family funerals. There were six sovereigns, six presidents and sixteen prime ministers present that day.

On the morning of the funeral, 30 January, Big Ben struck at 9.45 a.m. as the coffin left Westminster, but thereafter remained silent for the rest of the day. The catafalque was carried upon the same gun-carriage that had been used for Queen Victoria in 1901. It was pulled through the streets of London by 104 Royal Navy bluejackets, a reminder of Churchill's two periods as first lord of the Admiralty. The sight as it left the Palace of

Westminster was likened by one spectator to that of a great warship leaving harbour. Other troops in the procession, which included detachments from no fewer than eighteen military units, marched with their rifles reversed. It took four majors of the Queen's Royal Irish Hussars (successor regiment of the 4th Hussars) to carry all Churchill's orders and decorations behind the gun carriage.

As the cortège passed the Cenotaph in Whitehall, one hundred flags carried by men and women of the wartime resistance movements of France, Denmark, Norway and Holland were raised in a final salute. After the coffin had passed, a group of Danish Underground fighters laid a wreath of lilies at the Cenotaph. When asked for their names by a journalist, one answered, before slipping back into the crowd, 'We were unknown at war; it must be the same now.'

Just as Churchill had promised, there were indeed some 'lively' hymns. His mother's birthplace, his friendship with President Roosevelt and his belief in the potency of the English-speaking peoples were reflected in the choice of 'The Battle Hymn of the Republic', while his personality and career were recalled by 'Who Would True Valour See' and 'Fight the Good Fight with All thy Might'. The coffin, hewn from English oaks of the Blenheim estate, took eight white-gloved Guardsmen to carry up the west steps of St Paul's. After the ceremony, it was carried out of the Cathedral to the withdrawal hymn 'O God, our Help in Ages Past'. The pageantry was solemn, superb, sublime. Churchill became the only commoner in history to receive a ninety-gun salute from the Royal Horse Artillery in St James's Park.

Some 350 million people watched the funeral on television worldwide; indeed the American audience was even larger than for President Kennedy's funeral fifteen months earlier. No fewer than 112 countries were represented; only Communist China refused to send a representative, and only the Republic of Ireland failed to broadcast the funeral live. After the ceremony, former President Eisenhower and Sir Robert Menzies delivered fine broadcasts.

The coffin was taken aboard the launch *Havengore*, and as it set off upstream sixteen Lightning aircraft swooped low in a flypast that recalled his founding of the RAF and his tribute to it during the Battle of Britain. London was still one of the world's greatest seaports in 1965, its docks served by many vast cranes stationed on the innumerable quays. When the *Havengore* sailed past, their operators dipped the jibs of each crane in turn, as though even these enormous cranes were bowing their heads in tribute to the nation's dead chieftain.

Foreign visitors were surprised to see the supposedly buttoned-up Britons crying in public. 'Not since the war has there been showed such emotion,' wrote the novelist Laurie Lee. An American historian who visited Britain specially for the spectacle recorded that 'in the crowd lived the spirit of 1940, there was a great democratic upsurge of Englishmen, with men in bowler hats and elegant women standing with the cockneys and stevedores'. The coffin was taken from *Havengore* at Festival Pier and then carried by the Grenadier bearer party into a motor hearse which was driven on to the concourse of Waterloo station, where the coffin was placed on a train. As it passed through the countryside, people standing in stations and fields took off their caps in respect. In Oxfordshire, Dr Rowse saw 'The Western sky filled with the lurid glow of winter sunset; the sun setting on the British Empire.'[67]

At Bladon, two wreaths were placed on the grave. 'To my darling Winston, Clemmie' read one handwritten note, and the other, 'From the Nation and Commonwealth, in grateful remembrance. Elizabeth R.' Clementine, in the opinion of everyone present and the words of one reporter, 'carried herself like a queen'. As she retired to bed after that exhausting, emotional day, she proudly told her daughter Mary, 'It wasn't a funeral, it was a triumph!'[68] When she died in December 1977, at the age of ninety-two, her ashes were strewn in his grave.

# Conclusion: 'Walking with Destiny'

*I have known finer and greater characters, wiser philosophers, more understanding personalities, but no greater man.*

President Dwight D. Eisenhower on Churchill, December 1954[1]

*He was a child of nature. He venerated tradition, but ridiculed convention.*

General Lord Ismay on Churchill[2]

*As one's fortunes are reduced, one's spirit must expand to fill the void.*

Churchill to Clementine from the trenches, 20 December 1915[3]

'Far too much has been and is being written about me,' Churchill told Prof Lindemann – and that was in the 1920s.[4] Despite all that literary activity (which has continued unabated), General Sir Alan Brooke wrote in August 1943, 'I wonder whether any historian of the future will ever be able to paint Winston in his true colours.'[5] In 1960, when he started writing his memoirs, Lord Ismay told President Eisenhower that an objective biography of Churchill could not be written until at least the year 2010. It was indeed not until the present decade that the last pieces of the archival jigsaw – King George VI's and Ivan Maisky's unexpurgated diaries, Lawrence Burgis's verbatim reports of the War Cabinet meetings, Churchill's children's private papers, and much more – finally became available to researchers. Fifty years after Churchill's death, it is at last possible to paint him in something approaching his true colours.

'To do justice to a great man,' Churchill himself wrote, 'discriminating criticism is necessary. Gush, however quenching, is always insipid.'[6] This book has not been short of criticism, which I hope has been discriminating.

In the year Churchill was born, General Sir Garnet Wolseley signed a treaty forcing the defeated King Koffee of the Ashanti to end human sacrifice; in the year he died, the spaceship Gemini V orbited the earth and the Beatles released 'Ticket to Ride'. In the nine decades between, we can see with hindsight that there were many times when Churchill's judgement could legitimately be called into question, including his opposition to votes for women, personally attending the Sidney Street Siege, his manner of sacking Admiral Bridgeman, appointing Jackie Fisher in the First World War and Roger Keyes in the Second, continuing the Gallipoli operation after March 1915, employing the paramilitary Black and Tans in Ireland, his brinkmanship during the Chanak Crisis, proposing the Ten Year Rule, rejoining the Gold Standard, supporting Edward VIII during the Abdication Crisis, mismanaging the Norway Campaign, scapegoating King Leopold III of the Belgians, assisting Greece in 1940–41, failing to appreciate the military capacity of the Japanese, describing the Italian peninsula as a 'soft underbelly', underestimating the capacity of Stuka aircraft against both ships and tanks, browbeating Stanisław Mikołajczyk to accept the Curzon Line as Poland's post-war frontier, pressing for the Dodecanese campaign in 1943, allowing the deportations of the Crimean Cossacks to Stalin and of anti-Tito Yugoslavs to Tito, making the 'Gestapo' speech during the 1945 general election campaign, instituting the system of 'overlords' and appeasing the trade unions in his Indian Summer premiership, remaining as prime minister after his stroke in 1953, and more besides. Yet as he told Clementine from the trenches of the Great War, 'I should have made nothing if I had not made mistakes.'[7] Several of these mistakes arose from his habit of insisting on seeing things for himself at first hand: this often got him into trouble, as in Natal, Sidney Street and Antwerp, but more usually it gave him important insights. 'It does not matter how many mistakes one makes in politics so long as one keeps on making them,' he once said to Lord Rosebery. 'It is like throwing babies to the wolves; once you stop, the pack overtakes the sleigh.'[8]

In his obituary of Churchill, Clement Attlee stated that 'Energy, rather than wisdom, practical judgement or vision, was his supreme qualification.'[9] Is that fair? Churchill's supposed lack of judgement was hung about his neck throughout his career, sometimes, as we have seen, with good reason. Yet when it came to all three of the mortal threats posed to Western civilization, by the Prussian militarists in 1914, the Nazis in the 1930s and 1940s and Soviet Communism after the Second World War, Churchill's judgement stood far above that of the people who had sneered at his. On those three vital junctures, Churchill's judgement proved right, while those around him were, to adapt one of his favourite poets, Rudyard Kipling, losing their heads and blaming it on him. Attlee himself was still opposing rearmament and conscription before the Second World War long after Churchill had called for both. Whose 'wisdom, practical judgement or vision' were the greater when it came to the things that truly mattered in the life of Britain, her Empire and Commonwealth?

It must be expected that someone who spent two-thirds of a century in the public eye, taking important decisions on many matters and opining on everything that came into his view, would make mistakes – sometimes serious ones – and many of his attitudes are not ones that are widely held today. Yet set against his failures and mistakes is a far longer and more important list of his successes. The Greek poet Archilochus wrote that 'A fox knows many things, but a hedgehog one important thing.' Churchill's detractors have depicted him as a hedgehog who made endless mistakes but got one important thing – Hitler and the rise of Nazism – right, almost by chance, on the law of averages. But they are mistaken. 'His judgments of the trends of history were uniformly perceptive and often profound,' Henry Kissinger wrote of Churchill. 'Before World War I, Churchill recognized that France was no longer capable of standing up to Germany alone and that Britain needed to abandon its historic isolation in favour of an alliance with France. In the 1920s, he wanted to involve Germany in building a world order by propitiating Berlin's resentments over the Treaty of Versailles.'[10] Churchill was also the man who got the Grand Fleet ready for the outbreak of war in 1914; the father of the tank; the initiator of much social legislation to alleviate the suffering of the grindingly poor of Edwardian Britain; a reforming, liberal home secretary; one of those who helped bring the Irish Free State into existence, and the creator of the state of Jordan. He settled Great War debts, preached magnanimity after the General Strike, wrote tax-cutting budgets and was the peacetime premier who built a million homes and abolished rationing. Above all, he was the first significant political figure to spot the twin totalitarian dangers of Communism and Nazism, and to point out the best ways of dealing with both. Churchill was a quintessential fox, who knew and did many things, not a hedgehog.

Churchill learned from his mistakes, and put the lessons to good use. The Dardanelles catastrophe taught him not to overrule the Chiefs of Staff; the General Strike and Tonypandy taught him to leave industrial relations during the Second World War to Labour's Ernest Bevin; the Gold Standard disaster taught him to reflate and keep as much liquidity in the financial system as the exigencies of wartime would allow. He also learned from his successes. The Great War cryptographic breakthroughs of the Admiralty's Room 40 taught him to back Alan Turing and the Ultra cryptanalysts; the anti-U-boat campaign of 1917 taught him the advantages of the convoy system; his advocacy of the tank encouraged him to promote the invention of new weaponry, pioneered by General Hobart and the MI(R) Directorate. He had long understood the superiority of the Mauser over the spear.

Churchill was right when he wrote that all his past life had been but a preparation for the hour and trial of his wartime premiership. His early mastery of the 'noble' English sentence, and his wide reading as a subaltern, enabled him to produce his magnificent wartime oratory. His time in Cuba taught him coolness under fire, and how to elongate his working day through siestas. His experience in the Boer War exposed him to the deficiencies of generals. His time as a pilot and as secretary of state for air made him a champion of the RAF long before the Battle of Britain. His writing of *Marlborough* prepared him for synchronized decision-making between allies. His penchant for always personally visiting the scenes of action, such as the Sidney Street Siege and Antwerp, prepared him for the morale-boosting visits around Britain during the Blitz. His fascination for science, fuelled by his friendship with Lindemann, led him to grasp the military application of nuclear fission. His writing about Islamic fundamentalism prepared him for the fanaticism of the Nazis. His prescient, accurate analysis of Bolshevism laid the ground for his Iron Curtain speech, and his introduction of National Insurance and old age pensions with Lloyd George before the First World War prepared him for accommodating the welfare state after the Second. Above all his experiences in the Great War – preparing the Navy, the Dardanelles debacle, his time in the trenches and as minister of munitions – all gave him vital insights that he put to use in the Second World War.

He was protean. One of Churchill's biographers, Robert Rhodes James, described him as a 'politician, sportsman, artist, orator, historian, parliamentarian, journalist, essayist, gambler, soldier, war correspondent, adventurer, patriot, internationalist, dreamer, pragmatist, strategist, Zionist, imperialist, monarchist, democrat, egocentric, hedonist, romantic'.[11] He was indeed all of those, but to them might also be added: butterfly-collector, big-game hunter, animal-lover, newspaper editor, spy, bricklayer, wit, pilot, horseman, novelist and crybaby (this last the Duke and Duchess of Windsor's nickname for him). In all of these, he was animated more by deep emotions than by rational analysis, which for much of his life left people believing that he lacked judgement. He believed passionately – and wrongly – that his father had been cruelly ill-used by the Tory Party, for example. He believed that his Free Trade principles justified crossing the floor of the Commons. He believed – again, incorrectly – that he would die young and so needed to cut corners in order to achieve greatness early. He passionately wanted to be a general, preferably another Napoleon. He profoundly believed – also probably wrongly – that he could have brought the Great War to an early and successful conclusion by forcing the Dardanelles Straits.

He loved Clementine and his children (even Randolph); he loved his (often sybaritic) pleasures too. He loved his friends – many of whom died early, and most of whom he rowed with at some stage or other – loyally. He viscerally hated Lenin, Trotsky and Hitler – but remarkably few others. Churchill was supremely egotistical, instinctively combative and prone to deliberate exaggeration, and he consistently underestimated the negative impression that these traits made on people. Readers will have noticed more than a few instances of Churchill's selfishness, insensitivity and ruthlessness in these pages. 'Absorbed in his own affairs,' wrote Commander Tommy Thompson, his personal assistant throughout the Second World War, 'he seemed to many people brusque, vain, intolerant and overbearing.'[12] He could also be idiosyncratic, stubborn and an interfering micromanager. Several of these failings he turned into strengths, however, and some were necessary to help him through the crises he faced in peace and war. He could be intensely lovable, too, of course, when taken on his own terms. Few top-rank politicians do not have a powerful ego, but in his case, and with his talents, it was not an unwarrantably inflated one.

Churchill's moods of deep gloom during this period, and at others during his life such as during the Gallipoli campaign, do not mean that he was a depressive, let alone a manic depressive, or bipolar. His sole reference to 'black dog' is discussed in Chapter 10; the myth of Churchill as a depressive is, like the equally pervasive myth that he was an alcoholic, without foundation. He was depressed by things that would make anyone depressed, and drank heavily, as other people did in the 1930s. (Nor did he inhale the smoke of the 160,000 cigars he is estimated to have consumed during his lifetime.) In his farewell speech to his battalion in the Great War, Churchill declared, 'Whatever else they may say of me as a soldier, at least nobody can say I have ever failed to display a meet and proper appreciation of the virtues of alcohol.'[13] Readers will surely agree with his own estimate about his drinking, that 'I have taken more out of alcohol than alcohol has taken out of me.'[14]

In a speech at the Grand Hall, Victoria, in July 1932, to celebrate the bicentenary of George Washington's birth, Churchill asked, 'As for courage, as for that personal and civic intrepidity which Washington showed in every situation, is it not needed as much today in the anxieties and perils of modern peace as it ever was in the fires of bygone war?'[15] With Hitler only six months from the chancellorship, it certainly was needed. Churchill himself displayed remarkable physical and moral courage throughout his life, for as he wrote in *Great Contemporaries*, 'Men and kings must be judged in the testing moments of their lives. Courage is rightly esteemed the first of human qualities because . . . it is the quality which guarantees all others.'[16] Apart from his obvious bravery on the battlefields of five wars before 1939, one of the ways in which his courage manifested itself was in the many journeys he made outside Britain during the Second World War – no fewer than twenty-five return trips, covering over 110,000 miles, far more travelling than any other wartime leader. Some were quick, hazardous trips across the Channel in 1940, 1944 and 1945, but others lasted weeks and involved crossing continents and oceans.[17] He did this in his middle to late sixties, overweight and unfit, often in uncomfortable, noisy, unpressurized planes and sometimes in considerable danger of crashing or being shot down. The list of prominent people who died on flights during the war includes Generals 'Strafer' Gott, Admiral Bertram Ramsay, Orde Wingate, General Władysław Sikorski, the Duke of Kent, Admiral Yamamoto, the actor Leslie Howard and Glenn Miller. Yet the journeys were worth the risks involved, as he ended up knowing the other world leaders much better than they knew each other. The only occasions on which Roosevelt, Stalin and Churchill were all together were at Teheran in 1943 and at Yalta in 1945. Yet Churchill and Roosevelt met on eleven occasions, and Churchill and Stalin on three, whereas Roosevelt and Stalin never met alone except on the margins of the two trilateral meetings. Churchill's travels during the Second World War provided the glue that held the Big Three together.

As well as being physically and morally courageous, Churchill was a remarkably magnanimous statesman, both to defeated enemy nations and to personal opponents. Fisher had tried to destroy him in May 1915, but he suggested his reappointment as first sea lord the next year and they exchanged friendly correspondence until Fisher's death. Bonar Law had insisted on his expulsion from the Admiralty, but they too retained good personal relations. Lord Alfred Douglas libelled him viciously over the communiqué after the Battle of Jutland, but Churchill said, 'Tell him from me that time ends all things.'[18] Lord Derby seriously misled the Committee of Privileges during Churchill's investigation into the Manchester Chambers of Commerce affair in 1934, but was forgiven. Colin Thornton-Kemsley attempted to have him deselected as MP for Epping after Munich, but on the outbreak of war Churchill wrote, 'so far as I am concerned the past is dead.'[19] He returned Eliot Crawshay-Williams's defeatist letter of 1940 'to burn and forget'.[20] Max Beaverbrook and Stafford Cripps were forgiven for their blatant jockeying for the premiership during the Second World War, and Lloyd George for waiting 'until Winston is bust'. Churchill's eulogies to Neville Chamberlain, Lloyd George and Stafford Cripps ignored past slights, rows and wrongs with great generosity. He offered

Cabinet posts to Leslie Hore-Belisha in 1945 and Clement Davies in 1951, who had voted to remove him as prime minister in the 'hinge of fate' year of 1942, as he did not believe in vengeance against domestic political opponents, but rather in what he called 'A judicious and thrifty disposal of bile'.[21] His many acts of kindness towards people from less privileged backgrounds were prompted by his natural compassion and a powerful sense of *noblesse oblige*. They were of a piece with his Tory Democrat views and were to be seen regularly throughout his life.

In all his passions, Churchill was more extreme and extravagant than his contemporaries, most of whom entered politics from a sense of social obligation, ambition, ideological conviction or just a desire to lead an interesting life. For Churchill it was nothing less than to vindicate a dead father and 'to lift again the tattered flag', as he put it. This gave him an advantage over them, especially when in 1940 and 1941 he had the opportunity to channel all his abilities, experience and passions into the destruction of 'that man'.

In May 1940 Churchill promised the British people 'blood, toil, tears and sweat', and he was ready to give all four – especially, as we have seen, the third. His passions and powerful emotions often summoned tears to his eyes; indeed like his humour he could use his lachrymosity almost as a political weapon on occasion. 'I blub an awful lot, you know,' he told Anthony Montague Browne, his last private secretary. 'You have to get used to it.'[22] Browne recalled that Churchill's tears would usually be induced by 'Tales of heroism . . . a noble dog struggling through the snow to his master would inspire tears. It was touching. I found it perfectly acceptable.' Churchill considered his lachrymosity to be almost a medical condition, telling his doctor that he dated it to his defeat by forty-three votes in the Westminster Abbey by-election of 1924. Yet there were plenty of times that he cried before that; a more accurate diagnosis was that he was an emotional, indeed sentimental Regency aristocrat born into a late Victorian age and class that instead prized the stiff upper lip. Every one of the eight admirals carrying Horatio Nelson's coffin in January 1806 had cried quite uninhibitedly.

The effect Churchill's father had upon him has been a central theme of this book. He wrote a two-volume life of Lord Randolph; his maiden speech was about him, and he mentioned him regularly in debates thereafter. His political career began as a conscious vindication of his father's, and he believed he was advancing Lord Randolph's Tory Democrat principles (which Lord Randolph had himself inherited from Benjamin Disraeli) even when he was in the Liberal Party starting the welfare state. His obsession with winning his father's approval was in no way lessened by Lord Randolph's death, as his short story from 1947, 'The Dream', made abundantly clear. He named his only son after him, adopted many of his personal mannerisms and even managed to die on the same date, the ultimate compliment, by which time he had far surpassed all his father's achievements. It would have been understandable if Churchill had seen himself in competition with his cold and distant father, but it is part of his greatness of character that instead he regarded himself as magnifying his father's ideas and promoting his principles. 'I am a child of the House of Commons,' he told the US Congress in December 1941. 'I was brought up in my father's house to believe in democracy. "Trust the people" – that was his message. I used to see him cheered at meetings and in the streets by crowds of working men way back in those aristocratic Victorian days when, as Disraeli said, the world was for the few, and for the very few.'[23]

Because of his family's early deaths, Churchill believed he did not have long to live, and the extraordinary number of close brushes that he had with death, both on and off battlefields, left him with a powerful sense of personal destiny. The reason that the Churchill Archive at Cambridge University is so extensive is that he kept everything, believing from an early age that he was going to be a great man taking great decisions at great moments in the history of what was then the greatest empire in history. He even kept his household bills from the Edwardian period (which tell us that he drank Pol Roger champagne from at least 1908). He kept correspondence relating to his pets, and about the gifts he received (including the wartime testing of his cigars after a large gift from the National Tobacco Commission of Cuba), as well as menus and seating plans. The sheer volume of papers and documents and speeches and publications left by Churchill has rightly been called 'one of the richest records of human undertaking'.[24]

Churchill's written output was similarly immense. He published 6.1 million words in thirty-seven books – more than Shakespeare and Dickens combined – and delivered five million in public speeches, not counting his voluminous letter- and memorandum-writing. Partly because he was such a polymath and so prolific, he also seemed to be a mass of contradictions. His Atlantic Charter proclaimed a belief in democracy that did not extend to Indian independence; he championed the weak, but briefly believed in eugenics; he was a duke's grandson who ended the peers' veto; he ordered the Combined Bomber Offensive and loved butterflies; he was a rugged soldier who wore silk underwear because of his 'sensitive cuticle'; he crossed the floor of the Commons, not once but twice. In politics, most of his seeming contradictions can be explained by the fact that his Tory Democrat principles of compassionate Conservatism were highly flexible, and could involve virtually anything within the generalized soubriquet *Imperium et Libertas*. The rest can be explained by his statement in 1927 that 'The only way a man can remain consistent amid changing circumstances is to change with them while preserving the same dominating purpose.'[25]

Thanking him for the gift of the second volume of *A History of the English-Speaking Peoples* in 1956, Lord Kilmuir wrote to Churchill, 'I have always believed that a living sense of history is a *sine qua non* of a politician.'[26] As an historian himself, it mattered immensely to Churchill how he would plead before what he called in his eulogy to Neville Chamberlain 'the grievous inquest of History'. Churchill wrote that the thirty-five years since leaving Sandhurst in 1895 had been 'An endless moving picture in which one was an actor'.[27] He knew he would be written about – not least by himself – and so was concerned not to fall 'below the level of events'. He was acting out scenes in his own drama, knowing that he would recount them for readers.[28] As his daughter Mary put it, 'He saw events and people, as on a stage, lit by his own knowledge of history and his burning sense of destiny and the march of events.'[29] In his obituary of Churchill, Clement Attlee wrote, 'He was, in effect, always asking himself, "What must Britain do now so that the verdict of history will be favourable?"'[30] As they reached Briare airfield on the way home from a conference with the French leaders in June 1940, Ismay pleaded that the divisions earmarked for reinforcing France should be unobtrusively delayed from embarking, as the French were clearly on the brink of surrender. 'Certainly not,' replied Churchill. 'It would look very bad in history if we were to do any such thing.'[31]

On that occasion Ismay was right, but on most other occasions Churchill's living sense of history, especially his capacity to use apposite analogies from Britain's past, served him and his country well. It allowed him to appreciate that the appeasers were acting outside the traditions of British foreign policy, which for centuries had been proactive, pugnacious and occasionally piratical in preventing any power gaining hegemony over the European continent. He could also place Britain's predicament in 1940–41 in its proper historical context, telling the British people that they had been there before in the past, and had ultimately prevailed. His speeches about how Drake had foiled the Armada and Nelson had destroyed the invasion threat posed by Napoleon were all the more powerful coming from a prime minister who was also an historian and biographer. His historical imagination was powerful, but it was also practical; it was intended to instruct and inform. This was true of every history book he wrote, and part of the reason why by his death he had sold more history books than any other historian in history.

It was also partly this living sense of history that encouraged him to try to replicate with Franklin Roosevelt the relationship that the Duke of Marlborough had enjoyed with Prince Eugene of Savoy during the War of Spanish

Succession. It was argued in the War Office in 1942 that nothing like the pooling of sovereignty implicit in the concept of the Combined Chiefs of Staff had ever happened before. Churchill knew otherwise, and as he had written in 1934 in his biography of his great ancestor's friendship with Eugene, 'Without this new fact at the allied headquarters the extraordinary operations which these chapters describe, so intricate, so prolonged, and contrary on so many occasions to the accepted principles of war, could never have been achieved.'[32]

The stresses of Churchill's relationship with Roosevelt can be truly measured through the litany of complaints he made to King George VI at their weekly Tuesday lunches, which make plain the depths of resentment Churchill felt towards his most important ally at key moments of the war. Yet both Churchill and the King were relieved and delighted when Roosevelt was re-elected president in November 1944, and the President's death the following April brought forth an almost unprecedented eulogy from Churchill, recorded in the King's diary. It was possible to feel disappointment and anger at the same time as admiration, and despite the private brickbats there is no reason to doubt Churchill when he said of Roosevelt on at least three occasions, 'I loved that man.'

Like Roosevelt, Churchill came from the highest echelon of his society. 'People will not look forward to posterity', he liked to quote Edmund Burke as saying, 'who never look backward to their ancestors.'[33] Churchill constantly looked back to his own. His aristocratic background sits uncomfortably today with his image as the saviour of democracy, but had it not been for the unconquerable self-confidence of his caste background he might well have tailored his message to his political circumstances during the 1930s, rather than treating such an idea with disdain. He never suffered from middle-class deference or social anxiety, for the simple reason that he was not middle class, and what the respectable middle classes thought was not important to the child born at Blenheim. Alec Douglas Home was the last aristocrat to have been prime minister, but he had a tiny majority, a completely different personality and lasted less than a year at No. 10. Churchill was the last aristocrat to rule Britain.

Yet, despite his aristocratic lineage, he was no snob. His closest friends came from a wide geographical and social background, including the sons of a Canadian priest (Max Beaverbrook), a Welsh schoolteacher (Lloyd George), an Irish builder (Brendan Bracken), a Birkenhead estate agent (F. E. Smith) and an Alsatian engineer (Prof Lindemann). He (wrongly) believed Smith to have had Gypsy blood.[34] It was true that he was also friendly with the dukes of Marlborough (his first cousin) and Westminster, but a true snob would not have taken his closest friends from such a wide social milieu. He was to put this great and wide capacity for friendship to good political use, as was demonstrated by the way the Other Club rallied to him in the Norway Debate in May 1940 and afterwards.

'I can see vast changes coming over a now peaceful world,' Churchill predicted to his friend Murland Evans; 'great upheavals, terrible struggles; wars such as one cannot imagine; and I tell you London will be in danger – London will be attacked and I shall be very prominent in the defence of London . . . I see into the future. This country will be subjected, somehow, to a tremendous invasion, by what means I do not know, but I tell you I shall be in command of the defences of London and I shall save London and England from disaster . . . I repeat – London will be in danger and in the high position I shall occupy, it will fall to me to save the capital and save the Empire.'[35] Churchill said those words not in 1931, 1921, 1911 or even 1901, but in 1891, when he was only sixteen years old. He had seen his destiny as a teenager, and achieved it. Aged sixty-five and considered by many – including Hitler – to be a hopeless has-been, he came to power and did exactly what he had prescribed for himself half a century earlier.

Even those who cannot bring themselves to think in terms of destiny must admit that Churchill was amazingly lucky, even in his defeats. This book is pitted with examples of occasions when defeat at the polls or some other setback plucked him out of tricky political situations and allowed him to reorientate himself, such as his defeats in three parliamentary elections between 1922 and 1924 which permitted him to move from the Liberals to the Conservatives, and MacDonald's decision not to appoint him to the Government in 1931, reaffirmed by Baldwin in 1935, which allowed him to denounce appeasement. 'I've done a lot of foolish things that turned out well, and a lot of wise things that have turned out badly,' he said in his CBS interview in New York in March 1932. 'The misfortune of today may lead to the success of tomorrow.'[36] The continual refusal of successive governments to employ him throughout the 1930s seemed devastating at the time, but later he felt that 'invisible wings' had protected him from complicity in policies with which he profoundly disagreed and which, it turned out, were greatly damaging for his country. The Wilderness Years were useful, but they hurt. 'To be so entirely convinced and vindicated in a matter of life and death to one's country,' he wrote, 'and not to be able to make Parliament and the nation heed the warning, or bow to the proof by taking action, was an experience most painful.'[37]

Churchill was preparing for a crisis like 1940 all his life, but the man and the moment only just coincided. If Hitler, who was fifteen years younger, had put off the Anschluss and Czech crises for a few years, Churchill would probably no longer have been in front-rank politics and able to make himself the one indispensable figure thereafter. Churchill was indispensable during the Second World War because he exuded a confidence in victory that no other senior figure did, and was able to provide something that Neville Chamberlain could not – hope.

The historian J. H. Plumb observed soon after Churchill's death that 'far more than Churchill the writer of history books' he was also 'the last great practitioner of the historic theme of England's providential destiny'.[38] This stemmed not just from his self-confidence, but from an innate belief in the British people – what he himself called the British 'race' – and their Empire which he was certain was the greatest force for good in the history of mankind. 'We in this small island have to make a supreme sacrifice to keep our place and status,' he told the boys of Harrow in 1952, 'the place and status to which our undying genius entitles us.'[39] Biological racism – the Social Darwinian belief that mankind is organized hierarchically by race, with the whites at the top – was considered scientific fact when Churchill was growing up in the late nineteenth century. Even solidly left-wing figures such as Beatrice Webb, Hugh Dalton and H. G. Wells subscribed to it, just as earlier in the century Karl Marx had too. Absurd though it might seem to us today, when Churchill was learning about the world it was taken for granted.

It is another uncomfortable truth that Churchill's lifelong belief in the superiority of the British people over all others ultimately served the cause of democracy well, convincing him of the correctness of fighting on against the Germans when several of those around him wanted to sue for peace. His constant references in his speeches to the British – he often said English – race could not have been made by any of the other possible premiers at the time. Simon, Halifax and Hoare, for example, had been the three principal leaders of the campaign for Dominion status for India and were – not coincidentally – three of the principal appeasers of Germany. They tended to shy away from a vernacular that was natural to Churchill, whose thinking encompassed both his memory, his historical knowledge and his racial and imperial assumptions. On occasion those assumptions let him down, as when they misled him about the fighting qualities of the Turks at Gallipoli and of the Japanese in 1941.

Churchill had fought Simon, Halifax and Hoare in the 1930s over India, and although he had comprehensively lost, he did not mind fighting them again over appeasement. Edmund Burke, whom Churchill read and quoted, wrote of 'prejudice' in *Reflections on the Revolution in France* that it 'does not leave the man hesitating in the moment of decision, sceptical, puzzled, and unresolved . . . Through just prejudice, his duty becomes a part of his nature.' Churchill's belief that the British were superior to every other nation in the world – including the Germans – was undoubtedly one of unquestioning prejudice, but it did not leave him hesitating in 1940 in the way that the crisis left others 'sceptical, puzzled, and unresolved'.

'Churchill has told me more than once over the years,' noted Ivan Maisky in his diary in May 1941, 'and I have no grounds not to believe him, that the British Empire is his alpha and omega.'[40] Churchill's belief in the British Empire was not just political but also spiritual. Sceptical as he was of Christianity, the Empire was his creed. He had created, largely from his reading of the Whig historians, a theory of historical progress that put the English-speaking peoples' adoption of Magna Carta, the Bill of Rights of 1689, the American Constitution and parliamentary institutions at the apogee of civilizational development, a progress that was being carefully and systematically extended to the parts of the world coloured pink on the imperial map. 'There was a strong element of altruism in the kind of imperialism for which Churchill stood,' stated Jock Colville, correctly.[41] This love of and belief in the Empire explains why on several occasions he took courses of action that damaged his own political career but which he thought right for the Empire, such as the doomed campaign to deny self-government to India in the early 1930s. He believed that the Empire was the reason that his era would be admired by future generations. His father had added Burma to the parts of the map coloured pink; he himself had fought on its Indian, Sudanese and South African battlefields; he travelled widely within it; at the Colonial Office he tried to improve it; several close friends like Max Beaverbrook and Jan Smuts hailed from it, and in the Second World War he insisted on a strategy that liberated the eastern parts of it from Japan by British rather than American forces. In his second premiership no part of the Empire was given its independence, and at the end of his life he nevertheless considered his career a failure for not having defended it successfully.

'The unsurpassed bravery of Indian soldiers and officers, both Moslem and Hindu, shine for ever in the annals of war,' wrote Churchill in his war memoirs. 'Upwards of two and a half million Indians volunteered to serve in the forces . . . The response of the Indian peoples, no less than the conduct of their soldiers, makes a glorious final page in the story of our Indian Empire.'[42] They are not the words of a man who hated Indians, as his detractors claim he did. But one cannot pick and choose with Churchill; one has to take him all or nothing ('*totus porcus*', as Fisher put it in a different context). The man who defied Hitler and proclaimed the virtues of Liberty was the same man who was nauseated by Mahatma Gandhi. One cannot simply deplore his obstinacy and bullheadedness, because those were equally on display over India in the 1930s and the Nazis in 1940: they are the same man and in his mind he was defending the same Empire. 'We would like genius to be discerning and moderate, to be a little bit more like the rest of us,' wrote the historian Manfred Weidhorn. 'Few geniuses have been so. Churchill had the vices of his virtues.'[43]

It is often argued by historians and biographers that Churchill should not have wasted his political capital over India in the 1930s, but should have used it arguing against appeasement instead. In fact his political credibility in 1940 was intimately bound up with the public's perception of him as someone who told unpopular truths as he saw them, followed his heart, stood up for the Empire and above all did not calculate like the other politicians did. The struggle against Indian self-government was a part of him just as much as the campaigns where he was on the winning side. The reason the public trusted and soon came to love him in 1940 was not because they believed he had been right in the past, but because they believed he had been consistently true to his beliefs, in a way many other, self-serving politicians who had held office throughout the 1930s had not been.

The important point about Churchill in 1940 is not that he stopped a German invasion that year, but that he stopped the British Government from making peace. If Churchill had not been prime minister, Halifax undoubtedly would have been, and he wanted at least to discover what Hitler's terms might be. Churchill was wrong to assume – or at least to claim to assume – that they would have been onerous. In fact they would probably have been very reasonable, as the Führer ultimately wanted to fight a one-front war against the USSR. Halifax was certainly not the semi-traitor he has sometimes been depicted as being: he simply could not see how Britain could possibly win once driven off the continent, when France was about to fall, the Soviet Union was a German ally, Italy was about to become another and the United States was in no mood to declare war on Germany. Halifax was merely a logical rationalist when the need was for a stubborn, emotional romantic. Churchill understood that a German victory in the East would have soon afterwards spelt disaster for Britain, and that signing an ignoble peace would have demoralized the British and destroyed their credibility with the Americans, as well as looking bad in history. Churchill could not offer the British a realistic plan for victory until Hitler invaded Russia, the Japanese attacked Pearl Harbor and Germany declared war against the United States in 1941, but he kept Britain in the war. In March 1916 he had described his own potential death in the trenches to Clementine as being 'an impoverishment of the war-making power of Britain which no one would ever know or measure or mourn'.[44] By 1940 it was clear that his contribution to Britain's war-making capacity was massive.

Churchill crucially refused to make peace, but was much criticized on other grounds. As Major-General John Kennedy put it, 'Only Churchill's magnificent and courageous leadership compensated for his deplorable strategic sense.'[45] According to this analysis, the Chiefs of Staff alone deserve credit for the strategy, and Churchill was at best an irritant and at worst a menace. This was certainly Brooke's view, as was clear from his diaries. Yet in September 1944, speaking to Jock Colville, Churchill likened the grand strategy of the Second World War to a bullfight. The operations in Africa and Italy 'were like the preliminaries, the Picadors, the *banderilleros*, etc. Then came Overlord, the Matador coming at the crucial moment to make the kill, waiting till the bull's head was down and his strength weakened.'[46] This 'Mediterranean strategy' was the correct one for the Western Allies to adopt, where Anglo-American strengths and successes could be best exploited, drawing away German strength and putting off the Second Front until it had a good chance of success.[47]

It was the strategy that Churchill set out to the Chiefs of Staff as he crossed the Atlantic in December 1941, and one with which they wholeheartedly agreed. It was furthermore the one he sold to the Americans in increasingly tense negotiations throughout 1942 and 1943, which Brooke could never have persuaded them to adopt on his own. Most of the fighting would be done on the Eastern Front, where four out of every five Germans killed in action perished. Yet it is untrue to say that Roosevelt and Stalin won the Second World War, while Churchill did not lose it.[48] In fact Churchill's and Brooke's strategy was a key component in winning the war, and in all the bitterness of Brooke's diaries it is easy to forget that on the true essentials of that strategy he and Churchill saw eye to eye and each badly needed the other in order to have it implemented. For all Brooke's planning of the Mediterranean strategy of 1943, it required Churchill to persuade the Americans of it. 'The accession of the United States makes amends for all,' he was to say during the Second World War, 'and with time and patience will give certain victory.'[49] He was able to say this partly because he knew the country far better than any other British politician of his day having visited twenty-eight of its forty-eight states.

Kennedy's criticism should also be considered beside the observation of Ian Jacob that 'If the Chiefs of Staff stood firm on something which they regarded as right, he fell in with their views.'[50] In his proposed attacks on Pantelleria, northern Sumatra, northern Norway and elsewhere, which the Chiefs of Staff opposed, they won rather than him. Similarly, they formally planned and approved the details of all the defeats such as Norway, Dakar, Greece and Singapore. For all that historians have concentrated on Brooke's strictures against Churchill, he also wrote after the war, 'I thank God that I was given an opportunity of working alongside of such a man, and of having my eyes opened to the fact that occasionally such supermen exist on this earth.'[51]

Churchill's mistakes must also be weighed as feathers in the balance against his other supreme contribution, the iron that he inserted into the British soul when it was most needed. In his speech on his eightieth birthday in Westminster Hall on 30 November 1954, he repeated a claim he had often made earlier, that 'It was a nation and race dwelling all round the globe that had the lion heart. I had the luck to be called upon to give the roar.'[52] But was that actually true? The pacifist movement was still strong during the Phoney War, and both the Communist Party and the British Union of Fascists opposed the war. Had Halifax negotiated a peace treaty with Hitler in the summer of 1940, there would have been a majority in both Houses of Parliament to approve it, and Royal Assent would not have been refused. Churchill was being unduly modest in Westminster Hall: it was much more the case that Churchill had the lion heart and also gave the roar, and in so doing taught the British people to rediscover the latent lionheartedness in themselves. Nine years later Churchill said that 'had I at this juncture faltered at all in the leading of the nation I should have been hurled out of office,' but he did not falter, and his leadership ensured that Britain fought on.[53]

In November 1938 Adolf Hitler sneered, 'Has the Almighty perhaps handed the key to democracy to such people as Churchill?'[54] The answer was yes. In 1897 Churchill had been mentioned in dispatches for his 'courage and resolution' and for having 'made himself useful at a critical moment'.[55] It was the same forty-three years later.

'The reasonable man adapts himself to the world,' George Bernard Shaw wrote in 'The Revolutionist's Handbook'; 'the unreasonable one persists in trying to adapt the world to himself. Therefore all progress depends on the unreasonable man.' The disregard for rules that got Churchill into endless trouble at school proved invaluable in 1940 when he rode roughshod over Whitehall promotion and procurement conventions, the concept of 'gentlemanly warfare', political and even royal protocol, War Office procedure and so on. Churchill's 'Action this day' approach differed profoundly from that of the Respectable Tendency of sober, conscientious, usually middle-class businessmen-politicians of all parties who dominated British politics between the fall of Lloyd George in 1922 and that of Neville Chamberlain in 1940. He didn't abide by what was known as 'form', an instinctively respectful behaviour inculcated by the public schools, Oxford and Cambridge, the BBC, the Civil Service, the Court, the City of London, the Church of England, the gentlemen's clubs and the political parties. With all of these Churchill had at best an ambivalent relationship, or none at all.

In that sense, Churchill was one of the greatest individualists of modern times, because he approached everything in life completely as an individual rather than as part of a group, from the moment he left his officers' mess in 1899 onwards. He despised school, never attended university or worked in trade or the Civil Service or the colonies, served in six regiments (so never became slavishly attached to any of them), was blackballed from one club and forced to resign from another, left both the Conservative and Liberal parties and was not in any meaningful sense a Christian. Despite being the son of a chancellor of the Exchequer and the grandson of a duke, he was a contrarian and an outsider. He even refused to subscribe to the clubland anti-Semitism that was a social glue for much of the Respectable Tendency, but instead was an active Zionist. The reason his contemporaries saw him as profoundly perverse is because he truly was.

He never minded being outnumbered either. In February 1927, speaking about trade union legislation in the Commons as chancellor of the Exchequer, he reminisced about the days when 'It was the fashion in the Army when a court-martial was being held and the prisoner was brought in, that he should be asked if he objected to being tried by the President or to any of those officers who composed the court-martial. On one occasion a prisoner was so insubordinate as to answer, "I object to the whole bloody lot of you." '[56] Churchill exhibited just such a sense of blanket defiance in the 1930s, refusing to be cowed by the almost complete unanimity of the British Establishment in appeasing Hitler and the Nazis. In the 1940s, this same attitude allowed him to think beyond the Establishment's way of waging war.

His extraordinary *esprit* was particularly displayed in the way he made jokes during the great crisis moments of his and his nation's life. When he was being appointed prime minister by the King in May 1940; when he was trying to persuade the French to fight on the following month at Tours; during both no-confidence debates of 1942, as well as on numerous occasions during his wartime speeches and in meetings with the Chiefs of Staff, Churchill made humorous, often self-deprecating remarks. Indeed the worse the situation got, the funnier he became. On being attacked by Leslie Hore Belisha over the failings of the A22 tank during the confidence motion in July 1942, he replied, 'As might be expected, it had many defects and teething troubles, and when these became apparent the tank was appropriately rechristened the "Churchill".'[57] Some decried his use of humour as flippant, others as a cynical weapon to win popularity, but in fact it reflected his extraordinary coolness under pressure, as well as his refusal to be cast down (at least for long) and his belief in the necessity of maintaining morale by showing confidence during crises. He was an epigrammatist to rival Oscar Wilde, Noël Coward and even Samuel Johnson, but unlike them he was witty while also leading his country during a world war.

Since the invention of the internet, a revisionist 'Black Legend' has attached to Churchill's name, in which he is held responsible for the sinkings of the

*Titanic* and *Lusitania*, massacring striking miners in Tonypandy, ordering the bombing and strafing of innocent Irish demonstrators, poison-gassing Iraqi tribesmen, promulgating anti-Semitism, deliberately not saving Coventry from destruction, assassinating Admiral Darlan, General Sikorski and several others, genocidally starving Bengalis during the Famine, and very much more. Mostly these arise from (sometimes wilful) misreadings of the original sources or from taking them wildly out of context, though some are just entirely invented. A return to the original archives and documents, as this book demonstrates, reveals them to be myths, but ones that will always exist in cyberspace.

In a survey of 3,000 British teenagers in 2008, no fewer than 20 per cent of them thought Winston Churchill to be a fictional character.[58] (In the same survey, 58 per cent thought Sherlock Holmes and 47 per cent thought Eleanor Rigby were real people.) Of course this is an indictment of the virtual excising of Churchill from the school curriculum, but in a sense it is also a tribute that people think of him, insofar as they know about him at all, as someone whose life story could not possibly be true, someone who has achieved the status of myth. It all seems so improbable that a single person could have lived such an extraordinary life. 'He is of the race of giants,' MacCallum Scott wrote of him, which must have seemed hagiographical in 1905, but four decades later looked extraordinarily prescient.[59] Scott ended that first biography with the words: 'He plays for high stakes, but his nerve is steady and his eye is clear. He will at any rate make a fight for it, and the fight will be something to have lived for and to have seen.'[60] That was as good as any of Churchill's own predictions.

'Man is spirit,' Churchill told the ministers of his Government just before his resignation in April 1955.[61] What he meant was that, given spirit – by which he meant the dash, intelligence, hard work, persistence, immense physical and moral courage and above all iron willpower that he himself had exhibited in his lifetime – it is possible to succeed despite material restraints. He himself succeeded despite parental neglect, the disapproval of contemporaries, a prison incarceration, a dozen close brushes with death, political obloquy, financial insecurity, military disaster, press and public ridicule, backstabbing colleagues, continual misrepresentation and even, from some quarters, decades of hatred, among countless other setbacks. With enough spirit, he believed that we can rise above anything, and create something truly magnificent of our lives. His hero John Churchill, Duke of Marlborough, won great battles and built Blenheim Palace. His other hero, Napoleon, won even more battles and built an empire. Winston Churchill did better than either of them: the battles he won saved Liberty.

# *Select Bibliography*

This is solely a list of the archives, books, articles and unpublished theses from which I have quoted. All of the books were published in London unless otherwise stated. The full bibliography can be found at www.andrew-roberts.net.

## Archives


| | |
|---|---|
| Viscount Addison | Bodleian Library, Oxford |
| A. V. Alexander | Churchill Archives Centre, Cambridge |
| Viscount Allenby | Liddell Hart Centre, King's College London |
| Julian Amery | Churchill Archives Centre, Cambridge |
| Leopold Amery | Churchill Archives Centre, Cambridge |
| Sir John Anderson, Viscount Waverley | Bodleian Library, Oxford |
| Lord Ashburnham | Parliamentary Archives, House of Lords, London |
| Herbert Asquith | Bodleian Library, Oxford |
| Joan Bright Astley | By kind permission of the late Mrs Astley |
| Clement Attlee | Bodleian Library, Oxford and Churchill Archives Centre, Cambridge |
| Stanley Baldwin | Cambridge University Library, Cambridge |
| Arthur Balfour | British Library, London |
| Harold Balfour | Parliamentary Archives, House of Lords, London |
| Group Captain Stephen Beaumont | Liddell Hart Centre, King's College London |
| Lord Beaverbrook | Parliamentary Archives, House of Lords, London |
| Ernest Bevin | Churchill Archives Centre, Cambridge |
| 2nd Earl of Birkenhead | By kind permission of Mr John Townsend |
| Sol Bloom | New York Public Library |
| Brendan Bracken | Churchill Archives Centre, Cambridge |
| Sir Edward Bridges | New York Public Library |

| | |
|---|---|
| Patrick Buchan-Hepburn, Lord Hailes | Churchill Archives Centre, Cambridge |
| Lawrence Burgis | Churchill Archives Centre, Cambridge |
| Sir Alexander Cadogan | Churchill Archives Centre, Cambridge |
| Sir Henry Campbell-Bannerman | British Library, London |
| Andrew Bonar Law | Parliamentary Archives, House of Lords, London |
| Violet Bonham Carter | Bodleian Library, Oxford |
| Lord Hugh Cecil, Lord Quickswood | Hatfield House, Hertfordshire |
| Lord Robert Cecil, Lord Cecil of Chelwood | British Library and Hatfield House, Hertfordshire |
| Austen Chamberlain | Cadbury Research Library, Birmingham University |
| Neville Chamberlain | Cadbury Research Library, Birmingham University |
| Joseph Chamberlain | Cadbury Research Library, Birmingham University |
| Clementine Churchill | Churchill Archives Centre, Cambridge |
| Randolph Churchill | Churchill Archives Centre, Cambridge |
| Lord Randolph Churchill | Cambridge University Library, Cambridge |
| Sarah Churchill | Churchill Archives Centre, Cambridge |
| Winston Churchill | Churchill Archives Centre, Cambridge |
| William Bourke Cockran | New York Public Library |
| Sir John Colville | Churchill Archives, Cambridge |
| Lt-Col. James Connell | Liddell Hart Centre, King's College London |
| Conservative Party | Bodleian Library, Oxford |
| Alfred Duff Cooper, 1st Viscount Norwich | Churchill Archives Centre, Cambridge |
| Lady Diana Cooper | Churchill Archives Centre, Cambridge |
| Wing Commander Maxwell Coote | Liddell Hart Centre, King's College London |
| Sir Stafford Cripps | Bodleian Library, Oxford |
| Sir Henry Page Croft | Churchill Archives Centre, Cambridge |
| Admiral Lord Cunningham | British Library, London |
| J. C. C. Davidson | Parliamentary Archives, London |
| Geoffrey Dawson | Bodleian Library, Oxford |
| William Deakin | Churchill Archives Centre, Cambridge |
| Field Marshal Sir John Dill | Liddell Hart Centre, King's College London |
| Charles Eade | Churchill Archives Centre, Cambridge |
| Anthony Eden | Cadbury Research Library, Birmingham University |
| General James Edmonds | Liddell Hart Centre, King's College London |
| Emrys Evans | British Library, London |

| | |
|---|---|
| King Edward VII | Royal Archives, Windsor |
| King Edward VIII | Royal Archives, Windsor |
| Admiral Lord Fisher | Churchill Archives Centre, Cambridge |
| Fladgate | Fladgate LLP, London |
| King George V | Royal Archives, Windsor |
| King George VI | Royal Archives, Windsor |
| Admiral J. H. Godfrey | Churchill Archives Centre, Cambridge |
| Sir (Percy) James Grigg | Churchill Archives Centre, Cambridge |
| Earl of Halifax | Private collection |
| Grace Hamblin | Churchill Archives Centre, Cambridge |
| General Sir Ian Hamilton | Liddell Hart Centre, King's College London |
| Pamela Harriman | By kind permission of Mrs Luce Churchill |
| Roy Harrod | British Library, London |
| Samuel Hoare, Lord Templewood | Cambridge University Library, Cambridge |
| Marian Holmes | By kind permission of Tom, Simon, Sarah and Joe Walker |
| Leslie Hore-Belisha | Churchill Archives Centre, Cambridge |
| Thomas Inskip, Lord Caldecote | Churchill Archives Centre, Cambridge |
| General Lord Ismay | Liddell Hart Centre, King's College London |
| Sir Ian Jacob | Churchill Archives Centre, Cambridge |
| Gladwyn Jebb, Lord Gladwyn | Churchill Archives Centre, Cambridge |
| Admiral Lord Jellicoe | British Library, London |
| Major-General John Kennedy | Liddell Hart Centre, King's College London |
| Admiral Lord Keyes | British Library, London |
| Sir Alan Lascelles | Churchill Archives Centre, Cambridge |
| Valentine Lawford | Churchill Archives Centre, Cambridge |
| Sir Shane Leslie | Churchill Archives Centre, Cambridge |
| Sir Basil Liddell Hart | Liddell Hart Centre, King's College London |
| Frederick Lindemann, Lord Cherwell | Nuffield College, Oxford |
| George Lloyd, Lord Lloyd | Churchill Archives Centre, Cambridge |
| Hugh Lunghi | Churchill Archives Centre, Cambridge |
| Oliver Lyttelton, Lord Chandos | Churchill Archives Centre, Cambridge |
| Harold Macmillan, 1st Earl of Stockton | Bodleian Library, Oxford |
| Ian Malcolm | Parliamentary Archives, House of Lords, London |
| David Margesson | Churchill Archives Centre, Cambridge |
| Sir Edward Marsh | Churchill Archives Centre, Cambridge |
| Sir Charles Masterman | Cadbury Research Library, Birmingham University |

| | |
|---|---|
| Lucy Masterman | Cadbury Research Library, Birmingham University |
| David Maxwell-Fyfe, Lord Kilmuir | Churchill Archives Centre, Cambridge |
| Paul Maze | Liddell Hart Centre, King's College London |
| Lady Alexandra Metcalfe | Private collection |
| Sir Oswald Mosley | Cadbury Research Library, Birmingham University |
| Oscar Nemon | Churchill Archives Centre, Cambridge |
| 1922 Committee | Bodleian Library, Oxford |
| Lord Normanbrook | Churchill Archives Centre, Cambridge |
| Lord Northcliffe | British Library, London |
| The Other Club | By kind permission of Sir Nicholas Soames MP |
| Sir Eric Phipps | Churchill Archives Centre, Cambridge |
| Admiral Sir Dudley Pound | Churchill Archives Centre, Cambridge |
| Lt-Gen. Sir Henry Pownall | Liddell Hart Centre, King's College London |
| Admiral Sir Bertram Ramsay | Churchill Archives Centre, Cambridge |
| Admiral Sir John de Robeck | Churchill Archives Centre, Cambridge |
| Field Marshal Sir William Robertson | Liddell Hart Centre, King's College London |
| 3rd Marquess of Salisbury | Hatfield House, Hertfordshire |
| 4th Marquess of Salisbury | Hatfield House, Hertfordshire |
| 5th Marquess of Salisbury | Hatfield House, Hertfordshire |
| Herbert Samuel | Parliamentary Archives, House of Lords, London |
| Duncan Sandys, Lord Duncan-Sandys | Churchill Archives Centre, Cambridge |
| Vincent Sheean | New York Public Library |
| Archibald Sinclair, Viscount Thurso | Churchill Archives Centre, Cambridge |
| Field Marshal Lord Slim | Churchill Archives Centre, Cambridge |
| F. E. Smith, 1st Earl of Birkenhead | By kind permission of Mr John Townsend |
| Lord (Christopher) Soames | Churchill Archives Centre, Cambridge |
| Admiral Sir James Somerville | Churchill Archives Centre, Cambridge |
| General Sir Louis Spears | Churchill Archives Centre, Cambridge |
| Frances Stevenson | Parliamentary Archives, House of Lords, London |
| John St Loe Strachey | Parliamentary Archives, House of Lords, London |
| Jo Sturdee, later Countess of Onslow | Churchill Archives Centre, Cambridge |
| R. W. Thompson | Liddell Hart Centre, King's College London |
| Lord Trenchard | Churchill Archives Centre, Cambridge |
| Lord Vansittart | Churchill Archives Centre, Cambridge |

| | |
|---|---|
| Cecil Vickers | By kind permission of Mr Hugo Vickers |
| Sir George Harvie Watt | Churchill Archives Centre, Cambridge |
| Ava, Viscountess Waverley | Bodleian Library, Oxford |
| Woodrow Wyatt | By kind permission of Hon. Petronella Wyatt |

## Books

Addison, Paul, *Churchill on the Home Front 1900–1955* 1992
——, *Churchill: The Unexpected Hero* 2004
eds. Addison, Paul, and Crang, Jeremy, *Listening to Britain: Home Intelligence Reports on Britain's Finest Hour – May to September 1940* 2010
Aldrich, Richard J., and Cormac, Rory, *The Black Door: Spies, Secret Intelligence and British Prime Ministers* 2016
Alexander, Earl, *The Memoirs of Field Marshal Earl Alexander of Tunis* 1962
Alldritt, Keith, *Churchill the Writer* 1992
Amery, L. S., *My Political Life: The Unforgiving Years* 1955
Andrew, Christopher, *Defence of the Realm* 2009
——, and Mitrokhin, Vasili, *The Mitrokhin Archive* 1999
Arnn, Larry P., *Churchill's Trial* 2015
Ashley, Maurice, *Churchill as Historian* 1968
Aspinall-Oglander, Cecil, *Roger Keyes* 1951
Asquith, Henry Herbert, *Memories and Reflections* 2 vols. 1928
Astley, Joan, *The Inner Circle*, 1971
Atkins, J. B., *Incidents and Reflections* 1947
Attenborough, Wilfred, *Churchill and the 'Black Dog' of Depression* 2014
Attlee, C. R., *As It Happened* 1954
Balfour, Arthur James, *Chapters of Autobiography* 1930
ed. Ball, Stuart, *Parliament and Politics in the Age of Baldwin and MacDonald*, 1992
——, *Conservative Politics in National and Imperial Crisis* 2014
Baring, Maurice, *Puppet Show of Memory* 1922
eds. Barnes, John, and Nicholson, David, *The Empire at Bay: The Leo Amery Diaries 1929–1945* 1988
Barnett, Correlli, *The Audit of War* 1986
Beaverbrook, Max, *Politicians and the War* 1928
ed. Becket, Ian, *The Memoirs of Sir James Edmonds* 2013
Beevor, Antony, *D-Day: The Battle for Normandy* 2014
——, *Arnhem: The Battle for the Bridges 1944* 2018
Beiriger, Eugene Edward, *Churchill, Munitions and Mechanical Warfare: The Politics of Supply and Strategy* New York 1997
Bell, Christopher M., *Churchill and Sea Power* 2013
——, *Churchill and the Dardanelles* 2017
Bell, Henry Hesketh, *Glimpses of a Governor's Life* 1946
Bennett, Richard, *The Black and Tans* 2001

Berlin, Isaiah, *Mr Churchill in 1940* 1949
Best, Geoffrey, *Churchill: A Study in Greatness* 2001
Bew, John, *Citizen Clem: A Biography of Attlee* 2016
Bew, Paul, *Churchill and Ireland* 2016
Birdwood, Field-Marshal Lord, *Khaki and Gown: An Autobiography* 1941
Birkenhead, 1st Earl of, *Contemporary Personalities* 1924
Birkenhead, 2nd Earl of, *The Prof in Two Worlds: The Official Life of Professor F. A. Lindemann, Viscount Cherwell* 1961
——, *Churchill 1874–1922* 1989
Birse, A. H., *Memoirs of an Interpreter* New York 1967
Black, Conrad, *Franklin Delano Roosevelt* 2003
Black, Jonathan, *Winston Churchill in British Art* 2017
Blake, Robert, *The Unknown Prime Minister: The Life and Times of Andrew Bonar Law* 1955
eds. Blake, Robert and Wm. Roger Louis, *Churchill* 1993
eds. Bland, Larry, and Stevens, S. R., *The Papers of George Catlett Marshall* vols. III, IV and V 1996
Bloch, Michael, *Operation Willi* 1986
Blunt, Wilfrid Scawen, *My Diaries* 2 vols. 1932
Bond, Brian, *The Diaries of Sir Henry Pownall* vols. I and II 1974
Booth, A. H., *The True Story of Winston Churchill* Chicago 1958
Boothby, Robert, *I Fight to Live* 1947
——, *My Yesterday, your Tomorrow* 1962
Borneman, Walter R., *MacArthur at War* 2016
Bossenbroek, Martin, *The Boer War* 2017
Bowra, Maurice, *Memories* 1966
Boyd-Carpenter, John, *Way of Life* 1980
Boyle, Andrew, *Poor, Dear Brendan* 1974
Brendon, Piers, *Winston Churchill* 2001
——, *Edward VIII* 2016
ed. Brett, Maurice, *Journals and Letters of Reginald, Viscount Esher* 4 vols. 1934
eds. Brock, Michael and Eleanor, *H. H. Asquith: Letters to Venetia Stanley* 1982
——, *Margot Asquith's Great War Diary 1914–1916* 2014
Brodhurst, Robin, *Churchill's Anchor: The Biography of Admiral of the Fleet Sir Dudley Pound* 2000
Brown, David, *The Grand Fleet* 1999
Browne, Anthony Montague, *Long Sunset* 1995
Bryant, Arthur, *The Turn of the Tide* 1957
——, *Triumph in the West* 1959
Buczacki, Stefan, *Churchill and Chartwell* 2007
Buell, Thomas, *Master of Sea Power*
Bullock, Alan, *Ernest Bevin* 2002
Butcher, Harry C., *Three Years with Eisenhower* 1946
Butler, David, *British Political Facts* 1994
Butler, R. A., *The Art of Memory* 1982

ed. Butler, Susan, *My Dear Mr Stalin: The Complete Correspondence of Franklin D. Roosevelt and Joseph V. Stalin* New Haven 2005

Calder, Angus, *The Myth of the Blitz* 1992

Callwell, Sir C. E., *Field Marshal Sir Henry Wilson* 2 vols. 1927

Campbell, John, *F. E. Smith, First Earl of Birkenhead* 1983

Cannadine, David, *The Decline and Fall of the British Aristocracy* 1992

——, *In Churchill's Shadow* 2002

——, *Heroic Chancellor: Winston Churchill and the University of Bristol* 2016

——, *Churchill: The Statesman as Artist* 2017

eds. Cannadine, David, and Quinault, Roland, *Winston Churchill in the Twenty-First Century* 2004

Carlton, David, *Churchill and the Soviet Union* 2000

Carr, John, *The Defence and Fall of Greece 1940–1941* 2013

Carter, Violet Bonham, *Winston Churchill: As I Knew Him* 1965

Cawthorne, Graham, *The Churchill Legend: An Anthology* 1965

Chandos, Oliver, *The Memoirs of Lord Chandos* 1962

Chaplin, Charlie, *My Autobiography* 1964

Chaplin, E. D. W., *Winston Churchill and Harrow* 1941

Charmley, John, *Churchill: The End of Glory* 1993

Chisholm, Anne and Davie, Michael, *Beaverbrook* 1992

*Churchill by his Contemporaries: An Observer Appreciation* 1965

Churchill, John, *Crowded Canvas* 1961

Churchill, Randolph S., *Twenty-One Years* 1964

——, The Official Biography:

Vol. I: *Winston S. Churchill: Youth 1874–1900* 1966

Vol. II: *Winston S. Churchill: Young Statesman 1901–1914* 1967

Churchill, Sarah, *A Thread in the Tapestry* 1967

——, *Keep on Dancing* 1981

Churchill, Winston S., *The Story of the Malakand Field Force* 1898

——, *The River War* 2 vols. 1899

——, *Ian Hamilton's March* 1900

——, *London to Ladysmith via Pretoria* 1900

——, *Savrola: A Tale of the Revolution in Laurania* 1900

——, *Mr Brodrick's Army* 1903

——, *For Free Trade* 1906

——, *Lord Randolph Churchill* 2 vols. 1906

——, *My African Journey* 1908

——, *Liberalism and the Social Problem* 1909

——, *The People's Rights* 1909

——, *The World Crisis* 5 vols. 1923–31

——, *My Early Life* 1930

——, *Thoughts and Adventures* 1932

——, *Marlborough: His Life and Times* 2 vols. Chicago 2002 (first published in 4 vols. 1933–8)

——, *Great Contemporaries* 1937

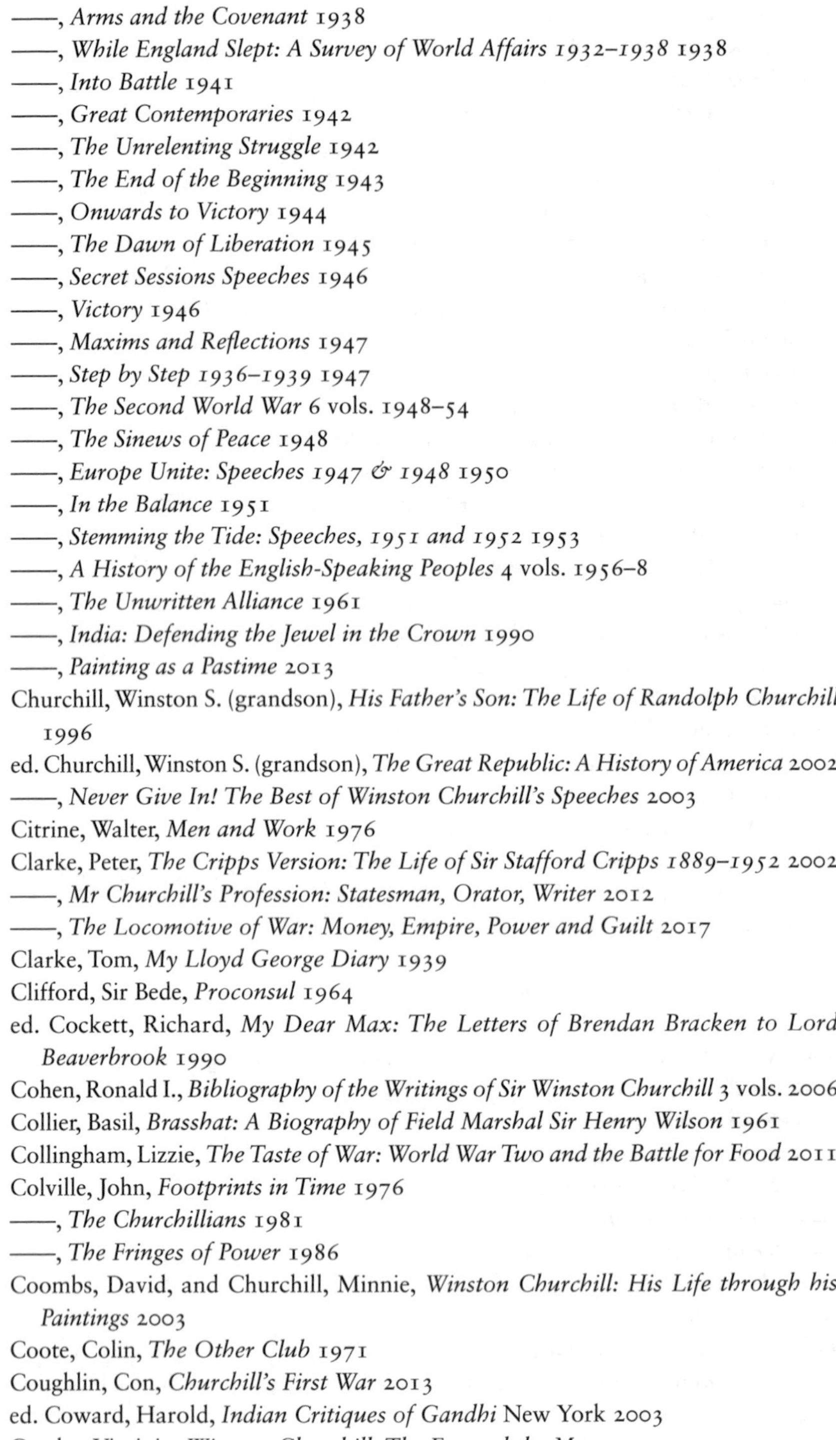


——, *Arms and the Covenant* 1938

——, *While England Slept: A Survey of World Affairs 1932–1938* 1938

——, *Into Battle* 1941

——, *Great Contemporaries* 1942

——, *The Unrelenting Struggle* 1942

——, *The End of the Beginning* 1943

——, *Onwards to Victory* 1944

——, *The Dawn of Liberation* 1945

——, *Secret Sessions Speeches* 1946

——, *Victory* 1946

——, *Maxims and Reflections* 1947

——, *Step by Step 1936–1939* 1947

——, *The Second World War* 6 vols. 1948–54

——, *The Sinews of Peace* 1948

——, *Europe Unite: Speeches 1947 & 1948* 1950

——, *In the Balance* 1951

——, *Stemming the Tide: Speeches, 1951 and 1952* 1953

——, *A History of the English-Speaking Peoples* 4 vols. 1956–8

——, *The Unwritten Alliance* 1961

——, *India: Defending the Jewel in the Crown* 1990

——, *Painting as a Pastime* 2013

Churchill, Winston S. (grandson), *His Father's Son: The Life of Randolph Churchill* 1996

ed. Churchill, Winston S. (grandson), *The Great Republic: A History of America* 2002

——, *Never Give In! The Best of Winston Churchill's Speeches* 2003

Citrine, Walter, *Men and Work* 1976

Clarke, Peter, *The Cripps Version: The Life of Sir Stafford Cripps 1889–1952* 2002

——, *Mr Churchill's Profession: Statesman, Orator, Writer* 2012

——, *The Locomotive of War: Money, Empire, Power and Guilt* 2017

Clarke, Tom, *My Lloyd George Diary* 1939

Clifford, Sir Bede, *Proconsul* 1964

ed. Cockett, Richard, *My Dear Max: The Letters of Brendan Bracken to Lord Beaverbrook* 1990

Cohen, Ronald I., *Bibliography of the Writings of Sir Winston Churchill* 3 vols. 2006

Collier, Basil, *Brasshat: A Biography of Field Marshal Sir Henry Wilson* 1961

Collingham, Lizzie, *The Taste of War: World War Two and the Battle for Food* 2011

Colville, John, *Footprints in Time* 1976

——, *The Churchillians* 1981

——, *The Fringes of Power* 1986

Coombs, David, and Churchill, Minnie, *Winston Churchill: His Life through his Paintings* 2003

Coote, Colin, *The Other Club* 1971

Coughlin, Con, *Churchill's First War* 2013

ed. Coward, Harold, *Indian Critiques of Gandhi* New York 2003

Cowles, Virginia, *Winston Churchill: The Era and the Man* 1953

ed. Cowley, Robert, *The Great War* 2004
Cowling, Maurice, *Religion and Public Doctrine in Modern England* vol. 2 1985
——, *The Impact of Hitler* 2005
Croft, Rodney, *Churchill's Final Farewell* 2014
ed. Cross, Colin, *Life with Lloyd George: The Diary of A. J. Sylvester 1931–45* 1975
Dalton, Hugh, *The Fateful Years: Memories 1931–1945* 1957
eds. Danchev, Alex, and Todman, Daniel, *Field Marshal Lord Alanbrooke: War Diaries 1939–1945* 2001
Dardanelles Commission, Part I: *Lord Kitchener and Winston Churchill* (2000)
——, Part II: *Defeat at Gallipoli* (2000)
Davenport-Hines, Richard, *Ettie: The Intimate Life and Dauntless Spirit of Lady Desborough* 2008
Davis, Richard Harding, *Real Soldiers of Fortune* 1906
de Gaulle, Charles, *The Complete War Memoirs* 1972
Dean, Joseph, *Hatred, Ridicule or Contempt* 1953
Deane, John R., *The Strange Alliance: The Story of our Efforts at Wartime Co-Operation with Russia* 1947
Dennis, Geoffrey, *Coronation Commentary* 1937
D'Este, Carlo, *Warlord: A Life of Winston Churchill at War* 2008
Dilks, David, *Sir Winston Churchill* 1965
——, *Neville Chamberlain*, 1984
——, *The Great Dominion: Winston Churchill in Canada 1900–1954* 2005
——, *Churchill and Company* 2012
ed. Dilks, David, *The Diaries of Sir Alexander Cadogan* 1971
——, *Retreat from Power: Studies in Britain's Foreign Policy of the 20th Century* vol. I 1981
Dimbleby, Jonathan, *The Battle of the Atlantic* 2015
Dix, Anthony, *The Norway Campaign and the Rise of Churchill* 2014
Djilas, Milovan, *Conversations with Stalin* 1962
Dockter, Warren, *Winston Churchill and the Islamic World* 2015
ed. Dockter, Warren, *Winston Churchill at the Telegraph* 2015
ed. Domarus, Max, *The Essential Hitler* 2007
Donaldson, Frances, *Edward VIII* 1974
Downing, Taylor, *Churchill's War Lab* 2010
Dugdale, Blanche, *Arthur James Balfour* vol. II 1936
Dundonald, The Earl of, *My Army Life* 1934
ed. Eade, Charles, *Churchill by his Contemporaries* 1955
Eden, Anthony, *Full Circle* 1960
——, *Facing the Dictators* 1962
——, *The Reckoning* 1965
Egremeont, Max, *A Life of Arthur James Balfour* 1980
'Ephesian' (Carl Eric Bechhofer Roberts), *Winston Churchill* 1927
eds. Esher, Oliver, and Brett, M. V., *Journals and Letters of Reginald Viscount Esher* 3 vols. 1938
ed. Evans, Trefor, *The Killearn Diaries* 1972

Farmelo, Graham, *Churchill's Bomb: A Hidden History of Science, War and Politics* 2013
Farrell, Brian, *The Defence and Fall of Singapore* 2005
Feiling, Keith, *The Life of Neville Chamberlain* 1946
ed. Fergusson, Bernard, *The Business of War: The War Narrative of Major-General Sir John Kennedy* 1958
Fenby, Jonathan, *Alliance: The Inside Story* 2006
ed. Ferrell, R. H., *The Eisenhower Diaries* 1981
Fisher, Lord, *Memories* 1919
Fishman, Jack, *My Darling Clementine: The Story of Lady Churchill* 1963
Fitzroy, Sir Almeric, *Memoirs* 2 vols. 1923
Fleming, Peter, *Invasion 1940* 1957
Foot, Michael, *Aneurin Bevan* vol. I 2009
Foot, M. R. D., *SOE* 1984
Forbes-Robertson, Diana, *Maxine* 1964
Fort, Adrian, *Prof: The Life and Times of Frederick Lindemann* 2003
——, *Wavell: The Life and Times of an Imperial Servant* 2009
Foster, R. F., *Lord Randolph Churchill* 1988
ed. Frank, Otto, *Anne Frank: The Diary of a Young Girl* 1997
Fraser, Lady Antonia, *My History: A Memoir of Growing Up* 2015
French, Sir John, *1914* 2009
Freudenberg, Graham, *Churchill and Australia* 2008
Gaddis, John Lewis, *On Grand Strategy* 2018
Gallup, George H., *The Gallup International Public Opinion Polls* 1976
Gardiner, A. G., *Pillars of Society* 1913
——, *Prophets, Priests and Kings* 1917
Gardner, Brian, *Churchill in his Time: A Study in a Reputation 1939–1945* 1968
George, William, *My Brother and I* 1958
Gibb, A. D., 'Captain X', *With Winston Churchill at the Front* 2016
Gilbert, Martin, *Winston Churchill: The Wilderness Years* 1981
——, *Churchill's Political Philosophy* 1981
——, *Churchill: A Life* 1991
——, *In Search of Churchill* 1994
——, *Churchill at War: His 'Finest Hour' in Photographs, 1940–1945* 2003
——, *Continue to Pester, Nag and Bite: Churchill's War Leadership* 2004
——, *D-Day* 2004
——, *Churchill and America* 2005
——, *Churchill and the Jews* 2007
——, *Winston Churchill and The Other Club* (privately published) 2011
——, *Churchill: The Power of Words* 2012
——, The Official Biography:
Vol. III: *Winston Churchill: The Challenge of War 1914–1916* 1971
*Companion Volume* III (in two parts)
Vol. IV: *Winston Churchill: World in Torment 1916–1922* 1975
*Companion Volume* IV (in three parts)

Vol. V: *Winston Churchill: The Coming of War 1922–1939* 1976
*Companion Volume* V (in three parts)
Vol. VI: *Winston Churchill: Finest Hour 1939–1941* 1983
*Churchill War Papers* (in three parts)
Vol. VII: *Winston Churchill: Road to Victory 1941–1945* 1986
*The Churchill Documents* vol. 17: *Testing Times* 2014
Vol. VIII: *Winston Churchill: 'Never Despair' 1945–1965* 1988

eds. Gilbert, Martin, and Arnn, Larry P., *The Churchill Documents* vol. 18: *One Continent Redeemed* 2015

——, *The Churchill Documents* vol. 19: *Fateful Questions* 2017

——, *The Churchill Documents* vol. 20: *Normandy and Beyond* 2018

——, *The Churchill Documents* vol. 21: *Shadows of Victory* 2018

Gillies, Donald, *Radical Diplomat: The Life of Archibald Clark Kerr, Lord Inverchapel* 1999

Gilmour, David, *Curzon* 1994

Gladwyn, Lord, *Memoirs* 1972

Golland, Jim, *Not Winston, Just William?: Winston Churchill at Harrow School* 1988

Gooch, John, *The Plans of War: The General Staff and British Military Strategy c. 1900–1916* 1974

ed. Gorodetsky, Gabriel, *The Grand Delusion: Stalin and the German Invasion of Russia* 1999

——, *The Maisky Diaries: Red Ambassador to the Court of St James's 1932–1943* 2015

——, *The Complete Maisky Diaries* 3 vols. 2018

Gough, Barry, *Churchill and Fisher at the Admiralty* 2017

Gough, General Sir Hubert, *Soldiering On* 1954

'Gracchus' [Michael Foot and Frank Owen], *Your MP* 1944

Graebner, Walter, *My Dear Mr Churchill* 1965

Greenberg, Joel, *Gordon Welchman* 2014

Gretton, Peter, *Former Naval Person: Winston Churchill and the Royal Navy* 1968

Griffiths, Richard, *What Did You Do during the War?* 2016

Grigg, John, *Lloyd George: War Leader 1916–1918* 2002

Grigg, P. J., *Prejudice and Judgment* 1948

ed. Guedalla, Philip, *Slings and Arrows: Sayings Chosen from the Speeches of the Rt Hon. David Lloyd George* 1929

Habsburg, Otto von, *Naissance d'un continent: une histoire de l'Europe* Paris 1975

Halle, Kay, *Winston Churchill on America and Britain* 1970

——, *Randolph Churchill: The Young Unpretender* 1971

——, *The Irrepressible Churchill* 2010

Hamilton, Ian, *Listening for the Drums* 1944

Hamilton, Nigel, *Monty*, vol. III: *The Field Marshal 1944–1976* 1986

——, *The Mantle of Command: FDR at War 1941–1942* 2014

Hancock, W. K., and Gowing, M. M., *British War Economy* 1949

Hanfstaengl, Ernst, *Hitler: The Missing Years* 1957

Hanson, Victor Davis, *The Second World Wars: How the First Global Conflict was Fought and Won* 2017

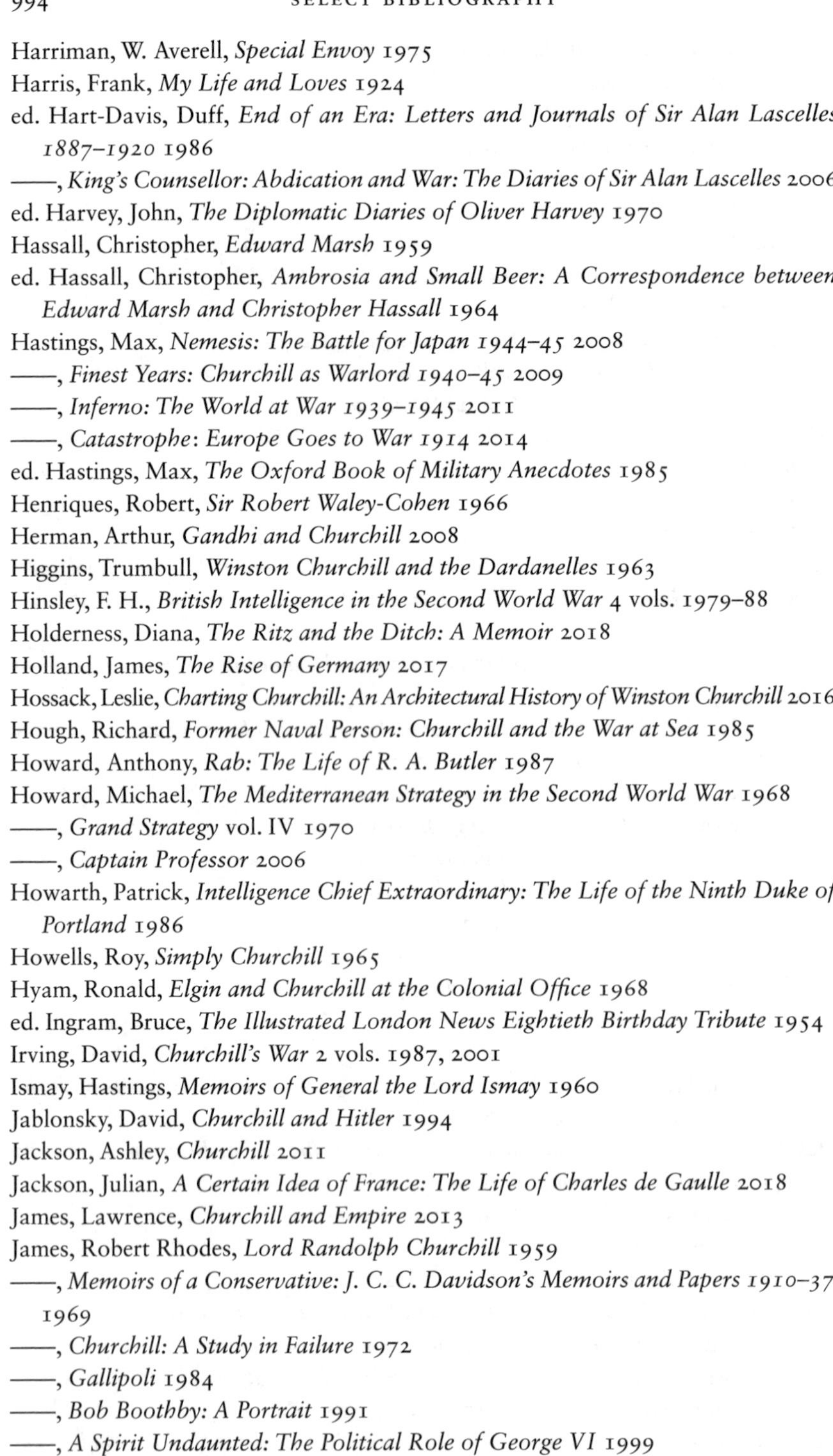


Harriman, W. Averell, *Special Envoy* 1975

Harris, Frank, *My Life and Loves* 1924

ed. Hart-Davis, Duff, *End of an Era: Letters and Journals of Sir Alan Lascelles 1887–1920* 1986

——, *King's Counsellor: Abdication and War: The Diaries of Sir Alan Lascelles* 2006

ed. Harvey, John, *The Diplomatic Diaries of Oliver Harvey* 1970

Hassall, Christopher, *Edward Marsh* 1959

ed. Hassall, Christopher, *Ambrosia and Small Beer: A Correspondence between Edward Marsh and Christopher Hassall* 1964

Hastings, Max, *Nemesis: The Battle for Japan 1944–45* 2008

——, *Finest Years: Churchill as Warlord 1940–45* 2009

——, *Inferno: The World at War 1939–1945* 2011

——, *Catastrophe*: *Europe Goes to War 1914* 2014

ed. Hastings, Max, *The Oxford Book of Military Anecdotes* 1985

Henriques, Robert, *Sir Robert Waley-Cohen* 1966

Herman, Arthur, *Gandhi and Churchill* 2008

Higgins, Trumbull, *Winston Churchill and the Dardanelles* 1963

Hinsley, F. H., *British Intelligence in the Second World War* 4 vols. 1979–88

Holderness, Diana, *The Ritz and the Ditch: A Memoir* 2018

Holland, James, *The Rise of Germany* 2017

Hossack, Leslie, *Charting Churchill: An Architectural History of Winston Churchill* 2016

Hough, Richard, *Former Naval Person: Churchill and the War at Sea* 1985

Howard, Anthony, *Rab: The Life of R. A. Butler* 1987

Howard, Michael, *The Mediterranean Strategy in the Second World War* 1968

——, *Grand Strategy* vol. IV 1970

——, *Captain Professor* 2006

Howarth, Patrick, *Intelligence Chief Extraordinary: The Life of the Ninth Duke of Portland* 1986

Howells, Roy, *Simply Churchill* 1965

Hyam, Ronald, *Elgin and Churchill at the Colonial Office* 1968

ed. Ingram, Bruce, *The Illustrated London News Eightieth Birthday Tribute* 1954

Irving, David, *Churchill's War* 2 vols. 1987, 2001

Ismay, Hastings, *Memoirs of General the Lord Ismay* 1960

Jablonsky, David, *Churchill and Hitler* 1994

Jackson, Ashley, *Churchill* 2011

Jackson, Julian, *A Certain Idea of France: The Life of Charles de Gaulle* 2018

James, Lawrence, *Churchill and Empire* 2013

James, Robert Rhodes, *Lord Randolph Churchill* 1959

——, *Memoirs of a Conservative: J. C. C. Davidson's Memoirs and Papers 1910–37* 1969

——, *Churchill: A Study in Failure* 1972

——, *Gallipoli* 1984

——, *Bob Boothby: A Portrait* 1991

——, *A Spirit Undaunted: The Political Role of George VI* 1999

ed. James, Robert Rhodes, *'Chips': The Diaries of Sir Henry Channon*, 1967

——, *Winston S. Churchill: His Complete Speeches* 8 vols. 1974
——, *Churchill Speaks* 1981
Jenkins, Roy, *Churchill* 2001
Jerrold, Douglas, *The Royal Naval Division* 1923
Johnsen, William T., *The Origins of the Grand Alliance* 2016
Johnson, Boris, *The Churchill Factor* 2014
Johnson, Paul, *Churchill* 2009
ed. Jolliffe, John, *Raymond Asquith: Life and Letters* 2018
Jones, Christopher, *No. 10 Downing Street* 1985
Jones, Thomas, *A Diary with Letters* 1954
Karslake, Basil, *1940: The Last Act: The Story of the British Forces in France after Dunkirk* 1979
Keegan, John, *The Second World War* 1997
——, *Intelligence in War* 2003
ed. Keegan, John, *Churchill's Generals* 1991
Kennedy, John, *The Business of War* 1957
ed. Kennedy, Paul, *Grand Strategies in War and Peace* New Haven 1991
Kersaudy, François, *Churchill and de Gaulle* 1982
——, *Norway 1940* 1990
Kershaw, Ian, *Hitler: Hubris 1889–1936* 1998
——, *Hitler: Nemesis 1936–1945* 2000
——, *Making Friends with Hitler: Lord Londonderry and Britain's Road to War* 2004
——, *To Hell and Back: Europe 1914–1949* 2015
Keynes, John Maynard, *The Economic Consequences of Mr Churchill* 1925
Kimball, Warren, *The Most Unsordid Act: Lend-Lease* Baltimore 1969
——, *Forged in War: Churchill, Roosevelt and the Second World War* 1997
ed. Kimball, Warren, *Churchill and Roosevelt: The Complete Correspondence* 3 vols. 1983
Klepak, Hal, *Churchill Comes of Age: Cuba 1895* 2015
Kotkin, Stepen, *Stalin: Waiting for Hitler* 2017
Lacouture, Jean, *De Gaulle: The Rebel 1890–1944* 1990
——, *De Gaulle: The Ruler 1945–1970* 1991
Laird, Stephen, and Graebner, Walter, *Hitler's Reich and Churchill's Britain* 1942
Lamb, Richard, *Churchill as War Leader: Right or Wrong?* 1991
Langworth, Richard, *A Connoisseur's Guide to the Books of Sir Winston Churchill* 1998
——, *Churchill and the Avoidable War* 2015
——, *Churchill: Myth and Reality* 2017
ed. Langworth, Richard, *Correspondence: Winston S. Churchill to Christine Lewis Conover* 1996
——, *Winston Churchill: The Dream* 2005
——, *Churchill in His Own Words* 2012
Layton, Elizabeth, *Mr Churchill's Secretary*
Leasor, James, *War at the Top* 1959
Lee, Celia, *Jean, Lady Hamilton* 2001
Lee, John, *A Soldier's Life: General Sir Ian Hamilton* 2000

Lee, John and Celia, *Winston & Jack: The Churchill Brothers* 2007
——, *The Churchills* 2010
Lees-Milne, James, *A Mingled Measure: Diaries 1953–1972* 1994
Lehrman, Lewis E., *Churchill, Roosevelt and Company* 2017
Leslie, Anita, *Train to Nowhere* 2017
Lewin, Ronald, *Churchill as Warlord* 1973
Lloyd George, David, *The Truth about the Peace Treaties* vol. I 1938
Lloyd George, Robert, *David & Winston: How the Friendship between Churchill and Lloyd George Changed the Course of History* 2005
ed. Lochner, Louis, *The Goebbels Diaries* 1948
Longford, Elizabeth, *Winston Churchill* 1978
Lough, David, *No More Champagne: Churchill and his Money* 2015
ed. Louis, William Roger, *More Adventures with Britannia* 1998
Lowenheim, Francis, et al., *Roosevelt and Churchill: Their Secret Wartime Correspondence* New York 1975
ed. Lowndes, Susan, *Diaries and Letters of Marie Belloc Lowndes 1911–1947* 1971
Lucy, Sir Henry, *The Balfourian Parliament* 1906
Lysaght, Charles Edward, *Brendan Bracken* 1979
Lysaght, Charles, and White, Trevor, *Churchill and the Irishman: The Unbelievable Life of Brendan Bracken* 2016
Macaulay, Thomas Babington, *The History of England from the Accession of James the Second* 5 vols. 1800–1859
McDonald, Iverach, *The History of the Times* vol. V 1984
McDonough, Frank, *Neville Chamberlain, Appeasement and the Road to War* 1998
McGinty Stephen, *Churchill's Cigar* 2007
McGowan, Norman, *My Years with Churchill* 1958
Macintyre, Ben, *SAS: Rogue Heroes: The Authorized Wartime History* 2016
eds. Mackenzie, Norman and Jeanne, *The Diary of Beatrice Webb* vol. II 1983
McMenamin, Michael, and Zoller, Curt J., *Becoming Winston Churchill* Westport, Conn. 2007
Macmillan, Harold, *Winds of Change* 1966
——, *The Blast of War* 1967
——, *Tides of Fortune* 1969
——, *Riding the Storm* 1971
——, *War Diaries: The Mediterranean 1943–1945* 1984
Makovsky, Michael, *Churchill's Promised Land* 2007
Mallinson, Allan, *Too Important for the Generals: Losing and Winning the First World War* 2016
ed. Marchant, James, *Winston Spencer Churchill: Servant of Crown and Commonwealth* 1954
Marder, Arthur, *From the Dreadnought to Scapa Flow: The Royal Navy in the Fisher Era 1904–1919* 5 vols. 1961
——, *Winston is Back* 1972
——, *From the Dardanelles to Oran: Studies of the Royal Navy in War and Peace 1915–1940* 1974

ed. Marder, Arthur, *Fear God and Dread Nought: The Correspondence of Admiral Lord Fisher* 3 vols. 1952–9
Marsh, Edward, *A Number of People: A Book of Reminiscences* 1939
Marsh, Richard, *Churchill and Macaulay* Ann Arbor 2015
——, *Young Winston Churchill and the Last Victorian Church of England Anti-Ritual Campaign* n.d.
Martin, Hugh, *Battle: The Life Story of the Rt Hon. Winston Churchill* 1932
Martin, Sir John, *Downing Street: The War Years: Diaries, Letters and a Memoir* 1991
Massie, Robert, *Castles of Steel: Britain, Germany and the Winning of the Great War at Sea* 2003
Masterman, Lucy, *C. F. G. Masterman: A Biography* 1939
Mayo, Katherine, *Mother India* 1935
Meacham, Jon, *Franklin and Winston: An Intimate Portrait of an Epic Friendship* 2003
Mee, Charles, *Meeting at Potsdam* New York 1975
Meehan, Patricia, *The Unnecessary War: Whitehall and the German Resistance to Hitler* 1992
ed. Middlemas, Keith, *Thomas Jones: Whitehall Diary* 3 vols. 1969–71
Middlemas, Keith, and Barnes, John, *Baldwin* 1969
ed. Midgley, Peter, *The Heroic Memory: Memorial Addresses to the Rt. Hon. Sir Winston Spencer Churchill Society, Edmonton, Alberta, 1965–1989* Edmonton 2004
Millard, Candice, *Hero of the Empire* 2016
Miller, Russell, *Boom: The Life of Viscount Trenchard* 2016
Milton, Giles, *The Ministry of Ungentlemanly Warfare: Churchill's Mavericks* 2016
Mitter, Rana, *China's War with Japan 1939–1945* 2013
Moggridge, D. E., *British Monetary Policy 1924–31: The Norman Conquest of $4.86* 1972
Montgomery, Viscount, *The Memoirs of Field Marshal Montgomery* 1958
Moran, Lord, *Winston Churchill: The Struggle for Survival* 1966
Morgan, Ted, *Churchill: The Rise to Failure 1874–1915* 1983
Morley, Lord, *Recollections* vol. II 1917
——, *Memorandum on Resignation* 1928
Mukerjee, Madhusree, *Churchill's Secret War: The British Empire and the Ravaging of India during World War II* 2010
ed. Muller, James W., *Churchill as Peacemaker* 1997
——, *Winston Churchill: Thoughts and Adventures* 2009
——, *Winston Churchill: Great Contemporaries* 2012
——, *Winston Churchill: The River War* 2017
Murray, Edmund, *I Was Churchill's Bodyguard* 1987
Nel, Elizabeth, *Mr Churchill's Secretary* 1958
——, *Winston Churchill by his Personal Secretary* 2007
Nichols, Beverley, *Verdict on India* 1944
——, *All I Could Never Be* 1949
Nicolson, Sir Arthur, *The First Lord Carnock* 1937
Nicolson Harold, *King George V* 1984

Nicolson, Nigel, *Alex: The Life of Field Marshal Earl Alexander of Tunis* 1973
ed. Nicolson, Nigel, *Harold Nicolson: Diaries and Letters* 3 vols. 1966–8
Niestlé, Axel, *German U-Boat Losses during World War II* 2014
Nolan, Cathal J., *The Allure of Battle: A History of How Battles Have Been Won and Lost* 2017
ed. Norwich, John Julius, *The Duff Cooper Diaries* 2005
——, *Darling Monster: The Letters of Lady Diana Cooper to her Son John Julius Norwich 1939–1952* 2013
Ogden, Christopher, *Life of the Party: The Life of Pamela Digby Churchill Hayward Harriman* 1994
Oliver, Vic, *Mr Showbusiness* 1954
Orange, Vincent, *Dowding of Fighter Command: Victor of the Battle of Britain* 2008
Ossad, Stephen L., *Omar Nelson Bradley* 2017
Overy, Richard, *The Air War 1939–1945* 1981
——, *The Bombing War: Europe 1939–1945* 2013
Owen, David, *Cabinet's Finest Hour: The Hidden Agenda of May 1940* 2016
Owen, Roderic, *Tedder* 1952
Pakenham, Thomas, *The Boer War* 1979
Parker, R. A. C., *Churchill and Appeasement*, 2000
ed. Parker, R. A. C., *Winston Churchill: Studies in Statesmanship* 2002
Pawle, Gerald, *The War and Colonel Warden* 1963
Pearson, John, *Citadel of the Heart: Winston and the Churchill Dynasty* 1991
Peck, John, *Dublin from Downing Street* 1978
Pelling, Henry, *Winston Churchill* 1974
Penn, Geoffrey, *Fisher, Churchill and the Dardanelles* 1999
Petrie, Sir Charles, *The Carlton Club* 1955
eds. Pickersgill, J. W., and Forster, D. F., *The Mackenzie King Record* vols. II and III 1968, 1970
Pilpel, Robert H., *Churchill in America* New York 1977
Pimlott, Ben, *Hugh Dalton: A Life* 1985
ed. Pimlott, Ben, *The Second World War Diary of Hugh Dalton* 1986
Ponting, Clive, *Churchill* 1994
Postan, M. M., *British War Production* 1952
Potter, John, *Pim and Churchill's Map Room* 2014
ed. Pottle, Mark, *Champion Redoubtable: The Diaries and Letters of Violet Bonham Carter 1914–1945* 1998
——, *Daring to Hope: The Diaries and Letters of Violet Bonham Carter 1946–1969* 1999
ed. Pottle, Mark, and Bonham Carter, Mark, *Lantern Slides: The Diaries and Letters of Violet Bonham Carter 1904–1914* 1996
Ramsden, John, *The Age of Churchill and Eden 1940–1957* 1995
——, *Man of the Century: Winston Churchill and his Legend since 1945* 2002
ed. Ranft, B., *The Beatty Papers* 2 vols. 1993
Read, Sir Herbert, *English Prose Style* 1928
Reade, Winwood, *The Martyrdom of Man* 1945

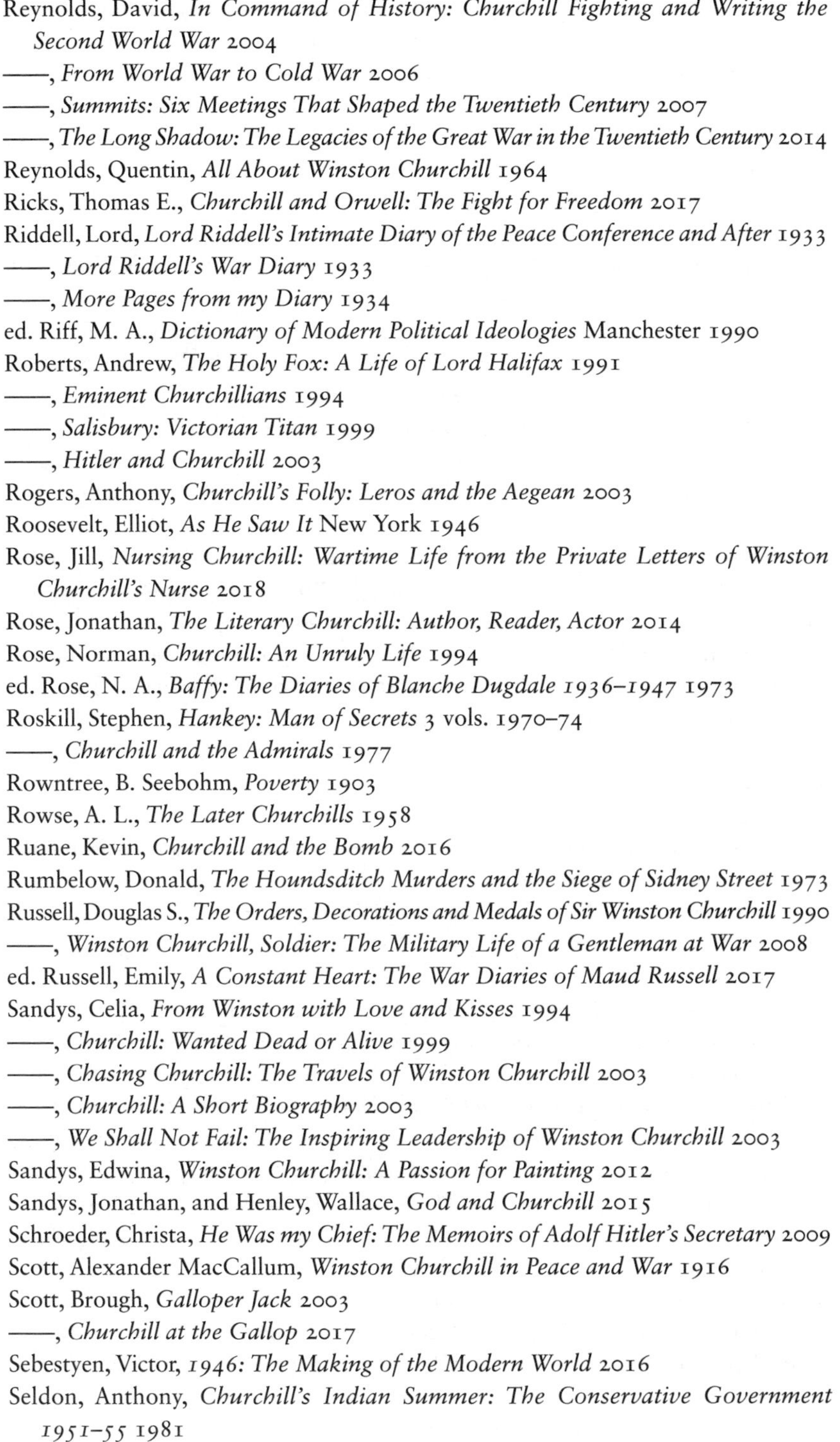


Reynolds, David, *In Command of History: Churchill Fighting and Writing the Second World War* 2004

——, *From World War to Cold War* 2006

——, *Summits: Six Meetings That Shaped the Twentieth Century* 2007

——, *The Long Shadow: The Legacies of the Great War in the Twentieth Century* 2014

Reynolds, Quentin, *All About Winston Churchill* 1964

Ricks, Thomas E., *Churchill and Orwell: The Fight for Freedom* 2017

Riddell, Lord, *Lord Riddell's Intimate Diary of the Peace Conference and After* 1933

——, *Lord Riddell's War Diary* 1933

——, *More Pages from my Diary* 1934

ed. Riff, M. A., *Dictionary of Modern Political Ideologies* Manchester 1990

Roberts, Andrew, *The Holy Fox: A Life of Lord Halifax* 1991

——, *Eminent Churchillians* 1994

——, *Salisbury: Victorian Titan* 1999

——, *Hitler and Churchill* 2003

Rogers, Anthony, *Churchill's Folly: Leros and the Aegean* 2003

Roosevelt, Elliot, *As He Saw It* New York 1946

Rose, Jill, *Nursing Churchill: Wartime Life from the Private Letters of Winston Churchill's Nurse* 2018

Rose, Jonathan, *The Literary Churchill: Author, Reader, Actor* 2014

Rose, Norman, *Churchill: An Unruly Life* 1994

ed. Rose, N. A., *Baffy: The Diaries of Blanche Dugdale 1936–1947* 1973

Roskill, Stephen, *Hankey: Man of Secrets* 3 vols. 1970–74

——, *Churchill and the Admirals* 1977

Rowntree, B. Seebohm, *Poverty* 1903

Rowse, A. L., *The Later Churchills* 1958

Ruane, Kevin, *Churchill and the Bomb* 2016

Rumbelow, Donald, *The Houndsditch Murders and the Siege of Sidney Street* 1973

Russell, Douglas S., *The Orders, Decorations and Medals of Sir Winston Churchill* 1990

——, *Winston Churchill, Soldier: The Military Life of a Gentleman at War* 2008

ed. Russell, Emily, *A Constant Heart: The War Diaries of Maud Russell* 2017

Sandys, Celia, *From Winston with Love and Kisses* 1994

——, *Churchill: Wanted Dead or Alive* 1999

——, *Chasing Churchill: The Travels of Winston Churchill* 2003

——, *Churchill: A Short Biography* 2003

——, *We Shall Not Fail: The Inspiring Leadership of Winston Churchill* 2003

Sandys, Edwina, *Winston Churchill: A Passion for Painting* 2012

Sandys, Jonathan, and Henley, Wallace, *God and Churchill* 2015

Schroeder, Christa, *He Was my Chief: The Memoirs of Adolf Hitler's Secretary* 2009

Scott, Alexander MacCallum, *Winston Churchill in Peace and War* 1916

Scott, Brough, *Galloper Jack* 2003

——, *Churchill at the Gallop* 2017

Sebestyen, Victor, *1946: The Making of the Modern World* 2016

Seldon, Anthony, *Churchill's Indian Summer: The Conservative Government 1951–55* 1981 ed. Self, Robert, *The Neville Chamberlain Diary Letters* vols. I, II, III and IV 2005

Shakespeare, Geoffrey, *Let Candles Be Brought In* 1949

Shakespeare, Nicholas, *Six Minutes in May: How Churchill Unexpectedly Became Prime Minister* 2017

ed. Shawcross, William, *Counting One's Blessings: Selected Letters of the Queen Mother* 2012

Sheean, Vincent, *Between the Thunder and the Sun* 1943

Sheffield, Gary, *The Chief: Douglas Haig and the British Army* 2011

Shelden, Michael, *Churchill: Young Titan* 2013

Sheridan, Clare, *Nuda Veritas* 1934

ed. Sherwood, Robert, *The White House Papers of Harry L. Hopkins* 2 vols. 1949

——, *Roosevelt and Hopkins* 2008

Shuckburgh, Evelyn, *Descent to Suez: Diaries 1951–56* 1986

Singer, Barry, *Churchill Style: The Art of being Winston Churchill* 2012

Sitwell, William, *Eggs or Anarchy: The Remarkable Story of the Man Tasked with the Impossible: To Feed a Nation at War* 2016

Skidelsky, Robert, *Oswald Mosley* 1975

——, *John Maynard Keynes*, vol. II: *The Economist as Saviour 1920–1937* 1992

——, *John Maynard Keynes*, vol. III: *Fighting for Britain 1937–1946* 2000

ed. Smart, Nick, *The Diaries and Letters of Robert Bernays* 1996

ed. Smith, Amanda, *Hostage to Fortune: The Letters of Joseph P. Kennedy* 2001

Snyder, Timothy, *Black Earth: The Holocaust as History and Warning* 2016

Soames, Mary, *A Churchill Family Album* 1982

——, *Winston Churchill: His Life as a Painter* 1990

——, *Clementine Churchill* 2002

——, *A Daughter's Tale* 2012

ed. Soames, Mary, *Speaking for Themselves: The Personal Letters of Winston and Clementine Churchill* 1999

Spears, Sir Edward, *Assignment to Catastrophe* 2 vols. 1954

Spence, Lyndsy, *The Mistress of Mayfair: Men, Money and the Marriage of Doris Delevingne* 2016

Stacey, Colonel C. P., *The Victory Campaign: Operations in North-West Europe 1944–1945* (Official History of the Canadian Army in the Second World War, vol. III) Ottawa 1966

Stafford, David, *Churchill and Secret Service* 1997

Stargardt, Nicholas, *The German War: A Nation under Arms 1939–45* 2015

Stelzer, Cita, *Dinner with Churchill: Policy-Making at the Dinner Table* 2013

Stewart, Andrew, *The First Victory: The Second World War and the East Africa Campaign* 2016

Strachan, Hew, *The First World War* 2003

ed. Stuart, Charles, *The Reith Diaries* 1975

Stuart, James, *Within the Fringe: An Autobiography* 1967

Symonds, Craig L., *Neptune: The Allied Invasion of Europe and the D-Day Landings 1944* 2014

Taylor, A. J. P., *Beaverbrook* 1970

ed. Taylor, A. J. P., *Lloyd George: A Diary by Frances Stevenson* 1971
——, *W. P. Crozier: Off the Record: Political Interviews* 1973
——, *My Darling Pussy: The Letters of Lloyd George and Frances Stevenson* 1975
Taylor, Robert Louis, *Winston Churchill: An Informal Study of Greatness* New York 1952
Templewood, Viscount, *Nine Troubled Years* 1954
Thomas, David, *Churchill: The Member for Woodford* 1995
Thompson, Julian, *Gallipoli* 2015
Thompson, Laurence, *1940* 1968
Thompson, R. W., *The Yankee Marlborough* 1963
——, *Churchill and Morton* 1976
Thompson, Walter, *I Was Churchill's Shadow* 1951
——, *Sixty Minutes with Winston Churchill* 1953
Thomson, George Malcolm, *Vote of Censure* 1968
ed. Thorne, Nick, *Seven Christmases: Second World War Diaries of Lt-Commander Vivian Cox* 2010
Thornton-Kemsley, Colin, *Through Winds and Tides* 1974
eds. Thorpe, Andrew, and Toye, Richard, *Parliament and Politics in the Age of Asquith and Lloyd George: The Diaries of Cecil Harmsworth MP* 2016
Tillett, Ben, *The Transport Workers' Strike 1911* 1912
Todman, Daniel, *Britain's War*, vol. I: *Into Battle 1937–1941* 2016
Tolppanen, Bradley, *Churchill in North America 1929* Jefferson, NC 2014
Tolstoy, Nikolai, *Victims of Yalta* 1977
Toye, Richard, *Lloyd George and Churchill: Rivals for Greatness* 2007
Travers, Tim, *Gallipoli 1915* 2001
Tree, Ronald, *When the Moon was High* 1975
Tunzelmann, Alex von, *Indian Summer: The Secret History of the End of an Empire* 2007
United States Department of State, *Foreign Relations of the United States, Diplomatic Papers, 1942*, vol. I: *General; the British Commonwealth; the Far East*, Washington, DC 1942
Udy, Giles, *Labour and the Gulag* 2017
Vickers, Hugo, *Cocktails and Laughter: The Albums of Loelia Lindsay (Loelia, Duchess of Westminster)* 1983
——, *Cecil Beaton* 1985
ed. Vincent, John, *The Crawford Papers: The Journals of David Lindsay, Twenty-Seventh Earl of Crawford and Tenth Earl of Balcarres during the Years 1892 to 1940* 1984
Waldegrave, William, *A Different Kind of Weather: A Memoir* 2015
*The War Book of Gray's Inn 1939–45* 2015
ed. Ward, Geoffrey C., *Closest Companion* New York 1995
Watt, Donald Cameron, *How War Came: The Immediate Origins of the Second World War 1938–1939* 2001
Watson, Alan, *Churchill's Legacy: Two Speeches to Save the World* 2016
Weeks, Sir Ronald, *Organisation and Equipment for War* Cambridge 1950

Weidhorn, Manfred, *Churchill's Rhetoric and Political Discourse* 1987
ed. Wheeler-Bennett, John, *Action This Day: Working with Churchill* 1968
Willans, Geoffrey, and Roetter, Charles, *The Wit of Winston Churchill* 1954
Williams, Susan, *The People's King: The True Story of the Abdication* 2004
Wilson, John, *CB: A Life of Sir Henry Campbell-Bannerman* 1973
Wilson, Stephen Shipley, *The Cabinet Office to 1945* 1975
ed. Wilson, Trevor, *The Political Diaries of C. P. Scott* 1970
Windsor, The Duke of, *A King's Story* 1953
Winterton, Lord, *Orders of the Day* 1953
ed. Wolf, Michael, *The Collected Essays of Sir Winston Churchill* 4 vols. 1974
Wright, Robert, *Dowding and the Battle of Britain* 1969
Wrigley, Chris, *Winston Churchill: A Biographical Companion* 2002
ed. Young, Kenneth, *The Diaries of Sir Robert Bruce Lockhart*, vol. II: *1939–1965* 1980
Ziegler, Philip, *King Edward VIII* 1990
Zoller, Curt, *Annotated Bibliography of Works about Sir Winston Churchill* 2004

## Articles and Theses

Addison, Paul, 'The Three Careers of Winston Churchill' *Transactions of the Royal Historical Society* vol. 11 2001
Adelman, Paul, 'The British General Election 1945' *History Review* issue 40 September 2001
Alkon, Paul, 'Imagining Scenarios: Churchill's Advice for Alexander Korda's Stillborn Film "Lawrence of Arabia"' *Finest Hour* no. 119 Summer 2003
Ball, Stuart, 'Churchill and the Conservative Party' *Transactions of the Royal Historical Society* vol. XI 2001
Barclay, Gordon, 'Duties in Aid of the Civil Power' *Journal of Scottish Historical Studies* forthcoming
Baxter, Colin, 'Winston Churchill: Military Strategist?' *Military Affairs* vol. XLVII no. 1 February 1983
Bell, Christopher M., 'Air Power and the Battle of the Atlantic' *Journal of Military History* vol. 79 no. 3 July 2015
Blake, Robert, 'Churchill and the Conservative Party' Crosby Kemper Lecture, Westminster College, Fulton, Mo. April 1987
Bose, Sugata, 'Starvation amidst Plenty: The Making of Famine in Bengal, Honan and Tonkin, 1942–45' *Modern Asian Studies* vol. 24 no. 4 October 1990
Bridge, Carl, 'Churchill, Hoare, Derby and the Committee of Privileges, April to June 1934' *Historical Journal* vol. 22 no. 1 1979
Cannadine, David, 'Churchill and the British Monarchy' *Transactions of the Royal Historical Society* vol. XI 2001
Capet, Antoine, 'Scientific Weaponry: How Churchill Encouraged the "Boffins" and Defied the "Blimps"' *Churchillian* Winter 2013
Charmley, John, 'Churchill's Darkest Hour: Gallipoli 100 Years On' *Conservative History Journal* vol. II issue 4 Autumn 2015

Churchill, Winston S., 'Man Overboard!' *Harmsworth Magazine* vol. 1 no. 6 1898–9

Cocks, Paul, 'The Improbable Three: Virtual History, Spirituality and the Meaning of May 1940' *Agora* vol. 51 no. 4 2016

Cohen, Eliot, 'Churchill at War' *Commentary* vol. 83 no. 5 May 1987

Colville, John, 'Churchill's England: "He Had No Use for Second Best"' *Finest Hour* no. 41 Autumn 1983

Coombs, David, 'Sir Winston Churchill, His Life and Painting: An Account of the Sotheby's Loan Exhibition' *Finest Hour* no. 100, Autumn 1998

Corfield, Tony, 'Why Chamberlain Really Fell' *History Today* vol. 46 issue 12 December 1996

Courtenay, Paul, 'The Smuts Dimension' Sixteenth International Churchill Conference 24 July 1999

Deakin, William, 'Churchill and Europe in 1944' Crosby Kemper Lecture, Westminster College, Fulton, Mo. March 1984

Devine, Richard, 'Top Cop in a Top Hat: Churchill as Home Secretary' *Finest Hour* no. 143 Summer 2009

Dilks, David, '"The Solitary Pilgrimage": Churchill and the Russians 1951–1955' Address to the Churchill Society for the Advancement of Parliamentary Democracy November 1999

——, '"Champagne for Everyone": The Greatness of Bill Deakin' *Finest Hour* no. 131 Summer 2006

——, 'The Queen and Mr Churchill' Address to Royal Society of St George, City of London Branch 6 February 2007

——, 'Churchill and the Russians, 1939–1955' Second World War Experience Centre Lecture, October 2016

Dockter, Warren, and Toye, Richard, 'Who Commanded History? Sir John Colville, Churchillian Networks and the "Castlerosse Affair"' *Journal of Contemporary History* March 2018

Encer, Craig, 'Churchill in Turkey 1910' *Finest Hour* no. 126 Spring 2005

Feldschreiber, Jared, '"Emotional Intelligence" in Churchill's View of Jewish National Sovereignty' *Churchillian* Autumn 2012

Foster, Betsy, 'The Statesmanship and Rhetoric of Churchill's Maiden Speech' *Finest Hour* no. 126 Spring 2005

Foster, Russ, 'Wellington, Waterloo and Sir Winston Churchill' *Waterloo Journal* vol. 38, no. 3 Autumn 2016

Gardiner, Nile, 'Forever in the Shadow of Churchill?: Britain and the Memory of World War Two at the End of the 20th Century' International Security Studies, Yale University, Occasional Paper No. 9 1997

Gilbert, Martin, 'What Did Churchill Really Think about the Jews?' *Finest Hour* no. 135 Summer 2007

——, 'Churchill and Bombing Policy' *Finest Hour* no. 137 Winter 2007–8

——, 'Churchill and Eugenics' *Finest Hour* no. 152 Autumn 2011

Hatter, David, 'The Chartwell Visitors Book' *Finest Hour* no. 130 Spring 2006

Hennessy, Peter, 'Churchill and the Premiership' *Transactions of the Royal Historical Society* vol. XI 2001

Herman, Arthur 'Absent Churchill, India's 1943 Famine Would Have Been Worse', *Finest Hour no.* 149, Winter 2010–11

Heyking, John von, 'Political Friendship in Churchill's *Marlborough*' *Perspectives on Political Science* vol. 46 2017

Ives, William, 'The Dardanelles and Gallipoli' *Finest Hour* no. 126 Spring 2005

Jacob, Ian, 'Principles of British Military Thought' *Foreign Affairs* vol. 29 no. 2 January 1951

——, 'The High Level Conduct and Direction of World War II' *RUSI Journal* vol. CI no. 603 August 1956

——, 'The Turning Point: Grand Strategy 1942–43' *Round Table* vol. 62 no. 248 October 1972

James, Robert Rhodes, 'Churchill, the Man' Crosby Kemper Lecture, Westminster College, Fulton, Mo. April 1986

Jones, R. V., 'Churchill as I Knew Him' Crosby Kemper Lecture, Westminster College, Fulton, Mo. March 1992

Karsh, Yousuf, 'The Portraits That Changed my Life' *Finest Hour* no. 94 Spring 1997

Keohane, Nigel, 'Sitting with the Enemy: The Asquith Coalition through a Conservative Lens' *Conservative History Journal* vol. II issue 4 Autumn 2015

Kimball, Warren, '"Beggar My Neighbor": America and the British Interim Finance Crisis, 1940–1941' *Journal of Economic History* vol. XXIX no. 4 December 1969

Langworth, Richard, 'Churchill and Lawrence' *Finest Hour* no. 119 Summer 2003

——, 'Feeding the Crocodile: Was Leopold Guilty?' *Finest Hour* no. 138 Spring 2008

——, 'Churchill and the Rhineland' *Finest Hour* no. 141 Winter 2008–9

——, 'Myth: "Churchill Caused the 1943–45 Bengal Famine"' *Finest Hour* no. 142 Spring 2009

——, 'Blood, Sweat and Gears' *Automobile* August 2016

Liddell Hart, Basil, 'Churchill in War' *Encounter* April 1966

Lippiatt, Graham, 'The Fall of the Lloyd George Coalition' *Journal of Liberal History* issue 41 Winter 2003

Mallinson, Allan, 'Churchill's Plan to Win the First World War' *History Today* vol. 63 no. 12 December 2013

Masterman, Lucy, 'Winston Churchill: The Liberal Phase' *History Today* vol. 14 nos. 11 and 12 November and December 1964

Mather, John H., 'Sir Winston Churchill: His Hardiness and Resilience' *Churchill Proceedings* 1996–7

——, 'Lord Randolph Churchill: Maladies et Mort' *Finest Hour* no. 93 Winter 1996–7

Maurer, John H., '"Winston Has Gone Mad": Churchill, the British Admiralty, and the Rise of Japanese Naval Power' *Journal of Strategic Studies* vol. 35 no. 6 2012

——, 'Averting the Great War? Churchill's Naval Holiday' *Naval War College Review*, vol. 67 no. 3 Summer 2014

Maynard, Luke, 'Tory Splits over Revolutionary Russia 1918–20' *Conservative History Journal* vol. II issue 4 Autumn 2015

Messenger, Robert, 'Churchill's Friends and Rivals' *New Criterion* October 2008

Muller, James W., '"A Good Englishman": Politics and War in Churchill's Life of Marlborough' *Political Science Reviewer* vol. 18 no. 1 1988

——, 'Churchill's Understanding of Politics' in eds. Mark Blitz and William Kristol, *Educating the Prince* Lanham, MD 2000

Newman, Hugh, 'Butterflies to Chartwell' *Finest Hour* no. 89 Winter 1995–6

Nicholas, Sian, 'Churchill's Radio Impostor' *History Today* vol. 51 issue 2 February 2001

O'Connell, John F. 'Closing the North Atlantic Air Gap' *Air Power History* 59 Summer 2012

Pearce, Robert, 'The 1950 and 1951 General Elections in Britain', *History Review* issue 60 March 2008

Phillips, Adrian, 'MI5, Churchill and the "King's Party" in the Abdication Crisis', *Conservative History Journal* vol. II issue 5 Autumn 2017

Philpott, William J., 'Kitchener and the 29th Division' *Journal of Strategic Studies* vol. 16 no. 3 September 1993

Plumb, John, 'The Dominion of History' Crosby Kemper Lecture, Westminster College, Fulton, Mo. May 1983

Powers, Richard, 'Winston Churchill's Parliamentary Commentary on British Foreign Policy, 1935–1938' *Journal of Modern History* vol. 26 no. 2 1954

Quinault, Roland, 'Churchill and Democracy' *Transactions of the Royal Historical Society* vol. XI 2001

——, 'Churchill and the Cunarders' *History Today* vol. 65 no. 8 August 2015

Ramsden, John, '"That will Depend on Who Writes the History": Winston Churchill as his own Historian' Inaugural Lecture at Queen Mary and Westfield College October 1996

——, 'How Winston Churchill Became "The Greatest Living Englishman"' *Contemporary British History* vol. 12 no. 3 Autumn 1998

Reynolds, David, 'Churchill's Writing of History' *Transactions of the Royal Historical Society* vol. XI 2001

——, 'Churchill the Historian' *History Today* vol. 55 no. 2 February 2005

Rowse, A. L., 'A Visit to Chartwell' *Finest Hour* no. 81, Fourth Quarter 1993

Sáenz-Francés San Baldomero, Emilio, 'Winston Churchill and Spain 1936–1945' in ed. David Sarias Rodríguez, *Caminando con el destino: Winston Churchill y España* Madrid 2011

Sandys, Edwina, 'Winston Churchill: His Art Reflects his Life' Crosby Kemper Lecture, Westminster College, Fulton, Mo. March 1993

'Scrutator', 'An Eye-Witness at the Dardanelles' *Empire Review* vol. XLVII no. 329 1928

Searle, Alaric, 'J. F. C. Fuller's Assessment of Winston Churchill as Grand Strategist, 1939–45' *Global War Studies* vol. 12 no. 3 2015

Smith, Richard W., 'Britain's Return to Gold' Harvard University thesis 1974

Soames, Mary, 'Winston Churchill: The Great Human Being' Crosby Kemper Lecture, Westminster College, Fulton, Mo. April 1991

Soames, Nicholas, 'Winston Churchill: A Man in Full' Address to the Churchill Society for the Advancement of Parliamentary Democracy November 1998

Sterling, Christopher, 'Getting There: Churchill's Wartime Journeys' *Finest Hour* no. 148 Autumn 2010

Strauss, Leo, 'Churchill's Greatness' *Weekly Standard* vol. 5 no. 3 January 2000

Tolppanen, Bradley P, 'Churchill and Chaplin' *Finest Hour* no. 142 Spring 2009

——, 'The Accidental Churchill' *Churchillian* Winter 2012

Vale, Allister, and Scadding, John, 'Did Winston Churchill Suffer a Myocardial Infarction in the White House at Christmas 1941?' *Journal of the Royal Society of Medicine* vol. 110 no. 12 2017

——, 'Winston Churchill . . . Treatment for Pneumonia in March 1886' *Journal of Medical Biography* https://doi.org/10.1177/0967772018754646

Vego, Milan, 'The Destruction of Convoy PQ17' *Naval War College Review* vol. 69 no. 3 Summer 2016

Warner, Geoffrey, 'The Road to D-Day' *History Today* vol. 34 issue 6 June 1984

Wrigley, Chris, 'Churchill and the Trade Unions' *Transactions of the Royal Historical Society* vol. XI 2001

Ziegler, Philip, 'Churchill and the Monarchy' *History Today* vol. 43 issue 3 March 1993

# *Notes*

## ABBREVIATIONS

### General

| | |
|---|---|
| AP | Avon Papers at Birmingham University Archives |
| BIYU | Borthwick Institute, York University |
| BL | British Library |
| Bod | Bodleian Library, Oxford |
| BU | Birmingham University Archives |
| CAC | Churchill Archives at Churchill College, Cambridge |
| CHAR | Chartwell Papers at the Churchill Archives, Cambridge |
| CHUR | Churchill Papers at the Churchill Archives, Cambridge |
| *CIHOW* | ed. Richard Langworth, *Churchill in His Own Words* 2012 |
| *CS* | ed. Robert Rhodes James, *Winston S. Churchill: His Complete Speeches*, published in New York in eight volumes in 1974 |
| CUL | Cambridge University Library |
| *CV* | *Companion Volumes* to the Official Biography (OB) |
| *CWP* | The three volumes of *Churchill War Papers* companion volumes published by Martin Gilbert between 1993 and 2000: |
| *CWP* I | *At the Admiralty* 1993 |
| *CWP* II | *Never Surrender* 1995 |
| *CWP* III | *The Ever-Widening War* 2000 |
| *FH* | *Finest Hour*, the quarterly magazine published by the International Churchill Society |
| FRUS | *Foreign Relations of the United States* |
| Hansard | House of Commons Parliamentary Debates |
| Hatfield | The Archives of the Marquesses of Salisbury and Cecil family at Hatfield House, Hertfordshire |
| JC | Joseph Chamberlain Papers at Birmingham University Archives |
| LHC | Liddell Hart Centre at King's College London |
| NA | National Archives at Kew |
| NC | Neville Chamberlain Papers at Birmingham University Archives |

| | |
|---|---|
| NYPL | New York Public Library |
| OB | The Official Biography of Sir Winston Churchill. Vols. I and II by Randolph S. Churchill and vols. III to VIII by (Sir) Martin Gilbert, published in eight volumes between 1966 and 1988: |
| OB I | *Winston S. Churchill: Youth 1874–1900* 1966 |
| OB II | *Winston S. Churchill: Young Statesman 1901–1914* 1967 |
| OB III | *Winston S. Churchill: The Challenge of War 1914–16* 1971 |
| OB IV | *Winston S. Churchill: World in Torment 1916–1922* 1975 |
| OB V | *Winston S. Churchill: The Coming of War 1922–1939* 1976 |
| OB VI | *Winston S. Churchill: Finest Hour 1939–1941* 1983 |
| OB VII | *Winston S. Churchill: Road to Victory 1941–1945* 1986 |
| OB VIII | *Winston S. Churchill: 'Never Despair' 1945–1965* 1988 |
| PA | Parliamentary Archives, House of Lords |
| RA | Royal Archives at Windsor Castle |
| *TCD* | The five volumes of *The Churchill Documents* edited by Martin Gilbert and Larry P. Arnn, published by Hillsdale College Press, Michigan: |
| *TCD* 17 | *The Churchill Documents* vol. 17: *Testing Times* 2014 |
| *TCD* 18 | *The Churchill Documents* vol. 18: *One Continent Redeemed* 2015 |
| *TCD* 19 | *The Churchill Documents* vol. 19: *Fateful Questions* 2017 |
| *TCD* 20 | *The Churchill Documents* vol. 20: *Normandy and Beyond* 2018 |
| *TCD* 21 | *The Churchill Documents* vol. 21: *Shadows of Victory* 2018 |
| *TLS* | *Times Literary Supplement* |
| WSC | Books by Winston S. Churchill (see below) |

## Churchill's Works

| | |
|---|---|
| *Arms* | *Arms and the Covenant* 1938 |
| *Balance* | *In the Balance* 1951 |
| *CE* | ed. Michael Wolf, *The Collected Essays of Sir Winston Churchill* 4 vols. 1974 |
| *Dawn* | *The Dawn of Liberation* 1945 |
| *Dream* | ed. Langworth, *The Dream* 2005 |
| *End* | *The End of the Beginning* 1943 |
| *GC* | *Great Contemporaries* 1937 |
| *HESP* | *A History of the English-Speaking Peoples* 4 vols. 1956–8 |
| *India* | *India: Defending the Jewel in the Crown* 1990 |
| *Liberalism* | *Liberalism and the Social Problem* 1909 |
| *L to L* | *London to Ladysmith via Pretoria* 1900 |
| *LRC* | *Lord Randolph Churchill* 2 vols. 1906 |
| *MAJ* | *My African Journey* 1908 |

| | |
|---|---|
| *Marl* | *Marlborough: His Life and Times* 2 vols. Chicago 2002 (first published in 4 vols. 1933–8) |
| *MEL* | *My Early Life* 1930 |
| *MFF* | *The Story of the Malakand Field Force* 1898 |
| *Onwards* | *Onwards to Victory* 1944 |
| *Painting* | *Painting as a Pastime* 1948 |
| *RW* | *The River War* 2 vols. 1899 |
| *Savrola* | *Savrola: A Tale of the Revolution in Laurania* 1900 |
| *Secret* | *Secret Sessions Speeches* 1946 |
| *Sinews* | *The Sinews of Peace* 1948 |
| *Stemming* | *Stemming the Tide: Speeches, 1951 and 1952* 1953 |
| *Step* | *Step by Step 1936–1939* 1947 |
| *Thoughts* | *Thoughts and Adventures* 1932 |
| *TSWW* | *The Second World War*, published in six volumes: |
| *TSWW* I | *The Gathering Storm* 1948 |
| *TSWW* II | *Their Finest Hour* 1949 |
| *TSWW* III | *The Grand Alliance* 1950 |
| *TSWW* IV | *The Hinge of Fate* 1951 |
| *TSWW* V | *Closing the Ring* 1952 |
| *TSWW* VI | *Triumph and Tragedy* 1954 |
| *Unite* | *Europe Unite: Speeches 1947 & 1948* 1950 |
| *Unrelenting* | *The Unrelenting Struggle* 1942 |
| *Unwritten* | *The Unwritten Alliance* 1961 |
| *Victory* | *Victory* 1946 |
| *WC* | *The World Crisis*, published in five volumes: |
| *WC* I | *1911–1914* 1923 |
| *WC* II | *1915* 1923 |
| *WC* III | *1916–18* Parts 1 and 2 1927 |
| *WC* IV | *The Aftermath 1918–1922* 1929 |
| *WC* V | *The Eastern Front* 1931 |
| *WES* | *While England Slept: A Survey of World Affairs 1932–1938* 1938 |

## 1. A Famous Name: November 1874–January 1895

1. WSC, *Marl* I p. 33 2. James, 'Churchill, the Man' p. 5 3. OB I p. 2 4. CAC EADE 2/2 5. Plumb, 'Dominion' p. 2 6. *CS* VII p. 6869 7. WSC, *Marl* I p. 740 8. BU Avon Papers 20/1/24 9. OB I p. 19 10. CAC EMAR 2 11. *CV* V Part 2 p. 820 12. Birkenhead, *Churchill* p. 115 13. Murray, *Bodyguard* p. 92 14. Browne, *Sunset* p. 118 15. *CV* I Part 1 p. 192 16. OB I p. 171 17. Marian Holmes's Diary p. 3 18. WSC, *TSWW* I p. 65 19. Carter, *Knew Him* p. 24 20. ed. Hart-Davis, *King's Counsellor* p. 93 21. *CV*

V Part 3 p. 1325 **22.** WSC, *MEL* p. 1 **23.** Ibid. p. 2 **24.** Ibid. p. 7 **25.** Gilbert, *A Life* p. 2 **26.** Sheridan, *Nuda Veritas* p. 14 **27.** Brendon, *Churchill* p. 8 **28.** Jenkins, *Churchill* p. 10 **29.** CAC CHAR 28/43/42 **30.** Ibid. **31.** Ibid. **32.** Ibid. **33.** WSC, *MEL* p. 3 **34.** CAC CHAR 28/44/2–8 **35.** Langworth, *Myth* p. 13 **36.** CAC CHAR 28/44/5–7 **37.** CAC CHAR 28/44/7 **38.** Baring, *Puppet Show* p. 71 **39.** Muller, 'Churchill's Understanding' p. 293 **40.** WSC, *MEL* p. 19 **41.** *CV* I Part 1 p. 221 **42.** WSC, *MEL* p. 87 **43.** Ibid. p. 9 **44.** Churchill, *Tapestry* p. 43 **45.** Jackson, *Churchill* pp. 14–15 **46.** CAC CHAR 28/44/9–10 **47.** *CIHOW* p. 519 **48.** Sandys, *From Winston* p. 70 **49.** Addison, *Unexpected* p. 12 **50.** *CS* VII p. 7357 **51.** Vale and Scadding, 'Pneumonia' p. 2 **52.** Ibid. passim **53.** James, *Lord Randolph Churchill* p. 207 **54.** WSC, *MEL* p. 12 **55.** Jablonsky, *Churchill and Hitler* p. 206 **56.** Foster, *Randolph* p. 216 **57.** Ibid. p. 270 **58.** CAC CHAR 28/11/42–3 **59.** Roberts, *Salisbury* p. 288 **60.** WSC, *LRC* II p. 301 **61.** RA GV/PRIV/GVD/1887: 8 August **62.** OB I p. 97 **63.** Gilbert, *A Life* p. 17 **64.** Colville, *Fringes* p. 444 **65.** ed. Eade, *Contemporaries* p. 18 **66.** WSC, *MEL* p. 27 **67.** Ibid. p. 52 **68.** Harrow School Archives Box H4/8 **69.** ed. Eade, *Contemporaries* p. 18 **70.** Jones, 'Knew Him' p. 3 **71.** WSC, *MEL* p. 15 **72.** *CIHOW* pp. 58–9 **73.** OB I p. 179 **74.** ed. Nicolson, *Diaries and Letters* III p. 268 **75.** ed. Eade, *Contemporaries* p. 19 **76.** Ibid. p. 20 **77.** Harrow School Archives Box H4/8 **78.** Gardiner, *Prophets* p. 235 **79.** Harrow School Archives Box H4/8 **80.** Ibid. **81.** Ibid. **82.** Ibid. **83.** Ibid. **84.** Ibid. **85.** Gilbert, *Search* p. 215 **86.** *CS* VIII p. 8425 **87.** ed. Eade, *Contemporaries* p. 19 **88.** Ibid. p. 18 **89.** *CV* I Part 1 p. 227 **90.** OB I p. 174 **91.** Ibid. p. 130 **92.** Ibid. p. 131 **93.** Ibid. p. 163 **94.** Ibid. pp. 163–4 **95.** Ibid. p. 164 **96.** Ibid. p. 165 **97.** Ibid. p. 167 **98.** *FH* no. 140 p. 18 **99.** OB I pp. 112–13 **100.** Ibid. **101.** WSC, *MEL* p. 17 **102.** Golland, *Not Winston* p. 31 **103.** WSC, *MEL* p. 24 **104.** Ibid. p. 30 **105.** Ibid. p. 18 **106.** Ibid. p. 29 **107.** Ibid. pp. 34–5 **108.** *CV* I Part 1 pp. 390–91 **109.** Blake, 'Conservative' p. 2 **110.** Mather, 'Maladies' pp. 24, 26 **111.** OB I p. 198 **112.** Ibid. p. 200 **113.** Birkenhead, *Contemporary Personalities* p. 113 **114.** WSC, *MEL* p. 34 **115.** Scott, *Churchill at the Gallop* passim **116.** *CV* I Part 1 p. 413 **117.** OB I pp. 219–20 **118.** WSC, *MEL* p. 43 **119.** *CV* I Part 1 p. 531 **120.** Browne, *Sunset* p. 122 **121.** WSC, *MEL* p. 42 **122.** Carter, *Knew Him* p. 27 **123.** Harrow School Archives Box H4/8 **124.** WSC, *MEL* p. 51 **125.** Searle, 'Fuller' p. 46 **126.** WSC, *MEL* p. 56 **127.** Churchill, *Crowded Canvas* p. 181 **128.** CUL Add 9248/4526 **129.** CUL ASH/B/32/6a and 6b **130.** WSC, *LRC* II p. 820 **131.** Gardiner, *Prophets* pp. 230–31 **132.** ed. Muller, *Thoughts* pp. 31–2

## 2. Ambition under Fire: January 1895–July 1898

**1.** WSC, *RW* I p. 37 **2.** Gardiner, *Prophets* p. 228 **3.** Lough, *Champagne* pp. 35–6 **4.** WSC, *MEL* p. 76 **5.** BL RP 6688/19 **6.** WSC, *MEL* p. 57 **7.** CAC CHAR 28/152A/53–4 **8.** OB I p. 259 **9.** Clarke, *Lloyd George Diary* pp. 97–8 **10.** ed. Muller, *Thoughts* pp. 49–50 **11.** McMenamin and Zoller, *Becoming Winston Churchill* p. 15 **12.** Gilbert, *Search* p. 269 **13.** Ibid. **14.** *New York Times* 27 March 1893 **15.** OB I pp. 282–3 **16.** *CV* I Part 1 p. 597 **17.** Ibid. p. 599 **18.** Ibid. p. 600 **19.** WSC, *MEL* p. 91 **20.** Ibid. p. 73 **21.** Russell, *Churchill's Decorations* p. 17 n. 17 **22.** WSC, *MEL* p. 96 **23.** Klepak, *Comes of Age* p. 129 **24.** WSC, *MEL* p. 75 **25.** Ibid. p. 75 **26.** Ibid. p. 78 **27.** ed. Midgley, *Heroic Memory* p. 12 **28.** Sandys, *Chasing Churchill* p. 33 **29.** WSC, *MEL* p. 79 **30.** Ibid. p. 107 **31.** *CV* I Part 1 p. 676 **32.** Ibid. **33.** WSC, *MEL* p. 91 **34.** Ibid. p. 116 **35.** Ibid. pp. 101–2 **36.** Jackson, *Churchill* p. 53 **37.** *Daily Telegraph* 9 October 1897 **38.** Marian Holmes's Diary p. 6 **39.** WSC, *MEL* pp. 98, 100 **40.** CAC CHAR 28/23/10–11 **41.** Birkenhead, *Personalities* p. 115 **42.** CAC CHAR 28/23/10–11 **43.** Bod Bonham Carter Papers 298/7 **44.** *CV* I Part 2 pp. 757–68 **45.** Ibid. p. 760 **46.** CAC Churchill's *Annual Register* 1874 p. 2 **47.** Ibid. p. 94 **48.** Ibid. 1875 pp. 48–9 **49.** Ibid. p. 51 **50.** Ibid. pp. 56, 119 **51.** Ibid. 1877 p. 64 **52.** *CV* I Part 2 p. 762 **53.** Ibid. p. 766 **54.** CAC Churchill's *Annual Register* 1881 pp. 58, 68, 72, 109 **55.** Ibid. 1885 pp. 119–20 **56.** Ibid. p. 134 **57.** *CV* I Part 2 p. 763 **58.** Ibid. p. 765 **59.** A reference to a chapter in William James, *The Varieties of Religious Experience* (1902) **60.** Cowling, *Religion and Public Doctrine* p. 285 **61.** WSC, *MEL* p. 103 **62.** OB VIII p. 1161 **63.** Best, *Greatness* p. 10 **64.** *CV* I Part 2 p. 697 **65.** Ibid. p. 1044 **66.** Lough, *Champagne* p. 68 **67.** WSC, *MEL* p. 119 **68.** Ibid. p. 114 **69.** WSC, *MFF* p. 9 **70.** *CV* I Part 2 p. 696 **71.** Ibid. **72.** *CS* I p. 27 **73.** Ibid. p. 28 **74.** WSC, *MEL* p. 185 **75.** Ibid. p. 110 **76.** *CV* I Part 2 p. 833; WSC, *MEL* p. 110 **77.** Coughlin, *First War* p. 207 **78.** *CV* I Part 2 p. 807 **79.** Gilbert, *A Life* p. 79 **80.** *CV* I Part 2 p. 793 **81.** WSC, *MEL* p. 119 **82.** Coughlin, *First War* p. xiv **83.** Gilbert, *A Life* p. 80 **84.** OB I pp. 355–6 **85.** *CV* Part 2 pp. 816–18 **86.** OB I p. 293 **87.** Gilbert, *A Life* p. 173 **88.** Gardiner, *Pillars* p. 62 **89.** *CV* I Part 2 p. 819 **90.** Ibid. **91.** Ibid. p. 820 **92.** Ibid. pp. 816–20 **93.** Ibid. p. 821 **94.** Ibid. **95.** Ibid. p. 839 **96.** Gilbert, *A Life* p. 86 **97.** *CV* I Part 2 p. 839 **98.** Ibid. p. 856 **99.** Gough, *Soldiering On* p. 62 **100.** OB I p. 371 **101.** *CV* I Part 2 p. 879 **102.** WSC, *MFF* pp. 117, 97 **103.** Ibid. p. 294 **104.** *The Times* 1 October 1897 **105.** Coughlin, *First War* p. 1 **106.** Ibid. p. 21 **107.** WSC *MFF* pp. 26–7 **108.** *CV* I Part 2 p. 936 **109.** WSC, *MEL* p. 137 **110.** Sheffield, *The Chief* p. 34 **111.** WSC, *WC* I p. 234 **112.** *CV* I Part 2 p. 971 **113.** WSC, *MEL* p. 149 **114.** Hatfield 3M/E41 **115.** WSC, *MEL* p. 151

## 3. From Omdurman to Oldham via Pretoria: August 1898–October 1900

**1.** WSC, *Savrola* p. 114 **2.** Riddell, *More Pages* p. 139 **3.** WSC, *MEL* p. 153 **4.** Jackson, *Churchill* p. 65 **5.** OB I p. 402; *CV* I Part 2 p. 968; WSC, *RW* II pp. 34–7 **6.** WSC, *MEL* p. 157 **7.** Ibid. p. 160 **8.** Ibid. p. 163 **9.** ed. Langworth, *Conover* p. 23 **10.** WSC, *RW* II pp. 72–3 **11.** WSC, *MEL* p. 166 **12.** My thanks to Ben Strickland; the original is in 17th/21st Lancers Museum **13.** WSC, *MEL* p. 171 **14.** Ibid. p. 172 **15.** Ibid. **16.** Ibid. p. 174 **17.** ed. Midgley, *Heroic Memory* p. 13 **18.** WSC, *MEL* p. 175 **19.** OB I p. 414 **20.** WSC, *MEL* pp. 192–3 **21.** WSC, *RW* II pp. 221, 222 **22.** Blunt, *Diaries* II p. 280 **23.** OB I pp. 438–9 **24.** Blunt, *Diaries* II p. 417 **25.** WSC, *MEL* p. 177 **26.** Moran, *Struggle* p. 556 **27.** *CV* I Part 2 p. 989 **28.** Lough, *Champagne* p. 68 **29.** Ibid. p. 56 **30.** Colville, *Churchillians* p. 112; Lough, *Champagne* p. 68 **31.** OB I pp. 438–9 **32.** CAC CHAR 28/26/5, CHAR 28/152B/168 **33.** Mather, 'Hardiness and Resilience' pp. 83–97 **34.** ed. Langworth, *Conover* p. 23 **35.** Ibid. p. 24 **36.** Hatfield House 3M/E41 **37.** WSC, *RW* I p. 156 **38.** Ibid. p. 116 **39.** Ibid. p. 6 **40.** Ibid. pp. 280–81 **41.** Ibid. p. 290 **42.** Davis, *Real Soldiers* p. 108 **43.** WSC, *RW* II p. 162 **44.** Ibid. pp. 248–50 **45.** Harrow School Archives Box H4/8 **46.** ed. Vincent, *Crawford* pp. 54–5 **47.** ed. Langworth, *Conover* p. 26 **48.** *CS* I p. 43 **49.** OB I p. 449 **50.** Ibid. p. 446 **51.** WSC, *MEL* p. 240 **52.** Ibid. **53.** ed. Langworth, *Conover* p. 25 **54.** BL Add MS 62516 **55.** OB I p. 449 **56.** BU JC10/9/70 **57.** Atkins, *Incidents* p. 122 **58.** Ibid. p. 123 **59.** Pakenham, *Boer War* p. 157 **60.** Atkins, *Incidents* p. 124 **61.** Ibid. p. 125 **62.** Ibid. p. 126 **63.** Pakenham, *Boer War* p. 171 **64.** Atkins, *Incidents* p. 128 **65.** Pakenham, *Boer War* p. 172 **66.** Ibid. p. 73 **67.** Ibid. p. 278 **68.** Ibid. p. 172 **69.** Scott, *Churchill* p. 43 **70.** Atkins, *Incidents* pp. 193–5 **71.** Courtenay, 'Smuts Dimension' p. 55 **72.** OB I p. 477 **73.** WSC, *L to L* p. 134 **74.** Pilpel, *America* p. 30 **75.** WSC, *MEL* p. 273 **76.** RA VIC/MAIN/W/25/92 **77.** OB I pp. 487–8 **78.** eds. Barnes and Nicholson, *Empire at Bay* p. 50 **79.** *Strand Magazine*, December 1923 **80.** WSC, *L to L* pp. 176–7 **81.** *CS* I p. 63 **82.** WSC, *L to L* pp. 195–7 **83.** *CS* I p. 405 **84.** Churchill, *Crowded Canvas* p. 106 **85.** *CS* I p. 63 **86.** Millard, *Hero* pp. 223–4 **87.** ed. Pottle, *Daring* pp. 317–18 **88.** *Natal Mercury*, 25 December 1899 p. 5; *FH* no. 88 p. 43 **89.** BL RP 6515 **90.** WSC, *MEL* p. 271 **91.** OB I p. 507 **92.** Dundonald, *Army Life* pp. 117–18 **93.** Ibid. p. 147 **94.** WSC, *L to L* p. 292 **95.** Jackson, *Churchill* p. 81 **96.** WSC, *L to L* p. 137 **97.** Ibid. p. 376 **98.** Bossenbroek, *Boer War* p. 208 **99.** WSC, *MEL* p. 341 **100.** Jackson, *Churchill* p. 82 **101.** Hamilton, *Listening* p. 248 **102.** Ibid. p. 249 **103.** ed. Langworth, *Conover* p. 18 **104.** ed. Eade, *Contemporaries* p. 69; WSC, *MEL* p. 139 **105.** WSC, *Savrola*

p. 42 **106.** ed. Eade, *Contemporaries* pp. 69–79 **107.** WSC, *Savrola* p. 344 **108.** *CV* I Part 2 p. 1162 **109.** BL Add MS 49694 fols. 20–21 **110.** James, *Failure* pp. 20–21 **111.** *CS* I p. 61 **112.** Millard, *Hero* p. 313 **113.** ed. Blake, *Churchill* p. 9 **114.** Hatfield 3M/E41 **115.** Gardiner, *Pillars* p. 61

## 4. Crossing the Floor: October 1900–December 1905

**1.** *CWP* I p. 833 **2.** WSC, *Marl* I p. 322 **3.** *CV* II pp. 1043–4 **4.** *CS* I p. 61 **5.** Hamilton, *Listening* p. 250 **6.** NYPL Churchill Papers Microfilm 1 **7.** Pilpel, *America* p. 36 **8.** *New York Times* 9 December 1900 p. 28; *FH* no. 149 p. 40 **9.** Pilpel, *America* pp. 36–7 **10.** Gilbert, *Churchill and America* p. 36 **11.** OB I pp. 542–3 **12.** Pilpel, *America* pp. 54–5 **13.** *CV* I Part 2 p. 1225 **14.** Ibid. p. 1231 **15.** *Daily Telegraph* 11 March 2016 **16.** Stuart, *Within* p. 124 **17.** Jackson, *Churchill* p. 280 **18.** WSC, *MEL* p. 377 **19.** Ibid. pp. 378–80 **20.** *CS* I pp. 65–6 **21.** Ibid. p. 66 **22.** Ibid. p. 65 **23.** Ibid. p. 68 **24.** Ibid. p. 70 **25.** Ibid. **26.** Lucy, *Balfourian Parliament* pp. 62–4 **27.** *CS* I p. 83 **28.** Ibid. p. 79 **29.** Ibid. p. 80 **30.** Ibid. p. 83 **31.** *CIHOW* p. 113 **32.** Mallinson, *Too Important* p. 28 **33.** BU JC/11/9/3 **34.** Halle, *Irrepressible* p. 61 **35.** *CS* I pp. 110, 107 **36.** *CV* II Part 1 pp. 104–5 **37.** Rowntree, *Poverty* pp. 304–5 **38.** *CV* II Part 1 p. 111 **39.** Ibid. **40.** eds. Mackenzie, Norman and Jeanne, *Diary of Beatrice Webb* II p. 287 **41.** Ibid. pp. 287–8 **42.** OB II p. 35 **43.** WSC, *GC* p. 178 **44.** James, *Failure* p. 16 **45.** ed. Eade, *Contemporaries* pp. 86–7 **46.** *CS* I p. 112 **47.** Halle, *Irrepressible* p. 50 **48.** Ibid. p. 49 **49.** Ramsden, 'Greatest' p. 13 **50.** WSC, *MEL* p. 385 **51.** OB II p. 47 **52.** BL Add MS 49694 fols. 39–40 **53.** Blake, 'Conservative' p. 4 **54.** *CS* I pp. 197–8 **55.** BL Add MS 49694 fols. 41–2 **56.** ed. Muller, *Thoughts* p. 10 **57.** *CS* I pp. 192–3 **58.** CAC EADE 2/2 **59.** *CS* I p. 215 **60.** Willans and Roetter, *Wit* p. 40 **61.** BL Add MS 62156 fol. 7 **62.** *Monthly Review* no. 13 November 1903 pp. 28–9 **63.** *CV* II Part 1 p. 243 **64.** Blunt, *Diaries* II p. 77 **65.** Gardiner, *Pillars* p. 58 **66.** *CS* I p. 221 **67.** Ibid. p. 224 **68.** Ibid. p. 236 **69.** Ibid. p. 237 **70.** Ibid. p. 259 **71.** Ibid. p. 261 **72.** Jackson, *Churchill* p. 93 **73.** Blake, 'Conservative' p. 4 **74.** Gardiner, *Prophets* p. 228 **75.** *CS* I p. 270 **76.** Ibid. pp. 272–3 **77.** Hansard vol. 133 cols. 958–1012 **78.** Jackson, *Churchill* p. 88 **79.** Carter, *Knew Him* p. 115 **80.** *CS* I p. 293 **81.** Ibid. p. 441 **82.** Carter, *Knew Him* p. 116 **83.** *CV* I Part 2 p. 104 **84.** George, *My Brother* p. 210 **85.** *CS* I p. 368 **86.** Carter, *Knew Him* p. 116 **87.** Pawle, *Warden* p. 179 **88.** Rowse, *Later Churchills* p. 454 **89.** James, *Failure* p. 21 **90.** *CIHOW* p. 408 **91.** ed. Muller, *Thoughts* p. 10 **92.** Birkenhead, *Contemporary Personalities* p. 118 **93.** OB II p. 92 **94.** Ibid. p. 93 **95.** *The Times* 31 May 1904 **96.** *Manchester Guardian* 31 May 1904 p. 5 **97.** Gilbert, *Churchill and the Jews* p. 1 **98.** Ibid. p. 13 **99.** Ibid. p. 3; *CV* II p. 975 **100.** CAC CHUR 1/55; Gilbert, *Churchill and the Jews* p. 14 **101.** Gilbert, *Churchill and the Jews* p. xvi **102.** Ibid. p. 9 **103.** Scott, *Churchill* p. 240 **104.** *CS* I p. 346 **105.** Ibid. p. 414 **106.** Ibid. pp. 416–17 **107.** Scott, *Churchill* pp. 1–2 **108.** *CV* II Part 1 p. 393 **109.** Gilbert, *A Life* p. 171; Petrie, *Carlton* p. 145 **110.** *CS* I p. 482 **111.** Ibid. p. 483 **112.** James, *Failure* p. 21 **113.** ed. Brett, *Esher* II p. 92 **114.** ed. Vincent, *Crawford* p. 83 **115.** *CS* I p. 503 **116.** Marsh, *Number* p. 149 **117.** Ibid.

## 5. Liberal Imperialist: January 1906–April 1908

**1.** WSC, *LRC* I p. 217 **2.** Brendon, *Churchill* p. 43 **3.** *CV* II Part 1 p. 423 **4.** WSC, *LRC* I p. 11 **5.** Foster, *Randolph* p. 383 **6.** D'Este, *Warlord* p. 74 **7.** Foster, *Randolph* p. 395 **8.** Ibid. **9.** Ibid. pp. 396–9 **10.** Ibid. **11.** Johnson, *Churchill* p. 26 **12.** WSC, *LRC* I p. 217 **13.** Ibid. II p. 489 **14.** Gilbert, *Churchill and the Jews* p. 13 **15.** *CS* I p. 553 **16.** Marsh, *Number* p. 150 **17.** *CS* I p. 523 **18.** Ibid. **19.** Ibid. pp. 530–31 **20.** Ibid. p. 545 **21.** Foster, *Randolph* p. 383 **22.** Lord Winterton in *The Illustrated London News Eightieth Birthday Tribute* p. 3 **23.** Hyam, *Elgin* p. 208; Gilbert, *A Life* p. 183 **24.** *CS* I p. 605 **25.** Gilbert, *Other Club* p. 203 **26.** *CS* I p. 658 **27.** *TCD* 18 p. 59 **28.** Courtenay,

'Smuts Dimension' pp. 55–6 **29.** RA GVI/PRIV/DIARY/COPY/1942: 14 October **30.** *CS* I p. 562 **31.** Ibid. p. 571 **32.** Best, *Greatness* p. 25 **33.** *CS* I p. 598 **34.** Marsh, *Number* pp. 151–2 **35.** Winterton, *Orders* p. 19 **36.** Wilson, *CB* p. 503 **37.** *National Review* no. 287 January 1907 p. 758 **38.** OB II p. 185 **39.** BU NC1/15/3/83 **40.** *CS* I p. 649 **41.** Ibid. p. 669 **42.** Ibid. p. 693 **43.** Morgan, *Rise to Failure* p. 202 **44.** OB II p. 196 **45.** Ibid. **46.** WSC, *Liberalism* p. 163 **47.** *CS* I p. 677 **48.** Ibid. pp. 674–7 **49.** Ibid. p. 677 **50.** Campbell, *FE* p. 461 **51.** *FH* no. 56 p. 17 **52.** OB V p. 374 **53.** Bod Bonham Carter Papers 298/6 **54.** Carter, *Knew Him* p. 15 **55.** Bod Bonham Carter Papers 298/7 **56.** Carter, *Knew Him* p. 19 **57.** RA VIC/MAIN/W/7/80 **58.** *CS* I p. 714 **59.** Ibid. p. 715 **60.** Ibid. p. 807 **61.** Ibid. pp. 808–9 **62.** George, *My Brother* p. 211 **63.** *CS* VII p. 7357 **64.** WSC, *MAJ* p. 101 **65.** Gardiner, *Prophets* p. 228 **66.** WSC, *MAJ* pp. 11–12 **67.** Ibid. pp. 121, 104 **68.** Ibid. p. 112 **69.** Ibid. p. 14 **70.** Ibid. p. 15 **71.** Ibid. p. 21 **72.** Ibid. p. 42 **73.** Ibid. p. 94 **74.** Ibid. **75.** Ibid. p. 84 **76.** Jackson, *Churchill* p. 101 **77.** Bell, *Glimpses* p. 167 **78.** Ibid. p. 168 **79.** Ibid. pp. 179–80 **80.** Ibid. p. 170 **81.** OB II pp. 228–9 **82.** Ibid. p. 51 **83.** Ibid. p. 46 **84.** Ibid. pp. 23–4 **85.** Ibid. pp. 25–6 **86.** Ibid. p. 127 **87.** Ibid. p. 27 **88.** Ibid. **89.** Ibid. p. 56 **90.** Ibid. pp. 56–7 **91.** RA VIC/MAIN/W/8/87 **92.** WSC, *MAJ* p. 60 **93.** Ibid. pp. 122–3 **94.** Ibid. p. 124; Marsh, *Number* p. 162 **95.** *CS* I p. 860 **96.** Ibid. p. 863 **97.** Ibid. p. 868 **98.** Ibid. p. 903 **99.** Ibid. **100.** *FH* no. 137 p. 58 **101.** Addison, *Unexpected* p. 43 **102.** Masterman, *Masterman* p. 97 **103.** Ibid. p. 98 **104.** Ibid. pp. 97–8 **105.** ed. Soames, *Speaking* p. 5; Birkenhead Papers 65/A3 **106.** Best, *Greatness* p. 28 **107.** Colville, *Fringes* p. 195 **108.** OB I p. 252 **109.** ed. Soames, *Speaking* p. 6 **110.** Birkenhead Papers 65/A3

## 6. Love and Liberalism: April 1908–February 1910

**1.** ed. Soames, *Speaking* p. 37 **2.** *CS* II p. 1099 **3.** Marsh, *Number* p. 163 **4.** *CS* I p. 944 **5.** Ibid. p. 945 **6.** ed. Soames, *Speaking* p. 7 **7.** Ibid. p. 8 **8.** Ibid. p. 9 **9.** OB II p. 451 **10.** RA GV/PRIV/GVD/1908 **11.** Ramsden, *Man of the Century* p. 39 **12.** ed. Soames, *Speaking* p. 9 **13.** *CS* I p. 1025 **14.** Ibid. p. 1027 **15.** Shelden, *Titan* p. 176 **16.** *CS* I p. 1041 **17.** Lough, *Champagne* p. 67 **18.** Carter, *Knew Him* p. 230 **19.** Singer, *Style* p. 54 **20.** *CIHOW* p. 579 **21.** Gilbert, *A Life* p. 195 **22.** *CS* II p. 1060 **23.** ed. Soames, *Speaking* p. 10 **24.** Marsh, *Number* p. 166 **25.** *The Times* 7 August 1908 p. 11; Tolppanen, 'Accidental' p. 10 **26.** Birkenhead Papers 65/A3 **27.** ed. Soames, *Speaking* p. 13 **28.** OB II p. 267 **29.** ed. Soames, *Speaking* p. 12 **30.** Ibid. p. 14 **31.** Ibid. **32.** Dilks, *Dominion* p. 31 **33.** Soames, *Clementine* p. 30. **34.** Ibid. p. 45 **35.** ed. Soames, *Speaking* p. 15 **36.** Ibid. p. 16 **37.** Ibid. p. 17 **38.** *CV* II Part 2 p. 810 **39.** Riddell, *More Pages* p. 1 **40.** Soames, *Clementine* p. 49 **41.** BU CFGM 4/1/2/4 **42.** *CV* II Part 2 p. 820 **43.** ed. Soames, *Speaking* p. 19 **44.** Birkenhead Papers 65/A3 **45.** Ibid. **46.** Best, *Greatness* p. 29 **47.** BU Lucy Masterman Papers CFGM 29/2/2/2 **48.** *CS* II p. 1099 **49.** Ibid. p. 1102 **50.** Ibid. p. 1105 **51.** OB II p. 322 **52.** *CS* I pp. 1151–2 **53.** 'Gracchus', *Your MP* p. 26 **54.** *CS* II p. 1252 **55.** *CV* II Part 3 p. 1874 **56.** Gilbert, 'Churchill & Bombing Policy' **57.** *CS* II p. 1257 **58.** James, *Failure* p. 35 **59.** ed. Soames, *Speaking* p. 21 **60.** *CS* II p. 1273 **61.** Nicolson, *Carnock* p. 23 **62.** *CS* II pp. 1254–5 **63.** Ibid. pp. 1258–9 **64.** ed. Soames, *Speaking* p. 23 **65.** Birkenhead Papers 65/A3 **66.** BU Lucy Masterman Papers CFGM 29/2/2/2 **67.** Toye, *Lloyd George and Churchill* p. 59 **68.** *CS* II p. 1322 **69.** Ibid. p. 1324 **70.** James, *Undaunted* p. 200 **71.** *CV* II Part 2 p. 908 **72.** Marsh, *Number* p. 167 **73.** ed. Vincent, *Crawford* p. 134 **74.** ed. Soames, *Speaking* p. 30 **75.** *CV* II Part 2 pp. 958–61 **76.** Blunt, *Diaries* II p. 289 **77.** *CS* II p. 1339 **78.** ed. Soames, *Speaking* p. 32 **79.** Ibid. p. 35 **80.** Ibid. p. 36 **81.** Ibid. pp. 37–8 **82.** Ibid. p. 37 **83.** Gilbert, *A Life* p. 210; *The Times* 15 November 1909 **84.** Gilbert, *A Life* p. 210; *The Times* 15 November 1909 **85.** Butler, *British Political Facts* p. 266 **86.** ed. Brett, *Esher* II pp. 404–5, 422–3 **87.** *CS* II p. 1382 **88.** Ibid. p. 1422 **89.** Ibid. p. 1424 **90.** Ibid. p. 1429 **91.** Addison, *Unexpected* p. 46 **92.** BU Lucy Masterman Papers CFGM 29/2/2/2 **93.** Birkenhead Papers 65/A3 **94.** Ibid. **95.** Colville, *Fringes* p. 444 **96.** OB II p. 365

## 7. Home Secretary: February 1910–September 1911

**1.** Donaldson, *Edward VIII* p. 78 **2.** Kersaudy, *Churchill and de Gaulle* p. 200 **3.** Lee, *Lady Hamilton* p. 197 **4.** OB II p. 418 **5.** Addison, *Home* p. 119 **6.** Blunt, *Diaries* II p. 416 **7.** OB II p. 418 **8.** Riddell, *More Pages* p. 29 **9.** Lee, *Lady Hamilton* p. 197 **10.** Blunt, *Diaries* II p. 461 **11.** Ibid. p. 288 **12.** Colville, *Fringes* p. 519 **13.** ed. Vincent, *Crawford* p. 153 **14.** Gilbert, *Other Club* p. 11 **15.** BU CFGM 29/2/2/2 **16.** ed. Soames, *Speaking* p. 50 **17.** Devine, 'Top Cop' p. 21 **18.** OB II p. 358 **19.** Addison, *Home* p. 128 **20.** Ibid. p. 132 **21.** Devine, 'Top Cop' p. 22 **22.** OB II p. 1453 **23.** *CS* II p. 1583 **24.** BU CFGM 29/2/2/2 **25.** *CS* II p. 1587 **26.** OB II p. 341 **27.** *CS* I p. 1598 **28.** OB II p. 373 **29.** Addison, *Home* p. 114 **30.** OB II p. 387 **31.** Devine, 'Top Cop' p. 23 **32.** Addison, *Unexpected* p. 52 **33.** OB II p. 391 **34.** CAC EADE 2/2 **35.** CAC EMAR 2 **36.** Higgins, *Dardanelles* p. 19 **37.** *CV* II Part 2 p. 1023 **38.** Blunt, *Diaries* II p. 336 **39.** Gilbert, 'Eugenics' p. 45 **40.** Bod Asquith Papers MS 12 fols. 224–8 **41.** Devine, 'Top Cop' p. 21 **42.** Ibid. **43.** ed. Eade, *Contemporaries* p. 369 **44.** Ibid. p. 367 **45.** Ibid. p. 370 **46.** James, *Failure* p. 38 **47.** *CS* II p. 1872 **48.** Hansard vol. 26 col. 1015 **49.** Tillett, *Transport Workers' Strike* p. 35 **50.** BU CFGM 4/2/3 **51.** OB II p. 399 **52.** Ibid. p. 400 **53.** Ibid. **54.** Ibid. p. 401 **55.** *CS* II p. 1630 **56.** Ibid. pp. 1630–31 **57.** BU CFGM 29/2/2/2 **58.** Ibid. **59.** Ibid. **60.** *CV* II Part 2 pp. 1030–33 **61.** *CS* I p. 794 **62.** Martin, *Battle* p. 85 **63.** Devine, 'Top Cop' p. 21 **64.** Martin, *Battle* p. 87 **65.** Ibid. p. 88 **66.** *CV* II Part 2 p. 1033 **67.** Ibid. **68.** Brendon, *Churchill* p. 58 **69.** *CV* II Part 2 p. 1033 **70.** BU CFGM 29/2/2/2 **71.** James, *Failure* p. 19 **72.** Rumbelow, *Houndsditch* p. 152 **73.** Hansard vol. 21 cols. 44–122 **74.** WSC, *Thoughts* p. 67 **75.** OB II p. 418 **76.** Ibid. p. 423 **77.** Ibid. **78.** *CS* II p. 1711 **79.** ed. Vincent, *Crawford* p. 179 **80.** *CS* II p. 1744 **81.** ed. Soames, *Speaking* p. 43 **82.** Gilbert, *Other Club* pp. 33, 31 **83.** Coote, *Other Club* p. 111 **84.** Gilbert, *Other Club* p. 239 **85.** Ibid. p. 70 **86.** CAC RDCH 1/2/46 **87.** Ibid. **88.** Interview with Minnie Churchill 7 November 2017 **89.** ed. Soames, *Speaking* p. 45 **90.** Ibid. p. 50 **91.** Ibid. p. 54 **92.** Ruane, *Bomb* p. 5 **93.** ed. Soames, *Speaking* p. 52 **94.** NA CAB 38/19/50 **95.** Mallinson, *Too Important* p. 26 n. 1 **96.** WSC, *WC* I p. 58 **97.** Collier, *Brasshat* p. 119 **98.** Mallinson, *Too Important* pp. 27–8 **99.** Ibid. p. 29 **100.** PA Lloyd George Papers C/3/15/12 **101.** Bod Bonham Carter p. 249

## 8. First Lord of the Admiralty: October 1911–August 1914

**1.** WSC, *WC* I p. 188 **2.** Ibid. pp. 13–14 **3.** Higgins, *Dardanelles* p. 31 **4.** Hough, *Former Naval Person* p. 47 **5.** Higgins, *Dardanelles* p. 15 **6.** WSC, *WC* I p. 73 **7.** *CV* II Part 3 p. 1929 **8.** Fisher, *Memories* pp. 209–14 **9.** Callwell, *Wilson* I p. 109 **10.** Jackson, *Churchill* p. 121 **11.** Roskill, *Hankey* I p. 104 **12.** Jackson, *Churchill* p. 128 **13.** WSC, *WC* I pp. 107–8 **14.** Brown, *Grand Fleet* p. 23 **15.** ed. Eade, *Contemporaries* p. 142 **16.** BU CFGM 29/2/2/2 **17.** ed. Marder, *Fisher Correspondence* I p. 437 **18.** Ibid. p. 469 **19.** *CV* II Part 3 p. 1549 **20.** BL Add MS 49694 fol. 84 **21.** Riddell, *More Pages* p. 82 **22.** Best, *Greatness* p. 46 **23.** ed. Nicolson, *Diaries and Letters* III p. 193; *CIHOW* p. 77 **24.** Hanson, *Wars* p. 149 **25.** Blunt, *Diaries* II p. 415 **26.** WSC, *WC* II p. 280 **27.** ed. Soames, *Speaking* p. 58 **28.** ed. Eade, *Contemporaries* p. 142 **29.** ed. Soames, *Speaking* p. 62 **30.** Carter, *Knew Him* p. 262 **31.** *CV* II Part 3 p. 1678 **32.** *CS* II p. 2042 **33.** RA PS/PSO/GV/C/G/414/18 **34.** Roskill, *Churchill and the Admirals* pp. 20–21; Hough, *Former Naval Person* pp. 36, 42–6 **35.** Gilbert, *Other Club* p. 48 **36.** Thompson, *Yankee* p. 180 **37.** BL Add MS 49694 fol. 62 **38.** RA PS/PSO/GV/C/F/285/1 **39.** RA PS/PSO/GV/C/F/285/5 **40.** *CV* II Part 3 p. 1665 **41.** RA PS/PSO/GV/C/F/285/13 **42.** Gretton, *Naval Person* p. 88 **43.** RA PS/PSO/GV/C/F/285/1 **44.** Massie, *Castles* p. 781 **45.** ed. Soames, *Speaking* p. 66 **46.** Addison, *Unexpected* p. 125 **47.** ed. Soames, *Speaking* p. 59 **48.** Ibid. p. 60 **49.** *CS* II p. 1907 **50.** Riddell, *More Pages* p. 37 **51.** Ibid. **52.** James, *Failure* p. 44 **53.** Bew, *Churchill and Ireland* passim **54.** OB II p. 473; Gilbert, *A Life* p. 250 **55.** *CS* II p. 1928 **56.** Maurer,

'Averting' p. 29 **57.** Ibid. **58.** WSC, *WC* II p. 112 **59.** Maurer, 'Averting' p. 29 **60.** WSC, *Step* p. 155 **61.** ed. Soames, *Speaking* p. 65 **62.** CAC CSCT 2/5/4 **63.** ed. Soames, *Speaking* p. 62 **64.** Soames, *Clementine* p. 93 **65.** Riddell, *More Pages* p. 51 **66.** Ibid. p. 103 **67.** CAC RDCH 1/2/46 **68.** ed. Nicolson, *Diaries and Letters* II p. 451 **69.** CAC NEMO 3/3 **70.** Riddell, *More Pages* pp. 130–31 **71.** BU CFGM 29/2/2/2 **72.** Ibid. **73.** OB II p. 554 **74.** Riddell, *More Pages* p. 131 **75.** George, *My Brother* p. 203 **76.** *CS* II p. 2110 **77.** Ibid. p. 2111 **78.** *CV* II Part 3 pp. 1744–5 **79.** OB II p. 557 **80.** RA GV/PRIV/GVD/1913, 18 September **81.** ed. Soames, *Speaking* p. 76 **82.** Gilbert, *Other Club* p. 52; Bew, *Churchill and Ireland* passim **83.** Gilbert, *Other Club* p. 53 **84.** Maurer, 'Averting' p. 33 **85.** Ibid. p. 30 **86.** *National Review* no. 369 November 1913 p. 368 **87.** Addison, *Unexpected* p. 63 **88.** Riddell, *More Pages* p. 186 **89.** ed. Soames, *Speaking* p. 78 **90.** Ibid. p. 79 **91.** Ibid. p. 80 **92.** Ibid. p. 82 **93.** Miller, *Boom* p. 98 **94.** Gilbert, *A Life* p. 259 **95.** ed. Soames, *Speaking* p. 89 **96.** Ibid. p. 90 **97.** Ibid. p. 91 **98.** Ibid. p. 92 **99.** Beaverbrook, *Politicians* p. 25 **100.** *CS* VIII p. 8137 **101.** Riddell, *More Pages* pp. 192–3 **102.** Ibid. p. 193 **103.** Henriques, *Waley-Cohen* p. 189 **104.** Ibid. pp. 189–90 **105.** Riddell, *More Pages* p. 197 **106.** Ibid. p. 198 **107.** Ibid. p. 199 **108.** *CS* III p. 2245 **109.** Ibid. p. 2251 **110.** Ibid. p. 2253 **111.** Scott, *Galloper* p. 145 **112.** *CS* III p. 2233 **113.** Amery, *My Political Life* I pp. 444–5 **114.** OB II p. 498 **115.** Blake, 'Conservative' p. 5 **116.** Scott, *Galloper* p. 147 **117.** Gough, *Soldiering On* p. 110 **118.** Blake, *Unknown Prime Minister* p. 189 **119.** ed. Vincent, *Crawford* p. 327 **120.** Ibid. p. 332 **121.** James, *Failure* p. 48 **122.** *Daily Mail* 6 April 1914 **123.** OB II pp. 499–500 **124.** eds. Thorpe and Toye, *Parliament* p. 157 **125.** *CS* III p. 2294 **126.** Fitzroy, *Memoirs* I pp. 290, 544 **127.** Bew, *Churchill and Ireland* passim **128.** WSC, *CE* I p. 275. **129.** Jackson, *Churchill* p. 136 **130.** WSC, *WC* I pp. 192–3 **131.** Gilbert, *A Life* p. 265 **132.** Morley, *Memorandum on Resignation* p. 4 **133.** Ibid. p. 5 **134.** George, *My Brother* p. 242 **135.** WSC, *WC* I pp. 212–13 **136.** ed. Soames, *Speaking* p. 96 **137.** Gilbert, *A Life* p. 269 **138.** ed. Soames, *Speaking* p. 96 **139.** Ibid. **140.** Ibid. p. 100 **141.** Hastings, *Catastrophe* p. 85 **142.** Ibid. p. 88 **143.** Gilbert, *Other Club* p. 54 **144.** RA GV/PRIV/GVD/1914: 29 July **145.** ed. Soames, *Speaking* p. 97 **146.** Beaverbook, *Politicians* p. 86 **147.** WSC, *WC* I pp. 216–17; ed. Eade, *Contemporaries* p. 142 **148.** BL Add MS 51073 fol. 99 **149.** Gilbert, *A Life* p. 274 **150.** *The Times* 4 August 1914 **151.** WSC, *WC* I p. 224 **152.** Gilbert, *A Life* p. 275 **153.** WSC, *WC* I p. 122 **154.** Lee, *Lady Hamilton* p. 114 **155.** Hastings, *Catastrophe* p. 115 **156.** Gilbert, *A Life* p. 275 **157.** Gardiner, *Pillars* pp. 58, 63 **158.** Ibid. pp. 57–8

## 9. 'This Glorious, Delicious War': August 1914–March 1915

**1.** *CS* III p. 2331 **2.** Ibid. p. 2343 **3.** ed. Roskill, *Hankey* I pp. 143–4 **4.** Hastings, *Catastrophe* p. 385 **5.** Callwell, *Wilson* I p. 163 **6.** ed. Taylor, *Lloyd George* p. 41 **7.** Riddell, *Intimate* p. 15 **8.** Jerrold, *Naval Division* p. xvii **9.** Ibid. p. xv **10.** Gilbert, *A Life* p. 279 **11.** Stafford, *Secret Service* p. 60 **12.** Hastings, *Catastrophe* pp. 364ff **13.** eds. Brock, *Asquith Letters* p. 203 **14.** Brendon, *Churchill* p. 64 **15.** *CV* III Part 1 p. 97 **16.** *CS* III p. 2331 **17.** Ibid. **18.** WSC, *Thoughts* p. 95 **19.** Ibid. p. 99 **20.** *TLS* 5 December 1997 p. 28 **21.** Hastings, *Catastrophe* p. 97 **22.** *CS* III p. 2337 **23.** ed. Eade, *Contemporaries* p. 143 **24.** Riddell, *War Diary* p. 14 **25.** Ibid. **26.** Olsen, 'Antwerp Expedition' p. 19 **27.** eds. Brock, *Asquith Letters* pp. 258, 262 **28.** Olsen, 'Antwerp Expedition' p. 36 **29.** eds. Brock, *Asquith Letters* p. 260 **30.** Mallinson, *Too Important* p. 72 **31.** Marder, *Dreadnought to Scapa* II p. 85; Addison, *Unexpected* p. 74 **32.** OB III pp. 111–12 **33.** *CV* III Part 1 p. 166 **34.** Mallinson, *Too Important* p. 72 **35.** Halle, *Irrepressible* p. 68 **36.** Olsen, 'Antwerp Expedition' p. 32 **37.** *Scribner's Magazine* January 1915 **38.** OB III p. 111n. **39.** Best, *Greatness* p. 56 **40.** eds. Brock, *Asquith Letters* p. 271 **41.** ed. Taylor, *Lloyd George* p. 5 **42.** OB III p. 124 **43.** *CV* III Part 1 p. 178 **44.** eds. Brock, *Asquith Letters* pp. 266–7; Asquith, *Memories* II pp. 45–6 **45.** PA Bonar Law 37/4/21 **46.** eds. Brock, *Asquith Letters* p. 275 **47.** *Morning Post* 23 October 1914 **48.** WSC, *Thoughts* pp. 11–12 **49.** ed. Eade, *Contemporaries* p. 145 **50.** ed. Vincent, *Crawford* p. 279 **51.** Massie, *Castles* p. 175n. **52.** RA GV/PRIV/

GVD/1914: 29 October; WSC, *WC* I p. 177 **53.** WSC, *WC* I p. 360; Brodhurst, *Anchor* p. 27 **54.** *CV* II Part 2 p. 932 **55.** Thompson, *Gallipoli* p. 3 **56.** ed. Wilson, *Scott* pp. 110–12 **57.** ed. Eade, *Contemporaries* p. 143 **58.** Strachan, *First World War* p. 77 **59.** *CS* III p. 2340 **60.** Ibid. p. 2348 **61.** *CV* III Part 1 p. 25 **62.** Travers, *Gallipoli* p. 20 **63.** *CV* III Part 1 p. 361 **64.** Strachan, *First World War* p. 113 **65.** Gooch, *Plans of War* p. 259 **66.** Strachan, *First World War* p. 113 **67.** Ibid. p. 114 **68.** Bew, *Citizen Clem* pp. 13, 86 **69.** ed. Cowley, *Great War* p. 182 **70.** OB III p. 233 **71.** Ibid. p. 236 **72.** Ibid. p. 234 **73.** *CV* III Part 1 pp. 377–8 **74.** WSC, *WC* II p. 71 **75.** NA CAB 41/1/12 **76.** Penn, *Fisher* p. 124 **77.** Ibid. **78.** eds. Brock, *Margot* p. 68 **79.** Penn, *Fisher* p. 124 **80.** WSC, *WC* II pp. 102, 121–2 **81.** Penn, *Fisher* p. 125 **82.** eds. Brock, *Asquith Letters* p. 375 **83.** Roskill, *Hankey* I p. 265 **84.** eds. Brock, *Asquith Letters* p. 374 n. 6 **85.** WSC, *WC* II p. 543; Penn, *Fisher* p. 126 **86.** *CS* III p. 2396 **87.** Penn, *Fisher* p. 127 **88.** Bell, *Dardanelles* p. 359 **89.** WSC, *WC* II p. 91 **90.** Bell, *Dardanelles* p. 85 **91.** eds. Brock, *Asquith Letters* p. 118 **92.** Ibid. p. 375 **93.** Ibid. p. 376 **94.** ed. Taylor, *Lloyd George* p. 21 **95.** Penn, *Fisher* p. 126 **96.** WSC, *WC* II p. 551 **97.** Marder, *Fear God* III p. 133 **98.** Ibid. pp. 141–2 **99.** PA LG/C/4/11/3 **100.** Ibid. **101.** ed. Taylor, *Lloyd George* p. 7 **102.** PA LG/C/4/11/3 **103.** Bell, *Dardanelles* p. 234 **104.** *CS* III p. 2397 **105.** ed. Brett, *Esher* III p. 212 **106.** OB III p. 273 **107.** James, *Failure* p. 71 **108.** Ibid. p. 70 **109.** ed. Brett, *Esher* III p. 217 **110.** ed. Pottle, *Champion* p. 25 **111.** Ibid. **112.** James, *Failure* p. 69 **113.** NA CAB 42/1/47 **114.** Philpott, '29th Division' pp. 384–407 **115.** WSC, *Thoughts* p. 12 **116.** BL Add MS 82379 fol. 1 **117.** Bell, *Dardanelles* p. 112 **118.** ed. Cowley, *Great War* p. 183 **119.** WSC, *WC* II p. 272

## 10. Gallipoli: March–November 1915

**1.** WSC, *Savrola* p. 317 **2.** WSC, *GC* p. 131 **3.** ed. Cowley, *Great War* p. 183 **4.** Thompson, *Gallipoli* p. 5 **5.** WSC, *WC* II p. 244 **6.** Ibid. I pp. 254–76; Bell, *Dardanelles* p. 356; Strachan, *First World War* p. 116; ed. Cowley, *Great War* p. 183 **7.** Roskill, *Hankey* I p. 168 **8.** Ives, 'Dardanelles and Gallipoli' p. 3 **9.** WSC, *WC* I pp. 254–76 **10.** John Lee in *Journal of Military History*, vol. 64, no. 2 April 2000 **11.** WSC, *RW* I p. 235 **12.** *CV* III Part 1 p. 559 **13.** James, *Failure* p. 75 **14.** ed. Roskill, *Hankey* I p. 182 **15.** Bell, *Dardanelles* p. 357 **16.** Thompson, *Gallipoli* p. 6 **17.** NA CAB 42/2/17 **18.** BU NC7/11/8/6 **19.** ed. Taylor, *Lloyd George* p. 41 **20.** BL Add MS 49694 fols. 108–10 **21.** Bell, *Dardanelles* p. 157 **22.** *The Times* 26 April 1915 **23.** NYPL Berg Collection Winston Churchill **24.** Jerrold, *Naval Division* p. xvii **25.** James, *Failure* p. 76 **26.** Lee, *Soldier's Life* p. 162 **27.** *Morning Post* 29 May 1915 **28.** Soames, *Clementine* p. 138; Charmley, 'Churchill's Darkest Hour' p. 47 **29.** eds. Brock, *Margot* pp. 107–8 **30.** Ibid. p. 108 **31.** Langworth, *Myth* pp. 69–73 **32.** *CV* III p. 501 **33.** WSC, *WC* III p. 166 **34.** eds. Brock, *Margot* pp. 109–10 **35.** Ibid. p. 113 **36.** Addison, *Unexpected* p. 78 **37.** French, *1914* p. 357 **38.** WSC, *WC* II p. 350 **39.** ed. Taylor, *Lloyd George* pp. 49–50 **40.** OB III p. 431; CAC FISR 1/24/35 **41.** OB III p. 884 **42.** ed. Cowley, *Great War* p. 121; eds. Brock, *Margot* p. 114 **43.** Brodhurst, *Anchor* p. 28 **44.** Marder, *Fear God* III p. 328 **45.** Nicolson, *George V* p. 263 **46.** ed. Taylor, *Lloyd George* p. 50 **47.** eds. Brock, *Margot* p. 116 **48.** Ibid. p. 84 **49.** James, *Failure* p. 54 **50.** ed. Taylor, *Lloyd George* p. 53 **51.** PA Bonar Law 37/2/33 **52.** eds. Brock, *Margot* p. 118 **53.** Carter, *Knew Him* p. 19 **54.** ed. Brett, *Esher* III p. 237 **55.** Hamilton, *Listening* p. 253 **56.** eds. Brock, *Margot* p. 118 **57.** Ibid. p. 120 **58.** ed. Taylor, *Lloyd George* p. 51 **59.** Ibid. **60.** Lee, *Lady Hamilton* p. 123 **61.** ed. Taylor, *Lloyd George* p. 52 **62.** Ibid. **63.** Ibid. **64.** Ibid. **65.** OB III p. 456. **66.** Bell, *Dardanelles* p. 186 **67.** *CV* III Part 2 p. 911 **68.** Bod Asquith Box 27 fols. 172–5 **69.** eds. Brock, *Margot* pp. 133–4 **70.** OB III p. 459; Soames, *Clementine* p. 142 **71.** Best, *Greatness* p. 71 **72.** OB III p. 457 **73.** *CV* III Part 2 pp. 922–4 **74.** Ibid. p. 924 **75.** Ibid. pp. 925–6 **76.** Ibid. pp. 925–7 **77.** Roskill, *Hankey* I pp. 174–5 **78.** RA GV/PRIV/GVD/1915: 22 May **79.** Carter, *Knew Him* pp. 427–8 **80.** WSC, *WC* I p. 234 **81.** Ibid. II pp. 374–5 **82.** James, *Failure* p. 80 **83.** *Observer* 23 May 1915 **84.** Soames, *Clementine* p. 142 **85.** CAC RDCH 1/2/46 **86.** Soames, *Painter* p. 20 **87.** Thompson, *Gallipoli* p.

32 **88.** *CS* III p. 2380 **89.** CAC THSO 1/1/2 **90.** ed. Taylor, *Lloyd George* p. 59 **91.** NA CAB 37/130/14 **92.** NA CAB 37/130/16 **93.** *CV* III Part 2 p. 1042 **94.** CAC CHAR 28/43/42 **95.** OB VIII p. 1154 **96.** Soames, *Painter* p. 24 **97.** WSC, *Thoughts* p. 336 **98.** *CIHOW* p. 458 **99.** Sandys, *From Winston* p. 141 **100.** WSC, *Thoughts* pp. 331–2 **101.** *CIHOW* p. 455 **102.** ed. Soames, *Speaking* p. 111 **103.** Lee, *Lady Hamilton* p. 129 **104.** CAC THSO 1/1/3 **105.** OB III p. 473 **106.** Soames, 'Human Being' p. 3; Birkenhead Papers 65/A3 **107.** ed. Soames, *Speaking* p. 53 **108.** Attenborough, *Black Dog* pp. 214–15 **109.** Ibid. pp. 212–13 **110.** *CV* IV Part 1 p. 8 **111.** CAC THSO 1/1/3 **112.** BU Austen Chamberlain C18/4/8 pp. 50–111 **113.** ed. Taylor, *Lloyd George* p. 57 **114.** Roskill, *Hankey* I p. 215 **115.** ed. Taylor, *Lloyd George* p. 59 **116.** Roskill, *Hankey* I p. 222 **117.** ed. Wilson, *Scott* p. 142 **118.** *CV* III Part 2 p. 1204 **119.** WSC, *WC* II p. 489 **120.** NA CAB 37/136/12 **121.** Roskill, *Hankey* I p. 232 **122.** ed. Taylor, *Lloyd George* p. 74 **123.** *CV* III Part 2 pp. 1249–50 **124.** ed. Taylor, *Lloyd George* p. 74 **125.** Roskill, *Hankey* I p. 230 **126.** *CV* III Part 2 p. 1255 **127.** *CS* III pp. 2400–401 **128.** Ibid. p. 2399 **129.** Ibid. p. 2401 **130.** WSC, *WC* II p. 4 **131.** WSC, *TSWW* II p. 3 **132.** ed. Soames, *Speaking* p. 149 **133.** D'Este, *Warlord* p. 295 **134.** CAC RCDH 1/2/46 **135.** Fraser, *My History* p. 109 **136.** *The Times* 16 November 1915

## 11. Plug Street to Victory: November 1915–November 1918

**1.** WSC, *Thoughts* p. 111 **2.** WSC, *WC* IV p. 304 **3.** Ibid. II p. 500 **4.** WSC, *Thoughts* p. 110 **5.** ed. Smart, *Bernays* p. 124 **6.** ed. Soames, *Speaking* p. 113 **7.** Ibid. p. 114 **8.** Ibid. pp. 114–15 **9.** Ibid. p. 115 **10.** Ibid. p. 114 **11.** WSC, *Thoughts* p. 110 **12.** ed. Soames, *Speaking* p. 123 **13.** OB III pp. 578–81 **14.** ed. Soames, *Speaking* p. 119 **15.** Ibid. p. 115 **16.** Ibid. p. 128 **17.** Jeffrey, *1916* pp. 15–16 **18.** Beckett, *Attlee* p. 61 **19.** ed. Soames, *Speaking* pp. 152–3 **20.** Ibid. p. 116 **21.** WSC, *Thoughts* p. 114 **22.** ed. Soames, *Speaking* pp. 118–19 **23.** WSC, *Thoughts* p. 116 **24.** ed. Soames, *Speaking* p. 119 **25.** WSC, *Thoughts* p. 116 **26.** ed. Soames, *Speaking* p. 119 **27.** Ibid. p. 133 **28.** Ibid. p. 124 **29.** ed. Pottle, *Champion* pp. 25–6 **30.** ed. Soames, *Speaking* p. 120 **31.** Ibid. **32.** Ibid. p. 121 **33.** Colville, *Fringes* p. 127 **34.** CAC SPRS 1/76 **35.** ed. Hunter, *Winston and Archie* passim **36.** ed. Soames, *Speaking* p. 132 **37.** WSC, *WC* II p. 87 **38.** ed. Soames, *Speaking* p. 132 **39.** Ibid. p. 130 **40.** Ibid. pp. 132–3 **41.** Ibid. p. 137 **42.** Ibid. p. 139 **43.** Ibid. pp. 141–2 **44.** Sheffield, *The Chief* p. 324 **45.** WSC, *WC* III Part 1 p. 193 **46.** ed. Soames, *Speaking* p. 142 **47.** Ibid. p. 143 **48.** Ibid. p. 148 **49.** *CV* III Part 2 p. 1354 **50.** Gibb, *Winston* p. 68 **51.** Ibid. p. 139 **52.** OB III p. 658 **53.** Gibb, *Winston* p. 106 **54.** Ibid. p. 117 **55.** Ibid. p. 115 **56.** ed. Soames, *Speaking* p. 156 **57.** Ibid. p. 143 **58.** CAC RCDH 1/2/46 **59.** ed. Soames, *Speaking* pp. 163–4 **60.** Ibid. p. 164 **61.** Gibb, *Winston* p. 71 **62.** ed. Soames, *Speaking* p. 166 **63.** Ibid. pp. 167–8 **64.** *CV* III Part 2 p. 1416 **65.** ed. Soames, *Speaking* p. 169 **66.** *Strand Magazine* March 1931; WSC, *Thoughts* p. 7 **67.** ed. Soames, *Speaking* p. 175 **68.** *CV* III Part 2 pp. 1432–3 **69.** George, *My Brother* p. 253 **70.** *CS* III p. 2410 **71.** eds. Brock, *Margot* p. 242; Gilbert, *Other Club* p. 63; Bod Dawson Papers 66/35–6 **72.** Bod Bonham Carter Box 323 pp. 45–6 **73.** Ibid. p. 47 **74.** Carter, *Knew Him* p. 454 **75.** Bod Bonham Carter Box 323 pp. 48–50 **76.** ed. Soames, *Speaking* p. 195 **77.** Ibid. p. 196 **78.** *CV* III Part 2 p. 1467 **79.** ed. Soames, *Speaking* p. 196 **80.** Ibid. p. 198 **81.** Ibid. p. 199 **82.** Ibid. p. 200 **83.** Ibid. p. 202 **84.** ed. Hart-Davis, *Era* pp. 196–7 **85.** *CS* III p. 2421 **86.** Ibid. p. 2341 **87.** WSC, *WC* III Part 1 p. 112; Hastings, *Catastrophe* p. 357 **88.** Dean, *Hatred, Ridicule* p. 40 **89.** Lee, *Lady Hamilton* p. 137 **90.** Hamilton, *Listening* pp. 253–4 **91.** ed. Roskill, *Hankey* I p. 286 **92.** WSC, *WC* III Part 1 p. 187 **93.** Best, *Greatness* p. 89 **94.** ed. Roskill, *Hankey* I p. 286 **95.** Bod Asquith Papers Box 129 fols. 15–17 **96.** WSC, *GC* p. 99 **97.** ed. Jolliffe, *Raymond* pp. 297–8 **98.** WSC, *WC* II p. 21 **99.** *Daily Mail* 3 October 1935 **100.** *CV* III Part 2 p. 1533 **101.** *CS* III p. 2485 **102.** Ibid. p. 2503 **103.** OB III pp. 801–2 **104.** Gilbert, *A Life* p. 367 **105.** *The Spectator* 2 September 1916 **106.** Keohane, 'Sitting' p. 56 **107.** James, *Davidson* pp. 53–4 **108.** Gilbert, *Other Club* p. 67 **109.**

Eden, *Reckoning* p. 277 **110.** WSC, *GC* p. 185 **111.** Dardanelles Commission Part I pp. 105–6 **112.** Ibid. p. 78 **113.** Ibid. p. 160 **114.** CAC FISR 8/12/4726 **115.** OB IV p. 10 **116.** NA CAB 19/1 **117.** *CS* III p. 2539 **118.** ed. Lowndes, *Belloc Lowndes* p. 80 **119.** WSC, *WC* III Part 1 p. 214 **120.** WSC, *Thoughts* p. 137 **121.** Other Club Betting Book **122.** OB IV p. 17 **123.** Ibid. pp. 5, 16–17 **124.** Gardiner, *Prophets* p. 228 **125.** ed. Brett, *Esher* IV p. 121 **126.** Birkenhead Papers 65/A3 **127.** Ibid. **128.** *Morning Post* 18 July 1917 **129.** *C V* IV Part 1 p. 107 **130.** Ponting, *Churchill* p. 207 **131.** Blake, *Unknown* p. 361 **132.** Beiriger, *Munitions* passim **133.** WSC, *WC* III Part 2 p. 300 **134.** Roskill, *Hankey* I p. 415 **135.** BL Add MS 48992 fol. 97 **136.** BL Add MS 82379 fols. 109–22; Brodhurst, *Pound* p. 38 **137.** Brodhurst, *Pound* p. 38 **138.** WSC, *WC* III p. 339 **139.** *History Today* January 2015 pp. 36–7 **140.** Birkenhead, *Contemporary Personalities* p. 121 **141.** OB IV p. 38 **142.** Jackson, *Churchill* p. 164 **143.** Churchill Museum, London **144.** Marsh, *Number* p. 252 **145.** Ibid. **146.** Ibid. p. 257 **147.** Ibid. p. 259 **148.** Ibid. p. 256 **149.** Sassoon, *Siegfried's Journey* p. 78 **150.** Ibid. p. 79 **151.** Ibid. **152.** Ibid. **153.** OB IV p. 268 **154.** Reynolds, *Long Shadow* p. 71 **155.** WSC, *WC* II p. 511 **156.** Lloyd George, *The Truth* p. 325 **157.** *CS* III p. 3011 **158.** Ibid. p. 2583 **159.** Miller, *Boom* p. 192 **160.** ed. Soames, *Speaking* p. 205 **161.** WSC, *WC* III Part 2 p. 293 **162.** RA GV/PRIV/GVD/1918: 19 April **163.** WSC, *WC* III Part 2 p. 410 **164.** Colville, *Fringes* p. 574 **165.** ed. Soames, *Speaking* p. 206 **166.** Ibid. **167.** ed. Muller, *Contemporaries* p. 297 **168.** Ibid. p. 298 **169.** Ibid. p. 299 **170.** Ibid. p. 300 **171.** Ibid. **172.** Gilbert, *A Life* pp. 389–90 **173.** WSC, *WC* III Part 2 p. 371 **174.** CAC THSO 1/1/26 **175.** Ibid. **176.** ed. Soames, *Speaking* p. 207 **177.** *The Lady* 20 April 1999 p. 49 **178.** Lee, *Lady Hamilton* pp. 198–9 **179.** *CS* III p. 2615 **180.** Ibid. **181.** Ibid. pp. 2613–16 **182.** CAC THSO 1/1/26 **183.** ed. Muller, *Contemporaries* p. 300 **184.** ed. Kimball, *Complete Correspondence* I p. 355 **185.** Roskill, *Hankey* I p. 424 **186.** Ibid. p. 425 **187.** ed. Soames, *Speaking* p. 214 **188.** Hassall, *Marsh* p. 456 **189.** WSC, *WC* IV p. 273 **190.** NA CAB 23/14 **191.** WSC, *WC* III Part 2 pp. 541–4 **192.** Ibid. II p. 6 **193.** Ibid. pp. 52–4 **194.** Ibid. p. 22 **195.** Ibid. p. 20

## 12. Coalition Politics: November 1918–November 1922

**1.** WSC, *CE* III p. 28 **2.** OB VII p. 1008 **3.** WSC, *MEL* p. 73 **4.** Ibid. p. 37 **5.** Marsh, *Number* p. 156 **6.** *CS* III p. 2615 **7.** *C V* IV Part 1 p. 422 **8.** *CS* III p. 2645 **9.** *The Times* 27 November 1918 **10.** WSC, *WC* IV p. 47 **11.** OB IV p. 278 **12.** Ibid. p. 179 **13.** Ibid. pp. 179–80 **14.** Hansard vol. 113 col. 72 **15.** Riddell, *Intimate* pp. 15–16 **16.** Borthwick Institute, York, Lord Halifax Diary 30 November 1941 **17.** Miller, *Boom* p. 241 **18.** CAC TREN 1 **19.** Ibid. **20.** Miller, *Boom* p. 235 **21.** Roskill, *Hankey* II p. 47 **22.** Callwell, *Wilson* II p. 165 **23.** *C V* IV Part 1 p. 479 **24.** Maynard, 'Tory Splits' p. 25 **25.** James, *Failure* p. 110 **26.** WSC, *WC* IV pp. 128–9 **27.** *CS* III p. 2671 **28.** Maynard, 'Tory Splits' p. 25 **29.** *CS* IV in speeches delivered on 3 January 1920, 28 July 1920, 20 September 1924, 21 October 1924, 27 October 1924, 29 November 1925, 19 June 1926, 22 June 1926 and 23 July 1927 **30.** 'Gracchus', *Your MP* p. 16 **31.** James, *Failure* p. 112 **32.** *CS* IV p. 2798 **33.** James, *Failure* p. 117 **34.** ed. Soames, *Speaking* p. 219 **35.** Ibid. p. 220 **36.** Hansard vol. 131 cols. 1725–30 **37.** *CS* III p. 3009 **38.** Ibid. p. 3010 **39.** *C V* IV p. 649 **40.** ed. Middlemas, *Whitehall Diary* I p. 86 **41.** CAC BRGS 1/2 **42.** WSC, *WC* IV p. 41 **43.** James, *Failure* p. 109 n. 1 **44.** Miller, *Boom* p. 243; CAC CHAR 1/132/12 **45.** CAC SPRS 1/76 **46.** Miller, *Boom* p. 243 **47.** James, *Failure* p. 119 **48.** *C V* IV Part 2 p. 869 **49.** Ibid. p. 870 **50.** Ibid. pp. 870, 871 **51.** Ibid. pp. 871–2 **52.** Ibid. pp. 873–4 **53.** Ibid. p. 907 **54.** Ibid. p. 874 **55.** Ibid. p. 918; James, *Failure* p. 121 **56.** *CS* III p. 2868 **57.** Ibid. p. 2871 **58.** WSC, *WC* IV p. 74 **59.** James, *Failure* p. 123 **60.** WSC, *WC* IV p. 377 **61.** WSC *MEL* pp. 60–61 **62.** Gilbert, *Other Club* p. 80 **63.** WSC, *WC* IV pp. 287, 289 **64.** *C V* IV Part 2 p. 1135 **65.** Bennett, *Black and Tans* p. 37 **66.** WSC, *WC* IV p. 290 **67.** *Illustrated Sunday Herald*, 8 February 1920 **68.** Ibid. **69.** Addison, *Unexpected* p. 99 **70.** Thompson, *Shadow* p. 17 **71.** Udy, *Labour* p.

52 72. Ibid. pp. 53–4 73. Roskill, *Hankey* II p. 173 74. *CV* IV Part 2 pp. 1260–61 75. Ibid. p. 1261 76. ed. Soames, *Speaking* p. 224 77. Ibid. p. 228 78. Ibid. p. 225 79. OB IV p. 528 80. ed. Soames, *Speaking* p. 230 81. *CV* IV Part 2 p. 1355 82. CAC SPRS 1/76 83. WSC, *GC* p. 117 84. LHC Coote Papers Box 1 85. Ibid. 86. Ibid. 87. *FH* no. 89 p. 17 88. ed. Eade, *Contemporaries* p. 164 89. *CS* VI p. 5715 90. *FH* no. 89 p. 16 91. LHC Coote Papers Box 1 92. Ibid. 93. Ibid. 94. Ibid. 95. OB IV p. 559 96. *CS* III p. 3085 97. Ibid. IV p. 3349 98. *FH* no. 90 p. 13 99. ed. Taylor, *Lloyd George* p. 210 100. Ibid. p. 219 101. Roberts, *Holy Fox* p. 13 102. ed. Soames, *Speaking* p. 281 103. *CV* IV Part 3 p. 1532 104. Ricks, *Orwell* p. 7 105. *CV* IV Part 3 p. 1525 106. CAC RDCH 1/2/46 107. Ibid. 108. ed. Soames, *Speaking* p. 239 109. Churchill, *Tapestry* p. 21 110. ed. Soames, *Speaking* p. 239 111. Ibid. p. 245 112. Jones, 'Knew Him' p. 7 113. Ibid. p. 8 114. Moran, *Struggle* p. 729 115. Churchill, *Tapestry* p. 37 116. Birkenhead, *Prof* p. 162 117. Cherwell Papers K62/2 118. ed. Soames, *Speaking* p. 238 119. *CS* III p. 3133 120. ed. Muller, *Thoughts* pp. 161–2 121. WSC, *WC* IV pp. 305–6 122. Ibid. p. 317 123. *CS* III p. 3199 124. Ibid. V p. 348 125. OB IV p. 499 126. *CV* IV Part 2 p. 1055 127. ed. Soames, *Speaking* p. 258 128. Gilbert, *A Life* p. 375 129. BL Add MS 52516 130. James, *Failure* p. 143 131. Nel, *Personal Secretary* p. 187 132. Roskill, *Hankey* II p. 287 133. ed. Vincent, *Crawford* p. 440 134. OB V p. 865 n. 1 135. Stuart, *Within* p. 85 136. *CIHOW* p. 409 137. Chisholm and Davie, *Beaverbrook* p. 190 138. OB IV p. 873 139. Bod Conservative Party Archive [CPA] PUB 229/2/16/fol. 11 140. ed. Soames, *Speaking* p. 264 141. Ibid. p. 265 142. ed. Muller, *Thoughts* p. 180 143. *CV* IV Part 3 p. 2161 144. Ibid. 145. *Strand Magazine* September 1931; ed. Muller, *Thoughts* p. 154

## 13. Redemption: November 1922–May 1926

1. *CS* IV p. 3871 2. *CIHOW* p. 518 3. CAC RDCH 1/2/46 4. Churchill, *Tapestry* p. 28 5. ed. Soames, *Speaking* p. 268 6. WSC, *WC* II p. vii 7. Bell, *Dardanelles* p. 369 8. Dugdale, *Balfour* II p. 337 9. WSC, *WC* I p. 322 10. ed. Taylor, *Darling Pussy* pp. 154, 161 11. OB V p. 7 12. Read, *Prose* p. 192 13. Bell, *Dardanelles* p. 369; LHC Edmonds Papers II/3/6 14. ed. Beckett, *Edmonds* p. 463 15. Ibid. 16. LHC Edmonds Papers II/3/passim 17. LHC Edmonds Papers II/3/16 18. Ibid 19. LHC Hamilton Papers 13/24 20. Riddell, *Intimate* p. 409 21. Colville, *Churchillians* p. 63 22. Bowra, *Memories* pp. 205–6 23. ed. Soames, *Speaking* p. 267 24. Dean, *Hatred, Ridicule* p. 41 25. Ibid. p. 45 26. Mather, 'Maladies' p. 28 27. ed. Soames, *Speaking* p. 271 28. Ibid. 29. Ibid. 30. Ibid. p. 239 31. Churchill, *Tapestry* p. 23 32. *CIHOW* p. 13 33. CAC HAMB 1/2/6 1/6 34. Soames, 'Human Being' p. 4 35. CAC HAMB 1/1/17; WSC, *TSSW* I p. 62 36. *FH* no. 130 pp. 34–6 37. ed. Soames, *Speaking* p. 259 38. Soames, 'Human Being' p. 3 39. Cherwell Papers K63/15 40. Cherwell Papers K63/16 41. Cherwell Papers K63/18 42. Peck, *Dublin from Downing Street* p. 71; *CIHOW* p. 534 43. Churchill, *Tapestry* p. 28 44. *CIHOW* p. 535 45. Soames, 'Human Being' p. 3; Pawle, *Warden* p. 119; Churchill, *Tapestry* p. 99 46. CAC HAMB 1/1/20 47. Churchill, *Tapestry* p. 27 48. Howells, *Simply Churchill* p. 123; CAC HAMB 1/1/17 49. Buczacki, *Chartwell* p. 188 50. *FH* no. 67 p. 4 51. CAC BRGS 1/2 52. ed. Soames, *Speaking* pp. 370, 371 n. 3 53. Ibid. p. 275 54. Lysaght and White, *Irishman* p. 36 55. Ibid. p. 14 56. ed. Cockett, *My Dear Max* p. 2 57. Ibid. p. 7 58. ed. Ball, *Conservative Politics* p. 407; ed. Pimlott, *Dalton Diary* p. 358 59. CAC BBKN 2/3 60. Stuart, *Within* p. 107; CAC NEMO 3/3 61. Stuart, *Within* p. 106 62. ed. Muller, *Thoughts* p. 13 63. *CS* IV p. 3399 64. Ibid. p. 3423 65. ed. Muller, *Thoughts* p. 13 66. *CS* IV p. 3396 67. *The Times* 18 January 1924 68. ed. Soames, *Speaking* p. 280 69. James, *Davidson* p. 194 70. Bod CPA PUB 229/1/2/fol. 9 71. Ibid. 72. CAC SPRS 1/76 73. James, *Failure* p. 153 74. WSC, *Thoughts* p. 13 75. *CS* VII p. 7315 76. Ibid. IV p. 3453 77. ed. Muller, *Thoughts* p. 274 78. Ibid. 79. Bod CPA PUB 229/4/9/fol. 56 80. OB V p. 57; CAC CHAR 2/136/4 81. Feiling, *Chamberlain* p. 110 82. OB V p. 59 83. Moran, *Struggle* p. 612 84.

OB V p. 60 **85.** ed. Soames, *Speaking* p. 290 **86.** ed. Middlemas, *Whitehall Diary* I p. 303 **87.** Cowles, *Era* p. 257 **88.** OB V p. 91 **89.** James, *Conservative* p. 213; ed. Middlemas, *Whitehall Diary* II p. 28 **90.** *CS* IV p. 3505 **91.** Halle, *Irrepressible* p. 53; Colville, *Fringes* p. 345 **92.** Birkenhead, *Contemporary Personalities* p. 113 **93.** Ibid. p. 114 **94.** Ibid. p. 115 **95.** *CS* VI p. 6862 **96.** James, *Failure* p. 158n; Grigg, *Prejudice* pp. 174–7 **97.** James, *Failure* p. 156 **98.** ed. Middlemas, *Whitehall Diary* I p. 307 **99.** BBC Broadcast 'Personality and Power' 24 November 1970 **100.** *CV* V Part 1 p. 305; CAC CHUR 18/2 **101.** *CV* V Part 1 p. 305; CAC CHUR 18/2 **102.** BU Austen Chamberlain Papers 51/67 **103.** *CV* V Part 1 p. 306 **104.** Ibid. p. 385 **105.** Ibid. p. 366 **106.** Maurer, 'Mad' p. 776 **107.** ed. Ranft, *Beatty Papers* II p. 277 **108.** NA FO 371/10634 and 371/10965/5787 **109.** Roskill, *Hankey* II p. 402 **110.** Maurer, 'Mad' passim **111.** Ibid. p. 793 **112.** Jackson, *Churchill* p. 189 **113.** WSC, *TSWW* I p. 20 **114.** *CV* V Part 1 p. 334 **115.** ed. Soames, *Speaking* p. 288 **116.** OB V p. 82 **117.** *CV* V Part 1 p. 339 **118.** *The Times* 6 March 1925 **119.** Rowse, *Later Churchills* p. 439 **120.** Roskill, *Hankey* II p. 411 **121.** *CV* V Part 1 p. 437; Grigg, *Prejudice* pp. 182–3 **122.** Skidelsky, *Economist as Saviour* pp. 199–200 **123.** Keynes, *Economic Consequences* p. 10 **124.** *CV* V Part 1 p. 412 **125.** *CS* IV p. 3599 **126.** Ibid. p. 3634 **127.** Smith, 'Return to Gold' p. 66 **128.** Moggridge, *Monetary Policy* p. 233 **129.** Smith, 'Return to Gold' p. 64 **130.** Grigg, *Prejudice* p. 185 **131.** Moran, *Struggle* p. 303 **132.** Hansard vol. 183 cols. 71–83 **133.** *CS* IV p. 3570 **134.** *CV* V Part 1 p. 473 **135.** ed. Guedalla, *Slings* p. 204 **136.** ed. Middlemas, *Whitehall Diary* I p. 316 **137.** BU AP 20/1/5/p118 **138.** BU AP 20/1/2/p217 **139.** *CV* V Part 1 p. 533 **140.** ed. Soames, *Speaking* p. 293 **141.** Gilbert, *Other Club* p. 92 **142.** *CS* IV p. 3821 **143.** Ibid. p. 3824 **144.** Ibid. p. 3849 **145.** ed. Soames, *Speaking* p. 295 **146.** Ibid. p. 297 **147.** Ibid. p. 298 **148.** *CS* IV pp. 3952–3 **149.** Middlemas and Barnes, *Baldwin* p. 411 **150.** James, *Davidson* p. 242 **151.** Brendon, *Edward VIII* p. 32 **152.** Blake, 'Conservative' p. 8 **153.** *British Gazette* 5 May 1926 **154.** James, *Failure* p. 172 **155.** James, *Davidson* p. 245 **156.** ed. Ball, *Conservative Politics* p. 39; James, *Davidson* p. 243 **157.** ed. Stuart, *Reith Diaries* p. 96 **158.** Charmley, *Glory* p. 219 **159.** ed. Middlemas, *Whitehall Diary* II p. 41 **160.** ed. Ball, *Conservative Politics* p. 28 **161.** *CV* V Part 1 p. 717 **162.** *New Statesman* 22 May 1926 **163.** Earl of Birkenhead Papers Box 1

## 14. Crash: June 1926–January 1931

**1.** WSC, *TSWW* I p. 21 **2.** *CV* V Part 1 p. 1444 **3.** CAC CHAR 1/196/30 and 39 **4.** *The Times* 26 February 1920 **5.** Marian Holmes's Diary **6.** *CS* IV p. 4034 **7.** Ibid. **8.** ed. Ball, *Conservative Politics* p. 76 **9.** Ibid. pp. 77–8 **10.** Ibid. p. 242 **11.** OB V p. 185 **12.** Ibid. p. 218 **13.** 'Ephesian', *Churchill* p. 267 **14.** ed. Soames, *Speaking* p. 302 **15.** Ibid. **16.** CAC RDCH 1/2/46 **17.** Toye, *Lloyd George and Churchill* p. 302 **18.** OB V p. 226 **19.** BL Add MS 82379 fol. 28 **20.** WSC, *WC* III Part 1 pp. 53–4 **21.** Ibid. Part 2 pp. 541–4 **22.** OB V p. 229 **23.** *CV* V Part 1 p. 1291 **24.** Ibid. p. 985 **25.** *CS* IV p. 4189 **26.** ed. Midgley, *Heroic Memory* p. 15 **27.** *CS* IV p. 4223 **28.** *CV* V Part 1 p. 1082 **29.** Addison, *Unexpected* p. 125 **30.** *CV* V Part 1 p. 1033 **31.** Ibid. p. 1342 **32.** ed. Roskill, *Hankey* II p. 455 **33.** Ibid. p. 456 **34.** ed. Ball, *Conservative Politics* p. 172 **35.** Ibid. p. 173 **36.** Ibid. p. 176 **37.** BL Add MS 51073 fol. 132 **38.** ed. Ball, *Conservative Politics* p. 176 **39.** *CV* V Part 1 p. 1154 **40.** ed. Ball, *Conservative Politics* p. 239 **41.** *CV* V Part 1 p. 1169; CAC CHUR 18/85 **42.** CAC RDCH 1/3/1 **43.** ed. Soames, *Speaking* p. 318 **44.** Ibid. p. 320 **45.** Ibid. p. 321 **46.** Ibid. p. 320 **47.** *CS* IV p. 4403 **48.** *CV* V Part 1 p. 280 **49.** Ibid. p. 1274; CAC CHUR 18/76 **50.** *CV* V Part 1 p. 1278; CAC CHUR 18/76 **51.** NA CAB 23/15 **52.** James, *Failure* p. 167 **53.** ed. Soames, *Speaking* pp. 327–8 **54.** *CV* V Part 1 p. 1333 **55.** ed. Soames, *Speaking* p. 325 **56.** Kershaw, *Making Friends* p. 306 **57.** ed. Soames, *Speaking* p. 328 **58.** *CV* V Part 1 pp. 1349–50 **59.** ed. Soames, *Speaking* p. 329 **60.** Ibid. **61.** Ibid. p. 331 **62.** Ibid. p. 332 **63.** Gilbert, *Other Club* p. 95 **64.** Other Club Betting Book **65.** WSC, *WC* IV p. 451 **66.** OB V p. 319 **67.** *CS* V p. 4575 **68.** OB V p. 325 **69.** Ibid. p. 1464 **70.** OB V p. 325 **71.** Bod

CPA PUB 229/5/10/fol. 73 **72.** Ibid. **73.** WSC, *MEL* p. 87 **74.** Cherwell Papers K64/7 **75.** ed. Middlemas, *Whitehall Diary* II pp. 186, 191 **76.** BU NC/7/11/22/1 **77.** eds. Barnes and Nicholson, *Empire at Bay* p. 48 **78.** Gilbert, *Search* p. 227; eds. Barnes and Nicholson, *Empire at Bay* p. 50 **79.** Gilbert, *Search* p. 227 **80.** OB V p. 373 **81.** eds. Barnes and Nicholson, *Empire at Bay* p. 49 **82.** Ibid. pp. 49–50 **83.** OB V p. 341 **84.** ed. Soames, *Speaking* p. 338 **85.** Gilbert, *A Life* p. 493 **86.** Churchill, *Crowded Canvas* p. 67 **87.** ed. Soames, *Speaking* p. 338 **88.** *C V* V Part 2 pp. 61–2 **89.** Churchill, *Crowded Canvas* p. 69 **90.** *C V* V Part 2 p. 96 **91.** Pilpel, *Churchill in America* p. 89 **92.** Chaplin, *Autobiography* p. 332 **93.** Tolppanen, 'Churchill and Chaplin' p. 17; Chaplin, *Autobiography* p. 335 **94.** OB V p. 348 **95.** CAC CHAR 1/208/92 **96.** ed. Soames, *Speaking* p. 345 **97.** Ibid. **98.** Ibid. p. 347 **99.** *CS* V p. 4980 **100.** Clarke, *Profession* p. xiv **101.** Vickers da Costa Ledger Nos. 9, 12, 13, 16 and 25 **102.** Lough, *Champagne* p. 187 **103.** Ibid. p. 158 **104.** Vickers da Costa Ledger No. 13 **105.** *News of the World* 20 June 1937 **106.** ed. Soames, *Speaking* p. 349 **107.** OB V p. 350 **108.** Stuart, *Within* p. 28 **109.** *New York Times* 26 October 1929 **110.** Lough, *Champagne* p. 199 **111.** Ibid. p. 199 **112.** ed. Pimlott, *Dalton Diary* p. 126 **113.** Blake, 'Conservative' p. 9 **114.** OB V p. 600 **115.** *C V* V Part 2 p. 1042 **116.** Mayo, *Mother India* pp. 285–6, 287–314, 346–62 **117.** Tirthankar Roy, book review in *Cambridge Review of International Affairs*, 2018 **118.** Mayo, *Mother India* pp. 139–64, 165–200, 226–42 **119.** *CS* V p. 4689 **120.** ed. Eade, *Contemporaries* p. 149 **121.** Ibid. **122.** James, *Failure* p. 168 **123.** *CS* V p. 4800 **124.** BL Add MS 71183 fol. 1 **125.** *CS* V pp. 4853–4 **126.** ed. Ball, *Conservative Politics* p. 334 **127.** Addison, *Home Front* p. 300; Clarke, *Lloyd George Diary* p. 95 **128.** Addison, *Home Front* p. 301 **129.** Gilbert, *Wilderness* p. 36 **130.** *Strand Magazine* April 1931; WSC, *GC* p. 163 **131.** Gilbert, *Other Club* pp. 100–101 **132.** *News of the World* 1 March 1936 **133.** Birkenhead Papers 65/A3 **134.** Ibid. **135.** ed. Ball, *Conservative Politics* p. 366 **136.** ed. Vincent, *Crawford* p. 542 **137.** *The Times* 20 October 1930 **138.** Ramsden, *Century* p. 205 **139.** CAC CHAR 8/286/1 **140.** *CIHOW* p. 195; WSC, *MEL* p. 346 **141.** WSC, *MEL* p. 81 **142.** Ibid. p. 59 **143.** Ibid. p. 75 **144.** Ibid. p. ix **145.** James, *Davidson* p. 356 **146.** Addison, *Unexpected* p. 134 **147.** Ibid. **148.** James, *Davidson* p. 355 **149.** Ibid. **150.** ed. Pottle, *Champion* p. 25 **151.** CAC SPRS 1/76

## 15. Into the Wilderness: January 1931–October 1933

**1.** *Sunday Chronicle* 8 November 1931 **2.** WSC, *TSWW* I p. 9 **3.** ed. Nicolson, *Diaries and Letters* I p. 67 **4.** *CS* V p. 4965 **5.** Ibid. p. 4971 **6.** Ibid. p. 4968 **7.** Ibid. p. 4972 **8.** Cherwell Papers K64/9–10 **9.** Cherwell Papers K64/14 **10.** Thomas, *Woodford* p. 55 **11.** *CS* V p. 4985 **12.** Thomas, *Woodford* p. 55 **13.** ed. Soames, *Speaking* p. 354 **14.** ed. Muller, *Thoughts* p. 9 **15.** *Strand Magazine*, March 1931; ed. Muller, *Thoughts* p. 10 **16.** *C V* V Part 2 pp. 282–3 **17.** James, *Davidson* p. 172 **18.** *CS* V p. 5007 **19.** Ibid. p. 5008 **20.** ed. Ball, *Conservative Politics* p. 417 **21.** *CS* V p. 5011 **22.** Ibid. p. 5017 **23.** Ibid. p. 5019 **24.** ed. Muller, *Thoughts* p. 15 **25.** *CS* V p. 5023 **26.** CAC EMAR 2 **27.** WSC, *TSWW* I p. 29 **28.** ed. Muller, *Contemporaries* p. 235 **29.** *CIHOW* p. 3 **30.** ed. Muller, *Contemporaries* p. 34 **31.** Wrigley, *Biographical Companion* p. 28 **32.** Bod CPA PUB 229/6/9/fol. 22 **33.** Ibid. **34.** *C V* V Part 2 p. 699 **35.** ed. Muller, *Thoughts* p. 200 **36.** Ibid. p. 199 **37.** Ibid. p. 289 **38.** Ibid. p. 294 **39.** Ibid. **40.** Ponting, *Churchill* p. 351; Jenkins, *Churchill* p. 457 **41.** ed. Muller, *Thoughts* p. 294 **42.** CAC THRS II 85/3 **43.** Tolppanen, 'Accidental' p. 12 **44.** WSC, *CE* IV pp. 90–91 **45.** *Daily Mail* 5 January 1932 **46.** Tolppanen, 'Accidental' p. 12 **47.** Ibid. **48.** CAC THRS II 85/3 **49.** Cherwell Papers K65/4 **50.** WSC, *CE* IV p. 94 **51.** My thanks to Henry and Benita Black for this information **52.** Clifford, *Proconsul* p. 188 **53.** Ibid. p. 189 **54.** CAC CHAR 1/400A/46 **55.** OB V p. 425 n. 1 **56.** *Chicago Tribune* 3 February 1932 **57.** Gilbert, *Churchill and America* p. 140 **58.** CAC CHAR 1/399A/66–79 **59.** Ibid. **60.** Ibid. **61.** *C V* V Part 2 p. 442 **62.** Ibid. p. 394n **63.** Lough, *Champagne* p. 478 n. 15 **64.** KCL Hamilton Papers 13/25 **65.** Other Club Betting Book **66.** *CS* V pp. 5193–4 **67.** eds. Blake and Louis, *Churchill* p. 21 **68.** *CV* V Part 2 p. 475 **69.** *CIHOW* p. 539 **70.** WSC, *TSWW* I p. 65 **71.** Hanfstaengl, *Hitler* p. 184. **72.** WSC, *TSWW* I p. 65 **73.** Ibid. **74.** *CS* V pp. 5199–200 **75.** ed. Smart, *Bernays* p. 30 **76.** Ibid. p. 45 **77.** Parker, *Appeasement* p. 320 **78.** *CS* VII p. 7251 **79.** LHC Liddell Hart Papers 1/171/22 **80.** *CS* V p. 5220 **81.** Hatfield House QUI Bundle 63 **82.** *CS* V p. 5220 **83.** OB V p. 457 **84.** *CS* V p. 5220 **85.** ed. Smart, *Bernays* p. 55 **86.** *CS* V p. 5236 **87.** ed. Eade, *Contemporaries* p. 23 **88.** *CS* V p. 5263 **89.** Ibid. **90.** Ibid. p. 5261 **91.** Ibid. p. 5268 **92.** Ibid. **93.** Ibid. p. 5267 **94.** ed. Smart, *Bernays* p. 85 **95.** OB V pp. 480–81 **96.** Other Club Dining Book vol. 1 **97.** Ibid. **98.** Ibid. **99.** Ibid. **100.** Gilbert, *Other Club* p. 116 **101.** Ibid. **102.** Muller, 'Good Englishman' pp. 89–90 **103.** OB I p. 198 **104.** *FH* no. 164 p. 19 **105.** Coote, *Other Club* p. 112 **106.** Ashley, *Historian* pp. 143–4 **107.** WSC, *Marl* I pp. 19, 132 **108.** Ibid. II p. 485 **109.** Ibid. I p. 774 **110.** Ibid. I p. 905 **111.** Ibid. pp. 740–41 **112.** Ibid. pp. 570–71 **113.** Ibid. p. 59 **114.** Ibid. p. 108 **115.** Ibid. II p. 135 **116.** Ibid. I p. 264 **117.** Ibid. **118.** ed. Soames, *Speaking* p. 370 **119.** WSC, *Marl* I p. 309 **120.** Ibid. **121.** *FH* no. 140 p. 43 **122.** Rose, *Literary Churchill* passim **123.** WSC, *Marl* I p. 364 **124.** Ibid. p. 773 **125.** Muller, 'Englishman' p. 86 **126.** Halle, *Irrepressible* p. 6. **127.** Ibid. **128.** *CV* V Part 2 p. 693

## 16. Sounding the Alarm: October 1933–March 1936

**1.** *CS* V p. 5377 **2.** Bod CPA PUB 227/7/9/fol. 40 **3.** James, *Davidson* p. 398 **4.** *CS* V p. 5297 **5.** ed. Smart, *Bernays* p. 87 **6.** Ibid. **7.** *CS* V pp. 5302–3 **8.** Todman, *Into Battle* p. 67 **9.** *CS* V p. 5324 **10.** Ibid. **11.** Ibid. p. 5325 **12.** ed. Smart, *Bernays* p. 119 **13.** Gilbert, *Wilderness* p. 106 **14.** *CS* V p. 5343 **15.** ed. Smart, *Bernays* p. 122 **16.** OB V p. 51 **17.** Bridge, 'Privileges' p. 217 **18.** Templewood, *Troubled Years* pp. 91–9 **19.** Bridge, 'Privileges' passim **20.** Hansard vol. 290 col. 1738 **21.** ed. Smart, *Bernays* p. 142 **22.** ed. Evans, *Killearn Diaries* p. 41 **23.** *CV* V Part 2 p. 843 **24.** Ibid. p. 678 **25.** *History of the Times* IV Part II p. 887 **26.** *CS* V p. 5377 **27.** Gilbert, *Wilderness* p. 113 **28.** Todman, *Into Battle* p. 68 **29.** Interview with Jasper Rootham 22 October 1988 **30.** ed. Gorodetsky, *Maisky Diaries* p. 28 **31.** Ibid. p. 50 **32.** ed. Soames, *Speaking* p. 360 **33.** ed. James, *Chips* p. 234 **34.** Forbes-Robertson, *Maxine* p. 208 **35.** Nichols, *All I Could* p. 101 **36.** Pearson, *Citadel* p. 234 **37.** ed. Soames, *Speaking* p. 362 **38.** Jackson, *Churchill* p. 234 **39.** Halle, *Irrepressible* p. 77 **40.** ed. Smart, *Bernays* p. 160 **41.** CAC MCHL 1/1/2 **42.** *CV* V Part 2 p. 923 **43.** *CS* V pp. 5434–5 **44.** BL Add MS 82379 fol. 47 **45.** Hansard vol. 295 col. 863 **46.** *CS* V p. 5443 **47.** Ibid. p. 5449 **48.** Ibid. **49.** Carter, *Knew Him* p. 149; ed. Russell, *Constant* p. 93 **50.** ed. Soames, *Speaking* p. 390 **51.** Ibid. **52.** Ibid. p. 366 **53.** Ibid. p. 368 **54.** Ibid. p. 366 **55.** Ibid. p. 370 **56.** Ibid. p. 376 **57.** Ibid. **58.** WSC, *CE* III p. 176 **59.** Soames, *Speaking* p. 374 **60.** Ibid. **61.** Ibid. p. 376 **62.** Ibid. p. 395 **63.** Spence, *Mistress* pp. 101–2 **64.** CAC CHOH/3/CLVL/Tape 2/Side 3 **65.** ed. Soames, *Speaking* pp. 415–16 **66.** Vickers, *Cocktails* p. 68 **67.** https://spectator.org/the-churchill-marriage-and-lady-castlerosse/ and also https://www.winstonchurchill.org/publications/churchill-bulletin/bulletin-117-mar-2018/an-affair-not-to-remember/ **68.** ed. Soames, *Speaking* p. 416 **69.** Sheean, *Thunder* pp. 78, 48 **70.** CAC CHAR 1/299/77 **71.** Dockter and Toye, 'Who Commanded History?' passim **72.** Piers Brendon in *FH* no. 180 p. 49 **73.** Spence, *Mistress* p. 179 **74.** ed. Muller, *Contemporaries* p. 289 **75.** James, *Davidson* p. 403 **76.** Cowling, *Impact of Hitler* p. 215 **77.** James, *Davidson* p. 403 **78.** Ibid. **79.** ed. Soames, *Speaking* pp. 390–91 **80.** *CS* V p. 5551 **81.** ed. Self, *Diary Letters* IV p. 119 **82.** WSC, *TSWW* I p. 96 **83.** Ibid. p. 110 **84.** Pawle, *Warden* p. 212 **85.** Todman, *Into Battle* p. 74 **86.** ed. Soames, *Speaking* p. 396 **87.** Ibid. p. 399 **88.** Ibid. **89.** *CS* VI p. 5592 **90.** *CV* V Part 3 p. 143 **91.** Hansard vol. 301 col. 666 **92.** *CIHOW* p. 249 **93.** CAC CHAR 2/235/79–86. **94.** *CV* V Part 2 pp. 1169–70. **95.** ed. Vincent, *Crawford* p. 562 **96.** OB V pp. 618–19 **97.** *CV* V Part 2 pp. 1244–5 **98.** *CS* VI p. 5662 **99.** Ibid. pp. 5653–56 **100.** Ibid. pp. 5662–3 **101.** Roskill, *Hankey* II p. 407 **102.** Cherwell Papers F8/1/1 **103.** Cherwell Papers F8/1/6 **104.** Hansard vol.

303 cols. 540–50 **105.** *CS* VI p. 5680 **106.** Ibid. p. 5681 **107.** Hansard vol. 305 col. 368 **108.** Bod CPA PUB 227/7/9/fol. 40 **109.** Ibid. **110.** WSC, *TSWW* I p. 141 **111.** OB V p. 587 **112.** ed. Muller, *Contemporaries* p. 258 **113.** *Strand Magazine* November 1935 **114.** ed. Soames, *Speaking* p. 402 **115.** Ibid. p. 408 **116.** CAC RDCH 1/3/1 **117.** ed. Soames, *Speaking* p. 407 **118.** Gilbert, *Wilderness* p. 13 **119.** Gilbert, *Churchill and the Jews* p. 136 **120.** Oliver, *Mr Showbusiness* p. 100 **121.** ed. Soames, *Speaking* p. 404 **122.** Ibid. p. 412 **123.** Ibid. **124.** Ibid. p. 410 **125.** RA EDW/PRIV/MAIN/A/2853 **126.** Todman, *Into Battle* p. 94

## 17. Apotheosis of Appeasement: March 1936–October 1938

**1.** WSC, *L to L* pp. 172–3 **2.** *CS* V p. 5721 **3.** Kershaw, *Nemesis* p. xxxv **4.** WSC, *TSWW* I pp. 153–4 **5.** *CS* V p. 5701 **6.** Gilbert, *A Life* p. 552 **7.** *CS* VI p. 5699 **8.** Ibid. p. 5701 **9.** Ibid. p. 5703 **10.** Ashley, *Historian* pp. 163–4 **11.** James, *Davidson* p. 410 **12.** ed. Soames, *Speaking* p. 414 **13.** WSC, *TSWW* I p. 156 **14.** ed. Self, *Diary Letters* IV p. 179 **15.** ed. Nicolson, *Diaries and Letters* I p. 251 **16.** Langworth, 'Rhineland' pp. 20–21 **17.** ed. Gorodetsky, *Maisky Diaries* p. 68 **18.** BU AC 41/3/77 **19.** *CS* V p. 5721 **20.** Ibid. **21.** Hansard, vol. 310 col. 2489 **22.** BL Add MS 51073 fols. 140–41 **23.** Ibid. fol. 142 **24.** Churchill, *Tapestry* p. 32 **25.** OB V p. 723 **26.** ed. Nicolson, *Diaries and Letters* p. 258 **27.** *CS* VI pp. 5734–5 **28.** Hansard, vol. 310 col. 2307 **29.** ed. Vincent, *Crawford* p. 570 **30.** ed. James, *Chips* p. 62 **31.** *CS* VI p. 5755 **32.** Ibid. p. 5757 **33.** OB V p. 741 **34.** ed. Gorodetsky, *Maisky Diaries* p. 70 **35.** Ibid. **36.** *CS* V p. 5765 **37.** Cherwell Papers F8/1/12 **38.** Cherwell Papers F8/1/14 **39.** Cherwell Papers F8/5/6 **40.** ed. Nicolson, *Diaries and Letters* II p. 266 **41.** Ibid. **42.** *CV* V Part 3 p. 113 **43.** Baldomero, 'Spain' passim **44.** WSC, *Step* pp. 38–40 **45.** *CS* VI p. 5783 **46.** Ibid. p. 5785 **47.** Ibid. p. 5717 **48.** Ibid. pp. 5718–19 **49.** Langworth, *Myth* p. 76 **50.** CAC SCHL 1/1/5 **51.** Ibid. **52.** ed. Soames, *Speaking* p. 404; Churchill, *Keep on Dancing* p. 47 **53.** PA LG/G/19/16/8 **54.** Gilbert, *A Life* p. 581 **55.** Addison, *Unexpected* p. 144 **56.** *News of the World* 26 May 1935; ed. Muller, *Contemporaries* p. 104 **57.** Browne, *Sunset* pp. 201–2 **58.** Alkon, 'Imagining Scenarios' p. 37 **59.** Ibid. p. 38 **60.** Ibid. p. 39 **61.** Ibid. **62.** Ibid. p. 41 **63.** *CS* VI p. 5801 **64.** CAC CHAR 2/260/93 **65.** Hansard vol. 317 cols. 309–19 **66.** *CS* VI p. 5809 **67.** Ibid. p. 5813 **68.** Coote, *Other Club* p. 86 **69.** *CS* VI p. 5813 **70.** Middlemas and Barnes, *Baldwin* p. 972 **71.** OB V p. 799 **72.** WSC, *TSWW* I p. 615 **73.** *CV* V Part 3 p. 1307 **74.** ed. Soames, *Speaking* pp. 418–19 **75.** ed. Vincent, *Crawford* p. 575 **76.** ed. Lowndes, *Diaries and Letters* p. 155 **77.** ed. Hart-Davis, *King's Counsellor* p. 270 **78.** Zeigler, 'Churchill and the Monarchy' passim **79.** ed. Hart-Davis, *King's Counsellor* p. 414 **80.** Williams, *People's King* passim **81.** Taylor, *Beaverbrook* p. 370 **82.** WSC, *TSWW* I pp. 217–18; *Daily Telegraph*, 11 March 1965; Citrine, *Men and Work* p. 357 **83.** ed. James, *Chips* p. 90 **84.** RA EDW/PRIV/MAIN/A/3045 **85.** ed. Hart-Davis, *King's Counsellor* p. 414 **86.** Stuart, *Within* p. 132 **87.** WSC, *MEL* p. 380 **88.** ed. James, *Chips* p. 95 **89.** Winterton, *Orders of the Day* p. 223 **90.** James, *Failure* p. 275 **91.** James, *Davidson* p. 415 **92.** ed. Nicolson, *Diaries and Letters* II p. 284 **93.** Bod CPA PUB 1922/3/109 **94.** *CS* VI p. 5822 **95.** *CV* V Part 3 p. 521 **96.** OB V p. 829 **97.** Windsor, *A King's Story* p. 373 **98.** OB V p. 828 **99.** Brendon, *Edward VIII* p. 64 **100.** Colville, *Fringes* p. 196 **101.** ed. James, *Chips* p. 116 **102.** James, *Boothby* pp. 166–7 **103.** Owen, *Cabinet* p. 47 **104.** Boothby, *Fight to Live* p. 164; McDonough, *Chamberlain* p. 108 **105.** ed. Soames, *Speaking* p. 431 n. 6 **106.** RA EDW/PRIV/MAIN/A/3098 **107.** RA PS/PSO/GVI/C/069/01 **108.** Bodleian MS Eng c 2708/42 **109.** OB V p. 834 **110.** ed. Soames, *Speaking* p. 420 **111.** Oliver, *Mr Showbusiness* p. 110 **112.** Ibid. p. 107 **113.** Ibid. p. 110 **114.** Ibid. p. 116 **115.** Ibid. p. 142 **116.** ed. Soames, *Speaking* p. 426 **117.** WSC, *Marl* I p. 243 **118.** CAC PJGG 2/4/55 **119.** *CIHOW* p. 254 **120.** *CS* VI p. 5826 **121.** *CV* V Part 3 pp. 604–5 **122.** Ibid. p. 616 **123.** https://richardlangworth.com/churchill-anti-semite/ **124.** *CS* VI p. 5850 **125.** *Guardian* 28 November 2002 **126.** WSC, *CE* II p. 395 **127.** *CS* VI p. 5854 **128.** ed. James, *Chips* p. 119 **129.** Gilbert, *Other Club*

p. 131 **130.** CAC RMSY 7/6 **131.** Ibid. **132.** Soames, *Clementine* p. 274 **133.** CAC CHAR 2/300/39 **134.** RA EDW/PRIV/MAIN/A/3266 **135.** RA EDW/PRIV/MAIN/A/3475 **136.** Gilbert, *Churchill and America* p. 157 **137.** ed. Soames, *Speaking* p. 341 **138.** *CS* VI p. 5857 **139.** Blake, 'Conservative' pp. 10–11 **140.** ed. Rose, *Baffy* p. 39 **141.** Dilks, *Dominion* p. 265 **142.** Halle, *Irrepressible* p. 134 **143.** *CS* VI p. 5858 **144.** Ibid. **145.** ed. Soames, *Speaking* p. 427 **146.** ed. Muller, *Contemporaries* p. 275 **147.** Ibid. p. xii **148.** Ibid. p. 10 **149.** Ibid. p. xxv **150.** Ibid. **151.** Ibid. p. xxvi **152.** Ibid. p. 59 **153.** WSC, *GC* p. 302 **154.** WSC, *Step* p. 156. **155.** ed. Muller, *Contemporaries* p. xxvi **156.** WSC, *CE* IV p. 397. **157.** WSC, *Step* p. 174 **158.** Interview with John Forster, Blenheim Archivist 22 March 2017 **159.** Gilbert, *Other Club* p. 133 **160.** Ibid. p. 134 **161.** Other Club Betting Book **162.** *CS* VI pp. 5908–9 **163.** WSC, *Step* pp. 189–90 **164.** WSC, *TSWW* I p. 199 **165.** Cherwell Papers K67/8 **166.** Sheean, *Thunder* p. 62 **167.** Ibid. pp. 61, 66 **168.** ed. Soames, *Speaking* p. 433 **169.** Ibid. **170.** WSC, *TSWW* I p. 201 **171.** Feiling, *Chamberlain* p. 306 **172.** BU AP 20/1/23 **173.** BU AP 20/1/21 **174.** ed. James, *Chips* p. 122 **175.** Blake, 'Conservative' p. 11 **176.** ed. Nicolson, *Diaries and Letters* I p. 377 **177.** CAC EMAR 2 **178.** *CS* VI p. 5924 **179.** Ibid. pp. 5925–7 **180.** Ibid. p. 5927 **181.** ed. Nicolson, *Diaries and Letters* I p. 332 **182.** Interview with Jasper Rootham 22 October 1988 **183.** ed. Gorodetsky, *Maisky Diaries* p. 107 **184.** Ibid. **185.** Ibid. p. 108 **186.** Ibid. **187.** Ibid. pp. 108–9 **188.** Ibid. p. 110 **189.** Hansard vol. 333 cols. 1405–46 **190.** *CS* VI p. 5943 **191.** WSC, *WES* p. 403; WSC, *Arms* pp. 465–6 **192.** ed. Smart, *Bernays* p. 348 **193.** WSC, *Arms* pp. 465–6 **194.** ed. Self, *Diary Letters* IV p. 312 **195.** McDonough, *Chamberlain* p. 60; Hansard vol. 332 cols. 235–47 **196.** *CS* VII p. 7326 **197.** ed. James, *Chips* p. 155 **198.** Bew, *Churchill and Ireland* p. 152 **199.** Amery, *My Political Life* III p. 245 **200.** Other Club Betting Book **201.** *CS* VI pp. 5955–6 **202.** WSC, *CE* II p. 185 **203.** Ibid. IV p. 438 **204.** Ibid. **205.** *CS* VI pp. 5972–3 **206.** Ibid. p. 5973 **207.** *FH* no. 179 p. 41 **208.** OB V p. 952 **209.** ed. Self, *Diary Letters* IV p. 332 **210.** Gilbert, *Other Club* p. 139 **211.** Gilbert, *Wilderness* p. 184 **212.** Ibid. **213.** *CV* V Part 3 p. 1117 **214.** CV V Part 3 p. 1119 **215.** Ibid. p. 1121 **216.** WSC, *Step* pp. 264–5 **217.** Kershaw, *Making Friends* p. 243 **218.** CAC INKP 1 p. 13 **219.** ed. Self, *Diary Letters* IV pp. 348–9 **220.** Langworth, *Avoidable War* p. 58; Meehan, *Unnecessary War* p. 178 **221.** ed. Rose, *Baffy* p. 104 **222.** Jenkins, *Churchill* p. 525 **223.** ed. Nicolson, *Diaries and Letters* I pp. 370–71 **224.** OB V p. 987 **225.** KCL Liddell Hart Papers 1/171/31 **226.** *Daily Telegraph* 12 March 1965 **227.** Ibid. **228.** WSC, *CE* IV p. 444 **229.** OB V p. 898 **230.** Gilbert, *Other Club* p. 140 **231.** Ibid. **232.** Cooper, *Old Men Forget* p. 241 **233.** Gilbert, *Other Club* p. 141 **234.** James, *Undaunted* p. 143 **235.** Hansard vol. 339 cols. 29–40 **236.** CAC DUFC 2/14 **237.** Hansard vol. 110 col. 1394 **238.** Ibid. col. 1397 **239.** *CS* VI p. 6004 **240.** Ibid. pp. 6004–5 **241.** Ibid. p. 6005 **242.** Ibid. p. 6007 **243.** Ibid. p. 6009 **244.** Ibid. p. 6008 **245.** Ibid. p. 6010 **246.** Ibid. pp. 6008–9 **247.** Ibid. p. 6011 **248.** Ibid. p. 6013; CAC CHAR 9/130/354–79 **249.** ed. James, *Chips* p. 173; ed. Barnes and Nicholson, *Empire at Bay* p. 527; Thomas, *Woodford* pp. 92–3 **250.** ed. Self, *Diary Letters* IV p. 351 **251.** Gardner, *Churchill in his Time* p. 11 **252.** Thomas, *Woodford* p. 93 **253.** ed. Self, *Diary Letters* IV pp. 351–2 **254.** ed. Muller, *Contemporaries* p. 297

## 18. Vindication: October 1938–September 1939

**1.** WSC, *Marl* I p. 919 **2.** *CS* VI p. 6030 **3.** Ibid. p. 6017 **4.** Ibid. p. 6016 **5.** Ibid. **6.** Ibid. p. 6017 **7.** Ibid. p. 6016 **8.** Griffiths, *What* p. 76 **9.** *CS* VI pp. 6018–19 **10.** Ibid. p. 6019 **11.** ed. Eade, *Contemporaries* p. 209 **12.** Ibid. p. 210 **13.** *CV* V Part 3 p. 1264 **14.** ed. Vincent, *Crawford* p. 591 **15.** Kershaw, *Making Friends* p. 260 **16.** Watt, *How War Came* p. 89 **17.** *CV* V Part 3 p. 1277 **18.** *CS* VI pp. 6020–21 **19.** *CV* V Part 3 p. 1280 **20.** *CS* VI p. 6047 **21.** ed. Self, *Diary Letters* IV p. 369 **22.** *CV* V Part 3 p. 1305 **23.** The letter is not in the companion volumes to the official biography but among Randolph's recently opened private papers: CAC RDCH 1/3/1 **24.** *CV* V Part 3 p. 1305 **25.** CAC RDCH 1/3/1 **26.** *CV* V Part 3 p. 1309 **27.** CAC DSND 11 **28.** Ibid. **29.** ed. Soames, *Speaking*

p. 443 **30.** Ibid. p. 442 **31.** *CV* V Part 3 p. 1316 **32.** Ibid. p. 1318 **33.** Ibid. p. 1325 **34.** Ibid. p. 1320 **35.** *CS* VI p. 6004 **36.** *CV* V Part 3 p. 1332 **37.** Ibid. p. 1213 n. 3 **38.** *New Statesman* 7 January 1939 **39.** ed. Soames, *Speaking* p. 446 **40.** Ibid. p. 448 **41.** *CV* V Part 3 p. 1345 **42.** ed. Soames, *Speaking* p. 449 **43.** Gilbert, *Search* p. 23 **44.** *CV* V Part 3 pp. 1349–50 **45.** Ibid. p. 1349 **46.** ed. Domarus, *Essential* p. 579 **47.** Hatfield House 5M/62/1 **48.** Thomas, *Woodford* p. 98 **49.** Ibid. **50.** Thornton-Kemsley, *Winds and Tides* p. 96 **51.** Thomas, *Woodford* p. 100 **52.** Ibid. p. 101 **53.** Ibid. p. 102 **54.** Ibid. p. 104 **55.** OB V pp. 1043 and 1043 n. 2 **56.** Ibid. p. 1044 **57.** *CS* VI p. 6082 **58.** Ibid. **59.** ed. Gorodetsky, *Maisky Diaries* p. 163 **60.** *CS* VI p. 6095 **61.** Ibid. **62.** Macmillan, *Winds* p. 592 **63.** ed. Self, *Diary Letters* IV p. 403 **64.** *CS* VI p. 6105 **65.** ed. Self, *Diary Letters* IV p. 407 **66.** Ibid. **67.** ed. James, *Chips* p. 194 **68.** Hansard vol. 346 col. 497 **69.** ed. James, *Chips* p. 195 **70.** WSC, *Step* p. 344 **71.** Addison, *Unexpected* p. 154 **72.** James, *Davidson* p. 424 **73.** Ibid. **74.** ed. Pickersgill, *Mackenzie King* p. 78 **75.** *CS* VI p. 6123 **76.** Ibid. pp. 6123–4 **77.** Ibid. p. 6125 **78.** ed. Nicolson, *Diaries and Letters* I p. 403 **79.** Ibid. **80.** OB V p. 866 **81.** Ibid. p. 1103 n. 1 **82.** ed. Gorodetsky, *Maisky Diaries* p. 206 **83.** ed. Self, *Diary Letters* IV p. 431 **84.** OB V p. 1081 **85.** Ibid. p. 1082 **86.** Gilbert, *Other Club* p. 148 **87.** Hansard vol. 350 col. 2440 **88.** ed. Self, *Diary Letters* IV pp. 437–43 **89.** Hatfield House 5M/62/1 **90.** *CS* VI p. 6151 **91.** Pawle, *Warden* p. 42 **92.** OB V p. 1101 **93.** Ibid. p. 1102 **94.** ed. Soames, *Speaking* p. 451 **95.** WSC, *TSWW* III p. 316 **96.** Thompson, *Shadow* p. 11 **97.** Ibid. p. 15 **98.** Ibid. p. 14 **99.** Ibid. **100.** Ibid. p. 16 **101.** Ibid. p. 17 **102.** Hansard vol. 351 col. 35 **103.** CAC INKP 2 p. 38 **104.** Watt, *How War Came* p. 580 **105.** Ibid. p. 579 **106.** *CV* V Part 3 p. 1603 **107.** Watt, *How War Came* p. 588 **108.** Pawle, *Warden* p. 81 **109.** WSC, *TSWW* I p. 319 **110.** Thompson, *Shadow* p. 19 **111.** *CS* VI p. 6152 **112.** Ibid. p. 6153 **113.** ed. Self, *Diary Letters* IV p. 445 **114.** Addison, *Unexpected* p. 154 **115.** WSC, *TSWW* I p. 320 **116.** Thompson, *Shadow* p. 20 **117.** Oliver, *Mr Showbusiness* p. 126 **118.** Ibid. pp. 126–7 **119.** ed. Vincent, *Crawford* p. 603 **120.** *Life* 3 September 1939 **121.** ed. Eade, *Contemporaries* p. 397 **122.** WSC, *TSWW* I p. 321 **123.** Pawle, *Warden* p. 19 **124.** OB V p. 1115 **125.** Ibid.

## 19. 'Winston is Back': September 1939–May 1940

**1.** WSC, *GC* p. 137 **2.** Longford, *Churchill* p. 205 **3.** Hanson, *Wars* p. 149 **4.** ed. Eade, *Contemporaries* p. 150 **5.** Ibid. p. 151 **6.** Ibid. **7.** Pawle, *Warden* p. 39; *CWP* I pp. 487, 914 **8.** Marder, *Dardanelles to Oran* p. 110 n. 10 **9.** Ibid. p. 110 **10.** Colville, *Fringes* p. 368 **11.** Brodhurst, *Pound* p. 133 **12.** BL Add MS 52565 **13.** NA ADM 205/4, ADM 199/1928 **14.** Brodhurst, *Pound* p. 132 **15.** *CWP* I p. 497 **16.** WSC, *TSWW* I p. 365; Brodhurst, *Pound* p. 132 **17.** Potter, *Pim* p. 1 **18.** Ibid. p. 2 **19.** Pawle, *Warden* p. 30 **20.** Ibid. **21.** Ibid. **22.** *The Churchillian* Spring 2014 **23.** Colville, *Fringes* p. 129 **24.** Fort, *Prof* p. 201 **25.** Pawle, *Warden* p. 31 **26.** RA GVI/PRIV/DIARY/COPY/1939: 5 September **27.** Fleming, *Invasion* p. 146 n. 1 **28.** ed. Self, *Diary Letters* IV p. 448 **29.** *CWP* I pp. 111–12 **30.** ed. Kimball, *Complete Correspondence* I p. 24 **31.** McGowan, *My Years* p. 120 **32.** CAC BRGS 1/3 **33.** Ibid. **34.** Roberts, *Holy Fox* p. 177 **35.** ed. Self, *Diary Letters* IV p. 448 **36.** ed. Eade, *Contemporaries* p. 150; CAC INKP 2 pp. 52–3 **37.** ed. James, *Chips* p. 220 **38.** Pawle, *Warden* p. 29 **39.** Ibid. **40.** Shakespeare, *Let Candles* pp. 230–32 **41.** CAC CHUR 19/3 **42.** Baxter, 'Military Strategist' p. 8 **43.** CAC INKP 2 p. 54 **44.** CV V Part 3 pp. 13–37; CAC INKP 2 p. 56 **45.** ed. Nicolson, *Diaries and Letters* II p. 37 **46.** Ibid. **47.** ed. James, *Chips* p. 222 **48.** ed. Vincent, *Crawford* p. 603 **49.** *CS* VI p. 6159 **50.** ed. Nicolson, *Diaries and Letters* II p. 37 **51.** Ibid. p. 36 **52.** Ibid. p. 38 **53.** *CS* VI p. 6161 **54.** Ibid. **55.** Davenport-Hines, *Ettie* p. 334 **56.** RA GVI/PRIV/DIARY/COPY/1939: 2 October **57.** Carlton, *Soviet Union* p. 1 **58.** ed. Nicolson, *Diaries and Letters* II p. 38 **59.** A recurring feature of the writings of the revisionist historians Maurice Cowling, Alan Clark and John Charmley **60.** Gilbert, *A Life* p. 627 **61.** ed. Russell, *Constant* p. 70 **62.** ed. Gorodetsky, *Maisky Diaries* p. 230 **63.** Ibid. **64.** Ibid. p. 231 **65.** Ibid. **66.** Ibid. p. 232 **67.** Ibid. **68.** RA GVI/PRIV/DIARY/COPY/1939: 9

October **69.** Roberts, *Holy Fox* p. 177 **70.** ed. James, *Chips* p. 223 **71.** Ibid. p. 224 **72.** CAC INKP 2 p. 77; Brodhurst, *Pound* p. 129 **73.** Thompson, *Shadow* p. 23 **74.** Colville, *Fringes* p. 310 **75.** Ibid. p. 170 **76.** Gilbert, *Other Club* p. 153 **77.** Thompson, *Shadow* p. 26 **78.** ed. Eade, *Contemporaries* p. 396 **79.** BU NC 18/1/1125 **80.** CAC INKP 2 pp. 78–9 **81.** Ibid. p. 79 **82.** Pawle, *Warden* p. 28 **83.** Halle, *Irrepressible* p. 159 **84.** ed. Eade, *Contemporaries* p. 150; Pawle, *Warden* p. 28; Gladwyn, *Memoirs* p. 96 **85.** ed. Taylor, *Crozier* p. 105 **86.** ed. Gorodetsky, *Maisky Diaries* p. 237 **87.** Ibid. p. 238 **88.** Ibid. p. 239 **89.** Gilbert, *Other Club* p. 155; Pawle, *Warden* p. 38; Thompson, *Shadow* p. 24 **90.** Pawle, *Warden* p. 40 **91.** CAC MCHL 1/1/2 **92.** Pawle, *Warden* p. 40 **93.** *CS* VI p. 6193 **94.** Ibid. **95.** Ibid. **96.** Thompson, *Shadow* p. 34 **97.** WSC, *TSWW* I pp. 432–3 **98.** ed. Eade, *Contemporaries* p. 396 **99.** Ibid. p. 398 **100.** RA GVI/PRIV/DIARY/COPY/1940: 16 January **101.** *CS* VI p. 6184 **102.** Ibid. **103.** ed. Self, *Diary Letters* IV p. 492 **104.** Roberts, *Holy Fox* p. 189 **105.** ed. Self, *Diary Letters* IV p. 492 **106.** CAC MCHL 1/1/2 **107.** *CS* VI p. 6185 **108.** Ibid. pp. 6185–6 **109.** Ibid. p. 6184 **110.** *CWP* I pp. 668–9 **111.** Ibid. p. 679 **112.** *CIHOW* p. 305 **113.** ed. Thorne, *Seven Christmases* p. 89 **114.** Niestlé, *U-Boat Losses* p. 188 **115.** Ibid. pp. 189–97 **116.** *CWP* I p. 1134 **117.** CAC GDFY 1/7/327–8 **118.** Waldegrave, *Weather* p. 193 **119.** *CS* VI pp. 6186–9 **120.** Ibid. p. 6187 **121.** Thompson, *Shadow* p. 32 **122.** Pawle, *Warden* p. 46 **123.** ed. Vincent, *Crawford* p. 613 **124.** ed. Dilks, *Cadogan* p. 252 **125.** CAC AVAR 5/4/1 **126.** Pawle, *Warden* p. 46 **127.** CAC GDFY 1/7/326 **128.** ed. Dilks, *Cadogan* p. 264 **129.** CAC CHAR 9/143/107–14 **130.** Ibid. **131.** ed. James, *Chips* p. 234 **132.** ed. Vincent, *Crawford* p. 614 **133.** Hansard vol. 358 cols. 411–529 **134.** *CWP* I p. 914 **135.** BU AP/20/1/20 **136.** Pawle, *Warden* p. 49 **137.** *CWP* I pp. 925–6 **138.** ed. Taylor, *Crozier* p. 155 **139.** Ibid. **140.** *CS* VI p. 6199 **141.** Ibid. p. 6200 **142.** Griffiths, 'What' pp. 66–7 **143.** BU AP/20/1/20 **144.** Gilbert, *Other Club* p. 158 **145.** ed. Russell, *Constant* p. 268 **146.** ed. Wheeler-Bennett, *Action* p. 250 **147.** Butler, *Facts* p. 268 **148.** Dix, *Norway* p. 206 **149.** Ibid. p. 83 **150.** CAC INKP 2 p. 104 **151.** Robert Blake in *TLS* 22 April 1994 **152.** ed. Eade, *Contemporaries* p. 153 **153.** Kersaudy, *Norway* passim; Shakespeare, *Six Minutes* passim **154.** Pawle, *Warden* p. 50 **155.** Marder, *Winston is Back* p. 54 **156.** WSC, *TSWW* I p. 495 **157.** Ibid. p. 480 **158.** Dix, *Norway* p. 204 **159.** BU AP/20/1/20 **160.** CAC INKP 2 p. 105 **161.** *CS* VI p. 6209 **162.** ed. Gorodetsky, *Maisky Diaries* pp. 270–71 **163.** RA GVI/PRIV/DIARY/COPY/1940: 17 April **164.** *CWP* I p. 1152 **165.** ed. Self, *Diary Letters* IV p. 520 **166.** Ibid. **167.** ed. Nicolson, *Diaries and Letters* II p. 73 **168.** RA GVI/PRIV/DIARY/COPY/1940: 24 April **169.** Gilbert, *Other Club* p. 156 **170.** ed. James, *Chips* p. 242 **171.** ed. Self, *Diary Letters* IV p. 522 **172.** ed. Nicolson, *Diaries and Letters* II p. 74 **173.** RA GVI/PRIV/DIARY/COPY/1940: 30 April **174.** ed. Self, *Diary Letters* IV pp. 526–7 **175.** *CWP* I p. 1169 **176.** ed. James, *Chips* p. 243 **177.** Colville, *Fringes* p. 115 **178.** ed. James, *Chips* p. 244 **179.** Ibid. **180.** CAC GLLD 5/9 Part I **181.** Dix, *Norway* p. 205 **182.** ed. Self, *Diary Letters* IV p. 527 **183.** Ibid. p. 528

## 20. Seizing the Premiership: May 1940

**1.** Scott, *Churchill* p. 153 **2.** ed. Muller, *Contemporaries* p. 141 **3.** Hansard vol. 360 col. 1290 **4.** Roberts, *Holy Fox* p. 196 **5.** Hansard vol. 360 cols. 1075, 1082 **6.** Ibid. col. 1081 **7.** Ibid. cols. 1093–4 **8.** Ibid. cols. 1173, 1296 **9.** Ibid. cols. 1127–8 **10.** Ibid. cols. 1129–30 **11.** Ibid. col. 1150 **12.** Ibid. col. 1165 **13.** Ibid. cols. 1252, 1263 **14.** Ibid. col. 1266 **15.** Ibid. col. 1281 **16.** Ibid. cols. 1282–3 **17.** Roberts, *Holy Fox* p. 265 **18.** Hansard vol. 360 col. 1283 **19.** Ibid. cols. 1307–8 **20.** ed. Nicolson, *Diaries and Letters* II p. 78 **21.** Ibid. pp. 78–9 **22.** ed. James, *Chips* p. 246 **23.** Ibid. **24.** Hansard vol. 360 col. 1361 **25.** Ibid. cols. 1361–2 **26.** ed. Gorodetsky, *Maisky Diaries* p 274 **27.** ed. Stuart, *Reith Diaries* p. 249 **28.** CAC ATLE 1/16 **29.** Amery, *My Political Life* p. 368 **30.** RA GVI/PRIV/DIARY/COPY/1940: 8 May **31.** CAC MCHL 1/1/2 **32.** ed. Gorodetsky, *Maisky Diaries* p. 275 **33.** Ibid. **34.** ed. Nicolson, *Diaries and Letters* II p. 79 **35.** ed. James, *Chips* p. 246 **36.** Colville, *Fringes* p. 310 **37.** Lysaght, *Bracken* p. 172 **38.** PA

BBKN 2/3 **39.** BIYU Halifax Diary **40.** Gilbert, *Other Club* p. 175 **41.** BU AP/20/1/20, AP 20/1/23 **42.** BU AP 20/1/23 **43.** BIYU Halifax Diary 9 May 1940 **44.** Roberts, *Holy Fox* p. 199 **45.** Feiling, *Chamberlain* p. 422 **46.** ed. Taylor, *Crozier* p. 175 **47.** Thompson, *1940* p. 91 **48.** CAC ATLE 1/16 **49.** Thompson, *1940* p. 87 **50.** Attlee, *As It Happened* p. 113 **51.** RA GVI/PRIV/DIARY/COPY/1940: 9 May **52.** ed. Dilks, *Cadogan* p. 280 **53.** WSC, *TSWW* I p. 523 **54.** Thompson, *1940* p. 85 **55.** PA BBK/G/11/11 **56.** Ibid. **57.** BU AP/20/1/20 **58.** ed. Smith, *Hostage to Fortune* p. 476 **59.** BIYU Halifax Diary 31 March 1942 **60.** ed. Evans, *Killearn Diaries* p. 234 **61.** Moran, *Struggle* p. 323 **62.** Stuart, *Within* p. 87 **63.** Pawle, *Warden* p. 53 **64.** RA GVI/PRIV/DIARY/COPY/1940: 10 May **65.** ed. Self, *Diary Letters* IV p. 407 **66.** Gilbert, *Search* p. 215 **67.** *CWP* I p. 1264 **68.** BU AP/20/1/20 **69.** *CV* VI Part 1 p. 1276 **70.** Roberts, *Holy Fox* p. 207 **71.** BU AP 20/1/23 **72.** CAC ATLE 1/16 **73.** ed. James, *Chips* p. 249 **74.** Ibid. **75.** RA GVI/PRIV/DIARY/COPY/1940: 10 May **76.** WSC, *TSWW* I p. 525 **77.** RA GVI/PRIV/DIARY/COPY/1940: 10 May **78.** Thompson, *Shadow* p. 37 **79.** CAC ATLE 1/16 **80.** Colville, *Fringes* p. 122 **81.** Ibid. **82.** Halle, *Irrepressible* p. 135 **83.** ed. James, *Chips* p. 248 **84.** Ibid. p. 250 **85.** Howard, *Rab* p. 94 **86.** Bod Dawson Papers 56/89 **87.** WSC, *TSWW* I pp. 526–7 **88.** Moran, *Struggle* p. 324

## 21. The Fall of France: May–June 1940

**1.** ed. Soames, *Speaking* p. 475 **2.** WSC, *TSWW* II p. 105 **3.** WSC, *RW* II p. 162 **4.** *CS* I p. 83 **5.** CS I pp. 197–8 **6.** *CV* II Part 3 p. 1874 **7.** *CS* III p. 2245 **8.** WSC, *TSWW* I p. 124 **9.** OB IV p. 38 **10.** WSC, *Thoughts* p. 264 **11.** WSC, *WC* III Part 1 p. 193 **12.** Jackson, *Churchill* p. 162 **13.** *CS* III p. 2331 **14.** Ibid. p. 2348 **15.** Ibid. V p. 5203 **16.** Ibid. III p. 2341 **17.** WSC, *Marl* II p. 485 **18.** Gilbert, *A Life* pp. 389–90 **19.** Jackson, *Churchill* p. 130 **20.** WSC, *Marl* I p. 774 **21.** *CS* V p. 5268 **22.** ed. Muller, *Contemporaries* p. 300 **23.** WSC, *TSWW* I p. 328 **24.** ed. Self, *Diary Letters* IV p. 530 **25.** Lysaght, *Bracken* p. 176 **26.** Dalton, *Fateful Years* p. 321; ed. Young, *Bruce Lockhart* p. 532; Lysaght, *Bracken* p. 176; ed. Gorodetsky, *Maisky Diaries* p. 280 **27.** Colville, *Fringes* p. 128 **28.** OB VI p. 454 **29.** ed. Gorodetsky, *Maisky Diaries* p. 239 **30.** ed. James, *Chips* p. 257; PA BBK G/11/11 **31.** Moran, *Struggle* p. 26 **32.** *CIHOW* p. 324 **33.** Ibid. **34.** Gilbert, *Other Club* p. 175 **35.** BU AP/20/1/20 **36.** ed. Stuart, *Reith Diaries* p. 251 **37.** Colville, *Fringes* p. 130 **38.** ed. Eade, *Contemporaries* p. 274 **39.** James, *Boothby* pp. 245–6 **40.** *CS* VI p. 6333 **41.** PA LG F/9/1/5 **42.** Harriman, *Special Envoy* p. 59 **43.** ed. Stuart, *Reith Diaries* p. 250 **44.** WSC, *TSWW* II p. 15 **45.** Boothby, *Fight to Live* p. 145 **46.** Bew, *Citizen Clem* p. 23 **47.** ed. Eade, *Contemporaries* pp. 68–9 **48.** Jacob, 'High Level' p. 365 **49.** WSC, *TSWW* II p. 20 **50.** Colville, *Fringes* p. 129 **51.** Soames, *Daughter's Tale* p. 153 **52.** Ismay, *Memoirs* p. 116 **53.** ed. James, *Chips* p. 252 **54.** ed. Nicolson, *Diaries and Letters* II p. 85 **55.** Foot, *Bevan* I p. 316 **56.** ed. Gorodetsky, *Maisky Diaries* p. 277 **57.** Blake, 'Conservative' p. 12 **58.** BIYU Halifax Diary 13 May 1940 **59.** Hansard vol. 360 cols. 1502 **60.** ed. Nicolson, *Diaries and Letters* II p. 85 **61.** *CS* VI p. 6219 **62.** ed. James, *Chips* p. 252 **63.** Hansard vol. 360 col. 1511 **64.** ed. Cross, *Life with Lloyd George* p. 281 **65.** ed. Gorodetsky, *Maisky Diaries* p. 521 **66.** ed. Dilks, *Cadogan* p. 283 **67.** Pawle, *Warden* p. 57 **68.** *CV* VI Part 2 p. 32 **69.** WSC, *CE* I pp. 394–5 **70.** Ibid. pp. 424–5 **71.** Wright, *Dowding* p. 10 **72.** Ibid. **73.** Lewin, *Warlord* p. 31 and n **74.** Ibid. p. 31 **75.** Wright, *Dowding* p. 112 **76.** Owen, *Cabinet* p. 97. **77.** ed. Dilks, *Cadogan* p. 264 **78.** ed. Kimball, *Complete Correspondence* I p. 37 **79.** Ibid. **80.** Ibid. **81.** Ibid. pp. 37–8 **82.** RA GVI/PRIV/DIARY/COPY/1940: 16 May **83.** ed. Harvey, *Diaries* p. 359 **84.** WSC, *TSWW* II p. 42 **85.** Owen, *Cabinet* pp. 97–8 **86.** Spears, *Assignment* I p. 148; Colville, *Fringes* p. 261; Ismay, *Memoirs* pp. 128–9 **87.** Spears, *Assignment* I p. 148 **88.** Colville, *Fringes* pp. 177, 261 **89.** Pawle, *Warden* p. 57 **90.** LHC Dill Papers 3/1/8 **91.** Ibid. **92.** ed. Dilks, *Cadogan* p. 285 **93.** Colville, *Fringes* p. 134 **94.** Ibid. p. 132 **95.** *CWP* II p. 62 **96.** Colville, *Fringes* p. 133 **97.** Ibid. **98.** Ibid. p. 134 **99.** Karslake, *1940* p. 82 **100.** ed. Dilks, *Cadogan* p. 285 **101.** Karslake, *1940* p. 83 **102.** ed. Nicolson, *Diaries* *and Letters* II p. 86 **103.** ed. Self, *Diary Letters* IV p. 531 **104.** Ibid. p. 532 **105.** Ibid. pp. 535–7 **106.** RA GVI/PRIV/DIARY/COPY/1940: 17 May **107.** Colville, *Fringes* p. 135 **108.** NA PREM 4/19/5 **109.** Colville, *Fringes* pp. 134–5 **110.** ed. Dilks, *Cadogan* p. 286 **111.** BU AP/20/1/20 **112.** Colville, *Fringes* p. 135 **113.** Ibid. **114.** *CS* VI pp. 6222–3 **115.** eds. Addison and Crang, *Listening to Britain* p. 12 **116.** ed. Dilks, *Cadogan* p. 287 **117.** ed. Kimball, *Complete Correspondence* I p. 40 **118.** Ibid. **119.** *CV* VI Part 2 p. 93 **120.** Colville, *Fringes* p. 136 **121.** *CWP* II p. 97 **122.** Colville, *Fringes* p. 137 **123.** Ibid. p. 138 **124.** PA BBK C/92 **125.** ed. Dilks, *Cadogan* p. 288 **126.** Colville, *Fringes* p. 177 **127.** WSC, *TSWW* V p. 635 **128.** Griffiths, 'What' pp. 97–8 **129.** eds. Blake and Louis, *Churchill* p. 422 **130.** Christopher Andrew in *Literary Review* June 2006 p. 16 **131.** Hinsley, *British Intelligence* I p. 160 and Appendix 6 **132.** eds. Blake and Louis, *Churchill* p. 410 **133.** ed. Dilks, *Cadogan* p. 288 **134.** Owen, *Cabinet* p. 116 **135.** Potter, *Pim* p. 5 **136.** Ibid. **137.** RA GVI/PRIV/DIARY/COPY/1940: 23 May **138.** *CWP* II pp. 138–9 **139.** WSC, *TSWW* II p. 53 **140.** *CWP* II p. 139 **141.** WSC, *TSWW* II p. 73 **142.** Ibid. **143.** Colville, *Fringes* p. 213 **144.** *FH* no. 136 p. 51 **145.** NA CAB 66/7 WP (40) 168 **146.** ed. Dilks, *Cadogan* p. 289 **147.** Ibid. p. 290 **148.** Ibid. **149.** Ibid. **150.** NA CAB 65/13 WM 142 (40) **151.** BU NC 2/24A; NA CAB 65/13 Confidential annexes **152.** BU NC 2/24A **153.** Owen, *Cabinet* p. 21 **154.** WSC, *TSWW* II p. 157 **155.** NA CAB 65/13 WM 142 **156.** Owen, *Cabinet* p. 127 **157.** *CWP* II p. 168 **158.** ed. Dilks, *Cadogan* p. 291 **159.** Langworth, 'Feeding the Crocodile' passim **160.** RA GVI/PRIV/DIARY/COPY/1940: 30 May **161.** Colville, *Fringes* p. 182; Habsburg, *Naissance* p. 175; RA GVI/PRIV/DIARY/COPY/1940: 30 May **162.** *CWP* II pp. 169–80 **163.** Colville, *Fringes* p. 141 **164.** ed. Dilks, *Cadogan* p. 291 **165.** Colville, *Fringes* p. 141 **166.** Ibid. **167.** *CS* VI p. 6224 **168.** RA GVI/PRIV/DIARY/COPY/1940: 28 May **169.** NA CAB 65/13 WM 145 (40) 1 **170.** OB VI p. 419 **171.** ed. Dilks, *Cadogan* p. 290 **172.** WSC, *TSWW* II p. 81 **173.** CAC BRGS 1/3 **174.** Reynolds, *World War* p. 82 **175.** *CWP* II pp. 182–3, 183 n. 2 **176.** Thompson, *Shadow* p. 56 **177.** Pawle, *Warden* p. 59; Browne, *Sunset* p. 204 **178.** Plumb, 'Dominion' p. 2 **179.** Colville, *Fringes* p. 344 **180.** Rowse 'Visit' pp. 8–13 **181.** WSC, *TSWW* II p. 88 **182.** Potter, *Pim* p. 6 **183.** Ibid. p. 11 **184.** LHC Dill Papers 3/1/8 **185.** Colville, *Fringes* p. 143 **186.** *CWP* II p. 200 **187.** ed. Harvey, *Diaries* p. 374 **188.** Thompson, *Shadow* p. 41 **189.** Karslake, *1940* p. 122 **190.** Pawle, *Warden* p. 59 **191.** ed. Harvey, *Diaries* p. 375 **192.** ed. Dilks, *Cadogan* p. 293 **193.** OB VI p. 449; NA PREM 7/2 **194.** Colville, *Fringes* p. 145 **195.** Karslake, *1940* p. 122 **196.** Colville, *Fringes* pp. 146–7 **197.** Holland, *Rise of Germany* p. 308 **198.** Jackson, *Churchill* p. 269; RA GVI/PRIV/DIARY/COPY/1940: 9 June **199.** Pawle, *Warden* p. 68 **200.** *CS* VI p. 6226 **201.** Ibid. p. 6227 **202.** Ibid. **203.** Ibid. p. 6229 **204.** Ibid. **205.** Ibid. p. 6230 **206.** ed. James, *Chips* p. 256 **207.** ed. Nicolson, *Diaries and Letters* II p. 93 **208.** Ibid. **209.** Ronald Golding to Richard Langworth, 1985 **210.** ed. Dilks, *Cadogan* p. 294 **211.** Colville, *Fringes* pp. 148–9 **212.** Ibid. p. 149 **213.** Gilbert, *D-Day* p. 24 **214.** Colville, *Fringes* p. 152 **215.** Ibid. p. 163 **216.** Pawle, *Warden* p. 62 **217.** Karslake, *1940* p. 173; LHC Dill Papers 3/1/8 **218.** *TCD* 19 p. 573 **219.** Pawle, *Warden* p. 62 **220.** RA GVI/PRIV/DIARY/COPY/1940: 12 June **221.** Pawle, *Warden* p. 63 **222.** RA GVI/PRIV/DIARY/COPY/1940: 12 June **223.** Ismay, *Memoirs* p. 139 **224.** Ibid. p. 140 **225.** Ibid.; LHC Ismay Papers 2/1/25 **226.** Ismay, *Memoirs* pp. 141–2 **227.** OB VI p. 522 **228.** Ismay, *Memoirs* p. 142 **229.** eds. Blake and Louis, *Churchill* p. 249 **230.** Colville, *Fringes* p. 175 **231.** RA GVI/PRIV/DIARY/COPY/1940: 12 June **232.** Colville, *Fringes* p. 154 **233.** Thompson, *Shadow* p. 55 **234.** Pawle, *Warden* p. 59 **235.** KCL Beaumont Papers Chapter 8 fol. 146 **236.** Pawle, *Warden* p. 64 **237.** ed. Dilks, *Cadogan* p. 298 **238.** Pawle, *Warden* p. 64 **239.** Thompson, *Shadow* p. 56 **240.** Pawle, *Warden* p. 64 **241.** Spears, *Assignment* II pp. 205–6; OB VI p. 507 **242.** CAC CHAR 23/2 **243.** PA BBK/D/480 **244.** Thomson, *Vote of Censure* p. 45 **245.** WSC, *TSSW* II p. 162 **246.** Pawle, *Warden* p. 65 **247.** ed. Russell, *Constant* p. 105 **248.** Thompson, *Shadow* p. 56 **249.** eds. Danchev and Todman, *War Diaries* p. 81 **250.** Jackson, *Churchill* p. 26 **251.** Pawle, *Warden* p. 119 **252.** *CIHOW* p. 534 **253.** ed. Dilks, *Cadogan* p. 299 **254.** Colville, *Fringes* p. 157 **255.** Ibid. p. 158 **256.** Ibid. **257.** Ibid. **258.** Ibid. **259.** Ibid. p. 161 **260.** Ibid. p. 504 **261.** Ibid. p. 160 **262.**

Ibid. **263.** Ibid. **264.** Roberts, *Holy Fox* p. 232 **265.** Ibid. **266.** Ibid. p. 161 **267.** Martin, *Downing Street* p. 11 **268.** ed. Dilks, *Cadogan* p. 304 **269.** Martin, *Downing Street* p. 6

## 22. The Battle of Britain: June–September 1940

1. Colville, *Fringes* p. 194 **2.** *Washington Post* 23 September 1940 **3.** Stuart, *Within* p. 34 **4.** WSC, *TSWW* II p. 451 **5.** Martin, *Downing Street* p. 14 **6.** *CS* VI p. 6232 **7.** Ibid. pp. 6238–9 **8.** Ibid. p. 6234 **9.** Fleming, *Invasion* p. 141 **10.** *CS* VI p. 6328 **11.** ed. Gorodetsky, *Maisky Diaries* p. 287 **12.** ed. Nicolson, *Diaries and Letters* II p. 97 **13.** RA GVI/PRIV/DIARY/COPY/1940: 19 June **14.** Colville, *Fringes* p. 165 **15.** Ibid. pp. 165–6 **16.** OB VI pp. 584–5 **17.** Aldrich and Cormac, *Black Door* p. 17 **18.** WSC, *TSWW* II p. 339 **19.** Jones, 'Knew Him' pp. 10–11 **20.** Jones, *Most Secret* pp. 107–8 **21.** Capet, 'Scientific' p. 4 **22.** Ibid. **23.** Colville, *Fringes* p. 197 **24.** ed. Dilks, *Cadogan* p. 307 **25.** James, *Davidson* p. 427 **26.** Colville, *Fringes* p. 170 **27.** RA GVI/PRIV/DIARY/COPY/1940: 25 June **28.** Bloch, *Operation Willi* passim **29.** RA GVI/PRIV/DIARY/COPY/1940: 25 June **30.** CAC MCHL 1/1/2 **31.** Colville, *Fringes* p. 172 **32.** ed. Soames, *Speaking* p. 454 **33.** Colville, *Fringes* p. 281 **34.** Ibid. pp. 172–3 **35.** Colville, 'Second' p. 7 **36.** Colville, *Fringes* p. 273 **37.** ed. Russell, *Constant* pp. 121–2 **38.** CAC MRGN 1/6/1 **39.** NA PREM 3/479 **40.** *CWP* II p. 436 **41.** Christie's Manuscripts Sales Catalogue 2003 **42.** Colville, *Fringes* pp. 186–7 **43.** Ibid. p. 178 **44.** Martin, *Downing Street* p. 13 **45.** Colville, *Fringes* p. 179 **46.** Ibid. pp. 179–80 **47.** Ibid. p. 180 **48.** Ibid. p. 182 **49.** ed. Harvey, *Diaries* p. 378 **50.** Bryant, *Turn of the Tide* p. 199 **51.** Montgomery, *Memoirs* p. 69 **52.** Pawle, *Warden* p. 70 **53.** Gallup, *Opinion Polls* p. 34 **54.** Colville, *Fringes* p. 217 **55.** Gallup, *Opinion Polls* pp. 34–61 **56.** Leasor, *War at the Top* p. 45 **57.** Holland, *Rise of Germany* p. 327 **58.** CAC CHUR 20/9; OB VI p. 705 **59.** Colville, *Fringes* p. 184 **60.** CAC CHAR 20/31A/16 and 30 **61.** CAC CHAR 20/31A/51 **62.** RA GVI/PRIV/DIARY/COPY/1940: 7 July **63.** Pawle, *Warden* p. 71 **64.** PA BBK/D/480 **65.** ed. Eade, *Contemporaries* p. 154 **66.** Ibid. **67.** Colville, *Fringes* pp. 183–4 **68.** CAC MCHL 1/1/2 **69.** Martin, *Downing Street* p. 14 **70.** CAC MCHL 1/1/2 **71.** ed. Nicolson, *Diaries and Letters* II p. 100 **72.** Colville, *Fringes* p. 185 **73.** Mitter, *China's War* pp. 221–2 **74.** CAC GLLD 519 part 1 **75.** ed. Dilks, *Cadogan* p. 311 **76.** ed. Rose, *Baffy* p. 173 **77.** WSC, *TSWW* II p. 238 **78.** Colville, *Fringes* p. 187 **79.** RA GVI/PRIV/DIARY/COPY/1940: 10 July **80.** Soames, *Clementine* p. 322 **81.** Martin, *Downing Street* p. 6 **82.** Fleming, *Invasion* p. 98 **83.** Colville, *Fringes* p. 189 **84.** Ibid. p. 190 **85.** ed. Norwich, *Monster* p. 38 **86.** Colville, *Fringes* p. 192 **87.** Ibid. **88.** Ibid. **89.** Ibid. pp. 192–3 **90.** Ibid. p. 193 **91.** Ibid. p. 194 **92.** Ibid. p. 195 **93.** Best, *Greatness* p. 187 **94.** *CS* VI p. 6247 **95.** Ibid. p. 6248 **96.** Ibid. p. 6249 **97.** eds. Addison and Crang, *Listening* p. 232 **98.** ed. Nicolson, *Diaries* II p. 102 **99.** Colville, *Fringes* p. 197 **100.** CAC MCHL 1/1/2 **101.** Colville, *Fringes* p. 197 **102.** *CWP* II pp. 532–3 **103.** Ibid. p. 533 **104.** Ibid. p. 534 **105.** ed. Eade, *Contemporaries* p. 211 **106.** Colville, *Fringes* p. 200 **107.** BU AP/20/1/20 **108.** WSC, *TSWW* III p. 663 **109.** ed. Midgley, *Heroic Memory* p. 42 **110.** WSC, *TSWW* III p. 660 **111.** ed. Pimlott, *Dalton Diary* p. 62 **112.** Colville, *Fringes*, p. 306; *New Statesman* 29 January 1965 **113.** Milton, *Ungentlemanly* p. 63 **114.** Foot, *SOE* p. 105 **115.** For criticisms of SOE see Keegan, *Intelligence in War* passim; Richard J. Aldrich in *Contemporary British History* Autumn 1997 pp. 159–60; Roger Fontaine in *History: Reviews of New Books* vol. 26 no. 4 1998 pp. 217–21, http://www.tandfonline.com/doi/abs/10.1080/03612759.1998.10528264 **116.** Milton, *Ungentlemanly* passim **117.** BU AP/20/1/20 **118.** eds. Danchev and Todman, *War Diaries* p. 100 **119.** BU AP/20/1/20 **120.** PA BBK C/92 **121.** eds. Addison and Crang, *Listening* p. 309 **122.** CAC BRGS 1/3 **123.** De Gaulle, *War Memoirs* p. 104 **124.** Colville, *Fringes* pp. 214–15 **125.** BA AP/20/1/20 **126.** RA GVI/PRIV/DIARY/COPY/1940: 16 July **127.** Colville, *Fringes* p. 223 **128.** Ibid. p. 219 **129.** Ibid. p. 220 **130.** Ibid. p. 223 **131.** Colville, *Churchillians* p. 143 **132.** Colville, *Fringes* p. 223 **133.** Ibid. p. 224 **134.** CAC MCHL 1/1/2 **135.** Martin, *Downing Street* p. 19 **136.** Colville, *Fringes*

p. 196 **137.** *CS* VI p. 6265 **138.** Ibid. p. 6267 **139.** Ibid. **140.** Ibid. p. 6269 **141.** Colville, *Fringes* p. 227 **142.** ed. Gorodetsky, *Maisky Diaries* p. 305 **143.** ed. Wheeler-Bennett, *Action* p. 257 **144.** *CS* I p. 365 **145.** CAC EADE 2/2 **146.** *CS* VII p. 7885 **147.** Colville, *Fringes* p. 258 **148.** BU AP/20/1/20 **149.** Ibid. **150.** Colville, *Fringes* p. 229 **151.** NA CAB 65/14 WM (40) 232 **152.** RA GVI/PRIV/DIARY/COPY/1940: 24 August **153.** Hancock and Gowing, *British War Economy* p. 234 **154.** Kimball, 'Beggar my Neighbour' p. 765 **155.** Colville, *Fringes* p. 232 **156.** Pawle, *Warden* p. 74 **157.** Colville, *Fringes* p. 230 **158.** OB VI p. 803 **159.** ed. Nicolson, *Diaries and Letters* II pp. 121–2 **160.** RA GVI/PRIV/DIARY/COPY/1940: 27 August **161.** Colville, *Fringes* p. 231 **162.** Ibid. pp. 232–3 **163.** ed. Wheeler-Bennett, *Action* p. 112 **164.** Colville, *Fringes* p. 233 **165.** Ibid. p. 238 **166.** Ibid. p. 234 **167.** Ibid. **168.** Ibid. p. 235 **169.** Ibid. p. 237 **170.** Ibid. pp. 234, 238 **171.** Ibid. p. 238 **172.** NA CAB 65/8 WM (40) 227 **173.** Colville, *Fringes* p. 223; ed. Kimball, *Complete Correspondence* I p. 60 **174.** ed. Eade, *Contemporaries* p. 154 **175.** RA GVI/PRIV/DIARY/COPY/1940: 3 September **176.** NA CAB 66/11 WP (40) 352 **177.** Stargardt, *German* pp. 111–12 **178.** *CS* VI p. 6275 **179.** Gilbert, *Other Club* p. 166 **180.** Skidelsky, *Fighting for Britain* p. 80

## 23. The Blitz: October 1940–January 1941

**1.** WSC, *TSWW* II p. 555 **2.** Ibid. p. 246 **3.** Gilbert, *Other Club* p. 166 **4.** Ismay, *Memoirs* p. 183 **5.** Ibid. pp. 183–4 **6.** WSC, *TSWW* II p. 308 **7.** Calder, *Myth of the Blitz* passim **8.** Colville, *Fringes* p. 231 **9.** Sitwell, *Eggs or Anarchy* passim **10.** Colville, *Footprints* p. 98 **11.** CAC CHOH/3/CLVL **12.** James, *Undaunted* p. 207 **13.** Ibid. p. 209 **14.** *CS* VI p. 6277 **15.** Ibid. **16.** CAC CHOH/3/CLVL **17.** ed. Gorodetsky, *Maisky Diaries* p. 311 **18.** WSC, *TSWW* II pp. 295–6 **19.** Martin, *Downing Street* p. 25 **20.** Ibid. **21.** WSC, *TSWW* II p. 297 **22.** *CS* VI p. 6283 **23.** Ibid. **24.** ed. Nicolson, *Diaries and Letters* II p. 114 **25.** Colville, *Fringes* p. 241 **26.** *CS* VI p. 6279 **27.** Martin, *Downing Street* p. 26 **28.** Colville, *Fringes* p. 243 **29.** Thompson, *Shadow* p. 63 **30.** Ibid. **31.** Colville, *Fringes* p. 243 **32.** Ibid. p. 245 **33.** Ibid. **34.** Ibid. **35.** Ibid. p. 246 **36.** Ibid. p. 248 **37.** RA GVI/PRIV/DIARY/COPY/1940: 1 October **38.** ed. Dilks, *Cadogan* p. 328 **39.** Colville, *Fringes* p. 249 **40.** ed. James, *Chips* p. 268 **41.** WSC, *TSWW* II pp. 436–7 **42.** RA GVI/PRIV/DIARY/COPY/1940: 1 October **43.** RA GVI/PRIV/DIARY/COPY/1940: 25 September **44.** RA GVI/PRIV/DIARY/COPY/1940: 24 September **45.** Colville, *Fringes* p. 252 **46.** *CWP* II p. 845 **47.** Ibid. p. 890 **48.** BU AP/20/1/20 **49.** Ibid. **50.** BU NC 20/1/202 **51.** PA FLS/5/6 **52.** Kennedy, *Business* p. 275 **53.** Ibid. p. 173 **54.** BU AP/20/1/20 **55.** Colville, *Fringes* p. 248 **56.** *CS* VI p. 6315 **57.** BA AP/20/1/20 **58.** *CS* VI pp. 6286–7 **59.** BU AP/20/1/20 **60.** OB VIII p. 308 **61.** Churchill, *His Father's Son* p. 183 **62.** WSC, *TSWW* II p. 439 **63.** *CS* VI p. 6295 **64.** *CV* II Part 1 p. 243 **65.** Colville, *Fringes* p. 262 **66.** Ibid. **67.** Ibid. p. 264 **68.** Ibid. p. 265 **69.** Ibid. p. 266 **70.** Ibid. p. 265 **71.** WSC, *TSWW* II p. 305 **72.** Ibid. p. 306 **73.** Martin, *Downing Street* pp. 30–31 **74.** CAC BRGS 1/2 **75.** Thompson, *Shadow* p. 59 **76.** CAC GLLD 519 part 1 **77.** RA GVI/PRIV/DIARY/COPY/1940: 15 October **78.** Ibid. **79.** Peck, *Dublin from Downing Street* p. 72 **80.** Jones, *No. 10 Downing Street* p. 138 **81.** Colville, *Fringes* p. 341 **82.** Pawle, *Warden* p. 82 **83.** Martin, *Downing Street* p. 29 **84.** Colville, *Fringes* p. 268 **85.** Hastings, *Finest Years* p. 102 **86.** Colville, *Fringes* p. 280 **87.** Pawle, *Warden* p. 80 **88.** Ibid. **89.** Ibid. p. 81 **90.** Colville, *Fringes* p. 270 **91.** Pawle, *Warden* p. 81 **92.** Thompson, *Shadow* p. 62 **93.** Ibid. **94.** Colville, *Fringes* p. 341 **95.** Thompson, *Shadow* p. 58 **96.** Ibid. p. 60 **97.** Ibid. **98.** Peck, *Dublin from Downing Street* p. 71 **99.** Thompson, *Shadow* p. 61 **100.** Colville, *Fringes* p. 244 **101.** LHC LH 15/15/1 **102.** Ibid. **103.** Martin, *Downing Street* p. 11 **104.** Colville, *Fringes* pp. 154–5 **105.** ed. Wheeler-Bennett, *Action* pp. 50–51 **106.** Pawle, *Warden* p. 101 **107.** ed. Wheeler-Bennett, *Action* p. 20 **108.** Stuart, *Within* p. 96 **109.** *FH* no. 84 p. 8 **110.** Thompson, *Shadow* p. 47 **111.** WSC, *TSWW* III p. 639 **112.** Ibid. II p. 560 **113.** CAC CHOH/3/CLVL **114.** Colville, *Fringes* p. 291 **115.** Marsh, *Number*

p. 246 **116.** Laird and Graebner, *Hitler's Reich* p. 55 **117.** WSC, *MEL* p. 95 **118.** Thompson, *Shadow* p. 44 **119.** Ibid. **120.** WSC, *TSWW* I p. 201 **121.** Singer, *Style* p. 172 **122.** Colville, *Fringes* p. 245 **123.** ed. Eade, *Contemporaries* p. 397 **124.** Peck, *Dublin from Downing Street* p. 76 **125.** Martin, *Downing Street* p. 8 **126.** *CS* VI p. 6297 **127.** *CIHOW* p. 485 **128.** Colville, *Fringes* p. 272 **129.** Ibid. p. 283 **130.** ed. Dilks, *Cadogan* p. 340 **131.** WSC, *WC* IV p. 302 **132.** *CS* VI p. 6341 **133.** Stuart, *Within* p. 90 **134.** Colville, *Fringes* p. 366 **135.** Ibid. p. 273 **136.** Ibid. **137.** Carr, *Fall of Greece* p. 38 **138.** Colville, *Fringes* p. 277 **139.** Tree, *When the Moon* p. 136 **140.** WSC, *TSWW* II p. 472 **141.** Colville, *Fringes* p. 284 **142.** Ibid. p. 283 **143.** Kimball, *Unsordid* p. 235 **144.** ed. Kimball, *Complete Correspondence* I p. 40 **145.** Colville, *Fringes* p. 278 **146.** OB VI pp. 949–50 **147.** Colville, *Fringes* p. 282 **148.** Ibid. p. 284 **149.** Ibid. p. 291 **150.** *CS* VI p. 6303 **151.** ed. Nicolson, *Diaries and Letters* II p. 125 **152.** WSC, *TSWW* II p. 489; CAC MCHL 1/1/2 **153.** WSC, *TSWW* II p. 501 **154.** Ibid. **155.** ed. James, *Chips* p. 276 **156.** Ibid. p. 273 **157.** Ibid. **158.** *CS* VI p. 6307 **159.** Ibid. **160.** ed. James, *Chips* p. 276 **161.** Colville, *Fringes* p. 292 **162.** *CIHOW* p. 331 **163.** ed. Nicolson, *Diaries and Letters* II p. 129 **164.** Stuart, *Within* p. 87 **165.** Tree, *When the Moon* p. 130; *FH* no. 165 pp. 38–41 **166.** *CIHOW* p. 518 **167.** Martin, *Downing Street* p. 33 **168.** CAC MCHL 1/1/2 **169.** *The Times* 28 August 1976; CAC SOAM 7/6c **170.** Martin, *Downing Street* p. 33 **171.** Colville, *Fringes* p. 295 **172.** *Standpoint* November 2015 p. 55 **173.** Langworth, *Myth* pp. 132–6 **174.** Colville, *Fringes* p. 297 **175.** Ibid. p. 299 **176.** Best, *Greatness* p. 198 **177.** ed. Kimball, *Complete Correspondence* I p. 103 **178.** Ibid. pp. 108, 100 **179.** WSC, *TSWW* III p. 35 **180.** BU AP/20/1/20 **181.** Pawle, *Warden* p. 95 **182.** Aspinall-Oglander, *Keyes* p. 399 **183.** Colville, *Fringes* p. 305 **184.** BU AP/20/1/20 **185.** RA GVI/PRIV/DIARY/COPY/1940: 10 December **186.** Colville, *Fringes* p. 312 **187.** ed. James, *Chips* pp. 278–9 **188.** *CS* VI p. 6317 **189.** Colville, *Fringes* p. 309 **190.** Ibid. p. 275 **191.** Ibid. p. 310 **192.** Ibid. pp. 215–16 **193.** Ibid. p. 216 **194.** Ibid. pp. 312–13 **195.** WSC, *TSWW* III p. 638 **196.** Pawle, *Warden* p. 77 **197.** Colville, *Fringes*, p. 319 **198.** Ibid. **199.** *CS* VI p. 6314 **200.** CAC CHOH/3/CLVL **201.** Colville, *Fringes* p. 321 **202.** RA GVI/PRIV/DIARY/COPY/1940: 24 December **203.** Colville, *Fringes* p. 322 **204.** BU AP/20/1/20 **205.** Birkenhead Papers 65/A3 **206.** BU AP/20/1/21 **207.** Martin, *Downing Street* p. 36 **208.** Ibid. **209.** Colville, *Fringes* p. 314 **210.** Martin, *Downing Street* p. 37 **211.** CAC MCHL 1/1/2 **212.** Colville, *Fringes* p. 323 **213.** Ibid. p. 325 **214.** Ibid. p. 327 **215.** RA PS GVI C 069/07 **216.** Hamilton, *Listening* p. 238 **217.** eds. Blake and Louis, *Churchill* p. 407 **218.** Ibid. p. 414 **219.** Ibid. p. 415 **220.** Ibid. **221.** *CS* VI p. 6328 **222.** ed. Wheeler-Bennett, *Action* p. 252 **223.** WSC, *TSWW* III p. 21 **224.** Pawle, *Warden* p. 92 **225.** Colville, *Fringes* p. 333 **226.** Ibid. **227.** Ibid. p. 394 **228.** ed. Sherwood, *Hopkins* I p. 242 **229.** Colville, *Fringes* p. 335 **230.** Ibid. **231.** Ibid. **232.** Ibid. **233.** ed. Dilks, *Cadogan* p. 349 **234.** Martin, *Downing Street* p. 40 **235.** Pawle, *Warden* p. 92 **236.** Martin, *Downing Street* p. 42 **237.** Gilbert, *A Life* p. 688

## 24. 'Keep Buggering On': January–June 1941

**1.** Churchill, *Marl* I p. 569 **2.** LHC Edmonds Papers II/3/53b **3.** *CS* VI p. 6337 **4.** ed. Nicolson, *Diaries and Letters* II p. 140 **5.** Colville, *Fringes* p. 340 **6.** *CS* VI p. 6333 **7.** Colville, *Fringes* p. 340 **8.** Ibid. p. 341 **9.** Ibid. **10.** Gallup, *Opinion Polls* p. 41 **11.** Colville, *Fringes* p. 341 **12.** Ibid. p. 342 **13.** Ibid. **14.** ed. Sherwood, *Hopkins* I p. 257 **15.** James, *Undaunted* p. 231 **16.** Colville, *Fringes* pp. 345–6 **17.** Ibid. p. 346 **18.** Ibid. p. 348 **19.** Ibid. p. 346 **20.** Ibid. **21.** Ibid. **22.** Ibid. p. 347 **23.** Ibid. pp. 347–8 **24.** Johnsen, *Origins* passim **25.** Potter, *Pim* p. 13 **26.** Colville, *Fringes* p. 349 **27.** RA GVI/PRIV/DIARY/COPY/1941: 4 February **28.** *CS* VI p. 6343 **29.** ed. Dilks, *Cadogan* p. 353 **30.** Colville, *Fringes* p. 355 **31.** *CS* VI p. 6344 **32.** Ibid. p. 6346 **33.** Ibid. p. 6351 **34.** RA GVI/PRIV/DIARY/COPY/1941: 8 and 9 February **35.** WSC, *TSWW* III p. 63 **36.** Kennedy, *Business* p. 79 **37.** Ibid. **38.** ed. Norwich, *Monster* p. 108 **39.**

Ibid. **40.** Martin, *Downing Street* p. 43 **41.** ed. Gorodetsky, *Maisky Diaries* p. 238 **42.** RA GVI/PRIV/DIARY/COPY/1941: 25 February **43.** Colville, *Fringes* p. 358 **44.** *CS* VI p. 6355 **45.** Colville, *Fringes* p. 361 **46.** Ibid. p. 360 **47.** Ibid. **48.** Ibid. p. 361 **49.** CAC EADE 2/2 **50.** Ibid. **51.** Ibid. **52.** Ibid. **53.** Ibid. **54.** Ibid. **55.** RA GVI/PRIV/DIARY/COPY/1941: 4 March **56.** *CS* VI p. 6505 **57.** eds. Danchev and Todman, *War Diaries* pp. 144–5 **58.** RA GVI/PRIV/DIARY/COPY/1941: 11 March **59.** ed. Dilks, *Cadogan* p. 431 **60.** Kimball, *Unsordid* p. 237 **61.** Pawle, *Warden* p. 141 **62.** ed. Dilks, *Cadogan* p. 364 **63.** ed. Thorne, *Seven Christmases* p. 134 **64.** Thompson, *Shadow* p. 21 **65.** CAC EADE 2/2 **66.** Colville, *Fringes* p. 366 **67.** ed. Thorne, *Seven Christmases* p. 107 **68.** Ogden, *Life of the Party* p. 128 **69.** Churchill, *Dancing* p. 58 **70.** CAC SCHL 1/2/1 **71.** ed. Eade, *Contemporaries* p. 155 **72.** WSC, *TSWW* III p. 107 **73.** Ibid. II p. 529 **74.** ed. Dilks, *Cadogan* p. 364 **75.** Pawle, *Warden* p. 98 **76.** WSC, *TSWW* III pp. 100–101 **77.** Ibid. p. 142 **78.** *CS* VI p. 6373 **79.** Colville, *Fringes* pp. 367–8 **80.** *CS* VI p. 6367 **81.** Ibid. **82.** Ibid. p. 6369 **83.** Colville, *Fringes* p. 368 **84.** Ibid. p. 369 **85.** Ibid. pp. 366–8 **86.** ed. Dilks, *Cadogan* p. 368 **87.** WSC, *TSWW* III p. 668 **88.** *FH* no. 140 p. 17 **89.** Colville, *Fringes* p. 372 **90.** Pawle, *Warden* p. 105 **91.** Stewart, *First* p. 104 **92.** Hinsley, *British Intelligence* I p. 395 **93.** Colville, *Fringes* p. 371 **94.** Kotkin, *Waiting for Hitler* pp. 850–51 **95.** RA GVI/PRIV/DIARY/COPY/1941: 8 April **96.** ed. Nicolson, *Diaries and Letters* II p. 162 **97.** *CS* VI p. 6377 **98.** Moran, *Struggle* p. 612; Cannadine, *Heroic Chancellor* passim **99.** Gilbert, *Search* p. 236 **100.** Colville, *Fringes* p. 373 **101.** Pawle, *Warden* p. 102 **102.** Ibid. p. 4 **103.** Ibid. p. 103 **104.** *CS* VII p. 6823 **105.** Ibid. VI p. 6377 **106.** Addison, *Unexpected* p. 169 **107.** Pawle, *Warden* p. 4 **108.** CAC BRGS1/2 **109.** ed. Dilks, *Cadogan* p. 372 **110.** RA GVI/PRIV/DIARY/COPY/1941: 23 April **111.** ed. James, *Chips* p. 301 **112.** Colville, *Fringes* pp. 432–3 **113.** Leasor, *War at the Top* p. 148 n. 1 **114.** *CS* VI p. 6381 **115.** Ibid. p. 6379 **116.** Ibid. **117.** Ibid. p. 6381 **118.** Ibid. p. 6385 **119.** Ibid. **120.** *CWP* III p. 556 **121.** Ibid. pp. 556–7; Farrell, *Defence and Fall* p. 399 **122.** ed. Wheeler-Bennett, *Action* p. 241 **123.** Ibid. p. 245 **124.** Ibid. p. 263 **125.** Ibid. pp. 248–9 **126.** Ibid. pp. 221–2 **127.** Peck, *Dublin from Downing Street* p. 69 **128.** BU AP/20/1/21 **129.** ed. Hassall, *Ambrosia* p. 165 **130.** Colville, *Fringes* p. 381 **131.** Ibid. p. 382 **132.** Ibid. p. 383 **133.** Ibid. p. 382 **134.** Ibid. **135.** Colville, 'Second' p. 7 **136.** *CS* VI p. 6387 **137.** ed. Eade, *Contemporaries* pp. 207, 212 **138.** Schroeder, *Chief* p. 55 **139.** RA GVI/PRIV/DIARY/COPY/1941: 6 May **140.** Ibid. **141.** NA CAB 69/2 DO (41) 24, 25 and 26 **142.** *CS* VI p. 6388 **143.** Ibid. p. 6390 **144.** Ibid. p. 6393 **145.** Ibid. p. 6396 **146.** Ibid. p. 6399 **147.** Colville, *Fringes* p. 384 **148.** ed. Gorodetsky, *Maisky Diaries* p. 354 **149.** Ibid. **150.** Pawle, *Warden* p. 107 **151.** Colville, *Fringes* p. 387 **152.** WSC, *TSWW* III p. 43; ed. Sherwood, *Hopkins* I p. 294; Addison, *Unexpected* p. 185 **153.** Colville, *Fringes* pp. 387–8 **154.** Pawle, *Warden* p. 108 **155.** OB VI p. 1087 **156.** RA GVI/PRIV/DIARY/COPY/1941: 13 May **157.** Ibid. **158.** Ibid.: 4 March **159.** eds. Blake and Louis, *Churchill* p. 421 **160.** Jackson, *Churchill* p. 284 **161.** Pawle, *Warden* p. 106 **162.** Colville, *Fringes* p. 389 **163.** BU AP/20/1/21 **164.** Colville, *Fringes* p. 391 **165.** Rowse 'Visit' pp. 8–13 **166.** Pawle, *Warden* p. 108 **167.** Ibid. p. 106 **168.** Oliver, *Mr Showbusiness* p. 143 **169.** Colville, *Fringes* p. 391 **170.** ed. Dilks, *Cadogan* pp. 380–81 **171.** BU AP/20/1/21 **172.** Potter, *Pim* p. 15 **173.** ed. Nicolson, *Diaries and Letters* II p. 169; Martin, *Downing Street* p. 50 **174.** RA GVI/PRIV/DIARY/COPY/1941: 27 May **175.** *CWP* III p. 750 **176.** RA GVI/PRIV/DIARY/COPY/1941: 5 June **177.** ed. James, *Chips* p. 307 **178.** ed. Dilks, *Cadogan* p. 386 **179.** RA GVI/PRIV/DIARY/COPY/1941: 10 June **180.** *CS* VI p. 6417 **181.** Ibid. p. 6426 **182.** Colville, *Fringes* p. 400 **183.** eds. Blake and Louis, *Churchill* p. 418 **184.** Pawle, *Warden* p. 118 **185.** ed. Dilks, *Cadogan* p. 389 **186.** BU AP/20/1/21 **187.** Gilbert, *Other Club* p. 176 **188.** Colville, *Fringes* p. 404 **189.** Ibid. **190.** Ibid. p. 405 **191.** *CS* VI p. 6428 **192.** Ibid. p. 6429 **193.** Ibid. p. 6431 **194.** Ibid. **195.** Colville, *Fringes* pp. 405–6 **196.** Ibid. p. 406 **197.** OB VI pp. 1122–3 **198.** ed. Hassall, *Ambrosia* p. 178 **199.** Colville, *Fringes* p. 405

## 25. 'Being Met Together': June 1941–January 1942

**1.** ed. Muller, *Contemporaries* p. xxix **2.** WSC, *Marl* I p. 775 **3.** RA GVI/PRIV/DIARY/COPY/1941: 24 June **4.** ed. James, *Chips* p. 308 **5.** *CS* VI p. 6432 **6.** Ibid. **7.** Ibid. p. 6438 **8.** Ruane, *Bomb* pp. 24–6 **9.** Farmelo, *Bomb* pp. 37–8; Ruane, *Bomb* passim **10.** Ruane, *Bomb* p. 26 **11.** Capet, 'Scientific' p. 9 **12.** Pawle, *Warden* p. 123 **13.** Colville, *Fringes* pp. 412–13 **14.** Ibid. p. 412 **15.** Ibid. **16.** *CS* VI p. 6450 **17.** Ibid. p. 6451 **18.** WSC, *TSWW* III p. 344 **19.** ed. Gorodetsky, *Maisky Diaries* p. 374 **20.** Kennedy, *Business* p. 80 **21.** CAC HARV 3/1/part 2 **22.** CAC HARV 1/1; BU AP 20/1/23 **23.** Colville, *Fringes* p. 415 **24.** WSC, *Unrelenting* p. 198 **25.** *Spectator* 22 October 2016 p. 33 **26.** Colville, *Fringes* p. 416 **27.** Ibid. p. 417 **28.** CAC EADE 2/2 **29.** Ibid. **30.** Ibid. **31.** Pawle, *Warden* p. 123 **32.** James, *Undaunted* p. 226 **33.** *CS* VI pp. 6460–61 **34.** ed. Gorodetsky, *Maisky Diaries* pp. 377–8 **35.** Colville, *Fringes* p. 423 **36.** Ibid. p. 424 **37.** CAC ACAD 7/2 **38.** Ibid. **39.** Martin, *Downing Street* p. 56 **40.** CAC ACAD 7/2 **41.** Pawle, *Warden* p. 126 **42.** WSC, *TSWW* III p. 381 **43.** Potter, *Pim* p. 18 **44.** ed. Stuart, *Reith Diaries* p. 283 **45.** Pawle, *Warden* p. 127 **46.** ed. Dilks, *Cadogan* pp. 396–7 **47.** Pawle, *Warden* p. 127 **48.** Martin, *Downing Street* p. 57 **49.** Pawle, *Warden* p. 126 **50.** ed. Dilks, *Cadogan* p. 396 **51.** Ibid. **52.** Potter, *Pim* p. 18 **53.** Pawle, *Warden* p. 127 **54.** CAC ACAD 7/2 **55.** WSC, *TSWW* I p. 345 **56.** ed. Ward, *Closest Companion* p. 141 **57.** WSC, *Marl* I p. 825 **58.** Colville, *Fringes* p. 624 **59.** WSC, *TSWW* III p. 724 **60.** CAC ACAD 7/2 **61.** WSC, *TSWW* III p. 384 **62.** Martin, *Downing Street* p. 58 **63.** CAC ACAD 7/2 **64.** Potter, *Pim* p. 21 **65.** Pawle, *Warden* p. 128 **66.** Martin, *Downing Street* p. 60 **67.** ed. Dilks, *Cadogan* p. 402 **68.** RA GVI/PRIV/DIARY/COPY/1941: 19 August **69.** Roberts, *Eminent Churchillians* pp. 256–8 **70.** Gretton, *Naval Person* pp. 300–301 **71.** *CS* VI p. 64 **72.** Snyder, *Black Earth* p. 146 **73.** *CS* VI p. 6477 **74.** WSC, *Unrelenting* pp. 310–11 **75.** Colville, *Fringes* p. 432 **76.** Ibid. p. 434 **77.** Ibid. p. 433 **78.** Ibid. p. 434 **79.** ed. Gorodetsky, *Maisky Diaries* p. 386 **80.** Ibid. **81.** Ibid. pp. 386–7 **82.** Ibid. p. 387 **83.** Ibid. pp. 386–7 **84.** Colville, *Fringes* p. 437 **85.** CAC BRGS 1/3 **86.** ed. Dilks, *Cadogan* p. 405 **87.** BA AP/20/1/21 **88.** Ibid. **89.** Martin, *Downing Street* p. 61 **90.** RA GVI/PRIV/DIARY/COPY/1941: 11 September **91.** Colville, *Fringes* p. 439 **92.** NA CAB 65/23 WM (41) 94 **93.** NA CAB 65/23 WM (41) 98 **94.** ed. Kennedy, *Grand Strategies* p. 59 **95.** Ibid. p. 60 **96.** BU AP/20/1/21 **97.** Colville, *Fringes* p. 439 **98.** *CIHOW* p. 548 **99.** Colville, *Fringes* p. 440 **100.** WSC, *TSWW* III p. 737 **101.** Colville, *Fringes* p. 441 **102.** Ibid. **103.** Ibid. p. 442 **104.** Pawle, *Warden* p. 134 **105.** Colville, *Fringes* p. 443 **106.** Ibid. **107.** NA PREM 8/724 **108.** LHC Dill Papers 3/1/12 **109.** Ibid. **110.** Colville, *Fringes* p. 275 **111.** Ibid. p. 443; CAC SCHL 1/2/1 **112.** *CS* VI p. 6495 **113.** Aspinall-Oglander, *Keyes* p. 409 **114.** Martin, *Downing Street* p. 64 **115.** RA GVI/PRIV/DIARY/COPY/1941: 7 October **116.** Pawle, *Warden* p. 133 **117.** Bryant, *Turn of the Tide* p. 261 **118.** eds. Blake and Louis, *Churchill* p. 423 **119.** BU AP/20/1/21 **120.** Ibid. **121.** Ibid. **122.** Ibid. **123.** ed. Kimball, *Complete Correspondence* I pp. 249–50 **124.** Farmelo, *Bomb* p. 195 **125.** Ibid. pp. 191–2 **126.** Churchill, *Twenty-One Years* p. 127 **127.** NA CAB 69/2 D (41) 64 **128.** eds. Danchev and Todman, *War Diaries* p. 192 **129.** Greenberg, *Welchman* p. 46 **130.** ed. Nicolson, *Diaries and Letters* II p. 189 **131.** CAC HARV 1/1 **132.** *CWP* III pp. 1391–2 **133.** *CS* VI p. 6499 **134.** Ibid. p. 6501 **135.** WSC, *Dawn* p. 24 **136.** ed. James, *Chips* p. 313 **137.** *CS* VI p. 6510 **138.** Colville, *Fringes* p. 188 **139.** eds. Todman and Danchev, *War Diaries* p. xvi **140.** WSC, *WC* III p. 193 **141.** Moran, *Struggle* p. 113 **142.** ed. Taylor, *Crozier* p. 142 **143.** *FH* no. 130 pp. 34–6 **144.** Howarth, *Intelligence Chief Extraordinary* p. 166 **145.** Macmillan, *War Diaries* p. 295 **146.** Martin, *Downing Street* p. 64 **147.** CAC BRGS **148.** CAC EADE 2/2 **149.** Ibid. **150.** Ibid. **151.** Ibid. **152.** Ibid. **153.** eds. Danchev and Todman, *War Diaries* p. 207 **154.** Sherwood, *Roosevelt and Hopkins* p. 349; Pawle, *Warden* pp. 143, 6–7; Martin, *Downing Street* p. 67 **155.** *CS* VI p. 6504 **156.** Hansard vol. 376 col. 1359 **157.** WSC, *TSWW* III pp. 542–3 **158.** CAC EADE 2/2 **159.** WSC, *TSWW* III pp. 539–40 **160.** Ibid.

p. 540 **161.** Ramsden, 'Historian' p. 14 n. 46 **162.** WSC, *End* p. 173 **163.** WSC, *TSWW* III p. 568 **164.** ed. Kimball, *Complete Correspondence* I p. 283 **165.** WSC, *TSWW* III p. 608 **166.** RA PS/PSO/GVI/C/069/12 **167.** ed. Nicolson, *Diaries and Letters* II p. 194 **168.** ed. James, *Chips* pp. 313–14 **169.** RA GVI/PRIV/DIARY/COPY/1941: 9 December **170.** RA GVI/PRIV/DIARY/COPY/1942: 23 January **171.** Pawle, *Warden* p. 144 **172.** WSC, *TSWW* IV p. 43 **173.** Pawle, *Warden* p. 144 **174.** *CS* VI p. 6533 **175.** CAC HARV 1/1 **176.** Ibid. **177.** Martin, *Downing Street* p. 68 **178.** OB VI p. 1274 **179.** RA GVI/PRIV/DIARY/COPY/1941: 12 December **180.** ed. Thorne, *Seven Christmases* p. 103 **181.** ed. Soames, *Speaking* p. 459 **182.** Ibid. **183.** Ibid. **184.** Martin, *Downing Street* p. 69 **185.** Pawle, *Warden* p. 146 **186.** ed. Thorne, *Seven Christmases* p. 104 **187.** ed. Soames, *Speaking* p. 460 **188.** ed. Thorne, *Seven Christmases* p. 104 **189.** *CWP* III p. 1633 **190.** Ibid. p. 1634 **191.** Ibid. p. 1635 **192.** Ibid. p. 1636 **193.** Ibid. p. 1639 **194.** Ibid. p. 1642 **195.** Ibid. **196.** Ibid. p. 1643 **197.** Ibid. p. 1650 **198.** ed. Thorne, *Seven Christmases* p. 111; CAC JACB 1/12 **199.** Stelzer, *Dinner with Churchill* p. 65 **200.** ed. Thorne, *Seven Christmases* p. 122 **201.** Pawle, *Warden* p. 151; Martin, *Downing Street* p. 69 **202.** Symonds, *Neptune* p. 33 **203.** Pawle, *Warden* p. 150 **204.** ed. Soames, *Speaking* p. 548 **205.** *CS* VI p. 6535 **206.** BIYU Halifax Diary 25 December 1941 **207.** Meacham, *Franklin and Winston* p. 86 **208.** *CS* VI p. 6537 **209.** Ibid. **210.** Ibid. p. 6539 **211.** Ibid. p. 6540 **212.** Moran, *Struggle* p. 16 **213.** Vale and Scadding, 'Myocardial Infarction' passim; Mather, 'Hardiness and Resilience' pp. 83–97 **214.** ed. Kennedy, *Grand Strategies* p. 53 **215.** NA CAB 80/33 COS (42) 77 **216.** *CS* VII p. 6776 **217.** WSC, *WC* II p. 22 **218.** Freudenberg, *Churchill and Australia* p. 1 **219.** Ibid. **220.** Hancock and Gowing, *British War Economy* pp. 367–8, 373; Postan, *Production* p. 247 **221.** Pawle, *Warden* p. 152 **222.** *CS* VI p. 6543 **223.** Ibid. p. 6545 **224.** Weidhorn, *Rhetoric* p. 134 n. 14 **225.** Karsh, 'Portraits' pp. 13–14 **226.** Pawle, *Warden* p. 152 **227.** Dilks, *Dominion* p. 220 **228.** WSC, *TSWW* III pp. 605–7 **229.** *CIHOW* p. 365 **230.** Pawle, *Warden* p. 153 **231.** Martin, *Downing Street* p. 72 **232.** Pawle, *Warden* p. 155 **233.** BIYU Halifax Diary 18 February 1942 **234.** Martin, *Downing Street* p. 73 **235.** BIYU Halifax Diary 18 February 1942 **236.** Martin, *Downing Street* p. 73 **237.** WSC, *TSWW* IV pp. 727–8 **238.** Bryant, *Turn of the Tide* p. 231

## 26. Disaster: January–June 1942

**1.** WSC, *TSWW* IV p. 78 **2.** ed. Nicolson, *Diaries and Letters* II p. 238 **3.** CAC BRGS 2/11 18 January 1942 **4.** Ibid. **5.** Ibid. **6.** Ibid. **7.** RA GVI/PRIV/DIARY/COPY/1942: 19 January **8.** *Manchester Guardian* 19 January 1942 **9.** ed. Dilks, *Cadogan* p. 429 **10.** OB VII p. 40 **11.** ed. Kimball, *Complete Correspondence* I p. 337 **12.** ed. James, *Chips* p. 317 **13.** ed. Nicolson, *Diaries and Letters* II p. 206 **14.** NA CAB 69/4/23 **15.** BU AP 20/1/22 **16.** WSC, *TSWW* II p. 15 **17.** CAC HARV 2/1 part 1 **18.** *CS* VI p. 6555 **19.** Ibid. **20.** Hansard vol. 377 col. 685 **21.** *CS* VI p. 6559 **22.** Ibid. p. 6565 **23.** Ibid. p. 6558 **24.** OB VII p. 51 **25.** *CS* VI p. 6571 **26.** ed. Nicolson, *Diaries and Letters* II p. 209 **27.** ed. Dilks, *Cadogan* p. 433 **28.** Ibid. p. 4 **29.** CAC BRGS 2/11 2 February 1942 **30.** WSC, *TSWW* IV p. 87 **31.** RA GVI/PRIV/DIARY/COPY/1942: 3 February **32.** ed. Dilks, *Cadogan* pp. 432–3 **33.** RA GVI/PRIV/DIARY/COPY/1942: 10 February **34.** Brodhurst, *Anchor* p. 208 **35.** ed. Dilks, *Cadogan* p. 433 **36.** ed. Nicolson, *Diaries and Letters* II p. 211 **37.** ed. Soames, *Speaking* pp. 463–4 **38.** ed. James, *Chips* p. 321 **39.** Overy, *Air War* pp. 122–5 **40.** LHC Kennedy Papers 4/2/4 **41.** *CS* VI p. 6587 **42.** Ibid. p. 6584 **43.** Ibid. p. 6585 **44.** Ibid. p. 6587 **45.** Ibid. **46.** ed. Nicolson, *Diaries and Letters* II p. 212 **47.** LHC Kennedy Papers 4/2/4 **48.** ed. Lochner, *Goebbels Diaries* p. 9 **49.** Pawle, *Warden* p. 163 **50.** Potter, *Pim* pp. 22–3 **51.** ed. Kennedy, *Grand Strategies* p. 55 **52.** OB VII p. 34 **53.** Other Club Betting Book **54.** James, *Undaunted* p. 224 **55.** RA GVI/PRIV/DIARY/COPY/1942: 16 February **56.** ed. Gorodetsky, *Maisky Diaries* p. 411 **57.** ed. James, *Chips* p. 322 **58.** *CS* VI p. 6597 **59.** Lloyd George, *David & Winston* p. 238 **60.** BIYU Halifax Diary 20 February 1942 **61.** ed. Hart-Davis,

*King's Counsellor* p. 210 **62.** Chisholm and Davie, *Beaverbrook* p. 429 **63.** CAC MRGN 1/4/8 **64.** CAC MRGN 1/4/9 **65.** ed. Nicolson, *Diaries and Letters* II p. 213 **66.** ed. Stuart, *Reith Diaries* p. 59 **67.** RA GVI/PRIV/DIARY/COPY/1942: 24 February **68.** Brodhurst, *Anchor* p. 208 **69.** CAC CHAR 20/53A/98–9 **70.** ed. Dilks, *Cadogan* p. 440 **71.** LHC Kennedy Papers 4/2/4 **72.** Ibid. **73.** ed. Nicolson, *Diaries and Letters* II p. 223 **74.** *Sunday Dispatch* 8 March 1942 **75.** CAC BRGS 2/11 9 March 1942 **76.** Ibid. **77.** RA GVI/PRIV/DIARY/COPY/1942: 21 March **78.** *CS* VII p. 7445 **79.** ed. Riff, *Dictionary* p. 170 **80.** ed. Coward, *Gandhi* p. 243 **81.** Tunzelmann, *Indian Summer* pp. 110–11 **82.** Herman, *Gandhi and Churchill* p. 446 **83.** Roberts, *Holy Fox* p. 72 **84.** RA GVI/PRIV/DIARY/COPY/1942: 10 March **85.** Ibid.: 17 March **86.** ed. Gorodetsky, *Maisky Diaries* p. 417 **87.** Ibid. p. 419 **88.** Ibid. p. 420 **89.** Ibid. p. 421 **90.** Ibid. **91.** CAC BRGS 2/12 23 March 1942 **92.** Borneman, *MacArthur at War* p. 173 **93.** Ibid. **94.** ed. Kimball, *Complete Correspondence* I p. 421 **95.** WSC, *TSWW* IV p. 202 **96.** Ibid. p. 454 **97.** CAC BRGS 2/12 30 March 1942 **98.** eds. Danchev and Todman, *War Diaries* p. 243 **99.** LHC Kennedy Papers 4/2/4 **100.** BU AP 20/1/22 **101.** Ibid. **102.** Hatfield House 5M/62/1 **103.** eds. Blake and Louis, *Churchill* p. 424 **104.** Roberts, *Masters and Commanders* pp. 137–66 **105.** ed. Kimball, *Complete Correspondence* I p. 446 **106.** Sherwood, *Roosevelt and Hopkins* pp. 530–31 **107.** WSC, *TSWW* IV p. 195 **108.** Lowenheim, *Wartime Correspondence* p. 204 **109.** WSC, *TSWW* IV p. 185 **110.** ed. Kimball, *Complete Correspondence* I pp. 448–9 **111.** NA CAB 69/4/59 **112.** NA CAB 69/4 COS Committee no. 118 14 April 1942 **113.** OB VII p. 89 **114.** NA CAB 69/4 Defence Committee no. 10 14 April 1942 **115.** NA CAB 69/4/61–2 **116.** WSC, *TSWW* IV pp. 289–90 **117.** Ismay, *Memoirs* p. 250 **118.** Moran, *Struggle* p. 35 **119.** eds. Danchev and Todman, *War Diaries* p. 248 **120.** Ibid. **121.** Ibid. p. 249 **122.** ed. Kimball, *Complete Correspondence* I p. 450 **123.** Pawle, *Warden* p. 168 **124.** ed. Kimball, *Complete Correspondence* I p. 523 **125.** Ibid. **126.** Ibid. pp. 458–9 **127.** ed. Nicolson, *Diaries and Letters* II p. 223 **128.** *CS* VI p. 6615 **129.** Ibid. **130.** ed. Nicolson, *Diaries and Letters* II p. 223 **131.** Ibid. p. 224 **132.** ed. James, *Chips* p. 327 **133.** ed. Soames, *Speaking* p. 464 **134.** Ibid. p. 465 **135.** Ibid. **136.** CAC RDCH 1/2/46 **137.** PA BBK C/92 **138.** Colville, *Fringes* p. 195 **139.** Fladgates Archives Moir Doc ch. II **140.** NA CAB 195/1 WM (42) 53rd **141.** WSC, *TSWW* IV p. 755 **142.** LHC Kennedy Papers 4/2/4 **143.** *CS* VI p. 6631 **144.** Ibid. p. 6633 **145.** Ibid. p. 6637 **146.** RA GVI/PRIV/DIARY/COPY/1942: 19 May **147.** Pawle, *Warden* p. 172 **148.** ed. Kimball, *Complete Correspondence* I p. 497 **149.** ed. Gorodetsky, *Maisky Diaries* p. 432 **150.** WSC, *TSWW* I pp. 288–9 **151.** ed. Dilks, *Cadogan* p. 450 **152.** RA GVI/PRIV/DIARY/COPY/1942: 28 May **153.** ed. Kimball, *Complete Correspondence* II p. 494 **154.** *FRUS*, 1942, III p. 594 **155.** WSC, *TSWW* V p. 66 **156.** RA GVI/PRIV/DIARY/COPY/1942: 30 June **157.** ed. Dilks, *Cadogan* p. 456 **158.** BU AP 20/1/22 **159.** James, *Undaunted* p. 238 **160.** RA PS/PSO/GVI/C/069/17 **161.** CAC BRGS 2/12 8 June 1942 **162.** Ibid. **163.** NA CAB 195/1 WM (42) 74th **164.** Ibid. **165.** LHC Kennedy Papers 4/2/4 **166.** eds. Danchev and Todman, *War Diaries* p. 279 **167.** LHC Kennedy Papers 4/2/4 **168.** *TCD* 17 p. 795 **169.** Pawle, *Warden* p. 173 **170.** Martin, *Downing Street* p. 81 **171.** WSC, *TSWW* IV p. 341 **172.** Reynolds, *Command* p. 334 **173.** Ibid. **174.** Ibid. p. 335 **175.** Ruane, *Bomb* p. 43 **176.** Ibid. pp. 44–5 **177.** LHC Kennedy Papers 4/2/4 23 June 1942 **178.** WSC, *TSWW* IV p. 344 **179.** Halle, *Irrepressible* p. 200 **180.** WSC, *TSWW* IV p. 344 **181.** ed. Ward, *Closest Companion* p. 167

## 27. Desert Victory: June–November 1942

**1.** *CS* VI p. 6661 **2.** WSC, *Marl* II p. 381 **3.** Birkenhead Papers 65/A3 **4.** ed. James, *Chips* p. 333 **5.** Gallup, *Opinion Polls* p. 61 **6.** CAC HARV 2/1 part 1 **7.** WSC, *TSWW* IV p. 347 **8.** CAC RDCH 1/3/1 **9.** eds. Danchev and Todman, *War Diaries* p. 271 **10.** ed. Dilks, *Cadogan* p. 429 **11.** ed. Hassall, *Ambrosia* pp. 220–21 **12.** WSC, *TSWW* IV p. 353 **13.** ed. James, *Chips* p. 334 **14.** Hansard vol. 381 col. 528 **15.** *CS* VI p. 6646 **16.**

Ibid. p. 6649 **17.** Ibid. p. 6657 **18.** Ibid. p. 6661 **19.** ed. Dilks, *Cadogan* p. 460 **20.** RA GVI/PRIV/DIARY/COPY/1942: 7 July **21.** ed. Gorodetsky, *Maisky Diaries* p. 440 **22.** Ibid. p. 442 **23.** Ibid. **24.** Ibid. p. 443 **25.** NA CAB 65/30 WM (42) 64 **26.** ed. Gorodetsky, *Maisky Diaries* p. 449 **27.** Ibid. p. 448 **28.** Vego, 'PQ17' p. 84 **29.** ed. Dilks, *Cadogan* p. 461 **30.** Ibid. p. 462 **31.** eds. Danchev and Todman, *War Diaries* p. 282 **32.** Jacob, 'Grand Strategy' p. 532 **33.** ed. Dilks, *Cadogan* p. 463 **34.** Jacob, 'Grand Strategy' p. 533 **35.** RA GVI/PRIV/DIARY/COPY/1942: 28 July **36.** Gallup, *Opinion Polls* pp. 61–113 **37.** ed. Wheeler-Bennett, *Action* p. 252 **38.** Eden, *Reckoning* p. 333 **39.** RA PS/PSO/GVI/C/069/19 **40.** Pawle, *Warden* p. 189 **41.** Ibid. **42.** ed. Dilks, *Cadogan* p. 466 **43.** Courtenay, 'Smuts' p. 59 **44.** ed. Keegan, *Churchill and his Generals* pp. 129–30 **45.** ed. Dilks, *Cadogan* p. 467 **46.** WSC, *TSWW* IV p. 414 **47.** ed. Evans, *Killearn Diaries* p. 245 **48.** Ibid. pp. 245–6 **49.** WSC, *TSWW* IV pp. 412–24 **50.** Keegan, *Churchill and his Generals* p. 11 **51.** ed. Nicolson, *Diaries and Letters* II p. 259 **52.** Ibid. **53.** ed. Wheeler-Bennett, *Action* p. 254 **54.** WSC, *TSWW* IV p. 412 **55.** *CS* VI p. 6751 **56.** ed. Dilks, *Cadogan* p. 469 **57.** ed. Soames, *Speaking* p. 467 **58.** Ibid. **59.** WSC, *Marl* I p. 569 **60.** ed. Soames, *Speaking* p. 467 **61.** Macintyre, *Rogue Heroes* p. 167 **62.** ed. Soames, *Speaking* p. 466; OB VII p. 172 **63.** CAC ACAD 7/2 **64.** Pawle, *Warden* p. 5 **65.** Ibid. p. 194 **66.** Owen, *Tedder* p. 171 **67.** Pawle, *Warden* p. 195; WSC, *TSWW* IV pp. 428–9 **68.** *FH* no. 140 p. 29 **69.** NA FO 800/300/50 p. 123 **70.** Owen, *Tedder* p. 171 **71.** CAC ACAD 7/2 **72.** Pawle, *Warden* p. 6 **73.** Ibid. pp. 6, 194 **74.** CAC ACAD 7/2 **75.** CAC KENN 4/2/4 p. 302 **76.** Gillies, *Radical* p. 131 **77.** WSC, *TSWW* IV p. 433 **78.** Ibid. p. 432; OB VII p. 178 **79.** Gillies, *Radical* p. 131 **80.** Pawle, *Warden* p. 5 **81.** *Daily Telegraph* obituary of Patrick Kinna 18 March 2009 **82.** NA FO 800/300/138–45 **83.** Ibid. **84.** Gillies, *Radical* p. 135 **85.** NA FO 800/300/138–45 **86.** Gillies, *Radical* p. 133 **87.** ed. Wheeler-Bennett, *Action* p. 255 **88.** CAC ACAD 7/2 **89.** Ibid. **90.** Birse, *Memoirs* p. 103; Moran, *Struggle* p. 63 **91.** Gillies, *Radical* p. 133; Pawle, *Warden* p. 194 **92.** Reynolds, *Command* p. 345 **93.** Ibid. p. 346 **94.** CAC CHUR 4/25A/21–3 **95.** CAC ISMAY 2/3/261/1 **96.** Reynolds, *Command* pp. 347–8, 503 **97.** Ibid. p. 348 **98.** eds. Danchev and Todman, *War Diaries* p. 313 **99.** Soames, *Speaking* p. 469 **100.** Martin, *Downing Street* p. 84 **101.** Stuart, *Within* p. 130 **102.** CAC EADE 2/2 **103.** Ibid. **104.** Andrew and Mitrokhin, *Mitrokhin Archive* p. 157 **105.** Dilks, 'Churchill and the Russians' p. 8 **106.** *CS* VI p. 6675 **107.** RA GVI/PRIV/DIARY/COPY/1942: 27 August **108.** *CS* VI p. 6665 **109.** Colville, *Fringes* p. 350 **110.** eds. Barnes and Nicholson, *Empire at Bay* p. 833 **111.** Herman, *Gandhi and Churchill* p. 498 **112.** *CS* VII p. 6995 **113.** CAC EADE 2/2 **114.** ed. Dilks, *Cadogan* p. 480 **115.** Ibid. p. 477 **116.** ed. Nicolson, *Diaries and Letters* II p. 241 **117.** Browne, *Sunset* p. 76 **118.** Gallup, *Opinion Polls* p. 62 **119.** Cripps Papers SC11/2/74, 75, 76, 81, 82 **120.** Cripps Papers SC11/2/84 **121.** ed. Nicolson, *Diaries and Letters* II p. 241 **122.** Ibid. p. 244 **123.** Martin, *Downing Street* p. 88 **124.** OB VII p. 239 **125.** PA BBK C/92 **126.** *CS* VI p. 6680 **127.** WSC, *End* p. 241 **128.** Ibid. p. 243 **129.** ed. Dilks, *Cadogan* p. 483 **130.** *TCD* 17 p. 1278 **131.** ed. Hart-Davis, *King's Counsellor* pp. 66–7 **132.** ed. Dilks, *Cadogan* p. 486 **133.** RA GVI/PRIV/DIARY/COPY/1942: 3 November **134.** James, *Undaunted* p. 223 **135.** RA GVI/PRIV/DIARY/COPY/1942: 3 November **136.** ed. Dilks, *Cadogan* p. 488 **137.** Lord Chalfont in ed. Hastings, *Anecdotes* p. 413 **138.** ed. Hassall, *Ambrosia* p. 259 **139.** ed. Dilks, *Cadogan* p. 489 **140.** ed. Nicolson, *Diaries and Letters* II p. 260 **141.** *CS* VI p. 6693

## 28. 'One Continent Redeemed': November 1942–September 1943

**1.** *CS* VI p. 6704 **2.** ed. Gorodetsky, *Maisky Diaries* p. 510 **3.** eds. Danchev and Todman, *War Diaries* p. 340 **4.** *CS* VI p. 6695 **5.** Ibid. **6.** Ibid. p. 6707 **7.** Ibid. p. 6701 **8.** Ibid. p. 6698 **9.** Ibid. p. 6702 **10.** Hinsley, *British Intelligence* I pp. 456–7 **11.** eds. Blake and Louis, *Churchill* p. 424 **12.** Ossad, *Bradley* p. 240 **13.** RA GVI/PRIV/DIARY/COPY/1942: 17 November **14.** Howard, *Grand Strategy* IV p. 231 **15.** WSC, *Secret* p. 81 **16.** Ibid. p. 83 **17.** Roosevelt, *As He Saw It* p. 73 **18.** Halle, *Irrepressible* p. 212 **19.**

Ibid. p. 213 **20.** ed. Hart-Davis, *King's Counsellor* p. 76 **21.** *TCD* 18 pp. 59–60 **22.** RA GVI/PRIV/DIARY/COPY/1943: 1 January **23.** Ibid.: 12 January **24.** Pawle, *Warden* p. 3 **25.** Colville, *Fringes* p. 461; OB VII p. 634 **26.** Ismay, *Memoirs* p. 287 **27.** *CS* VII p. 6893 **28.** ed. Soames, *Speaking* p. 473 **29.** Ibid. p. 475 **30.** Ibid. **31.** WSC, *TSWW* IV p. 622 **32.** Rogers, *Folly* p. 25 **33.** Ibid. p. 24 **34.** NA CAB 120/77 **35.** CAC BRGS 1/3 **36.** NA CAB 120/77 **37.** ed. Gorodetsky, *Maisky Diaries* p. 482 **38.** NA CAB 120/77 **39.** Ibid. **40.** Ibid. **41.** *CS* VII p. 6741 **42.** eds. Danchev and Todman, *War Diaries* p. 379 **43.** Sandys, *Chasing Churchill* p. 159 **44.** BU AP 20/1/23 **45.** Stuart, *Within* p. 157 **46.** PA BBK/D/480 **47.** *CS* VII p. 6742 **48.** Ibid. p. 6749 **49.** Ibid. p. 6751 **50.** Ibid. p. 6752 **51.** ed. Nicolson, *Diaries and Letters* II p. 279 **52.** RA PS/PSO/GVI/C/069/29 **53.** ed. Nicolson, *Diaries and Letters* II p. 284 **54.** Rose, *Nursing Churchill* p. 158 **55.** Ibid. p. 159 **56.** Ibid. p. 164 **57.** *New York Times* 22 January 2006 **58.** *CS* VII p. 6760 **59.** Ibid. p. 6762 **60.** Ibid. p. 6763 **61.** Ibid. p. 6765 **62.** Marian Holmes's Diary p. 1 **63.** ed. Hart-Davis, *King's Counsellor* p. 117 **64.** eds. Danchev and Todman, *War Diaries* p. 389 **65.** Ibid. pp. 389–90 **66.** ed. Eade, *Contemporaries* p. 155 **67.** Howard, *Grand Strategy* IV p. 369 **68.** Dilks, 'Churchill and the Russians' p. 11 **69.** *CS* III p. 2771 **70.** ed. Nicolson, *Diaries and Letters* II p. 291 **71.** ed. Gorodetsky, *Maisky Diaries* p. 509 **72.** Ibid. p. 510 **73.** BU AP 20/1/23 **74.** RA PS/PSO/GVI/C/069/31 **75.** BU AP 20/1/23 **76.** RA PS/PSO/GVI/C/069/34 **77.** Roskill, *Admirals* pp. 229–30; O'Connell, 'Air Power Gap'; Dimbleby, *Battle of the Atlantic* passim **78.** Bell, 'Air Power' p. 693 **79.** Ibid. p. 717 **80.** Ibid. p. 718 **81.** Sterling, 'Getting' p. 14 **82.** CAC CHAR 20/111 **83.** ed. Soames, *Speaking* p. 481 **84.** WSC, *Victory* p. 174 **85.** *CS* VII p. 6775 **86.** Ibid. p. 6782 **87.** Kennedy, *Business* p. 274 **88.** ed. Gorodetsky, *Maisky Diaries* p. 481 **89.** Ibid. **90.** WSC *TSWW* IV p. 727 **91.** Sterling, 'Getting' p. 13 **92.** ed. Soames, *Speaking* p. 484 **93.** WSC *TSWW* IV p. 730 **94.** ed. Soames, *Speaking* p. 484 **95.** Ibid. **96.** ed. Gorodetsky, *Maisky Diaries* p. 522 **97.** *Stars and Stripes* 7 June 1943 **98.** eds. Danchev and Todman, *War Diaries* p. 416 **99.** Eden, *Reckoning* p. 389 **100.** *Stars and Stripes* 7 June 1943 **101.** Martin, *Downing Street* p. 104 **102.** eds. Danchev and Todman, *War Diaries* pp. 420–21 **103.** RA GVI/PRIV/DIARY/COPY/1943: 6 April **104.** OB VII p. 437 **105.** Gilbert, *Other Club* p. 168 **106.** Overy, *Bombing War* p. 408 **107.** Rose, *Nursing Churchill* p. 152 **108.** Weeks, *Organisation and Equipment* p. 8 **109.** NA CAB 195/1 WM (43) 92nd **110.** Ibid. **111.** Ibid. **112.** Ibid. **113.** WSC, *Onwards* p. 136 **114.** Jacob, 'High Level' p. 367 **115.** RA VI/PRIV/DIARY/COPY/1943: 29 June **116.** *TCD* 18 p. 1811 **117.** WSC *TSWW* IV pp. 651–2 **118.** Martin, *Downing Street* p. 109 **119.** ed. Eade, *Contemporaries* p. 155 **120.** ed. Kennedy, *Grand Strategies* p. 64 **121.** Marian Holmes's Diary p. 3 **122.** Lamb, *War Leader* p. 225 **123.** WSC *TSWW* V p. 572 **124.** Ibid. **125.** BU AP 20/1/23 **126.** ed. Hart-Davis, *King's Counsellor* p. 138 **127.** Kersaudy, *Churchill and de Gaulle* p. 248; ed. Nicolson, *Diaries and Letters* II p. 303 **128.** ed. Hart-Davis, *King's Counsellor* p. 231 **129.** BU AP 20/1/23 **130.** Ibid. **131.** Ibid. **132.** ed. Hart-Davis, *King's Counsellor* p. 143 **133.** Ibid. **134.** ed. James, *Chips* p. 345 **135.** Mukerjee, *Churchill's Secret War* passim; Langworth, *Myth*, pp. 149–54; Herman, 'Absent Churchill'; Mitter, *China's War with Japan* p. 273; https://winstonchurchill.hillsdale.edu/did-churchill-cause-the-bengal-famine/ **136.** James, *Churchill and Empire* p. 304; Fort, *Wavell* p. 361 **137.** Fort, *Wavell* p. 362 **138.** *TCD* 19 p. 414 **139.** CAC CHUR 23/11; Langworth, *Myth* p. 150 **140.** NA CAB 65/41 14 February 1944 **141.** *TCD* 19 p. 755 **142.** Fort, *Wavell* p. 364 **143.** Collingham, *Taste of War* p. 148 **144.** eds. Barnes and Nicholson, *Empire at Bay*, pp. 933–4 **145.** Browne, *Sunset* p. 133 **146.** James, *Churchill and Empire* p. 184 **147.** NA CAB 65/41 7 February 1944 **148.** *TCD* 19 p. 1543 **149.** Herman, 'Absent Churchill' p. 51 **150.** *TCD* 19 p. 2554 **151.** ed. Kimball, *Complete Correspondence* III p. 117 **152.** *FH* no. 142 p. 35 **153.** https://winstonchurchill.hillsdale.edu/churcills-secret-war-bengal-famine-1943/ **154.** ed. Hart-Davis, *King's Counsellor* p. 143 **155.** Ibid. **156.** BU AP 20/1/23 **157.** Gilbert, *Search* p. 225 **158.** Marian Holmes's Diary pp. 3–4 **159.** BU AP 20/23 **160.** *CS* VII p. 6811 **161.** ed. Nicolson, *Diaries and Letters* II pp. 308–9 **162.** BU AP 20/23 **163.** OB VII p. 467 **164.** WSC, *TSWW* V p. 583 **165.** Martin, *Downing Street* p. 110 **166.** Dilks, *Dominion* p. 265 **167.**

OB VII p. 469 **168.** ed. Kimball, *Complete Correspondence* II pp. 389–402 **169.** eds. Danchev and Todman, *War Diaries* pp. 441–2 **170.** Jacob, 'Grand Strategy' p. 534 **171.** eds. Danchev and Todman, *War Diaries* pp. 447, 450–51 **172.** WSC, *TSWW* V pp. 83–4 **173.** OB VII p. 484 **174.** CAC CHUR 20/152 **175.** ed. Dilks, *Cadogan* p. 559 **176.** Pawle, *Warden* p. 150: Pilpel, *America* p. 199; ed. Midgley, *Heroic Memory* pp. 25–6 **177.** ed. Hart-Davis, *King's Counsellor* p. 158 **178.** Ibid. **179.** BU AP 20/23 **180.** Martin, *Downing Street* p. 116 **181.** *CS* VII pp. 6823–4 **182.** WSC, *Onwards* p. 185 **183.** *CS* VII p. 6824 **184.** Ibid. **185.** Ibid. p. 6825 **186.** Ibid. p. 6827 **187.** *CIHOW* p. 139

## 29. The Hard Underbelly: September 1943–June 1944

**1.** eds. Danchev and Todman, *War Diaries* p. 680 **2.** Churchill, *Tapestry* p. 69 **3.** Soames, *Clementine* p. 340 **4.** Martin, *Downing Street* p. 116 **5.** BA AP 20/23 **6.** *CS* VII p. 6839 **7.** Ibid. **8.** Ibid. p. 6840 **9.** Ibid. **10.** ed. Nicolson, *Diaries and Letters* II p. 321 **11.** BA AP 20/23 **12.** RA GVI/PRIV/DIARY/COPY/1943: 23 September **13.** Wilson, *Cabinet Office* p. 45 **14.** OB VII p. 710 **15.** Marian Holmes's Diary p. 5 **16.** eds. Danchev and Todman, *War Diaries* p. 459 **17.** Hamilton, *Mantle of Command* passim **18.** RA PS/PSO/GVI/C/069/340 **19.** RA GVI/PRIV/DIARY/COPY/1943: 14 October **20.** WSC, *TSWW* V p. 280 **21.** CAC CHUR 20/122 **22.** CAC EADE 2/2 **23.** Ibid. **24.** Ibid. **25.** Moran, *Struggle* p. 122 **26.** Brodhurst, *Anchor* p. 5 **27.** Potter, *Pim* p. 38 **28.** *CS* VII p. 6869 **29.** Ibid. p. 6871 **30.** Ibid. **31.** ed. Midgley, *Heroic Memory* p. 23 **32.** Marian Holmes's Diary p. 5 **33.** ed. Hart-Davis, *King's Counsellor* p. 176 **34.** Baxter, 'Strategist?' p. 8 **35.** Churchill, *Tapestry* p. 59 **36.** CAC BRGS 1/2 **37.** Churchill, *Tapestry* p. 58 **38.** LHC Kennedy 4/2/5 **39.** Ibid. **40.** ed. Soames, *Speaking* p. 485 **41.** CAC SCHL 1/1/7 **42.** Ibid. **43.** WSC, *TSWW* V p. 635 **44.** Ibid. p. 637 **45.** Churchill, *Tapestry* p. 62 **46.** Martin, *Downing Street* p. 127 **47.** Churchill, *Tapestry* pp. 62–3 **48.** CAC SCHL 1/1/7 **49.** eds. Danchev and Todman, *War Diaries* p. 478 **50.** CAC SCHL 1/1/7 **51.** Ibid. **52.** ed. Soames, *Speaking* p. 487 **53.** Ibid. **54.** Churchill, *Tapestry* p. 63 **55.** Ibid. **56.** Ibid. **57.** Ibid. p. 64 **58.** Ibid. **59.** Martin, *Downing Street* p. 122 **60.** Moran, *Struggle* p. 141 **61.** WSC, *TSWW* V p. 330 **62.** ed. Soames, *Speaking* p. 489 **63.** ed. Sherwood, *Hopkins* II p. 772 **64.** Ibid. p. 774 **65.** *TCD* 19 p. 999 **66.** WSC, *TSWW* V p. 338 **67.** NA CAB 120/113 **68.** Ibid. **69.** ed. Hart-Davis, *King's Counsellor* p. 194 **70.** Stelzer, *Dinner with Churchill* pp. 105–13 **71.** Churchill, *Tapestry* p. 65 **72.** CAC SCHL 1/1/7 **73.** Ibid. **74.** OB VII p. 586 **75.** NA CAB 120/120 **76.** ed. Evans, *Killearn Diaries* p. 267 **77.** Churchill, *Tapestry* p. 67 **78.** Eden, *Reckoning* p. 429 **79.** *CIHOW* p. 184 **80.** eds. Danchev and Todman, *War Diaries* p. 493 **81.** *CIHOW* p. 510 **82.** Thompson, *Sixty* p. 77 **83.** WSC, *TSWW* V p. 373 **84.** Martin, *Downing Street* p. 124 **85.** CAC SCHL 1/8/1 **86.** Martin, *Downing Street* p. 132 **87.** Colville, *Fringes* p. 457 **88.** Martin, *Downing Street* p. 132 **89.** CAC BRGS 1/3 **90.** Martin, *Downing Street* p. 1303 **91.** Major Buckley recollections in Astley Papers **92.** Bryant, *Triumph in the West* pp. 93–4 **93.** Colville, *Fringes* p. 463 **94.** CAC CHUR 20/179 **95.** Colville, *Fringes* p. 464 **96.** ed. Norwich, *Monster* pp. 165–6 **97.** Marian Holmes's Diary pp. 5, 20 **98.** OB VII p. 646; ed. Rose, *Baffy* p. 211 **99.** Martin, *Downing Street* p. 134 **100.** Colville, *Fringes*, p. 465 **101.** Colville, 'Second' p. 6; Potter, *Pim* p. 47 **102.** ed. Nicolson, *Diaries and Letters* II pp. 344–5 **103.** WSC, *Dawn* p. 53 **104.** RA GVI/PRIV/DIARY/COPY/1944: 18 January **105.** Butcher, *Three Years* p. 404 **106.** WSC, *TSWW* V p. 426 **107.** Ibid. p. 432 **108.** Colville, *Fringes* pp. 674–5 **109.** OB VII p. 663 **110.** Colville, *Fringes* p. 476 **111.** CAC BRGS 2/19 **112.** CAC CHUR 20/156 **113.** Meacham, *Franklin and Winston* p. 274 **114.** eds. Danchev and Todman, *War Diaries* p. 525 **115.** Colville, *Fringes* p. 475 **116.** *CS* VII p. 6893 **117.** Colville, *Fringes* p. 476 **118.** Ibid. **119.** WSC, *Dawn* p. 54 **120.** RA GVI/PRIV/DIARY/COPY/1944: 7 March **121.** WSC, *TSWW* V pp. 521, 542–3; OB VII p. 706 **122.** CAC CHAR 20/188A/64–5 **123.** CAC CHAR 20/188A/67–8 **124.** Reynolds, *Command* pp. 403–4 **125.** eds. Danchev and Todman, *War Diaries* p. 533 **126.** LHC ALAB 6/3/9 **127.** Ibid. **128.** CAC CHAR

20/188B/128 **129.** LHC ALAB 6/3/10 **130.** *CS* VII p. 6907 **131.** Ibid. p. 6916 **132.** ed. Hart-Davis, *King's Counsellor* p. 209 **133.** ed. Frank, *Anne Frank Diary* p. 239 **134.** ed. James, *Chips* p. 391 **135.** ed. Nicolson, *Diaries and Letters* II p. 358 **136.** RA GVI/PRIV/DIARY/COPY/1944: 28 March **137.** CAC CAB 69/6 DO (44) 6 **138.** Cohen, 'Churchill at War' pp. 40–49 **139.** WSC, *WC* II p. 21 **140.** eds. Danchev and Todman, *War Diaries* p. 537 **141.** WSC, *TSWW* V p. 618 **142.** Ibid. **143.** James, *Within* p. 112 **144.** Marian Holmes's Diary p. 9 **145.** Ibid. p. 11 **146.** Colville, *Fringes* p. 486 **147.** eds. Bland and Stevens, *Marshall Papers* IV p. 405 **148.** Ibid. **149.** Reynolds, *Command* p. 393 **150.** *CS* VII p. 6921 **151.** Colville, *Fringes* p. 485 **152.** ed. Russell, *Constant* p. 245 **153.** ed. Hart-Davis, *King's Counsellor* p. 230 **154.** eds. Danchev and Todman, *War Diaries* p. 544 **155.** ed. Fergusson, *Business of War* p. 328 **156.** CAC BRGS 2/20 **157.** RA PS/PSO/GVI/C/069/47 **158.** James, *Undaunted* p. 256 **159.** RA PS/PSO/GVI/C/069/34 **160.** James, *Undaunted* p. 257 **161.** Ibid. p. 258 **162.** RA PS/PSO/GVI/C/069/45 **163.** RA GVI/PRIV/DIARY/COPY/1944: 3 June **164.** BL Cunningham Add Mss 52577/28 **165.** CAC LWFD 2/7 **166.** Beevor, *D-Day* p. 21 **167.** CAC BRGS 2/21 **168.** Ibid. **169.** Marian Holmes's Diary p. 11 **170.** ed. Soames, *Speaking* p. 496 **171.** eds. Barnes and Nicholson, *Empire at Bay* p. 986 **172.** CAC BRGS 2/21 **173.** eds. Barnes and Nicholson, *Empire at Bay* pp. 986–7 **174.** BL Cunningham Add Mss 52577/8 **175.** Djilas, *Conversations with Stalin* p. 61 **176.** Macmillan, *Blast* p. 423 **177.** Potter, *Pim* p. 50 **178.** Pawle, *Warden* p. 302; ed. Soames, *Speaking* p. 497; OB VII p. 794

## 30. Liberation: June 1944–January 1945

**1.** *CS* VI p. 6657 **2.** Colville, *Fringes* p. 510 **3.** *CS* VII p. 6947 **4.** ed. Nicolson, *Diaries and Letters* II p. 375 **5.** *CS* VII p. 6972 **6.** WSC, *TSWW* V p. 67 **7.** Stacey, *Victory Campaign* III pp. 119, 652 **8.** WSC, *Dawn* p. 120 **9.** BU AP 20/1/24 **10.** OB VII p. 807 **11.** eds. Danchev and Todman, *War Diaries* p. 557 **12.** Martin, *Downing Street* p. 152 **13.** Ibid. p. 153 **14.** BL Cunningham Add Mss 52577/32 **15.** RA GVI/PRIV/DIARY/COPY/1944: 13 June **16.** Hansard vol. 400 cols. 2293–300 **17.** Nicolson, *Alexander* p. 259 **18.** Bryant, *Triumph in the West* p. 223 **19.** *CIHOW* pp. 290–91 **20.** CAC HARV 4/1/part 2 **21.** *CS* VII p. 6957 **22.** Potter, *Pim* p. 51 **23.** OB VII p. 841 **24.** Ibid. **25.** eds. Blake and Louis, *Churchill* p. 426 **26.** Ibid. **27.** *Spectator* 8 February 2014 p. 11 **28.** ed. Hart-Davis, *King's Counsellor* p. 240 **29.** Marian Holmes's Diary p. 12 **30.** Ibid. **31.** Ibid. p. 14 **32.** WSC, *TSWW* VI p. 50 **33.** eds. Bland and Stevens, *Marshall Papers* IV p. 498 **34.** ed. Kimball, *Complete Correspondence* III pp. 212–13 **35.** Ibid. p. 223 **36.** RA GVI/PRIV/DIARY/COPY/1944: 4 July **37.** ed. Hart-Davis, *King's Counsellor* p. 240 **38.** OB VII p. 843 **39.** ed. Hart-Davis, *King's Counsellor* p. 240 **40.** Gilbert, *Churchill and the Jews* p. 211 **41.** Ibid. **42.** NA PREM 4/51/10 **43.** Gilbert, *Churchill and the Jews* pp. 212–13 **44.** NA PREM 4/51/10 **45.** Gilbert, *Churchill and the Jews* p. 213 **46.** NA FO 371/39454 **47.** OB VII p. 847 and n. 1 **48.** Ibid. p. 847 **49.** Gilbert, *Churchill and the Jews* pp. 189–90 **50.** ed. Harvey, *Diaries* p. 249 **51.** *CS* VII p. 7376 **52.** eds. Danchev and Todman, *War Diaries* p. 566 **53.** Bew, *Citizen Clem* p. 316 **54.** BL Cunningham Add Mss 52577/42 **55.** BU AP 20/1/24 **56.** Marian Holmes's Diary pp. 13–14 **57.** Colville, *Fringes* p. 419 **58.** Deakin, '1944' p. 19 **59.** *CS* VII p. 6996 **60.** Ibid. p. 6982 **61.** Martin, *Downing Street* p. 157 **62.** CAC BRGS 2/2 **63.** WSC, *TSWW* VI p. 124 **64.** *CS* VII p. 6977 **65.** Ibid. p. 6982 **66.** ed. Soames, *Speaking* p. 498 **67.** OB VII pp. 887–8 **68.** ed. Soames, *Speaking* p. 501 **69.** Churchill, *Father's Son* p. 264 **70.** CIHOW p. 285 **71.** ed. Soames, *Speaking* p. 500 **72.** WSC, *TSWW* VI p. 96 **73.** ed. Soames, *Speaking* p. 501 **74.** Ibid. **75.** WSC, *TSWW* VI pp. 106–7 **76.** OB VII p. 915 **77.** Colville, *Fringes* p. 506; Martin, *Downing Street* p. 158; BL Cunningham Add Mss 52577 **78.** BL Cunningham Add Mss 52577/60 **79.** Colville, *Fringes* p. 507 **80.** WSC, *TSWW* VI p. 607 **81.** BL Cunningham Add Mss 52577/94 **82.** BU AP 20/1/24 **83.** Colville, *Fringes* p. 509 **84.** CAC SCHL 1/2/1 **85.** BL Cunningham Add Mss 52577/70 **86.** Ibid. **87.** Colville, *Fringes* p. 511 **88.** eds. Danchev and Todman, *War Diaries* p. 590 **89.** Colville, *Fringes* p. 511 **90.**

eds. Danchev and Todman, *War Diaries* p. 590 **91.** Potter, *Pim* p. 53 **92.** Colville, *Fringes* p. 513 **93.** eds. Pickersgill and Forster, *Mackenzie King Record* II p. 67 **94.** Ibid. **95.** LHC ALAB 6/1/5/p236 **96.** WSC, *TSWW* VI p. 132 **97.** Buell, *Master of Sea Power* pp. 470–71 **98.** Deakin, '1944' p. 6 **99.** OB VII p. 914 **100.** Deakin, '1944' p. 6 **101.** Colville, *Fringes* p. 513 **102.** CAC SCHL 1/2/1 **103.** Martin, *Downing Street* p. 161 **104.** OB VII p. 965 **105.** Ibid. p. 967 **106.** Beevor, *Arnhem* passim **107.** Colville, *Fringes* p. 574 **108.** CAC CHUR 20/148 **109.** Colville, *Fringes* p. 516 **110.** BL Cunningham Add Mss 52577/75 **111.** Colville, *Fringes* p. 517 **112.** Lacouture, *De Gaulle* I p. 575 **113.** *CS* VII p. 6991 **114.** Ibid. p. 6996 **115.** Ibid. **116.** CAC HARV 4/1/part 2 **117.** CAC BRGS 2/22 **118.** RA PS/PSO/GVI/C/069/51 **119.** OB VII p. 968 **120.** ed. Hart-Davis, *King's Counsellor* p. 261 **121.** OB VII p. 992 **122.** NA PREM 3/434/2 **123.** WSC, *TSWW* VI p. 198 **124.** Deakin, '1944' p. 11 **125.** Ibid. **126.** ed. Soames, *Speaking* p. 506 **127.** Ibid. **128.** OB VII p. 1015 **129.** Dilks, *Churchill & Company* p. 195 **130.** Moran, *Struggle* p. 200 **131.** RA PS/PSO/GVI/C/069/52 **132.** Deane, *Strange Alliance* p. 245 **133.** CAC BRGS 2/22 **134.** Deane, *Strange Alliance* p. 155 **135.** Martin, *Downing Street* p. 167 **136.** RA GVI/PRIV/DIARY/COPY/1944: 24 October **137.** *CS* VII p. 7015 **138.** *CS* VII p. 7023 **139.** ed. Nicolson, *Diaries and Letters* II p. 409 **140.** Gilbert, *Churchill and the Jews* p. 223 **141.** Ibid. pp. 224–5 **142.** *CS* VII pp. 7034–5 **143.** ed. Evans, *Killearn Diaries* p. 318 **144.** ed. Russell, *Constant* p. 268 **145.** Ibid. **146.** CAC LWFD 2/7 **147.** ed. Nicolson, *Diaries and Letters* II p. 412 **148.** *CS* VII p. 7031 **149.** Pamela Harriman Papers 13 November 1944 **150.** Best, *Greatness* pp. 198–9 **151.** BL Cunningham Add Mss 52577/102 **152.** Hancock and Gowing, *British War Economy* p. 367 **153.** ed. Kimball, *Complete Correspondence* III p. 421 **154.** Ibid. p. 409 **155.** Colville, *Fringes* p. 528 **156.** ed. Hart-Davis, *King's Counsellor* p. 274 **157.** WSC, *TSWW* VI p. 632 **158.** Colville, *Fringes* p. 533 **159.** WSC, *TSWW* VI p. 252 **160.** Ibid. p. 311 **161.** *CS* VII p. 7052 **162.** Ibid. p. 7055 **163.** Ibid. p. 7059 **164.** ed Hart-Davis, *King's Counsellor* p. 277 **165.** ed. Soames, *Speaking* p. 508 **166.** Pawle, *Warden* pp. 338–9 **167.** ed. Hart-Davis, *King's Counsellor* p. 282n **168.** Information from Mark Foster-Brown, grandson of Rear Admiral Roy Foster-Brown **169.** Colville, *Fringes* p. 540 **170.** OB VII p. 1121 **171.** Colville, *Fringes* p. 552 **172.** Ibid. p. 540 **173.** NA CAB 120/169 **174.** ed. Hart-Davis, *King's Counsellor* p. 281 **175.** NA PREM 3/208 **176.** ed. Hart-Davis, *King's Counsellor* p. 278 **177.** ed. Wheeler-Bennett, *Action* p. 258 **178.** Ibid. **179.** Hastings, *Finest Years* pp. 528–9 **180.** ed. Soames, *Speaking* p. 541 **181.** BL Cunningham Add Mss 52577/109 **182.** OB VII p. 1138 **183.** ed. Kimball, *Complete Correspondence* III p. 502 **184.** Papers of Joseph E. Davies, Library of Congress Box 16 **185.** *CS* VII p. 7100 **186.** McDonald, *The Times* V pp. 121–2 **187.** Ibid. p. 122 **188.** *CS* VII p. 7102 **189.** OB VII p. 1151 **190.** Colville, *Fringes* p. 555

## 31. Victory and Defeat: January–July 1945

**1.** WSC, *Marl* II p. 603 **2.** Colville, *Fringes* p. 537 **3.** OB VII p. 664 **4.** Martin, *Downing Street* p. 175 **5.** Ibid. p. 178 **6.** Ibid. p. 179 **7.** ed. Soames, *Speaking* p. 512 **8.** Ibid. **9.** Martin, *Downing Street* p. 179 **10.** ed. Soames, *Speaking* p. 513 **11.** Gladwyn, *Memoirs* p. 153 **12.** Churchill, *Tapestry* p. 76 **13.** Ibid. **14.** Martin, *Downing Street* p. 179 **15.** CAC SCHL 1/1/8 **16.** CAC LWFD 2/8 **17.** Ibid. **18.** Gladwyn, *Memoirs* p. 153 **19.** Ibid. p. 155 **20.** CAC LWFD 2/8 **21.** Gladwyn, *Memoirs* p. 153 **22.** OB VII p. 1189 **23.** CAC LWFD 2/8 **24.** Gilbert, *A Life* p. 823 **25.** CAC LWFD 2/8 **26.** *CS* VII p. 7293 **27.** Tolstoy, *Victims of Yalta* p. 96 **28.** Ibid. p. 430 **29.** ed. Soames, *Speaking* p. 517 **30.** NA PREM 4/78/1 **31.** Gilbert, *A Life* p. 818 **32.** Ibid. p. 820 **33.** Ibid. p. 821 **34.** Churchill, *Tapestry* p. 80 **35.** CAC LWFD 2/8 **36.** WSC, *TSWW* VI p. 352 **37.** CAC LWFD 2/8 **38.** CAC BRGS 1/2 **39.** Churchill, *Tapestry* p. 83 **40.** Martin, *Downing Street* p. 185 **41.** Ibid. p. 177 **42.** CAC BRGS 1/3 **43.** WSC, *TSWW* VI p. 348 **44.** ed. Evans, *Killearn* p. 325 **45.** ed. Soames, *Speaking* p. 518 **46.** Martin, *Downing Street* p. 186 **47.** CAC BRGS 1/3 **48.** Gilbert, *A Life* p. 825 **49.** Ibid. **50.** ed. Evans, *Killearn Diaries* p. 325 **51.** Ibid. p. 331 **52.** ed. Soames, *Speaking* p. 518 **53.** CAC BRGS 1/3 **54.** *Daily*

*Telegraph* obituary of Patrich Kinna 18 March 2009 **55.** Colville, *Fringes* p. 562 **56.** Ibid. **57.** Ibid. **58.** Ibid. p. 563 **59.** Ibid. **60.** RA GVI/PRIV/DIARY/COPY/1945: 28 February **61.** ed. Pimlott, *Dalton Diary* p. 835 **62.** *CS* VII p. 7117 **63.** ed. Nicolson, *Diaries and Letters* II p. 437 **64.** WSC, *TSWW* VI p. 638 **65.** eds. Danchev and Todman, *War Diaries* pp. 667–8 **66.** Taylor, *Winston Churchill* p. 388 **67.** Colville, *Footprints* p. 187 **68.** RA GVI/PRIV/DIARY/COPY/1945: 25 March **69.** eds. Danchev and Todman, *War Diaries* p. 678 **70.** Leslie, *Train to Nowhere* p. 210 **71.** Colville, *Fringes* p. 579 **72.** OB VII p. 1257 **73.** WSC, *TSWW* VI p. 434 **74.** Ibid. **75.** Ibid. p. 437 **76.** RA GVI/PRIV/DIARY/COPY/1945: 13 March **77.** ed. Soames, *Speaking* p. 521 **78.** Colville, *Fringes* p. 581 **79.** *CS* VII pp. 7138–9 **80.** Marian Holmes's Diaries p. 21 **81.** WSC, *TSWW* VI p. 409 **82.** Colville, *Fringes* p. 582 **83.** CAC BRGS 2/24 **84.** Colville, *Fringes* p. 582 **85.** ed. Butler, *Dear Mr Stalin* p. 315 **86.** ed. Soames, *Speaking* p. 523 **87.** Colville, *Fringes* p. 583 **88.** Courtenay, 'Smuts' p. 61 **89.** Colville, *Fringes* p. 585 **90.** WSC, *TSWW* VI p. 640 **91.** ed. Pottle, *Champion* p. 314 **92.** Colville, *Fringes* p. 587 **93.** Potter, *Pim* p. 62 **94.** Thompson, *Shadow* p. 153 **95.** BU AP 20/25 **96.** WSC, *TSWW* VI p. 399 **97.** OB VII p. 1294 **98.** ed. James, *Chips* p. 402 **99.** *CS* VII p. 7139 **100.** Ibid. p. 7141 **101.** Ibid. p. 7149 **102.** ed. Soames, *Speaking* p. 528 **103.** *TCD* 21 p. 658 **104.** WSC, *TSWW* VI pp. 642–3 **105.** Colville, *Fringes* p. 592 **106.** Ibid. p. 596 **107.** *CS* VII p. 7149 **108.** ed. Soames, *Speaking* p. 529 **109.** Ibid. p. 524 **110.** Marian Holmes's Diaries p. 21 **111.** ed. Soames, *Speaking* p. 530 **112.** Ibid. **113.** Colville, *Fringes* p. 596 **114.** Potter, *Pim* p. 62 **115.** Marian Holmes's Diaries p. 22 **116.** *CS* VII p. 7153 **117.** ed. James, *Chips* p. 402 **118.** OB VII p. 1345 **119.** ed. Nicolson, *Diaries and Letters* II p. 458 **120.** eds. Danchev and Todman, *War Diaries* p. 688 **121.** Ibid. **122.** *CS* VII p. 7154 **123.** OB VII p. 1348 **124.** *CS* VII pp. 7156–7 **125.** Ibid. p. 7158 **126.** WSC, *TSWW* VI p. 667 **127.** Marian Holmes's Diaries p. 22 **128.** Peck, *Dublin from Downing Street* p. 68 **129.** Colville, *Fringes* p. 599 **130.** Ibid. **131.** Ibid. p. 601 **132.** Ibid. p. 474 **133.** ed. Nicolson, *Diaries and Letters* II p. 347 **134.** OB VIII p. 7 **135.** NA CAB 120/691 **136.** Ibid. **137.** Ibid. **138.** Dalton, *Fateful Years* p. 462 **139.** BU AP 20/25 **140.** Stuart, *Within* p. 138 **141.** *TCD* 21 p. 1530 **142.** *CS* VII p. 7172 **143.** Harrow School Archives Box H4/8 **144.** Soames, *Clementine* p. 382 **145.** Colville, *Fringes* p. 606 **146.** CAC EADE 2/2 **147.** ed. Lowndes, *Belloc Lowndes* p. 260 **148.** Bod CPA PUB 229/8/8/fol. 73 **149.** Ibid. **150.** ed. Hart-Davis, *King's Counsellor* p. 336 **151.** CAC SCHL 1/1/7 **152.** eds. Danchev and Todman, *War Diaries* p. 702 **153.** Colville, *Fringes* p. 610 **154.** Ibid. **155.** eds. Pickersgill and Forster, *Mackenzie King* III p. 236 **156.** WSC, *TSWW* VI p. 545 **157.** Ibid. pp. 545–6 **158.** *CS* VII p. 7211 **159.** Mee, *Potsdam* p. 164 **160.** *CIHOW* p. 375 **161.** BU AP 20/25; ed. Dilks, *Cadogan* p. 765 **162.** ed. Soames, *Speaking* p. 532 **163.** Churchill, *Tapestry* p. 86 **164.** Marian Holmes's Diaries p. 25 **165.** Gilbert, *Other Club* p. 191 **166.** Potter, *Pim* p. 66; WSC, *TSWW* VI p. 583; ed. Soames, *Speaking* p. 536 n. 3 **167.** ed. Wheeler-Bennett, *Action* p. 262 **168.** Moran, *Struggle* p. 307 **169.** ed. Hart-Davis, *King's Counsellor* p. 342 **170.** Ibid. p. 343 **171.** RA GVI/PRIV/DIARY/COPY/1945: 26 July **172.** *CIHOW* p. 41 **173.** CAC BRGS 1/3 **174.** Eden, *Reckoning* p. 551 **175.** Hatfield House QUI Bundle 63 **176.** Pamela Harriman Papers 1/8/1945 **177.** Pawle, *Warden* p. 7

## 32. Opposition: August 1945–October 1951

**1.** ed. Soames, *Speaking* pp. 512–13 **2.** WSC, *Unite* p. 347 **3.** Churchill, *Tapestry* pp. 18–19 **4.** CAC EADE 2/2 **5.** Ramsden, 'Greatest' p. 9 **6.** Gilbert, *Search* p. 307; CAC CHUR 2/495 **7.** Hatfield House QUI Bundle 63 **8.** Marian Holmes's Diaries p. 25 **9.** WSC, *Marl* III p. 25 **10.** ed. Muller, *Contemporaries* p. 301 **11.** Colville, *Fringes* p. 428 **12.** Marian Holmes's Diaries p. 25; RA PS/PSO/GVI/C/069/34 **13.** Stuart, *Within* p. 139 **14.** Ibid. **15.** Woodrow Wyatt Papers 9 April 1946 **16.** WSC, *TSWW* VI p. 224 **17.** *CS* VII p. 7211 **18.** Ibid. **19.** OB VIII p. 249 **20.** *CS* VII p. 7211 **21.** Ibid. p. 7213 **22.** Ibid. p. 7214 **23.** Ibid. pp. 7214–15 **24.** ed. Soames, *Speaking* p. 535 **25.** Mather, 'Hardiness and Resilience' pp. 83–97 **26.** Churchill, *Tapestry* p. 95 **27.** Ibid. p. 98 **28.** ed. Soames, *Speaking* p. 541 **29.**

*CS* VII p. 7235 **30.** Ibid. p. 7269 **31.** ed. Nicolson, *Diaries and Letters* III p. 82 **32.** Colville, 'Second' p. 7 **33.** *CS* VII p. 7417 **34.** *CIHOW* p. 550 **35.** Ibid. **36.** Gilbert, *A Life* p. 864 **37.** *CS* VII pp. 7283–4 **38.** Ibid. p. 7285 **39.** Halle, *America and Britain* pp. 34–5 **40.** CAC ONSL 2 part 2 **41.** *CIHOW* p. 321 **42.** Earl of Birkenhead Papers 65/A3 **43.** *CS* VII p. 7286 **44.** Ibid. p. 7287 **45.** Ibid. p. 7289 **46.** Ibid. **47.** Ibid. p. 7290 **48.** Ibid. pp. 7292–3 **49.** Ibid. **50.** Gladwyn, *Memoirs* p. 185 **51.** Hatfield House 5M/62/1 **52.** Sebestyen, *1946* p. 185 **53.** Ramsden, 'Historian' p. 22 **54.** ed. Wheeler-Bennett, *Action* p. 258 **55.** Pilpel, *America* p. 225 **56.** Hatfield House 5M/62/1 **57.** OB VIII p. 341 **58.** Stuart, *Within* p. 147 **59.** *CS* VII p. 7317 **60.** Ibid. p. 7377 **61.** Ibid. p. 7443 **62.** Ibid. p. 7447 **63.** Ibid. p. 7386 **64.** Ibid. p. 7549 **65.** CAC CHUR 2/174/146, CHUR 2/100/57-8, CHUR 2/43/214 **66.** WSC, *Sinews* p. 134 **67.** *CS* VII p. 7379 **68.** Ibid. p. 7382 **69.** Gladwyn, *Memoirs* p. 218 **70.** *CS* VII p. 7765 **71.** ed. Eade, *Contemporaries* p. 433 **72.** Newman, 'Butterflies at Chartwell' p. 39 **73.** Hatfield House QUI Bundle 63 **74.** Churchill, *Crowded Canvas* p. 181 **75.** WSC, *Dream* p. 59 **76.** Howard, *Rab* p. 156 **77.** *CS* VII p. 7525 **78.** PA DR/182 **79.** *CS* VII p. 7545 **80.** Hansard vol. 443 col. 1848 **81.** Woodrow Wyatt Papers **82.** *CS* VII p. 7566 **83.** Ibid. p. 7571 **84.** Ramsden, 'Greatest' p. 18 **85.** OB VIII p. 364 **86.** WSC, *Dream* p. 10 **87.** OB VIII p. 364 **88.** Ibid. p. 365 **89.** Ibid. **90.** Ibid. p. 366 **91.** Ibid. p. 368 **92.** Ibid. **93.** Ibid. p. 369 **94.** Ibid. p. 370 **95.** Ibid. **96.** Ibid. **97.** Ibid. p. 371 **98.** Ibid. **99.** Ibid. p. 372 **100.** Ibid. **101.** Ibid. p. 367 **102.** CAC BRDW/V/2/9 **103.** WSC, *Dream* p. 12 **104.** OB VIII p. 331 **105.** Reynolds, *Command* p. 405 **106.** Soames, *Life as a Painter* p. 180 **107.** CAC SCHL 1/1/9 **108.** Graebner, *My Dear* pp. 77–8 **109.** Ibid. p. 25 **110.** ed. Soames, *Speaking* p. 548 **111.** CAC LASL 8/7/2 **112.** CAC ONSL 2 part 2 **113.** *CS* VII p. 7587 **114.** OB VIII p. 315 **115.** WSC, *Marl* II pp. 1036, 754 **116.** WSC, *MEL* p. 346 **117.** ed. James, *Chips* p. 426 **118.** WSC, *TSWW* I pp. 26, 615 **119.** Hatfield House 5M/62/1 **120.** Ashley, *Historian* p. 163 **121.** Reynolds, *Long Shadow* p. 317 **122.** *CS* VII p. 7679 **123.** Ibid. p. 8123 **124.** Boothby, *My Yesterday* p. 212 **125.** *CS* VII p. 7709 **126.** *The Times* 11 November 1948 **127.** Ibid. **128.** *CS* VII p. 7774 **129.** Soames, *Churchill Family Album* p. 370 **130.** Halle, *Irrepressible* p. 285 **131.** OB VIII p. 613 **132.** Halle, *Irrepressible* p. 285 **133.** *CS* VII p. 7777 **134.** Pilpel, *America* p. 235 **135.** *CS* VII p. 7797 **136.** Ibid. **137.** Ibid. **138.** Ibid. p. 7799 **139.** Ibid. p. 7803 **140.** Ibid. p. 7807 **141.** *CIHOW* p. 500 **142.** Moran, *Struggle* p. 334 **143.** PA DR/182 **144.** ed. Soames, *Speaking* p. 553 **145.** ed. James, *Chips* p. 439 **146.** *CS* VII p. 7883 **147.** *CIHOW* p. 552 **148.** McGowan, *Years* p. 96 **149.** ed. Soames, *Speaking* p. 453 **150.** Ibid. **151.** *CS* VIII p. 7927 **152.** WSC, *Balance* p. 201 **153.** *CS* VII p. 7944 **154.** CPA LCC 1/1/6 p. 6 **155.** ed. James, *Chips* p. 442 **156.** *CS* VIII p. 7985 **157.** Ibid. p. 7987 **158.** Ibid. p. 8360 **159.** Ramsden, 'Historian' p. 4 **160.** Ibid. p. 10 **161.** Booth, *True* pp. 135–6 **162.** Hatfield House Papers **163.** Hansard vol. 476 cols. 2157–8 **164.** Ibid. col. 2156 **165.** Best, *Greatness* p. 285 **166.** ed. Pottle, *Daring* p. 55 **167.** ed. Nicolson, *Diaries and Letters* III p. 178 **168.** Gilbert, *Other Club* p. 203 **169.** Courtenay, 'Smuts' passim **170.** WSC, *TSWW* IV p. 611 **171.** Jackson, *Churchill* p. 358 **172.** *CS* VIII p. 8143 **173.** ed. James, *Chips* p. 451 **174.** OB VIII p. 511 **175.** *CS* VIII p. 8170 **176.** Ibid. p. 8196 **177.** Ibid. p. 8226 **178.** Bod CPA LCC 1/1/6 p114 **179.** Woodrow Wyatt Papers **180.** *CS* VIII p. 8253 **181.** Ibid. p. 8283 **182.** Pearce, '1950 and 1951 Elections' passim **183.** Ibid. **184.** WSC, *Savrola* p. 344

## 33. Indian Summer: October 1951–April 1955

**1.** Jones, 'Knew Him' p. 11 **2.** Colville, *Fringes* p. 632 **3.** Roberts, *Eminent Churchillians* pp. 243–85 **4.** Gilbert, *Other Club* p. 107 **5.** Colville, *Fringes* p. 127 **6.** Interview with Christopher Clement-Davies 1 March 2017 **7.** Seldon, *Indian Summer* pp. 102–6 **8.** Colville, *Fringes* p. 644 **9.** Macmillan, *Tides* p. 491 **10.** Browne, *Sunset* p. 437 **11.** Halle, *Irrepressible* p. 312 **12.** ed. Midgley, *Heroic Memory* p. 30 **13.** ed. James, *Chips* p. 461 **14.** Willans and Roetter, *Wit* pp. 18–19 **15.** ed. Midgley, *Heroic Memory* p. 30 **16.** Colville, *Fringes* p. 635 **17.** *CIHOW* p. 88 **18.** Ramsden, *Age* p. 99 **19.** Colville, *Fringes* pp. 632–3 **20.** Shuckburgh, *Descent* p. 62 **21.** Ibid. p. 66 **22.** Colville, *Fringes* p. 635

**23.** Ismay, *Memoirs* p. 457 **24.** NA CAB129/48C(51)32 **25.** *CS* VIII p. 8481 **26.** *CIHOW* p. 550 **27.** Macmillan, *Tides* p. 493 **28.** *CS* VIII p. 8310 **29.** Colville, *Fringes* p. 310 **30.** Butler, *Art of Memory* p. 137 **31.** WSC *TSSW* I p. 21 **32.** *CS* VIII p. 8317 **33.** Colville, *Fringes* p. 637 **34.** Ibid. **35.** Ibid. p. 639 **36.** Dilks, 'Solitary' pp. 10–11 **37.** WSC, *Stemming* pp. 226–7 **38.** *CS* VIII p. 8327 **39.** Ibid. p. 8333 **40.** Shuckburgh, *Descent* p. 75 **41.** Interview with Sir Edward Ford **42.** *FH* no. 135 p. 51 **43.** Colville, *Fringes* p. 640 **44.** *CS* VIII p. 8338 **45.** OB VIII p. 697; Moran, *Struggle* p. 372 **46.** Murray, *Bodyguard* p. 145 **47.** *CS* VIII p. 8342 **48.** ed. Hart-Davis, *King's Counsellor* p. 430 **49.** Moran, *Struggle* pp. 425, 429 **50.** Mather, 'Hardiness and Resilience' pp. 83–97 **51.** Colville, *Fringes* p. 642 **52.** ed. Hart-Davis, *King's Counsellor* p. 406 **53.** Cawthorne, *Legend* p. 32 **54.** Boyd-Carpenter, *Way of Life* pp. 90–91 **55.** OB VIII p. 714 **56.** Hansard vol. 498 col. 204 **57.** Lyttelton, *Chandos* p. 168; Hansard vol. 500 cols. 32–3 **58.** Hansard vol. 501 col. 529 **59.** Colville, *Fringes* p. 648 **60.** Ibid. p. 649 **61.** Hansard vol. 501 cols. 1366–7 **62.** Colville, *Fringes* p. 651 **63.** Ibid. **64.** Hansard vol. 503 col. 1978 **65.** CAC NEMO 3/3 **66.** Gilbert, *A Life* p. 916 **67.** Ruane, *Bomb* p. 214 **68.** Ibid. p. vii **69.** Colville, *Fringes* p. 676 **70.** Ibid. p. 654 **71.** Ibid. **72.** *CS* VIII p. 8435 **73.** Hansard vol. 503 col. 286 **74.** Colville, *Fringes* pp. 657–8 **75.** Ibid. p. 658 **76.** Ibid. p. 659 **77.** Ibid. **78.** ed. Ferrell, *Eisenhower Diaries* pp. 222–3 **79.** Colville, *Fringes* p. 661 **80.** Ibid. p. 662 **81.** Ibid. p. 665 **82.** Ibid. p. 663 **83.** Ibid. **84.** Ibid. **85.** Colville, 'Second Best' p. 7 **86.** *CS* VIII p. 8455 **87.** Dilks, 'Solitary' p. 13 **88.** Hatfield House 5M/E41 **89.** Hansard vol. 515 cols. 897–8 **90.** ed. Hart-Davis, *King's Counsellor* p. 344 n. 1 **91.** Hansard vol. 514 col. 1757 **92.** *CIHOW* p. 352 **93.** ed. Hart-Davis, *King's Counsellor* p. 399 **94.** CAC LASL 8/7/6/25A/21 **95.** Dilks, 'Solitary' p. 14 **96.** Colville, *Fringes* p. 668 **97.** Mather, 'Hardiness and Resilience' pp. 83–97 **98.** Macmillan, *Tides* p. 516 **99.** Colville, *Fringes* p. 668n **100.** NA CAB 128/26/36 **101.** Cherwell Papers K70/6 **102.** Colville, *Fringes* p. 669; Cherwell Papers K70/6 **103.** NA CAB 128/26/38–44 **104.** NA CAB 128/26/37 **105.** Colville, *Fringes* p. 668 **106.** Ibid. p. 669 **107.** Ibid. p. 670 **108.** Hatfield House 5M/E41. **109.** Moran, *Struggle* pp. 425–6; *Sunday Express* 22 May 1966 **110.** *Sunday Express* 10 and 22 May 1966 **111.** Moran, *Struggle* p. 444 **112.** Ibid. pp. 419–20 **113.** Clarke, *Cripps Version* p. 538 **114.** Colville, *Fringes* p. 672 **115.** Ibid. p. 675 **116.** Moran, *Struggle* p. 486 **117.** Rose, *Unruly*, p. 336 **118.** Moran, *Struggle* p. 477 **119.** *British Medical Journal* vol. 310 10 June 1995 p. 1537 **120.** *CS* VIII p. 8496 **121.** Ibid. **122.** Moran, *Struggle* p. 528 **123.** CAC HAIS 4/3 **124.** *CS* VIII p. 8515 **125.** Hansard vol. 518 col. 1803 **126.** Colville, *Fringes* pp. 674–5 **127.** ed. Soames, *Speaking* p. 576 **128.** Colville, *Fringes* p. 682 **129.** Ibid. p. 683 **130.** Ibid. **131.** Ibid. **132.** Ibid. p. 685 n. 1 **133.** ed. Hart-Davis, *King's Counsellor* p. 430 **134.** Moran, *Struggle* pp. 540–41 **135.** Lady Soames to Richard Langworth in September 2005 **136.** Best, *Greatness* p. 315 **137.** Norman Brook diaries, *Sunday Telegraph* 5 August 2007 **138.** Roberts, *Eminent Churchillians* pp. 217–41 **139.** Addison, *Unexpected* p. 233 **140.** Norman Brook diaries, *Sunday Telegraph* 5 August 2007 **141.** Woodrow Wyatt Papers **142.** Colville, *Fringes* p. 691 **143.** *FH* no. 122 p. 15 **144.** Colville, *Fringes* p. 693 **145.** Halle, *Irrepressible* p. 305 **146.** *CIHOW* p. 32 **147.** Ibid. p. 93 **148.** Hatfield House 5M/E41 **149.** Colville, *Fringes* p. 702 **150.** Ibid. **151.** Ibid. p. 703 **152.** CAC BRGS 1/3 **153.** Colville, *Fringes* p. 703 **154.** ed. Soames, *Speaking* p. 587 **155.** Colville, *Fringes* p. 705 **156.** WSC, *Unwritten* p. 202 **157.** Fladgate Archives Moir Doc ch. III **158.** Browne, *Sunset* p. 171 **159.** CAC SCHL 1/2/1 **160.** Soames, *Clementine* p. 549 **161.** *CS* VIII pp. 8608–9 **162.** Fladgate Archives Moir Doc ch. III **163.** Ibid. **164.** Ramsden, 'Greatest' p. 15; Brendon, *Churchill* p. xx **165.** CAC NEMO 3/3 **166.** BU AP 20/25 **167.** *CS* VIII p. 8625 **168.** Ibid. p. 8633 **169.** Colville, *Fringes* p. 706 **170.** Ibid. p. 705 **171.** ed. Soames, *Speaking* p. 590 **172.** Colville, *Fringes* p. 706 **173.** ed. Soames, *Speaking* p. 590 **174.** Colville, *Fringes* p. 706 **175.** Ibid. **176.** Ibid. p. 707 **177.** Ibid. **178.** Ibid. p. 708 **179.** Ibid. **180.** Ibid. **181.** OB VIII p. 1123 **182.** Ibid. **183.** Ibid. **184.** *CV* I Part 2 p. 839 **185.** Seldon, *Indian Summer* passim **186.** Gilbert, *Churchill's Political Philosophy* passim **187.** Colville, *Fringes* p. 709 **188.** OB VIII p. 327 **189.** Ibid. p. 704 **190.** CAC HAMB 1/1/8 **191.** Ibid. **192.** ed. Midgley, *Heroic Memory* p. 29

## 34. 'Long Sunset': April 1955–January 1965

**1.** WSC, *Marl* II p. 1036 **2.** WSC, *Savrola* p. 35 **3.** ed. Marchant, *Servant* p. 141 **4.** Interview with Francis Maude 26 July 2016 **5.** Rowse 'Visit' pp. 8–13 **6.** Ibid. **7.** Ibid. **8.** Ibid. **9.** Browne, *Sunset* p. 305 **10.** Colville, *Fringes* pp. 526–7 **11.** ed. James, *Chips* p. 396 **12.** OB V p. 441 **13.** Ashley, *Historian* p. 210 **14.** Reynolds, 'Churchill the Historian' **15.** WSC, *HESP* IV pp. 182, 263 **16.** *CIHOW* p. 522 **17.** Browne, *Sunset* p. 120 **18.** ed. Soames, *Speaking* p. 604 **19.** Halle, *Irrepressible* p. 313 **20.** *New York Times* 22 April 1956 **21.** WSC, *HESP* I pp. 95, 99 **22.** CAC KLMR 6/9 **23.** ed. Soames, *Speaking* p. 610 **24.** OB VIII p. 1123 **25.** Moran, *Struggle* p. 748 **26.** Colville, *Fringes* p. 392 **27.** Macmillan, *Riding* p. 175 **28.** Lees-Milne, *Mingled Measure* p. 68 **29.** Browne, *Sunset* pp. 166–7 **30.** ed. Soames, *Speaking* p. 619 **31.** Gilbert, *Other Club* p. 216 **32.** ed. Soames, *Speaking* p. 622 **33.** CAC CHOH/3/CLVL **34.** Colville, *Churchillians* p. 123 **35.** Howells, *Simply Churchill* p. 61 **36.** Lysaght, *Brendan* p. 349 **37.** Gilbert, *Other Club* p. 218 **38.** Sandys, *Chasing Churchill* p. 1 **39.** ed. Soames, *Speaking* p. 627 **40.** Halle, *Irrepressible* p. 337; ed. Midgley, *Heroic Memory* p. 30 **41.** Sandys, *Chasing Churchill* p. 1 **42.** Ibid. p. 9 **43.** Ibid. p. 13 **44.** Ibid. p. 14 **45.** *CIHOW* p. 368 **46.** PA BBK/3/70 **47.** ed. Soames, *Speaking* p. 632 **48.** CIHOW p. 341 **49.** WSC, *Unwritten* p. 324 **50.** Bod CPA PUB 229/12/7/fol. 44 **51.** *CS* VIII p. 8707 **52.** *CIHOW* p. 530; Churchill, *Tapestry* p. 17 **53.** *CIHOW* p. 161 **54.** ed. Soames, *Speaking* p. 635 **55.** Murray, *Bodyguard* p. 202 **56.** Gilbert, *A Life* p. 957 **57.** *FH* no. 117 p. 7; Browne, *Sunset* pp. 273–4; OB VIII p. 1337 **58.** CAC CHAR 28/26/5 **59.** Soames, 'Human Being' p. 8 **60.** ed. Soames, *Speaking* p. 646 **61.** Browne, *Sunset* p. 325 **62.** Soames, *Clementine* p. 535 **63.** Ramsden, *Man of the Century* p. 3 **64.** *Commentary Magazine* 1 October 1966. **65.** The best account of the funeral is to be found in Croft, *Final Farewell* p. 62 **66.** *The Times* 25 January 1965 **67.** Rowse, *Memories* p. 12 **68.** Soames, *Clementine* p. 545

## Conclusion: 'Walking with Destiny'

**1.** eds. Blake and Louis, *Churchill* p. 406 **2.** Ismay, *Memoirs* pp. 269–70 **3.** *CV* III Part 2 p. 1339 **4.** Cherwell Papers K70/4 **5.** eds. Danchev and Todman, *War Diaries* pp. 450–51 **6.** WSC, *RW* II p. 375 **7.** ed. Soames, *Speaking* p. 149 **8.** OB II p. 34 **9.** *Churchill by his Contemporaries*, https://winstonchurchill.hillsdale.edu/clement-attlee-part-2/ **10.** *New York Times Book Review* 16 July 1995 **11.** ed. Muller, *Peacemaker* p. 6 **12.** Pawle, *Warden* p. 179 **13.** Taylor, *Winston Churchill* p. 291 **14.** ed. Eade, *Contemporaries* p. 248 **15.** *CS* V p. 5197 **16.** WSC, *GC* p. 137 **17.** Sterling, 'Getting' p. 10 **18.** Dean, *Hatred, Ridicule* p. 45 **19.** OB V p. 1115 **20.** Christie's Manuscripts Sales Catalogue 2003 **21.** ed. Eade, *Contemporaries* p. 433 **22.** Browne, *Sunset* p. 119 **23.** *CS* VI p. 6537 **24.** Arnn, *Churchill's Trial* p. xiv **25.** *Pall Mall Magazine* July 1927; WSC, *Thoughts* p. 23 **26.** CAC KLMR 6/9 **27.** WSC, *MEL* p. 73 **28.** Rose, *Literary Churchill* passim **29.** Soames, 'Human Being' p. 4 **30.** ed. Eade, *Contemporaries* pp. 14–35 **31.** Ismay, *Memoirs* p. 142 **32.** WSC, *Marl* II p. 331 **33.** *CS* VIII p. 8321 **34.** ed. Muller, *Contemporaries* p. 189 **35.** Gilbert, *Search* p. 215 **36.** CAC CHAR 1/399A/66–79 **37.** WSC, *TSWW* I p. 96 **38.** Reynolds, 'Churchill the Historian' **39.** *CS* VIII p. 8422 **40.** ed. Gorodetsky, *Maisky Diaries* p. 353 **41.** CAC CHOH/3/CLVL **42.** WSC, *TSWW* IV p. 182 **43.** WSC, *India* pp. xxxix–xl **44.** *CV* III Part 2 p. 1467 **45.** Kennedy, *Business* p. 115 **46.** Colville, *Fringes* p. 507 **47.** Baxter, 'Military Strategist' p. 9; Howard, *Mediterranean Strategy* pp. 31–2 **48.** *FH* no. 140 p. 31 **49.** OB VI p. 1274 **50.** Jacob, 'High Level' p. 373 **51.** eds. Danchev and Todman, *War Diaries* p. 713 **52.** *CS* VIII p. 8608 **53.** WSC, *TSWW* II p. 88 **54.** ed. Eade, *Contemporaries* p. 209 **55.** Gilbert, *A Life* p. 79 **56.** *CS* IV p. 4143; *CIHOW* p. 72 **57.** *CS* VI p. 6655 **58.** http://www.telegraph.co.uk/news/uknews/1577511/Winston-Churchill-didnt-really-exist-say-teens.html **59.** Scott, *Churchill* p. 2 **60.** Ibid. p. 266 **61.** OB VIII p. 1123.

# Index

**(1) "ATLANTIC CHARTER" MEETING**
**H.M.S. "Prince of Wales"**

**1941, August** *4th, Scapa. 9th-12th, Little Placentia Bay, Newfoundland. 16th, Hval Fjord, Iceland. 18th, Scapa.*

**(2) 1st "WASHINGTON CONFERENCE"**
**Visiting Ottawa and Pompano. H.M.S. "Duke of York" (to Hampton Roads). B.O.A.C. Flying Boat "Berwick" (from Norfolk, home)**

**December** *13th, Clyde. 22nd, Hampton Roads (thence by U.S. Navy Plane). 22nd-28th, Washington (26th, Addressed Joint Session of the Senate and the House of Representatives of the U.S.). 29th-31st, Ottawa (by Rail. 31st, Addressed Joint Session of the Canadian Senate and House of Commons).*

**1942, January** *1st-5th, Washington. 5th-10th, Pompano (by U.S. Army Plane and Rail, to and from West Palm Beach, thence by Road). 11th-14th, Washington. 15th, Norfolk (by Rail). 15th-16th, Bermuda. 17th, Plymouth.*

**(3) 2nd "WASHINGTON CONFERENCE"**
**Visiting Hyde Park and Camp Jackson. B.O.A.C. Flying Boat "Bristol"**

**June** *17th, Stranraer. 18th-19th, Washington. 19th-20th, Hyde Park (by U.S. Navy Plane and Rail). 21st-23rd, Washington. 24th, Camp Jackson (by Rail and U.S. Army Plane). 24th-25th, Washington. 26th, Baltimore, Botwood. 27th, Stranraer.*

**(4) 1st "MOSCOW CONFERENCE"**
**Visiting Cairo, Teheran and the El Alamein Front. R.A.F. Ferry Command Liberator "Commando"**

**August** *2nd, Lyneham, Gibraltar. 3rd-11th, Cairo (5th and 8th, El Alamein). 11th, Teheran. 12th-16th, Moscow. 16th-17th, Teheran. 17th-23rd, Cairo (19th-20th, El Alamein). 24th, Gibraltar, Lyneham.*

**(5) "CASABLANCA CONFERENCE"**
**Visiting Cairo, Adana, Cyprus, Tripoli and Algiers. R.A.F. Transport Command Liberator "Commando"**

**1943, January** *12th, Lyneham. 12th-24th, Casablanca. 24th-25th, Marrakech (by Road). 26th-30th, Cairo. 30th-31st, Adana. 31st-February 1st, Nicosia.* **February** *1st-3rd, Cairo. 3rd-5th, Tripoli. 5th-7th, Algiers. 7th, Lyneham.*

**(6) 3rd "WASHINGTON CONFERENCE"**
**Visiting Algiers and Tunisia. H.M.T. "Queen Mary" (to New York). B.O.A.C. Flying Boat "Bristol" (Washington-Gibraltar). R.A.F. York (to Algiers and Tunisia, then home)**

**1943, May** *5th, Clyde. 11th, New York (thence by Rail). 11th-26th, Washington (14th-17th, "Shangri La"—by Road. 19th, Addressed Joint Session of the Senate and the House of Representatives of the U.S.). 26th, Botwood. 27th-28th, Gibraltar. 28th-June 1st, Algiers.*

**June** *1st-2nd, Tunis (1st, Carthage, Tebourba. 2nd, Hammam Lif, Hammamet, Grombalia). 2nd-4th, Algiers. 4th, Gibraltar. 5th, Northolt.*

**(7) 1st "QUEBEC CONFERENCE"**
**Visiting Hyde Park, Washington and Boston. H.M.T. "Queen Mary" (to Halifax). H.M.S. "Renown" (from Halifax, home)**

**August** *5th, Clyde. 9th, Halifax (thence by Rail). 10th-31st, Quebec (12th-14th, Hyde Park, by way of Niagara Falls—by Rail. 25th-31st, Lac des Neiges—by Road).*

**September** *1st-11th, Washington (6th, Boston, Harvard College—by Rail). 12th, Hyde Park (by Rail, thence by Rail). 14th, Halifax. 19th, Clyde.*

**(8) "CAIRO CONFERENCE"—"TEHERAN CONFERENCE"**
**Homeward journey broken at Carthage and Marrakech through illness. H.M.S. "Renown" (to Alexandria). R.A.F. York (to Cairo, Teheran, Carthage, Marrakech and Gibraltar). H.M.S. "King George V" (from Gibraltar, home)**

**November** *12th, Plymouth. 15th, Gibraltar. 16th, Algiers. 17th-19th, Malta. 21st, Alexandria. 21st-27th, Cairo. 27th-December 2nd, Teheran.* **December** *2nd-11th, Cairo. 11th-27th, Tunis (Carthage). 27th-January 14th, Marrakech.*

**1944, January** *14th-15th, Gibraltar. 17th, Plymouth.*

**(9) "NORMANDY"**

**June** *12th,* TOUR OF THE BEACHES. *H.M.S. "Kelvin." Portsmouth, Normandy Beach-head, Creully, Courseulles, Portsmouth. Toured Beaches by Dukw and Jeep.*

**July** *20th-23rd,* TOUR OF THE LIBERATED AREAS. *20th, Heston to Cherbourg in U.S. Army Dakota, thence to Arromanches by Road and M.T.B. 20th-23rd, Arromanches (lived on board H.M.S. "Enterprise"). Visited Caen and Tilly by Road, and toured R.A.F. Airfields in captured Storch Aircraft. 23rd, Northolt (in R.A.F. Dakota).*

**1944, August** *7th,* FLYING VISIT. *From Northolt in R.A.F. Dakota, returning to Northolt.*

**(10) ITALY, THE ITALIAN FRONTS AND THE SOUTH OF FRANCE INVASION COAST**
**R.A.F. York (to Naples, and from Naples, home)**

**August** *10th, Northolt. 11th, Algiers. 11th-14th, Naples. 14th-16th, Ajaccio (by Dakota. Lived on board H.M.S. "Royal Scotsman" and H.M.S. "Largs." 15th, To the Gulf of St. Tropez and thence along the Invasion Coast in H.M.S. "Kimberley"). 16th-17th, Naples. 17th, Cassino (by Road). 17th-19th, Siena (by Dakota). 19th, Cecina, Leghorn, Siena (by Dakota and Road). 20th, San Casciano (proceeding vicinity Florence), Siena (by Road). 21st-23rd, Rome (by Dakota). 23rd-25th, Siena (by Dakota). 25th-27th, Loretto, Iesi, Monte Maggiore, Iesi (by Dakota and Road). 27th-28th, Naples. 28th-29th, Rabat. 29th, Northolt.*

**(11) 2nd "QUEBEC CONFERENCE"**
**H.M.T. "Queen Mary" (to Halifax, and from New York, home)**

**September** *5th, Clyde. 10th, Halifax (thence by Rail). 11th-17th, Quebec (thence by Rail). 18th-19th, Hyde Park. 20th, New York (by Rail). 25th, Clyde.*

**(12) 2nd "MOSCOW CONFERENCE"**
**Visiting Cairo and Naples. R.A.F. York**

**October** *8th, Northolt, Naples. 8th-9th, Cairo. 9th-10th, Moscow. 19th-20th, Sarabuz (19th, Simferopol—by Road). 20th-21st, Cairo. 21st-22nd, Naples. 22nd, Northolt.*